lonely planet

Costa Rica

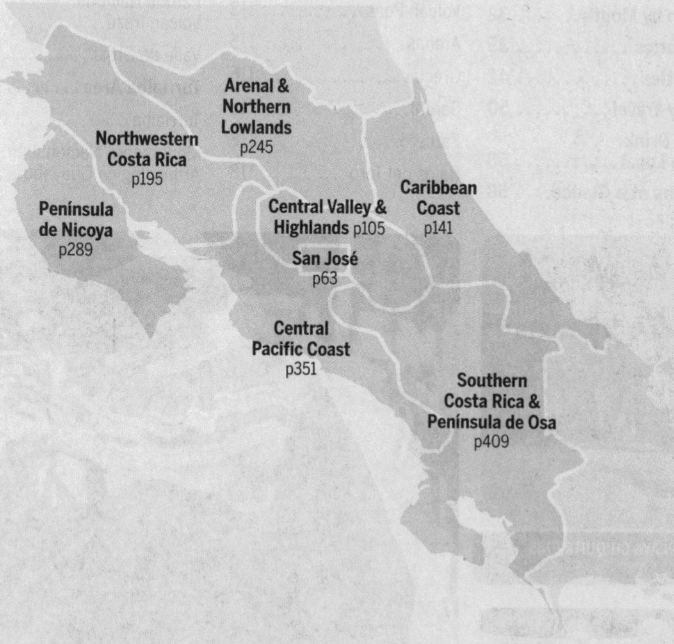

Jade Bremner, Ashley Harrell,
Brian Kluepfel, Mara Vorhees

PLAN YOUR TRIP

DAMSEA/SHUTTERSTOCK ©

PLAYA CHIQUITA P185

MARK KOSTICH/GETTY IMAGES ©

THREE-TOED SLOTH P495

ON THE ROAD

CARA KOCH/SHUTTERSTOCK ©

Contents

COSTA RICAN INDEPENDENCE DAY P34

ON THE ROAD

MAREK STEFUNKO/ALAMY STOCK PHOTO ©

HONEYCREEPER, PUERTO VIEJO DE SARAPIQUI P284

INSPIRED BY MAPS/SHUTTERSTOCK ©

CATARATA LA CANGREJA P233

Contents

EHTESHAM/SHUTTERSTOCK ©

SQUIRREL MONKEY P495

LINDSAY FENDT/ALAMY STOCK PHOTO ©

ENVISION FESTIVAL, UVITA P401

UNDERSTAND

SURVIVAL GUIDE

COVID-19

We have re-checked every business in this book before publication to ensure that it is still open after the COVID-19 outbreak. However, the economic and social impacts of COVID-19 will continue to be felt long after the outbreak has been contained, and many businesses, services and events referenced in this guide may experience ongoing restrictions. Some businesses may be temporarily closed, have changed their opening hours and services, or require bookings; some unfortunately could have closed permanently. We suggest you check with venues before visiting for the latest information.

SPECIAL FEATURES

Right: Catarata del Toro (p118)

WELCOME TO

Costa Rica

On a clear day at the summit of Cerro Chirripó, you can see both the Caribbean Sea and the Pacific Ocean in one sweeping 360-degree view, from sea to shining sea. I love how this little country contains a world's worth of adventures, landscapes and life in all its forms. Whether I have a week or a year, it's never enough time to experience everything Costa Rica has to offer.

By Mara Vorhees, Writer
For more about our writers, see p544

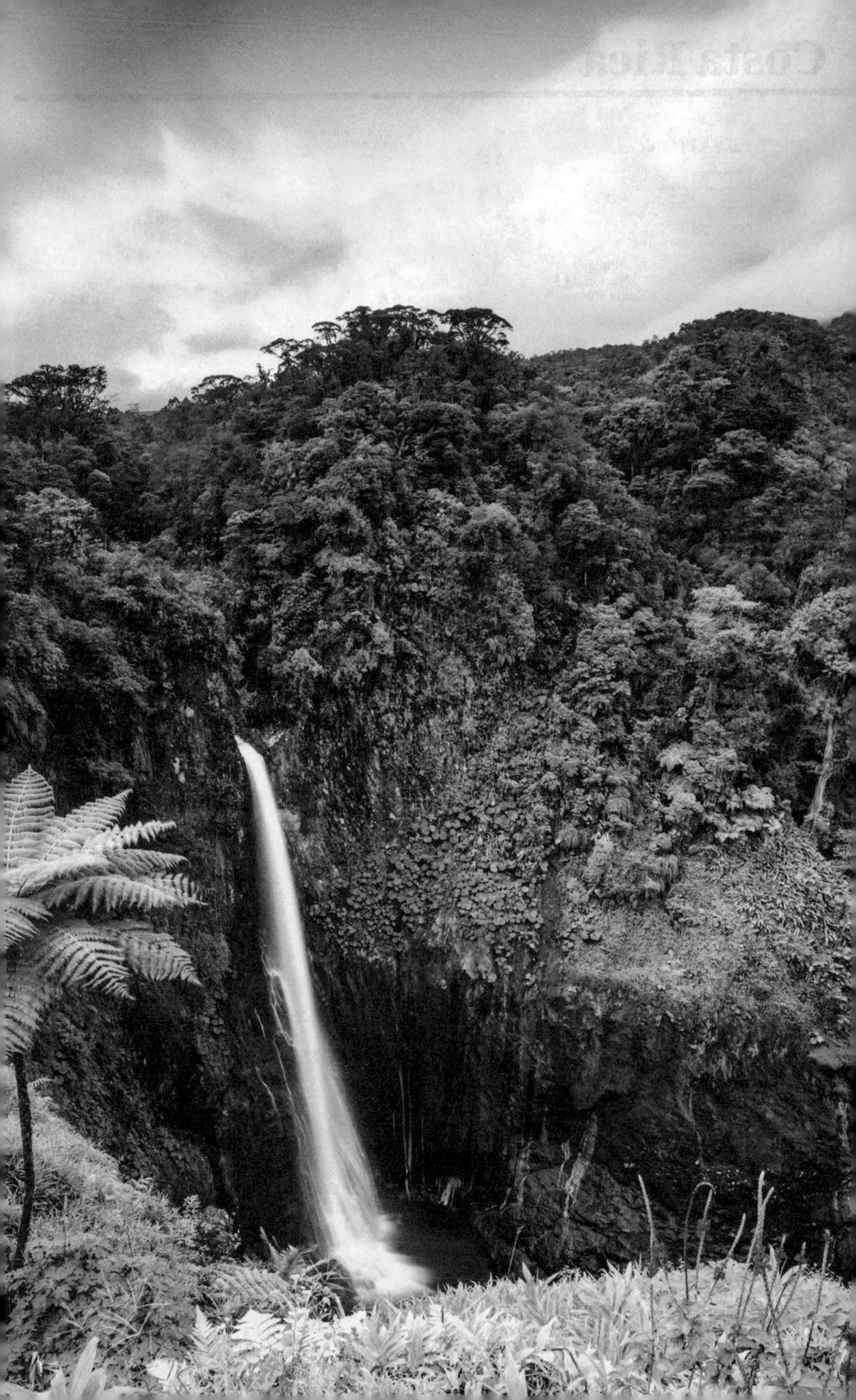

Costa Rica

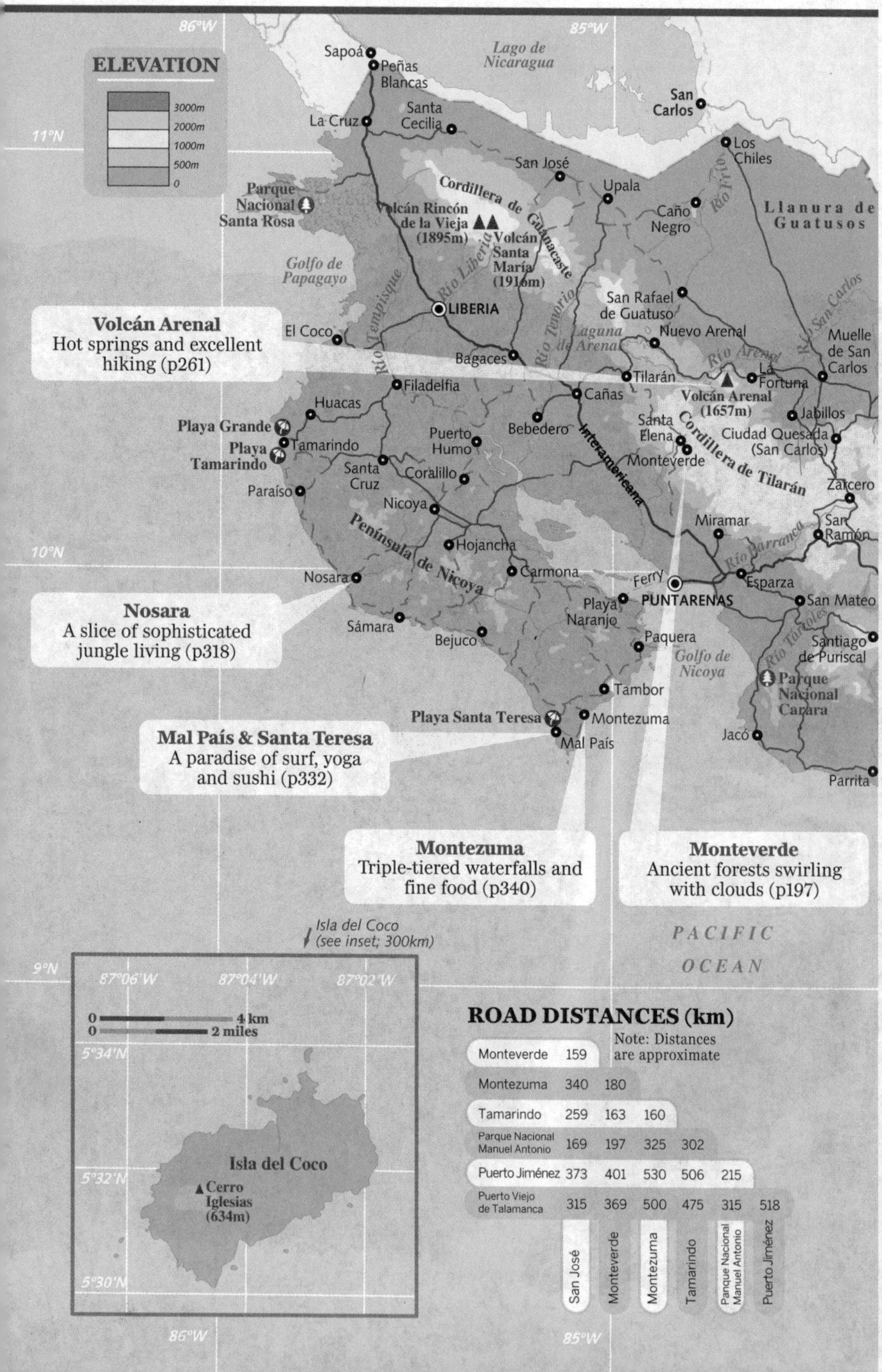

ROAD DISTANCES (km)

Note: Distances are approximate

	San José	Monteverde	Montezuma	Tamarindo	Parque Nacional Manuel Antonio	Puerto Jiménez
Monteverde	159					
Montezuma	340	180				
Tamarindo	259	163	160			
Parque Nacional Manuel Antonio	169	197	325	302		
Puerto Jiménez	373	401	530	506	215	
Puerto Viejo de Talamanca	315	369	500	475	315	518

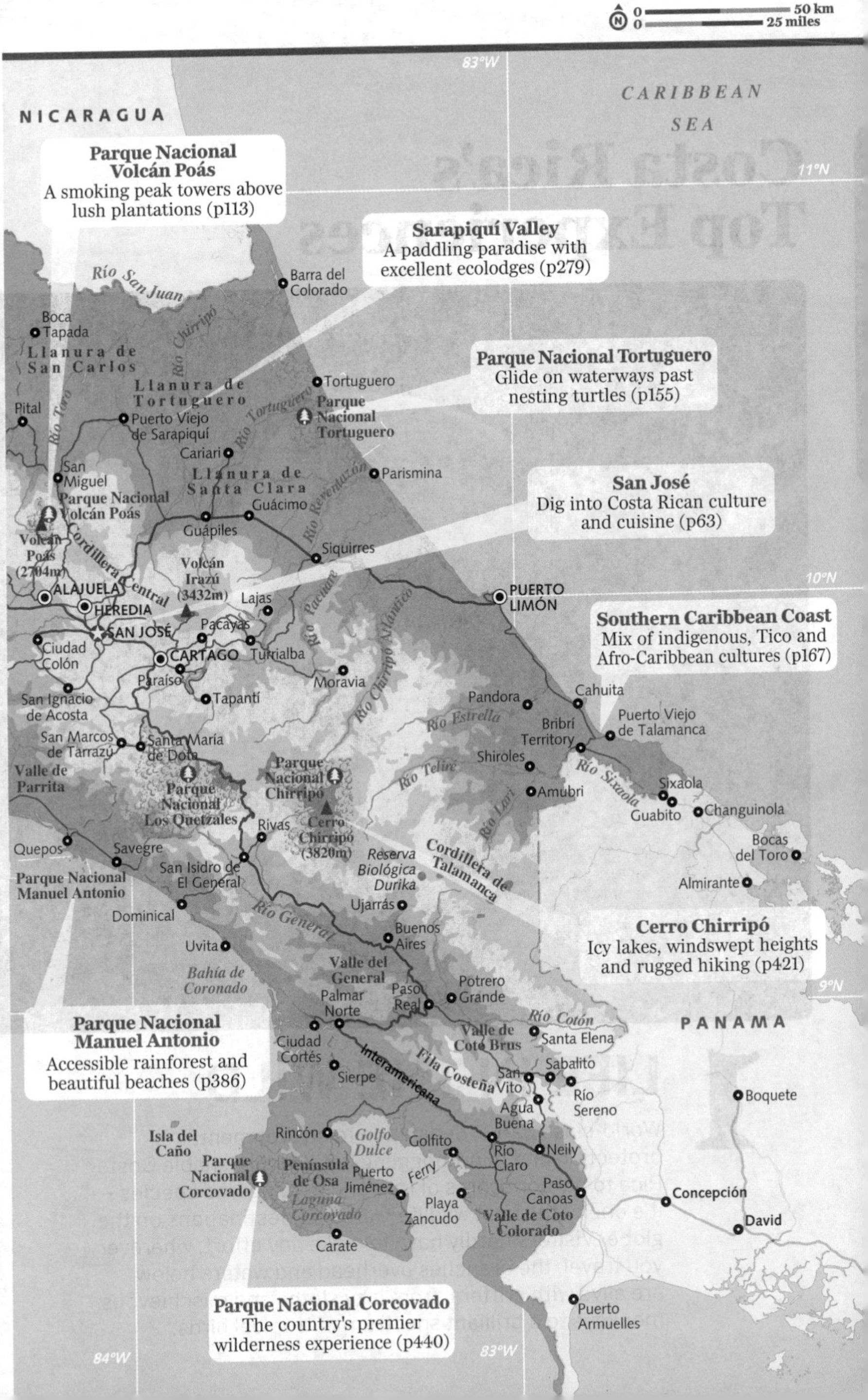
0 50 km
0 25 miles
83°W
84°W
11°N
10°N
9°N
NICARAGUA
CARIBBEAN SEA
PANAMA
Parque Nacional Volcán Poás
A smoking peak towers above lush plantations (p113)
Sarapiquí Valley
A paddling paradise with excellent ecolodges (p279)
Parque Nacional Tortuguero
Glide on waterways past nesting turtles (p155)
San José
Dig into Costa Rican culture and cuisine (p63)
Southern Caribbean Coast
Mix of indigenous, Tico and Afro-Caribbean cultures (p167)
Cerro Chirripó
Icy lakes, windswept heights and rugged hiking (p421)
Parque Nacional Manuel Antonio
Accessible rainforest and beautiful beaches (p386)
Parque Nacional Corcovado
The country's premier wilderness experience (p440)
Río San Juan
Río Chirripó
Río Toro
Río Tortuguero
Río Reventazón
Río Pacuare
Río Chirripó Atlántico
Río Estrella
Río Telire
Río Sixaola
Río Lari
Río General
Río Cotón
Barra del Colorado
Boca Tapada
Llanura de San Carlos
Llanura de Tortuguero
Llanura de Santa Clara
Tortuguero
Parque Nacional Tortuguero
Pital
Puerto Viejo de Sarapiquí
Cariari
Parismina
San Miguel
Parque Nacional Volcán Poás
Volcán Poás (2704m)
Guápiles
Guácimo
Cordillera Central
Volcán Irazú (3432m)
Siquirres
ALAJUELA
HEREDIA
SAN JOSÉ
Lajas
Pacayas
PUERTO LIMÓN
Ciudad Colón
CARTAGO
Turrialba
Paraíso
Moravia
Tapantí
San Ignacio de Acosta
Pandora
Cahuita
Puerto Viejo de Talamanca
Bribrí Territory
San Marcos de Tarrazú
Santa María de Dota
Shiroles
Amubri
Valle de Parrita
Parque Nacional Los Quetzales
Parque Nacional Chirripó
Cerro Chirripó (3820m)
Sixaola
Guabito
Changuinola
Rivas
Quepos
Savegre
San Isidro de El General
Reserva Biológica Durika
Cordillera de Talamanca
Bocas del Toro
Almirante
Parque Nacional Manuel Antonio
Dominical
Ujarrás
Buenos Aires
Uvita
Bahía de Coronado
Valle del General
Potrero Grande
Paso Real
Palmar Norte
Ciudad Cortés
Valle de Coto Brus
Santa Elena
Sierpe
Interamericana
Fila Costeña
San Vito
Sabalito
Río Sereno
Agua Buena
Boquete
Isla del Caño
Rincón
Golfo Dulce
Golfito
Río Claro
Neily
Parque Nacional Corcovado
Península de Osa
Puerto Jiménez
Ferry
Playa Zancudo
Paso Canoas
Concepción
Laguna Corcovado
Valle de Coto Colorado
David
Carate
Puerto Armuelles

Costa Rica's Top Experiences

1 LIFE IN THE WILD

World-class parks, dedication to environmental protection and mind-boggling biodiversity enable Costa Rica to harbor scores of rare and endangered species – it's one of the best wildlife-watching destinations on the globe. Visitors hardly have to make any effort; wherever you travel, the branches overhead and waters below are alive with critters, from lazy sloths and mischievous monkeys to a brilliant spectrum of tropical birds.

Parque Nacional Corcovado

Muddy, muggy and intense, this vast rainforest (pictured right) is no walk in the park, but the further in you go, the better it gets: the country's best wildlife-watching, most desolate beaches and most vivid adventures lie down Corcovado's seldom-trodden trails. p442

Parque Nacional Tortuguero

Canoeing Tortuguero's jungle-clad canals is a boat-borne safari: you can get up close with shy caimans, river turtles, manatees, monkeys and sloths. Sandwiched between extravagantly green wetlands and the wild Caribbean Sea, this is among the premier places in Costa Rica to spot wildlife. p155

Above: Turtles, Parque Nacional Tortuguero

Monteverde & Santa Elena

Costa Rica's premier cloud forest destination is a haven for bird life, including some rare high-altitude species that you're unlikely to see in other parts of the country. Keep your eyes peeled for the three-wattled bellbird, the resplendent quetzals, and dozens of species of hummingbirds. p213

Above: Cloud forest, Monteverde (p197)

Far left: Keel-billed toucan

2 HIGH-VOLTAGE VOLCANOES

There's nothing like a spectacular, steaming, swirling mountain to flaunt the sheer power and perils of this amazing planet. Whether you prefer to peer over the edge into the center of the earth or admire the view from afar (perhaps while soaking in a naturally heated pool), Costa Rica can provide. Five active volcanoes show off their geothermal magnificence with impressive crater lakes, bubbling fumaroles, solidified lava flows and steamy springs.

Volcán Poás

An hour northwest of the capital, Poás (pictured below) is a fairy-tale land of verdant mountains and hydrangea-lined roadsides, strawberry farms and coffee plantations. The volcano itself is a spectacular, sulfurous behemoth – the most accessible volcanic crater in the country. p113

ALEXILENA/SHUTTERSTOCK ©

MACDUFF EVERTON/GETTY IMAGES ©

KRYSSIA CAMPOS/GETTY IMAGES ©

Volcán Arenal

While the molten night views are gone, this mighty, perfectly conical giant (pictured above right) is still worthy of a pilgrimage. Shrouded in mist or bathed in sunshine, Arenal has trails to explore, waterfalls to swim in and hot springs to soak in. p261

Volcán Irazú

Arrive early to the massive Volcán Irazú to get a glimpse of the volcano's impressive craters and turquoise lake (pictured above left) before the clouds – and crowds – roll in. Intrepid explorers can scout out the volcanic-ash landscape and even hike up to the impressive 3432m summit. p129

3 CATCHING WAVES

Point break, beach break, reef break, left, right: whether or not these terms mean something to you, no worries. Costa Rica's patient instructors and forgiving beaches welcome the beginner, but for the experienced there are challenges aplenty. The bath-like waters mean no wetsuits are required, and rental shops and requisite gear are easy to come by. Hey, they didn't film *Endless Summer II* here for nothing, dude.

FOTOS593/SHUTTERSTOCK ©

KRYSSIA CAMPOS/GETTY IMAGES ©

JEN EDNEY/GETTY IMAGES ©

Mal País & Santa Teresa

In these twin surf towns, the waves are near-ideal in shape, color and temperature. Out of the water, it's pure yogic paradise and foodie bliss. Best of all, the hills are lush and the coastline long – a perfect backdrop for multi-hued sunsets. p333

Above left: Santa Teresa

Playa Grande

This is a tiny town with dirt roads and a wilderness beach (pictured top right), but the reliable beach breaks draw hordes of surfers. Luckily, it's a long beach that never seems too crowded. Head to either end to catch one of two main beach breaks. p301

Dominical

Countless foreigners and Ticos alike come to Dominical (pictured bottom right) to surf and can't bring themselves to leave. And no wonder... besides the sweet point and beach breaks, the town offers a laid-back vibe, a sophisticated dining scene and a locally made, thirst-quenching microbrew. p394

4 HEAD IN THE CLOUDS

At elevations above 1000m, Costa Rica's tropical environment takes on a completely different character. The so-called cloud forest is shrouded in mist, draped with mossy vines, gushing with creeks, blooming with life and nurturing rivulets of evolution. Above 2500m, the landscape morphs into *páramo*, a grassy, shrubby highland. It's not the Costa Rica of postcards, but these intriguing ecosystems are rich with plant and animal life and ripe with opportunities for adventure.

Bosque Nuboso Monteverde

Turning their back on the Korean War in the 1950s, the Quakers came, saw, and protected this 105-sq-km cloud-forest paradise (pictured below) straddling the continental divide. They're still here, teaching and living modestly, while Monteverde and neighboring preserves still offer a misty escape to a mysterious Neverland. p213

WORLD_XPLORER/SHUTTERSTOCK ©

MARCO DIAZ SEGURA/SHUTTERSTOCK ©

JURATEBUVIENE/SHUTTERSTOCK ©

Cerro Chirripó

The two-day trek to the rugged peak of Cerro Chirripó (pictured above left) rewards hikers with views of windswept rocks and icy lakes, as well as a chance to see both the Caribbean Sea and the Pacific Ocean in a full and glorious panorama from 3820m up. p421

San Gerardo de Dota

The rushing Savegre River and the cloudy Talamanca Mountains provide the backdrop for this picturesque village, popular for walking, fishing and especially birding. The flamboyantly colored resplendent quetzal is often sighted in the surrounding avocado trees. p412

Above right: Emerald toucanet, San Gerardo de Dota

5 SPYING ON SEA TURTLES

Under cover of darkness, on beaches on both the Caribbean and the Pacific coasts, sea turtles labor to build their nests and lay their eggs; meanwhile, tiny *tortuguitas* crack their eggs and make the perilous journey to the sea. Costa Rica is home to four different endangered species: olive ridley, leatherback, green and hawksbill. Witnessing the millennial-old ritual of these majestic creatures is a truly wondrous experience.

Refugio Nacional de Vida Silvestre Ostional

Olive ridley turtles (pictured below) arrive en masse – sometimes by the thousands – to build their nests on the beach at Ostional. This incredible *arribada* takes place approximately monthly during the rainy season. p323

JHVEPHOTO/SHUTTERSTOCK ©

Parque Nacional Tortuguero

From March to October all four species nest here, but it is the most important breeding ground of the green turtle (pictured above). Tortuguero is also the birthplace of the turtle conservation movement. p155

Parque Nacional Marino Las Baulas de Guanacaste

Las Baulas protects the beach at Playa Grande, nesting ground for leatherback turtles (pictured right). These massive creatures come to shore from October to March. p301

6 WATERFALL SWIMMING

KRYSSIA CAMPOS/GETTY IMAGES ©

DAVID MCMANUS/SHUTTERSTOCK ©

KEVIN SCHAFER/GETTY IMAGES ©

You'll hear it before you see it – the roar of the water, crashing over rocks and into pools below. Despite this foreshadowing, the moment of visual contact is always a show-stopper, when you spot the sparkling cascade of water, cutting through the forest green and tumbling over reddish rocks. Costa Rica is replete with breathtaking waterfalls, many with inviting pools to cool off in the waters below.

Montezuma Waterfalls

A 40-minute river hike leads to three levels of gorgeous, rushing water, each with its own adventurous swimming option, whether it's a relaxing dip or a thrilling leap of faith. p340

Llanos de Cortés

This wonderful, wide cascade of water (pictured above) is a favorite for its picture-perfect beach and swimming area, its supremely climbable rocks and – not the least – its easy access. p239

Viento Fresco

A 1.3-km trail (and 400-some steps) connects these four delightful waterfalls, each with its own plunge pool. Viento Fresco is an excellent break en route between La Fortuna and Monteverde. p270

7 RIDING THE WHITE WATER

Dedicated adrenaline junkies can cover some heart-pounding river miles in Costa Rica. Just pick a river, any river. They all offer fun runs, with rapids ranging from Class I to Class V, and all have smooth stretches that allow rafters to take in the luscious jungle scenery and animal life amid the glorious gorges. All you need is a lifejacket, a helmet and a good amount of chutzpah.

KEVIN SCHAFER/GETTY IMAGES ©

PAFNUTI/SHUTTERSTOCK ©

Río Sarapiquí

This frothing, serpentine river (pictured top left) is a paddlers' paradise. When you're not on the water, nearby ecolodges and forest preserves invite you into that looming, wild and muddy jungle. p282

Río Pacuare

Near Turrialba, the wild Río Pacuare (pictured bottom left) offers the country's best white water, with rapids up to and including Class V. Ecoaventuras is an excellent option for multiday adventures. p136

Río Savegre

The gentler rapids of the Río Savegre (pictured above) pick up in the rainy season, when the shores are draped with lush rainforest, ensuring a scenic backdrop for your adventure. p375

8 TREETOP ADVENTURES

TG23/SHUTTERSTOCK ©

HENK BOGAARD/SHUTTERSTOCK ©

MARCO DIAZ SEGURA/SHUTTERSTOCK ©

Steady those knocking knees and let go! Few things are more purely joyful than clipping onto a high-speed, high-altitude cable and zooming through the teeming jungle canopy. But of course there are other less terrifying ways to explore the treetops. Costa Rica offers opportunities for serious tree climbing, by power of one's own strength, and even for tree sleeping – as in spending the night in a fantastic dream-come-true treehouse.

Ziplining

There are ziplines throughout the country, but the best place to try it is Monteverde (pictured left), where the forest is alive, the mist fine and swirling, and the afterglow worth savoring. p201

Tree Climbing

Test your grit on the *original* jungle gym. It's a 70ft strangler fig with a viewing platform near the top at Psycho Tours in Cabo Matapalo. To get there, pick your own route (or root) and climb! p446

Treehouse Living

All around the country, there are incredible opportunities for guests to sleep in real, monkey-approved treehouses. One favorite is Finca Bellavista, an entire community of treehouses immersed deep in the rainforest. p457

Left: Treehouse, Boca Tapada (p278)

9 BEACH BUMMING

There's a lot of talk about adventure in Costa Rica, but sometimes, a vacationer just needs to lounge on a glorious sandy beach, dip toes in the water and relax. Fortunately, this country is blessed with 800 miles of coastline on two different oceans, and some of those miles are perfect for beach bumming. So don't forget to build an adventure recovery day into your itinerary.

Southern Caribbean Coast

From Cahuita to Manzanillo, the Southern Caribbean coast is a string of sweet beaches, each more inviting than the last. Cahuita's wild black-sand Playa Negra doesn't draw many surfers, making it great for swimming. p167

Below: Beach, Manzanillo (p189)

Playa Sámara

There's something about Playa Sámara (pictured above) that makes it hard to resist. Might it be the picturesque crescent of sand, spanning two rocky headlands and dotted with welcoming beach bars? p325

Parque Nacional Manuel Antonio

Despite the visitors, this remains a gem, where capuchin monkeys (pictured right) scurry across idyllic beaches and pelicans dive-bomb the clear waters. Playa Gemelas is a gorgeous, often overlooked hidden beach. p386

10 COFFEE: BEANS TO BREW

Along the scenic back roads of the Central Valley and highlands, the hillsides are a patchwork of agriculture and coffee shrubbery. If you're curious about the magical brew, tour one of the coffee plantations and learn how Costa Rica's golden bean goes from plant to cup. Tastings are always included! Bonus: coffee beans are a pretty perfect souvenir, so here's your chance to stock up.

Café Britt Finca

In the Central Valley, the charming town of Barva is a sort of coffee brewing center, home to the country's most famous coffee producer and largest exporter, Café Britt. p125

Santa Elena

Local farmers are growing a large variety of crops, including the holy coffee bean. Many are keen to show off their operation, which often include sustainable practices. p197

Mi Cafecito

In the foothills of Volcán Poás, Mi Cafecito is a perfect place for a pit stop. Stop for a caffeine boost and stay for a lesson in organic coffee farming. p279

Need to Know

For more information, see Survival Guide (p505)

Currency
Costa Rican colón (₡)
US dollar ($)

Language
Spanish, English

Visas
Most nationalities do not need a visa for stays of up to 90 days. Check requirements at www.costarica-embassy.org.

Money
US dollars are accepted almost everywhere and dispensed from many ATMs; carry colones for small towns and bus fares. Credit cards are widely accepted.

Cell Phones
3G and 4G available; US plans require international roaming.

Cheap prepaid SIM cards widely available.

See www.opensignal.com/networks for details of cellular providers.

Time
Central Standard Time (GMT/UTC minus six hours)

When to Go

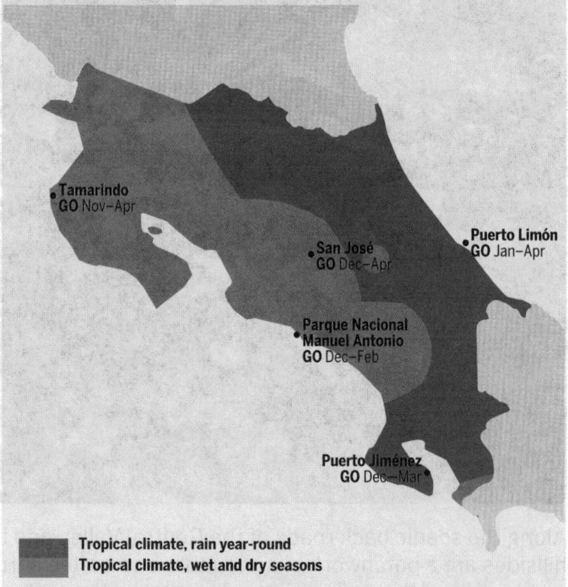

High Season
(Dec–Apr)

- 'Dry' season still sees some rain; beach towns fill with domestic tourists on weekends.
- Accommodations should be booked well ahead; some places enforce minimum stays.

Shoulder
(May–Jul)

- Rain picks up and the stream of tourists starts to taper off.
- Many accommodations offer lower prices.
- Roads are muddy and rivers begin to rise; off-the-beaten-track travel is challenging.

Low Season
(Aug–Nov)

- Rainfall is highest, but Pacific swells bring the best surfing conditions.
- Rural roads can be impassable due to river crossings.
- Accommodations prices lower significantly.
- Some places close entirely; check before booking!

Useful Websites

Anywhere Costa Rica (www.anywhere.com/costa-rica) Excellent overviews of local destinations; run by a well-reviewed tour agency.

Essential Costa Rica (www.visitcostarica.com) The Costa Rica Tourism Board website has planning tips and destination details.

Yo Viajo (www.yoviajocr.com) Enter two destinations anywhere in the country and view the bus schedule and fare.

The Tico Times (www.ticotimes.net) The website of Costa Rica's English-language newspaper; its searchable archives can help with trip planning.

Lonely Planet (www.lonelyplanet.com/costa-rica) Destination information, hotel bookings, traveler forum and more.

My Tan Feet (www.mytanfeet.com) Tips and travel stories from a Tico–expat couple living in Costa Rica.

Important Numbers

Costa Rica's country code	☎506
International access code	☎011
International operator	☎00
Emergency	☎911

Exchange Rates

Australia	A$1	₡477
Canada	C$1	₡512
Eurozone	€1	₡753
Japan	¥100	₡562
New Zealand	NZ$1	₡445
UK	£1	₡874
USA	US$1	₡617

For current exchange rates, see www.xe.com.

Daily Costs

Budget: Less than US$50

- Dorm bed: US$8–20
- Meal at a *soda* (inexpensive eatery): US$5–8
- DIY hikes : free
- Travel via local bus: US$2 or less

Midrange: US$50–150

- Basic room with private bathroom: US$40–80 per night
- Meal at a restaurant geared toward travelers: US$5–12
- Travel on an efficient 1st-class shuttle van like Interbus: US$50–60

Top End: More than US$150

- Upscale lodges and boutique hotels: from US$80 per night
- Meal at an international fusion restaurant: from US$20
- Guided wildlife-watching excursion: from US$40
- Short domestic flight: from US$100
- 4WD rental for local travel: from US$60 per day

Opening Hours

The following are high-season hours; hours will generally shorten in the shoulder and low seasons. Generally, sights, activities and restaurants are open daily.

Banks 9am–4pm Monday to Friday, sometimes 9am–noon Saturday

Bars and clubs 8pm–2am

Restaurants 7am–9pm; upscale places may open only for dinner, and in remote areas the small *sodas* might open only at specific meal times

Shops 9am–6pm Monday to Saturday

Arriving in Costa Rica

Aeropuerto Internacional Juan Santamaría (San José) Buses from the airport to central San José (about US$1.50, 20 minutes to one hour, hourly) run all day. Taxis (from US$30, 20 minutes to one hour) depart from the official stand. Interbus runs between the airport and San José accommodations (adult/child US$19.50/9). Many rental-car agencies have desks at the airport; book ahead.

Aeropuerto Internacional Daniel Oduber Quirós (Liberia) Buses run to the Mercado Municipal (around US$1, 30 minutes, hourly) between 5am and 9pm Monday to Saturday, less frequently on Sunday. Taxis between the airport and Liberia are about US$20. A few of the major rental firms have desks at the airport; make reservations in advance.

Getting Around

Air Inexpensive domestic flights between San José and popular destinations such as Puerto Jiménez, Quepos and Tortuguero will save you the driving time.

Bus Very reasonably priced with extensive coverage of the country, but travel can be slow and with infrequent service.

Shuttle Private and shared shuttles such as Interbus and Gray Line provide door-to-door service between accommodations popular destinations and allow you to schedule to your needs.

Car Cars can be rented at international airports and in major tourist destinations. A 4WD vehicle is advantageous (and essential in some parts of the country); avoid driving at night.

For much more on **getting around**, see p520

First Time Costa Rica

For more information, see Survival Guide (p505)

Checklist

- Check the validity of your passport and visa requirements
- Get necessary travel vaccinations and medications
- Purchase travel insurance
- Check airline restrictions on oversized luggage like surf boards or other equipment
- Research your credit card's policy on rental-car insurance.
- Procure an international cell phone plan

What to Pack

- Latin American Spanish phrasebook
- Sunglasses, sun hat and mineral sunscreen
- Hiking sandals or water shoes
- Refillable water bottle
- Insect repellent with DEET
- Waterproof case for phone
- Flashlight or headlamp
- Rain poncho
- Binoculars
- First-aid kit
- Small day pack

Top Tips for Your Trip

- In Costa Rica things can take longer than expected. Learn to relax into delays, make space for leisurely meals and don't overschedule.
- Avoid driving at night: pedestrians, animals and potholes are difficult to see on the largely unlit roads. Watch out for impatient drivers passing on two-lane roads; tailgating is a national custom.
- If you need directions, ask a few different people before you leave.
- It's often cash-only and ATM-free in remote areas; keep a stash of colones or dollars.
- Ticos use a lot of local slang; even experienced Spanish speakers might need time to adjust.

What to Wear

Coastal areas are sunny, hot and humid, calling for a hat, shorts and short sleeves, but you'll want to pack a sweater and lightweight jacket for high-elevation destinations. If you plan to hike up Chirripó, bring lots of layers and a hat and gloves. While hiking through the rainforest is often a hot and sweaty exercise, long sleeves and lightweight, quick-drying pants help keep the bugs away. A rain poncho comes in handy in several places.

Sleeping

Book ahead if you're visiting during high season; this is especially important during the Christmas, New Year and Easter (Semana Santa) holidays, when prices skyrocket.

Hotels and lodges These range from small, family-run affairs to boutique and larger establishments.

Guesthouses and B&Bs There's a variety of B&Bs throughout the country, reflecting the diversity of the landscape as well as the proprietors.

Hostels You'll find great hostels in the more popular tourist locales, some of high quality with excellent amenities.

Apartments and villas All levels of short-term rental apartments, villas and, increasingly, entire homes are available.

Eating

A handful of finer restaurants merit a reservation. Keep 'Tico time' in mind and all will be cool when you dine out.

Sodas Basic cafeteria-type eateries with plenty of economical set-meal rice dishes and soups.

Chains Bigger cities have international and local chains like McDonald's and KFC, with wi-fi and other modern amenities.

Cafes Most tourist towns have a couple of cafes with good Tico coffee drinks and a smattering of sandwiches.

International Busier towns feature sushi, Italian, French and other international fare.

Bar food Most bars serve *bocas* (snacks), and many have Western options like burgers.

Bargaining

➡ A high standard of living along with a stream of international tourist traffic means that the Latin American tradition of haggling is uncommon in Costa Rica.

➡ Negotiating prices at outdoor markets is acceptable, as is bargaining when arranging informal tours or hiring long-distance taxis.

Tipping

Guides Tip guides US$5 to US$20 per person per day. Tip the tour driver about half of what you tip the guide.

Hotels Tip the bellhop/porter US$1 to US$5 per service and the housekeeper US$1 to US$2 per day in top-end hotels; less in budget places.

Restaurants Bills usually include a 10% service charge. If not, you might leave a small tip.

Taxis Tip only if special service is provided.

DAVID HASTILOW/GETTY IMAGES ©

Guacamole with plantain chips

Etiquette

While Ticos are very laid-back as a people, they are also very conscientious about being *bien educado* (polite). Maintaining a respectful demeanor and a smile will go a long way.

Asking for help Say *disculpe* (translated as 'sorry') to get someone's attention, and *perdón* (also translated as 'sorry') to apologise.

Visiting indigenous communities Ask permission to take photos, particularly of children, and dress more modestly than you would at the beach.

Surfing Novices should learn the etiquette of the lineup, not drop in on other surfers, and be aware of swimmers in their path.

Hitchhiking Picking up hitchhikers in rural areas is common. If you get a ride from a local, offer a contribution towards the cost of the fuel.

Topless sunbathing It isn't customary for women to sunbathe topless in public.

Language

Spanish is the national language of Costa Rica, and knowing some very basic phrases is not only courteous but also essential, particularly when navigating through rural areas. That said, a long history of North American tourists has made English the country's unofficial second language. With the exception of basic *sodas* (inexpensive eateries), local buses, and shops catering exclusively to locals, travelers can expect bilingual menus, signs and brochures. For more, see the Language chapter, p526.

What's New

The biggest attractions in Costa Rica are as old as the trees. In fact, they are the trees. But there's always something new and innovative going down in this forward-thinking country, from trendy eating and drinking venues to progressive social and environmental policies – even as the country struggles to recover from the economic fallout of the global pandemic.

Best in Travel

Costa Rica was awarded sixth place in Lonely Planet's list of top 10 countries to visit in 2020 for its focus on sustainability and wellness. Costa Ricans understand the importance of preserving their slice of tropical paradise and have found a way to invite others in while living in harmony with their neighbors – from leafcutter ants to jaguars. Recent efforts towards achieving carbon neutrality are a concrete example of this commitment.

Reducing Carbon Emissions

Costa Rica now produces 98% of its electricity from renewable sources, including hydro, solar and geothermal. However, an oil-reliant transportation infrastructure creates about 40% of the country's emissions. The country's latest emissions-reduction plan aims to change this by building a new electric train line in San José and switching to electric buses around the country. The goal is to cut in half the number of cars in urban areas by 2040 (which is going to be a challenge, considering that the number of cars in the country doubled in the past decade, according to the *Tico Times*).

Creative Containers

Taking recycling to the next level, entrepreneurs are using old shipping containers for new businesses. The containers are afford-

LOCAL KNOWLEDGE

WHAT'S HAPPENING IN COSTA RICA

Mara Vorhees, Lonely Planet writer

In a country where tourism provides nearly 10% of all jobs, the global pandemic has had a severe effect on the Costa Rica economy. International borders closed for nearly five months, and travel from the US was restricted longer than that. According to the central bank, hotel and restaurant business shrank by some 40% in 2020. There is not much optimism that the situation will improve drastically in 2021, although the Minister of Tourism was hopeful that the country's focus on nature tourism would aid its recovery.

Prior to the pandemic, Costa Rica was touting its new plan (as of 2019) to achieve 'zero net emissions' and eliminate its carbon footprint by 2050. While this is significantly later than the previously stated goal of 2021, at least they have a plan – which is more than most other countries in the world.

Whether Costa Rica can stick to the plan is another question. The economy relies heavily on tourism – even more so since implementing a 13% value-added tax on tourism services. But tourism demands better airports and better roads; upgrades that seem to be in direct conflict with reducing carbon emissions.

And therein lies the challenge: achieving and maintaining that delicate balance between development and conservation. Costa Rica does not have it all figured out, but the awareness is there – and growing – that this country's most valuable natural resource is the nature itself, and it must be protected and preserved.

able, environmentally friendly and nearly indestructible. You'll find them around the country, containing hotels (p320), restaurants (p403) and even a yoga retreat (p396).

Stop Animal Selfies

In 2019 the government launched its latest ecotourism campaign, #stopanimalselfies, to make travelers aware that direct contact with wild animals is harmful: if you're close enough to take a selfie, you're too close. This should not be surprising to travelers, who would have noted the signs everywhere forbidding handling, feeding or otherwise harassing wildlife. But sometimes it takes a hashtag to get through to people.

Infrastructure Upgrades

In a move to create jobs and promote tourism, several domestic airports are receiving upgrades. There are shiny new terminals – some complete, some in the works – at Bahía Drake, Guápiles, San Isidro and Tortuguero, as well as remodeling and expansion in Golfito, Palmar Sur and Puerto Jiménez.

Meanwhile, the country is being paved like never before, with smooth new roads to Monteverde, El Castillo and Boca Tapada and a four-lane superhighway between between Guápiles and Puerto Limón (Ruta 4). A brand new bridge over the Sixaola River will soon connect the border town Sixaola with Guabito, Panama. And another new slab of asphalt will soon bisect El Castillo and connect drivers to the cloud forests of Monteverde. What does this mean for the prized ecosystems and promise of carbon neutrality? Only time will tell.

Food Markets

These inviting 'markets' are less about shopping for produce, and more about grabbing a bite to eat or a drink from a range of trendy restaurants and craft beer bars. In some cases you can also browse the handiwork of local artists or catch some live music.

- Container Platz, San José (p90)
- Mercado La California, San José (p91)
- El Mercadito, Tamarindo (p308)
- El Garden, Portrero (p298)

Craft Beer

Not that we don't enjoy a cold Imperial lager on occasion, but the arrival of craft beer in Costa Rica is truly worth celebrating. You'll find it at nearly every corner

LISTEN, WATCH, FOLLOW

For inspiration and up-to-date news, visit www.lonelyplanet.com/costa-rica/articles.

The Costa Rica Experience Popular podcast about expat life in Costa Rica.

Twitter @Visit_CostaRica Official feed of Costa Rica's Tourism Board.

Voz de Guanacaste (www.vozdeguanacaste.com) Articles on current events, culture, and environmental and human-rights issues.

Costa Rican Times (www.costaricantimes.com) Local news, entertainment and sports.

FAST FACTS

Food Trend Food markets

Life Expectancy 79.8

Number of orchid species 1400

Pop 5.09 million

(pub) of the country, and experimentation with local ingredients continues unabated. *Maracuya* (passion fruit) ale, anyone?

- Hoppy's Place, San José (p93)
- Casa House of Beers, San José (p91)
- Cerveceria Independiente, Playa Potrero (p298)
- La Selva Brewery, Cabuya (p340)
- Fuego Brew Co, Dominical (p398)

LGBTIQ+ Rights

In 2018, the Inter-American Court on Human Rights mandated the legalization of same-sex marriage and adoption rights, as well as the recognition of non-cisgender identities. The Supreme Court ruled that the country's ban on same-sex marriage was unconstitutional, and gave the legislature 18 months to reform the law. Same-sex marriage became legal in 2020. But it's not without opposition: polls show that about 60% of the population are against the change.

Accommodations

Find more accommodation reviews throughout the On the Road chapters (from p61)

PRICE RANGES

The following price ranges refer to a standard double room with bathroom, in high season. Unless otherwise stated, a combined tourism and sales tax of 13% is included in the price.

$ less than US$60

$$ US$60–US$150

$$$ more than US$150

Accommodations Types

Apartments and villas Typically including a kitchen and several bedrooms, long-term rentals can be an excellent option for families.

B&Bs and guesthouses Usually midrange to top-end accommodations, often run by resident European and North American expats.

Camping Most major tourist destinations have at least one campground, usually offering toilets, cold-water showers and kitchen facilities. There are also excellent camping facilities at many national parks.

Hostels The hostel scene has gone upscale in many tourist towns, with 'resort hostels' offering amenities like bars, pools and private rooms. Compared to other destinations in Central America, hostels in Costa Rica tend to be fairly expensive, though the quality of service and accommodations is unequaled.

Hotels and lodges A huge range of options, varying dramatically in size, location and atmosphere. It's always advisable to ask to see the room before committing to a stay, especially in budget lodgings, as rooms within a single hotel can vary greatly. The term *cabina* (cabin) is a catch-all, covering a wide range of prices and amenities, from very rustic to very expensive.

Best Places to Stay

Best on a Budget

Costa Rica is not the cheapest place in Central America for shoestring travelers. The upside is that the higher prices reflect higher quality. Budget travelers can expect resort hostels, jungle hostels and ecohostels that offer a fantastic experience for the money. The main tourist towns offer lodgings in all price categories, but off-the-beaten-track destinations have fewer budget options.

- Flutterby House, Uvita (p401)
- Buddha House, Jacó (p366)
- Pensión Santa Elena), Monteverde & Santa Elena (p205
- Playa Grande Surf Camp, Playa Grande (p301)
- Osa Jungle Hostel, Puerto Jiménez (p449)
- Bolita Rainforest Hostel, Dos Brazos (p452)

Best for Families

Costa Rica is a dream come true for adventurous kids longing to live in a treehouse, sleep in the jungle or wake up to the waves. There are countless opportunities for kids of all ages to live out their wildest fantasies. The best part is that many of these accommodations also offer a degree of comfort and luxury, that will likely be appreciated by some members of the family.

- Tree Houses Hotel, Ciudad Quesada (p278)
- Chira, Monteverde & Santa Elena (p208)
- Río Perdido, Volcán Miravalles Area (p224)
- Rafiki Safari Lodge, Quepos (p388)
- Fiesta Resort, Puntarenas (p356)
- Naguala Jungle Lodge, Bahía Drake (p435)

INVICTUS SARL/ALAMY STOCK PHOTO ©

Evergreen Lodge (p163), Tortuguero Village

BLEND IMAGES - JEREMY WOODHOUSE/GETTY IMAGES ©

Reserva Biológica Bosque Nuboso Monteverde (p213)

Best for Solo Travelers

There's no shortage of folks traveling solo in Costa Rica, and a plethora of ways to meet them. The easiest (and cheapest) way is to stay in hostels; there are plenty of more upscale lodgings that offer family dining and other aspects of community living. Alternatively, join a tour or a volunteer project for an introduction to like-minded travelers.

- Fauna Luxury Hostel, San José (p82)
- Gringo Pete's, La Fortuna (p255)
- Canaima Chill House, Santa Teresa (p337)
- Cascada Verde, Uvita (p401)
- Casa Mariposa, San Gerardo de Rivas (p420)
- Yoga Farm, Pavones (p460)

Best Eco Accommodations

This is where Costa Rica truly excels, with myriad opportunities to stay in a wild, natural setting while minimizing your impact there. Steps taken by ecofriendly lodgings might include: natural construction from repurposed materials, recycling and minimizing waste, obtaining power from renewable sources and engaging and supporting the local community.

- Hotel Sí Como No, Manuel Antonio (p381)
- Tierra Madre Eco Lodge, Interamericana Norte (p240)
- Mundo Milo Ecolodge, Playa Junquillal (p313)
- Finca Bellavistax, Parque Nacional Piedras Blancas (p313)
- Playa Nicuesa Rainforest Lodge, Golfo Dulce (p459)

Booking

Book ahead during the high season; this is especially important during the Christmas, New Year and Easter (Semana Santa) holidays. Prices skyrocket during those weeks. Some lodgings close during the months of September and October, or even longer, especially in the Península de Osa and the Golfo Dulce.

Lonely Planet (www.lonelyplanet.com/costa-rica/hotels) Find independent reviews, as well as recommendations on the best places to stay – and then book them online.

Costa Rica Innkeepers Association (www.costaricainnkeepers.com) A nonprofit association of B&Bs, small hotels, lodges and inns.

Escape Villas (www.villascostarica.com) High-end accommodations across Costa Rica – most near Parque Nacional Manuel Antonio – that are suitable for families and honeymooners looking for luxury.

Go Visit Costa Rica (www.govisitcostarica.com) Lots of information to help you plan your trip, including booking hotels, ecolodges and vacation rentals around the country.

Month by Month

TOP EVENTS

Las Fiestas de Palmares, January

Envision Festival, February

Vuelta al Lago Arenal, March

Costa Rican Independence Day, September

Whale & Dolphin Festival, September

Fiesta de los Diablitos, December

January

Every year opens with a rush, as North American and domestic tourists flood beach towns to celebrate. January sees dry days and occasional afternoon showers.

Fiesta de la Santa Cruz

Held in Santa Cruz in the second week of January, this festival centers on a rodeo and *Toros a la Tica* (bullfights). It also includes the requisite religious procession, music, dances and a beauty pageant.

See p500 for information on bullfighting in Costa Rica.

Las Fiestas de Palmares

In the second half of the month, the tiny town of Palmares (p121) turns into carnival central, with carnival rides, bullfighting, live music, a horse parade and plenty of boozing.

February

February is the perfect month, with ideal weather and no holiday surcharges. The skies above Nicoya are particularly clear, and it's peak season for some species of nesting turtle to do their thing.

Envision Festival

Held in Uvita in late February, this is a festival (p401) with a consciousness-raising, transformational bent, bringing together fire dancers, performance artists, yoga, music and spiritual workshops. Also takes place during the first week of March in Dominical.

Carrera Chirripó

This grueling race (p419) from San Gerardo de Rivas to Crestones Base Lodge and back (34km) takes place at the end of February, with up to 225 participants. If you're trekking up the mountain you may be disheartened (or inspired) to know that the fastest person covered the distance in three hours and nine minutes.

March

Excellent weather continues through the early part of March, though prices shoot up during Semana Santa (the week leading up to Easter) and North American spring break, aka Holy Week and Unholy Week.

Día del Boyero

A colorful parade (p74), held in Escazú on the second Sunday in March, features colorfully painted *carretas* (oxcarts, the national symbol) and includes a blessing of the animals. Plaid shirt and cowboy hat optional.

Vuelta al Lago Arenal

They say that it's virtually impossible to circumnavigate this lake under your own locomotion. But *they* have never participated in the two-day Vuelta al Lago Arenal (p270), an annual event in March, when some 4000 cyclists do just that.

Feria de la Mascarada

During the Feria de la Mascarada (p125), begun in 2002, people don massive colorful masks (weighing up to 20kg) to dance and parade around the town square of Barva. Usually held during the last week of March.

April

Easter and Semana Santa can fall early in April, which means beaches fill and prices spike. Nicoya and Guanacaste are dry and hot, with little rain.

Día de Juan Santamaría

Commemorating Costa Rica's national hero (the main airport is named for him), who died in battle against American colonist William Walker's troops in 1856, this day of celebration (p110) on April 11 includes parades, concerts and dances.

Festival de las Artes (FIA)

This multidisciplinary, multiday festival (p74) featuring international artists takes place all across San José and usually happens in March or April, but the month can vary.

May

Attention, budget travelers: wetter weather begins to sweep across the country in May, heralding the country's low season. So, although conditions are pleasant, prices can be expected to drop.

Día de San Isidro Labrador

On May 15 visitors can taste the bounty of San Isidro and neighboring villages during the nation's largest agricultural fair, in honor of the growers' patron saint.

June

The Pacific Coast gets fairly wet during June, which makes for good surfing. The beginning of the 'green season,' this time of year has lots of discounted rates.

Walter Ferguson International Calypso Festival

One weekend each summer (p169) Cahuita hails centenarian Walter Gavitt Ferguson (b 1919), the 'Calypso King' who invented the local style of music you hear often around town. *Calypso Limonese* has been declared a national cultural heritage, and Walter personifies 'living legend.'

July

July is mostly wet, particularly on the Caribbean coast, but the month also occasionally enjoys a brief dry period that Ticos call *veranillo* (summer). Expect rain, particularly late in the day.

National Surfing Championship

Local surfers head to Jacó for this much publicized national competition on the waves (p371). Can also be held in August.

Fiesta de La Virgen del Mar

Held in Puntarenas and Playa del Coco on the Saturday closest to July 16, the Festival of the Virgin of the Sea involves colorful, brightly lit regattas and boat parades.

Día de Guanacaste

Celebrates the 1824 annexation of Guanacaste from Nicaragua. There are rodeos, bullfights, cattle shows and general bovine madness. It takes place on July 25.

August

It's the middle of the rainy season, but the mornings can still be bright and sunny. Travelers who don't mind some rain will find great hotel and tour deals.

La Virgen de los Ángeles

The patron saint of Costa Rica, the Black Virgin or Black Madonna, is celebrated with an important religious procession from San José to Cartago on August 2.

September

The Península de Osa gets utterly soaked during September, which is the heart of the rainy season and what Ticos refer to as the *temporales del Pacífico*. It's the cheapest time to visit the Pacific.

Whale & Dolphin Festival

Uvita officially kicks off whale-watching season with a lively, responsibly organized, week-long festival (p401), featuring dolphin- and whale-watching tours, as well as a fun run and a mountain bike race.

Costa Rican Independence Day

With events all over the country, Costa Rica's Independence Day is a fun party. The center of the action is the relay race that passes a 'Freedom Torch' from Guatemala to Costa Rica. The torch arrives at Cartago on the evening of the 14th (the eve of the holiday), when the nation breaks into the national anthem.

October

Many roads become impassable as rivers swell and rain continues to fall in one of the wettest months in Costa Rica. Lodges and tour operators are sometimes closed until November.

Día de la Raza

Columbus' historic landing on Isla Uvita has traditionally inspired a small carnival (p150) in Puerto Limón on October 12, with street parades, live music and dancing.)

November

The weather can go either way in November. Access to Parque Nacional Corcovado is difficult after several months of rain, though the skies are usually clear by month's end.

Día de los Muertos

Families visit graveyards and have religious parades in honor of the dead in this lovely and picturesque festival on November 2.

La Ruta de los Conquistadores

On the first weekend in November, this three-day mountain-biking race (www.larutadelosconquistadores.com) goes from coast to coast, traversing steamy rainforest, scorching banana plantations and chilly mountain ranges.

December

Although the beginning of the month is a great time to visit – with clearer skies and relatively uncrowded attractions – things ramp up toward Christmas and reservations become crucial.

Festival de la Luz (Festival of Light)

San José comes to life as it marks the beginning of the Christmas season on the second Saturday of the month, with marching bands, spectacular floats, and various colorful light displays and artworks throughout downtown (www.festivaldelaluz.cr).

Jacó Christmas Carnival

The whole town comes out for this family-friendly, mega-festive Christmas celebration (p366) with more brass bands than you've ever seen. Troupes parade in various outfits along the main street through town, creating a merry spirit as they go with dances, loud brass classics, Christmas songs and even rock numbers.

Fiesta de los Diablitos

Men booze up and don wooden devil masks and burlap sacks, then re-enact the fight between the indigenous and the Spanish. (In this rendition, Spain loses.) Held in Boruca (p425) from December 30 to January 2 and in Rey Curré from February 5 to February 8.

Las Fiestas de Zapote

In San José between Christmas and New Year's Eve, this weeklong celebration (p75) of all things Costa Rican (including rodeos, cowboys, carnival rides, fried food and booze) draws tens of thousands of Ticos to the bullring in the suburb of Zapote every day.

Itineraries

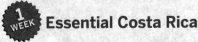

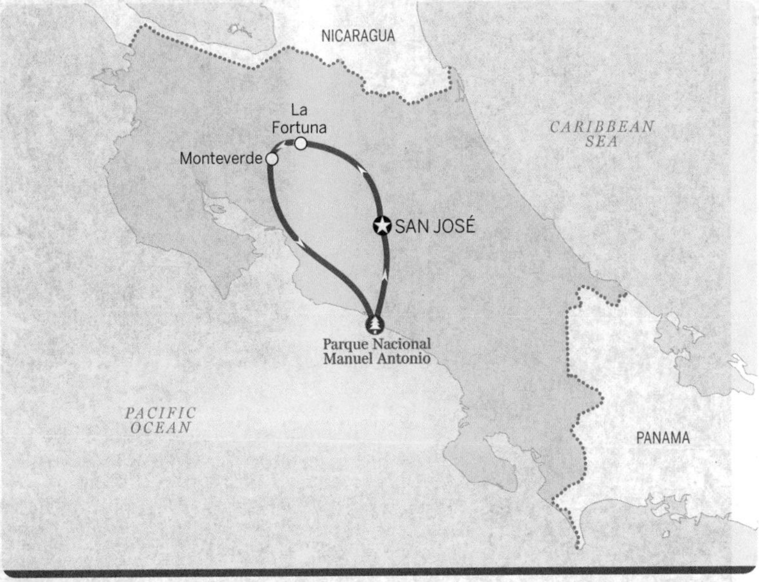

1 WEEK Essential Costa Rica

This is the trip you've been dreaming about: a romp through paradise with seething volcanoes, tropical parks, warm-water beaches and ghostly cloud forests.

From **San José**, beeline north to **La Fortuna**. After an invigorating forest hike on the flanks of Volcán Arenal, take a dip in a majestic waterfall or soak in the country's best hot springs. Then do the classic jeep-boat-jeep run across Lake Arenal to **Monteverde**, where you can get up close and personal with bats, bugs and butterflies. Fly through the clouds on a canopy tour and keep your eyes peeled for the elusive quetzal on your walk through the Bosque Nuboso Monteverde.

Next up: some well-earned beach time. Spend half a day busing to Quepos, the gateway to **Parque Nacional Manuel Antonio**. A full day in the park starts with a jungle hike, where you're likely to encounter monkeys, sloths and iguanas. End your hike with a picnic and a dip in the park's perfect waters. Bus back to San José in time to catch your flight home.

Top: Catarata Río Fortuna (p249)

Bottom: Jacó (p363)

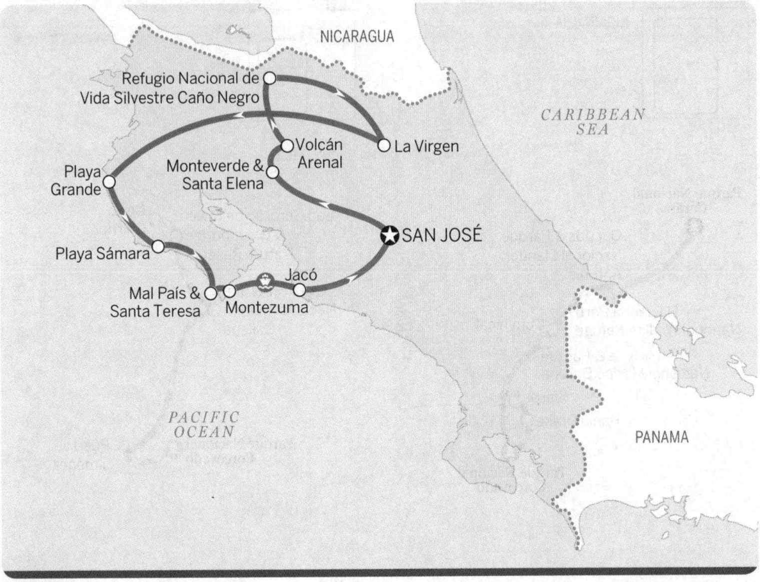

2 WEEKS

Northern Costa Rica

Tiptoe cloud-forest bridges and feel the lava bubbling below hot springs, then wander the quiet swampy lowlands, vibrant with irds, before basking in the bath-warm Pacific.

From **San José** your first stop is **Monteverde & Santa Elena**. Here, you can watch mist roll over dense forest in the Bosque Nuboso Monteverde or the Reserva Santa Elena. Don't miss the chance to dare dizzying ziplines and aerial walkways at Selvatura.

Now, hop on a bus for **Volcán Arenal**, the country's biggest active volcano. Though it's not spitting lava, Arenal remains an incredible sight. Admire the view and look for wildlife in the national park, or hike to the fantastic Catarata Río Fortuna for a cooling waterfall dip. Finish your hikes with a soak in the hot springs.

Leave the tourists behind and head north to the lowland ecolodges of **Refugio Nacional de Vida Silvestre Caño Negro**. Here you will encounter bird and animal life galore, especially if you opt for a boat tour on the local waterways. Then pick up the pace again, making your way to **La Virgen** to raft the white water of the Río Sarapiquí.

The last leg of your trip is dedicated to beach time, and there's no better place to spend it than the Península de Nicoya. The options are many, and each beach has its own attractions, although all of them boast killer surf. **Playa Grande** is a long beach with a long break and (during nesting season) hordes of nesting leatherback turtles. Continue south to **Playa Sámara**, a perfect destination for families and non-surfers. Finally, head all the way to the southern tip of the peninsula for amazing swells and restorative yoga at **Mal País** and **Santa Teresa**.

From **Montezuma** take the fast boat to **Jacó**, where you can enjoy some last rays of sunshine and a decadent meal before returning to San José.

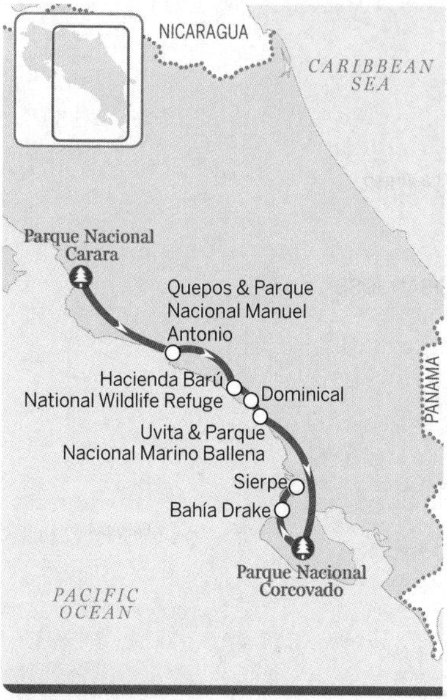

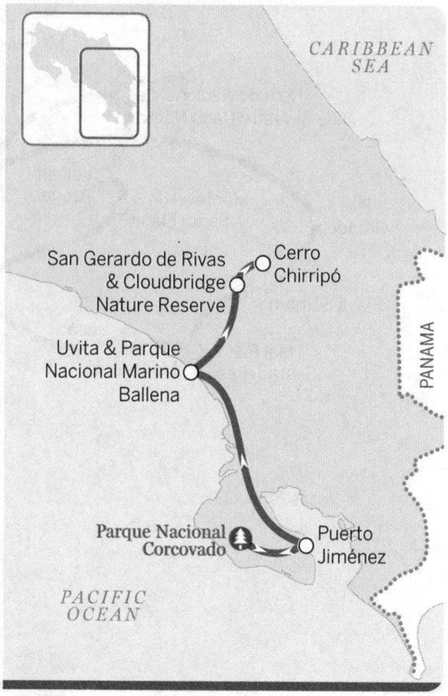

2 WEEKS Pacific Coast Explorer

Kick off your exploration in **Parque Nacional Carara**, home to enchanting scarlet macaws, and spend a few hours hiking the coast. Head south to **Quepos**, a convenient base for the country's most popular national park, **Parque Nacional Manuel Antonio**. Sweeping down to meet the sea, the rainforest here provides a refuge for rare animals, including the endangered squirrel monkey.

Continue south to **Hacienda Barú National Wildlife Refuge** for sloth spotting, then head further south to **Dominical** in search of waves. For deserted beach wandering, continue to **Uvita**, where you can look for whales spouting offshore at **Parque Nacional Marino Ballena**.

On the far-flung Península de Osa, journey through **Parque Nacional Corcovado**, the country's top national park for wildlife viewing. Emerge at the northern end in lush and remote **Bahía Drake** to swim in paradisiacal coves in the dripping rainforest. Return to civilization by boat through Central America's longest stretch of mangroves, arriving in **Sierpe** to see mysterious stone spheres left by ancient peoples.

2 WEEKS Southern Costa Rica

The best itinerary for adventurers, Southern Costa Rica represents the wilder side of the country.

Either head down the Pacific coast or fly into **Puerto Jiménez**, gateway to Península de Osa. Here you can spend a day or so kayaking the mangroves and soaking up the charm.

Parque Nacional Corcovado is the crown jewel of the country's national parks. Spend a few days exploring jungle and beach trails with a local guide, whose expert eyes will spot tapirs and rare birds; trekkers willing to get down and dirty can tackle a through-hike of the park.

Return to Puerto Jiménez and travel up the Pacific Costanera Sur to **Uvita**, where you can surf, snorkel and look for whales at **Parque Nacional Marino Ballena**.

Then it's off to the mountains. Link together buses for **San Gerardo de Rivas**, where you can spend a day acclimating to the altitude and hiking through the **Cloudbridge Nature Reserve**. End the trip with an exhilarating two-day adventure to the top of **Cerro Chirripó**, Costa Rica's highest peak.

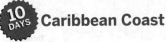

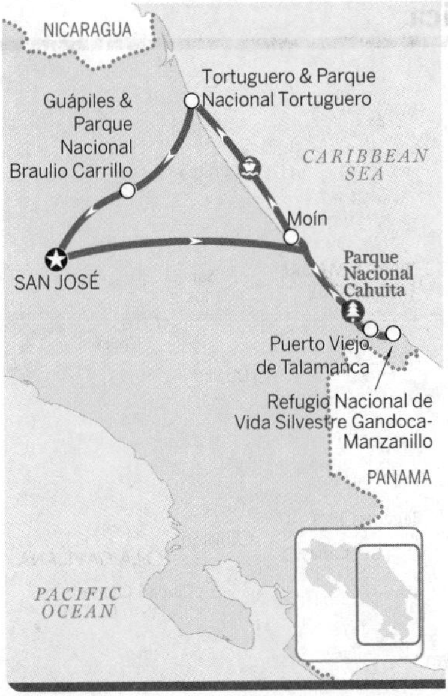

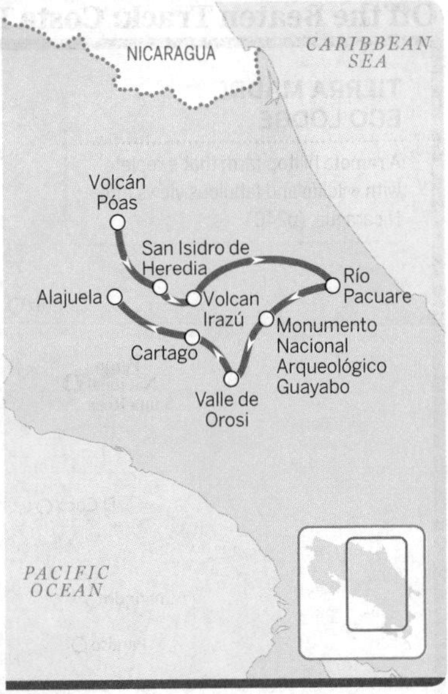

10 DAYS Caribbean Coast

Latin beats change to Caribbean rhythms as you explore the 'other Costa Rica.'

Hop on an eastbound bus out of **San José** to Cahuita, capital of Afro-Caribbean culture and gateway to **Parque Nacional Cahuita**. Decompress in this mellow village before moving on to **Puerto Viejo de Talamanca**, this coast's center for nightlife, cuisine and all-round positive vibes.

Rent a bicycle and ride to Manzanillo, jumping-off point for snorkeling, kayaking and hiking in **Refugio Nacional de Vida Silvestre Gandoca-Manzanillo**.

Heading north, grab a boat from **Moín** to travel up the canal-ribboned coast to **Tortuguero**. In season you can spy on nesting green and leatherback turtles. But it's worth a visit any time of year to canoe the mangrove-lined canals of **Parque Nacional Tortuguero**, Costa Rica's mini Amazon.

After spotting your fill of wildlife, head inland via water taxi and bus through the tiny town of Cariari to **Guápiles**. This is an ideal base for gazing at open farmland and exploring **Parque Nacional Braulio Carrillo** before returning to San José.

10 DAYS Central Valley

The Central Valley circuit centers on volcanoes, waterfalls and strong coffee. Begin the scenic route by glimpsing into the crater of the active **Volcán Póas**, with its turquoise lake.

Move on to **San Isidro de Heredia** for a close encounter with rescued baby sloths and toucans, and a taste of the region's chocolate history. Hike around slumbering **Volcán Irazú** and peer right into its crater. Known as 'the collosus', at 3432m it's the highest volcano in Costa Rica. With geological and culinary wonders covered, raft along the **Río Pacuare**, one of the country's best white-water runs.

Next, visit **Monumento Nacional Arqueológico Guayabo**, the country's only significant archaeological site, protecting ancient petroglyphs and aqueducts. Finally, swing south into the **Valle de Orosi**, Costa Rican coffee country, and take the caffeinated 32km loop passing the country's oldest church and endless green hills. End on a spiritual note at Costa Rica's grandest colonial-era temple, the Basílica de Nuestra Señora de Los Ángeles in **Cartago**, before finishing in **Alajuela**.

Off the Beaten Track: Costa Rica

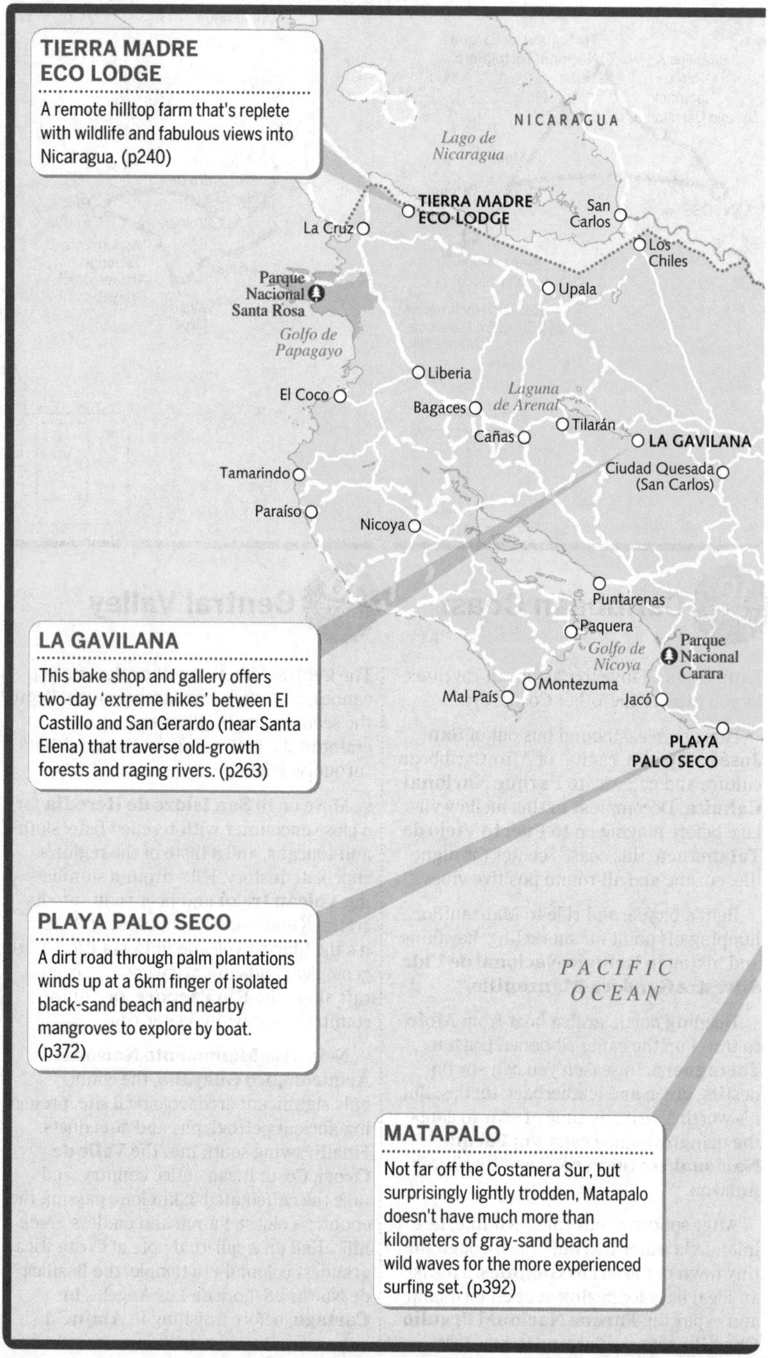
TIERRA MADRE ECO LODGE
A remote hilltop farm that's replete with wildlife and fabulous views into Nicaragua. (p240)
LA GAVILANA
This bake shop and gallery offers two-day 'extreme hikes' between El Castillo and San Gerardo (near Santa Elena) that traverse old-growth forests and raging rivers. (p263)
PLAYA PALO SECO
A dirt road through palm plantations winds up at a 6km finger of isolated black-sand beach and nearby mangroves to explore by boat. (p372)
MATAPALO
Not far off the Costanera Sur, but surprisingly lightly trodden, Matapalo doesn't have much more than kilometers of gray-sand beach and wild waves for the more experienced surfing set. (p392)
NICARAGUA
Lago de Nicaragua
TIERRA MADRE ECO LODGE
San Carlos
La Cruz
Los Chiles
Parque Nacional Santa Rosa
Upala
Golfo de Papagayo
Liberia
El Coco
Laguna de Arenal
Bagaces
Tilarán
Cañas
LA GAVILANA
Ciudad Quesada (San Carlos)
Tamarindo
Paraíso
Nicoya
Puntarenas
Paquera
Golfo de Nicoya
Parque Nacional Carara
Montezuma
Mal País
Jacó
PLAYA PALO SECO
PACIFIC OCEAN

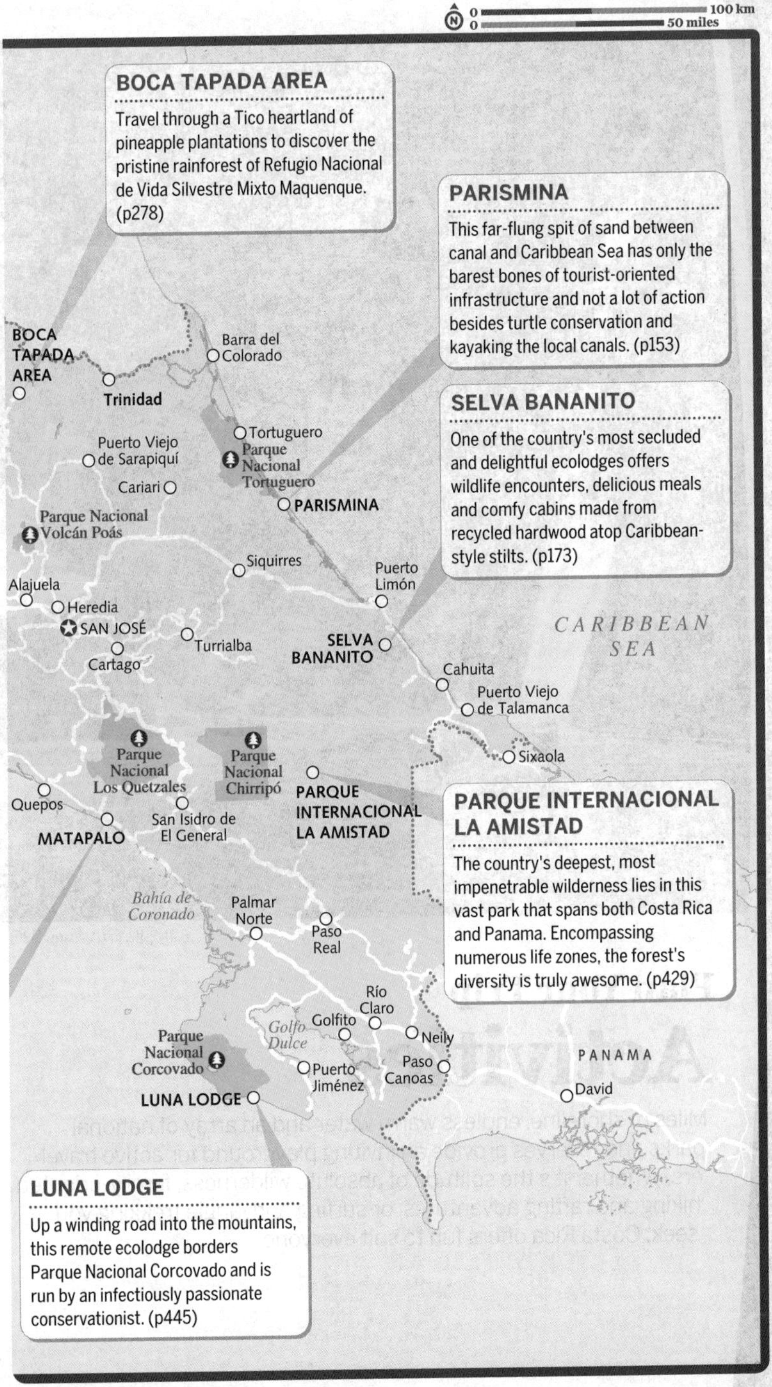

BOCA TAPADA AREA

Travel through a Tico heartland of pineapple plantations to discover the pristine rainforest of Refugio Nacional de Vida Silvestre Mixto Maquenque. (p278)

PARISMINA

This far-flung spit of sand between canal and Caribbean Sea has only the barest bones of tourist-oriented infrastructure and not a lot of action besides turtle conservation and kayaking the local canals. (p153)

SELVA BANANITO

One of the country's most secluded and delightful ecolodges offers wildlife encounters, delicious meals and comfy cabins made from recycled hardwood atop Caribbean-style stilts. (p173)

PARQUE INTERNACIONAL LA AMISTAD

The country's deepest, most impenetrable wilderness lies in this vast park that spans both Costa Rica and Panama. Encompassing numerous life zones, the forest's diversity is truly awesome. (p429)

LUNA LODGE

Up a winding road into the mountains, this remote ecolodge borders Parque Nacional Corcovado and is run by an infectiously passionate conservationist. (p445)

Rafting the Río Pacuare (p136)

Plan Your Trip

Activities

Miles of shoreline, endless warm water and an array of national parks and reserves provide an inviting playground for active travelers. Whether it's the solitude of absolute wilderness, family-oriented hiking and rafting adventures, or surfing and jungle trekking you seek, Costa Rica offers fun to suit everyone.

KEVIN SCHAFER/GETTY IMAGES ©

When to Do What

Costa Rica is a year-round outdoor activity destination. Seasonal rains or lack thereof will affect some activities – to varying degrees – but most are viable at any time of year.

Dry Season (December to April)

Trails are not as muddy during the dry season, which makes for easier hiking, mountain biking and horseback riding. These months also see strong and steady winds for windsurfing and kitesurfing.

Rainy Season (May to November)

White-water rafting is best when the rivers are high, which is from June to October.

Year-round

Heavy rains and river run-off affect visibility for snorkeling near the shore, but off-shore snorkeling and diving can be good year-round. There are also waves to ride all year long, but choose your destination wisely. Surf's up on the Pacific Coast in the late rainy season, while the Caribbean surfers are riding high from November to May.

Hiking & Trekking

Hiking opportunities around Costa Rica are seemingly endless. With mountains, canyons, dense jungles, cloud forests and two coastlines, this is one of Central America's best and most varied hiking destinations.

Hikes come in a wide spectrum of difficulty. At tourist-packed destinations shorter trails are clearly marked and sometimes paved. This is fantastic if you're traveling with kids or aren't confident about route finding. For long-distance trekking there are many more options throughout the country.

Opportunities for moderate hiking are typically plentiful in most parks and reserves. For the most part, you can rely on signs and maps for orientation, though it helps to have some navigational experience. Good hiking shoes, plenty of water and confidence in your abilities may enable you to combine several shorter day hikes into a lengthier expedition. Tourist-information centers at park entrances are great resources for planning your intended route.

Costa Rica's top challenges are scaling Cerro Chirripó (p421) and traversing Corcovado (p440), both of which normally take at least two days of hiking. In these cases, lodges in the parks mean that camping is not required. Penetrating deep into the heart of La Amistad (p429) – another off-the-beaten-track adventure – does require camping. While Chirripó can be undertaken independently, local guides are required for most of La Amistad and for all of Corcovado.

Surfing

Point and beach breaks, lefts and rights, reefs and river mouths, warm water and year-round waves make Costa Rica a favorite surfing destination. For the most part, the Pacific coast has bigger swells and better waves during the latter part of the rainy season, but the Caribbean cooks from November to May. Basically, there's a wave waiting to be surfed at any time of year.

For the uninitiated, lessons are available at almost all of the major surfing destinations – especially popular towns include Jacó, Dominical, Playa Sámara and Tamarindo on the Pacific coast. Surfing definitely has a steep learning curve, and it can be dangerous if the currents are strong. With that said, the sport is accessible to children and novices, though it's advisable to start with a lesson. Always inquire locally about conditions before you paddle out.

Throughout Costa Rica waves are big (though not massive), and many offer hollow and fast rides that are perfect for intermediates. As a bonus, Costa Rica is one of the few places on the planet where you can surf two different oceans in the same day. Advanced surfers with plenty of experience can contend with some of the world's most famous waves. The top ones include Ollie's Point and Witch's Rock, off the coast of the Sector Santa Rosa (p235) of the Área de Conservación Guanacaste (featured in *Endless Summer II*); Mal País and Santa Teresa (p332), with a groovy scene to match the powerful waves; Playa Hermosa (p333), whose bigger, faster curls attract a more determined (and experienced) crew of wave chasers; Pavones (p459), a legendary long left across the sweet waters of the Golfo Dulce; and the infamous Salsa Brava in Puerto Viejo de Talamanca (p176), for experts only.

Wildlife-Watching & Birding

Costa Rica's biodiversity is legendary, and the country delivers unparalleled opportunities for birding and wildlife-watching. Most people are already familiar with the most famous, yet commonly spotted, animals. You'll recognize monkeys bounding through the treetops, sloths clinging to branches and toucans gliding beneath the canopy. Young children, even if they have been to the zoo dozens of times, typically love the thrill of spotting creatures in the wild. Keeping checklists is a fun way to add an educational element to your travels.

A quality pair of binoculars is highly recommended and can really make the difference between far-off movement and a veritable face-to-face encounter. Most guides carry a spotting scope, which they will set up when they sight a bird or creature, so that clients can get a good look and even take photographs.

FRANCESCO RICCARDO IACOMINO/GETTY IMAGES ©

Kayaking in Parque Nacional Tortuguero (p156)

TOP SPOTS TO SEE WILDLIFE

Parque Nacional Corcovado (p440) At the heart of the Península de Osa, this is the country's richest wildlife area.

Parque Nacional Tortuguero (p155) Canals and waterways provide excellent birdwatching.

Refugio Nacional de Vida Silvestre Caño Negro (p272) Expansive wetlands provide a refuge for reptiles and avians.

Monteverde & Santa Elena (p197) These reserves provide unique insight into the cloud-forest ecosystem.

Boca Tapada Area (p278) The steamy rivers near the Nicaraguan border are a birder's and fisher's delight.

Río Tárcoles (p360) Top spot for crocodile spotting and cruising on birdwatching tours.

How to Make it Happen

Costa Rica is brimming with wildlife at every turn, but sometimes it takes an experienced guide to help you notice it.

Aratinga Tours (www.aratinga-tours.com; tours from US$1935) Some of the best bird tours in the country are led by Belgian ornithologist Pieter Westra.

Tropical Feathers (☎2771-9686; www.costaricabirdingtours.com; 10-day tours from US$3959)

SHELLYGRAPHY/SHUTTERSTOCK ©

Yoga (p49)

Local owner and guide Noel Ureña has two decades of experience leading birding tours.

Birding Eco Tours (in USA 937-238-0254; www.birdingecotours.com; 9-day tours around US$4000) An international bird-tour company with highly entertaining and qualified guides in Costa Rica.

Windsurfing & Kitesurfing

Laguna de Arenal (p265) is the nation's undisputed windsurfing (and kitesurfing) epicenter. From December to April winds are strong and steady, averaging 20 knots in the dry season, often with maximum winds of 30 knots, and windless days are a rarity. The lake has a year-round water temperature of 18°C (64°F) to 21°C (70°F), with 1m-high swells.

For warmer water and equally consistent winds, try Playa Copal (p241) in the less visited Bahía Salinas.

White-Water Rafting & Kayaking

White-water rafting has remained one of Costa Rica's top outdoor pursuits since the '80s. Ranging from family-friendly Class I riffles to nearly unnavigable Class V rapids, the country's rivers offer highly varied experiences.

First-time runners are catered for year-round, while seasoned enthusiasts arrive en masse during the wildest months from June to October. There is also much regional variation, with gentler rivers located near Manuel Antonio along the central Pacific coast, and world-class runs along the Río Pacuare near Turrialba in the Central Valley. Since all white-water rafting in Costa Rica requires the presence of a certified guide, you will need to book trips through a reputable tour agency. No matter the run, you'll get totally soaked and tossed about, so bring your sense of adventure, but no fancy clothes or jewelry.

The tiny village of La Virgen in the northern lowlands is the unofficial kayaking capital of Costa Rica and the best spot

ASCENT XMEDIA/GETTY IMAGES ©

Canopy tour, La Fortuna (p253)

to hook up with other paddlers. The neighboring Río Sarapiquí has an impressive variety of runs that cater to all ages and skill levels.

With 1228km of coastline, two gulfs and plentiful mangrove estuaries, Costa Rica is also an ideal destination for sea kayaking. This is a great way for paddlers to access remote areas and catch glimpses of rare birds and wildlife. Access varies considerably, and is largely dependent on tides and currents.

How to Make it Happen

June to October are considered peak season for river rafting and kayaking, though some rivers offer good runs all year. Government regulation of outfitters is not particularly stringent , so ask lots of questions about your guide's water safety, emergency and medical training.

River kayaking can be organized in conjunction with white-water-rafting trips if you are experienced; sea kayaking is popular year-round.

Aguas Bravas (p282) Near Chilamate, this is the top outfitter on Costa Rica's best white water.

Exploradores Outdoors (p176) This outfit offers one- and two-day trips on the Ríos Pacuare, Reventazón and Sarapiquí.

Green Rivers (p282) A young and fun Sarapiquí-based outfit working out of the Posada Andrea Cristina.

Pineapple Tours (p395) Exciting half-day kayaking trips go through caves and mangrove channels.

H2O Adventures (p375) Arranges two- and five-day adventures on the Río Savegre.

Ríos Tropicales (Map p76; ☎2233-6455, in USA 866-722-8273; www.riostropicales.com; Calle 38 btwn Avs 3 & 5, San José; day tours from $96) Multiday adventures on the Río Pacuare and two days of kayaking in Tortuguero.

Canopy Tours

The most vibrant life in the rainforest takes place at canopy level, but with trees extending 30m to 60m in height, the average human has a hard time getting a look at what's going on up there. You will find canopy tours everywhere in Costa Rica, most of which include zipline cables and hanging bridges. The most elaborate facilities also have 'Superman' cables (allowing you to fly like the Man of Steel) and 'Tarzan' swings. Canopy tours originated in Costa Rica in Monteverde (p201), and you'll still find the biggest selection of operations there.

TOP SPOTS TO RIDE WATER

Turrialba (p136) Home to the country's most popular rafting rivers, the Pacuare and Reventazón.

La Virgen (p282) The base town for rafting and kayaking on the Río Sarapiquí.

Parque Nacional Tortuguero (p156) Boasts 310 sq km of wildlife-rich and kayak-friendly lagoons and canals.

Golfo Dulce Explore the mangroves by kayak, setting off on tours from Puerto Jiménez (p447) or north of town in La Palma (p453).

Surfer's Map

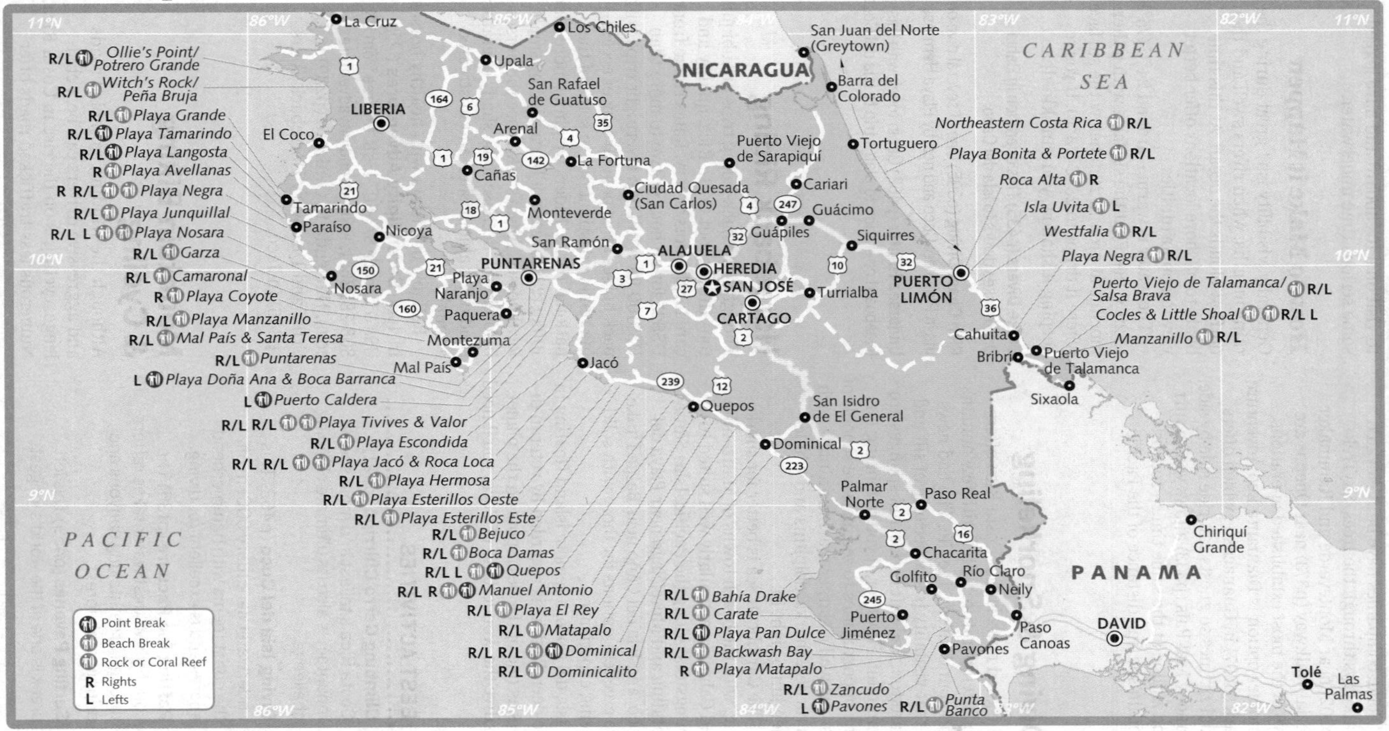
0 100 km
0 50 miles
CARIBBEAN SEA
PACIFIC OCEAN
NICARAGUA
PANAMA
R/L Ollie's Point/ Potrero Grande
R/L Witch's Rock/ Peña Bruja
R/L Playa Grande
R/L Playa Tamarindo
R/L Playa Langosta
R Playa Avellanas
R R/L Playa Negra
R/L Playa Junquillal
R/L L Playa Nosara
R/L Garza
R/L Camaronal
R Playa Coyote
R/L Playa Manzanillo
R/L Mal País & Santa Teresa
R/L Puntarenas
L Playa Doña Ana & Boca Barranca
L Puerto Caldera
R/L R/L Playa Tivives & Valor
R/L Playa Escondida
R/L R/L Playa Jacó & Roca Loca
R/L Playa Hermosa
R/L Playa Esterillos Oeste
R/L Playa Esterillos Este
R/L Bejuco
R/L Boca Damas
R/L L Quepos
R/L R Manuel Antonio
R/L Playa El Rey
R/L Matapalo
R/L R/L Dominical
R/L Dominicalito
R/L Bahía Drake
R/L Carate
R/L Playa Pan Dulce
R/L Backwash Bay
R Playa Matapalo
R/L Zancudo
L Pavones
R/L Punta Banco
Northeastern Costa Rica R/L
Playa Bonita & Portete R/L
Roca Alta R
Isla Uvita L
Westfalia R/L
Playa Negra R/L
Puerto Viejo de Talamanca/ Salsa Brava R/L
Cocles & Little Shoal R/L L
Manzanillo R/L
La Cruz
Los Chiles
Upala
San Rafael de Guatuso
LIBERIA
El Coco
Arenal
La Fortuna
Cañas
Tamarindo
Paraíso
Nicoya
Monteverde
Ciudad Quesada (San Carlos)
Puerto Viejo de Sarapiquí
San Juan del Norte (Greytown)
Barra del Colorado
Tortuguero
Cariari
Guácimo
Guápiles
Siquirres
San Ramón
ALAJUELA
HEREDIA
SAN JOSÉ
CARTAGO
Turrialba
PUERTO LIMÓN
PUNTARENAS
Playa Naranjo
Paquera
Nosara
Montezuma
Mal País
Jacó
Quepos
San Isidro de El General
Dominical
Palmar Norte
Paso Real
Chacarita
Golfito
Río Claro
Neily
Puerto Jiménez
Pavones
Paso Canoas
Cahuita
Bribrí
Puerto Viejo de Talamanca
Sixaola
Chiriquí Grande
DAVID
Tolé
Las Palmas
Point Break
Beach Break
Rock or Coral Reef
R Rights
L Lefts

Some companies have built elevated walkways through the trees. SkyTrek (p202) near Monteverde and Rainmaker Aerial Walkway (p373) near Quepos are two of the most established operations. Another option is Diamante Eco Adventure Park (p297) in Guanacaste, which offers dual ziplines so guests can ride side by side. Canopy Mal País (p333) allows you to surf and zipline at the same time – sort of! – within spitting distance of the Pacific.

Diving & Snorkeling

The good news is that Costa Rica offers body-temperature water with few humans and abundant marine life. The bad news is that visibility is low because of silt and plankton, and soft corals and sponges are dominant. However, if you're looking for fine opportunities to see massive schools of fish, as well as larger marine animals such as turtles, sharks, dolphins and whales, then jump right in.

The Caribbean Sea is better for snorkeling, with the beach towns of Manzanillo and Cahuita particularly well suited to youngsters. Along the Pacific, Islas Santa Catalina and Murciélago near Playa del Coco, and Isla del Caño near Bahía Drake are excellent options for those with solid diving experience.

Isla del Coco, a remote island floating in the deep Pacific, is regarded by veteran divers as one of the best spots on the planet. To dive the wonderland of Coco, you'll need to visit on a liveaboard and have logged some serious time underwater.

How to Make it Happen

Generally, visibility isn't great during the rainy months, when rivers swell and their outflow clouds the ocean. At this time, boats to offshore locations offer better viewing opportunities.

The water is warm – around 24°C (75°F) to 29°C (84°F) at the surface, with a thermocline at around 20m below the surface where it drops to 23°C (73°F). If you're keeping it shallow, you can skin-dive.

Drake Divers (p435) This operation in Bahía Drake takes divers to Isla del Caño.

Rich Coast Diving (p395) One of several dive outfits in Playa del Coco and nearby Playa Hermosa.

Undersea Hunter (p462) Get in touch with this liveaboard operation to plan a trip to Isla del Coco.

BEST ACTIVITIES

Climbing Cerro Chirripó (p421) Costa Rica's tallest and most scenic mountain is also its ultimate climbing challenge.

Diving Isla del Coco (p462) This underwater sanctuary 500km off the coast teems with hammerhead sharks and is excellent for diving.

Rafting Río Pacuare (p136) The country's wildest water takes rafters through breathtaking canyons and dripping rainforest.

Surfing Pavones (p459) This left break is one of the world's longest.

Horseback Riding

Though horseback-riding trips are ubiquitous throughout Costa Rica, quality and care for the horses vary. Rates range from US$25 for an hour or two to more than US$100 for a full day. Overnight trips with pack horses are a popular way of accessing remote destinations in some of the national parks. Riders weighing more than 100kg (220lb) cannot be carried by small local horses. Always ask to see the horses beforehand, because some shady operators send out malnourished and mistreated animals.

Reliable outfitters with healthy horses include **Serendipity Adventures** (☎in USA & Canada 877-507-1358, toll free from UK 808-281-8681; www.serendipityadventures.com), Hacienda El Cenizaro (p239) in La Cruz, and Discovery Horseback Tours (p366) in Jacó.

Mountain Biking & Cycling

Although the winding, potholed roads and aggressive drivers can be a challenge, cycling is on the rise in Costa Rica. Numerous less-trafficked roads offer

ETHAN DANIELS/SHUTTERSTOCK ©

Diving, Parque Nacional Isla del Coco (p462)

plenty of adventure – from scenic mountain paths with sweeping views to rugged trails that take riders through streams and past volcanoes.

The best long-distance rides are along the Pacific coast's Interamericana, which has a decent shoulder and is relatively flat, and on the road from Montezuma to the Reserva Natural Absoluta Cabo Blanco on the southern Península de Nicoya.

Mountain biking has taken off in recent years and some tour operators can organize guided rides, including Ecoaventuras (p135) in Turrialba, Aventuras del Sarapiquí (p282) in Chilamate, and Green Rivers (p282) in Puerto Viejo de Sarapiquí.

Near Arenal there are trail networks at Sky Adventures (p263) in El Castillo and Arenal 1968 (p261). Near Volcán Miravalles, Río Perdido (p224) also has an extensive network of biking trails on its gorgeous grounds.

Yoga

Something about yoga and Costa Rica just go together: whether people come here solely to relax or to beat up their bodies in the surf or on the trails, nothing seems to be a better cure-all than a session on the mat. Along the beaches, schools are catering to this need better than ever (and the fantastic views at many places are part of the allure). Drop in for a class or stay for a week; you'll leave with body and mind refreshed. Some favorites include the following:

- Bodhi Tree (p320)
- Anamaya Resort (p344)
- Casa Zen (p336)
- Yoga Studio at Nautilus (p336)
- Danyasa Yoga Arts School (p395)
- Blue Osa Yoga Retreat (p450)

Plan Your Trip

Family Travel

With such a dizzying array of experiences and close encounters in Costa Rica – wildlife, waves, ziplines and volcanoes – the biggest challenge might be choosing where to go. Fortunately, each region has its attractions, and kids of all ages will find epic adventure awaiting them.

Keeping Costs Down

Accommodations

Many hostels and budget lodgings have accommodations that are suitable for families with children. Lodges and resorts often offer discounts up to 50% for children under 12 years old. Look also for family packages, which include activities that are appealing for children.

Transportation

Children under the age of 12 receive discounts of up to 25% on domestic flights. Children under two usually fly free (provided they sit on a parent's lap). If you're renting a car, you're better off bringing your own infant car seat, as they are not always available or in good repair at the car rental agencies.

Eating

Consider renting accommodations with kitchen facilities (shared or private) to avoid eating out all the time. Children's menus are not common at local restaurants.

Activities

Some tour companies and nature reserves offer reduced rates for children and students, normally 25% to 50% off the full price.

Children Will Love...

Wildlife-Watching

Parque Nacional Manuel Antonio (p388) Tiny and easily accessible; a walk through this park usually yields sightings of squirrel monkeys, iguanas and coatis.

Parque Nacional Cahuita (p174) Seeing white-faced capuchins is almost guaranteed along the beach trail.

Parque Nacional Tortuguero (p155) Boat tours through Tortuguero's canals uncover wildlife all around, but staying in any jungle lodge outside the village will reveal the same.

Refugio Nacional de Vida Silvestre Ostional (p323) One of Costa Rica's truly magical experiences is watching sea turtles lay their eggs under the cover of night.

Refugio Nacional de Vida Silvestre Caño Negro (p272) Spy on birds, iguanas and caimans on a boat trip through the waterways of this national park.

Animal Sanctuaries

Frog's Heaven, Horquetas (p286) A frog-lover's heaven, this tropical garden is filled with all sorts of brightly colored (and transparent!) amphibians, including the iconic red-eyed tree frog.

Ecocentro Danaus, La Fortuna (p248) Walk the trails to look for monkeys and sloths, visit a pond with caimans and turtles, delight in the butterfly garden and watch frogs in the ranarium (frog pond).

Jaguar Centro de Rescate, Playa Chiquita (p186) No jaguars were here at the time of research, but other attractions include howler monkeys, baby sloths, colorful snakes, raptors and frogs.

Alturas Wildlife Sanctuary, Dominical (p394) Meet various rescued critters here, from macaws and monkeys to Bubba the famous coatimundi.

Beaches

Playa Pelada, Nosara area (p318) This low-key beach has little wave action and big, intriguing boulders.

Playa Carrillo, near Sámara (p329) South of family-friendly Sámara, this beach can be all yours during the week and convivially crowded with Tico families on the weekends.

Parque Nacional Marino Ballena, Pacific coast (p404) A yawning stretch of white-sand, jungle-fringed beach, a sand spit shaped like a whale's tail at low tide, and the chance to see whales spouting offshore.

Playa Manzanillo, Mal País & Santa Teresa (p333) Beautiful, jungle-backed beach from here to Punta Mona (about as far south as you can go before you have to start bushwhacking).

Aquatic Adventures

One Love Surf School, Puerto Viejo de Talamanca (p177) One of many surf schools that offers lessons designed for little ones. Kids' lessons are also offered at beginner beaches in Jacó and Playa Tamarindo.

Parque Nacional Volcán Póas, Central Valley (p113) Peer into a volcano's crater at this national park with plenty of trails suitable for children (and even strollers).

Canopy Tours, Monteverde (p201) Kids as young as five years old can fly across the tree tops on a zipline, while younger children can explore the treetops on hanging bridges.

Llanos de Cortés, Bagaces (p239) The water is cool but refreshing at this beautiful waterfall pool, which is easy to reach and safe for swimming.

Edible Experiences

Tree House Restaurant & Cafe, Monteverde (p210) Gourmet dining at the top of a 100-year-old fig tree.

Finca Köbö, La Palma (p453) Learn all about the production of cacao and the making of chocolate, then sample the goods.

Antojos de Maiz, San Isidro (p417) Try a *chorreada*, a sweet corn pancake topped with a dollop of sour cream.

Region by Region

San José

The capital is not Costa Rica's biggest draw in general, especially for families. Those who find themselves with time to kill in the capital will appreciate a decent variety of lodgings and restaurants, as well as a few kid-friendly museums and animal sanctuaries. See San José for Kids (p94) for details.

Central Valley & the Highlands

Peer into the center of highly active Volcán Poás (p113) – where a turquoise lake fills the crater. Wander the peculiar, blobby formations of abstract topiary in the sleepy hillside town of Zarcero (p118) and hand-feed hummingbirds and toucans at La Paz Waterfall Gardens (p114) before feeling the spray from five mighty cascades.

Arenal & the Northern Lowlands

La Fortuna (p248) is nonstop fun. Ziplining? Frog watching? Chocolate tasting? You'll run out of time before you run out of stuff to do. Finish with a safari float on the Sarapiquí (p282), a mellow day trip which allows you to relax on the rapids and check out the wildlife on the shore and in the trees.

Caribbean Coast

The mild waves on the reefs of Cahuita (p167) and Manzanillo (p189) are a perfect spot for first-time snorkelers: the colors of the fish and coral will wow them. A must-stop for animal lovers is the Jaguar Rescue Center (p186), while Ara Manzanillo's (p191) macaws are great – and green – too.

Northwest Costa Rica

The mysterious and ghostly cloud forests of Monteverde (p197) pique children's imaginations about the creatures that live there, while the area's specialty sanctuaries allow up-close observation. Monteverde is also a great place to try activities like ziplining and tree climbing. Elsewhere, the region steams with volcanoes and hot springs, which are accessible and fun to explore at Parque Nacional Rincón de la Vieja (p232) and Río Perdido (p224).

Península de Nicoya

Excellent beaches and family-friendly resorts make the Península de Nicoya an ideal destination for families. Tamarindo (p303) is the place for kids (and their folks) to take surfing lessons, while Refugio Nacional de Vida Silvestre Ostional (p323) offers the opportunity to see a turtle *arribada* (mass nesting), one of the country's most amazing and accessible wildlife experiences.

Central Pacific Coast

Easy trails lead past spider monkeys and sloths to great swimming beaches at Parque Nacional Manuel Antonio (p386), a busy but beautiful piece of coastal rainforest. Close encounters with prehistoric giants await on the Río Tárcoles, home to around 2000 crocodiles. At Marino Ballena (p404), Uvita's national park with a sandbank in the shape of a whale's tail, families can watch the annual migration of humpbacks.

Southern Costa Rica & Península de Osa

It's not easy to get here, but families who make the long journey will be rewarded with easy waterfall hikes, deserted beaches, mangrove boat tours and the country's best snorkeling. Enjoy the clouds without the crowds in lesser-known cloud-forest destinations like San Gerardo de Dota (p412) and San Gerardo de Rivas (p419).

Useful Resources

Lonely Planet Kids (www.lonelyplanet.com/kids) Loads of activities and great family-travel blog content.

Book: Let's Explore Jungle (https://shop.lonelyplanet.com) An activity book for ages five and up, jam-packed with facts, puzzles and pictures about tropical rainforests.

Book: First Words Spanish (https://shop.lonelyplanet.com) A beautifully illustrated introduction to the Spanish language for ages five to eight.

Two Weeks in Costa Rica (www.twoweeksincostarica.com) Travel tips from an expat couple and their two kids.

Kids' Corner

Say What?

Hello.	Hola. *o·la*
Goodbye.	Adiós. *a·dyos*
Thank you.	Gracias. *gra·syas*
My name is...	Me llamo... *me ya·mo ...*

Did You Know?

- Sloths come down from trees once a week to poop.
- Costa Rica has about 750,000 insect species.

Have You Tried?

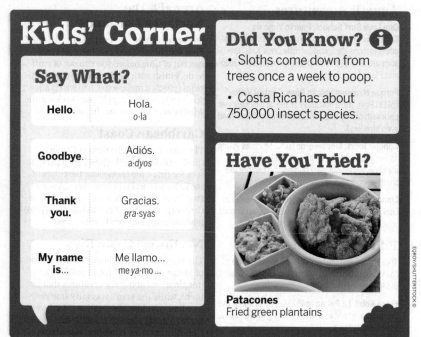

Patacones
Fried green plantains

EQROY/SHUTTERSTOCK ©

JEF_M/GETTY IMAGES ©

Dish including *gallo pinto* (fried rice and beans)

Plan Your Trip

Eat & Drink Like a Local

Traditional Costa Rican fare, for the most part, is comfort food, consisting largely of beans and rice, fried plantains, and the occasional slab of chicken, fish or beef. Recently locals have started to experiment more with the country's fresh, exotic and plentiful produce. The results have been inspiring and delicious.

The Year in Food

Food festivals are concentrated at the end of the rainy season, but the tropical Eden that is Costa Rica produces exotic and incredible fruits and vegetables and sells them in farmers markets year-round.

Rainy season (October and November)

Deliciously ripe mangoes and *mamon chino* (rambutan) abound, plus agricultural celebrations such as the Fiesta del Maíz (Festival of Corn) and the Feria Nacional de Pejibaye (National Peach Palm Market) take place.

Christmas (December)

Tamales, prepared with masa (corn meal soaked in lime), pork, potatoes and garlic and steamed in banana leaves, become a very big deal at this time of year.

Coffee harvest (September to January)

Many seasonal laborers from Nicaragua head down to pick *grano de oro* (the golden grain).

Food Experiences

Cheap Treats

Guanabana Also known as soursop, this sweet and sticky fruit should be purchased wherever you find it, and eaten with your hands.

Patí A flaky, Caribbean-style turnover filled with meat, onions, garlic and spicy goodness.

Street mango Sold in plastic bags with salt, lime juice and sometimes chili powder, this is the ultimate refreshment.

Pipa fría Find a vendor with a machete and an ice chest and they'll hack off the top of a coconut, stick a straw in it, and you're good to go, with a frosty, sweet treat.

Pejivalle The roasted peach-palm fruit is a roadside standard, delicious warm and salted, although Ticos like to add a dab of mayonnaise.

Dare to Try

Museo de Insectos (p72) This bug museum has its own kitchen, where guests are served meal worms and crickets with lots of salt and oregano.

Mondongo Tripe intestines are a *campesino* (farmer) favorite in Costa Rica, and they are served surprisingly spicy.

Meat on a stick Is it pork? Chicken? Beef? Who cares. On roadsides and at local fiestas, this mysterious Tico delicacy is just as good as it smells, even after the vendor uses a brush to apply spicy sauce.

Green Treats

Sibu Chocolate (p126) In San Isidro de Heredia, the history of chocolate illuminates and satisfies.

Feria Verde de Aranjuez (p96) San José's 'green market,' and an all-around winner for breakfast, produce, smoothies, everything.

Punta Mona (p192) The sprawling garden at this secluded eco-retreat near Manzanillo has one of the world's largest collections of edible tropical plants.

Costa Rica Cooking (p251) Help to whip up your own meal at this cooking school in La Fortuna, based on local and almost entirely organic produce.

Local Specialties

Breakfast for Ticos is usually *gallo pinto* (literally 'painted rooster'), a stir-fry of last night's rice and beans. When combined, the rice gets colored by the beans, and the mix obtains a speckled appearance. Served with eggs, cheese or *natilla* (sour cream), *gallo pinto* is cheap, filling and sometimes downright tasty. If you plan to spend the whole day surfing or hiking, you'll find that *gallo pinto* is great energy food.

Considering the extent of the coastline, it's no surprise that seafood is plentiful, and fish dishes are usually fresh and delicious. While it's not traditional Tico fare, *ceviche* is on most menus, usually made from *pargo* (red snapper), *dorado* (mahi-mahi), octopus or tilapia. The fish is marinated in lime juice with some combination of chilis, onions, tomatoes and herbs. Served chilled, it is a delectable way to enjoy fresh seafood. Emphasis is on 'fresh' here – it's raw fish, so if you have reason to believe it's not fresh, don't risk eating it. Sushi is also finding a foothold in many towns.

Food is not heavily spiced, unless you're having traditional Caribbean-style cuisine. Most local restaurants will lay out a bottle of Tabasco-style sauce, homemade salsa or Salsa Lizano, the Tico version of Worcestershire sauce and the 'secret' ingredient in *gallo pinto*. Some lay out a tempting jar of pickled hot peppers as well.

Most bars also offer the country's most popular *boca* (snack), *chifrijo,* which derives its name from two main ingredients: *chicharrón* (fried pork) and *frijoles* (beans). Diced tomatoes, spices, rice, tortilla chips and avocado are also thrown in for good measure. Fun fact about *chifrijo:* in 2014 a restaurant owner named Miguel Cordero claimed he officially invented it. He brought lawsuits against 49 businesses (including chain restaurants KFC and Spoon) and demanded a cool US$15 million in damages. So far he has not been able to collect.

Caribbean cuisine is the most distinctive in Costa Rica, having been steeped in indigenous, *criollo* (Creole) and Afro-Caribbean flavors. It's a welcome cultural change of pace after seemingly endless *casados*. Regional specialties include *rondón* (whose moniker comes from 'rundown,' meaning whatever the chef can run down), a spicy seafood gumbo; Caribbean-style rice and beans, made with red beans, coconut milk and curry spices; and *patí,* the Caribbean version of an *empanada* (savory turnover), the best street food, bus-ride snack and picnic treat.

MARCOS HONMA/GETTY IMAGES ©

Ceviche (fish marinated in lime juce with seasonings)

How to Eat & Drink

When to Eat

Breakfast for Ticos is taken in the early morning, usually from 6am to 8am, and consists of *gallo pinto*. Many hotels offer a tropical-style continental breakfast, usually toast with butter and jam, accompanied by fresh fruit. American-style breakfasts are also available in many eateries.

A midday lunch (served between 11:30am and 2:30pm) at most *sodas* (lunch counters) usually involves a *casado* (set meal; literally, 'married'), a cheap, well-balanced plate of rice, beans, meat, salad and sometimes *plátanos maduros* (fried sweet plantains) or *patacones* (twice-fried plantains), which taste something like french fries.

For dinner (6pm to 9pm), a *casado* is on offer at most restaurants. Upscale Tico establishments may serve *lomito* (a lean cut of steak) and dishes like *pescado en salsa palmito* (fish in heart-of-palm sauce). Some of the more forward-thinking eateries in San José may drop an experimental vegetable plate in front of you.

Where to Eat

The most popular eating establishment in Costa Rica is the *soda*. These are small, informal lunch counters dishing up a few daily *casados*. Other popular cheapies include the omnipresent fried- and rotisserie-chicken stands.

A regular *restaurante* is usually higher on the price scale and has slightly more atmosphere. Many *restaurantes* serve *casados,* while the fancier places refer to the set lunch as the *almuerzo ejecutivo* (literally 'executive lunch').

For something smaller, *pastelerías* and *panaderías* are shops that sell pastries and bread, while many bars serve *bocas* ('mouthfuls'; snack-sized portions of main meals).

THE GALLO PINTO CONTROVERSY

No other dish in Costa Rica inspires Ticos quite like their national dish of *gallo pinto*, that ubiquitous medley of rice, beans and spices. You might even hear Costa Ricans refer to themselves as *'más Tico que gallo pinto'* (literally, 'more Costa Rican than *gallo pinto*'). Exactly what type and amount of this holy trinity makes up authentic *gallo pinto* is the subject of intense debate, especially since it is also the national dish of neighboring Nicaragua.

Both countries claim that *gallo pinto* originated on their soil. Costa Rican lore holds that the dish and its iconic name were coined in 1930 in the neighborhood of San Sebastián, on the southern outskirts of San José. Nicaraguans claim that it was brought to the Caribbean coast of their country by Afro-Latinos long before it graced the palate of any Costa Rican.

The battle for the rights to this humble dish doesn't stop here, especially since the two countries can't even agree on the standard recipe. Nicaraguans traditionally prepare it with small red beans, whereas Costa Ricans swear by black beans. And let's not even get into the subtle complexities of balancing cilantro, salt and pepper.

Nicaragua officially holds the world record for making the biggest-ever pot of *gallo pinto*. On 15 September, 2007, a seething vat of it fed 22,000 people, which firmly entrenched Nicaragua's name next to *gallo pinto* in the *Guinness Book of World Records*. Costa Rica responded in 2009 by cooking an even more massive vat of the stuff, feeding a small crowd of 50,000. Though the event was not officially recognized as setting any records, that day's vat of *gallo pinto* warmed the hearts and bellies of many a proud Tico.

Vegetarians & Vegans

Costa Rica is a relatively comfortable place for vegetarians to travel. Rice and beans, as well as fresh fruit, are ubiquitous, but there's a lot more than that. The Happy Cow has a handy list of veggie restaurants nationwide (www.happycow.net/north_america/costa_rica). Visit farmers markets to sample what's in season: Costa Rica is a growers' paradise.

Most restaurants will make veggie *casados* on request and many places are now including them on the menu. These set meals usually include rice and beans, cabbage salad and one or two selections of variously prepared vegetables or legumes.

With the high influx of tourism, there are also many specialty vegetarian restaurants or restaurants with a veggie menu in San José and in tourist towns, and even vegans will find some options in these places. Lodges in remote areas that offer all-inclusive meal plans can accommodate vegetarians with advance notice.

Gluten-free, macrobiotic and raw-food-only travelers will have a tougher time, as there are fewer outlets accommodating those diets, although this is slowly changing. If you intend to keep to your diet, it's best to choose lodgings where you can prepare food yourself. Many towns have *macrobióticas* (health-food stores), but the selection varies. Fresh vegetables can be hard to come by in isolated areas and are often quite expensive, but farmers markets are cropping up throughout the country.

Habits & Custom

When you sit down to eat in a restaurant, it is polite to say *buenos días* (good morning), *buenas tardes* (good afternoon) or *buenas noches* (good evening) to the waitstaff and any people you might be sharing a table with – and it's generally good form to acknowledge everyone in the room this way. It is also polite to say *buen provecho*, which is the equivalent of *bon appetit*, at the start of the meal.

GUSTAVO MIRANDA HOLLEY/GETTY IMAGES ©

JALVAREZG/GETTY IMAGES ©

Top: *Casado* (cheap set meal)

Bottom: Cocoa fruit

Regions at a Glance

Where will your passion take you? Wildlife-watchers will be in heaven in Costa Rica, with an array of biospheres supporting a multitude of colorful species, including rare and beautiful birds, rainbow-hued frogs and nesting sea turtles. Surfers need no introduction to the plentiful and varied surf spots, and even rookies will find plenty of beginner breaks. If surfing's not your thing, you can take to the ocean, lakes or rivers in kayaks or white-water rafts. Hikers can traverse the thick, humid jungle of remote Corcovado, summit the country's highest peak, Cerro Chirripó, or just meander through cloud forests, around the rims of steaming volcanoes and along beachside trails on day hikes.

RAINER LESNIEWSKI/ALAMY STOCK PHOTO ©

BARRY VINCENT/ALAMY STOCK PHOTO ©

PAULA JONES/GETTY IMAGES ©

Top: Teatro Nacional (p65), San José
Centre: *Ceviche* with cassava and *pejibaye* chips
Bottom: Parque Nacional Marino Ballena (p404)

San José

Culture
Entertainment
Food

Museums

Gritty San José offers little in the way of architectural beauty, but it's what's on the inside that counts. This is the only place in Costa Rica with a dense concentration of museums, exhibiting everything from pre-Columbian gold frogs to the hottest multimedia installations by local contemporary artists.

Live Music

This is where you come to catch chamber music, international touring bands and up-and-coming local talent. The National Theater is a solid place to start.

Fine Restaurants

Argentinian, vegetarian, Asian-fusion and classic French cuisine shine in superb San José venues, bringing welcome diversity to *gallo pinto*–weary palates.

p63

Central Valley & Highlands

Geography
Adventure
Landscapes

Highland Countryside

Costa Rica's picturesque highlands are often overlooked in favor of its beaches. But here cows wander along twisting mountain roads, and villages boast organic farmers markets and parks with psychedelic topiaries.

White-Water Rafting

World-class white water awaits on the Río Pacuare, which is well worth a run for its cascade of thrilling rapids through a stunningly beauteous jungle gorge.

Volcanoes

Volcanoes here range from the wild and moderately active (Turrialba) to the heavily trafficked (Poás), showing off crater lakes and misty moonscapes. If you're lucky, one may send up smoke during a visit.

p105

Caribbean Coast

Culture
Ecology
Turtles

Afro-Caribbean Flavor

Set apart geographically and culturally from the rest of Costa Rica, the Caribbean coast has a distinct Afro-Caribbean feel of its own. Taste it in the coconut rice, hear it in the *patois* and live it in superchill Cahuita.

Wildlife

The waterlogged coast along the Caribbean teems with sloths, three of Costa Rica's four monkey species, crocodiles, caimans, poison-dart frogs, manatees, tucuxi dolphins and over 375 bird species.

Nesting Beaches

On this wild coast, turtle nesting is a serious business. In Parismina and Tortuguero leatherback, green and hawksbill turtles return to their natal beaches to nest – a breathtaking sight.

p141

Northwestern Costa Rica

Places to Stay
Outdoors
Landscapes

Ecolodges

The number of independent ecolodges means you can choose from cute B&Bs to spectacular working *fincas* (farms) or biological stations ensconced in forest, all far from the madding crowd.

Volcanoes

The Cordillera de Guanacaste is a volcanic mountain range that stretches across the country's northwestern corner, offering steaming peaks, soaking pools and hiking trails for adventurers to explore.

Cloud Forests

Northwestern cloud forests – studded with cathedral trees that sprout dozens of species and shelter valuable watersheds – birthed the ubiquitous canopy tour. You'll be in awe of *bosques* (forests) on volcanic slopes along the wild coast, peering over the continental divide.

p195

Arenal & Northern Lowlands

Culture
Wildlife
Outdoors

Local Perspective

This is where you'll discover real-life Costa Rica – face to face with cows and pigs on working *finca* homestays, on tours through rainforest preserves, and while paddling inky lagoons or mocha rivers with resident guides.

Birds

The humid swamps and lowland hills are thick with vegetation and teeming with hundreds of species of bird, from storks and egrets to toucans and macaws.

Water Sports & Fishing

Whether you plan to paddle frothing white water shadowed by looming forest, carve inland lakes by kayak, or hop in a motorboat to spot caimans or reel in tarpon, this is your Neverland.

p245

Península de Nicoya

Outdoors
Food
Yoga

Surfing & Diving

It's almost impossible to believe that there are so many waves on one spectacular peninsula, for novices and veterans alike. Below the surface, don't expect Caribbean clarity, but the mantas, bull sharks and pelagics will bend your brain.

Food

The creative kitchens that dot this coast source ingredients from local *fincas* and fishers, and dishes are prepared with *savoir faire*. Nicoya is one of the world's 'blue zones', with many residents living into their 90s and beyond thanks in part to the traditional diet.

Yoga

Nosara and Santa Teresa are standout locations with multiple studios, many with hard-to-beat vistas.

p289

Central Pacific Coast

Outdoors
National Park
Beaches

Surfing

From pros-only Playa Hermosa to beginner-friendly Dominical, the famous breaks of the Pacific coast bring blissful swells and tons of variety.

Parque Nacional Manuel Antonio

Manuel Antonio, Costa Rica's smallest and most popular national park, is a kid-friendly, beach-lined delight. Sure, there are crowds of people, but they're outnumbered by monkeys, coatis and tropical birds.

Parque Nacional Marino Ballena

It's a bit of a hike to get to Parque Nacional Marino Ballena, but those lucky few who find themselves on its empty beaches can scan the sparkling horizon for migrating whales. There's even a whale and dolphin festival in September.

p351

Southern Costa Rica & Península de Osa

Mountain Peak
Outdoors
Culture

Cerro Chirripó

Scaling ancient trails to the windswept peak of Chirripó is an adventure into a wholly different Costa Rica. The sunrise view from above the clouds is the brilliant highlight of this two-day excursion.

Hiking

Among the world's most biologically intense patches of green, this area represents a whopping 2.5% of the planet's biodiversity. Hiking Corcovado is a sublime trip into untamed tropical rainforest.

Indigenous Costa Rica

Travel deep into the Talamanca mountains or the Osa jungle to see how Costa Rica's indigenous citizens keep the country's ancient traditions alive.

p409

On the Road

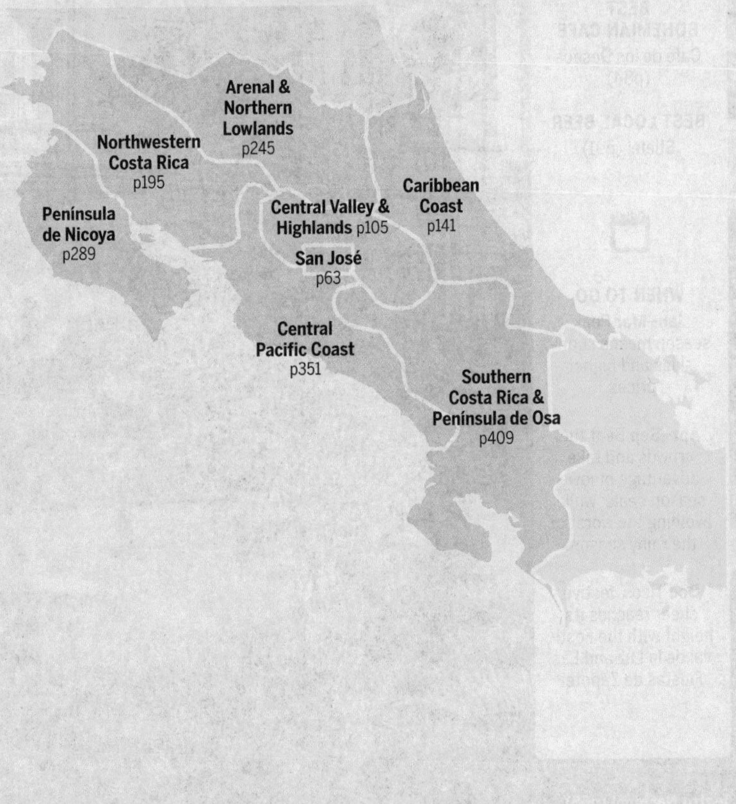

Arenal & Northern Lowlands p245
Northwestern Costa Rica p195
Caribbean Coast p141
Península de Nicoya p289
Central Valley & Highlands p105
San José p63
Central Pacific Coast p351
Southern Costa Rica & Península de Osa p409

AT A GLANCE

POPULATION
344,851

FAST FACT
Approximately one third of the country's population lives in the metropolitan San José area.

BEST URBAN BIRDING
Barrio Bird Walking Tours (p73)

BEST BOHEMIAN CAFE
Café de los Deseos (p84)

BEST LOCAL BEER
Stiefel (p91)

WHEN TO GO

Jan–Mar Peak season means sunny skies and higher prices.

Apr–Sep Beat the crowds and take advantage of low-season deals, while avoiding the worst of the rainy season.

Dec Ticos' festive cheer reaches its height with the Festival de la Luz and Las Fiestas de Zapote.

Teatro Nacional (p65)
MILOSK50/SHUTTERSTOCK ©

San José

San José – aka Chepe – is the intellectual, cultural and culinary capital of Costa Rica (and its actual capital). Jazz pours out of uptown cafes while poets recite at bookstores, hotels and museums alike. Old-school workers' *cantinas* nestle side by side with modern fusion eateries; student bars jostle with artisanal breweries; and there's a bevy of lovely urban parks. Take your time exploring historical neighborhoods such as Barrio Amón, where colonial mansions have been converted into contemporary art galleries, and Barrio Escalante, the city's gastronomic epicenter. Stroll with shoppers at the farmers market, bump elbows at the bustling Mercado Central, join the Sunday crowds in Parque Metropolinato La Sabana and dance at the city's vibrant clubs.

INCLUDES

San José Highlights

1 Teatro Nacional (p95) Savoring classical music and dance in the beaux-arts interior.

2 Feria Verde de Aranjuez (p96) Scouring the lively farmers market for local treats.

3 Barrio Amón (p67) Wandering around colonial mansions converted into coffee shops and art galleries.

4 Estadio Nacional de Costa Rica (p95) Attending a soccer match or concert in this clam-shaped arena.

5 Museo del Jade (p65) Exploring the vast universe of carved stone treasures.

6 Barrio Escalante (p72) Indulging your taste buds at fine restaurants and bars.

7 Museo de Oro Precolombino y Numismática (p66) Admiring Costa Rica's artistic and indigenous traditions.

8 Mercado Central (p66) Absorbing the riot of colors, sounds and smells in this labyrinth of foodstuffs.

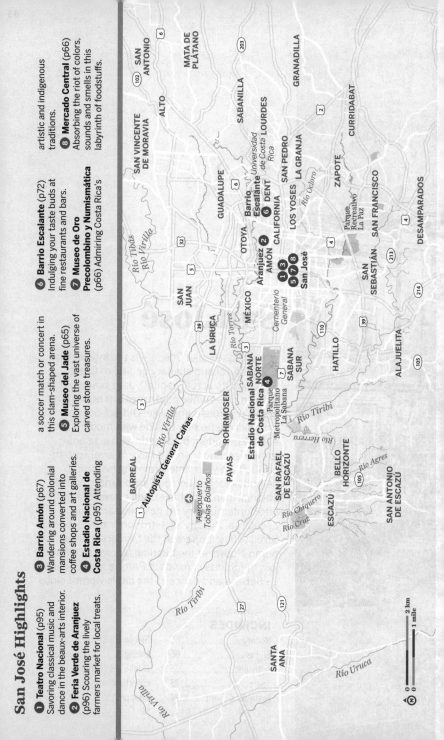

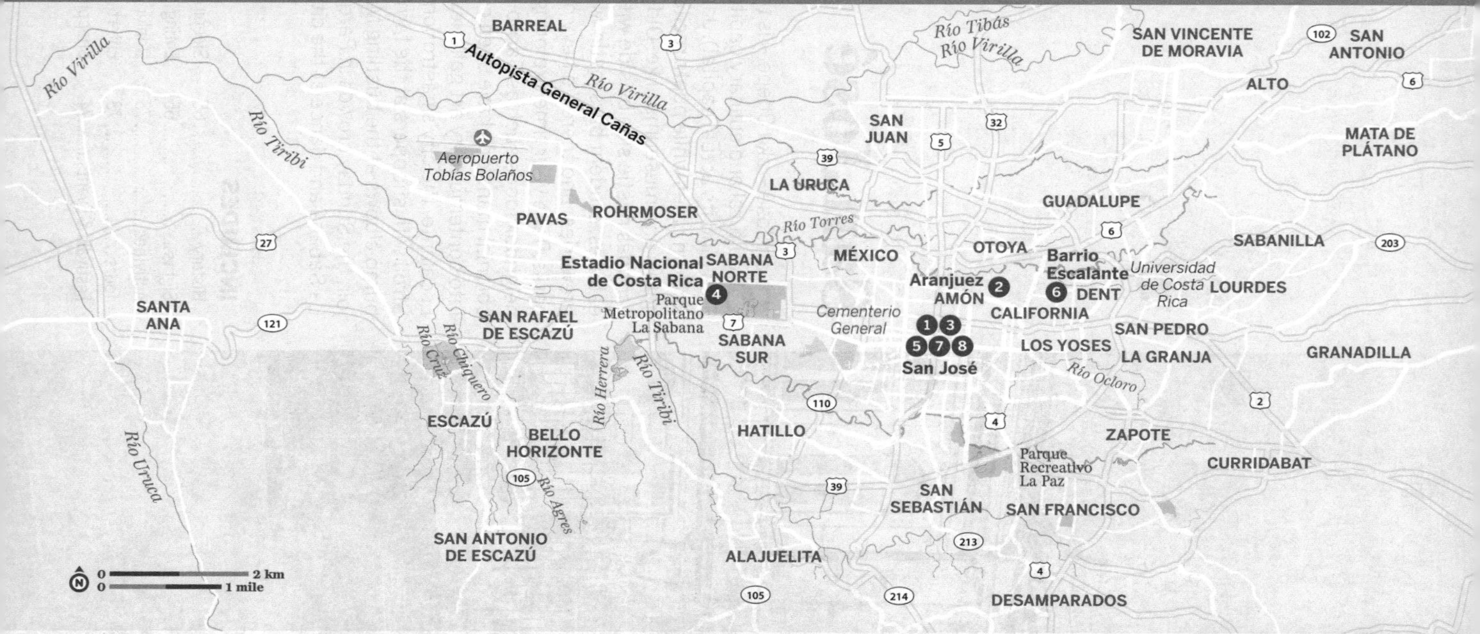

History

For much of the colonial period, San José played second fiddle to the bigger and relatively more established Cartago, a city whose origins date from 1563 and which, during the colonial era, served as the provincial capital. Villanueva de la Boca del Monte del Valle de Abra – as San José was first known – was not founded until 1737, when the Catholic Church issued an edict that forced the populace to settle near churches (attendance was down).

The city remained a backwater for decades, though it did experience some growth as a stop in the tobacco-trading route during the late 18th century. Following independence in 1821, rival factions in Cartago and San José each attempted to assert regional supremacy. The struggle ended in 1823 when the two sides faced off at the Battle of Ochomongo. San José emerged the victor and subsequently declared itself capital.

Despite its new status, the city remained a quiet agricultural center into the 20th century. The calm was shattered in the 1940s, when parts of San José served as a battlefield in the civil war of 1948, one of the bloodiest conflicts in Costa Rica's history. Out of that clash, José Figueres Ferrer of the Partido Liberación Nacional (National Liberation Party) emerged as the country's interim leader, signing a declaration that abolished the army at the armory that now serves as the Museo Nacional.

The rest of the 20th century would see the expansion of the city from diminutive coffee-trading outpost to sprawling urban center. In the 1940s San José had only 70,000 residents. Today the greater metro population stands at over 2 million. Recent years have been marked by massive urban migration as Ticos (Costa Ricans) and, increasingly, Nicaraguans have moved to the capital in search of economic opportunity. As part of this, shantytowns have mushroomed on the outskirts, and crime is increasingly becoming a part of life for the city's poorest inhabitants.

The city remains a vital economic and arts hub, home to important banks, museums and universities – as well as the everyday outposts of culture: live-music spaces, art centers, bookstores and the corner restaurants where *josefinos* (people from San José) – or even less formally, *chepeños* (Chepe is a nickname for people named José, hence the city's moniker *El Chepe*) – gather to chew over ideas.

Sights

Central San José

★Teatro Nacional NOTABLE BUILDING
(Map p72; ☎2010-1110; www.teatronacional.go.cr; Av 2, btwn Calles 3 & 5; ⊙9am-5pm, Mon-Fri) On the southern side of the Plaza de la Cultura resides the Teatro Nacional, San José's most revered building. Constructed in 1897, it features a columned neoclassical facade flanked by statues of Beethoven and famous 17th-century Spanish dramatist Calderón de la Barca. The lavish marble lobby and auditorium are lined with paintings depicting various facets of 19th-century life. Performances throughout the year (p95). The hourly **tours** (☎ext 1114 2010-1100; www.teatronacional.go.cr/Visitenos/turismo; US$11, children under 12 free; ⊙hourly between 9am-4pm) here are fantastic. And if you're looking to rest your feet, there's an excellent onsite cafe (p85).

The theater's most famous painting is *Alegoría al café y el banano,* an idyllic canvas showing coffee and banana harvests. The painting was produced in Italy and shipped to Costa Rica for installation in the theater, and the image was reproduced on the old ₡5 note (now out of circulation). It seems clear that the painter never witnessed a banana harvest because of the way the man in the center is awkwardly grasping a bunch (actual banana workers hoist the stems onto their shoulders).

Conveniently, a few city walking tours start here, too.

★Museo del Jade MUSEUM
(Map p72; ☎2521-6610; www.museodeljadeins.com; Plaza de la Democracia; adult/child under 6yr US$15/free; ⊙10am-5pm) This museum houses the world's largest collection of American jade (pronounced '*ha*-day' in Spanish), with an ample exhibition space of five floors offering seven exhibits. There are nearly 7000 finely crafted, well-conserved pieces, from translucent jade carvings depicting fertility goddesses, shamans, frogs and snakes to incredible ceramics (some reflecting Maya influences), including a highly unusual ceramic head displaying a row of serrated teeth. Interesting indigenous

SAN JOSÉ IN...

One Day

Begin with a peek inside the city's most beautiful building, the 19th-century **Teatro Nacional** (p65), and an espresso at the theater's atmospheric **cafe** (p85) before heading into the nearby **Museo de Oro Precolombino y Numismática** to peruse its trove of pre-Columbian gold treasures.

Take lunch within the city's gastronomic hub **Barrio Escalante** on the terrace of **Kalú Café & Food Shop** (p89), or try the open-air options at the **Mercado La California** (p91). Wander historical **Barrio Amón** (p###), with stops at **Galería Namu** (p96) and **eÑe** (p96), then end your afternoon sampling Costa Rican microbrews at **Stiefel** (p91) or sipping a cocktail at the fabulous **Café de los Deseos** (p84).

Two Days

Start your second day with a primer on Costa Rican history at the **Museo Nacional de Costa Rica**, then cross **Plaza de la Democracia** (p70) to the state-of-the-art **Museo del Jade** (p65). After a stroll through the neighboring **Mercado Nacional de Artesanía** (p97) for handicrafts, head northwest to the **Mercado Centra** to shop for Costa Rican coffee, cigars and cheap snacks.

In the evening, grab dinner at Barrio Amón's finest, **Restaurante Silvestre** (p86), then venture east for a drink at the rooftop bar at **Hotel Presidente** (p77) en route to catching a local band and brews at either the magical **Steinvorth Building** (p85) or **Mundoloco** (p94).

history is on display too. The museum cafe, **Grano Verde**, serves sandwiches, salads and smoothies.

Children aged five and under have free entry to the museum, and many of the interactive displays are designed with them in mind. Buy a three-museum pass (US$33; covers this one, Museo de Oro Precolombino y Numismática and Museo Nacional) to save money if you plan to visit all – it has no expiration date.

★Museo de Oro Precolombino y Numismática MUSEUM

(Map p72; ☎2243-4202; www.museosdelbancocentral.org; Plaza de la Cultura, Avs Central & 2, btwn Calles 3 & 5; adult/student/child US$13/8/free; ⏰9:15am-5pm) This three-in-one museum houses an extensive collection of Costa Rica's most priceless pieces of pre-Columbian gold and other artifacts, including historical currency and some contemporary regional art. The museum, located underneath the Plaza de la Cultura, is owned by the Banco Central and its architecture brings to mind all the warmth and comfort of a bank vault. The interactive 360-degree videography display of Bribrí cultural hierarchy in the basement is worth the admission price alone.

Security is tight; visitors must leave bags at the door.

★Mercado Central MARKET

(Map p72; www.facebook.com/Mercado-Central-de-San-José-Costa-Rica-132271433523797; Avs Central & 1, btwn Calles 6 & 8; ⏰6:30am-6pm Mon-Sat) Though *josefinos* mainly do their shopping at chain supermarkets, San José's crowded indoor markets retain an old-world, authentic feel. This is the main market, lined with vendors hawking everything from spices and coffee beans to *pura vida* souvenir T-shirts. It's all super cheap, and likely made in China or Nicaragua (not the coffee beans, though).

In December Mercado Central sometimes has extended hours and is open on Sundays. While browsing, try a La Sorbetera ice cream cone (p87), or a quick *ceviche* at Poseidon (p87).

Museo Nacional de Costa Rica MUSEUM

(Map p68; ☎2257-1433; www.museocostarica.go.cr; Calle 17, btwn Avs Central & 2; adult/student/child US$11/6/free; ⏰8:30am-4:30pm Tue-Sat, 9am-4:30pm Sun) Entered via a beautiful glassed-in atrium housing an exotic butterfly garden, this museum provides a quick survey of Costa Rican history. Exhibits of pre-Columbian pieces from ongoing digs, as well as artifacts from the colony and the early republic, are all housed inside the old Bellavista Fortress, which historically served as the army headquarters and saw fierce fighting (hence the pockmarks) in the 1948 civil war.

It was here that President José Figueres Ferrer announced, in 1949, that he was abolishing the country's military. Among the museum's many notable pieces is the fountain pen that Figueres used to sign the 1949 constitution.

Don't miss the period galleries in the northeast corner, which feature turn-of-the-20th-century furnishings and decor from when these rooms served as the private residences of the fort's various commanders.

Museo de los Niños & Galería Nacional MUSEUM

(Map p68; ☎2258-4929; www.museocr.org; Calle 4; adult/child US$4.50/4; ⌚8am-4:30pm Tue-Fri, 9:30am-5pm Sat & Sun; 👪) If you're wondering how to get your young kids interested in art and science, this unusual museum – actually two museums in one – is an excellent place to start. Housed in an old penitentiary built in 1909, it's part children's museum and part art gallery. Small kids will love the hands-on exhibits related to science, geography and natural history, while grown-ups will enjoy the unusual juxtaposition of contemporary art in abandoned prison cells. You'll find it north of Av 9.

Barrio Amón AREA

(Map p72) Northwest of Plaza España, this pleasant, historical neighborhood is home to a cluster of 19th-century *cafetalero* (coffee grower) mansions. Recently many of the area's historical buildings have been converted into hotels, cafes, bars and offices, making this a popular district for an architectural stroll. You'll find everything from art deco concrete manses to brightly painted tropical Victorian structures in various states of upkeep.

Plaza de la Cultura PLAZA

(Map p72; Avs Central & 2, btwn Calles 3 & 5) This architecturally unremarkable concrete plaza in the heart of downtown is usually packed with locals slurping ice-cream cones and admiring the wide gamut of San José street life: juggling clowns, itinerant vendors and cruising teenagers. It is perhaps one of the safest spots in the city as there's a police tower stationed at one corner. It's bordered by the Museo Nacional.

Museo de Arte y Diseño Contemporáneo MUSEUM

(MADC; Map p72; ☎2257-7202; www.madc.cr; cnr Av 3 & Calle 15; US$3, 1st Tue of the month free; ⌚9:30am-5pm Tue-Sat) Commonly referred to as MADC, the Contemporary Art & Design Museum is housed in the historical National Liquor Factory building, which dates from 1856. It's just across from the Parque Nacional. Modern photography, painting, and other exhibits are the norm.

Centro Nacional de la Cultura LANDMARK

(Cenac; Map p72; ☎2255-3190; www.mcj.go.cr; Calle 11A; ⌚8am-4pm Mon-Fri) Housed in the historical National Liquor Factory, this cultural center contains the museum of art and design, a video museum, a gallery and two theaters.

TEOR/éTica GALLERY

(Arte y pensamiento; Map p72; ☎2233-4881; www.teoretica.org; cnr Calle 7 & Av 11, Casa 953, Barrio Amón; ⌚11am-6pm Wed-Fri, 10am-4pm Sat) FREE This contemporary-art museum is the brick-and-mortar gathering space for the TEOR/éTica Foundation, a nonprofit organization that supports Central American art and culture. Housed in a pair of vintage mansions across the street from one another, each elegant room exhibits cutting-edge works from Latin America and the rest of the world.

Parque Nacional PARK

(Map p68; Avs 1 & 3, btwn Calles 15 & 19) One of San José's nicest green spaces, this shady spot lures retirees to read newspapers and young couples to smooch coyly on concrete benches. At its center is the Monumento Nacional, a dramatic 1953 statue that depicts the Central American nations driving out North American filibuster William Walker. The park is dotted with myriad monuments devoted to Latin American historical figures, including Cuban poet, essayist and revolutionary José Martí, Mexican independence figure Miguel Hidalgo and 18th-century Venezuelan humanist Andrés Bello.

Across the street, to the south, stands the **Asamblea Legislativa** (Legislative Assembly;

San José

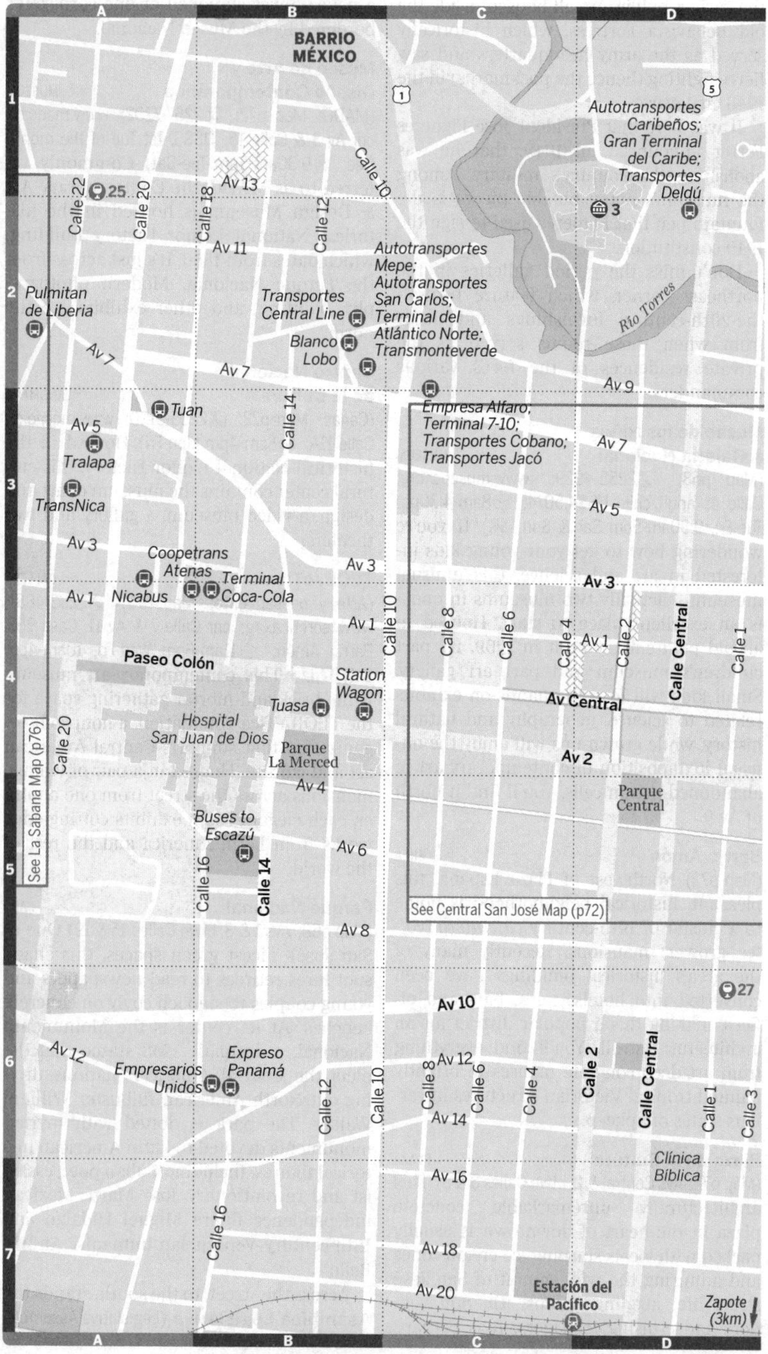
A
B
C
D
1
2
3
4
5
6
7
BARRIO MÉXICO
Autotransportes Caribeños; Gran Terminal del Caribe; Transportes Deldú
3
25
27
Calle 22
Calle 20
Calle 18
Calle 12
Calle 10
Av 13
Av 11
Pulmitan de Liberia
Transportes Central Line
Autotransportes Mepe; Autotransportes San Carlos; Terminal del Atlántico Norte; Transmonteverde
Blanco Lobo
Río Torres
Av 7
Av 9
Tuan
Calle 14
Empresa Alfaro; Terminal 7-10; Transportes Cobano; Transportes Jacó
Av 5
Tralapa
TransNica
Av 3
Coopetrans Atenas
Terminal Coca-Cola
Nicabus
Av 1
Calle 8
Calle 6
Calle 4
Calle 2
Calle Central
Calle 1
Paseo Colón
Station Wagon
Tuasa
Av Central
Hospital San Juan de Dios
Parque La Merced
Av 2
Parque Central
Av 4
See La Sabana Map (p76)
Buses to Escazú
Av 6
Calle 16
See Central San José Map (p72)
Av 8
Av 10
Av 12
Expreso Panamá
Empresarios Unidos
Av 14
Calle 3
Clínica Bíblica
Av 16
Av 18
Av 20
Estación del Pacífico
Zapote (3km)

0 500 m
0 0.25 miles
E
F
G
H
1
2
3
4
5
6
7
32
108
BARRIO TOURNON
Moravia (6km)
See Los Yoses, Barrio Escalante & San Pedro Map (p81)
BARRIO ARANJUEZ
BARRIO AMÓN
BARRIO OTOYA
Av 13
Av 11
Av 9
Av 7
Av 3
Av 1
Av Central
Av 2
Av 6
Av 8
Av 10
Av 12
Av 14
Av 16
Av 18
Calle 3A
Calle 3
Calle 5
Calle 7
Calle 9
Calle 11
Calle 13
Calle 13A
Calle 15
Calle 17
Calle 19
Calle 21
Parque Morazán
Parque España
Estación del Atlántico
BARRIO LA CALIFORNIA
Transtusa
Supreme Court of Justice
Supreme Court of Justice Complex
Lumaca
Terminal Tracopa
1
2
4
5
6
7
8
9
10
11
12
13
14
15
16
17
18
19
20
21
22
23
24
26
28
29
30
31
32
33
34
35

San José

Sights

1 Asamblea Legislativa G4
2 Estación del Ferrocarril de Costa Rica H4
3 Museo de los Niños & Galería Nacional D2
4 Museo Nacional de Costa Rica G5
5 Parque Nacional G4
6 Spirogyra Jardín de Mariposas F2

Sleeping

7 Casa Botanica de Aranjuez H2
8 Casa Ridgway F6
9 Costa Rica Backpackers H5
10 Costa Rica Guesthouse H5
11 Hostel Casa del Parque G4
12 Hostel Shakti F6
13 Hotel Aranjuez H2
14 Hotel Posada del Museo G5
15 Kaps Place H3

Eating

16 Café de los Deseos G2
17 Café del Barista H3
Kaps Cafe .... (see 15)
18 La Terrasse G3
19 La Ventanita Meraki G4
20 Maza Bistro G4
Restaurante Shakti .... (see 12)
21 Restaurante Silvestre E3
22 Talentum E2
23 Tin Jo F5

Drinking & Nightlife

24 Antik G6
25 Castro's A1
26 Craic Irish Pub H5
27 La Avispa D6
28 La Bohemia E6
29 La Concha de la Lora H4
Mercado La California .... (see 29)
30 Pucho's Bar F6

Entertainment

31 Arenas Skate Park F6
Auditorio Nacional .... (see 3)
32 Cine Magaly H4
33 El Cuartel de la Boca del Monte H4
34 El Sótano E3

Shopping

35 Feria Verde de Aranjuez G2

Map p68; Ave Central, btwn Calle 15 & 17), which also bears an important statue: this one a depiction of Juan Santamaría – the young man who helped kick Walker out of Costa Rica – in full flame-throwing action.

A creative walker could easily connect Parque Francia (p72), Parque Nacional, Parque España, and Parque Morazán along Avenida 3, stopping at cafes and bookshops along the way.

Spirogyra Jardín de Mariposas GARDENS
(Map p68; ☎2222-2937; www.butterflygardencr.com; Barrio Amón; adult/child US$7/5; ⏲9am-2pm Mon-Fri, to 3pm Sat & Sun; ; to El Pueblo) Housing more than 30 species of butterfly – including the luminescent blue morpho – in plant-filled enclosures, this small butterfly garden is a great spot for kids. Visit in the morning to see plenty of fluttering. The garden is 150m east and 150m south of Centro Comercial El Pueblo, which can be reached on foot (about a 20- to 30-minute walk from downtown), by taxi or bus.

Plaza de la Democracia PLAZA
(Plaza de la Democracia y de la Abolición del Ejército; Map p72; Avs Central & 2, btwn Calles 13 & 15) Between the Museo Nacional (p66) and the Museo del Jade (p65) is the stark Plaza de la Democracia, which was constructed by President Óscar Arias in 1989 to commemorate 100 years of Costa Rican democracy. The concrete plaza is architecturally dull, but some of its elevated terraces provide decent views of the mountains surrounding San José (especially at sunset). On its western flank is an open-air crafts market (p97).

Catedral Metropolitana CATHEDRAL
(Map p72; ☎2221-3820; Avs 2 & 4, btwn Calles Central & 1) East of Parque Central, the Renaissance-style Catedral Metropolitana was built in 1871 after the previous cathedral was destroyed in an earthquake. The graceful neoclassical interior has colorful Spanish-tile floors, stained-glass windows, and a Christ figure that was produced by a Guatemalan workshop in the late 17th century. On the north side of the nave, a recumbent Christ that dates back to 1878 draws devout Ticos, who arrive here to pray and deposit pleas scribbled on small slips of paper.

Estación del Ferrocarril de Costa Rica HISTORIC BUILDING
(Estación Atlántico; Map p68; ☎2542-5800; www.incofer.go.cr; cnr Av 3 & Calle 21) Less than a

block east of Parque Nacional (p67) is San José's historical train station to the Atlantic, built in 1908. Nowadays offering weekday train service to Heredia, Belén and Cartago, it's a remarkable example of tropical architecture, with swirling art nouveau–inspired beams and elaborate stonework along the roofline. Hulking iron horses of yore litter the yard.

Parque Morazán PARK

(Map p72; Avs 3 & 5, btwn Calles 5 & 9) Parque Morazán is named for Francisco Morazán, the 19th-century general who attempted to unite the Central American nations under a single flag (he was executed by firing squad for his troubles). Once a notorious center of prostitution, the park is now beautifully illuminated in the evenings. At its center is the **Templo de Música** (Music Temple) – a replica of the Temple of Love in Versailles – the unofficial symbol of San José.

You'll find it southwest of Parque España.

Parque Central PARK

(Map p72; Avs 2 & 4, btwn Calles Central & 2) The city's central park is more of a run-down plaza than a park. At its center is a grandiose bandstand that looks as if it was designed by Mussolini: massive concrete arches support a florid roof capped with a ball-shaped decorative knob.

Parque España PARK

(Map p72; Avs 3 & 7, btwn Calles 9 & 11) Surrounded by heavy traffic, Parque España may be small, but it becomes a riot of birdsong every day at sunset when the local avian population comes in to roost. In addition to being a good spot for a shady break, the park is home to an ornate statue of Christopher Columbus that was given to the people of Costa Rica in 2002 by his descendants, commemorating the quincentenary of the explorer's landing in Puerto Limón.

There's a wonderful beer hall (p91) across the way.

Mercado Borbón MARKET

(Map p72; ☎2223-3512; www.facebook.com/mercadoborbon; cnr Av 3 & Calle 8; ⏲5am-5pm Mon-Sat) The Mercado Borbón is a true sensory experience of sights and smells, and you might catch the daily hand-truck race among the workers. The focus is on produce, though it sells a bit of everything. Be aware: the streets can get sketchy around the Borbón. Keep a close watch on your bag.

Edificio Metálico LANDMARK

(Map p72; cnr Av 5 & Calle 9) One of downtown San José's most striking buildings, this century-old two-story metal edifice on Parque España's western edge was prefabricated in Belgium, then shipped piece by piece to San José. Today it functions as a school and local landmark.

Casa Amarilla HISTORIC BUILDING

(Map p72; Av 7, btwn Calles 11 & 13) On Parque España's northeast corner, this elegant colonial-style yellow mansion (closed to the public) houses the Foreign Affairs Ministry. The ceiba tree in front was planted by John F Kennedy during his 1963 visit to Costa Rica. If you walk around to the property's northeast corner, you can see a graffiti-covered slab of the Berlin Wall standing in the rear garden.

The building, initially the Central American Court of Justice, was built with funds donated by Andrew Carnegie in 1910. There's a nice tribute to tango legend Carlos Gardel adjacent (on the 'Paseo Argentino') as well as some cute cafes, gift shops, and a groovy bookshop.

La Sabana & Around

Parque Metropolitano La Sabana PARK

(Map p76) Once the site of San José's main airport, this 72-hectare green space at the west end of Paseo Colón is home to a regional art museum, a lagoon and various sporting facilities – most notably Costa Rica's National Stadium (p95). During the day, the park's paths make a relaxing place for a stroll, a jog or a picnic.

Museo de Arte Costarricense MUSEUM

(Map p76; ☎2256-1281; www.mac.go.cr; Parque Metropolitano La Sabana; ⏲9am-4pm Tue-Sun; 👪) FREE This Spanish-style structure served as San José's main airport terminal until 1955. The remodeled museum features regional art, a sculpture garden, a huge (150 sq m) bas-relief mural of Costa Rican history from pre-Columbian times to 1940 by French artist Luis Féron Parizot, and other exhibits. Located at the east entrance of Parque La Sabana.

Central San José

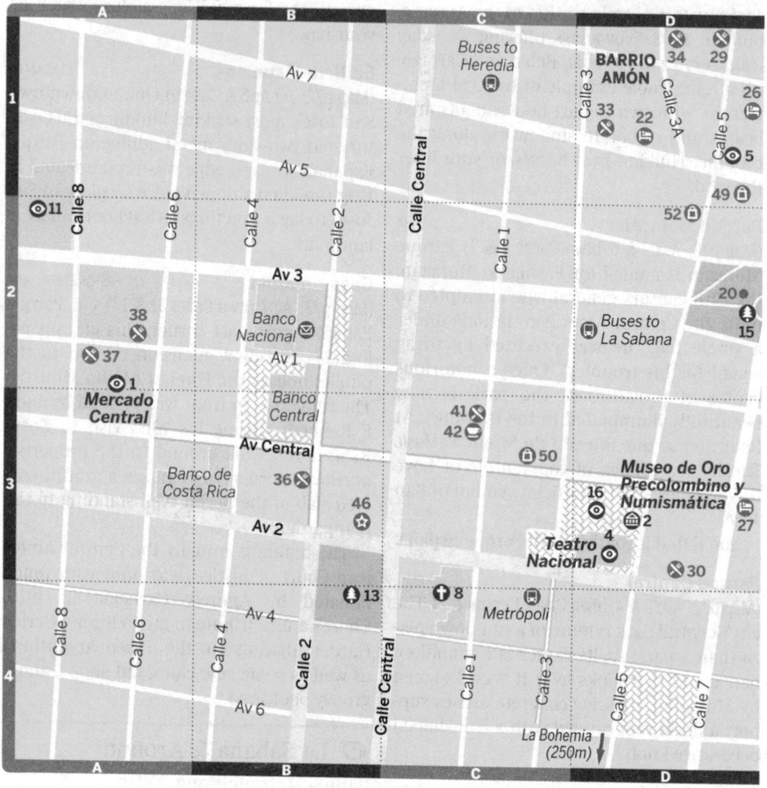

Museo de Ciencias Naturales La Salle MUSEUM

(☎2232-1306; www.museolasalle.ed.cr; Sabana Sur; adult/child US$2/1.60; ⏰8am-4pm Mon-Sat, 9am-5pm Sun; 👪) Ever wanted to see a spider-monkey skeleton or a herd of stuffed tapirs? This natural-history museum near Parque La Sabana's southwest corner has an extensive collection of taxidermic animals and birds from Costa Rica and far beyond, alongside animal skeletons, minerals, preserved specimens and a vast new collection of butterflies. Kids in particular will appreciate this place (it has dinosaurs!).

◉ Los Yoses, Barrio Escalante & San Pedro

Barrio Escalante AREA

(Map p81) Formerly a residential enclave, the streets of this increasingly hip neighborhood are now lined with dozens of restaurants, cafes, bakeries and bars. The largest concentration stretches along Calle 33 and has been dubbed Paseo Gastronómico La Luz (La Luz Restaurant Promenade) in honor of a small grocery store that used to stand on the street's corner.

Parque Francia PARK

(Map p81; Av 5 & Calle 29, Barrio Escalante) A lovely little space of former farmland, bordered by a French cafe and French-Spanish bookstore, as well as some restaurants. There are trees providing shade and plenty of grass and benches to sit on.

Museo de Insectos MUSEUM

(Insect Museum; Map p81; ☎2511-5318, 2511-8551; www.facebook.com/insectosucr; University of Costa Rica, San Pedro; US$3; ⏰8am-noon & 1-4:45pm Mon-Fri) Reputedly Central America's largest insect museum, this place has an extensive collection assembled by the Facultad de Agronomía (agronomy faculty) at the

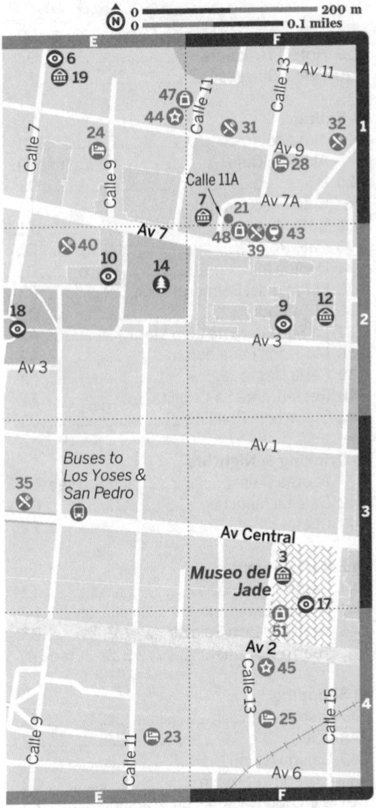

Universidad de Costa Rica. After viewing the specimens, visitors are invited to a room with a kitchen to sample meal worms, scarabs and crickets. A little salt and oregano does wonders.

Curiously, the museum is housed in the basement of the music building, a brutalist structure painted an incongruous shade of pink.

Escazú & Santa Ana

Refugio Herpetologico de Costa Rica ANIMAL SANCTUARY
(☎2282-4614; www.refugioherpetologico.com; Carretera John F Kennedy, Santa Ana; adult/child US$20/10; 9am-4:30pm Tue-Sun) Costa Rica is full of wild reptiles, but for people who prefer meeting things with scales under controlled circumstances, there's the Refugio Herpetologico. On display are a bunch of snakes, turtles, caimans and a large crocodile, which can be viewed through a window as it swims underwater. There are also some resident spider and capuchin monkeys, plus a couple of ocelots.

Activities

Parque Metropolitano La Sabana (p71) has a variety of sporting facilities, including tennis courts, volleyball, basketball and baseball areas, jogging paths and soccer pitches. Beyond that, you can also hike to a bunch of awesome windmills and learn salsa.

Tours

The city is small and easily navigable. If you're looking for a walking tour that will guide you to key sites, there are plenty on offer.

★Barrio Bird Walking Tours WALKING
(Map p72; ☎6280-6169; www.toursanjosecostarica.com; tours from adult/child US$32/10) Knowledgeable and engaging guides show visitors San José's famous and not-so-famous sights, providing history and insight on the city's architecture, markets and urban art. Specialized tours also cater to foodies and culture enthusiasts.

ChepeCletas TOURS
(Map p72; ☎8849-8316; www.chepecletas.com) This dynamic Tico-run company offers excellent private tours focusing on history, culture, food markets, coffee and nightlife. Its ever-changing menu of offerings also includes informative walks around San José on Saturday mornings (US$10), and free bike tours on Wednesdays at 7pm and occasionally on Sunday mornings: you'll need to rent a city bike (p102) for this option.

Costa Rica Art Tours TOURS
(☎8359-5571, in USA 877-394-6113; www.costaricaarttours.com; per person US$150) This small outfit conducts private tours that offer an intimate look at artists in their studios, where you can view (and buy) the work of local painters, sculptors, printmakers, ceramicists and jewelers. Lunch and pick up from San José city hotels are included in the price. Reserve at least a week in advance. Discounts are available for groups.

Central San José

Top Sights
1 Mercado Central ... A2
2 Museo de Oro Precolombino y Numismática ... D3
3 Museo del Jade ... F3
4 Teatro Nacional ... D3

Sights
5 Alianza Francesa ... D1
6 Barrio Amón ... E1
7 Casa Amarilla ... F1
8 Catedral Metropolitana ... C4
9 Centro Nacional de la Cultura ... F2
10 Edificio Metálico ... E2
11 Mercado Borbón ... A2
12 Museo de Arte y Diseño Contemporáneo ... F2
13 Parque Central ... B4
14 Parque España ... E2
15 Parque Morazán ... D2
16 Plaza de la Cultura ... D3
17 Plaza de la Democracia ... F3
18 Templo de Música ... E2
19 TEOR/éTica ... E1

Activities, Courses & Tours
20 Barrio Bird Walking Tours ... D2
21 ChepeCletas ... F1
Teatro Nacional ... (see 4)

Sleeping
22 Hostel Pangea ... D1
23 Hotel Colonial ... E4
24 Hotel Don Carlos ... E1
25 Hotel Fleur de Lys ... F4
26 Hotel Kekoldi ... D1
27 Hotel Presidente ... D3
28 Selina San José ... F1

Eating
29 Alma de Amón ... D1
Alma de Café ... (see 4)
30 Bò ... D3
31 Café Miel Garage ... F1
32 Café Mundo ... F1
33 Café Rojo ... D1
34 De Acá ... D1
35 El Patio del Balmoral ... E3
36 El Tostador ... B3
37 La Sorbetera de Lolo Mora ... A2
38 Mariscos Poseidon ... A2
39 Perla Negra ... F2
40 Restaurante La Criollita ... E2
41 Steinvorth Building ... C3

Drinking & Nightlife
Azotea Calle 7 ... (see 27)
42 Café La Mancha ... C3
43 Stiefel ... F2

Entertainment
44 Centro de Cine ... E1
45 El Lobo Estepario ... F4
46 Teatro Melico Salazar ... B3
Teatro Nacional ... (see 4)

Shopping
47 Distrito Carmen ... E1
48 eÑe ... F2
49 Galería Namu ... D1
50 Librería Lehmann ... C3
51 Mercado Nacional de Artesanía ... F4
52 Mora Books ... D2

Carpe Chepe TOURS
(☎8347-6198; www.carpechepe.com; guided pub crawls US$25; ⊙8pm Fri & Sat) For an insider's look at Chepe's nightlife, join one of these Friday- and Saturday-evening guided pub crawls, led by an enthusiastic group of young locals. A shot is included at each of the four bars visited. There are other offerings as well, including a hop-on, hop-off nightlife bus, food tours, a craft-beer tour and free walking tours of San José. Note that the tours may not run on time and can feel a bit disorganized.

Festivals & Events

Día del Boyero CULTURAL
On the second Sunday of March, Escazú holds this popular event honoring Costa Rica's *boyeros* (oxcart drivers). Dozens of attendees from all over the country decorate traditional, brightly painted carts and form a colorful (if slow) parade.

Día de San José RELIGIOUS
(St Joseph's Day; ⊙19 Mar) San José marks the day of its patron saint with mass in some churches.

Festival de las Artes PERFORMING ARTS
(FIA; ☎2248-3240; www.facebook.com/festivaldelasartescr; ⊙Mar or Apr) About every other year, San José becomes host to this citywide arts showcase that features theater, music, dance and film. It's usually held for two weeks in March or April, but the month can vary. Keep an eye out for information in the daily newspapers.

International Book Fair LITERATURE
(www.feriadellibrocostarica.com; Antigua Aduana; ⊙May) For 40 years, thousands of bibliophiles have descended on Costa Rica's capital for this massive, multiday literary event, which includes readings, book sales and presentations from internationally renowned authors.

Desfile de los Boyeros CULTURAL
(Oxcart Parade; Paseo Colón; ⌚Nov) This parade of oxcarts down Paseo Colón, from Parque Metropolitano La Sabana to the Plaza de la Democracia, is a celebration of the country's agricultural heritage.

Festival de la Luz RELIGIOUS
(Festival of Light; www.festivaldelaluz.cr; ⌚Dec) The second Saturday of December brings San José's big Christmas parade, marked by marching bands from around the country, elaborate costumes and floats, and an absurd amount of plastic 'snow.'

Las Fiestas de Zapote CULTURAL
(www.facebook.com/fiestasdezapoteSJO; Zapote; ⌚late Dec-early Jan) Between Christmas and New Year, this week-long celebration of all things Costa Rican draws tens of thousands of Ticos to the bullring in the suburb of Zapote, just southeast of San José.

Sleeping

Accommodations in San José run the gamut of simple but homey hostels to luxurious boutique retreats. If you're flying into or out of Costa Rica from here, it may be more convenient to stay in Alajuela, as the town is minutes from the international airport.

Reservations are recommended in the high season (December through April), particularly the two weeks around Christmas and Semana Santa (Holy Week, the week preceding Easter).

Central San José

Most of downtown's better sleeping options are located east of Calle Central, many of them in historical Victorian and art deco mansions. Most of the top-end hotels accept credit cards.

★ **Hostel Casa del Parque** HOSTEL $
(Map p68; ☎2233-3437; www.hostelcasadelparque.com; Calle 19, btwn Avs 1 & 3; dm US$14, d with/without bathroom US$49/39; 📶) A 1936 vintage art deco manse houses this cozy, welcoming spot on the northeastern edge of Parque Nacional. Five large, basic private rooms (two are gigantic, with bathrooms), a newer seven-bed dormitory and an older 10-bed dormitory upstairs have parquet floors and simple furnishings. Enjoy some sun on the plant-festooned outdoor patio and dig into the shared kitchen.

The bilingual owner is a good source of local dining information, but the adjacent Maza Bistro (p86) is a good choice if you don't feel like leaving.

Selina San José HOSTEL $
(Map p72; ☎4052-5147; www.selina.com/san-jose; cnr Calle 13 & Av 9; dm US$10-15, r from US$60; ❄📶) Ensconced in a rad space within the centrally located Barrio Otoya, this hostel is part of the Selina backpacker empire now stretching across the lower Americas. Seemingly overnight, it has become the go-to hangout for young travelers. It's loud here, and people like it that way.

Beds are comfy and the space is inspired, with a reception desk built out of an old Volkswagon.

Casa Ridgway GUESTHOUSE $
(Map p68; ☎2222-1400, 2233-6168; cnr Calle 15 & Av 6A; incl breakfast dm US$17, s/d without bathroom US$24/38; P🚭📶) A small, peaceful guesthouse on a quiet side street run by the adjacent Friends' Peace Center, a Quaker organization promoting social justice and human rights. There is a small lounge, a communal kitchen and a lending library filled with books about Central American politics and society. No smoking or alcohol is allowed, with quiet hours from 10pm to 6am.

Costa Rica Backpackers HOSTEL $
(Map p68; ☎2221-6191; www.costaricabackpackers.com; Av 6, near Calle 21; dm US$9-14, d without bathroom US$35; P@📶🏊) This popular hostel has 19 basic but clean dormitories and 14 private rooms (shared bathroom) surrounding a spacious hammock-filled garden and a free-form pool. Two bars, a restaurant and chill-out music enhance the inviting, laid-back atmosphere. Other benefits include a communal kitchen and TV lounge, free luggage storage, internet access, an onsite travel agency and low-cost airport transfers (US$26).

Hostel Shakti HOSTEL $
(Map p68; ☎2221-4631; cnr Av 8 & Calle 13; dm/s/d incl breakfast US$18/30/40; P@📶) A lovely little guesthouse using bold colors and natural materials to create an oasis of calm and comfort amid the chaos of San José. Three dorms and four private rooms are dressed up with eclectic furnishings and colorful bedding. There is a fully equipped kitchen, but you might not need it as the onsite restaurant (p85) is healthy, fresh and amazing.

La Sabana

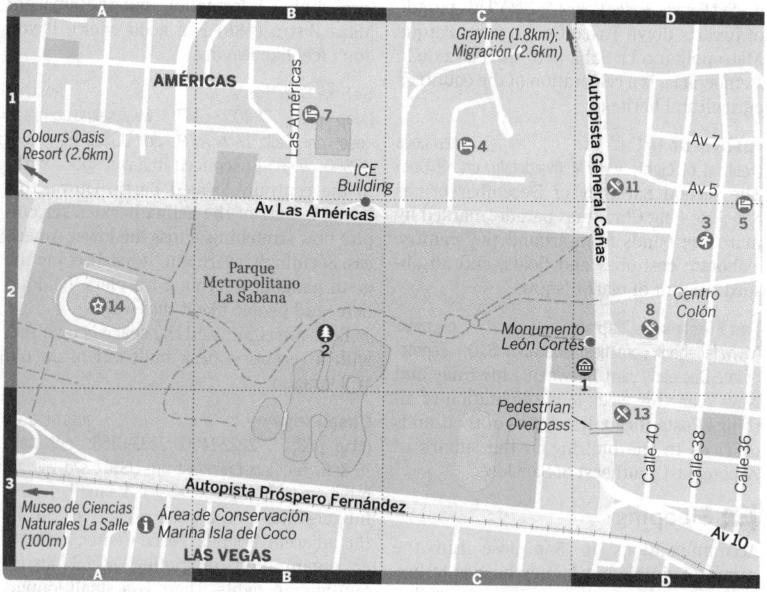

La Sabana

Sights

1 Museo de Arte Costarricense D2
2 Parque Metropolitano La Sabana B2

Activities, Courses & Tours

3 Ríos Tropicales D2

Sleeping

4 Apartotel La Sabana C1
5 Gaudy's D2
6 Hotel Grano de Oro E3
7 Mi Casa Hostel B1

Eating

8 Las Mañanitas D2
9 Lubnan F3
10 Machu Picchu E2
11 Más X Menos D1
12 Palí F2
Restaurante Grano de Oro .... (see 6)
13 Soda Tapia D3

Entertainment

14 Estadio Nacional de Costa Rica A2
15 Sala Garbo E3

Hostel Pangea HOSTEL $
(Map p72; ☎2221-1992; www.hostelpangea.com; Av 7, btwn Calles 3 & 3A, Barrio Amón; dm US$14, d with/without bathroom US$45/34, ste from US$55; P @ 🛜 ≋) This industrial-strength hostel – 25 dorm beds, 25 private rooms, and five cushy suites – has been a popular twentysomething backpacker hangout for years. It's not difficult to see why: it's smack in the middle of the city and has a pool and a rooftop restaurant-lounge/speakeasy-style bar with stellar views. Needless to say, it's a party spot. Wristband-controlled entry.

Rooms are tidy, mattresses firm and the shared bathrooms enormous and clean. The five suites (one Presidential) have king-size beds and flat-screen TVs. Other perks include free internet, luggage storage and 24-hour airport shuttles (from US$12 shared). They've got a sister hostel in La Fortuna.

Hotel Posada del Museo GUESTHOUSE $
(Map p68; ☎2258-1027; cnr Calle 17 & Av 2; s/d/tr/q incl breakfast US$40/51/65/79; @ 🛜) Managed by an amiable multilingual couple, this architecturally intriguing vintage inn (1928) is diagonally across from the Museo Nacional. French doors line the entrances

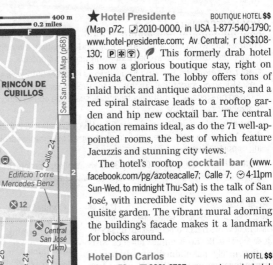

to each of the rooms, no two of which are alike. Some rooms accommodate up to four people, making this a family-friendly option. Light sleepers, take note: the hotel is adjacent to the train tracks.

Bells' Home Hospitality HOMESTAY **$**

(2225-4752, 8499-4738; www.homestay-thebells.com; s/d incl breakfast US$35/60) This recommended agency is run by the bilingual Marcela Bell, who has operated the business for more than 30 years. She can arrange stays in more than a dozen homes around San José, including her own. Each one has been personally inspected and they are all close to public transportation. Dinner US$10.

Costa Rica Guesthouse GUESTHOUSE **$**

(Map p68; 2223-7034; www.costa-rica-guesthouse.com; Av 6, btwn Calles 21 & 25; d incl breakfast with/without bathroom US$50/40, extra person US$15; P @ wifi) This 1904 guesthouse has simple, graceful rooms with spacious bathrooms and hallways lined with Spanish tiles. Furnishings are basic (creaky beds), but it's a tranquil, couples-friendly spot. There's a small internet lounge, an outdoor patio adorned with epiphytes and an enclosed parking area out back. Laundry service (per kg US$3) is available. More expensive rooms have televisions and bathrooms.

★Hotel Presidente BOUTIQUE HOTEL **$$**

(Map p72; 2010-0000, in USA 1-877-540-1790; www.hotel-presidente.com; Av Central; r US$108-130; P air-con wifi) This formerly drab hotel is now a glorious boutique stay, right on Avenida Central. The lobby offers tons of inlaid brick and antique adornments, and a red spiral staircase leads to a rooftop garden and hip new cocktail bar. The central location remains ideal, as do the 71 well-appointed rooms, the best of which feature Jacuzzis and stunning city views.

The hotel's rooftop **cocktail bar** (www.facebook.com/pg/azoteacalle7; Calle 7; 4-11pm Sun-Wed, to midnight Thu-Sat) is the talk of San José, with incredible city views and an exquisite garden. The vibrant mural adorning the building's facade makes it a landmark for blocks around.

Hotel Don Carlos HOTEL **$$**

(Map p72; 2221-6707; www.doncarloshotel.com; Calle 9, btwn Avs 7 & 9; incl breakfast s/d US$79/90, ste s/d US$80/90 family US$100; P @ wifi) Built around an early-20th-century house that once belonged to President Tomás Guardia, this quiet, welcoming Barrio Amón inn exudes a slightly campy colonial-era vibe. Its 32 rooms surround a faux-pre-Columbian sculpture garden with a sundeck. All rooms have cable TV, a lockbox and a hairdryer; upstairs units are generally nicer than the mustier ones downstairs. The family room sleeps four. There's also a cheesy gift shop.

Don't miss the Spanish-tile mural, just outside the onsite restaurant, which beautifully depicts central San José in the 1930s, as well as the Don Quixote murals on the property next door.

Casa Botanica de Aranjuez HISTORIC HOTEL **$$**

(Art Hotel; Map p68; 8326-9321; www.facebook.com/pg/casabotanicaaranjuez; Calle 19, btwn Av 11 & 13; r US$35-100; wifi) Set in a century-old wooden home in Barrio Aranjuez, this charming place to stay is owned by botanist Christian and adorned with his personal art collection. There are five uniquely decorated units of varying sizes, and three apartments with private or shared kitchens. There's also a basement gallery/event space where San José's movers and shakers are known to gather.

VOLUNTEERING

For travelers who want an experience beyond a vacation, there are dozens of not-for-profit organizations in San José that gladly accept volunteers.

Central American Service Expeditions (☎8839-0515; www.serviceexpeditions.com) A Costa Rican nonprofit that creates custom volunteer opportunities for families and teens focused on sustainability. Projects include sea turtle conservation and visits to the Bribrí indigenous community.

Educational Travel Adventures (☎in USA & Canada 866-273-2500; www.etadventures.com) Arranges a wide variety of volunteer trips, conservation projects and service learning opportunities.

United Planet (☎in USA 1-617-874-8041; www.unitedplanet.org) Places volunteers in programs working on global health, education and the environment.

Hotel Aranjuez HOTEL **$$**
(Map p68; ☎2256-1825; www.hotelaranjuez.com; Calle 19, btwn Avs 11 & 13; d incl breakfast US$45-95; P@🛜) This Barrio Aranjuez hotel consists of five nicely maintained vintage homes, strung together with a labyrinth of gardens and connecting walkways. The 35 spotless rooms come in various configurations, all with a lockbox and cable TV. The hotel's best attribute is the lush garden patio, where a legendary breakfast is served every morning (open to nonguests by reservation).

Though the architecture can be a bit creaky and the walls thin, the service is efficient and the hotel is a solid family-friendly option. Rooms in the newer apartment-building annex half a block away lack the charm and sense of community of the main hotel, but annex guests still have access to the bounteous breakfast and pleasant common areas across the street.

The swanky 11-47 restaurant opened in 2018 and is open daily (6pm to 9:30pm; mains US$10 to US$20). Like the hotel itself, the restaurant's menu is a fusion of various entities.

Luz de Luna BOUTIQUE HOTEL **$$**
(Map p81; ☎2225-4919; www.luzdelunahotelboutique.com; Calle 33, btwn Avs 3 & 5; r US$46-75; ❄🛜) A converted old mansion, this boutique hotel, restaurant and cafe is in the heart of Escalante's Paseo Gastronómico district and its up-and-coming restaurants. Foodies who like to relax will appreciate this sanctuary and self-described 'lunar complex' for its lush gardens, hardwood floors and pre-Columbian masks. All rooms now have air-con, some have balconies, and a new bar opened in 2019.

Owner Silvia sometimes hosts poetry readings. The attached Luna Roja restaurant is charming.

Kaps Place GUESTHOUSE **$$**
(Map p68; ☎2221-1169; www.kapsplace.com; Calle 19, btwn Avs 11 & 13; incl breakfast s US$40-50, d/tr US$60/70, apt US$100-140; P@🛜) On a residential street in Barrio Aranjuez, this homey guesthouse has 30 rooms of various configurations spread over two buildings. Guests have access to patios decorated in colorful mosaics, plus three shared kitchens, a games room with ping-pong, foosball tables, and a big-screen TV lounge. Monthly rates available.

Recently the owner opened Kaps Cafe (p86), a lovely little eatery catering to both guests and nonguests.

Hotel Fleur de Lys HOTEL **$$**
(Map p72; ☎2223-1206; www.hotelfleurdelys.com; Calle 13, btwn Avs 2 & 6; incl breakfast r from US$78, junior/master ste US$136/166; P🚭❄@🛜) Impeccably maintained, this century-old, bright-pink Victorian mansion houses 30 spotless wood-paneled rooms with firm beds, ceiling fans and wicker furnishings. A small bar provides a welcome cocktail; live music on Fridays. The staff is attentive and the location central (note the proximity of the train tracks). German, French and English spoken. One room has air-con, another an attractive balcony.

Hotel Colonial HOTEL **$$**
(Map p72; ☎2223-0109; www.hotelcolonialcr.com; Calle 11, btwn Avs 2 & 6; s/d/ste incl breakfast US$73/73/113; P❄@🛜≋) An intricately carved baroque-style carriage door and an arched poolside promenade usher guests into this 1940s Spanish-style inn.

The 16 rooms and one suite are either whitewashed or painted an earthy mustard-yellow, with dark-wood furnishings and bright bedspreads. Those on higher floors have sweeping views of the city and outlying mountains. Three ground-level rooms are wheelchair accessible.

The parking is not onsite, but a short distance from the hotel.

Hotel Kekoldi HOTEL **$$**
(Map p72; ☎2248-0804; www.kekoldi.com; Av 9, btwn Calles 5 & 7; r incl breakfast US$67-88; 📶) This airy art deco building in Barrio Amón has 10 high-ceilinged rooms of various sizes, painted in pastel shades and equipped with cable TV. The best ones face the backyard and are drenched in natural light; interior rooms are less appealing. Common spaces include a cheerful breakfast room and garden. Mustiness can be common in hotels of all classes in Costa Rica; you're in the tropics. Sometimes opening a window just for a bit can do the trick, but don't be shy about requesting a different room if the mustiness lingers

La Sabana & Around

You'll find everything from hostels to vintage B&Bs in the neighborhoods that surround Parque Metropolitano La Sabana.

Gaudy's HOSTEL **$**
(Map p76; ☎2248-0086; www.backpacker.co.cr; Av 5, btwn Calles 36 & 38; dm US$14, r with/without bathroom US$39/35; P@📶) Popular with shoestring travelers for years, this homey hostel inside a sprawling modernist house northeast of Parque La Sabana has 13 private rooms and three dormitories. The owners keep the design scheme minimalist and the vibe mellow, with professional service and well-maintained rooms. There's a communal kitchen, a TV lounge, a pool table and a courtyard strung with hammocks.

Mi Casa Hostel HOSTEL **$**
(Map p76; ☎2231-4700; www.micasahostel.com; Las Américas; incl breakfast dm US$21, r with/without bathroom from US$47/40; P@📶) This converted modernist home in La Sabana has polished-wood floors, vintage furnishings and over a dozen eclectic guest rooms to choose from, including one large dorm and another room that's wheelchair-accessible. Mellow communal areas are comfortably furnished and the shared kitchen is clean and roomy. There is a pleasant garden, a pool table, free internet and a laundry service.

They also have locations in Playa Cocles and Playa Grande, if you're headed that way.

Colours Oasis Resort BOUTIQUE HOTEL **$$**
(☎2296-1880, USA & Canada 866-517-4390; www.coloursoasis.com; cnr Triángulo de Pavas & Blvr Rohrmoser; d US$70-150; 📶🏊) This longtime LGBTIQ-friendly hotel occupies a sprawling Key West–style complex in the elegant Rohrmoser district (northwest of La Sabana). Rooms and mini-apartments have modern furnishings and impeccable bathrooms. Facilities include a TV lounge, pool, sundeck and Jacuzzi, as well as an international restaurant, ideal for evening cocktails. Book directly to save.

TALK LIKE A TICO

San José is loaded with schools that offer Spanish lessons (either privately or in groups) and provide long-term visitors to the country with everything from dance lessons to volunteer opportunities. Well-established options include the following:

Costa Rican Language Academy (Map p81; ☎2280-1685, in USA 866-230-6361; www.spanishandmore.com; Calle Ronda, Barrio Dent)

Institute for Central American Development Studies (ICADS; ☎2225-0508; www.icads.org; Calle 87A, Curridabat; month-long courses with/without homestay US$1990/915)

Personalized Spanish (☎2278-3254, USA 786-245-4124, WhatsApp 8543-7152; www.personalizedspanish.com; Tres Ríos)

Already speak Spanish? To truly talk like a Tico, check out the Costa Rica Idioms app, available for iOS. It's quite basic but defines local lingo and uses each term in a sentence. *Tuanis, mae!* (Cool, dude!)

Apartotel La Sabana HOTEL $$
(Map p76; ☎2220-2422, USA & Canada 877-722-2621; www.apartotel-lasabana.com; Calle 48; d/apt incl breakfast from US$105/159; P ❄ @ 📶 🏊) This lovely, well-maintained apartment complex 150m north of Rostipollos has 32 units in various configurations that draw long-term business travelers as well as families. Apartments (with or without kitchen) are accented with wood furnishings and folk art. The interior courtyard has a nice pool, and free shuttle service is offered from the airport (to the airport costs US$8).

★**Hotel Grano de Oro** BOUTIQUE HOTEL $$$
(Map p76; ☎2255-3322; www.hotelgranodeoro.com; Calle 30, btwn Avs 2 & 4; d US$180-372, ste US$390-593; P ⊖ @ 📶) It's easy to see why honeymooners love it here. Built around a sprawling early-20th-century Victorian mansion, this elegant inn has 39 demure 'Tropical Victorian' rooms with wrought-iron beds and rich brocade linens. Some rooms boast private courtyards with gurgling fountains, and a rooftop garden terrace offers two bubbling Jacuzzis. The whole place sparkles with tropical flowers and polished-wood accents. If you want to experience the Costa Rica of a gilded age, this is the place to do it.

The restaurant (p88) is incredible.

Los Yoses, Barrio Escalante & San Pedro

If you ask for directions to your accommodations, note that locals use several prominent landmarks when giving directions, including Spoon restaurant, the Fuente de la Hispanidad fountain and Más X Menos supermarket.

★**Hostel Siesta** HOSTEL $
(Map p81; ☎2234-1091, USA 1-813-750-8572; Av 8, btwn Calles 39 & 41; dm US$13, d from US$32; 📶) For pure positive energy, you won't find a nicer hostel in San José. Now under new ownership, this restful spot, in a hip area of Los Yoses just a block south of Av Central, feels extremely homey, thanks to frequent backyard BBQs, a living room with piano and guitar, and a fully equipped kitchen. Formerly known as Hostel Bekuo.

The airy modernist structure has nine colorful rooms (including four dormitories, one female-only) with high-quality beds and mattresses, along with large tiled bathrooms, an expansive TV lounge dotted with beanbags, and an interior courtyard slung with hammocks. Yet this remains a place where you can get a good night's sleep; quiet time is respected from 10pm onwards.

Hostel Urbano HOSTEL $
(Map p81; ☎2281-0707; www.hostelurbano.com; Calle 39, near Av 8; dm US$12, d with/without bath US$45/35; @ 📶) Within easy walking distance of the university and its nightlife, yet right on the bus line into downtown San José, this immaculate hostel has a coffee shop right next door. Guests feel instantly welcome, with its open floor plan, spacious backyard, pool table, modern internet facilities, Netflix and a kitchen-dining area nice enough for a dinner party.

Smaller rooms, which are often rented out as private doubles, are ideal for groups of three or four friends traveling together. Even the larger 12- and 16-bed dorms manage not to feel claustrophobic, thanks to the thoughtful placement of well-constructed modern bunks.

Lost In Costa Rica Hostel HOSTEL $
(formerly Hostel Casa Yoses; Map p81; ☎8880-0402; www.lostincostaricahostel.com; Av 8, Los Yoses; incl breakfast dm US$10-11, d with/without bathroom US$35/29, q US$69; P @ 📶) This Spanish Revival–style house (1949) perched on a Los Yoses hill was completely re-done by Jose Maria and family in 2019, complete with new four-poster beds and a spectacular set of murals by a visiting Cuban artist. Perks include dance, yoga and crossfit classes, a nocturnal fire pit, and pool table.

Hotel 1492 B&B $
(Map p81; ☎2225-3752, 2280-6265; www.hotel1492.com; Av 1, btwn Calles 29 & 33; r incl breakfast from US$58; P 📶) On a quiet Barrio Escalante side street you'll find this 10-room B&B in a Spanish-style house built in the 1940s by the Volio family. The rooms vary in size, but all are nicely accented, with Portuguese tile work and some original furnishings. Breakfast is served in a charming rear garden.

Hotel Ave del Paraíso HOTEL $$
(Map p81; ☎2225-8515, 2283-6017; www.hotelavedelparaiso.com; Paseo de la Segunda Republica; s/d incl breakfast US$73/84; @ 📶) 🍃 Decorated with beautiful mosaic tiles and a yard full of interesting art, this hotel run by an artsy family is set back from

Los Yoses, Barrio Escalante & San Pedro

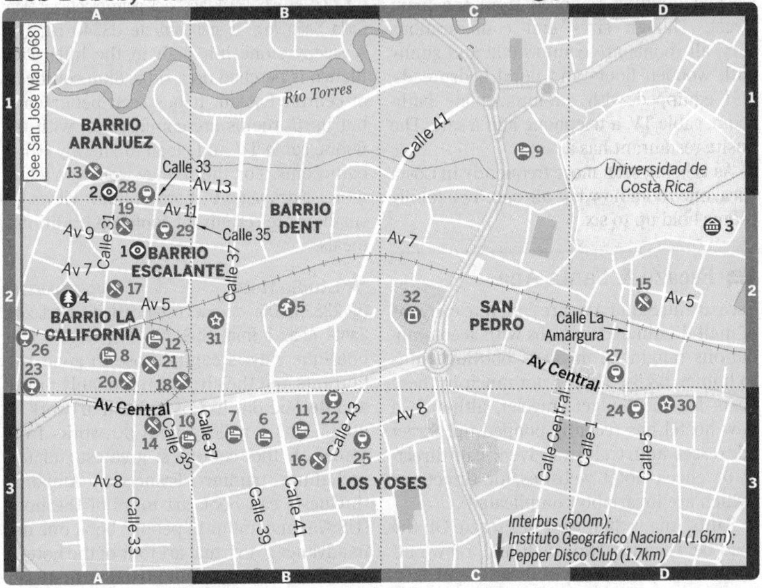

Los Yoses, Barrio Escalante & San Pedro

Sights
1 Barrio Escalante ... A2
2 Cooperación Española Cultura ... A1
3 Museo de Insectos ... D2
4 Parque Francia ... A2

Activities, Courses & Tours
5 Costa Rican Language Academy ... B2

Sleeping
6 Hostel Siesta ... B3
7 Hostel Urbano ... B3
8 Hotel 1492 ... A2
9 Hotel Ave del Paraíso ... C1
10 Hotel Le Bergerac ... A3
11 Lost In Costa Rica Hostel ... B3
12 Luz de Luna ... A2

Eating
13 Al Mercat ... A1
Café Kracovia ... (see 9)
14 Capra Vegano ... A3
15 El Buho ... D2
16 El Portón Rojo ... B3
17 Kalú Café & Food Shop ... A2
18 Lolo's ... A2
Olio ... (see 12)
19 Saúl Bistro ... A2
20 Sikwa ... A2
21 Sofia Mediterráneo ... A2

Drinking & Nightlife
22 Bar Río ... B3
23 Casa House of Beers ... A2
24 La Gata Candonga ... D3
25 Roots Cool and Calm ... B3
26 Sasta Pub ... A2
27 Terra U ... D2
28 Un Lugar Resto-bar ... A1
29 Wilk ... A2

Entertainment
30 Mundoloco ... D3
31 Teatro Eugene O'Neill ... B2

Shopping
Kiosco SJO ... (see 17)
32 Mall San Pedro ... C2

the busy street just far enough to permit a good night's sleep. The wonderful restaurant and bar, Café Kracovia (p88), is owned by the same family. The university is just a two-minute walk east. Partially solar powered.

Hotel Le Bergerac BOUTIQUE HOTEL $$
(Map p81; 2234-7850; www.bergerachotel.com; Calle 35, btwn Avs Central & 8; d incl breakfast standard/superior/deluxe/grande US$111/134/162/179; P ❄ @ ☜) This Los Yoses standard-bearer features 25 rooms, most

with a private garden patio, in a whitewashed building removed from the main street. Though sizes and configurations vary, all rooms are comfortable and sunny with wooden floors and floral bedspreads, and equipped with an immaculate bathroom, cable TV, a telephone and a safe. The onsite restaurant has a bar.

As is being seen more frequently in Costa Rica, one room now has air-con. Two family rooms hold up to six.

Escazú & Santa Ana

Escazú and Santa Ana are concrete canyons of mall-dominated suburbs with accommodations ranging from sleek boutique inns to homey B&Bs. There's not much in these parts for the budget traveler, although a new hostel has recently popped up. Street addresses aren't always given; call directly or check hotel websites for directions (which are invariably complicated).

Santa Ana is 3km west of Escazú. On the road between the two you'll find a few out-of-the-way spots to stay and eat.

Tiger's Den B&B $

(☎8667-3591, 4033-4632, USA 415-251-8676; www.tigersdenbnb.com; La Paco, San Rafael de Escazú; r per person US$30-35; ❄📶) This comfy B&B in residential Escazú is a quiet, homey escape run by Tiger, an attentive former nutritionist and personal trainer who makes art and cooks brilliantly (meals US$10). Guests here are frequently medical and dental tourists, and Tiger can cater to their diets. Prices drop for longer stays, and the host prefers a minimum three-night commitment.

Ask Tiger for directions, or consult the rather specific ones on her website.

Fauna Luxury Hostel HOSTEL $

(Map p83; ☎2289-5020; www.faunahostel.com; Av 30 & Calle 138, Escazú; dm US$10-15, d US$35-50; P❄) From cigarette-shaped 'pods' to dorms and private rooms, this former luxury hotel has made an easy transition to luxe hostel. There are wonderful airy common spaces for cooking and playing ping-pong and pool, and a spectacular view of the city from the rooftop. Odd statuary and other art abound; perks include yoga classes and cheap shuttles downtown and to the airport.

Hotel Mirador Pico Blanco HOTEL $

(☎2289-6197; www.facebook.com/picoblancoinn; Calle Salitrillos; d standard/ste US$40/50; P) A sleepy stone inn high in the hills, Pico Blanco is perched on a ridge 3km southeast of central Escazú. It has seen better days, but its 15 rooms are comfortable, with tile floors, cable TV and clean, if slightly worn, bathrooms. For the money, you won't find more extravagant metropolitan views. A small onsite restaurant cooks up traditional meals.

★Studio Hotel BOUTIQUE HOTEL $$

(☎2282-0505; www.costaricastudiohotel.com; Santa Ana; r from US$120; P❄📶🏊) This boutique stay is comfy, close to good restaurants and the airport, reasonably priced and decked out in Costa Rican artwork. It doubles as a gallery, with 90 works from some of the country's greatest talents, including painter Francisco Amighetti. Guests can book art tours of the hotel (US$75, maximum 12 people, book one day in advance). A virtual art tour of the hotel is available on the website; try that first! The third floor bar-pool area provides a cozy and splendid view of the area.

It's located 50m north of the Red Cross (Cruz Roja).

Posada El Quijote B&B $$

(☎2289-8401; www.quijote.cr; Calle del Llano; incl breakfast d standard/superior/deluxe/studio apt US$85/95/109/109; P⊖❄📶🏊) This Spanish-style hillside *posada* (guesthouse) rates as one of the area's top B&Bs. Homey standard rooms have wooden floors, throw rugs, cable TV and hot-water bathrooms; superior and deluxe units have a patio or a private terrace. Guests can drink at the honor bar, then soak up sweeping Central Valley views from the patio, the new pool, or the fireplace.

A backyard swing set and trampoline make this place especially fun for families with kids. A 2019 makeover included installation of new floors, flat-screen televisions, updated bathrooms, and air-con. Popular with medical tourists.

Costa Verde Inn INN $$

(☎2228-4080, in USA 1-800-773-5013; www.costaverdeinn.com; Av 34, Escazú; s/d/tr incl breakfast US$68/73/80, d apt from US$90; P@📶🏊) This homey stone inn is surrounded by gardens that contain a hot tub, fireplace,

Escazú

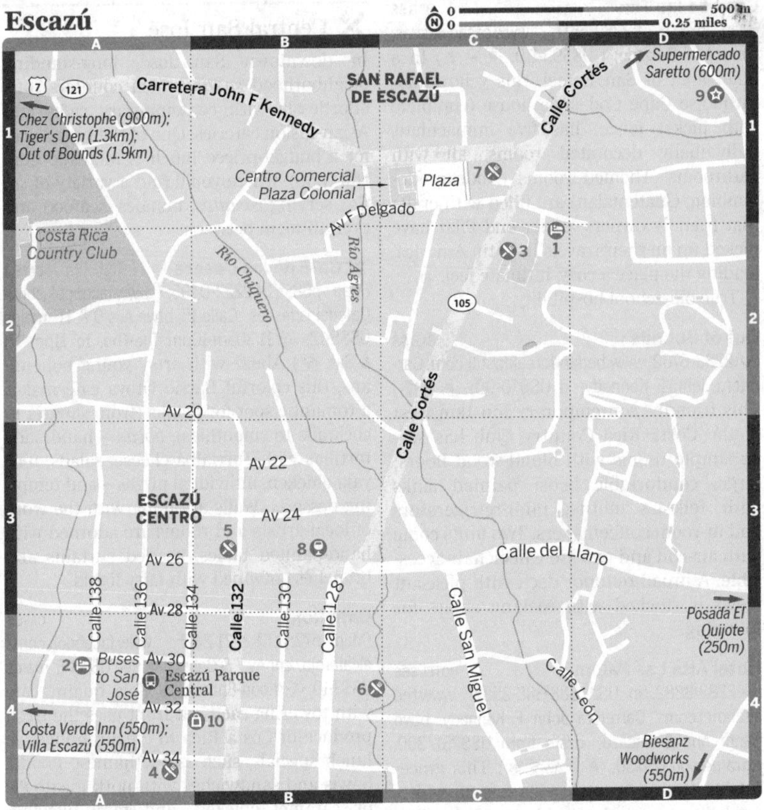

a mosaic-tiled swimming pool, a BBQ area and a sundeck with wi-fi. Sixteen rooms of various sizes have queen- or king-size beds, comfy rocking chairs and folk-art accents. Six apartments come with a fully equipped kitchen. A generous Tico breakfast is served on the outdoor terrace.

Weekly and monthly rates are available.

Villa Escazú B&B **$$**
(☎2289-7971; www.hotels.co.cr/villaescazu; Av 36; d incl breakfast US$65, apt US$300-325 week; P 📶) This wooden chalet with a wrap-around veranda is surrounded by gardens and fruit trees. The two quaint wood-paneled rooms feature local artwork, comfy couches and a shared bathroom. Breakfast is served on the outdoor balcony. There's a two-night minimum stay in the B&B and a five-night minimum in the apartments: reserve well in advance. It's 900m west of Banco Nacional.

Escazú

Sleeping
1 Casa de las Tías C2
2 Fauna Luxury Hostel A4

Eating
3 Automercado C2
4 Buena Tierra A4
5 Casona de Laly B3
6 La Posada de las Brujas B4
7 Más X Menos C1

Drinking & Nightlife
8 Pub B3

Entertainment
9 Little Theatre Group D1

Shopping
10 Sin Domicilio Fijo B4

Casa de las Tías B&B $$
(Map p83; 2289-5517; www.casadelastias.com; Av F Delgado; r US$95-110;) In a quiet area of San Rafael, this yellow-and-turquoise Cape Cod–style house (complete with picket fence) has five immaculate, individually decorated rooms, all with bathrooms. Themed rooms (Andean, Colombian, Guatemalan) are filled with crafts that friendly owners Xavier and Pilar have picked up on their travels in Latin America, lending the place a cozy, intimate feel.

True old-school hospitality.

Out of Bounds B&B $$
(2288-6762; www.bedandbreakfastcr.com; Carretera John F Kennedy; d US$70-90;) This friendly, contemporary inn 1km west of the Costa Rica Country Club has seven simple rooms with blond-wood floors; large, comfortable beds; painted sinks with folk-art motifs; mini-refrigerators and in-room coffeemakers. Two units come with air-con and two are wheelchair accessible. A broad outdoor deck with pleasant views is stocked with rocking chairs for lounging.

Hotel Alta Las Palomas HOTEL $$$
(2282-8882, in USA 888-388-2582; www.thealtahotel.com; Carretera John F Kennedy, btwn Santa Ana & Escazú; d/ste from US$231/300, extra person US$30;) This graceful Mediterranean-style villa has 23 whitewashed rooms decked out in terracotta tiles, contemporary wood furnishings and expansive bathrooms equipped with hair dryers and robes. Upstairs balconies offer stunning views of the surrounding hills, and the on-site restaurant, La Luz, serves up fresh Mediterranean fare in an elegant setting. An upstairs parlor often hosts classical music performances.

Eating

From humble corner stands dishing out gut-filling *casados* (set meals) to contemporary bistros serving fusion everything, in cosmopolitan San José you'll find the country's best restaurant and cafe scene. Dedicated foodies should check out the options in Los Yoses and San Pedro, as well as Escazú and Santa Ana.

Top-end restaurants are often busy on weekend evenings; make a reservation.

Central San José

In downtown San José, long-standing neighborhood *sodas* (lunch counters) mix effortlessly with contemporary cafes and Asian-fusion eateries. One of the best places for a budget-priced lunch is Mercado Central (p66), where you'll find a variety of *sodas* serving *casados*, tamales, seafood and everything in between.

★**Café de los Deseos** CAFE $
(Map p68; 2222-0496; www.facebook.com/Cafedelosdeseos; Calle 15, btwn Avs 9 & 11; mains US$5-12; 11:30am-10pm Tue-Thu, to 11pm Fri & Sat;) Abuzz with artsy young bohemians, this colorful Barrio Otoya cafe makes a romantic spot for drinks (from sangria to cocktails to smoothies), *bocas* – handmade tortillas with Turrialba cheese, salads, teriyaki chicken, individual pizzas – and tempting desserts. Walls are hung with the work of local artists and rooms are adorned with hand-painted tables, beaded curtains and branches entwined with fairy lights.

Café Rojo CAFE $
(Map p72; 2221-2425; www.facebook.com/elcaferojo; cnr Av 7 & Calle 3; coffee US$3-5, mains US$7-10; noon-8pm;) This quaint cafe with towering cacti out front uses the fresh produce of Costa Rica to create innovative lunch specials, such as Vietnamese noodle bowls and sandwiches with pork meatballs or caramel chicken, and mind-blowingly delicious Asian-inspired salads. Vegans will find plenty to like here, as will coffee enthusiasts.

All the flavorings and syrups for drinks are homemade, and the iced ginger coffee is divine.

Restaurante La Criollita COSTA RICAN $
(Map p72; 2256-6511; Av 7, btwn Calles 7 & 9; breakfast from US$3, casados US$8-10; 6am-9pm Mon-Fri, until 4pm Sat, 8am-5pm Sun) This homey local spot, popular with office types, dishes out a changing menu of simple Costa Rican specialties, such as stewed chicken or grilled fish. The setting is pleasant and the service efficient, and you can order a glass of Chilean or Spanish wine (US$4) to accompany your meal.

Café Miel Garage CAFE $
(Map p72; www.cafemielgarage.com; Av 9, btwn Calle 11 & 13; coffee US$2-5, pastries US$2; 9am-6pm Mon-Sat, 1-6pm Sun) This tiny cafe opened

to such wild success in 2014 that the owners quickly opened another nearby. What's its secret? In addition to adorable and homey interiors, it's the artisanal products from the chefs and bakers. The mushroom *empanadas* are divine, as is the locally sourced coffee.

La Ventanita Meraki FAST FOOD $
(Map p68; ☎2221-8016; www.facebook.com/laventanitameraki; cnr Av 3 & Calle 21; mains US$5-8; ⏰6pm-midnight Tue-Thu, to 2am Fri-Sun) Ventanita means 'little window' in Spanish and Meraki means 'artistry' in Greek. Together it's an accurate moniker for this hole-in-the-wall, to-go window across from downtown's train station that serves innovative street food. Expect elaborate spins on typical fare, plus sandwiches such as Pumpkin Butter Cheese Madness, and Twinkie *frito* (fried Twinkie) for dessert.

Opens and closes late, for the bar crowd.

Restaurante Shakti VEGETARIAN $
(Map p68; cnr Av 8 & Calle 13; mains US$5-10; ⏰7:30am-6pm Mon-Fri, to 5pm Sat; 🖉) This informal neighborhood health-food outpost has simple, organic-focused cooking and freshly baked bread and other niceties. Favorites include veggie burgers, along with various fish and chicken dishes, but most people come for the vegetarian *plato del día* (meal of the day) – only US$6 for soup, salad, main course and fruit drink (or US$8 with coffee and dessert thrown in).

You'll find it below the hostel of the same name (p75).

Alma de Café CAFE $
(Map p72; ☎2010-1119; www.teatronacional.go.cr/Cafeteria; Teatro Nacional, Av 2, btwn Calles 3 & 5; mains US$6-11; ⏰9am-7pm Mon-Sat, to 6pm Sun) One of the most beautiful cafes in the city, this spot evokes early 20th-century Vienna. It's a perfect place to sip a cappuccino, enjoy a crepe or quiche and take in the lovely ceiling frescoes and rotating art exhibitions. The coffee concoctions – such as the chocolate *alma de cafe*, spiked with cinnamon and clove – are an excellent midday indulgence.

Talentum CAFE $
(Restaurante Tournant; Map p68; ☎2256-6346, restaurant 2248-9523; www.galeriatalentum.com; Av 11, btwn Calles 3 & 3A; lunch specials US$8-12; ⏰restaurant noon-4pm Mon & Tue, noon-10pm Wed-Fri, 1-10pm Sat, gallery 11am-6pm Mon-Sat) This vibrant, quirky cultural space/gallery in a renovated mansion sports local artwork inside and out. There's cozy seating on vintage couches, plus tables made from old sewing machines and an outdoor deck; it's a fun place for a midday break. The ever-changing cultural agenda includes book signings, films, anatomical drawing classes and occasional live music.

Perla Negra CAFE $
(Map p72; ☎2222-8272; cnr Av 7 & Calle 13; mains US$6, cakes US$1.50-3; ⏰10:30am-7:30pm Mon-Fri, noon-7:30pm Sat; 📶🖉🐾) This petite cafe in Barrio Amón retains the stained glass windows from an earlier incarnation and adds a Chaplinesque touch, though it's now owned by the small Perla Negra chain. It's a perfect place to work over a flavored espresso, latte or affogato (ice cream topped with espresso), then stay for a fresh salad, delicious omelette or 'monster brownie.'

De Acá CAFE $
(Mini Mercado y Vegan Cafe; Map p72; ☎7014-3221; Calle 3A, btwn Av 9 & 11, Barrio Amón; desserts & smoothies US$5-6, mains US$7-9; ⏰11:30am-7pm; 🖉) A vegan cafe with the best cappuccino in Barrio Amón, wonderful views from the top two floors connected by winding staircases, and a nice shop with animal-friendly products on the first floor. For the thirsty a raft of tasty smoothies are on the menu, as well as a 'liquid tiramisu.' A smattering of cakes, calzones, empanadas, and tacos satisfy the hungry.

Café del Barista CAFE $
(Map p68; ☎2221-4712; www.facebook.com/CafeDelBarista; Av 9, btwn Calles 19 & 21; mains US$5-7; ⏰7am-6pm Mon-Fri) This corrugated-roofed, warehouse-like space in Barrio Aranjuez brews up a great cup of gourmet coffee (US$2 to US$3) and makes a halfway decent cinnamon roll too. House-brewed beer makes every hour a happy hour.

Steinvorth Building FOOD HALL $$
(El Stein; Map p72; www.edificiosteinvorth.com; Calle 1 btwn Avs Central & 1) Food court! American burger bar! Brewpub/pizzeria! Performance space/movie theater/lecture hall! The Stein, seized from German immigrants during WWII and restored by noted Tico architect Julian Mora in 2008, is a cool bit of Chepe architecture, lit from within by a massive skylight. It's a place where something seems to be happening at any given time, from weekday coffee to Friday-night jazz.

Bò CATALAN $$
(Map p72; ☎2222-1003; Av 2 & Calle 7; sausages US$6-7; ⏰5pm-midnight) Bò is a play on words involving the Catalan word for 'good' and '*botifarra*', their signature *salchicha* (sausage similar to a hot dog). Josep offers up a dozen varieties of the savory stuffed skin: Philly cheese-steak to Korean kimchi-style are on offer, but you'll die for the original (*laia*), which needs no toppings at all.

A stunning interior designed by a Pritzker-winning architect only makes things better. Local jazzers often end up here in impromptu, cava-drenched sessions.

It's located 150m east of the National Theater.

Maza Bistro BISTRO $$
(Map p68; ☎2248-4824; www.facebook.com/MazaBistro; Calle 19; mains US$10-12, brunch US$10-12; ⏰9am-5pm Tue-Sun; 🌿) At this charming, alfresco restaurant attached to Hostel Casa del Parque (p75), brunch is served all day, with dishes such as *huevos pochados* (poached eggs with hollandaise sauce) and braised beef shank *au jus* with pickled vegetables and a fried egg. The burgers combine three kinds of meat and are also a hit, along with daily veggie options (think pumpkin sandwiches).

You'll find it on Parque Nacional.

Café Mundo ITALIAN $$
(Map p72; ☎2222-6190; cnr Av 9 & Calle 15; mains US$8-36; ⏰11am-10:30pm Mon-Fri, 5-11:30pm Sat; 🌿) This longtime Italian cafe and expat favorite is set on a sprawling terrace in a vintage Barrio Otoya mansion with a green exterior. It's a perfect spot to enjoy a glass of wine and good (if not earth-shattering) pizzas and pastas within sight of a splashing outdoor fountain. Don't miss the good-value *plato del día* (US$10) at weekday lunchtime.

El Patio del Balmoral INTERNATIONAL $$
(Map p72; ☎2222-5022; www.balmoral.co.cr; Av Central, btwn Calles 7 & 9; mains US$8-27; ⏰4-10pm Tue-Sat) Filled with chattering gringos and suited Ticos, this all-purpose cafe-restaurant is a good place to chill out while taking in the pedestrian action on Av Central. The upstairs terrace bar hosts live bands on Friday nights.

Alma de Amón LATIN AMERICAN $$
(Map p72; ☎4700-2637; www.facebook.com/AlmadeAmon; Calle 5, btwn Avs 9 & 11; small plates US$6-9, large plates US$10-18; ⏰6am-10pm Mon-Wed, to midnight Thu-Sat, 6-11am Sun) With dishes from nearly a dozen Latin countries, this open-air restaurant is a solid Barrio Amón option. Popular menu items include *patacon pisao* (a Venezuelan dish with fried plantains) and *rondón vegano* (a healthier version of traditional Caribbean stew with tumeric and coconut). The bartender shakes up spicy, delicious cocktails; 'El Chapulin' has tequila, ginger beer, lime and sugar-cane syrup.

El Tostador CAFE $$
(Map p72; ☎4056-5604; cnr Av Central & Calle 2; mains US$8-20; ⏰9am-7pm) A sleek, monochromatic cafe with excellent views of the ornate Correo Central building (p98), this multilevel spot near the heart of San José's pedestrian zone is perfect for coffee drinks (including delicious iced mochas) and pastries. Try the *empanadas* or breakfast burritos, which go well with the cafe's homemade hot sauce. Lovers beware: heed the 'no makeout' (*escenas romanticas*) signs.

One of the many El Tostador chains in town and around Costa Rica.

Kaps Cafe CAFE $$
(Map p68; ☎2221-1169; www.kapsplace.com; Calle 19, btwn Avs 11 & 13; mains US$7-15; ⏰7am-7pm Mon-Sat, from 11am Sun; 📶) A lovely little eatery linked to the eponymous hostel (p78), with yummy coffee plus creative pastries and sandwiches. Especially great carrot cake.

Tin Jo ASIAN $$
(Map p68; ☎2257-3622, 2221-7605; www.tinjo.com; Calle 11, btwn Avs 6 & 8; mains US$11-19; ⏰11:30am-2:30pm & 6-10pm Mon-Thu, til 11pm Fri, noon-3:30pm & 6-11pm Sat, noon-9pm Sun; 🌿) The interiors of this popular standard-bearer are a riot of pan-Asian everything, just like the menu. Themed salons – from Chinese to Indian to Japanese – reflect the diverse food choices. Expect a wide range of fare from various regions – from kung pao shrimp to crunchy shrimp rolls to pad thai – as well as an extensive vegetarian menu.

Reservations recommended.

Restaurante Silvestre COSTA RICAN $$$
(Cothnejo Fishy Cantina; Map p68; www.restaurantesilvestre.com; Av 11, near Calle 3A, Barrio Amón; mains US$20-30, tasting menu US$60; ⏰6-11pm Mon-Sat) Chef Santiago has created a sensation upstairs with his six-course tasting menu. Equally enjoyable and more

relaxed, the downstairs *cantina* serves variations on traditional *cantina* food: succulent bone marrow, white beans with pork skin, *pulpo vigorón* (crispy octopus) on a creamy cassava croquette, and *pejibaye* (peach palm) chips. Plenty of romantic corners to get lost in.

Must try: the Tico Mule.

La Terrasse
FRENCH $$$

(Map p68; ☑8939-8470; www.restaurantlaterrasse.blogspot.com; Calle 15, btwn Avs 9 & 11; mains US$17-32; ⊗noon-2pm & 7-10pm Tue-Fri, 7-10pm Sat, noon-2pm Sun) Hidden away in the living room of a 1927 Barrio Otoya home, this intimate French restaurant regularly welcomes well-heeled locals with something to celebrate. Talented chef Patricia reveals her fine sensibilities in thick, creamy soups and cheeses, hearty meat dishes and imaginative presentation. Her husband, the gracious Gerald, plays host. Order French wine and a few dishes to share.

By reservation only, payment in cash or bank transfer.

✖ La Sabana & Around

There's a good mix of upscale international cuisine and fast food around the park. Supermarkets include **Más X Menos** (Map p76; ☑2248-1396; www.masxmenos.co.cr; cnr Autopista General Cañas & Av 5; ⊗7am-midnight Mon-Sat, to 10pm Sun; P) and **Palí** (Map p76; ☑2256-5887; www.maxipali.co.cr; Paseo Colón, btwn Calles 24 & 26; ⊗8am-8pm Mon-Sat, 8:30am-6pm Sun; P).

Soda Tapia
SODA $

(Map p76; ☑2222-6734; www.facebook.com/sodatapia; cnr Av 2 & Calle 42; mains US$4-10, desserts US$2-7; ⊗6am-2am Sun-Thu, 24hr Fri & Sat; P☻) An unpretentious '50s-style diner with garish red-and-white decor, this place is perpetually filled with couples and families noshing on grilled sandwiches and generous *casados*. If you have the nerve, try the monstrous 'El Gordo,' a pile of steak or chicken with onions, cheese, lettuce, bacon and tomato served on Spanish bread. Save room: ice cream and fruit sundaes are the specialty.

La Sorbetera de Lolo Mora
DESSERTS $

(Map p72; ☑2256-5000; www.facebook.com/Lolomora1901; Mercado Central, Avs Central & 1, btwn Calles 6 & 8; desserts US$2-5; ⊗9:30am-5:30pm Mon-Sat) Head to the main market for dessert at this century-old local favorite that

serves up fresh sorbet and cinnamon-laced frozen custard. Do as the locals do and also order *barquillos* (cylindrical sugar cookies that are perfect for dipping).

Mariscos Poseidon
SEAFOOD $

(Map p72; ☑2221-8589; Mercado Central Annex; mains US$5-12; ⊗9am-6pm Mon-Fri, to 5pm Sat) The congenial Doris runs this narrow blue-and-yellow seafood joint in the northern wing of the central market (p66). The *ceviche mixto* appetizer (fish, shrimp and octopus marinated in lime juice) is tasty and cheap, as are the generous portions of seafood-studded rice. Find it in a narrow passage outside and across Avenida 1 from the main market.

Lubnan
LEBANESE $$

(Map p76; ☑2257-6071; www.facebook.com/lubnancr; Paseo Colón, btwn Calles 22 & 24; mains US$8-25; ⊗11am-3pm & 6pm-midnight Tue-Fri, noon-4pm & 6-11pm Sat, 11am-5pm Sun; P) This atmospheric Lebanese place is a great date spot, with creamy hummus, flavorful tabbouleh and an array of succulent meats – some cooked, some deliciously raw. Waiters wear fezzes and a live belly-dancing performance goes down every Thursday at 8pm. A cave-like ambiance with pillowy seats enhances the *1001 Nights* feeling.

Machu Picchu
PERUVIAN $$

(Map p76; ☑2222-7384; www.facebook.com/restaurante.machu.picchu; Calle 32, btwn Avs 1 & 3; mains US$9-22; ⊗11am-10pm Mon-Sat, to 6pm Sun; P☏☻) This locally renowned Peruvian restaurant does Andean right. A popular spot for a leisurely Sunday lunch, it has a broad menu featuring Peruvian classics such as *pulpo al olivo* (octopus in olive sauce), *ají de gallina* (a nutty chicken stew) and *causa* (chilled potato terrines stuffed with shrimp and avocado). The pisco sours here are deliciously powerful.

Las Mañanitas
MEXICAN $$

(Map p76; ☑2248-1593; Calle 40, btwn Paseo Colón & Av 3; mains US$6-17; ⊗11:30am-10pm Mon-Sat) At this authentic Mexican place near the park, well-rendered specialties include tacos in sets of four – corn tortillas accompanied by chicken, steak, sea bass or *carne al pastor* (spiced pork). Fans of *mole poblano* (central Mexico's famous chili and chocolate sauce) will also want to try it here, as the restaurant's owner Oscar hails from Puebla.

Restaurante Grano de Oro FUSION $$$

(Map p76; 2255-3322; www.hotelgranodeoro.com; Calle 30, btwn Avs 2 & 4; lunch mains US$15-29, dinner mains US$19-42; 7am-10pm) Known for its Costa Rican–fusion cuisine, this stately, flower-filled restaurant is one of San José's top dining destinations. The menu features unusual specialties such as sea bass breaded with toasted macadamia nuts, or seared duck crowned with caramelized figs. There's an encyclopedic international wine list. For dessert, don't miss the coffee-cream mousse. Dinner reservations recommended.

Los Yoses, Barrio Escalante & San Pedro

Succulent Turkish sandwiches, Mediterranean pastas, vegan tacos, wood-fired pizzas – you can find every type of cuisine imaginable in this corner of the city. Just north of Los Yoses, Calles 33 and 35 in Barrio Escalante are prime foodie destinations, boasting several fine restaurants within a few city blocks.

Capra Vegano VEGAN $

(Map p81; Av Central, near Calle 35, Los Yoses; mains US$5-6; noon-9pm Mon-Sat) Just down the street but a million miles away from Starbucks in look, feel, and taste, this hole-in-the-wall offers wholesome and delicious plates of tacos and giant cups of delicious coffee. Gay friendly and welcoming to all.

★Olio MEDITERRANEAN $$

(Map p81; 2281-0541; www.facebook.com/Restaurante.olio; cnr Calle 33 & Av 3; tapas from US$7, dishes US$12-22; 11:30am-11pm Mon-Wed, to midnight Thu & Fri, 5pm-midnight Sat;) This cozy, Mediterranean-flavored gastropub in a century-old brick building in Barrio Escalante serves a long list of tempting tapas (many veggie), including divine stuffed mushrooms, goat-cheese croquettes and pastas. The enticing drinks list includes homemade sangria and a decent selection of beers and wine. It's a romantic spot for a date, with imaginative, conversation-worthy quirks of decor and beautiful patrons.

Café Kracovia CAFE $$

(Map p81; 2253-9093; www.cafekracovia.com; Paseo del la Segunda Republica; snacks US$4-10, mains US$8-14; 10:30am-9pm Mon, to 11pm Tue-Sat;) With several distinct spaces – from the low-lit, intimate basement to the outdoor garden courtyard – this hip cafe has something for everyone. Contemporary artwork and a university vibe create an appealing ambiance for lunching on crepes, wraps, salads, sweet and savory Polish pierogi and craft beer. It's 500m north of the Fuente de la Hispanidad, just past the university entrance.

Saúl Bistro MEDITERRANEAN $$

(Map p81; 2228-8685; www.saulemendez.com/cr/gastronomia/saul-bistros; cnr Av 9 & Calle 31, Barrio Escalante; appetizers US$10-16, mains US$11-25; 7am-10pm Mon-Thu, to midnight Fri-Sun) There are life-sized plastic zebras in the dining room at this snazzy Escalante open-air restaurant. An extension of Saúl Mendez, the Guatemala-based empire of men's fashion, the restaurant is adorned with curious art, bubbling fountains and vertical gardens. It serves delicious Mediterranean cuisine, savory crepes, fine wines and exquisite cocktails.

Lolo's PIZZA $$

(La Cava de Lolo; Map p81; 2283-9627; pizzas US$14-24; 6pm-midnight Mon-Sat) Fans of bohemian chic will appreciate this quirky pizzeria, hidden in a mustard-yellow house (No 3396) along the railroad tracks north of Av Central in Barrio Escalante. The vibrantly colorful, low-lit interior, hung with an eclectic collection of armor and other medieval bric-a-brac, creates an artsy, romantic setting for sangria and pizzas fired up in the bright-red oven out back.

Sikwa COSTA RICAN $$

(Map p81; cnr Calle 33 & Av 1, Barrio Escalante; mains US$10-16, appetizers US$7; noon-10pm) Pablo Bonilla's intention is no less than to rescue indigenous cuisine in his homeland. Sikwa ('outsider') is an interesting take on Costa Rican indigenous food, with an 'ancestral tasting menu' (US$50) of six courses and a fascinating blue-corn-and-ginger drink called *cichleme*.

Ambient (sometimes annoying) music, simple brick facade.

El Buho VEGETARIAN $$

(Map p81; 2224-6293; www.facebook.com/ElBuhoVegetariano; Av 5; mains US$10-18; 11:30am-6pm Mon-Fri;) Drawing health-food devotees from the nearby university and further afield, this buzzing San Pedro eatery just off Calle de la Amargura serves a variety of vegan, vegetarian and gluten-free treats, from eggplant croquettes and stir-fries to mushroom casseroles to passionfruit cookies. It's 25m east of Calle 3.

El Portón Rojo PIZZA **$$**

(Map p81; ☎2224-4872; www.elportonrojo.com; cnr Av 10 & Calle 43; pizzas small US$8-10, large US$16-18; ⏲noon-3pm & 5:30-11pm Tue-Sat, 5:30-11pm Mon, noon-5pm Sun) Serving up some of the best pizza and sangria in the Los Yoses area, this hip restaurant doubles as a gallery. Funky local art sells right off the brick walls, and a steady influx of customers from the local hostels keeps things lively.

Kalú Café & Food Shop INTERNATIONAL **$$$**

(Map p81; ☎2253-8367, 2253-8426; www.kalu.co.cr; cnr Calle 31 & Av 5; mains US$15-21; ⏲noon-7pm Tue-Fri, 9am-7pm Sat-Sun; ✎) Sharing a sleek space with Kiosco SJO (p96) in Barrio Escalante, chef Camille Ratton's exceptional cafe serves a global fusion menu of soups, salads, sandwiches, pastas and unconventional delights such as the fish taco trio filled with mango-glazed salmon, red-curry prawns and macadamia-crusted tuna. Don't miss the mind-meltingly delicious passion-fruit pie (US$7, but you only live once).

Sofia Mediterráneo MEDITERRANEAN **$$$**

(Map p81; ☎2224-5050; www.facebook.com/SofiaMediterraneo; cnr Calle 33 & Av 1; mains US$12-28; ⏲6-11pm Mon & Wed-Fri, noon-11pm Sat, noon-5pm & 6:30-9pm Sun; ✎) This Barrio Escalante gem serves a superb mix of authentic Mediterranean specialties, including house-made hummus, tortellini, grilled lamb and a rotating selection of daily specials, accompanied by sweet, delicate baklava for dessert. The restaurant doubles as a community cultural center where owner Mehmet Onuralp hosts occasional themed dinners featuring musicians, chefs and speakers from around the world.

Al Mercat GASTRONOMY **$$$**

(Map p81; ☎2221-0783; http://almercat.com; Av 13, Barrio Escalante; mains US$15-30, bocas US$8-10; ⏲noon-5pm Tue & Wed, noon-5pm & 6:30-10pm Thu-Sat, noon-3pm Sun; ✎) Inspired by Tico author Aquileo Echeverria, Cordon Bleu alumnus Jose González serves market-fresh produce, often from his own *finca*. Family-style dishes of corn and sweet potato *chalupas* or grilled vegetables with smoked cheese are fresh and flavorful; both vegetarians and carnivores are well served. The service is impeccable and the atmosphere is enlivened by vertical gardens.

The chef has recently added smaller and less expensive plates to the menu, such as tacos and *ceviche*.

Escazú & Santa Ana

These two suburbs are home to a great many upmarket restaurants, as well as some fine farmers markets and plenty of gourmet grocery stores, including **Automercado** (Map p83; ☎2588-1812; Atlantis Plaza, Calle Cortés, San Rafael de Escazú; ⏲7am-10pm Mon-Sat, 8am-9pm Sun), **Más X Menos** (Map p83; ☎2228-2230; Centro Comercial Escazú, Carretera John F Kennedy, San Rafael; ⏲6:30am-midnight Mon-Sat, to 10pm Sun) and **Supermercado Saretto** (☎7209-1512; www.saretto.cr; Av Central, Escazu, 100m west of Peri Anonos; ⏲8am-9pm).

Buena Tierra CAFETERIA **$**

(Map p83; ☎2288-0342; cnr Calle 134 & Av 34; mains US$6-8; ⏲9am-5:30pm Mon-Fri, 8am-noon Sat; ✎) This friendly organic cafe and health-food store in Escazú Centro has tree-trunk tabletops and huge windows. The sandwiches are sublime and the coffee is delicious. The cafe also organizes a Wednesday-morning organic farmers market (8am to 11am).

Chez Christophe BAKERY **$**

(☎2228-2512; www.facebook.com/ChezChristopheCR; Calle Convento; pastries US$2-5; ⏲7am-7pm Tue-Sat, 8am-7pm Sun) If you have a hankering for a coffee éclair, croque monsieur or plain (but transcendent) croissant, linger here. French *tostadas* are reserved for Sunday, but every other day this authentic French bakery offers freshly baked breads and pastries, as well as espresso and a full breakfast and lunch menu. Across the street from Centro Comerical El Paco in Escazû.

★**Maxi's By Ricky** CARIBBEAN **$$**

(☎2282-8619; www.facebook.com/Restaurant.Maxi; Calle San Rafael, Santa Ana; appetizers US$5-8, mains US$10-20; ⏲noon-10:30pm) If you can't get to the Caribbean coast, the 'yard' vibe here is a good substitute. Manzanillo native Ricky transported his lip-smacking restaurant to the Central Valley so *josefinos* could feast on the traditional rice-n-beans, Caribbean chicken and *rondón* soup. The small plates (*bocas*) are a perfect chance for everybody to try a little of everything. Delish!

It's tricky to find: ask locally for directions. If you get too chill (literally), there's an outdoor fireplace.

alTapas Bar TAPAS $$

(☎2282-4871; www.facebook.com/tapeandorico; Radial Santa Ana, Santa Ana; tapas US$10-25; ⏲5pm-2am Tue-Thu, noon-2pm Fri & Sat, noon-10pm Sun; 📶) Owned by four brothers, this Spanish tapas restaurant is over-the-top hospitable, offering guests a complimentary glass of *cava* (sparkling Catalonian wine) and a flavorful mini-croquette at the start of the meal, best followed by dishes such as octopus in garlic and expertly prepared paella. Consider finishing with a *creme de catalan,* sister to France's crème brûlée, with a digestive of blueberry/anis spirits.

It's 150m north of the Red Cross, next to Studio Hotel.

Los hermanos Puigcorbé have opened a downtown bar as well, Bó (p86), just near the National Theater, echoing the 21st century architectural sensibilities of one of the brothers. It offers Catalan sausage (*bottefarra*) and other *bocas* (appetizers).

Container Platz GASTRONOMY $$

(☎6050-1045; www.facebook.com/ContainerPlatz; Calle 5, Santa Ana; mains US$6-15; ⏲noon-10pm Mon-Thu, 11am-midnight Fri & Sat, 11am-8pm Sun) In this innovative gastronomic experiment, 20 mini-businesses representing Latin American and world flavors have sprung to life in brightly painted shipping containers in Santa Ana. It earns high marks for innovation and reasonably priced, artisanal fast food, with everything from a circus-themed nacho place to a churros factory and a 'hummuseria' that serves its house-made hummus with delectable pita triangles.

Communal picnic tables foster a sense of camaraderie, as does the craft-beer container and play area for kiddies. Hours vary slightly by business.

La Posada de las Brujas COSTA RICAN $$

(Map p83; ☎2228-1645; https://laposadadelasbrujas.business.site; off Av 30, btwn Calles San Miguel & 128, Escazú; mains US$6-24; ⏲11am-midnight Tue-Sat, to 10pm Sun; 🅿👪) This open-air steak house is one of Escazú's finest family options. Spacious indoor and outdoor seating accommodates large groups, and big eaters are well served with heaped plates of rice, beans, fried plantains and a meat of their choice. The trampolines will be big hits with kids.

Casona de Laly COSTA RICAN $$

(Map p83; ☎2288-1507; www.lacasonadelalycr.com; cnr Av 26 & Calle 1, Escazú; US$7-34; ⏲11am-11pm Mon-Sat, to 9pm Sun; 🅿) All four branches of this Escazú staple have the same delicious Costa Rican menu that everybody has always showed up for, including hearty *casados,* grilled meats and luscious seafood soup. There's a multicolored light-up sign outside, along with a small parking lot, a bunch of flat-screens and a small bar in the corner.

The other three Lalys are in neighboring suburbs, but this original location remains the favorite.

Tiquicia COSTA RICAN $$

(Mirador Tiquicia; ☎2289-7330; www.miradortiquicia.com; Calle Cuesta Grande, Escazú; bocas US$5-17, mains US$13-23; ⏲noon-11pm Tue-Thu, to midnight Fri & Sat, to 9pm Sun) This long-running hilltop restaurant 5km south of Escazú Centro serves up bounteous platters, accompanied by live folk music on weekends. Yes, the food is only so-so, but you're not here to eat, you're here to admire the extravagant views of the Central Valley. It's tricky to find; call for directions.

🍷 Drinking & Nightlife

Chepe's artsiest, most sophisticated drinking venues are concentrated north and east of the center, in Barrio Amón and Barrio Escalante. For a rowdier, younger scene, head to Barrio la California or Calle la Amargura (p92).

Best for cityscapes and cocktails are the rooftop bar at Hotel Presidente (p77) and the upstairs terrace at El Patio del Balmoral (p86). The people-watching rocks at Café de los Deseos (p84) in Barrio Otoya and at Mercado La California.

🍷 Central San José

On weekends, the streets of La California in central San José are packed with 20-something revelers puffing cigarettes and pondering where to head for the next *chili guaro* (an increasingly popular shot with sugar-cane liquor, hot sauce and lime juice). Meanwhile, young professionals hit up the fancier cocktail bars.

★ Casa House of Beers CRAFT BEER
(Map p81; ☎ 8345-4100; Av Central btwn Calle 27 & 27A; ⏲ 6pm-midnight Mon-Thu, until 2am Fri-Sat) On the other side of Av Central from the rowdier college bars, this two-level house has about two dozen beers on tap to satisfy the thirstiest of hop-starved pilgrims. Programmed music fills downstairs while live bands and DJs thrash away on the second floor. Good, relatively cheap food (sausage, pizza) too. Magnificently decrepit.

★ Stiefel PUB
(Map p72; ☎ 8850-2119; www.facebook.com/StiefelPub; Av 5; ⏲ 11:30am-2pm & 6pm-2am Mon-Sat) Two dozen-plus Costa Rican microbrews on tap and an appealing setting in a historical building create a convivial buzz at this pub half a block from Plaza España. Grab a pint of Pelona or Maldita Vida, Malinche or Chichemel; better yet, order a flight of four miniature sampler glasses and try 'em all.

La Bohemia CAFE
(Map p68; Calle 5 near Av 12; ⏲ 5pm-midnight) Old-school San José *cantina* La Bohemia is a traditional gathering place of poets and *guitarristas*, whose spirits still sometimes trouble the night air. Cheap beer, regular company, and three appetizers which the bartender has memorized (meatballs, garbanzos, and *ceviche*): no menu and no tie required. Take a taxi after dark. Featured in the book *300 Cantinas of Costa Rica*.

Café La Mancha CAFE
(Map p72; ☎ 2221-5591; www.facebook.com/pg/cafelamancha; Steinvorth building, Calle 1; ⏲ 10am-7pm Mon-Sat) Hidden away in a courtyard within the historical Steinvorth building (p85), this new third-wave coffee shop is the passion project of a local photographer with a fondness for the golden bean. From *cortado* (espresso mixed with warm milk) to Chemex, La Mancha offers all the latest in coffee technology and even holds coffee-related workshops. Coffee US$3 to US$5

Mercado La California BEER GARDEN
(Map p68; www.facebook.com/MercadoLaCalifornia; Calle 21; ⏲ 6pm-3:30am Thu-Sat, 4pm-1:30am Sun) Inspired by Madrid's 'Mercado San Miguel,' El Mercadito (as the locals say) is a recent addition to the up-and-coming Barrio La California. The line regularly snakes down the block from the entrance to this nightlife plaza's food kiosks, cocktail stands and craft-beer vendors, and the people in that line are often stunning to behold.

Antik CLUB
(Map p68; www.antik.cr; Av 10 near Calle 21, Casa Matute; cover US$10; ⏲ 11:30am-3pm & 6-11pm Tue-Thu, 11:30am-3pm & 6pm-6am Fri, 6pm-6am Sat) Set in a historical mansion that once belonged to a Venezuelan general, Antik offers a tri-level experience, with a basement catering to the EDM crowd, a main level pizza restaurant and an upper floor featuring

LGBTIQ+ VENUES

San José is home to Central America's most thriving LGBT+ scene. As with other spots, admission charges vary depending on the night and location (from US$5 to US$10). Some clubs close on various nights of the week (usually Sunday to Tuesday) and others host women- or men-only nights; inquire ahead or check individual club websites for listings.

Many clubs are on the south side of town, which can get rough after dark: take a taxi. However, a new joint inside the trendy Steinvorth Building (p85), **BomBóm**, has opened up on the 3rd floor. Other trending spots include **Club Teatro** (Av 16 near Calle 2), **Neon Ice** near Parque Francia (Calle 31 near Av 7), plus **Venue** and **PopPop** in La California (Av 2 near Calle 19).

A lesbian disco bar that has been in operation for more than four decades, **La Avispa** (The Wasp; Map p68; ☎ 2223-5343; www.laavispa.com; Calle 1, btwn Avs 8 & 10; ⏲ 8pm-6am Thu-Sat, 5pm-6am Sun) has a bar, pool tables and a boisterous dance floor that's highly recommended by travelers.

The gay men's bar **Pucho's Bar** (Map p68; ☎ 2256-1147; cnr Calle 11 & Av 8; ⏲ 8pm-2am Tue-Sat) is more low-rent (and significantly raunchier) than some; you'll find scantily clad go-go boys and over-the-top drag shows.

DRINK RESPONSIBLY

Be safe. Enterprising thieves sometimes lurk around popular nightspots, waiting to relieve drunken party people of their wallets. Never drink from a glass of unknown provenance. When leaving a bar late at night, keep your wits about you and take a taxi.

Latin dance rhythms and a sweet balcony with city views. There are a couple of bars offering craft beer and excellent, reasonably priced cocktails.

Craic Irish Pub PUB

(Map p68; cnr Av 2 & Calle 25A, 100m south of Nicaraguan Embassy; 6pm-2am Mon-Sat) The faux-Irish theme here extends to posters of sporting heroes past, including boxer Barry McGuigan and footballer Liam Brady. There's also Guinness, if only in the bottle. The wooden underfooting is so flimsy you may fear breaking the floorboards. Lively indeed.

La Concha de la Lora BAR

(Map p68; 2222-0130; www.facebook.com/laconchalora; Calle 21 btwn Avs Central & 1; 9pm-5am Tue & Thu-Sun) An enthusiastic young crowd packs in here nightly for foosball, good bar snacks, DJs spinning everything from Latin music to Jimi Hendrix, and occasional live bands and reggae nights. Low cover charges (free to US$6) help maintain the upbeat mood.

La Sabana & Around

★Castro's CLUB

(Map p68; 2256-8789; www.castrosbar.wixsite.com/castros; cnr Av 11a & Calle 22; 1pm-4am) Chepe's oldest dance club, this classic Latin American disco in Barrio México draws crowds of locals and tourists to its large dance floor with a dependable mix of salsa, *cumbia* (Colombian dance tunes) and merengue. And it's a three-in-one: sports bar, karoake bar, and disco: pick your poison (so to speak).

Los Yoses, Barrio Escalante & San Pedro

Calle La Amargura (Sorrow St) is the more poetic name for Calle 3, north of Av Central. However, it should be called Calle de la Cruda (Street of Hangovers) because it has the highest concentration of bars of any single street in town, and many of these are packed with customers (mainly university students) even during daylight hours. Places come and go, but **Terra U** (Map p81; 2283-7728; www.facebook.com/TerraUSanPedro; Calle La Amargura; 10:30am-2:30am Mon-Sat, 3pm-2am Sun) is a long-time party spot. The area gets rowdy in the wee hours: watch out for drunks and pickpockets.

Wilk BREWERY

(Map p81; www.facebook.com/wilkcraftbeer; cnr Calle 33 & Av 9; 4pm-1am Tue-Sat) Named Wilk (Wolf) in honor of its former life as the Polish embassy, this Escalante pub attracts a mixed Tico/gringo crowd who share an appreciation for craft brews and seriously delicious burgers (veggie included). More than a dozen craft beers include concoctions from Costa Rica Craft Brewing and Treintaycinco. On occasion, a local brewmaster invents a new beer, live.

Sasta Pub PUB

(Map p81; 8460-2063; Av 3 near Calle 25, Escalante, by the railroad tracks; 5pm-midnight Tue-Sun) The passing trains will shake or stir your martini just fine in this quaint replica of an English Pub. British pop from various eras politely rattles the sepia-toned pub-themed pictures on the wall. Cute, small and fun.

Un Lugar Resto-bar BAR

(Map p81; 2225-3979; www.facebook.com/barunlugar; Calle 33 btwn Avs 11 & 13; 5:30pm-midnight Mon-Thu, 5pm-2:30am Fri & Sat) This small wood-lined bar in Barrio Escalante serves as a neighborhood hangout that draws artsy types and young professionals for cold beer and *bocas*. Dark burgundy walls, heavy rock music...you get the vibe. The *patacones* (twice-fried platano chips, with chimichurri and salt) are divine.

Roots Cool and Calm BAR

(The House of Reggae; Map p81; 2253-1953; www.facebook.com/rootscoolandcalm; Av 8; 7:30pm-2:30am Mon-Sat, to midnight Sun) This cool, crowded Los Yoses bar brings in DJs from as far afield as Puerto Viejo on the Caribbean coast. It's a sweet spot to get a beer and leave with red-rimmed eyes.

Bar Río BAR

(Map p81; ☎2225-8371; Av Central; ⏰4-10pm Mon, 4pm-1am Tue-Thu, 2pm-2am Fri & Sat, 2-10pm Sun) Just west of Calle 43 and the Fuente de la Hispanidad (the official boundary between Los Yoses and San Pedro), this large, popular bar has live bands some nights and TVs showing the current game. It's a good spot to watch the rush-hour traffic crawl by: a place to start, but not finish, the evening.

Escazú & Santa Ana

If you're looking for a spicy cocktail and some house music, 8ctavo Rooftop (p94) is where the beautiful people partake. Escazú also has a few dive bars sprinkled around its main plaza, but few are particularly appealing.

Hoppy's Place BREWERY

(Brewpub and Grill; ☎8849-8732; info@hoppysplace.com; Calle 5, Escazú; ⏰5-11pm Tue-Thu, to midnight Fri-Sat, 1-9:30pm Sun) Voluble owner/brewer Alberto Sancho's encyclopedic knowledge of all things hoppy and his passion for classic rock make this a very, very fun place indeed. And his homemade *chili guaro* is off the hook. The bar and chairs, fabricated from recycled wood, lend a homey touch. At least a dozen beers on tap. Don't worry, be Hoppy.

It's across from Container Platz (p90).

Pub BAR

(Map p83; ☎2288-3062; www.facebook.com/thepubcr; Centro Comercial Montescazú, Av 26, btwn Calles 128 & 130; ⏰4pm-2am Mon-Sat) This small, friendly pub has a list of about a dozen international beers, more than a dozen local brews and a selection of shots. Well-priced happy-hour drink specials keep things hopping, and a greasy bar menu is available to soak up the damage.

Entertainment

Pick up *La Nación* on Thursday for listings (in Spanish) of the coming week's attractions. The free publication *GAM Cultural* (www.gamcultural.com) and the website San José Volando (www.sanjosevolando.com) are also helpful guides to nightlife and cultural events.

Cinema

Many cinemas show recent Hollywood films with Spanish subtitles and an English soundtrack. Occasionally films are dubbed over in Spanish *(doblado* or *hablado en español)* rather than subtitled; ask before buying a ticket. Movie tickets cost about US$4 to US$5, and generally Wednesday is cheaper. Check newspaper listings or individual theater websites for schedules.

There are bigger multiplexes in Los Yoses and San Pedro, while the most modern theaters are in Escazú.

Centro de Cine CINEMA

(Map p72; ☎2242-5200; www.centrodecine.go.cr; cnr Calle 11 & Av 9) This pink Victorian mansion houses the government-run film center and its vast archive of national and international flicks. Festivals, lectures and events are held here and in outside venues; check the website for current events.

Sala Garbo CINEMA

(Map p76; ☎2222-1034, 6351-1799; www.salagarbo.com; cnr Av 2 & Calle 28) Art-house and classic film screenings.

Cine Magaly CINEMA

(Map p68; ☎2222-7116, box office 2223-0085; www.cinemagaly.com; Calle 23 btwn Avs Central & 1; ⏰bar noon-10pm Mon-Sat, 1-10pm Sun) Screens the latest releases in a large renovated theater, along with independent films in English. The attached Kubrick Gastro Bar serves up delicious salads, pizza, desserts and an assortment of flavored teas.

CULTURAL CENTERS

Alianza Francesa (Map p72; ☎2257-1438; www.alianzafrancesacostarica.com; cnr Calle 5 & Av 7; French course US$350; ⏰8am-6pm Mon-Sat) The Alliance has French classes, a small library and rotating art exhibits in a historical Barrio Amón home.

Cooperación Española Cultura (CCECR; Centro Cultural de España en Costa Rica; Map p81; ☎2257-2919; www.ccecr.org; Rotonda del Farolito, Barrio Escalante; ⏰8am-7pm Mon-Fri) One of the city's most vibrant cultural institutions, this Spanish-run center offers a full roster of events. There is also an audiovisual center and a lending library.

Live Music

The best spots to see live, local music in San José are El Lobo Estepario, Mundoloco and El Sótano. Internationally renowned DJs frequently appear at 8ctavo Rooftop. Another happening place for tunes is **La Gata Candonga** (Map p81; ☎6012-7692; www.facebook.com/lagatacandongacr; cnr Av Central & Calle 63, San Pedro, across from AM/PM; ⏲noon-10pm), a food market and music hall in San Pedro. The Steinvorth Building (p85) downtown has jazz on Fridays from 5pm to 7pm, and sometimes other music as well.

★Mundoloco LIVE PERFORMANCE

(Map p81; ☎2253-4125; www.facebook.com/MundolocoRestaurante; Av Central, San Pedro; ⏲4pm-2:30am Mon-Thu, from noon Fri & Sat, noon-1:30am Sun) Grab a craft beer and some vegetarian grub, such as stuffed mushrooms, at this cute San Pedro restaurant and bar. Then head to the spacious and comfortable back room for the entertainment, which rotates through stand-up comedy, dance performances and live music of all kinds. There are great acoustics here: it's an ideal place to catch a local band.

El Sótano LIVE MUSIC

(Map p68; ☎2221-2302; www.amonsolar.com; cnr Calle 3 & Av 11; ⏲5pm-2am Mon, Tue & Thu-Sat) One of Chepe's most atmospheric nightspots, Sótano is named for its cellar jazz club, where people crowd in for frequent performances including intimate jam sessions. Upstairs in the same mansion, a cluster of elegant rooms with high ceilings have been converted into a gallery space, a stage and a dance floor where an eclectic mix of groups play live gigs.

El Lobo Estepario LIVE MUSIC

(Map p72; ☎2256-3934; www.facebook.com/loboesteparioocr; Av 2; ⏲4pm-1am Sun-Thu, to 2am Fri & Sat) This artsy, two-story dive attracts some of the top local talent for live music gigs. The blackboard ceiling fills with messages and drawings nightly. And for literary fans, what could be cooler than a bar with bookshelves named for a Hermann Hesse novella? Serves up good vegetarian fare too.

Jazz Café Escazú LIVE MUSIC

(☎2253-8933; www.jazzcafecostarica.com; Autopista Prospero Fernandez, Escazú; cover US$6-13; ⏲6pm-2am Mon-Sat) Now with only a single location in the suburb of Escazú, Jazz Café nonetheless continues to impress. Countless performers have taken to the stage here, including legendary Cuban bandleader Chucho Valdés and Colombian pop star Juanes. It's across from Hospital CIMA.

8ctavo Rooftop LIVE MUSIC

(☎4055-0588; www.facebook.com/8voRooftop; Autopista Próspero Fernández, Hotel Sheraton San José; ⏲6-10pm Tue & Wed, to 3am Thu-Sat) See and be seen at this swanky rooftop lounge, where international DJs regularly perform. If you want to show up early and dine first, this place is also a hit for the city views, the eclectic menu and the spicy cocktails.

SAN JOSÉ FOR KIDS

Chances are if you're in Costa Rica on a short vacation you'll be headed out to the countryside fairly quickly. But if you're going to be hanging out in San José for a day – or two or three – with your kids, know that it's not a particularly kid-friendly destination. There is lots of traffic and the sidewalks are crowded and cracked, making it difficult to push strollers or drag toddlers around.

Although the city offers relatively few things specifically for children, there are a few activities they will likely enjoy.Near Parque La Sabana, the Museo de Ciencias Naturales La Salle (p72) will impress youngsters with its astounding array of skeletons and endless cases full of stuffed animals, while the Museo de los Niños (p67) is a sure hit for children, with plenty of hands-on exhibits. Young nature-lovers will enjoy getting up close to butterflies at the Spirogyra Jardín de Mariposas (p70). Just a little further afield (an easy day trip from San José) is the wonderful zoo and wildlife-rescue center Zoo Ave (p#), where you can enjoy native birds and monkeys in a more naturalistic setting.

If you're spending more than a week in the city, note that many Spanish-language academies offer special custom-made lessons for teens.

Pepper Disco Club LIVE MUSIC
(☎2224-1472; www.facebook.com/pepperdiscoclub; Av 34, Zapote) This club is *the* place to see heavy metal, punk and ska bands. Its salsa dancing nights are also good.

El Cuartel de la Boca del Monte LIVE MUSIC
(Map p68; ☎2221-0327; www.facebook.com/elcuartelcr; Av 1 btwn Calles 21 & 23; ⏲11:30am-2pm Mon-Fri, 6pm-midnight Tue-Thu, 6pm-2am Fri, Sat & Mon) This atmospheric old Barrio La California bar has long drawn cheek-by-jowl crowds for live bands. Friday is a good night to visit, as is Monday, when ladies get free admission and the band cranks out a crazy mix of calypso, salsa, reggae and rock. It's popular with university students.

Auditorio Nacional CONCERT VENUE
(Map p68; ☎2105-0509, 2105-0511 ext 511; http://auditorionacional.museocr.org; Museo de los Niños, Calle 4) A grand stage for concerts, dance, theater and plays. Affiliated with the Centro Costarricense de Ciencia y Cultura.

Arenas Skate Park LIVE MUSIC
(Map p68; ☎8813-7544; www.facebook.com/ArenasSkatePark; Calle 11, btwn Avs 10 & 12; ⏲9am-8pm) On Friday and Saturday nights, punk shows (Guttermouth, Voodoo Glow Skulls!) are all the rage at this skate park in Barrio Soledad.

Theater

There is a wide variety of theatrical options in San José, including some in English. Local newspapers list current shows. Most theaters are not very large, so performances tend to sell out; get tickets as early as possible.

★ **Teatro Nacional** THEATER
(Map p72; ☎2010-1100; www.teatronacional.go.cr; Av 2 btwn Calles 3 & 5) Costa Rica's most important theater stages plays, dance, opera, classical concerts, Latin American music and other major events. The main season runs from March to November, but there are performances throughout the year.

Teatro Melico Salazar THEATER
(Map p72; ☎2233-5172, 2257-6005, box office 2295-6032; www.teatromelico.go.cr; Av 2 btwn Calles Central & 2) A restored 1920s theater with regular fine-arts performances, including music, theater, ballet and other forms of dance.

BULLFIGHTING

Bullfighting is traditional and fights are held seasonally in the southern suburb of Zapote over the Christmas period. Members of the public, who are often drunk at such events, are encouraged to participate in the action. The bull isn't killed in the Costa Rican version of the sport; however, many bulls are taunted, kicked and otherwise injured as a result of the fights, and animal welfare groups are keen to see the fights stopped.

Teatro Eugene O'Neill THEATER
(Map p81; ☎2207-7554; www.centrocultural.cr; Calle 37) This theater hosts performances sponsored by the Centro Cultural Costarricense Norteamericano, a cultural center that promotes ties between Costa Rica and the United States. It's north of Avenida Central, in San Pedro.

Little Theatre Group PERFORMING ARTS
(Map p83; ☎8858-1446; www.littletheatregroup.org) This English-language performance troupe has been around since the 1950s and presents several plays a year. They perform in venues around town; call or go online to find out when and where the works will be shown.

Sport

Estadio Nacional de Costa Rica STADIUM
(Map p76; Parque Metropolitano La Sabana) Costa Rica's graceful, modernist 35,000-seat national soccer stadium, constructed with funding from the Chinese government and opened in 2011, is the venue for international and national Division 1 *fútbol* (soccer) games. Its predecessor in the same spot in Parque Metropolitano La Sabana (p71) hosted everyone from Pope John Paul II to Bruce Springsteen and soccer legend Pelé over its 84-year history.

Casinos

There are casinos in several of the larger hotels. Most of these are fairly casual, but in the nicer spots it's advisable to ditch T-shirts in favor of a button-down shirt as there may be a dress code. Be advised that casinos are frequented by sex workers, so be wary if you're suddenly the most desirable person in the room.

WORTH A TRIP

BIESANZ WOODWORKS

Located in the hills of Bello Horizonte in Escazú, the workshop of **Biesanz Woodworks** (☑2289-4337; www.biesanz.com; Calle Pedrero 33; ⊗8am-5pm Mon-Fri Jan-Dec, 9am-3pm Sat Dec-Apr) can be difficult to find, but the effort is well worth it. This shop is one of the finest woodcrafting studios in the nation, run by celebrated artisan Barry Biesanz. His bowls and other decorative containers are exquisite and take their inspiration from pre-Columbian techniques.

🔒 Shopping

Whether you're looking for indigenous carvings, high-end furnishings or a stuffed sloth, San José has no shortage of shops, running the gamut from artsy boutiques to tourist traps stocked full of tropical everything. Haggling is not tolerated in stores (markets are the exception).

For the country's finest woodcrafts, it is absolutely worth the trip to Biesanz Woodworks.

★**Feria Verde de Aranjuez** MARKET
(Map p68; www.facebook.com/FeriaVerde; Barrio Aranjuez; ⊗7am-12:30pm Sat) For a foodie-friendly cultural experience, don't miss this fabulous Saturday market, a meeting place for San José's artists and organic growers since 2010. You'll find organic coffee, artisanal chocolate, tropical-fruit ice blocks, produce, leather, jewelry and more at the long rows of booths set up in the park at the north end of Barrio Aranjuez.

Feria Verde is also held in Barrio Colón on Tuesdays from 1pm to 7pm.

Sin Domicilio Fijo ARTS & CRAFTS
(Map p83; ☑2289-9461; www.facebook.com/sindomiciliofijo; cnr Av 32 & Calle Central; ⊗8am-7pm Tue-Sat, to 4pm Sun) In downtown Escazú, this art and design shop is ensconced in a 150-year-old house with adobe walls, near the southwest corner of Escazú's church. It's full of unique handicrafts that make ideal gifts, from dainty footwear to kitchen adornments. There's also a lovely open-air cafe that serves up fresh coffee and tasty meals.

Distrito Carmen ART
(Casa de Carmen; Map p72; ☑6090-6425, 2256-0337; www.distritocarmen.com; cnr Calle 11 & Av 9) Cool design store where you can pick up interesting art, clothing, jewelry and other odds and ends created by a couple of dozen local artists.

Mora Books BOOKS
(Map p72; ☑8383-8385; www.facebook.com/MORA-Books-276174472445975; Calle 5 btwn Avs 5 & 7; ⊗11am-7pm) Dog-eared paperbacks in mostly English but also Spanish, French and German teeter in precarious towers atop crammed shelves at this chaotic jumble of a used bookstore. The best place in town for stocking up on reading material for the road. Hours are hit and miss.

Kiosco SJO ARTS & CRAFTS
(Map p81; ☑2253-8426; www.kalu.co.cr; cnr Calle 31 & Av 5; ⊗10am-8pm Tue-Fri, 10am-7pm Sat, 10am-4pm Sun) 🍃 With a focus on sustainable design by Costa Rican artisans, this sleek shop in Barrio Escalante stocks handmade jewelry, hand-tooled leather bags, original photography, stuffed animals, fashion and contemporary home decor by established designers. It's pricey, but everything you find here will be of exceptional quality. It's part of Kalú Café (p89).

eÑe ARTS & CRAFTS
(Tienda eÑe; Map p72; ☑2222-7681; www.facebook.com/esquina13y7; cnr Av 7 & Calle 11A; ⊗10am-6:30pm Mon-Sat) This hip little design shop across from Casa Amarilla (p71) sells all manner of pieces crafted by Costa Rican designers and artists, including clothing, jewelry, handbags, picture frames, zines and works of graphic art.

Galería Namu ARTS & CRAFTS
(Map p72; ☑2256-3412, in USA 800-616-4322; www.galerianamu.com; Av 7, btwn Calles 5 & 7; ⊗9am-6:30pm Mon-Sat year-round, 11am-4pm Sun Dec-Apr) The Bribrí word for jaguar, Namu fair-trade gallery brings together artwork and cultural objects from a diverse population of regional ethnicities, including Boruca masks, finely woven Wounaan baskets, Guaymí dolls, Bribrí canoes, Chorotega ceramics, traditional Huetar reed mats, and contemporary urban and Afro-Caribbean crafts. It can also help arrange visits to remote indigenous territories in different parts of Costa Rica.

Multiplaza Escazú MALL
(☎4001-7999; www.facebook.com/MultiplazaCostaRica; Autopista Próspero Fernández; ⏲10am-9pm Mon-Sat, to 8pm Sun) Costa Rica's most stylish and massive shopping mall has everything you need (or don't). If you're coming from San José, the mall can be reached by taking any bus marked 'Escazú Multiplaza'.

Mercado Nacional de Artesanía MARKET
(Crafts Market; Map p72; Plaza de la Democracia, Avs Central & 2, btwn Calles 13 & 15; ⏲8am-7pm) A touristy open-air market that sells everything from handcrafted jewelry and Bob Marley T-shirts to elaborate woodwork and Guatemalan sarongs.

Librería Lehmann BOOKS
(Map p72; ☎2522-4848; www.librerialehmann.com; Av Central btwn Calles 1 & 3; ⏲8am-6:30pm Mon-Fri, 9am-5pm Sat, 11am-4pm Sun) Good selection of English-language books, maps and guidebooks (including Lonely Planet). There are a half-dozen branches around town.

Mall San Pedro MALL
(Map p81; ☎4001-7999; www.tumallsanpedro.com; Boulevard Los Yoses) This busy four-story mall (often used as a landmark) houses a multiscreen cinema, a food court, a video arcade and the usual mix of clothing, phone and other retailers. It's northwest of Fuente de la Hispanidad.

Orientation

San José's center is arranged in a grid with avenidas (avenues) running east to west and calles (streets) running north to south. Av Central is the nucleus of the downtown area and is a pedestrian mall between Calles 6 and 9. The downtown has several loosely defined barrios (neighborhoods); those of greatest interest to tourists are north and east of Plaza de la Cultura, including Barrio Amón, Barrio Otoya, Barrio Aranjuez, Barrio Escalante and Barrio La California. The central area is home to innumerable businesses, hotels and cultural sites, while the area immediately west of downtown is home to San José's central market and many of its bus terminals.

Slightly further west of downtown is La Sabana, named for its huge and popular park where many *josefinos* spend their weekends jogging, swimming, picnicking or attending soccer matches.

A few kilometers southwest is the affluent outer suburb of Escazú, really three neighborhoods in one: Escazú Centro with its peaceful central plaza and unhurried Tico ambiance; the US expatriate enclave of San Rafael, dotted with strip malls, top-end car dealerships, tract housing and chain restaurants; and San Antonio, a hillside mix of humble rural homes, sprawling estates and spectacular views. Still further west is the up-and-coming enclave of Santa Ana, another expat favorite with oodles of green space, a fantastically warm and dry climate and new businesses galore.

East (and within walking distance) of the center are the contiguous neighborhoods of Los Yoses and San Pedro, the former a low-key residential area with some nice accommodations, the latter home to the tree-lined campus of the UCR, the country's most prestigious university. Marking the dividing line between Los Yoses and San Pedro is a traffic circle graced by a large fountain known as the Fuente de la Hispanidad (a frequently referenced local landmark). North of Los Yoses is Barrio Escalante, home to some of San José's trendiest bars and restaurants.

Information

DANGER & ANNOYANCES

Though Costa Rica has the lowest crime rate of any Central American country, crime in urban centers such as San José is a problem. The most common offense is opportunistic theft (eg pickpocketing and mugging). Keep a streetwise attitude, leave your car empty of valuables in a guarded lot and never put your bag in the overhead racks on a bus. Be aware that sex workers are known for sleight-of-hand, and that they often work in pairs.

Neighborhoods covered by Lonely Planet are generally safe during the day, though you should be especially careful around the Coca-Cola

TOURIST POLICE

The establishment in 2007 of the *policía turística* (tourist police; you'll see them patrolling in pairs around San José, on foot, bicycle and even horseback) has helped prevent petty crimes against foreigners. These officers can be helpful in the event of an emergency since most of them speak at least some English.

If you find yourself the victim of a crime, you'll have to file a report in person at the **Organismo de Investigacíon Judicial** (☎2222-1365, 2295-3000; Calle 19 btwn Avs 6 & 8; ⏲24hr) in the Supreme Court of Justice building on the south side of downtown.

bus terminal and the red-light district south of Parque Central, particularly at night. Be advised that adjacent neighborhoods can vary greatly in terms of safety; inquire locally before setting out.

Gridlocked traffic, gigantic potholes, noise and smog are unavoidable components of the San José experience. Most central hotels are subject to street noise, no matter how nice they are. Be skeptical of touts and taxi drivers who try to sell you tours or tell you that the hotel you've booked is a crime-infested bordello. Many of them will say anything to steer you to the places that pay them commissions.

EMERGENCY

Fire	☎118
Red Cross	☎128
Traffic Police	☎2523-3300, 2222-9245, 2222-9330

INTERNET ACCESS

Most accommodations, eateries and even bars offer free wi-fi and/or guest computers.

MEDICAL SERVICES

Clínica Bíblica (☎WhatsApp 8529-2100, I 2522-1000; www.clinicabiblica.com; Av 14, btwn Calles Central & 1; ⊙24hr) The top private clinic downtown has a 24-hour emergency room; doctors speak English, French and German.

Hospital Calderón Guardia (☎2212-1000; www.ccss.sa.cr/hospitales?v=9; cnr Calle 17 btwn Avs 7 & 9; ⊙24hr) A public hospital in central San José.

Hospital CIMA (☎2208-1000, in USA 1 (855) 782-6253; www.hospitalcima.com; Autopista Próspero Fernández; ⊙24hr) For serious medical emergencies, head to this hospital in San Rafael de Escazú. Its facilities are the most modern in the greater San José area.

Hospital La Católica (☎2246-3000; www.hospitallacatolica.com; Vía 109, Guadalupe; ⊙24hr) Pricey private clinic geared toward medical-tourism patients from abroad.

Hospital San Juan de Dios (☎2547-8000; www.ccss.sa.cr/hospitales?v=25; cnr Paseo Colón & Calle 14) Free public hospital open 24 hours; expect long waits.

POST

Correo Central (Central Post Office; Map p72; ☎2202-2900; www.correos.go.cr; Calle 2, btwn Avs 1 & 3; ⊙6:30am-6pm Mon-Fri, to noon Sat) Post office in a gorgeous historical building near the center of town. Express and overnight services.

TOURIST INFORMATION

Canatur (Cámara Nacional de Turismo; ☎2234-6222; www.canatur.org; ⊙7am-10pm) The Costa Rican National Chamber of Tourism provides information on member services from a small stand next to international baggage claim.

ℹ Getting There & Away

San José is the country's transportation hub, and you may pass through the capital a number of times throughout your travels (whether you want to or not).

AIR

International flights leave from Juan Santamaría (SJO) airport outside Alajuela.

Aeropuerto Internacional Juan Santamaría (☎2437-2400; www.fly2sanjose.com) Handles international flights in its main terminal. Domestic flights on **Sansa** (☎2290-4100; www.flysansa.com) depart from the Sansa terminal.

Aeropuerto Tobías Bolaños (☎2232-2820; Pavas) In the San José suburb of Pavas; services private charter and a few domestic flights.

BUS

Bus transportation in San José can be bewildering. There is no public bus system and no central terminal. Instead, dozens of private companies operate out of stops scattered throughout the city. Many bus companies have no more than a stop (in this case pay the driver directly); some have a tiny office with a window on the street; others operate from bigger terminals servicing entire regions.

Note that bus schedules and prices change regularly. Pick up a copy of the free (but not always up-to-date) booklet *Itinerario de Buses* from San José's downtown tourist office, or download a PDF version from www.visitcostarica.com (most easily located in your search engine by typing 'Costa Rica Itinerario de Buses').

The website www.yoviajocr.com is helpful for finding the schedule and cost of buses from San José to other destinations in the country. Buses are crowded on Friday evening and Saturday morning and packed to the gills at Christmas and Easter.

For buses that run infrequently, it is advisable to buy tickets in advance.

Bus Terminals

Collectively, the following five San José terminals serve Costa Rica's most popular destinations. Chances are you'll be passing through one or more of them during your trip. Be aware that theft is common in many bus terminals. Stay alert, keep your valuables close to you and don't stow anything important (such as passports and money) in the overhead racks or luggage compartment of a bus.

Gran Terminal del Caribe (Calle Central) This roomy station north of Av 13 is the central departure point for all buses to the Caribbean coast.

Terminal 7-10 (☎2519-9740; www.terminal7-10.com; cnr Av 7 & Calle 10) This newer bus terminal is a base for routes to Nicoya, Nosara, Sámara, Santa Cruz, Tamarindo, Jacó, Monteverde, La Fortuna and a few other places. The four-story facility has a food court, shopping center and parking lot. Although it's located in the *zona roja*, historically a dangerous area of the city, police have stepped up their patrols to reduce crime.

Terminal Coca-Cola (Map p68; Av 1 btwn Calles 16 & 18) A well-known landmark. Numerous buses leave from the terminal and the four-block radius around it to points all over Costa Rica, in particular the Central Valley and the Pacific coast. This is a labyrinthine station with ticket offices scattered all over. Also located in the *zona roja*.

Terminal del Atlántico Norte (cnr Av 9 & Calle 12) A small, rather decrepit terminal serving the Southern Caribbean and Puerto Jiménez.

Terminal Tracopa (Map p68; ☎2221-4214; www.tracopacr.com; Calle 5 btwn Avs 18 & 20) Buses to southwestern destinations including Neily, Dominical, Golfito, Manuel Antonio, Palmar Norte, Paso Canoas, Quepos, San Isidro de El General, San Vito and Uvita.

Domestic Bus Companies

Alfaro (www.empresaalfaro.com) Nicoya, Playa Sámara and Playa Tamarindo.

Autotransportes Caribeños (Grupo Caribeños; ☎2222-0610; www.facebook.com/grupocaribenos; Gran Terminal del Caribe, Calle Central) Northeastern destinations including Puerto Limón, Guápiles, Cariari, Siquirres and Puerto Viejo de Sarapiquí; the Caribeños group encompasses several smaller companies (including Empresarios Guapileños and Líneas del Atlántico), all of which share the same terminal and customer-service phone number.

Autotransportes Mepe (☎2257-8129; www.mepecr.com; cnr Av 9 & Calle 12, Terminal del Atlántico Norte) Southern Caribbean destinations including Cahuita, Puerto Viejo de Talamanca, Manzanillo, Bribrí Territory and Sixaola.

Autotransportes San Carlos (☎2255-4300; www.terminal7-10.com; Terminal 7-10, cnr Av 7 & Calle 10) La Fortuna, Ciudad Quesada and Los Chiles.

Blanco Lobo (Grupo Blanco; Map p68; ☎2257-4121; www.grupoblanco.cr/rutas; cnr Av 9 & Calle 12, Terminal del Atlántico Norte) Puerto Jiménez.

Coopetrans Atenas (Map p68; ☎2446-5767; www.coopetransatenas.com; Av 1, btwn Calles 16 & 18, Terminal Coca-Cola) Atenas.

Deldu (www.facebook.com/transportedeldu) Peñas Blancas.

Empresa Alfaro (☎2222-2666; www.empresaalfaro.com; cnr Av 7 & Calle 10, Terminal 7-10) Nicoya, Nosara, Sámara, Santa Cruz and Tamarindo.

INTERNATIONAL BUSES FROM SAN JOSÉ

DESTINATION	COMPANY	COST (US$)	DURATION (HR)	DEPARTURES
David (Panama)	Tracopa	20	8½	7:30am, noon
Guatemala City (Guatemala)	Tica Bus	86	48	3am, 6am, 7am, 12:30pm
Managua (Nicaragua)	Tica Bus	29-42	9	3am, 6am, 7:30am, 12:30pm
	TransNica	28	8½	2am, 4am, 5am, 9am, noon
	Central Line	29	8½	4:30am, 10am
	Nicabus	26	8	4:30am, 6:30am
Panama City (Panama)	Expreso Panamá	40	14	noon
	Tica Bus	42-58	16	noon, 11:55pm
San Salvador (El Salvador)	Tica Bus	65	20	3am, 6am, 7:30am, 12:30pm
Tegucigalpa (Honduras)	TransNica	57	16	2am

Empresarios Unidos (Map p68; ☎2221-6600; www.eupsacr.com; cnr Av 12 & Calle 16, Los Ángeles) San Ramón and Puntarenas.

Lumaca (Map p68; ☎2552-5280; www.autotransporteslumaca.com; Av 10, btwn Calles 5 & 7) Cartago.

Metrópoli (Map p72; ☎2530-1064; www.facebook.com/busesmetropoli.metropoli; Av 2, btwn Calles 1 & 3) Volcán Irazú.

Musoc (☎2222-2422; Calle Central, btwn Avs 22 & 24, across from Women's Hospital) San Isidro de El General and Santa María de Dota.

Pulmitan de Liberia (Map p68; ☎2222-0610; www.facebook.com/Pulmitan-de-liberia-235807189780829; Calle 24, btwn Avs 5 & 7) Northwestern destinations including Cañas, Liberia, Playa del Coco and Tilarán.

Station Wagon (Map p68; ☎2441-1181; Av 2, btwn Calles 10 & 12) Alajuela and the airport.

Tracopa (www.tracopacr.com) Dominical, Uvita, Golfito, Palmar, Paso Canoas, Quepos, Manuel Antonio and San Isidro de El General.

Tralapa (Map p68; ☎2223-5876; Av 5, btwn Calles 20 & 22) Several Península de Nicoya

DOMESTIC BUSES FROM SAN JOSÉ

DESTINATION	COMPANY	COST (US$)	DURATION (HR)	DEPARTURES
Cahuita	Mepe	9.00	4	6am, 8am, 10am, noon, 2pm, 4pm, 6pm
Cañas	Pulmitan	5.67	3½	11:40am, 1:30pm, 3:30pm
Cariari	Caribeños	3.14	2½	6:30am, 9am, 10am, 10:30am, 1pm, 3pm, 4:30pm, 6pm, 7pm
Cartago	Lumaca	1.13	1	every 10min
Ciudad Neily	Tracopa	14.21	6½-7½	9 daily from 5am-6:30pm
Ciudad Quesada	San Carlos	3.34	3	hourly
Dominical & Uvita	Tracopa	11.13	4½-5½	6am, 6:45am, 8:30am, 10:15am, 11am, 12:15pm, 1pm, 2pm 3pm, 6:40pm
Golfito	Tracopa	14.21	6½	6:30am, 7am, 3:30pm
Grecia	Tuan	2.11	1	half-hourly
Guápiles	Caribeños	2.67	1¼	hourly 5:30am-7:30pm
Jacó	Transportes Jacó	4.66	2½	6am, then every 2hr 7am-5pm
La Fortuna/Guatuso	San Carlos	4.95	4	5am, 8:40am, 11:50pm, 2:45pm
Liberia	Pulmitan	7.62	4½	hourly 6am-8pm
Los Chiles	San Carlos	5.60	5	7:10am, 11:40am, 3:30pm, 7:10pm
Manzanillo	Mepe	11.55	5	noon
Monteverde/Santa Elena	Transmonteverde	5.46	4½	6:30am, 2:30pm
Montezuma/Mal País	Cobano	12.50	5½-6	6am, 2pm
Nicoya	Alfaro	9.69	5	5:30, 7:30am, 10am, noon, 1pm, 3pm, 5pm
Palmar	Tracopa	10.32	6	13 daily
Paso Canoas	Tracopa	13.81	7-8	13 daily
Peñas Blancas	Deldú	8.98	6	9 daily
Playas del Coco	Pulmitan	9.06	5½	8am, 2pm, 4pm

destinations, including Playa Flamingo, Playa Hermosa, Playa Tamarindo and Santa Cruz.

Transmonteverde (☎2645-7447; www.transmonteverde.com; Terminal 7-10, cnr Av 7 & Calle 10) Monteverde.

Transportes Cobano (☎2221-7479; www.facebook.com/TransCobano; Terminal 7-10, cnr Av 7 & Calle 10) Montezuma and Mal País.

Transportes Deldú (Calle Central, Gran Terminal de Caribe) Peñas Blancas (Nicaraguan border).

Transportes Jacó (☎2290-2922; www.transportesjacoruta655.com; Terminal 7-10, cnr Av 7 & Calle 10) Jacó.

Transtusa (Map p68; ☎4036-1800; www.transtusacr.com; Calle 13, btwn Avs 6 & 8) Cartago and Turrialba.

Tuan (Terminal de Buses Grecia; Map p68; ☎2494-2139, 2258-2004; Barrio Mexico, cnr Av 5 & Calle 18A) Grecia.

Tuasa (Map p68; ☎2442-6900; Av 2, btwn Calles 12 & 14) Alajuela and the airport.

DESTINATION	COMPANY	COST (US$)	DURATION (HR)	DEPARTURES
Playa Flamingo	Tralapa	8.03	6	8am, 10:30am, 3pm
Playa Nosara	Alfaro	8.11	6	5:30am
Playa Sámara	Alfaro	7.54	5	noon
Playa Hermosa	Tralapa	8.90	5	3:30pm
Playa Tamarindo	Alfaro	9.51	5	11:30am, 3:30pm
Playa Tamarindo	Tralapa	8.92	5	7am, 4pm
Puerto Jiménez	Blanco Lobo	15	8	8am, noon
Puerto Limón	Caribeños	5.64	3	hourly
Puerto Viejo de Sarapiquí	Caribeños	4.47	2½	10 daily
Puerto Viejo de Talamanca	Mepe	10.55	4½	6am, 8am, 10am, noon, 2pm, 4pm, 6pm
Puntarenas	Empresarios Unidos	4.57	2½	hourly
Quepos/Manuel Antonio	Tracopa	8.10	3½	every 1-2hr
San Isidro de El General	Musoc	6.41	3	hourly 4:30am-6:30pm
San Isidro de El General	Tracopa	5.73	3	hourly 5:30am-6:30pm
San Vito	Tracopa	13.36	7	6am, 8:15am, noon, 12:15pm, 4pm
Santa Cruz	Alfaro	9.05	5	7 daily
Santa Cruz	Tralapa	9.05	5	9am, noon, 2pm, 6pm
Santa María de Dota	Musoc	4.16	2	6am, 9am, 12:30pm, 2:30pm, 3pm, 5pm, 7:30pm
Sarchí	Tuan	2.15	1½	11:55pm
Siquirres	Caribeños	3.16	2	hourly
Sixaola/Bribrí Territory	Mepe	10/12.94	5½	6am, then hourly 8am-7pm
Tilarán	Pulmitan	7.81	4	7:30am, 9:30am, 12:45pm, 3:45pm, 6:30pm
Turrialba	Transtusa	2.76	2	every 45 min
Volcán Irazú	Metrópoli	9.10 (round trip)	2	8am, 5:15pm

International Bus Companies

International buses get booked up fast. Buy your tickets in advance – and take your passport.

Expreso Panamá (Map p68; ☎2221-7694; www.expresopanama.com; cnr Av 12 & Calle 16, Terminal Empresarios Unidos) Panama City (Panama).

Nicabus (Map p68; ☎2221-2581; www.nicabus.com.ni; cnr Av 1 & Calle 20) Managua (Nicaragua).

Tica Bus (Map p76; ☎2296-9788; www.ticabus.com; cnr Transversal 26 & Av 3) Nicaragua, Panama, El Salvador and Guatemala.

TransNica (Map p68; ☎2223-4242; www.transnica.com; Calle 22, btwn Avs 3 & 5) Nicaragua and Honduras.

Transportes Central Line (Map p68; ☎2221-9115; www.transportescentralline.com; Av 9) Managua (Nicaragua).

Shuttle Buses

Grayline (☎2220-2126, WhatsApp 8854-9496; www.graylinecostarica.com; Av 31) and **Interbus** (☎4100-0888; www.interbusonline.com; Av 20) shuttle passengers in air-conditioned minivans from San José to a long list of popular destinations around Costa Rica. They are more expensive than the standard buses, but they offer door-to-door service and can get you there faster.

Getting Around

Central San José frequently resembles a parking lot – narrow streets, heavy traffic and a complicated one-way system mean that it is often quicker to walk than to take the bus. The same applies to driving: if you rent a car, try to avoid downtown. If you're in a real hurry to get somewhere that's more than 1km away, take an Uber or a taxi; note that Uber is technically illegal here, but everyone uses it.

If traveling by bus, you'll arrive at one of several bus terminals sprinkled around the western and southern parts of downtown. Some of this area is walkable provided you aren't hauling a lot of luggage and are staying nearby. But if you're arriving at night, take a taxi, since most terminals are in dodgy areas.

BUS

Local buses are useful to get you into the suburbs and surrounding villages, or to the airport. Most buses run between 5am and 10pm and cost between US$0.40 and US$1.10.

La Sabana For buses heading west from San José towards La Sabana (US$0.40), head for the convenient downtown stop at the southeast corner of **Av 3 and Calle 3** (Map p72). Buses returning from Parque La Sabana to downtown follow Paseo Colón, then go over to Av 2 at the San Juan de Dios hospital. They then go three different ways through town before eventually heading back to La Sabana. Buses are marked Sabana–Estadio, Sabana–Cementerio or Cementerio–Estadio. These buses are a good bet for a cheap city tour.

Los Yoses & San Pedro Catch eastbound buses to Los Yoses and San Pedro (US$0.50) from the northeast corner of **Av Central and Calle 9** (Map p72). These buses run east along Av 2 and then switch over to Av Central at Calle 29. (Many are easily identifiable by the big sign that says 'Mall San Pedro' on the front window.)

Escazú Buses southwest to Escazú (US$0.65 to US$0.80, 15 to 25 minutes) leave from two different locations: **Av 6** (Map p68) between Calles 14 and 16 (south of the Hospital San Juan de Dios), and Calle 16 between Avs 1 and 3 (near the Coca-Cola terminal). Buses for Santa Ana are on the same block. Buses labeled 'San Antonio de Escazú' climb the hill south of Escazú and end near the Iglesia San Antonio de Escazú; those labeled 'Escazú Centro' end in **Escazú's Parque Central** (Map p83; Calle 136); others, labeled 'Guachipelín', go west on the Carretera John F Kennedy and pass the Costa Rica Country Club. All go through San Rafael.

Heredia Regular buses leave from Calle 1 between Av 7 and Av 9 (Map p72).

BICYCLE

A new bike-sharing app, **Omni** (☎WhatsApp 7236-9499; www.omni.cr), has appeared on the Chepe scene, and with the use of a cell phone, credit card, and a bit of moxie you can be tooling the city streets for about US$1 per hour. There are designated drop-off and pick-up points (see the website), but you can also leave the bike where you wish, once you've signed off. City-dwellers seem to have taken to the app, with thousands of rentals and, shockingly, bike-friendly lanes have been designated in some neighborhoods. Download the app (which is in Spanish) from the website.

CAR

It is not advisable to rent a car just to drive around San José. The traffic is heavy, the streets are narrow and the meter-deep curbside gutters make parking nerve-wracking. In addition, break-ins are frequent, and leaving a car – even in a guarded lot – might result in a smashed window and stolen belongings.

If you are renting a car to travel throughout Costa Rica, there are more than 50 car-rental agencies – including many of the global brands – in and around San José. Travel agencies and upmarket hotels can arrange rentals; you can also arrange rentals online and at the airport. Note: If you book a rental car online and the low cost seems too good to be true, it is. Rental agencies are notorious for tacking on hundreds of dollars in mandatory insurance when you arrive. They are also known to lie about this over the phone.

One excellent local option is **Wild Rider** (☎2258-4604, in USA/Canada (800) 721-9821; www.wild-rider.com; Diagonal 16 near Calle 34; ⊙8am-6pm). It has a fleet of reasonably priced 4WD vehicles (from US$380 per week in high season, including all mandatory insurance coverage). There's a discount of up to 40% for long-term rentals (four weeks or more). Reserve well in advance.

MOTORCYCLE

Costa Rica Motorcycle Rentals (www.costaricamotorcyclerental.com; per day US$85-125) rents KTM and Kawasaki motorcycles and can deliver the them to your hotel in San José, or an agreed-upon pick up point, such as the airport or downtown San José.

TAXI

Red taxis can be hailed on the street day or night, or you can have your hotel call one for you.

Marías (meters) are generally used, though a few drivers will tell you they're broken and try to charge you more – especially if you don't speak Spanish. Not using a meter is illegal. The rate for the first kilometer should automatically appear when the meter starts up (at the time of research, the correct starting amount was 610 colones). Make sure the *maría* is operating when you get in, or negotiate the fare up front. Short rides downtown cost US$2 to US$4. There's a 20% surcharge after 10pm that may not appear on the *maría*.

You can hire a taxi and a driver for half a day or longer; it is best to negotiate a flat fee in advance. Uber has also become popular (though technically illegal), and some savvy Ticos use a third level of transport, the *pirata* (pirate taxi) when in a jam.

AT A GLANCE

POPULATION
Alajuela: 293,601

FAST FACT
At 3432m, Volcán Irazu (p129) is the tallest volcano in the country.

BEST BIRDING
Rancho Naturalista (p137)

BEST WATERFALL
Catarata del Toro & the Blue Falls (p118)

BEST TOPIARY
Parque Francisco Alvarado (p118)

WHEN TO GO

Dec–Apr Perfect weather due to high altitudes and land-locked location.

Jun–Dec Expect bargain prices and afternoon rain showers.

Jun–Oct The rainy months are prime for white-water rafting.

Valle de Orosi (p129)
SATHISH JOTHIKUMAR/SHUTTERSTOCK ©

Central Valley & Highlands

It is on the coffee-cultivated hillsides of the Central Valley that you'll find Costa Rica's heart and soul. This is the geographical center of the country, but also its cultural and spiritual core. It is here that coffee built a prosperous nation and here that picturesque highland villages still gather for centuries-old fiestas. It is also here that you'll get to fully appreciate country cooking: artisanal cheeses, steamy corn cakes and freshly caught river trout. Quaint and quirky agricultural towns invite leisurely detours, but it's not all cows and coffee – world-class rapids, resplendent quetzals and close encounters with active volcanoes all show off the rich landscape in which Costa Rica's character is rooted.

INCLUDES

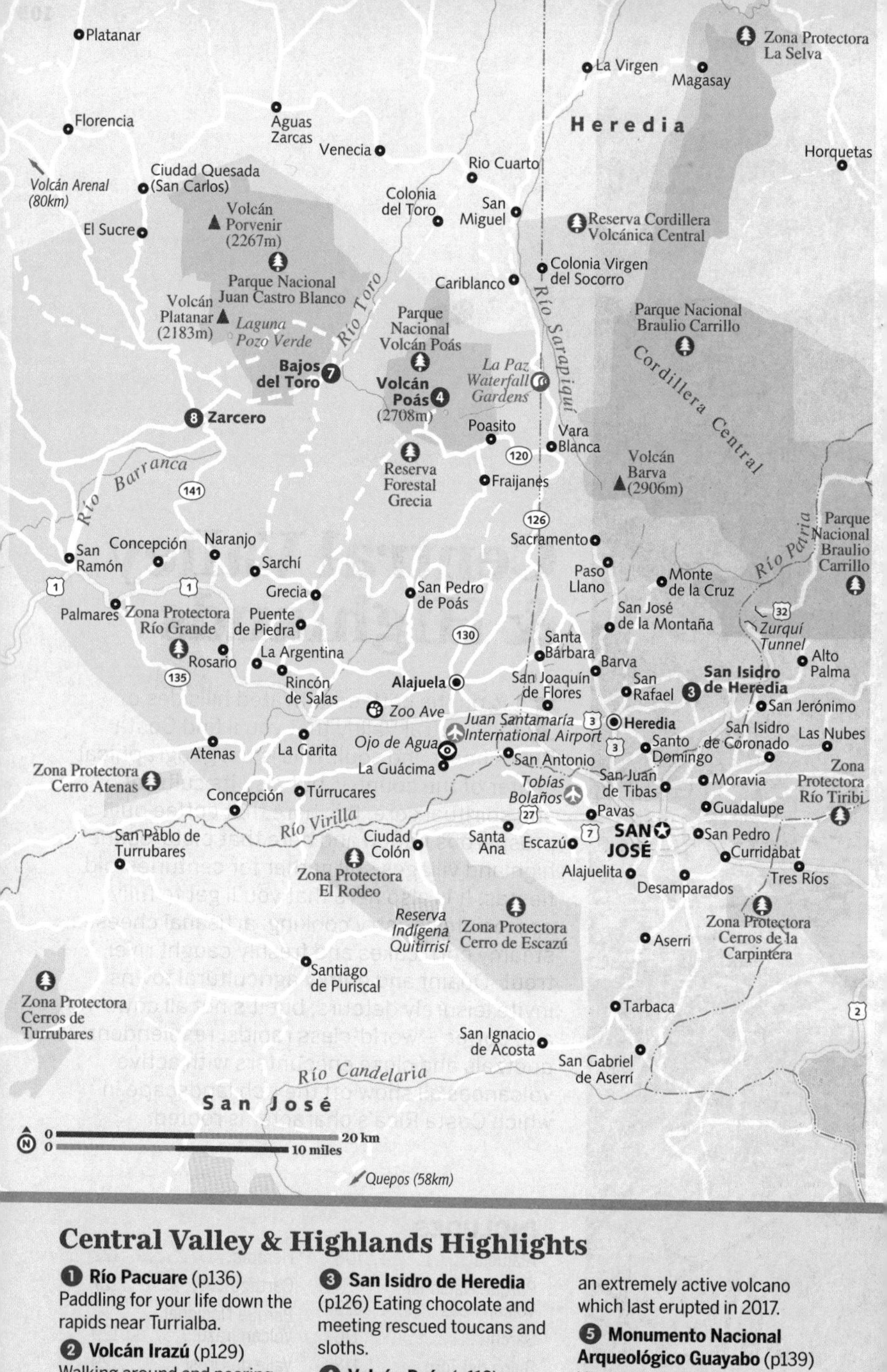

Central Valley & Highlands Highlights

1 Río Pacuare (p136)
Paddling for your life down the rapids near Turrialba.

2 Volcán Irazú (p129)
Walking around and peering into the mammoth crater.

3 San Isidro de Heredia (p126) Eating chocolate and meeting rescued toucans and sloths.

4 Volcán Poás (p113)
Getting frighteningly close to an extremely active volcano which last erupted in 2017.

5 Monumento Nacional Arqueológico Guayabo (p139)
Viewing Costa Rica's ancient archaeological site.

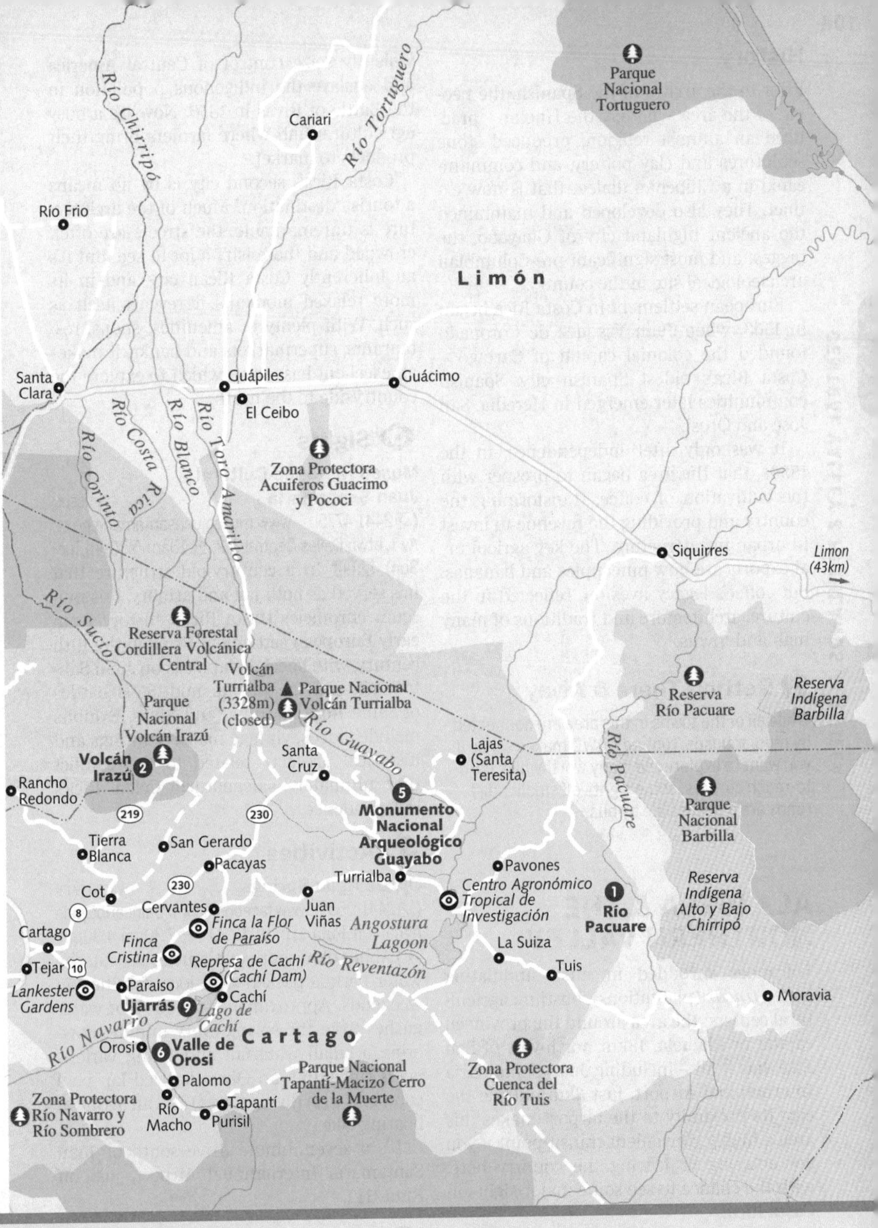

6 Valle de Orosi (p129) Exploring wilderness, culture and coffee *fincas* in this beauteous valley.

7 Bajos del Toro (p118) Birdwatching beside a rushing river or hiking to waterfalls.

8 Zarcero (p118) Winding along scenic mountain roads and trippy topiary hedges.

9 Ujarrás (p134) Lazing beside the ruins of a 17th-century church.

History

Prior to the arrival of the Spanish, the people of the area – largely the Huetar – practiced an animist religion, produced stone sculptures and clay pottery, and communicated in a Chibchan dialect that is now extinct. They also developed and maintained the ancient highland city of Guayabo, the biggest and most significant pre-Columbian archaeological site in the country.

European settlement in Costa Rica began in 1563, when Juan Vásquez de Coronado founded the colonial capital of Cartago – Costa Rica's oldest Spanish city. Spanish communities later emerged in Heredia, San José and Orosi.

It was only after independence, in the 1830s, that the area began to prosper with the cultivation of coffee, transforming the country and providing the revenue to invest in urban infrastructure. The key agricultural exports are now pineapples and bananas, but coffee's legacy lives on, reflected in the culture, architecture and traditions of many highland towns.

Getting There & Away

While all of the towns in this area are connected by regular buses, renting a 4WD makes sense if you want to explore the many worthwhile, hard-to-reach corners; some sights off smaller dirt roads are inaccessible by bus.

ALAJUELA & THE NORTHERN VALLEY

Volcanoes shrouded in mist, undulating coffee *fincas* (plantations), bustling agricultural centers: the area around the provincial capital of Alajuela, 18km northwest of San José, has it all – including Juan Santamaría International Airport, just 3km outside the city. Its proximity to the airport makes this area a highly convenient transit point if you are entering or leaving the country here, with the chance to see some major sights in Costa Rica.

Alajuela

POP 43,000

Alajuela was home to one of the country's most famous figures: Juan Santamaría, the humble drummer boy who died putting an end to William Walker's campaign to violently seize control of Central America and enslave the indigenous population in the Battle of Rivas in 1856. Now it's a busy agricultural hub where farmers bring their products to market.

Costa Rica's second city is by no means a tourist 'destination.' Much of the architecture is unremarkable, the streets are often crowded and there isn't a lot to see. But it's an inherently Costa Rican city, and in its more relaxed moments it reveals itself as such. With plenty of amenities, shops, restaurants, supermarkets and banks, it makes an excellent base from which to explore the countryside to the north.

Sights

Museo Histórico Cultural Juan Santamaría MUSEUM

(2441-4775; www.museojuansantamaria.go.cr; Av 1, btwn Calles Central & 2; 10am-5:30pm Tue-Sun) FREE In a century-old structure that has served as both jail and armory, this museum chronicles Costa Rican history from early European settlement through the 19th century, with special emphasis on Juan Santamaría and the pivotal mid-1850s battles of Santa Rosa, Sardinal and Rivas. Exhibits include videos, vintage maps, paintings and historical artifacts related to the conflict that ultimately safeguarded Costa Rica's independence.

Activities

Ojo de Agua Springs WATER PARK

(2441-0655; www.facebook.com/BalnearioOjodeAgua; off Ruta 111; US$2.70; 7:30am-4:30pm;) About 6km south of Alajuela, this kitschy water park is packed with local families on weekends. Approximately 20,000L of water gushes from the spring every minute, powering a small waterfall and filling various pools (including an Olympic-sized lap pool complete with diving tower) and an artificial boating lake.

It's a seven-minute drive south of Juan Santamaría International Airport, just off Ruta 111.

Courses

Intensa LANGUAGE

(2442-3843, WhatsApp 8866-1059, in USA & Canada 866-277-1352; www.intensa.com; cnr Av 6 & Calle 2; 1 week group tuition 4-6hr per day US$270, with homestay US$475, private 1 week tuition 3hr per day $370, with homestay US$575; 8am-8pm Mon-Fri) Schools in Alajuela and Heredia

Alajuela

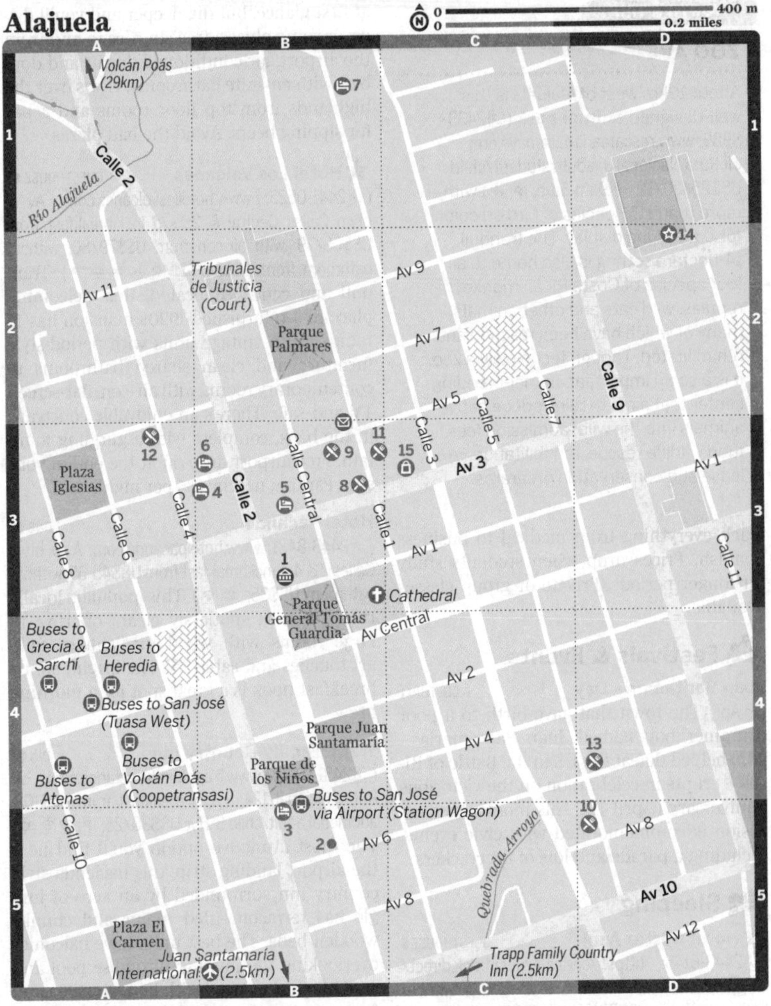

Alajuela

Sights
1 Museo Histórico Cultural Juan Santamaría ... B3

Activities, Courses & Tours
2 Intensa ... B5

Sleeping
3 Alajuela Backpackers Hostel ... B5
4 Hotel Cortez Azul ... B3
5 Hotel Los Volcanes ... B3
6 Hotel Pacandé ... B3
7 Vida Tropical B&B ... B1

Eating
8 Café Delicias ... B3
9 El Chante Vegano ... B3
10 El Hop ... D5
11 Jalapeños Central ... B3
12 Kurkuma ... A3
13 Pesqueria da Limonta ... D4

Entertainment
14 Estadio Morera Soto ... D2

Shopping
15 Goodlight Books ... C3

WORTH A TRIP

ZOO AVE

About 10km west of Alajuela is this well-designed **animal park** (☎2433-8989; www.rescateanimalzooave.org; off Ruta Nacional 3; adult/student/child US$25/20/10; ⏰9am-5pm; P 👪) with more than 115 species of bird on colorful, squawking display. The tranquil 14-hectare setting is also home to all four species of Costa Rican monkey, reptiles, wild cats and other animals, many of which have been rescued and rehabilitated. Though technically a zoo, it is also an important animal-breeding center that aims to reintroduce native animals into the wild; admission fees fund wildlife rescue, rehabilitation, release and conservation programs.

teach everything from medical to business Spanish. Prices drop when students study for longer periods. Private or group classes available.

Festivals & Events

Juan Santamaría Day CULTURAL

(⏰Apr) The town that gave birth to a poor drummer boy named Juan Santamaría – who helped defeat the US in the Battle of Rivas – erupts in celebration on the victorious anniversary (April 11). This momentous occasion is commemorated with civic events, including a parade and lots of firecrackers.

Sleeping

★Hotel Cortez Azul GUESTHOUSE $

(☎2443-6145; https://cortez-azul-cr.book.direct/en-gb; Av 5 btwn Calles 4 & 2; d with/without bathroom from US$27/23; ❄ 📶 🐾) Great-value, friendly guesthouse. Clean, well-finished, light and airy doubles, some with beds made out of wooden pallets, some with shared bathrooms. Rooms facing the road are louder. The simple all-you-can-eat breakfast (bread and jam, fruit and cereal) is served in a lovely garden with fake grass and hammocks. There's a shared kitchen and a library. Nearby parking costs US$6 per stay.

Alajuela Backpackers Hostel HOSTEL $

(☎2441-7149; www.alajuelabackpackers.com; cnr Av 4 & Calle 4; dm US$13-16, r/ste from US$55/62; ❄ @ 📶) This gloomy four-story place with cookie-cutter rooms feels a tad institutional at first glance, but dig deeper and you'll discover some pluses: free shuttles to and from the airport, air-conditioned dorms and doubles with en-suite bathrooms, views over the highlands from top floor rooms and a bar for sipping beers. Avoid the bad pizzas.

★Hotel Los Volcanes GUESTHOUSE $$

(☎2441-0525; www.hotellosvolcanes.com; Av 3, btwn Calles Central & 2; s/d incl breakfast from US$68/79, with air-con from US$79/80, without bathroom from US$34/51; P 🚭 ❄ @ 📶) Tranquil and centrally located, this welcoming place in a refurbished 1920s mansion has 15 rooms, from vintage units with period-style furniture and clean shared bathrooms to contemporary rooms with air-con, flat-screen TV and safe. There's an enjoyable courtyard in the back, complete with a gurgling fountain. Free airport drop-off at the end of your stay. Parking nearby ($5 per night).

Hotel Pacandé B&B $$

(☎2443-8481; www.hotelpacande.com; Av 5, btwn Calles 2 & 4; r incl breakfast from US$45-65, without bathroom US$35; @ 📶) This popular, locally run option is spotlessly clean, offering 10 large rooms with wood furnishings, folk-art touches and cable TV. The bright, sunny breakfast nook is a great spot for a morning brew.

Trapp Family Country Inn INN $$

(☎2431-0776; www.trappfamilycostarica.com; off Ruta Nacional 124; r incl breakfast from US$108, additional adult/child 5-11yr US$30/25; P @ 📶 🏊) The most attractive option you'll find near the airport landing strip, this hacienda-style country inn surrounded by an acre of jungle has terracotta-tiled rooms and chunky wooden beds. The best units have balconies overlooking the inviting turquoise pool and verdant garden laced with bougainvillea and fig trees. Despite its remote feel, it's a convenient 2km from the airport. Transfers are included.

Vida Tropical B&B B&B $$

(☎2443-9576; www.vidatropical.com; Calle 3; s/d incl breakfast US$45/55, without bathroom US$35/45; P @ 📶 🐾) In a quiet residential neighborhood a five-minute walk north of downtown Alajuela, this friendly house has snug, simple guest rooms awash with bright murals; two share a bathroom. The well-tended backyard is perfect for catching some sun in a hammock, and laundry service is available ($5 per load; free with two-night stay).

★**Tacacori Ecolodge** BUNGALOW **$$$**
(☎2430-5846; www.tacacori.com; Calle Burios; d/tr incl breakfast from US$133/155) This peaceful retreat sitting on a verdant hillside high above Alajuela has four spacious bungalows with enchanting furnishings, floral motifs, modern fixtures and abundant ecofriendly touches (solar-powered hot water, LED lighting, dual-flush toilets). It's only a 40-minute drive up to Volcán Poás from here and around 20 minutes to the airport.

Xandari Resort Hotel & Spa HOTEL **$$$**
(☎2443-2020; www.xandari.com; Calle Burios; d/q incl breakfast from US$316/483;) With spectacular bird's-eye views of the Central Valley, this romantic spot is set on a 40-acre plantation with 24 spacious villas (sleeping two to six people). Units come with ceiling fans and are tastefully decorated in vibrant tropical colors, with hand-woven textiles and garden-view showers. The grounds have 4km of trails, five waterfalls, three pools, a spa with a Jacuzzi, and an organic restaurant (p112).

Hotel Buena Vista HOTEL **$$$**
(☎2442-8595, in US 855-817-3732; www.hotelbuenavistacr.com; Ruta Nacional 130; d/ste/villa incl breakfast from US$145/202/242;) About 5km north of Alajuela, this whitewashed Mediterranean-style hotel, perched on a mountaintop, has panoramic views of the nearby volcanoes. The best of the tastefully decorated rooms have private balconies with valley views. Villas also offer private balconies along with wood-beamed ceilings and minibar. A small trail leads down through a coffee *finca* to the main road.

Eating

★**Jalapeños Central** MEXICAN **$**
(Comida Tex-Mex; ☎2430-4027; www.facebook.com/JalapenosCentralig; Calle 1, btwn Avs 3 & 5; mains US$6-8; ⏲11:30am-9pm Mon-Sat, to 8pm Sun) Offering the best Tex-Mex in the country, this popular, cozy spot will introduce some spice to your diet. The simple and fresh burritos, chimichangas and enchiladas come in a meal deal or on their own, and regardless should be devoured with some of the house-made guacamole and salsa, and washed down with a salty margarita or a giant Coronarita.

Kurkuma BURGERS **$**
(☎4080-2300; cnr Calle 4 & Av 7; mains $6-12; ⏲noon-9:30pm Tue-Sun;) Thick, juicy tuna or beef burgers are served up with herby fries in this casual and welcoming place in the north of the city, with red booths and world flags decorating the walls. Those on a budget should order the excellent value *casados* (set meals). It stocks two dozen imported beers, from Samuel Adams and Estrella to Voll-Damm strong lager.

El Chante Vegano VEGETARIAN **$**
(☎2440-3528; Av 5 btwn Calles 1 & Central; mains US$7-11; ⏲noon-8pm Tue-Sat, to 4pm Sun;) This healthy eatery specializes in organic food. Vegan treats include Buffalo cauliflower tacos, falafel pitas and portobello-mushroom burgers, plus there are many other delights such as acai bowls, pasta, pizzas and veggie sandwiches. All are served on an open-air, street-facing patio and all the decoration inside is recycled.

Café Delicias CAFE **$**
(☎2431-4722; www.cafedelicias.com; cnr Calle 1 & Av 3; mains US$5-10; ⏲7am-8pm;) For breakfast, *bocas* (appetizers), and a variety of *típico* (traditional Costa Rican dishes), centrally located Café Delicias is a reliably good place to dine or enjoy a coffee accompanied by one of its rich desserts.

★**Pesqueria da Limonta** SEAFOOD **$$**
(☎2430-3572; cnr Av 6 & Calle 5; mains US$12-16; ⏲noon-4pm Sun, noon-9pm Mon, 11:30am-9pm Tue-Thu, 11:30am-10pm Fri, noon-10pm Sat) Set in an atmospheric villa with a sophisticated patio lit by fairy lights, Pesqueria da Limonta is the best dining experience in town, serving up fresh and beautifully presented seafood dishes with Costa Rican and Italian flair. Mains include Parmigiano gratin shrimps, perfectly tangy *ceviche* (seafood marinated in lemon or lime juice, garlic and seasonings) and Caribbean salmon. The seafood salads are superb, and there are succulent beef cuts for non-seafood-eaters.

★**La Casona del Maíz** COSTA RICAN **$$**
(☎2433-5363; www.facebook.com/lacasonadelmaizcr; Intersection of Autopista Bernardo Soto & Ruta Nacional 3, La Garita; mains US$9-19; ⏲5:30am-9pm Sun-Thu, to 10pm Fri & Sat;) Hugely popular among Tico families who come to enjoy proper country cooking, this casual place is on the road to Atenas, 9km east of Alajuela. The menu is heavy on grilled meats and corn dishes, though there are veggie *casados* too. The *chorreadas* (savory corn pancakes) are excellent. Grab an insanely good dulce de leche coconut bar at the counter. It's just north of the Interamericana.

El Hop AMERICAN $$
(☎2101-0264; www.facebook.com/elhopcr; El Patio, Calle 5 btwn Avs 8 & 6; dishes $8-12; ⏰5pm-10pm Tue, noon-3pm & 6pm-10pm Wed & Thu, noon-11pm Fri & Sat, noon-9pm Sun) Open-plan gastropub serving top grub and beer. The kitchen rustles up adventurous dishes like seafood cocktails (with poached octopus and shrimp), plus ultra-thin-crust pizzas that will keep you coming back. Bases come topped with classic pepperoni or more unusual toppings like mozzarella cheese with caramelized red onion and avocado. The drinks list has good craft beers and cocktails.

Xandari INTERNATIONAL $$$
(☎2443-2020; www.xandari.com; Xandari Resort Hotel & Spa, Calle Burios; mains US$12-32; ⏰7-10am, noon-4pm & 6-8pm;) If you want to impress a date, you can't go wrong at this elegant restaurant with incredible views. The menu is a mix of Costa Rican and international dishes, with plenty of vegetarian options. The restaurant utilizes the resort's homegrown organic produce, supplemented by locally grown organic produce where possible – it all makes for tasty and feel-good gourmet meals.

☆ Entertainment

Alajuela's own soccer team, La Liga (Liga Deportiva Alajuelense), has been around for more than 100 years. Over its lifetime, the club has won 29 national championships and the team plays at **Estadio Morera Soto** (☎2289-0909; www.lda.cr; Av Parque; tickets from US$8) at the northeastern end of town on Sunday during *fútbol* (soccer) season.

Shopping

Goodlight Books BOOKS
(☎2430-4083; Av 3 btwn Calles 1 & 3; ⏰noon-6:30pm Tue-Sat) Bookaholics, rejoice! Alajuela has one of the best English-language bookstores in the country (if not Central America). Well-organized Goodlight offers thousands of used and new books, a worthwhile stock of difficult-to-find volumes on Costa Rica, a growing supply of Spanish-language titles and a sizable array of books in other European languages.

ℹ Information

Banco Nacional (Calle 2; ⏰8:30am-3:30pm Mon-Fri) The most centrally located ATM can be found in the main square opposite the church.

Hospital San Rafael (☎2436-1001; Alameda Tomás Guardia; ⏰24 hours) Alajuela's hospital is a three-story building south of Av 10.

Post office (☎2443-2653; cnr Av 5 & Calle 1; ⏰8am-5pm Mon-Fri, to noon Sat)

ℹ Getting There & Away

Taxis charge between US$6 and US$10 (depending on destination) for the five- to 10-minute drive from Juan Santamaría International Airport (p515) into Alajuela.

There is no central bus terminal; instead, a number of small terminals and bus stops dot the southwestern part of the city. Note that there are two Tuasa terminals – **east** (☎2442-6900; Calle 8 btwn Avs Central & 1) and **west** (Calle 8 btwn Avs Central & 1) – right across the street from each other. From there, **buses to Grecia and Sarchí** (cnr Calle 10 & Av 1) are a block west; **buses to Atenas** (Calle 10 btwn Avs Central &

BUSES FROM ALAJUELA

DESTINATION	COMPANY	COST (US$)	DURATION	FREQUENCY
Atenas	Coopetransatenas	2	1hr	every 30min-1hr 5:50am-10:30pm Mon-Fri (7am-10:30pm Sat & Sun)
Grecia	Transportes Tuan	2	1hr	roughly half-hourly 5am-10pm
Sarchí	Transportes Tuan	2	1-1.5hr	roughly half-hourly 6am-10:20pm
Heredia	Tuasa	1.50	45min	every 15min 5:30am-10pm
Juan Santamaría International Airport	Tuasa	1.50	15min	every 10-30min, 24hr
San José	Tuasa	1.50	45min	every 10-30min, 24hr
Volcán Poás	Coopetransasi/ Tuasa	5 round trip	50min-1hr	departs 9:15am, returns 2:30pm

2) are one block west and one block south; and **buses to Volcán Poás** (☎2442-6900; Calle 8 btwn Avs Central & 2) are a block south. **Buses to San José via the airport** (Av 4 btwn Calles 2 & 4) leave from in front of the Parque de los Niños, on the opposite side of the street.

Coopetransasi (☎2449-6040, 2449-5141) offers routes around Costa Rica. Bus times are subject to change at any time; check with local bus companies for up-to-date schedules before your journey.

Parque Nacional Volcán Poás

Just 37km north of Alajuela by a winding and scenic road is **Parque Nacional Volcán Poás** (☎2482-1226; www.sinac.go.cr; Ruta Nacional 120; adult/child 12yr & under US$15/5, parking US$3.50; ⏲8am-2pm, last entry 1:20pm; P), the home of an impressive 2708m-high active volcano. Violent eruptions hadn't taken place for more than 60 years when rumblings began in 2014; there were further significant eruptions in April and June 2017, and the park did not open again until August 2018.

It's now once again possible to peer into the 260m-deep crater and the turquoise lake at its center. Visitors can watch the steaming, bubbling cauldron belch sulfurous gases into the air. However, hiking trails are now off-limits and visits are restricted to 20 minutes at the crater. Advance bookings are essential.

The winding drive up to Poás is equally spectacular. Without cloud cover, it offers magnificent views over the green central valleys below. Pair a morning trip to the volcano with an afternoon jaunt to La Paz Waterfall Gardens for an abundance of exotic wildlife and a series of rushing waterfalls.

Activities

The Walk to the Crater

Visits take roughly 45 minutes. On arrival, guests are provided with a hard hat in case of debris and ash spewing from the volcano, and given a safety briefing (in Spanish only) in an auditorium. A ranger outlines the volcanic activity in the area, what to do during an evacuation, and the potential poisonous gases in the air, which are likely to most affect people with asthma or existing breathing problems. After the briefing, your group walks (self-guided) around 750m uphill along a paved pathway (roughly 20 minutes) to the viewpoint, which looks into the whopping 360m-diameter crater. There's a strong eggy smell of sulfur in the air and you may find that as you get closer to the crater your throat feels sore and you begin to cough. Officials explain that the gases in the air are checked regularly. If they rise to a certain level your group will be asked to leave the viewpoint. If you are struggling to breathe you may use one of the masks provided – the best advice is to walk back to the visitor center.

It's common to see dramatic smoke plumes rising from the crater. Be aware that cloud cover is also common, and many travelers make the winding drive up to the summit (roughly an hour from Alajuela) only to find they can't see a thing through the mist. Your best chance of a clear crater sighting is early in the morning. There are no refunds for bad weather conditions, and trails around the volcano are now off-limits. It can get chilly at the crater, so bring warm clothes, comfortable walking shoes and water.

Tours

Hacienda Alsacia FOOD & DRINK
(☎2103-4282; www.starbuckscoffeefarm.com/en; tours adult/child under 6yr $30/free; ⏲8:30am-6pm Mon-Fri, 8am-6pm Sat & Sun) The only farm in the world owned by coffee giants Starbucks is at the bottom of Volcán Poás. Visitors can join a 90-minute tour to learn the processes from crop to cup on this 240-hectare property, before sampling coffee in a flashy tasting room and cafe. Find it 15km north of Alajuela on the way to Volcán Poás.

Corso Dairy Farm FOOD & DRINK
(☎4002-1430; Ruta Nacional 120; tours incl lunch adult/child US$11/8; ⏲tours 9am, 11am and 1:30pm) With a farm-to-table restaurant, shop and dairy-farm tour, families and cheese fans will enjoy this stop before or after visiting Volcán Poás. Tours navigate 2km of trails, as a guide teaches about local geology and the methods of growing crops like strawberries, blackberries and blueberries. Kids can have a go at milking the cows.

Sleeping & Eating

Poás Lodge B&B $$
(☎2482-1091; www.poaslodge.com; Ruta Nacional 120; r incl breakfast US$75-95; P 📶) Run by

WORTH A TRIP

LA PAZ WATERFALL GARDENS

This polished storybook **garden complex** (☎2482-2720, reservations 2482-2100; www.waterfallgardens.com; Ruta National 126; adult/under 13yr US$45/29; ⏰8am-5pm; P 👪) just east of Volcán Poás offers the most easily digestible cultural experience in the Central Valley. Guests walk 3.5km of well-maintained trails to five jaw-droppingly scenic waterfalls, and can also wander around zoo-like displays including a butterfly conservatory, get up close to hummingbirds and hand-feed toucans. Tour a serpentarium and ranarium (frog garden), witness wild cats eating meals, and devour a plate of your own at one of the park's restaurants.

American expats Leah and Matthew Lentz, this roadside hotel perched high on Poás' slopes at 2186m (only 4km south of the park entrance) has a cozy, welcoming vibe. The restaurant's wraparound windows offer gorgeous sunset perspectives and views down the slopes of the volcano. Downstairs, four simple and pleasant rooms have satellite TV, wi-fi and stunning views.

★Peace Lodge LODGE $$$
(☎2482-2720; www.waterfallgardens.com; Ruta Nacional 126; r standard/deluxe from US$559/666, villa/deluxe villa from US$989/1230, additional adult/child US$45/23; P 📶 🏊) Feel like you've stepped into a fairy tale at this over-the-top lodge, with its exquisite villas boasting majestic valley views, fireplaces, private decks with Jacuzzis, and huge bathrooms with waterfall showers. Guests get free access to the La Paz Waterfall Gardens next door – an animal-rescue center with hiking trails, five giant waterfalls and a trout pond.

This highly imaginative setting, with its multiple pools and interactive animal experiences (toucan and hummingbird feeding), will have kids over the moon. Disappointingly, breakfast is not included in the pricey room rate (add an extra $20/12 for adult/child).

Poás Volcano Lodge LODGE $$$
(☎2482-2194; www.poasvolcanolodge.com; Vara Blanca; r incl breakfast from US$125; P @ 📶) For sophisticated, contemporary class in an idyllic rural setting, stay at this high-altitude property. Suites combine rusticity and elegance; the best have a balcony and private garden and/or fireplace. Spacious common areas include a games room and a library. There's more than 3km of hiking over three trails for quetzal sightings and views of the volcano.

★Freddo Fresas BREAKFAST, SOUP $
(☎2482-2800; Poasito; dishes breakfast US$3-7, lunch US$8-16; ⏰7am-4pm) This homey spot looks as though it was built from oversize Lincoln logs. It's known for heavenly strawberry smoothies (milky ones beat watery ones) and large, piping-hot breakfasts that fuel some serious hikes. For those returning from lofty elevations, a wide soup selection warms the soul, and the *casados* are good too. Find Freddo's a couple of blocks north of the cemetery.

El Churrasco Hotel Restaurante COSTA RICAN $
(☎2482-2135; www.hotelelchurrasco.com; Ruta Nacional 120; mains US$8-12; ⏰8am-8pm; P 📶) On the way up to Volcán Poás, this rustic restaurant serves tasty, authentic Costa Rican cuisine. Ingredients are sourced locally and the *casados* and mixed rice dishes are full of flavor. The house specializes in steak, with nine cuts on offer. Pair your succulent slab with everything from creole tomato sauce to Roquefort cheese.

Colbert Restaurant FRENCH $$
(Restaurante Frances Colbert; ☎8301-1793, 2482-2776; www.colbert.co.cr; Vara Blanca; mains US$8-32; ⏰noon-7pm Fri-Tue) At this charming restaurant 6km east of Poasito, the menu is loaded with traditional French items such as onion soup, house-made pâté, beef fillet, rabbit in mustard sauce and chocolate mousse (a French recipe using chocolate from Costa Rica). A good wine list is strong on vintages from South America and France.

ℹ Information

At Parque Nacional Volcán Poás there's a ranger station, cafeteria, souvenir shop and restrooms.

Daily visitor numbers are strictly controlled by a convoluted online booking system (via www.sinac.go.cr), requiring an initial registration with ID, then payment. Advance booking on the website is essential or you may be turned away at the gate. Upon purchasing a ticket, you sign a waiver of liability outlining the increase in toxic volcanic gases at the crater (sulfur dioxide, sulfuric acid, hydrochloric acid and carbon dioxide). The booking system has been known to crash so book well in advance of your visit, and download your confirmation in advance as cellphone signal is scarce on the volcano. Check the park opening status before you visit; temporary closures have been known to happen due to ash and gas emissions.

Getting There & Away

Volcán Poás is located 30km from Alajuela via a scenic mountain drive through pretty hillside towns along Ruta Nacional 120. Numerous local companies offer daily tours to the volcano (around US$40 to US$100). Tour companies will help with the complicated ticket booking process (advanced reservations and ID required) and arrange transport up to the volcano. It's much cheaper, and nearly as easy, to visit the volcano on the daily Coopetransasi bus from Alajuela (US$5 return, 50 minutes to 1 hour, departs 9:15am). On any given visit there may be cloud cover; the best option is to visit early in the morning but, unfortunately, there is only one bus in the morning, which arrives at around 10am.

To beat the clouds, your best bet is to hire a car (from US$40 per day) or take a taxi (roughly US$35 from Alajuela or US$50 to US$60 from San José) and arrive near the park's entrance. The road (Ruta 120) from Alajuela to the volcano is well signposted.

Atenas

POP 5000

This small village, on the historic *camino de carretas* (oxcart trail) that once carried coffee beans as far as Puntarenas, is best known for having the most pleasant climate in the world – according to none other than *National Geographic*. It's not too heavy on sights, but it's a good base from which to explore the Central Valley and springtime is always in the air. The central square is a lovely spot to take in Costa Rican life.

Sights & Activities

Atenas Railway Museum MUSEUM

(Estacion de Tren Rio Grande; 9am-6pm Sat & Sun) FREE Trains first pulled in at this atmospheric, now-abandoned station more than a century ago and continued until the 1990s, when the remaining freight engines were replaced by trucks. The first steam locomotive bellowed along here in 1898. The green and white building (though rebuilt in the 1930s) still looks the part, decked out with wooden boards, vintage signage and a tin roof. The stone slab floors are completely original, dating back to the 1890s.

The museum, notorious for its irregular opening hours, is a jumble of donated vintage train memorabilia, from signals and wheels to lanterns, ticket punches, agricultural tools and old photos. The best attraction is outside on the track: a rusty blue AEG locomotive, made in Berlin in 1928.

Take a 0.5km hike to the northeast, along the creepy, jungle-fringed, abandoned railroad. Local houses line the old tracks and wild chickens roam around. You'll quickly come to an epic photo opportunity: a grand, arched steel bridge with vast views of the verdant valley below. There are no barriers preventing onlookers from walking onto the bridge, but it is hazardous, so don't.

Aventuras Costa Rica ADVENTURE SPORTS

(8320-2429; www.aventurascr.com; Casa Catuca, cnr Av 3 and Calle Central; bike tours from US$40, bike rental per day US$40; 9:30am-5pm) This friendly outfit runs local day trips and bespoke tours around the local area and beyond. It specializes in biking tours, and the staff know some great secret(ish) sights in the local area. They will create an itinerary for you around most adventures you can dream up, from volcano visiting, Manuel Antonio nature spotting and beach going, to rafting, ziplining and chocolate tours.

Sleeping & Eating

Vista Atenas B&B B&B $$

(2446-4272; www.vistaatenasbnb.com; near Ruta Nacional 3; r incl breakfast US$85-90, studio not incl breakfast from $95;) Soak up dreamy valley views that include four volcanoes – and sometimes smoking craters – in the distance. Located in a residential area 5km outside Atenas is this B&B with comfy, bright rooms and self-catering cabins, plus a gorgeous communal swimming-pool terrace. Ecofriendly touches include spring water pumped and heated using solar power. Breakfast is made using organic ingredients. Kitchenettes are available.

★ **El Balcón del Café** CAFE $

(2446-8592; www.balcondelcafe.com; Av 5; breakfast from US$3.50, lunch mains from US$8; 8am-6pm Mon-Sat) The best place in town for breakfast is inside this little lime-green house decorated with black-and-white vintage photos. It serves up full Tico, American and German breakfasts, the latter with tasty German bread, proper Swiss cheese, ham, eggs, juice and coffee or tea. Other international delights include quiche lorraine and schnitzel for lunch, plus irresistible homemade cakes and pastries.

Restaurant La Trocha del Boyero COSTA RICAN $$
(☎8650-0528, 2446-0533; Calle Abel Rodríguez; casados US$9, mains US$9-18; ⊙noon-9pm Tue-Sun; 📶) Tico families and local expats crowd the pleasant deck here for the variety of *casados* on offer, fresh trout (in season), sirloin and heaped bowls of *chifrijo* (rice and beans with fried pork, corn chips and fresh tomato salsa). It's located on a road off the main road towards Alajuela before the monument. Look for a sign at the turnoff.

Getting There & Away

Coopetransatenas (☎2446-5767) buses run from Atenas to Alajuela (around US$2, 45 to 60 minutes, every 30 minutes to 1½ hours from 5am to 8:15pm), with one change in La Garita. Coopetransatenas and **Tracopa** (☎2221-4214; www.tracopacr.com) buses run to San José (around US$2, 1¼ hours, four daily from 8:10am to 8pm). Schedules are subject to change; contact the local bus companies for up-to-date route times.

The Atenas area is quite spread out, and best navigated by car.

Grecia

POP 15,500

The village of Grecia – known as the 'Cleanest Little Town in Latin America' – is centered on pleasant **Parque Central**, anchored by one of the most charming churches in Costa Rica. It's a sleepy place with no 'tourist' attractions but makes for a pleasant base from which to explore the Central Valley.

Sights

Catedral de la Mercedes CHURCH
(☎2494-1616; www.parroquiadegrecia.com; Calle 1 btwn Avs León Cortés Castro & Ismael Valerio; ⊙8am-noon & 2pm-5pm Mon-Fri, 8am-noon Sat, masses held Sun) At the heart of town you'll find the incredibly quaint Catedral de la Mercedes, a red metal structure that was prefabricated in Belgium and shipped to Costa Rica in 1897 – and resembles a gingerbread church. It has an airy nave, bright Spanish-tile floors and a Gothic-style altar covered in marble.

Sleeping & Eating

Mangífera Hostel HOSTEL $
(☎2494-6065; Av León Cortés Castro; dm/d from US$12/38, d without bathroom US$34; P📶) This cozy hostel, with wooden floors and a friendly ambiance, feels instantly welcoming. Located on the northern side of Parque Central, it has eight rooms, three of which are dorms. There's a shared kitchen and a small garden with a hammock from which to watch hummingbirds feed. Laundry service is available.

Siglos Crepería DESSERTS $
(☎2102-7306; Calle 3 btwn Avs León Cortés Castro and Ismael Valerio; crepes from $5; ⊙11am-8pm Wed & Thu, to 9pm Fri-Sun) Need a sweet fix? Head to Siglos, a small creperie serving decadently indulgent brownies, and French-style thin pancakes smothered in chocolate or fruit. All freshly made.

Café Delicias CAFE $$
(☎2494-2093; www.cafedelicias.com; Av Ismael Valerio; breakfasts from US$4, sandwiches US$4-7, mains US$5-15; ⊙7am-9pm; 📶) For breakfast, rich coffee drinks, pastries, sandwiches and plate meals (from chicken fajitas to steak), hit this enjoyable spot near the southwestern corner of Parque Central.

La Casa De Miguel GRILL $$
(☎2444-6767; Av León Cortés Castro btwn Calles 5 & 3; mains US$8-18; ⊙11am-9pm Tue-Thu, to 10pm Fri & Sat, to 5pm Sun) For a more leisurely sit-down meal, join locals here and choose from an extensive menu of international dishes, including six types of *ceviche* to start, plus pastas, steak and seafood- or chicken-based mains. There's an imported-wine list, but bottles are hit and miss.

Getting There & Away

Buses for San José and Sarchí stop at the TUAN bus terminal, 150m north of Grecia's central plaza. Bus schedules are subject to change; check timetables with local bus companies before your departure.

San José Around US$2, one hour, at least half-hourly from 4:30am to 8:30pm.

Sarchí, connecting to Naranjo Around US$1, 30 minutes, half-hourly from 4:50am to 10pm.

Sarchí

POP 7000

Welcome to Costa Rica's most famous crafts center, where artisans produce the ornately painted oxcarts and leather-and-wood furnishings for which the Central Valley is known. You'll know you've arrived because many places are covered in the colorful signature geometric designs – even city hall. Yes, it's a tourist trap, but it's a pretty one. The town is stretched out along a road that weaves through hilly countryside.

Most people come for a couple of hours of shopping and call it a day, but if you have time on your hands it's possible to meet different artisans and custom-order a creation.

In Sarchí Norte you'll find the heart of the village, including a twin-towered church, some restaurants and *pulperías* (corner stores), and what is purported to be the world's largest oxcart (photo op!).

Sights

Jardín Botánico Else Kientzler GARDENS

(☎2454-2070; www.elsegarden.com; Sarchí Norte; adult/child US$6.50/5; ⏰8am-4pm; 👪) This well-tended botanical garden 400m north of Sarchí stadium has 2km of trails winding through more than 2000 types of clearly labeled plants, including local tropical plants and those from around the world. See succulents, fruit trees, palms, heliconias and orchids on show. Regular yoga workshops, plant fairs and talks also take place in the grounds.

Sleeping & Eating

Hotel Paraíso Río Verde BUNGALOW $$

(☎2454-3003; San Pedro de Sarchí; bungalows from US$60; P📶🏊) A 5km detour northeast of Sarchí, this spot in the highland village of San Pedro enjoys panoramic vistas of coffee plantations and volcanoes Poás, Barva and Irazú. Spacious bungalows come with kitchenettes. On an unnamed road, finding this place is tricky so booking is essential – the owners provide GPS coordinates or meet you beside the giant oxcart in Sarchí's plaza.

Super Mariscos SEAFOOD $$

(☎2454-4330; Ruta Nacional 118; mains US$7-29; ⏰11am-10pm Wed-Mon; P📶) Forgive appearances: Super Mariscos looks dated and plays melodic pan pipes on the stereo, but it serves very good *ceviche,* rice dishes and seafood galore, plus pasta and a few beef dishes. You can order most items in a small or large size, depending on your appetite.

Getting There & Away

If you're driving from San José, from the Interamericana take the signed exit to Grecia and from there follow the road north to Sarchí. If you're coming from the west, take the turnoff north to Naranjo then head east to Sarchí.

Buses arrive and depart from Sarchí Norte, running to:

Alajuela Around US$2, one to 1½ hours, every 15 to 30 minutes from 5am to 10pm.

Grecia Around US$1, 30 minutes, half-hourly from 5am to 10pm.

San José Around US$2.50, 1½ to 2¾ hours, around every 30 minutes from 5am to 10pm, with a change in Alajuela.

Bus schedules are subject to change; check with local bus companies for up-to-date times before departure.

SHOPPING SARCHÍ

Most travelers come to Sarchí for one thing only: *carretas*, the elaborate, colorfully painted oxcarts that are the unofficial souvenir of Costa Rica – and the official symbol of the Costa Rican worker. In Sarchí they come ready for the road (oxen sold separately) or in scaled-down versions. But the area produces plenty of other curios: leather-and-wood furniture (including incredible rocking chairs that collapse for shipping), wooden tableware and trinkets emblazoned with the colorful mandala design popularized by the *carretas*.

There are dozens of vendors, and prices and quality vary, so it pays to shop around. Workshops are usually open from 8am to 5pm daily; they accept credit cards and US dollars, and can arrange international shipping. Two of the most respected and popular spots are the **Fábrica de Carretas Eloy Alfaro** (☎2454-4131; www.souvenirscostarica.com; Sarchí Norte; ⏰8am-5pm) and the **Fábrica de Carretas Joaquín Chaverri** (☎2454-4411; Sarchí Sur; ⏰8am-5pm) or get mini versions at the **Coopearsa** (☎2454-4050; www.coopearsarl.com; Av Central, near Calle 4; ⏰8am-6pm, butterfly farm 10am-4pm) gift shop, which has a butterfly farm behind it.

Zarcero

POP 4300

North of Naranjo, the road winds for 20km until it reaches Zarcero's 1736m perch at the western end of the Cordillera Central. This is a gorgeous location: the mountains look as if they've been lifted from landscape paintings and the climate is famously fresh. But the real reason you're here is to see the country's most surreal shrubbery at Parque Francisco Alvarado.

Sights

★Parque Francisco Alvarado PARK

(btwn Avs Central & 2) In front of the Church of San Rafael, this park was a normal plaza until the 1960s, when a gardener named Evangelisto Blanco became inspired to shave the ordinary topiary into a bizarre series of trippy, abstract shapes. Over the years these morphed into fanciful creatures, weird blobby creations and tunnels of arches you can walk through. Bring your camera.

Sleeping

Hotel Zarcero HOTEL $

(☎2463-4141; Calle 1, north of Av 1; s/d/tr from US$25/29/38) A couple of blocks up from the church, Hotel Zarcero is the only place to stay in town. There are 15 basic rooms with locally made furnishings.

Rancho Amalia FARMSTAY $$

(☎2463-2401, 8994-4288; www.ranchoamalia.com; Ruta National 141; d cabin US$89, extra person $18; ⏰Nov-May, groups year-round; P 📶) Attention, horse people: this family-owned mountaintop ranch just 10 minutes' drive south of Zarcero is your dream. On offer are four charming and well-constructed cabins with fireplaces, TVs and full kitchens, a dining hall and elegant stables. The property's horses carry guests across the hillside, through forests and over scenic pastureland surrounded by wildflowers and views of the Central Valley.

Eating

Zarcero is a hub for Costa Rican organic farming. You can find unusual varieties of pesticide-free produce around town, and the surrounding mountains are perfect for a picnic. While eating-out options are scarce, there are a couple of quick-bite bakeries and *sodas,* such as **Soda Rosa** (☎2463-2442; Calle Central; mains $3-5; ⏰6am-6pm), plus stands selling fresh cashews, honey, sweets and *queso palmito* (a locally made cheese with a delicate taste; it goes well with fresh tomatoes and basil) on the road into Zarcero.

Getting There & Away

Transportes Zarcero (☎2451-4080) and TUAN run daily direct buses to San José (around US$2, two hours, with one change in Alajuela) about every 30 minutes daily between 5am-3pm. All buses stop along the main street south of the square. Bus timetables are subject to change.

Bajos del Toro

A gorgeous road snakes northeast out of Zarcero, climbing steeply through hillsides dotted with family dairy farms, then plunging abruptly into the stunning valley of the Río Toro, surrounded by the lower reaches of the area's cloud-forest ecosystem. If you were looking for a little piece of Costa Rica where everybody knows everybody, then look no further. This small town (full name: Bajos del Toro Amarillo) is rural idyll at its finest.

There are no banks. Bring all the cash you'll need.

Sights

★Catarata del Toro & the Blue Falls WATERFALL

(☎2476-0800, 8399-7476; www.catarata-del-toro.com; Ruta Nacional 708; waterfall entry adult/child US$14/7, Blue Falls entry 2-person minimum light trail US$15, full trail US$50, combo tours from US$25; ⏰7am-3pm, entry to Blue Falls until 2pm Mon-Sat) Find a beautiful 90m-tall waterfall that cascades into a volcanic crater (free for overnight guests) and two trail options through virgin forest (one 4.5km out-and-back option, and one 6km route) to turquoise swimming holes and the Blue Falls of Costa Rica. There's also a restaurant where you can recharge after your hike while watching hummingbirds fly around. Or make a night of it in one of the wood-paneled rooms (from US$65 per night) tucked under A-frame-style eaves.

Reservations are required for the longer trail with seven waterfalls on it.

Sleeping & Eating

There are a few places to rest your head in the area, and they're very popular. Be sure to show up with a reservation.

OFF THE BEATEN TRACK

PARQUE NACIONAL JUAN CASTRO BLANCO

This 143-sq-km **national park** (admission by donation) was created to protect the slopes of Volcán Platanar (2183m) and Volcán Porvenir (2267m) from logging and mining. The headwaters for five major rivers originate here, making this one of the most important watersheds in the country.

While federally protected, much of the park is still privately owned by plantation families – only those parts that have already been purchased by the government are technically open to travelers.

From the **visitor center** (Montaña Sagrada Natural Reserve; 8815-7094; apanajuca@gmail.com; 8am-4pm Fri-Sun) a 2km trail climbs through pastureland, then descends to Pozo Verde, a green lake surrounded by mountains. A rougher trail continues 3.5km to Las Minas, an abandoned mine site (only hikeable with a guide). Shorter trails include the Universal Trail (only half a kilometer) and the 1.5km Canto de Las Aves (Birdsong) trail.

The park is frequented by anglers as the five rivers are brimming with trout. The limited infrastructure and very little tourist traffic mean your chances of spotting rare wildlife (quetzals, black guans, curassows) are higher than average. Guides can be arranged through tour agencies and hotels in the area.

Sleeping & Eating

Albergue Pozo Verde (2460-8452; www.alberguemonterreal.com; d incl breakfast from US$66;) is the only accommodation near the park.

Tucked into a pretty valley about 1km before the park headquarters, **Restaurante El Congo** (2460-8452; www.alberguemonterreal.com; mains US$8-10; 5am-5pm;) is the area's sole place to eat.

Getting There & Away

The park entrance is located at the end of a rough 10km road from El Sucre, 20km north of Zarcero. The road is passable for skilled drivers in 2WD vehicles until the final descent; if you don't have a 4WD, park on the hilltop 300m before the visitor center.

Bosque de Paz LODGE $$$
(Bosque de Paz Cloud Forest Lodge & Biological Reserve; 2234-6676; www.bosquedepaz.com; Ruta Nacional 741; d incl breakfast US$218-246, ste incl breakfast US$318;) A birdwatcher's paradise, this 10-sq-km reserve straddles an important wilderness corridor between Parque Nacional Volcán Poás and Parque Nacional Juan Castro Blanco, with more than 22km of trails in old-growth forest and an orchid garden. The dozen spacious, terracotta-tiled rooms, within earshot of a rushing river, feature large windows with forest views. Vegan diets can be accommodated. Reservations recommended.

El Silencio LODGE $$$
(2476-0627, reservations 2231-6122; www.elsilenciolodge.com; ste/villas incl breakfast US$380-786;) Secluded outside of town, this upscale lodge from the Relais & Châteaux group comprises luxuriously designed *cabina* suites with private deck, rocking chairs, a Jacuzzi and fine mountain views, plus six-person villas with gas fireplaces and full kitchens. There's also a spa, 8km worth of trails (leading to stunning waterfalls) and a health-conscious restaurant serving meals using organic produce grown onsite.

Soda Restaurante Nené COSTA RICAN $
(2476-0130, 2476-0631; mains US$8-14; 9am-5pm Sat & Sun) Just south of town, tucked back slightly from the main road, this simple green shack of a restaurant is flanked by well-stocked trout ponds. Catch your own fish, then enjoy it fried or grilled with garlic at the rustic picnic-bench-style tables. Chicken, squid and tuna fried rice also available. Hours can be irregular, so call ahead.

Getting There & Away

Driving north from the Interamericana through Zarcero, take a right immediately after the church and continue northeast about 15km. Alternatively, take the road due north from Sarchí's central plaza. Both roads are almost entirely paved but involve stomach-churning steep climbs and hairpin turns requiring some skillful driving; a 4WD makes all the difference to your nerves but isn't obligatory. There's currently no direct bus service to the area. A taxi from Alajuela and San José costs around US$30.

San Ramón

POP 11,000

The pretty colonial town of San Ramón is no wallflower in the pageant of Costa Rican history. The 'City of Presidents and Poets' has sent five men to the country's highest office, including Rodrigo Carazo, who built a tourist lodge a few kilometers to the north.

Another of Costa Rica's beloved presidents, José Figueres Ferrer, is paid homage in a museum and edifying culture and history center just north of the city's central park.

Sights & Activities

San Ramón Regional Museum MUSEUM
(☎2447-7137; www.so.ucr.ac.cr/museo-regional-de-san-ramon; Av 1 Juan Santamaria; ⌚10am-6pm Tue-Sat) FREE On the northern edge of San Ramón park, this informative museum run by the University of San Ramón covers the cultural heritage of the area with a number of exhibition rooms around a central courtyard. Here you can peruse local art, a historic timeline, explanations about local geology and economic information, and see local plant-life in the pleasant courtyard. Kids will love the colorful *gigantes* (big masks worn during festivities). Info boards are in Spanish only.

Bosque Nuboso El Cocora NATURE CENTER
(☎7236-6417; www.facebook.com/elcocora; Hwy 70, San Luis; adult/child under 12 US$10/5; ⌚9am-4:30pm) This short trail around a nice garden is a pretty, if a little pricey, place to stretch your legs on the way to the high cloud forest or Lands in Love hotel. There's a butterfly garden, around a dozen hummingbird species, plus a fishpond and a lake on the grounds. At the entrance you'll get a birders checklist.

Costa Rica Eco Bungee ADVENTURE SPORTS
(☎8344-0123; www.facebook.com/ecobungee; Hwy 702; bungee/zipline/sky swing US$75/69/35; ⌚8am-4pm) Daredevils can throw themselves off an 80m-high platform with a bungee attached to their ankles or chest in this spectacular rainbow hotspot – a transitional forest valley consisting of both rain and cloud forest. Not up for leaping into the valley? Go on a 2km hike around the area along a number of bridges hanging throughout the forest.

Other activities at the center include 12 ziplines (the longest of which is 550 meters) and a sky swing. The owners are currently building a treehouse, where visitors will be able to sleep overnight. Discounts are available if you book more than one activity and all participants are free to visit the butterfly tent.

Sleeping

★Casa Amanecer B&B $$
(☎2445-2100; www.casa-amanecer-cr.com; off Ruta Nacional 704; s/d incl breakfast from US$68/75 extra person US$25; P📶) 🌿 A 10-minute drive northeast of San Ramón, this sleekly designed, secluded B&B, owned by welcoming host Helen, offers five contemporary rooms with polished concrete floors and orthopedic beds. Tasty veggie breakfasts are served on the breezy shared terrace opposite a green lawn. Two friendly dogs and a cat live on the property.

Lands in Love LODGE $$
(Tierras Enamoradas; ☎2447-9331, in USA 1-408-215-1000; www.landsinlove.com; Hwy 702; d incl breakfast from US$113; P📶🏊🐾) 🌿 Midway between San Ramón and La Fortuna, this well-signposted lodge is run by animal lovers (they care for hundreds of them here). The 33 eclectic rooms have bright floral motifs and guests can enjoy a lounge, an outdoor swimming pool, a Jacuzzi and a plethora of adventure activities – from trails around the property to a canopy tour and horseback riding.

The Lands in Love restaurant is worth a stop alone. It serves a mix of delicious Israeli, vegetarian and vegan dishes. Try the super-fresh salads or the very creative meat-substitute dishes like the BLT (without real pork), mock-meatballs in spicy tomato sauce, and the 'Cafe de Paris' steak minus the beef.

Hotel La Posada INN $$
(☎2445-7359, 2447-3131; www.posadahotel.net; Av 9; s/d/tr US$60/80/105, breakfast per person US$10; P❄@📶) 🌿 Well-maintained rooms surround a lush, plant-filled courtyard at

this pleasant inn, 400m north of the church. Rooms are somewhat baroque-looking, outfitted with massive handcrafted beds that lie somewhere on the design continuum between Louis XIV and African safari. All have minifridges and cable TV; more expensive units have hot tubs. Some units are wheelchair-accessible, and a few have air-conditioning.

★Villa Blanca Cloud Forest Hotel & Nature Reserve LODGE $$$

(☎2461-0300, in USA 1-877-288-0664; www.villablanca-costarica.com; Calle Villa Blanca; d US$111-275, child under 6yr free; P@≈) Occupying a cloud-forest aerie, this private reserve is centered on a lodge and dairy ranch once owned by ex-president Rodrigo Carazo. Its 35 free-standing *casitas* (little houses) come with wi-fi, private terrace, minibar and TV. Guests won't be bored with a restaurant, spa, yoga center and movie theater screening films nightly, plus a schedule of activities including dance, tree planting, and cooking lessons.

The surrounding 800 hectares of primary and secondary cloud forest offers trails and excellent wildlife-spotting opportunities. Bilingual naturalist guides are available for morning and evening cloud-forest walks (US$34), and birdwatching (US$34) and quetzal-spotting (US$110) tours. Certified at the highest level of sustainability, the lodge composts, recycles and follows energy-efficient practices. The turnoff north of San Ramón is well signposted from the Interamericana, but a 4WD is recommended for the 9km-long potholed road. A taxi from San Ramón costs about US$35.

Eating & Drinking

Merak Fusion FUSION $

(☎2447-3470; cnr Av 8 & Calle 1; mains from US$7; ⊙7-10pm Fri & Sat; ≈) With hardwood floors and simple, clean decor, Merak is a gastronomic restaurant with flavors that cross continents. Creations include the likes of Portobello mushrooms with blue cheese; Caribbean squid; marlin and garlic; and shrimp skewers. The menu changes weekly. Find it southeast of the church.

Frusty Helados Artesanales ICE CREAM $

(☎6125-7576; Calle 1, btwn Avs 4 & 6; ice pops from US$2; ⊙11am-6pm Mon-Sat, 1-5pm Sun) Delicious handmade ice pops, using fruit from the local area, are sold here. Choose a flavor from blackberry, guava, passion fruit, coconut, strawberry, green mango and more.

Restaurante Nazca PERUVIAN $$

(☎2445-5005; Calle 1 btwn Avs 2 & 4; mains $8-16; ⊙11:30am-11pm) In a somewhat soulless tiled dining room with chunky wooden tables and obligatory splashes of color, this restaurant serves up Peruvian specials like fried *ceviche* and stuffed potatoes with meat, chicken or shrimp. The rice dishes could pass as Costa Rican. With a lack of quality dining options in town, meals here will certainly satisfy your hunger.

Gastrobar Octubre 29 BAR

(☎2447-6000; www.facebook.com/octubre29gastrobar; Av Central; ⊙4-11pm Tue-Thu, to midnight Fri & Sat, noon-10pm Sun) On the second floor, overlooking the square, this vibrant space decorated with papier-mâché trees, bright floral wall art and patterned tiles is the hippest hangout spot in town. It serves up local beers from San Ramón, craft brews and other artisanal drinks, plus decent tapas, pizzas, hamburgers and pasta (menu items from US$10).

Getting There & Away

San Ramón is served by half-hourly direct and indirect buses (around US$3, 1½ hours, between 4:05am and 10:15pm) to San José's Empresarios Unidos terminal (p100). Direct and indirect buses also head north to Zarcero via Ciudad Quesada (around US$5, three hours, 12 daily from 5:55am to 7:30pm). Bus stops are just northwest of Parque Central; contact **Coopatrac** (☎2460-0638) for information. Bus schedules are liable to change, check with the local bus providers for up-to-date times.

WORTH A TRIP

FIESTAS DE PALMARES

This two-week **extravaganza** (⊙mid-Jan) has been running for more than 30 years. It features carnival rides, a *tope* (horse parade), fireworks, big-name bands, small-name bands, exotic dancers, fried food, *guaro* (a local firewater made from sugarcane) tents and more merry Ticos than you've ever seen. One of the country's biggest events (crowds can reach hundreds of thousands), it's covered widely on national TV.

HEREDIA AREA

At the southern point of the province, only 11km north of San José, a quaint university city sits in the shadow of the dormant Volcán Barva. Established in 1706, Heredia is known as the 'City of Flowers' due to its verdant flora, which thrive in the area's temperate climate and sporadic rain showers. Dotted with colonial architecture, it's a popular choice for those wanting to learn Spanish.

There's a mini tech industry in Heredia – Intel opened two new business units in 2015 and employs just shy of 3000 people, who focus on engineering, information security and product life cycle. However, the region's most notable industry is still coffee. Base yourself here for an easy gateway to one of Costa Rica's largest swaths of highland forest, Parque Nacional Braulio Carrillo.

❶ Getting There & Away

Buses are a reliable, cheap bet in and around Heredia. Rent a car for more flexibility.

Heredia

POP 138,600

During the 19th century, La Ciudad de las Flores (the City of the Flowers) was home to a *cafetalero* (coffee grower) aristocracy that made its fortune exporting Costa Rica's premium blend. Today the historic center retains some of this well-bred air, with a leafy main square and low-lying buildings, reflecting the Spanish-colonial architectural style.

Although only 11km from San José, Heredia is – in personality – removed from the grit and grime of the capital. Universidad Nacional keeps things a touch bohemian, and on any afternoon you're bound to find the local bars and cafes abuzz with young folk idling away their time.

Heredia is also the most convenient base from which to explore the little-visited Volcán Barva, within the Parque Nacional Braulio Carrillo.

◉ Sights

Casa de la Cultura MUSEUM
(☑2261-4485; www.facebook.com/casagonzalezflores.mcj.cr; cnr Calle Central & Av Central; ⊗8am-6pm Mon-Fri, 9am-6pm Sat & Sun) FREE Occupy-

ing a privileged position on the corner of the plaza just north of the church, this low-lying Spanish structure dates back to the late 18th century. At one point it served as the residence of President Alfredo González Flores, who governed from 1913 to 1917. It is beautifully maintained and now houses permanent historical displays as well as rotating art exhibits.

At the time of research, the building was closed for refurbishment and to renovate the original mosaics in the corridor and main hall. The building will reopen on completion, but call ahead before you visit.

El Fortín TOWER
(Av Central) This tower, constructed in 1876 by order of the provincial governor, is the official symbol of Heredia. It was declared a national historic monument in 1974. It sits in a lovely park with a children's play area, near the main square.

🎓 Courses

Centro Panamericano de Idiomas LANGUAGE
(CPI; ☑2265-6306, in USA 1-877-373-3116; www.cpi-edu.com; Calle Cementerio; 1-week private lessons from US$600, 20hr group tuition from US$460, 1-week homestay from US$200) Based in San Joaquín de Flores, just outside Heredia, this popular school also has a teen camp and family programs. There's a maximum of four students per class. There are also campuses in other parts of the country.

Intercultura LANGUAGE
(☑2260-8480; www.interculturacostarica.com; cnr Calle 10 & Av 4; private lessons from US$26, 20hr group tuition per week from US$200, with 1-week homestay incl meals US$530) Arranges language lessons, volunteer opportunities and offers activities from cooking to dance classes. You can also study at their campus on the beach in Sámara.

🛌 Sleeping

Hotel Las Flores HOTEL $
(☑2261-8147; www.hotel-lasflores.com; Av 12 btwn Calles 12 & 14; s/d US$17/32; 🅿🛜) A bit of a walk from the action, this spotless no-frills, family-run place has basic, brightly painted rooms with TVs and hot-water showers. Those who want privacy on a tight budget can't go wrong. There's a basic snack restaurant onsite.

Heredia

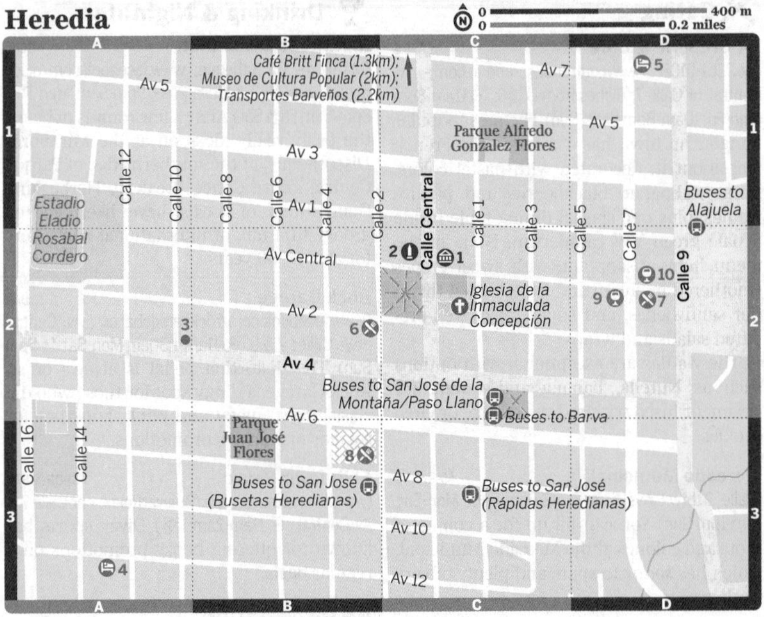

Heredia

Sights
1 Casa de la Cultura C2
2 El Fortín C2

Activities, Courses & Tours
3 Intercultura A2

Sleeping
4 Hotel Las Flores A3
5 Hotel Valladolid D1

Eating
6 Coffee Break by Herbarium B2
7 Creperie & Café D2
8 Mercado Municipal B3

Drinking & Nightlife
9 El Bulevar Relax D2
Miraflores Disco Club .... (see 6)
10 Rock Garage D2

Hotel Valladolid HOTEL $$
(☎2260-2905, 2260-2912; www.hotelvalladolid.net; cnr Calle 7 & Av 7; s/d/tr incl breakfast US$75/87/99, extra person US$30; P❄@📶) This business hotel on a quiet street has 12 bright, clean and businesslike tiled rooms with dated decor, wi-fi, safes, cable TV and private bathrooms with hot water. Credit cards accepted.

Hotel Chalet Tirol INN $$
(☎2267-6223, 2267-6222; www.hotelchaleteltirol.com; nr Camino de El Sol and Camino de Los Cipreses; r US$86-115; P📶🐾) Once serving as the backdrop for a German beer advert, this charming hotel channels the gingerbread quaintness and romance of the Austrian Alps. Somehow, with its stellar mountain views, it works. Cute suites and chalets of various sizes have cable TV and room service; some have Jacuzzis and fireplaces. Find the hotel northeast of Heredia, 3km north of Castillo Country Club.

Hotel Bougainvillea HOTEL $$$
(☎2244-1414, in USA 866-880-5441; www.hb.co.cr; Calle Peligro, Santo Domingo; d incl breakfast from US$131; P⊖@📶🏊) 🍃 Set on four beautiful hectares about 6km outside town, this top hotel is surrounded by an expansive, well-manicured garden dotted with old trees, orchids, stunning flowers and statues. The crisp, slightly dated but very comfortable rooms have balconies with views of mountains or the city, and several private trails wind by the swimming pool and tennis courts, through forest and orchards.

Eating

★Creperie & Café CAFE $
(☎2261-5108; www.entrenouscreperie.com; Av Central, nr Calle 7; dishes from US$6; ⏰11am-8pm Mon-Fri, 10am-8pm Sat & Sun) The most popular hangout in town has a cute/kitschy French feel about it, decorated with pastel colors, floral wallpaper, blackboards and picture frames, plus one special dining table inside a pale green VW campervan. None of the menu items disappoint, with sweet crepes smothered in cream and fruit, loaded three-tier sandwiches, and super fresh, well-prepared salads and wraps.

The waffles are exceptional with options such as Nutella, banana and vanilla ice cream, or fused with red velvet cake or Oreo cookies.

Mercado Municipal MARKET $
(Calle 2 btwn Avs 6 & 8; ⏰6am-6pm Mon-Sat, 7am-1pm Sun) You can fill up for a couple of thousand colones at the Mercado Municipal, which has *sodas* to spare and plenty of very fresh groceries.

Coffee Break by Herbarium CAFE $
(☎2261-6191; www.facebook.com/herbariumcoffeebreak; cnr Av 2 & Calle 2; mains from US$4.50; ⏰7am-7:30pm Mon-Sat, 9am-7:30pm Sun) A simple, casual, counter-service cafe at the southwestern side of the park, selling typical breakfasts, coffee, salads and sandwiches (including chicken, ham, and cheese), plus quiches, omelets and pancakes. Good for a quick snack.

Drinking & Nightlife

Miraflores Disco Club CLUB
(Miraflores Discotheque; www.facebook.com/discomiracr; cnr Av 2 & Calle 2; ⏰9pm-5am Mon-Thu, 8pm-6am Fri & Sat) After a few rounds of beers, the party really kicks off at the Miraflores Discotheque, at the southern edge of Parque Central above Coffee Break by Herbarium. Generations of locals have been getting groovy to a mix of international beats here for around 50 years.

Rock Garage BAR
(www.facebook.com/rockgaragebar.cr; Av Central btwn Calles 7 & 9; ⏰11am-1:30am Mon-Sat, to 5pm Sun) The distortion pedal is always on at Rock Garage, a dingy spot for those who dig classic rock, metal and punk. Look out for two-for-one drinks promotions.

El Bulevar Relax SPORTS BAR
(www.facebook.com/pg/BulevarRelax; cnr Calle 7 & Av Central; ⏰11am-2am; 📶) Divey sports bar known for offering boozy promotions on a regular basis.

Information

BCR (Av Central; ⏰5am-10pm) Has an ATM dispensing US dollars.

Hospital San Vicente de Paul (☎2562-8100; www.facebook.com/hospitaldeheredia; Calle 12; ⏰24hr) South of Av 14.

Getting There & Away

There is no central bus terminal; buses leave from stops scattered between the university and the Mercado Central.

The San José–bound **Rápidas Heredianas** bus stops on Av 8 between Calle Central and Calle 1 and is the best option if you're transferring to

BUSES FROM HEREDIA

DESTINATION	COMPANY	COST (US$)	DURATION (MIN)	FREQUENCY
Alajuela	Tuasa	1	45	every 15min 6am-10:30pm
Barva	Transportes Barveños LTDA	1	15	every 15min 4:55am-11pm
San José	Busetas Heredianas	1	30	every 5-10min 5am-11pm
San José	Rápidas Heredianas	1	30	every 15min-2hr midnight-11:50pm
San José de la Montaña/Paso Llano (for Volcán Barva)	Rápidas Heredianas	1	60	every 10min-1hr 4:50am-5:30pm

a Caribbean-bound bus, as it drops you near San José's Terminal Caribeña. The other bus to San José can be found two blocks **west** (Av 8 btwn Calles 2 & 4). **Buses to Barva** (Calle 1 btwn Avs 4 & 6), as well as **buses to San José de la Montaña/Paso Llano** (Calle 1 btwn Avs 4 & 6), can be found due north of the San José Rápidas Heredianas buses near the main drag, Av 4. **Buses to Alajuela** leave from the corner of Av 1 and Calle 9 on the northeastern side of town. Schedules are subject to change, contact the local bus companies for up-to-date information.

Barva

POP 35,000

Surrounded by picturesque mountains only 2.5km north of Heredia, the historic town of Barva is a settlement dating back to 1561. Declared a national monument, the town center is dotted with low-lying 19th-century buildings and is centered on the towering Iglesia San Bartolomé, constructed in 1893. The surrounding area was once popular with the Costa Rican elite: Cleto González Víquez (1858–1937), twice president of Costa Rica (he built the original National Library), was born and raised here. It's a perfect spot for a lazy afternoon stroll.

◎ Sights

Museo de Cultura Popular MUSEUM
(☑ 2260-1619; www.museo.una.ac.cr; Santa Lucía; ☉ 10am-5pm Sun, group reservations 8am-4pm Mon-Sat) **FREE** Housed in a restored 19th-century farmhouse 1.5km southeast of Barva, this tiny museum surrounded by well-labeled gardens is run by the Universidad Nacional. Visitors can tour rooms full of antique furniture, textiles, ceramics and other period pieces. The museum is open by reservation only for groups Monday to Friday, when an admission fee is charged for different group sizes.

On Sundays, visitors can try 'gourmet' Tico food at the onsite restaurant La Fonda.

☞ Tours

Café Britt Finca TOURS
(☑ 2277-1600; www.coffeetour.com; off Calle Central; adult/concession with lunch US$40/35 without lunch US$26/21; ☉ 8am-5pm, 1½hr tours 9am, 11am, 1:15pm & 3:15pm) Costa Rica's most famous coffee roaster offers a 90-minute bilingual tour of its plantation that includes coffee tasting and a comedic stage play about the history of coffee (kids will likely

enjoy it). More in-depth tours are available, as are packages including transport from San José; reserve ahead. Drivers won't be able to miss the many signs between Heredia and Barva.

Large onsite restaurant La Casita serves a decent buffet lunch (US$15 including salad, soup, mains and dessert). The gift shop and cafe sells coffee, chocolate, drinks and pastries, plus Costa Rica–themed gifts.

✯ Festivals & Events

Feria de la Mascarada CULTURAL
In the last week of March, Barva hosts the Feria de la Mascarada, a tradition with roots in the colonial era. Participants don massive colorful masks (some weighing 20kg), and gather to dance and parade around the town square. Demons and devils are frequent subjects, but celebrities and politicians also feature (you haven't lived until you've seen a 6m-tall Celia Cruz).

🛏 Sleeping

★ Finca Rosa Blanca INN $$$
(☑ 2269-9392, in USA 305-395-3042; www.fincarosablanca.com; Calle Rosa Blanca, Santa Bárbara; d incl breakfast from US$375, extra person adult/child US$51/25; 🅿@🛜🏊) ✇ Set amid a stunning hillside organic coffee plantation 6km northwest of Barva, this honeymoon-ready, Gaudí-esque confection of suites and villas is cloaked in fruit trees that shade private trails. The 14 sparkling-white adobe rooms with wood-beamed ceilings and private balconies are lavishly appointed; one tops a tower with 360-degree views, reached by a winding staircase made from a tree trunk.

Rooms come with minifridges and coffee from the plantation. In the grounds, you can shower in an artificial waterfall, take a moonlit dip in the pool or Jacuzzi, and have an organic coffee scrub at the spa. Fuel up at the hotel's bar and restaurant; it has magnificent views and serves fresh local produce, including eggs from the chicken coop in the garden for breakfast and Costa Rican or fusion dishes like the catch of the day with herby yogurt and creole salad. Credit cards accepted.

At 9am and 1pm, Finca Rosa Blanca offers a 2½-hour tour of its picturesque, 12-hectare organic coffee plantation, processing plant and roasting house. Guests hike the fields, learn about the processes and taste the delicious results. Nonguests can pay US$40 per person for the same tour.

KID-FRIENDLY CENTRAL VALLEY

Family-friendly attractions abound in the Central Valley. Here are a few spots guaranteed to please kids and adults alike.

Parque Francisco Alvarado (p118) In Zarcero, kids will love zigzagging through rows of bushes sculpted into stegosauruses and other fantastic shapes in these topiary gardens.

Rafting in Turrialba (p136) Outfitters lead trips on the Río Pejibaye, a not-too-rough, Class II river that teenagers will love.

Zoo Ave (p110) In La Garita, stroll the grounds alongside peacocks and giant lizards, visit monkeys or take the canopy tour at this zoo and animal-rescue center.

Parque Nacional Tapantí-Macizo Cerro de la Muerte (p132) Mostly easy hiking trails lead down to sandy beaches where kids can splash in a boulder-strewn river.

Getting There & Away

Buses travel about every 15 minutes between Heredia and Barva (about US$1, 15 minutes), picking up and dropping off in front of Barva's church. Routes from Barva to Heredia start at 4:45am and run until 11pm. The route (422) is operated by **Transportes Barveños** (2262-1839; Av Cleto González Víquez).

San Isidro de Heredia

POP 17,000

This scenic, agrarian town northeast of San José offers all the lush greenery of the neighboring Parque Nacional Braulio Carillo, along with undulating drives over the countryside and a couple of the Central Valley's most enjoyable tours.

Light afternoon showers nearly every day make San Isidro de Heredia the rainbow capital of Costa Rica, and a fantastic place to grow (and eat) just about anything.

Sights

Toucan Rescue Ranch ANIMAL SANCTUARY

(2268-4041; www.toucanrescueranch.org; off Ruta Nacional 112; classic ranch walk adult/child 6-10yr/under 6yr US$35/17/free, 'Slothies & Coffees' adult/child 6-10yr/under 6yr $60/30/free; tours by appointment 9am & 2pm Mon-Sat) More than a decade ago, Leslie Howle and her husband, Jorge Murillo, started taking in sick and injured toucans. The couple eventually ended up with a menagerie of animals in need of care, from owls and sloths to monkeys and an oncilla. Guests can tour their picturesque grounds as part of a 2½-hour 'Slothies & Coffees' tour, or on a two-hour classic ranch walk to see parrots, macaws, owls, sloths, spider monkeys and weasels. Call for directions.

Tours

★**Sibu Chocolate** FOOD & DRINK

(2268-1335; www.sibuchocolate.com; Calle Bombacho nr Calle Zurquí; half-day tours US$28; tours 10am Tue-Sat, restaurant 11am-6pm Tue-Sat, to 4pm Sun) This divine chocolate tour (1½ hours) explains the culture surrounding Costa Rica's most decadent export. See cacao's story brought to life as you sample fine pre-Columbian-inspired hot chocolate and other treats. This storybook operation is located just 20 minutes north of downtown San José, around 1.5km off the highway to Guápiles. Tours have a four-person minimum; call ahead.

Lunch (dishes from US$12, afternoon tea from US$9) and sumptuous hot chocolate can be enjoyed on the restaurant terrace, surrounded by lush gardens – the desserts are to die for. A shop sells goodies to take home. Ingredients, such as herbs,- for flavoring the chocolate and the restaurant's recipes, are grown organically at the facility.

Sleeping & Eating

Toucan Rescue Ranch B&B **$$$**

(2268-4041; www.toucanrescueranch.org; off Ruta Nacional 112; guesthouse for 1-4 people incl tour & breakfast US$750; P) The local animal-rescue center also provides the best lodgings in town, with two adorable and well-constructed guesthouses just a short walk from the sloths, toucans and other exotic recovering creatures. It's an incredibly serene setting, with a backdrop of rainforest and rolling hills, and is conveniently located just 35 minutes from San José's international airport.

★ Casa Antigua Café & Restaurante

COSTA RICAN $

(☎2268-3366; Ruta Nacional 112; mains from US$7.50; ⊙noon-7pm Thu, to 9pm Fri, 8am-9pm Sat, 8am-7pm Sun) Breakfast, lunch and dinner are served in this atmospheric, century-old colonial clapboard house with hardwood floors, painted ceilings, stained-glass windows, period furniture and jazz on the stereo. Order an espresso and a slice of exquisite cake or enjoy breakfast, *casados*, pastas, wraps, hamburgers, crepes and sandwiches in the unique individual dining rooms; some are private, like you're hosting a dinner party.

It's on the road east out of San Isidro on the way to San Josécito.

Bromelias del Río

CAFETERIA $$

(☎2236-8574; www.facebook.com/cafeteriayrestaurantebromeliasdelrio; Ruta Nacional 112; mains US$9-33, pastries from US$2; ⊙8am-7pm) By a tropical garden and a mountain stream, this bakery-restaurant tempts with spiked coffee drinks (hot mocha with Baileys and chocolate syrup), crepes and salad, plus decadent sandwiches – some piled high with *lomito* (tenderloin). Share a main plate and save room for a dulce de leche dessert. It's 50m off Hwy 32 at the Santa Elena exit to San Isidro.

Casa Azul

SPANISH $$

(☎8376-6493, 2268-6908; Calle Trapiche, San Josécito; mains US$12-22; ⊙6pm-10pm Wed-Fri, noon-10pm Sat, noon-3pm Sun) Tucked away just off Hwy 32 in a quaint little blue house adorned with blue curtains, antiques and hardwood floors, this Spanish–Costa Rican fusion restaurant is one of the Central Valley's most romantic spots. Popular dishes include paella, stone-baked pizza, Gorgonzola chicken and mouthwatering medallions of *lomito* (tenderloin) that pair well with a bottle of cabernet.

ℹ Getting There & Away

Transportes Arnoldo Ocampo SA buses for San José leave from a stop 100m east of San Isidro de Heredia's central plaza. Buses for Heredia leave from in front of the **MegaSuper supermarket** (www.megasuper.com; cnr Av Central and Calle 1; ⊙8am-10pm), 100m east of the Catholic church. Schedules are subject to change; check current route times with local bus companies.

San José Under US$1, 20 minutes, roughly half-hourly from around 5am to 9pm Monday to Saturday, 5:30am to 9:30pm Sunday.

Heredia Under US$1, 15 minutes, roughly every 20 minutes from 4:50am to 10:15pm.

CARTAGO AREA

The riverbank setting of the city of Cartago was handpicked by Spanish governor Juan Vásquez de Coronado, who said that he had 'never seen a more beautiful valley.' Cartago was founded as Costa Rica's first capital in 1563, and Coronado's successors endowed the city with fine colonial architecture. However, the city was destroyed during a 1723 eruption of Volcán Irazú, and any remaining landmarks were toppled by earthquakes in 1841 and 1910.

Although the city was relegated to backwater status when the seat of government moved to San José in 1823, the surrounding area, particularly the Orosi Valley, flourished during the days of the coffee trade. Today, much of the region continues to be devoted to coffee production. Although unpretty Cartago no longer has the prestige of a national capital, it remains a vital commercial hub – not to mention the site of some of the country's most important religious monuments.

ℹ Getting There & Away

Bus stops are scattered around Cartago (p128) and routes connect to Turrialba, Orosi and San José. Train services run between San José's Estación del Pacífico and Cartago's downtown station.

Cartago

POP 160,500

Cartago exists mainly as a commercial and residential center, though the beauty of the surrounding mountains helps take the edge off smoggy modern life. As in other commercial towns, expect plenty of functional concrete structures. Two worthy exceptions, however, are the striking ruins of the Santiago Apóstol Parish, an ancient site home to a number of churches since 1575, and the bright white Basílica de Nuestra Señora de Los Ángeles. The latter is visible from many parts of the city – it stands out like a snowcapped mountain above a plain of one-story edifices. The city is thrown briefly into the spotlight every August, when pilgrims from every corner of the country descend on the basilica to say their prayers.

Sights

Basílica de Nuestra Señora de Los Ángeles CHURCH
(www.santuarionacional.org; Calle 15, btwn Avs Central & 1; Mass 6am, 9am, 11am, 6pm daily, plus 4pm Sat & Sun) Cartago's most important site, and Costa Rica's most venerated religious shrine, this basilica exudes Byzantine grace, with fine stained-glass windows, hand-painted interiors and ornate side chapels featuring carved-wood altars. Dating from the 1630s, the structure retains an unharmed central relic: La Negrita (the Black Virgin), a small representation of the Virgin Mary, that was found on this spot on August 2, 1635.

As the story goes, when the woman who discovered the statuette tried to take it with her, it miraculously reappeared back where she'd found it. Twice. So the townspeople built a shrine around her. In 1824 she was declared Costa Rica's patron Virgin. The statuette now resides on a gold, jewel-studded platform at the main altar. Each August 2, on the anniversary of the statuette's miraculous discovery, pilgrims from every corner of the country (and beyond) walk the 22km from San José to the basilica. Many of the penitents complete the last few hundred meters of the pilgrimage on their knees.

Las Ruinas de la Parroquia RUINS
(Iglesia del Convento; Calle Central btwn Avs Central & 2; hours vary) FREE This now-ruined church was built in 1575 as a shrine to St James the Apostle. It was destroyed by the 1841 earthquake, rebuilt a few years later and then destroyed again in the 1910 earthquake. Today only the outer walls remain, but the pretty garden inside 'the ruins' is a pleasant spot for a stroll and some people-watching. Legend has it that the ghost of a headless priest wanders here.

Sleeping & Eating

Los Ángeles Lodge B&B $
(2591-4169, 2551-0957; hotel.los.angeles@hotmail.com; Av 1 btwn Calles 13 & 15; s/d incl breakfast US$35/50;) Although it looks a little seedy from the outside, it's clean and comfortable inside, with balconies overlooking the Plaza de la Basílica. While slightly overpriced, it's the only decent choice in the area with hot showers and breakfast made to order. Check-in takes place in La Puerta del Sol restaurant to the right. It can be noisy in the evening.

La Dulce Armonía CAFE $
(2551-5354; Av Central; menu items from US$5.50; 2-7pm Mon, to 8pm Tue-Sun) Cartago's most welcoming cafe is a lovely spot for a recharge with a mini library inside. Patrons can peruse the many (mostly Spanish) books at their leisure. The menu is basic, with crepes and sandwiches, plus super-sweet desserts named after local sights and places, like the Irazú-Turrialba ice cream and Orosi chocolate cake.

La Puerta del Sol COSTA RICAN $$
(2551-0615; Av 1 btwn Calles 13 & 15; mains US$5-15; 9am-10pm Mon-Fri, to 11pm Sat, to 8pm Sun) Located downstairs from Los Ángeles Lodge and decorated with vintage photos of Cartago, this cheery no-frills restaurant has been around since 1957 and serves myriad reasonably priced Tico specialties, from *ceviche* to *casados*, along with breakfasts (rice, beans and eggs), chicken salads, pastas, burgers and sandwiches.

Information

Banco de Costa Rica (Av Central btwn Calles 5 & 7) and **Banco Popular** (Av 2; 8:45am-4:30pm Mon-Fri, 8:15-11:30am Sat) have ATMs.

Hospital Max Peralta (2550-1999; www.ccss.sa.cr/hospitales; Av 6 btwn Calles 2 & 4; 24hr) Emergency and medical services.

Getting There & Away

BUS

Bus stops are scattered around town. Destinations include:

Orosi (Autotransportes Mata Irola) About US$1, 45 minutes, every 15 to 30 minutes between 5:15am and 10:25pm; departs from Calle 3 between Avs 2 and 4.

San José (Lumaca) About US$1.50, 50 minutes, every 15 minutes between 4:35am and 11pm; departs from the terminal on Calle 6 between Avs 3 and 7.

Turrialba (Transtusa) US$1.60, 80 minutes, every 20 minutes to an hour between 6:15am and 11pm weekdays (less frequently on weekends); departs from Av 4 between Calles 5 and 7.

TRAIN

Train services run between San José's Estación del Atlantico and Cartago's downtown **station** (Av 3, btwn Calles 4 & 6; Mon-Sat). The one-hour trip costs around US$1. Trains run Monday to Friday from 5:30am to 6.30pm every 30 minutes to an hour in a schedule weighted toward morning and afternoon commuting hours. On

Saturday trains run to San José every hour until 1:30pm. See www.incofer.go.cr for up-to-date timetable info.

Parque Nacional Volcán Irazú

Looming on the horizon 19km northeast of Cartago, 3432m Irazú – which derives its name from the indigenous word *ara-tzu* (thunder point) – is the largest and highest active volcano in Costa Rica and one of the few you can currently walk around. In 1723 the Spanish governor of the area, Diego de la Haya Fernández, watched helplessly as the volcano unleashed its destruction on the city of Cartago (one of the craters is named in his honor). Since the 18th century, 15 major eruptions have been recorded. At the time of research the volcano was slumbering peacefully.

The summit is a bare landscape of volcanic-ash craters. The principal crater is 1050m across, 300m deep and has a turquoise lake; the adjacent Diego de la Haya Crater is 690m across and 80m deep; and the shallowest, Playa Hermosa Crater, is being colonized by sparse vegetation. There's also a pyroclastic cone, consisting of rocks fragmented by volcanic activity. With a telescope and no cloud cover, it's possible to see Lago de Nicaragua (Lake Nicaragua) from this stunning scene.

Tours

Tours are arranged by a variety of San José operators and cost US$70 and above for a half-day, and from US$100 for a full day combined with lunch and visits to sights such as the Lankester Gardens (p130) or the Orosi Valley.

Tours from hotels in Orosi (US$30 to US$50) can also be arranged – these may include lunch and visits to the basilica in Cartago or sights around the Orosi Valley.

Eating

Restaurant 1910 COSTA RICAN **$$**
(☎2536-6063; Ruta Nacional 219; mains US$11-26; ⏰8am-9pm Mon-Thu, to 10pm Fri & Sat, to 6:30pm Sun; P 📶) Set in a green-and-cream clapboard house with a glass-walled deck, this cozy restaurant serves a long list of overpriced Tico specialties. But it's worth a stop alone to see photographs documenting the 1910 earthquake that completed the destruction of colonial Cartago. Find it on the road to Irazú (Ruta 219), 300m north of the Christ statue marking the Guayabo turnoff.

Tico families come on Sundays for the all-you-can-eat buffet (US$21, 11:30am-3pm).

Information

The **ranger station** (☎2299-5800; Ruta Nacional 219; ⏰8am-3:30pm) at the park's entrance, 1km before the summit, is where you pay for admission (US$15) and parking (US$2). There's a small shop selling snacks and souvenirs inside the park, plus restroom facilities.

Getting There & Away

A daily bus to Irazú (roughly US$10) departs from San José at 8am near Hotel Costa Rica on Av 2 and arrives at the summit around 10am. A return bus leaves from the volcano at 12:30pm, transferring in Cartago at 1:45pm and arriving in San José at 2:35pm.

A round-trip taxi from Cartago to the summit will cost about US$50; negotiate with drivers to allow you an hour to explore up top (this may cost you more).

If you're in a group, renting a car is the best deal as you can get to the park early, before the skies cloud over and the crowds arrive (weekends are particularly busy, when hour-long queues into the park are common). From Cartago, take Hwy 8, which begins at the northeastern corner of the plaza and continues 31km to the summit. The road is well signposted.

Valle de Orosi

This straight-out-of-a-storybook river valley is famous for mountain vistas, a lake formed by a hydroelectric facility, a truly wild national park and coffee – lots and lots of coffee. A well-paved 32km loop winds through a landscape of rolling hills terraced with coffee plantations and valleys dotted with pastoral villages, all set against the backdrop of volcanoes Irazú and Turrialba. If you have a rental car (or good legs for cycling) you're in for a treat, though it's still possible to navigate most of the loop via public buses.

The loop road starts 8km southeast of Cartago in Paraíso, heads south to Orosi, then doubles back northeast and west around the artificial Lago de Cachí, passing the historic church at Ujarrás en route back to Paraíso. Alternatively, from Orosi you can branch south into Parque Nacional Tapantí-Macizo Cerro de la Muerte, an end-of-the-road national park with superb river and mountain scenery.

Getting There & Away

Autotransportes Mata Irola (☎2533-1916) runs buses (roughly US$1) every 30 minutes to Paraíso (20 minutes) from 4:15am to 8pm weekdays, 5:30am to 9pm Saturday and 5:30am to 10pm Sunday; and to Cartago (45 minutes) from 4:15am to 8pm weekdays, 5:30am to 9pm Saturday and 5:30am to 10pm Sunday. From Cartago you can transfer for buses to San José. The main bus stops sit along Orosi's main street, next to the square.

Paraíso Area

Though the village of Paraíso isn't all that its name implies, it does lead to the wonderful Valle de Orosi. The area's attractions include the tranquil Lankester Gardens, the spectacular Mirador de Orosi, and natural hot pools.

Sights

Mirador de Orosi VIEWPOINT
(Ruta Nacional 224; ⏲8am-4:30pm) FREE Heading south from Paraíso toward Orosi you'll hit Mirador de Orosi, a big green space with a jaw-dropping scenic overlook complete with BBQ facilities, cultivated flowerbeds, toilets and a secure parking lot. Bring your camera, and food for a picnic.

Lankester Gardens GARDENS
(☎2511-7939; www.jbl.ucr.ac.cr; Calle Lankester, Paraíso Area; adult/student US$10/7.50; ⏲8:30am-4:30pm) The University of Costa Rica runs the exceptional 11-hectare Lankester Gardens, started as a private garden by British orchid enthusiast Charles Lankester in 1917, then turned over to the university for public administration in 1973. Orchids are the big draw here: there are more than 1000 varieties, at their showiest in April. The garden is wheelchair accessible. Find it about 5km west of Paraíso on the road to Cartago.

There's also a Japanese garden, as well as areas full of bromeliads, palms, heliconias and other tropical plants. Guided tours around the garden in English and Spanish are available by prior arrangement.

Activities

Finca La Flor de Paraíso VOLUNTEERING
(☎2534-8003; www.fincalaflor.org; volunteering per day US$25, yoga retreat from US$75, lodges per person incl meals US$50) Immerse yourself in the Central Valley's rural culture with a stay at Finca La Flor de Paraíso, outside Cartago. This not-for-profit organic farm operated by the Association for the Development of Environmental and Human Consciousness (Asodecah) has a volunteer program that will allow you to get your hands dirty on projects related to agriculture, reforestation, animal husbandry and medicinal-herb cultivation.

Tours

Finca Cristina TOURS
(☎2574-6426, in USA 203-549-1945; www.cafecristina.com; Hwy 224; guided tours US$15; ⏲9am & 2pm by appointment) Finca Cristina, 2km east of Paraíso on the road to Turrialba at the end of a short dirt track, is an organic coffee farm producing 15 tons of coffee per year. Linda and Ernie have been farming in Costa Rica since 1977, and a two-hour tour of their microprocessing plant is a fantastic introduction to the processes of growing, harvesting and roasting.

Getting There & Away

Autotransportes Mata Irola runs buses back and forth between Orosi and Paraíso (around US$1, 20 minutes, every 30 minutes), making multiple stops en route. Buses run from Paraíso between 5:40am and 10:50pm weekdays and from 5:55am Saturday and Sunday.

Orosi

POP 10,000

Named for a Huetar chief who lived here at the time of the Spanish invasion, Orosi charmed colonialists in the 18th century with its perfect climate, rich soil and wealth of water – from lazy hot springs to bracing waterfalls. So, with the typical attitude of the day, the colonists violently seized the land from Orosi. Today the area remains ridiculously picturesque – and it's a good spot to revel in beautiful scenery and a small-town atmosphere.

Sights

Iglesia de San José Orosi CHURCH
(☎2533-3051) Orosi is one of the few colonial-era towns to survive Costa Rica's frequent earthquakes, which have thankfully also spared the photogenic village church. Built in the mid-1700s, it is the oldest religious site still in use in the country. The church's roof is a combination of thatched cane and ceramic tiling, while the carved-wood altar is adorned with religious paintings of Mexican origin.

Museo de Arte
Religioso San José Orosi MUSEUM

(☑2533-3051; adult/child under 12yr US$1/0.50; ⊙1-5pm Tue-Sat, 9am-5pm Sun) Adjacent to Orosi's church, this small museum housed in a former convent displays interesting examples of Spanish-colonial religious art and artefacts, some of which date back to the 17th century.

⚞ Activities

Cicle Orosi CYCLING

(☑2533-3322; Ruta Nacional 224; bike rental US$30 per day; ⊙10am-noon & 1-7pm) The place to pick up a rental mountain bike for exploring the area. All bikes are in good condition and the store sells all the cycling gadgets you might need for a serious biking adventure.

Monte Sky HIKING

(☑2228-0010, 8382-7502; www.facebook.com/MonteSkyME; off Ruta Nacional 408; admission US$8, overnight stay from with/without meals US$45/24; ⊙8am-4pm Tue-Sun) About 5km south of Orosi, high in the hills off the road to Tapantí, this 536-hectare private reserve teems with 290 bird species and offers four hiking trails with waterfalls and jaw-dropping vistas. Admission includes use of all cabin facilities, including kitchen and BBQ area. Call for directions; a 4WD is essential for the 3.5km dirt road up to the cabin.

⮂ Courses

Montaña Linda runs one of the most affordable Spanish-language schools in the country; check the website for current prices and schedules. Located 300m south of Orosi's plaza.

⌷ Sleeping

★ Montaña Linda HOSTEL $

(☑2533-3640; www.montanalinda.com; dm US$10, guesthouse s/d/tr/q with bathroom US$32/32/38/44, without bathroom US$16/24/36/48; P @ ⋒) A short walk southwest of Orosi's bus stop, this welcoming, chilled-out budget option has three tidy dorms and private rooms with twins, doubles or a double with a bunk, all surrounding a homey terrace with flowers and hammocks. Shared bathrooms have hot showers. Owners provide an exceptional information packet highlighting local attractions (hot springs, waterfalls and more) in the area.

Orosi Lodge INN $$

(☑2533-3578; www.orosilodge.com; d/tr US$74/85, chalet d US$112, extra person US$15; P ⋒) This quiet haven has bright rooms with wood-beamed ceilings, tile floors, minibar, coffeemaker and free organic coffee. Most rooms face a lovely garden courtyard with a fountain, and one is wheelchair accessible. Next door is a two-story, three-bedroom chalet that sleeps up to five.

Rancho Río Perlas RESORT $$$

(☑2533-3341; www.rio-perlas.com; Ruta Nacional 405; d/cabin/ste incl breakfast from US$115/125/215; P ⋒ ☒) With trout-filled lakes, a system of thermal waters (including a hot-spring swimming pool) and 2km of hiking trails, this picturesque mountain resort is a top sanctuary for locals and visitors looking to escape city life. Rooms are large; the best offer artificial fireplaces and Jacuzzi tubs. A conference center, spa and chapel make this a popular spot for weddings and other events.

⚒ Eating

Panadería Suiza BAKERY $

(☑8706-6777; www.costarica-moto.com/caf-y-panaderia-suiza; pastries from US$1, breakfast US$5-7; ⊙6am-4pm Tue-Sat, to noon Sun) Starting at the crack of dawn, ebullient expat Franzisca serves simple breakfasts (bread, butter, jam and coffee) at her main-street bakery, 100m south of Banco Nacional. Extras include eggs, cheese and ham. Also on offer are cakes, sweet and savory pastries, and fresh wholegrain breads.

Cafetería & Galeria De Arte CAFE $

(☑2201-6665; mains from US$5; ⊙1-8pm Tue-Sun) Decorated with artworks, black chairs and blackboards displaying the specials, this pleasant cafe sits right on the southwestern corner of the square and sells crepes with homemade ice cream, sandwiches, smoothies and plenty of coffee. Pull up a seat on the veranda and watch village life go by.

★ Pizzeria a la leña il Giardino PIZZA $$

(☑2533-2022; www.facebook.com/pizzeriailgiardino; pizzas from US$10; ⊙3-9pm Tue-Thu, noon-9pm Fri-Sun) This cute country-style pizzeria has a proper stone pizza oven where the chef makes tasty thin-crust pizzas. The mozzarella, tomato and basil is spot on as are the hearty pastas. The place is decorated with hardwood paneling and farm equipment.

THERMAL SPRINGS

Being in a volcanic region means that Orosi has the perk of thermal springs. Though not nearly on the scale of the steaming-hot waters found near Fortuna, Orosi does offer a pair of warm-water pool complexes. **Balneario de Águas Termales Orosi** (☑2533-2156; www.balnearioaguastermalesorosi.com; US$6; ☺7:30am-4pm Wed-Mon) is the more centrally located of the two, with four pools of varying size flanked by grassy expanses and a shaded bar-restaurant terrace. **Los Patios** (☑2533-3009; Ruta Nacional 224; US$5.50; ☺8am-4pm Tue-Sun) is a larger, weathered complex 1.5km south of town, whose waters include a 43°C (110°F) therapeutic pool suitable for adults only.

Out front is a pretty garden in which to sample some of the many craft beers on offer.

Onde su Agüela Parrilla 100% COSTA RICAN $$
(☑8525-5372; Ruta Nacional 224; breakfast from US$4, mains US$6-25; ☺7am-8pm Mon-Wed, to 10pm Thu-Sun) For excellent grilled meats and a lovely ambiance, come to this open-air restaurant decorated with fairy lights, colored wooden chairs, pop-art portraits of iconic musicians, and killer tracks on the stereo. There's tasty *ceviche*, seafood and eight different steak cuts to choose from, served with two sides (mash, stuffed peppers, or a mix of veggies).

The shrimp mixed rice is full of flavor – drizzle the excellent homemade salsa picante over it. Service is top-notch and the welcoming owner, Joanna, speaks English.

Bar y Restaurante Coto COSTA RICAN $$
(☑2533-3032; mains US$8-21; ☺9am-10pm) Established in 1952, this family-run eatery on the north side of the soccer field dishes out good *típico* food (particularly the whole fried fish) in a wood-beamed dining room with open-air seating. It's a great place to enjoy mountain views and the goings-on about town.

ℹ Information

OTIAC (Orosi Tourist Information; ☑2533-3640; ☺9am-4pm Mon-Fri, 11am-5pm Sun; ☎) is run by multilingual long-term residents Toine and Sara. This helpful organization functions as an information center, cafe, cultural hall and book exchange. It can help arrange tours and is a good source of information about volunteer and teaching opportunities. Find it 200m south of the park and one block west of the main road. Hours can be irregular; if the center is closed call the phone number for assistance.

ℹ Getting There & Away

The drive into Orosi is a pretty one, as Ruta 224 from Paraiso snakes down the valley with gorgeous views of the mountains.

Autotransportes Mata Irola (p130) buses run between Orosi and Paraíso (roughly US$1, 20 minutes, every 30 minutes from 4:15am to 8pm weekdays and 5:30am to 9pm on weekends).

Services to Cartago (roughly US$1, 45 minutes) run from 4:30am to 8pm weekdays, 5:30am to 9pm Saturday and 8:30am to 10pm Sunday. From Cartago you can transfer for buses to San José.

The main bus stop sits along Orosi's main street, next to the square.

Parque Nacional Tapantí-Macizo Cerro de la Muerte

Protecting the lush northern slopes of the Cordillera de Talamanca, this 580-sq-km **national park** (☑2206-5615; adult/child 6-12yr US$10/5; ☺8am-4pm; P♿) is the wettest in Costa Rica. Known simply as Tapantí, the park protects wild and mossy country that's fed by literally hundreds of rivers. Waterfalls abound, vegetation is thick and the wildlife is prolific, though not always easy to see because of the rugged terrain. In 2000 the park was expanded to include the infamous Cerro de la Muerte (Mountain of Death), a precipitous peak that marks the highest point on the Interamericana and the northernmost extent of *páramo*, a highland shrub and tussock-grass habitat – most commonly found in the Andes – that shelters a variety of rare bird species. There are easy trails here for families.

◎ Sights

El Mirador VIEWPOINT
Around 70 steps (approx 10 to 15 minutes up) lead to a viewing platform overlooking the vast verdant hillsides, with a trickling waterfall in the distance. There are picnic benches and restrooms here.

Activities

Walking and nature spotting are the main ways to spend your time here. Rain gear is advisable year-round.

Wildlife-Watching

More than 300 bird species have been recorded in the park, including hummingbirds, parrots, toucans, trogons and eagles. The birdwatching opportunities here are world class: it's possible to spot hundreds of varieties in this small area. Though rarely sighted due to the thick vegetation, monkeys, coatis, pacas, tayras and even pumas, ocelots and oncillas are present.

Hiking

A well-graded dirt road runs into the park from the information center, dead-ending at a *mirador* (viewing platform) that affords broad views across the valley. Three signed trails branch off from this road.

Sendero La Catarata HIKING

This fun hike runs 1km (around 20 to 30 minutes one way) along a moderate gravel trail, descending into the valley and through the forest, over small bridges and brooks leading to Rio Grande de Orosí. Then it goes along riverside boulders to a waterfall view in the distance. There are restrooms at the trail entrance.

Sendero Oropendola HIKING

This easy and very pleasant 1.2km walk along flat, stone-bordered gravel pathways leads down to the Rio Grande de Orosí. It has 13 picnic areas, clean water and restrooms. Swimming is not allowed in the river. Ask rangers about potential swimming holes before you set off. There are occasionally safe areas when currents are mild.

Sendero Natural Arboles Caidos HIKING

If you want a workout and a good nature-spotting opportunity, this difficult 3km (roughly 1½ hours up and down) hill trail will get seasoned hikers warmed up. It's not very well maintained and runs through thick, lush, humid forest. The path is rocky, with slippery tree roots, it's often muddy, with fallen branches and occasional large steps up.

There are no views, but you'll likely have the place – plus the birdsong and sounds of the forest – all to yourself. At the end of the trail you'll hit the main road to the park, from here it's roughly a five- to 10-minute walk back to the trailhead and your car. Not recommended for kids.

Sleeping & Eating

There's not much in the way of accommodation here. Head to Orosi, only a 25-minute drive away.

For food, your best bet is a packed lunch, or it's a short drive to Orosi for several good restaurants.

Information

Visitors receive a simple trail map upon paying fees at the park entrance, which doubles as the **Information Center** (☎2206-5615; ⏲8am-4pm). It contains a small museum with stuffed animals including a sloth and wild cats, plus insects and butterflies in cabinets. There's information about the surrounding natural environment, from pumas and tamanduas to the collared peccary.

Getting There & Away

With your own car you can drive the 11km from Orosi to the park entrance; about halfway along, near the town of Purisil, the route becomes a bumpy gravel road (4WD recommended but not required).

Renting a bike in Orosi (p131) is another good option; the ride to the park takes about an hour. Buses (about US$1, 30 minutes) only make it as far as Purisil, 5km from the entrance; they leave Orosi at 7:15am, 11:45am, 1:45pm and 4:45pm and return at 8am, noon and 3pm. Taxis charge about US$20 to US$30 one way from Orosi to the park.

Orosi to Paraíso

From Orosi, a scenic loop circles the artificial Lago de Cachí. The lake was created following the construction of the Represa de Cachí (Cachí Dam), which supplies San José and the majority of the Central Valley with electricity. About 3km past the dam, at the foot of a long, steep hill, you'll find the abandoned village of Ujarrás and the ruins of its 17th-century church.

Sights

Dreamer's House GALLERY

(Casa del Soñador; ☎8955-7779; Ruta Nacional 224; ⏲9am-5pm) FREE This artisanal woodworking studio is run by Hermes and Miguel Quesada, sons of renowned Tico carver Macedonio Quesada. The brothers maintain the *campesino* (peasant farmer) tradition of whittling gnarled coffee-wood branches into ornate religious figures and whimsical characters. Their workshop displays sculptures from mystical faces and masks to abstract carvings of all sizes, with pieces available for purchase (from US$10). The studio is on the main road, 1.5km south of the dam.

Ruins of Ujarrás RUINS
(2299-5918; off Ruta Nacional 224; 8am-4:30pm) FREE The village of Ujarrás was damaged by an 1833 flood and then abandoned. All that remains are the crumbling walls of **Iglesia de Nuestra Señora de la Limpia Concepción**, a 1693 stone church once home to a miraculous painting of the Virgin. According to folklore, the relic refused to be moved, forcing clerics to build a church around it. But after floods and earthquakes, the painting conceded to move to Paraíso, leaving the church ruins in a rambling park.

Every year, usually on the Sunday closest to April 14, there is a procession of 3000 to 4000 people from Paraíso to the ruins, where Mass, food and music help celebrate the day of La Virgen de Ujarrás. The church's grassy grounds are a popular picnicking spot on Sunday afternoon, but go in the middle of the week and chances are you'll have them all to yourself. There are restroom facilities in the park.

To reach the village, turn left off the main road at the 'Ujarrás' sign and wind about 1km gently downhill, passing the well-signposted Restaurant La Pipiola en route.

Activities

Escalada Cachí CLIMBING
(8610-9849, 8867-8259; www.escaladacachi.com; Ruta Nacional 225; from US$30; 8am-4pm by appointment) A fun climbing spot with 39 routes for different abilities. The fee includes equipment rental, as much climbing as you can crank out, and a soak in a lovely river-diverted pool afterwards. Book 24 hours ahead of your visit and bring your own lunch/snacks. It also has an eight-person bungalow and camping area (US$16 per person including access to trails).

Located on a challenging dirt road off Rte 225 (near the cemetery) when heading north of the town of San Jeronimo, the climbing wall can be tricky to find as the small sign is faded. To avoid getting lost, call ahead for directions (though note that the route requires a 4WD and a lot of skill) or to get picked up. Alternatively, park where the dirt road branches off and hike the 2.2km down, but don't leave anything in your car.

Sleeping & Eating

★ **Hotel Quelitales** BUNGALOW $$$
(2577-1919, 2577-2222; www.hotelquelitales.com; d incl breakfast from US$75, ste incl breakfast US$125-200; P) Secluded and quiet, this off-the-beaten-path collection of 10 clean, contemporary-chic bungalows features spacious rooms with wooden floors, ultra-comfy mattresses, pops of color, indoor and outdoor solar-powered rain showers and private decks (some with waterfall views). Walls display large canvases of the hummingbirds, ladybugs, toucans and other critters for whom the cabins are named. The onsite restaurant serves delicious trout and other Tico specialties.

Activities on offer include 2km of surrounding trails and canyoning down the waterfall, plus more relaxing endeavors – yoga, massage and meditation sessions. Birdwatchers will be in their element – it's possible to spot more than 370 species in this area (including more than 30 species of hummingbird). Guests can hire a birdwatching guide (half-/full day US$80/120). Find it off Ruta Nacional 224, past the village of Finca Krieg.

La Casona del Cafetal COSTA RICAN $$
(2577-1414; www.lacasonadelcafetal.com; mains US$9-17, Sunday buffet adult/child US$23/14; 11:30am-5pm, to 4pm Sun;) It's all about the beautiful setting at this charming restaurant situated in the middle of a coffee plantation, with calming views of the Lago de Cachí. Specialties include fresh river trout and coffee-laced desserts, plus crepes and flans. It's especially popular with local families on all-you-can-eat buffet on Sundays. There's a small playground, as well as short trails around the lagoon.

The restaurant is near the town of Cachí, on the left-hand side of the road about 2km past the dam as you head southeast.

Getting There & Away

This stretch is best explored by car, bicycle, scooter or motorcycle – and it's worth exploring, as this is beautiful countryside. After Ujarrás, the route continues west for a few more kilometers to rejoin the main road at Paraíso.

TURRIALBA AREA

In the vicinity of Turrialba, at an elevation of 650m above sea level, the Río Reventazón gouges a mountain pass through the Cordillera Central. In the 1880s this geological quirk allowed the 'Jungle Train' between San José and Puerto Limón to roll through, and the mountain village of Turrialba grew prosperous from the coffee trade. Later, the first highway linking the capital to the coast exploited this same quirk. Turrialba thrived.

Things changed by the early 1990s, however, when the straighter, smoother Hwy 32 through Guápiles was completed and an earthquake shut down the railway for good. Suddenly Turrialba found itself off the beaten path. Even so, the area remains a key agricultural center, renowned for its strong coffee, ubiquitous cheese and Central America's best white-water rafting. To the north, the area is home to two worthy sites: the majestic and highly active Volcán Turrialba (best seen from a distance) and the ancient archaeological site of Guayabo.

Getting There & Away

Regular and reliable buses serve the Turrialba area. But if you'd like the freedom to explore these twisting mountain roads, renting a car is a great idea.

Turrialba

POP 32,000

When the railway shut down in 1991, commerce slowed, but Turrialba nonetheless remained a regional agricultural center where local coffee planters could bring their crops to market. And with tourism on the rise in Costa Rica in the 1990s, this modest mountain town soon became known as the gateway to some of the best white-water rafting on the planet. By the early 2000s, Turrialba was a hotbed of international rafters looking for Class V thrills. For now, the Río Pacuare runs on, but raft now before it's too late.

Activities

Centro Agronómico Tropical de Investigación GARDENS

(Catie; Center for Tropical Agronomy Research & Education; ☎2556-2700; www.catie.ac.cr/productos-y-servicios/catienatura; Ruta Nacional 10; adult/student/child 8-12yr US$10/8/6, children under 7yr free with two adults, guided tours US$26-50; ⏰7am-4pm) Catie's sprawling grounds, 2km east of Turrialba, encompass 10 sq km dedicated to tropical agricultural research and education. Agronomists from all over the world recognize this as one of the most important centers in the tropics. Reservations are required for one of several guided tours which pass through laboratories, greenhouses, a seed bank, experimental plots and one of the most extensive libraries of tropical-agriculture literature in the world. Alternatively, pick up a map and take a self-guided walk.

Ecoaventuras OUTDOORS

(☎8868-3938, 2556-7171; www.ecoaventuras.co.cr; Calle 6; white-water rafting from US$70, mountain biking Turrialba Valley from US$70) Ecoaventuras offers white-water rafting on the Ríos Pacuare and Pejibaye, along with horseback riding (from US$50) and mountain biking (prices depend on tour length and rider experience). Three-day rafting experiences include all meals, accommodations, equipment and a zipline tour (enquire for prices).

PARQUE NACIONAL VOLCÁN TURRIALBA

Before 2015 Volcán Turrialba's last major eruption was in 1866. At the time of research the 3328m volcano was very active, having belched chemicals and spewed multiple times in 2017, 2018 and 2019. The **park** (pnvolcanturrialba@gmail.com) was most definitely closed and the capital put on high alert. At the time of writing, there was no information as to when it may reopen. Warning signs forbade visitors from driving further than 8km shy of the summit along Ruta 417, just beyond the turn off to **Volcán Turrialba Lodge** (☎8383-6084, 2273-4335; www.facebook.com/turrialbalodge; d cabinas US$30 per person per night; Ⓟ). The exclusion zone may be larger or smaller during your visit. Check with locals before you attempt to drive on the volcano and avoid it altogether if you suffer from respiratory or heart conditions. The best place to see Volcán Turrialba may be from afar. Views are best in the mornings, before the clouds pass over.

DON'T MISS

WHITE-WATER RAFTING IN THE CENTRAL VALLEY

The Turrialba area is a major center for white-water rafting. Traditionally the two most popular rafting rivers have been the **Río Reventazón** and the **Río Pacuare**, but the former has been dramatically impacted by a series of hydroelectric projects, including a huge 305-megawatt dam currently under construction.

As a result, most organized expeditions from Turrialba now head for the Río Pacuare, which arguably offers the most scenic rafting in Central America. The river plunges down the Caribbean slope through a series of spectacular canyons clothed in virgin rainforest, through runs named for their fury and separated by calm stretches that enable you to stare at near-vertical green walls towering hundreds of meters above.

The Pacuare can be run year-round, though June to October are considered the best months. The highest water is from October to December, when the river runs fast with huge waves. March and April are when the river is at its lowest, although it's still challenging.

Lower Pacuare

With Class II–IV rapids, this is the more accessible run: 28km through rocky gorges, past an indigenous village and untamed jungle.

Upper Pacuare

Classified as Class III–IV, but a few sections can go to Class V, depending on conditions. It's about a two-hour drive to the put-in, after which you'll have the prettiest jungle cruise on earth all to yourself.

Costa Rica Ríos RAFTING
(☎2556-8664, in USA & Canada 888-434-0776; www.costaricarios.com) Offers well-organized and highly enjoyable week-long rafting trips in and around the Turrialba area, which must be booked in advance. An eight-day kayaking and canoeing trip costs US$1699 per person (based on double occupancy), while the adventure-tour package, including rafting, ziplining, snorkeling, surfing and mountain biking, costs US$2899 per person (also based on double occupancy).

Courses

Spanish by the River LANGUAGE
(Spanish at Locations; ☎2556-7380, in USA 1-877-268-3730; www.spanishatlocations.com; Ruta Nacional 10; 20/30hr per week group US$225/300, 10/20hr per week private $225/360, homestay/hostel bed per night US$22/14) A five-minute bus ride from Turrialba, this school offers accommodation along with Spanish classes for students at varying levels of fluency. Courses are also offered with adventure packages. Try Spanish with rafting, mountain biking, kayaking and birdwatching.

Adventure Education Center LANGUAGE
(☎in USA 800-237-2730; www.adventurespanishschool.com; off Calle 6; 1 week with group/intensive group US$310/360) Combine Spanish classes and white-water rafting at this friendly Turrialba school with classrooms on stilts overlooking tropical gardens. It offers standard Spanish and also medical Spanish. A standard week's group language instruction entails 16 hours of lessons with a class size of up to six. The intensive course is 20 hours.

Tours

Tico's Rafting Adventure RAFTING
(☎2556-1231; www.ticoriver.com; Ruta Nacional 230; 1-day rafting $80) This friendly adventure outfit runs one- to three-day rafting trips on an 18-mile stretch of the Río Pacuare. The route has stretches of calm water, linked with thrilling Class IV rapids. Day trips are roughly eight hours long, with four hours of paddling. Lunch is included, and served next to two waterfalls.

Overnight trips offer the chance to be fully immersed in the beautiful canyon and do some hiking.

Explornatura RAFTING
(☎2556-0111, in USA & Canada 866-571-2443; www.explornatura.com; Av 4, btwn Calles 2 & 4; canyoneering and canopy/rafting US$75/85) Solid adventure outfit offering rafting, mountain-biking and horseback-riding tours, plus coffee, dairy farm, and archeological site tours.

Sleeping

In Town

★Casa de Lis Hostel HOSTEL $

(☎2556-4933; www.hostelcasadelis.com; Av Central; dm/d/tr US$14/55/65, under 3yr free; P 📶) Hands down Turrialba's best value sleep, this sweet, centrally located place is a traveler's dream. Spotless dorms and doubles with comfy mattresses and reading lamps are complemented by a fully equipped kitchen, a volcano-view roof terrace, a pretty back garden, fantastic information displays and a friendly atmosphere. There's free tea and coffee in the mornings, a book exchange and board games.

Secure parking is available for two cars on a first come, first served basis. It's near Calle 2.

Hotel Wagelia HOTEL $$

(☎2556-1566; www.hotelwageliaturrialba.com; Av 4, btwn Calles 2 & 4; d incl breakfast from US$85; P 📶) Simple, modern and clean rooms come with cable TV and face a quiet interior courtyard. A restaurant serves Tico specialties, while the pleasant terrace bar is a good place for a drink and has wi-fi.

Turrialba B&B B&B $$

(☎2556-6651; www.turribb.com; Calle 1; d/tr incl breakfast from US$74/84; P ❄ 📶) For a bit of tranquility in downtown Turrialba (a rare commodity!), this B&B has a lovely garden patio with pool table and hammocks. Rooms are spacious with pops of color and hardwood furniture. The living room has a TV and a good collection of paperbacks. There's also a shared kitchen and a small bar. It's north of Av 6.

Turrialba Borders

Wagelia Espino Blanco Lodge LODGE $$

(☎2556-0616; www.wageliaespinoblancolodge.com; r incl breakfast US$120, extra person US$15; P 📶) 🍃 High above Turrialba, this 10-bungalow ecolodge sits on 30 hectares of forest land. The quaint and well-constructed cabins have hot water and rechargeable lamps but no electricity, TVs or distractions from the serenity of the place. Sit back in your personal hammock and take in the surrounding nature. The grounds have a small amphitheater, a poets' corner and seven hiking trails.

A charming restaurant serves a buffet (advance booking required). The lodge runs three- to four-hour nature tours for US$40 per person, plus staff can book other activities for guests. There's wi-fi in the bar but not in the rooms. From Turrialba, the lodge is about a 20-minute drive north up winding Hwy 230. The roads can be tricky – call for directions.

Turrialtico Lodge LODGE $$

(☎2538-1111; www.turrialtico.com; near Ruta Nacional 10; d/tr/q incl breakfast from US$64/87/98; P 📶) Commanding dramatic, sweeping views of the Río Reventazón valley, this old farmhouse 9km east of Turrialba (off the highway to Siquirres) offers 18 attractive, wood-paneled rooms decorated with local artwork. Rooms in the reception building share a large terrace and sitting area, and a pleasant open-air restaurant (open 7am to 10pm, mains US$7 to US$16) serves up country cooking.

★Rancho Naturalista LODGE $$$

(☎2100-1855, 8704-3217; www.ranchonaturalista.net; near Ruta Nacional 414; r per person incl 3 meals from US$152; P @) About 1.3km south of Tuis and 900m above sea level, this small lodge on 50 hectares of land is a must-stay for birdwatchers. More than 450 species have been recorded in the area (250 from the lodge's balcony alone). The 15 homey rooms are divided between the lodge and a cluster of private *casitas,* surrounded by pretty landscaped grounds.

Sit on the big wooden veranda with a coffee and watch hummingbirds approach the many feeders. Delicious meals include organic beef and pork from the cows and pigs raised onsite. Staff are friendly and the lodge has knowledgeable, eagle-eyed billingual private guides, who can be booked from US$70 in the morning and US$50 in the afternoon (price per trip for up to five people) to accompany you along the surrounding trails, or you can walk them yourself.

Casa Turire HOTEL $$$

(☎2531-1111, 2531-1309; www.hotelcasaturire.com; near Ruta Nacional 225; d/ste/master ste US$186/288/452, additional person US$28-55, child under 3yr free, child 4-12yr US$28; P ❄ @ 📶 🏊) 🍃 This elegant three-story plantation inn with manicured lawns and an inner courtyard has 16 well-appointed rooms with high ceilings, wood floors and wrought-iron beds; a massive master suite comes with a

Jacuzzi and excellent views of the coffee and macadamia-nut plantations in the distance.

Adding icing to the cake are spa services (from US$30), a restaurant and bar, horseback riding, birdwatching, and kayaking on the onsite lake. A kids' pool and playground will please younger visitors. Take the La Suiza/Tuis turnoff from Hwy 10, head south for 2.3km, then follow signs an additional 1.4km down a dirt road to the hotel.

Eating

Maracuyá CAFE $

(2556-2021; www.facebook.com/maracuya2012; Calle 2; frozen coffee from US$2, mains from US$8; 2-9:30pm Wed-Mon;) This bright-walled cafe north of Av 10 serves up one of the best coffee treats in the country – a frozen caffeine concoction with gooey *maracuyá* (passion fruit) syrup and crunchy seeds. Dishes include veggie panini, burritos, chicken burgers, and Latin American favorites such as *patacones* (fried plantains).

La Feria COSTA RICAN $

(2556-0386; www.facebook.com/RestauranteLaFeria; Calle 6; mains US$3-14; 11am-9:30pm Wed-Mon, to 3pm Tue;) This unremarkable-looking eatery has friendly service and excellent, reasonably priced home cooking. Sometimes the kitchen gets a bit backed up, but the hearty *casados* (typical dishes with beans, rice, a small salad and a choice of protein) are well worth the wait. Caribbean chicken, salads, pasta and red snapper are also available. Find it north of Av 4.

Restaurant Betico Mata BARBECUE $

(2556-2006; Ruta Nacional 10; mains from US$7; 11am-11pm) This carnivores' delight is just south of town on the road to Juan Viñas. It's perched on a hill with open-air views, and you can't beat the good-value *casados* and meat fillets. It all goes smashingly well with an ice-cold beer. Friendly host Kenneth speaks great English.

★ **Wok & Roll** ASIAN $$

(2556-6756; Calle 1; mains US$10-16; 11am-10pm Wed-Mon) Pan-Asian cuisine fills the menu at this casual eatery with half a dozen wooden tables near the main square. Enjoy sushi rolls and sashimi, teriyaki or sweet-and-sour chicken, Thai curry, wontons and other Asian favorites, plus tempura ice cream for dessert. Wash it all down with homemade mint lemonade and honey-sweetened jasmine tea. Takeout available.

More Than Words THAI, ITALIAN $$

(2556-1362; www.facebook.com/morethanwords888; Av 6; small/large pizzas from US$8/15, mains from US$10; 11am-10pm Tue-Thu, to 11pm Fri, noon-11pm Sat & Sun) Dishes are satisfying at this restaurant opposite the church in the main square, with a large bar at its center. The diverse menu has freshly made pizzas, pasta dishes, New York steaks and interesting creations like *wantacos* (a hybrid wanton-taco stuffed with marinated chicken and salad). Service can be leisurely; grab a game at the pool table after you order.

Drinking & Nightlife

Loco's Bar and Restaurant BAR

(2556-3500; www.facebook.com/locosrestauranteybar; Av 4; 3pm-midnight Sun-Thu, to 2am Fri & Sat) Where rafters finish with a cool beer after an adrenaline-fueled day on the rivers. Things might get lively later with brightly colored cocktails, but it's a decent late-lunch and dinner spot, too (dishes from US$4). The hamburgers are mega, with a super-thick patty and dense, freshly made bun. The flatbreads, wraps and *papas fritas* (chips) hit the spot too.

Respira & Koko CAFE

(8995-2918; Av 6; noon-7pm) Turrialba's trendy youth hang out at this industrial-chic cafe with corrugated-iron roof, exposed beams and open-plan garden featuring pleasant decking and an artificial lawn. Respira & Koko is ideal for watching the world go by. As you do, order from a whole range of coffee-based drinks, plus savory crepes and snacks (menu items from US$4). It's on Turrialba's main square.

Information

Banco de Costa Rica (cnr Av Central & Calle 3; 9am-4pm Mon-Fri) Has 24-hour ATMs dispensing dollars and colones.

There's no official tourist office, but most hotels and rafting outfits can organize tours, accommodation and transportation throughout the region.

Getting There & Away

A modern bus terminal is located on the western edge of town off Hwy 10.

San José via Paraíso and Cartago About US$3, two hours to 2 hours 20 minutes, every 15 to 30 minutes, 4:30am to 9pm Monday to Saturday and 5am to 9pm Sunday.

Siquirres, for transfer to Puerto Limón About US$2.50, two hours, every 30 minutes to two hours, 5:30am to 6:15pm weekdays, 6am to 7pm Saturday and 6am to 6pm Sunday.

Monumento Nacional Arqueológico Guayabo

Nestled into a patch of stunning hillside forest 19km northeast of Turrialba is the largest and most important archaeological site in the country. **Guayabo** (☎2559-1220; US$6; ⊙8am-3:30pm) is composed of the remains of a pre-Columbian city that was thought to have peaked at some point in 800 CE, when it was inhabited by as many as 20,000 people. Today visitors can walk an interpretive trail and examine the remains of petroglyphs, residential mounds, a roadway and an impressive aqueduct system – built with rocks that were hauled in from the Río Reventazón along a cobbled 8km road. Amazingly the cisterns still work, and (theoretically) potable water remains available at the site. In 1973, as the site's importance became evident, Guayabo was declared a national monument, with further protections established in 1980. The site occupies 232 hectares, most of which remain unexcavated. It's a small place, so don't go expecting Mayan pyramids, but it's a fascinating visit nonetheless.

Activities

The site currently protects the last remaining pre-montane forest in the province of Cartago, and although mammals are limited to mainly squirrels, armadillos and coatis, there are plenty of good birdwatching opportunities here. Particularly noteworthy among the avifauna are the oropendolas, which colonize the monument by building sack-like nests in the trees. Other birds include toucans, woodpeckers and brown jays – the latter are unique among jays in that they have a small inflatable sac in their chest, which causes the popping sound that is heard at the beginning of their raucous calls.

Tours

Guided tours (☎8534-1063; www.usurecr.org; guided tour 1-3 people US$20, 4-9 people US$35, 10-20 people US$50) are available from the monument's front desk. In high season English-speaking guides may be available with advance notice.

Information

Across the road from the ticket office there are restrooms, a small shop selling snacks, plus an information center that provides an overview of what the pre-Hispanic city may have looked like.

Getting There & Away

Head north out of Turrialba on Ruta 230 and make a right on to Ruta 415. The road is well signposted, and the site is roughly 20km from Turrialba along winding roads. All but the last 3km is paved; a 4WD is recommended, though not required if you take it slowly. There's another entrance from the north of the site (3km longer) off Rte 230 northwest of Turrialba.

Buses leave from Turrialba to Guayabo at 11:15am daily; the return bus to Turrialba departs at 4pm. The journey takes around one hour and costs US$2. A taxi will cost around US$30 to Guayabo from Turrialba.

AT A GLANCE

POPULATION
Puerto Limón: 60,148

FAST FACT
Costa Rica is the fourth-largest exporter of bananas in the world.

BEST CARIBBEAN COOKING
Taylor's Place (p164)

BEST BEACH
Playa Negra (p167)

BEST BEACH BAR
Salsa Brava (p184)

WHEN TO GO

Dec–Mar The biggest swells draw surfers to the southern Caribbean.

Mar–Oct Turtle-nesting season means egg-laying and hatching spectacles in Tortuguero.

May–Dec Off season for tourism, so prices may be discounted.

Playa Cocles **(p185)**

Caribbean Coast

It takes a bit of effort to travel here to see the nesting turtles of Tortuguero, raft the Río Pacuare or dive the reefs off Manzanillo, but you'll be glad you made the trip. Nature has thrived on this rugged and rustic coast – herons and egrets share the vast network of canals with caimans and sloths, while pelicans and frigate birds glide above the surf like prehistoric planes. Kitchens serve up Afro-Caribbean delights such as jerk chicken, grilled snapper and *rondón* (spicy seafood gumbo); increasingly, Europeans are bringing their own flavors to the party, too. All life forms slow down here, from turtles crawling to the sea to land-bound *homo sapiens* adapting to the equatorial sun. Listen to the lilt of patois; vibe to the rhythms of reggae and calypso in rum-soaked bars.

INCLUDES

Caribbean Coast Highlights

1. **Parque Nacional Tortuguero** (p155) Sliding silently through jungle canals in search of wildlife, or volunteering to protect endangered sea turtles.
2. **Río Pacuare** (p176) Rafting the country's most extreme river.
3. **Puerto Viejo de Talamanca** (p176) Sampling the culinary scene, lazing on the beach and partying.
4. **Punta Uva** (p185) Surfing or diving at Punta Uva's pristine, tucked-away cove.
5. **Cahuita** (p167) Chilling out in rustic bliss, soaking up the Caribbean Creole culture and visiting Cahuita National Park.
6. **Manzanillo** (p189) Snorkeling the teeming reefs and adventuring through the dripping jungle.
7. **Parque Nacional Braulio Carrillo** (p145) Witnessing the dramatic meeting of the murky Río Sucio and the crystal-clear Río Honduras.
8. **Bribrí Territory** (p183) Visiting cacao farms and indigenous villages.

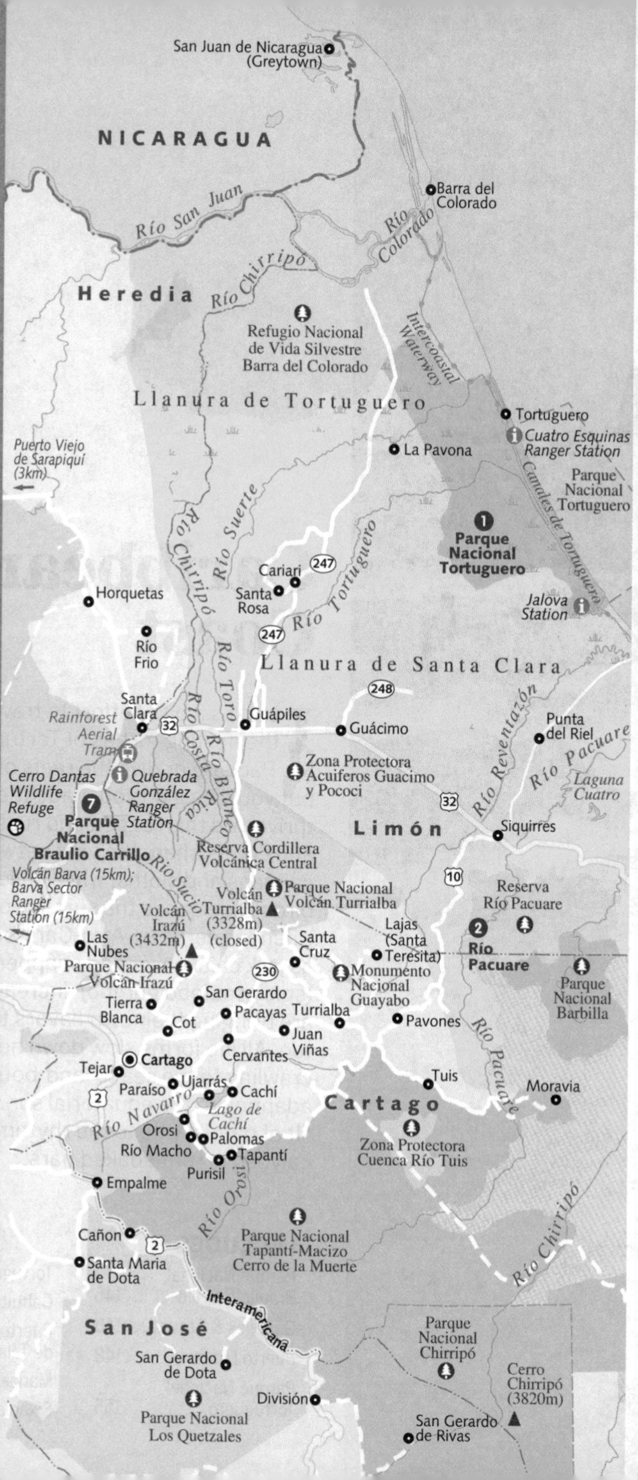

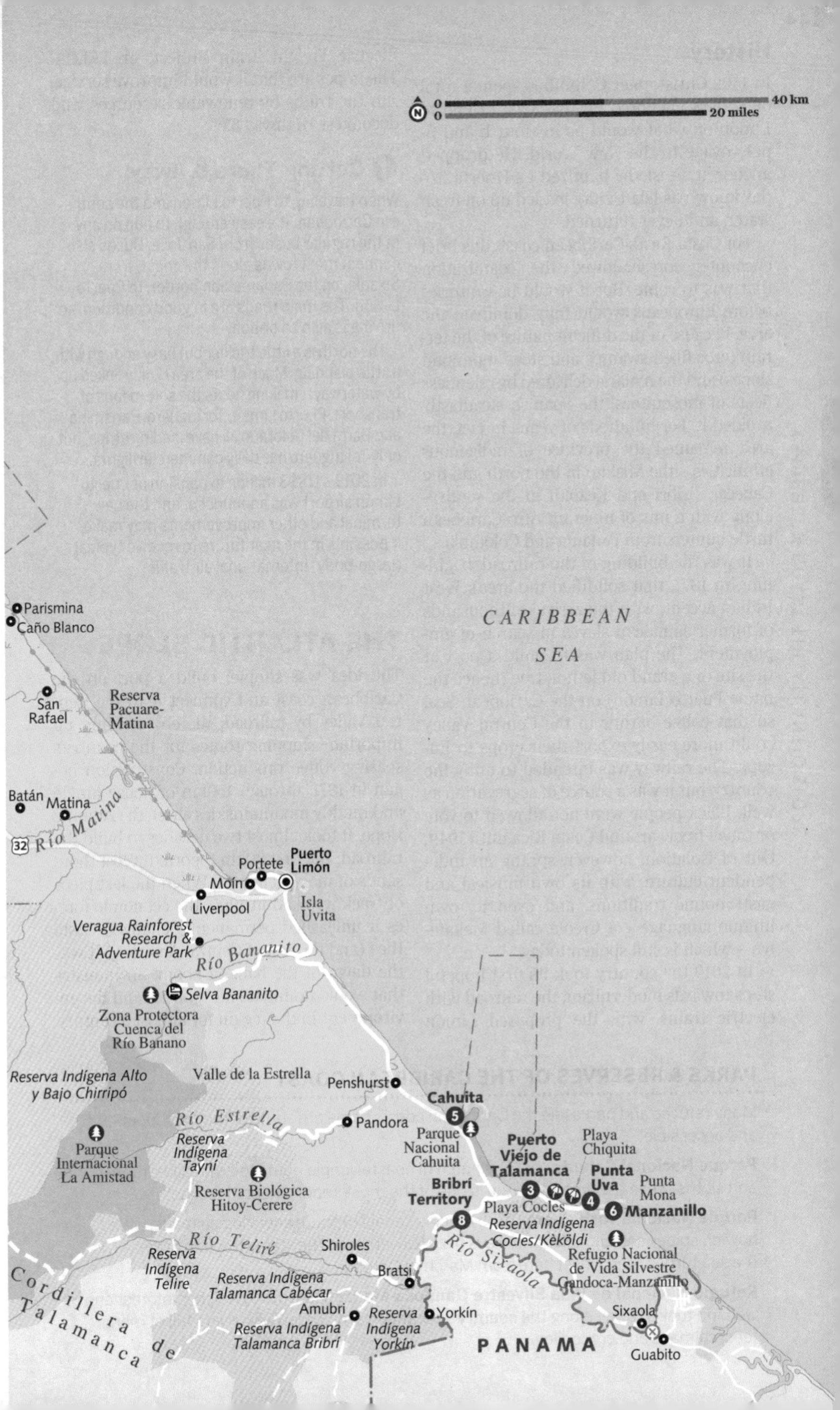

0
40 km
0
20 miles
CARIBBEAN SEA
Parismina
Caño Blanco
San Rafael
Reserva Pacuare-Matina
Batán
Matina
Río Matina
32
Portete
Puerto Limón
Moín
Liverpool
Isla Uvita
Veragua Rainforest Research & Adventure Park
Río Bananito
Selva Bananito
Zona Protectora Cuenca del Río Banano
Reserva Indígena Alto y Bajo Chirripó
Valle de la Estrella
Penshurst
Cahuita
5
Río Estrella
Pandora
Parque Nacional Cahuita
Parque Internacional La Amistad
Reserva Indígena Tayní
Reserva Biológica Hitoy-Cerere
Puerto Viejo de Talamanca
Playa Chiquita
Punta Uva
Punta Mona
3
4
6
Manzanillo
Bribrí Territory
8
Playa Cocles
Reserva Indígena Cocles/Kèköldi
Río Telirė
Shiroles
Río Sixaola
Refugio Nacional de Vida Silvestre Gandoca-Manzanillo
Reserva Indígena Telire
Bratsi
Reserva Indígena Talamanca Cabécar
Cordillera de Talamanca
Amubri
Reserva Indígena Yorkín
Yorkín
Sixaola
Reserva Indígena Talamanca Bribrí
PANAMA
Guabito

History

In 1502 Christopher Columbus spent a total of 17 days anchored off the coast of Puerto Limón on what would be his fourth and final voyage to the New World. He dropped anchor at an isle he baptized La Huerta (today known as Isla Uvita), loaded up on fresh water, and never returned.

For Costa Rica's Caribbean coast, this brief encounter foreshadowed the colonization that was to come. But it would be centuries before Europeans would fully dominate the area. Because of the difficult nature of the terrain (croc-filled swamps and steep mountain slopes) and the malaria delivered by relentless fleets of mosquitoes, the Spanish steadfastly avoided it. For hundreds of years, in fact, the area remained the province of indigenous ethnicities – the Miskito in the north and the Cabécar, Bribrí and Kèköldi in the south – along with a mix of itinerant Afro-Caribbean turtle hunters from Panama and Colombia.

It was the building of the railroad, beginning in 1871, that solidified the area's West Indian accent, with the arrival of thousands of former Jamaican slaves in search of employment. The plan was to build a port at the site of a grand old lemon tree (hence the name Puerto Limón) on the Caribbean Sea, so that coffee barons in the Central Valley could more easily export their crops to Europe. The railway was intended to unify the country, but it was a source of segregation as well. Black people were not allowed to vote or travel freely around Costa Rica until 1949. Out of isolation, however, sprang an independent culture, with its own musical and gastronomic traditions, and even its own unique language – a Creole called Mekatelyu – which is still spoken today.

In 2019 the country took its first hopeful steps towards modernizing the railroad with electric trains, with the proposed Limón Electric Freight Train Project, or TELCA. The hopes are that it would improve service, run the trains by renewable resources, and decongest Highway 32.

Getting There & Away

When traveling to Puerto Limón and the southern Caribbean, it's easy enough to hop on any of the regular buses from San José. Buses also connect most towns along the coast, from Sixaola, on the Panamanian border, to Puerto Limón. The main roads are in good condition, so driving is also an option.

The north is a little trickier but easy enough with a little planning. Much of the area is only linked up by waterways, making boats the sole means of transport. Puerto Limón, Tortuguero, Parismina and Barra del Colorado all have landing strips, but only Tortuguero has daily commercial flights.

In 2019 a US$3 million expansion of Puerto Limón airport was announced, and the new terminal and other improvements may make it possible in the near future to receive typical (large-body) international air traffic.

THE ATLANTIC SLOPE

The idea was simple: build a port on the Caribbean coast and connect it to the Central Valley by railroad, thereby opening up important shipping routes for the country's soaring coffee production. Construction began in 1871, through 150km of dense jungle and muddy mountainsides along the Atlantic slope. It took almost two decades to build the railroad; the first 30km reportedly cost thousands of men their lives. When the last piece of track was laid in 1890, the economic forces it unleashed permanently changed Costa Rica (and the rest of Central America). It was the dawn of the banana boom, an industry that would dominate life, politics and the environment in the region for almost a century.

PARKS & RESERVES OF THE CARIBBEAN COAST

Many refuges and parks line the Caribbean coast. These are some of the most popular and accessible:

Parque Nacional Cahuita (p174) A patch of coastal jungle home to armadillos, monkeys and sloths, while the protected reef is one of the most important on the coast.

Parque Nacional Tortuguero (p155) Jungle canals obscure snoozing caimans, while howler, spider and capuchin monkeys traipse overhead. The star attraction, however, is the sea turtles, which nest here from March to October.

Refugio Nacional de Vida Silvestre Gandoca-Manzanillo (p190) A rich rainforest and wetland tucked away along the country's southeastern border, with rivers full of manatees, caimans and crocodiles.

Today, the railroad is no longer (though plans are afoot to revive it). Likewise, banana production is not as mighty as it was, supplanted in many areas by pineapples and African oil palms.

Parque Nacional Braulio Carrillo

Enter this underexplored national **park** (☎2266-1883, 2206-5500; www.sinac.go.cr; adult/child US$12/5; ⊙8am-3:30pm) and you'll have an idea of what Costa Rica looked like prior to the 1950s, when 75% of the country's surface area was still covered by forest. Here, steep hills cloaked in impossibly tall trees are interrupted only by canyons and cascading rivers. It has extraordinary biodiversity due to the range of altitudes, from steamy 2906m cloud forest alongside Volcán Barva to lush, humid lowlands on the Caribbean slope. Its most incredible feature, however, is that the southernmost point of this massive park is only 30 minutes north of San José.

History

Braulio Carrillo was created in the 1970s as a unique compromise between conservationists and developers. At the time, the government had announced a plan to build a new highway that would connect the capital to Puerto Limón. Back then, San José's only link to its most important port was via a crumbling railroad or a slow rural road through Cartago and Turrialba. The only feasible route for the new thoroughfare was along a low pass between the Barva and Irazú volcanoes – an area covered in primary forest. Conservationists were deeply worried about putting a road (and any associated development) in an area that served as San José's watershed. So a plan was hatched: the road would be built, but the 475 sq km of land to either side of it would be set aside as a national park. Thus, in 1978, Parque Nacional Braulio Carrillo was born.

Doubling the width of the highway which passes through the park may have some effect on its wildlife. The project, designed to help ease the flow of traffic from the ports of Moín and Limón and begun by a Chinese company in 2018, has faced massive delays.

Activities

Birdwatching in the park is excellent, and commonly seen species include parrots, toucans and hummingbirds; quetzals can be seen at higher elevations, primarily in the Barva sector. Other rare but sometimes sighted birds include eagles and umbrella birds.

Mammals are difficult to spot due to the lush vegetation, though deer, monkeys and *tepezcuintle* (pacas, the park's mascot) are frequently seen. Jaguars and ocelots are present but seldom seen.

Volcán Barva HIKING
(☎2266-1883; ⊙8am-3:30pm) Climbing Volcán Barva is a strenuous adventure along a remote but reasonably well-maintained trail. Because of its relative inaccessibility, there's a good chance you'll be alone. Begin at the western entrance of the park, north of Heredia. From there, a 3km signposted track climbs to the summit, where you'll see a lake inside the crater.

VOLUNTOURISM

Near Monte de la Cruz, in the Barva sector, the **Cerro Dantas Wildlife Refuge** (☎8866-7380, 2274-1997; www.cerrodantas.co.cr) is an education facility that is always seeking volunteers to help out with administrative, maintenance and research duties.

Tours

Rainforest Adventures ECOTOUR
(☎2257-5961, USA 1-866-759-8726; www.rainforestadventure.com; adult/student & child tram US$65/33, combo tram/zipline tour US$99/65; ⊙7:30am-2pm; 👪) Rainforest Adventures and its aerial tram allow you to visit the heights of the forest canopy in a gondola. The 2.6km ride takes roughly two hours, affording unusual plant-spotting and birdwatching opportunities. The fee includes a guide, which is helpful since the density of the vegetation can make observing animals difficult.

Information

The park's three most accessible hiking trails originate at **Quebrada González ranger station** (☎2206-5500; park entry adult/child US$12/5; ⊙8am-4pm) in the park's northeastern corner; find it on Hwy 32 (the San José–Guápiles highway), a 25-minute drive from Guápiles. It has safe parking, toilets, drinking water and a ranger-staffed info booth. For security reasons, don't leave your car parked anywhere along the main highway.

People who want to climb Volcán Barva on a day trip or camp overnight can stop by the **Barva Sector ranger station** (☎2266-1883; park

OFF THE BEATEN TRACK

LA DANTA SALVAJE

West of Guápiles, in a secret volcanic-mountain-range location, a 45-minute 4WD trip and a three-hour hike lead to this fabulous 410-hectare **rainforest reserve** (☎8332-8045, 2750-0012; www.ladantasalvaje.com; 3-night packages per person US$400), set in a Parque Nacional Braulio Carrillo buffer zone (altitude 800m). You'll sleep in an atmospheric lodge with no electricity. Rates include transport from Guápiles, meals, jungle hiking, wildlife-spotting and splashing in rivers. Reserve ahead. There's a minimum of six people and a maximum of 12.

entry adult/child US$12/5; ⏲8am-3:30pm), in the southwest of the park, 3km north of Sacramento.

Getting There & Away

Frequent buses between San José and Guápiles can drop you off at the Quebrada González ranger station, but the trip back is more challenging. While it's possible to flag a bus down on busy Hwy 32, your luck will depend on the driver's discretion and how full the bus is.

Drivers can reach the Barva station by following the decent paved road north from Heredia through Barva village to San José de la Montaña, Paso Llano and Sacramento. From Sacramento, a signposted, 4WD-only trail leads 3km north to the entrance. It is not advisable to drive this stretch in the rain, as the road is a mess of car-swallowing potholes. Public buses from Heredia will only get you as far as Paso Llano, 7km from the park entrance. For a day trip without your own vehicle, you'll need to take an early bus from Heredia. Make sure you're catching a bus that goes all the way to Paso Llano, or you'll be left more than 15km from the park's entrance.

Guápiles & Around

POP 28,448

Guápiles, at the base of the northern foothills of the Cordillera Central, is also a heavy intersection for Costa Rican truck traffic: the newly widened four-lane highway is testament to that. It serves as a transportation center for the Río Frío banana-growing region and also makes a potential base from which to explore Parque Nacional Braulio Carrillo – the entrance is a 20-minute drive away – or go ziplining or tramming through the canopy with Rainforest Adventures (p145).

Though often just an overnight stop for those on their way to Tortuguero, if you zoom by too quickly you'll miss the chance of staying at an old-school ecolodge or visiting the workshop of a bamboo master, or perhaps miss out on an interesting community tourism project.

Sights

Copetillo Birdwatching/ Donde Cope NATURE CENTER
(Cope Arte; ☎7136-5472; www.copeartcr.com; La Unión de Guápiles; US$10; ⏲hours vary) Guapileño artist-photographer Cope (co-pay) has converted this former tilapia farm into a paradise of hummingbirds, tanagers and other birds, with a convenient blind to take excellent photos. You can sit and have coffee or lunch, and even hike some of his trails. Located 2 km after crossing the Río Frío toward Limón; make a right.

Sleeping

Ruta del Agua HOMESTAY $
(ASIREA, Asociación de Industriales, Reforestadores y Dueños de Finca de la Zona Atlántica; ☎2710-7416; www.facebook.com/asirea.asociacion) Since 1987 the Asociación para el Desarrollo Sostenible de la Región Atlántica has worked in building sustainable tourism here. Now they've developed a small network of hotels, restaurants, and other locally owned businesses in the Guápiles/Guácimo area, including everything from yoga centers to waterfall hikes. The office is just a short distance southeast of Hotel Suerre off the Ruta Vieja.

Hotel y Cabinas de Tropico HOTEL $
(☎2710-1882; d from US$30; P❄📶) This motel-style abode isn't glamorous – it's on a side road off Guápiles' main highway (Rte 32) and is frequented by traveling vendors making deals in town, but you can't beat it on price or facilities. Clean, simple rooms – some have air-con, some have TV and some have refrigerators; some have all three. The front desk sells snacks, as well as canned beer and Cuba Libres, and serves free coffee.

It's a 15-minute walk or five-minute drive into the center of town. Rooms with fan but no air-con are a few dollars less.

Casa Río Blanco B&B B&B $$
(☎2710-4124, 8570-8294; www.casarioblanco.com; s/d/tr/q incl breakfast US$85/85/100/115; P📶) 🍃 At one of Costa Rica's original ecolodges, Herbie and Annette offer four hillside cabins on two hectares above the

murmuring Río Blanco. Devoid of cable TV and air-con, it's a throwback to earlier days when ecotourism was all about unplugging (there *is* limited wi-fi).

Croaking frogs and flickering lightning bugs provide late-night entertainment; daytime diversions include the swimming hole and day trips to Tortuguero.

Dinner from mostly organic produce, vegetarian or meat-based, costs US$15.

Eating

Soda Yurifer COSTA RICAN $

(☎2710-1721; cnr Calle 5 & Av 8A; casados US$6-10; ⏲24hr; 📶) It has lime-green walls and a cafeteria feel, but this clean, simple *soda* (lunch counter) sells good, cheap *casados* (with chicken, Mexican-style meat or pork, or fajita style), and fried rice with shrimp, beef or both. Ask for some pickled vegetables in a large chili jar to garnish your rice. Find it south of Av Central.

Restaurante El Yugo de Mi Tata COSTA RICAN $

(☎2711-0090; mains US$5-10; ⏲24hr) It doesn't look like much, but there's a reason this joint is truck-stop heaven. Strategically placed just below Hwy 32's tortuous climb into Parque Nacional Braulio Carrillo (p145; 13km west of Guápiles), it's the perfect stop before or after a visit to the national park. A huge and fabulous array of tasty, affordable buffet-style food is available round the clock.

Shopping

Artistry in Bamboo ARTS & CRAFTS

(☎8614-5451; www.brieri.com; Río Blanco; ⏲call for appointment) For three decades and across several countries, expat master craftsman Brian Erikson has been fashioning wonderful things out of bamboo. You may have even seen some of his work in the high-end homes and hotels of Costa Rica. A nice stop on your way back to San José, and home. He's just down the street from Casa Río Blanco B&B.

Orientation

The center of town is about 1km north of Hwy 32, reached by a pair of well-marked turnoffs on either side of Taco Bell. Guápiles' two major streets are one way, running parallel to each other east and west. Most of the services, restaurants, shops and ATMs are on the loop that these streets make through the busy downtown.

Getting There & Away

Guápiles' modern bus terminal is 800m north of the main highway from the western Taco Bell turnoff.

Siquirres

POP 20,640

The steamy lowland town of Siquirres has long served as an important transportation hub. It sits at the intersection of Hwy 32 (the main road that crosses the Atlantic slope to Puerto Limón) and Hwy 10, the old road that connects San José with Puerto Limón via Turrialba.

Siquirres is a good stop en route to Parismina in which to find an ATM – there are none in Parismina (or Tortuguero).

History

Even before the highways bisecting the town were built, Siquirres was a significant location, for it was here in the early 20th century that the lines of segregation were drawn. At the time, black people were barred from traveling west of the town without special permission. Accordingly, any train making its way from Limón to San José was required to stop here and change its crew: black people working as conductors and engineers would change places with their Spanish counterparts and the train would continue on its route to the capital. This ended in 1949, when a new constitution outlawed racial discrimination.

Today Siquirres still marks the place where Costa Rica takes a dip into the Caribbean – and not just geographically. This is

BUSES FROM GUÁPILES

DESTINATION	COST (US$)	DURATION	DEPARTURES
Puerto Limón via Guácimo & Siquirres (Tracasa)	5	1-2hr	hourly 4:50am-7:10pm, from 5:30am Sun
Puerto Viejo de Sarapiquí (Guapileños, Caribeños)	2	1hr	5:30am, 8am, 9am, 10:30am, noon, 2:30pm, 4pm & 6:30pm
San José (Guapileños)	2.60	1¼hr	every 15-30min 5am-7:30pm

where Costa Rican *casados* give way to West Indian *rondón* and where Spanish guitar is replaced with the strains of calypso.

Sleeping & Eating

Pacuare Lodge LODGE $$$

(☎4033-0060, in USA & Canada 1-800-963-1195; www.pacuarelodge.com; Packages per person from US$1725;) There are two ways into this dream of an ecolodge, both equally adventurous. Most arrive at its remote location on the Río Pacuare by raft, via a thrilling 45-minute guided paddle. Others take a 7km dirt path (accessible via the hotel's 4WD) to the river, and then climb into a rickety cable car that crosses the water to the lodge.

Outdoor enthusiasts will love the elegant private bungalows overlooking the river, with hardwood floors, solar-heated showers and thatched roofs; some have infinity pools. Most (aside from family rooms) have no electricity or walls, only screens – all the better to immerse yourself in nature. Activities include guided hikes, ziplining, canyoning and meeting nearby indigenous communities. Unwind at the spa or eat dinner in the treetops on an elevated canopy terrace.

The lodge is currently participating in a panther program: 40 motion-sensor cameras are set up around the reserve to capture wild-cat activity, and there's a learning center with video footage of recent sightings.

A new 20m infinity pool enhances the experience.

Package deals include transportation to and from San José, a bilingual guide, a rafting tour or ground transportation to the lodge, equipment, meals, most drinks and a hike.

Pacuare River Bar & Grill COSTA RICAN $

(☎7016-3147; www.facebook.com/pacuareriverbar; bar food US$2-8; 11am-midnight) This Colorado-style bar and restaurant is on Hwy 10 between Turrialba and Siquirres. Enter the laid-back roadhouse through swing doors, grab a drink at the bar, decorated with a snakeskin and bull horns, and tuck into tangy *ceviche* (seafood marinated in lemon), fresh beef fajitas or buffalo wings.

Look for the kayaks out front. Former owner Kirk now runs the rafting business Pacuare River Lodge.

WORTH A TRIP

CENTRO TURÍSTICO LAS TILAPIAS

Enthusiastic owner Chito is a passionate naturalist who spent 20 years building and introducing wildlife into a 5km canal system just outside Siquirres. **Centro Turístico Las Tilapias** (☎8398-1517, 2768-9293; 30min canal tours from US$10, cabinas d with fan/air-con US$45/50; 9am-7pm; P) is now teeming with exotic nature, from birds, turtles and sloths to monkeys, frogs and more; Chito runs tours around his thriving canal network. There's also a tasty restaurant-bar here and some charming rustic *cabinas* perched above a lagoon and the canals. Take a taxi (US$3) or ask locals for careful directions, as it's tricky to find.

Getting There & Away

Siquirres has two main bus terminals. The one on the southeastern corner of the park serves **Limón** (US$2.40; 1hr; every 20-40min 5am-8:10pm Mon-Sat, 5:30am-8.10pm Sun) and **San José** (US$3; 2hr; every 30min-2½hr 2am-6:50pm). Buses for **Turrialba** (US$2.30; 1hr 50 min; every 1-1½hr 5:30am-7pm Mon, Fri & Sat. every 2hr 5:30am-6.30pm Tue-Thu, every 1-1½hr 6am-7pm Sun) leave from a separate terminal on the north side of the park.

There are hourly Tracasa buses to **Guápiles** from 5:40am 7pm.

Puerto Limón

POP 60,148

Puerto Limón is the biggest city on Costa Rica's Caribbean coast, the capital of Limón province, and a hardworking port that sits removed from the rest of the country. Cruise ships deposit passengers here between October and May, but around these parts, business is measured by truckloads of fruit, not busloads of tourists: don't expect any pampering.

Nonetheless, Limón can be a good base for adventurous urban explorers. There's a couple of wonderful restaurants, and the Regional Heritage Museum, a tribute the the multi-ethnic mix on which the city was built, sits above the post office; it was being re-done in late 2019. There's hope that a remodel of the airport will bring in more international flights.

Puerto Limón

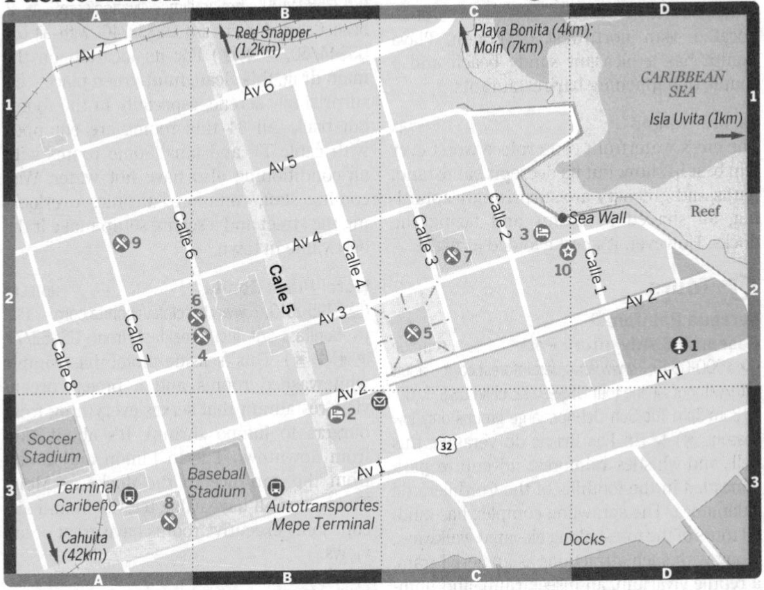

Puerto Limón

Sights

1 Parque Vargas ... D2

Sleeping

2 Hotel Miami ... B3
3 Park Hotel ... C2

Eating

4 Caribbean Kalisi Coffee Shop ... B2
5 Central Market ... C2
6 Macrobiótica Bionatura ... B2
7 Más X Menos ... C2
8 Palí ... A3
9 Soda El Patty ... A2

Entertainment

10 Tsunami Sushi ... C2

History

Until the 1850s the most frequent visitors to Limón were pirates (replaced today by cruise-ship tourists), who used the area's natural deep-water bays as hideouts. At the time, the country's main port was in Puntarenas, on the Pacific coast, but when the railroad arrived in the late 19th century Limón blossomed into a full-blown trade hub. The city ultimately served as the key export point for the country's newest agribusiness: bananas.

Beginning in 1913, a series of blights shut down many Caribbean *fincas* (farms) and a large portion of the area's banana production moved to the southern Pacific coast. Afro-Caribbean workers, however, couldn't follow the jobs, as they were forbidden to leave the province. Stranded in the least-developed part of Costa Rica, many turned to subsistence farming, fishing or managing small-scale cacao plantations. Others organized and staged bloody strikes against the powerful United Fruit company. Fed up with the status quo, Limón provided key support to revolutionary José Figueres during the 1948 civil war. This act was rewarded the following year when Figueres, who was then president, enacted a constitution that granted black people full citizenship and the right to work and travel freely throughout Costa Rica.

Even though segregation was officially dismantled, Limón continues to live with its legacy. The province was the last to get paved roads and the last to get electricity (areas south of the city weren't on the grid until the late 1970s), and the region has chronically higher crime and unemployment rates than the rest of the country.

Sights

Playa Bonita BEACH

Located 4km northwest of Limón, Playa Bonita has a pleasant sandy beach and a couple of happening bar-restaurants.

Parque Vargas PARK

The city's waterfront centerpiece won't ever win best in show, but its decrepit bandstand, paths and greenery are surprisingly appealing, all shaded by palms and facing the docks. However, it's best avoided at night.

Tours

Veragua Rainforest Research & Adventure Park ECOTOUR

(4000-0949; www.veraguarainforest.com; adult with/without zipline tour US$99/72, child US$75/60; 8am-3pm Tue-Sun Oct-Apr, large groups only low season;) In Las Brisas de Veragua, this bells-and-whistles rainforest adventure park is nestled in the foothills of the Cordillera de Talamanca. The sprawling complex has guided tours of the forest along elevated walkways, along with such attractions as an aerial tram, a reptile vivarium, an insectarium, and hummingbird and butterfly gardens. Since 2016 solar panels provide 90% of the park's power.

There's also a zipline canopy tour. Installations include a cafeteria and gift shop. Many of the attractions are wheelchair accessible. To get here, take the signed turnoff south from Hwy 32 at Liverpool, 12km west of Puerto Limón.

Festivals & Events

Día de la Raza CULTURAL

(Columbus Day; Oct 12) When the city can afford it, Puerto Limón celebrates Día de la Raza with a boisterous week of *Carnaval* festivities, including live music, dancing and a big Saturday parade. During this time, book hotels in advance.

Festival Flores de la Diáspora Africana CULTURAL

(www.facebook.com/festivaldiasporacr; late Aug) While this celebration of Afro-Caribbean culture centers on Puerto Limón, the festival sponsors events throughout the province and in San José. It held its 20th iteration in 2018.

Sleeping

Limón offers nothing remotely upscale; it has only budget and midrange business-like options. For something more appealing, head to nearby Playa Bonita.

Hotel Miami HOTEL $

(2758-0490; hmiamilimon@yahoo.com; Av 2, btwn Calles 4 & 5; s/d US$32/40, with air-con US$44/60;) For its location on the main drag, this clean, mint-green place feels surprisingly serene, especially in the rooms out back. All 34 tidy rooms are equipped with cable TV and fans. Some rooms with air-conditioning also have hot water. Welcoming staff, common balconies overlooking the street and a secure setup make it the best value in town.

Hotel Playa Bonita HOTEL $$

(2795-1010; www.hotelplayabonita.com; Playa Bonita; s/d incl breakfast from US$52/77;) This seaside hotel has simple whitewashed rooms and a breezy ocean-view restaurant that serves everything from burgers to jumbo shrimp. It's about 5km from downtown Puerto Limón and 2.5km from the entrance to the docks at Moín. The rooms all have cable television and air-con; some executive rooms have great ocean views.

Park Hotel HOTEL $$

(2798-0555; Av 3, btwn Calles 1 & 2; d incl breakfast US$81;) Downtown Limón's most attractive hotel has 32 rooms in a faded yellow building that faces the ocean. Tiled rooms are tidy and sport clean bathrooms with hot water; superior and deluxe units come with ocean views and balconies. The hotel also houses the swankiest restaurant in the town center.

Eating

Find cheap meals at the *sodas* in the **central market** (Av 2 btwn Calles 3 & 4; 6am-8pm Mon-Fri). You can get groceries at the large **Más X Menos** (cnr Av 3 & Calle 3; 7am-9pm, to 8pm Sun), or at the **Palí** (cnr Calle 7 & Av 1; 8am-9pm Fri-Mon, to 8:30pm Tue-Thu) next to the Terminal Caribeño.

Soda El Patty CARIBBEAN $

(2798-3407; cnr Av 5 & Calle 7; patí US$1.50, mains US$2-5; 7am-7pm Mon-Sat) This beloved nine-table Caribbean eatery, with soccer memorabilia on the walls, serves up delicious *patí* (flaky beef turnovers stuffed with onion, spices and Panamanian peppers), along with sweet plantain tarts and heaping plates of rice-and-beans (the spicier, more flavorful version of the country's traditional *casado*).

Macrobiótica Bionatura VEGETARIAN $
(2798-2020; Calle 6, btwn Avs 3 & 4; 8am-6:15pm Mon-Fri, to 5:15pm Sat;) This macrobiotic grocery store sells healthy vegetarian foods, vitamins and some things made of soy.

★Caribbean Kalisi Coffee Shop CARIBBEAN $$
(2758-3249; Calle 6, btwn Avs 3 & 4; mains from US$10; 7am-8pm Mon-Sat, 8am-3pm Sun) Belly up to the cafeteria-style counter at this friendly family spot and cobble together a plate of coconut rice, red beans and whatever Caribbean meat and veggies are cooking. Miss Roena Brown's oxtail stew is simply to die for, washed down with a glass of sorrel (Jamaican hibiscus-ginger drink). The chewy cassava pudding ain't bad, either.

If you cook for the president, your food must be damned good. Check the pictures of Roena with former Costa Rican head of state Laura Chinchilla.

Red Snapper CARIBBEAN $$
(2758-7613; near Calle Los Miranda; mains US$15-25; 11am-10pm;) Head honchos for Limón's new port project (p152) often lunch at this scenic Caribbean restaurant perched on a mountainside overlooking the city and coastline. The open-air dining room has some TVs and a convivial vibe, making it an ideal spot to catch a soccer game and devour a whole fried fish.

The local Humphreys family purchased it recently from the former Italian owner. It's on a lane near Calle Los Miranda, and can be tricky to find.

Reina's SEAFOOD $$
(2795-0879; mains US$9-15; 9am-8pm) On the beach at Playa Bonita, Reina's has loud music, good vibes and plenty of *mariscos* (seafood) plus a laundry list of cocktails.

Drinking & Nightlife

Rough bars are dotted around Parque Vargas and a few blocks west. The more appealing **Tsunami Sushi** (2758-8628; Av 3, btwn Calles 1 & 2; 11am-2am Fri & Sat, 11:30am-11:45pm Tue-Thu) has a good cocktail list and live music. There are better Caribbean towns to go out in. Playa Bonita might be a bit more welcoming.

Information

SAFE TRAVEL

Though police presence has ramped up noticeably in recent years, pickpockets can be a problem, particularly in the market and along the sea wall. People also get mugged here, so stick to well-lit main streets at night, avoiding the sea wall and Parque Vargas. If driving, park in a guarded lot overnight and remove everything from the car (as you would in the rest of the country).

It's worth noting that most of the violent incidents recorded in Limón relate to organized crime and those involved in drug and human trafficking, and do not affect travelers.

INTERNET ACCESS

The internet connection is reasonably good in Limón. Most guesthouses have wi-fi.

BUSES FROM PUERTO LIMÓN

DESTINATION	COST (US$)	DURATION (HR)	TERMINAL	DEPARTURES
Bribrí	4	2.5	Autotransportes Mepe Terminal	hourly 5am-7pm
Cahuita	3	1-1½	Autotransportes Mepe Terminal	Mon-Fri hourly 5:30 am-7pm
Guápiles (Tracasa)	4	1½	Terminal Caribeño	frequent 5am-6:20pm
Manzanillo	5	2	Autotransportes Mepe Terminal	Mon-Fri every 1-2hr 5am-5:15pm
Puerto Viejo de Talamanca	4	1½-2	Autotransportes Mepe Terminal	Mon-Fri every hr 5am-7pm
San José (Autotransportes Caribeños)	6	3	Terminal Caribeño	every 30min-1hr 4:30am-7pm
Siquirres (Tracasa)	3	1	Terminal Caribeño	hourly 5am-7pm
Sixaola	5.50	3	Autotransportes Mepe Terminal	hourly 5am-7pm

NEW INFRASTRUCTURE FOR CARIBBEAN PORTS

Two major new infrastructure developments will certainly shape the future of Limón.

The construction of a US$1-billion container port in Moín was completed in February 2019 by the multinational corporation APM. The Dutch-based company will control the port for 30 years.

Still in process, but facing delays is a Chinese-and-Costa Rican–financed US$495-million initiative to widen a 107km section of Hwy 32 between Río Frío and downtown Limón to four lanes, including 26km of bike paths.

While it's estimated that 80% of the country's exports make their way through the Caribbean ports, it is unclear whether the economic benefits of these projects will be shared by the local population. Indeed, plans for the container port sparked massive protests in Limón and Moín by dockworkers-union members, who fear that privatization of the port will undermine rather than improve their standard of living. Others believe that it will bring jobs and infrastructure to the area – only time will tell.

A demonstration of the port's potential took place in November 2019, when the *MSC Sara Elena* docked at Moin, the largest container ship to ever berth in Costa Rica, measuring 300m long and with a capacity of 8000 shipping containers.

MEDICAL SERVICES

Hospital Tony Facio (☎2758-2222) Serves the entire province. It's northeast of the center.

MONEY

If you're traveling onward to Parismina or Tortuguero, Limón is a good opportunity to get cash and phonecards (neither village has an ATM).

Banco de Costa Rica (☎2211-1111; cnr Av 2 & Calle 1; ⏲9am-4pm Mon, to 6pm Tue-Fri, 8:30am-3:30pm Sat) Exchanges US dollars and has an ATM.

Scotiabank (cnr Av 3 & Calle 2; ⏲9am-5pm Mon-Fri, to 1pm Sat) Exchanges cash and has a 24-hour ATM that dispenses US dollars.

POST

Post office (Correos de Costa Rica; Calle 4, btwn Avs 1 & 2; ⏲8am-5pm Mon-Fri, to noon Sat)

Getting There & Away

Puerto Limón is the transportation hub of the Caribbean coast, particularly with the recent widening of the San José–Limón (Hwy 32) artery.

Cruise ships dock in Limón, but smaller passenger boats bound for Parismina and Tortuguero use the port at Moín, about 7km west of town.

Buses from all points west arrive at **Terminal Caribeño** (Av 2, btwn Calles 7 & 8), just west of the baseball stadium. Buses to all points south depart from the **Autotransportes Mepe Terminal** (☎2758-1572; Calle 6, btwn Avs 1 & 2), on the eastern side of the stadium. Note that buses are less frequent on the weekends.

Moín

Most visitors come to Moín for connections to Parismina or Tortuguero. Located 8km northwest of Puerto Limón, the town is a transportation dock for trucks and boat transfers along the connecting canals and rivers.

Tours

All Rankin's Tours BOATING
(☎2709-8101, WhatsApp 8815-5175; www.allrankinslodge.com; round trips to Tortuguero from US$70) For leisurely boat rides to Tortuguero, choose these tours run by longtime resident Willis Rankin. He can spot a bevy of wildlife en route, but the pretty journey alone is worth the trip. Willis also offers deals for his once-rustic lodge (which recently added a swimming pool) near Tortuguero's airstrip.

Tortuguero Wildlife Tour & Transportation BOATING
(William Guerrero, TUCA; ☎8371-2323, 2798-7027; www.tortuguero-wildlife.com; one-way tours to Tortuguero from US$35) Small, well-regarded company run by master sloth-spotter William Guerrero and his wife. It's ideal if you want a leisurely ride to Tortuguero with plenty of pit stops to see wildlife and have lunch.

Getting There & Away

BOAT

The journey by boat from Moín to Tortuguero can take anywhere from three to five hours. It's worth taking your time. As you wind through these jungle canals on an Indiana Jones–style adventure, you're likely to spot howler monkeys, crocodiles, two- or three-toed sloths and an amazing array of wading birds, including roseate spoonbills.

Tourist-boat schedules exist in theory only and change frequently depending on demand. If you're feeling lucky, you can just show up in Moín in the morning and pay a premium to get on one of the outgoing tour boats (there's often at least one departure at 10am). You're better off reserving, though, particularly during slower seasons when boats don't travel the route on a daily basis. If the canal becomes blocked by water hyacinths or logjams, the route might be closed altogether. Call ahead for departure times and reservations.

One-way fares generally run between US$35 and US$45 to Tortuguero, US$70 to US$80 round-trip, and between US$30 and US$60 one way/round-trip to Parismina. Benjamín Gómez is a recommended guy to look for at the docks (phone 8928-0857). Try in Tortuguero (p165) for additional operators.

BUS

Tracasa buses to Moín from Puerto Limón (roughly US$1, 20 minutes) depart from Terminal Caribeño hourly from 5:30am to 6:30pm (less frequently on Saturday and Sunday). Get off the bus before it goes over the bridge.

Caribe Shuttle and **Tropical Wind** (☎8327-0317, 8313-7164; Moín; one way/return US$35/70) operate almost-daily shuttles between Tortuguero and Moín in high season.

NORTHERN CARIBBEAN

This is the wettest region in Costa Rica, a network of rivers and canals that is home to diminutive fishing villages and slick sportfishing camps, raw rainforest and all-inclusive resorts – not to mention plenty of wading birds and sleepy sloths.

Most significantly, the area's long, wild beaches serve as the protected nesting grounds for three kinds of sea turtle. More green turtles are born here than anywhere else in the world.

Parismina

For a sense of what Costa Rica's Caribbean coast was like prior to the arrival of mass tourism, jump ship at this sleepy coastal fishing village, wedged between the Canales de Tortuguero and the Caribbean Sea.

Parismina is also a great place to view turtles and aid in their conservation while avoiding the crowds of Tortuguero. Though fewer turtle species and numbers nest here, it's possible to spot leatherbacks. greens and hawksbills. There's also a turtle hatchery at which volunteers can help guard the eggs. Sportfishing is the other traditional tourist draw in this area.

Activities

Aside from turtle spotting, you can hike, horse ride and learn about coconuts here at Green Gold Ecolodge. Río Parismina Lodge (p154) organizes package sportfishing expeditions from the USA.

Asociación Salvemos Las Tortugas de Parismina VOLUNTEERING
(ASTOP, Save the Turtles of Parismina; ☎2798-2220, 8357-2862; www.parisminaturtles.org; by arrangement Mar-Sep) This grassroots turtle-protection organization has strong community support and employs former poachers as 'turtle guides.' It maintains a guarded turtle hatchery on a section of 6km beach. Travelers can volunteer as guards to patrol the beaches alongside local turtle guides. Day volunteers pay a one-time US$50 registration fee, then US$10 per patrol (five-patrol minimum).

ASTOP also organizes homestays (US$40 per night including three meals and patrols; US$20 without meals) and can arrange horseback-riding trips, bike rentals, turtle-watching tours and wildlife-viewing excursions by boat.

Turtle Love VOLUNTEERING
(☎8704-0505; http://turtleslove.org; Parismina) A team of biologists working south of the Pacuare river mouth (ASTOP patrols the northern part), Turtle Love protects and monitors 5km of nesting beach for green, leatherback, and hawksbill turtles, and has cut down significantly on poaching in this area. They can arrange homestays for volunteers. President Renato Bruno has received international recognition for his work.

Sleeping & Eating

Green Gold Ecolodge LODGE $
(☎8697-2322, 8647-0691; dm adult/child US$20/10, incl 3 meals US$50/30) About 3km south of the dock, this simple solar- and generator-powered retreat, steps from the beach and surrounded by 36 hectares of jungle, is an authentic rainforest hideaway. Run by the charming (and bilingual) Jason and Juliana, it has rustic but comfortable facilities including eight screened-in upstairs

rooms (some with dorm beds), a shared open-air kitchen and shared bathrooms.

Jason can arrange hiking, horse riding, fishing and coconut tours. To get there, walk around 40 minutes from the village, arrange for a truck ride from town (around US$10) or arrive by private boat (US$15 from Caño Blanco); reservations recommended. BBQ meals can be arranged.

Río Parismina Lodge LODGE **$$$**
(☎in USA 800-338-5688, in USA 210-824-4442; www.riop.com; 3-day acommodation and fishing packages from US$2600;) Top-of-the-line spot on 20 hectares of jungle, with swimming pool, Jacuzzi, English-speaking guides, and both river and ocean boats. Meals, beverages, internal charter flights, boat, guide, equipment, lures and daily laundry service included in rates.

A true fisher's delight: four world-record snook have been caught here.

Soda Rancho La Palma SODA **$**
(☎8550-7243; casados US$7; ⏲6am-8pm Mon-Sat) Right next to the dock, no-nonsense doña Amelia serves up fresh, tasty fish and meat *casados,* plus rice and beans cooked in a coconut Creole-style sauce. She also keeps the small plaster statue of the Virgin that is paraded during a boat procession in July.

ℹ Information

There are no banks or post offices in Parismina. Credit cards and wire transfers are sometimes accepted, but better to make sure you bring enough cash.

There's not much in the way of public internet access in Parismina. If you want good service, it's best to connect to a national phone company such as Kolbi for more reliable wi-fi.

You can usually buy phone cards in town, but they sometimes sell out.

ℹ Getting There & Away

Parismina is only accessible by boat or charter flight.

The only scheduled boat service is to Caño Blanco (for transfer to Siquirres). Water taxis (US$2, 10 minutes) leave from the Parismina dock at 5:30am, 1:30pm and 5:30pm on weekdays, and at 5:30am, 9am, 1:30pm and 5:30pm on weekends. A bus will be waiting at Caño Blanco's dock to continue the journey to Siquirres (US$2.20, two hours); you'll wait roughly 10 minutes for it to leave. There are toilet facilities and a snack shop at Caño Blanco. The boat and bus drivers only accept the local currency: colones.

For journeys from Siquirres to Parismina, walk to the smaller bus terminal, 200m from the main terminal toward the football pitch, next to the bakery La Castellana, and take the bus to Caño Blanco (US$2.20, two hours); it leaves at 4:30am, 7am, noon and 3:15 pm. On arrival at Caño Blanco a boat should be waiting at the dock and will take you to Parismina (US$2.60, 15 minutes).

If you are in, or going to, Tortuguero (via Moín), it's possible to reserve a seat on one of the tourist boats that travel between the two destinations, but planning is essential. Note that it may take 24 to 48 hours to secure transportation (around US$25 to US$35), as Parismina is not a regular stop. Call one of the boat companies in Moín or Tortuguero directly, or ask the friendly folk at Soda Rancho La Palma to help you book.

From Tortuguero direct to Parismina, Costa Rica Roots Tours (www.costaricarootstours.com) has a boat leaving the main dock at 1pm (US$12, one hour).

TURTLE BEACH TRAGEDY

The Caribbean's turtle-conservation community suffered a devastating blow on the night of May 30, 2013, when 26-year-old Costa Rican environmentalist Jairo Mora Sandoval was murdered while patrolling a stretch of Moín beach near Puerto Limón.

While many communities along the coast have successfully engaged former poachers in guiding and conservation work, turtle eggs continue to be prized on the black market for their supposed aphrodisiac qualities. The remote section of beach where Sandoval was working is insalubrious, with a history of drug running.

Mora's death sparked strong international and domestic protest, with calls for a beefed-up police presence and stronger conservation measures. In 2016, maximum sentences were given to four poachers found guilty of the murder. The saga has been devastating to Costa Rica's sea-turtle conservation movement, but some bold activists still patrol the beaches on the Caribbean coast.

In 2013 the environmental group Sea Shepherd Conservation Society named one of their boats *MY Jairo Mora Sandoval* in the activist's honor.

Around Tortuguero

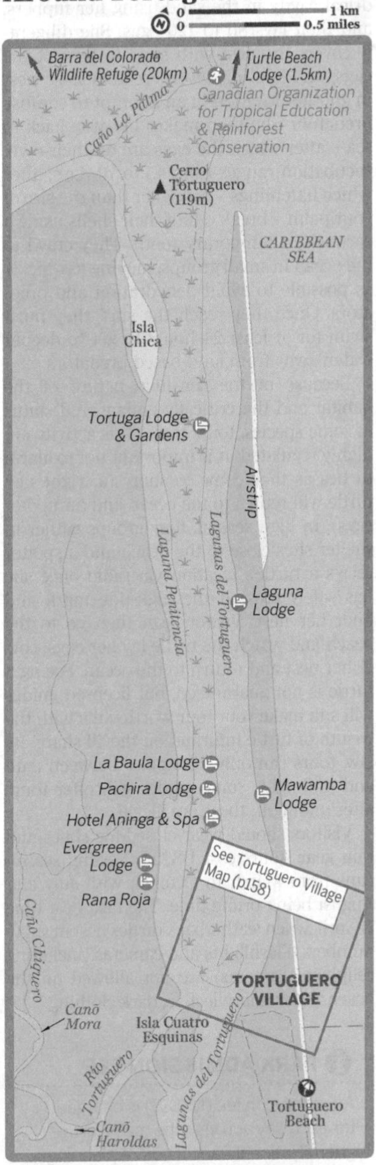

Parque Nacional Tortuguero

Humid **Tortuguero** (☎2709-8086; www.acto.go.cr; US$15; ⏰6am-6pm, last entry 4pm) is a 311-sq-km coastal park that serves as the most important breeding ground of the green sea turtle. With annual rainfall of up to 6000mm, it is one of the wettest areas in the country. The protected area extends into the Caribbean Sea, covering about 52 sq km of marine habitat. In other words, plan on spending quality time in a boat.

The famed **Canales de Tortuguero** are the introduction to this park. Created to connect a series of lagoons and meandering rivers in 1974, this engineering marvel allowed inland navigation between Limón and coastal villages in something sturdier than a dugout canoe. Regular flights service the village of Tortuguero – but if you fly in, you'll be missing half the fun. The leisurely taxi-boat ride, through banana plantations and wild jungle, is equal parts recreation and transportation; and yes, you'll get a bit wet!

Activities

Most visitors come to watch sea turtles lay eggs on the wild beaches. The area is more than just turtles, though: Tortuguero teems with wildlife. You may find sloths and howler monkeys in the treetops, tiny frogs and green iguanas scurrying among buttress roots, plus mighty tarpons, alligators and endangered manatees swimming in the waters.

Turtle-Watching

The area attracts four of the world's seven species of sea turtle, making it a crucial habitat for these massive reptiles. It will come as little surprise, then, that these hatching grounds gave birth to the sea-turtle-conservation movement. The Caribbean Conservation Corporation (now Sea Turtle Conservancy; p162), the first program of its kind in the world, has continuously monitored turtle populations here since 1959. Today green sea turtles are increasing in numbers along this coast, but the leatherback, hawksbill and loggerhead are in decline. (Numbers are difficult to divine because the turtles only lay eggs every two to three years.)

Most female turtles share a nesting instinct that drives them to return to the beach of their birth (their natal beach) in order to lay their eggs. (Only the leatherback returns to a more general region instead of a specific beach.) During their lifetimes, they will usually nest every two to three years and, depending on the species, may come ashore to lay eggs 10 times in one season. Often, a turtle's ability to reproduce depends on the ecological health of this original habitat.

The female turtle digs a perfect cylindrical cavity in the sand using her flippers, and then lays 80 to 120 eggs. She diligently covers the nest with sand to protect the eggs, and she may even create a false nest in another location in an attempt to confuse predators. She then makes her way back to sea – after which the eggs are on their own. Incubation ranges from 45 to 70 days, after which hatchlings – no bigger than the size of your palm – break out of their shells using a caruncle, a temporary tooth. They crawl to the ocean in small groups, moving as quickly as possible to avoid dehydration and predators. Once they reach the surf, they must swim for at least 24 hours to get to deeper water, away from land-based predators.

Because of the sensitive nature of the habitat and the critically endangered status of some species, tours to see this activity are highly regulated. It is important not to alarm turtles as they come to shore (a frightened turtle will return to the ocean and dump her eggs). In high season, tour groups gather in shelter sites close to the beach and a spotter relays a turtle's location via radio once she has safely crossed the high-tide mark and built her nest. Visitors can then go to the beach and watch the turtle lay her eggs, cover her nest and return to the ocean. Seeing a turtle is not guaranteed, but licensed guides will still make your tour worthwhile with the wealth of turtle information they'll share. By law, tours can only take place between 8am and midnight. Some guides will offer tours after midnight; these are illegal.

Visitors should wear closed-toe shoes and rain gear. Tours cost US$25. Nesting season runs from March to October, with July and August being prime time. The next best time is April, when leatherback turtles nest in small numbers. Flashlights and cameras (including cellphone cameras) are not allowed on the beach. Wear nonreflective, dark clothing.

> **PARK ADMISSION FEE**
>
> An admission fee (US$15) is charged for each day you visit the main Tortuguero National Park. If you're planning multiple activities within the park, you can save a few colones by concentrating them in a single day; for example, if you go out on a boat tour in the early morning, then hike the walking trail that same afternoon, meaning you'll only pay the admission fee once.

Other Wildlife-Watching

More than 400 bird species, both resident and migratory, have been recorded in Tortuguero – it's a birdwatchers' paradise. Due to the wet habitat, the park is especially rich in waders, including egrets, jacanas and 14 types of heron, as well as species such as kingfishers, toucans and the great curassow (a type of jungle peacock known locally as the *pavón*). The great green macaw is a highlight, most common from December to April, when the almond trees are fruiting. In September and October, look for flocks of migratory species such as eastern kingbirds, barn swallows and purple martins.

Certain species of mammal are particularly evident in Tortuguero, especially mantled howler monkeys, the Central American spider monkey and the white-faced capuchin. If you've got a reliable pair of binoculars and a good guide, you can usually see both two- and three-toed sloths. In addition, normally shy neotropical river otters are reasonably habituated to boats. Harder to spot are timid West Indian manatees and dolphins, which swim into the brackish canals looking for food. The park is also home to big cats such as jaguars and ocelots, but these are savvy, nocturnal animals – sightings are very rare.

Most wildlife-watching tours are done by boat. To get the best from Tortuguero, go out following a heavy rain, when all the wildlife comes out to sunbathe. It is also highly recommended to take tours by canoe or kayak – these smaller, silent craft will allow you to get into the park's less trafficked nooks and crannies.

Boating

Four aquatic trails wind their way through Parque Nacional Tortuguero, inviting waterborne exploration. **Río Tortuguero** acts as the entranceway to the network of trails. This wide, beautiful river is often covered with water lilies and is frequented by aquatic birds such as herons, kingfishers and anhingas – the latter of which is known as the snakebird for the way its slim, winding neck pokes out of the water when it swims.

Caño Chiquero and **Canõ Mora** are two narrower waterways with good wildlife-spotting opportunities. According to park regulations, only kayaks, canoes and silent electric boats are allowed in these areas (boatmen claim that these are sometimes blocked and not well maintained by the parks service). Caño Chiquero is thick with vegetation, especially red *guácimo* trees and epiphytes. Black turtles and green iguanas like to hang out here. Caño Mora is about 3km long but only 10m wide, so it feels as if it's straight out of *The Jungle Book*. **Caño Haroldas** is actually an artificially constructed canal, but that doesn't stop the creatures – such as Jesus Christ lizards and caimans – from inhabiting its tranquil waters.

Canoe rental and boat tours are available in Tortuguero village (p159).

Hiking

Behind Cuatro Esquinas ranger station, the well-trodden **main trail** is a muddy, 2km out-and-back hike that traverses the tropical humid forest and parallels a stretch of beach. Green parrots and several species of monkey are commonly sighted here. The short trail is well marked. Rubber boots are required and can be rented at hotels and near the park entrance.

A second hiking option, **Cerro Tortuguero Trail**, is also available. To reach the trailhead, guests have to take a boat to the town of San Francisco, north of Tortuguero village, where they will disembark at another ranger station and buy a ticket (US$7, plus US$4 for the 15- to 20-minute round-trip boat ride). The trail – now a plank-covered, easy-to-navigate walkway – then takes visitors 1.8km (480 steps!) up a hill for a view of the surrounding lagoon, forest and ocean (it's the highest point on the Caribbean coast). You can arrange a local guide (from US$35) at the docks to take you on the trip.

Information

Park headquarters is at **Cuatro Esquinas** (2709-8086; www.acto.go.cr; 6am-4pm), just south of Tortuguero village. This is a helpful ranger station with maps and info. For canoe tours from this station, new rules limit the number of boats and the amount of time they spend on the canals. Boats are permitted in the park between 6am and 3pm. Reserve early for the canal tour, especially in high season.

Warning: boats follow each other in a copy-cat pattern, so you may not feel very tranquil for very long, particularly with large groups in pursuit of wildlife sightings.

Jalova Station (6am-4pm) is on the canal at the southern entrance to the national park; it's accessible from Parismina by boat. Although fewer tourists stop here, there's a small visitors center, a short nature trail and a bathroom.

TURTLE MOTHER

The legend of Turtle Mother was born on Cerro Tortuguero, the highest point on the Caribbean coast. A stone carved into the shape of a turtle was said to turn its head inland each year to signal the arrival of the nesting season. Modern-day research indicates that rock carvings in the highlands of Central America, including here, register powerful magnetic readings, and that turtles indeed use magnetic fields to return to their natal beaches. For further reading, check out *Search for the Great Turtle Mother* by Jack Rudloe.

Getting There & Away

The park entrance is a short walk south of the village of Tortuguero (the most common entry point) and is also accessible by boat from Parismina.

Tortuguero Village

POP 906

Located within the confines of Parque Nacional Tortuguero, accessible only by air or water, this bustling little village with strong Afro-Caribbean roots is best known for attracting hordes of sea turtles (the name Tortuguero means 'turtle catcher'). While peak turtle season is in July and August, the park and village attract travelers year-round.

Activities

Boating & Canoeing

Nonmotorized boat transport offers the best chance of spotting wildlife while exploring the waterways. Numerous businesses rent kayaks and canoes and offer boat tours.

Hiking

Hikers can follow a self-guided trail (adjacent to Cuatro Esquinas ranger station) that runs parallel to the beach via a well-worn coastal path north from the village to the airport, or walk the beach during daylight hours. Other hiking opportunities exist in and around the park but require the services of a guide. Note: night hiking in the national park is not allowed, although there are guided night walks available in Tortuguero village.

Tortuguero Village

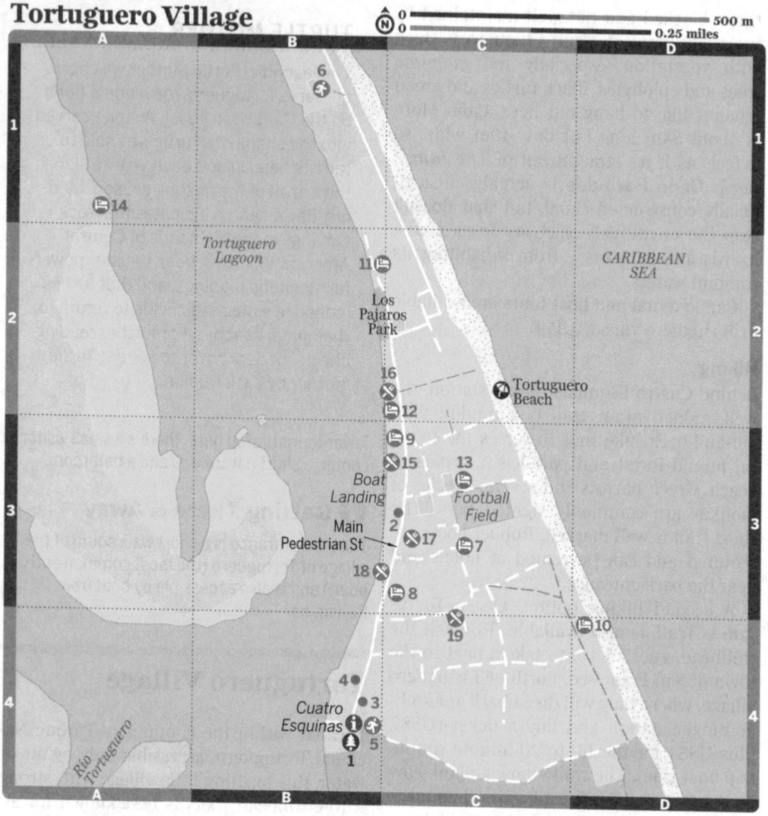

Tortuguero Village

Sights
1 Parque Nacional Tortuguero B4

Activities, Courses & Tours
2 Asociación de Guías de Tortuguero C3
3 Casa Cecropia B4
4 Castor Hunter Thomas B4
5 Jenifor Masaje B4
6 Sea Turtle Conservancy B1
Tortuguero Keysi Tours .... (see 17)

Sleeping
7 Aracari Garden Hostel C3
8 Cabinas Tortuguero C3
9 Casa Marbella C3
10 El Icaco D4
11 Hotel Miss Junie B2
12 Hotel River View C2
13 La Casona C3
14 Toucan & Tarpon Lodge A1

Eating
15 Budda Cafe C3
16 Dorling Bakery C2
17 Mi Niño C3
Miss Junie's .... (see 11)
18 Sunrise Restaurant B3
19 Taylor's Place C4

Spas

Jenifor Masaje SPA
(☎8317-9035, 8881-2006; massages $65-75, manicure/pedicure $30-50) Tortuguero local Jenifor is well schooled in various massage techniques including deep tissue, hot rocks, neck and back, for those afternoons following a morning of kayaking along the canals. From La Taberna head 50m south, 25m east, then a further 100m south: you can't miss it! Mani-pedi combos fix nails broken by stray canoe paddles.

Tours

Guides post signs all over town advertising their services for canal tours and turtle walks. The most convenient places to arrange tours are at local hotels and at the official Asociación de Guías de Tortuguero kiosk.

Note that a 6am tour isn't always best, because *everyone* goes out then. Maybe sleep in and go at 8am, when the boat traffic has died down a bit.

Tinamon Tours TOURS
(☎8842-6561; www.tinamontours.de; 2½hr hikes from US$25) Zoologist and 20-plus-year Tortuguero resident Barbara Hartung offers hiking, canoeing, cultural and turtle tours in German, English, French or Spanish. Tour packages, including two nights' accommodations, breakfast, a canoe tour and a hike, start at US$100 per person. Note that you'll need to pay the US$15 entrance fee for park (p155) hikes.

Riverboat Francesca Nature Tours FISHING
(☎2226-0986; www.tortuguerocanals.com; 2-day nature packages from US$225, per hour US$65-75) A highly recommended company run by Modesto and Fran Watson, Riverboat Francesca offers sportfishing (river and ocean) as well as wildlife-viewing tours through the national park.

Castor Hunter Thomas TOURS
(☎8870-8634; www.castorhunter.blogspot.com; nature tours per person from US$35) Excellent local guide and lifelong Tortuguero resident Castor Hunter Thomas has led hikes, turtle tours and canoe tours for more than 20 years. There's also a cool restaurant right next to his house.

Casa Cecropia FOOD & DRINK
(☎8829-8523, 2709-8196; www.facebook.com/casacecropia; 2hr tour US$25; ⊙tours 10:30am & 4pm) At the entrance to Tortuguero National Park (p155) a little hut offers the perfect indoor activity if it's raining. Biologist Rafael teaches the history of chocolate, including how it's produced, and even lets you have a go at peeling and grinding cacao beans. Then you get to gobble some chocolate and try a delicious chocolatey drink.

Asociación de Guías de Tortuguero TOURS
(☎2767-0836; www.asoprotur.com; ⊙6am-7pm) The most convenient place to arrange tours is at the official Asociación de Guías de Tortuguero kiosk by the boat landing. Made up of scores of local guides, the association offers tours in English, French, German and other languages. Although guides are all certified to lead tours in the park, the quality of the tours can vary.

Note that tour departure times can vary with the weather.

Rates at the time of research were US$30 per person for a two-hour turtle tour and US$25 for a canoe tour. Other options include two-hour walking (US$20 to US$25), birdwatching (US$35) and fishing (from US$80, minimum two people) tours. Tours also involve an extra US$15 admission fee to the park (not required for the fishing tour). A newish tour offers a view from Cerro Tortuguero (US$35).

Sleeping

Tortuguero has accommodation options in different places around its waterways; be aware that at the more secluded hotels you may need a boat to get into the main village. The most upscale lodges and *cabinas* (cabins) are outside the main village. In the village itself you'll find simpler *cabinas* charging US$20 and up for a private room. Recently, some swank has been added to existing accommodations, such as air-con, televisions and swimming pools.

In Tortuguero Village

★**Hotel Miss Junie** CABINA $
(☎2709-8029; www.iguanaverdetours.com/lodge.htm; incl breakfast s/d standard US$50/55, superior US$65/75; 📶) Tortuguero's longest-established lodging, Miss Junie's is set on spacious palm-shaded grounds strewn with hammocks and wooden armchairs. Spotless wood-paneled rooms in a tropical plantation-style building are tastefully decorated with wood accents and bright bedspreads. Upstairs balconies overlook the sea or lagoon; the restaurant (p164) downstairs serves delicious food. It's at the northern end of the town's main street. Kayak rental is available.

Aracari Garden Hostel HOSTEL $
(☎2767-2246; www.aracarigarden.com; dm US$13, r US$30-45; 📶) This tangerine-colored hostel on the south side of the soccer field has eight sparkling rooms and relaxing shared spaces surrounded by fruit trees. A new building features two additional rooms with common kitchen and bathroom. There's free coffee, a shared open-air kitchen, book exchange and hammocks. The ocean is 50m away: you can feel it in your bones.

Turtles of the Caribbean

One of the most moving experiences for visitors to the Caribbean coast is turtle-watching on its wild beaches. Witnessing the return of a massive turtle to its natal beach and its laborious nesting ritual is solemn and magical. Four species of sea turtle – green, leatherback, hawksbill and loggerhead – nest along this coast, and all of them are endangered or threatened.

A Population in Peril

It takes many years for sea turtles to mature and reproduce, so their populations are vulnerable to environmental hazards such as pollution and poaching. Conservation efforts, including guarding hatchlings from predators and providing incentives for local communities to protect turtles and their eggs, are crucial to their survival. Volunteer opportunities are plentiful along the Caribbean coast. Tasks range from beach patrols, data collection and tagging, to moving eggs to hatcheries and hatchling release.

Planning a Tour

Due to the sensitive habitat and critically endangered status of some species, turtle-nesting tours are highly regulated. Groups must be accompanied by licensed guides, who ensure that the turtles are able to lay their eggs in peace and that nests are not disturbed. Nesting season runs from March to October. July and August are the most active months for green turtles; leatherback turtles arrive in April.

Depending on when you visit, you may find yourself watching a mother hauling herself onto the beach, laboriously digging a nest with her flippers and hatching dozens of ping-pong-ball-sized eggs,

INGA SPENCE/GETTY IMAGES ©

ANDIPANTZ/GETTY IMAGES ©

KEVIN WELLS PHOTOGRAPHY/SHUTTERSTOCK ©

1. Studying turtle eggs
2. Leatherback turtle hatchlings
3. Young green sea turtle, Parque Nacional Tortuguero (p155)

or a parade of new hatchlings on their determined and endearingly clumsy crawl back to the sea.

Turtle-watching tours can be arranged through the Asociación Salvemos Las Tortugas de Parismina, and by licensed guides in Tortuguero village. US-based nonprofit See Turtles (www.seeturtles.org) aims to protect nesting areas globally, and offers three different tours in Costa Rica.

It is crucial that you avoid the 'hatchling tours' sometimes promoted October through December in Tortuguero. These are most often people who have illegally disturbed nests in order to 'surprise' visitors with hatchling sightings.

Doing Time for the Turtles

There are many volunteering opportunities to help protect sea turtles and the many other creatures inhabiting the Caribbean coast. Most require a minimum commitment of a week. A few options:

Asociación Salvemos Las Tortugas de Parismina (p153) Small, locally run group.

Turtle Love (p153) Another group in Parismina; it organizes homestays.

Latin American Sea Turtles Association (LAST; p162) Grassroots NGO working north of the Río Pacuare river mouth.

Turtle Rescue Cahuita (p172) Consortium who patrols its patch of the breeding ground.

Canadian Organization for Tropical Education and Rainforest Conservation (p162) Canadian not-for-profit with a research station in Tortuguero.

Sea Turtle Conservancy (p162) Longtime organization with a research station in Tortuguero.

VOLUNTEERING FOR TURTLES

Canadian Organization for Tropical Education & Rainforest Conservation (COTERC; ☑2709-8052; www.coterc.org; dm per week incl 3 meals per day US$310) This not-for-profit organization operates the Estación Biológica Caño Palma, 8km north of Tortuguero village. Its small biological research station runs a volunteer program in which visitors can assist with upkeep of the station and ongoing research projects, including sea-turtle and bird monitoring, mammal, caiman and snake monitoring, and also a community program.

Latin American Sea Turtles Association (LAST; formerly Asociación Widecast; ☑in San José 2236-0947; www.latinamericanseaturtles.com) This grassroots NGO offers volunteer opportunities on turtle-protection projects in Pacuare (just southeast of Tortuguero) and on the Osa Peninsula. Participants can assist in patrols, hatchery maintenance, and research and beach clean-up efforts. Rates (US$40 per day) include training, accommodations, all equipment and three meals per day. Boat transfers are not included.

Sea Turtle Conservancy (STC; ☑2297-5510, in USA 352-373-6441; www.conserveturtles.org; museum US$2.50; ◷10am-noon & 2-5pm) Just past Miss Junie's at the north end of town, Tortuguero's original turtle-conservation organization (founded in 1959) operates a research station, visitors center and museum. Exhibits focus on all things turtle related, including a video about the local history of turtle conservation. STC (formerly Caribbean Conservation Corporation) also runs a highly reputable volunteer program.

La Casona
CABINA $
(☑2709-8092; d incl breakfast with fan/air-con US$30-35/45; ❇@☲❇) Cute rooms with rustic touches, fans and hot showers surround a lovely garden at this family-run spot. Sit back and relax in one of the hammocks and watch hummingbirds, butterflies, iguanas and frogs visit the garden. It's on the north side of the soccer field. Some rooms have air-con, and a new pool was added in 2019.

Casa Marbella
B&B $
(☑2709-8011, 8833-0827; http://casamarbella tortuguero.com; r incl breakfast US$45-65, extra person US$10; ❇@☎) In the heart of the village, with a spacious and delightful canal-side deck, this B&B owned by naturalist Daryl Loth is a convenient in-town option. Thirteen simple, well-lit rooms come with ceiling fans (two have air-con), super-clean bathrooms and hearty breakfasts served overlooking the water. Street noise, however, even in this little burg, can be a problem.

El Icaco
HOTEL $
(☑2709-8044; www.hotelelicaco.com; s/d/tr/q US$25/35/40/50 with air-con d/q US$60/80; ❇☎☲) This simple lodging offers clean, brightly painted rooms and friendly service. The beachfront location is ideal, and there are plenty of hammocks from which to enjoy it. The hotel also offers access to an off-site swimming pool (200m away), along with rental housing for groups and families. Cash only. Breakfast (US$7) is available by prior arrangement.

The owners also run Los Amigos, just down the road where the pool is.

Cabinas Tortuguero
CABINA $
(☑8839-1200, 2709-8114; dm US$10, r US$25-35; ☎) Down a side street between the boat landing and the park entrance, you'll find eight quaint bungalows surrounding a tidy garden at this popular budget spot. Rooms have hardwood floors and fans, plus hammocks, a shared kitchen and a laundry service.

Its owners also own Tortuguero Adventures on the beach which has a new guesthouse with two swanky rooms with air-con, flatscreens, tubs, shared kitchen and fridges, all overlooking the water (US$85 to US$95)

Hotel River View
HOTEL $
(☑2767-0444; s/d/tr/q US$25/50/75/100; ❇☎) In a prime location on the main street, eight simple, immaculate rooms with TVs and air-con sit perched above the river. A communal balcony overlooks the water's edge. Breakfast can be arranged in the restaurant downstairs, which is also home to Dorling Bakery (p164).

🛏 Outside the Village

★ Rana Roja
LODGE $$
(☑2709-8260, 8730-2280; www.ranarojalodge.com; r/cabins per person incl breakfast US$65/75, r/cabins per person incl 3 meals US$85/90; @☎☲) ✐ On the opposite side of the canal from Tortuguero village, this jungle hideaway is good value. The immaculate rooms are con-

nected by elevated walkways; some rooms have private terraces and rockers, and all have tiled floors, hot showers and awesome nature views – iguanas, deer and herons are frequently spotted.

Free kayaks are available, and the saltwater pool has a slide. The restaurant serves a nightly buffet.

Toucan & Tarpon Lodge CABINA **$$**
(☎8408-4239; www.toucanandtarpon.com; s/d/tr/q incl breakfast US$56/67/72/78) Just across the river from Tortuguero village, this place has three simple *cabinas* with solar electricity and Guatemalan textiles. Each room sleeps between two and five people; there are no fans, but the big windows are well ventilated with screens. Other amenities include delicious homemade breakfasts, a communal kitchen with a well-stocked spice cabinet, a ping-pong table and free canoe use.

Half-day fishing trips can be arranged for US$350, including refreshments.

La Baula Lodge LODGE **$$**
(☎2767-0101, 2711-3030; www.labaulalodge.com; s/d incl breakfast US$70/87; @) North of town and across the river, this laid-back, long-running lodge has an unpretentious atmosphere. Rooms have hardwood floors, ceiling fans and hot-water showers. In high season the outdoor dining area features live *marimba* (xylophone) and Caribbean guitar music. A 300m trail in the grounds offers the chance to spot exotic birds, spider monkeys, iguanas and snakes.

Turtle Beach Lodge LODGE **$$$**
(☎2241-1419, after hours 8837-6969; www.turtlebeachlodge.com; 1-night, 2-day all-incl packages per person s/d/tr/q/child US$311/268/247/229/97;) Reached by an Indiana Jones–style boating adventure, this isolated lodge – surrounded by 70 hectares of tropical gardens and rainforest – is flanked by beach and river. Spacious wood cabins have tile floors, hardwood furniture and huge screened windows. Guests can explore the network of jungle trails, kayak the adjacent canal, or lounge around the turtle-shaped pool or thatch-roofed hammock hut.

Tortuga Lodge & Gardens LODGE **$$$**
(☎2257-0766, 2709-8136; www.tortugalodge.com; r US$238-268, ste US$338-368;) This elegant lodge is set amid 20 serene hectares of private gardens, directly across the canal from Tortuguero's airstrip. The 27 demure rooms channel a 19th-century safari vibe, with creamy linens, handmade textiles, vintage photos and broad terraces that invite lounging. The grounds come equipped with private trails and a riverside pool, bar and restaurant.

Hotel Aninga & Spa LODGE **$$$**
(☎2222-6840, 2222-6841; www.aningalodgetortuguero.com; 2-night packages per person s/d US$359/338;) Sitting 1km north of the village on the opposite side of the canal, Hotel Aninga has a cluster of stilted bungalows connected by a series of boardwalks, along with a bar and a restaurant serving buffet food including Caribbean chicken, beef and pork, veggies and salad, plus pasta.

Nonguests can make appointments at the spa for massages (US$65 to US$120) and other treatments. National Park fee of US$15 not included in tour rate.

Evergreen Lodge LODGE **$$$**
(☎2222-6841; www.evergreentortuguero.com; 2-night packages per person s/d/tr US$299/245/234;) This pleasant place has a rustic feel, with 66 rooms and private bungalows with fans and hot water surrounded by jungle greenery. Guests have access to a pool area, Tortuguero's only canopy tour (US$35), a 1km trail, kayaks and an upstairs bar overlooking the river.

Laguna Lodge LODGE **$$$**
(☎2253-1100, 2709-8082; www.lagunatortuguero.com; s/d/tr per person incl meals, transfers, tours & activities US$298/267/258;) This expansive lodge, liberally decorated with gorgeous mosaic art and trim, has 106 graceful rooms with high ceilings and wide decks lined with Sarchí-made leather rocking chairs. It also has a buffet restaurant, three bars (canal-side, in the rainforest, and poolside), a massage room, a soccer pitch and a Gaudí-esque reception with a giant conch shell on the roof.

Mawamba Lodge LODGE **$$$**
(☎2293-8181, 2709-8181; www.mawamba.com; 2 nights incl meals, transfers & standard tours s/d/tr per person US$363/338/310;) With pool tables, foosball, a mosaic swimming pool, and butterfly and frog gardens, this lodge sits between the canal and Tortuguero's main turtle-nesting beach, within walking distance of town. Simple wood-paneled rooms have firm beds, good fans and spacious bathrooms with hot water. All are fronted by wide verandas with hammocks and rocking chairs.

Pachira Lodge LODGE $$$
(☎2256-7078, 2257-2242; www.pachiralodge.com; 2-night packages per person s/d US$299/245;) A sprawling compound set on 14 hectares of land, this 88-room hotel with a turtle-shaped pool is a popular family spot. Pristine, brightly painted clapboard bungalows with shared terraces house blocks of rooms that sleep up to four. Cribs and children's beds are available. Rates include transfers, a welcome cocktail and three local tours.

Eating

One of Tortuguero's unsung pleasures is its cuisine: the homey restaurants lure you in with steaming platters of Caribbean-style food, plus international options including pizza and pasta. Most use local produce.

★**Taylor's Place** CARIBBEAN $
(☎8319-5627; mains US$7-14; ⊙6-9pm) Low-key atmosphere and high-quality cooking come together beautifully at this backstreet eatery southwest of the soccer field. The inviting garden setting, with chirping insects and picnic benches spread under colorful paper lanterns, is rivaled only by friendly chef Ray Taylor's culinary artistry. House specialties include beef in tamarind sauce, grilled fish in garlic sauce, and avocado-and-chicken salad.

Mi Niño CARIBBEAN $
(☎8460-5262; mains US$3.50-9, smoothies US$3-4; ⊙7am-10pm;) Juan and Carole are getting high marks for their vegetarian and vegan offerings, as well as coastal specialties such as pasta in Caribbean sauce and garlic shrimp. To capitalize on their success, they're also offering a more romantic setting uptown in the former Tutti locale called Mi Niño Spot II, with the same menu.

Dorling Bakery BAKERY $
(☎2767-0444; pastries US$2, breakfast US$4-5; ⊙5am-8:30pm Mon-Sat, to noon Sun) Thanks to its predawn opening time, this is a good spot to pick up homemade banana bread, lemon-and-orange cake or cinnamon rolls before an early-morning flight or canal tour. The owner, Ricardo, also has some rooms upstairs to rent at Hotel River View (p162).

Budda Cafe EUROPEAN $
(☎2709-8084; www.buddacafe.com; mains US$7-9, pizzas US$7-9; ⊙1-9pm Tue-Sun;) Ambient club music, Tibetan prayer flags and a river view give this trendy cafe a tranquil vibe. It's a pleasant setting for pizzas, salads, cocktails and crepes (savory and sweet). Grab a table outside for a prime view of the boats going by and, if you're lucky, the yellow-bellied flycatchers zipping across the water.

★**Miss Junie's** CARIBBEAN $$
(☎2709-8029; www.iguanaverdetours.com/lodge.htm; mains US$11-16; ⊙7-9am, noon-2:30pm & 6-9pm) Over the years Tortuguero's best-known and most delicious Caribbean eatery has grown from a personal kitchen to a full-blown restaurant. Prices have climbed accordingly, but the menu remains true to its roots: jerk chicken, filet mignon, whole snapper and coconut-curry mackerel with rice and beans. It's at the northern end of the main street.

Sunrise Restaurant CARIBBEAN $$
(mains US$10-12; ⊙11am-9pm) Between the dock and the national park, this cozy log-cabin-like place will lure you in with the delicious smoky aroma of grilled chicken and pork ribs. It also serves seafood pasta, fajitas, salad, breakfast and a full Caribbean menu at lunch and dinnertime, plus a handful of luscious cocktails (caipirinha, pina colada).

LOCAL KNOWLEDGE

STREET FOOD

Beat restaurant prices and mix with the locals by indulging in some Tortuguero street food.

A must-have here is the 'Coco Loco,' a delicious coconut-rum drink by Sonia (near the weird statues), who's handy with her machete (a warning to non-payers). Don't forget to ask for the surplus coconut meat after you've slurped your drink down!

When night falls, head to the dock for chicken skewers or tortillas with cheese and sour cream (US$1 to US$1.50), from one of the vendors set up there.

Information

The community's website, Tortuguero Village (www.tortuguerovillage.com), is a solid source of information, listing local businesses and providing comprehensive directions on how to get to the Tortuguero area.

Immediately to the left of the boat landing, the local tour guides' association (p159) is also a good source of tourist information, as is **Tortuguero Keysi Tours** (☎8579-9414; ⊙5:30am-6pm).

Most accommodations have wi-fi, but connectivity can be iffy during heavy rains.

There's no longer an ATM here: stock up on cash in La Pavona, Guápiles or Puerto Limón.

Getting There & Away

If you're coming from San José, the two most convenient ways to get to Tortuguero are by air or all-inclusive bus-boat shuttles – though budget travelers can save money by taking public transportation.

If you're coming from the southern Caribbean, your best bets are with private boat operators from Moín or shuttle deals from Cahuita and Puerto Viejo.

AIR

The small airstrip is 4km north of Tortuguero village. Sansa (www.flysansa.com) has regular high-season flights, and charter flights land here regularly.

BUS & BOAT

The classic public-transit route to Tortuguero is a bit of a faff, taking four to six hours, but is by far the cheapest option. You'll travel by bus from San José to Cariari and then La Pavona, and then by boat from La Pavona to Tortuguero. Alternatively, Tortuguero is easily accessible by private boat from Moín (three to four hours).

From San José & Cariari

From San José's Gran Terminal del Caribe, buy a ticket at the window for one of the early buses (6:10am or 9am) to Cariari (around US$4, two to three hours). In Cariari, buy another ticket from the bus-station window to catch a local **Coopetraca** (☎2767-7137, 2767-7590; www.facebook.com/coopetraca) bus (US$2.20, 11:30am and 3pm) to La Pavona (one to two hours), where you'll transfer onto the boat (US$3.50, 1pm and 4:30pm) to Tortuguero (around one hour).

On the trip back, boats leave Tortuguero for La Pavona daily at 5am, 9am, 11am and 2pm or 3pm, connecting with Cariari-bound buses at the La Pavona dock.

Note that there is not really an official boat and you can negotiate with the water taxis at any hour you arrive.

From Moín

Moín–Tortuguero is primarily a tourist route. While there isn't a scheduled service, boats do cruise these canals frequently. When running, boats typically depart at 10am in either direction, charging US$35 to US$45 for the three- to four-hour trip (about US$75 for a round-trip journey). With notice, these same boats can stop in Parismina (one way from either Tortuguero or Moín for US$25 to US$35). Bear in mind that it may take 24 to 48 hours to secure a seat – especially in the low season. For onward transportation beyond Moín, catch a local bus (around US$1, 20 to 30 minutes) to Puerto Limón's bus terminal.

SHUTTLE SERVICES

If you prefer to leave the planning to someone else, convenient shuttle services can whisk you to Tortuguero from San José, Arenal-La Fortuna or the southern Caribbean coast in just a few hours. Shuttle companies typically offer minivan service to La Pavona or Moín, where waiting boats take you the rest of the way to Tortuguero. This is a relatively inexpensive, hassle-free option, as you only have to buy a single ticket, and guides help you negotiate the van-to-boat transfer.

Caribe Shuttle (☎2750-0626; www.caribeshuttle.com) Shuttles from Puerto Viejo (US$75, five hours), San José (US$50, six hours) and Arenal-La Fortuna (US$60, six hours).

Exploradores Outdoors (p176) More expensive package deals that include transport from San José, Puerto Viejo or Arenal-La Fortuna, a mid-journey Río Pacuare rafting trip, and accommodation in Tortuguero.

Pleasure Ride (p185) Shuttles from Puerto Viejo (from US$75, around 1½ hours) and Cahuita (from US$70, around one hour).

Jungle Tom Safaris (☎2221-7878; www.jungletomsafaris.com) Offers one-way shuttles between Tortuguero and San José (US$62). All-inclusive one- and two-night packages (US$135 to US$206) can also include shuttles from Cahuita (US$70), Puerto Viejo (US$70) and Arenal-La Fortuna (US$70), as well as optional tours.

Ride CR (☎2469-2525; www.ridecr.com) Shuttles from Arenal-La Fortuna (US$55). Minimum two passengers.

Riverboat Francesca Nature Tours (p159) Shuttles from San José to Tortuguero via Moín (from US$75, including lunch) as well as package deals including accommodations.

Terraventuras (p177) Overnight shuttle packages from Puerto Viejo (US$99) or daily departure shuttle (US$65).

Willie's Tours (p169) Shuttles from Cahuita (from US$60; two-person minimum).

All Rankin's Tours (p152) Round-trip shuttles to Tortuguero from Moín, including excellent nature guides (from US$70).

Getting Around

Water Taxi Friendly Colombian boatman Ariel (heir to compatriot Enrique, aka *El Pelón*; The Bald Guy) will ferry you around the local waterways.

Guzman's Water Taxi (8798-9191) a third-generation family of river rats, offers service to various locations. Prices vary depending on the trip: go down to the *muelle* (pier) in your bargaining shoes.

Barra del Colorado

At 904 sq km, including the frontier zone with Nicaragua, Refugio Nacional de Vida Silvestre Barra del Colorado, or 'Barra' for short, is the biggest national wildlife refuge in Costa Rica. It is also one of the most remote – commercial airlines suspended service to the area in 2009.

The area has long been a favorite of sportfishers, who arrive to hook gar, tarpon and snook. The Ríos San Juan, Colorado and Chirripó all wind through the refuge and out to the Caribbean Sea through a soggy wetland habitat made up of marshes, mangroves and lagoons. Here you'll find West Indian manatees, caimans, monkeys, tapirs and three-toed sloths, plus countless species of waterbird.

Activities

Fishing

Fishing is the bread and butter of area lodges, which can also organize custom wildlife-watching excursions along mangroves, lagoons and canals (from US$40).

Anglers go for tarpon from January to June and snook from September to December. Fishing is good year-round, however, and other catches include barracuda, mackerel and jack crevalle, all inshore; or bluegill, guapote (rainbow bass) and machaca in the rivers. There is also deep-sea fishing for marlin, sailfish and tuna, though this is probably better on the Pacific. Area lodges are experts at arranging fishing trips; dozens of fish can be hooked on a good day, so 'catch and release' is an important conservation policy of all the lodges.

> **NICARAGUA: NO-GO ZONE**
>
> The northern border of the refuge is the Río San Juan, which is also the border with Nicaragua. This is a little-used border crossing. Barra del Colorado has a police checkpoint but does not have a Costa Rican immigration office of its own: you would have to go to Limón to secure the proper permits (paying the trip back and forth, plus a US$60 fee). Virtually nobody crosses here since the two countries got mixed up in a dispute over some spits of land in the San Juan River.

Tours

Roberto Abram BOATING

(☎8818-8749; 1hr Tortuguero canal tours from US$35) A recommended guide who can be contacted through Casa Marbella (p162) in Tortuguero village; he also leads local river trips originating in Barra del Colorado.

Sleeping

Most of the area's lodging is west of the airstrip, on the south side of the river. Río Colorado Lodge is accessible on foot. Other lodges will have a boat waiting when you arrive with a reservation. There are also a few basic family-run *cabinas* between the airstrip and the beach, charging roughly US$30 to US$45 per night.

Río Colorado Lodge LODGE $$$

(☎2232-8610, in USA 800-243-9777; www.riocoloradotarponfishing.com; fishing packages incl lodging & meals per day US$775; ❄📶) This 18-room lodge is housed in a rambling tropical-style building with breezy rooms connected by covered walkways; there's also a pool table and deck with satellite TV. Rooms are built on stilts sprawling along the banks of the Colorado. While remote, style isn't lacking: rooms are air-conditioned with private tile baths and hot showers. There are daily maid and free laundry services.

Daily rate includes lodging, meals, an eight-hour guided fishing trip and happy hour.

Silver King Lodge LODGE $$$

(☎8447-5988, in USA 877-335-0755; www.silverkinglodge.com; 3-day packages per person US$3085; ❄@📶🏊) This sportfishing lodge caters to couples, families and friends. Twelve huge hardwood rooms have cane ceilings and *muchos* amenities. Covered walkways lead to a pool, Jacuzzi and sauna. Bounteous meals are served buffet style and an open-air bar whips up cocktails. Rates include equipment, fishing license, air transport to and from San José and one cigar per day. No joke. Call for single rates and group discounts (10+).

Getting There & Away

The cheapest, but most difficult, way to Barra del Colorado is public bus-boat transportation from Cariari. Coopetraca (p165) buses go from Cariari to the village of Puerto Lindo (roughly US$5, 2½ hours, 4am and 2pm), then you transfer to the boat for Barra del Colorado (around US$6, 20 minutes). Boat and bus drivers will only accept colones.

A much easier and more scenic way to reach Barra del Colorado is by chartering a boat from Tortuguero. The 90-minute trip starts at US$100 per boat (the price goes up or down depending on gas prices, season and number of passengers). A recommended guide is Roberto Abram in Tortuguero village; he also does local trips around Tortuguero's waterways.

That said, most folks intent on a remote fishing trip arrive by air charter from San José, arranged by individual lodges.

SOUTHERN CARIBBEAN

The southern coast is the heart and soul of Costa Rica's Afro-Caribbean community. Jamaican workers arrived in the middle of the 19th century, and stayed to build the railroad and work for the United Fruit corporation. In this area's interior, some of the country's most prominent indigenous cultures have managed to remain intact despite centuries' worth of incursions: they principally inhabit the Cocles/Kèköldi, Talamanca Cabécar and Bribrí territories.

Naturally, this fascinating cultural bubble couldn't remain isolated forever. Since the 1980s the southern coast has seen the arrival of surfers, backpackers and adventurous families on holiday – many of whom have stayed, adding European, Middle Eastern, and North American flavors to the cultural stew. For the traveler it's a rich and rewarding experience – with lovely beaches to boot.

Reserva Biológica Hitoy-Cerere

One of Costa Rica's most rugged and rarely visited reserves, 99-sq-km **Hitoy-Cerere** (☎2206-5516; US$5; ⊙8am-4pm) sits at the edge of the Cordillera de Talamanca, characterized by varying altitudes, evergreen forests and rushing rivers. This may be one of the wettest reserves in the park system, inundated with 4000mm to 6000mm of rain annually. Be aware that the river can wash away bridges; check with a guide before you visit.

The reserve is surrounded by some of the country's most remote indigenous reserves, which you can visit with a local guide. This virgin habitat is also home to jaguars.

Although there's a ranger station with bathrooms at the reserve entrance, there are no other facilities nearby. A 9km trail leads south to a waterfall, but it's steep, slippery and poorly maintained. When rivers are high, some crossings may be impassable. Jungle boots are recommended.

Activities

Richard Robinson HIKING
(☎8750-9261) Cahuita-based nature guide Richard Robinson works with other guides to take adventurous hikers into Reserva Biológica Hitoy-Cerere; he also leads snorkeling trips, and hikes in Parque Nacional Cahuita (p174).

Getting There & Away

By car (4WD essential) from Cahuita, the journey will take roughly two hours. Head west on Rte 234 towards Finca Concepción – you'll drive on a series of dirt roads passing a spectacular banana plantation. Head through Finca Concepción village past the football field, then take a left at the crossroads and continue to the right. The ranger station will be at the end of a challenging dirt road. Leave your name in the visitors book – you'll likely be the only one there.

Cahuita

POP 652

Even as tourism has mushroomed on Costa Rica's southern coast, Cahuita – a bit Puerto Viejo lite – has managed to hold onto its laid-back Caribbean vibe. Dirt roads remain off the main highways, many of the older houses rest on stilts, and chatty neighbors still converse in Mekatelyu.

Cahuita proudly claims the area's first permanent Afro-Caribbean settler: a turtle fisherman named William Smith, who moved his family to Punta Cahuita in 1828. Now his descendants (and a few Europeans) run the charming restaurants and brightly painted bungalows that hug this idyllic stretch of coast.

Situated on a pleasant point, the town itself has a waterfront but no beach. For that, most folks make the five-minute jaunt up the coast to Playa Negra or southeast into neighboring Parque Nacional Cahuita.

Sights

★**Playa Negra** BEACH
At the northwestern end of Cahuita, Playa Negra is a long, black-sand beach flying the *bandera azul ecológica,* a flag that indicates that the beach is kept to the highest

Cahuita

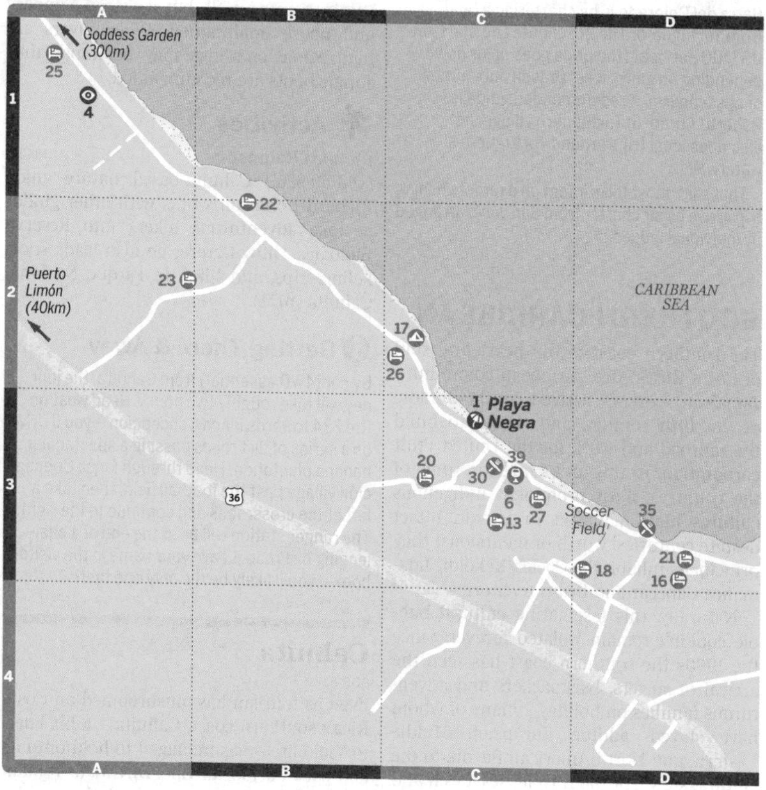

ecological standard. This is undoubtedly Cahuita's top spot for swimming and is never crowded. When the swells are big, this place also has a good beach break for beginner surfers.

Playa Blanca BEACH

At the entrance to the national park, this beach is a good option for swimming.

Tree of Life GARDENS

(☎2755-0014, 8317-0325; www.treeoflifecostarica.com; adult/child US$20/10; ⊙tour 11am Tue-Sun Nov-Mar & Jul-Aug) This lovingly maintained wildlife center and botanical garden 3km northwest of town rescues and rehabilitates animals while promoting conservation through educational programs. The rotating cast of residents typically includes kinkajous, peccaries, sloths, monkeys and toucans. There are excellent English-language signs. It's also possible to volunteer here.

Tours

Snorkeling, horseback riding, national-park hiking, chocolate tours and visits to nearby indigenous territories are standard offerings.

Centro Turístico Brigitte HORSEBACK RIDING

(☎2755-0053; www.brigittecahuita.com; Playa Negra) Behind Reggae Bar (p173), this well-signposted backstreet spot does it all, but specializes in horseback tours (hour to full day, US$35 to US$110) and surf lessons (US$40 including board use). Brigitte also rents bicycles (US$9) and offers laundry service (US$12 a load).

There are also a couple of fully equipped *cabinas* and two private single rooms, as well as a good brekkie (you'll go mad for the banana pancakes).

Cahuita Tours TOURS

(☎2755-0101, 2755-0000; www.cahuitatours.com; ⊙7:30am-noon & 2-5pm) One of the most established agencies in town. Offers snor-

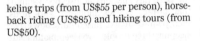

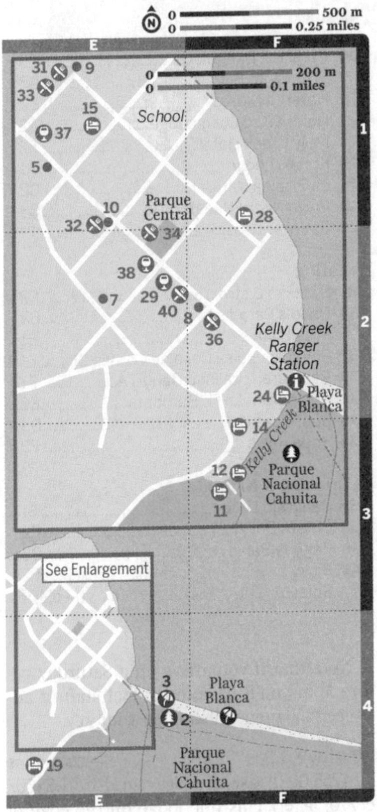

keling trips (from US$55 per person), horseback riding (US$85) and hiking tours (from US$50).

Snorkeling House TOURS

(☎8361-1924; www.snorkelinghouse.com; snorkeling tours from US$30) Local tour guide and conservationist Fernando Brown launches his excellent snorkeling tours in the national park from Miss Edith's (p173), his family's restaurant. The tour includes a couple of stops where reef sharks, rays and numerous fish are often spotted, and concludes with a fresh fruit snack.

Mister Big J's TOURS

(☎2755-0060; www.cahuita.cr/paseos-a-caballo; horseback riding from US$30; ⏲8am-7:30pm) Offers horseback riding, hiking, snorkeling and other local tours.

Roberto's Tours FISHING

(Aventuras Roberto Tours; ☎8457-8407, 2755-1148; aventurasrobertotour@gmail.com; full-day fishing tours from US$300-500) Specializes in sportfishing tours *and* has a restaurant for cooking up your catch.

Willie's Tours TOURS

(☎8917-6982, 2755-1024; www.williestourscostarica.com; tours from US$30; ⏲8am-6pm Mon-Sat) A full-service tour agency that can also arrange further-flung tours and transport. Options include white-water rafting (US$99), a traditional Bribrí lunch and chocolate-making tour (US$59), a Parque Nacional Cahuita (p174) hike (US$40) and snorkeling (US$30). Twice-daily shuttle to Bocas del Toro, Panama (US$33).

Festivals & Events

Walter Ferguson International Calypso Festival MUSIC

(⏲Jul) One weekend each summer Cahuita hails centenarian Walter Gavitt Ferguson (b 1919), the 'Calypso King' who invented the local style of music you hear often around town in places such as Reggae Bar and Coco's. Ferguson's unique Calypso Limonese has been declared a national cultural heritage, and Walter personifies 'living legend.'

Find out more about Walter at http://walterferguson-tapehunt.mozello.com.

Sleeping

There are two general areas to stay in Cahuita: the town center (near the national park) and the quieter area north of town along Playa Negra. If you're journeying between Playa Negra and the center at night, the road is generally tranquil, save the dust from passing cars (and the one taxi in town).

In the Center

Cabinas Tito BUNGALOW $

(☎2755-0286, 8880-1904; www.cahuita-cabinas-tito.com; d/tr/q US$46/60/70, 5-person house with kitchen US$120; P, wi-fi) Only 200m northwest of Cahuita, surrounded by extensive gardens, this quiet oasis offers six brightly painted, clean and simple *casitas,* plus a family-friendly Caribbean-style house with a kitchen. There's also a resident sloth named Lola, who's been living with her offspring on the property for years, as well as a three-toed cousin named Alexandra.

Cabinas Riverside CABINA $

(☎6064-0825, 8893-2252; d with/without kitchen US$30/25; P) This tidy budget place just around the corner from Kelly Creek ranger

Cahuita

station (p175) offers nine simple rooms with mosquito nets and hot showers; five units that are a bit more expensive also come with kitchens. The grassy yard abuts a swampy area perfect for spotting caimans, monkeys and sloths.

Cabinas Smith 1 & 2 CABINA $
(☎2755-0157, 2755-0068; d with fan/air-con US$34/45; P ❄ 📶) These clean rooms spanning two properties between the main drag and the waterfront are run by a friendly older couple with deep local roots. Eight units adjacent to the owners' home have flatscreens, air-con, and fridge; five fan-cooled units around the corner are primarily of interest to the budget minded. All share a guest kitchen.

Miss Joyce makes you feel right at home.

Spencer Seaside Lodging CABINA $
(☎2755-0027; s US$18-22, d US$28-32; P) Rooms at this long-standing, locally owned spot are surprisingly well kept for a budget option – and nothing else at this price level can match the seaside setting within two blocks of the town center with national-park views. Upstairs units have better views as well as a shared terrace strung with hammocks. There is a shared kitchen.

Note that if you arrive on a Saturday before 5pm you'll have to contact staff in advance to arrange picking up your key.

★ **Alby Lodge** BUNGALOW $$
(☎2755-0031; www.albylodge.com; d/tr/q US$60/65/70; P 📶) This fine lodge on the edge of the park has spacious landscaped grounds that attract howler monkeys and birds. Four palm-thatched, raised bungalows (two sleeping three people, two sleeping four) are spread out, allowing for plenty of privacy. High ceilings, mosquito nets (and coils) and driftwood details make for pleasant jungle decor. Rooms also have safes and fans. Cash only.

A *rancho* (thatched gazebo) has excellent communal kitchen facilities and an honesty bar with water, beer and Coke. The comical collection of canines will elicit a laugh or two.

Kelly Creek Hotel CABINA $$
(☎2755-0007; http://kellycreekhotel.com; d standard/duplex US$50/80, extra person US$10; P 📶) Just outside the national-park entrance, sloths and caimans linger. Draw closer and find five graceful wood *cabinas,* some with new bathrooms, that have high ceilings, cream-colored linens and mosquito nets. Local artwork adorns the reception area, and

the restaurant serves continental breakfast (US$7.50). French owner Erica has put some spit and polish into Kelly Creek, and it shows.

Bungalows Aché BUNGALOW **$$**
(☎2755-0119; www.bungalowsache.com; bungalows s/d/tr US$75/80/95; P ☎) In Nigeria Aché means 'Amen,' and you'll likely say the same thing when you see these three spotless polished-wood bungalows nestled into a grassy yard bordering the national park. Each octagonal unit comes with lockbox, mini fridge, coffeemaker and small private deck with hammock. You can also rent a nearby two-bedroom house if the bungalows are full.

Ciudad Perdida BUNGALOW **$$**
(☎2755-0303; www.ciudadperdidaecolodge.com; d incl breakfast US$127-254, additional person US$28; P) In a shady, peaceful spot bordering the national park, great-tailed grackles roam the landscaped gardens of this lodge offering cute one- and two-room candy-colored wood bungalows. All include hammocks, ceiling fans and air-con, cable TV, refrigerators and safe boxes. One house has a Jacuzzi, some have kitchens.

The hotel is a sister business of Cahuita Tours (p168).

Playa Negra & Around

Camping María CAMPGROUND **$**
(☎2755-0091; campsites per person US$8; P) Well-spaced campsites share a gorgeous section of waterfront near the northern end of Playa Negra, shaded by coconut palms and fruit trees. Campers have access to rudimentary cooking facilities, bathrooms with cold-water showers, hammocks, a tree swing and a BBQ area. There are power outlets throughout for phone charging. No pets.

There's one private room (US$20) and one cabin (US$40), with wi-fi and TV.

★ **Playa Negra Guesthouse** BUNGALOW **$$**
(☎2755-0127; www.playanegra.cr; d/q US$76/90, d with air-con US$104; P) Owned by a delightful Quebecoise couple, this meticulously maintained place offers four charming rooms in a Caribbean-style plantation house, complemented by three kitchen-equipped storybook cottages. Tropical accents include colorful mosaics in the bathrooms and cozy wicker lounge furniture on the private verandas. A lovely pool, honor bar and BBQ area are tucked into the well-manicured garden dotted with fan palms.

Pierre may offer to take you on a local hike or you can just check out the resident wildlife.

Casa Marcellino CABINA **$$**
(☎2755-0390, 8351-1198; www.casamarcellino.com; d US$102-125, q US$129-142;) In a peaceful garden setting, just inland down a side road between Cahuita and Playa Negra, you'll find this charming cluster of four spotless wood cabins with fully equipped kitchens. All units have bathtubs, plus spacious porches with hammocks and retractable awnings. Superior rooms have larger tubs, air-con, queen-size beds and bigger porches. For monthly and weekly rates, call direct.

El Encanto B&B B&B **$$**
(☎2755-0113; www.elencantocahuita.com; s/d/tr/studio/ste incl breakfast US$97/133/145/145/240; P) This pleasant B&B, only about 200m northwest of downtown Cahuita, is set in landscaped grounds dotted with easy chairs and hammocks. Demure bungalows have high ceilings, tile floors and firm beds draped in colorful textiles; some have air-con. The studio and upstairs apartment both have fully equipped kitchens, and there's an onsite spa.

Cabinas Iguana CABINA **$$**
(☎2755-0005; http://cabinas-iguana.com; d/tr/q US$73/90/107, 5/6 people US$124/135, d without bathroom US$33; P) Set back from the beach on the road marked by the Reggae Bar (p173), this family-run spot features rather worn but nicely shaded simple wood cabins with kitchens. There are televisions, but no air-con. Cabins are of various sizes and are nestled into forested grounds with abundant wildlife. The pool's a pretty place to spot nature.

La Piscina Natural CABINA **$$**
(☎2755-0146; www.piscina-natural.com; d US$65; P) Run by Cahuita native Walter and expatriate former schoolteacher Patty, this chilled-out gem of a spot near Playa Negra's northern end is a self-proclaimed 'Caribbean Paradise.' The small rooms share access to a huge kitchen and open-air lounge, but the lush grounds, the hammocks next to the gorgeous waterfront and the rock-fringed natural ocean-water pool really make this place special.

The owners suggest booking directly to save money.

Hotel La Diosa BUNGALOW **$$**
(☎2755-0055; www.hotelladiosa.net; d incl breakfast US$90-120, extra person US$20; P ❄ ☎ ≋) This relaxing spot on Playa Negra offers six well-constructed bungalows. Some have Jacuzzi tubs and oceanfront terraces; all have air-con. The grounds include a tranquil pool, a *palapa*-topped restaurant and a meandering walkway to the beach. This is the spot for some serious R&R.

You can inquire with owner Jackie about volunteering with **Turtle Rescue Cahuita** (☎8919-2967; www.leetchi.com/c/sauvez-les-tortues-luth), which has had great success in hatching and releasing turtles.

Kenaki Lodge BUNGALOW **$$$**
(☎2755-0485; www.kenakilodge.com; d incl breakfast/bungalow US$90/250; P ☎) Opposite Playa Grande, this appealing place is the creation of expat Isabelle and Costa Rican tae kwon do master Roberto. Bright, high-ceilinged rooms and elegant bungalows with satellite TV and modern kitchen fixtures surround a spacious landscaped yard and a wooden breakfast deck. Yoga and tae kwon do sessions are available in the open-air dojo.

An extra bed in a room or bungalow is US$20, while an extra person for breakfast is US$10 (children aged six to 11 pay half price for both).

Coral Hill Bungalows BUNGALOW **$$**
(☎2755-0479, USA (1) 314-488-3519; www.coralhillbungalows.com; d US$100; ☎) Popular with honeymooners, these three immaculate private bungalows in a wildlife-friendly garden setting feature tropical decor: polished-wood floors, bamboo beds, mosquito nets, hand-painted ceramic sinks, local art, blackout curtains, and porches with hammocks and leather rocking chairs. Luxuries include rain showers and fresh flowers. Follow signs from Reggae Bar. There's a minimum two-night stay.

Hotel Suizo Loco Lodge BUNGALOW **$$**
(☎2755-0349; www.suizolocolodge.com; incl breakfast s/d/tr from US$87/130/145, ste from US$143; P ☎ ≋) Eleven immaculate whitewashed bungalows have queen-size beds and folk-art decor at this serene family-friendly lodge (cribs available). All units have safes, mini fridges, solar-heated showers and small private terraces. The perfectly landscaped grounds contain an impressive mosaic-tile pool with a swim-up bar. Plus, there's a tropical/European restaurant. It's around 2km northwest of Cahuita's main center.

Goddess Garden Eco Resort LODGE **$$$**
(☎2755-0070; www.thegoddessgarden.com; d 5-night packages incl 3 meals daily US$1090; P ☎ ≋) Surrounded by old-growth jungle (including an awe-inspiring 'Goddess Tree'), this place at the end of the Playa Negra road is geared toward larger groups and yoga enthusiasts, but independent travelers looking for a peaceful, meditative five- to seven-day immersive experience are also welcome. Rates include four free yoga classes, a one-hour massage and a hike in Cahuita National Park.

Eating

The town offers some of the best Caribbean fare around, some delicious Italian and French cuisine, and a handful of nice cafes. There are good options near Playa Negra, too.

Soda Kawe COSTA RICAN **$**
(☎2755-0233; casados US$6; ⊙5:30am-7pm) This humble spot on Cahuita's main street (a few hundred metres from the Kelly Creek national park entrance) serves delicious, reasonably priced *casados* cooked over a wood fire, plus hearty breakfasts. Also offers *ceviche* (seafood marinated in lemon or lime juice, garlic and seasonings), fried rice dishes and fresh fruit juice.

★**Restaurant Italiano CahuITA** PIZZA **$$**
(☎2755-0179; pizzas US$11-20; ⊙4-9.30pm Fri-Wed; ☎) Giuseppe and Eliza of Ravenna, Italy, famed for its Byzantine mosaics, bring an artistic touch to their kitchen. Start with a *bruschetta mixta* and graduate to the four-cheese gnocchi. Wash it down with a blood-red Montepulciano. Or enjoy a surf serenade while you wait for your thin-crusted beauty to emerge from the wood-fired oven. Grilled meats and gluten-free options available.

★**Barakka Bistro** BISTRO **$$**
(☎2755-0145; www.facebook.com/barakkabistrocahuita; mains US$12-20; ⊙noon-9:30pm Tue-Sun) Enjoy some of the best French and Italian fare in town: the Florentina crepe is stuffed with spinach, cream, chicken and cheese and has an egg cooked into its center, and Barakka (the Italian half of the marriage) makes a fine pesto from macadamia, not pine, nuts. Those who like it raw may opt for the ever-fine tartare or carpaccio.

The baked fish of the day and the croque monsieur with béchamel sauce, ham and Emmental cheese are also winners. Finish up with the homemade tiramisu. The desserts are the creation of Barakka's sister,

OFF THE BEATEN TRACK

SELVA BANANITO

At the foot of Cerro Muchito, this 12-sq-km family-run **farm** (☎2253-8118, 8375-4419; www.selvabananito.com; d all-incl from US$120, extra person US$10;) has dedicated three decades to developing sustainable ecotourism. While there's no beach access, there's plenty to keep adventurous travelers occupied: tree climbing, birdwatching, waterfall hiking and horseback riding. Rates include activities, three meals and transportation from San José; minimum three-night stay.

The owners employ solar energy, recycled hardwood and biodegradable products. They are deeply committed to preserving the Limón watershed and have installed camera traps around their property to record the movements of wild cats and other fauna. They aim to become a wildlife corridor that will allow jaguars to move freely between here and the coast.

For those driving to the lodge, the turnoff is just south of the Río Vizcaya crossing (about 19km south of Limón). The lodge is about 11km inland on a bumpy, often wet dirt road, suitable for 4WD only. You can also arrange transport from the town of Bananito (US$40).

who runs the **Pan y Azucar** pastry shop near the bus terminal. Barakka was the first business in town to support Turtle Rescue Cahuita.

Palenque Luisa Casa de Carnes STEAK $$
(☎7039-9689; mains US$6-16; ⊙noon-10pm Mon-Sat) In the corner veranda of an old house, this cozy, candle-lit spot specializes in delicious red-wine-covered filet mignon, tenderloin and T-bone steaks. You'll also find plenty of other savory treats, including chicken in jalapeño or coconut sauce, pork chops, grilled seafood and *ceviche*. Honeymooners may opt for the *viagra rondón* – a stimulating seafood stew certain to raise your sensibilities.

Chao's Paradise CARIBBEAN $$
(☎6098-4864; seafood mains US$9-15; ⊙noon-10pm;) Follow the wafting smell of garlic and simmering sauces to this highly recommended Playa Negra open-air restaurant-bar, where chef Norman has been serving up fresh catches cooked in spicy 'Chao' sauce for more than 20 years. Other dishes include shrimp and octopus in Caribbean sauce, and beef in red-wine sauce. Also has a pool table. Right next to the Reggae Bar.

Restaurant La Fé Bumbata SEAFOOD $$
(☎8323-3497; dishes US$6-14; ⊙8:30am-11pm sometimes closed Sunday) Give chef/owner Walter a 'bum-bah-tah' and he'll shout back 'pata-boom-boom!' While his secret language remains so, there's no mystery why folks come to this reasonably priced spot: tasty meals – from pancakes to sandwiches to whole snapper. There's a laundry list of Tico and Caribbean items, but the main draw is anything doused in the restaurant's spicy and delicious coconut sauce.

Sobre Las Olas SEAFOOD $$
(☎2755-0109; pastas US$15-18, mains US$15-30; ⊙noon-10pm Wed-Mon;) Garlic shrimp, seafood pasta and grilled fish of the day come accompanied by crashing waves and sparkling-blue Caribbean vistas at this sweet spot. Cahuita's top option for romantic waterfront dining, it's only a 400m walk northwest of Cahuita, on the road to Playa Negra. Even the menu looks fancy.

Miss Edith's CARIBBEAN $$
(☎2755-0248; mains US$6-16; ⊙7am-10pm;) This long-standing restaurant serves a slew of Caribbean specialties and a number of vegetarian options, such as coconut-milk-and-ginger curry. The service may be laid-back, and some dishes aren't spectacular, but the spicy jerk chicken and potatoes stewed in garlic are worth the wait. The fresh passionfruit, lemon-ginger-mint and pineapple juices are good too.

Drinking & Nightlife

Reggae Bar BAR
(⊙noon-10pm;) The place to be on Friday nights in Cahuita: anybody who's anybody in the expat community shakes their thang here as the rum and Red Stripe flow. Live music ranges from calypso to reggae until the DJs take over. The last Friday of the month is particularly lively.

Coco's Bar BAR
(www.facebook.com/cocosbar.cahuita; noon-late) At the main intersection, you can't miss it: painted Rasta red, gold and green and cranking the reggaetón up to 11. On Saturday nights there's calypso music.

Cangrejo Loco COCKTAIL BAR
(Crazy Crab; Main St; 6-10pm) The Crazy Crab is a big supporter of live music including the inimitable 'Latin Hendrix,' who has to be seen to be believed. Two-for-one drinks seems to be the rule and not the exception.

Ricky's SPORTS BAR
(2755-0323; 11am-10pm Wed-Mon) The former Cafe Cahuita is finding an identity as a sports bar, although the rather tepid nachos are not so sporty. There's also live music weekends.

Splash BAR
(10am-8pm) This day-drinking spot has an outdoor bar with its own swimming pool and often hosts roots and reggae nights, private parties and other special events.

Information

The town's helpful website, www.cahuita.cr, has lodging and restaurant information. Keep in mind the listings are of places who are paying for advertising on the website.

Most cafes, bars, hotels, and restaurants have wi-fi. Connectivity in Cahuita can be fizzy, due to proximity (or lack thereof) to cell towers, and the muggy weather. Have another Cuba Libre while you're waiting for Instagram to load!

Banco de Costa Rica (9am-4pm Mon-Fri) at the bus terminal has an ATM.

Getting There & Around

Autotransportes Mepe buses arrive and depart at the bus terminal 200m southwest of Parque Central. Ticket office open 7am to 6pm.

The best way to get around Cahuita – especially if you're staying in Playa Negra – is by bicycle. Several places rent bikes, including Mister Big J's (p169) in Cahuita and Centro Turístico Brigitte (p168) in Playa Negra. Most places charge between US$7 and US$10 per day.

Parque Nacional Cahuita

This small but beautiful **park** (2755-0302, 2755-0461; US$5; Kelly Creek entrance 6am-5pm, Puerto Vargas entrance 8am-4pm) – just 10 sq km – is one of the more frequently visited national parks in Costa Rica. It's bursting with wildlife (p176) and easily walkable from town, which provides attractive accommodation. It also has the unusual combination of white-sand beach, coral reef and coastal rainforest, so you can spot an abundance of exotic species on land and underwater all in one day.

Sunday is not the best day to visit as weekends bring large groups, sometimes in buses, to the park. Also avoid the cruise-ship crowd if possible. The park is best enjoyed early on weekdays.

Activities

Hiking

An easily navigable 8km **coastal trail** leads through the jungle from Kelly Creek to Puerto Vargas. At times the trail follows the beach; at other times hikers are 100m or so away from the sand. At the end of the first beach, Playa Blanca, hikers must ford the dark Río Suarez, which bisects Punta Cahuita. Inquire about conditions before you set out: this river is generally easy enough to wade across, but during periods of heavy rain it can become impassable since it serves as the discharge for the swamp that covers the point. Respect the red flag: it means crossing is unsafe and could be the difference between life and death, not just a ruined phone.

BUSES FROM CAHUITA

DESTINATION	COST (US$)	DURATION (HR)	DEPARTURES
Manzanillo	2.40	1	6am, 9:30am, 11:30am, 1:45pm, 4pm, 6:15pm
Puerto Limón	2.40	1½	hourly 6:30am-8:30pm
Puerto Viejo de Talamanca	1.50	½	half-hourly 6am-8:30pm
San José	9	4-5	every 1-2hr 6am-4pm
Sixaola	4	2	hourly 6:30am-8:30pm

The trail continues around Punta Cahuita to the long stretch of Playa Vargas. It ends at the southern tip of the reef, where it meets up with a road leading to the Puerto Vargas ranger station. Once you reach the ranger station, it's another 1.5km along a gravel road to the park entrance.

Note that sometimes a more interesting walk for nature-lovers can begin here at Puerto Vargas early in the morning and go in the opposite direction. It's less crowded than the other section and if you get terribly bored, there's a cool mini-golf course. There's also an 'official' fee here; the Kelly Creek entrance is by voluntary donation (but don't be cheap).

From Puerto Vargas you can hike the 3.5km back to Cahuita along the coastal highway or catch a ride going in either direction. Buses will stop if you flag them down. They pass around every 30 minutes in each direction; fares are about US$1 – bring change in local currency.

Prepare for more crowded conditions on weekends, particularly Sundays.

Guided Nature Walks HIKING
(☎8412-8355; ludrickenrriquemcloud@hotmail.com) Friendly local guide Ludrick McLoud offers fascinating nature walks through Cahuita National Park and snorkeling trips off the coast. He can also arrange guides to Gandoca-Manzanillo wildlife refuge (p190) and Hitoy-Cerere biological reserve (p167).

Swimming

Almost immediately upon entering the park you'll see the beautiful 2km-long **Playa Blanca** stretching along a gently curving bay to the east. The first 500m of beach may be unsafe for swimming, but beyond that the waves are usually gentle (look for green flags marking safe swimming spots). The rocky Punta Cahuita headland separates this beach from the next one, **Playa Vargas**. It is unwise to leave clothing or other belongings unattended when you swim.

Snorkeling

Parque Nacional Cahuita contains one of the last living coral reefs in Costa Rica. While the reef represents some of the area's best snorkeling, it has suffered damage over the years from earthquakes and tourism-related activities. In an attempt to protect the reef from further damage, snorkeling is only permitted with a licensed guide (p167). The going rate to accompany one person is about US$35.

Parque Nacional Cahuita

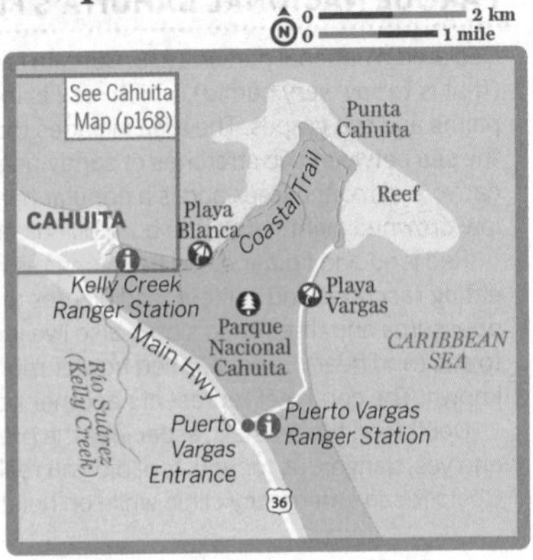

Conditions vary greatly, depending on the weather and other factors. In general, the drier months in the highlands (February to April) are best for snorkeling on the coast, as less runoff results in less silt in the sea. Conditions are often cloudy at other times.

Wear a shirt *and* sunblock while snorkeling to avoid sunburn.

Eating

Right next door to the park, Cahuita offers a wide selection of good Caribbean, Italian and seafood restaurants.

Information

Kelly Creek Ranger Station (☎2755-0461; admission by donation; ⌚6am-5pm) Restrooms are available at the park's northern entrance.

Puerto Vargas Ranger Station (☎2755-0302; US$5; ⌚8am-4pm) Near the park's southern entrance.

Getting There & Away

It's possible to flag down a local bus traveling on the main road from either end of the park. Buses pass roughly every 30 minutes and will drop you 3.5km away at the other end of the park; fares are about US$1.

Buses to San José (about US$9, four hours, every two hours 6am to 4pm) and Puerto Limón (about US$2.40, 1½ hours, hourly 6:30am to 8:30pm) leave from Cahuita's main bus terminal.

PARQUE NACIONAL CAHUITA'S FLORA & FAUNA

Declared a national park in 1978, Cahuita is meteorologically typical of the entire coast (that is to say: very humid), which results in dense tropical foliage, as well as coconut palms and sea grapes. The area includes the swampy **Punta Cahuita**, which juts into the sea between two stretches of sandy beach. Often flooded, the point is covered with cativo and mango trees and is a popular hangout for birds such as the green ibis, the yellow-crowned night heron, the boat-billed heron and the rare green-and-rufous kingfisher.

Red land and fiddler crabs live along the beaches, attracting mammals such as crab-eating raccoons and white-nosed *pizotes* (coatis). White-faced capuchins, southern opossums and three-toed sloths also live in these parts. The mammal you are most likely to see (and hear) is the mantled howler monkey, which makes its bellowing presence known. The coral reef represents another rich ecosystem, abounding with sea life.

Don't feed the animals, especially the precocious raccoons. It's dangerous for them, and yes, dangerous for you, too: did you really want to get a rabies vaccine or go to a Costa Rican emergency clinic while on holiday?

Puerto Viejo de Talamanca

This burgeoning party town is no longer just a destination for intrepid surfers; it's bustling with tourist activity. Street vendors tout Rasta trinkets and Bob Marley T-shirts, stylish eateries serve global fusion, and intentionally rustic bamboo bars pump dancehall and reggaetón. It can get downright hedonistic, attracting revelers wanting to marinate in ganja and *guaro* (a local firewater made from sugarcane).

Real-estate agents have found out that this place exists, too, so its existential Rasta isolation is fading but hanging on like a surfer to the last wondrous curl of the day. The main road out to Playa Cocles and beyond is absolutely teeming with international restaurants, many of fine quality.

Sights

Aiko-logi WILDLIFE RESERVE

(☎8997-6869, 2750-2084; www.aiko-logi-tours.com; day tours incl transport & lunch US$60, overnight stays per person incl meals US$120; P) Nestled into the Cordillera de Talamanca, 15km outside Puerto Viejo, this private 135-hectare reserve is centered on a former *finca*, on land fringed with dense primary rainforest. It's ideal for birdwatching, hiking and splashing around in swimming holes. Day tours from Puerto Viejo (or Cahuita) can be arranged, as can overnight tent-platform stays and yoga classes. Reserve in advance.

Finca La Isla GARDENS

(☎8886-8530, 2750-0046; www.costaricaorganicsfarm.com; self-guided/guided tours US$6/12; ⏲10am-4pm Fri-Mon; P) West of town, this farm and botanical garden has long produced organic pepper and cacao, along with more than 150 tropical fruits and ornamental plants. Birds and wildlife, including sloths, poison-dart frogs and toucans, abound. Informative guided tours (minimum three people) include admission, fruit tasting and a glass of fresh juice; alternatively, buy a booklet (US$1) and take a self-guided tour. The farm also makes its own chocolate (three-hour workshop US$32).

Activities

Exploradores Outdoors RAFTING

(☎2222-6262; www.exploradoresoutdoors.com; 1-day rafting trips incl lunch & transportation from US$99) This outfit – an excellent source of general information on local activities – offers one- and two-day trips on the Ríos Pacuare and Reventazón. Staff can pick you up and drop you off in Cahuita, Puerto Viejo, San José or Arenal; you're free to mix and match your pick-up and drop-off points. It has an office in the center of Puerto Viejo.

Om at Cashew Hill YOGA

(☎2750-0001, 2750-0256; http://omatcashewhill.com; Calle 213; 5-night retreats from US$1250;) On a lush hillside five minutes above town is this chill yoga retreat center with three to four drop-in classes for US$14 each and 200-hour teacher training sessions. In December 2019 it expanded its reach beyond groups, so folks not specifically on yoga retreats can stay for US$100 a night and participate in two classes.

Surfing

Find one of the country's most infamous waves at Salsa Brava (p180) – a shallow reef break that's most definitely for experts only. It's a tricky but thrilling ride over sharp coral. Salsa Brava offers both rights and lefts, although the right is usually faster. Conditions are best with a southeasterly swell.

For a softer landing, try the beach break at Playa Cocles (p185), where the waves are consistent, the white water is abundant for beginners, and the wipeouts are more forgiving. Cocles is about 2km east of town. Conditions are usually best early in the day, before the wind picks up. Meanwhile, Punta Uva (p185) has a fun, semi-fickle right-hand point for intermediates, and you can't beat the setting.

Waves in the area generally peak from December to February, but you might get lucky during the surfing mini-season between June and July. From late March to May, and in September and October, the sea is at its calmest.

Several surf schools around town charge US$40 to US$50 for two-hour lessons. Locals on Playa Cocles rent boards from about US$20 per day.

One Love Surf School SURFING
(☎8719-4654; https://onelovecostarica.wordpress.com/about; 2hr surf lesson US$50) Julie Hickey and her surfing sons, Cedric and Solomon McCrackin, specialize in beginners' surf lessons, reiki (one hour US$60) and Thai massage. Cedric has represented Costa Rica in international competitions and is a patient instructor.

Julie also offers massage and reiki courses from US$300. Drop-in yoga (9am weekdays) is US$10.

Caribbean Surf School & Shop SURFING
(☎8357-7703; 2hr lesson US$55) Lessons by super-smiley surf instructor Hershel Lewis are widely considered the best in town. He also teaches paddleboarding. You can find the school on Facebook.

Hiking

There are superb coastal hiking opportunities within easy reach. Parque Nacional Cahuita (p174) is 17km north of Puerto Viejo, and Refugio Nacional de Vida Silvestre Gandoca-Manzanillo (p190) is 13km south. There is also a nice waterfall hike near the Bribrí indigenous community, signposted from the main highway.

Courses

Spanish School Pura Vida LANGUAGE
(☎2750-0029; www.spanishschool-puravida.com; 1/2/3/4 weeks Spanish lessons US$226/429/627/814) Located at the Hotel Pura Vida (p179), this school offers everything from private hourly tutoring (US$20) to intensive five-hours-a-day multiweek courses.

Tours

Tour operators generally require a minimum of two people on any excursion. Rates may be discounted for larger groups. Gecko Trail Costa Rica can help you book.

Gecko Trail Costa Rica TOURS
(☎2756-8159, in USA & Canada 415-230-0298; www.geckotrail.com; ⏲tours per adult from US$28) This full-service agency arranges local tours as well as transportation, accommodation and excursions throughout Costa Rica, including horseback riding, hikes, rafting, hot-spring visits and spa days. It has an administrative office in Puerto Viejo (inside the Pleasure Ride building; p185), but bookings are made by phone and online.

Terraventuras TOURS
(☎2750-0750; www.terraventuras.com; ⏲7am-7pm) Offers overnight stays in Tortuguero (US$99), a cultural tour to an indigenous reserve (US$75) and a Caribbean cooking class (US$55), along with the usual local tours. It also has its very own 23-platform, 2.1km-long canopy tour (US$59), complete with Tarzan swing.

Caribe Shuttle TOURS
(☎2750-0626; www.caribeshuttle.com/puerto-viejo-tours; tours from US$55) This company offers a wide variety of tours in the Puerto Viejo area, and excursions to Bocas del Toro (Panama) and Tortuguero. It also provides transport to San José, northwestern Costa Rica and San Juan del Sur (Nicaragua).

Sleeping

Puerto Viejo has a little bit of everything. Many budget spots have private hot-water bathrooms and everywhere has wi-fi, though the signal throughout this region is a bit iffy. Rates are generally discounted slightly if you pay in cash.

Kaya's Place GUESTHOUSE $
(☎2750-0690; www.kayasplace.com; d with/without air-con from US$55/35; P❄📶) Across from the beach at Puerto Viejo's western edge, this cool guesthouse has colorful basic

Puerto Viejo de Talamanca

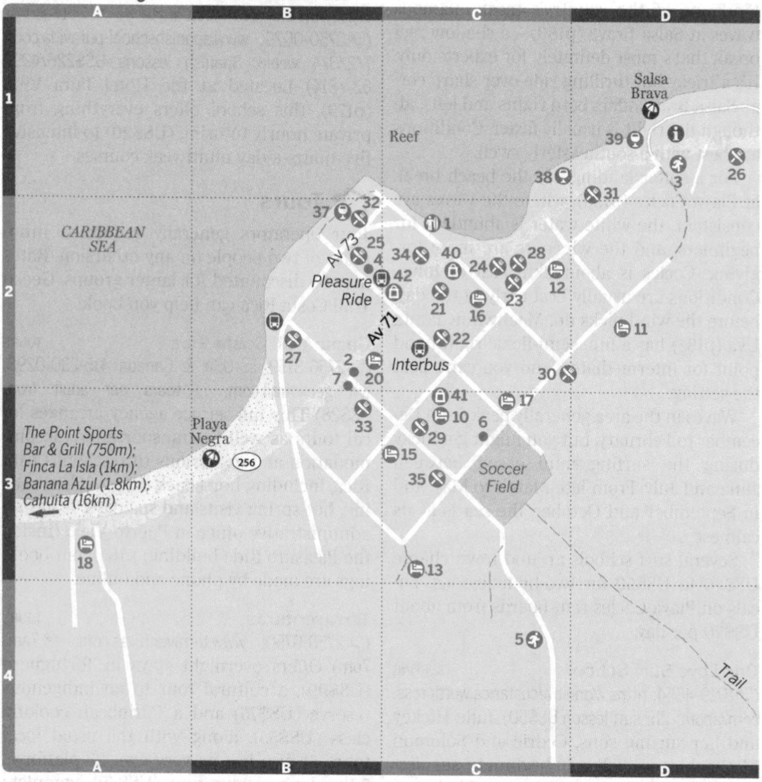

rooms, including spacious garden rooms with air-con and hot-water bathrooms. Some older units have been combined into larger, more modern accommodations. The property also includes a private cabin and three apartments. A 2nd-floor deck is filled with hammocks with ocean views.

The bar and restaurant serves breakfast (from US$5), plus *casados,* homemade pizzas and excellent craft beer. There's a brewery onsite with a slew of local flavors (lemon wheat, watermelon pale ale). There's also a free pool table.

Cabinas Tropical CABINA **$**
(☎2750-2064; https://hotelcabinastropical.com; s/d/tr US$45/50/60; P ⊖ ❄ ☰) Ten spacious rooms – two with air-con – decorated with varnished wood and shiny tiles surround a primly landscaped garden at the eastern end of town. The comfortable quarters are just part of the appeal: biologist owner Rolf Blancke leads excellent hikes, birdwatching excursions and rainforest tours. Ask about the collection of rare plants from around the world.

La Ruka Hostel HOSTEL **$**
(☎2750-0617; http://larukahostel.com; dm US$10-12, r with/without bathroom US$60/46; P ☰) If the sign reading 'Welcome all sexes, races, colors, religions, languages, shapes and sizes' doesn't lure you in, the friendly greeting from owners Dannie and Dave will. East of town, this hostel has common areas, a shared kitchen, plus a BBQ area, book exchange, and surfboard and snorkel rental.

Hotel Puerto Viejo CABINA **$**
(☎2750-0620; d US$40, r per person without bathroom US$17; P @ ☰) This crash pad launched by surfer Kurt Van Dyke has been around for 30 years, and consists of a warren of wooden rooms in the middle of town. Units are basic but clean and come equipped with strong fans. There's a huge shared kitchen and a bar with a mellow vibe, where the talk is often all about waves.

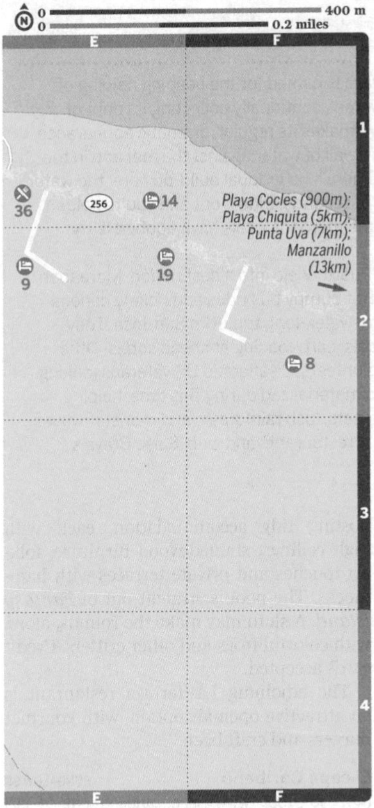

Hotel Pura Vida HOTEL $
(☎2750-0002; www.hotel-puravida.com; s/d/tr US$52/58/70, without bathroom US$40/45/57; P 📶) This inn opposite the soccer field doubles as a Spanish school (p177) and offers midrange amenities. Breezy, immaculate rooms feature polished wood, bright linens and ceramic-tile floors; many have charming views of the surrounding village. Showers are heated using solar power, and there's a lounge with easy chairs and hammocks. Breakfast (US$8), snacks and chilled beer are available.

A family unit for up to five people is available for US$105.

Jacaranda Hotel & Jungle Garden CABINA $
(☎2750-0069; www.cabinasjacaranda.net; s/d/tr from US$35/45/60, air-con extra US$15; P ❄ 📶) In a blooming garden intersected by mosaic walkways, this place near the soccer field has 12 simple wood *cabinas* (sleeping one to four people) with ceramic-tile floors and murals of flowers. There's a small shared kitchen and patio. Yoga classes (US$10) are available.

Puerto Viejo de Talamanca

Activities, Courses & Tours
1 Caribbean Surf School & Shop C2
2 Caribe Shuttle B2
3 Exploradores Outdoors D1
4 Gecko Trail Costa Rica B2
5 Om at Cashew Hill C4
6 Spanish School Pura Vida C3
7 Terraventuras B2

Sleeping
8 Blue Conga Hotel F2
9 Bungalows Calalú E2
10 Cabinas Guaraná C3
11 Cabinas Tropical D2
12 Casa Verde C2
13 Coco Loco Lodge C3
14 Escape Caribeño E1
15 Hostel Pagalú C3
16 Hotel Puerto Viejo C2
Hotel Pura Vida ..... (see 6)
17 Jacaranda Hotel & Jungle Garden C3
18 Kaya's Place A3
19 La Ruka Hostel E2
20 Lionfish Hostel B2

Eating
21 Bikini Restaurant & Bar C2
22 Bread & Chocolate C2
23 Café Rico C2
24 Chile Rojo C2
25 Como en mi Casa Art Café B2
26 De Gustibus D1
27 DeeLite Ice Cream Shop B2
28 KOKi Beach C2
29 MegaSuper C3
30 Miss Lidia's Place C2
31 Mopri D1
32 Pan Pay B2
33 Sel & Sucre B3
34 Soda Riquisimo C2
35 Soda Shekiná C3
36 Stashu's con Fusion E1

Drinking & Nightlife
37 Johnny's Place B2
38 Lazy Mon C1
39 Salsa Brava D1

Shopping
40 Choco C2
41 Lulu Berlu Gallery C3
42 Organic Market C2

LOCAL KNOWLEDGE

SALSA BRAVA

One of the best breaks in Costa Rica, Salsa Brava is named for the heaping helping of 'spicy sauce' it serves up on the sharp, shallow reef, continually collecting its debt of fun in broken skin, boards and bones. The wave makes its regular, dramatic appearance when the swells pull in from the east, pushing a wall of water against the reef and in the process generating a thick and powerful curl. There's no gradual build-up here: the water is transformed from swell to wave in a matter of seconds. Ride it out and you're golden. Wipe out and you may rocket into the reef. Some mordant locals have dubbed it 'the cheese grater.'

Interestingly, this storied wave helped turn Puerto Viejo into a destination. More than 30 years ago the town was barely accessible. But bumpy bus rides and rickety canoes didn't dissuade dogged surfers from making the week-long trip from San José. They camped on the beach and shacked up with locals, carb-loading at cheap *sodas*. Other intrepid explorers – biologists, Peace Corps volunteers, disaffected US veterans looking to escape the fallout of the Vietnam War – also materialized during this time, helping spread the word about the area's luminous sunsets, lush rainforests and monster waves. Today Puerto Viejo has a fine paved road, global restaurants and wi-fi. Salsa Brava's ferocity, however, remains unchanged.

Lionfish Hostel
HOSTEL **$**

(☑ 2750-2143; http://thelionfishhostel.com; dm US$24, r with/without bathroom US$64-54; P 🛜) Right in the center of the action, this hostel is tops for party people. It was started by local surfers and appeals to like-minded adventurers. The dorms are basic and can be stuffy, basic rooms a bit less so. Facilities include shared kitchen, fans, lockers and hot water. A fried-chicken joint on the first level keeps patrons well fed.

Hostel Pagalú
HOSTEL **$**

(☑ 2750-1930; www.pagalu.com; dm US$12-13, d with/without bathroom US$36/30; P 🛜) A contemporary hostel with clean, airy doubles and dorms, the latter with lockers and bunkside reading lamps. There's also a shared open-air kitchen and a quiet lounge with tables and hammocks, plus a supply of coffee, tea and spring water for refilling your bottle.

Cabinas Guaraná
CABINA **$**

(☑ 2750-0244; www.hotelguarana.com; s/d/tr/q US$35/45/57/62; P ❄ @ 🛜) Right in town, amid a flourishing tropical garden, brightly painted concrete *cabinas* – some with air-con – come with vibrant walls, wooden furniture and colorful folk tapestries. Each one has a small private terrace with hammock. There are mosaics throughout the property, plus a spacious shared kitchen.

Casa Verde
CABINA **$$**

(☑ 2750-0015; d US$78-96, extra person US$20; P ❄ 🛜 ⛱) This 17-room wonder features tiled walkways winding through gardens

hosting tidy accommodation, each with high ceilings, stained-wood furniture, folk-art touches and private terraces with hammocks. The pool is straight out of *Fantasy Island*. A sloth may make the rounds, along with colorful frogs and other critters. Credit cards accepted.

The adjoining La Terraza restaurant is an attractive open-air option, with gourmet burgers and craft beer.

Escape Caribeño
BUNGALOW **$$**

(☑ 2750-0103; www.escapecaribeno.com; d incl breakfast garden view US$111, ocean view US$135; P ❄ @ 🛜) Charming owners keep these bungalows spotless. Some bungalows sit on the beach side, others in the garden across the road, 500m east of town toward Playa Cocles. More expensive units are in lovely Caribbean-style structures with hardwood walls (others are brick); all units have stocked mini fridges, satellite TV, fans and hammocks.

Banana Azul
LODGE **$$**

(☑ 2750-2035; www.bananaazul.com; incl breakfast cabinas from US$109, r & ste US$149-222; P 🛜 ⛱) Removed from town, this romantic hotel sits astride a blissfully tranquil black-sand beach. Jungle-chic decor (white linens, mosquito nets, bromeliads in the showers) is complemented by fine ocean vistas from upstairs terraces. Of the 22 rooms, the best is the corner Howler Suite, with multidirectional views. There's also a restaurant-bar, and bike and boogie-board rentals. No children under 16.

Coco Loco Lodge BUNGALOW $$
(☎2750-0281; www.cocolocolodge.com; d with/without air-con US$92-112/85, 5-person house US$188; P@wi-fi pool) You'll find various options at this quiet hotel. The most charming are the palm-thatched bungalows, featuring shining wooden floors, mini fridges and coffee makers. All have private terraces with hammocks, offering views of the expansive garden. One large accommodation in the main house is equipped with a kitchen; the unit above it is ideal for a family. Credit cards accepted.

Breakfast is US$11. A new pool follows a growing trend on the Caribbean coast.

Bungalows Calalú BUNGALOW $$
(☎2750-0042; www.bungalowscalalu.com; d/tr US$55/65, d/tr/q with kitchen & air-con US$90/105/120; P air-con wi-fi pool) A lovely tropical-garden setting, a swimming pool and convenient parking are among the appealing features at this cluster of six bungalows within easy walking distance of town. Cheaper fan-cooled units have private front porches where you can listen to the chorus of chirping birds every morning. Larger family-friendly units come with air-con and kitchen.

Blue Conga Hotel B&B $$
(☎2750-0681; www.hotelblueconga.com; d incl breakfast US$75-95; P wi-fi pool) This backstreet B&B 1km east of town has simple rooms in a two-story, tropical-style building. Best value are the airy upstairs units, with high ceilings, clerestory windows, canopy beds with mosquito nets, handcrafted lamps, private terraces, coffee makers and refrigerators. Rooms downstairs are less inspiring. Breakfast is served on a lovely open-air garden deck beside the pool.

Eating

With the most diverse restaurant scene on the Caribbean coast, Puerto Viejo has the cure for *casado* overkill. You'll find everything from sushi to homemade pizza.

Groceries are stocked at the incongruous chain-store **MegaSuper** (☎2750-0187; ⏲8am-9pm). Don't miss the Saturday organic market (p184).

A wonderful regional chocolate shop (p184) opened in 2019.

★**Café Rico** CAFE $
(☎2750-0510; caferico.puertoviejo@yahoo.com; breakfast US$6-8; ⏲7am-noon Sat-Wed; wi-fi) Roger from Hounslow West, England will sort you out with house-roasted coffee, homemade ginger-lemonade, and a massive concoction called the Ana Rosa which features a fried egg, Canadian bacon, fried potatoes, avocado and cheese. This cozy garden cafe, which could double as a library, also serves healthier breakfasts (yogurt and strawberries, omelets).Other services include wi-fi, book exchange, laundry and bike rentals.

★**Bread & Chocolate** CAFE $
(☎2750-0723; www.breadandchocolatecr.com; cakes US$3.50-4, meals US$7-11; ⏲6:30am-6:30pm Wed-Sat, to 2:30pm Sun; vegetarian) Ever had a completely homemade PB&J, with bread, peanut butter and jelly all made from scratch? That and more can be yours at this dream of a cafe, serving sandwiches, soups and salads, and (of course) the treat that gives it its name: chocolate. Served as truffles, bars, cakes, tarts and covered nuts, and in cookies (gluten-free available).

Coffees are served in individual French presses; mochas come deconstructed so you have the pleasure of mixing your own homemade chocolate, steamed milk and coffee. Everything else – from the gazpacho to the granola to the biscuits – is lovingly and skillfully made in-house.

Soda Riquisimo CARIBBEAN $
(☎2750-0367; US$4.50-9; ⏲7am-10pm; wi-fi) Typical Caribbean dishes, such as jerk chicken served with salad, beans, rice and plantain, are done well at this simple *soda* off the main strip. A musical mélange fills in the background and the atmosphere is friendly enough, but in this touristy town you can't beat these prices. Packs out on weekends. Also serves toast, omelets and fruit for breakfast.

Como en mi Casa Art Café VEGETARIAN $
(☎6069-6337; www.facebook.com/Comoenmicasaartcafe; mains US$3.50-6; ⏲8am-4pm Wed-Mon, kitchen to 2:30pm; vegetarian) Owned by a friendly bohemian expat couple, this charming vegetarian cafe champions the slow-food movement and makes everything from scratch, from the jams and the hot sauces to the gluten-free pancakes. Popular items include raw cakes, homemade lentil-bean burgers, and gluten-free avocado wraps, smoothies and chocolate brownies. The walls are covered in local art.

Soda Shekiná CARIBBEAN $
(☎2750-0549; mains US$6-10; ⏱breakfast 7:30-11:30am, lunch & dinner 11:30am-9pm Thu-Sun) Delicious pancake and fruit breakfasts and Caribbean home cooking can be found at this backstreet eatery with wooden slab tables on an open-air terrace. Lunch and dinner mains are served with coconut rice and beans, salad and caramelized fried bananas. It's just west of the soccer field.

They may closer earlier on Sunday (5pm) if there's not a crowd.

De Gustibus BAKERY $
(☎2756-8397; www.facebook.com/degustibusbakery; baked goods from US$1; ⏱6:45am-6pm Thu-Tue) This bakery on Puerto Viejo's main drag draws a devoted following with its fabulous focaccia, along with slices of pizza, apple strudels, profiteroles and all sorts of other sweet and savory goodies. Eat in or grab a snack for the beach.

Sel & Sucre FRENCH $
(☎2750-0636; meals US$4-10; ⏱noon-9:30pm Tue-Sun;) Dark coffee and fresh-fruit smoothies offer a nice complement to the menu of savory and sweet crepes. These delights are all prepared by chef Sebastien Flageul, who also owns the hostel next door (dorm US$12, double US$30 to US$35). Service can be slow, but it's worth it; use the cash machine across the street while you wait.

DeeLite Ice Cream Shop ICE CREAM $
(Gelateria Artigianale Italiana; ☎2750-3226; gelati from US$3, menu items US$1-7; ⏱8am-10pm Wed-Mon;) Directly across from the bus stop, this authentic *gelateria* has up to 80 flavors on rotation, including non-dairy and vegan options. It's the perfect place to cool off after a long, hot bus ride. It also serves crepes, banana splits, pancakes, paninis, pastries and hot and cold drinks.

Pan Pay BAKERY $
(☎2750-0081; www.panpaypuertoviejo.com; dishes US$3-6; ⏱7am-5pm Mon & Tue, to 9pm Wed-Sun) This popular corner spot on the beachside road in town is excellent for strong coffee, freshly baked goods and hearty wedges of fluffy Spanish omelet served with crisp tomato bread. There are sandwiches and other light meals, but it's the flaky chocolate croissants that'll make you want to jump out of bed in the morning.

★ **Mopri** SEAFOOD $$
(☎2756-8411; mains US$9-20; ⏱noon-10pm;) You'd never know it from Mopri's dingy facade and cheap plastic tables, but this place serves some of the best seafood in Puerto Viejo. Choose your star ingredient – whole snapper, calamari, lobster or prawns – then choose your sauce – Caribbean, Mopri's garlic butter, curry, jalapeño or lip-smacking salsa. Last, pile on the sides – rice, fried potatoes, plantains, salad, veggies or beans.

It also has a kids' menu and pasta dishes for non-fish eaters, plus wine, beer, juice and coffee to wash it all down.

Stashu's con Fusion FUSION $$
(☎2750-0530; mains US$10-16; ⏱5-10pm Thu-Tue;) Stroll 250m out of town toward Playa Cocles to this romantic low-lit patio cafe serving creative cuisine that combines elements of Caribbean, Indian, Mexican and Thai cooking. Tandoori chicken and macadamia- and coconut-encrusted tilapia are just a couple of standouts. There are excellent vegetarian and vegan items. Owner-chef Stash Golas is an artist inside the kitchen and out.

The Lotus Garden hotel, behind the restaurant, has two nice pools and cozy rooms; readers will gravitate to David's Library, adjacent to the main dining area.

Miss Lidia's Place CARIBBEAN $$
(☎2750-0598; dishes US$7-20; ⏱1-9pm Tue-Sat, 11:30am-8pm Sun) A long-standing favorite for classic Caribbean flavors, Miss Lidia's enters its third decade of pleasing palates and satisfying the stomachs of locals and tourists alike. Lidia's rice-and-beans with anything on the side (chicken, shrimp) is excellent. The *hiel* (Jamaican lemon-ginger drink) will cool the fieriest of souls.

Chile Rojo ASIAN $$
(☎8396-3247; US$7-13; ⏱noon-11pm;) Craving sushi? Head to this open-air Asian joint on Puerto Viejo's main street overlooking the beach and boats. Bonus raw-fish varieties include soy-infused Hawaiian-style tuna *poke*, and *ceviche*. Meanwhile, cooked dishes include Thai curries, whole red snapper and yellowfin tuna. Vegetarians can tuck into Middle Eastern delights such as tabouleh, fattoush salad and falafel burgers.

Bikini Restaurant & Bar FUSION $$
(☎2750-3061; mains US$5.50-14; ⏱5.30-11pm;) If frozen mojitos (US$3.50) are your

WORTH A TRIP

VISITING INDIGENOUS COMMUNITIES

At least two indigenous groups occupied the territory on the Caribbean side of the country from pre-Columbian times. The Bribrí people tended to inhabit lowland areas, while the Cabécar people made their home high in the Cordillera de Talamanca. Over the last century members of both ethnic groups have migrated to the Pacific side. But many have stayed on the coast, intermarrying with Jamaican immigrants and even working in the banana industry. Today the Bribrí tend to be more acculturated, while the Cabécar are more isolated.

The groups have distinct languages (which are preserved to some degree), though they share similar architecture, weapons and canoe style. They also share the spiritual belief that the planet – and the flora and fauna contained within it – are gifts from Sibö (God). *Taking Care of Sibö's Gifts*, by Juanita Sánchez, Gloria Mayorga and Paula Palmer, is a remarkable record of Bribrí history and available online.

Making It Happen

There are several reserves on the Caribbean slopes of the Cordillera de Talamanca, including the Talamanca Cabécar territory (which is more difficult to visit) and the Bribrí territory, where locals are more equipped to handle visitors.

The most interesting destination is **Yorkín**, in the Reserva Indígena Yorkín. Only reachable by boat, the village is situated on the Río Yorkín, bordering Panama. Immersive day, one-night and two-night tours (from US$210 per person including meals, transfers and experiences) entail travel via dugout canoe followed by local demonstrations of roof thatching, the uses of medicinal plants, and basket-weaving. You can tuck into a Bribrí-style lunch and learn the chocolate-making process (eating some samples for dessert). An optional hike in the highlands is also possible. It's a rewarding experience, well worth the time and effort to get there.

Alternatively, you can do day trips (US$59) to the **territory of the Kèköldi** (a tiny group ethnically related to the Bribrí), where you'll go on a 2½-hour nature-spotting hike to the village and enjoy a traditional lunch cooked over a log fire by members of the community. It's also possible to arrive there on foot and just pay the US$4 fee to visit the community and check out exhibits such as the green iguana farm. Many Puerto Viejo companies offer this tour.

The Watsi community, within the Bribrí territory just outside of Puerto Viejo, offers an interesting day-long experience including chocolate-making, learning about medicinal plants, and lunch. Contact shaman Luís or his wife Ana. They can pick you up in town.

Visiting these territories independently can be done, but with care; Kèköldi and Bribrí territories are close to Puerto Viejo and are easy day trips, but the community should be contacted in advance. Note, however, that some of the spots are difficult to reach and in most cases villages do not have the infrastructure to accommodate streams of tourists. During your visit bear in mind that these are people's private homes and work spaces, not tourist attractions.

Terraventuras (p177) in Puerto Viejo runs day tours to Bribrí territory (US$80 per person) that include a meeting with an Awa (a Bribrí doctor), who will demonstrate medicinal customs and do a purification ceremony. Willie's Tours (p169) in Cahuita does day, one-night and two-night trips to Yorkín and a day trip to the Kèköldi territory which includes a waterfall hike and chocolate-making experience (five hours, US$57).

thing, get thee to Bikini. This hip restaurant and bar attracts a crowd of revelers with its affordable cocktails and varied menu. Caribbean dishes, pasta, salads, curries and sushi all pair well with strong drinks and a convivial atmosphere. There are also 32 vegan and vegetarian options.

KOKi Beach LATIN AMERICAN **$$$**
(☎2750-0902; http://kokibeach.blogspot.com.au; mains US$10-43; ⊙5-11pm Tue-Sun; 📶) A high-end favorite for drinks and dinner, this sleek restaurant at the eastern end of town cranks up the lounge music and sports an interior furnished almost entirely from local river stones and an abandoned Hone

Creek house. The yucca fries are a nice starter, and you can pick your own lobster. Produce comes from local organic suppliers when possible. It's sometimes closed in the low season.

Drinking & Nightlife

Restaurants often metamorphose into rollicking bar scenes after the tables are cleared. For excellent people-watching over beer, try Bikini Restaurant & Bar. (p182) If you want to see and be seen, hit Koki Beach (p183), or eat the catch of the day at Mopri (p182).

Salsa Brava BAR

(www.facebook.com/SalsaBravaBeachBar; ⏲9am-2am Fri-Sun) Specializing in tacos, Caribbean bowls and sweet plantain fries, this popular spot is the perfect end-of-day cocktail stop – hit happy hour from 4pm to 6pm and you'll also catch two-for-one mojitos to enjoy while taking in the sunset over the Salsa Brava surf break. On Friday and Sunday the bar brings in DJs for popular reggae nights. Cocktails from US$5.

Lazy Mon CLUB

(☎2750-2116; www.thelazymon.com; signature cocktails from US$5; ⏲noon-2:30am) Run by brothers Khalil and Abasi and their friend Rocky, Puerto Viejo's most dependable spot for live music draws big crowds, plays reggae, and serves two-for-one cocktails (4pm to 7pm); sometimes there's even a 'crappy hour' (10pm to midnight). Try Jamakin' Me Crzy, a potent mix of vanilla vodka, orange liquor, mango and coconut cream.

Look for the Stanford's sign on the beach (the former business in this locale).

The Point Sports Bar & Grill SPORTS BAR

(☎2756-8491; Playa Negra; ⏲10:30am-11:30pm; wi-fi) The Point is a truly trashy dive bar, complete with video games, and a few TVs showing sports from around the world. Just look for the pirate flag. New ownership's direction was uncertain in late 2019.

Johnny's Place CLUB

(☎2750-2000; www.facebook.com/JohnnysPlacePuertoViejo; ⏲11am-7pm Mon, Thu & Fri, to 2am Wed, Sat & Sun) The place shut down briefly and reopened under new ownership as a high-end attempt at selling *ceviche*, salads, mixed rice and grilled fish (meals US$5 to US$18). There's a bar with fancy cocktails. There are still DJs, dancing and occasional revelry: it's an expat must-stop on Wednesdays.

Entertainment

Guerrilla Cinema CINEMA

(Playa Chiquita) The pop-up movie experience has found a new home at the newly opened Paradise Bar 2.0, right on the beach. Have a drink and catch a movie.

Shopping

Choco CHOCOLATE

(☎6363-4274; www.cho.co.cr; Calle 217) Québécois partners Martin and Nelson have turned this tidy air-conditioned shop into a must-stop for local Talamanca chocolates (five different brands). There are chocolate-making classes, tours of local cacao *fincas*, and pairings of beer, wine or Costa Rican rums and chocolates...yum. To call this just a chocolate shop would be like calling Willy Wonka's establishment just a factory.

Lulu Berlu Gallery ARTS & CRAFTS

(☎2750-0394; ⏲9am-9pm) On a backstreet parallel to the main road, this gallery carries folk art, jewelry, ceramics, embroidered purses and mosaic mirrors, among many other one-of-a-kind, locally made items.

Organic Market MARKET

(⏲6am-noon Sat) Don't miss the weekly organic market, where local vendors and growers sell snacks typical of the region, particularly tropical produce and chocolate. Arrive before 9am or the best stuff will be long gone.

Information

SAFE TRAVEL

Be aware that though the use of marijuana (and harder stuff) is common in Puerto Viejo, it is nonetheless illegal.

As in other popular tourist centers, theft can be an issue. Stay aware, use your hotel safe, and if staying outside town avoid walking alone late at night.

INTERNET ACCESS

Most bars, cafes, guesthouses and hotels have wi-fi.

MONEY

Banco de Costa Rica (⏲9am-4pm Mon-Fri) Two ATMs here work on Plus and Visa systems, dispensing both colones and dollars. Sometimes they run out of cash on weekends, and they can be finicky; if one machine won't let you withdraw cash, try the other.

Banco Nacional (9am-4pm Mon-Fri, ATM 6am-10pm daily) Just off the main street near the bridge into town. Dispenses colones only.

TOURIST INFORMATION

Costa Rica Way (2750-3031; www.costaricaway.info; 8am-6pm) Operates a tourist-information center near the waterfront east of town, and lists hotel and restaurant info on its website and accompanying magazine, *Caribbean Way*. It is also a for-profit tour operator.

Puerto Viejo Satellite (www.puertoviejosatellite.com) A good place to look for info on local lodgings, eating and activities.

Getting There & Around

BICYCLE

A bicycle is a fine way to get around town, and pedaling out to beaches east of Puerto Viejo is one of the highlights of this corner of Costa Rica. You'll find rentals all over town for about US$10 per day.

BUS

All public buses arrive at and depart from the bus stop along the beach road in central Puerto Viejo. The ticket office is diagonally across the street.

SHUTTLE

An ever-growing number of companies offer convenient van shuttles from Puerto Viejo to other tourist hot spots around Costa Rica and down the coast to Bocas del Toro (Panama). For an exhaustive list, see Gecko Trail's very helpful website (www.geckotrail.com). The following companies operate out of Puerto Viejo:

Caribe Shuttle (p177) Serves Bocas del Toro (Panama), San José and Tortuguero.

Gecko Trail Costa Rica (p177) Standard shuttle service to San José and Tortuguero; also offers good-value Adventure Connection packages.

Interbus (4100-0888, WhatsApp 6050-6500; www.interbusonline.com; Mon-Sat) Serves Arenal-La Fortuna, San José, Siquirres and Puerto Viejo de Sarapiquí.

Pleasure Ride (2750-0290, 2750-2113; www.pleasureridecr.com) Operates tours and transportation in the Caribbean, as well as reliable private vans to the rest of the country. It also runs an Airport Express to and from San José.

Playa Cocles, Playa Chiquita & Punta Uva

A 13km road winds east from Puerto Viejo through rows of coconut palms, alongside coastal lodges and through lush lowland rainforest before coming to a dead end at the sleepy town of Manzanillo. Though well paved, the road is narrow, so if you're driving, take your time and be alert for cyclists and one-lane bridges.

Sights

★ **Punta Uva** BEACH

Off a dirt road marked by Punta Uva Dive Center (p186) is a quiet, idyllic cove that could double for a scene in the film *The Beach*. There are usually a couple of locals renting out surfboards on the sand, and the reef to the right of the cove is excellent for snorkeling and surfing (but not at the same time!). When the waves are up, this spot creates a forgiving peeling right-hand wave that's suitable for intermediates.

★ **Playa Cocles** BEACH

Playa Cocles has waves for surfers who aren't keen to break skin and bones at nearby Salsa Brava (Costa Rica's biggest break; p180). Instead, it has steep lefts and rights, which break (and often dump) on the steep sandy beach. During the right tide and swell, the best wave breaks are near the island offshore, producing a mellow left-hand longboarder's ride over a deep reef. Conditions best from December to March, and early in the day before winds pick up.

The organized lifeguard system helps offset the dangers of the frequent riptides.

BUSES FROM PUERTO VIEJO

DESTINATION	COST (US$)	DURATION	DEPARTURES
Bribrí/Sixaola	1.50/3.35	30/90min	hourly 6:30am-7:30pm
Cahuita/Puerto Limón	1.50/3.60	45min/2hr	hourly 5:30am-8:15pm
Manzanillo	1.30	30min	every 2hr 6:30am-6:45pm; less frequent on weekends
San José	10.90	5hr	4:50am, 7:30am, 9am, 11am, 1pm & 4pm

Jaguar Centro de Rescate WILDLIFE RESERVE
(2750-0710; www.jaguarrescue.foundation; Playa Chiquita; 1½hr tours adult/child under 10yr US$20/free; tours 9:30am & 11:30am Mon-Sat;) Named in honor of its original resident, a jaguar, this well-run wildlife-rescue center in Playa Chiquita now focuses mostly on other animals, including sloths, crocodiles, anteaters, snakes and monkeys. Founded by zoologist Encar and her late partner Sandro, a herpetologist, the center rehabilitates orphaned, injured and rescued animals for reintroduction into the wild whenever possible (40% success rate).

Volunteer opportunities (US$350 including accommodation) are available with a one-month minimum commitment. You can also tour the Punta Uva release center, where many of the Center's success stories are returned to their natural habitat.

Activities

The region's biggest draws are surf, sand, wildlife-watching and tanning.

Indulgence Spa SPA
(2750-0536; www.lacostadepapito.com/spa; Playa Cocles; treatments from US$25, massages US$60-85; 11am-6pm Mon-Sat) The southern Caribbean's best day spa. It's located at La Costa de Papito.

Punta Uva Dive Center DIVING
(2759-9191; www.puntauvadivecenter.com; shore/boat dives from US$85/95) Offers fun dives, night dives, PADI courses, snorkeling tours (US$55), SUP tours (US$75) and kayak hire (US$10 per hour). Clearly signposted off the main road in Punta Uva.

Tours

Chocolate Forest Experience TOURS
(8341-2034, 2750-0504; www.caribeanscr.com; Playa Cocles; tours US$28; 8:30am-6pm Mon-Sat, tours 10am Mon, 10am & 2pm Tue, Thu & Fri, 2pm Sat) Playa Cocles–based chocolate producer Caribeans leads tours of its sustainable cacao forest and chocolate-creation lab, accompanied by gourmet chocolate tastings. There's also a shop with a refrigerated chocolate room where visitors can try several varieties of chocolate flavor. This is a 1.5km walking tour of moderate difficulty.

Sleeping

This stretch of coastline features some of the most charming and romantic accommodations in the country.

Playa Cocles

The broad, 2km-long white-sand Playa Cocles lies within easy walking distance east of Puerto Viejo (1.5km away), offering proximity to the village and its many restaurants but plenty of peace and quiet too.

El Tucán Jungle Lodge CABINA $
(2750-0026; www.eltucanjunglelodge.com; s/d/tr/q US$48/58/68/78;) Only 1km off the road, this jungle retreat feels miles from anywhere, making it ideal for birdwatchers. Four clean wooden *cabinas* on the banks of the Caño Negro share a broad patio with hammocks, from which you can observe a plethora of wildlife. Upon request the welcoming owners serve breakfast (US$8) and organize walks in the area.

Two additional houses (US$65 to US$70) across the road from El Tucán offer more room and privacy. Bathrooms have beautiful mirrors reflecting the Ndbele culture of South Africa, where the owners once lived. Irena's artistic touch is everywhere.

Physis B&B $$
(2750-0941, 8866-4405; www.physiscaribbean.net; incl breakfast d US$118, tr US$130-156;) Comforts abound at this four-bedroom B&B, tucked down a Playa Cocles side road and managed by transplanted Pittsburghers Juliet and Matthew. There are free Netflix movies in the smaller downstairs units, satellite TV in the honeymoon suite, and sound systems, dehumidifiers, air-con, mini fridges and wi-fi throughout. The pretty garden has water features; nature scenes adorn the bright external walls.

Finca Chica BUNGALOW $$
(2750-1919; www.fincachica.com; bungalows US$70-140;) These four stand-alone wooden cabins range from a two-person bungalow to an amazing three-story structure known as 'La Casita del Río' that sleeps up to six. All have full kitchens; three have spacious living and dining areas. It's tucked down a dead-end dirt driveway a few hundred meters off the main road (past Physis).

At the time of research, the smallest *casita* was being expanded to match the grandeur of the others.

La Costa de Papito BUNGALOW $$
(☑2750-0080; www.lacostadepapito.com; d incl breakfast US$128, additional adult/child US$19/10; P 🔊) Relax in rustic comfort in the sculpture-studded grounds of this popular Cocles outpost, which has timber-and-bamboo bungalows decked out with hand-carved furniture, stone bathrooms straight out of *The Flintstones* and roomy porches draped with hammocks and a table area. The restaurant serves Caribbean specialties, while the rustic, palm-thatched Indulgence Spa offers massage and spa treatments.

The attentive owners were replacing mattresses in late 2019.

Hotel Isla Inn CABINA $$
(☑2537-9338, 2750-0109; www.hotelislainn.com; d/f/master ste incl breakfast US$100/215/245; P ❄ 🔊 🏊) Opposite the lifeguard tower at the main hub of Playa Cocles lies this efficient wooden lodge with expansive rooms, some sleeping up to five and a few with killer ocean views. All rooms are equipped with air-con, cable TV, hot shower, coffeemaker, fridge and handmade wooden furnishings crafted from the slightly curved outer boards that are discarded during lumber processing.

Azánia Bungalows BUNGALOW $$
(☑2750-0540; www.azania-costarica.com; d incl breakfast US$118, additional person US$25; P @ 🏊) Eleven spacious but dark thatch-roofed bungalows are brightened up by colorful linens at this charming inn set on landscaped jungle grounds. Nice details include woven bedspreads, well-designed bathrooms and wide-plank hardwood floors. A free-form pool and a Jacuzzi nestle into the greenery, and there's an Argentine restaurant and bar. Rooms sleep up to four people and all have cable television.

🏖 Playa Chiquita

It isn't exactly clear where Playa Cocles ends and Playa Chiquita begins, but conventional wisdom applies the latter name to a series of beaches 4km to 6km east of Puerto Viejo.

La Kukula BUNGALOW $$
(☑2750-0653; www.lakukulalodge.com; d incl breakfast US$124-144; 🏊) 🍃 Six tastefully

spaced 'tropical contemporary' bungalows bring guests close to nature with natural ventilation (super-high ceilings, screen walls) and open jungle views from the rain showers. The wood-decked pool is great for bird- and frog-watching. For larger groups a house, divided into two apartments with private kitchen and pool, sleeps up to ten (you can rent one or both apartments).

The delicious breakfast features homemade bread and marmalade.

Tierra de Sueños BUNGALOW $$
(☑2750-0378; http://tierradesuenoslodge.com; bungalows incl breakfast US$95-153; P 🔊) 🍃 True to its name ('land of dreams'), this blissful garden retreat comprises seven adorable wood bungalows with mosquito nets and private decks. The quiet, tropical atmosphere is complemented by regular yoga (US$8/10 for guests/nonguests) on an open-air platform. Laundry (US$10 per load) is available, as is wi-fi. The bungalows sleep two to five.

★ Tree House Lodge BUNGALOW $$$
(☑2750-0706; www.costaricatreehouse.com; d US$225-399, extra adult/child US$50/25; P) 🍃 Adventurers who like their lodgings whimsical will love these five open-air *casitas*, including a literal 'tree house' and the Casa Cristal two-storey cabin built around a living sangrillo tree, complete with a mini-golf course around the trunk. All have kitchens, BBQs, spacious decks with easy chairs and hammocks, and private paths leading to a small white-sand beach.

The houses sleep up to five and have mosquito nets; five have Jacuzzis.

The owner is a founder of the Iguana Verde Foundation, an effort to save the endangered green iguana. There's a huge breeding area on the grounds (*Jurassic Park*, anyone?) and informational tours are available (US$15).

Shawandha Lodge BUNGALOW $$$
(☑2750-0018; www.shawandha.com; d incl breakfast US$170, additional person US$40; P ❄ @ 🔊 🏊) Immersed in greenery, with frogs, agoutis and other tropical critters close by, this upscale lodge has 14 private, spacious, nature-themed bungalows painted in earth tones and equipped with large mosaic-tiled bathrooms. A meticulously maintained thatched *rancho* serves as an open-air lounge, and there's a French-Caribbean

restaurant. A private path across the road leads to the beach.

At the time of research, a new pool and additional cabins were slated to open soon.

Punta Uva

In calm seas, Punta Uva has one of the region's most swimmable beaches. It's a quiet spot, embraced by a palm-lined cove. To find the turnoff to the point (about 7km east of Puerto Viejo), look for the Punta Uva Dive Center sign.

Wal-aba Eco Lodge HOSTEL $
(2750-0147; tw per person with bathroom US$30, dm/s/d without bathroom US$18/24/48; P Wi-fi) Funky, colorful and relatively cheap for Punta Uva, this ramshackle collection of open-air dorms, private rooms (including an 'attic' double reached by a ladder) and 3 casitas is surrounded by a flowery garden and managed by friendly staff. Guests share ample kitchen facilities, hot and cold showers, and a creaky-floored communal area with games, books and rental bikes.

★ **Cabinas Punta Uva** CABINA $$
(8876-0568, 2759-9180; www.cabinaspuntauvapuertoviejo.com; cabinas with/without private kitchen US$120/65; P) Steps from idyllic Punta Uva, this cluster of *cabinas* with tiled bathrooms, polished-wood verandas, hammocks and a shared open-air kitchen is hidden down a dead-end street in a verdant garden setting. Fall asleep to the sound of crashing waves and chirping insects and wake up to the roar of the resident howler monkeys.

★ **Korrigan Lodge** BUNGALOW $$
(2759-9103; www.korriganlodge.com; s/d incl breakfast US$125/135; P) *Korrigan* is a Breton word for a fairy or gnome, and maybe that was the impetus for this otherworldly lodge, nestled into a patch of Talamanca jungle. Four thatch-roofed wood-and-concrete bungalows come with minibar, safe, fan, modern bathroom and private terrace with hammock. Guests have access to free bikes. Organic breakfast is served in an open-air *rancho* surrounded by gardens.

We hear that in addition to *korrigans*, sometimes jaguars roam the grounds (but only at night, promise). Patrick and Irena hail from Luxembourg.

Villas del Caribe HOTEL $$
(2233-2200, 2750-0202; www.villasdelcaribe.com; incl breakfast d US$95, villas US$120-165 std/superior r US$110/140; P) With a prime location near the beach, this resort offers lovely, brightly painted rooms, comfortable beds, sitting areas and roomy bathrooms with Spanish tiles. Junior villas also come with kitchenettes, while the two-story villas have ocean views, king-size beds, kitchens and BBQs. All have private decks with hammocks. Most villas have air-conditioning. Wi-fi is available throughout.

Casa Viva BUNGALOW $$$
(2750-0659; https://casavivalodge.com; 1-bedroom house US$100, 2-bedroom bungalow $158-214; P Wi-fi) Beautifully handcrafted by a master carpenter, these enormous, fully furnished hardwood houses, each with tiled shower, kitchen and wraparound veranda, all have direct beach access – an ideal spot in which to chill out in a hammock and observe the local wildlife. Venezuelan architect/owner Ricardo was making it all bigger and better in late 2019. Three rooms have air-con.

Eating

Playa Cocles is close to the lively eating options of Puerto Viejo; after that, the pickings get slim until you approach Punta Uva, which has a cluster of fantastic restaurants.

★ **Selvin's Restaurant** CARIBBEAN $$
(Blanca and Selvin's Cabinas y Restaurante; 2750-0664; www.selvinpuntauva.com; Punta Uva; mains US$12-18; noon-8pm Thu-Sun) Selvin has been serving Caribbean food since 1982. His place is considered one of the region's best, specializing in shrimp, sautéed lobster in butter, garlic and onion, T-bone steak, a terrific *rondón* (seafood gumbo) and a succulent chicken *caribeño* (chicken stewed in a spicy Caribbean sauce). Those with a sweet tooth will enjoy the organic chocolate bar and coconut candy.

Pita Bonita MIDDLE EASTERN $$
(2756-8173; Playa Chiquita; US$7.50-13.50; noon-9pm Mon-Sat) For Turkish coffee, hummus and the best pita bread in the Caribbean, this Israeli-owned spot is the place. There's also creamy *moutabal* (a roasted-aubergine and tahini dip), spicy *shakshuka* (a Middle Eastern dish with poached eggs

and tomato sauce) and fresh tabouli (tomatoes, parsley, mint, bulgur, lemon juice and onion). Find the open-air restaurant across from Tree House Lodge (p187).

There's a good selection of liquor, beer and wines too.

Pura Gula INTERNATIONAL $$
(☑ 8634-6404; Punta Uva; mains US$6-16; ⊙ 5-10pm Mon-Sat; ✐) Raquel and Matias completely revamped the menu here at the end of 2019, keeping old faves including Pad Thai but including mouth-watering delights such as *lomito* (beef) and *carpaccio de atún* (tuna carpaccio). The menu is mostly organic with a few vegan options. Everything's served on a pleasant open-air deck, just off the main road between Playa Chiquita and Punta Uva.

El Refugio ARGENTINE $$$
(☑ 2759-9007; Playa Grande; mains US$12-25; ⊙ noon-2pm, 5:30-9pm Thu-Tue) This Argentine-owned restaurant with five tables is renowned for its rotating menu of three appetizers, five main dishes and three desserts. New offerings get chalked up on the board daily, anchored by perennial favorites such as red tuna in garlic, *bife de entraña* with chimichurri (skirt steak in a marinade of parsley, garlic and spices) and *dulce de leche* crepes. Reserve ahead.

La Pecora Nera ITALIAN $$$
(☑ 2750-0490; Playa Cocles; mains US$20-30; ⊙ 5:30-10pm Tue-Sun; ✐) If you're looking to splurge on a fancy meal during your trip, do it at this romantic eatery run by Ilario Giannoni. On a lovely candlelit patio, deftly prepared Italian seafood and pasta dishes are served alongside unusual offerings such as the delicate *carpaccio di carambola:* transparent slices of starfruit topped with shrimp, tomatoes and balsamic vinaigrette.

There is an extensive wine list, but you can't go wrong with the well-chosen and relatively inexpensive house wines.

❶ Getting There & Away

Buses heading from Puerto Viejo to Manzanillo will stop at Playa Cocles, Playa Chiquita or Punta Uva on request. Alternatively, it's an easy and pleasant 30- to 40-minute slow cycle from Puerto Viejo to Punta Uva (bike hire is roughly US$10 per day). Most motorists are respectful but you should ride close to the shoulder so they can pass if necessary. Don't cycle without strong bike lights after dark, as these roads are not lit.

Manzanillo
POP 251

Chilled-out Manzanillo has long been off the beaten track. This little town is a vibrant outpost of Afro-Caribbean culture and has remained pristine, thanks to the 1985 establishment of the Refugio Nacional de Vida Silvestre Gandoca-Manzanillo, which includes the village and imposes strict regulations on regional development.

Activities are of a simple nature, *in* nature: hiking, snorkeling and kayaking reign supreme. As elsewhere, ask about riptides before heading out.

🏃 Activities

Bad Barts SNORKELING
(Dive Shop & Adventures; ☑ 8333-9688, 2750-3091; www.facebook.com/badbartsmanzanillo; ⊙ 8am-5pm Tue-Sun) Near the bus stop in Manzanillo, this outfit rents kayaks, boogie boards and bicycles. Hours can vary; call ahead.

🛏 Sleeping

Cabinas Manzanillo CABINA $
(☑ 8327-3291, 2759-9033; s/d/tr US$50/50/100; ⓟ❋🛜) Run by the ever-helpful Sandra Castillo and Pablo Bustamante, these eight *cabinas* at Manzanillo's western edge are so clean you could eat off the tile floors. The cheery rooms have big beds, impressive indigenous masks, industrial-strength ceiling fans, TVs, safes and spacious bathrooms with hot water. There's air-con in some rooms and a shared kitchen.

From Maxi's Restaurant (p190), travel 300m west toward Punta Uva, then make a left onto the signposted dirt road.

Congo Bongo BUNGALOW $$
(☑ 2759-9016; www.congo-bongo.com; bungalows US$132-195, extra person US$15; ⓟ❋🛜) Just 1km outside Manzanillo, Dan from Amsterdam has created a whimsical pop-art paradise of repurposed and recycled materials. Eight *cabinas*, surrounded by dense forest (formerly a cacao plantation) offer fully equipped kitchens and plenty of living space, including open-air terraces and strategically placed hammocks perfect for wildlife-watching. A network of trails leads to the beautiful beach. Two-night minimum stay.

Bowing to market forces, two *cabinas* now have air-con. Guests are encouraged to book direct.

Sumaqtikaq Cabins GUESTHOUSE **$$**
(☎8860-9331, 2261-8186, 2759-9146; www.cabinas-sumaqtikaq.com; incl breakfast cabins for 2-3 people US$70, 5 people US$100; P 📶) The best option for groups, this guesthouse with indigenous art and a pretty garden has two double rooms, a room sleeping five and a two-story house sleeping 11. Facilities include shared kitchen, BBQ, and laundry service. Some rooms have refrigerators, mosquito nets and hammocks. Tours to the nearby Gandoca-Manzanillo wildlife refuge can be arranged here.

Almonds & Corals Lodge BUNGALOW **$$$**
(☎2271-3000, in USA 1-888-373-9042; www.almondsandcorals.com; ste incl breakfast US$205-235; P @ 📶 ❄) Buried in the jungle, this beachfront spot is popular with honeymooners (splurge on the master suite!). Its 24 green palm-roofed bungalows with netted walls are connected by wooden boardwalks. Accommodation features four-poster beds, Jacuzzis (in some), and patios with hammocks from which to enjoy nature's serenade. A breakfast buffet is included; other meals can be purchased at the restaurant.

Wi-fi is available in the lobby/restaurant only.

Eating

Maxi's Restaurant CARIBBEAN **$$**
(Mr. Maxie's; ☎2759-9086; mains US$10-19, lobster US$20-60; ⊙noon-10pm; 📶) Manzanillo's most famous restaurant draws a tourist crowd with large platters of grilled seafood, *pargo rojo* (whole red snapper), *ceviche*, pork-and-rice, steak and pricey Caribbean-style lobster. Service can be slow, but the open-air upstairs dining area is a wonderful seaside setting for a meal and a beer with views of the beach and the street below.

At the end of the road into town (where buses arrive).

Check the Euro soccer scarves on the wall – your team just might be there.

Cool & Calm Cafe CARIBBEAN **$$**
(mains US$12-26; ⊙11am-10pm Thu-Tue) Directly across from Manzanillo's western beachfront, this front-porch eatery plies visitors with fine Caribbean cooking – from snapper to shrimp to chicken to lobster, roasted over coconut husks – with extras such as veggie curry thrown in for good measure. Owner Andy offers Caribbean cooking classes and a 'reef-to-plate' tour where, in certain seasons, you dive for your own lobster or fish. Andy catches the lobster and prepares his outrageous lobster *caribeño* daily.

Getting There & Away

Buses to Puerto Limón via Puerto Viejo depart from Manzanillo at 5am, 7am, 10am, noon, 2pm, 4pm and 6pm (to Puerto Limón roughly US$5, 2½ hours; to Puerto Viejo US$1.50, 30 minutes). Buses from Puerto Limón to Manzanillo (via Puerto Viejo) depart at 5:30am, 6:30am, 8:30am, 10:30am, 12:30pm, 5:30pm and 6:30pm. This schedule varies slightly on Sundays and holidays.

Autotransportes Mepe also runs one direct bus daily between Manzanillo and San José (about US$13, five hours), leaving Manzanillo at 7am. The bus from San José to Manzanillo departs at noon.

Refugio Nacional de Vida Silvestre Gandoca-Manzanillo

This little-explored **refuge** (REGAMA; ☎2759-9100; US$6; ⊙8am-4pm) protects nearly 70% of the southern Caribbean coast, extending from Manzanillo all the way to the Panamanian border. It encompasses 50 sq km of land plus 44 sq km of marine environment. The peaceful, pristine stretch of sandy white beach – one of the area's main attractions and the center of village life in Manzanillo – stretches from Punta Uva in the west to Punta Mona (p192) in the east. Offshore, a 5-sq-km coral reef is a teeming habitat for lobsters, sea fans and long-spined urchins.

Activities

Hiking

A coastal trail heads 5.5km east out of Manzanillo to Punta Mona. The first part of this path, which leads from Manzanillo to Tom Bay (about a 90-minute walk), is well trammeled and clearly marked and doesn't require a guide. Once you pass Tom Bay, however, the path gets murky and it's easy to get lost, so ask about conditions before you set out, or hire a local guide. It's a rewarding walk with amazing scenery, as well as excellent (and safe) swimming and snorkeling at the end.

Another, more difficult, trail (12km) leaves from just west of Manzanillo and skirts the southern edges of the Pantano Punta Mona, continuing to the small community of **Gandoca**. This trail is not commonly walked, as most people access Punta Mona and Gandoca by boat or from the park entrance at the northern edge of the refuge, which is located on the road to Sixaola. If you want to try to hike this, be sure to hire a guide.

A third trail ('La Trocha') in the reserve takes visitors through thick forest. Parts of this trail were previously dangerous or difficult to access, but now some sections are covered with a boardwalk made of wood and plastic. Again, however, it's best to use a local guide.

Snorkeling & Diving

The undersea portion of the park cradles one of the two accessible living coral reefs in the country. Comprising five types of coral, the reefs begin in about 1m of water and extend 5km offshore to a barrier reef that local fishers have long relied on and researchers have only recently discovered. This colorful undersea world is home to some 400 species of fish and crustaceans. Punta Mona is a popular destination for snorkeling, though it's a trek, so you may wish to hire a boat. Otherwise, you can snorkel offshore at Manzanillo at the eastern end of the beach; the riptide can be dangerous here, so inquire about conditions before setting out.

Conditions vary widely, and visibility can be adversely affected by weather changes.

Kayaking

You can explore some of the area's waterways by kayak. Paddle out to the reef, and on clear days you'll be able to gaze right into the water and see marine life. If you have kids in tow, head along the coastline west or east of Manzanillo village for shorter paddles.

Dolphin-Watching

In 1997 a group of local guides in Manzanillo identified tucuxi dolphins, a little-known species previously not found in Costa Rica, and began to observe their interactions with bottlenose dolphins. A third species – the Atlantic spotted dolphin – is also common in this area. This unprecedented activity has attracted the attention of marine biologists and conservationists, who are following these animals with great interest.

You also may be lucky enough to spot another wonderful sea mammal, the ponderous 'sea cow' or manatee.

Note that in Costa Rica it is illegal to swim with dolphins; be sure to keep a distance from the animals and refrain from touching or bothering them.

Turtle-Watching

Marine turtles – especially leatherback but also green, hawksbill and loggerhead – nest on the beaches between Punta Mona and the Río Sixaola. Leatherbacks nest from March to July, with a peak in April and May. The hawksbill (or Carey) may hang around until September. Local conservation efforts are under way to protect these nesting grounds, as the growth of the area's human population has led to increased theft of turtle eggs.

During turtle season, no flashlights, fires or camping are allowed on the beach. All tourists must be accompanied by a local guide to minimize disturbance of the nesting turtles.

Tours

You could explore the refuge on your own, but without a guide you'll likely miss out on the incredible diversity of medicinal plants, exotic birds and earthbound animals. Most guides charge US$35 to US$40 per person per trek, depending on the size of the group. Ask at Maxi's in Manzanillo.

Recommended local guides include **Florentino Grenald** (☎8841-2732; 4hr tours per person from US$40), who used to serve as the reserve's administrator, and **Abel Bustamante** (☎2759-9043). Abel is the only officially government-licensed guide in Manzanillo.

Ara Manzanillo BIRDWATCHING

(☎8971-1436; www.aramanzanillo.org; $10; ⏲tour 3pm) Few things in nature compare with the beauty of a great green macaw in full flight, multicolored tail feathers shining in the sun. On this once-a-day educational/photo-op tour, you'll hear these raucous, cawing birds before you see them! Though wild, these birds are accustomed to a daily snack around 3pm.

Ara has had great success with its artificial nest-box program for the *lapa verde* (great green macaw): 24 chicks have been born in recent years. The 45 others introduced through breeding have boosted the local population of the endangered bird, which numbers fewer than 400 in Costa Rica.

Sleeping & Eating

Pack snacks for a day hike, or call ahead to Punta Mona (p192) to make reservations for lunch there. After a hike, grab a fruit smoothie and tasty Caribbean food at Cool & Calm Cafe in Manzanillo, a short walk north of the refuge entrance.

GETTING TO PANAMA

Welcome to Costa Rica's most entertaining border crossing! An old railroad bridge spans the churning waters of the Río Sixaola, connecting Costa Rica with Panama amid a sea of agricultural plantations. Oversize buses and trucks used to ply this route – making for a surreal scene whenever one of them came clattering along the wood planks, forcing pedestrians to scatter to the edges. Today there's a parallel bridge for motor-vehicle traffic, but pedestrians still get the fun of walking across the old bridge.

From here, most travelers make for Bocas del Toro, a picturesque archipelago of jungle islands that's home to lovely beaches and endangered red frogs. It's easily accessible by regular water taxi from the docks at Almirante.

The border is open 7am to 5pm (8am to 6pm in Guabito, Panama, which is an hour ahead of Costa Rica), though one or both sides may close for lunch at around 1pm. At the entrance to the bridge, on the right-hand side, pay the US$8 Costa Rican departure tax (in dollars or colones) and get your exit stamp at the **Costa Rican immigration office** (www.migracion.go.cr/SitePages/Directorio.aspx; 7am-5pm). It's best to bring cash in case the electronic machine is not working. Once you're over the bridge, stop at Panamanian immigration to get your passport stamped (at time of research, no entry tax was required). Note that in Panama you will be required to show proof of onward travel out of Panama, or another Central American country, to your home country, such as a copy of your plane ticket home. To cross, you'll need a passport valid for more than six months; sometimes proof of at least US$500 in your bank account is also required, although it's not often requested at the Sixaola border. Be prepared with a copy of a recent bank statement or ATM receipt. A copy of your passport – in addition to the real one, of course – is always a good idea, too. Personal cars (not rentals) can cross here. Be aware that sometimes lines here can be long; plan your onward travel accordingly.

Guabito has no hotels or banks, but in a pinch you can exchange colones at the market across the street. From the border, half-hourly buses (about US$2, one hour) run to Terminal Piquera in Changuinola, where you can transfer to one of the frequent buses to Almirante (roughly US$2, 45 minutes) for the water taxi. Alternatively, from Guabito you can take a collective taxi (per person around US$10, one hour) straight to Almirante. From this point, hourly water taxis (per person US$6, 25 minutes) make the trip to Bocas del Toro between 6:30am and 6pm.

For a more streamlined, if slightly more expensive, trip to Bocas del Toro, take one of the daily shuttles from Cahuita or Puerto Viejo de Talamanca (it's US$33 with Caribe Shuttle, p177; some operators charge as little as US$25). A day round trip into Panama is possible with any of the shuttle companies. Most do not include the US$16 Costa Rican exit/entry tax in their pricing

★**Punta Mona** CABINA **$$**
(www.puntamona.org; cabinas per person incl meals US$90; @) Accessible via a two-hour trek or a 15-minute boat ride, this 35-hectare organic farm and retreat 5km southeast of Manzanillo is a thriving experiment in permaculture design and sustainable living. More than 200 varieties of fruit and nut trees and hundreds of edible greens, roots, veggies and medicinal plants grow here. Vegetarian meals are included in the rate.

At the time of research Punta Mona was one of the largest sources of useful plants in the world, and Norman Brooks, who set the place up, was also establishing the world's first eco-versity here. He continues to host yoga retreats and a jungle camp. To arrange accommodation and transportation, email ahead of your visit. Day trips with lunch are also possible in this paradise setting; boat taxis cost roughly US$50.

Nature Observatorio TREEHOUSE **$$$**
(8628-2663; www.natureobservatorio.com; overnight package adult/child US$200/120) Located 25m up a tree within the Gandoca-Manzanillo wildlife refuge (p190), this observation deck and tree house allows guests to experience life in the canopy of an old-growth forest. The open-air, two-storey accommodation features hammocks and comfy beds from which monkeys, kinkajous and toucans are regularly spotted. To reach the platform, guests must climb the tree (harnesses provided).

The owner, an ardent conservationist, collects his customers in Manzanillo at 1pm each day and leads them on a 45-minute hike to the tree, which he helps them to scale on a rope ladder. Dinner and breakfast are delivered up the tree in a basket. The entire deck is 60 sq m and includes two units sleeping two people each.

Information

An excellent photo book on the area, with commentary in Spanish and English, is *Refugio Nacional de Vida Silvestre Gandoca-Manzanillo* by Juan José Puccí, available locally and online.

The park office has maps, available after you register at the park entrance and make your donation.

Getting There & Away

Buses to Manzanillo drop off in front of Maxi's Restaurant (p190). From there it's about 1km to the refuge entrance. A bridge allows guests to enter the park without having to wade through the water at high tide. Another good option for accessing different areas of the park is to hire a boat.

Sixaola

POP 1823

This is the end of the road – literally. Bumpy tarmac leads to an old railroad bridge over the Río Sixaola that serves as the border crossing into Panama. There's no good reason to stay in Sixaola, but if you get stuck, head for safe, clean **Cabinas Sanchez** (Cabinas Sanchez-Salazar; ☎2754-2126; d/tr US$20/30; ❄📶).

Getting There & Away

The bus terminal is just north of the border crossing, one block east of the main drag.

Buses to San José (about US$14, six hours) run hourly from 6am to 1pm, and at 3pm, 4pm and 7pm, with a change in Puerto Limón (about US$7, three hours from Sixaola). All buses pass Bribrí Territory and Cahuita.

There are also regular buses to Puerto Viejo (about US$3, one hour), running hourly between 6am and 7pm Monday to Saturday, and every two hours on Sunday.

AT A GLANCE

POPULATION
Liberia: 56,900

FAST FACT
The forests around Monteverde are home some 500 species of orchids, including many endemic species.

BEST CLOUD FOREST ADVENTURE
El Tigre Waterfalls (p203)

BEST GLAMPING
Chira (p208)

BEST FOOD TRUCK
Pollo Frito La Casona (p243)

WHEN TO GO

Dec–Apr Costa Rica's driest province (Guanacaste) gets very little rain, as well as strong winds in Bahía Salinas.

May–Nov Fewer tourists and prices for accommodations are reduced.

Sep–Oct Humpback whales migrate up the coast, putting on a spectacular, splashy show.

Catarata de Río Celeste (p221)

Northwestern Costa Rica

What did you come to Costa Rica for? To lounge on pristine beaches and ride glorious waves? To hike up volcanoes and soak in geothermal springs? To spy on birds and monkeys and get lost among ancient trees? The northwestern corner of Costa Rica packs in all this and more. Unlike any other part of the country, Guanacaste – in the far northwest – is a wide, flat expanse of grasslands and dry tropical forest, where savanna vistas are broken only by windblown trees. Further east, the Cordillera de Guanacaste rises majestically out of the plains in a line of sputtering, steaming volcanic peaks that beg exploration. Further south, higher altitudes create misty, mystical cloud forests, teeming with life. Whatever you came to Costa Rica for, here it is.

INCLUDES

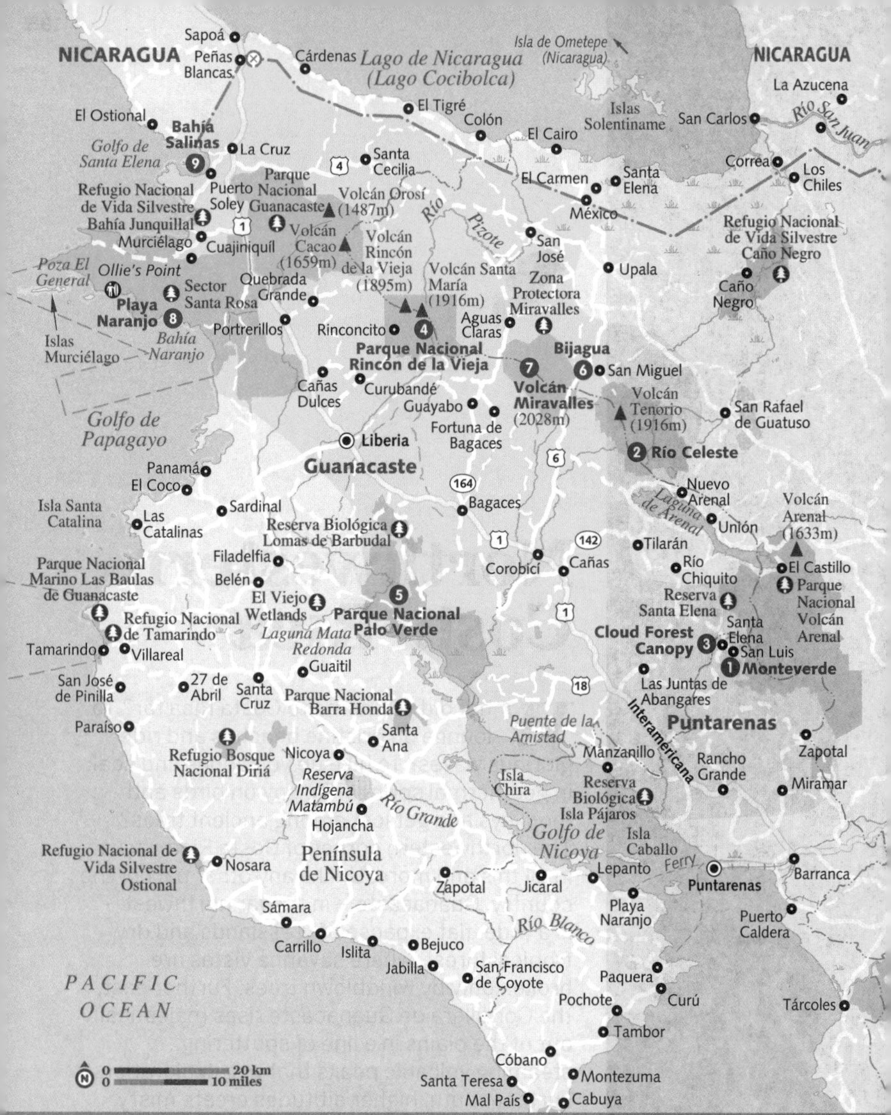

Northwestern Costa Rica Highlights

1 Monteverde Spotting the resplendent quetzal through the mist at nearby reserves.

2 Río Celeste (p221) Hiking to tumbling waterfalls alongside a Gatorade-blue river.

3 Cloud Forest Canopy Tours (p201) Making like a monkey zipping through trees.

4 Parque Nacional Rincón de la Vieja (p232) Trekking past waterfalls and volcanic vents.

5 Parque Nacional Palo Verde (p226) Expanding your bird list at Costa Rica's largest wetland sanctuary.

6 Bijagua (p218) Playing tourist in this verdant town.

7 Hot Springs & Mud Pots (p227) Painting yourself with mud in Rio Perdido's springs.

8 Playa Naranjo (p237) Surfing the legendary beach break at Witch's Rock.

9 Bahía Salinas (p240) Catching wind on one of Central America's breeziest beaches.

Getting There & Away

More and more visitors are flying directly into Liberia's Aeropuerto Internacional Daniel Oduber Quirós (p232), a convenient international airport that makes for quick escapes to both northwestern Costa Rica and the beaches of the Península de Nicoya. Liberia is also a major transportation center for buses traveling the Interamericana, from the border with Nicaragua to San José. Regular buses also connect the Península de Nicoya to hubs such as Santa Cruz and Nicoya and coastal points beyond.

This is a heavily touristed region, and entrepreneurs have picked up on the need for more transportation options. If you're looking for a ride that's cheaper than a rented car and more comfortable (and faster) than a public bus, you'll probably be able to find a shuttle. Several companies ply the most popular routes.

If you do opt to rent, consider a 4WD vehicle (or at least one with high clearance), particularly during the rainy season.

MONTEVERDE & AROUND

Spread out on the slopes of the Cordillera de Tilarán, this area is a sprawling chain of villages, farms and nature reserves. The biggest population center – the village of Santa Elena – runs seamlessly uphill into next-door neighbor Cerro Plano and then tiny Monteverde, which borders its namesake reserve.

The Reserva Biológica Bosque Nuboso Monteverde (Monteverde Cloud Forest Reserve; p213) is the most famous one, but there are public and private properties of all shapes and sizes – from tiny family *fincas* (farms) to the vast Bosque Eterno de los Niños (Children's Eternal Rainforest; p203) – that blanket this whole area in luscious green. As a result, there are trails to hike, birds to spot, waterfalls to swim in and adventures to be had at every turn.

Monteverde & Santa Elena

POP 6750

Strung between two lovingly preserved cloud forests, this slim corridor of civilization consists of the Tico village of Santa Elena and the Quaker settlement of Monteverde, each with an eponymous cloud forest reserve. The cloud forests are premier destinations for everyone from budget backpackers to families and well-heeled retirees.

On a good day, the Monteverde area is a place where you can be inspired about the possibility of a world in which organic farming and alternative energy sources are the norm; on a bad day, it can feel like Disneyland in Birkenstocks. Take heart in the fact that the local community continues to fight the good fight to maintain the fragile balance between nature and commerce.

PARKS & RESERVES OF NORTHWESTERN COSTA RICA

Northwestern Costa Rica has a wealth of parks and reserves, ranging from little-visited national parks to the highlight on many visitors' itineraries, Monteverde Cloud Forest.

Parque Nacional Palo Verde (p226) Stay at the research station and take a guided tour to see some of the 300-plus bird species recorded in this rich wetland.

Parque Nacional Rincón de la Vieja (p232) Peaceful, muddy isolation can be found just outside of Liberia, where bubbling thermal activity abounds.

Refugio Nacional de Vida Silvestre Bahía Junquillal (p238) A small and peaceful protected site, this refuge has a beach backed by mangrove swamp and tropical dry forest.

Reserva Biológica Bosque Nuboso Monteverde (p213) Costa Rica's most famous cloud forest, Monteverde receives a steady stream of visitors but hasn't lost its magic.

Reserva Biológica Lomas de Barbudal (p232) In March, you might be lucky enough to catch the yellow blooms of the corteza amarilla tree in this tropical dry forest reserve.

Reserva Santa Elena (p216) With fewer crowds and a higher elevation than neighboring Monteverde, this is a mistier and more mysterious place to experience the cloud forest.

Sector Santa Rosa (p235) Access legendary surf, hike through the largest stand of tropical dry forest in Central America and visit a historical battle site.

Sector Murciélago (p236) Brave the notorious roads to explore deserted beaches, or catch a boat to surf the country's most celebrated break.

Monteverde & Santa Elena

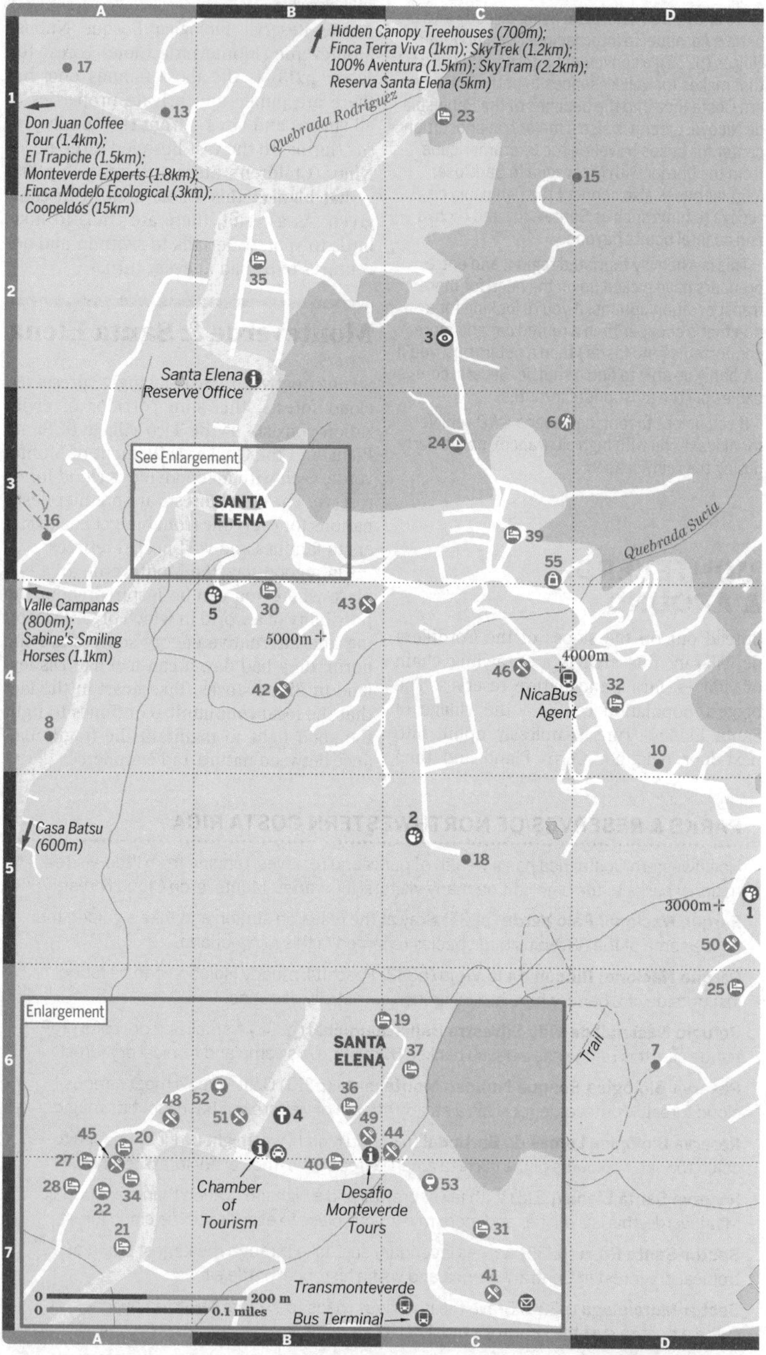

A
B
C
D
1
2
3
4
5
6
7
Hidden Canopy Treehouses (700m); Finca Terra Viva (1km); SkyTrek (1.2km); 100% Aventura (1.5km); SkyTram (2.2km); Reserva Santa Elena (5km)
Don Juan Coffee Tour (1.4km); El Trapiche (1.5km); Monteverde Experts (1.8km); Finca Modelo Ecological (3km); Coopeldós (15km)
Quebrada Rodríguez
Santa Elena Reserve Office
See Enlargement
SANTA ELENA
Quebrada Sucia
Valle Campanas (800m); Sabine's Smiling Horses (1.1km)
5000m
4000m
NicaBus Agent
3000m
Casa Batsu (600m)
Trail
Enlargement
SANTA ELENA
Chamber of Tourism
Desafío Monteverde Tours
Transmonteverde Bus Terminal
0 200 m
0 0.1 miles

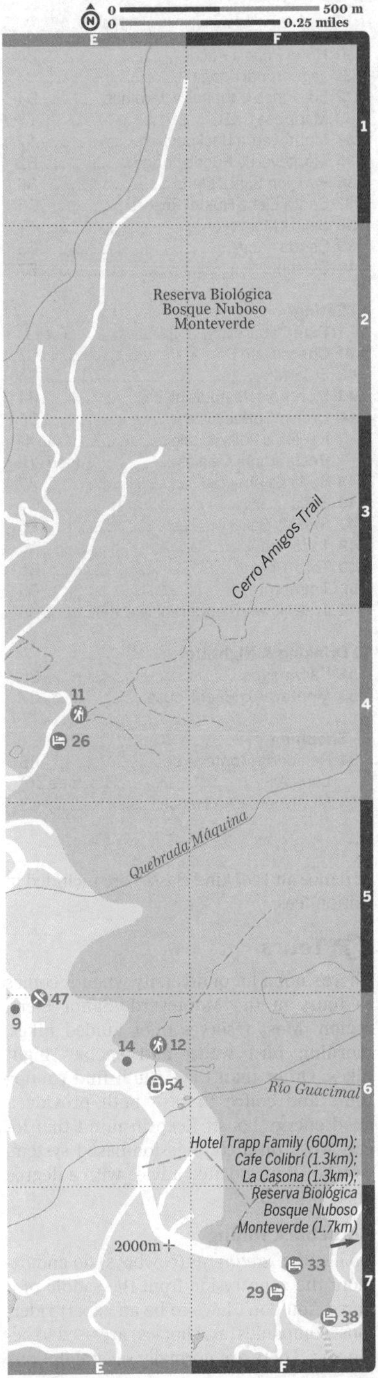

Sights

The sights in Monteverde and Santa Elena are mostly geared to bringing the wildlife a little closer, whether it's bats, butterflies, frogs, snakes or flowers. These stops can be entertaining and educational – especially for children – but it's even more rewarding when you see these creatures in the wild. And you're in the wild now, so go out there and see it.

Ranario — ZOO

(Monteverde Frog Pond; ☎2645-6320; Santa Elena; per attraction US$15.50, package ticket for frogs and insects US$20; ⏲9am-8:30pm) Returning to its former glory as the Ranario, or Frog Pond (it's changed names a few times), this place also features an insect house. The frogs are still the highlight – 28 species reside in transparent enclosures lining the winding indoor jungle paths. Sharp-eyed guides point out frogs, eggs and tadpoles with flashlights. Your ticket entitles you to two visits, so come back in the evening to see the nocturnal species.

Butterfly Garden — ZOO

(Jardín de Mariposas; ☎2645-5512; www.monteverdebutterflygarden.com; Cerro Plano; adult/student/child US$17.50/13.50/5.50; ⏲8:30am-4pm) Head here for everything you ever wanted to know about butterflies. There are four gardens representing different habitats; they're home to more than 40 species. Up-close observation cases allow you to witness the butterflies as they emerge from the chrysalis (if your timing is right). Other exhibits feature the industrious leafcutter ant and a tarantula hawk specimen (the wasp that eats tarantulas!) and lots of scorpions. Kids love this place, and knowledgeable naturalist guides truly enhance the experience with an enlightening hour-long tour (complimentary with admission).

Bat Jungle — ZOO

(☎2645-9999; www.batjungle.com; Monteverde; adult/child US$17/14; ⏲9am-6pm) The Bat Jungle in Monteverde is a small but informative exhibit, with good bilingual educational displays and a habitat housing almost 100 free-flying bats. Make a reservation for your 45-minute tour to learn about echolocation, bat wing aerodynamics and other amazing flying-mammal facts.

The bats are on a reversed day/night schedule so they are most active from 9am to 5pm.

Monteverde & Santa Elena

Sights

1 Bat Jungle D5
2 Butterfly Garden C5
3 El Arbol Hueco C2
4 Iglesia B6
5 Ranario B4

Activities, Courses & Tours

6 Aguti Reserve C3
7 Bosque Eterno de los Niños D6
8 Caballeriza El Rodeo A4
Caburé Chocolate Tour .... (see 1)
9 Café de Monteverde E6
10 Centro Panamericano de Idiomas D4
11 Cerro Amigos E4
12 Curi-Cancha Reserve E6
13 Horse Trek Monteverde A1
14 Monteverde Institute E6
15 Original Canopy Tour D1
16 Pasión Costa Rica A3
Reserva Bajo del Tigre .... (see 7)
17 Santa Maria Night Walk A1
18 Valle Escondido C5

Sleeping

19 Arco Iris Ecolodge C6
20 Cabinas & Hotel Vista al Golfo A6
21 Cabinas Eddy A7
22 Camino Verde B&B A7
23 Capulín Cabins & Farm C1
24 Chira C3
Cloud Forest Lodge .... (see 15)
25 El Bosque D6
26 Hotel Belmar E4
27 Hotel Claro de Luna A7
28 Hotel El Atardecer A7
29 Hotel Fonda Vela F7
30 Hotel Poco a Poco B4
31 Jaguarundi Lodge C7
32 Los Pinos Cabañas y Jardines D4
33 Mariposa B&B F7
34 Monteverde Backpackers A7
35 Monteverde Rustic Lodge B2
36 Pensión Santa Elena B6
37 Santa Elena Hostel Resort C6
38 Selina Monteverde F7
39 Senda Lodge C3
40 Sleepers B7

Eating

Café Caburé .... (see 1)
41 Choco Café Don Juan C7
42 El Jardín B4
43 Morpho's Restaurant B4
44 Orchid Coffee C6
Raulito's Pollo Asado .... (see 4)
Restaurante Celajes .... (see 26)
45 Soda La Amistad A7
46 Sofia C4
47 Stella's Bakery E6
48 Taco Taco A6
49 Toro Tinto B6
50 Tramonti D5
51 Tree House Restaurant & Café B6

Drinking & Nightlife

52 Bar Amigos B6
53 Monteverde Beer House C7

Shopping

54 Heladería Monteverde E6
Luna Azul .... (see 36)
55 Monteverde Art House C3

Courses

Monteverde Institute LANGUAGE

(☎2645-5053; www.monteverde-institute.org; Monteverde; week-long courses US$390, homestay per day incl meals US$25.50) This nonprofit educational institute in Monteverde offers interdisciplinary courses in Spanish, as well as more specialized programs in tropical ecology, conservation and ecotourism, among other topics. Courses are occasionally open to the public, as are volunteer opportunities in education and reforestation.

Centro Panamericano de Idiomas LANGUAGE

(CPI; ☎2265-6306; www.cpi-edu.com; Cerro Plano; week-long classes from US$460; ⏲8am-5pm) Specializes in Spanish-language education, with courses geared toward families, teenagers, medical professionals and retirees. For fun: optional cultural activities such as dance and cooking classes are included in tuition fees.

Tours

There's not a lot of diversity when it comes to tours in the Monteverde/Santa Elena region. Most reserves offer guided hikes, morning bird walks and spooky night hikes. Other than that, you'll find canopy tours and coffee tours – both provide a good energy boost! Keep in mind that locals work on a commission-based system, so take all unsolicited advice with a degree of skepticism.

Horseback Riding

Do like the *sabaneros* (cowboys) do and explore the countryside from the saddle of a horse. You don't have to be an expert rider; most companies (and horses) are used to beginners. There are normally several options for routes and duration, ranging from two hours to full days.

Sabine's Smiling Horses HORSEBACK RIDING
(☎8385-2424; www.horseback-riding-tour.com; rides per hour US$25; ⏲tours at 9am, 11am & 3pm) Conversant in four languages (in addition to equine), Sabine will make sure you're comfortable on your horse, whether you're a novice rider or an experienced cowboy. Her long-standing operation offers a variety of treks including a popular waterfall tour (three hours) and a magical full-moon tour (monthly), and she keeps Arabian horses for endurance riding. Multiday rides must be booked well in advance.

Horse Trek Monteverde HORSE RIDING
(☎English 8359-3485, Spanish 8379-9827; www.horsetrekmonteverde.com; Ruta 606, Santa Elena; 2-/5hr tour US$49/85; ⏲7am-7pm Mon-Fri, 10am-6pm Sat-Sun) Owner and guide Marvin Anchia is a Santa Elena native, a professional horse trainer and an amateur naturalist who offers an excellent, intimate horseback-riding experience. Choose between scenic two-hour and all-day rides on the outskirts of town where few other tourists venture, and multiday cowboy experiences. The horses are well cared for, well trained and a joy to ride.

Caballeriza El Rodeo HORSEBACK RIDING
(☎2645-5764; elrodeo02@gmail.com; Santa Elena; from US$45; ⏲8am-4:30pm) Based at a local *finca,* this outfit offers tours on private trails through rainforest, coffee plantations and grasslands, with plenty of pauses to spot wildlife and admire the fantastic landscapes. The specialty is a sunset tour to a spot overlooking the Golfo de Nicoya. *¡Que hermoso!* (How beautiful!)

Canopy Tours

Wonder where the whole canopy tour craze was born? Santa Elena is the site of Costa Rica's first ziplines, today eclipsed in adrenaline by dozens of imitators who have followed, some of which are right here in town. You won't be spotting any quetzals or coatis as you whoosh your way over the canopy, but if you came to Costa Rica to fly, this is the absolute best place to do it. If you want to explore the treetops at your own pace, several outfits also have systems of hanging bridges and tree-climbing adventures. Transportation from your lodging is usually included.

Original Canopy Tour ADVENTURE
(☎2645-5243; www.theoriginalcanopy.com; adult/student/child US$45/35/25; ⏲tours 7:30am, 10:30am & 2:30pm) The storied zipline tour that started the trend. With 10 cables, a Tarzan swing, a climb up the center of an old fig tree and a thrilling rappel, it's a lot of fun. Your adrenaline rush may not be as big as at some of the other canopy tours, but you'll enjoy smaller groups and more emphasis on the natural surroundings.

Selvatura ADVENTURE
(☎4001-7899, toll free in USA 1-800-771-1803; www.selvatura.com; canopy tour US$55, walkways US$39, animal exhibits US$6-17; ⏲tours at 8:30am, 11am, 1pm & 2:30pm) One of the bigger games in town, Selvatura has 13 cables, 15 platforms and a Tarzan swing over a stretch of incredibly beautiful primary cloud forest. In addition to the cables, it features eight hanging bridges on its 'Treetop Walkways' and extras including a hummingbird garden, a butterfly garden and an amphibian and reptile exhibition.

Finca Modelo Ecologica ADVENTURE
(☎2645-5581; www.familiabrenestours.com; La Cruz; treetop/canyoning/combo US$45/79/113; ⏲tours at 8am, 11am, 2pm & 5:30pm) The Brenes family *finca* offers a number of unique and thrilling diversions. The masterpiece is the two-hour canyoning tour, which descends six glorious waterfalls, the highest of which is 40m. No experience necessary, just an adventurous spirit. The treetop tour involves climbing a 40m ficus tree, using ropes and rappels to go up and down.

100% Aventura ADVENTURE
(☎2645-6388; www.aventuracanopytour.com; Ruta 619, Santa Elena; canopy tour adult/child from US$57/46, bridges from US$40/34; ⏲tours 8am, 11am, 1pm & 3pm) Aventura boasts the longest zipline (nearly 1600m!) in Latin America. The nine cables are supplemented with a Tarzan swing, a 15m rappel and two Superman ziplines that make you feel as if you really are flying. It also has a network of suspension bridges, laced through secondary forest. Reservations required. You can also do ATV and horseback tours.

Monteverde Extremo ADVENTURE
(☎4001-8295, 8305-0126; www.monteverdeextremo.com; Santa Elena; canopy tour US$50, bungee US$80, Tarzan swing US$44; ⏲8am-4pm) This place has a canopy ride that allows you

to fly Superman-style through the air, the highest and most adrenaline-addled Tarzan swing in the area, and a bungee jump from 150m. One way or another, you will scream. Located in secondary forest, the views are marvelous but they herd some pretty big groups through here, so it's not exactly a nature experience.

SkyTrek ADVENTURE
(Sky Adventures; ☎2479-4100, toll free USA 1-844-468-6759; www.skyadventures.travel/skytrek; Santa Elena; adult/student/child SkyWalk US$41/33/28, SkyTrek US$84/70/58; ⏲8am-3pm, SkyWalk to 2pm) This seriously fast canopy tour, zooming over swatches of primary forest, consists of eight platforms attached to steel towers spread out along a road. Speeds reach up to 64km/h, which is probably why SkyTrek was the first canopy tour with a real brake system. **SkyWalk** is a 2km-long guided tour over six suspended bridges.

The newest attraction within the Sky Adventures park is an arboreal tree-climbing adventure (adult/student/child US$42/34/29). It involves scaling four trees (the tallest is 20m) that are outfitted with handholds and straps. As you climb, you are belayed in harnesses that ensure safety and allow for an easy rappel back to the ground.

You can book online or at the office in Santa Elena, beside the town's Catholic church. The park is located up near the Reserva Santa Elena (p216).

SkyTram CABLE CAR
(☎2479-4100, toll free USA 1-844-468-6759; www.skyadventures.travel/skytram; Santa Elena; adult/student/child US$48/40/33; ⏲8am-3pm) Owned by SkyTrek, SkyTram is a wheelchair-accessible gondola that floats gently over the cloud forest. On a clear day you can see from the volcanoes in the east to the Pacific in the west. Packages are available if you're also interested in the SkyTrek (canopy tour) and SkyWalk (hanging bridges).

Guided Hikes

In addition to the two biggies anchoring this area at the north and south, Monteverde and Santa Elena are home to dozens of smaller private reserves. The Monteverde (p213) and Santa Elena (p216) reserves are special – very special – because they are essentially the only cloud forest reserves in the area. But if you want to immerse yourself in nature, get some exercise, spot some monkeys, admire a scenic vista or cool off in a waterfall, there are countless places to do so (most of which will be significantly less crowded than the Monteverde reserve).

THE TALE OF THE GOLDEN TOAD

Once upon a time in the cloud forests of Monteverde, there lived the *Bufo periglenes* (golden toad), also known as the *sapo dorado*. Because this bright burnt-yellow, exotic little toad was sporadically seen scrambling amid the Monteverde leaf litter – the only place in the world where it appeared – it became something of a Monteverde mascot. Sadly, the golden toad has not been seen since 1989 and is now believed to be extinct.

In the late 1980s unexplained rapid declines in frog and toad populations all over the world spurred an international conference of herpetologists to address these alarming developments. Amphibians, once common, were becoming rare or had already disappeared, and the scientists scrambled to find the reason for the sudden demise of so many species in so many different habitats.

Ultimately, they decided the main culprit was the worldwide spread of chytridiomycosis disease (caused by the fungus *Batrachochytrium dendrobatidis*, in case you were wondering), which some scientists believe climate change has been fueling. There's also the global issue of habitat loss, an equally bleak story.

According to the Global Amphibian Assessment, 42% of the world's 7993 known amphibians are currently threatened with extinction. In response to this dire statistic, an international coalition of zoos and wildlife conservation organizations have jointly established **Amphibian Ark** (www.amphibianark.org), an attempt to 'bank' as many species as possible in the event of further die-offs. We may never know what happened to the golden toad, but as one of the first warning signs that the ecosystem is off balance, its mysterious disappearance might have given a chance for survival to other amphibian species.

LOCAL KNOWLEDGE

NATURE FOR NADA

Tired of paying a premium to hike up mountains and stroll through forest canopies? Here are two fantastically free ways to enjoy Monteverde's natural wonderland.

El Arbol Hueco

There's no sign, no website, and last we checked, nobody was collecting any money for this delightful roadside attraction. It's simply a hollowed-out fig tree (or, rather, a few interlocking ones) that happens to have 'branches' creating an easy-to-use ladder. You can shimmy up the center of the tree and then your friend can take a sweet photo of you from the bottom, for the 'gram.

Do wait your turn and climb carefully, as there's no safety equipment. To get there, take the road heading north of Santa Elena for about 600m, and you'll see a small, unmarked trail heading west. The tree is only 25m from the road.

Cerro Amigos

Take a hike up to the highest peak (1842m) in the area for good views of the surrounding rainforest and, on a clear day, Volcán Arenal, 20km away to the northeast. Behind Hotel Belmar (p208) in Cerro Plano, take the dirt road going downhill, then the next left. The trail ascends roughly 300m in 3km.

Note that this trail does not connect to the trails in the Monteverde reserve (p213).

★El Tigre Waterfalls OUTDOORS
(☎8391-9625; www.eltigrewaterfalls.com; US$79; ⏲tour begins 7:30am) For the able-bodied and adventure-minded, this is Monteverde's best new jungle trek. The 4½-hour journey into 60 hectares of forestland involves a little of everything: some hiking here, a hanging bridge-crossing there, some horseback riding here, a river plunge there. The rough and mostly virgin territory brims with wildlife, and is often remembered by travelers as the vacation's highlight.

A knowledgeable guide and transport are included. Lunch can be purchased at the end of the tour.

Bosque Eterno de los Niños HIKING
(Children's Eternal Rainforest, BEN; ☎4001-4866; https://acmcr.org/contenido/; adult/child US$15/10, guided night hike US$24/20, transportation per person US$5; ⏲8am-5pm, night hike 5:30pm; 👪) What became of the 1980s efforts of a group of Swedish schoolchildren to save the rainforest? Only this enormous 2300-sq km reserve – the largest private reserve in the country. It's mostly inaccessible to tourists, with the exception of the well-marked 4.5km Sendero Bajo del Tigre (p204), which is actually a series of shorter trails. Make reservations in advance for the popular two-hour night hikes.

At the entrance there's an education center for children and a fabulous vista over the reserve.

The Estación Biológica San Gerardo, reachable by a rather gnarly 2½-hour trail from Reserva Santa Elena (p216), is managed by BEN and has dorm bunk beds for researchers and students, but you may be able to stay overnight with prior arrangements.

Aguti Reserve HIKING
(☎4000-3385; www.agutimonteverde.com; US$15; ⏲7am-3:30pm) Open since 2018, this is Monteverde's newest private reserve. Its 4km network of trails make figure eights up and down a mountainside, looping through *matapalo* trees (strangler figs) over hillside lookouts and, if you're lucky, past the reserve's curious spokescreature – the agouti. It sort of looks like a giant rabbit got busy with a hamster. The other solid find here is the three-wattled bellbird, a migratory species with a piercing call and a ridiculous mustache.

Tours of the reserve are also on offer, including guided walks (from US$35), night hikes (from US$25) and birdwatching excursions (from US$65).

Curi-Cancha Reserve HIKING
(☎8448-8283, 2645-6915; www.reservacuricancha.com; entrance US$15, night tour US$20, natural history tour US$20, bird tour US$70; ⏲7am-3pm, guided hike 5:30-7:30pm) Bordering Monteverde but without the crowds, this lovely private reserve on the banks of the Río Cuecha is popular among birders. There is

PAVING THE WAY

A 1983 feature article in *National Geographic* billed the Monteverde and Santa Elena area as the place to view one of Central America's most famous birds – the resplendent quetzal. Suddenly, hordes of tourists armed with tripods and telephoto lenses started braving Monteverde's notoriously awful access roads, which came as a huge shock to its Quaker community. In an effort to stem the tourist flow, local communities lobbied to stop developers from paving the roads. It worked for a while, but eventually, the lobby to spur development bested the lobby to limit development. After several years of delays and broken contract agreements since the project first began in 2017, the paving of the main access road was finally completed in early 2020. The better road will inevitably mean more visitors, and this precious experiment in sustainable ecotourism will undergo a whole new set of trials.

about 8km of well-marked trails, a hummingbird garden and a view of the continental divide and the Golfo de Nicoya. Make reservations for the guided hikes, including the early-morning bird walks and specialized three-hour natural history walks.

Reserva Bajo del Tigre HIKING
(☎2645-5200; https://acmcr.org/contenido; adult/child US$15/10, guided night hike US$24/20, transportation per person US$5; ⊙8am-5pm, night hike 5:30pm; 👪) This section of the Bosque Eterno de los Niños (p203) is the only bit that's really accessible to the public. It's a sweet slice of forest with a small children's center, 3.3km of walking trails and a lookout platform with views to the gulf.

Pasión Costa Rica HIKING
(☎8304-7161; www.pasioncostarica.com; tours US$35-130) Guacimal-born Marcos Méndez has an encyclopedic knowledge of Costa Rica's flora and fauna, and leads engaging tours around the area, specializing in smaller groups and customized tours. He's been a guide for more than 20 years, and you might say, the *pasión* shines through. Tour times are flexible and include transportation.

Santa Maria Night Walk HIKING
(☎2645-6548; www.nightwalksantamarias.com; Santa Elena; US$25; ⊙tour 5:45pm) Night walks are popular around these parts, mainly because 80% of the cloud forest creatures are nocturnal. This one takes place on a private Santa Elena *finca* with a 10-hectare swathe of primary and secondary forest. Expert guides point out active nocturnal wildlife, ranging from snakes and spiders to sloths and kinkajous. Flashlights provided.

Valle Escondido HIKING
(Hidden Valley; ☎2645-5156; www.valleescondidopreserve.com; Cerro Plano; day entry US$16, night tour adult/child US$26/16; ⊙6am-4:30pm, night tour 5:30pm) Reserve in advance for the popular two-hour guided night tour, then come back the next day to explore the reserve on your own. Located behind Monteverde Inn in Cerro Plano, the well-marked trail winds through a deep canyon into an 17-hectare reserve, passing wonderful vistas and luscious waterfalls.

It's recommended for birding and wildlife-watching during the day, when it's quiet with few tourists.

Food & Drink

Café de Monteverde FOOD & DRINK
(☎2645-7546, 2645-7550; www.cafedemonteverde.com; Monteverde; tour adult/child US$30/15; ⊙coffee tasting 7am-6pm, tours 8:30am, 1:30pm & 3pm) 🍃 Stop by the shop in Monteverde to take a crash course in coffee and sample the delicious blends. You can also sign on for the 2½-hour tour on sustainable agriculture, which visits organic *fincas* implementing techniques such as composting and solar energy. Learn how coffee growing has helped shape this community and how it can improve the local environment.

Kind of makes you want to pour yourself another cup! Transport is an extra US$5 per person.

El Trapiche FOOD & DRINK
(☎2645-7650; www.eltrapichetour.com; Santa Elena; adult/child US$35/13; ⊙tours 10am & 3pm Mon-Sat, 3pm Sun) Visit this picturesque family *finca* in Santa Elena, where they grow coffee, sugarcane, bananas and plantains. See the coffee process firsthand, take a ride in a traditional ox cart, and try your hand at making sugar. There are lots of samples along the way, including sugarcane liquor, sugarcane toffee and – of course – delicious coffee. Kids love this one.

Caburé Chocolate Tour FOOD & DRINK
(☎2645-5020; www.cabure.net; Monteverde; US$15; ⏲tours 1pm & 4pm Mon-Sat) Bob, the owner of the Caburé chocolate shop in Monteverde, shares his secrets about the magical cacao pod and how to transform it into the food of the gods. There are plenty of opportunities for taste testing along the way, and you'll try your hand at making truffles.

Don Juan Coffee Tour FOOD & DRINK
(☎2645-6858, 2645-7100; www.donjuancr.com/monteverde; Santa Elena; adult/child US$33/14, night tour US$37/19; ⏲tours 8am, 10am, 1pm, 3pm & 5:30pm) Don Juan's three-in-one tours cover all your favorite vices (okay, maybe not *all* your favorites, but three of the good ones). It's a pretty cursory overview of how sugarcane is harvested and processed, how cacao beans are transformed into dark, decadent chocolate, and how coffee happens, from plant to bean to cup.

Sleeping

Santa Elena and Monteverde are lined with lodgings, from fun hostels and friendly farmstays to sumptuous mountain lodges. Accommodations are packed into village streets and spread out on the forested hills around town.

With many accommodations and transport options, Santa Elena appeals to budget travelers. Midrange and high-end visitors might consider Cerro Plano, Monteverde or further afield for closer interaction with nature (a vehicle – preferably 4WD – may be required).

Santa Elena

★**Pensión Santa Elena** HOSTEL $
(☎2645-5051; www.pensionsantaelena.com; incl breakfast d US$37-47, d without bathroom US$28, ste US$47-65, apt US$65; P@📶) This full-service hostel right in central Santa Elena is a perennial favorite, offering budget travelers top-notch service and *pura vida* hospitality. Each room is different, with something to suit every budget. The 'grand' rooms in the annex feature perks including superior beds, stone showers and iPod docks. There are also four family lofts with bunk beds, and apartments with kitchens.

Sleepers HOSTEL $
(☎8305-0113; www.sleeperssleepcheaperhostels.com; dm/s/d incl breakfast US$12/23/28) Downstairs it looks like a friendly restaurant, but it's actually a crowded communal kitchen, where happy travelers prepare and share meals. Upstairs it looks like a modern motel, but it's actually a hostel, where guests surf the web and catch a breeze on the balcony. Rooms are spotless, with en suite bathrooms. You'll find it in central Santa Elena.

A special rooftop 'suite' (US$30) has the best view in the place.

Camino Verde B&B B&B $
(☎2645-6849; www.hotelcaminoverde.com; incl breakfast, d standard from US$50, superior US$65; P📶) This travelers' nest offers an assortment of spacious rooms with wood ceilings and tile floors. A newer addition contains more expensive (and recommended) superior rooms with whitewashed walls and contemporary furnishings. There's a sweet little restaurant and a rambling garden. Rocking chairs are scattered about the porch, offering a perfect spot to soak up the scenic view.

Monteverde Backpackers HOSTEL $
(☎2645-5844; www.monteverdebackpackers.com; dm incl breakfast US$12-15; 📶) Small and friendly, Monteverde Backpackers is part of the Costa Rica Hostel Network. The dorms are clean and comfy enough, the showers are hot, the location in Santa Elena is quiet and management is helpful. Freebies include coffee, hammocks and a sunset hike. Breakfast is DIY, so you can make 'em how you like 'em (eggs, that is). Accommodation is in dorms only.

Cabinas Eddy CABINA $
(☎2645-6635; www.cabinas-eddy.com; incl breakfast d US$40-60, without bathroom US$30; P@📶) This budget spot continues to get rave reviews for its amazing breakfasts, attentive service and delightful manager Eddy (son of Freddy). The rooms are spotless, as is the fully equipped communal kitchen. The balcony is a great place to relax with a cup of free coffee and take in the view.

You'll find Freddy in the barbershop downstairs, should you need a trim.

Cabinas & Hotel Vista al Golfo CABINA $
(☎2645-6682, 2645-6321; www.cabinasvistaalgolfo.com; incl breakfast dm US$14, r with/without bathroom from US$37/30, ste US$50; P 📶) This bright, kitschy lodge is well kept, the showers are hot and the owners will make you feel right at home. On a clear day the upstairs balconies have great views of the Golfo de Nicoya. There's a communal kitchen, and the common space is furnished with beanbags. The 'suite' in the blue house next door is worth the step up in price.

★ Casa Batsu B&B $$
(☎2645-7004; www.casabatsu.org; d incl breakfast from US$100; P 📶) Carlos and Paula remodeled their family farmhouse, filled it with art, jazz and delicious food, and then opened their doors to share the love. Five rooms are furnished with pillow-strewn beds and striking stone showers. You'll enjoy the decadent breakfasts, for sure, but do make a reservation for dinner one night (mains US$25 to US$30 with a drink included), as Carlos is an amazing chef.

Batsu is the indigenous Bribrí word for hummingbird.

Finca Terra Viva FARMSTAY $$
(☎8380-4437; www.terravivacr.com; d/casita incl breakfast US$56/102; P @ 📶) 🍃 A 121-hectare working dairy *finca* surrounded by lush forest, this unique place offers guests an authentic rural experience, while raising environmental consciousness. Try your hand at feeding baby cows, hike on trails through farm and forest and observe the measures the carbon neutral farm is taking to minimize its environmental footprint.

Night tours, as well as a dairy and cheese-making experience, are available to guests for US$30 per person (minimum of four). Terra Viva is about 3km north of town on the road toward Reserva Santa Elena.

Capulín Cabins & Farm CABINA $$
(☎2645-6719; www.cabinascapulin.com; cabinas US$60-100; P 📶) Observe traditional farm life, hike the trails to spot birds and monkeys or just swing in a hammock and watch the show in the sky. There are nine comfortable cabins of varying sizes – some with kitchens and some with fantastic views to the gulf. This Tico family couldn't be more generous in sharing knowledge of the area.

Valle Campanas FARMSTAY $$
(☎2645-5631; www.vallecampanas.com; incl breakfast, d US$90, f US$126-138; P 📶) Four humble cabins are scattered around this family-run coffee and sugar plantation. The functional cabins have shiny kitchens, wide porches with hammocks and plenty of polished wood. Trails wind around the grounds, allowing guests to observe a working *finca*. It produces eggs, milk, honey and fresh fruits, all of which you'll sample in the scrumptious breakfasts.

Monteverde Rustic Lodge LODGE $$
(☎2645-6256; www.monteverderusticlodge.com; d/tr/q incl breakfast US$85/113/135; P 📶) Funny thing about the Rustic Lodge: it's not that rustic. The tree-trunk posts and furnishings play along with the theme, but remodeled rooms are spotless, comfortable and even upscale. Decorated in subtle earth tones, the 14 rooms have tiled floors, floral curtains and lots of stained wood. The shared balcony overlooks a blooming garden. Small, quiet, atmospheric.

Jaguarundi Lodge LODGE $$
(☎2645-5216; www.jaguarundilodge.com; d incl breakfast from US$70; P 📶) All the dorms in this former hostel have been replaced by double rooms. It's akin to a well-appointed mountain lodge but only 200m from town; you might expect the resident troops of howler and capuchin monkeys to accompany you to the pub next door.

Santa Elena Hostel Resort HOSTEL $$
(☎2645-7879; www.costaricahostels.net; dm US$13, d from US$62; P 📶) With fish in the koi pond and monkeys and coatis on the rooftops, this hostel seems like a fan-cooled paradise. The shady grounds are strung with hammocks for sunny days, and there's a big stone fireplace for cool nights. The rooms have stained-wood walls and high sloped ceilings. It's worth asking for a room with a private balcony.

A bar, kitchen and onsite restaurant make this even more of a one-stop shop. If it seems eerily familiar to a hostel in La Fortuna, that's because the same guy owns this one.

Arco Iris Ecolodge LODGE $$
(☎2645-5067; www.arcoirislodge.com; s/d/tr budget from US$35/45/55, standard US$72/95/105, superior US$110/125/140; P 📶) This clutch of pretty cabins is on a little hill

overlooking Santa Elena and the surrounding forests. Rooms vary in size and style, but all are quite lovely, with lots of stained wood, rainforest showers and private terraces. The honeymoon cabin is a two-level dream. A small system of private trails winds through the property, one to a majestic Pacific lookout.

Attentive owner Susana sees to it that the site remains impeccable.

Hotel Claro de Luna B&B **$$**
(☎2645-5269; www.hotelclarodeluna.com; d incl breakfast US$75-110; P 📶) This graceful old mahogany gingerbread-style house in Santa Elena is surrounded by gorgeous gardens bursting with heliconias, orchids and other tropical blooms. Rooms are simple and homey, with muted colors and floral quilts. Unfortunately, sound travels easily in this old house, so get a deluxe annex room if you can. Some even have Jacuzzi-style bathtubs.

Hotel El Atardecer LODGE **$$**
(☎2645-5462; www.atardecerhotel.com; s/d/tr/q incl breakfast US$45/70/90/100; P 📶) This attractive two-story wooden lodge is located away from the main drag in Santa Elena, guaranteeing a good night's rest. Surrounding a spacious courtyard restaurant, the musty yet ample tiled rooms have high, beamed ceilings, wood paneling and good mattresses. The selling point is the shared balcony, a magnificent place for – you guessed it – the sunset.

If there's no room at *this* inn, the owner's daughter runs El Amanecer down the block; it's similarly named, built and priced (double/triple US$65/75).

★Hidden Canopy Treehouses BOUTIQUE HOTEL **$$$**
(☎2645-5447; www.hiddencanopy.com; d US$299-449; P ❄ 📶 🏊) The accommodations are perched on stilts (not in trees) but, goodness, everything else is perfect. Floor-to-ceiling windows encase this opulent forest retreat, while multihued hardwood floors and ceilings and tree-root furnishings highlight the natural surrounds. Spacious chalets of varying layouts offer private decks overlooking the Gulf of Nicoya, along with Jacuzzis, canopy beds and waterfall showers.

If you can stand to leave the chalet, there's a lovely shared den and breakfast nook, a terraced pool system and a relaxing spa, all connected by an elevated boardwalk. Your worldly host Jennifer has gone to great lengths to satisfy, constantly making small adjustments based on feedback.

Cloud Forest Lodge LODGE **$$$**
(☎2645-5058; www.cloudforestlodge.com; s/d/tr/q incl breakfast from US$90/110/133/155; P @ 📶) Sleep in the clouds – this hilltop lodge is up there, surrounded by 28 hectares of primary and secondary forest. There are trails to walk, species to check off your bird list and gulf views to marvel at. The wooden cabins are spacious and comfortable but hardly luxurious, though you'll enjoy the view from your private porch.

The Original Canopy Tour (p201) is right here at the lodge, which is about 2km from the main road, and 4km from Santa Elena. It's a pleasant walk into town, but you'll get your exercise on the way back uphill.

Hotel Poco a Poco HOTEL **$$$**
(☎2645-6000; www.hotelpocoapoco.com; d incl breakfast US$209-389, f $367; P @ 📶 🏊) 🍃 There's a lot to love about Poco a Poco. There's the spa, of course, but the restaurant is also excellent, and the contemporary architecture is striking. The whole place is family friendly, with a small playground, kiddie pool and ceramic critters peeking out in unexpected places. Rooms show off a sophisticated style, but you'll pay more for the upper-floor views.

It's earned four out of five leaves in the government's sustainable tourism rating system.

🛏 Monteverde & Cerro Plano

Selina Monteverde HOSTEL **$**
(☎7146-7986; www.selina.com/costa-rica/monteverde; dm/d/tr from US$9/62/100; P ❄ 📶) An outlier in the Selina chain for its quiet location right up against the cloud forest, Selina Monteverde appeals to the backpacker or young family looking to socialize until a reasonable hour, then get up and see nature. Accommodations are basic with artful touches, and the six-, eight-, and 10-bed dorms – all with access to the property's hot tub, fire pit, yoga studio, hip restaurant and co-working space – offer excellent value.

E-bike rentals (per hour from US$5) are a great way to get from here to Bosque Nuboso Monteverde (p213) and back.

Los Pinos Cabañas y Jardines LODGE $$
(☎2645-5252; www.lospinos.net; Cerro Plano; d standard/superior US$105/165, family cabinas US$195-270; P 📶) 🍃 Fifteen freestanding cabinas are scattered around the forested gardens of this 8-hectare property, which once formed part of the family *finca*. Each *cabaña* affords plenty of privacy, plus a fully equipped kitchen and small terrace. The grounds have tons of birdlife, a playground, a scenic lookout, walking trails and organic and hydroponic gardens. Awesome option for families.

Family cabins have three rooms, while superior rooms have fireplaces and wraparound balconies. Los Pinos also garnered the coveted elite status in the sustainable tourism ratings, along with the *Bandera Azul* (Blue Flag) for sustainability.

The cabinas lack some basic niceties such as storage.

El Bosque CABINA $$
(☎2645-5158; www.bosquelodgecr.com; Monteverde; d/tr/q incl breakfast from US$95/110/125; P 📶) 🍃 On the edge of the Bosque Eterno de los Niños (p203) in Monteverde, this place is a pleasant surprise. Wooden duplex solar-powered cabins are surrounded by tropical gardens and primary forest, with many kilometers of trails to get lost on. Wildlife abounds – keep your eyes open for agoutis, coatis, capuchin monkeys and amazing birds. Walking distance to pastries and pizza.

Mariposa B&B B&B $$
(☎2645-5013; www.mariposabb.com; Monteverde; incl breakfast s/d/tr/q US$43/68/82/93, apt d/q US$97/125; P 📶) Just 2km from the Monteverde reserve (p213), this friendly place has nice rooms with stained-wood walls, terracotta floors, writing desks and beamed ceilings, not to mention a sweet local family looking after guests. It's nestled in the forest, with a sunny terrace for observing wildlife or just savoring a cup of local joe. The traditional Tico breakfast is a highlight.

★Chira TENTED CAMP $$$
(☎8824-1189; www.chiraglamping.com; tent from US$217; P 📶) An imaginative treetop glamping experience involving geodesic dome tents on platforms overlooking the cloud forest. Kids will love the family tents, which come with turbo slides from the outside into the sleeping area, while parents will appreciate the fully equipped kitchen and the private hot tub. The honeymoon tent's all-glass shower is also a real bonus.

Blow-dryers, a free minibar, bathrobes, slippers, yoga mats and more are all part of the deal. Oh, and there's a popular restaurant that delivers seven-course meals (adult/child US$88/55) to an elevated, all-glass deck in the treetops. Glamorous camping, indeed.

Senda Lodge LODGE $$$
(☎4001-6349, toll free from USA 866-380-4032; www.sendamonteverde.com; d from US$280; P 📶) 🍃 This resurrected collection of bungalows has been freshened up with contemporary decor and local art, and surrounded by newly planted foliage. Add to that a tasty restaurant, a fire pit and a hanging bridge, plus the neighboring Aguti Wildlife Reserve (to which guests have complimentary tickets; p203), and you've got one dreamy stay.

Hotel Belmar HOTEL $$$
(☎2645-5201; www.hotelbelmar.net; Cerro Plano; r from US$281, ste from US$407; P @ 📶 ≋) 🍃 Every room at the Belmar boasts views of forest or gulf – or both! The gorgeous light-filled rooms are decked out with handcrafted furniture and high-thread-count linens. There are spectacular sunset views from the private balconies – the higher you go, the more spectacular they are. Other perks include yoga classes, spa services and a fabulous **restaurant** (☎2645-5201; www.hotelbelmar.net/restaurant-monteverde-celajes; mains US$15-22; ⏲6:15-10am & noon-9pm; P 🖉) 🍃 with those same jaw-dropping views.

Incidentally, this place is a *real* eco-resort, boasting five leaves from the country's sustainable tourism program. Solar-heated water, biodigested energy and rainwater harvesting are just a few of the sustainable practices at the Belmar.

Hotel Trapp Family HOTEL $$$
(☎2645-5858; www.trapphotelmonteverde.com; Monteverde; incl breakfast, d US$147, ste US$164 add person $35; P 📶) 🍃 Here's some contemporary luxury in the midst of the cloud forest. The 20 spacious rooms have high wooden ceilings, big bathrooms and fabulous views from picture windows overlooking gardens or cloud forest. The Trapp family extends their renowned hospitality, promising warmth no matter what the weather.

You can't get much closer to the Monteverde reserve than here (it's less than 1km from the entrance). The trade-off, of course, is that it's far away from everything else.

There's an elegant restaurant, with an additional breakfast-only nook.

Hotel Fonda Vela LODGE $$$
(☎2645-5125; www.fondavela.com; Monteverde; d/ste incl breakfast from US$141/229; P @ ☎ ≋) With unique architectural styling and around 14 hectares of trail-laced grounds, this long-standing lodge had, at the time of research, recently been purchased by deep-pocketed Sky Adventures and was soon to undergo considerable changes and upgrades. Plans included two restaurants and a bar, and it was likely the birding trails, pool and Jacuzzi would be open daily to the public.

Located about 2km from the Monteverde reserve (p213).

Eating

The kitchens of Santa Elena and Monteverde offer high quality but poor value. You'll be delighted by the organic ingredients, local flavors and international zest, but not by the high price tags. Even the local *sodas* (places serving counter lunches) and bakeries are more expensive than they ought to be. Santa Elena has the most budget options.

Santa Elena

Orchid Coffee CAFE $
(☎2645-6850; www.orchidcoffeecr.com; mains US$8-12; ⏰7am-8pm; ☎ ✎) Feeling peckish? Go straight to this lovely Santa Elena cafe, filled with art and light. Grab a seat on the front porch and take a bite of heaven. It calls itself a coffee shop, but there's a full menu of traditional and nontraditional breakfast items, sweet and savory crepes, interesting and unusual salads and thoroughly satisfying sandwiches.

Taco Taco MEXICAN $
(☎2645-7900; www.tacotaco.net; mains US$5-8; ⏰11am-10pm; ☎) A wildly popular terrace restaurant offering tasty Tex-Mex tacos, plus burritos and quesadillas filled with shredded meats like chicken and *carnitas* (pork). There's also slow-roasted short rib, roasted veggies and battered mahi-mahi. The only difficulty is deciding what to eat (though you really can't go wrong). When the place is slammed, service can be painfully slow.

Raulito's Pollo Asado CHICKEN $
(☎8308-0810; mains US$4-5; ⏰8am-11pm) Scrappy street dogs and chatty *taxistas* (taxi drivers) vie for attention at this porcelain-countered wonder. Golden, crispy chicken morsels are transferred from the spit to your plate with a heap of rice, fries, salad or *gallo pinto* (rice and beans). Wash it down with an icy *horchata* (rice milk and cinnamon drink) and still walk away with some beer money.

Soda La Amistad SODA $
(☎2645-6108; mains US$6-9; ⏰11am-9:30pm; ✎) Friendly and family run, this is a well-loved *soda* that's convenient if you're staying along this side road. You'll find typical, tasty *casados* (a meat selection with beans, rice and salad), burgers, pasta and a list of handy translations on the menu. Herbivores will appreciate the veggie options, which include one burger and a *casado*. These folks know their stuff (and it's cheap).

★**Choco Café Don Juan** CAFE $$
(☎2645-7444; www.facebook.com/chococafedonjuan; mains US$7-15; ⏰8am-8pm; ☎ ✎) This little cafe roasts beans from its coffee farm (Don Juan; p205) and uses fancy machinery (La Marzocco!) to serve up the best cup of joe in Monteverde. The food is also excellent, with healthy salads and heaping plates of pasta, fish, chicken and steak, plus delicious baked goods for dessert. There's great porch seating, but the indoor environs are downright dainty.

Toro Tinto STEAK $$
(☎2645-6252; www.facebook.com/torotintocr; mains $15-25; ⏰6-10pm) This Argentine steakhouse will warm your cloud-soaked soul with its cozy atmosphere and open kitchen. Then it'll sate your hunger with steaks that are perfectly cut and grilled to order, plus unexpected specials and delicious desserts. The wine selection is good – mostly Chilean and Argentine – but pricey.

Morpho's Restaurant INTERNATIONAL $$
(☎2645-7373; www.morphosrestaurant.com; mains US$8-20; ⏰11am-9:15pm; ✎) In new digs with a killer sunset view, this double-decker restaurant is a favorite in Santa Elena for its varied menu combining local ingredients with gourmet flair. There is a good number of vegetarian options (salads, soups, pastas,

etc), but do take note that the 'veggie burger' is really just an egg sandwich. Arrive early for a prime table on the terrace.

Happy hour two-for-one drinks last from 3:30pm to 5pm.

El Jardín INTERNATIONAL **$$$**
(2645-5057; www.monteverdelodge.com; Monteverde Lodge, mains US$12-24; 7am-10pm;) The menu at this fine-dining establishment is wide ranging, always highlighting the local flavors. But these are not your typical *tipica* (traditional plates). A case in point: the beef tenderloin marinated for five hours in a coffee liquor and served with cashew butter and mashed casava. The setting – with windows to the trees – is lovely and the service is superb.

Romantics can opt for a private table in the garden.

Tree House Restaurant & Café CAFE **$$$**
(2645-5751; www.treehouse.cr; mains US$15-22; 11am-10pm;) It's a fine line between hokey and happy. But this restaurant – built around a hundred-year-old *higuerón* (fig) tree – definitely raises a smile. There's a menu of well-prepared if overpriced standards, from carpaccio to burgers to *comida tipica* (regional specialities). The service is spot-on. It's a lively space to have a bite, linger over wine and occasionally catch live music.

Cold? Try the Chocolate Tree House, a devilish dash of coffee with chocolate-flavored liqueurs.

Monteverde & Cerro Plano

Stella's Bakery BAKERY **$$**
(2645-5560; Monteverde; mains US$8-15; 6:30am-6pm;) A bakery for birders. Come in the morning for strong coffee and sweet pastries, or later for rich, warming soup, and sandwiches on homemade bread. Plates such as the huevos rancheros satisfy, especially with a heap of passion fruit cheesecake for dessert. Whenever you come, keep on eye on the bird feeder, which attracts tanagers, motmots and an emerald-green toucanet.

Café Caburé CAFE **$$**
(2645-5020; www.cabure.net; Monteverde; lunch US$6-12, dinner US$14-18; 9am-9pm Mon-Sat;) This Argentine cafe above the Bat Jungle (p199) specializes in creative and delicious everything, from sandwiches on homemade bread and fresh salads, to more elaborate fare such as sea bass in almond sauce or filet mignon with chimichurri. Save room for dessert: the chocolate treats are high art. There's hot chocolate, an Argentine brownie and (yes!) the cafe's Chocolate Tour (p205).

Tramonti ITALIAN **$$**
(2645-6120; www.tramonticr.com; Monteverde; mains US$10-16; 11:30am-9:30pm;) Tramonti offers authentic Italian fare, specializing in fresh seafood, hearty pastas and wood-fired pizzas. With a greenery-filled dining room twinkling with lights, the ambiance is relaxed yet romantic. If you're up in Monteverde and don't feel like venturing into town, this is a real crowd pleaser. Several pizzas and pastas are suitable for vegetarians.

There's a decent selection of wines from Italy and Argentina.

Sofia FUSION **$$**
(2645-7017; Cerro Plano; mains US$14-18; 11:30am-9:30pm;) With its Nuevo Latino cuisine – a modern fusion of traditional Latin American cooking styles – Sofia has established itself as one of the best places in town. Our faves include plantain-crusted sea bass, seafood chimichanga, and beef tenderloin with roasted red pepper and cashew sauce. The ambiance is enhanced by groovy music, picture windows, romantic candle lighting and potent cocktails.

Drinking & Nightlife

Nightlife in these parts generally involves a guided hike and nocturnal critters, but since these misty green mountains draw artists and dreamers, there's a smattering of regular cultural offerings. When there's anything going on, you'll see it heavily advertised around town. You'll also see some action at the bars in Santa Elena, especially during the dry season.

Monteverde Beer House BEER GARDEN
(2645-7675; www.facebook.com/monteverdebeerhouse; Santa Elena; 10am-10pm;) It's not a brewery – contrary to the sign – but it does offer a selection of local craft beers. There's a shady deck out back and smiling servers on hand; it's a perfect atmosphere for kicking back after a day of adventures.

The Middle Eastern food (mains US$6 to US$10) is hit or miss, but if you're hungry, go for the *shakshuka* (baked eggs in a tomato and pepper sauce).

Bar Amigos BAR
(☎2645-5071; www.baramigos.com; Santa Elena; ⊙11:40am-2am) With picture windows overlooking the mountainside, this Santa Elena mainstay evokes the atmosphere of a ski lodge. But there are DJs, karaoke and pool tables plus sports on the screens. This is the one consistent place in the area to let loose, so there's usually a good, rowdy mix of Ticos and tourists.

The food, such as the *chifrijo* (rice and pinto beans with fried pork and capped with fresh tomato salsa and corn chips), is surprisingly good.

Shopping

★**Luna Azul** JEWELRY
(☎2645-6638; www.facebook.com/lunaazulmonteverde; Santa Elena; ⊙10am-7pm) In a new home next to Pensión Santa Elena (p205), this cute gallery and gift shop is packed to the gills with locally made jewelry, clothing, soaps, sculpture and macramé, among other things. The jewelry in particular is stylish and stunning, crafted from silver, shell, crystals and turquoise.

Monteverde Art House ARTS & CRAFTS
(Casa de Arte; ☎2645-5275; www.facebook.com/monteverde.arthouse; Cerro Plano; ⊙9am-6pm Mon-Sat, 10am-6pm Sun) You'll find several rooms stuffed with colorful Costa Rican artistry here. The goods include jewelry, ceramic work, Boruca textiles and traditional handicrafts. There's a big variety of offerings, including some paintings and more contemporary work, but it's mostly at the crafts end of the arty-crafty spectrum. Great for souvenirs.

Heladería Monteverde FOOD & DRINK
(☎2645-6889; Monteverde; ⊙8am-5pm) Formerly the Monteverde Cheese Factory, this business was started in 1953 by Monteverde's original Quaker settlers. It produced everything from a creamy Gouda to a very nice sharp white cheddar, as well as other dairy products such as yogurt and, more importantly, ice cream and milk shakes. Now owned by the Mexican giant Sigma Alimentos, the shop still sells products made with the original recipes.

Don't miss the chance to sample Monte Rico cheese, a Monteverde original. Sadly, tours of the facility are no longer offered.

Information

EMERGENCY

Police (☎2645-7074; Santa Elena)

INTERNET ACCESS

Nearly all hotels and hostels have wi-fi, while some accommodations also offer computers with internet access.

MEDICAL SERVICES

Consultorio Médico (☎2645-7778; Cerro Plano; ⊙24hr) A block east of the restaurant Sofia.

MONEY

Banks and ATMs are clustered in the downtown quadrant of Santa Elena.

Banco de Costa Rica (Cerro Plano; ⊙9am-4pm Mon-Fri)

Banco Nacional (Santa Elena; ⊙8:30am-3:45pm Mon-Fri)

Banco Popular (☎2542-3390; Centro Comercial Plaza Monteverde, Santa Elena; ⊙8:45am-4:30pm Mon-Fri)

POST

Correos de Costa Rica (Santa Elena; ⊙8am-5pm Mon-Fri, to noon Sat) Across from the shopping mall.

TOURIST INFORMATION

Most hotels, hostels and guesthouses are eager to assist their guests, whether by booking tours or making transportation arrangements.

Chamber of Tourism (☎2645-6565; www.exploremonteverde.com; Santa Elena; ⊙8am-7pm) This office promotes its member hotels and tour companies, so it's not necessarily an unbiased source. It also gives out maps and has information on bus schedules.

Monteverde Info (www.monteverdeinfo.com) This comprehensive website is chock full of information, with listings for hotels, tours, restaurants, transportation and more.

Getting There & Away

All visitors must arrive on wheels via one of three access roads, whether in a private vehicle or a bus. A longstanding project to pave the main route through Guacimal was completed in 2020. Lots of travelers get between Monteverde and Arenal via a taxi-boat-taxi route.

BUS

Most buses stop at the **bus terminal** (Santa Elena) across from the Centro Comercial mini-mall on the hill above downtown Santa Elena, and do not continue to Monteverde; you'll have to walk or take a taxi if that's where you plan to stay. On the trip in, keep all bags at your feet and not in the overhead bin. Note that the bus to Tilarán does not leave from the terminal, but from downtown Santa Elena, just meters down the street from the Vitosi pharmacy.

If you're traveling to Managua or Grenada in Nicaragua, you can make arrangements to meet the international bus en route on the Interamericana in Lagartos with:

Monteverde Experts (☎2645-7263; www.monteverdeexperts.com; Ruta 606; ⏲7am-5pm) Agent for TicaBus.

NicaBus Agent (☎2221-2679; www.nicabus.com.ni) At the bus terminal across from the Centro Comercial mini-mall.

CAR

While most Costa Rican communities regularly request paved roads in their region, preservationists in Monteverde have done the opposite, and most roads around here are shockingly rough. Even if you arrive on the newly paved road via Guacimal, you'll still want a 4WD to get to the more remote lodges and reserves.

There are three roads from the Interamericana. Coming from the south, the first well-signed turnoff is at Rancho Grande (18km north of the Puntarenas exit). The first stretch of this route (from Sardinal to Guacimal) was paved in 2011. The remaining 17km (from Guacimal to Santa Elena) was finished in early 2020. The drive now takes about 2½ hours if there's no traffic.

A second, shorter road goes via Juntas, but it's not paved except for the first few kilometers.

Finally, if coming from the north, drivers can take the paved road from Cañas via Tilarán and then take the rough road from Tilarán to Santa Elena.

If you're coming from Arenal, consider taking the lakeside route through Tronadora and Río Chiquito, instead of going through Tilarán. The roads are rougher, but the panoramas of the lake, volcano and surrounding countryside are magnificent.

There are two gas stations open for business in the area, one of which is in Cerro Plano.

TAXI-BOAT-TAXI

The fastest route between Monteverde–Santa Elena and La Fortuna is via a taxi-boat-taxi combo (from US$25, four hours, departs 8am and 2pm), which can be arranged through almost any hotel or tour operator – including **Monteverde Tours** (☎2645-5874; www.monteverdetours.com; Santa Elena; ⏲7:30am-6pm Mon-Sat, 10am-6pm Sun) – in either town. A 4WD minivan can pick you up at your hotel and take you to Río Chiquito, meeting a boat that crosses Laguna de Arenal, where a van on the other side continues to La Fortuna. This is increasingly becoming the primary transportation between La Fortuna and Monteverde as it's incredibly scenic, reasonably priced and saves half a day of rough travel.

TAXI

Taxis wait in front of the Chamber of Tourism (p211; next to the **Catholic Church** and chicken stand) in Santa Elena to take travelers to the reserves (about US$12) or other out-of-town destinations.

Bosque Nuboso Monteverde

Here is a virginal forest dripping with mist, dangling with mossy vines, sprouting with ferns and bromeliads, gushing with creeks, and nurturing rivulets of evolution. When

BUSES FROM MONTEVERDE

DESTINATION	COMPANY	COST (US$)	DURATION (HR)	DEPARTURES
Las Juntas	Transmonteverde	2.50	1½	4:20am, 3pm
Puntarenas via Las Juntas via Sardinal via Lagartos	Transmonteverde	3.50	3	4:20am, 5:30am, 6am, 3pm
Reserva Monteverde (Monteverde Cloud Forest Reserve)	Transmonteverde	1.15	15min	Departs 6:15am, 7:30am, 9:30am, 1:20pm, 3pm; returns 6:40am, 8:30am, 11am, 2pm, 4pm
San José	Tilarán Transportes	5	3-4	5:30am, 2:30pm
Tilarán, with connection to La Fortuna	local bus	3	2½ (7 total)	5am, 7am, noon, 4pm

Quaker settlers first arrived here in the 1950s, they agreed to preserve about a third of their property to protect this watershed. The community later joined forces with environmental organizations to purchase 328 hectares adjacent to the already preserved area. This was called the **Reserva Biológica Bosque Nuboso Monteverde** (Monteverde Cloud Forest Wildlife Biological Reserve; ☎2645-5122; www.cloudforestmonteverde.com; adult/student/child under 6yr US$25/12/free; ⏲7am-4pm), which the Centro Científico Tropical (Tropical Science Center) began administering in 1975. Nowadays the reserve totals 41.25 sq km.

Due to its fragile environment, the reserve allows a maximum of 250 people at any given time; during the dry season this limit is usually reached by 10am. Assure your admission by making advance reservations for a spot on a tour. Otherwise, be an early bird and arrive before the gates open.

Activities

Hiking

Visitors should note that the reserve's walking trails can be muddy, even during the dry season, and several of them were damaged during recent hurricanes. Some trails have closed, but many good options remain.

You're essentially walking around in a cloud, so don't bother complaining; just bring rain gear and suitable boots. Many of the trails have been stabilized with concrete blocks or wooden boards, but unpaved trails deeper in the preserve turn sloppy during the rainy season.

There are 10km of marked and maintained trails – take a photo of the map at the entrance. The most popular trails to the east of the reserve entrance include the following:

Sendero Bosque Nuboso A popular 1.9km interpretive walk through the cloud forest that begins at the ranger station (park entrance); it's paralleled by the more open, 2km **El Camino**, a favorite of birdwatchers.

Sendero Cuecha The trail begins at the reserve entrance and continues for 1km to a waterfall. You can take **Sendero Tosi** (800m) to return.

The gorgeous **Chomogo Trail** (1.8km) lifts hikers to 1680m, the park's highest point.

The trail to the **Mirador La Ventana** (elevation 1550m) is moderately steep and leads further afield to a wooden deck overlooking the continental divide. To the west, you can see the Golfo de Nicoya and the Pacific on clear days. To the east, you can see the Peñas Blancas valley and the San Carlos plain. Even on wet, cloudy days it's magical, especially when the winds are howling and fine swirling mist washes over you in waves.

All over these woods, in hidden pockets and secluded gullies, that mist collects into rivulets that gather into threads that stream into a foaming waterfall, visible from **Sendero Cascada.** From here the pools form a gushing river, best glimpsed from **Sendero Río** or **Sendero Cuecha.** There's a 100m-long suspension bridge about 1km from the ranger station on **Sendero Wilford Guindon.** Like a miniature Golden Gate suspended in the canopy, you can feel it rock and sway with each step.

Note that backcountry camping is no longer allowed.

Wildlife-Watching

Monteverde is a birdwatching paradise, with the list of recorded species topping out at more than 400. The resplendent quetzal is most often spotted during the March and April nesting season, though you may get lucky any time of year. Keep your ears open for the three-wattled bellbird, a kind of cotinga that is famous for its distinctive call. If you're keen on birds, a specialized bird tour is highly recommended.

For those interested in spotting mammals, the cloud forest's limited visibility and abundance of higher primates (human beings) can make wildlife-watching quite difficult. That said, there are some commonly sighted species including coatis, howler monkeys, capuchins, sloths, agoutis and squirrels (as in actual squirrels, not the squirrel monkey). Most animals avoid the main trails, so get off the beaten track.

Tours

Although you can (and should) hike around the reserve on your own, a guide will provide an informative overview and enhance your experience. Make reservations at least a day in advance for park-run tours. The English-speaking guides are trained naturalists; proceeds benefit environmental education programs in local schools. The reserve can also recommend excellent guides for private tours.

1

Life in the Cloud Forest

To explore the Monteverde cloud forest is to arrive at the pinnacle of Costa Rica's continental divide. A blast of swirling, misty euphoria surrounds you, where lichen-draped trees soar, exotic birds gossip, and orchids and bromeliads bloom. Life is abundant, throbbing and palpable.

Two Forests, Two Ecosystems

Warm, humid trade winds from the Caribbean sweep up forested slopes to the Reserva Biológica Bosque Nuboso Monteverde (p213), where they cool and condense into clouds that congregate over the nearby Reserva Santa Elena (p216). The two forests are each rich in diversity and oxygen, but the slight temperature and topographical differences mean that each has its own unique ecosystem.

Cloud Flora

The most abundant life form in the cloud forest, epiphytes seem to take over the trees they are growing on, yet these clever plants are not parasites and they do not harm their hosts; they get their nutrients from the floating mist, which explains their exposed roots. Look closely and you'll see that one tree might be covered in dozens of epiphytes. This is one of the major reasons that cloud forests can claim such biodiversity: in Monteverde it's estimated that epiphytes represent almost 30% of the flora species.

The biggest family of epiphytes is the orchids, with nearly 550 species (the greatest diversity of orchids on the planet). Most amazingly, this figure includes some 34 endemic species – those that do not exist anywhere else.

DMITRIYBURLAKOV/GETTY IMAGES ©

JONATHAN GREGSON/LONELY PLANET ©

JONATHAN GREGSON/LONELY PLANET ©

1. Walking in the Reserva Biológica Bosque Nuboso Monteverde (p213)
2. Rufous-tailed hummingbird
3. Orchid *(Oerstedella endressii)*

Cloud Birds

Playing an important role in the pollination of orchids and other blooming plants, hummingbirds are among the most visible of the cloud-forest creatures. Their unique ability to fly in place, backwards and upside down allows them to drink on the fly, as it were. There are some 30 species buzzing around; check them out at Cafe Colibrí (p216), just outside the Monteverde reserve.

You'll hear the three-wattled bellbird long before you see it, as the male's distinctive song is supposedly one of the loudest bird calls on earth. As you might guess, the male has three long wattles hanging from its beak.

The most famous cloud-forest resident is the resplendent quetzal. This beauty is as colorful and exotic as its name suggests, and males have long plumes of jade green and electric blue. Quetzals move seasonally between elevations, but if you're in the right place at the right time, a good bird guide should be able to find one.

Quaker Connection

The Quakers were the original conservationists here. In the early 1950s, about a dozen pacifist farming families decided to leave the US so that they would not be drafted to fight in the Korean War. They settled in this remote perch and called it Monteverde (literally, 'Green Mountain'). They have been actively involved in protecting this unique environment ever since. *Walking with Wolf*, by Kay Chornook, tells the story of one of these pioneers, Wolf Guindon, who helped establish the Cloud Forest Preserve.

DON'T MISS

RESERVA SANTA ELENA

The exquisitely misty 310-hectare **Reserva Santa Elena** (Reserva Bosque Nuboso Santa Elena; ☎2645-7107, 2645-5390; www.reservasantaelena.org; entrance adult/student US$16/9, guided hike US$33; ⏲7am-4pm) offers a completely different cloud forest experience from Monteverde (p213). Cutting through the veiled forest, the reserve's 12km of dewy trails see much less traffic, retaining a magic that is sometimes missing at Monteverde. A recently upgraded observation tower in the reserve offers views all the way to the Arenal and Miravalles volcanoes (on a clear day). Open since 1992, Santa Elena was one of the first community-managed conservation projects in the country.

The reserve has a simple restaurant, coffee shop and gift store. Note that all proceeds go toward managing the reserve, as well as to environmental education programs in local schools.

The reserve itself is about 6km northeast of the village of Santa Elena; the **reserve office** (Colegio Técnico Profesional de Santa Elena; ⏲7am-5pm Mon-Fri) is in town. A private **shuttle service** (☎8725-4335; US$4 return) offers transportation to the reserve with pickups from hotels, departing at 6am, 8:30am, 10:30am and 12:30pm. Return trips from the reserve are at 9am, 11am, 1pm and 4pm. You can book the service by phone or directly through your hotel.

Birdwatching Tours BIRDWATCHING
(☎2645-5122; tours incl entry fee US$85; ⏲tours depart 6am) These guided bird walks usually last four to five hours, checking off as many as 40 species of birds out of a possible 400. There's a three-person minimum, six-person maximum. Book in advance through the reserve office.

Natural History Tours OUTDOORS
(☎2645-5122; adult/student incl entry fee US$45/32; ⏲tours depart 7:30am, 11:30am & 1:30pm) These tours start with an informative 10-minute orientation, followed by a 2½- hour walk in the woods. You'll learn all about the characteristics of a cloud forest and identify some of its most unique flora. Your ticket is valid for the entire day; you can continue to explore on your own when the tour is over.

Reservations required (book through the reserve office), two-person minimum.

Night Tours OUTDOORS
(☎2645-5122; www.cloudforestmonteverde.com; with/without transportation US$29/23; ⏲tours depart 6pm) Two-hour night tours of the reserve offer the opportunity to observe the 70% of regional wildlife that has nocturnal habits. Frogs, bats and other night critters are increasingly active as the sun sets. Tours are by flashlight (bring your own for the best visibility). Arrange this tour in advance by at least the morning of the tour.

Sleeping & Eating

La Casona LODGE $$
(☎2645-5122; www.cloudforestmonteverde.com; r incl three meals & reserve admission per person adult/child US$93/54) At the entrance to the reserve, this mountain lodge is usually used by researchers and student groups, but it's open to tourists when there's room. The 12 plain private rooms feel rather institutional, but they're clean and comfortable – and you can't get any closer to the park. Your hard-earned cash directly contributes to protecting the cloud forest.

Cafe Colibrí CAFE $
(☎2645-7768; sandwiches US$5-7; ⏲7am-4:30pm) Just outside the reserve gates, the 'Hummingbird Cafe' is a top-notch spot to refuel after a hike in the woods. The drinks will warm your body, but the sound of dozens of hummingbirds in the garden will delight your heart. Many say the sandwiches are just OK; come for the coffee (US$2) and hummingbirds. Great photo ops.

An identification board shows the nine species that you're likely to see.

Information

The visitors center, adjacent to the reserve gift shop, is where you can get information and buy trail guides, maps and bird and mammal lists, as well as souvenirs and postcards. Leave your passport to rent a pair of binoculars (US$12).

The reserve is managed by the Centro Científico Tropical and supported by donations through the Friends of Monteverde Cloud Forest (www.friendsofmonteverde.org).

The annual rainfall here is about 3000mm, though parts of the reserve reportedly get twice as much. It's usually cool, with high temperatures around 18°C (64°F); wear appropriate clothing. It's important to remember that the cloud forest is, unsurprisingly, often cloudy.

Getting There & Away

Transmonteverde (2645-7447; Bus Terminal, Santa Elena) buses (US$1.15, 15 minutes) depart for the reserve from the Santa Elena bus terminal at 6:15am, 7:30am, 9:30am, 1:20pm and 3pm. Buses return from the reserve at 6:40am, 8:30am, 11am, 2pm and 4pm. You can flag down the buses from anywhere on the road between Santa Elena and the reserve – inquire at your lodgings about what time they will pass by. Taxis are also available for around US$12.

Private vehicles can park in a lot across from Selina Monteverde (p207), where a free shuttle picks up about every 15 minutes. It's a five-minute ride on an e-bike (available at Selina) or the shuttle, or a 25-minute walk (and the birdwatching on this stretch is magnificent). Ambitious travelers can walk all the way from Santa Elena (6km) – look for paths that run parallel to the road.

INTERAMERICANA NORTE

Despite Tico speed demons and lumbering big rigs, the Interamericana offers a wide-angle view of the region. The main artery connecting San José with Managua runs through kilometers of tropical dry forest and neat roadside villages to the open Guanacaste grasslands, where savanna vistas are broken only by windblown trees. Along the way, thin, mostly earthen roads branch off and wander up the slopes of hulking volcanoes shrouded in cloud forest, skirt hidden waterfalls and meander into vast estuaries that kiss pristine bays.

Getting There & Away

The 50km stretch of road between Cañas and Liberia has undergone a huge, US$200 million improvement in recent years. There are additional lanes, overpasses and on-off ramps that have made driving easier (and much faster) along this stretch. The only downside is that some formerly easy turns into towns have been complicated by the overpasses.

Your destination is probably not on the Interamericana itself, but somewhere off of it. Once you leave the highway, you may wish you had a 4WD.

If you're traveling by bus, you are likely to have to break your journey (to change buses) in Cañas, Bagaces, Liberia or La Cruz.

Montes de Oro

Northeast of Puntarenas, Montes de Oro is a gold-mining district that's tucked into the slopes and valleys of the Cordillera de Tilarán. A good number of day-trippers come up from Puntarenas and other coastal towns to fly through the trees on one of the country's biggest canopy tours. Otherwise, this area is largely off the beaten track, with few facilities catering to independent travelers; you'll need your own vehicle (a 4WD, of course) and a sense of adventure. In the district capital **Miramar**, you'll discover a real Tico town that's largely untouched by tourism. And if you make it all the way up to **Zapotal**, at 1500m above sea level, you'll have unparalleled views all the way down to the Golfo de Nicoya and a cloud forest of your very own.

Activities

Colinas Verdes Zapotal HIKING
(8829-0619, 2639-8516; www.colinasverdescr.com; Jabonal; tours from US$10) You'll find a little bit of magic amid the clouds at Colinas Verdes, set on 35 hectares of emerald-green hills and misty skies. Much of the property has been set aside for conservation and reforestation, but you'll find 4km of biking/hiking trails winding their way through the forest, with five hanging bridges, four short zipline cables and countless stunning vistas.

Adventure Park and Hotel Vista Golfo ADVENTURE SPORTS
(2260-6823, 8382-3312; www.adventureparkcostarica.com; Tajo Alto; canopy tour from US$89) Just when you thought you had arrived in a place where no tourist had gone before... there's a flag-waving, adrenaline-rushing, scream-inducing adventure park, catering to busloads of day-trippers from the coast. It offers purportedly one of the biggest canopy tours in the country, with 25 cables and 11 waterfalls (some dip-worthy). There's also a rope obstacle course through the trees.

The place is definitely fun, but the big groups may be a detractor. If you don't have your own wheels, the adventure park can bus you in from Puntarenas, Jacó, Guanacaste, or even San José. It's located on the grounds of the Hotel Vista Golfo, about 7km north of Miramar, in Tajo Alto.

Sleeping

There are a few lovely places to stay around Miramar and Zapotal, but they are all small and this region is remote, so make sure to book in advance so you're not stranded.

Hotel Vista Golfo HOTEL **$$**
(2260-6823, 8382-3312; www.adventureparkcostarica.com; Tajo Alto; d/tr/q incl breakfast from US$87/98/110; P) This onsite lodging at Adventure Park (p217) is a pleasant place with a tranquil mountain setting that's perfect for getting a little fresh air. Comfortable rooms have traditional decor and private terraces, some with sweeping views of the Golfo de Nicoya. Located 7km due north of Miramar.

Getting There & Away

The town of Miramar is the capital of this district and the main population center. It's 6km north of the Interamericana on a good paved road. The small village of Zapotal is a further 16km northeast, and it's a rough road into the clouds.

Autotransportes Miramar buses connect Miramar to San José (US$4, 2½ hours, four daily). Nonetheless, this is a difficult area to navigate without your own car. Be advised that the roads here are frequently washed out during the rainy season, so a 4WD is highly recommended.

Volcán Tenorio Area

Part of the Área de Conservación Arenal (ACA), Parque Nacional Volcán Tenorio (p221) is a cool, misty and magical place highlighted by cloud forests and the icy-blue Río Celeste; the region is known locally by the river's name. The park entrance is located just north of Bijagua (pronounced 'bee-hag-gwa'); the town, which leads the way in rural community tourism, is the main base for visiting this natural wonder.

Getting There & Away

About 7km north of Cañas, Hwy 6 branches off the Interamericana and heads north toward Upala, passing through the small town of Bijagua. From Bijagua, there is a graded dirt road on the right that leads 9km to the entrance of Parque Nacional Volcán Tenorio. If you're coming from the east, you can also reach the park from Hwy 4, coming up from La Fortuna. If you have your own wheels, it's a doable day trip from Liberia, Cañas or La Fortuna.

If you don't have your own wheels, you can catch a bus from Liberia (US$4), San José or Upala (US$2.50) to Bijagua, then book a tour locally or catch a taxi (US$50 to US$75 round-trip) to the park entrance.

Bijagua

POP 5200

The only sizable town in the Tenorio sphere is Bijagua, a small farming community that's strung out along Hwy 6, halfway between the Interamericana and the bigger town of Upala. It's a gem.

Bijagua is a leader in rural community tourism. It all started with the Heliconias Rainforest Lodge, managed by a cooperative of local families. That spirit continues in small-scale tours that mimic – on a more charming level – the night tours and chocolate tours of more established tourism centers.

Now the 'graduates' of Heliconias have founded their own businesses, and a growing entrepreneurial spirit along with a genuine down-to-earth Tico vibe make this a wonderful place to base yourself while visiting the nearby hot spots of Tenorio, Palo Verde, and La Fortuna.

Sights

Finca Verde Lodge FARM
(www.fincaverdelodge.com/activities; day/night tour US$14/18, 4-person minimum; tours 8:30am-4pm; P) Sloths, frogs, snakes, butterflies and prolific birdlife inhabit the gorgeous grounds of this *finca*, worth a visit to see the methods of a working organic farm. It's located on a rather rough road a few kilometers southeast of the main highway.

Activities & Tours

★ Heliconias Rainforest Lodge BIRDWATCHING, HIKING
(Hanging Bridges; 2466-8483; www.heliconiascr.com; US$14; 8am-5pm) Get a different perspective on the forest from this trail of hanging bridges. It's a beautiful spot – rife with butterflies, birdlife and even tapirs – and you're likely to have the trail to yourself. It's located about 4km from the main road. A new family took over administration of the

OFF THE BEATEN TRACK

LE ENSEÑADA LODGE & WILDLIFE REFUGE

A wonderfully remote 400-hectare working cattle ranch and salt farm, **La Enseñada Lodge & Wildlife Refuge** (2289-6655; www.laensenada.net; Km 155 Interamericana, Abangaritos; s/d/tr/q US$55/65/75/89, meals US$8-18;) is an incredible setting for birding, horseback riding and good old-fashioned R&R. Rustic but comfortable wooden bungalows face the Golfo de Nicoya, and have private solar-heated bathrooms and patios with hammocks. There's also a restaurant, a romantically rickety jetty and a terrific trail network.

Containing primary and secondary forest (a rarity in this part of the country), as well as mangrove swamps at the mouth of the Río Abangares, this property has been declared a national wildlife refuge. Boat tours to the mangroves (minimum six people, per person US$35) offer the chance to glimpse dozens of bird species, caimans and crocs, while horseback tours (US$35) take you through the tropical dry forest.

lodge and bridges in 2018, making major improvements to both.

The cabins (d incl breakfast US$79-201) are dreamy, and there's also a good restaurant open daily from 11am to 7:30pm.

Jorge Soto BIRDWATCHING
(Bijagua Birdwatching; 8314-9784; www.facebook.com/Bijagua-Birdwatching-515266105581477; half-/full-day tours from $70/110) Jorge is an independent bird guide who is recognized as one of the top guys in this part of the country. He can cater trips to your needs (and life lists!). He doesn't have an office, but you can inquire for him at the Heliconias Rainforest Lodge or at Casitas Tenorio.

Bijagua Rainforest Tours OUTDOORS
(2466-8242, 8998-2954; www.bijaguarainforesttours.com; 7am-5pm) Bijagua resident Marlon Brenes and his team have been working this patch of northern Costa Rica for more than a decade. Knowledgeable and efficient, they're well connected to local sustainable tourism efforts and also offer wider-ranging trips to sights including Caño Negro.

Its guesthouse, **Casa Natural View** (d US$85, two-night minimum), is just down the hill from Casitas Tenorio.

Frog's Paradise WILDLIFE-WATCHING
(8634-7402; US$20; 5:30pm-dark) With a flashlight and a walking stick, you'll accompany Miguel on a nocturnal prowl around former cattle grazing turf, now a wildlife wonderland. You'll likely see some of the 20 regional frog species, and maybe owls, fruit-eating bats, sleeping birds, creeping insects and the things that eat them. There are phosphorescent mushrooms, too.

Chocolate Tree Tour FOOD & DRINK
(8309-5826, 2470-8061; www.treechocolate.com; 1½hr tour US$18; 8am-4pm) Gerardo Solorzano will guide you around his *finca*, which produces cacao and many other crops. But you want the chocolate, right? You'll see the entire process – cutting, fermentation, drying, roasting, husking – and end on a happy note with a cup of hot or cold chocolate.

Located 4km off Ruta 6, after making the right turn just past Super Ale's *soda*, 8km north of Bijagua.

Sleeping

There's a shortage of budget options, but little Bijagua has a pretty good range of places to stay. You'll find them on the main road, Hwy 6, or nestled into the hills east or west of town.

★ **Casitas Tenorio B&B** B&B $$
(8312-1248, 8439-9084; www.casitastenorio.com; d incl breakfast US$110-210;) This sweet family-run farm has six spare but gracious *casitas* (cottages) surrounded by wildlife. Tico/Aussie couple Donald and Pip are committed to rural community tourism. The charm of this place is experiencing life on the farm – you can milk the cows on the morning dairy tour – and exploring the fruit-tree-laden grounds. Your breakfast comes straight from the chickens!

It's 2km southeast from Bijagua, on the road to Heliconias Rainforest Lodge. Donald also takes visitors on tours of **Tapir Valley** (www.tapirvalley.com), a private property on the road to the national park, where you can see – you guessed it – tapirs and other critters.

Cataratas Bijagua Lodge LODGE $$
(☎8937-4687; www.cataratasbijagua.com; d/tr/q incl breakfast US$79/95/113; P 📶) Warner and his sons have turned the family's dairy farm into a beautiful ecolodge, with seven rustic cabins set on gorgeous jungle grounds with views of both Tenorio and Miravalles. The wildlife-filled property is ripe for exploring, with a river trail leading to a private waterfall. Located 2km west of Bijagua; look for the turnoff near the Casita del Maiz.

Warner and Carla don't speak much English, so brush up on your Spanish.

Hotel Cacao HOTEL $$
(☎8337-4032, 2466-6142; www.hotelcacaoriocеleste.com; d incl breakfast with/without air-con from US$56/46; P ❄ 📶) Set in a yellow concrete building, this motel-style place has spacious rooms with new tiles and wooden beds plus a few decorative flourishes such as hanging masks and pottery. There's plenty of deck seating with lovely views of Volcán Miravalles. Onsite laundry (for a fee), shared kitchen and nice hot showers. It's located 300m northwest of the main highway.

At the time of research, there was new *soda* under construction across the street.

Sueño Celeste B&B $$
(☎2466-8221; www.sueno-celeste.com; Km 28, Hwy 6; bungalow incl breakfast d/tr/q US$139/169/199; P 📶 ≋) This cute B&B at the southern end of Bijagua has a collection of stylish bungalows with polished-concrete floors, frilly bed linens, beamed ceilings and molded-concrete rain showers, scattered around a garden plot with Volcán Tenorio views. Seven new rooms were recently added, and there's also a toasty hot tub.

The fastidious Belgian owners will make sure you're oriented and informed during your stay; one of them paints all the cool nature-themed murals!

★**Finca Mei Tai** B&B $$$
(☎8411-7801; www.finca-meitai.com; d/tr/q incl breakfast from US$112/135/157; P 📶 ≋) Set on 40 hectares of forest and pastures 3km west of Bijagua, this family *finca* is crisscrossed by 3.5km of trails and dotted with farm animals. The two guest rooms and family chalet have an abundance of natural light, local hardwoods and graceful details. Eric and Cecile are constantly improving the property; the lastest addition is a tropical salon with an outdoor kitchen.

To get here, take the turnoff across from Pizzeria Barrigon.

Celeste Mountain Lodge LODGE $$$
(☎2278-6628; www.celestemountainlodge.com; s/d/tr/q incl all meals US$165/210/250/290; P 📶) Innovative and sustainable, this contemporary, open-air, hilltop lodge in the shadow of Tenorio is stunning. The 18 rooms are small but stylish, with wooden shutters that open onto immobilizing vistas. Winding through labyrinthine gardens, a trail is laid with geotextile (no more muddy shoes!), making for soundless hiking and prime birdwatching. The price includes meals at the excellent gourmet restaurant.

Hot water comes from solar power, and cooking gas is partially produced by kitchen waste. The lodge is located about halfway down the new access road from Bijagua to Tenorio, and about 4km east of town.

Origins Lodge LODGE $$$
(☎4001-5356; www.originslodge.com; d US$850; 📶 ≋) In the mood to have your mind blown? Splurge on this absurdly cool resort in the middle of nowhere. Accommodations are the most stylish hobbit huts imaginable, with teardrop-shaped living rooftops and private, fire-heated hot tubs on the terraces overlooking Lago de Nicaragua. Meals are prepared by a rotating cast of Michelin-grade French chefs, and majestic horses seem omnipresent.

Activities include nature tours, horseback rides, yoga sessions and spa treatments. Don't miss the night walk.

From Bijagua you'll head northwest on a bumpy road into an abyss of farmland and, after about 45 minutes, a stone wall with the letter 'O' will appear. Few humans have ventured through these gates, and the density of wildlife on the property proves it.

Tenorio Lodge LODGE $$$
(☎2466-8282; www.tenoriolodge.com; s/d/tr incl breakfast from US$70/140/205; P @ 📶) On a lush hilltop 1km south of Bijagua, this lodge has 12 romantic and roomy bungalows featuring orthopedic beds, stone or wood floors and floor-to-ceiling windows with amazing views of Volcán Tenorio. On the 7-hectare property you'll find a restaurant, two ponds, a heliconia garden, fruit

trees galore and two hot tubs to luxuriate in after a long day of hiking.

The lodge's sustainability efforts include using solar heating for hot water, using biodegradable shampoos and soaps, watering the crops with waste water, and drying clothes naturally rather than with a dryer.

Eating

Sprinkled along Hwy 6, Bijagua has the requisite *sodas*, a pizzeria and a few other places to eat in addition to hotel restaurants. It's mostly pretty standard stuff.

Poro COSTA RICAN $
(☎2466-6478; mains US$5-10; ⊙11am-10pm) The finest local restaurant in Bijagua, offering tasty regional dishes like *olla de carne* (meat soup), *lengua en salsa* (tongue in sauce) and fried pork (including the entrails and the head) at excellent prices. Less adventurous options include *casados* and seafood, all of which goes well with a fruit smoothie or a glass of wine.

Getting There & Away

About 6km northwest of Cañas, a paved road branches off the Interamericana and heads north to Upala, passing between Volcán Miravalles to the west and Volcán Tenorio to the east. Smack dab in the middle of these mighty volcanoes sits Bijagua. It's about 40km north of Cañas and 27km south of Upala. There is no gas station here: fill your tank before you arrive.

Buses between San José and Upala stop in Bijagua (US$9, six daily), and there are local buses (US$3, 45 minutes) making the circuit from Cañas to Upala, stopping here. There are also frequent services to Bagaces (US$3, one hour), from where you can continue to the thermal baths of Volcán Miravalles.

A relatively new road bisecting the Parque Nacional Volcán Tenorio has made driving from La Fortuna a relatively straight shot (two to 2½ hours). A bus from there requires a transfer in Cañas.

Parque Nacional Volcán Tenorio

They say that when God finished painting the sky blue, he washed his paintbrushes in the Río Celeste. The heavenly blue river and its waterfalls and lagoons – found in **Parque Nacional Volcán Tenorio** (☎4040-0941; www.sinac.go.cr; adult/child US$12/5; ⊙8am-4pm, last entry 2pm) – are among the most spectacular natural phenomena in Costa Rica, which is probably why the park is known to locals simply as Río Celeste.

Established in 1976, this magical 189 sq km national park remains a blissfully pristine rainforest teeming with wildlife. Soaring 1916m above the cloud forest is the park's namesake, Volcán Tenorio, which consists of three peaked craters: Montezuma, Tenorio I (the tallest) and Tenorio II.

Your first stop will be the Puesto El Pilón ranger station at the park entrance. Take a photo here of the English or Spanish hiking map.

Activities

A well-signed trail begins at the ranger station parking lot (park entrance) and winds 1.5km through the rainforest until you reach an intersection. Turn left and climb down a very steep but sturdy staircase to the **Catarata de Río Celeste**, a milky-blue waterfall that cascades 30m down the rocks into a fantastically aquamarine pool.

It's 400m further to the **Mirador** (lookout point), where you'll have gorgeous views of Tenorio from the double-decker wooden platform. Further on is the technicolor **Pozo Azul** (Blue Lagoon). The trail loops around the lagoon for 400m until you arrive at the confluence of rivers known as **Los Teñideros** (The Stainers). Here two small rivers – one whitish blue and one brownish yellow – mix together to create the blueberry milk of Río Celeste.

Note that swimming is strictly prohibited everywhere along this trail. The nearby hot springs were closed after some tourists were burned in 2011. Hiking to the volcano crater is also prohibited.

Allow two to three hours to complete the entire hike. It's about a 5km round-trip, but parts of the trail are steep and rocky. The trail is wet and muddy year-round. Good hiking shoes or boots are a must; you can rent boots for US$4 at the park entrance. After your hike, you'll find an area to wash your footwear near the trailhead.

For visitors looking for something a bit more adrenaline pumping, quite a few adventure-tourism operators have popped up in this area. They mainly offer river tubing and horseback rides along stretches of the river just outside of the park.

LOCAL KNOWLEDGE

CERRO PELADO

Down a modest country lane just south of Cañas, a local farmer has for the last decade been welcoming in-the-know visitors to an unofficial and utterly majestic mountain hike on his expansive property. Dubbed **Cerro Pelado** (☎8838-3645), which means 'bare hill,' this dormant volcano is particularly amazing to scale at sunrise or sunset, as its panoramic views of undulating hilltops and grassy lowlands extend from the Gulf of Nicoya to the peaks of La Fortuna to the wind turbines of Tilarán. Some folks go up there to stargaze, others to camp. It's also possible to hike to three waterfalls, a pond and a basic cabin for overnight stays (per person US$4).

But mostly people show up with their headlamps to summit Cerro Pelado at sunrise. You'll need your own wheels, as there's no public transport, but a 4WD won't be necessary. Drive 3.5km south of Cañas on Hwy 1 and then head east on Road 926 through the village of Jabilla. After continuing on a dirt road for about 30 minutes, you'll see signs for the parking lot.

Regardless of what time you arrive, the attraction's gatekeeper Wilbert Barrantes will be there to greet you. He charges around US$4 for parking, and US$5 per person for entry. Walking sticks and bathrooms are available at the entrance, and after that you're on your own.

There's an initial uphill slog for about a kilometer, and thereafter you'll be sauntering over the mountain ridge with beauty in all directions. It's about 2km more of gradual climbs and descents to reach the top, with every turn offering a lovely new perspective.

Note that during windier months (November through January) the hike becomes treacherous, as there aren't any guardrails. Fires are no longer allowed because in 2018 a campfire spread and killed two people. In 2019 Wilbert Barrantes was still in the process of obtaining all the permits to bring his attraction into full compliance with the law; call ahead before setting out.

Sleeping & Eating

There are some sweet places to stay along the road to the national park, ranging from friendly budget *cabinas* to swanky mountain lodges. If you really want to get away from it all, there are a few lodges north of the park in the vicinity of the village of San Miguel.

La Carolina Lodge LODGE $$
(☎2466-6393; www.lacarolinalodge.com; per person incl meals US$100-140; P 📶) Flanked by a roaring river and tucked into the trees on the volcano slope, this isolated lodge is also a working cattle ranch. Cabins are rustic and romantic. The river is delicious for swimming, and a wood-fired hot tub is luxurious for soaking. Room rates include guided hikes and cow milking. Horseback rides in the surrounding countryside are US$18 per person.

Amazing organic meals featuring poultry and meat from the farm are cooked over an outdoor wood-burning stove.

The lodge is about 1.3km west of the charming ranching hamlet of San Miguel; turn off the highway 5km north of Bijagua and follow the signs. It's a rough road from here to the national park; don't say we didn't warn you!

Posada Cielo Roto CABIN $$
(☎2466-6049; www.cielorotocostarica.com; per person incl 3 meals US$79) Six wood cabins perched on the northern slope of Volcán Tenorio offer traditional Tico living, where dinner is cooked over a wood stove and guests gather around the fireplace. Gregarious Mario goes out of his way to extend the warmest of welcomes. A two-night stay includes a horseback riding outing on the property. Cash only.

To get here, take the turn to San Miguel that is signposted 5km north of Bijagua. The *posada* (guesthouse) is about 10km east on a sometimes brutal road. 4WD highly recommended.

Catarata Río Celeste Hotel HOTEL $$
(☎8938-9927, 2201-0176; www.catarataarioceleste.com; d/bungalow/ste US$70/91/121; P 📶 ❄) About 1.5km from the park entrance, this family-run property is spread out over

landscaped grounds. There are six simple tiled rooms that share a hammock-strung terrace, as well as one suite and four more luxurious bungalows with Jacuzzis, outdoor showers and volcano views. Many different tours are on offer, including river tubing, horseback riding and a night hike.

A pleasant open-air restaurant regularly attracts tour groups.

Cabinas Piuri HOTEL **$$**

(☎8706-0617, 8699-6858; www.facebook.com/cabinaspiuri; s/d incl breakfast US$30/50, planetarium r US$60, ste US$80; P 📶) About 1km past the park entrance, this unusual property is perched on a gorgeous slice beside the milky-blue Río Celeste (Piuri is the indigenous name for the river). Accommodations vary from colorful *cabinas* with king-size beds to an egg-shaped 'planetarium.' Soak in an inviting natural stone dipping pool on the river banks or take this unique opportunity to swim in the magnificent river itself.

The spacious breakfast area has expansive views.

Posada Río Celeste La Amistad CABINA **$$**

(☎8978-2676, 8356-0285; www.posadarioceleste.com; d incl breakfast US$50-75; P ❄) This homey property offers eight clean, rustic rooms (but with cable TV!) and hearty home-cooked meals, all on a family farm in a rural community 1km northeast of the park entrance. Blooming gardens lead to a 'Surprises Trail' which offers a Tarzan swing and river swimming among other delights (US$6 for nonguests). Staff can also organize hiking and horseback riding.

Even if you're not staying here, this is a perfect pit stop for lunch after hiking in the park. There's no menu: Wilbur and Vilma will serve up whatever they have cooking on their stove. Portions are huge and prices are reasonable.

Rio Celeste Hideaway HOTEL **$$$**

(☎2206-4000; www.riocelestehideaway.com; d incl breakfast US$400; P 📶) Five-star elegance, about 1.5km from the park gate. Huge, 90-sq-m thatched *casitas* with wooden floors, pastel paintwork and antique furnishings are sprinkled among the lush landscaped grounds. Beds are covered with canopies and draped in 300-thread-count sheets. Even the bathrooms are luxurious here, with soaking tubs, outdoor showers and twin sinks.

Delicias del Tenorio SODA **$**

(☎6033-5037; US$5-10; ⊙noon-9pm; 📶) Want a *casado* or hot coffee to warm you up after a long walk in the park? Local chef Christian will whip you up some *lomito* (grilled steak) or a chicken fillet with beans and rice, and then you can hike the short trail behind his restaurant for free. It leads to a calm stretch of Río Celeste where you can swim (US$4 for those who don't eat at the restaurant).

ℹ Getting There & Away

There's no bus to the national park. The closest you can get is Bijagua, from where you can book a tour at almost any hotel, or take a taxi for US$50 to US$75 round-trip.

The main access road is a 30km road that connects Bijagua (Hwy 6) and Guatuso (Hwy 4), indicated by a small brown sign just north of the Agro Logos hardware store. This road has been graded in recent years and is now paved, passing many lodgings along the way. The entrance to the national park is about 9km from Bijagua and 21km from Guatuso – not a bad day trip from La Fortuna (about a two-hour drive).

Five kilometers north of Bijagua is a gravel road to San Miguel. The only real reason to take this goat path is if you're staying at La Carolina or Cielo Roto lodges. Turning left at the San Miguel intersection will bring you to La Carolina Lodge (1.3km). It's about 10km to Cielo Roto from the turnoff (2km past San Miguel village).

WORTH A TRIP

BIG CATS

Las Pumas (El Centro de Rescate Las Pumas; ☎2669-6044; www.centrorescatelaspumas.org; Corobicí; adult/child US$12/8; ⊙8am-4pm) is a wild-animal shelter, which was founded in the 1960s by the late Lilly Hagnauer, a Swiss environmentalist. It's one of the largest shelters of its kind in Latin America, housing big cats including pumas, jaguars, ocelots, jaguarundis and margays, plus badgers, turtles, monkeys, peccaries, toucans and other birds that have been orphaned or injured. The ideal time to visit is between 2pm and 3pm, also known as feeding time. It's located 4.5km north of Cañas on the Interamericana, near Corobicí.

Cañas

If you're cruising north on the Interamericana, Cañas is the first town of any size in Guanacaste, Costa Rica's driest province. *Sabanero* (cowboy) culture is evident on the sweltering streets, where full-custom pickup trucks share the road with swaggering cowboys on horseback. It's a dusty, typically Latin American town, where almost everyone struts slowly and businesses shut down for lunch. It's all centered around the Parque Central, a large bull ring and the decidedly atypical **Catholic church** (cnr Calle Central & Av Central; hours vary).

Although you're better off basing yourself in livelier Liberia or the more scenic Bijagua, Cañas is a good place to organize rafting trips on the nearby Río Corobicí or for exploring Parque Nacional Palo Verde (p226).

Most visitors can accomplish everything they want to do in Cañas in just a few hours, so there's no real need to spend the night. But should you care to linger (or if you really can't drive any longer), there are some decent accommodations. The places in town are functional but not fabulous; by contrast, **Hotel Hacienda La Pacífica** (2669-9393; www.pacificacr.com; d/apt incl breakfast US$110/149; P ❄ @ ☎ ≋), north of Cañas, is atmospheric indeed.

Getting There & Away

All buses arrive and depart from **Terminal Cañas** (La Cañera; Calle Central btwn Avs 11 & 13) at the northern end of town. There are a few *sodas* and snack bars. You can store your bags at the desk.

Volcán Miravalles Area

Volcán Miravalles (2028m) is the highest volcano in the Cordillera de Guanacaste, and although the main crater is dormant, the geothermal activity beneath the ground has led to its development as a hot springs destination. Miravalles isn't a national park or refuge, but the volcano itself is afforded a modicum of protection by being within the Zona Protectora Miravalles.

North of Fortuna de Bagaces, the government-run Proyecto Geotérmico Miravalles is an ambitious project that uses geothermal energy to produce electricity, primarily for export to Nicaragua and Panama. It also produces about 13% of Costa Rica's electricity. A few bright steel tubes from the plant snake along the flanks of the volcano, adding an eerie, alien feel to the remote landscape.

Activities

Volcán Miravalles and other volcanoes are critical sources of renewable energy for Costa Rica. But the geothermal energy visitors crave comes in liquid form: most of the area's hot springs are north of the tiny village of La Fortuna de Bagaces (not to be confused with La Fortuna de Arenal). Some of the country's best mountain biking trails can also be found in this region.

★ **Río Perdido** HOT SPRINGS
(2673-3600, toll free USA 1-888-326-5070; www.rioperdido.com; San Bernardo de Bagaces; day pass adult/child US$40/30, spa treatment US$55-95) This fabulous facility, set amid an otherworldly volcanic landscape, is a wonderful place to soak in Miravalles' soothing waters. The day pass allows access to miles of hiking and mountain-biking trails complete

BUSES FROM CAÑAS

DESTINATION	COMPANY	COST (US$)	DURATION (HR)	FREQUENCY
Liberia	Reina del Campo	3	1	frequent, 4:30am-8:30pm
San José	Autotransportes Tilarán	5	3½	6 daily, 4am-5pm
Tilarán	Autotransportes Tilarán	1	40min	5 daily, 5am-4:50pm
Upala	Transnorte de Upala	3	1½	8 daily, 4:30am-5:30pm

with waterfalls and panoramic views, plus the thermal river and hot springs, where temperatures range from 32°C (90°F) to 46°C (115°F).

Stay the night in eco-chic bungalows (double from US$275). The bungalows are contemporary and cool, with polished-concrete floors, bold patterns and raised terraces facing the forest. Some newer, more spacious units feature floor-to-ceiling windows, outdoor showers and a minimalist approach to design.

There's also swim-up bar, hanging bridges and glorious views all around.

Las Hornillas HOT SPRINGS
(☎8839-9769, 2100-1233; www.hornillas.com; La Fortuna de Bagaces; tours incl lunch US$35-55; ⏲8am-5pm) On Miravalles' southern slopes, Las Hornillas has a lunar landscape, with bubbling pools and fumaroles. Hike to see the volcanic action up close, soak in thermal pools or try out horseback riding. An additional tour involves a tractor ride followed by a walk across hanging bridges through the forest to reach a series of spectacular waterfalls.

Spend the night in one of the rustic cabins (d US$110) on the property, and you can soak in the pools by the light of the silvery moon.

Thermomania HOT SPRINGS
(☎2673-0233; www.thermomania.net; adult/child US$12/10; ⏲8am-10pm) The biggest complex in the area feels like a Tico mini Disneyland, and unsurprisingly families love it. There are more than a dozen thermal pools ranging from lukewarm to warm, a swim-up bar, a large waterpark (with several long slides) and a sauna. Kids will be thoroughly entertained, while adults can soak and relax or take the geothermal energy tour.

The property also contains a spa, restaurant, canopy tour and children's castle.

Guests who camp (per person US$18) or stay in the 40 log cabin rooms (per person US$38) have free access to the pools during their stay. Rooms have a TV and cold-water bathroom.

El Guayacán HOT SPRINGS
(☎2673-0349; www.termaleselguayacan.com; La Unión; adult/child US$7.50/5.50; ⏲8am-10pm) Just behind Thermomanía – the road sign is not terribly obvious – this is a family *finca* that's hissing and smoking with vents and mud pots. There are eight thermal pools and one cold pool with a waterslide. You can also ride a zipline or take a guided tour of the fumaroles (stay on the trail!).

Yökö Termales HOT SPRINGS
(☎2673-0410; www.yokotermales.com; Miravalles; adult/child US$10/8; ⏲7am-10pm) Four hot springs and a larger pool with a small waterslide and waterfall, in an attractive meadow at the foot of Miravalles. The views are magnificent, but there's little shade around the pools (though one has a true 'wet' bar, Jacuzzi, and sauna). The 12 canary-tinted rooms (including breakfast US$40 to US$150) are an OK, but far from magical, sleeping option.

Tours

Many tour companies offer organized trips to the various hot springs, sometimes with additional activities such as hiking, horseback riding and ziplining. Packages include transportation from Bahía Salinas, Liberia or the northern Península de Nicoya.

Canyon Adventure ADVENTURE
(☎2673-3600; www.rioperdido.com; San Bernardo de Bagaces; adult/child US$60/50) You've done canopy tours, but have you tried a canyon tour? This new take on a tried-and-true adventure will have you zipping from platform to platform, most of which are mounted on rocks or canyon walls. The route is challenging and fun, with five ziplines plus a series of bridges, swings and steel cables. One of Rio Perdido's many attractions.

Canyon Adventure also gives full access to the thermal river, hot springs and hiking trails.

Getting There & Away

Volcán Miravalles is 27km northeast of Bagaces. Head north on a paved road through the communities of Salitral and Torno, where the road splits. Take the left-hand fork to reach Guayabo, with a few *sodas* and basic *cabinas;* to the right, you'll find Fortuna de Bagaces, with easier access to the hot springs. The road reconnects north of the two towns and continues toward Upala.

There are hourly buses connecting Bagaces with Guayabo and Fortuna de Bagaces (US$1, 45 minutes). Make sure to take the bus that passes the *termales* (ask the driver); there are two routes and one bypasses them completely. There are also direct buses here from Liberia.

When returning, it's easier to go to *el cruce* (the road crossing) 1km north from Thermomania (p225), because all the buses back toward civilization stop there; only a few a day turn down the road that goes directly past the hot springs.

Parque Nacional Palo Verde

The 198 sq km **Parque Nacional Palo Verde** (☎2206-5965, 2680-6596; adult/child US$12/5; ⏰8am-4pm) is a wetland sanctuary in Costa Rica's driest province. It lies on the northeastern bank of the mouth of the Río Tempisque and at the head of the Golfo de Nicoya. All the major rivers in the region drain into this ancient intersection of two basins, which creates a mosaic of habitats, including mangrove swamps, marshes, grassy savannas and evergreen forests. A number of low limestone hills provide lookouts over the park, and the shallow, permanent lagoons are focal points for wildlife. The park derives its name from the abundant *palo verdes* (green trees), small shrubs that are green year-round. The park is contiguous in the north with the Refugio de Vida Silvestre Dr Rafael Lucas Rodríguez Caballero and the Reserva Biológica Lomas de Barbudal (p232).

The mosquitoes are legendary in this place. By all means, bring insect repellent!

Activities

Hiking

You can explore the park's well-maintained trails on your own or accompany an OTS (Organization for Tropical Studies) guide on their regular three-hour guided walk (adult/child US$34/23). Contact OTS ahead of time if you'd like a guided walk, which takes place sometime between 8am and 3pm, depending on conditions. Pick up a map at the park entrance.

From the entrance, the first trailhead you'll reach is for the **Sendero Roco**, which is a short, steep climb (570m) up to a scenic viewpoint over the lagoon. On a clear day you can see the Río Tempisque to the Golfo de Nicoya. Next along, the **Sendero Mapache** traverses three distinct habitats in a short 710m. See if you can tell the difference between the deciduous lowland, limestone and evergreen forests.

For the most adventurous hikers, **Sendero El Guayacán** cuts through the heart of the park and offers striking views of the lagoon and Tempisque plains. And at the far end of the park, beyond the ranger station, you can hike 1400m along the **Sendero La Cantera** to reach a splendid lookout that takes in the whole area.

No matter which trail you choose, remember that it gets fiercely hot in the dry season – carry ample water, wear a sun hat and avoid hiking at midday.

Wildlife-Watching

Palo Verde has the greatest concentrations of waterfowl and shorebirds in Central America; over 300 bird species have been recorded here. Birdwatchers come to see the large flocks of herons (including rare black-crowned night herons), storks (including the endangered jabirú), spoonbills, egrets, ibises, grebes and ducks. Forest birds, including scarlet macaws, great curassows, keel-billed toucans and parrots, are also common. Frequently sighted mammals include deer, coatis, armadillos, monkeys and peccaries, as well as the largest population of jaguarundis in Costa Rica. There are also numerous reptiles in the wetlands including crocodiles that are reportedly up to 5m in length.

The dry season (December to March) is the best time to visit, as flocks of birds tend to congregate in the remaining lakes and marshes. The trees also lose their leaves, allowing for clearer viewing. Mammals are occasionally seen around the watering holes. That said, the entire basin swelters during the dry season, so bring adequate sun protection. During the wet months large portions of the area are flooded and access may be limited.

If you'd like some help spotting and identifying furred and feathered creatures, OTS offers guided bird walks and night tours.

Tours

To fully appreciate the size and topography of the park, it's worth organizing a boat trip (per person adult/child from US$51/40) down the Río Tempisque, a wide, brown, brackish river contained on either side by mangroves. Arrangements can be made through OTS.

Boat tours depart from the dock in Puerto Chamorro, which is on the main park road, 2km from the ranger station. If you arrive early enough, you may be able to show up and find a free spot on an outgoing boat. You can also hire a boatman from Puerto

DON'T MISS

HOTTEST THERMAL POOLS

Costa Rica's volcano-powered thermal pools and mud pots provide plenty of good, clean fun for beauty queens and would-be mud wrestlers.

Hot Springs Río Negro (p233) On the slopes of Volcán Rincón de la Vieja, with several pools in a jungle setting.

Río Perdido (p224) Thermal pools, hanging bridges and low-key luxury characterize this thermal canyon experience near Volcán Miravalles.

Borinquen Mountain Resort & Spa (p234) The pinnacle of indulgent dirt exists in the remote heights of Rincón de la Vieja. If mineral mud is not your thing, you can opt instead for a skin treatment of coconut, cappuccino or chocolate.

Humo, which is reachable by the 'Rosaria' bus from Nicoya.

Tour operators on the Península de Nicoya and in La Fortuna bring tour groups to Palo Verde, but if you can get here on your own, you'll save plenty of money by arranging everything yourself.

El Viejo Wetlands ACTIVITY CENTER
(Hacienda el Viejo; ☎2296-0966; www.elviejowetlands.com; incl lunch boat/cultural tour US$70/35; ⏲7am-5pm) Bordering Parque Nacional Palo Verde, this impressive facility is operated by a successful sugarcane family that has devoted 20 sq km to a wetlands refuge. In addition to hiking, biking and boat tours (some of which enter the national park), they also do a sugarcane demonstration; you'll make *'agua de sapo'* ('toad water') from lime, ginger and sugarcane.

Meals are served in the historic and atmospheric *casona* (mansion).

The main entrance is about 15km south of Filadelfia. Head southeast out of town on Calle 5 and follow the signs. El Viejo can also provide transportation from anywhere on the northern Península de Nicoya.

Sleeping & Eating

OTS Hacienda Palo Verde Research Station LODGE $$
(☎ext 1340 2524-0607; www.tropicalstudies.org; r incl meals per adult/child from US$84/36; P ☎) Run by the OTS (Organization for Tropical Studies), this station conducts tropical research and teaches university graduate-level classes. But it also has rustic cabins with bunk beds and fans, which are rented out to 'natural history visitors.' The research station is on a well-signed road 8km from the park entrance.

Getting There & Away

The main road to the entrance, usually passable by ordinary cars year-round, begins from a signed turnoff from the Interamericana, opposite Bagaces. The 28km gravel road has tiny brown signs that direct you when the road forks. Once inside the park, another 8km brings you to the limestone hill, Cerro Guayacán (and the OTS Hacienda Palo Verde Research Station), from where there are great views; 2km further are the Palo Verde park headquarters and ranger station. You can drive through a swampy maze of roads to the Reserva Biológica Lomas de Barbudal (p232) without returning to the Interamericana, but be sure to ask rangers about road conditions.

Buses connecting Cañas and Liberia can drop you in Bagaces, opposite the turnoff to the park, but still a good distance away. If you're staying at the Palo Verde Research Station, the staff may be able to pick you up, but be sure to make advance arrangements.

You can take the 'Rosaria' bus from Nicoya to Puerto Humo, and then bargain with local boatmen to take you to Puerto Chamorro, the dock where all the boat tours leave, just 2km from the ranger station.

Liberia

POP 56,900

The sunny rural capital of Guanacaste has long served as a transportation hub to Nicaragua, as well as being the standard-bearer of Costa Rica's *sabanero* (cowboy) culture. Today, tourism is fast becoming a significant contributor to the economy. With a recently expanded international airport, Liberia is a safer and more chilled-out Costa Rican gateway than San José.

Most of the historic buildings in the town center are in need of a paint job, though the 'White City' is pleasant, with a good range of

Liberia

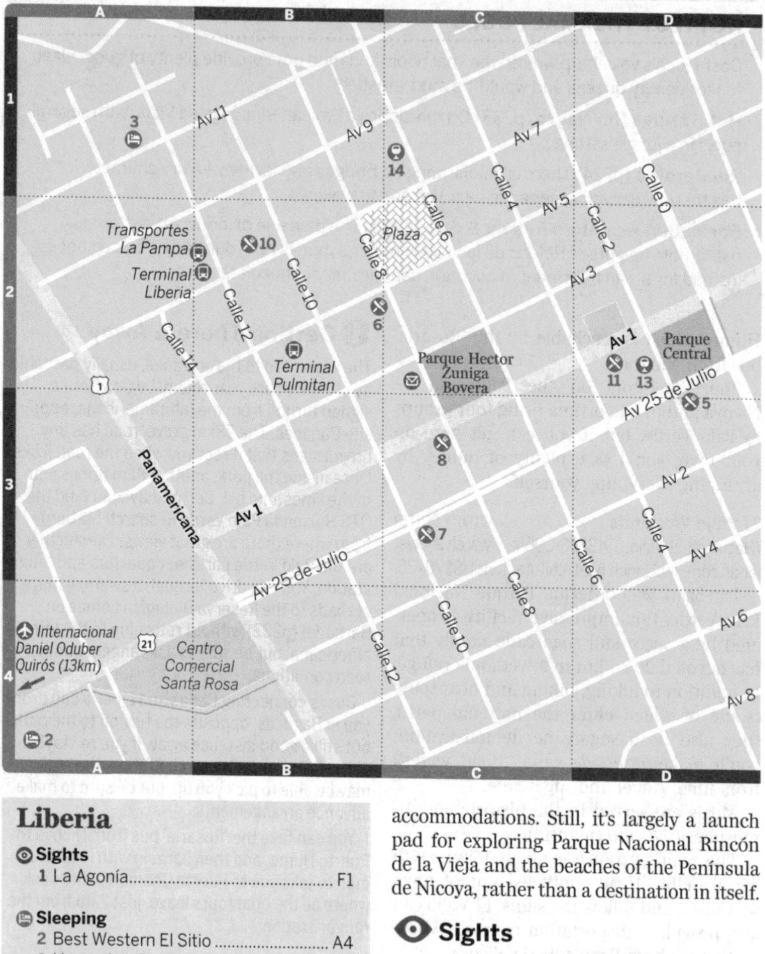

Liberia

Sights

1 La Agonía F1

Sleeping

2 Best Western El Sitio A4
3 Hospedaje Dodero A1

Eating

4 Café Liberia E3
5 Casa de Calá D3
6 Donde Pipe B2
7 Jauja C3
8 Los Comales C3
9 Mariajuana E1
10 Market B2
11 Masala D2
12 Pizza Pronto E3

Drinking & Nightlife

13 Guana's D2
14 La Selegna C1
15 Palermo House E2

accommodations. Still, it's largely a launch pad for exploring Parque Nacional Rincón de la Vieja and the beaches of the Península de Nicoya, rather than a destination in itself.

Sights

The blocks around the intersection of Av Central and Calle Real contain several of Liberia's oldest houses, many dating back about 150 years. Locals harbor a long-term dream to pedestrianize Calle Real (south of the park), the historic thoroughfare into and out of the city, to replicate places like nearby Grenada in Nicaragua.

Ponderosa Adventure Park WILDLIFE RESERVE
(☎2288-1000, WhatsApp 8460-1750; www.ponderosaadventurepark.com; half-/full-day package US$48/63, safari US$35; ⊙8am-5pm) Wildebeests, zebras, giraffes and other African animals are right at home in the dry Guanacaste heat, as you can see at this private

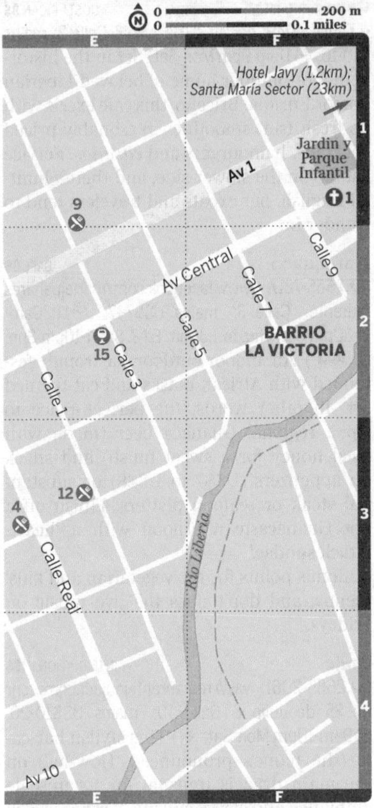

wildlife reserve. The safari tour allows you to get up close and personal with the (sort of) wild animals. Kayaking, ziplining and horseback riding are also on offer.

The park is in El Salto, about 11km south of town on the Interamericana, halfway to Bagaces.

La Agonía CHURCH

(La Iglesia de la Ermita de Nuestro Señor de la Agonía; cnr Av Central & Calle 9; variable) With whitewashed walls and twin pillars flanking the front door, La Agonía typifies the Spanish colonial architecture that earned Liberia its 'White City' nickname. This is the city's oldest church, built in 1825. There is supposedly an art and culture exhibit inside, but it's difficult to say for sure, as the doors are usually locked tight.

Check at the house next door to the church for opening hours; if you can't go in, at least check out the massive yellow iguana statue in the park.

Sleeping

Budget and midrange options abound though they are fairly uninspiring, and there are also a couple of high-end international chain hotels near the airport. Demand picks up considerably during the dry season, and reservations are strongly recommended over weekends and holidays. During the rainy season, most of the midrange and top-end hotels give discounts.

Hospedaje Dodero HOSTEL $

(2665-4326, 8729-7524; www.hospedajedodero.yolasite.com; Av 11, btwn Calles 12 & 14; dm US$12, s US$17-19, d US$25-30;) This place is clean, has super service and is close to the bus station. All rooms have shared bathrooms; some have air-con. There's a communal outdoor kitchen overlooking a small yard filled with flowers and hung with hammocks. It's nothing fancy, but it's very friendly.

Hotel Javy HOTEL $$

(2666-9253; www.hoteljavy.com; cnr Av 19 & Calle 19; d incl breakfast US$56; P) On the outskirts of Liberia, this charming stay offers light-filled and comfortable rooms, firm beds, and enormous, traditional breakfasts. Furnishings are incongruously formal and bathrooms are spotless. The location, about 2km northeast of Parque Central and 200m north of the IPEC, is not convenient, particularly without a car.

Best Western El Sitio HOTEL $$

(2666-1211; www.bestwestern.com; d from US$80; P) It's nothing special, but if you've got a night to burn in Liberia this chain property is comfortable enough and conveniently located just off the Interamericana. Rooms are functional with all the usual amenities, though the grounds are actually pretty appealing, with lots of tropical flora, a gym, two pools (one adults only) and a hot tub.

There was once a casino, but during research it was closed.

Eating

Liberia has a good selection of restaurants, both in town and on the road to the airport. If you've been on the road for weeks and are dying for it, 'modernized' Liberia has some chain fast-food joints near the highway. If you're taking the bus, pick up some snacks for the road at the **market** (Av 7, btwn Calles 10 & 12; 6am-7pm Mon-Sat, to noon Sun) next to Terminal Liberia.

Donde Pipe CAFE $

(2665-4343; www.dondepipe.com; cnr Calle 8 & Av 5; mains US$7-11; 7am-6pm;) This little cafe is a local favorite, thanks to free wi-fi, strong coffee and scrumptious sweets and breakfasts. In addition to cafe fare, the menu features local specialties such as *chifrijos* (rice and pinto beans with fried pork, fresh tomato salsa and corn chips) and tamales, plus fresh fruit juices.

Friendly staff, air-con and a block from the bus station: need we say more?

Los Comales COSTA RICAN $

(2665-0105; cnr Av 1 & Calle 8; dishes US$4-8; 6:30am-9pm Mon-Thu & Sat, 6:30am-7pm Fri, 7:30am-2pm Sun) This convivial and popular local spot is run by a women's collective. Come for traditional Guanacaste fare such as *arroz de maís* (rice with chicken and corn). Lunchtime is crowded which means slow service. There's a dozen fresh juices and *batidos* (fruit shakes made with milk or water) to wet your whistle.

★Masala INDIAN $$

(4703-0477; www.facebook.com/IndianFoodLiberia; 50m west of Parque Central; US$9-17; 11:30am-10pm;) Liberia is not a city where you'd expect to find any Indian restaurant, let alone the best one in the country. But here it is! Start with some crispy warm samosas, and continue with a bold tandoori dish or a sinus-clearing curry lapped up with a decadent slice of garlic naan. The authentic flavors here hail from across India, with an emphasis on the north.

The owner couldn't be nicer, and there are lots of delicious veggie options and a children's menu.

★Café Liberia FUSION $$

(2665-1660; Calle Real btwn Avs 2 & 4; mains US$9-14; 9am-9pm Tue-Sat, 4:30pm-9pm Mon;) This beautifully restored colonial-era building has heavy wooden furniture and frescóed ceilings, creating a romantic ambiance for enjoying rich coffee and gourmet fare. French chef Sebastien and his Tica wife Ligia have taken staple foods to new levels: super-fresh *ceviche* is served with warm, fresh-baked tortilla chips, and the lasagna and crepes are top-notch.

The courtyard hosts occasional live events, including a Latin dance party and BBQ on certain Saturdays.

Casa de Calá COSTA RICAN $$

(2101-4049; cnr Av 25 de Julio & Calle 2; mains $10-16; 11am-9pm Mon-Sat) Set in the historic indoor-outdoor home of beloved Liberian doctor Enrique Briceño, this cafe excels with its fresh fruit smoothies, reasonably priced cocktails, hamburgers and *casados*. Service can be on the slower side, and there's limited English, but expats and travelers tend to wander in.

Mariajuana CAFE $$

(2665-7217; www.facebook.com/mariajuanarestaurante; Calle 3; mains US$7-17; 11:30am-11:30pm Sun-Thu, to 1:30am Fri & Sat, 1-10pm Sun;) An indoor-outdoor gastropub festooned with African masks and cat-themed art. In other words, the perfect place to sip a regional Guanaca beer (made with local honey for a sweet finish) and snack on appetizers (US$7 to US$8) or substantial steak or seafood platters. Finish off a hot Guanacaste afternoon with a 'heart-attack sundae.'

Bonus points for the vegetarian and kids' menus, and don't miss the live music on Fridays.

Jauja INTERNATIONAL $$

(2665-2061; www.restaurantejaujacr.com; cnr Av 25 de Julio & Calle 10; mains US$10-20; 9am-10pm Mon-Sat;) This stylish bar-cafe (the name's pronounced 'How-ha') on the main drag is unusual for its upscale ambiance and classy cuisine. Service is also excellent. Look for wood-fired pizza, tender steaks from grass-fed cattle, and burgers on home-baked buns. It's popular with the local professional set, as well as tourists and expats.

Pizza Pronto PIZZA $$

(2666-2098; cnr Av 4 & Calle 1; mains US$10-18; noon-3pm & 4-10pm) This very cute old-world pizzeria, where the wood is stacked next to the smoking courtyard oven, keeps it romantic and simple – just pizza, pasta and salads. The pizzas are delish, ranging from the recommended vegetarian option to the not-so-recommended taco pizza. You can choose from a list of more than 30 pizzas or create your own.

Drinking & Nightlife

There is no shortage of watering holes from the main square on down to the Interamericana. It's up to you to decide if you want to drink at the sports bar, the cocktail bar, the cowboy bar or the art cafe. What kind of mood are you in?

★La Selegna BAR

(☎2666-0029; Calle 6; ⊙noon-midnight) Liberia's best *sabanero* hangout is this family-owned *cantina*, serving cheap Pilsen since 1970. It's a fun place to watch sports or people, there's a jukebox and the food is surprisingly tasty. Try the *chifrijo* appetizer 'mixed,' with both beef tips, pork rinds and beans, and be sure to douse it in the house *chilero* (hot sauce).

Palermo House COCKTAIL BAR

(☎2240-3325; cnr Av Central & Calle 3; ⊙4pm-midnight Mon-Thu, 10am-midnight Fri-Sun) This tropical garden, lush with greenery, is one of the city's more pleasant places for a drink. There's also sports and music videos on the big screen, but the volume is usually turned down so patrons can enjoy the tranquil atmosphere. The menu offers very tasty pub grub and Tico fare (shared appetizers US$10).

Guana's SPORTS BAR

(☎2665-0105; Calle 2 btwn Avs 25 de Julio & 1; ⊙11am-2am) Facing Parque Central, this open-air bar has cold beer, decent pizza and football on the big screen. The place picks up on weekends, when the party spills out into the courtyard and onto the sidewalk. Chuck back a cold Imperial and people watch to your heart's content.

Information

MEDICAL SERVICES

Hospital Dr Enrique Baltodano Briceño (☎2690-9700, emergencies 2666-0318; Ruta 918) Behind the stadium on the northeastern outskirts of town.

MONEY

Banco de Costa Rica (☎2666-9002; cnr Calle Real & Av 1; ⊙8:30am-4pm Mon-Fri)

Banco Nacional (☎2690-9053; Av 25 de Julio btwn Calles 6 & 8; ⊙8:30am-7pm Mon-Fri)

POST

Post Office (Correos de Costa Rica; ☎2666-1649; cnr Av 3 & Calle 8; ⊙8am-5pm Mon-Fri, to noon Sat)

BUSES FROM LIBERIA

DESTINATION (COMPANY)	COST (US$)	DURATION (HR)	TERMINAL	FREQUENCY
Cañas (Reina del Campo)	2	1½	Liberia	Half-hourly, 5:25am-9:30pm
Curubandé (Tranbasa)	2	40min	Liberia	6:40am, noon, 5pm
La Cruz/Peñas Blancas (Tranbasa)	2.50	1½-2	Liberia	frequent, 5am-6:30pm
Nicoya, via Filadelfia and Santa Cruz (La Pampa)	3	1½	Liberia	Half-hourly, 4:30am-8:30pm
Playa Flamingo and Brasilito (La Pampa)	3	1½	Liberia	7 daily, 6:10am-6pm
Playas del Coco (Pulmitan)	1.50	1	Pulmitan	frequent, 5am-8pm
Playa Hermosa (La Pampa)	1.50	1½	Liberia	9 daily, 4:40am-5:30pm
Playa Tamarindo (La Pampa)	3	2	Liberia	13 daily, 3:50am-6:10pm
Puntarenas (Reina del Campo)	3	3	Liberia	9 daily, 5am-3:30pm
San José (Pulmitan)	8	4	Pulmitan	14 daily, 3:05am-8pm

OFF THE BEATEN TRACK

RESERVA BIOLÓGICA LOMAS DE BARBUDAL

Forming a cohesive unit with Palo Verde, the 26 sq km **Reserva Biológica Lomas de Barbudal** (hours vary) is a tropical dry forest reserve that's famous for its huge diversity of resident bees. If that doesn't make you want to come here, maybe the endangered gumbo-limbo and rosewood trees and giant anteaters will be more appealing. Hike here in March or April and the *corteza amarillas* may be in full yellow bloom.

In any case, Lomas de Barbudal is an accessible option for off-the-beaten-track independent hiking. A small **visitors center** (hours vary) with maps and other information is sporadically open. You can explore the reserve on several different hiking trails; a short jaunt along the Río Cabuya leads to a *poza* (watering hole) that lures lots of wildlife in the dry season. There's also a trail leading to a scenic waterfall.

The turnoff to Lomas de Barbudal from the Interamericana is 14km southeast of Liberia and 12km northwest of Bagaces. From here it's 6km to the entrance of the reserve on a rough, unpaved road. Some steep sections may require 4WD in the rainy season.

Getting There & Away

AIR

Located 12km west of Liberia, **Aeropuerto Internacional Daniel Oduber Quirós** (LIR; 2666-9600; www.lircr.com) serves as the country's second international airport, providing easy access to all those beautiful beaches without the hassle of San José. In January 2012 it unveiled its sleek and modern US$35 million terminal, and in 2018 the expansion project was finally complete.

The majority of international flights go to the USA and Canada, though there are some flights on Copa Air (to Panama) and Thompson Airways (London) and KLM (Amsterdam). Domestic flights mainly go to San José.

There's a number of car-rental desks at the airport near the exit if you haven't made a reservation in advance. Taxis from Liberia to the airport are about US$25, or you can catch a bus (US$1, 30 minutes, hourly) in front of the Mercado Municipal; it runs from 4am to 7pm.

Sansa (Aeropuerto Internacional Daniel Oduber Quirós 2668-1017, reservations 2290-4100; www.flysansa.com) flies from Liberia to San José, Tambor, Tamarindo, Nosara, La Fortuna and Costa Esmeralda (Nicaragua). Newer airlines Green Airways (www.costaricagreenair.com) and Aerobell Airlines (www.aerobell.com) have announced plans to serve Liberia's airport in the future.

BUS

Buses arrive and depart from **Terminal Liberia** (Av 7 btwn Calles 12 & 14) and **Terminal Pulmitan** (Av 5 btwn Calles 10 & 12).

CAR

Liberia lies on the Interamericana, 234km north of San José and 77km south of Peñas Blancas on the border with Nicaragua. Hwy 21, the main artery of the Península de Nicoya, begins in Liberia and heads southwest. A dirt road leads 25km from Barrio La Victoria to the Santa María entrance of Parque Nacional Rincón de la Vieja; the partially paved road to the Las Pailas entrance begins from the Interamericana, 5km north of Liberia.

It's generally hard to find street signs here, and locals still give directions using nearby locales and distances ('100 meters, then turn left at the pulperia'), rather than actual street names.

There are more than a dozen car-rental agencies in Liberia, most of which have desks at the airport. Most companies will drop off your car at your hotel upon request.

Adobe (2667-0608, in USA 855-861-1250; www.adobecar.com; 8am-5pm) is one of the cheapest and best rental companies in Costa Rica. The pick-up and drop-off is 10 minutes west of the airport.

Parque Nacional Rincón de la Vieja

Given its proximity to Liberia – really just a hop, a skip and a few bumps away – this 160 sq km **national park** (2661-8139; www.acguanacaste.ac.cr; adult/6-12yr/under 5yr US$15/5/free; 8am-4pm Tue-Sun, no entry after 3pm) feels refreshingly uncrowded and remote. The name (which translates as 'old lady's nook') comes from its steamy main attraction, the active Volcán Rincón de la Vieja (1895m). The park also covers several other peaks in the same volcanic range, including the highest, Volcán Santa María (1916m). Exhaling geothermal energy, the park bubbles with multihued fumaroles, tepid springs and steaming, flatulent mud pots, as well as a young and feisty *volcancito* (small volcano). All of these can be visited on foot via well-maintained (but often steep) trails. Note the Las Pailas sector is closed on Monday.

Activities

Hiking

From the Santa María ranger station (p235), there are more than 12km of hiking trails, one of which leads to hot springs. Since some rather strong eruptions in 2011, the trek to the summit of Rincón de la Vieja has not been open to the public.

Catarata La Cangreja HIKING

A four-hour, 5.1km (each direction) hike leads to Catarata La Cangreja, where falls drop 50m from a cliff into a small lagoon, though swimming is no longer allowed. The trail winds through forest past massive strangler figs, then to open savanna spiked with yucca on the volcano's flanks, where views stretch to the Palo Verde wetlands and the Pacific beyond.

Sendero Las Pailas HIKING

A circular trail known as Sendero Las Pailas – about 2.5km in total – takes you east of Las Pailas ranger station (p235), past boiling mud pools *(las pailas)*, sulfurous fumaroles and a *volcancito* (small volcano). This is the most popular (and most crowded) section of the park, as it's an easy but worthwhile trail with a lot to see.

A plan to pave part of this trail has come to fruition, allowing those in wheelchairs to enjoy about 600m of it.

Thermal Springs

There's no better way to recover from a grueling hike than by soaking in thermal springs. Many of the springs are reported to have therapeutic properties – always a good thing if you've been hitting the *guaro cacique* (sugarcane liquor) a little too hard.

In the Sector Santa María a trail leads 3km west through the 'enchanted forest,' past the lovely **Catarata Bosque Encantado** (Enchanted Forest Falls) to sulfurous hot springs. Don't soak in them for more than about half an hour (some people suggest much less) without taking a dip in the nearby cold springs, 2km away, to cool off. If you want real-deal, volcano-created thermal pools, here they are – it doesn't get more 'natural' than this.

On the fringes of the park there are several private facilities that have thermal pools with varying temperatures: no hiking required. Many companies and hotels offer tours to these sites from Liberia.

Hot Springs Río Negro HOT SPRINGS

(☎2690-2900; www.guachipelin.com; adult/child US$20/15; ⏰9am-6pm) Set in the dry forest along the Río Negro, this magical place is managed by the Hacienda Guachipelín (p235). Ten natural, stone-crafted hot pools are accessed by a lovely wooded trail, with hanging bridges leading to pools on either side of the raging river. Pools range in temperature from 40°C (104°F) to 57°C (135°F).

About 1km from the Las Pailas ranger station (p235), turn toward Rincon de la Vieja Lodge and the Santa María sector. The hot springs will be on your right.

Simbiosis Spa SPA

(☎2690-2900; www.guachipelin.com; day pass US$35, treatment from US$50; ⏰9am-5pm) A short jaunt from the park entrance, this spa takes advantage of the volcanic activity happening right on the property. Guests can see the boiling mud pools that are the source of their mud bath, and there are five pools (three warm, two cool) and a range of massage options.

Tours

Lodges in the area can arrange tours such as horseback riding, mountain biking, guided waterfall and hot-spring hikes, rappeling, rafting and tubing on the lesser-known Río Colorado, and – everyone's favorite cash-burner – canopy tours. Tours are offered by Borinquen Mountain Resort (p234), Buena Vista del Rincón (p234), Canyon de la Vieja Adventure Lodge and Hacienda Guachipelín (p235). Transportation from Liberia may also be provided, if needed.

Canyon de la Vieja Adventure Lodge ADVENTURE

(☎2665-5912; www.thecanyonlodge.com/activities; rapelling US$15, other activities US$35-45) On the bank of the crystal-blue Río Colorado, this sprawling lodge operates a full-service spa, with cool and warm pools, mud baths, massage and other treatments. The river current is strong, but the swimming hole is glorious for cooling off on a hot day (unfortunately, there's not much shade). The lodge also offers horseback riding, tubing, rafting and canopy tours.

FLORA & FAUNA OF RINCÓN DE LA VIEJA

The park was created in 1973 to protect a vital watershed that feeds 32 rivers and streams. Its relatively remote location means that wildlife, rare elsewhere, is out in force here, with the major volcanic crater making for a rather dramatic backdrop to the scene. Volcanic activity has occurred many times since the late 1960s, though the most recent eruptions (in 2019) have all been relatively small. The volcano remains active but does not present any danger – ask locally for the latest news, as volcanoes do act up. Note that the crater itself is off-limits, as the eruptions have made it unsafe.

Elevations in the park range from less than 600m to 1916m, meaning visitors pass through a variety of habitats as they ascend the volcanoes, though the majority of the trees in the park are typical of those found in dry tropical forests throughout Guanacaste. The park is home to the country's highest density of Costa Rica's national flower, the increasingly rare purple orchid *(Cattleya skinneri)*, locally known as *guaria morada*.

The lodge is 8km north of Liberia. Accommodation (single/double including breakfast US$85/105) is also available.

Sleeping & Eating

There is a rustic cafe near the park entrance to Las Pailas that will serve you a sandwich or sell you a bottle of water. It's not much, so you're better off coming prepared with a picnic and plenty of water. Otherwise, your eating options are mostly restricted to the hotels. There are a few *sodas* in Curubandé, if you want to change it up.

El Sol Verde CAMPGROUND **$**
(☎2665-5357; www.elsolverde.com; campsite US$10, tent houses US$30, d/q US$53/72; P Wi-Fi) The feisty Dutch couple here offer three Spanish-tiled, wood-walled rooms. Alternatively, bed down in the camping area, where there are a few furnished tent houses, a shared outdoor kitchen, solar-heated showers and plenty of space to pitch your own tent. The mural-painted terrace is a lovely place to relax. It's in Curubandé village.

You'll find hiking, swimming and wildlife in the immediate vicinity.

Casa Rural Aroma de Campo HOTEL **$$**
(☎2665-0008, reservations 7010-5776; www.aromadecampo.com; incl breakfast s/d/tr/q from US$59/83/112/129; P Wi-Fi pool) Near the village of Curubandé, this serene, epiphyte-hung, hammock-strung oasis has six rooms with polished hardwood floors, open bathrooms, colorful wall art, mosquito nets and a classy rural sensibility. Scattered around the property, six additional prefab containers have bold colors and glass walls for better immersion in the forested setting. Delicious meals are served family style in the courtyard.

Warning: the pet parrot is an early riser.

Buena Vista del Rincón LODGE **$$**
(☎2690-1414; www.buenavistadelrincon.com; d incl breakfast US$90-110; P Wi-Fi pool) Part cattle ranch, part adventure lodge, this expansive place is set on 809 hectares in the park's western sector. On the grounds are three waterfalls, thermal pools, a canopy tour, hanging bridges and a thrilling 420m mountain waterslide. Choose between rustic stained-wood rooms and more private log cabins with glorious views. This lodge caters to package tourists big time.

Accessible via the village of Cañas Dulces. The resort's sustainable practices include composting, environmental education classes and using methane gas for cooking and to run the laundry's dryers.

Rinconcito Lodge LODGE **$$**
(☎8536-5915, 2206-4833; www.rinconcitolodge.com; San Jorge; incl breakfast s/d US$61/82, superior d US$99; P Wi-Fi pool) Just 3.5km from the Santa María sector of the park, this affordable option has attractive, rustic cabins that are surrounded by some of the prettiest pastoral scenery imaginable. The cheaper rooms are small, but they are clean and fresh. The lodge also offers hiking, horseback riding and ziplining tours.

Located in San Jorge on Ruta 918, near El Tanque.

Borinquen Mountain Resort & Spa RESORT **$$$**
(☎2690-1900; www.borinquenresort.com; d incl breakfast US$188-307; P A/C Wi-Fi pool) The area's most luxurious resort is located on the western flank of the park. It features nicely appointed bungalows with private decks and jaw-dropping mountain views. Hot springs, mud baths and natural saunas are surrounded by greenery. A treatment at the

elegant **Anáhuac Spa** (9am to 5pm) – suspended over the steaming jungle – is the icing on this decadent mud pie.

The resort is accessible via the village of Cañas Dulces. It's 15km past the village on the main road to the entrance, and then another 3km from the entrance to the resort.

All the expected adventure tours are on offer here.

Hacienda Guachipelín HOTEL **$$$**
(☎2690-2900; www.guachipelin.com; d/tr/q incl breakfast from US$115/145/175; P❄@🛜🏊) This appealing 19th-century working cattle ranch is set on 13 sq km of primary and secondary forest. The 79 rooms are spacious and comfortable with traditional wood furniture and wide, welcoming verandas. Many of the rooms have lovely views of the volcano and surrounding grounds. You'll appreciate the welcome drink at check-in. It's 10km from the park entrance.

Be warned that the onsite 'adventure center' makes this place feel a little like a vacation factory, catering largely to package tourists who descend for organized horse tours, in-house canopy tours and guided hikes in the national park.

Information

The two main entrances to the park each have their own ranger station, where you sign in, pay admission and get free maps. Most visitors enter through **Las Pailas ranger station** (☎2666-5051; www.acguanacaste.ac.cr; ⏲8am-4pm Tue-Sun) on the western flank, where most of the trails begin. The **Santa María ranger station** (☎2666-5051; www.acguanacaste.ac.cr; ⏲7am-4pm), to the east, is in the Hacienda Santa María, a 19th-century *rancho* that was reputedly once owned by US President Lyndon Johnson. This is your access point to the sulfurous springs.

Getting There & Away

The Las Pailas sector is accessible via a good 20km road that begins at a signed turnoff from the Interamericana, 5km north of Liberia. It's paved for the first part of the drive past Curubandé. If you're not staying at the Hacienda Guachipelín, you'll have to pay (US$1.50 per person) to drive on its private road, which takes you to the park entrance.

The Santa María ranger station, in the east, is accessible via a rougher gravel road beginning at Barrio La Victoria in Liberia. Head east on Av 11, go around the stadium and continue north on Ruta 918 for about 20km to the park entrance.

While both roads are passable by regular cars throughout the dry season, a 4WD is required during the rainy season and is highly recommended at all other times. To travel between the two sectors you needn't double back to Liberia: one kilometer from the Las Pailas park entrance is the turn toward the Río Negro hot springs (p233) and the Sector Santa María.

There's no public transportation to the park entrances, but the Transbasa 523 bus travels from Liberia to Curubandé three times daily in each direction (US$2, 40 minutes). Any hotel in Liberia can arrange transport to the park for around US$20 per person. Otherwise, you can take a 4WD taxi from Liberia for about US$40 to Las Pailas, or US$65 to Santa María, each way.

The road to Cañas Dulces and beyond, toward Buena Vista Lodge and Borinquen Mountain Resort & Spa, is well signed about 11.5km north of Liberia, where it intersects with the Interamericana. Note that there is no access to the park from this side, so you'll have to go all the way back to the Interamericana and enter through Las Pailas.

Sector Santa Rosa

Established in 1971 as a national park, the **Sector Santa Rosa** (☎2666-5051; www.acguanacaste.ac.cr; adult/child US$15/5; ⏲8am-4pm) is now a part of the much larger Área de Conservación Guanacaste (ACG). This sprawling area was established to protect the largest remaining stand of tropical dry forest in Central America. With its primordial acacia thorn trees and tall jaragua grass, this rare landscape resembles the African savanna, though closer inspection reveals more American species of plants, including cacti and bromeliads.

Aside from the startlingly dry landscape, Santa Rosa has some legendary surf breaks, important nesting beaches for several species of sea turtle, and deep historical gravitas. Difficult access means that most of the Santa Rosa sector is fairly empty, though it can get reasonably busy on weekends in the dry season, when Ticos flock to the park in search of their often hard-to-find history.

Sights

Santa Rosa was the site of game-changing battles from three different eras, ranking it among the country's most significant

OFF THE BEATEN TRACK

SECTOR MURCIÉLAGO

Encompassing the wild northern coastline of the Península Santa Elena, Sector Murciélago (Bat Sector) is where you'll find the isolated white-sand beach of **Playa Blanca** and the trailhead for the **Poza el General** watering hole, which attracts birds and animals year-round.

Sector Murciélago is not accessible from the Sector Santa Rosa: to get to the northern Sector Murciélago, you'll need to turn off the Interamericana near the police checkpoint that is 10km north of Santa Rosa. After 8km, bear left at the village of Cuajiniquíl. Continue on the gravel road for another 9km, passing such historic sights as the former hacienda of the late Nicaraguan dictator Anastasio Somoza (it's currently a training ground for the Costa Rican police) and the airstrip that was used by Lieutenant Colonel Oliver North to 'secretly' smuggle goods to the Nicaraguan Contras in the 1980s. Continue straight until you cross a river, then hang a right and keep going straight over two more rivers until you reach the village of Murciélago and the park entrance.

Continue on a dirt road to the remote bays and beaches of El Hachal (5km), Bahía Santa Elena (8km) and Bahía Playa Blanca (17km). A 4WD is a must, and even then the road may be impassable in the wet season. Also, signage is nonexistent. Have fun!

historical sites. This history is commemorated with a museum and a monument.

Monumento a los Héroes MONUMENT

(incl in park admission) Climb up the steep staircase behind La Casona to reach a lookout point with a stunning view of three volcanoes. The monument itself was built to honor the heroes of the two important battles that took place in this vicinity – the defeat of William Walker's *filibusteros* in 1856 and the repelling of a separate Nicaraguan invasion in 1919.

La Casona MUSEUM

(☎2666-5051; www.acguanacaste.ac.cr; incl in park admission; ⊙8-11:30am & 1-4pm) La Casona is the main edifice of the old Hacienda Santa Rosa. The battle of 1856 was fought around this building. There are wonderful displays detailing (in English and Spanish) the old gold-rush route, William Walker's evil imperial plans and the 14-minute battle breakdown. There are also exhibits on the region's natural history. La Casona is located near the park headquarters (both are about 7km from the park entrance) in the Sector Santa Rosa (p235).

The original building was burned down in 2001 by poachers who were involved in another war, this one with park rangers. The rebuilt building has smoke alarms.

Two hiking trails leave from behind the museum.

Activities

Hiking

Several hiking trails originate near the park headquarters (7km from the park entrance), including a gentle hike to the **Mirador Valle Naranjo**, with spectacular views of Playa Naranjo.

From the southern end of Playa Naranjo there are two hiking trails: **Sendero Carbonal** is a 5km trail that swings inland along the mangroves and past Laguna El Limbo, where the crocs hang out; **Sendero Aceituno** parallels Playa Naranjo for 13km and terminates near the estuary across from Witch's Rock.

The main road is lined with short trails to small waterfalls and other photogenic natural wonders.

Surfing

The majority of travelers are here for one reason only: the chance to surf the near-perfect, world-class beach break at Playa Naranjo, **Witch's Rock** (Roca Bruja). This break is famous for its fast, hollow 3m rights. There are also fun lefts when it isn't pumping. Near **Playa Portrero Grande**, you'll find the best right in all of Costa Rica, the famous surf break Ollie's Point.

The breaks can get busy in the dry season, but clear out in the wet months from July through December when the beach access road is impassable. Diehards still arrive by boat, though.

★Ollie's Point — SURFING

Surfers make pilgrimages to this isolated beach, near Playa Portrero Grande, to find the best right in all of Costa Rica. This famous surf break offers a nice, long ride, especially with a southern swell. The bottom here is a mix of sand and rocks, and the year-round offshore is perfect for tight turns and slow closes.

Ollie's Point is only accessible by boat from Playas del Coco or Tamarindo. Or you can do as Patrick and Wingnut did in *Endless Summer II* and crash-land your chartered plane on the beach (ahem, not actually recommended).

Shortboarding is preferred.

Playa Naranjo — SURFING

A spectacular beach in the southernmost part of the Sector Santa Rosa (p235), Playa Naranjo attracts wave riders who come to surf the legendary beach break at **Witch's Rock** (Roca Bruja), famous for its 3m curls (not recommended for beginners). Be careful of rocks near the river mouth and crocodiles near the estuary, a rich feeding ground during tide changes.

Wildlife-Watching

The wildlife in Santa Rosa is both varied and prolific, especially during the dry season, when trees lose their leaves and animals congregate around the remaining water sources. More than 250 bird species have been recorded here, including the raucous white-throated magpie-jay, unmistakable with its long crest of manically curled feathers. The forests contain parrots and parakeets, trogons and tanagers; as you head down to the coast you'll be rewarded with sightings of various coastal birds.

Dozens of bat species have been identified in Santa Rosa. Other mammals you'll have a reasonable chance of seeing include deer, coatis, peccaries, armadillos, coyotes, raccoons, three kinds of monkey and a variety of other species – about 115 in all. There are also more than 30,000 insect species, including about 4000 moths and butterflies (bring insect repellent).

Reptiles include lizards, iguanas, snakes, crocodiles and four species of sea turtle. The olive ridley sea turtle is the most numerous, and during the July to December nesting season tens of thousands of turtles make their nests on Santa Rosa's beaches, especially Playa Nancite. From August to

SANTA ROSA IN HISTORY

This stretch of coast is famous among Ticos as a national stronghold. Costa Rica has been invaded three times, and the enemy has always surrendered in Santa Rosa.

The best known of these incidents is the Battle of Santa Rosa, which took place on March 20, 1856, when Costa Rica was invaded by the soon-to-be-self-declared president of Nicaragua, an uppity American named William Walker. Walker was the head of a group of foreign pirates and adventurers known as the 'Filibusters' that had already seized Baja and southwest Nicaragua and were attempting to gain control over all of Central America. In a brilliant display of military prowess, Costa Rican president Juan Rafael Mora Porras managed to assemble a ragtag group of fighters and surround Walker's army in the main building of the old Hacienda Santa Rosa, known as La Casona. The battle was over in just 14 minutes, and Walker was forever driven from Costa Rican soil.

Santa Rosa was also the site of battles between Costa Rican troops and invading forces from Nicaragua in the 20th century. The first – in 1919 – was a somewhat honorable attempt to overthrow the Costa Rican dictator General Federico Tinoco. Then, in 1955, Nicaraguan dictator Anastasio Somoza led a failed coup d'état. Today you can still see Somoza's abandoned tank, which lies in a ditch beside the road just beyond the entrance to the park.

The area's military history didn't end with Somoza. In the 1980s US Marine lieutenant-colonel Oliver North illegally sold weapons to Iran and used the profits to fund the Nicaraguan Contras during the Sandinistas–Contra war. The troops' staging area was just north of Santa Rosa at Playa Potrero Grande (near the famous surf break now known as Ollie's Point).

December, *arribada* (mass arrival) takes place about once a month and lasts for four days. During September and October especially, as many as 8000 of these 40kg turtles come ashore at same time. Playa Nancite is strictly protected and at the time of research no tourists were permitted to enter.

Sleeping

The **Santa Rosa research station** (Centro de Investigación del Bosque Tropical Seco; 2666-5051; www.acguanacaste.ac.cr/biodesarrollo/centro-de-investigacion-y-estaciones-biologicas/centro-de-investigacion-del-bosque-tropical-seco; dm US$15) is usually occupied by visiting researchers. There's a shady developed campground nearby, with picnic benches, grills, flushing toilets and cold-water showers. Playa Naranjo (p237) also has a campground with pit toilets but no potable water – bring your own, and don't expect complete solitude: everyone shares one sandy, flat basin, only moderately sheltered from gusty winds by thin trees. Camping at both sites costs US$4 per person per day

Santa Elena Lodge LODGE **$$**
(2679-1038; Cuajiniquíl; s/d incl breakfast US$55/85; P❄📶) Retired fisherman Manuel offers a fine deal in the quaint village of Cuajiniquíl (Kwah-hee-nee-kil). The eight-room house is convenient to Santa Rosa (p235) and Murciélago (p236) parks and nearby beaches. The lovely cedar used to remodel the old home give it a solid feel, while details such as the book exchange make you feel right at home.

Getting There & Away

Access to the Sector Santa Rosa (p235) park entrance is on the western side of the Interamericana, 35km north of Liberia and 45km south of the Nicaragua border. The well-signed main park entrance can be reached by public transportation: take any bus between Liberia and the Nicaraguan border and ask the driver to let you off at the park entrance. Rangers can help you catch a return bus. You can also arrange private transportation from the hotels in Liberia for about US$20 to US$30 per person round trip.

From the entrance it's another 7km to park headquarters, where you'll also find the museum (p236) and the campgrounds. This office administers the Área de Conservación Guanacaste (ACG).

From this complex, a very rough track leads down to Playa Naranjo (p237), 11km away. Even during the dry season this road is only passable with a high-clearance 4WD, and you must sign an eerie waiver at the park entrance stating that you willingly assume all liability for driving here. The park also requires that you be completely self-sufficient should you choose to undertake the trip, which means bringing all your own water and knowing how to do your own car repairs. During the rainy months (May to November) the road is open to hikers and horses but closed to vehicles. If you want to surf here, it's infinitely easier to gain access to the beach by hiring a boat from Playas del Coco or Tamarindo.

Refugio Nacional de Vida Silvestre Bahía Junquillal

Overlooking the Bahía Junquillal, just north of the Sector Murciélago, this 505-hectare **wildlife refuge** (2200-9484; www.acguanacaste.ac.cr; US$15; 8am-5pm) is part of the vast Área de Conservación Guanacaste. The quiet bay and beautiful protected beach offer gentle swimming and snorkeling opportunities, making this a popular destination for Tico families on weekends and holidays. On a clear day you'll see Volcán Orosí in the distance.

Activities

Two short trails (totaling 1.7km) hug the coast, traversing dry tropical forest. They lead to a marine bird lookout in one direction and to the mangroves in the other. Keep your eye out for pelicans and frigate birds, as well as capuchin monkeys, coatis and other scavengers.

Sleeping

There is a campground (per person US$19) near the ranger station, which is a few hundred meters past the park entrance. Very popular among domestic tourists, it's outfitted with brick grills and picnic tables at every site. There are also bathrooms and cold showers. If you don't care to camp, the nearest accommodations are 7km north, in Bahía Salinas.

Eating

There is no food for sale in the refuge, but you'll find several seafood *sodas* in the nearby village of Cuajiniquíl.

Information

The Refugio Nacional de Vida Silvestre Bahía Junquillal is administered from the ACG park headquarters at Santa Rosa (p236), but there will likely be a ranger at the beach to greet you and collect the admission fee.

Getting There & Away

From the Interamericana, turn off at the police checkpoint, following the signs about 8km to Cuajiniquíl. Don't go into Cuajiniquíl: just before you reach the village, turn right, remaining on the paved road to continue 4km to the park entrance. You'll know you're getting close when that glorious cobalt bay appears from out of nowhere on your left.

If you're coming from Bahía Salinas, take the paved road that heads south from El Soley. It hugs the coast, depositing you at the park in a mere 7km.

La Cruz

POP 11,060

La Cruz is the closest town to the Peñas Blancas border crossing with Nicaragua, and is the principal gateway to Bahía Salinas, Costa Rica's premier kitesurfing destination. La Cruz itself is a fairly sleepy provincial town set on a mountaintop plateau, with lots of Tico charm and magical views of an epic, windswept bay. El Mirador or the neighboring bar are good stops to stretch your legs and widen your worldview.

Sights

El Mirador Centro Turistico VIEWPOINT
(8840-1381) FREE Don't cruise through La Cruz without stopping at this oddly shaped 'tourist and cultural center' on the western edge of town. You might stumble across an exhibit or a concert, but the main attraction is the jaw-dropping 180-degree view of Bahía Salinas. You can also peek into Nicaragua from here.

Note that opening hours can be inconsistent, and a longstanding cafe here closed in 2019. At the time of research, plans to build another were afoot.

Tours

Hacienda El Cenizaro ADVENTURE
(8630-5050; www.haciendaelcenizaro.com; Ruta 935; tours from US$99; 8am-5pm) On the road to Bahía Salinas, this attractive hacienda sits back from the road, overlooking its farmland spotted with bulls. It's an atmospheric location to hop on a horse or an ATV. Horseback tours traverse the tropical dry forest, but ATVs carry you to new heights for splendid bay views. They share their trails with Bike House (p242).

The ranch is about 3.5km downhill from the El Mirador Centro Turistico on Ruta 935.

LLANOS DE CORTÉS

If you're pressed for time and in search of a quick, easy waterfall visit, **Llanos de Cortés** (adult/child US$7/4; 8am-4pm; P) will do nicely. From the entrance, which is now guarded, you'll scramble down a steep trail to reach the spectacular 28m-high, 12m-wide waterfall, which you'll hear before you see. The falls drop into a tranquil pond with a white sandy beach that's good for swimming and sunbathing. It was once possible to swim under the fall and hike behind it, but new rules now prohibit this.

Sleeping & Eating

There's a handful of conspicuous places to eat on the Interamericana, but it's better to wait until you drive down into Bahía Salinas for a more relaxed meal.

Hotel Amalia Inn INN $
(8830-3139, 2679-9618; www.hotelamalialacruz.weebly.com; Calle Central; s/d with fan US$25/35, with air-con US$40/50; P) This yellow stucco house on a cliff isn't a bad place to spend the night. Its eight homey rooms are furnished rather randomly and have attractive brick floors and wooden ceilings. Walls in the meandering house are hung with modernist paintings by Lester Bounds, husband of founder Amalia (neither still alive). The shared terracotta terraces and backyard have stupendous bay views.

Hotel Casa del Viento HOTEL $$
(2679-8060; www.facebook.com/casadelvientocr; s/d/q US$32/52/93; P) With lovely wall murals and a breezy restaurant at the top of the hill in town, this is a great place for a beer in the evenings. Fan-cooled rooms are crowded and mostly clean; those on the 2nd level have air-con, more light and outstanding views. There's a common mini-kitchen and monkey-viewing platform out back.

★**Tierra Madre Eco Lodge** FARMSTAY $$
(☎8705-4249; www.tierramadre.co.cr; s/d incl breakfast US$90/133, s/d all-incl US$134/224; P ☰ ☒) Totally worth the hour-long trip from La Cruz, this off-the-grid hilltop permaculture farm has views to Nicaragua and beyond. The farm's 65 hectares brim with wildlife, and a stay in one of the three rustic chalets means lounging by the pool, strolling the gardens, and feasting on home-cooked meals featuring little-known fruits and veggies, farm-fresh eggs, and fish from a nearby lake.

The Belgian expat hosts manage the farm without motorized machinery or chemicals, and the results are deliciously sustainable. At the time of research, they had plans to install a geodesic glamping tent.

All-inclusive rates cover excursions like guided hiking and fishing on the property, along with discounts on activities further afield (Santa Rosa National Park, a sailing trip in Bahía Salinas, etc). The lodge provides complimentary transport from La Cruz, and from either of the main airports for a fee. Depending on weather conditions, you'll be brought in by a 4WD or on horseback!

Drinking & Nightlife

Mirador Punta Descartes COCKTAIL BAR
(☎2679-9015; www.facebook.com/MiradorPuntaDescartes; Calle Central near Av Central; ⊙8am-10pm) Don't come for the food, but do come for the drinks and spectacular view over the bay in an easy chair. Whether you're watching a fiery sunset or a slashing lightning storm, it's a memorable experience, particularly with a tequila sunrise (sunset?) in hand.

Information

BANKS

Change money in town to avoid the high rates at the border.

Banco Nacional (☎2212-2000; ⊙8:30am-3:45pm Mon-Fri) At the junction of the short road into the town center.

Banco Popular (☎2681-4600; ⊙8:45am-4:30pm Mon-Fri, 8:15-11:30am Sat) In the town center, just south of the Catholic church.

MEDICAL SERVICES

Cruz Roja (☎2679-9004, emergency 2679-9146; ⊙office 7:30am-5pm Mon-Fri, emergency 24 hrs) A small clinic just north of the town center on the road towards the border.

Getting There & Away

The bus station is located on the western edge of town, just north of the road to Bahía Salinas (near Hotel Casa del Viento; p239). A **Transportes Deldú counter** (☎2222-0610; www.facebook.com/transportedeldu; Ruta 935; ⊙6am-5:30pm) down the street from the terminal sells tickets and stores luggage. Transportes Deldú services run only to the Peñas Blancas border with Nicaragua; to catch a TransNica bus through to Managua, you'll need to flag down a bus on the Interamericana.

The following services depart from La Cruz.

Peñas Blancas US$1, 45 minutes, frequent departures from 5:45am to 5:30pm.

Playa Jobo US$2, 30 minutes, departs four times daily from 8:30am to 5:40pm from the bus terminal.

San José via Liberia US$7, five hours, departs hourly from 5am to 10pm.

Bahía Salinas

Welcome to the kitesurfing capital of Costa Rica, where giddy riders shred beneath magnificent rainbows that arch over a wide bay extending all the way to Nicaragua. The destination has a deconstructed nature – communities congregate on empty beaches clumped with tropical forests that are home to howler monkey tribes and linked by dirt roads. The result is a pleasingly *tranquilo,* rural vibe.

Bahía Salinas is a stunning, under-the-radar destination even if you don't ride wind. But maybe not for long. The glorious sands of Playa Jobo are no longer deserted after the opening of a gigantic, 447-room all-inclusive resort. The road heading south is already partially paved and more development will likely follow.

Activities

If wind isn't your thing, head around the point to **Playa Jobo** – a perfect, 300m-wide horseshoe bay with calm water – or **Playa Rajada,** on the southernmost arm of Salinas. Rajada is ruggedly gorgeous and sheltered enough to be almost placid. In September and October, humpback whales often congregate here.

Boating

Boats can be rented in the village of El Jobo or at one of the local resorts to visit Isla Bolaños, a seabird refuge home to the brown pelican (visits are restricted to April

LAS FIESTAS DE GUANACASTE

Guanacastecos love their horses almost as much as they love their fiestas. And what better way to get the best of both worlds than with a *tope* (horse parade)? In addition to the *tope*, these traditional holiday fiestas are a mix of Western rodeo and country fair, complete with cattle auctions, food stalls, music, dancing, drinking and, of course, bull riding. (In Costa Rica the bulls are never killed, so watching the berserk helmetless, bareback bucking-bronco action is usually gore-free.) In the aftermath, the local drunks and young machos jump into the ring to act as volunteer rodeo clowns.

Though the bull riding usually draws the biggest crowds, the main event is the *tope* itself, where you can see the high-stepping gait of the *sabanero*'s (cowboy's) horse; this demands endurance and skill from both horse and rider.

Topes are also a great place to catch the region's traditional dance, known as the *punto guanacasteco*. The women wear long flowing skirts meant to resemble traditional handcrafted, hand-painted oxcart wheels. The old-fashioned courtship dance is frequently interrupted by young men, who shout rhyming verses to try to win over a love interest. The dance and accompanying music are fast paced, full of passion and fun to watch.

Topes usually occur on Costa Rican civic holidays, though you can bet on finding big parties during Semana Santa (the week before Easter), the week between Christmas and New Year, and on July 25, the anniversary of Guanacaste's annexation.

through November to avoid disturbing nesting seabirds). Ask around about fishing and diving trips to Isla Despense, Isla Caballo and Islas Murciélago, with its resident bull sharks.

Kitesurfing

Bahía Salinas is an internationally known mecca for kitesurfers between November and April, and the wind continues to howl consistently even through May, June and July. The shape of the hills surrounding the bay funnels the winds into a predictable pattern (though it can be gusty, ranging from 20 to 40 knots), and the sandy, protected beaches make this a great place for both beginners and experienced riders.

It's important to remember that there are inherent dangers to kiting (namely the risk of losing a limb – yikes!), so seek professional instruction if you're not experienced. The Professional Air Sports Association (PASA) and the International Kiteboarding Organization (IKO) have set standards for beginner instruction. You'll need to take a nine-hour certification course to rent gear and safely go out on your own.

The road follows the curve of the bay to the consistently windy **Playa Copal**, an incredibly wide, beige beach backed by scrubby manzanillo trees with views across the sea all the way to Nicaragua. It does get incredibly windy here; though picturesque, this is not the place for beach bumming. The entrance to the beach is marked by signs near Kiteboarding Costa Rica.

Kiteboarding Costa Rica KITESURFING
(☎8652-2973; www.kiteboardingcostarica.com; Playa Copal; lessons per hr US$45-65; ⏰Nov-Sep) This highly regarded kitesurfing school operates out of the KiteHouse (p242) at the western end of Playa Copal. IKO-certified instructors speak Spanish, French and English. If you've already got your certification and are confident about your abilities, you can also just rent equipment here.

Kitesurf School 2000 KITESURFING
(☎2676-1042, 8826-5221; Playa Papaturro; lessons per hr US$35-45; ⏰8am-10pm) Make reservations in advance to take lessons or rent gear at the area's original kite shop (IKO certified). Formerly known as Kitesurf 2000, it's located at the Blue Dream Hotel (p242), 250m from Papaturro. Lessons are available in Spanish, English and Italian. Cash only.

Mountain Biking

It's not just kitesurfers who can get their kicks in Bahía Salinas – this is also mountain biking territory. Explore back roads, beaches and the single-track cross-country area with Bike House (p242).

GETTING TO NICARAGUA

Crossing the border into Nicaragua at **Peñas Blancas** is a highly variable experience, sometimes taking a half hour or less, sometimes taking many hours. Here's what you need to know:

- Peñas Blancas is a busy border crossing (open 6am to midnight), which can be a major hassle at peak times. Avoid crossing the border shortly before closing time and in the days leading up to major holidays.
- Make sure you have at least six months' validity on your passport. If your passport is about to expire, you will be denied entry into Nicaragua.
- Car rental companies in Costa Rica won't allow you to take the vehicle out of the country. Leave your car in one of the nearby guarded parking areas (assuming you're coming back, of course). Don't leave any valuables in the car.
- Costa Rica charges a US$9 land exit fee; be sure to have this in cash.
- The border posts are about 1km apart. If you're on an international bus (TicaBus), you'll get a lift between posts. Otherwise, you'll have to hoof it. Hordes of generally useless touts will offer to 'guide' you through the simple crossing – let them carry your luggage if you like, but agree on a fee beforehand.
- Entering Nicaragua costs $12, and leaving Nicaragua costs US$3, which must be paid in US dollars. You'll also be charged US$1 to enter the state of Rivas.
- You may be asked to show a proof of exit, such as a return bus ticket or a flight reservation out of Nicaragua.
- There are no banks at the border, but there are plenty of money changers hanging around. Rates will be not be to your advantage, obviously.

There's a fairly fabulous duty-free shop waiting for you in Sapoá, the Nicaraguan equivalent of Peñas Blancas. Relax with your purchases on the 45-minute bus ride to Rivas (departing every 45 minutes or so). Rivas is a quiet transport hub, though its well-preserved 17th-century center is worth exploring. If you're good at bargaining (and you will have to bargain hard), there are taxis waiting on the Nicaraguan side of the border to whisk you to Rivas (US$30).

Sleeping & Eating

Bike House B&B $

(8704-7486; www.thebikehousecostarica.com; cabina incl breakfast from US$45;) This friendly B&B caters to travelers who prefer their adventure with two wheels on the ground. Accommodations are simple and sweet, with a shady common porch with hammocks. Owner Carole prepares delicious food using organic local ingredients. She can also help make arrangements for kitesurfing if you want to give it a try.

Carole leads a variety of half-day (US$75 per person) and full-day (US$145 per person) and custom multiday cycling trips in the area. A week-long, all-female camp combines biking, yoga and surfing. The Bike House is about 200m west of the Tempatal school.

Blue Dream Hotel HOTEL $

(8826-5221; Playa Papaturro; dm US$26, standard d US$35, bungalow d US$44, ste US$90;) This friendly hotel offers marvelous views over Playa Papaturro from every room on its terraced hillside. Lodgings range from simple and comfortable rooms with Spanish tiles to more spacious chalet-style suites with private balconies. All have access to a hammock-strung garden. The chef serves a hearty breakfast and amazing old-country fare.

There's a guitar on hand and a funny blue-eyed dog. Kitesurf School 2000 (p241) is located here.

★KiteHouse GUESTHOUSE $$

(8652-2978; www.kiteboardingcostarica.com; Playa Copal; dm US$20-25, cabina US$55-70, villa from US$95; Nov-Sep;) This excellent operation has taken over the western end of Playa Copal, with a wide range of accommodations, kiteboarding lessons and rentals (the same family runs Kiteboarding Costa Rica; p241), and a hilltop **restaurant** (8am to 9pm). Every sleeping option – from dorm room to villa – has a terrific view of the beach. The rooms also have kitchenettes; there are few other places to eat.

★Pollo Frito La Casona CHICKEN $
(☎8882-3736; fried chicken US$5; ⏰10am-9pm) This family-owned, roadside food truck serves up lip-smacking fried chicken that would rival any such business in San José, along with some other fun surprises: giant emu eggs from the attached farm (which you can tour), for instance. The fried-chicken cook, Roy, is a super nice guy and has a wealth of information about the area.

His family also runs a campground (US$7 per person per night) beside the truck with flush toilets and hot showers.

El Fogon de Juanita SODA $
(☎2676-1200; Playa Copal; mains US$8-10; ⏰8am-9pm; 📶) The former Blue Dream chef has opened her own place down the road, to rave reviews. Specializing in pastas (lasagna is a fave) and pizzas, Juana also conjures up a flavorful *arroz* (rice dish) or two. For tips on riding the waves, her son Mauricio, a kiteboarding instructor, is often just a shout away.

ℹ Getting There & Away

BUS

Buses (US$1.10) make the 30-minute run between the La Cruz bus terminal and the village of Jobo several times a day in either direction. A taxi to the beaches costs about US$25.

CAR

From La Cruz, the road is paved at first, but gravel for the last 9km. It leads down from the lookout point in La Cruz past the small coastal fishing community of Puerto Soley, at the eastern end of Playa Papaturro.

If you're driving from the south, there's a paved route to El Soley. Instead of driving all the way to La Cruz, turn off the Interamericana near the police checkpoint, following signs to Cuajiniquíl. After about 8km, just before the village, bear right toward Junquillal (don't go into the village). The paved road follows the coast about 12km north to El Soley, from where you'll pick up the gravel road from La Cruz.

AT A GLANCE

POPULATION
La Fortuna: 15,400

FAST FACT
The 1968 explosions of Volcán Arenal were the first time the volcano erupted in more than 400 years.

BEST WATERFALL
Viento Fresco (p270)

BEST ECOLODGE
Maquenque Eco-Lodge (p279)

BEST LOCAL EATS
La Ventanita (p264)

WHEN TO GO

Jan–Apr Slightly less rain (although there's no dry season in the lowlands); clearer skies and less mud.

Feb Fun *sabanero* (cowboy) street festival in La Fortuna.

Jul–Dec Run the rivers any time of year, but they flow faster in the second half.

White-water rafting, Río Sarapiquí (p282)
JOHN COLETTI/GETTY IMAGES ©

Arenal & Northern Lowlands

The sleeping giant of Volcán Arenal doesn't provide the fireworks of yore, but rambling around its perimeter and neighboring lake – where the wind and water can transport you – is still the top draw in the country. La Fortuna, at the base of the mountain, is the jumping-off point (often literally) for a bushel of activities, from hiking to hot springs. It also boasts a tasty range of restaurants, and modest-to-magnificent sleeping quarters for all budgets. Beyond bustling Fortuna, out past the banana and pineapple plantations, is where you get down, figuratively and literally, with the locals: swimming, rafting, fishing and birding the inky rivers and lagoons, finding repose in remote lodges and homestays, and immersing yourself in the quietude of the swampy lowlands.

INCLUDES

Arenal & Northern Lowlands Highlights

❶ **Parque Nacional Volcán Arenal** (p261) Taking in striking views of the volcano's cloud-ringed cone.

❷ **Eco Termales Hot Springs** (p249) Soothing your weary muscles in volcano-heated pools.

❸ **El Castillo** (p262) Marveling at sweeping lake or volcano views from this charming village.

❹ **Proyecto Asis** (p277) Visiting an animal rescue center for orphaned or injured wild animals.

❺ **Venado Caves** (p271) Getting down and dirty while exploring the underworld.

❻ **Refugio Nacional de Vida Silvestre Caño Negro** (p272) Exploring the lagoons, counting caimans and spying on spoonbills.

❼ **Boca Tapada** (p278) Falling asleep to the symphony of cicadas, frogs and birds in this remote corner of the country.

❽ **Río Sarapiquí** (p282) Experiencing thrills and chills while riding the rapids.

❾ **Wildlife-Watching** (p281) Spotting howlers, sloths, peccaries and all manner of birdlife in the grounds of your ecolodge.

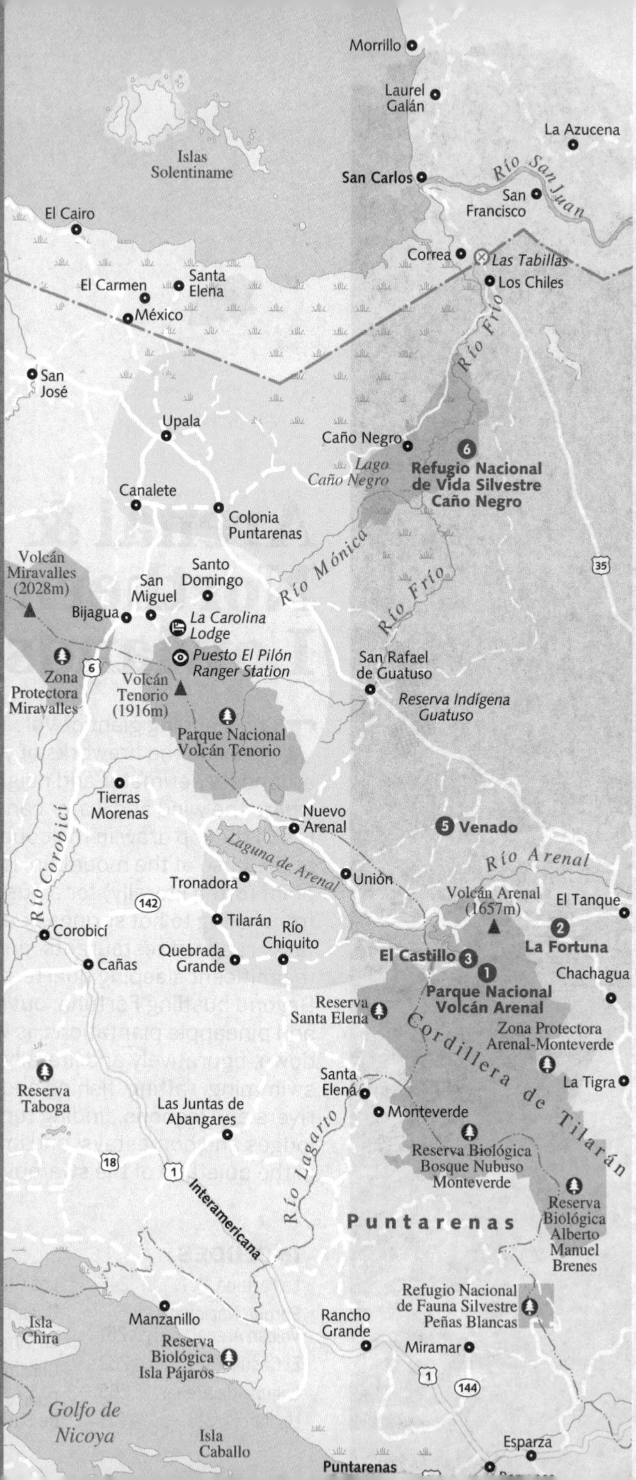

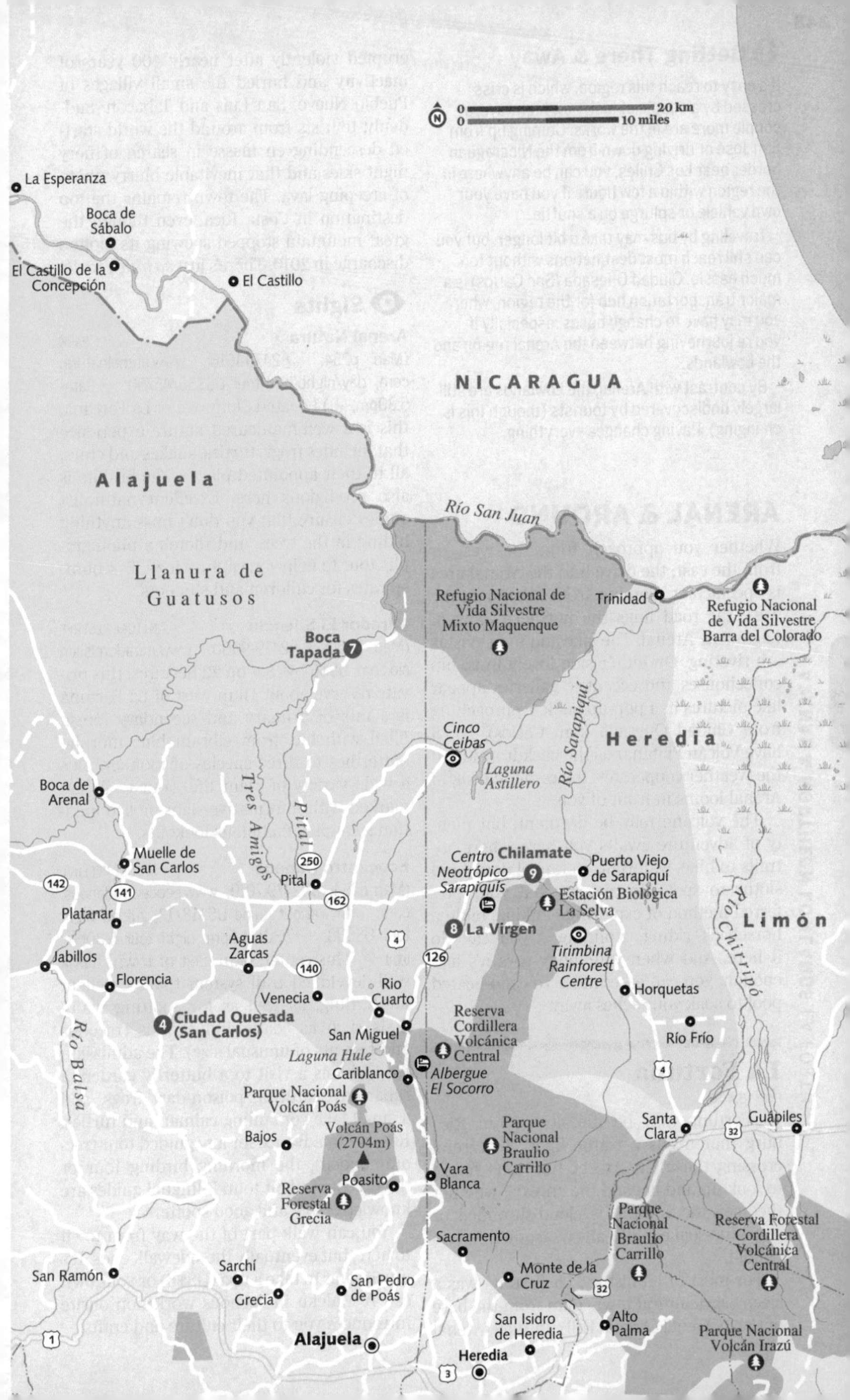
0 20 km
0 10 miles
N
La Esperanza
Boca de Sábalo
El Castillo de la Concepción
El Castillo
NICARAGUA
Alajuela
Río San Juan
Llanura de Guatusos
Refugio Nacional de Vida Silvestre Mixto Maquenque
Trinidad
Refugio Nacional de Vida Silvestre Barra del Colorado
Boca Tapada
7
Cinco Ceibas
Laguna Astillero
Río Sarapiquí
Heredia
Boca de Arenal
Tres Amigos
Pital
Muelle de San Carlos
250
Centro Neotrópico Sarapiquís
Chilamate
9
Puerto Viejo de Sarapiquí
142
141
Pital
162
Estación Biológica La Selva
Platanar
8 La Virgen
Tirimbina Rainforest Centre
Río Chirripó
Limón
Aguas Zarcas
4
126
Jabillos
140
Florencia
Rio Cuarto
Venecia
Horquetas
4 Ciudad Quesada (San Carlos)
Reserva Cordillera Volcánica Central
Río Frío
San Miguel
Río Balsa
Laguna Hule
Cariblanco
Albergue El Socorro
4
Parque Nacional Volcán Poás
Volcán Poás (2704m)
Parque Nacional Braulio Carrillo
Santa Clara
Guápiles
32
Bajos
Vara Blanca
Poasito
Reserva Forestal Grecia
Parque Nacional Braulio Carrillo
Reserva Forestal Cordillera Volcánica Central
Sacramento
San Ramón
Sarchí
Monte de la Cruz
32
Grecia
San Pedro de Poás
San Isidro de Heredia
Alto Palma
Parque Nacional Volcán Irazú
1
Alajuela
Heredia
3

Getting There & Away

It's easy to reach this region, which is criss-crossed by a couple of fast, new highways; a couple more are in the works. Coming up from San José or driving down from the Nicaraguan border near Los Chiles, you can be anywhere in the region within a few hours if you have your own vehicle or splurge on a shuttle.

Traveling by bus may take a bit longer, but you can still reach most destinations without too much hassle. Ciudad Quesada (San Carlos) is a major transportation hub for the region, where you may have to change buses, especially if you're journeying between the Arenal region and the Lowlands.

By contrast with Arenal, the Lowlands are still largely undiscovered by tourists (though this is changing). Paving changes everything.

ARENAL & AROUND

Whether you approach from the west or from the east, the drive into the Arenal area is spectacular. Coming from Tilarán in the west, the road hugs the northern bank of Laguna de Arenal. The lake and forest vistas are riveting. On either side lovely inns, hip coffeehouses and eccentric galleries appear like pictures in a pop-up book. Approaching from Ciudad Quesada (San Carlos), you'll have Volcán Platanar as the backdrop, and if the weather cooperates, the resolute peak of Arenal looms in front of you.

The volcano may be dormant, but plenty of adventure awaits you here. There are trails to hike, waterfalls to rappel down and sloths to spot. No matter what your preferred method of exploring – hiking, biking, horseback riding, ziplining – you can do it here. And when your body says it's had enough, you can ease into a volcano-heated pool to soak your aches away.

La Fortuna

POP 15,400

La Fortuna may be the next Costa Rica burg that needs a traffic light. Be careful crossing the main streets, but don't forget to look up and beyond the crowds: whether the majestic volcano is cloud-shrouded or sunshine-soaked, it's always something to behold.

For most of its history, La Fortuna was a sleepy agricultural town, 6km from the base of Cerro Arenal (Arenal Hill). In 1968, Arenal erupted violently after nearly 400 years of inactivity and buried the small villages of Pueblo Nuevo, San Luís and Tabacón. Suddenly, tourists from around the world started descending en masse in search of fiery night skies and that inevitable blurry photo of creeping lava. The town remains the top destination in Costa Rica, even though the great mountain stopped spewing its molten discharge in 2010. There's just *so much* to do.

Sights

Arenal Natura PARK

(Map p254; 2479-1616; www.arenalnatura.com; day/night/bird tour US$36/45/50; 8am-5:30pm;) Located 6km west of La Fortuna, this is a well-manicured nature experience that includes frogs, turtles, snakes and crocs, all in their appointed places. The birdlife is also prodigious here. Excellent naturalist guides ensure that you don't miss anything hiding in the trees, and there's a photography tour to help you capture it all. Discounted rates for children and students.

Mirador El Silencio NATURE RESERVE

(Map p254; 2479-9900; www.miradorelsilencio.com; US$6) Set on 22 hectares, this private reserve about 11km west of La Fortuna is a mix of primary and secondary forest, filled with life, from vibrant blue morpho butterflies to three species of monkey, plus a wide variety of plant life. Four trails are marked with informative signs, not to mention a couple of fabulous lookouts.

Ecocentro Danaus NATURE RESERVE

(Map p254; 2479-7019; www.ecocentrodanaus.com; with/without guide US$18/12, guided night tour US$38; 7:30am-5pm, night tour 5:30pm;) This center, 4km east of town, has a well-developed trail system that's excellent for birding, as well as for spotting mammals such as coatis and agoutis (racoons and rodents of unusual size). The admission fee includes a visit to a butterfly garden, a ranarium featuring poison-dart frogs, and a small lake containing caiman and turtles. Reserve in advance for any guided tour (recommended), the morning birding tour or the excellent night tour. Bilingual guides are knowledgeable and good spotters.

You can walk part of the way from town to here, but eventually the sidewalk ends. It's much safer to take a taxi (US$6) or your own car. A Maleku indigenous workshop onsite introduces you to their culture and crafts.

PARKS & RESERVES OF ARENAL & THE NORTHERN LOWLANDS

In addition to the famous volcano, there are several notable refuges and parks in the Northern Lowlands, offering opportunities for low-key, crowd-free boat tours and wildlife-watching.

Parque Nacional Volcán Arenal (p261) Centered on the perfect cone of the eponymous volcano, the clouds will sometimes disperse, revealing the hulking giant.

Parque Nacional Braulio Carrillo (p281) The northern sector of Costa Rica's largest park has basic infrastructure. Accessible trails in the Sector Quebrada Gonzalez and Volcán Barva areas are less-visited marvels.

Refugio Nacional de Vida Silvestre Caño Negro (p272) The lagoons of Caño Negro attract a wide variety of birds year-round, though prime time for birdwatchers is between January and March.

Refugio Nacional de Vida Silvestre Mixto Maquenque Though there isn't much in the way of infrastructure at this refuge, lodges in Boca Tapada can organise tours to take you into this remote rainforest.

Catarata Río Fortuna WATERFALL

(La Fortuna Waterfall; Map p254; www.catarata lafortuna.com; Diagonal 301; US$15; ⌚8am-5pm; P) You can glimpse the sparkling 70m ribbon of clear water that pours through a sheer canyon of dark volcanic rock arrayed in bromeliads and ferns with minimal exertion. But it's worth the climb down to see it from the jungle floor. Though it's dangerous to dive beneath the thundering falls, a series of perfect swimming holes with spectacular views tile the canyon in aquamarine. Early arrival is recommended: the parking lot fills quickly. Don't leave any valuables in your car.

The waterfall is located at the end of the main road (Ruta 301) going uphill from La Fortuna.

Activities

Hot Springs

Beneath La Fortuna the lava is still rolling and heating countless bubbling springs. There are free natural hot springs in the area that any local can point you toward (ask about 'El Chollín'). If you're after a more comfortable experience, consider one of the area's resorts.

★ **Eco Termales Hot Springs** HOT SPRINGS

(Map p254; ☎2479-8787; www.ecotermales fortuna.cr; Via 142; with/without meal US$72/44; ⌚10am-4pm & 5pm-10pm; 🚻) Everything from the natural circulation systems in the pools to the soft lighting is understated, luxurious and romantic at this gated, reservations-only complex about 4.5km northwest of town. Lush greenery surrounds the paths that cut through these gorgeous grounds. Numbers are managed to maintain the serene, secluded ambiance.

Cocktails – served while you soak – come highly recommended (at an additional cost). The add-on lunch is a traditional Tico offering (rice, beans, meat) and includes dessert and coffee.

Paradise Hot Springs HOT SPRINGS

(Map p254; www.paradisehotspringscr.com; Via 142; adult/child US$28/16, with/without meal US$45/27; ⌚11am-9pm) This low-key place has one lovely, large pool with a waterfall and several smaller, secluded pools, surrounded by lush vegetation and tropical blooms. The pools vary in temperature (up to 41°C/104°F), some with hydromassage. Paradise is much simpler than the other larger spring settings, but there are fewer people, and your experience is bound to be more relaxing and romantic.

Lockers and towels are included with admission. There's a classy dark-wood restaurant, and a snazzy 16-room hotel with all the frills was added to the mix in 2018 (doubles from US$200). Paradise can be found about 4.8 km uphill (west) of downtown La Fortuna.

Springs Resort & Spa HOT SPRINGS

(Map p254; ☎2401-3313, in USA 954-727-8333; www.thespringscostarica.com; 2-day admission US$65; ⌚8am-10pm; 🚻) If you're looking for a luxurious hot-spring experience (even Will Smith stayed here while filming a movie), the Springs features 28 free-form pools with varying temperatures, volcano views, landscaped gardens, waterfalls and swim-up bars, including a jungle bar with a waterslide. The whole scene is human-made, yet

La Fortuna

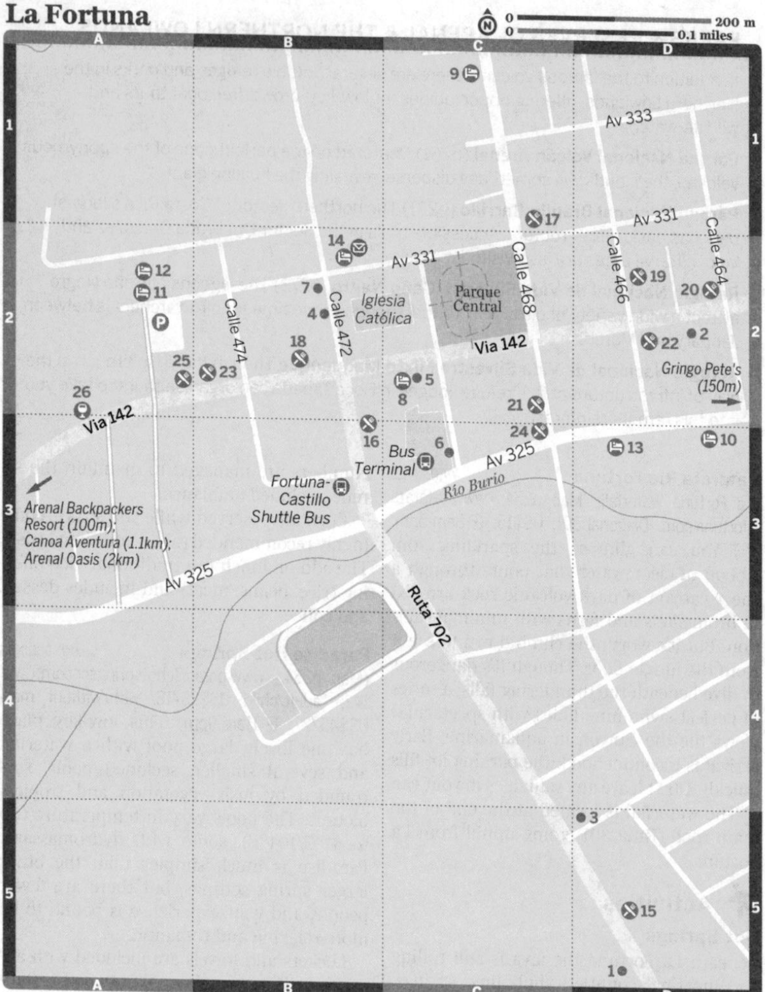

lovely. The formerly rough 3km road from La Fortuna is now paved.

Bigger packages including activities such as tubing and horseback riding, in addition to the Springs, start at US$150. The resort rooms definitely come at Hollywood prices.

Baldi Hot Springs HOT SPRINGS

(Map p254; ☎2479-9917; www.baldihotsprings.cr; with/without buffet US$63/41; ⏲9am-10pm; 👪) Big enough to have something for everyone, Baldi, 4.5km northwest of town, has 25 thermal pools ranging in temperature from 32°C (90°F) to a scalding 67°C (153°F). There are waterfalls and soaking pools for chill-seekers and 'Xtreme' slides for thrill-seekers, plus a good-size children's play area. At night, thumping music and swim-up bars attract a young party crowd (drinks US$10).

Injuries have been reported on occasion at the all-cement slides, so please do take care and watch your head. Extreme sports and alcohol make for strange bedfellows (and hospital bills).

Tabacón Hot Springs HOT SPRINGS

(Map p254; ☎2519-1999; www.tabacon.com; day pass incl lunch & dinner adult/child US$115/40; ⏲10am-10pm) 🍃 Some say it's cheesy and some say it's fun (we say it's both). Broad-leaf

La Fortuna

Activities, Courses & Tours
1 Alberto's Horse Tours ... D5
2 Aventuras Arenal ... D2
3 Bike Arenal ... D5
4 Desafío Adventure Company ... B2
5 Jacamar Naturalist Tours ... C2
6 Red Lava Tours ... C3
7 Wave Rafting ... B2

Sleeping
8 Downtown Inn ... C2
9 Hotel Arenal Rabfer ... C1
10 Hotel Monte Real ... D3
11 La Choza Inn ... A2
12 La Fortuna Suites ... A2
13 Selina La Fortuna ... D3
14 Sleeping Indian Guesthouse ... B2

Eating
15 Café Mediterraneo ... D5
16 Chifa La Familia Feliz ... B3
17 Kappa Sushi ... C1
18 Lava Lounge ... B2
19 Orgánico Fortuna ... D2
20 Plan B Sandwicheria ... D2
21 Rainforest Café ... C2
22 Restaurant Don Rufino ... D2
23 Soda Mima ... B2
24 Soda Víquez ... C3
25 Spec-Taco-Lar ... A2

Drinking & Nightlife
26 La Fortuna Pub ... A2

palms, rare orchids and other tropical blooms part to reveal a 40°C (104°F) waterfall pouring over a fake cliff, concealing constructed caves complete with camouflaged cup holders. Lounging across each well-placed stonelike substance are overheated tourists of various shapes and sizes, relaxing.

Note that an absolutely free hot spot on the river is located just 50m south of this property, much to the consternation of Tabacón. Officially tour companies can no longer go there, and you'd be best advised to visit only during daylight hours.

Hiking

Although it's not currently active, Volcán Arenal is the big draw here. There is a well-marked trail system within the park, and several private reserves on its outskirts. Waterfalls, lava flows and crater lakes are all worthy destinations that you can reach without a guide.

In November 2017, four Dutch tourists were injured, a couple severely, when they were caught in a landslide in the off-limits area (within 4km of the crater) of Volcán Arenal. It took more than a day to rescue them and their Costa Rican guide from the mountain. So, quite literally – don't go there.

Courses

★ **Costa Rica Cooking** COOKING
(Map p254; ☎2479-1569; www.costaricacooking.com; per person full day/bocas US$125/75) Scott's culinary adventures focus on Costa Rican food with a modern twist, starting with a Tico mojito. Recipes include *ceviche*, *patacones* (fried green plantains) and other Costa Rican staples sourced from local and sometimes organic ingredients. Menus vary but always involve three courses (there is a shorter *bocas* – appetizers – class). Enjoy the stunning view from Scott's new third-floor kitchen.

Farm-to-table and food presentation classes are also available, as are vegetarian and vegan options. Located inside Gecko's Waterfall Grill (p258), just before the La Fortuna waterfall.

Scott also runs the **Costa Rica Dog Rescue** (Map p254; ☎2479-1569; www.crdogrescue.com; US$30-60 donation) next door.

Tours

Tour companies run rampant here, each seeking their bit of 'fortune'. Commissions are big business, so shop around and keep in mind that you can actually do many of the activities on offer on your own – or by booking directly with the service provider. Tour companies offer many combo packages (canopy tour, guided hike, horseback riding etc) with a dip in the hot springs. Make sure you understand exactly what's included, especially admission fees to parks and springs.

Operators also offer a slew of pricey tours to distant destinations, such as Caño Negro, Río Celeste and Venado Caves. (A word of caution: some unscrupulous dealers here sell 'Caño Negro' tours but don't actually go there – they go to Los Chiles.) If you're short of time, this can be a fine option, though you'll save yourself a ton of money (and probably have a much better experience) if you actually go to the place and organize a tour upon arrival.

★Don Olivo Chocolate Tour TOURS
(☎6110-3556, 2469-1371; http://chocolatedonolivo.wixsite.com/chocolatedonolivo; Via 142; tour US$25; ⏲8am, 10am, 1pm & 3pm; 👪) Let don Olivo's heirs, Otto and Maynor, take you around their *finca*, showing off various fruits, herbs and – of course – cacao plants. The process of turning this funny fruit into the decadent treat that we all know and love is truly fascinating. Bonus: lots of taste-testing along the way. Finish with a piping hot coffee and scrumptious hot chocolate.

Located about 5km east of town on the main road, Via 142, just before the town of Tanque. The tour includes transportation from your hotel.

Down to Earth TOURS
(Map p254; ☎2479-8568; www.godowntoearth.org; Diagonal 301; tour US$35; ⏲8am-8pm, tours 8am, 10am, 1pm, 3pm) On the road up to La Fortuna waterfall (p249), this strolling tour is all about coffee, which is brewed from single-origin beans from the owner's farm in the Dota Tarrazu Valley. There's no food here, just coffee – smooth, strong and revitalizing. Matias explains the history of the world through coffee, for cognoscenti and novices alike. You'll even get to plant some.

The tour itself lasts two hours, so you'll need the java jolt at the end.

Alberto's Horse Tours HORSEBACK RIDING
(Map p250; ☎2479-9043, 2479-7711; www.facebook.com/albertoshorses; Ruta 702; US$85; ⏲8:30am-1:30pm) Alberto and his son lead popular horseback-riding trips to the Catarata Río Fortuna. It's a three- or four-hour trip, but you'll spend about an hour off your horse, when you hike down to the falls for a swim or a photo op. Beautiful setting, beautiful horses. Cash only. Located on Ruta 702, about 2km south of town.

Red Lava Tours HIKING
(Map p250; ☎2479-8004; www.redlavatouristservicecenter.com; Volcano Valley Hike/Monteverde Overnight Hike: US$70/125) The helpful staff at this place, next to the bus terminal, speak six languages (including Italian, German and Dutch). They offer unique alternatives to the standard tours (such as a rustic overnight trek to Monteverde), and seem to have great fun doing so. Also the place to buy bus tickets; staff know the routes backward and forward.

Bike Arenal CYCLING
(Map p250; ☎2479-9020, WhatsApp 8854-9020; www.bikearenal.com; cnr Ruta 702 & Av 319A; rental per day/week US$15/150, half-/full-day tour US$75/110; ⏲7am-6pm) This outfit offers a variety of bike tours for all levels of rider, including a popular ride around the lake and a half-day ride to El Castillo. E-bikes are good for the torturous inclines around these parts. Make advance arrangements for rental and an English-speaking bike mechanic will bring the bicycle to you. Bike-hike combos available. It's on the road south out of town (702).

PureTrek Canyoning CANYONING
(Map p254; ☎2479-1313, USA toll-free 1-866-569-5723; www.puretrekcanyoning.com; 4hr tour incl transportation & lunch US$105; ⏲7am-10pm; 👪) 🍃 The reputable PureTrek leads guided rappels down three waterfalls, one of which is 50m high. Also included: rock climbing and a 'monkey drop,' which is actually a zipline with a rappel at the end of it. High marks for attention to safety and high-quality gear. It gets some big groups, but does a good job keeping things moving.

Check in at PureTrek headquarters, in a tree house 6km west of town. Combo trips including ATV, pedalboard and farm-to-table food options are available.

Arenal Mundo Aventura ADVENTURE
(Map p254; ☎2479-9762; www.arenalmundoaventura.com; adult/child canopy tours US$70/53, hiking US$55/39, Maleku cultural experience US$36/20; ⏲8am-1:30pm; 👪) An all-in-one adventure park, this place offers various guided hikes, rappelling and horseback riding, as well as a canopy tour. It also hosts performances of indigenous Maleku dance and song. It's 2km south of La Fortuna, on the road to Chachagua.

Desafío Adventure Company ADVENTURE
(Map p250; ☎2479-0020; www.desafiocostarica.com; Calle 472; tours from US$65; ⏲6:30am-9pm) This tour agency has the widest range of tours in La Fortuna – everything from paddling trips on the Río Balsa, horse-riding treks to Volcán Arenal, adventure tours rappelling down waterfalls, safari floats on the Sarapiquí and mountain-bike expeditions. It can also arrange your transfer to Monteverde and Guanacaste.

Nature Tours

Arenal Oasis WILDLIFE
(Map p254; ☎2479-9526; www.arenaloasis.com; night/bird walks US$40/65, child under 12 half price; ⏲bird walk 6:45am & 2pm, night tour 5:45pm) This wild frog sanctuary, created by the Rojas Bonilla family, is home to some 35 species of croaking critters. The frogs are just the

beginning of this night walk, which continues into the rainforest to see other nocturnal animals. If you're more of a morning person, it also does birdwatching tours. Reservations recommended. Located 3km from La Fortuna's center. Hotel pick-up costs US$10.

This is part of the Arenal Oasis (p257) hotel, located just southwest of town on the way to the waterfall (p249).

Aventuras Arenal TOURS
(Map p250; ☎2479-9133; www.aventurasarenal.com; Via 142; kayaking, safari float or volcano hike US$63, horse riding from US$89; ⏲7am-8pm) Around for more than 25 years, this outfit organizes a variety of local day tours on bike, boat and horseback. It also does trips further afield, including to Caño Negro and Río Celeste.

Jacamar Naturalist Tours HIKING
(Map p250; ☎2479-9767; www.arenaltours.com; Via 142, Parque Central; river safari/birdwatching US$59/68; ⏲7am-9pm) Recommended for its variety of naturalist hikes, including Volcán Arenal, waterfall and hanging bridges. The guides are knowledgeable.

Rainforest Canopy Tours

Canopy Tours CANOPY TOUR
(Map p254; ☎2479-1100; www.arenalparaisoresort.com; Arenal Paraíso Resort, Via 142; tours US$50; ⏲8am-5pm; 👪) A dozen cables zip across the canyon of the Río Arenal, giving a unique perspective on two waterfalls, as well as the rainforest canopy. Also includes admission to the resort's swimming pool and 13 thermal pools, which are hidden among the rocks and greenery on the hillside.

Located on Via 142, uphill and west of La Fortuna town.

Athica Canopy CANOPY TOUR
(Arenal Canopy Adventure; Map p254; ☎2479-1405; www.arenalcanopy.com; Via 142; canopy tour adult/child US$55/45, canopy/horseback combo adult/child US$75/68; ⏲8am, 10:30am, 1pm & 3pm) This canopy tour offers a new perspective on Volcán Arenal and the surrounding conservation area. There are 10 cables and 14 platforms, as well as the ever-popular Tarzan swing. It's also possible to add on a two-hour horse-riding trip.

Canopy Los Cañones CANOPY TOUR
(Map p254; ☎2479-1047, WhatsApp 8986-1000; www.hotelloslagos.com; Hotel Los Lagos; US$55) 🍃 Located at the Hotel Los Lagos, the Canopy Los Cañones has 12 cables over the rainforest, ranging from 50m to 500m long. The price includes admission to a frog farm, crocodile farm, butterfly farm, hot springs, natural pools and waterslides, all on the hotel grounds. Located about 6km west of La Fortuna, just off Via 142.

Ecoglide CANOPY TOUR
(Map p254; ☎2479-7120; www.arenalecoglide.com; US$75; ⏲canopy tours at 8am, 10am, 1pm & 3pm; 👪) Ecoglide features 11 cables, 13 platforms and a 'Tarzan' swing. You can combine this with other tours, such as birdwatching, a night walk, and rafting. Located about 5km west (uphill) from La Fortuna.

Kayaking, Canoeing & Rafting

La Fortuna is not a river-running hub like other parts of the country, but a few companies offer canoeing and kayaking. If you wish to go white-water rafting, some outfits – such as the Sarapiquí-based Aguas Bravas (p282) – take groups to run the Sarapiquí and other distant rivers; some also offer the option to get dropped afterwards in San José or on the Caribbean coast – a good way to have some fun on a travel day.

Wave Rafting RAFTING
(Map p250; ☎2479-7262; www.waveexpeditions.com; cnr Calle 472 & Av 331; river trips US$65-100; ⏲6am-9pm) Wave Expeditions runs the wild Ríos Toro and Sarapiquí, as well as the mellower Balsa, in both rafts and tubes. There's also hiking, horseback riding, canopy, canyoning and chocolate tours on offer, through second-party tour companies.

Canoa Aventura CANOEING
(Map p254; ☎2479-8200; www.canoa-aventura.com; Via 142; canoe or kayak trip from US$59; ⏲6:30am-10pm) 🍃 This long-standing family-run company specializes in canoe and float trips (leisurely trips aimed at observation and relaxation) led by bilingual naturalist guides. Most are geared toward wildlife- and birdwatching. Canoa is the sister company of the Maquenque Lodge (p279) in Boca Tapada and can arrange an overnight stay there.

Sleeping

La Fortuna

La Fortuna's tourist infrastructure has overflowed out of town, meaning there are also plenty of lodges strung out along the roads heading south and west. With Parque Nacional Volcán Arenal at their doorstep, many of these places on the outskirts have hiking

Around La Fortuna

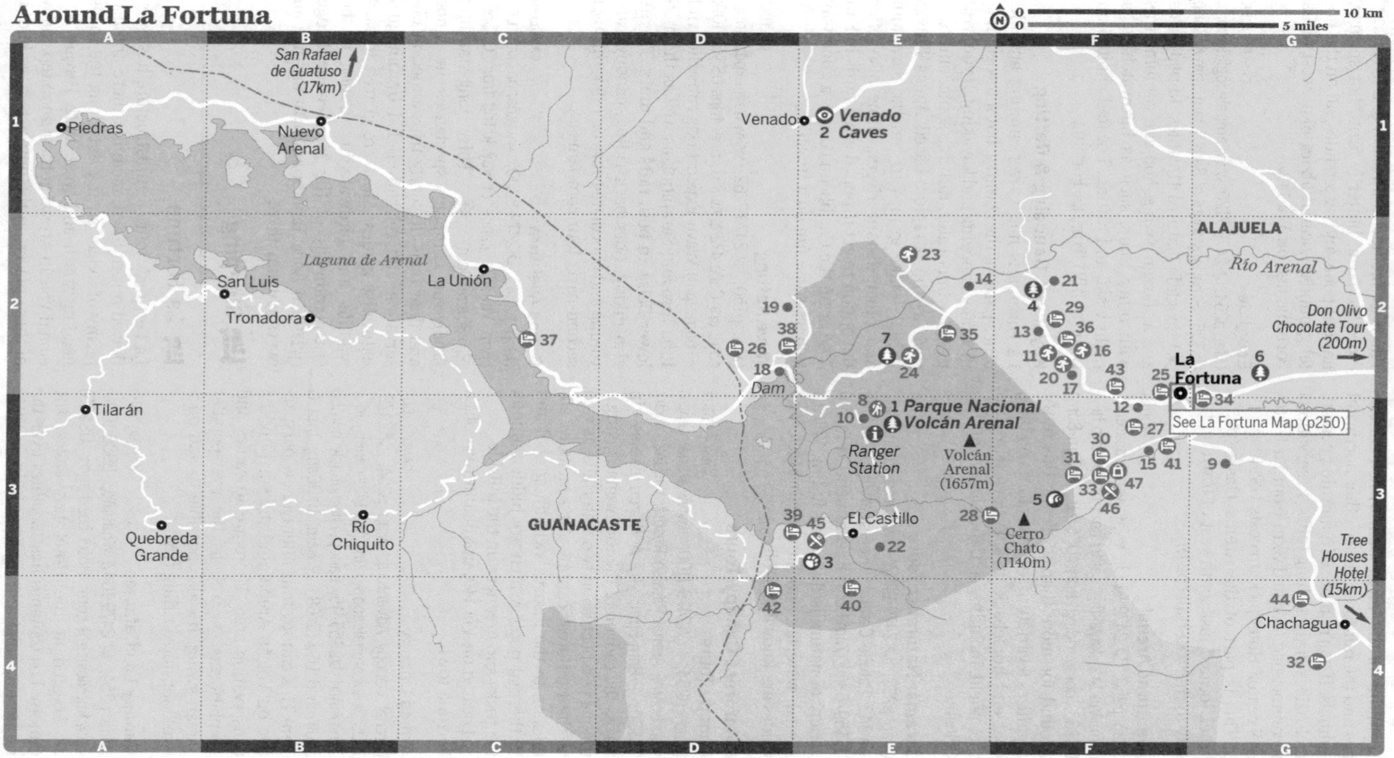

Around La Fortuna

Top Sights
1 Parque Nacional Volcán Arenal............E3
2 Venado Caves.......................................E1

Sights
3 Arenal EcoZoo......................................E3
4 Arenal Natura.......................................F2
5 Catarata Río Fortuna...........................F3
6 Ecocentro Danaus.................................G2
El Castillo-Arenal Butterfly Conservatory.............................(see 3)
7 Mirador El Silencio...............................E2

Activities, Courses & Tours
8 Arenal 1968...E3
9 Arenal Mundo Aventura.......................G3
Arenal Oasis...............................(see 27)
10 Arenal Wilberth Stables......................E3
Athica Canopy.................................(see 7)
11 Baldi Hot Springs................................F2
12 Canoa Aventura...................................F3
13 Canopy Los Cañones...........................F2
14 Canopy Tours.......................................E2
Costa Rica Cooking....................(see 46)
Costa Rica Dog Rescue..............(see 46)
15 Down to Earth......................................F3
16 Eco Termales Hot Springs...................F2
17 Ecoglide..F2
18 Fishing Lake Arenal.............................D2
La Gavilana...................................(see 3)
19 Mistico Hanging Bridges......................D2
Original ATV................................(see 10)
20 Paradise Hot Springs...........................F2
21 PureTrek Canyoning.............................F2
Rancho Adventure Tours...........(see 42)
22 Sky Adventures....................................E3
23 Springs Resort & Spa..........................E2
24 Tabacón Hot Springs............................E2
Waterfall Trail.............................(see 28)

Sleeping
25 Arenal Backpackers Resort..................F2
26 Arenal Lodge..D2
27 Arenal Oasis...F3
28 Arenal Observatory Lodge..................E3
29 Arenal Volcano Inn...............................F2
Cabinas Los Tucanes...................(see 3)
30 Casa Luna Hotel & Spa.........................F3
31 Catarata Eco-Lodge..............................F3
32 Chachagua Rainforest Ecolodge.........G4
Essence Arenal............................(see 3)
33 Green Lagoon.......................................F3
34 Gringo Pete's..G3
35 Hotel Campo Verde..............................E2
36 Hotel El Silencio del Campo.................F2
37 La Mansion..C2
38 Lost Iguana...D2
39 Majestic Lodge......................................D3
40 Nepenthe...E4
41 Rancho Cerro Azul................................F3
42 Rancho Margot.....................................D4
43 Roca Negra del Arenal..........................F2
44 Villas Josipek.......................................G4

Eating
45 Fusion Grill..E3
46 Gecko's Waterfall Grill..........................F3
La Ventanita..................................(see 45)
Pizza John.....................................(see 39)

Drinking & Nightlife
Howlers Bar & Grill........................(see 39)

Shopping
47 Neptune's House of Hammocks...........F3

trails, hot springs and volcano views right on the property, but restaurants and other facilities are limited.

Sleeping Indian Guesthouse GUESTHOUSE $
(Map p250; ☎8446-9149, 2479-8431; sleepingindianguesthouse@gmail.com; Av 331, near Calle 442; d incl breakfast US$45;) Named for the nearby mountain formation *(indio dormido)*, this delightful 2nd-storey guesthouse's five sweet, fan-cooled rooms have lofty ceilings, tile floors, colorful paint jobs and big windows. The spacious common area includes a fully equipped kitchen, balconies with volcano views, and a homey living room well stocked with books and games. Manager Heidy's artwork graces many of its walls.

Earplugs are provided to the noise-sensitive; breakfast is served at the Lava Lounge (p259).

Gringo Pete's HOSTEL $
(Map p254; Calle 460A; dm US$8, r without/with bathroom US$10/12;) 'Quiet, clean and cheap,' said one guest, and the prices are indeed pretty sweet. Books, a chess set and groovy red couches populate the common area; the kitchen is spacious and clean. Set in a quiet space a few blocks from the town center, with birdfeeder and BBQ, Pete's mantra is 'bed and breakfast: you make both.' Definitely old-school hosteling.

Pete's is the purple house with the amusing signage at the end of the block. There's a second location two blocks west of the bus terminal, which has more private rooms.

La Choza Inn INN $
(Map p250; ☎2479-9091, 2479-9361; www.lachozainnhostel.com; Av 331; incl breakfast dm US$9-15, s/d US$36/42;) With all the budget

'resorts' in town, it's refreshing to find a charming, old-fashioned, family-run inn, where facilities are basic but staff are always accommodating. Take your pick from the dark palm-wood dorms or the attractive doubles boasting volcanic views from the balcony. A clean common kitchen and one-time free transport to Tabacón hot springs are other perks. Air-con is US$10 extra.

Arenal Backpackers Resort HOSTEL $
(Map p254; ☎2479-7000; www.arenalbackpackersresort.com; Via 142; dm US$14-18, tent s/d US$35/44, r s/d US$55/86; P ❄ @ 📶 🏊) The original hostel-resort in La Fortuna, this self-proclaimed 'five-star hostel' with volcano views is pretty cushy. Sleep on orthopedic mattresses and take hot showers in your en suite bathroom (even in the dorms). A step up from the dorms are the raised tents, which have double beds and electricity (but no proper walls; you'll hear your neighbors loud and clear).

The main attraction is the landscaped pool with swim-up bar. You'll be in a traveler's party bubble here.

Selina La Fortuna HOSTEL $
(Map p250; ☎800-1022-463; www.selina.com/la-fortuna; Av 325; dm/tent US$16/69, d US$99-110; P ❄ 📶 🏊) The big-gun Central American hostel chain's locale in La Fortuna offers the 'bubble option' some seek: with everything at hand, you never have to leave the premises. Options range from dorms to luxurious tents to high-end hotel rooms. There's a swimming pool, bar and small movie theater/chill-out room.

No bracelet is needed to enter, as is *de rigueur* in hostel culture.

La Fortuna Suites GUESTHOUSE $$
(Map p250; ☎8328-7447; www.lafortunasuites.com; Av 331A; d incl breakfast from US$85; P ❄ 📶) Here's a chance to luxuriate in some high-end amenities (Apple TV and Netflix, for example) at budget prices. We're talking high-thread-count sheets and memory-foam mattresses, custom-made furniture and flat-screen TVs, gourmet breakfast on the balcony and killer views. Despite all these perks, guests agree that the thing that makes this place special is the hospitality shown by the hosts.

Located 300m west of Parque Central, behind La Choza Inn. If you can, get the suite with terrace access.

Hotel Monte Real HOTEL $$
(Map p250; ☎2479-9357; www.montereal hotel.com; Av 325, btwn Calles 464 & 466; d/ste incl breakfast US$99/123; P ❄ 📶 🏊) A smart, modern property on the edge of the Río Burio. This location combines the convenience of town with the rusticity of the forest – meaning lovely gardens and wildlife on your doorstep. Spacious rooms have Spanish-tile floors, stained-wood ceilings and sliding glass doors; some have a private balcony. The night guard can show you the *ranario* (frog pond).

A new onsite restaurant bordering the river was completed in 2019.

Downtown Inn BOUTIQUE HOTEL $$
(Map p250; ☎4000-2027; www.fortunadowntowninn.com; Main Sq, Via 142; d incl breakfast US$80; P ❄ 📶 🏊) The old Bromelia Hotel, right off the main square, features two dozen smart rooms, most with terraces overlooking the pool. You might not want a room facing the square, although the windows seem well insulated. A quality Fortuna lodging option. Car parking is 100m away.

La Parilla de Maria Bonita, an interesting, pricey Lebanese/steak joint (mains US$16 to US$30), is the onsite dining option.

Hotel Arenal Rabfer HOTEL $$
(Map p250; ☎2479-9187; www.arenalrabfer.com; Calle 468; s/d/tr/q incl breakfast US$75/87/101/113; P ❄ 📶 🏊) This place is set up around a pebbled pool area and shady palm garden. Rooms are spacious with high, slanted ceilings and crisp white paint. Located on a quiet side street, two blocks from the action. A lovely family owns it. A newly attached restaurant-bar ups the volume, so avoid the front wing.

West of La Fortuna

The road to the Arenal turnoff is lined with places to stay, ranging from quaint *cabinas* to luxurious lodges. Most of the area's high-end accommodations are located along this stretch. It's not convenient if you don't have your own transportation.

★**Roca Negra del Arenal** GUESTHOUSE $$
(Map p254; ☎2479-9237; www.hotelrocanegradelarenal.com; d/q US$80/110; P ❄ 📶 🏊) What makes this gem of a guesthouse so special? It's the paradisiacal setting, 2km from town. The gorgeous tiled pool and Jacuzzi are surrounded with tropical gardens bursting with blooms and buzzing with bees and birds, from parrots to peacocks. The spacious rooms have stained-wood accents, huge tile bathrooms and semiprivate terraces facing the garden (complete with rockers). Breakfast is US$7.

Arenal Oasis BUNGALOW $$
(Map p254; ☎2479-9526, 2479-8472; www.arenaloasis.com; d incl breakfast US$88; P 📶) Located just 3.5km from the center of La Fortuna but surrounded by vegetation and wildlife, this place is truly an oasis. The accommodations are in dark but cozy log-cabin bungalows (with bathtubs) that have private porches facing the rainforest. It's a family-run operation that truly offers a personal touch.

Located to the west of town; turn off at the cemetery. This is the site of a popular night frog-watching tour (p252), too. A larger 'villa' accommodates families.

Hotel Campo Verde BUNGALOW $$
(Map p254; ☎2479-1080; www.hotelcampoverde.com; d/ste incl breakfast from US$105/115; P 📶) A darling family-owned property, 9km west of town. Canary-yellow wooden bungalows have vaulted beamed ceilings, two queen beds, lovely drapes and chandeliers, and a tiled patio blessed with two waiting rockers. Book the bungalows at the foot of the mountain, where the views are unbeatable and connect to 2km of trails. Spring for a king bed or Jacuzzi for US$10.

Hotel El Silencio del Campo LODGE $$$
(Map p254; ☎2479-7055; www.hotelsilenciodelcampo.com; villas incl breakfast US$205-270; P ❄ 📶 🏊) This lovely lodge about 5km west of town has 23 stand-alone cabins that are luxurious without being showy. The property's pièce de résistance, though, is the hot spring – for guests only – with half a dozen decadent pools in a range of temperatures. Guests can also experience life on a working farm and feast on fresh eggs for breakfast.

Arenal Volcano Inn INN $$$
(Map p254; ☎2479-1122, in USA 1-315-215-0460; www.arenalvolcanoinn.com; incl breakfast s/d from US$132/145, deluxe US$154/168, ste US$218/232; P ❄ 📶 🏊) Resembling a gated suburban community, this lodging has sidewalks winding through perfectly manicured lawns, connecting the red-tile-roof bungalows and swimming pool. The bungalows open to private terraces that face the mighty mountain. Inside, clean white walls and linens are complemented by dark stained-wood trimmings, with all the amenities you'd expect.

South of La Fortuna

Just a few kilometers south of town, a partially paved road trundles to the base of Cerro Chato; hotels dot either side of it. Further flung is the village of Chachagua, 12km south along the road to San Ramón. Crisscrossed by local rivers, this authentic, agrarian market *pueblo* is an antidote to the touristy brouhaha of La Fortuna. Note that the crater of Cerro Chato remains closed to tourism, and no tour companies can legally offer tours there.

Rancho Cerro Azul BUNGALOW $$
(Map p254; ☎2479-7360; www.ranchocerroazul.com; d US$95-145; P ❄ 📶) Nine cute, shingled cabins face the parking lot but back up to the forest, with private porches overlooking the trees. A 200m trail leads to the rushing river, with the volcano beyond. The cabins have woody interiors and stylish details. They're simple, natural, beautiful and comfortable and have cable TV. The superior and deluxe cabins are roomier and have king beds.

Located on the road to La Fortuna waterfall (p249), just before Down to Earth (p252).

Catarata Eco-Lodge LODGE $$
(Map p254; ☎2479-9522; www.cataratalodge.com; s/d incl breakfast US$84/88; P ❄ 📶 🏊) Set at the base of Cerro Chato and surrounded by forest, this place is ideal if you want to get away from it all (but not *too* far away; you're still just 4km from town). The decent little Spanish-tile and wood rooms have air-con and TV, and hammocks strung on the terrace. The restaurant is basic, but handy.

Villas Josipek CABINA $$
(Map p254; ☎2479-9555; www.villasjosipekcr.com; Ruta 702; s/d/tr/q US$85/85/130/140; P ❄ 📶 🏊) Just north of Chachagua village, these immaculate, simple wooden cabins with full kitchens and volcano views are surrounded by private rainforest trails that penetrate the Bosque Eterno de Los Niños. Four newer cabins uphill lack garden ambiance but are more modern.

Ask your hosts, Jorge and Sioni, to point out the sloth that sometimes inhabits the guarumo tree near the lobby. Within the grounds, you can take an 800m stroll through the Jardín Botánico Josipek, home to rose gardens, rainforest and medicinal plants, as well as a labyrinth and a giant plastic brontosaurus.

Villas Josipek is about 10km south of La Fortuna proper.

★ **Finca Luna Nueva** LODGE $$
(☎2468-4006; www.fincalunanuevalodge.com; San Isidro; d incl breakfast from US$140; @ 📶 🏊) Bordering the Bosque Eterno de Los Niños, this special place started as a spice farm then blossomed into an ecolodge. It's

a pretty impressive amalgam of sustainability and luxury, featuring lovely *casas* built from reclaimed wood, a new adobe 'mud' house, ozonated swimming pool, solar-heated Jacuzzi, huge medicinal plant garden and an amazing restaurant, supplied by the onsite organic farm.

Located about 17km south of La Fortuna, in the village of San Isidro.

Green Lagoon HOTEL **$$**
(Map p254; ☎2479-7700; www.greenlagoon.net; d US$124-150, villa US$350-750; P 📶) Perched high above the Catarata Río Fortuna, this 'wellbeing resort' is great for birders and frog-lovers – especially with a naturalist on hand to point out specimens. The rooms are fairly plain, but comfortable. The 'wellness' is covered by spa services, a garden, a yoga space and a vegetarian restaurant. Spring for a superior with a balcony if you can.

At the La Fortuna waterfall (p249) parking lot, turn right up the unpaved drive. Top-range villas come with their own pool.

Chachagua Rainforest Ecolodge LODGE **$$$**
(Map p254; ☎2468-1020; www.chachaguarainforesthotel.com; d/bungalow incl breakfast US$149/209; P ❄ 📶) On a private reserve that abuts the Bosque Eterno de Los Niños, this place includes an organic farm and fishing ponds (catch and cook!). Explore on hiking trails or on horseback. The rooms are good quality, and the stylish, spacious bungalows are gorgeous. Two come with private porches and Jacuzzis. New hot-springs and *pozos* (swimming holes) installed in 2019.

To get here, drive 11km south of La Fortuna. On the southern side of Chachagua, fork right off the main road and follow the signs on a 2km dirt track (may require a 4WD in the rainy season).

Casa Luna Hotel & Spa HOTEL **$$$**
(Map p254; ☎2479-7368; www.casalunahotel.com; d/tr/q incl breakfast from US$170/180/200; P ❄ @ 📶) The snazziest joint on the rustic road toward La Fortuna waterfall (p249), this walled complex initially seems like a gated community. Once inside, you'll see that the landscaped gardens and adobe-style lodgings are lovely. Wooden doors open into elegant split-level duplexes with private patios, as well as four deluxe rooms and two junior suites. Green improvements include an organic garden which stocks the kitchen, and solar panels.

There's a full menu of spa treatments, and attentive service.

Eating

Unless you're eating exclusively at *sodas* (cheap lunch counters), you'll find the restaurants in La Fortuna to be more expensive than in other parts of the country. But there are some excellent, innovative kitchens, including a few that are part of the farm-to-table movement. The restaurants are mostly clustered in town, but there are also places to eat on the road heading west.

Soda Mima SODA **$**
(Map p250; Off Via 142; mains US$5; ⏰6am-8pm Mon-Sat, to noon Sun) Though nothing fancy from afar, the love radiates outward from Mari and Alvaro's kitchen to warm your belly and your heart. Cheap, delicious *casados* (set meals) and *gallo pintos* (rice and beans) are standard fare; add some eye-watering *chilera* (peppers distilled in vinegar) from the big jar if you dare.Customer artworks in various languages adorn the walls, the most fitting of which reads: 'Don Alvaro Rocks.'

In the parking lot behind Cafeto Chill Out and the Pollo Fortuneño restaurant. Friday is *olla* (special soup/stew) day.

Spec-Taco-Lar TEX-MEX **$**
(Map p250; tacos & burritos US$6-10; ⏰6am-10pm) The best place in town, hands down. Cesar cranks up weepy *ranchera* music while you drink in the atmosphere: a troika of sombreros and painted skulls complete the faux-Tex-Mex motif. But the food is why you're here, and it's show-stopping: from incredible street corn with chipotle-and-cheese toppings, to standard tacos and burritos with five home-made salsas, you can't miss.

If you're looking to get your drink on, stick around after dinner.

Gecko's Waterfall Grill INTERNATIONAL **$**
(Map p254; ☎2479-1569; www.facebook.com/geckogourmet; mains US$6-10; ⏰11am-5pm) What began as a snack counter on the last pass before La Fortuna waterfall (p249) has turned into a full-blown fusion excursion by Scott, famous for his love of food and dogs. The new menu has received rave reviews – why not stop by after a dunk in the river?

Plan B Sandwicheria SANDWICHES **$**
(Map p250; cnr Calle 464 & Via 142; US$2-4; ⏰10am-11pm Mon-Sat, from noon Sun) You forgot to eat or pack a lunch before your hike? Plan B. Cheap, filling sandwich and omelette fillings at this corner stand include chicken, three cheeses, and the old standby, peanut butter and jelly.

Rainforest Café CAFE $
(Map p250; ☎2479-7239; Calle 468; mains US$7-10; ⏰7am-10pm; 📶🖉) We know it's bad form to start with dessert, but the irresistible sweets at this popular spot are beautiful to behold and delicious to devour. There's also a full menu of coffees, including some tempting specialty drinks (such as Mono Loco: coffee, banana, milk, chocolate and cinnamon).

Soda Víquez SODA $
(Map p250; ☎2479-8772; cnr Calle 468 & Av 325; mains US$6-10; ⏰8am-10pm; 🖉) Travelers adore the local flavor that's served up at Soda Víquez (in all senses of the expression). It's a super-friendly spot, offering tasty *típico* (traditional dishes), especially *casados,* rice dishes and fresh fruit *batidos* (shakes). Prices are reasonable and portions ample. 'Friendship is born from our service' is their motto – need we say more?

Kappa Sushi SUSHI $
(Map p250; Calle 468, btwn Av 331 & Av 333; sushi & rolls US$7-11; ⏰noon-10pm; 🖉) When you're surrounded by mountains and cattle farms, who's thinking of sushi? Well, you should. The fish is fresh (you're not *that* far from the ocean) and the preparations innovative. The dragon roll (shrimp tempura, avocado, and eel sauce) is a favorite. Enjoy the view of Arenal while you feast on raw fish – or go for the veg options.

Kappa is a combination of the owners' names, Kattya and Pablo.

Orgánico Fortuna VEGETARIAN $$
(Map p250; ☎8572-2115; www.organicofortuna.com; Calle 466; mains US$9-15; ⏰9am-7pm Mon-Sat) A lovely little family operation that preaches better living through better eating, and the proof is in the pudding (or maybe the falafel). Delicious, locally sourced ingredients are used and offerings are prepared with care: smoothies, a tasty organic roast coffee (Cerro del Fuego) with almond milk, and even gluten-free bread and other options.

Café Mediterraneo ITALIAN $$
(Map p250; ☎2479-7497; Ruta 702; mains US$10-15; ⏰11:30am-10pm) This delightful osteria is worth the trip, cooking up homemade pasta and pizza such as the Arenal: bacon, egg, ham, mushroom and basil. Customers rave about the personable service and decadent desserts such as Nutella on pizza dough. Strangely, it also offers Texas-bred Angus beef, while a herd of highly affronted Tico cattle stare from across the road.

Located just after Bike Arenal (p252) and before El Establo bar, on the road out of the town center.

Chifa La Familia Feliz FUSION $$
(Map p250; ☎8469-6327; Calle 472; mains US$8-15; ⏰11am-10pm; 📶🖉👪) If you're looking for a change of taste – a *real* change from *casados* and pizza – check this out. *Chifa* is Peruvian Chinese fried rice, and chef Martin Gonzalez also whips up *causas* (yellow-potato dishes), *ceviches*, and *anticuchos* (skewers) with equal enthusiasm and skill. He goes out of his way to welcome and satisfy all comers.

Lava Lounge INTERNATIONAL $$
(Map p250; ☎2479-7365; www.facebook.com/lavaloungecostarica; Via 142; mains US$10-15, specials US$23-25; ⏰7am-10:30pm; P📶🖉) This open-air restaurant has become a go-to spot for a post-activities lunch or dinner. There are pizzas and pasta, wraps and salads, and loads of vegetarian options. The reggae throbs nonstop under a *palapa* (thatched) roof. Add colorful cocktails, hip service and occasional DJ/live music, and the place is pretty irresistible.

Owner/chef Scott also runs Gecko's Waterfall Grill and Costa Rica Dog Rescue (p251).

Restaurant Don Rufino INTERNATIONAL $$$
(Map p250; ☎2479-9997; www.donrufino.com; cnr Via 142 & Calle 466; mains US$16-40; ⏰11:30am-9:30pm) The vibe is trendy at this indoor-outdoor grill. The highlight is the perfectly prepared grilled meats: the New York Steak with mushrooms is to die for. If you're cutting back, go for Grandma's BBQ chicken (with chocolate, wrapped in a banana leaf) or a house favorite, the *kobocha* squash risotto with grilled chicken breast and chimichurri-glazed shrimp.

Drinking & Nightlife

La Fortuna Pub PUB
(Map p250; www.facebook.com/lafortunapub; Via 142; ⏰2pm-midnight Sun-Thu, to 1am Fri-Sat) Just uphill from the town center, this place is all about Tico artisanal beers, offering a dozen different home-country bottled *cervezas*. It also brews in small batches that disappear quickly, so watch its Facebook page for the next arrival. A standard pub-food menu satisfies, while Friday's open mic often devolves into a boozy karaoke session.

Shopping

Neptune's House of Hammocks HOMEWARES

(Neptuno Casa de Hamaca; Map p254; ☎2479-8269; Diagonal 301; ⊙8am-6pm) On the road to La Fortuna Waterfall (p249), Rastaman Daniel been watching the tourist traffic come and go for more than a decade while he and Yesenia weave magic hammocks (US$40 to US$50) and swinging chairs. Take a breather and test one out.

Information

MEDICAL SERVICES

Centro Medico Sanar (☎2479-9420; www.facebook.com/cmsanarfortuna; cnr Calle 464 & Av 331; ⊙8am-8:30pm) Medical consultation, ambulance services and pharmacy.

MONEY

Line up to get some colones (or dollars) at banks all around town.

BAC San José (cnr Av 331 & Calle 466; ⊙9am-6pm Mon-Fri, to 1pm Sat)

Banco de Costa Rica (Via 142; ⊙9am-4pm Mon-Fri)

Banco Nacional (cnr Calle 468 & Av 331; ⊙8:30am-3:45pm Mon-Fri)

Banco Popular (☎2479-9422; cnr Via 142 & Calle 460A; ⊙8:45am-4:30pm Mon-Fri, 8:15-11:30am Sat)

POST

Correos de Costa Rica (Map p250; Av 331; ⊙8am-5:30pm Mon-Fri, 7:30am-noon Sat) Northwest of the Parque Central.

Getting There & Away

BUS

The **bus terminal** (Map p250; Av 325) is on the river road. Keep an eye on your bags as this is a busy transit center, as well as on buses between Monteverde and La Fortuna, as you would on any public bus. Avoid placing it in the space above the seats.

TAXI-BOAT-TAXI

The fastest public transit route between Monteverde and La Fortuna is the taxi-boat-taxi combo (formerly known as jeep-boat-jeep, which sounds sexier but it was the same thing). It is actually a minivan with the requisite yellow '*turismo*' tattoo, which takes you to Laguna de Arenal, meeting a boat that crosses the lake, where a 4WD van on the other side continues to Monteverde. It's a terrific transportation option that can be arranged through almost any hotel or tour operator in La Fortuna or Monteverde (US$25, four hours).

This is now the first transportation choice for many traveling between La Fortuna and Monteverde as it's incredibly scenic and reasonably priced.

Getting Around

BICYCLE

Biking is a reasonable option to get around town and reach some of the top tourist attractions. The challenging 7km ride from town to the waterfall (p249) is a classic. Arrange to rent a bike from Bike Arenal (p252) and they'll drop it off at your hotel.

BUSES FROM LA FORTUNA

DESTINATION	COMPANY	COST (US$)	DURATION (HR)	FREQUENCY
Ciudad Quesada (San Carlos)	Auto-Transportes San José–San Carlos	3	1-1½	20 daily, 4:30am to 7pm
San José*	Auto-Transportes San José–San Carlos	5	4½	12:45pm, 2:45pm
San Ramon via Chachagua	Carbaches	4	2½	5:30am, 9am, 1pm, 4pm
Tilarán, with connection to Monteverde**	Auto-Transportes Tilarán, departs from the Parque Central	6	3½	8:30am, 12:30pm, 5pm

* Alternatively, take the bus to Ciudad Quesada, from where there are frequent departures to San José. However, you'll pay more doing so.

** To reach Monteverde/Santa Elena (US$12 total [2 buses], six to eight hours), take the 8:30am or 12:30pm to Tilarán, where you'll have to wait a few hours for the onward bus to Santa Elena.

A great and friendly source of bus information for the entire country is Red Lava Tours (p252), located right next to the terminal. Manager Sonia is known to locals as the 'Google of La Fortuna.'

CAR

La Fortuna is easy to access by public transportation, but nearby attractions such as the hot springs, Parque Nacional Volcán Arenal and Laguna de Arenal demand internal combustion (or a tour operator). A day trip to Río Celeste, Caño Negro or Venado Caves might also merit renting a car for the day.

Adobe Rent a Car (☎2479-7202; www.adobecar.com; Av 325; ⏲8am-5pm)

Alamo (☎2479-9090; www.alamocostarica.com; cnr Via 142 & Calle 472; ⏲7:30am-5:30pm)

Parque Nacional Volcán Arenal

For most of modern history, Volcán Arenal was just another dormant volcano surrounded by fertile farmland. But for about 42 years – from its destructive explosion in 1968 until its sudden subsidence in 2010 – the volcano was an ever-active and awe-striking natural wonder, producing menacing ash columns, massive explosions and streams of glowing molten rock almost daily.

The fiery views are gone for now, but **Arenal** (Map p254; ☎2461-8499; adult/child US$15/5; ⏲8am-4pm, last entrance 2:30pm) is still a worthy destination, thanks to the dense forest covering its lower slopes and foothills, and its picture-perfect conical shape up top (often shrouded in clouds, but still). The Parque Nacional Volcán Arenal is part of the Area de Conservación Arenal, which protects most of the Cordillera de Tilarán. This area is rugged and varied, rich with wildlife and laced with trails.

Activities

Hiking

From the ranger station (which has trail maps available; p262), you can hike the **Sendero Los Heliconias**, a 1km circular track that passes by the site of the 1968 lava flow. A 1.5km-long path branches off this trail and leads to an overlook. The **Sendero Las Coladas** also branches off the Heliconias trail and wraps around the volcano for 2km past the 1993 lava flow before connecting with the **Sendero Los Tucanes**, which extends for another 3km through the tropical rainforest at the base of the volcano. To return to the parking area, you'll have to turn back – you'll get good views of the summit on the way.

From the park headquarters (2km down the road from the ranger station) is the 1.3km **Sendero Los Miradores**, which leads down to the shores of the volcanic lake and provides a good angle for volcano viewing. Also from park headquarters, the **Old Lava Flow Trail** is an interesting and strenuous lower-elevation trail following the flow of the massive 1992 eruption. The 4km round trip takes two hours. If you want to keep hiking, combine it with the **Sendero El Ceibo**, a scenic 1.8km trail through secondary forest.

There are additional trails departing from Arenal Observatory Lodge (p262) and on a nearby private reserve.

Waterfall Trail HIKING

(Map p254; www.arenalobservatorylodge.com; Arenal Observatory Lodge; day pass US$10) This scenic hike departing from Arenal Observatory Lodge (p262) is an easy 2km round-trip hike to a 12m waterfall. The terrain starts out flat then descends into a grotto where you'll find the thundering gusher. You'll feel the mist long before you see its majesty.

Arenal 1968 HIKING

(Map p254; ☎2462-1212; www.arenal1968.com; El Castillo–La Fortuna road; trails US$15, mountain-bike park US$15; ⏲7am-10pm) This private network of trails along the original 1968 lava flow is right next to the park entrance. There's a *mirador* (lookout) that on a clear day offers a picture-perfect volcano view. It's 1.2km from the highway turnoff to the park, just before the ranger station (p262).

The 16km of mountain-bike trails, separate from the lava hiking trails, lets you see the park in a different way.

Tours

In addition to hiking, it's also possible to explore the park on a tour on horseback, mountain bike or ATV.

Arenal Wilberth Stables HORSEBACK RIDING

(Map p254; ☎2479-7522; www.arenalwilberthstable.com; 1/2hr US$40/65; ⏲7:30am, 11am & 2:30pm) Horseback-riding tours depart from these stables at the foot of Arenal. The ride takes in forest and farmland, as well as lake and volcano views. The stables are opposite the entrance to the national park; there's also an office in La Fortuna, next to Arenal Hostel Resort.

Original ATV ADVENTURE

(Map p254; ☎2479-7522; www.originalarenalatv.com; rental per hr US$60-90, tour per person US$95-105; ⏲7:30am, 11am & 2:30pm) This wild 2½-hour ATV ride takes place on a private farm near the national park, with volcano views all around. Along the way, you can cool off (and clean off) with a dip in the river. Located across from the park entrance; there's also an office in La Fortuna, at the Arenal Hostel Resort. Price includes transportation from your hotel.

Sleeping

Arenal Observatory Lodge LODGE $$$
(Map p254; 2479-1070, reservations 2290-7011; www.arenalobservatorylodge.com; d/tr/q without bathroom US$100/$115/130, with bathroom from US$140/155/185;) High on the Arenal slopes, this sprawling lodge is the only accommodation in the national park. Rooms range from La Casona's rustic doubles without bathrooms (but with nice views from the porch), to junior suites with king-size beds, local art and huge picture windows framing the volcano. The rooms (which have paper-thin walls) could stand a bit of improvement, as could the night-time lighting.

There's a decent international restaurant on the grounds (there's hardly anywhere else to eat in the area). There's also a small museum, with exhibits on the history, volcanology and hydrology of Arenal. Rates include access to the swimming pool and hiking trails, as well as a free guided walk each morning.

Information

The **ranger station** (Map p254; 2461-8499; adult/child US$15/5; 8am-4pm) is on the western side of the volcano. The complex housing the station includes an information center and parking lot. From here, trails lead 3.4km toward the volcano.

Getting There & Away

To get to the ranger station by car, head west from La Fortuna for 15km, then turn left at the 'Parque Nacional' sign and take the 2km good dirt road to the entrance on the left side of the road. You can also take an 8am bus toward Tilarán (ask the driver to drop you off at the park) and catch the 2pm bus back to La Fortuna.

If you are heading to Arenal Observatory Lodge, continue driving on the dirt road. About 3km past the ranger station you will come to a small one-lane bridge and parking area. After crossing the bridge you'll reach a fork in the road; left goes to the lodge and right goes to the village of El Castillo. Turn left and continue 2.6km to reach the lodge. This steep, hard-packed gravel and partially paved road is fine for most vehicles, but a 4WD is recommended.

A taxi from La Fortuna to either the lodge or El Castillo will cost about US$30.

El Castillo

POP 300

Just an hour around the bend from La Fortuna, the tiny mountain village of El Castillo is a beautiful, bucolic, and bumpy alternative. This picturesque locale, created as a relocation zone after the great eruption of 1968, has easy access to Parque Nacional Volcán Arenal and amazing, up-close views of the looming mountain. A recently paved road makes getting here a lot smoother than in the past.

There are hiking trails and swimming holes. There are also a few worthy attractions, including a butterfly house and an eco-zoo. The only thing El Castillo doesn't have is a sidewalk. And maybe that's a good thing.

Sights

Arenal EcoZoo ZOO
(El Serpentario; Map p254; 2479-1059; El Castillo–La Fortuna road; adult/child US$15/12, with guide US$23/16; 8am-7pm) This snake house offers a hands-on animal experience, as in, handling and milking a venomous snake. It's home to a red-tailed boa (one of the largest snakes in the world), as well as frogs, amphibious lizards, iguanas, turtles, scorpions, tarantulas and butterflies. Good photo ops! Ask about feeding time if you want to see snakes devouring bugs, frogs and even other snakes. Located on the main road uphill from the lake, which connects to La Fortuna.

El Castillo-Arenal Butterfly Conservatory WILDLIFE RESERVE
(Map p254; 2479-1149; www.butterflyconservatory.org; El Castillo–La Fortuna road; adult/student US$17/12; 8am-4pm) More than just a butterfly conservatory (although it has one of the largest butterfly exhibitions in Costa Rica). Altogether there are six domes (recreating the butterflies' natural Costa Rican habitat), a ranarium, an insect museum, a medicinal herb garden, and an hour's worth of trails through a botanic garden and along the river. The birding is also excellent here, and there are wonderful volcano views. The conservatory is located on the main road uphill from the lake.

The conservatory is wheelchair accessible, and it has multilingual docents.

Tours

La Gavilana
TOURS

(Map p254; ☎8433-7902, 2479-1747; www.gavilana.com; El Castillo–La Fortuna road; 1hr/half-day Food Forest hike from US$30/75; ⊙by appointment) The culinary adventurers here offer a Food Forest trail hike to their farm near the Río Caño Negro. Additional adventures on offer include a fermentation workshop, while artistic types can join Hannah in the mural painting class. All classes are by appointment only.

The office is on the main road uphill from the lake. The time spent on the hike can vary between one and three hours (US$30 per person) and half a day. Both include lunch.

Sky Adventures
CANOPY TOUR

(Map p254; ☎2479-4100; www.skyadventures.travel; adult/child Sky Walk US$39/27, Sky Tram US$48/33, Sky River Drift US$81/64, Sky Limit US$84/n/a, Sky Trek US$84/58; ⊙7:30am-4pm) El Castillo's entry in the canopy-tour category has ziplines (Sky Trek), a floating gondola (Sky Tram) and a series of hanging bridges (Sky Walk). It's safe and well run; visitors tend to leave smiling. A unique combo, Sky River Drift combines a zipline with tree-climbing and river tubing, while Sky Limit combines ziplining with rappel and other high-altitude challenges. There's also mountain biking on the property.

Located uphill from the lake and the El Castillo–La Fortuna road, just past the Arenal Tropical Gardens.

Rancho Adventure Tours
ADVENTURE

(Map p254; ☎8302-7318; www.ranchomargot.com; Rancho Margot; farm tour US$35, other tours US$55) Rancho Margot offers a good selection of guided tours, including horseback riding on the southern side of Laguna de Arenal, lake kayaking and touring the ranch itself to learn about the workings of a sustainable farm. A half-day tour of the ranch, with lunch, costs US$50. Located where the El Castillo–La Fortuna road intersects with Rancho Margot Rd.

Sleeping

For a tiny place, El Castillo has an impressive range of accommodations, from funky budget lodgings to charming B&Bs to expansive ecolodges. You'll find them clustered in the village, up on the hillside, and strung out along the lake shore. If you've got your tent, you can pitch it for free on the lakefront – take the dirt track just across from the church – and enjoy the best views in town. Majestic (p264) also has campsites across from Essence Arenal, up the hill, which have a fee, but come with bathrooms and security.

Essence Arenal
HOSTEL $

(Map p254; ☎2479-1131; www.essencearenal.com; d with/without bathroom US$65/40, additional person US$12, tents US$30-48; P@🛜≋) Perched on a 22-hectare hilltop with incredible volcano and lake views, this boutique hostel is the best cheap sleep in the region. Bed down in a basic but clean room or a fancy tent, done up with plush bedding and wood furnishings (some have terraces). It's an eclectic, positive-energy place, offering group hikes, yoga classes and good vibes.

Guests participate in the loving preparation of vegetarian meals (with ingredients sourced from its own organic farm) that will delight even the most hardcore carnivore; the restaurant is open between 7am and 8pm. At time of research there were plans for a new yoga deck and pool, along with two new rooms.

Cabinas Los Tucanes
HOTEL $

(Map p254; ☎2479-1076; www.arenalcabinaslostucanes.com; El Castillo–La Fortuna road; d/tr/q US$55/65/80; 🛜) Here you'll find huge, bright, spotless and spacious rooms, with plain decor but fabulous vistas from the picture windows. The top-floor rooms catch a nice breeze off the terrace; you'll pay extra for the view but it's money well spent. Fanny takes care of this place, and you will be well looked after. Breakfast US$5. Situated uphill from the lake.

★Rancho Margot
LODGE $$

(Map p254; ☎8302-7318; www.ranchomargot.org; cnr El Castillo–La Fortuna road & Rancho Margot Rd; incl meals dm per person US$80, bungalow US$190-299; P🛜≋) Part resort lodge, part organic farm, Rancho Margot is 61 hectares of cinematic loveliness, set along the rushing Río Caño Negro and surrounded by rainforested mountains. There are comfortable dorm-style bunkhouse accommodations but, if your budget allows, spring for a beautiful teak-furnished bungalow, blessed with views of hulking mountains, weeping jungle and a placid lake.

Prices include a two-hour guided tour of the farm and daily yoga classes. Hiking trails and (free) hot springs are at hand. Prices are more attractive if you stay three nights or more. Located where the El Castillo–La Fortuna road meets Rancho Margot Rd.

Majestic Lodge
RENTAL HOUSE **$$**

(Map p254; ☑ 8703-1561, 2479-1085; www.majesticpropertiescrc.com; El Fósforo–El Castillo road; entire lodge US$600; P ❈ ◉ ☳) This eight-room lodge overlooks Laguna de Arenal, and has a stone swimming pool, and Jacuzzi. It must be rented out entirely – no individual rooms are available. One of the rental options from Majestic Properties (which owns several El Castillo accommodations), the lodge serves as a rental office for the others too. 'Pie in the Sky' *cabinas* up the road have fully equipped kitchens.

At the time of research, Majestic also planned to open an information center at the town entrance.

Nepenthe
B&B **$$**

(Map p254; ☑ 8892-5501; www.nepenthe-costarica.com; d incl breakfast from US$135; P ❈ ◉ ☳) South of El Castillo, the highlight here is the spectacular, spring-fed infinity pool overlooking Laguna de Arenal. Lodge-like cabins are simple – tiled numbers with colorful artisanal accents, set in a gentle arc of a ranch-style building. Hammocks on the patio allow you to take it all in. Incredible views, but you may need a 4WD to reach it – seriously.

Some cabins have fully equipped kitchens. A separate house is available for up to 12 people.

The B&B's aptly named Phoenix restaurant is in its fourth incarnation.

🍴 Eating & Drinking

Though eating options are limited, there are some good restaurants here. In addition to the few places in the village, some lodgings on the outskirts have recommended restaurants. There are more choices over in La Fortuna.

★ La Ventanita
CAFE **$**

(Map p254; ☑ 2479-1735; El Castillo–La Fortuna road; mains US$4-6; ⊙ 11am-9pm; ☑) 'La Ventanita' refers to the 'little window' where you place your order. Soon, you'll be devouring the best *chifrijo* (rice-and-pinto-beans bowl with fried pork, fresh salsa and corn chips) in the province, along with a nutritious, delicious *batido* (fruit shake). It's typical food with a twist – pulled pork and bacon burritos, for example. Desserts include flan and carrot cake.

California expat Kelly is a wealth of information about the area, so ask away. He rents little motorbikes at economical prices, by the hour: a cool way to see the area.

Pizza John
PIZZA **$$**

(Map p254; pizzas US$11-19, calzones US$6-10; ⊙ noon-8pm) Old John may have passed away, but his recipes and legacy live on with his widow Myra, who still whips up delicious pizzas, calzones and homemade ice cream to beat the band, including wonders such as chocolate-ginger and Costa Rican coffee. The garden setting – orchids, fragrant rosemary – is a plus, too.

Fusion Grill
FUSION **$$**

(Map p254; ☑ 2479-1949; www.fusiongrillrestaurant.com; El Castillo–La Fortuna road; mains US$12-20; ⊙ 7am-10pm) Set in an open-air dining room with incredible volcano views, Fusion Grill shows off a little swank (at least, more than other restaurants in El Castillo). Chef Adrian Ramirez whips up a mean *parillada mixta* (mixed grill), but your favorite part of the meal might be the specialty desserts such as pineapple or banana flambé. Located uphill from the lake

The Ramirez family also rents 16 basic but functional rooms (including flat-screen TVs) for US$50.

Howlers Bar & Grill
BAR

(Map p254; ☑ 2479-1785; www.facebook.com/howlersbarandgrill; ⊙ 11:30am-8:30pm Tue-Sun) It stays open late if there's demand, and sometimes there's karaoke. The American-style pub grub is excellent, as is the cold draught beer. It's a popular place for the expat community to congregate. Part of the Majestic Lodge property.

ℹ Getting There & Away

El Castillo is located 8km past the entrance to Parque Nacional Volcán Arenal. The newly paved road has made driving here much easier.

There is one public bus coming and going to La Fortuna: it departs La Fortuna at 7am, and returns to the town at 5pm.

A private **shuttle bus** (Map p250; ☑ 8887-9141; Calle 472; US$10) runs from the Super Christian #1 in La Fortuna (45 minutes, US$10) at 9am, 1:30pm and 6:30pm. The shuttle runs from El Castillo to Fortuna at 8am, 10am and 4pm. Although this is a frequent service for workers, contact the father and son drivers Arturo and Luis in advance; their van will be either white, grey or green. This shuttle bus can also drop you at the entrance to the national park for US$4.

A new bridge (approved in 2019) crossing the Rancho Margot property is destined to cut the journey to Monteverde nearly in half, with vehicles able to avoid circling Laguna de Arenal.

Laguna de Arenal

About 18km west of La Fortuna you'll arrive at a 750m-long causeway across the dam that created Laguna de Arenal, the largest lake in the country at 88 sq km. Arenal and Tronadora were submerged during its 1979 creation, but the lake now supplies valuable water to Guanacaste, sport fish such as rainbow bass and hydroelectricity for the region. High winds also produce power with the aid of huge steel windmills, though windsurfers and kitesurfers frequently steal a breeze or two.

Circling the lake is one of the premier road trips in Costa Rica. The road is lined with odd and elegant businesses; strong winds and high elevations give the lake a temperate feel and the scenic views of lakeside forests and Volcán Arenal are about as romantic as they come.

🏃 Activities

Laguna de Arenal offers scores of secluded bays and coves to explore as well as a forested island. You'll usually find a kayak concession set up on the dam's western end, but take care because when the wind kicks in it can be a nightmare to make it back. This is also a popular route for cycling (inquire at Bike Arenal, p252), and the area has a few other attractions.

Mistico Hanging Bridges CANOPY TOUR
(Puentes Colgantes de Arenal; Map p254; ☑ 2479-8282; www.misticopark.com; adult/child US$24/free, tours US$36-47; ⊙ 7:30am-4:30pm, tours 6am, 9am & 2pm) Unlike the fly-by view you'll get on a zip-line canopy tour, a walk here allows you to explore the rainforest and canopy at a more natural and peaceful pace, via six suspended bridges and 10 traditional bridges. All are accessible from a single 3km trail that winds through a tunnel and skirts a waterfall.

The longest swaying bridge is 97m long and the highest is 25m above the ground. Reservations are required for guided birdwatching tours or informative naturalist tours. The Tilarán bus can drop you off at the entrance, but it's a 3km climb from the bus stop. There are also loads of tours from La Fortuna, and you can book directly at Mistico's office, 25m north of Banco Nacional.

Arrive early for peace and the best chance to see wildlife.

Fishing Lake Arenal FISHING
(Marc El Belga; Map p254; ☑ 8389-2989; www.fishinglakearenalcr.com; sunset/half-/full-day tours US$150/275/400) For more than two decades Marc, aka 'Marc el Belga' ('the Belgian'), has been helping visitors find the big ones in the depths of Arenal: rainbow bass, machaca and the delicious guapote. It's hard to miss him. There is an extra charge per person after two people.

Arenal Kayaks KAYAKING
(☑ 2694-4336; www.arenalkayaks.com; 2hr tour US$35) Take a two-hour guided paddle on Laguna de Arenal, including wildlife-watching and swim stops. Longer tours can be customized for the fit paddler. Hotel pick-up included.

Represa Arenal

Forget for a moment that there are always ecological issues associated with dams and revel in the fact that this one created a rather magnificent lake (it took a village, or two, in the exchange). In the absence of wind, the glassy surface of Represa Arenal (Arenal Dam) reflects the volcano and the surrounding mountains teeming with cloud forest. Formerly, crowds congregated to admire the view and snap photos. Safety reasons have compelled the authorities to clear this area to avoid traffic snarls, so it's not recommended to stop for the obligatory selfie any longer.

🛏 Sleeping

Arenal Lodge LODGE $$
(Map p254; ☑ 2479-1881, toll-free in US 1-800-716-2698; www.arenallodge.com; incl breakfast d standard/superior US$115/120, f US$150, ste US$180; ℗✳🛜🏊) Arenal Lodge is at the top of a steep 2.5km ascent, and the entire lodge offers views of Arenal and the surrounding cloud forest. Standard rooms are just that, but the spacious junior suites are tiled and have wicker furniture and a picture window or balcony with volcano views.

The grounds are crisscrossed by hiking trails, and the lodge also has a Jacuzzi, billiards room, restaurant and private stables. Just off Ruta 142.

Lost Iguana RESORT $$$
(Map p254; ☑ 2479-1557; www.lostiguanacr.com; r/ste/casita incl breakfast US$275/299/525; ℗✳@🛜🏊) This resort, just 1.5km from the dam, is set among lush rainforest and rushing streams with glorious views at every turn. Luxurious rooms have private

WORTH A TRIP

WINDSURFING

Consistent winds blow across northwestern Costa Rica, and this consistency attracts wind riders. Laguna de Arenal is rated one of the best windsurfing spots in the world; kitesurfers flock here too. From late November to April, **Tico Wind** (☎8383-2694, 2692-2002; www.ticowind.com; SUP/kitesurf/windsurf rental per day US$40/99/109, windsurfing lessons per hr US$50) sets up camp on the lake shore and offers lessons in both. It has state-of-the-art boards and sails, with equipment to suit varied wind conditions. The launch is located 15km west of Nuevo Arenal. The entrance is by the big white chain-link fence with 'ICE' painted on it – there's a blue-and-white sign announcing 'Windsurf Lessons Fun!' Follow the dirt road 1km to the shore. It gets a little chilly on Laguna de Arenal, but rentals usually include wetsuits, as well as harnesses and helmets.

balconies looking out on Arenal, plus beds with Egyptian cotton sheets, a terracotta wet bar and an invaluable sense of peace and privacy.

Upgrade to a suite for a Jacuzzi or outdoor rain shower. Also on the grounds: a romantic restaurant, a gorgeous bi-level pool with swim-up bar, and the well-equipped Golden Gecko Spa.

Getting There & Away

The Represa Arenal (Arenal Dam) is about 18km west of La Fortuna. It's an easy drive if you have your own vehicle. If not, there are plenty of tour operators (or taxis) who will bring you to this corner of the region. You can also wait for the bus to Tilarán, which runs twice a day.

Nuevo Arenal

POP 2600

A rest stop for travelers heading to Tilarán and points beyond, Nuevo Arenal is certainly a pleasant (and cheap) place to spend the night. The tiny downtown has a gas station, two banks, a supermarket and a bus stop near the park. It even has a rickety old *plaza de toros* (bullring).

In case you were wondering what happened to old Arenal, it's about 27m below the surface of Laguna de Arenal. In order to create a large enough reservoir for the dam, the Costa Rican government had to make certain, er, sacrifices, which ultimately resulted in the forced relocation of 3500 people. Today the humble residents of Nuevo Arenal don't seem to be fazed by history, especially since they now own premium lakeside property.

Sleeping

There are a few budget options right in town, in addition to the expat-owned properties that line the lake.

Aurora Inn HOTEL $

(☎2694-4245; r US$24; P @ ☎) You'd never know it from the street, but these rooms are rather sweet, spotless and spacious wood-cabin-like constructions with lovely lake views and vaulted beamed ceilings. It could use a bit of freshening up, though. Located on the eastern side of the square, across from the sports field, it's one of the only budget options on Laguna de Arenal.

The attached restaurant does decent pizza. The property was for sale at the time of research.

★**La Ceiba Tree Lodge** LODGE $$

(☎2692-8050, 8313-1475; www.laceibalodge.com; s/d/tr/q from US$65/90/115/135; P ❄ ☎) About 22km west of the dam, this lovely, laid-back lodge overlooks a magnificent 58m ceiba tree. Seven spacious Spanish-tile rooms are hung with original paintings and fronted by Maya-inspired carved doors. Each room has rustic artifacts, polished-wood ceilings and vast views of Laguna de Arenal. The tropical gardens and spacious terrace make this mountaintop spot a tranquil retreat. Three 'comfort rooms' with queen beds and nicer bathrooms cost US$30 extra.

Owner Dirk founded one of Costa Rica's first beer gardens, the Maya Lounge, in San José, before heading to the countryside of Arenal.

Agua Inn B&B $$

(☎2694-4218; www.aguainn.com; Ruta 142; d incl breakfast US$80; P ☎ ≋) The sound of the rushing river will lull you to sleep at this intimate B&B on the banks of the Río Cote. This gorgeous property is designed for total relaxation, with a jungle-shaded pool and private lake trail. Four simple rooms feature soothing tones and plush linens (100%

cotton, please!). A shared balcony provides a lovely view over the property.

Lucky Bug B&B
B&B $$

(☑2694-4515; www.luckybugcr.net; d/ste incl breakfast from US$100/125; ℗📶🌊) Set on a rainforest lagoon 3km west of Nuevo Arenal, the five blissfully isolated bungalows at the Lucky Bug feature works and decorative details by local artisans. Here are blond-wood floors, wrought-iron butterflies, hand-painted geckos, mosaic washbasins and end tables. Each room is unique and captivating. There's a rainforest trail in the grounds and kayaks for use on the lagoon.

The onsite Caballo Negro Restaurant features hearty German fare (think *spätzel* and schnitzel). The fabulously quirky Lucky Bug Gallery features the handiwork of co-owner Monika and others.

Villa Decary
B&B $$

(☑2694-4330, in US or Canada 1-800-556-0505; www.villadecary.com; r US$125, casitas US$160-185; ℗✳📶) This country inn 2km east of Nuevo Arenal is an all-round winner, offering epic views and unparalleled hospitality. Rooms feature bright serape bedspreads and original artwork, and have balconies with vistas of the woodland below and the lake beyond. *Casitas* (sleeping four) have full kitchens. Birds and botany are why the owners came here; you'll see a lot of both.

Decary also boasts one of the best collections of palm trees in Costa Rica, which explains why it's named for a French botanist who discovered a new species of palm.

And where else would they store your pillows in a humidity-free closet until you arrive?

La Mansion
INN $$$

(Map p254; ☑2692-8018; www.lamansionarenal.com; d/ste incl breakfast from US$175/295; ℗📶🌊) About 15.5km east of Nuevo Arenal, the cottages, pool and restaurant at La Mansion enjoy amazing lake views. The large split-level rooms feature king-size beds, private terraces and mural-painted walls. The fabulous infinity lap pool is surrounded by a relaxing patio and an ornamental garden featuring indigenous pottery. Or jump in the Jacuzzi to wind down. Lovely all around.

With a bar shaped like the bow of a ship, onsite restaurant Le Bistro is a romantic spot for lunch or dinner, with panoramic views from the dining room and outdoor patio. It has a substantial menu of well-prepared European food (four different *croques*!). There's quite a show at sunset.

✖ Eating

Nuevo Arenal is a surprising little foodie Shangri-la, with enough eating options to keep you out of the kitchen for at least a week. In addition to the charming (and quite delicious) places in town, you'll also find one of the country's top-rated restaurants in a charming and disarming 'gingerbread' house on the lake shore.

★ Casa Italia
SICILIAN $$

(☑8333-4792; Nuevo Arenal; mains US$12-22; ⊙noon-9pm Thu-Tue) Charming Christian, from the Sicilian highlands, has created a lakeside wonder, featuring both open-air and indoor dining. Southern Italian specialties such as arancini (rice balls) with his special *sugu* (sauce), and pizzas with pesto, tuna and other toppings, set the table for scrumptious tiramisu or panna cotta, which you'll try unsuccessfully to resist. Add a glass of Montepulciano: perfection.

Tinajas Arenal
CAFE $$

(☑8926-3365, 2694-4667; www.facebook.com/LasTinajaArenal; mains US$9-17; ⊙9am-9:30pm; 📶🌊🍴) 🍴 With glorious sunsets and a dock for boat access, this is a hidden gem. The chef – who works in tandem with his talented mom Cinia – has created a menu of traditional favorites and new surprises, using fresh seafood and organic ingredients grown right here.

The big new thing is the Black Angus Texan beef (steaks US$30 to US$40), which sits well alongside one of the bottles of Chilean or Argentine wine (US$30 to US$50 a bottle). Sample the refreshing cocktail *a la casa, limon hierba* (lemonade with mint).

You will find it at the southern end of Nuevo Arenal, turn off the main road and follow the signs.

Los Platillos Voladores
ITALIAN $$

(☑2694-5005; www.facebook.com/losplatillos voladores; mains US$6-14; ⊙noon-8pm) The plates really do fly out of this carry-out joint right in the center of Nuevo Arenal, which gets raves for its homemade pasta. It's mostly Italian – the eggplant Parmesan is delectable – and Emi's homemade lasagnas and raviolis come well recommended, as does the fresh *mozzarella di bufala* from nearby Upala. Enjoy the views of the lake from the patio.

In an effort to scare off tourists, the sign outside reads 'the worst restaurant in the world.' Don't believe it for a minute.

Moya's Place CAFE $$
(☎2694-4001; Ruta 142; mains US$8-16; ⊙11am-9pm) Murals, masks and other indigenous-inspired art adorn the walls at this friendly cafe. Take your pick from the delicious sandwiches, well-stuffed wraps and burritos, and tasty thin-crust pizza (the Canadian 'Eh' features bacon, ham, mushroom and onion). Ticos and expats gather here to eat, drink and laugh. The food is good and the beer is cold.

Las Delicias SODA $$
(☎8320-7102; mains US$5-14, breakfast US$5-6; ⊙7am-9pm; 📶) A cheap and cheerful *soda* near the top of the hill as you approach town, with ample wooden-table seating. It does Western-style breakfasts, pasta dishes, quesadillas and grilled steaks, but it's known for Berta's *casados*. More adventurous eaters may sample the marlin and tuna fillets, fresh from the waters off Puntarenas.

Tom's Pan BAKERY $$
(German Bakery; ☎2694-4547; www.facebook.com/tomspangermanbakery; Ruta 142; mains US$9-16; ⊙8am-4:30pm Mon-Sat; P 📶) Better known as the 'German bakery,' thanks to the signs that litter the lake road, this landmark is a famous rest stop for road-trippers heading to/from Tilarán. Its breads, strudels and cakes are all homemade, and it also has wursts, potato salad and pretzels, and more than 20 beers, Tico and German (Erdinger) alike. Cash only.

★Gingerbread Hotel & Restaurant INTERNATIONAL $$$
(☎2694-0039, 8351-7815; www.gingerbreadarenal.com; Ruta 142; mains US$25-40; ⊙5-9pm Tue-Sat; 🍷) Larger-than-life chef Eyal turns out transcendent meals from the freshest local ingredients (some from the gardens outside). Favorites include mushrooms smothered in cream sauce, tuna poke and (occasionally) local lamb and duck. Enormous, juicy burgers. It's big food that goes down well. Reservations recommended.

If you want to sleep where you eat, book one of the sweet boutique rooms upstairs or adjacent to Gingerbread, each showcasing fabulous murals and other artwork by local creatives.

ℹ Getting There & Away

Nuevo Arenal is 27km west of the dam, or an hour's drive from La Fortuna. There's not much public transportation in these parts, except the twice-daily bus that runs between La Fortuna and Tilarán.

West End of Laguna de Arenal

The hamlet of Piedras anchors the western end of Laguna de Arenal. It's more of an intersection than a town, but it has attracted a group of expats who appreciate the spectacular lakefront scenery and the proximity to Tilarán. This is also where most of the windsurfing takes place.

Sleeping

There's plenty of good karma at this end of the lake, where you can stay in one of two uplifting yoga lodges.

★Living Forest B&B $$
(☎8708-8822, 7031-3239; www.livingforestlakearenal.com; d with bathroom US$70, dm/d/tr/q without bathroom US$40/55/75/85; P 📶 🏊) Interior designer, massage therapist, yogi and free spirit: Johanna Harmala has combined these traits to create this inviting, inspiring retreat on the banks of the Río Sabalito, about 15km west of Nuevo Arenal. The jewel-toned rooms are furnished with attractive walnut beds, with shared or private access to beautiful open-air stone bathrooms. Minimum two-night stay; rates for longer stays are negotiable.

There's a swimming hole, as well as yoga and spa services, and a variety of feel-good workshops throughout the year.

Mystica Lodge LODGE $$
(☎2692-1001; www.mysticacostarica.com; incl breakfast d US$110-160, villa US$195; P @ 📶) Here's an invitation to relax and reconnect – with nature, your body and your breath. Comfortable, colorful rooms have Spanish-tile floors, woven bedspreads, wooden accents and an inviting front porch with volcano views. Yoga and meditation classes are held in a gorgeous sheltered hardwood yoga space overlooking a gurgling creek, and there's a tree-house healing center for Reiki and massage.

The organic garden supplies many of the ingredients for breakfast and dinner. The pizzas from the unique wood-burning oven are a fave among guests.

Eating & Drinking

There are only a few restaurants strung out along the western end of Laguna de Arenal, but they are varied and the food is delicious. You'll have no problem finding a lunch stop to please everyone in the car.

Equus Bar-Restaurant BARBECUE $$

(☎8389-2669; mains US$6-14; ⏰11am-midnight) Follow your nose to this authentic stone-built tavern, 14.5km west of Nuevo Arenal, where the meat is cooked in an open fire pit, producing decadent, delicious aromas. Take a seat at a wooden-slab picnic table and dig in. A local favorite, this place has been run by the same family for more than a quarter of a century.

Every two or three months, Equus turns into a live-music venue/disco – The Pukka Waiku – featuring music from *ranchero* to reggae. Check their Facebook for details.

Café y Macadamia CAFE $$

(☎2692-2000; www.facebook.com/cafeymacadamia; pastries & coffee US$2-4, mains US$6-13; ⏰8am-5pm; P 📶) Kind of a tourist trap. The souvenir shop is a turnoff, and US$4 is a lot for a muffin, even if the banana macadamia muffins *are* accompanied by a cup of Tico coffee and a spectacular view over Laguna de Arenal. About 15km west of Nuevo Arenal, this is a convenient pit stop: the lot fills with buses and bikes.

Lake Arenal Hotel & Brewery BREWERY

(☎2695-5050; www.lakearenalhotel.com; just off Ruta 142; ⏰11am-9pm; 📶) If you like beer, consider staying at the only hotel (that we're aware of) that has an onsite microbrewery, mixing up the hops and barley to bring you eight delicious and unusual beers, such as the Jungle Dunkle and Piña Blonde. Drink it while feeling the lake breezes and admiring the views at the top-floor restaurant, which serves standard pub grub.

High season features live music between Thursday and Sunday. The hotel and brewery are located just off Route 142, before you reach the village of Tejona.

The hotel itself has 21 rooms (single/double including breakfast from US$55/75, dorms US$20) which are acceptable, considering the location, though curtains are tissue-paper thin. You'll pay more for lake views and private patios. There's also a tennis court, skatepark and solar-powered Jacuzzi.

Getting There & Away

There's not much public transportation in these parts, except the twice-daily bus that runs between La Fortuna and Tilarán. Pledras is where you can get off the bus to reach the destinations around here, but you'll need a taxi from there to travel out to them. Although for some stops on the bus route, you can ask the driver to let you off.

LOCAL KNOWLEDGE

THE SCENIC ROUTE

If you're driving between Arenal and Monteverde, consider taking the scenic route through Tronadora and Río Chiquito instead of driving through Tilarán. The distance is a bit longer and the roads are a bit rougher, but the marvelous vistas are well worth it. Look for the turnoff to Río Chiquito about 1km east of Tronadora. Note: if you go this route, there are no gas stations between Nuevo Arenal and Santa Elena, and the gas gets guzzled on the rough mountain roads. Make sure you fill up when you can.

San Luis & Tronadora

San Luis and Tronadora are tiny twin communities on the southern side of Laguna de Arenal. They are the last outposts of civilization before the landscape gets swallowed by eternal rainforest (the Children's Eternal Rainforest – Bosque Eterno de Los Niños – to be exact) further south and east. The 'old' Tronadora did in fact get swallowed up by Arenal's waters when the dam was built.

A small contingent of travelers trickles through here – mostly windsurfers and wanderers – but this wild and windy corner of the lake feels blissfully undiscovered.

Sleeping & Eating

Monte Terras B&B $$

(☎2693-1349; www.monteterras.com; d incl breakfast US$85; P 📶) Set amid a blooming, bird-filled garden in Tronadora, here you'll find a handful of comfy *cabinas*, each with high ceilings, polished concrete floors, colorful paint jobs and tropical artwork. Dutch/Tica partners Kees and Griselda go out of their way to make sure their guests are content. Be warned that this place is really windy from December to March. It's about 70 km from La Fortuna on Ruta 142.

Brisas Del Lago SODA $

(☎2695-3363; San Luis; mains US$6-11; ⏰11am-10pm Tue-Sat, from 1pm Sun; P 📶) If you don't mind a little detour, here is your lunch stop between Monteverde and Arenal. Simple Tico fare is done with panache at this dressed-up *soda*. It marinates chicken breasts in its own BBQ sauce, skewers Thai-style shrimp and slathers up teriyaki chicken. The garlic fish is sensational. Just past the Catholic church in the community of San Luis.

Getting There & Away

On the southern side of Laguna de Arenal, the main lake road (Ruta 142) takes a sharp turn south to head toward Tilarán. If you take the northbound road instead, it quickly turns to gravel and descends into San Luis and, 3km further, Tronadora.

Tilarán

POP 8700

Near the southwestern end of Laguna de Arenal, the small town of Tilarán has a laid-back charm thanks to its long-running status as a regional ranching center. It's also the main commercial center for the growing community of expats along the shores of Arenal.

Most visitors, however, are just passing through, traveling between La Fortuna and Monteverde.

Waiting here for the next bus? Enjoy an ice cream under the peach-colored spaceship-like structure in the main plaza while admiring the modernistic church, which rivals the beauty in nearby Cañas. Or catch a lift (or walk) up to the Puente de Vista, with ocean views, dominated by a huge cross.

Sights

★Viento Fresco WATERFALL

(☎2695-3434; Ruta 145, Campos del Oro; adult/child US$16/12, horseback tour US$55/45; ⏰7:30am-5pm) If you're traveling between Monteverde and Arenal, there's no good excuse for skipping this stop. Viento Fresco is a series of five cascades, including the spectacular Arco Iris (Rainbow Falls), which drops 75m into a refreshing shallow pool that's perfect for swimming. There are no crowds or commercialism to mar the natural beauty of this place. You'll probably have the falls to yourself, especially if you go early in the day.

Add on a horseback riding tour or grab lunch at the restaurant to support this family-run operation. It's located 11km south of Tilarán on the road to Santa Elena (a US$15 cab ride from Tilarán).

The 1.3km of trails are maintained, but the stone steps can be slippery, especially after a rainfall, and only the reasonably fit can hike to the bottom and back.

Festivals & Events

Vuelta al Lago Arenal SPORTS

(www.vueltaallagoarenal.com; ⏰Mar) They say that it's virtually impossible to circumnavigate the lake under your own steam. But *they* have never participated in the Vuelta al Lago Arenal, an annual event in March, when some 4000 cyclists do just that. It takes two days – one off-road and one on – to complete the 148km route. Most participants camp along the route.

Transportation of camping equipment is provided but participants are responsible for their own provisions.

Sleeping & Eating

Right in the center of town, you'll find a few restaurants catering to the drive-through traffic between La Fortuna and Monteverde. Cheaper meals can be found in the *mercado* (market) beside the bus terminal, or pop into the supermarket across from the park.

Hotel Wilson Tilarán HOTEL $

(☎2695-5043; Calle 2; s/d without bathroom US$14/22, with bathroom US$20/26; P) This is as cheap as they come, and rooms are tiny and cleanish. If you can get one of the rooms toward the back, this is a decent budget choice on the western side of Parque Central – and just a half block from the bus terminal. It's a typical no-frills Wilson hotel, but with flat-screen TVs.

There's a retro bar, Encuentro, on the street front, which opens at midnight (not recommended).

BUSES FROM TILARÁN

DESTINATION	COMPANY	COST (US$)	DURATION (HR)	FREQUENCY
Cañas	Transporte Villana	1	40min	15 daily Mon-Sat, 5am-7:45pm (8 daily Sun)
Monteverde/Santa Elena	TransMonteverde	3	2½	7am, 12:15pm, 3:30pm, 4pm
La Fortuna	TransMonteverde	5	3	7am, noon, 3:30pm
San José	Pulmitan	8	4	5am, 7am, 9:30am, 2pm daily; 5pm Sun only

WORTH A TRIP

VENADO CAVES

Two kilometers northeast of Venado (Spanish for 'deer') along a good dirt road, the **Venado Caves** (Cavernas de Venado; Map p254; 2478-8008, 8653-2086; www.cavernasdelvenadocr.com; adult/child US$28/25, photographer US$20; 8am-3pm, last admission 2:30pm) are an adventurous excursion into an eight-chamber limestone labyrinth that extends for almost 3km. A bilingual guide leads small groups (up to seven) on two-hour tours through the darkness, squeezing through narrow passes and pointing out the most interesting rock formations (an altar, a papaya) while dodging bugs and bats (12 species in all – the vampires have darker poop from their iron-rich blood diet). Rubber boots, headlamps and helmets – plus a shower afterwards – are provided.

You'll definitely want to bring a change of clothes. It's better to spring for their photographer to take some snaps (US$20) than to lose your precious phone in the murky waters. Trust us.

Any tour operator in La Fortuna can arrange this trip for you. If you're driving yourself, the caves are well signed from Hwy 4. One bus at 9am comes straight here from La Fortuna (US$2.75, one hour). Otherwise, other Upala-bound buses can drop you at Jicarito, 9km from the caves. From the Jicarito *cruz* (crossing) it's simple to catch a lift uphill from one of the local farmers. Cash only if paying at the caves. There's also a pool and restaurant here.

Hotel Cielo Azul HOTEL $$
(2695-4000; www.cieloazulresort.com; d incl breakfast US$75; P) Situated 500m before town, when coming from Nuevo Arenal, this hillside property has 12 rooms with tiled floors, whitewashed walls and new bathrooms. There's a good-size pool, heated by solar panels, with a waterslide and a pretty spectacular vista. A convenient jumping-off point for lake or volcano activities.

A newer suite with Jacuzzi and microwave goes for US$150.

Hotel Guadalupe HOTEL $$
(2695-5943; www.hotelguadalupe.co.cr; Av 4, near Calle 1; s/d incl breakfast US$42/60; P) This modern hotel attracts traveling business types, who tuck themselves into simple rooms dressed up with jewel tones and tiled floors. Service is friendly and efficient. There is a decent restaurant onsite, plus a swimming pool and kids' pool. Bigger family rooms are available, but only some rooms have air-con. Exercise bikes and a ping-pong table complete the poolside entertainment.

Getting There & Away

Tilarán is 24km east of the Interamericana at Cañas, and 75km east of La Fortuna via the paved but winding lake road. The route from Tilarán to Santa Elena and Monteverde is paved for the first stretch, but then it becomes steep, rocky and rough. Just drive carefully on the bumpy bits.

BUS

Buses arrive and depart from the terminal half a block west of Parque Central. Be aware that Sunday afternoon buses to San José can sell out as much as a day in advance. There is also a direct bus service to Puntarenas (US$3, two hours, 6am).

NORTHERN LOWLANDS

In the far reaches of the Northern Lowlands, the vast, steamy stretches of pineapple and banana plantations intermingle with rainforest, wetlands and some undisturbed wilderness. Once a hotbed for Contras and *contrabandistas* (smugglers), this sector is now crisscrossed by swift highways, well trafficked by trucks laden with fresh-picked fruit and hefty cattle on their way to market. Many travelers cruise right through, heading to the Caribbean coast. But those who venture off the highway and brave the bumpy roads will be rewarded. The waterways along the Nicaraguan border provide habitats for an enormous diversity of bird life. Keep your eyes peeled, and you may even spot the rare great green macaw, which is making a comeback in these parts.

Upala

POP 6100

Just 9km south of the Nicaraguan border in the northwestern corner of this region, Upala is a small *ranchero* town with a bustling market and plenty of good *sodas*.

Most visitors are Costa Rican businesspeople who come to negotiate for a few dozen calves or a truckload of grain. You may change buses here going between the Volcán Tenorio area and the Caño Negro, but there's no reason to linger.

Sleeping & Eating

Cabinas Maleku CABINA $
(2470-0142; Av 3; d with/without air-con US$32/20; P ❄ 📶) Wrapping around a gravel parking lot, set just off the main plaza, these cute and comfortable *cabinas* are blessed with mosaic-tile patios decorated with hand-painted Sarchí-style wooden chairs and plenty of potted plants. It's a cheerful cheapie, for sure. There's an attached *soda* too.

Hotel Wilson Aeropuerto HOTEL $
(2470-3636; www.hoteleswilson.com/upala; d incl breakfast US$50; P ❄ 📶 🏊) This is a business-motel-style facility with a popular bar and restaurant and a big (temperate water) Jacuzzi-fed swimming pool. The 63 rooms are plain but clean, with mostly wood furniture and linoleum floors, plus other appreciated amenities. You'll need a car to reach this location, or derring-do if you're walking the 1.5km from town.

Rancho Don Horacio COSTA RICAN $
(2470-3222; Av 7; mains US$6-9; 11am-11pm) If you need a place to rest your weary feet while awaiting the next bus (the terminal's just 300m away) you can't do much better than Horacio's. The decorations, as they are, consist of soccer paraphernalia and Elvis bric-a-brac. The menu leans on ocean fish and local beef. Fun, lively family joint with televised *fútbol* on every wall.

Trivia: it's named for a local pilot who died doing some aerial daredevilry after a few too many *cervezas*.

Getting There & Away

From Upala, the well-maintained, paved Hwy 6 runs south via Bijagua, intersecting with the Interamericana just north of Cañas. Hwy 4, also paved, runs in a more southeasterly direction to Muelle de San Carlos (near La Fortuna). A rough, unpaved road, usually passable to all cars, skirts the Refugio Nacional de Vida Silvestre Caño Negro on the way to Los Chiles, the former official border crossing with Nicaragua.

Confusingly, there are two bus terminals – the new inter-regional one (built after Hurricane Otto in 2016) lies 1.5km from the center; the other (municipal) is nearer the main square. Most buses go through both, and also stop on the main plaza. For long-distance buses (ie San José or Nicaragua), your best bet is the new terminal. Taxis congregate here too.

Destinations include:

Ciudad Quesada (San Carlos) US$4.86, 2½ hours, 10 daily, 3:30am to 6pm

San José (via Bijagua and Cañas) US$9, five hours, 4:30am, 5:15am, 9:10am, 9:30am and 2pm

Caño Negro US$2.50, two hours, 4am, noon and 4:30 pm Mon-Sat, noon only Sun

Some of the San Carlos buses pass through Guatuso.

Refugio Nacional de Vida Silvestre Caño Negro

Part of the Area de Conservación Arenal-Huetar Norte, this remote, 102-sq-km **refuge** (2471-1309; www.sinac.go.cr; US$5; 8am-4pm) has long lured anglers seeking that elusive 18kg snook, and birders hoping to glimpse rare waterfowl. During the dry season water levels drop, concentrating the birds (and fish) in photogenically (or tasty) close quarters. From January to March, avian density is world class.

The Río Frío is a table-flat, swampy expanse of marsh and lagoon that is similar in appearance, if not size, to other famous wetlands such as the Florida Everglades or the Mekong Delta. North of town, it's a slender river that carves through looming forest. During the wet season, the river breaks its banks to form one immense 800-hectare lake. By April it has almost completely disappeared – until the May rains begin. This cycle has continued without fail for millennia, and the small fishing communities around the its edges adapt to each seasonal nuance.

Activities

Caño Negro is regarded among birdwatchers as one of the premier destinations in Central America. During the dry season, the sheer density of birds in the park is astounding, but the variety of species is also impressive. At last count, more than 300 species of bird live here at least part of the year. In the winter months, there are huge congregations of migratory ducks, as well as six species of kingfisher, herons, cormorants, three types of egret, ibises, rails, anhingas, roseate spoonbills, toucans and storks. The refuge is also one of the reliable sites in Costa Rica for neotropic cormorants, Nicaraguan grackles and lesser yellow-headed vultures.

Conspicuous reptiles include the spectacled caiman, green iguana and striped basilisk. Howler monkeys, white-faced capuchins and two-toed sloths are common. Despite incursions from poachers, pumas, jaguars and tapirs have been recorded here in surprising numbers.

Caño Negro is also home to an abundance of river turtles, which were historically an important part of the Maleku diet. Prior to a hunt, the Maleku would appease the turtle god, Javara, by fasting and abstaining from sex. If the hunt was successful, the Maleku would later celebrate by feasting on smoked turtle meat and consuming large quantities of *chicha,* a spirit derived from maize. And, well, they probably had some sex too.

Mosquitoes in Caño Negro are damn near prehistoric. Bring bug spray or suffer the consequences.

Tours

Hiring a local guide is quick, easy and full of advantages – you'll pay less, you'll be supporting the local economy and you'll have more privacy when you're out on the water. If you're spending the night in the area, your lodge can make arrangements for a tour. Otherwise, there are a few local outfits with an office (or at least a sign) in the village center, or just walk down to the pier early in the morning.

Sportfishing trips can also be arranged through the lodges. Be sure to inquire about obtaining a seasonal fishing licence, which is normally required. (Bring your passport.)

Chambita's Tours BIRDWATCHING
(☎8412-3269; www.facebook.com/chambita.romero; half-/full-day birding tour 2 people US$80/140) Barnaby Romero Hernandez, known locally as 'Chambita', is a rising star in the naturalist community, well respected for his vast birding knowledge. He also leads fishing trips on the river. He doesn't have a fixed office but can be reached by phone or his Facebook page.

Pantanal Tour BOATING
(www.facebook.com/pantanal.toursa) Join Marlon Castro and Juan Ríos for sportfishing or ecological tours of the lagoon (two-hour tour US$50 for two people; bigger groups US$20 per person). Boats hold up to 28 people. They also lead horse-riding trips and kayaking outings. The office is located just before the church as you walk into town.

Also offers lodgings (US$40 with fan, US$60 with air-con).

Paraíso Tropical BOATING
(☎8823-4026 WhatsApp, 2471-1621; https://paraisotropicalcanonegro.business.site; kayak/horse/boat tours US$10/30/50; ⏲8am-4pm) Joel Sandoval Bardos does a variety of nature tours around the refuge, including a two-hour boat tour of the lagoon (up to four people). There is no office, but a WhatsApp should do the trick.

Joel guided a trip on the Río Frío in 2014 that bagged a world-record 14.5kg tropical gar.

Sleeping & Eating

Caño Negro is a small village, meaning all the lodges have easy access to the lagoon.

Kingfisher Lodge CABINA $
(☎2471-1116; www.kingfisherlodgecr.com; r US$40-60; P ⊖ ❄) Located about 400m from the village center, these rustic *cabinas* surround a well-kept lawn; all have heavy wood furniture, hammock-strung porches and air-con. Your host, don Antonio, is an absolute charmer. The reception is located 400m to the east, in a house at the opposite end of the main town square.

A two-hour river tour for up to four people costs US$60.

Hotel de Campo Caño Negro LODGE $$
(☎2471-1012; www.hoteldecampo.com; s & d incl breakfast US$95; P ❄ ☜ ≋) Set in an orchard of mango and citrus trees next to the 'Chapel' lagoon, this friendly hotel is a fisher's and birdwatcher's paradise. After angling for tarpons or spying on spoonbills, relax in the ceramic-tiled *casitas,* decked out with vaulted beamed ceilings and tasteful bedding. The stylish restaurant serves top-notch Italian fare and seafood.

Boats, guides, kayaks and fishing equipment are all available for hire. Owner Mauro will proudly lead you around his tropical 'botanical garden' of more than 25 orchid and 150 tree species.

★ Caño Negro Natural Lodge LODGE $$$
(Hotel Natural Lodge Cano Negro; ☎8547-0437, 2471-1426; www.canonegrolodge.com; d incl breakfast US$160; P ❄ ☜ ≋) Perched on land that becomes a virtual island in the Río Frío during the rainy season, this lodge

is surprisingly upscale. Well-appointed rooms have sliding glass doors, wooden and wrought-iron furnishings, and tiny terraces facing the garden. Relax in the pool or Jacuzzi or stroll the leafy grounds. Just off the main road before Caño Negro's main plaza.

Staff can make arrangements for boat tours of the lagoon. There's a lovely patio restaurant serving freshly prepared meals (US$10 to US$16) and a friendly bartender who will bend your ear as you bend your elbow. Lunch and dinner are extra, but worth the price.

Buses will stop at the 'front door.' If you are driving on Ruta 35 towards Los Chiles, exit the highway 8km before Los Chiles when you see the signs for the lodge.

Information

Visitors to the park should stop at the **ranger station** to pay their admission fee. It's located on the western edge of the village, near the Kingfisher Lodge, but is not always attended. Note that there are no banks or gas stations in town.

Getting There & Away

Thanks to improved roads, tour operators are able to offer relatively inexpensive trips to Caño Negro from all over the country. However, you don't need them to explore the river. It's much more intriguing and rewarding to rent some wheels (or hop on a bus), navigate the rutted road into the rural flatlands and hire a local guide from Caño Negro village. It's also a lot cheaper, and it puts money directly into the hands of locals, thus encouraging communities in the area to protect wildlife.

The village of Caño Negro and the entrance to the park lie on the rough road connecting Upala and Los Chiles, Ruta 138, which is passable to all cars during the dry season. However, this road is frequently washed out during the rainy season, when a 4WD is required.

During the rainy season and much of the dry season, you can also catch a boat to and from Los Chiles, but this is only by private reservation – at Paraíso Tropical (p273) in Caño Negro, or at the dock in Los Chiles – for US$200.

In addition, the following bus routes serve Caño Negro village:

Los Chiles (US$2, one hour) Departing Los Chiles at 5am and 2pm; departing Caño Negro at 6:30am, 1pm and 6pm.

Upala (US$2.50, 2½ hours) Departing Upala at 4am, 11:30am and 4pm; departing Caño Negro at 6:30am, 1pm and 3pm.

Los Chiles

POP 9900

Seventy kilometers north of Muelle on a smooth, paved road through the sugarcane, and just 6km south of the Nicaraguan border, lies the sweltering farming and fishing town of Los Chiles. Arranged around a soccer field and along the banks of the leisurely Río Frío, the humid lowland village was originally settled by merchants and fisherfolk who worked on the nearby Río San Juan, much of which forms the border.

With the opening of the new border crossing at Las Tablillas, travelers to and from Nicaragua hardly ever pass through Los Chiles, but it remains an enjoyable water route to Caño Negro.

Tours

Los Chiles is a nice alternative base to organize boat trips to Caño Negro. Inquire at Restaurante Heliconia about these trips. Otherwise just head to the dock, where you can hire boat captains to take you up the lovely, chocolatey Río Frío during the dry season and all the way into Lago Caño Negro during the rainy season.

Three- to four-hour trips cost about US$70 for a small group. If possible, make arrangements a day in advance and get an early start in the morning: the earlier out, the more you'll see.

Sleeping & Eating

With the new border crossing at Las Tablillas, it's usually possible to cruise right by Los Chiles without spending the night (there's nothing to hold you here, trust us). If that doesn't work for you, you'll find a limited selection of hotels in town.

Hotel y Restaurante Carolina CABINA $
(2471-1151; Av 2A, near Calle 5; r from US$30; P ❄ wifi) This friendly family-run option gets good reviews for attentive staff, spotless rooms and above-average local food. It's near the main highway, just four blocks south of the bus terminal. There is no attendant on Sundays, so you'll have to phone to see a room.

Restaurante Heliconia COSTA RICAN $
(2471-2096, 8307-8585; Av Central (Av 0), near Calle 4; mains US$6-10; 6am-10pm) Across from the immigration office and next to Hotel Wilson Tulipán, this is a decent option for lunch or a smoothie. It also provides

GETTING TO NICARAGUA

If you're heading north to Nicaragua, be thankful for the 2015 construction of the Puente Santa Fe, a bridge that crosses the Río San Juan just north of the Nicaraguan border. As a result, there is now a border crossing at **Las Tablillas**, 6km north of Los Chiles:

- The border crossing at Las Tablillas (open 8am to 5pm) now handles a good amount of the Costa Rica–Nicaragua traffic, so you might encounter some lines depending on when you decide to cross.
- Hourly buses connect Los Chiles and Las Tablillas (US$1, 10 minutes). Or, get the bus directly from San José or Ciudad Quesada (San Carlos). These buses run daily.
- You will have to pay a Costa Rica land exit fee of US$8 at immigration, payable by credit or debit card only (no cash).
- After walking across the border, you'll go through Nicaraguan immigration. The entrance fee is US$12, payable in cash only (US dollars or cordobas). It's good to have small bills (US$1 and US$5) because change is hard to come by.
- After exiting immigration, you can catch a boat up the river or hop on a bus or a *collectivo* to San Carlos (bus US$2.50, *collectivo* US$2.20, 40 minutes).

If you are entering Costa Rica from Nicaragua, you can take an hourly bus to Los Chiles or Ciudad Quesada or catch the direct bus to San José, which departs at 2:30pm.

The old-fashioned river route to cross the border, for the adventurous types, is unfortunately no longer an option.

information on tours and transportation; ask Mayra or Oscar about boat trips to Caño Negro.

Information

Banco Nacional (☎2212-2000; Av 1, btwn Calles 0 (Calle Central) & 1; ⊙8:30am-3:45pm Mon-Fri) Close to the central park and soccer field, changes cash and has a 24-hour ATM.

Cruz Roja (Red Cross; ☎2471-2025, 2471-1037; cnr Calle 2 & Av 1; ⊙24hr) Located at the northwestern corner of the plaza.

Getting There & Away

BOAT

The boat docks are about 1km west of the bus terminal. With the opening of the land border at Las Tablillas, this river border is pretty sleepy; as of 2019, it was no longer possible to cross the border by boat. You can take a Río Frío tour from one of the boat captains, such as the ever-amiable Alejandro Alesandro (%7245-2643; US$70, four hours).

BUS

All buses arrive and leave from the **terminal** (Av 1, near Calle 5) behind Soda Pamela, near the intersection of Hwy 35. **Chilsaca** (☎2460-1886; www.chilsaca.com; Plaza San Carlos) has 16 daily buses to Ciudad Quesada (US$2.25, two hours) from 4:30am to 6pm; you can transfer here for La Fortuna. Autotransportes San Carlos (p99) has two daily buses to San José (US$6, five hours), departing at 5am and 3pm. There are also three departures to Caño Negro (US$4, 40 minutes) at 5am, noon and 4:30pm. Timetables are subject to change, so always check ahead.

CAR

You're likely to get here via Hwy 35 from Muelle. Skid marks and reptilian roadkill break up the beautiful monotony of orange groves, sage-blue pineapple fields and dense sugarcane plantations. More scenic (and bumpier) is the road running for 50km from Upala, through Caño Negro.

San Rafael de Guatuso

POP 8600

Centrally located off Hwy 4, the small town of San Rafael de Guatuso is the main population center of this agricultural area. The humble town is a decent base for exploring the fantastic Venado Caves to the south and is nearly equidistant to the blue waters of Río Celeste and the Parque Nacional Volcán Tenorio to the west, Arenal to the south and Caño Negro to the north. The area is also home to the few remaining indigenous Maleku, who reside in *palenques* (indigenous settlements) near here.

Sleeping & Eating

Cabinas Los Almendros CABINA $
(☎8887-0495; cabinaslosalmendros@gmail.com; Av 12, near Av 10; s/d/tr incl breakfast US$35/40/50; P❄📶) A cute family-run motel with well-maintained rooms, lovely bedding and cute curtains. Each room is named after a different jungle beast or bird, complete with hand-carved wooden sculptures. Set on the edge of town behind the Banco Nacional, this is easily the best choice in Guatuso.

The folk at Los Almendros can provide information on tours to the Maleku reservation and Río Celeste (Parque Nacional Volcán Tenorio).

Soda La Suyapa SODA $
(☎2464-0402; Hwy 4, near Calle 1A; mains US$4-8; ⊙6am-8pm) Recommended by locals as the best *soda* in this humble town, La Suyapa offers a fresh take on the traditional. *Casados* come with noodles and potato salad unless you request otherwise. *Bebidas* include options such as fresh-pressed carrot juice and fresh-squeezed lemonade. There are also burgers and excellent fried chicken. Soda La Suyapa is located right off the highway.

Getting There & Away

Guatuso lies on Hwy 4, midway between Upala and Muelle de San Carlos (about 40km from each). Buses leave frequently for Ciudad Quesada, where you can connect to La Fortuna. There is also one daily bus to Tilarán (three hours, 7:30pm) via Nuevo Arenal, and three daily buses to San José (five hours, 8am, 11:30am and 3pm).

From Guatuso, a paved road covers the 21km to the entrance of Parque Nacional Volcán Tenorio and onward to Bijagua. It's a smooth ride with stunning views.

Muelle de San Carlos

POP 4900

This small crossroads village – locally called Muelle – was once an important dock (hence the name) as it's the most inland spot from which the Río San Carlos is navigable. These days it's sugarcane country and serves as a rest stop for truckers and travelers. It's only 27km east of La Fortuna. Come for the iguanas!

Sights

Centro Turistico Las Iguanas BRIDGE
(Iguana Bridge; ☎2462-1107; www.facebook.com/LasIguanasSanCarlos) This bridge is a popular spot for tourists en route from La Fortuna to Caño Negro. Countless iguanas hang out in the bamboo and trees above the river, providing some great photo ops. Walk across the bridge to see how many you can count – but watch your step! The bridge is 1.8km north of the main intersection in Muelle, where Ruta 35 takes a sharp turn to cross the river.

Sleeping & Eating

Turismo Rural de Juanilama AGRITURISMO $
(Comunidad Agroecológica Juanilama; ☎8706-3914; www.turismoruraljuanilama.org; Juanilama, off Hwy 35; US$35, tours US$15-20; 📶) Seven kilometres north of Santa Rosa de Pocosol, off Hwy 35, is this opportunity to be part of rural life. This cooperative, female-driven effort took root more than 15 years ago and now involves 90 local families. You stay in one of the comfortable and modern family homes: you may even end up watching Tico *telenovelas* (soap operas) over breakfast.

While here, you can take a hike in the 19-hectare reserve, learn about the crops and various home remedies, and make a bit of sugarcane water. Options include a tour of the dairy, a cooking class and a walk to the waterfalls.

Tilajari Resort Hotel RESORT $$
(☎2462-1212; www.tilajari.com; d incl breakfast from US$116; P❄@📶) This country club turned luxury resort has well-landscaped grounds overlooking the Río San Carlos and comfortable, well-appointed rooms. Amenities include racquetball and tennis courts, restaurant, pool, sauna, spa and butterfly garden, plus access to the neighboring 400-hectare private rainforest reserve with several trails. The resort is 800m west of the intersection at Muelle, on the road to Ciudad Quesada.

The facilities are a bit dated but the place offers good value for the price.

Subasta Ganadera Sancarleña STEAK $$
(☎2462-1000; www.subastasganaderascr.com; mains US$4-12; ⊙bar & restaurant 10am-11pm) Overlooking a bull pen, this place is bustling with hungry *campesinos* (farmers). It has an expansive menu of local dishes,

WORTH A TRIP

PROYECTO ASIS

It's an animal rescue center. It's a volunteer project. It's Spanish classes. **Proyecto Asis** (2475-9121; www.institutoasis.com; adult/child US$35/20, incl volunteering half-day US$58/35, full-day US$93/55; tours 8:30am & 1pm Mon-Fri) is a community-based organization doing a lot of good, and you can help. The introductory experience is a two-hour tour of the wildlife rescue center, but it's worth springing for the half- or full-day 'volunteering' experience, which includes hands-on interaction with the animals. You'll see monkeys and birds, as well as *pizotes* (coatis), peccaries and more. Close-toed shoes are obligatory; bug repellent is recommended.

Most the animals have been seized from private hands (it's illegal in Costa Rica to have wild animals as pets) and some, but not all, are returned to the wild. There are also wild, uncaged animals onsite, such as birds – including a growing colony of boat-billed herons, toucans and manakins – plus caimans and bats. Keep a sharp eye out.

Asis also offers homestays in the local community. It's located in Jabillo, about halfway between Ciudad Quesada and La Fortuna. Any Fortuna–Quesada bus which passes through Chachagua (US$2.80, 40 min) can drop you here; just ask the driver. Asis can also arrange a taxi for you. Reserve at least a day in advance.

and is a great spot for a cold beer. Come for lunch on Tuesday or Thursday to see the cattle auction. It's 100m north of the gas station.

Getting There & Away

A 24-hour gas station lies at the main intersection of Hwy 4 (which connects Ciudad Quesada and Upala) and Hwy 35 (running from San José to Los Chiles). Buses pass through en route to all of those destinations.

Ciudad Quesada (San Carlos)

The official name of this small city is Ciudad Quesada (sometimes abbreviated to 'Quesada'), but all the locals know it as San Carlos, and local buses often list San Carlos as the destination. We'd like to think the 'cheesy' name stems from its position as the country's number one dairy supplier, but it might just have been someone's name.

It's long been a bustling ranching and agricultural center, known for its *talabaterías* (saddle shops). Although San Carlos is surrounded by pastoral countryside, the city has developed into the commercial center of the region. The main reason to enter the city is to change buses..

Activities

Ciudad Quesada is not exactly a destination in itself. But if you're driving this way, why not stop for a soak? Popular with Tico families, the thermal pools here are an affordable and pleasant alternative to the overdone, overpopulated springs in La Fortuna. The hot springs and resorts are located about 8km east of town, heading toward Aguas Zarcas.

El Tucano Resort & Thermal Spa HOT SPRINGS
(2460-6000; www.eltucanoresort.com; Ruta 140, La Marina de San Carlos; US$20; spa & thermal pools noon-10pm;) A posh but aging resort, set amid gorgeous primary forest. Thermal springs feed three pools of varying temperatures – perfect for soaking away your ills. The spring-fed river that streams through the property creates warm, delightful rapids. It's family friendly and the pools are open late. Frequented much more by Ticos than foreigners.

The spacious colonial-style rooms (doubles US$120 to US$135; suites US$145 to US$200) enjoy forest views from the terrace.

Termales del Bosque HOT SPRINGS
(2460-4740; http://hoteltermalesdelbosque.com; Ruta 140; adult/child US$12/6; 8am-10pm) Luxury here is low-key, with therapeutic soaking available in seven natural hot- and warm-water springs. The stone pools are surrounded by lush greenery and built into the riverbank, in a forested valley populated by morpho butterflies. About 10km east of Ciudad Quesada on Ruta 140, just down the road from El Tucano.

Sleeping & Eating

Apart from the plethora of chain restaurants, you'll find a few decent local *sodas* near the park. The restaurants at the resort are also good options (albeit more expensive).

Tree Houses Hotel HOTEL **$$**
(☎2475-6507; www.treehouseshotelcostarica.com; Ruta 141, Florencia de Santa Clara; d incl breakfast US$135-220, extra person US$20; P❄☎) Fulfil your childhood fantasy with a couple of nights in an awesome treetop hideout. With solid wood construction and big windows facing the rainforest, the comfortable cabins have all the ground-level amenities you would expect (including air-con), plus fabulous wrap-around porches that bring you even closer to the birds and monkeys. About 17km northwest of Ciudad Quesada (San Carlos).

Rates include a guided hike in the surrounding 36-hectare forest preserve. Assuming you have your own vehicle, it's within striking distance of the activities around Arenal, but removed from the hullabaloo. It's 300m north of the cemetery in Santa Clara. A two-night minimum stay is required.

Getting There & Away

Terminal Quesada is about 1km from the town center. Taxis (US$1) and a twice-hourly bus (US$0.50) make regular runs between town and the terminal, or you can walk if you don't mind hauling your luggage uphill. Popular bus routes from Ciudad Quesada are listed below.

Boca Tapada Area

This has long been an off-the-beaten-track destination for adventurous souls. However, that's all changing with the inevitable paving of Costa Rica. On the roads that pass pineapple fields and packing plants, your fellow travelers will be local residents going about their day-to-day business. And at the end of the road, you'll be rewarded with a luxuriant bit of rainforest replete with the sounds of frogs and rare birds, and an inkling of the symbiosis that can happen when humans make the effort. Local lodges offer tours into the Refugio Nacional de Vida Silvestre Mixto Maquenque.

Sleeping

Mi Pedacito de Cielo LODGE **$$**
(☎8308-9595, 7177-0708; www.pedacitodecielo.com; s/d/tr incl breakfast US$73/91/110; P☎) Perched above Río San Carlos, 'My Little Piece of Heaven' is a rustic retreat, and don Marco is keeping apace with the times, paving the parking area, adding internet and doubling the number of bungalows to 30 in recent years. Super-friendly service and don Marco's excellent home-cooked meals are perks. Situated 36km north of Pital, just off the main road.

Bungalows have river and rainforest views. There are hiking trails in the attached 300-hectare reserve. Three plusher rooms with all the modern trappings such as air-con are located 2km away from the lodge proper, next to beautiful Laguna Vicripalma (named for Mario's children). It's walking or driving distance to dinner, but right at the

BUSES FROM CIUDAD QUESADA

DESTINATION	COMPANY	COST (US$)	DURATION (HR)	FREQUENCY
Aguas Zarcas	Transportes Pital	0.90	45min	10 daily, 7:15am-7:15pm
La Fortuna	Transpisa	2.60	1½-2	16 daily, 4:30am-10pm
Los Chiles	Chilsaca	5	2	14 daily, 4:15am-7:30pm; direct bus 3pm
Puerto Viejo de Sarapiquí	Transportes Linaco	4	2	8 daily, 4:40am-6:30pm
San José	Autotransportes San José-San Carlos	3.50	2½	daily 5am-7:30pm
Upala	Transportes Upala/Transpisa	4	3	9 daily, 4:25am-10:10pm

foot of the reserve. It now offers opportunities for photography and fishing in magical Laguna Cureña, just up the road.

Swing in the hammock-chair and listen to the rainforest come alive.

Laguna del Lagarto Lodge LODGE **$$**
(☎7216-4190, 2289-8163; www.lagarto-lodge-costa-rica.com; s/d/tr US$65/75/85; P) Surrounded by virgin rainforest, this outpost is legendary among birders. Basic screened rooms share large, hammock-strung verandas. It's not fancy, but it's wild and lovely, with feeders and fruit attracting toucans, tanagers and more. The lodge is about 35km north of Pital on the main road, and then about 2km from the turnoff for the lodge.

There are 16km of trails, and canoes to explore the surrounding lagoons, where caimans dwell and Jesus Christ lizards make tracks across the water's surface. Breakfast costs $10 extra.

★**Maquenque Eco-Lodge** LODGE **$$**
(☎2479-7785; www.maquenqueecolodge.com; incl breakfast s/d/tr from US$111/138/164, tree houses s/d/tr US$167/207/246; P) Set on 80 glorious bird-filled hectares, 20 unique bungalows (including five gobsmacking tree houses) overlook a lagoon and tropical garden; additional tree houses are perched in nearby rainforest. To get here, you'll have to cross the San Carlos River in one of the lodge's boats; arrange your boat crossing ahead of time.

Prices include a guided rainforest hike, a student-led tour of a local school and use of canoes on the lagoon, as well as the opportunity to support sustainable tourism by planting a tree in the rainforest (by request). There's also a tour of the *finca* where many of the vegetables you'll eat for supper are grown. A new pergola and changing rooms for the pool are other improvements.

The place is a birders' (and photographers') paradise, with countless species flocking to feeders and fruit trees in the grounds. In addition to birds, encountering a roving band of coatis might make your day, too.

ℹ Getting There & Away

Getting to Boca Tapada can be an adventure in itself. The nearest town of note is Pital, north of Aguas Zarcas. About 2km north of Pital, take a right at the fork (after the bus stop) and follow the signs. After the town of Saino, the last 15km are a tad rough and bumpy. Even this bit of fun should be muted; at the time of research, the road was due to be paved.

Buses reach Boca Tapada on a 1½-hour trip from Pital, departing Pital at 10:30am and 4:30pm. Leaving Boca Tapada, the buses to Pital depart at 5:30am and 12:30pm (the early bus goes past the lodges; for the second bus, check with your lodge). You can reach Pital on frequent buses from Ciudad Quesada (US$2, 1½ hours) or four daily buses from San José (US$4, four hours).

The lodges can also arrange transfers from La Fortuna or San José.

SARAPIQUÍ VALLEY

This flat, steaming stretch of *finca*-dotted lowlands was once part of the United Fruit Company's vast banana holdings. Harvests were carried from the plantations down to Puerto Viejo de Sarapiquí, where they were shipped downriver on boats destined for North America. In 1880 a railway connected rural Costa Rica with the port of Puerto Limón, and Puerto Viejo de Sarapiquí became a backwater. Although it's never managed to recover its former status as a transport route, the river has again shot to prominence as one of the premier destinations in the country for kayakers and rafters. With the Parque Nacional Braulio Carrillo as its backyard, this is also one of the best regions for wildlife-watching, especially considering how easy it is to get here.

San Miguel

POP 2300

Coming from San José or Alajuela, Hwy 126 curves up the slopes of the Cordillera Central, leaving behind the urban bustle and passing Volcán Poás before descending again into pastureland. This is *campesino* country where the plodding hoofbeat of cattle is about the speed of life, as the hard-to-spot rural speed bumps will remind you if you take those curves too quickly. You're off the beaten track now, and if you're self-driving, you may as well linger; there are few Costa Rican corners quite this beautiful and unheralded.

☞ Tours

Mi Cafecito FOOD & DRINK
(☎2476-0215; www.micafecitocoffeetour.com; tour US$24; ⊙8am-5pm) About 5km south of San Miguel, in the foothills of Volcán Poás, Mi Cafecito makes for the perfect coffee break if

you're heading to/from the Sarapiquí Valley. Including more than 200 small farmers, this co-op shows off the whole process of growing, harvesting and roasting coffee beans, especially using organic farming practices.

The walk through the farm also yields expansive views of the gorgeous Sarapaquí Valley.

Even if you don't want to take a tour, there is a big shady cafe where you can get a cup o' Joe (and food too). A package tour includes lunch.

Sleeping & Eating

The best lunch stop near San Miguel is 5km south of town at Mi Cafecito (p279). In town, there is at least one *soda* that promises breakfast, as well as birdwatching, tourist information, *cabañas* and clean bathrooms.

★ **Albergue El Socorro** FARMSTAY $$
(☎8820-2160; www.alberguelsocorrosarapiqui.com; per person incl meals US$75; P @) Albergue El Socorro is a small family *finca*, located 1000m above sea level on a plateau surrounded by a magnificent knife's edge of green mountains, tucked between the looming Cerro Congo and Volcán Poás. There are three cozy A-frame cabins, from where guests can explore trails through the rainforest, discover waterfalls, swim in rivers or help on the dairy farm.

The owner was born and raised here, but in 2009 a massive earthquake struck the area, destroying the road to San Miguel along with his home and dairy. This wonderful family rebuilt the ranch from scratch and incorporated a tourism component, which provides a rare opportunity to slow down and experience authentic rural Tico living. This is the real *pura vida*. From San Miguel, turn off Hwy 126 east onto Calle a El Socorro, just before the cemetery if you're headed north, and then head south.

Getting There & Away

From Ciudad Quesada (San Carlos), Hwy 140 heads east for about 40km before terminating sharply when it runs into Hwy 126. This intersection – in the hills of the Cordillera Central – is where San Miguel is. You can't miss the sharp turn as the two highways merge and continue north for 12km toward La Virgen. If you're coming from La Virgen, it's about 15km south of downtown.

La Virgen

POP 2250

Tucked into the densely jungled shores of the wild and scenic Río Sarapiquí, La Virgen was the premier kayaking and rafting destination in Costa Rica for more than a decade. But the tremendous 2009 earthquake and landslide altered the course of the river and flattened the town's tourist economy. Some businesses folded, others relocated to La Fortuna, and a few held on. Now independent kayakers are starting to come back and there are a couple of river outfitters offering exhilarating trips on the Class II–IV waters of the Río Sarapiquí.

As well as tourism, La Virgen's economy has long relied on fruit exports, and the town remains dependent on its nearby pineapple fields.

Sights

Dave & Dave's Nature Park BIRDWATCHING
(☎506 2761 0801; www.sarapiquieco-observatory.com; US$40; ⏲by guided tour only) Father and son Dave and Dave greet all comers to this 4.5-hectare reserve on the Río Sarapiquí, 200m north of the cemetery. You don't have to be a birder to get great glimpses or photos from the two viewing platforms, with feeders attracting toucans, trogans, tanagers and 10 species of hummingbird. Follow one of the Daves on a trail system that winds through secondary forest all the way down to the river. A welcome bonus is the free coffee.

There are no scheduled tour hours, but one of the Daves should be able to help you upon arrival.

Snake Garden ZOO
(☎2761-1059; adult/child US$22/16; ⏲9am-5pm) Come face to face with 50 species of reptile and amphibian, including poison-dart frogs, rattlesnakes, crocs and turtles. The star attraction is a gigantic 80kg Burmese python. In addition, you'll see every freshwater turtle Costa Rica has to offer, plus a butterfly garden. It's 200m north of the cemetery.

Sleeping

There are cheap digs in town, or consider staying in one of the more interesting lodges on the road to Puerto Viejo.

Tirimbina Rainforest Center & Lodge LODGE $$

(☎2761-0333, 2761-0055; www.tirimbina.org; incl breakfast dm from US$65, r US$95-117, day pass US$18; P❄@☎) Situated 2km from La Virgen, this is a working environmental research and education center. The spacious accommodations are located at the lodge or at a more remote field station; dorms without bathrooms, as well as doubles, are on offer. Tirimbina reserve has over 9km of trails; tours include birdwatching, an educational bat program, night walks and a recommended chocolate tour.

The 345-hectare private reserve is connected to the nearby Sarapiquís Rainforest Lodge by two long suspension bridges. The island between is not open to the public. Esteemed international bat researcher Bernal Rodriguez Herrera of the University of Costa Rica does much of his work here.

Hacienda Pozo Azul BUNGALOW $$

(☎2761-1360, 2438-2616; www.haciendapozoazul.com; s/d/tr incl breakfast & dinner US$98/123/155; P@☎) Near La Virgen's southern end, Pozo Azul features stylish (and screened in) 'tent suites' scattered on the edge of the tree line, all on raised polished-wood platforms and dressed with plush bedding. At night, the frogs and wildlife sing you to sleep as raindrops patter on the canvas roof. There's a site for bonfires and a riverside basketball court.

Pozo Azul also has a bar-restaurant near the highway with a lovely riverside veranda, though it caters mostly to big tour groups. Either drive or catch a ride from the staff to get to the campgrounds, 3km from the main reception area.

Sarapiquís Rainforest Lodge LODGE $$

(☎2761-1415; www.sarapiquis.com; d with/without breakfast US$110/85; P❄@) About 2km north of La Virgen, this ecolodge offers bat-proof lighting and an education in environmental conservation and pre-Columbian culture. Modeled after a 15th-century pre-Columbian village, the *palenque*-style thatched-roof buildings contain sparse, spacious rooms, with huge solar-heated bathrooms and shared circular balconies. The restaurant incorporates ingredients used in indigenous cuisine. A stunning infinity pool stretches into the rainforest.

Eating & Drinking

El Chante SODA $

(☎2761-0032; www.facebook.com/restauranteelchante; mains US$8-12; ⏰11am-11pm) This La Virgen favorite has welcoming service and the food is tasty and filling. The place is popular (and it has televisions); it can get loud, and now that Heiner's opened a large cocktail bar in the back, your eardrums are guaranteed a pounding as strong as your hangover tomorrow. About 800m south of 'downtown' La Virgen, on the highway.

Bar & Cabinas El Río BAR

(☎2761-0138; ⏰noon-10pm) At the southern end of town, turn off the main road and make your way down to this atmospheric riverside hangout, set on rough-hewn stilts high above the river. Locals congregate on the upper deck to sip cold beers and nosh on filling Tico fare (mains US$6 to US$9).

This place also has A-frame bungalows (with fan/air-con US$15/20) near the road.

Getting There & Away

La Virgen lies on Hwy 126, about 8km north of San Miguel and 17km west of Puerto Viejo de Sarapiquí. It's a paved but curvy route (especially heading south, where the road starts to climb into the mountains). Buses ply this route from San José via San Miguel to Puerto Viejo, stopping in La Virgen along the way. Local buses run hourly between La Virgen and Puerto Viejo de Sarapiquí (US$1, 30 minutes) from 6am to 8pm.

The newish Vuelta Kooper Chilamate Hwy, aka Hwy 4, connects Sarapiquí Valley to Muelle and beyond, cutting the trip to La Fortuna to about one hour.

Chilamate & Around

The narrow, paved Hwy 4 runs for about 15km between La Virgen and Puerto Viejo, connecting a few farming villages such as the don't-blink-or-you'll-miss-it hamlet of Chilamate. On the northern side, the road is lined with small businesses, prosperous family *fincas* and acres upon acres of pineapple plantations. On the southern side is the wild Río Sarapiquí, providing a dramatic landscape for a handful of excellent ecolodges.

Beyond the river, these lodges are surrounded by their own private reserves of primary and secondary forest, crisscrossed

RUNNING THE SARAPIQUÍ

The Río Sarapiquí isn't as wild as the white water on the Río Pacuare near Turrialba, but it will get your heart racing. Even better, the dense jungle that hugs the riverbank is lush and primitive, with chances to glimpse wildlife from your raft.

You can run the Sarapiquí year-round, but December offers the biggest water. The rest of the year, the river fluctuates with rainfall. The bottom line is: if it's been raining, the river will be at its best. Where once there were nearly a dozen outfitters in the La Virgen area, now there are just a handful, but all offer roughly the same Class II–IV options at similar prices. (Class IV has some restrictions in terms of experience and costs more).

Aguas Bravas (2292-2072, 2761-1645; www.aguasbravascr.com; rafting trips US$65-80, safari float US$65; 9am-5:30pm) This well-established rafting outfit has set up shop along Río Sarapiquí (complete with onsite hostel). Aguas Bravas has two tours on offer: take a gentle safari float to spot birds, iguanas, caimans and other wildlife, or sign up to splash through 14km of 'extreme rapids' on the San Miguel section of the river. Both include lunch and snack. It now offers a curious nighttime 'Ant Tour' (US$15) which traces the life cycle of the ubiquitous leaf-cutter ants.

Aventuras del Sarapiquí (2766-6768; www.sarapiqui.com; river trips US$60-95) This highly recommended outfitter offers land, air and water adventures. In addition to white-water rafting (both Class II and III/IV trips), you can also fly through the air on a 12-cable canopy tour, or stay down to earth with horseback riding, mountain biking or hiking. Mellower options include canoeing the Rio Puerto Viejo, tubing and a motorboat tour. Save money and combine two of the tours in one package (US$109). Situated just off the highway. For the Class IV rapids, a minimum of four experienced people are required.

Sarapiquí Outdoor Center (SOC; 2761-1123; www.costaricaraft.com; 2/4hr rafting trip US$65/90, guided kayak trips from US$90) David Duarte is the local paddling authority. In addition to its own rafting excursions, SOC offers kayak rental, lessons and clinics. Located about 18km southwest of Sarapiquí, off Hwy 126.Indie paddlers should check in for up-to-date river information. If you need somewhere to sleep before you hit the water, you can crash in the simple rooms (from US$25) or camp in one of the all-inclusive tents (from US$15) – no equipment necessary. There's now a handy restaurant to satiate clients who have worked up an appetite on their adventure.

Green Rivers (2766-5274; www.sarapiquigreenrivers.com; tours US$60-85;) Operating out of Posada Andrea Cristina B&B (p284), this outfit is run by the ever-amiable Kevín Martínez and his wife, Evelyn. Offers a wide variety of rafting and kayaking tours, from family-friendly floats to adrenaline-pumping rapids-surfing rides. Natural history and bird tours, too. New offers include mountain biking and trekking.

by hiking trails. And beyond that, the landscape merges seamlessly into the unexplored northern reaches of Parque Nacional Braulio Carrillo (p145). Technically, travelers cannot access the park from here, but nothing stops the wildlife – an enormous diversity of birdlife and even mammals such as monkeys, kinkajous and peccaries – from sneaking out and spying on unsuspecting passers-by.

The whole region – from La Virgen to Puerto Viejo – is defined by the Río Sarapiquí. Several of the river-running companies have set up shop east of town.

Tours

While agriculture remains the primary money-maker in the region, tourism also has a role to play in the local economy. Entrepreneurial local farmers supplement their agricultural activities with farm tours, allowing visitors a view into Tico rural lifestyles, sustainable farming practices, and the ins and outs of producing delicious food.

Costa Rica Best Chocolate FOOD & DRINK
(8501-7951, 8816-3729; adult/child US$34/23; tours 8am, 10am, 1pm & 3pm) Where does chocolate come from? This local Chilamate family can answer that question for you,

starting with the cacao plants growing on their farm. The two-hour demonstration covers the whole chocolate-making process, with plenty of tasting along the way. Buy one of their four artisanal bars at tour's end. About 5km west of downtown Puerto Viejo, on the main highway.

Organic Paradise Tour FOOD & DRINK
(☎2761-0706; www.organicparadisetour.com; adult/child US$35/14; ⊙tours 8am, 10am, 1pm & 3pm) Take a bumpy ride on a tractor-drawn carriage and learn everything you ever wanted to know about pineapples (and peppers). The two-hour tour focuses on the production process and what it means to be organic; it also offers real insight into Costa Rican farm culture, as well as practical tips such as how to choose your pineapple at the supermarket.

The tour is educational and surprisingly entertaining. And, of course, you get to sample the goods (a midday piña colada? Why not?). Located 1km from the Chilamate school and 4km north of the main highway – follow the signs for 'Tour de Piña/Organic Paradise Tour.'

Sleeping & Eating

This scenic stretch of Hwy 126 and Hwy 4 is home to a few excellent ecolodges. Good news for budget travelers: you don't have to stay at them to take advantage of their private trails and other interesting attractions.

Isla del Río HOSTEL $
(☎2766-6525; www.aguasbravascr.com; dm US$15, r with/without bathroom US$50/40; P 📶) After riding the rapids, you can hunker down at this riverside hostel, operated by Aguas Bravas. It's a clean, basic setup with solid wooden beds, clean bathrooms and hearty breakfasts (US$6). There are trails for exploring, as well as an outdoor hangout area where you can lounge in a hammock, listen to the rushing river and recall your rafting adventure.

Rooms can be rented as dorms or as privates. On the main highway about 6km west of Puerto Viejo.

★Chilamate Rainforest Eco Retreat LODGE $$
(☎2766-6949; www.chilamaterainforest.com; incl breakfast dm US$30-35, s/d/tr/q US$90/113/135/155; P 📶) Family-run and family-friendly, this inviting and innovative retreat is dedicated to protecting the environment and investing in community. Built on 20 hectares of secondary forest, the basic, solar-powered cabins are full of character, with handcrafted furniture and natural air cooling. Rates include one guided 90-minute walk at 8am. Located just off the main highway, about 5km west of Puerto Viejo.

Two larger rooms with kitchenettes (US$140 to US$160) hold up to seven people. The restaurant serves incredible breakfast and dinner buffets, using local, organic ingredients. Covered flat walkways allow you to move between buildings in the complex without ever getting wet (after all, this is the rainforest!). Behind the cabins, 6km of paths wind through the jungle, where you're likely to spot sloths, monkeys, toucans, frogs, snakes and more. And when you can't take the heat, head to the nearby river swimming hole, complete with Tarzan swing from the bridge.

La Quinta de Sarapiquí Lodge LODGE $$
(☎2761-1052; www.laquintasarapiqui.com; d/tr/q US$125/140/155; P ❄ 📶 🏊) At this family-run lodge on the banks of the Río Sardinal, covered paths crisscross the landscaped garden, connecting thatched-roof, hammock-strung rooms. Swim in the pretty mineral pool or the nearby swimming hole; stroll through the frog house, caiman enclosure and butterfly garden; or hike trails through secondary forest. Your rocking chair will face the garden or river. Breakfast US$10.

Even if you're not staying here, you can get a day pass (US$15) to explore the animal exhibits and hiking trails. A new offer is the El Patio tour of the free-range, hormone-free and free-thinking pigs, chickens and lamb at the *finca* up the hill. Farm-to-table lives and breathes here – your morning eggs or evening lamb chops didn't travel far.

Selva Verde Lodge LODGE $$$
(☎2761-1800, in USA & Canada 1-800-451-7111; www.selvaverde.com; incl breakfast d US$155, bungalow d US$170; P ❄ 📶 🏊) This former *finca* in Chilamate is now an elegant lodge protecting 200 hectares of rainforest. Choose to stay at the river lodge, elevated above the forest floor, or in a private bungalow, tucked away in the nearby trees. Rooms have shiny wooden floors, solar-heated showers and wide verandas with forest views. All rooms have recently been expanded and air-con has been added.

Fortunate guests may get one of two rooms right on the river.

There are three walking trails through the grounds (one requires a guide) and into the premontane tropical wet forest, as well as a botanical garden, various boat tours on Río Sarapiquí and an onsite Italian kitchen overseen by humorous San Remo expat don Graziano.

Rancho Magallanes COSTA RICAN $
(2766-5606; chicken US$5-12; 10am-10pm) Rancho Magallanes is a sweet roadside restaurant with a wood-burning brick oven where it roasts whole chickens and serves them quite simply with tortillas and banana salsa. You can dine with the truckers by the roadside or in the more upscale riverside dining area, painted with colorful jungle scenes.

Getting There & Away

Any bus between La Virgen and Puerto Viejo de Sarapiquí can drop you off at the entrances to the ecolodges along Hwy 4, while a taxi from La Virgen will cost from US$8 to US$10.

Puerto Viejo de Sarapiquí

POP 9600

At the scenic confluence of the Ríos Puerto Viejo and Sarapiquí, this was once the most important port in Costa Rica. Boats laden with fruit, coffee and other commercial exports plied the Sarapiquí as far as the Nicaraguan border, then turned east on the Río San Juan to the sea.

Today the palm-shaded market town has made concessions to the new economy, with the local polytechnic high school offering students advanced tourism, ecology and agriculture degrees. The school even has its own reserve, laced with trails. Visitors, meanwhile, can choose from any number of activities in the surrounding area, such as birdwatching, rafting, kayaking, boating and hiking.

Tours

Oasis Nature Tours BOATING
(2766-6108, 2766-6260, 8816-6462; www.oasisnaturetours.com; full-day tour incl transportation from San José US$85-100, 2hr safari boat tour US$35) This is one of several companies running boat tours on the local rivers. Also offers ziplining, rafting and other guided adventures. Make a right out of the bus terminal, look for the sign marking an alley, then go down the alley and into the blue house.

Anhinga Tours BOATING
(2766-5858, 8346-1220; www.anhinga.jimdo.com; Av 7; tours per person US$25) This local outfit takes travelers out to explore the Río Sarapiquí and its tributaries. Located in one of the last houses on the left as you walk toward the river – it's a blue house with an awning, and is not always attended.

Sleeping

This stretch of jungle boasts quite a range of accommodations, from budget bunks in town designed for local long-term plantation workers to several excellent lodges on the outskirts.

Cabinas Laura CABINA $
(2766-6316; s/d US$25/30; P ❄ @) On the road to the pier, behind Banco Nacional, this place is quiet and cheap. The 22 rooms are simple but spotless, with shiny tiles, wooden furnishings and cable TV. Tica hostess Lilliana can show you to the hanging bridge which connects to some trails behind the property.

Posada Andrea Cristina B&B B&B $$
(8341-0493, 2766-6265; www.andreacristina.org; d incl breakfast US$64; P) On the edge of town and at the edge of the forest, this charming B&B is a rough-around-the-edges gem. Breakfast with the birds can't be beat, and night brings the enchanting symphony of the frog colony. Quaint cabins all have high beamed ceilings, colorful paint jobs and private terraces. There's also a tree house, built around a thriving inga tree.

Your delightful host, Alex Martínez, is also a birding guide, and bakes a mean loaf of bread. Because Green Rivers (p282) is based here, you can make this a base for a few days of differing sorts of adventures.

Hotel Gavilán HOTEL $$
(2234-9507; www.gavilanlodge.com; d/tr/q from US$70/85/100; P ❄) Sitting on a 100-hectare reserve just across the Sarapiquí from 'downtown', this former cattle *hacienda* is a birdwatching haven, with 5km of private trails. The rooms could really use a fresh coat of paint and some TLC, but the river views from some of them may make you forget all that.

WORTH A TRIP

CINCO CEIBAS

Finca Pangola (11 sq km) contains a swathe of dense, green primary rainforest, home to some of the country's oldest and largest trees. Including, yes, five glorious ceiba trees that you'll see as you walk 1.2km along the raised wooden jungle boardwalk. The stroll is paired with horseback riding, kayaking or an ox-cart ride for a carefully choreographed adventure.

Cinco Ceibas (2476-0606; www.cincoceibas.com; full-day tour incl lunch US$70-125) offers transportation for day-trippers from San José or La Fortuna. If you have your own wheels, it's a one-hour drive on mostly gravel roads from La Virgen. From the highway north of town, take the turn off to Pueblo Nuevo.

Hotel Ara Ambigua HOTEL $$
(2766-7101; www.hotelaraambigua.com; s/d/tr/q incl breakfast from US$95/95/112/128; P) About 1km west of Puerto Viejo, this countryside retreat (named for the great green macaw) offers oddly formal but well-equipped rooms, set on gorgeous grounds. There are birds buzzing in the luscious, blooming gardens, poison-dart frogs in the *ranario* (frog pond) and caimans in the small lake. There are three swimming pools (no caimans there).

Even if you're not staying here, the onsite restaurant, La Casona, is an excellent place to grab lunch and spy on your feathered friends.

Eating

Many of the lodgings in and around Puerto Viejo have onsite restaurants or provide meals. Otherwise, there are several *sodas* in Puerto Viejo de Sarapiquí and a supermarket at the western end of town. A couple of interesting restaurants are along the highway between Puerto Viejo and La Virgen (not your typical *sodas*).

Restaurante El Bambú COSTA RICAN $$
(Hotel El Bambú, Calle Central; mains US$8-12; 8am-10pm) Heaping helpings of Costa Rican food and other items dominate the menu: three different vegetarian pastas are on offer, as well as steaks, rice-and-beans with Caribbean chicken, sandwiches and a giant burger. The open-air *palapa* encourages you to linger and enjoy.

Restaurante y Pizzeria La Casona PIZZA $$
(2766-7101; www.hotelaraambigua.com; meals US$8-16; 8am-10pm) The restaurant at Hotel Ara Ambigua is particularly recommended for its oven-baked pizza and traditional homemade cuisine served in an open-air *rancho* (small house). If you're looking for something beyond the pizza/*casado* routine, try the tangy Frida Kahlo chicken.

Information

Banco Nacional (2766-5658; Av 7; 8:45am-4:30pm Mon-Fri) Near the dock.

Banco de Costa Rica (Calle Central; 9am-4pm Mon-Fri) At the entrance to the town.

Cruz Roja (administration 2764-2424, emergency 2766-6212; Av 4) provides medical care.

Getting There & Away

The **bus terminal** (Calle Central; 5am-7pm) is right across from the park, near Hotel El Bambú. Local buses run hourly between La Virgen and Puerto Viejo de Sarapiquí (US$1, 30 minutes) from 5am to 8pm.

Ciudad Quesada (Transportes Guapileños) US$3, two hours, departs nine times daily from 4:40am to 7pm.

Guápiles (Transportes Guapileños) US$2, two hours, departs 11 times daily from 5:30am to 7pm.

Río Frío 16 departures daily from 6am to 7pm.

San José (Autotransportes Sarapiquí and Empresarios Guapileños) US$4.90, two hours, departs 11 times daily from 5am to 5:30pm.

Estación Biológica La Selva

Not to be confused with Selva Verde Lodge in Chilamate, Estación Biológica La Selva is a working biological research station equipped with laboratories, experimental plots, a herbarium and an extensive library. The station is usually teeming with scientists and students researching the nearby private reserve.

The area protected by La Selva is 16 sq km of premontane wet tropical rainforest, much of which is undisturbed. It's bordered to the south by the 476-sq-km Parque Nacional Braulio Carrillo, creating a protected area large enough to support a great diversity of life. More than 886 bird species have been recorded here, as well as 120 mammal species (including 70 species of bat and five species of big cat), 1850 species of vascular plants (especially from the orchid, philodendron, coffee and legume families) and thousands of insect species – with 500 types of ant alone.

Tours

OTS La Selva Research Station HIKING
(☎ext 1340 2524-0607, in USA 919-684-5774; www.tropicalstudies.org/portfolio/la-selva-research-station; guided hike US$40, birdwatching hike US$50; ⏲guided hike 8am & 1:30pm, birdwatching hike 5:45am) Reservations are required for three-hour guided hikes with a bilingual naturalist guide. You'll head across the hanging bridge and into 57km of well-developed jungle trails, some of which are wheelchair accessible. Unguided hiking is forbidden, although you'll be allowed to wander a bit after your guided tour. You should also make reservations for the popular (early!) guided birdwatching hikes.

Sleeping & Eating

OTS La Selva Research Station LODGE $$
(☎2766-6565; www.tropicalstudies.org/portfolio/natural-history-visitors-la-selva; per person incl meals US$90-95; P wifi) Very basic but clean rooms equipped with twin beds, bathrooms, fans and balconies overlooking the forest. Prices include meals and two daily guided hikes. You'll walk about 15 minutes into the forest to reach your rainforest retreat – but even the wi-fi reaches out here, if the bats decide not to block the signal with their sonar.

Getting There & Away

Public buses between Puerto Viejo and Río Frío/Horquetas can drop you off along the highway, which is 1km from the entrance to La Selva. Alternatively, catch a taxi from Puerto Viejo (US$5.00), which is about 4km away.

Horquetas & Around

South of Puerto Viejo de Sarapiquí, pineapple plantations line Hwy 4 and sprawl all the way to the marshes and mangroves of the Caribbean coast. To the west, the rugged hills of the Cordillera Central mark the northeastern boundary of Parque Nacional Braulio Carrillo. Most travelers on this scenic stretch of highway are either heading to the Caribbean coast or to the Central Valley. However, some are pulling off the road to inhale *orejas* ('ears' in Spanish; huge discs of fried dough with sugar and syrup), and drink in some of the area's off-the-beaten-track destinations, such as a remote mountaintop retreat bordering the national park, a birder's and botanists' delight of heliconias and hummers.

Sights & Activities

Heliconia Island GARDENS
(☎2764-5220; www.heliconiaisland.com; self-guided/guided tours US$10/18; ⏲8am-5pm; P family) Down a rugged road and across the hanging bridge is home to more than 80 varieties of heliconias, tropical flowers, plants and trees. The 2 hectare island overlooking the Río Puerto Viejo is also a refuge for 228 bird species, including the sought-after dusky-faced tanager. Since the original owners sold up, the gardens are not as spectacular, though still great for birding.

Located about 5km north of Horquetas, across the road from the pueblo of Las Chaves (ask the bus driver to let you off there).

Guests can BBQ on a terrace overlooking the river and stay in immaculate raised cabins (d/q/apt from US$85/110/126) with stone floors and breezy balconies (one with bunk beds for families of four to six).

Frog's Heaven GARDENS
(Cielo de Ranas; ☎8891-8589, 2764-2724; www.frogsheaven.org; Horquetas; adult/child US$25/12; ⏲8am-8pm; family) The frogs hop free in this lovely tropical garden, a perfect habitat for more than 28 species. On bilingual guided tours you're likely to see old favorites such as the red-eyed tree frog and poison-dart frogs, as well as some lesser-known exotic amphibians, such as the translucent glass frog and the wrinkly Mexican tree frog. Come for the twilight tour (5pm) to see a whole different frog world. Find it diagonally across from the church.

It has opened a new area featuring snakes such as the fer-de-lance, eyelash pit viper, and false coral.

This place is also excellent for birding and has a mirador dedicated to photographing avian life. Reservations recommended.

Las Arrieras Nature Reserve BIRDWATCHING
(☎8510-4236; arrierasreserve@gmail.com; Horquetas; entrance US$5, full-day tour US$40) University of Costa Rica biologist David Segura offers informative birding and naturalist tours on his property, Las Arrieras ('the

army ants') Nature Reserve. He's just downhill from Yatama Ecolodge, and you can camp here, too (US$10).

Palmitour TOUR
(☎2764-1495; www.tourcert.org/en/community/palmitour; tour and lunch US$35) Stop here for a short tour of an organic palm plantation and to sample a menu consisting only of items made from hearts of palm, including lasagna, *ceviche* and flan. It caters to larger groups, but the short tour, hosted by doña Maria, is interesting. Cool birds, too. Reserve ahead. Located 800 meters north of the entrance to Ticari.

Sleeping & Eating

The tricky thing about the lodges in Horquetas is that they're not exactly in Horquetas. They use this address because it is the nearest vestige of civilization – but these lodges are out there. Make reservations and follow instructions on how to get there. And don't forget your sense of adventure (and humor), because you're going to need it.

There are not any noteworthy places to eat in Horquetas, but you'll find some good choices just 12km up the road in Puerto Viejo de Sarapiquí.

Yatama Ecolodge LODGE $$
(☎7015-1121; www.yatamaecolodge.com; per person incl 3 meals US$80) Willing to forgo some creature comforts for the chance to commune with the rainforest? At Yatama, you'll amble along wooden walkways above the forest floor, sleep in primitive wooden cabins with solar-fed electricity, and slog through the mud to glimpse frogs, birds and bugs. You'll eat three hearty meals cooked by a villager, and revel in the forest's vibrancy.

Staff pick you up in Horquetas to make the treacherous 45-minute drive up to the edge of the Parque Nacional Braulio Carrillo. Some intrepid *caballeros* ride horses all the way up from town: a wonderful way to connect with the landscape (not literally, we hope).

Yatama provides the rubber boots – you bring the repellent and adventurous spirit. One guided walk per day is included, and a neighboring biologist offers great tours.

Sueño Azul Resort RESORT $$$
(☎2764-1000; www.suenoazulresort.com; d US$165-198, extra person US$20; P❄📶🏊) Sueño Azul has a stunning perch at the confluence of the Ríos Sarapiquí and San Rafael. The vast property has hiking trails, a suspension bridge, a canopy tour and a waterfall, as well as a stable of gorgeous horses. The facility itself is looking worse for wear, but rooms are comfortable enough, with log beds and river views.

The restaurant, unfortunately, is overpriced and uninspiring.

Getting There & Away

About 12 smoothly paved kilometers from Puerto Viejo de Sarapiquí is the village of Horquetas. Taking a bus from Puerto Viejo de Sarapiquí, it's about 15 minutes (500 colones) to the village of Las Chaves, which is where you'll get off for Heliconia Island. Horquetas is another bit down the road. From Horquetas it's another 15km to Hwy 32, which connects San José to the Caribbean coast and bisects Parque Nacional Braulio Carrillo on the way to San José.

AT A GLANCE

POPULATION
Nicoya: 13,334

FAST FACT
An *arribada* (mass turtle nesting) at Playa Ostional sometimes sees as many as 300,000 olive ridley turtles nesting on the beach.

BEST SWIMMING BEACH
Playa Carrillo (p329)

BEST SURFING BEACH
Playa Santa Teresa (p332)

BEST BEACH BAR
Banana Beach (p338)

WHEN TO GO

Dec–Apr More sunshine, more surfers, more traffic, higher prices.

May–Nov Lower accommodation rates and fewer tourists.

Sep–Oct Increased rain causes rivers to swell; whales are migrating.

Península de Nicoya

Maybe you've come to the Península de Nicoya to sample the sapphire waters that peel left and right, curling into perfect barrels up and down the coast. Or perhaps you just want to hunker down on a pristine patch of sand and soak up some sun. By day, you might ramble down rugged roads, fording rivers and navigating ridges with endless coastal views. By night, you can spy on nesting sea turtles or take a midnight dip in the luxuriant Pacific. In between adventures you'll find no shortage of boutique bunks, tasty kitchens and indulgent spas to shelter and nourish body and soul. Whether you come for the thrills or just to chill, the Nicoya peninsula delivers. You'll find that the days (or weeks, or months) drift away on ocean breezes, disappearing all too quickly.

INCLUDES

Península de Nicoya Highlights

❶ Montezuma (p340) Hiking to wilderness beaches from a boho backpacker enclave.

❷ Mal País and Santa Teresa (p332) Surfing luscious breaks and feasting on farm-fresh cooking.

❸ Playa Grande (p301) Catching swells by day; spotting leatherback turtles by night.

❹ Playas San Miguel & Coyote (p330) Time traveling to a lesser-explored coast.

❺ Nosara (p318) Blissing out on waves and wellness in a secluded paradise.

❻ Refugio Nacional de Vida Silvestre Curú (p346) Kayaking and swimming in bioluminescent waters.

❼ Playa Sámara (p325) Beach hopping, craft shopping and mingling with friendly expats.

❽ Refugio Nacional de Vida Silvestre Ostional (p323) Marveling at the mass arrival of nesting olive ridley turtles.

❾ Playas del Coco (p292) Partying like a rock star and diving with rays and sharks.

❿ Playa Junquillal (p312) Witnessing a technicolor sunset with locals on a stunning beach.

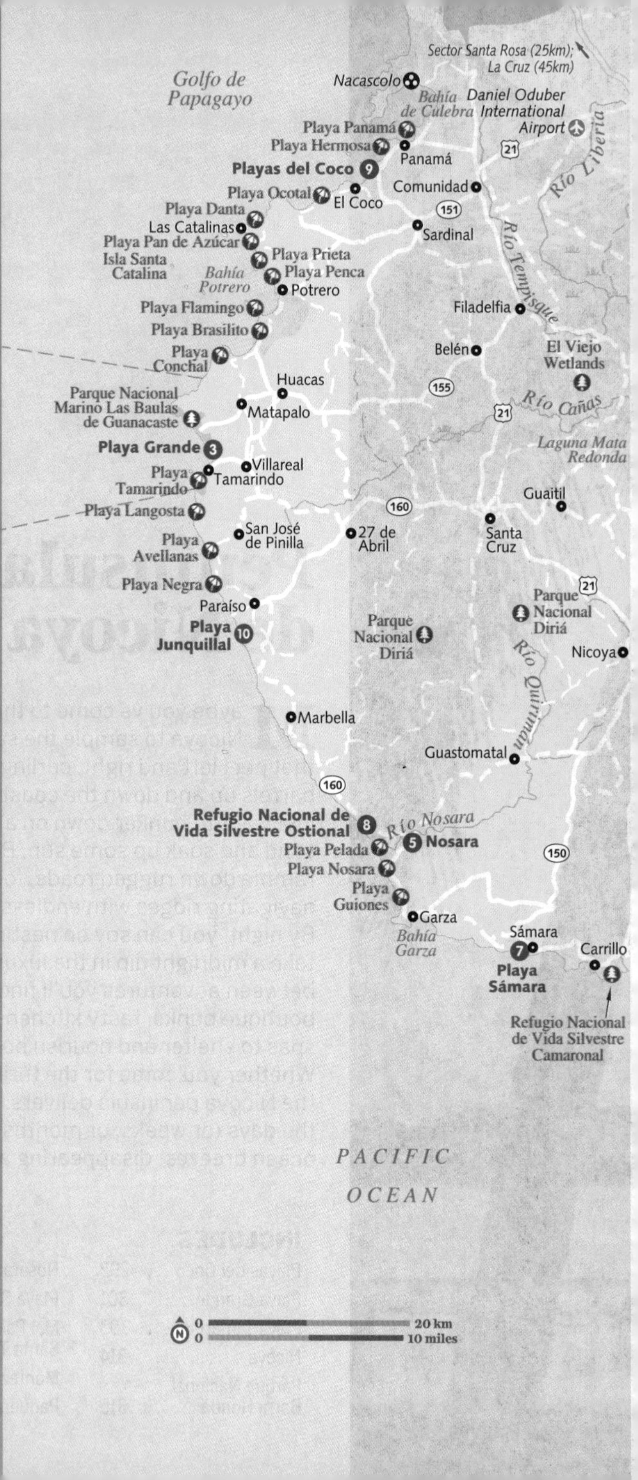

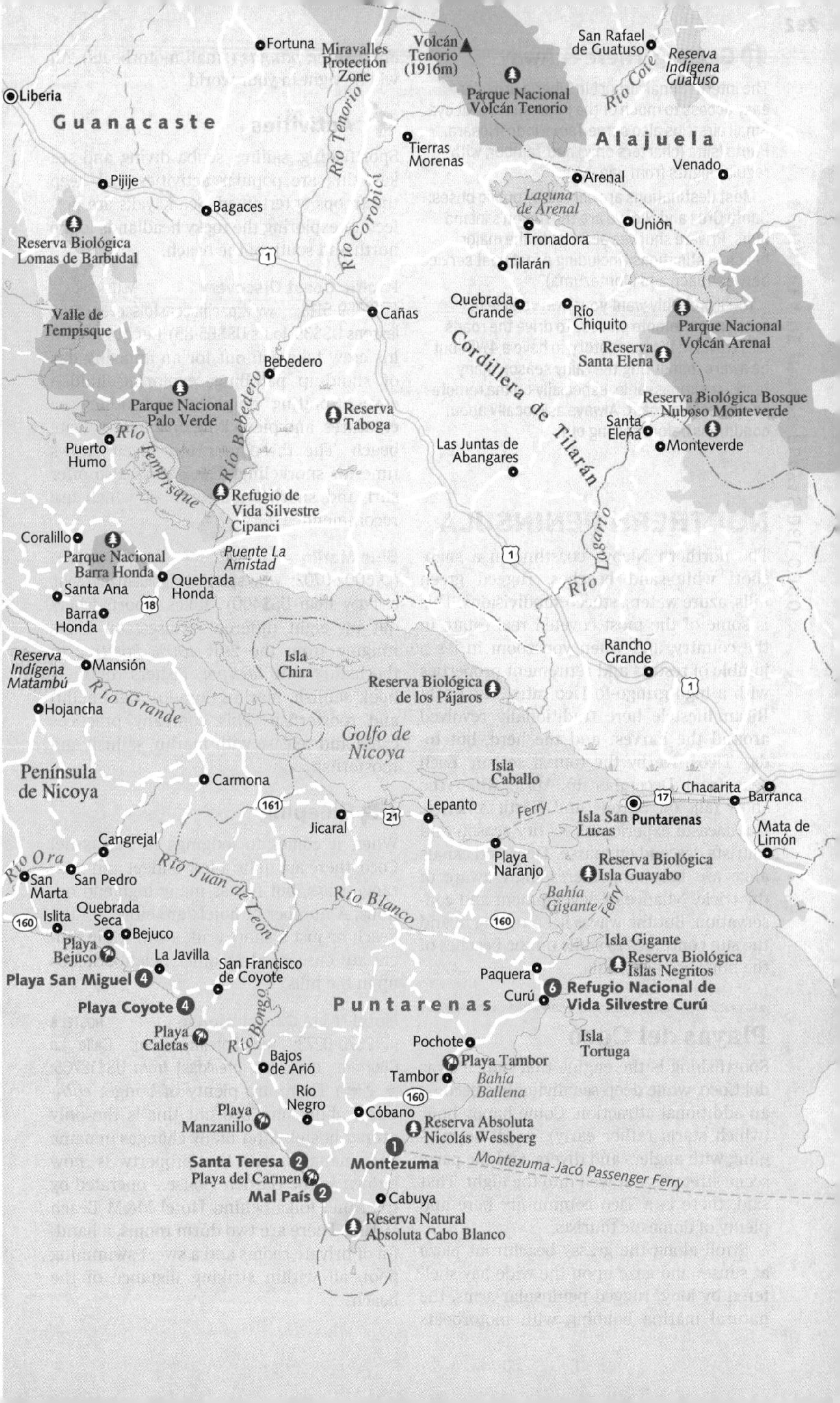
Fortuna
Miravalles Protection Zone
Volcán Tenorio (1916m)
San Rafael de Guatuso
Reserva Indígena Guatuso
Río Cote
Liberia
Parque Nacional Volcán Tenorio
Guanacaste
Río Tenorio
Tierras Morenas
Alajuela
Pijije
Río Corobicí
Arenal
Venado
Bagaces
Laguna de Arenal
Unión
Tronadora
Reserva Biológica Lomas de Barbudal
1
Tilarán
Quebrada Grande
Río Chiquito
Valle de Tempisque
Cañas
Parque Nacional Volcán Arenal
Cordillera de Tilarán
Reserva Santa Elena
Bebedero
Parque Nacional Palo Verde
Reserva Taboga
Reserva Biológica Bosque Nuboso Monteverde
Río Bebedero
Santa Elena
Monteverde
Río Tempisque
Puerto Humo
Las Juntas de Abangares
Refugio de Vida Silvestre Cipanci
Coralillo
Parque Nacional Barra Honda
Puente La Amistad
Río Lagarto
Quebrada Honda
Santa Ana
18
Barra Honda
Rancho Grande
Reserva Indígena Matambú
Mansión
Isla Chira
Reserva Biológica de los Pájaros
Río Grande
Hojancha
Golfo de Nicoya
Península de Nicoya
Isla Caballo
Carmona
Chacarita
17
Barranca
161
21
Lepanto
Ferry
Isla San Lucas
Puntarenas
Jicaral
Mata de Limón
Cangrejal
Playa Naranjo
Río Ora
Reserva Biológica Isla Guayabo
San Marta
San Pedro
Río Juan de Leon
Bahía Gigante
Ferry
Río Blanco
160
Quebrada Seca
Islita
Bejuco
Isla Gigante
Playa Bejuco
La Javilla
Reserva Biológica Islas Negritos
San Francisco de Coyote
Paquera
Playa San Miguel 4
6 Refugio Nacional de Vida Silvestre Curú
Curú
Playa Coyote 4
Puntarenas
Playa Caletas
Río Bongo
Isla Tortuga
Pochote
Bajos de Arió
Playa Tambor
Tambor
Bahía Ballena
Río Negro
Playa Manzanillo
Cóbano
Reserva Absoluta Nicolás Wessberg
1 Montezuma
Montezuma-Jacó Passenger Ferry
Santa Teresa 2
Playa del Carmen
Mal País 2
Cabuya
Reserva Natural Absoluta Cabo Blanco

Getting There & Away

The international airport in Liberia provides easy access to much of the Península de Nicoya. Small airstrips also serve Tamarindo, Nosara, Punta Islita (charters only) and Tambor, with regular flights from San José.

Most destinations are served by public buses; Santa Cruz and Nicoya are the region's inland hubs. Private shuttles also run to the major beach destinations (including a fast boat service between Jacó and Montezuma).

You'll probably want your own vehicle to reach more remote places. To drive the roads less traveled it's mandatory to have a 4WD, but be aware that during the rainy season many roads are impassable, especially on the remote southwestern coast. Always ask locally about conditions before setting out.

NORTHERN PENINSULA

The northern Nicoya coastline in a snapshot: white-sand beaches, rugged green hills, azure waters, stucco subdivisions. This is some of the most coveted real estate in the country, and when you zoom in it's a jumble of resorts and retirement properties with a high gringo-to-Tico ratio. The Costa Rican lifestyle here traditionally revolved around the harvest and the herd, but today Ticos live by the tourist season. Each year from December to April, when the snow falls on Europe and North America, Guanacaste experiences its dry season and tourists descend en masse. Ticos and expats alike are becoming increasingly aware of the tricky balance of development and conservation. But the waves keep rolling in and the sun continues to smile on the beaches of the northern peninsula.

Playas del Coco

Sportfishing is the engine that built Playas del Coco, while deep-sea diving has become an additional attraction. Come happy hour (which starts rather early), you'll be mingling with anglers and divers, and the party scene stretches out well into the night. That said, there is a Tico community here and plenty of domestic tourists.

Stroll along the grassy beachfront plaza at sunset and gaze upon the wide bay sheltered by long, rugged peninsular arms, the natural marina bobbing with motorboats and fishing *pangas* (small motorboats). All will be right in your world.

Activities

Sportfishing, sailing, scuba diving and sea kayaking are popular activities that keep the troops entertained. Sea kayaks are perfect for exploring the rocky headlands to the north and south of the beach.

Pacific Coast Discovery WATER SPORTS
(☎8359-5118; www.pacificcoastdiscovery.com; lessons US$35, tours US$65-85) Let Jorge and his crew take you out for an amazing day of stand-up paddling, exploring hidden coves, spotting dolphins and other sea creatures, and picnicking on a near-private beach. The three-hour tour even allows time for snorkeling. These guys also offer surf and snorkel tours, all of which are recommended.

Blue Marlin FISHING
(☎6002-0702; www.sportfishingbluemarlin.com; half-day from US$400) Takes sportsfishers out on eight different cruises, on boats ranging from the 29ft *100% Positive* to the luxury 55ft *Jackpot*. Fishers routinely hook sailfish, marlin, dorado (mahi-mahi) and roosterfish. This company practices catch and release with marlin, sailfish and roosterfish.

Sleeping

When it comes to lodgings in Playas del Coco, there are quite a few budget and midrange stays, but not as many high-end options. A number of hotels are either on the beach or just a short walk away, while others are ensconced in quiet neighborhoods up in the hills.

Hotel M&M Garden House HOSTEL $
(☎2670-0273; www.hotelmym.com; Calle La Chorrera; dm/d incl breakfast from US$18/65; ❄📶🏊) There are plenty of budget *cabinas* (cabins) in Coco but this is the only proper hostel. After many changes in name and management, the property is now known as the Garden House – operated by the same folks behind Hotel M&M Beach House. There are two dorm rooms, a handful of private rooms and a sweet swimming pool, all within striking distance of the beach.

PARKS & RESERVES OF THE PENÍNSULA DE NICOYA

Most of Nicoya's parks and reserves lie along the shoreline, with several stretching out to sea to protect marine turtles and their nesting sites.

Parque Nacional Barra Honda (p315) Best in the dry season; you can go spelunking in an underground limestone cave.

Parque Nacional Marino Las Baulas de Guanacaste (p301) Crucial to the survival of the leatherback, this park protects one of the turtle's major Pacific nesting sites.

Refugio Nacional de Vida Silvestre Ostional (p323) Olive ridley turtles converge in *arribadas* (mass nestings) at Ostional.

Refugio Nacional de Vida Silvestre Camaronal (p330) This out-of-the-way refuge has good surf and protects the nesting grounds of four marine-turtle species.

Refugio Nacional de Vida Silvestre Curú (p346) A privately owned reserve and an unexpected oasis of diverse landscapes.

Reserva Natural Absoluta Cabo Blanco (p342) Costa Rica's first protected wilderness area is at the peninsula's cape.

Villa del Sol HOTEL **$$**

(☎2670-0085, in Canada 514-400-9101; www.villadelsol.com; Calle La Chorrera; d incl breakfast US$65-85, apt US$85-105; P ❄ @ ☜ ≋) About 1km north of the town center, this leafy, tranquil property attracts monkeys, iguanas and a good variety of birdlife, in addition to happy travelers lounging in hammocks. The main building has stylish rooms with sunset-view balconies. In the back building, studio apartments (sleeping four) offer excellent value. Walk to the beach in five minutes.

Hotel M&M Beach House HOTEL **$$**

(☎2670-1212; www.hotelmym.com; s/d/tr/q incl breakfast from US$40/53/67/80; P ☜) A romantic beachfront hacienda with a wooden balcony overlooking the boardwalk. Fan-cooled rooms have ceramic tiled floors, beamed ceilings and cold-water showers. This simple place is one of the only beachfront properties in Coco. And if the beach is not your thing, you can take a dip in the pool at sister property Hotel M&M Garden House.

Pato Loco Inn GUESTHOUSE **$$**

(☎2670-0145; www.patolocoinn.com; d from US$78; P ❄ ☜ ≋ 🐾) Mary Cox and parrot Simon offer a warm welcome, with a wide range of rooms, a friendly bar and the best American breakfast in town (think biscuits and gravy). Rooms are freshly painted and furnished with new linens and curtains and as well as artwork by the owner. They also recently had flatscreen TVs installed. Stop by for beers and shoot the breeze with expats.

Hotel Chantel BOUTIQUE HOTEL **$$**

(☎8848-3883; www.facebook.com/ChantelSuites; d incl breakfast from US$60, apt from US$70; P ❄ ☜ ≋ 🐾) Perched on a cliff overlooking the coast, this intimate hotel is a step up from other local lodgings. Eleven rooms feature tasteful wood and wicker furniture, contemporary artwork and private terraces with stunning vistas of Playas del Coco. The elegant infinity pool and the breezy rooftop restaurant Lookout (p294) share the same panoramic view.

★**Rancho Armadillo** HOTEL **$$$**

(☎8336-9645; www.ranchoarmadillo.com; d incl breakfast standard US$204, deluxe US$244-278; P ❄ ☜ ≋) Near the entrance to town, this private estate is on a hillside about 600m off the main road (mostly paved), with ocean views to remind you where you are. It's set on 2 hectares with plenty of wildlife, and the six rooms are decorated with individually crafted furniture, hand-woven tapestries and local artwork. Self-catering gourmands will appreciate the professional kitchen.

The expat owner Rick is a hoot, a certified executive chef and a super nice guy who used to teach culinary arts in Detroit. Should a guest request it, he'll whip up a five- to seven-course meal for US$35 per person.

Hotel La Puerta del Sol HOTEL **$$$**

(☎2670-0195; www.lapuertadelsolhotel.com; d/ste incl breakfast US$124/159; P ❄ ☜ ≋) This unpretentiously luxurious Mediterranean-inspired hotel is a short walk from the town and the beach, but a world away from the traffic and the noise. There are three large suites, an apartment and eight huge pastel-colored rooms, with polished brick and concrete floors, king-sized beds and private terraces. The grounds are lush with blooming tropical flowers surrounding a glorious pool.

In 2019 the hotel debuted Garden Bar, a snazzy new drinking spot and event space that hosts live music and other entertainment on a nightly basis.

Eating

Coco's main drag is lined with places to eat, but it's hard to distinguish one from another on this noisy, crowded street. Our favorite places are on the beach (of course) or tucked away in the quieter corners of town. Not surprisingly, it excels at seafood.

Soda La Teresita COSTA RICAN $
(☎2670-0665; mains US$5-10; ⊙10am-10pm) At the crossroads of the main drag and the beach, this place can't be beaten for people watching in Coco. It's also your best bet for lunch, whether you're hankering for a *torta* (sandwich), a traditional *casado* (set meal) or Teresita's hearty breakfasts. Soda La Teresita has been here more than 40 years – so they must be doing something right!

Lookout SEAFOOD $$
(☎8755-7246; www.thelookoutcoco.com; oysters US$2-3, small plates US$6-15; ⊙noon-10pm Tue-Sun;) So many things to love about the Lookout: sustainably harvested Pacific oysters, locally brewed craft beers, and a small but intriguing menu of snacks, *ceviches* (seafood marinated in lemon or lime juice, garlic and seasonings) and sandwiches (though a number of items are frequently unavailable). Don't miss the avocado fries!

Then there's the incredible view, with the Golfo de Papagayo and the Cordillera de Guanacaste in the distance. Located on the top floor of the Hotel Chantel (p293).

La Dolce Vita PIZZA $$
(☎2670-1384; www.facebook.com/ladolcevitacostarica; mains US$15-20; ⊙noon-3pm & 5-10pm Thu-Tue;) Set in the Pueblito Sur open-air mall/food court about 500m north of the main drag, this is the local expat choice for oven-fresh pizza in Playas del Coco. The setting brings to mind suburban USA, but you can't argue with the tuna or octopus carpaccio. It also serves a range of pastas, distinctive seafood dishes and grilled meats.

★**Villa Italia** ITALIAN $$$
(☎8337-8105; www.villaitaliacostarica.com; mains US$16-22, couples menu US$75; ⊙6-10pm Mon-Sat;) Hidden away on a quiet residential block just west of the bus station, this small guesthouse contains the best Italian restaurant in Playas del Coco, and possibly all of Guanacaste. The owners have roots in Tuscany and Venetia, and to resurrect their family recipes they combine imported ingredients from Italy with fresh produce, fish and beef from local farms and fishing boats.

The set 'couples dinner' highlights the best of the menu, featuring crispy *crostone (*open-faced toast*)*, a delicate caprese salad, two handmade pasta dishes and an outrageous *straccetti di filetto* (beef strips) dish. There's also a full vegetarian menu, and everything pairs nicely with the Italian wines.

Restaurante Donde Claudio y Gloria SEAFOOD $$$
(☎2670-0256; www.facebook.com/RestauranteDondeClaudioYGloria; Calle La Chorrera; breakfast US$5-10, lunch US$10-20, mains US$14-24; ⊙8am-9pm;) Founded by Playas del Coco pioneers Claudio and Gloria Rojas, this casual, beachfront seafood restaurant has been a local landmark since the late 1950s. The setting is perfect – breakfast, lunch or dinner – for watching beach goings-on. Food is consistently good (though pricey). Service can be slow, but you're in no hurry, right?

Owner Javier rents a few rooms at the property next door.

Drinking & Nightlife

Coco has become more of a party town in recent years, and has developed a bit of a reputation for its drug culture. But there are also things like the Coco Night Market, a family-friendly, Wednesday evening event featuring hula hoops and produce shopping.

Bambu BAR
(☎2670-0711; www.facebook.com/bamboobeachbarcoco; ⊙11am-11pm;) A chilled-out beach bar with front-row seats for the ongoing sand volleyball action or, even better, a killer sunset. This open-air bar offers beach-accented gastropub fare (appetizers US$5 to US$10, mains US$8 to US$16, pizzas US$16

DEEP DIVES

The northern peninsula is one of the best and most easily accessible dive destinations in the country, though visibility varies greatly (9m to 15m, and sometimes up to 20m). Typical dive sites include the following:

- Volcanic rock pinnacles near the coast
- Isla Santa Catalina (about 20km to the southwest)
- Islas Murciélago (40km to the northwest, near the tip of Península Santa Elena)

There is no colorful hard coral such as you would see at a reef, but the sites make up for it with abundant marine life. Plenty of turtles and pelagics meander through, including mantas, sharks and whales. You'll be lost in huge schools of smaller tropical fish. These waters are sometimes home to humpback whales, who can be heard underwater during calving season (January to March) and seen during migration season (June and July).

Isla Santa Catalina and Islas Murciélago both host migrant manta rays from December to late April, and Murciélago is also known for its regular sightings of resident bull sharks.

Rocket Frog Divers (2670-1589; www.scuba-dive-costa-rica.com; 2-tank dives depending on location US$85-165; 7am-5pm) is an awesome dive shop on the Hotel Colono Beach property, with access to 22 local dive sites. They'll also motor you out to the Islas Catalinas to dive with mantas and the Bat Islands to dive with bull sharks. A fleet of six dive boats includes the 36ft, purpose-designed *Pacific Express*, which promises to make it to distant dive sites in half the time of other vessels.

Dutch outfit **Rich Coast Diving** (2670-0176; www.richcoastdiving.com; 2-tank dives from US$95, Open Water courses US$575; 7am-6pm) is one of the largest dive operations in Coco. They offer the regular range of local dives (good for spotting sharks, rays and schools of fish) as well as more expensive trips to the Islas Catalinas and Murciélagos. CDC certified by PADI.

to US$28), ice-cold beers and hand-crafted cocktails, not to mention service with a smile. Happy-hour specials nightly from 3pm to 7pm.

Coconutz CRAFT BEER
(2670-1982; www.coconutzbar.com; 9am-2am) A neighborhood sports bar that's also home to Angry Goats Brewing, one of the first microbreweries in Guanacaste. Surfboards dangle from the hardwood rafters, and the bar regularly hosts live music, karaoke and movie nights.

Information

Police (2670-0258) On Calle La Chorrera.

Getting There & Away

It's easy to get to Playas del Coco, which is 25km from Liberia airport; the journey takes only an hour or so by bus.

San José buses arrive and depart from the **main terminal**, about 100m north of Pato Loco Inn (p293). Buses for Liberia, Filadelfia and, very rarely, Playa Panamá, stop next to the red awning and benches opposite the Hard Rock Cafe.

Liberia US$1.50, one hour, departs half-hourly from 5am to 11pm.

San José US$9, five hours, departs 4am, 8am and 2pm. Serviced by Pulmitan (p100).

Playa Hermosa

Playa Hermosa (Beautiful Beach) is a lovely, wide and languid sheltered bay, framed by headlands and sprinkled with coconut palms and olive trees. It's only 5.5km (by road) north of Playas del Coco (and development is springing up rapidly along this entire coastline) but Hermosa feels more tranquil and remote.

Activities

North Pacific Tours FISHING
(8398-8129; www.northpacifictours.com; fishing trips from US$450, surfing trips from US$400) This fish and surf operation knows where to find the biggest fish and the biggest breaks. Captain Mauricio and first mate Daniel will take you on their 26ft fishing boat, *Don Manual,* for coastal fishing, snorkeling and/or

surfing. Split-charters available. Trips vary in length from half to full days.

BA Divers DIVING
(☎2672-0032; www.badivers.cr; Ruta 159, Sardinal; 2-tank dives incl equipment from US$126; ⏱7am-5pm) BA's very experienced and efficient crew will take you out on one of their five boats to hit the local dive sites around Playa Hermosa. Longer trips to the Bat Islands and Islas Catalinas also on offer. Located on the road leading into Playa Hermosa, after the large water tank.

Sleeping

Congo's Hostel & Camping HOSTEL $
(☎2672-1168; campsites US$9, dm/d US$15/35; P❄📶) This friendly budget option is on the second beach-access road, just one block from the beach. It's a ramshackle but relaxed place, offering hammocks, secure parking (US$2) and an open-air communal kitchen. The four-bed dorm room has metal beds with worn mattresses and a bathroom, and there are a couple of newer private cabinas as well.

La Gaviota Tropical BOUTIQUE HOTEL $$$
(☎2672-0011; www.lagaviotatropical.com; r/ste incl breakfast from US$185/275; P❄📶🏊) It's ingenious: a vertical hotel. All five huge suites – fully equipped and impeccably decorated – face the glorious sea. Climb to the top floor to cool off in the small but spectacular infinity pool. Downstairs, you can enjoy an excellent meal at restaurant **Roberto's** (☎8833-8580; mains US$15-20; ⏱7am-10pm; 📶), or walk a few steps to the sand.

Bosque del Mar HOTEL $$$
(☎2672-0046; www.bosquedelmar.com; d/tr/q US$248/282/316; P❄@📶🏊) Perched on the sand at the southern end of the beach, this lovely all-suite hotel offers a stunning location. Guests relish the gorgeous gardens, private terraces and contemporary design elements. Pay more for beachfront suites, which allow you to enjoy ocean views while soaking in your own open-air hot tub. Get here via the first beach-access road.

Hotel El Velero HOTEL $$$
(☎2672-1015, 2672-0036; www.costaricahotel.net; d US$150; P❄📶🏊) Just steps from the beach, this resort hotel has 21 spacious rooms decorated with woodwork, bamboo beds with colorful bedspreads, wicker ceiling fans and granite washbasins. Ask for a seafront room on the 2nd floor for optimal views.

Eating

La Casita del Marisco SEAFOOD $$
(☎2672-0226; ceviches & soups US$8-10, mains US$10-15; ⏱11:30am-9:30pm) Near the north end of town, this rather hidden, unassuming place has Ticos and gringos alike raving about the soups, *ceviches* and all things fishy. And you've got a great view of the famous Monkey Head rock in the bay: what could be better? Go the whole hog and treat yourself to a lobster. It's located across from Las Brisas condominiums.

Aqua Sport COSTA RICAN $$
(☎2672-0151; www.facebook.com/aquasportcr; mains US$10-20; ⏱11am-9pm; 📶) This colorful, fun beach bar is an excellent place to pass an evening feasting on burgers or fish tacos and swilling beers. Or sample the Peruvian specialties, such as *lomo saltado* (salted pork), *diabla* shrimp (spicy with tomato sauce) and, of course, *ceviche*. Take a seat in the giant green rocking chair and chill.

Ginger MEDITERRANEAN $$$
(☎2672-0041; www.gingercostarica.com; tapas US$7-14; ⏱5-10pm; 🍸) On the east side of the main road, you'll see this stunner cantilevered into the trees. This is not the restaurant you would expect to find in an unassuming beach village. The chic ambience complements a gourmet list of Asian- and Mediterranean-inspired tapas, fresh-fruit cocktails and a decent wine list. Reservations recommended for dinner during busy seasons.

Getting There & Away

BUS

Buses to Liberia and San José depart from the main road on the northern end of the beach and make a stop in Sardinal.

Liberia Operated by **La Pampa** (Map p228; ☎2665-7520); US$1.25, 1¼ hours, eight per day from 6:10am to 7:10pm.

San José Operated by Tralapa (p100); US$9, six hours, departs 5:10am.

CAR

Coming from Liberia, you'll drive west for 14km, crossing the steel bridge and entering the

DIAMANTE ECO ADVENTURE PARK

Short trip? Here's how to check most of your Costa Rica boxes at one adventure park. **Diamante** (☑2105-5200; www.diamanteecoadventurepark.com; Playa Matapalo; packages from US$48; ☺8:30am-4:30pm) offers nearly every activity in the book, including all-terrain vehicle (ATV) tours, hiking, horseback riding, kayaking, snorkeling, stand-up paddling, surfing and ziplining. The state-of-the-art, dual-zipline system lets you race your friends and family members, and includes the longest ride in the country (Superman-style, naturally). There's also an animal sanctuary and a botanical garden. And if you need a rest after your adventures, head for the hammock-strung beach.

village of Comunidad. Before the El Lagar Do It Center, turn right and drive another 1.6km. Turn left at the sign for Playa Panamá. Continue 11km and turn left onto the road that will take you into Hermosa. The entire route is paved, albeit winding.

If you have some time, it's worth exploring the beaches along the Golfo de Papagayo. Playa Panamá is right in the middle of the gulf with mangroves on one side, and a placid bay that feels almost like a lake. In between are the rustic Playa Bonita and Playa Buena.

Playa Ocotal

There is not much of a town here – just a few vacation rentals and an attractive resort. That's one reason it feels like a rustic outpost amid the condo-mania of the northern peninsula. The beach is gray and wooded, populated by mischievous magpie-jays, while the picturesque northernmost corner is dotted with small, brightly painted fishing boats rocking on the tide as wide-winged brown pelicans glide around them and kids cavort on the sand. The water is warm and placid, and you can snorkel around the rocks at the southern end.

Playa Ocotal is about 4km southwest of Playas del Coco by paved road and it's worth a trip simply to eat at Father Rooster

🛏 Sleeping & Eating

Los Almendros Ocotal　　APARTMENT $$
(☑2670-1560; www.losalmendrosocotal.com; studio/condo/villa US$82/181/237; 🅿✳@ 🛜⛲) Perched on the hillside just above the beach, these studios and apartments are a great option for divers, beach bums and self-caterers. Studios sleep two (no beach view, unfortunately), condos sleep four and villas sleep six. There are three shared pools, while fancier units have private Jacuzzis downstairs at the foot of the beach.

Father Rooster Bar & Grill　　PUB FOOD $$
(☑2670-1246; www.fatherrooster.com; mains US$10-20; ☺11am-10pm; 🛜) This colorful gastropub by the sea serves up tasty sandwiches and US pub fare, as well as top-notch (though expensive) cocktails. Try the Tica Linda, a wicked mix of Cacique, juice and grenadine. You can't beat the location, whether you sit at a table on the shaded terrace or in a hammock under the palms. *¡Pura vida!*

❶ Getting There & Away

There's no public transportation serving Playa Ocotal. It's around 4km away from Playas del Coco by road; a taxi should cost under US$10.

Beaches South of Playa Ocotal

Although they're lined up in a row, **Playas Danta**, **Pan de Azúcar**, **Potrero**, **Flamingo**, **Brasilito** and **Conchal** have little in common. The beaches range from gray sand to white sand to crushed seashells, with a wide variety of development along the way. It's gratifying to know that even here – along this busy strip of coastline – it's still possible to find a pretty *playa* without another soul on it.

Coming from the north, it's tempting to take the road from Sardinal to Potrero. Keep in mind there's a reason why locals call this route the 'Monkey Trail.' The first 8km of gravel road leading to the small town of Nuevo Colón is fine, but the second half is pretty brutal, and should only be tackled in dry season with a 4WD. The Monkey Trail begins 5km west of El Coco; turn right at the Castrol Oil sign and follow the signs for Congo Trail Canopy Tour. At the T-intersection in Nuevo Colón, turn left, bear left at the fork and continue for 5km until you reach Congo Trail Canopy. From there, it's a hair-raising 6km drive to Bahía Potrero.

To avoid the rough roads, return to the main peninsular highway from Playas del Coco, then head south through Filadelfia and on to Belén (a distance of 18km), from where a paved road heads 25km west to Huacas. Take the road leading north until you hit the ocean in Brasilito. If you turn right and head north, you'll pass Playa Flamingo and Bahía Potrero before reaching Playa Pan de Azúcar. If you make a left instead and head south, you will end up at Playa Conchal.

Potrero

Several beaches – largely undeveloped – are strung along this low-key bay. Playa Prieta is a gorgeous black-sand beach, with crystal-blue waters and lush green vegetation. The small cove is ideal for swimming, sunbathing and strolling. To the south, the gorgeous white-sand beach at Playa Penca curves around another little cove, where stand-up paddle-boarders ply the sheltered turquoise bay toward gleaming offshore islets. Further south is the more developed 'town' beach, Playa Potrero, and there's a small fishing village just beyond the northern end.

Sleeping

Pitaya Lodge HOTEL **$$**
(2654-4154; www.pitayalodge.com; d from US$75; P ❄ ☰ ≋) Oddly situated on the main drag north of Potrero, this little place (named for the popular dragon fruit) is set up like a roadside motel – a strip of rooms facing the pool, facing the road. That said, it has a boutique feel, with batik fabrics adorning earth-toned walls. It's a 15-minute walk to Playa Penca.

Bahía del Sol BOUTIQUE HOTEL **$$$**
(2654-4671; www.bahiadelsolhotel.com; d/ste incl breakfast from US$232/332, 4-person ste US$491; P ❄ @ ☰ ≋) With a prime beachfront location at Playa Potrero, this luxurious spot gets high marks for four-star laid-back elegance. Large, tropically themed rooms surround a pool with a swim-up bar and a garden with hammocks and day beds. Out front, the lawn leads to the upscale hotel restaurant, Nasu, and a beach peppered with *palapas* (shelters with thatched, palm-leaf roofs and open sides).

Eating & Drinking

Options for eating and drinking line Ruta 911 (the main road), especially at the northern end of town.

Cerveceria Independiente CRAFT BEER
(8464-0935; www.independiente.cr; El Garden; 10am-8pm Mon-Sat, noon-8pm Sun) Anchoring Playa Potrero's gastronomy park (El Garden), this expat-owned brewery excels at sours, stouts and gose-style beers. And once the friendly owners have lured you into their beer garden, you might as well give the surrounding street snacks a taste. The thin-crust pizza from the wood-fired oven is superb, as are the pork skewers from Gritanga.

Beach House BAR
(2654-6203; www.beachhousecr.com; 8am-9pm; ☰) It's hard to resist this colorful shack on the beach offering cold fruity cocktails and glorious sunset views. You'd expect seafood and pub fare, but there's also live music on Sundays. The 'you hook it, we cook it' special is on offer for fishing folk at a US$10 surcharge.

Getting There & Away

Departing Potrero, buses begin their route on the southeast corner of the soccer field. All buses go via Flamingo.

San José Operated by Tralapa (p100); US$10, six hours, departs 2:30am, 8:15am and 2:45pm.

Santa Cruz Operated by Folklórica; US$3, two hours, departs 16 times per day from 5am to 10:15pm.

Playa Flamingo

This sugary, postcard-worthy white-sand and shell beach is glorious. Kissed by a serene blue sea with the rugged keys of the Catalinas floating off in the distance, Flamingo attracts a local Tico scene along with package tourists. Turn your nose up at the tourist developments if you must, but keep them at your back and admire the ocean in front of you.

Sleeping & Eating

Mariner Inn INN $$

(2654-4156; www.marinerinn.com; d from US$60;) In an overdeveloped beach town filled with overpriced, cheesy resorts, this centrally located, eight-room inn is exceptional for its basic rooms at a reasonable rate. The upstairs bar, Scooter's, has good pub fare and a pool.

Surf Box CAFE $$

(8349-9773; www.facebook.com/surboxcr; mains US$9-14; 7:30am-9pm Mon-Sat, to 2:30pm Sun;) A cozy little restaurant serving up all the best après-surf goodies: a hulking breakfast burrito; tropical tacos with grilled shrimp and mango; a Brazilian acai bowl with almonds, chia and granola. The smoothies and coffee are also fabulous, as is the garden patio, decked out with surf boards, tropical foliage and a bamboo fence.

Coco Loco SEAFOOD $$

(2654-6242; www.cocolococostarica.com; mains US$9-30; 11am-10pm) In-the-know locals mix with clueless tourists at this undeniably perfect beach bar, where the cocktails are strong, the seafood is on point and the sunset view is killer. Crowd favorites include the tuna tacos and the steak, which comes on a sizzling hot lava rock.

Getting There & Away

Buses depart from the traffic circle near the town entrance and travel via Brasilito. Some also head north into Potrero and then turn around. Schedules change often, so ask locally about departure times as well as the best place on the road to wait for the bus.

San José Operated by Tralapa (p100); US$10, six hours, departs 2:45am, 8:30am and 3pm.

Liberia Operated by La Pampa (p296) US$2, two hours, departs 5am, 12:30pm, 4pm.

Santa Cruz Operated by **Folklórica** (2680-3161; cnr Calle 7 & Av 3, Santa Cruz); US$3, two hours, departs 16 times per day from 5am to 10:15pm.

Playa Brasilito

Brasilito's *pueblo* (village) has a town square, a beachfront soccer pitch, a pink-washed *iglesia* (church) and a friendly Tico community. While there is a beach, we recommend taking the a short stroll along the sea to sugary Conchal nearby.

Sleeping

Hotel Quinta Esencia B&B $$

(2654-5455; www.hotel-quintaesencia.net; d incl breakfast US$80;) An artistic vibe pervades this chilled-out lodging, built around the trees on the northern edge of Brasilito. The comfortable guest rooms feature driftwood, bamboo and neutral tones, accented by ribbons of color. Co-owner Stephanie is an artist, and you'll see her work scattered about the premises. There's a lot of love (and a few cute cats and dogs) here.

Hotel Brasilito HOTEL $$

(2654-4237; www.brasilito.com; r US$30-80;) On the beach side of the plaza, this basic hotel offers simple, clean rooms with wood floors and ceiling fans, lined up along a wide balcony. Sea-view rooms cost a little more, but are worth the splurge. Otherwise, the patio's hammocks are ideal for soaking up the sunset. Budget rooms (no air-con) are also available.

Conchal Hotel HOTEL $$

(2654-9125; www.conchalcr.com; d incl breakfast US$90-115;) This bougainvillea- and palm-dappled lodge is a sweet retreat. Spacious rooms are fitted with unique design touches, such as beamed ceilings and wrought-iron furniture. Enjoy the lovely gardens while lounging poolside or from the privacy of your patio. A simple but scrumptious continental breakfast is served at the Papaya Restaurant, which is also recommended for other meals.

Eating

Camarón Dorado SEAFOOD $$

(Golden Shrimp; 4700-0070; www.facebook.com/camarondoradoseafoodygrill; cnr of Plaza Deportes; fish platters US$15-35, children's plates US$7-9; 11am-9pm;) Conveniently located on the corner where the main square meets the beach, this local favorite has been serving up fresh seafood for years. A new owner as of 2018 hasn't changed the winning formula, and the sign still says it all: 'lunch and dinner on the beach.'

Papaya Restaurant SEAFOOD $$$

(2654-9125; www.conchalcr.com; mains US$16-22; 6:30am-8:30pm Thu-Tue;) Vegetarians and seafood lovers, rejoice! For the

LOCAL KNOWLEDGE

THIS BEACH TOWN IS DIFFERENT

Las Catalinas is an unusual new town on the Nicoya Peninsula's Playa Danta, and lately it has drawn international attention for abiding by principles of a unique city planning movement, 'new urbanism.' What are those principles, you ask? For starters, the town is carless. Additionally, it prioritizes environmentally friendly design and mixed-use structures, pairing up private and public spaces to encourage frequent socializing. The place resembles a Spanish-colonial version of Italy's Cinque Terre, though this isn't one of the principles.

Entering the town, guests ditch their cars and walk along a tranquil beachfront lined with restaurants, an outdoor adventure outfitter, an upscale grocery, a beach club, a day spa and several shops. The 85 villas constructed thus far feature dramatic archways, magnificent courtyards and lavish interiors, and the development is surrounded by hiking paths and mountain-biking trails. Playas Danta and Dantita are footsteps away, and the blissful Playa Pan de Azúcar is a short drive south.

Travelers can take advantage of these attractions on a day-trip, and it's also possible to stay the night in one of Las Catalinas' **vacation homes** (2654-4600; www.lascatalinascr.com; Playa Danta; house from US$250; P ❄ ☎ ≋) . A new boutique stay, **Santarena Hotel** (2654-4600; www.santarenahotel.com; d from US$425; P ❄ ☎ ≋), recently opened up within the community. Other nearby hotels are also excellent options.

Casa Chameleon (2103-1200; www.casachameleonhotels.com/las-catalinas; Playa Danta; d incl breakfast from US$697; P ❄ ☎ ≋) is a glamorous hilltop boutique is an adults-only dream stay, with just 21 posh villas (and private saltwater plunge pools) overlooking some of the country's most jaw-dropping coastline. The opulent grounds are replete with exotic touches by way of Morocco and Indonesia, and the yoga deck, fire-lit infinity pool and Costa Rican restaurant are all fabulous. If you're gonna splurge on a honeymoon or couples' getaway, you certainly won't be sorry you did it here.

Luxury at **Hotel Sugar Beach** (2654-4242; www.sugar-beach.com; d/ste incl breakfast from US$174/277; P ❄ @ ☎ ≋) is simple and understated: floor-to-ceiling windows, private balconies and stunning views are just a few of the upsides, though the property and style are somewhat dated. A walking path winds through lovely landscaped grounds, down to the sweet sands of Pan de Azúcar. The hotel rates highly in its sustainable practices, for example, its efforts to protect nesting sea turtles.

former, there are all-day breakfasts, power salads and falafel wraps. For the latter, there are seafood salads and jumbo shrimp. Come during the day for big burritos and flatbread sandwiches, or come at night for fancier fare – and (sometimes) live music. The brightly painted second-story restaurant is in the Conchal Hotel (p299).

Getting There & Away

All buses to and from Playa Flamingo and Potrero (US$3) travel through Brasilito (originating in Liberia, Santa Cruz or San José). There are three daily buses to San José. Buy tickets in advance at the **Tralapa Agencia** (2573-0074; 8am-5pm Mon-Fri, to 3pm Sat & Sun) at the north end of Brasilito, across from the sports field (the bus stops are here, too).

Playa Conchal

Just 1km south of Brasilito is Playa Conchal, a gorgeous stretch of palm-backed sea and sand. Conchal rates among Costa Rica's most beautiful beaches. The name comes from the billions of *conchas* (shells) that wash up on the beach, and are gradually crushed into coarse sand. The shallows drift from an intense turquoise to sea-foam green deeper out – a rarity on the Pacific coast. If you have snorkeling gear, this is a great place to use it.

The beach is often packed with locals, tourists and countless vendors, but on weekdays during low season Playa Conchal is pure paradise. The further south you stroll, the wider, sweeter and more spectacular the beach becomes.

You can walk to Conchal from Brasilito depending on the tide and, sometimes, the amount of rain (the gully between the two beaches may flood, but local guys with off-road vehicles will ferry you across, for a price).

Playa Grande

Playa Grande is a wide, gorgeous beach, famous among conservationists and surfers alike. By day, offshore winds create steep and powerful waves. By night, an ancient cycle continues, as leatherback sea turtles bearing clutches of eggs follow the ocean currents back to their birthplace. The beach stretches from the Tamarindo estuary, around a dome rock – with tide pools and superb surf fishing – and on to equally grand Playa Ventanas. Even confident swimmers should obey riptide signs, as people have drowned here.

Since 1991 Playa Grande has been part of the Parque Nacional Marino Las Baulas de Guanacaste, protecting one of the world's most important leatherback nesting areas. At night it's only possible to visit the beach on a guided tour.

Sights

Parque Nacional Marino Las Baulas de Guanacaste NATIONAL PARK
(☎2653-0470; turtle tours incl park admission US$27; ⊙office 8am-noon & 1-4pm, tours 6pm-2am) Las Baulas national marine park encompasses the entire beach at Playa Grande, as well as the adjacent land and 220 sq km of ocean. This is one of the world's most important nesting areas for the critically endangered *baula* (leatherback turtle). In the evenings from October to March, rangers lead tours to witness the turtles' amazing cycle of life.

Activities

Surfing

Surfing is the main motivation for coming to Playa Grande, and it is indeed spectacular. There are two main beach breaks – one at either end of the beach – especially in the window that begins three hours before high tide and ends three hours after. Unfortunately, when the surf's up the breaks get crowded, so chat up some locals to learn their secrets.

Playa Grande Surf Camp SURFING
(☎2653-1074; www.playagrandesurfcamp.com; board rental per day US$20, 2hr lessons US$40) In addition to board rentals and surf lessons, this outfit also offers surf packages which include accommodations, and can arrange transportation to the best breaks on the peninsula. Located in the southern part of Playa Grande.

Frijoles Locos Surf Shop SURFING
(☎2652-9235; www.frijoleslocos.com; board rental 2hr/day/weekly from US$8/25/100, 1½hr lessons from US$40; ⊙9am-6pm) An all-purpose surf shop where you can rent surfboards and sign up for lessons. This place also rents just about everything you need to guarantee a great day at the beach, including bikes, snorkel gear, boogie boards and paddleboards, shade tents and even two great apartments (US$165). Enjoy!

Wildlife-Watching

Playa Grande is a wilderness beach, nearly surrounded by mangrove swamps. Protected by the Tamarindo Wildlife Sanctuary (in addition to the Las Baulas national park), this place is teeming with wildlife – and not only turtles. Local guides lead canoe expeditions in the Tamarindo estuary, where you can spot crocs, monkeys, anteaters and *pizotes* (coatis), not to mention a stunning variety of birds.

Black Turtle Tours WILDLIFE
(☎8534-8664; Hotel Las Tortugas; canoe tour US$30, Playa Mina turtle tour US$25 Nov-Jul) Paddle a canoe through the saltwater jungle that dominates the Tamarindo Wildlife Sanctuary, at the southern end of Playa Grande. This maze of mangroves – including five different species – is home to a spectacular array of flora and fauna. Your guide, Jonathan, will help you spot it.

Sleeping

Lodgings are located at the two ends of Playa Grande. At the northern end you'll find the heart of the village, with Hotel Las Tortugas (p302), the main beach entrance, the ranger station and the bulk of facilities. At the southern end a handful of guesthouses can be found within the Palm Beach Estates development, where there's another beach access point. Further south is Hotel Bula Bula (p302) and the boats to Tamarindo.

★Playa Grande Surf Camp CABINA $
(☎2653-1074; www.playagrandesurfcamp.com; dm US$35, d US$36-100; P❄📶🏊) Aside from offering boards, lessons and trips, the surf camp is also a great budget-accommodations option. Three cute, thatched, A-frame *cabinas* have private porches and hammocks, just steps from the beach. There are also two breezy elevated *cabinas* that sleep two. Surf packages available. A yummy restaurant and an outdoor shared kitchen up the ante.

La Marejada Hotel BOUTIQUE HOTEL $$
(☎2653-0594, in USA & Canada 800-559-3415; www.hotelswell.com; r US$100; ❄📶🏊) Hidden behind a bamboo fence, this stylish nest has eight elegantly understated rooms with stone-tile floors, rattan and wooden furnishings, and queen beds. There's not a lot of space here, but it's well kept by the owner, who also runs Sugar's Monkey next door. Surf lessons, massage services and yoga are offered onsite, not to mention an excellent restaurant.

Indra Inn GUESTHOUSE $$
(☎8706-4302, 2653-4834; www.indrainn.com; r incl breakfast US$65-90; P❄📶) It's not too fancy at Indra Inn, but the grounds are blooming with fruit trees and hung with hammocks. Rooms are freshly updated (the old bar has been converted into four rooms) and are simply decorated. Owners Matt, Natalia and Dante are charming hosts.

Hotel Las Tortugas HOTEL $$
(☎2653-0423; www.lastortugashotel.com; d economy US$30, d standard US$100-250, apt US$40-125; P❄@📶🏊) 🍃 Local hero and granddad of Playa Grande, Louis Wilson was instrumental in the designation of the national park. Abutting the beach, his hotel was carefully designed to keep ambient light away from the turtle-nesting area. Rooms are quirky and comfortable and, best of all, about 15 steps from the waves. There's also a fabulous hot tub.

Apartments (500m inland), some with kitchenettes and private porches, offer more space and amenities. Discounts available for longer stays.

Hotel Cantarana INN $$$
(☎2653-0486; www.hotel-cantarana.com; Palm Beach Estates; r incl breakfast US$110-130; P❄📶🏊) This is a lovely, intimate inn nestled into the semi-gated Palm Beach Estates. Spacious and luxurious rooms each have a private terrace overlooking the glittering pool and gorgeous gardens. A highlight is the restaurant, set on the 2nd-floor terrace amid the treetops. Open for breakfast and dinner, the kitchen creates tasty concoctions from local ingredients.

Hotel Bula Bula HOTEL $$$
(☎2653-0975; www.hotelbulabula.com; r incl breakfast US$175; P❄📶🏊) At the southern end of town, Hotel Bula Bula has decked out its rooms with king-size beds, tropical paint jobs and whimsical local art. The grounds are gorgeous and the front porch is well equipped with rattan rockers. Most importantly: cocktails. The Great Waltini's hardwood bar puts out some seriously potent drinks, including rum yummies, margaritas and the mysterious Siberian.

Monday Mexican Nights crank up the fiesta a notch or two.

Eating & Drinking

When the sun sets, Playa Grande is a pretty sleepy place. But on Wednesday from 6pm to 9pm, the Las Olas Beach Club hosts a community night market with food, drinks and live music. There's also some after-hours fun at **Kike's** (☎2653-0834; www.facebook.com/KikesPlace; ⏲7am-11pm), Hotel Bula Bula, and **Rip Jack Inn** (☎2653-1636, in USA 800-808-4605; www.ripjackinn.com; d from US$113; P❄📶🏊), and a lot more action across the estuary in Tamarindo.

Taco Star MEXICAN $
(tacos US$4; ⏲9:30am-6:30pm) Three words: beachfront taco stand. Hefty beef and veggie tacos and fresh fruit *batidos* (shakes) will sustain you for a full day of sun and surf. Can't beat it.

★Pots & Bowls HEALTH FOOD $$
(☎4701-2394; www.facebook.com/potsandbowls; bowls US$7-14; ⏲8am-5pm; 📶) If you love potted plants, and you love eating nutritious food out of a bowl, this is your dream stop in Playa Grande. Bowls are divided into sweet (acai, chia pudding, tropical spirulina) and salty (*casados*, cauliflower rice, tuna poke), and they pair exceedingly well

with the cold-pressed juice and strong cups of coffee.

The adorable, roadside restaurant has a thatched roof above some outdoor picnic tables, and inside there's a store hawking household items, clothing and (of course) potted plants.

Cafe Del Pueblo ITALIAN $$$
(☎2653-2315; mains US$10-19; ⏲5-10pm Mon-Sat) Just east of town is this open-air Italian restaurant. The thin-crust pizzas get good reviews, and regulars rave about the innovative seafood preparations, tender steaks and homemade pasta dishes. Dine under the stars on the patio. Reservations recommended on weekends.

Information

Playa Grande Clinic (☎2653-2767, 24hr emergency 8827-7774; www.facebook.com/pgclinic) If you get rolled too hard in the surf and need a doctor, find this clinic next to Kike's Place.

Getting There & Away

The Folklórica (p299) bus between Santa Cruz and the coastal towns stops at Playa Grande twice daily, at 7am and 3pm. But the road is paved so it's also an easy drive.

Alternatively, catch a boat across the estuary from Tamarindo to the southern end of Grande (around US$2 per person). The boat is free if you arrange in advance (by 2pm) to eat dinner at Hotel Bula Bula. Otherwise, just pop up on the beach – the boatmen will see you.

Note: tourists have been attacked and one surfer lost his lower leg to a croc in the estuary – take the boat and don't try crossing on the cheap.

Playa Tamarindo

POP 6375

If Patrick and Wingnut from the 1994 surfing movie *Endless Summer II* surfed a time machine to present-day Tamarindo, they'd definitely wipe out. A quarter-century of hedonism has transformed the once-dusty burg into 'Tamagringo,' whose perennial status as Costa Rica's top surf and party destination has made it the first and last stop for legions of tourists.

Despite its party-town reputation, Tamarindo offers more than just drinking and surfing. It forms part of Parque Nacional Marino Las Baulas de Guanacaste, and the beach retains an allure for kids and adults alike. Foodies will find some of the best restaurants in the country. There's a thriving market on Saturday mornings and fierce competition has kept the price of lodgings somewhat reasonable. Its central location makes it a great base for exploring the northern peninsula.

Activities

Costa Rica Stand-Up Paddle Adventures ADVENTURE SPORTS
(☎8780-1774; www.costaricasupadventures.com; board rental from US$30, lessons/tours from US$65/115) Here's your chance to do sun salutations on a stand-up paddleboard. If yoga's not your thing and you prefer to just paddle, you can do that too. Lessons take place right on the beach at **Nogui's** (☎2653-0029; mains US$12-24; ⏲6am-10pm), while tours go out to ride the surf or explore the flat waters of the estuaries.

TAMARINDO'S LANGUAGE SCHOOLS

Use your vacation time wisely by learning Spanish. There are several language schools in Tamarindo, all of which offer weeklong intensive courses at various levels. Packages usually include 'homestay' accommodations with a Tico family. Here's a Tamarindo special: 'Spanish & Surf' packages that include language classes, surf lessons, accommodations and board rentals.

Coastal Spanish Institute (☎2653-2673; www.coastalspanish.com; per week from US$270) This Spanish school is right on the beach in downtown Tamarindo (which may make it more difficult to concentrate on your grammar and vocabulary). It specializes in weekly surf and Spanish packages, which include 20 hours of Spanish classes and six hours of surf instruction, as well as board rental.

Instituto de Wayra (☎2653-0359; www.spanish-wayra.co.cr; per week from US$310; ⏲7am-5:30pm Mon-Fri, 10am-4pm Sun) A Spanish program that offers small class sizes and an immersive experience. The school recommends (and arranges) homestays so students have more opportunities to polish up their language skills.

Playa Tamarindo

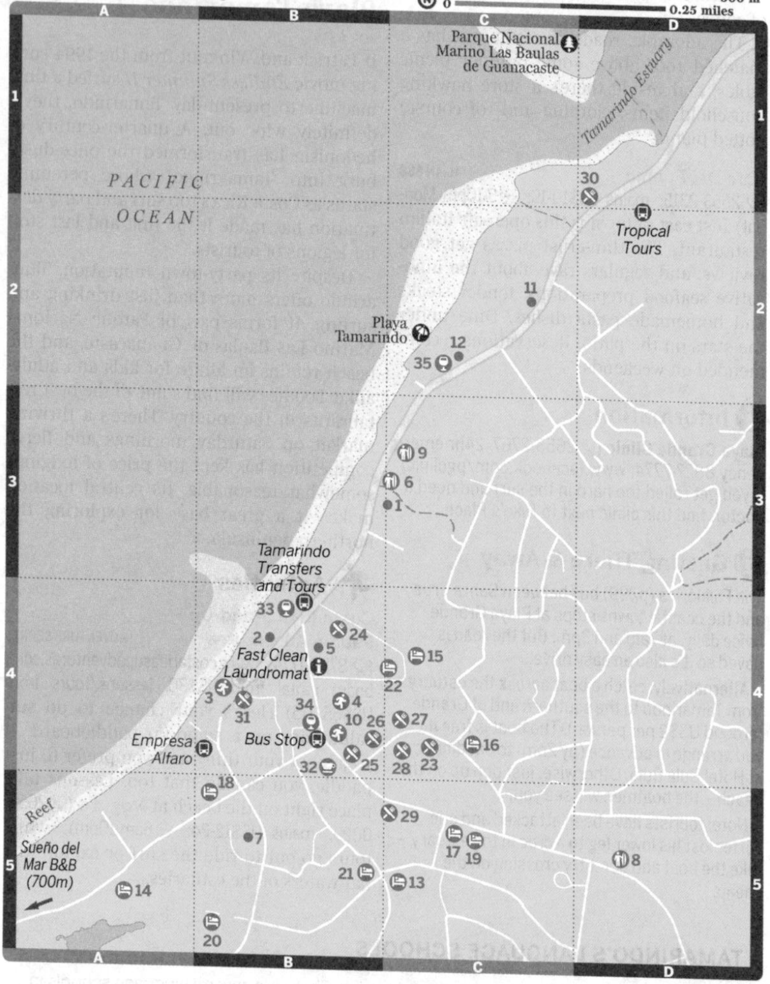

Ser Om Shanti Yoga Studio YOGA

(☎8591-6236; www.seryogastudio.com; Plaza Tamarindo, 2nd floor; classes from US$16) There's a full schedule of daily hatha and vinyasa yoga classes, as well as Pilates and restorative yoga. It all takes place in a bright, airy studio on the top floor of Plaza Tamarindo.

E-Bike Costa Rica MOUNTAIN BIKING

(☎8458-7963; www.ebikecostarica.com; rental per day/week US$40/200; ⏲10am-6pm) Well, some days you don't feel like pedaling. No problem! You can hire electric bikes and skateboards here that operate with a few flicks of the wrist, and travel up to 70km on one battery charge. Don't forget the helmet, though.

Located below Ser Om Shanti yoga studio, and next to El Niño Parque.

Surfing

Tamarindo's most popular wave is a medium-sized right that breaks directly in front of the Tamarindo Diria hotel, where the waters are full of virgin surfers learning to pop up. There is also a good left that's fed by the river mouth, though be advised that crocodiles are occasionally sighted here, particularly when the tide is rising (which is, coincidentally, the best time to surf).

Playa Tamarindo

Activities, Courses & Tours

1	Blue Trailz	C3
2	Coastal Spanish Institute	B4
3	Costa Rica Stand-Up Paddle Adventures	B4
4	E-Bike Costa Rica	B4
5	Freedive Costa Rica	B4
6	Iguana Surf	C3
7	Instituto de Wayra	B5
8	Kelly's Surf Shop	D5
9	Matos Surf Shop	C3
10	Ser Om Shanti Yoga Studio	B4
11	Tamarindo Diving	C2
12	Witch's Rock Surf Camp	C2

Sleeping

13	Beach Bungalows	C5
	Blue Trailz Hostel	(see 1)
14	Boho Tamarindo	A5
15	Hotel Luamey	C4
16	Hotel Mahayana	C4
17	La Botella de Leche	C5
18	Ocho Artisan Bungalows	B5
19	Pura Vida Hostel	C5
20	Tamarindo Backpackers	B5
21	Tamarindo Bay Boutique Hotel	B5
22	Villas Macondo	C4

Eating

23	Dragonfly Bar & Grill	C4
24	El Mercadito	B4
25	Falafel Bar	B4
26	Green Papaya	B4
27	Jolly Roger	C4
28	La Baula	C4
29	La Bodega	C5
	Nogui's	(see 3)
30	Pangas Beach Club	D1
31	Surf Shack	B4
	Utopia	(see 19)

Drinking & Nightlife

32	Café Tico	B4
33	El Be!	B4
34	Sharky's	B4
35	Volcano Brewing Company	C2

More advanced surfers will appreciate the bigger, faster and less crowded waves at neighboring beaches: Playa Langosta, on the other side of the point; Playas Avellanas, Negra and Junquillal to the south; and Playa Grande to the north.

There are countless surf schools offering lessons and board rental in Tamarindo. Surf lessons hover at around US$45 for 1½ to two hours, and most operators will let you keep the board for a few hours beyond that to practice. Note that lessons and rentals are now taxed at 13%.

★ Iguana Surf SURFING
(☎2653-0091, 2653-0613; www.iguanasurf.net; board rental per day/week US$20/120, group/semiprivate/private lessons US$45/65/80; ⌚7:30am-6pm) Iguana Surf has been giving lessons since 1989, so they probably know what they're doing. Excellent for couples, families or anyone, really. The two-hour lesson includes a rash guard and locker, in addition to the surfboard. After your lesson, board rentals are half-price.

Matos Surf Shop SURFING
(☎2653-0845; www.matossurfshop.com; Sunrise Commercial Center; board rental per day US$10; ⌚8am-7pm) In addition to giving lessons and renting boards, this place also offers surf photography and video (in case you wanted to star in your own version of *Endless Summer*). Tamarindo's cheapest rates for board rental and sales. There is another outlet in Playa Grande.

Kelly's Surf Shop SURFING
(☎2653-1355; www.kellyssurfshop.com/en; board rental per day/week from US$10/90, group/semiprivate/private lessons from US$45/65/90; ⌚9am-6pm) One of the best surf shops in the area, Kelly's has a terrific selection of newish boards that it rents out by the day or week. Premium boards cost a bit more. Staff are super-informative, with lessons, advice and other recommendations to get you out on the waves. You can also rent bikes here.

Blue Trailz SURFING
(☎2653-1705; www.bluetrailz.com; board rental per day US$15, group/semiprivate/private surf lessons US$45/60/80; ⌚7am-7pm) Blue Trailz offers surf lessons and board rental, as well as more comprehensive surf packages. The experienced and amiable surf instructors come highly recommended. There's a hostel (p306) at the back, if you're inclined to stay after your lesson.

Witch's Rock Surf Camp SURFING
(☎2653-1238; www.witchsrocksurfcamp.com; 1-week package from US$973; ⌚6am-10pm) Weeklong packages include lessons, board rental and a place to stay on the beach. Excursions to Witch's Rock and Ollie's Point are also available. *Endless Summer* surf legend Robert August shapes boards here.

Diving

Tamarindo is a surf town, but that doesn't mean there's nothing to see below the waves. Enticing dive sites in the vicinity include the nearby Cabo Velas and the Islas Catalinas.

Freedive Costa Rica DIVING
(☎8353-1290; www.freedivecostarica.com; Plaza Conchal; free-diving training from US$60, spearfishing US$140; ⊙7:30am-6:30pm) Owner Gauthier Ghilain claims free diving is 'the most natural, intimate and pure form of communion with the underwater world.' It requires no bulky gear and minimal training. He promises a safe and super-fun environment in which to learn how to explore the deep blue sea. Spearfishing, scuba diving and 'sea-scooter snorkeling' are also on offer.

Tamarindo Diving DIVING
(☎8583-5873; www.tamarindodiving.net; 2-tank dive US$115; ⊙7am-5:30pm) It's called Tamarindo Diving, although trips actually depart from Playa Flamingo and head out to the Islas Catalinas. (It's a trade-off: you'll spend more time on the road but less time on the boat motoring to your destination.) Turtles, dolphins and whales are often spotted from the boat, while eagle rays, sharks and manta rays are lurking below the surface.

Tours

There are tour agencies all around town, offering surf lessons of course, but also boat tours, canopy tours, snorkeling trips, ATV rentals, sea kayaking and stand-up paddling. Bike and board rental is also easy to find.

Sleeping

Tamarindo is packed with lodging options in all price ranges, including all manner of hostels, guesthouses and high-end resorts. Although the center can feel a bit oppressive, with crowded streets and nonstop heat, it's not that hard to escape the hullabaloo by staying on the south side of town. Things quiet down pretty quickly when you leave the main drag. Prices drop significantly outside of high season.

Tamarindo Backpackers HOSTEL $
(☎4033-4583; www.tamarindobackpackershostel.com; dm US$15-20, d with/without bathroom US$50/40; P❄@🛜🏊) This attractive yellow hacienda has a great vibe that welcomes all comers. Private rooms (mostly with shared bathroom) are excellent value, with Spanish-tiled floors, mural-painted walls, beamed ceilings and TVs. The dorms are quite clean but otherwise unspectacular. Outside, hammocks are strung in the tropical gardens and around a small pool. It's a five-minute walk to the beach.

La Botella de Leche HOSTEL $
(☎2653-0189; www.labotelladeleche.com; dm US$10-20, d US$40-60; P❄@🛜🏊) With a relaxed vibe, this congenial spot – aka 'the Bottle of Milk' – is recommended for its warm and attentive management, plus fully air-conditioned rooms and dormitories. Stenciled walls pretty up the otherwise plain rooms. Facilities include a shared kitchen, surfboard racks, hammocks and a TV lounge. A yoga and fitness studio was added in 2018.

Pura Vida Hostel HOSTEL $
(☎2653-2464, 8368-3508; www.puravidahostel.com; dm US$18-20, d US$60; ❄@🛜) Inside this leafy compound are dorms and private rooms accented by trippy murals and mirrored mosaics. The vibe is friendly and chill, especially in the common kitchens and *rancho* (small house-like building), furnished with hammocks and rocking chairs. It sometimes organizes open-mic nights and live music in keeping with the rock-star-themed rooms. Bikes and boards are available for rent, too.

Blue Trailz Hostel HOSTEL $
(☎2653-1705; www.bluetrailz.com/tamarindo-hostel; dm/r US$15/65; ❄@🛜) Across the street from the beach, this immaculate and intimate hostel is popular among the surfer set. Budget travelers appreciate the clean, cool dorms (with air-con) as well as the attentive service from the staff. Guests get reduced rates on boards and lessons at the Blue Trailz (p305) surf shop out front. Sweet.

Villas Macondo HOTEL $$
(☎2653-0812; www.villasmacondo.com; s/d/tr from US$50/65/75, with air-con US$75/87/97, apt US$130-175; P❄@🛜🏊) Although it's only 200m from the beach, this establishment is an oasis of serenity in an otherwise frenzied town – it's also one of the best deals around. Beautiful modern villas with private hammocks and patios surround a solar-heated pool, tropical garden and communal kitch-

en. Larger apartments have their own kitchens and are ideal for families.

Extra credit for naming it after Garcia-Marquez' fictional town.

Beach Bungalows B&B $$
(☎8800-0011; www.tamarindobeachbungalows.com; d incl breakfast from US$100; P Wi-Fi pool) Shaded by palms, these teak, stilted bungalows feel like a luxurious retreat. In each one, the raised living quarters are rich yet rustic, while the area below is an open-air poolside chill-out lounge. Guests enjoy a decadent breakfast, as well as free use of bikes, a gas grill and a common kitchen. Not exactly on the beach, but why quibble?

Three-night minimum stay in high season.

Hotel Mahayana HOTEL $$
(☎2653-1154; www.hotelmahayana.com; d from US$65; P A/C Wi-Fi pool) The Mahayana is a sweet retreat, away from the hustle and bustle of the main drag. Spotless, citrus-painted rooms have high ceilings, big windows and private terraces (with hammocks). The courtyard contains a small pool and an outdoor kitchen, which is at your disposal.

★**Ocho Artisan Bungalows** BOUTIQUE HOTEL $$$
(☎8365-9666; www.ochoartisansbungalows.com; bungalow/casita from $350/500; P A/C Wi-Fi) A slice of paradise just a block off the main drag. Meander through the jungle-like grounds' inlaid wooden paths to any of seven bungalows (plus two *casitas*) with pristine patios, or trundle over to the outdoor bar overlooking the beach. The stately and roomy habitations, comfortable for up to four, shine with newness; even the *mosquiteros* (mosquito nets) look fancy.

Tamarindo Bay Boutique Hotel BOUTIQUE HOTEL $$$
(☎2653-2692; www.tamarindobayhotel.com; d incl breakfast from US$165; A/C Wi-Fi pool) Here's a romantic getaway for adults only, and it helps to like dogs (there are three sweet rescues on the property). Slick modern rooms on the recently expanded and revamped property have king- or queen-sized beds and rain showers. Our favorite feature is the swimming pool, complete with multicolored LED lighting and recycled plastic decking. The open-air breakfast terrace is a treat, too.

Hotel Luamey BOUTIQUE HOTEL $$$
(☎2653-1510; www.hotelluamey.com; d from US$155; P A/C Wi-Fi pool) Simply exquisite, this boutique hotel is an oasis of serenity and beauty in the midst of Tamarindo chaos. Spacious *cabaña* suites are decorated in soothing earth tones, with dark wood furnishings, stone showers and private patios (where breakfast is served). Service is very accommodating. Yoga and surf classes offered. Culinary tours, too.

Sueño del Mar B&B B&B $$$
(☎2653-0284; www.sueno-del-mar.com; d US$220, casitas US$260-310; P A/C @ Wi-Fi pool) This secluded B&B on Playa Langosta is set in a stunning faux-adobe Spanish-style *posada* (guesthouse). The rooms have four-poster beds, artfully placed crafts and open-air garden showers, while the romantic honeymoon suite has a wraparound window with sea views.

There's private beach access beyond the pool and tropical garden, where guests (and in-the-know nonguests) take their exquisite three-course breakfast. No children allowed.

Boho Tamarindo B&B $$$
(☎8709-5674; www.boho-tamarindo.com; d from US$330; P A/C Wi-Fi) This elegant boutique B&B opened in late 2018 and became an insta-favorite thanks to the intimate atmosphere, convenient (yet secluded) location and fabulous hosts. The eight immaculate rooms feature private patios and all the modern comforts (but no TVs), and surround an inviting pool. The homemade French

SUNDAY FUNDAY

Dubbed **Sunday Funday** (www.beachandpoolcrawl.com; tickets from US$40; ⏲noon-8pm Sun), Tamarindo's beach and pool crawl convenes weekly at Sharky's (p309) as long as 15 people have signed up. Once participants are good and sozzled, they board a retired school bus and cruise along the coast, hitting up secret pool parties with DJs, hidden beach throw-downs involving volleyball and margaritas, and sunset watch spots featuring live entertainment and a beach bonfire. It's a pretty rad way to meet fellow travelers.

breakfasts are another huge selling point – yes, that means *croque monsieur*.

The hosts are a wealth of information about the area, and they provide complimentary bikes and snorkel gear.

Eating

★El Mercadito FOOD HALL $
(☎8727-5227; www.facebook.com/mercaditodetamarindo; mains US$5-12; ⊙11am-11pm; ✎) Travelers with diets and preferences that differ from their companions' will appreciate the wide range of offerings at this breezy, buzzing artisanal food marketplace. Options include poke, pizza, arepas, hamburgers, tacos and vegan dishes, and pagers conveniently let everybody know when their food is ready.

The atmosphere is enlivened by a large bar and stage illuminated with fairy lights, along with events like tango dancing and bingo.

★La Bodega CAFE $
(☎8395-6184; www.labodegatamarindo.com; Hotel Nahua; mains US$6-8; ⊙7am-3pm Mon-Sat, to noon Sun; 📶✎) This delightful cafe and shop specializes in freshly brewed java, but also serves fresh, local and organic foods. For breakfast it does amazing things with eggs, while lunch is a daily changing menu of sandwiches and salads. At any time of day, you can't go wrong with its banana bread or lemon scones.

Surf Shack BURGERS $
(☎2653-2346; www.facebook.com/surfshacktamarindo; mains US$5-10; ⊙11am-9pm Fri-Wed; 📶) If you are craving a big bad burger, Surf Shack has you covered with a good selection of patties, thick-cut onion rings and irresistible milkshakes. Tin-can walls and surfboard decor create a laid-back vibe, enhanced by the drinks coming from the bar. It's steps from the beach; the sea breeze is the perfect accompaniment to anything you order.

Falafel Bar LEBANESE $
(☎2653-1268; www.facebook.com/tamarindofalafelbar; mains US$5-10; ⊙10am-11pm Wed-Mon; ✎) When you get tired of *casados*, head to this Middle Eastern cafe for all the faves: shakshuka, shawarma, falafel, tabbouleh, hummus and kebabs. The pita bread is made fresh daily. Fresh juice and coffee in the morning; a real 'bar' at night.

Green Papaya MEXICAN $$
(☎2652-0863; www.facebook.com/Gr33nPapaya; mains US$8-15; ⊙11am-10pm Tue-Sun; ❄📶✎) Swing on up to the bar, grab a tree-stump stool, and prepare to sample some fantastic fare. The mahi-mahi tacos are perfection in a tortilla, while non-meat-eaters will appreciate the multiple veggie options including enchiladas in creamy chipotle sauce. You'll go loco for the Chocolate Lovers dessert. Everything is fresh and friendly – don't miss it.

Utopia FRENCH $$
(☎2275-4375, 7073-3584; ⊙7am-10pm) Pastry chef Hervé is out to impress with dishes including creamy chicken vol-au-vent, *moules marinière* (mussels in white wine) and a passel of veggie dishes. But the best is saved for last, with unholy black-and-white chocolate mousse and other delectables. Thursday is Latin night, with salsa and merengue dancing. It's next to Pura Vida Hostel (p306).

Jolly Roger GASTROPUB $$
(☎8451-6927; www.bestwingscostarica.com; wings US$11; ⊙2-10pm Thu-Mon; ❄) These chicken wings are so darn good, people plan their days around them. The meaty, oversized wings are a perfect combo of crunchy and tender, but it's the 24 different sauces that truly set these apart. Hot honey garlic! Spicy maple brown sugar! Hot sugarcane! Bring lots of friends and try them all. Cauliflower substitutes available.

There are sister restaurants in Dominical and Manuel Antonio.

La Baula PIZZA $$
(☎2653-1450; www.facebook.com/PizzeriaLaBaula; mains US$12-16; ⊙5:30-10:30pm; ✎) The best pizza in Tamarindo, by some accounts. This casual open-air restaurant has 28 different pizzas with a wide variety of toppings, as well as salads. It's also one of the most family-friendly restaurants in town, with a playground to keep the kids entertained. The open-air, woodsy setting requires insect repellent.

★Pangas Beach Club SEAFOOD $$$
(☎2653-0024; www.facebook.com/PangasTamarindo; mains US$15-28; ⊙noon-10pm Mon-Sat, 10am-10pm Sun) Tamarindo's best restaurant, and an ideal place for marking a special occasion. It's perched on the sand where an estuary meets the sea, with candle-lit tables

beneath swaying palm and ficus trees hung with glowing lamps. The seafood is freshly caught and expertly prepared, particularly the mouthwatering grilled octopus. The ribeye served searing on a hot lava rock is equally delightful.

Dragonfly Bar & Grill ASIAN $$$

(☎2653-1506; www.dragonflybarandgrill.com; mains US$15-22; ⏰5:30-10pm; P 📶 ✎) Beloved for its refined menu and its upscale tiki-bar atmosphere, this open-air dining room has twinkling lights and lanterns, with a subtle dragonfly motif throughout. The eclectic menu leans Asian, but fuses international elements. Go for the goodness-filled Buddha bowl or the fiery Thai beef served on glass noodles. Desserts such as *tres leches* (three-milk pudding) are also divine.

Drinking & Nightlife

The main drag in Tamarindo has the festive feel of spring break, with well-oiled patrons spilling out onto the beach, drinks in hand. Almost every hour is happy hour, all around you. If you're not sure where to start, go for sundowners at any bar on the beachfront strip – if you can wait that long.

Café Tico CAFE

(☎8861-7732; www.facebook.com/cafeticotamarindo; ⏰7am-3pm Mon-Sat, 8am-1pm Sun; 📶) Walk in. Take a deep breath. Smell the magic brewing? On the wall it says, 'good days start with coffee.' Sip it on the shady patio while snacking on a homemade pastry. Or a breakfast burrito. Or an omelette. *Pura vida.*

Sharky's SPORTS BAR

(☎8729-8274; www.sharkysbars.com; ⏰11:30am-2:30am) If you want to catch the big game, look no further than Sharky's. Besides nine screens showing sports, there are burgers, wings and lots of beer. There's a nightly lineup of fun and games, including karaoke night on Tuesday and ladies' night on Saturday. The motto is *'un zarpe mas?'* (one last drink?). Get ready to get your drink on.

El Be! BAR

(☎8804-0042; www.facebook.com/ElBeClubTamarindo; ⏰10am-11pm Tue, Wed & Fri, to 2:30am Thu, Sat & Sun) Formerly Le Beach Club, this place has changed languages (and added an exclamation point!) but the cool vibe remains the same. Lounge on beach beds or hammocks and listen to the DJ's tunes. Happy hour (5pm to 7pm) features drinks specials, live jazz and fabulous sunsets. Occasionally fire dancers perform after dark.

Volcano Brewing Company BEER GARDEN

(www.volcanobrewingcompany.com; ⏰11am-11pm) Beer on the beach is never a bad thing, and when it's Tico home brew, even better. The 15 varieties of *cerveza* are a bit pricey, but consider the location. Just stare into the Pacific over your plastic cup of Gato Malo (Bad Cat) stout – and if your inner volcano starts rumbling, you can order from the restaurant next door.

You'll find it right next to Witch's Rock Surf Camp (p305).

Information

BAC (Plaza Conchal; ⏰9am-6pm Mon-Fri, to 1pm Sat)

Banco de Costa Rica (Plaza Conchal; ⏰24hr) 24-hour ATM.

Beachside Clinic (☎2653-9911; www.facebook.com/beachsideclinic; ⏰24hr) A respected medical clinic near Tamarindo, in Huacas.

Fast Clean Laundromat (☎8935-5664; Plaza Conchal; ⏰7am-7pm) Get your clothes washed, dried and folded.

Getting There & Away

Surfers and other beach party people flock to Tamarindo by air, bus and car.

BUSES FROM TAMARINDO

DESTINATION	COMPANY	PRICE (US$)	DURATION (HR)	DEPARTURES
Liberia	La Pampa	2.50	2½	12 times per day, 3:30am-6:30pm
San José	Alfaro	10	5½	3am & 5:30am
San José	Tralapa	11	6	7:30am & 2pm
Santa Cruz	Tralapa	2	1½	6am, 8:30am & noon

AIR

The airstrip is 3km north of town; a hotel bus is usually on hand to pick up arriving passengers. During high season, **Sansa** (☎2290-4100; www.flysansa.com; Tamarindo Airport) has up to four daily flights to and from San José, and **Skyway** (www.skywaycr.com) offers five flights a week. If you book early or go for the promotional fares, you can sometimes get discounts.

BUS

The **Empresa Alfaro** (☎2222-2666; www.empresaalfaro.com) office is near the beach, while other buses depart from the **bus stop** in front of Pacific Park.

Private shuttle buses offer a faster (albeit more expensive) option. **Tamarindo Transfers and Tours** (☎2653-0505; www.tamarindotransfersandtours.com; Centro Comercial Galerías del Mar; ⊙8am-8pm) provides comfortable and convenient transfers from Tamarindo to destinations around the country, including both airports. **Tropical Tours** (☎2640-1900, 2640-0811; www.tropicaltourshuttles.com) has daily shuttles that connect Tamarindo to San José, as well as to several destinations in the southern part of the Nicoya Peninsula.

CAR & TAXI

By car from Liberia, take Hwy 21 to Belén, then Hwy 155 via Huacas to Tamarindo. A taxi costs around US$100 to or from Liberia.

Amazingly, there's no gas station here. For that, you'll have to drive 15 paved kilometers to Huacas, hang a right and go up the hill. The gas station is 4km ahead, on the right.

Getting Around

If you choose your lodgings wisely, there's no need for a car, as you can walk to the beach and book tours for other outings in the area.

AVOIDING TROUBLE IN TAMARINDO

Like a few other Tico beach towns with a young surfer crowd, Tamarindo has a bit of a nocturnal drug culture, a by-product of the country's place as a way station on the South America–North America trade route. The casual stroller will be approached with offers for drugs (and sometimes women) after the sun goes down. It's an annoyance at best, and you'll definitely want to pass on those offers; it's still illegal if you get caught with drugs.

Playas Avellanas & Negra

These popular surfing beaches have some of the best, most consistent waves in the area, made famous in the surf classic *Endless Summer II*. The killer waves have led to one section being nicknamed 'Little Hawaii.'

Playa Avellanas is an absolutely stunning, pristine sweep of pale golden sand. Backed by mangroves in the center and with two gentle hillsides on either end, it has plenty of room for surfers and sunbathers to have an intimate experience even when there are lots of heads in town.

Playa Negra is also undeniably romantic. Though the sand is a bit darker and the beach is broken up by rocky outcrops, gorgeous dusty back roads link tide pools of shredders who picked this place to exist (and surf) peacefully.

Activities

The waves at Playa Avellanas are decent for beginners and intermediate surfers. Little Hawaii is the powerful and open-faced right featured in *Endless Summer II*, while the beach break barrels at low tide. Still, advanced surfers who aren't long-boarders get restless here, so they go to Playa Negra, which is blessed by a world-class right that barrels. Further south is Playa Tortuga, a little-known but epic break for advanced surfers only. The waves are best between April and November, but start getting good in March.

Avellanas Surf School SURFING

(☎7105-2619; www.avellanas-surf-school.com; board rental per day US$20, lessons adult/child US$55/65; ⊙8am-5pm) Mauricio Ortega is a local guy who loves to surf and wants to share his expertise and lifestyle with anyone who cares to partake. He and his wife Dialan run this highly rated surf school, and rent out a handful of cabins and villas close to the waves. It's next to Lola's (p312).

Playa Negra SUP Wave Riders WATER SPORTS

(☎8702-7894; www.playanegrasupwaveriders.com; lessons US$70-80, tours US$60-70) In less than two hours, you'll learn how to stand up and paddle, either by touring the flats of the local estuary or by heading out on the open ocean waves. If you already know what you're doing, rental boards are also available. ASI certified.

LOCAL KNOWLEDGE

NO STRAW CHALLENGE

A Canadian boy living in Avellanas, Max Machum, was inspired to try to eliminate plastic drinking straws from restaurants when he heard the Leatherback Project's director describe how he had to remove a straw from a turtle's nose to save its life. His ambitious idea was picked up by Lola's (p312), who invested in biodegradable, environmentally friendly straws, and by other local restaurants.

There's a national conversation in Costa Rica about how to eliminate plastics entirely – and it got its start here. You can spread the word and also specifically ask not to be given a straw when ordering drinks. More information is available at www.nostrawchallenge.com.

Sleeping

There's not really a village here – just a series of surf-oriented lodgings strung out along the road that connects the two beaches. That said, there's a nice range of sleeping options, from hippy surf camps to more sophisticated guesthouses and villas. If you prefer to sleep out under the stars, you'll find a few places to string a hammock or pitch a tent at the southern end of Playa Avellanas.

Casa Surf GUESTHOUSE $
(2652-9075; www.casa-surf.com; Playa Avellanas; dm US$15; P) Casa Surf looks a bit tired but still tropical, with a bamboo exterior and palm-thatched roof. Inside, you'll find simple, clean rooms – brightly painted and clean enough – with shared access to a bathroom and a kitchen. The upstairs hammock deck is an enticing place to spend an afternoon (or a night). Also available: bike rental, book exchange and a community guitar.

Offers an excellent-value surf, sleep and eat option (US$30), which includes breakfast and surfboard rental. Highly personalized lessons with video analysis are available from onsite surf operation, School of Stoke (from US$60). Plans are afoot to add and air-conditioning in the dorms and private rooms with en suite bathrooms.

Kon-Tiki HOSTEL $
(2652-9117; www.facebook.com/kontikiplayanegra; Playa Negra; r without bathroom per person US$20; P) Along the road from Avellanas, this low-key and inviting place has a rambling collection of colorful cabins on stilts, and is highly popular with surfers and howler monkeys. Bathroom facilities are shared. In the middle of it all is a rickety pavilion where guests swing in hammocks and devour pizza and other affordable fare.

A popular new bar serves creative cocktail infusions and hosts live music on the regular.

Las Avellanas Villas APARTMENT $$
(8705-0714; www.lasavellanasvillas.com; Playa Avellanas; d from US$120; P) Thoughtfully designed, these stunning *casitas* are oases of tranquility and balance, with private teak terraces, polished-concrete floors, indoor greenery, open-air showers and large windows streaming with natural light. For practical matters, there are surfboard racks and hammocks (of course). Full kitchens make this option perfect for families or groups. The grounds are about 800m from the beach.

Café Playa Negra GUESTHOUSE $$
(2652-9351; www.cafeplayanegra.com; Playa Negra; s/d/tr/q incl breakfast US$55/75/90/100; P@) These stylish, minimalist digs upstairs from the cafe have polished-concrete floors, elevated beds dressed with colorful bedspreads, and other artistic touches. There's a shared deck with comfy hammock chairs and an inviting swimming pool. The downstairs cafe, open all day (closed Tuesday, though), is worth a stop no matter where you are sleeping. Sample delectable sandwiches and Peruvian seafood dishes.

Playa Negra Surf Lodge CABINA $$
(2652-9270; www.playanegrasurflodge.com; Playa Negra; incl breakfast s/d/tr/q US$80/80/90/100, studio US$80;) The quaint *cabinas* here are set around a gorgeous tropical garden teeming with hummingbirds, butterflies and parakeets. Simple rooms have freshly painted walls and a few artistic details. Guests also have access to a shared terrace and plenty of hammocks. Don't skip out on lunch at the onsite Jalapeño Eatery & Market (p312). Studios have private kitchens.

Eating

A legendary beach cafe that's named after a pig: that's the main eating destination in these surfer outposts. There are also some low-key markets and one renowned restaurant worth the trip into Negra.

Jalapeño Eatery & Market MEXICAN $
(☎2652-9270; www.playanegrasurflodge.com/restaurant-jalapeno; Playa Negra; mains US$7-10; ⊙8am-4pm Mon-Sat) There's something special about this glorified taco bar. Ingredients are all organically produced or locally sourced. Tortillas are hand-rolled; hot sauce and other condiments are house-made; chickens and eggs come from the neighbor's farm. Even the fish is usually speared by the chef/owner (so don't complain if it takes longer than you expected.)

Lola's on the Beach CAFE $$$
(www.facebook.com/playaavellana; Playa Avellanas; mains US$14-19; ⊙11am-5pm Tue-Sun; P ᯤ) Hang out at this stylish beach cafe while waiting for the waves. Slanted wood chairs are planted in the sand beneath thatched umbrellas. A tree-stump bar overlooks an open kitchen, where the beachy cuisine is tops. Kudos for its determined efforts to recycle cooking oils and not use any plastics (you'll get a paper straw).

In case you're wondering, Lola was an enormous and lovable pig, aka the 'Queen of Avellanas.' She has since passed, but her legacy lives on in 'little' Lolita!

★**Villa Deevena** FUSION $$$
(☎2653-2328; www.villadeevena.com; Playa Negra; mains US$19-45; ⊙7am-2:30pm & 5:30-9pm; P ❄ ᯤ) Foodies drive from all over Guanacaste to sample the fare at this otherworldly restaurant, the brainchild of chef/owner Patrick Jamon (let the jokes begin: *jamon* means 'ham' in Spanish). Start off with a fresh-fruit-juice cocktail while you peruse the masterful menu: perfect preparations of seafood, slow-roasted meats and one-of-a-kind desserts. Reservations recommended.

The property also offers simple but elegant luxury at its minimalist two- to four-person bungalows (double occupancy US$130). Swish accommodations – decorated with hardwood and soothing tones – surround the glittering saltwater pool.

TURTLES

Olive ridley turtles nest in Junquillal from July to November, with a peak in numbers from August to October, but there are fewer than at the refuges; Junquillal is also an important nesting site for leatherbacks. Though the area is not officially protected, conservation groups such as **Asociacion Vida Verdiazul** (☎2658-7251; www.facebook.com/pg/asociacion.vida.verdiazul; Beach Rd, at the roundabout) have teamed up with local communities to protect the nesting sites and eliminate poaching.

Getting There & Away

BUS

A public bus travels between Santa Cruz and Playas Avellanas and Negra twice a day. The outbound bus leaves Negra at around 6am and 1:45pm each day, and takes about 1½ hours. There are sometimes shuttles between Tamarindo and these beaches, and various surf camps also organize trips.

CAR

From Tamarindo, drive 5km inland to the village of Villareal, and turn right on to the dirt road. This road becomes progressively worse as you get further from Tamarindo and may require a 4WD. If you're not coming from Tamarindo, drive west from Santa Cruz on the paved highway, through 27 de Abril to Paraíso, then follow the signs to the beach of your choice. As always, do not leave valuables in your car, especially at the beaches.

Playa Junquillal

Hard to pronounce and almost as difficult to find, Junquillal (say 'hoon-kee-yal') is a 2km-wide gray-sand wilderness beach that's absolutely stunning and mostly deserted. To the south, a dome boulder crumbles into a jutting rock reef and beyond that is a vast, 200-hectare estuary carved by the Río Nandamojo. To the north is a narrow rise of bluffs sprouting clumps of palm trees. Sunsets are downright surreal, with blinding golds, molten oranges and shocking pinks. The sea does swirl with fierce rip currents, however, and when it gets big, surfers descend from Negra. Even when the surf isn't high, it's dangerous out there. Don't let kids or even intermediate swimmers venture out alone.

With far more Ticos than tourists, Junquillal has an inviting authenticity unique in the northern peninsula. The nearest town is 4km inland at Paraíso.

Sleeping

El Castillo Divertido HOTEL $
(☎8351-5162, 2658-8428; s US$20-40, d US$30-60; P 📶) This colorful castle, decked out with crenellated walls and carved masks, is just 400m from the beach, offering panoramic views from its rooftop bar. Take advantage of the one-of-a-kind boat and kayaking tours (US$40 per person) through the Río Nandamojo and surrounding mangroves. On certain Friday nights, guests are invited to partake of drinks and delicious grilled meat at a sunset BBQ.

★ **Mundo Milo Ecolodge** BUNGALOW $$
(☎2658-7010; www.mundomilo.com; d incl breakfast US$75-85; P ❄ 📶 🏊) The area's most creative nest is this unique ecolodge, where attention to detail is paramount. Choose from five skylit bungalows (four with air-con, one fan-cooled), each surrounded by lush vegetation and styled after a different world region (Africa, Mexico, Persia). The pool is an artful arc overlooking dry tropical woodland, with monkeys howling, birds chanting and waves crashing in the distance.

Lieke, your hostess, is a wonderful cook.

Eating & Drinking

Aside from the hotel restaurants, your best option for eating is to head to nearby Paraíso, though there a few small spots on the beach. **Lochito's** (☎8806-5216; Ruta 928; mains $8-12; ⊙4-10pm Tue-Sat, noon-10pm Sun), a small roadside joint on the road into town, is popular with locals. The best spot for a sunset *cerveza* is **Junquillal Eco Resort** (☎2249-9839; www.junquillalecoresort.com).

Getting There & Away

BUS

Buses depart from Junquillal to Santa Cruz (US$2, 1½ hours) at 6am, 9am, 12:30pm and 4:30pm; you can catch the bus anywhere along the main road. Buses from Santa Cruz to Junquillal depart from the Mercado Municipal at 5am, 10am, 2:30pm and 5:30pm.

CAR

If you're driving, it's about 16km by paved road from Santa Cruz to 27 de Abril, and another smooth 17km into town.

> **LOCAL KNOWLEDGE**
>
> **GUAITIL**
>
> An interesting excursion from Santa Cruz, Guaitil is a small artisanal potter community, where attractive ceramics are made from local clays, using earthy reds, creams and blacks in pre-Columbian Chorotega style. Ceramics are sold outside the potters' houses and also in San Vicente, 2km beyond Guaitil. If you ask, you can watch part of the potting process, and local residents will be happy to give you a few lessons for a small fee. You might also find traditional foods, such as corn tamales and *rosquillos* (cheese rings) here.

From Junquillal, it's possible to drive 35km south to Nosara via the legendary surf spot of Marbella. However, this is a rough dirt road, and 4WD and high clearance are recommended. In the rainy season, it may be impassable regardless of what you drive. There are no gas stations on the coastal road and little traffic, so ask locally before setting out. It's easier to reach beaches south of Junquillal from Nicoya.

Santa Cruz

POP 16,400

Santa Cruz is an important regional administrative center, and a good base for visiting Guaitil. At certain times of the year you can also witness the Guanacaste bull-riding tradition in the city's bullring. In Costa Rica the bull is never killed, but brave (or foolhardy!) citizens take their chances dodging them in the ring.

Sleeping & Eating

There are countless *sodas* (cheap lunch counters) and Chinese diners in town, though nothing stands out. It's not a bad lunch stop, but there are more diverse offerings in the coastal towns.

Hotel La Pampa HOTEL $
(☎2680-0586; Av 5 btwn Calles 2 & Central; s/d from US$36/40; P ❄ 📶) A good budget option, this peach-tinted hotel is 50m west of the Plaza de Los Mangos. It isn't all that inspiring from the outside, but the rooms are clean and modern, providing a decent place to lay your head.

La Calle de Alcalá HOTEL $$
(☎2680-0000, 2680-1515; www.hotellacallede alcala.com; Av 7 btwn Calles 1 & 3; s/d/ste US$57/77/130; P❄📶🏊) With its stucco arches and landscaped garden around a pool, this hotel gets points for design. Carved wooden doors open into small tiled rooms with rattan furnishings. It's one block due east of the bus terminal; a convenient stopover option.

Getting There & Away

Santa Cruz is 57km from Liberia and 25km south of Filadelfia on the main peninsular highway. A paved road leads 16km west to 27 de Abril, from where dirt roads continue to Playa Tamarindo, Playa Junquillal and other beaches. There's a gas station off the main intersection with the highway.

CENTRAL PENINSULA

Long the political and cultural heart of Guanacaste, the inland region of the central peninsula looks and feels palpably more 'Costa Rican' than the beach resorts of the northern coast. Over generations, the dry tropical forest has been cut down to make way for the *sabaneros'* cattle, but stands of forest remain, interspersed between *fincas* (farms) and coastal villages, sometimes backing stretches of wild, empty beaches. Though the areas around Sámara and Nosara are developing steadily, many foreigners who are drawn to the rugged coastline are active in its conservation. The central peninsula remains rife with secluded beaches, small villages and endless possibilities for getting 'off the map.'

Nicoya

POP 13,334

A hub between the beaches and ranches, the big cities and *pueblitos* (little towns), Nicoya (23km south of Santa Cruz) offers a blast of Tico time. Truckers, road-trippers and locals converge around a grid, packed with commerce and crowned with a gorgeous *iglesia* (church) that makes the leafy Parque Central worth a loiter.

Sleeping & Eating

Mundiplaza Hotel HOTEL $
(☎2685-3535; Calle 3; s/d US$30/40; ❄📶) Right in the center of Nicoya, this is a perfectly pleasant place to spend the night. With colorful paint jobs (a few could use some touching up) and tiled bathrooms, it's relatively clean and well maintained. The shared balcony has striking views to the Nicoya hills, though the road noise can be excessive.

Cafe Daniela SODA $
(☎2686-6148; www.facebook.com/cafedaniela; Calle 3; mains US$6-10; ⏲7am-9:30pm Mon-Sat; ✎) A popular *soda* serving appetizing *comida típica* (typical local food) such as *gallo pinto* (stir-fry of rice and beans) in the morning, and fish, beef, chicken and veggie *casados* (set meals) later on. Coffee, yummy cakes and other baked goods are also on offer, and it's all served in bright tiled environs.

Information

Banco de Costa Rica (Calle Central; ⏲9am-4pm Mon-Fri)

Banco Popular (Calle 3; ⏲8:30am-4:30pm Mon-Fri, to 11:30am Sat) Also has a 24-hour ATM at Hospital La Anexión.

Hospital La Anexión (☎2685-5066, 2685-8400; ⏲24hr) The peninsula's main hospital is on the north side of Nicoya.

Getting There & Away

Most buses arrive at and depart from the **bus terminal** (Calle 5) southeast of Parque Central.

BUSES FROM NICOYA

DESTINATION	COMPANY	COST (US$)	DURATION (HR)	DEPARTURES
Liberia	Transportes La Pampa	2	2	Every 30-60min, 7am-8:30pm
Playa Nosara	Empresa Traroc	3.40	2	4:45am, 10am, 12:30pm, 3:30pm & 5:30pm Mon-Sat. No early bus Sun
Sámara & Playa Carrillo	Empresa Traroc	3	1½	10 daily, 5am-8pm
San José	Empresa Alfaro	6.80	5	9 daily

Parque Nacional Barra Honda

Parque Nacional Barra Honda is situated about halfway between Nicoya and the mouth of the Río Tempisque. The main attraction of this inland park is a massive underground system of caverns composed of soft limestone, carved by rainfall and erosion over a period of about 70 million years. Speleologists have discovered 42 caverns, some reaching as deep as 200m, though to date only 19 have been fully explored. There have also been discoveries of pre-Columbian remains dating to 300 BCE.

In addition to the caverns there's a plethora of wildlife around. More than 80 bird species have been sighted, as well as bat populations, anteaters and armadillos.

Sights

Parque Nacional Barra Honda Caverns CAVE

(☎2659-1551; www.sinac.go.cr; adult/child US$12/5, guided tour incl park admission US$33; ⊙trails 8am-3pm, caverns to 1pm;) This 23-sq-km national park protects a system of 42 caverns. The only cave with regular public access is the 41m-deep La Terciopelo, which features incredible speleothems (calcite figures that rise and fall in the cave's interior). It's quite the underground art museum, and its stalagmites, stalactites and a host of beautiful formations have evocative names such as fried eggs, organ, soda straws, flowers and shark's teeth. Call the ranger station one day in advance to arrange the four-hour guided tour.

Unlike some caverns in other places, Barra Honda is not developed for wide-scale tourism, which means that it feels less like a carnival attraction and more like a scene from *Indiana Jones*. So, don your yellow miner's hat and sturdy boots, and be prepared to get down and dirty. The descent involves ladders and ropes, so you should be reasonably fit; children must be at least 12 years old. A small *'cuevita'* is appropriate for children under 12.

Tourists must be accompanied by a guide into the cave, and may hike or spelunk at any time of year, provided that the park rangers have determined it is safe. As always, carry several liters of water and let the rangers know where you are going. Sneakers or, preferably, boots are necessary if you will be caving. You will also need a 4WD vehicle to drive from the ranger station to the parking area near the caves. The last allowable descent into the caves is at 1pm.

> **WHY NICOYA?**
>
> One theory has it that Nicoya was named after an indigenous Chorotega chief, Nicoa, who welcomed Spanish conquistador Gil González de Ávila in 1523 (a gesture he regretted). A second theory is that it derives from the Nahuatl words *necoc iāuh*, meaning 'on both sides is water(s),' describing the town's location between two rivers. Regardless, following Ávila's arrival, the Chorotega were wiped out by the colonists, though many Nicoyans still proudly claim their indigenous heritage.

Activities

The Barra Honda hills have a few well-marked hiking trails through deciduous, dry tropical forest. Before or after visiting the cave you can hike 3.5km to the top of Cerro Barra Honda, which has a *mirador* (lookout point) with a view of Río Tempisque and Golfo de Nicoya. You won't need a guide to hike the trails.

Getting There & Away

To reach Barra Honda by public transportation, take a bus from Nicoya to Santa Ana (US$1, twice daily except Sunday), which will get you within striking distance (about 1km away). Alternatively, take a taxi from Nicoya for about US$20 round trip. You can arrange for your driver to pick you up at a specified time.

If you have your own vehicle, take the peninsular highway south out of Nicoya toward Mansión and make a left on the access road towards Puente La Amistad. Continue for 1.5km and make a left on the signed road to Barra Honda. The dirt road will take you to the village of Barra Honda then wind to the left for another 6km, passing Santa Ana, before ending at the national park gate. The road is clearly marked, and there are several signs along the way indicating the direction of the park. After the village of Barra Honda, the road is unpaved, but in good condition.

If you are coming to the park from Puente La Amistad, you will see the access road to Barra Honda signed about 16km after leaving the bridge.

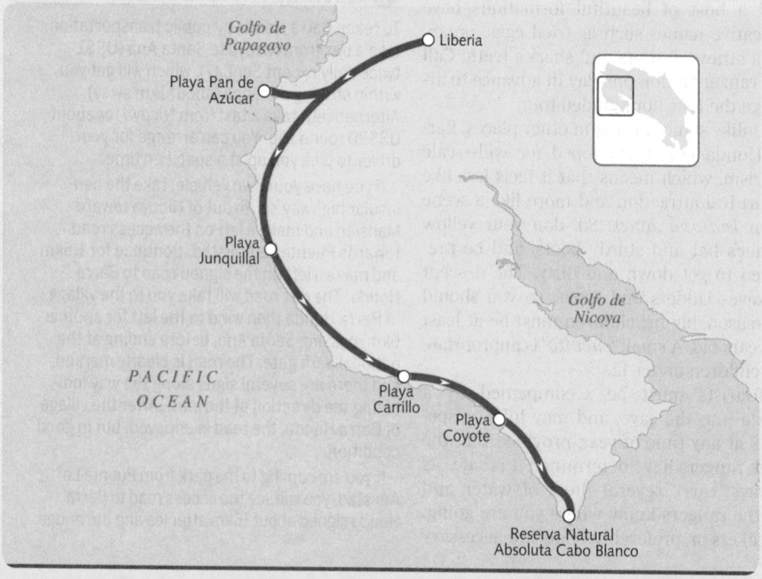
Golfo de Papagayo
Liberia
Playa Pan de Azúcar
Playa Junquillal
Golfo de Nicoya
PACIFIC OCEAN
Playa Carrillo
Playa Coyote
Reserva Natural Absoluta Cabo Blanco

MARCIN ROSZKOWSKI/SHUTTERSTOCK ©

JODIE ELLENOR/ALAMY STOCK PHOTO ©

Top: Playa Carrillo (p329)
Bottom: Halloween crab, Reserva Natural Absoluta Cabo Blanco (p342)

1 WEEK Undiscovered Nicoya

When it comes to beautiful beaches, Península de Nicoya is richly blessed indeed. Development here is uneven, which means there are plenty of hidden nooks, secluded coves and pristine paradises that remain unexploited.

Of course, you can't just take a direct flight to paradise; you have to work for it. In Costa Rica that usually means hiring a 4WD for some brutally bumpy roads, and perhaps fording a river or two. (NB: This itinerary is not recommended during rainy season.)

From **Liberia** (p227), your first destination is **Playa Pan de Azúcar**, accessible via the infamous Monkey Trail. It's a rough ride but you won't care once you reach this jigsaw of rugged cliffs and clandestine coves. The closest place to sleep is the Hotel Sugar Beach (p300) – a sweet choice.

Heading south, you'll pass through resort towns like Playa Flamingo and fishing villages like Playa Brasilito. The main road detours inland, so you can buzz right by Tamarindo. It's not until you reach **Playa Junquillal** (p312) that you'll feel you're really out there. And you are: unless the surf's up, this wild beach is often deserted.

Keep moving south, skipping Nosara and Sámara, but stopping at **Playa Carrillo** (p329), a white-sand beauty, framed by granite and backed by towering palms. Locals descend from the village to watch sunset – join them.

The area between Carrillo and Santa Teresa remains one of the peninsula's most isolated and wonderful stretches of coastline. Tackle the rugged roads and you'll be rewarded with miles of abandoned beaches backed by forest-covered hills. **Playa Coyote** (p330) is at once desolate and divine. Don't miss sundowners at El Barco (p332).

Your final stop is the **Reserva Natural Absoluta Cabo Blanco** (p353), a nature reserve that covers the entire tip of Península de Nicoya. The evergreen forests and wilderness beaches here are mostly empty of visitors – a perfect ending to your tour of Undiscovered Nicoya.

Nosara Area

Nosara is a cocktail of international surf culture, stunning back-road topography, moneyed expat mayhem and yoga bliss.

Here, three beaches are stitched together by a network of swerving, rutted earth roads that meander over coastal hills and kiss the coast just west of the small village of Nosara. Inland are remnant pockets of luxuriant dry forest that attract birds and other wildlife. The area has seen little logging, partly because of the nearby wildlife refuge, but also because of a dusty, bumpy access road, despite years of discussion about paving it.

The area is spread out, so your own wheels are a plus. Eight kilometers inland, Nosara is where you'll find gas, as well as the airport. Most accommodations and restaurants are in Playa Pelada and Playa Guiones, but you'll also find some gems up in the hills and down secluded side roads.

Sights

Playa Garza BEACH

From the south, the first beach you'll hit is Playa Garza, still a sleepy Tico fishing village with an arc of pale brown sand, and headlands on either side of the rippling bay. Fishing boats bob offshore and there's a point break to the north side. There are a few *cabinas* and *sodas* here, lots of sand space, and precious few tourists.

Playa Guiones BEACH

Nosara's most developed beach is also a stunner, with a wide, generous arc of marbled sand (and a few pebbles and shells mixed in), excellent beach breaks and plenty of wide open space. It's an easygoing place for surfers, surf dogs and surf babies – you might just see unattended strollers lodged in the wet sand at low tide.

Playa Pelada BEACH

North of Guiones, Playa Pelada is a family gathering place for sunset, swimming and surfing, though the waves can get a bit rough. On the northern end, the foaming sea crashes relentlessly against sheared-away boulders, but skilled surfers tend to congregate up there for a beach break. Pelada also offers two alluring beachside restaurants and the fishing-village intimacy that Guiones lacks.

Refuge for Wildlife ANIMAL SANCTUARY

(☎2682-5049; www.refugeforwildlife.org; Nosara; requested donation per person US$50; ⏱by appointment) Make an appointment to visit this animal rescue center. Brenda Bombard is an incurable animal lover who has devoted two decades to caring for injured and abandoned howler monkeys. Two-hour tours are highly educational, sharing information about the habits of howler monkeys and the center's efforts to rescue and release them (with an impressive 85% success rate). Volunteer opportunities available.

As the Refuge isn't open to the public without an appointment, they will contact you with directions once your appointment is made.

Sibu Sanctuary ANIMAL SANCTUARY

(☎8413-8889; www.sibusanctuary.org; US$65; ⏱tours 10:30am) Reservations are required to visit this wildlife sanctuary, set on 50 glorious acres of jungle and garden. The sanctuary is dedicated to rescuing, rehabilitating and eventually releasing howler monkeys who have been injured or abandoned. The educational visits include a guided tour of the grounds as well as some time observing (but no interaction with) the primates, as the point is to keep them wild. The fee supports the good work of this private center.

Reserva Biológica Nosara NATURE RESERVE

(☎2682-0035; www.lagartalodge.com/en/nature-reserve.html; US$10, private tour incl admission $38; ⏱8am-4pm, guided tours 6:30am & 3pm) The private 35-hectare reserve behind Lagarta Lodge (p320) has trails leading through a mangrove wetland down to the river and beach. Stop in the Lagarta lobby to pick up a map of a two-hour self-guided tour. This is a great spot for birding, reptile-spotting and other wildlife-watching. Boat tours of the mangroves are also available. Access is free to Lagarta guests.

Activities

Playa Ponies HORSEBACK RIDING

(☎2682-5096; www.playaponies.org; Playa Pelada; 1½hr/2hr/half-day tours US$50/60/120; 👪) Carrie and Neno want to take you riding on jungly trails and windswept beaches, with special routes designed for families with children. From the 'five corners' of Pelada, head north 500m on Hwy 160, then turn left. Alternatively, they can meet you at the Mobil station.

Tica Massage SPA

(☎2682-0096; www.ticamassage.com; Playa Guiones; massages US$40-100; ⏲9am-6pm Mon-Sat, to 5pm Sun) After a hard day of surfing, treat yourself to a spa treatment at Tica Massage, in the Heart of Guiones Wellness Center. Services cater especially to surfers; or opt for a foot massage, a face massage or an invigorating 'Sea Glow' massage.

Miss Sky ADVENTURE

(☎2682-0969; www.misskycanopytour.com; Nosara; adult/child 5-12yr US$75/50; ⏲tours 8am & 1:30pm) Miss Sky's ziplines run from mountainside to mountainside above a pristine private reserve. If you can keep your eyes open, you'll be rewarded with glorious views of forest, sea and sky.

Buceo Gavilana DIVING

(☎2656-8051; www.buceogavilana.com; Playa Garza; 2-tank dive with/without rental equipment US$120/100) Tucked into a country lane off Playa Garza, Frenchman Didier Halbart's dive shop is the only game in town. Diving with this passionate seafarer is a boutique experience – he'll get you at your hotel, provide the gear, load it onto his dive boat and assess the conditions to determine which of the two dozen dive sites you'll visit.

Surfing

★Surf Simply SURFING

(☎in USA 305-505-7135; www.surfsimply.com; 1-week all-incl package s/d US$6562/11,784) A high-end, all-inclusive surf camp that takes care of everything from airport transfers and luxury lodgings to meals and highly methodical trainings, all for a maximum of a dozen students each week. Video feedback and theory supplement in-water coaching sessions. The camp is crazy popular; book at least a year in advance.

Safari Surf SURFING

(☎2682-0113, in US or Canada 866-433-3355; www.safarisurfschool.com; Olas Verdes Hotel, Playa Guiones; 1-week packages from US$1680; ⏲6am-10pm) This all-inclusive surf school offers one-week packages, complete with lodging, meals, surf lessons and gear, as well as some extra activities (depending on the package). Different packages cater to budget travelers and women, in addition to the 'signature' Tortuga package. The quality of surf instruction is universally praised.

Coconut Harry's SURFING

(☎2682-0574; www.coconutharrys.com; Playa Guiones; board rental per day US$15-35, lessons adult/child private US$65/55 group $55/45; ⏲10am-5pm) At the main intersection in Guiones, this popular surf shop offers top-notch private lessons, as well as board rental and stand-up paddleboard rental. Conveniently, there's a second location near the main break at Playa Guiones (open 7am to 5pm).

Juan Surfo's Surf Shop SURFING

(☎2682-1081; www.juansurfosurfshop.com; Playa Guiones; surf/SUP board rental per day US$15/20, lessons per hr group/private US$40/65; ⏲7am-6pm Mon-Sat, to 4:30pm Sun) Juan Surfo is a highly recommended Tico surf teacher who gives lessons at Playa Guiones. His shop offers the regular rentals, transportation and surf tours, as well as some rooms for rent in a nearby house. Located on the northern loop road, 200m from the beach.

Yoga

Pilates Nosara YOGA

(☎8663-7354; www.pilatesnosara.com; Playa Guiones; from US$12) Located in a beautiful studio at Bodhi Tree (p320), this school offers Pilates mat and equipment classes (daily during the high season), as well as Balanced Body teacher training and retreats. Turn off from the first Guiones access road.

Nosara Wellness YOGA

(☎8812-1232; www.nosarawellness.com; Playa Pelada; drop-in classes from US$12, private sessions from US$60) This wellness center in Pelada offers everything from massage and acupuncture to pilates and yoga. If that's all too mainstream for you, sign up for a session of aerial yoga or 'yamuna body rolling.' Located just off the main road (Ruta 160) connecting Nosara to Play Pelada and northern points.

Harmony Healing Centre YOGA

(☎2682- 4114; www.harmonynosara.com/relax/yoga; drop-in class US$17; ⏲8am-6pm) Whether you're into vinyasa, yin, kunalini or aerial yoga, the Harmony Hotel's Healing Centre has you covered. The open-air yoga studio and its jungly surrounds are breathtaking, and after-class treats include massages at the spa or healthy smoothies at the juice bar. The attached hotel is laid-back and luxurious (and very pricey).

Sleeping

The main access roads to Playa Guiones are lined with hostels, hotels, guesthouses and more. Some of the Playa Pelada options are up in the hills, away from the beach. Prices outside of high season can be 20% lower or better, as in much of the country.

Selina HOSTEL $

(☎2215-2997; www.selina.com; incl breakfast dm from US$35, d/q from US$230/330; P ❄ 📶 🐾) This member of the mighty Selina hostel chain has really outdone itself. The expansive, jungle-shrouded property is defined by dreamy thatched-roof villas and multilevel pools, hammock gardens and bamboo design features. Dorm rooms and privates all feature a modern, Instagram-ready design, and social events, tours and activities run the gamut. There's also a co-working space equipped with high-speed internet.

Our only complaint: ensconced in the no-man's land between Guiones and Pelada, this place isn't on the beach. But during research a forest trail to Playa Pelada was under construction.

4 You Hostal HOSTEL $

(☎2682-1316; www.4youhostal.com; Playa Guiones; dm/s/d/bungalow from US$20/34/44/60; P 📶) A good, clean option close to the Guiones action. The high-end minimalist design makes this evolutionary hostel feel luxurious. Within one dorm are three private pods with walls that don't quite reach the soaring ceiling, allowing for extra privacy. Additional perks include Balinese furniture, a spotless community kitchen and lovely terraces.

Nosara Beach Hostel HOSTEL $

(☎2682-0238; Playa Guiones; dm US$23, d with/without air-con 85/75; ❄ 📶) 🍃 Lounge in a hammock on the breezy porch, overlooking iguana-frequented gardens, just steps from the surf. You have a stone shower to wash away the sand and a comfy wooden bunk to crash on. There's a big communal kitchen, a spacious TV room and – bonus – foosball. In 2019, the owner was adding four new apartments with air-con and hot water.

The vibe is super chill, and 40 solar panels provide electricity for part of the day. Look for the sign on the surfboard at the South Guiones beach entrance.

★Villa Mango B&B B&B $$

(☎2682-1168; www.villamangocr.com; Playa Pelada; s/d/tr/q incl breakfast US$77/88/105/120, air-con US$10; P ❄ 📶 🏊) At this B&B in the trees set high on a hillside with views of both bays, you can't help but relax. The seven spacious rooms have a Mediterranean flair, with gorgeous views and rustic stone and wood details. Lounge on the luxurious terrace, swim in the saltwater pool or take a short stroll down to the isolated stretch of beach.

The owner, Agnes, is delightful. Reserve if you're visiting in high season.

Bodhi Tree HOTEL $$

(☎2682-0256; www.bodhitreeyogaresort.com; Playa Guiones; incl breakfast and yoga dm from US$135, bungalow from US$423, 4-person ste US$954; P ❄ 📶 🏊) Set on a lush hillside, this yoga resort is traversed by a gurgling river, complete with waterfall. The setting is gorgeous and serene – perfect for reconnecting with your breath, your body and the nature around you. The most affordable accommodations are simple, offering comfortable beds and ample storage space, as well as shared bathrooms with stone sinks and open-air showers.

Yoga classes are held in a magnificent open-air studio with 360-degree canopy views (all rates include one daily yoga class). Pilates, spin, aerial yoga and barre drop-in classes are also available on the property. Free electric shuttles and bikes to town, and the popular juice bar and two restaurants are open to nonguests.

Green Sanctuary GUESTHOUSE $$

(☎8320-9822; www.hotelgreensanctuary.com; Playa Guiones; d/tr incl breakfast US$95/139; ❄ 📶 🏊) It's a 700m hike to the beach, but that's the only complaint about this spot in the woods. A stone path winds through the trees, connecting units made from old cargo containers; each has its own terrace, complete with hammock, and is surprisingly private. A yoga deck and relaxing pool round out the offerings.

Take the southernmost access road from the beach and head all the way up the hill.

★Lagarta Lodge LODGE $$$

(☎2682-0035; www.lagartalodge.com; Playa Pelada; ste US$390-499; P ❄ 📶 🏊) 🍃 Completely transformed by a recent renovation, 'the Lizard' now offers 26 stunning suites overlooking the ocean and rivers, at the northern end of Pelada. The balcony restaurant is worth a visit just for the spectacular sea and sunset views. One night here might cost what your plane ticket did, but you'll never forget it.

The owners make an effort to contribute to local community education and conservation efforts. The adjacent Reserva Biologica Nosara (p318) is free for guests to wander, and the onsite spa and restaurant envelop you further in the lap of luxury. An onsite tour company can help arrange further-flung adventures.

Costa Rica Yoga Spa LODGE **$$$**
(2682-0012, in USA 888-533-6461; www.costaricayogaspa.com; Nosara; dm from US$180, ste from US$338, additional person US$180; P wi-fi) This gorgeous mountaintop retreat takes care of all of the details, providing delightful accommodations, farm-to-table vegetarian meals (included), yoga classes and beach transport. There's also a new sweat lodge, along with ceremonies and workshops involving the psychedelic shrub iboga. Shared rooms with bunkbeds offer less privacy but still feature teak furniture and balconies with views.

About 5km north of Nosara village. There is a two-night minimum stay for private rooms, and a three-night minimum for shared rooms.

Gilded Iguana HOTEL **$$$**
(2215-6950; www.thegildediguana.com; d from US$270; P) Nosara's first bar opened in 1984 and was the go-to for expat wave chasers. Today a chic hotel of the same name stands around that original structure, and it's still the go-to for surfers (albeit those with slightly deeper pockets). The 30 sleek and modern units feature outdoor showers, gorgeous terraces and convenient surfboard closets.

It also has amenities for days, including a tasty Mediterranean–Costa Rican fusion restaurant, a fancy surf club, a spa, a gym and a mountain-biking shop.

Eating

Rosi's Soda Tica SODA **$**
(2682-0728; Playa Guiones; mains US$3-6; 8am-3pm Mon-Sat) Now with two prominent locations, this is the favorite *soda* in Guiones and it's a damn good one. It's a perfect spot for breakfast, whether it's banana pancakes or huevos rancheros. At lunchtime, Rosi keeps it real with *casados* and the like. It takes time, but you can't rush perfection. The 'downtown' location is on the main drag.

★El Local GASTROPUB **$$**
(2682-0258; Gardens Hotel, Playa Guiones; mains US$11-15; 7:30am-10pm) Construct a hardwood *rancho* and paint the whole thing white. Dangle fairy lights. Add tropical plants. Serve playful dishes made with fresh local ingredients, (mostly vegetables). Provide craft beer. Hire talented, fun local bands. Put a sign explaining what you've done near the road.

Ah, if only it were all as simple as El Local makes it seem, we'd all run amazing restaurants.

La Peruana FOOD TRUCK **$$**
(8338-3169; www.facebook.com/peruanacr; mains US$13-16; noon-10pm) So you've been craving *tallarin saltado* (a Peruvian–Chinese fusion stir fry) since Lima, and who says you shouldn't have it at an outdoor picnic table in a remote Costa Rican beach town? Yes, it can be accompanied by red snapper *tiradito* (thinly sliced raw fish) and washed down with a Pisco sour, or a cacao colada, or any number of creative cocktails.

It's all made possible by this adorable Peruvian fusion food truck with cheerful, multicolored paneling and effervescent service.

Burgers & Beers BURGERS **$$**
(2682-5558; www.facebook.com/burgersandbeerscr; Playa Guiones; mains US$14-16; noon-10pm Tue-Sun) Take your pick from six burgers and you'll get a plump, juicy patty of goodness, served on a fresh bun with big French-fry wedges. There's also a veggie burger and fish of the day, as well as a dozen craft beers on tap. Located on the north beach-access road.

El Chivo MEXICAN **$$**
(2682-0887; www.elchivo.co; Playa Pelada; mains US$12-20; 11am-10pm Mon-Thu, to midnight Fri, 9am-11pm Sat, 9am-10pm Sun) A groovy roadside joint in the middle of the Pelada wilderness. Tacos are a favorite – try the Korean BBQ pork belly or the *suadero* (beef). Like any upstanding Mexican place, bargain Taco Tuesday is mandatory. But there's also chimichurri-style steak and gut-busting 'wet' burritos (with cheese/sour cream) and a long list of tequilas and local beers, set among skull-and-wrestling-mask decor.

Beach Dog Café CAFE $$
(☎2682-1293; www.facebook.com/beachdogcafe; Playa Guiones; lunch mains US$6-10, dinner mains US$12-15; ⌚8:30am-10pm Mon-Sat, to 3:30pm Sun; P 📶 ✍) Just steps from the beach, this cafe, conjoined with a new cocktail lounge called Spirit, serves decadent and delicious food. Try banana-bread French toast for breakfast, or uber-popular fish tacos for lunch. Dinner is served every night but Sunday, and it hosts live music on Thursday through Saturday.

La Luna INTERNATIONAL $$$
(☎2682-0122; Playa Pelada; mains US$16-29; ⌚7am-10pm) On the beach, this trendy restaurant-bar has cushy couches right on the sand, perfect for sunset drinks. The interior is equally appealing, with soaring ceilings, a gorgeous hardwood bar and walls adorned with work by local artists. Asian and Mediterranean flourishes round out the eclectic menu, and the views (and cocktails) are intoxicating. Call ahead for reservations.

Marlin Bill's SEAFOOD $$$
(☎2682-0458; Playa Guiones; meals US$15-25, burgers US$7-15; ⌚11am-10pm Mon-Sat) Across the main road from 'downtown' Guiones, this old-timers' restaurant has views all the way to the ocean. The casual, open-air patio is a perfect place to feast on grilled tuna, *ceviche* and other fresh seafood. Bill is famous for his burgers, and he'll cook up your fresh catch as well.

Drinking & Nightlife

Nosara is far from a party town, but depending on the night, you can hear live music and get your groove on at **Kaya Sol** (☎2682-1459; www.kayasol.com; Playa Guiones; d US$139, apt US$250; ❄ 📶 🏊), Beach Dog Café, the Gilded Iguana (p321) or El Local (p321). On weekends after dark, head to **Tropic Revolution** (☎2682-0140; Nosara; ⌚10pm-2am Fri & Sat) for Latin dancing with locals.

Bar Olga's BAR
(☎8404-6316; www.facebook.com/BarOlgas; Playa Pelada; ⌚10am-10pm) The *other* beachfront establishment on Pelada is an old-fashioned beach bar, offering traditional Tico fare, cheap beer and the occasional pig roast. The place does not pretend to be anything other than what it is: an open-air *palapa* (thatched shelter) blasting everything from reggae to ranchero under a rusty tin roof, with a large open space that easily becomes a dance floor.

Pilos Bar BAR
(Playa Garza; ⌚11am-8pm) At this laid-back beach bar, the thing to do is grab a wooden barstool in the sand, crack a local beer, devour a whole fried fish and watch the sun dip behind Playa Garza. The man responsible for every aspect of this sublime experience is the enchanting local artist and bar owner, Pilo. He even catches (and cooks) the fish.

Before you go, wander inside to view Pilo's throne-like driftwood chairs and whimsical art.

Information

Banco Popular (☎2682-0011; Playa Guiones; ⌚8:45am-4:30pm Mon-Fri, 8:15-11:30am Sat)

Frog Pad (☎2682-4039; www.thefrogpad.com; Villa Tortuga, Playa Guiones; ⌚7:30am-6:30pm Mon-Sat, 10am-6pm Sun; 📶) An all-purpose stop for information, supplies and communication. Dave can answer any question – ever. You can also rent beach gear (surf boards, beach chairs, snorkel kits, you name it) or buy sunscreen, bug spray, sporting equipment, and the like).

Police (☎2682-1215; Nosara)

Getting There & Away

You can get here by airplane or bus, and there are many accommodations options close to the beach; so you don't really need your own vehicle in Nosara. That said, it's a sprawling area so you'll appreciate a car if you intend to explore the environs.

AIR

Sansa (www.flysansa.com) and **Aerobell** (www.aerobell.com) offer daily flights to Nosara during the high season.

BUS

Local buses depart from the *pulpería* (corner grocery store) by the soccer field. Traroc (p329) buses depart for Nicoya (US$3.50, two hours) at 5am, 6am, 7am, noon and 3:30pm. A direct bus to San José departs every day at 12:30pm from the **Alfaro bus stop** in Nosara village center.

To get to Sámara, take any bus out of Nosara and ask the driver to drop you off at *'la bomba de Sámara'* (Sámara gas station). From there, flag down one of the buses traveling from Nicoya to Sámara.

CAR

From Nicoya, a paved road leads toward Playa Sámara. About 5km before Sámara, turn onto a windy, bumpy (and, in the dry season, dusty) dirt road to Nosara village (4WD recommended). This road was much improved, but not paved as of 2019, so cross your fingers, folks. It's also possible (in the dry season) to drive north to Ostional and Junquillal, though you'll have to ford a few rivers. Ask around before trying this in the rainy season, when the Río Nosara becomes impassable.

There is a gas station in Nosara village, and a couple of rental car agencies in the area:

Economy Rent a Car (☎2299-2000; www.economyrentacar.com; Playa Guiones; ⏱8am-6pm)

National (☎2242-7878; www.natcar.com; Playa Guiones; ⏱8am-5pm)

Refugio Nacional de Vida Silvestre Ostional

This 85 sq km coastal **refuge** (☎2683-0400; www.sinac.go.cr; adult/child US$12/2, turtle tours incl admission US$20) extends from Punta India in the north to Playa Guiones in the south, and includes the beaches of Playa Nosara and Playa Ostional. It was created in 1984 to protect the *arribadas* (mass nestings of the olive ridley sea turtles), which occur from from July to December (peaking in September and October). Ostional is one of two main nesting grounds for this turtle in Costa Rica, along with Playa Nancite in Parque Nacional Santa Rosa.

Outside of *arribada,* Ostional is mostly deserted. But there is 5km of unbroken beach here, sprinkled with driftwood and swaying coconut palms. It's an ideal spot for surfing and sunbathing, birding and beachcombing.

Activities

Surfing

Surfers catch some good lefts and rights here during mid to high tide. Otherwise, this stretch of sea is notorious for strong currents and isn't suitable for swimming (unless you're green and have flippers).

Wildlife-Watching

Ostional is rife with sea creatures, even in addition to the turtles. Rocky Punta India at the northwestern end of the refuge has tide pools that abound with marine life, such as sea anemones, urchins and starfish. Along the beach, thousands of almost transparent ghost crabs go about their business, as do the bright-red Sally Lightfoot crabs.

The sparse vegetation behind the beach consists mainly of deciduous trees and is home to iguanas, crabs, howler monkeys, *pizotes* and many birds. Near the southeastern edge of the refuge is a small mangrove swamp where there is good birdwatching.

Tours

Mass arrivals of nesting turtles occur every three or four weeks during the rainy season (usually on dark nights preceding a new moon) and last about four nights (larger ones can last more than week). It's possible to see turtles in lesser numbers almost any night during nesting season. In the dry season a fitting consolation prize is the small number of leatherback and green turtles that also nest here.

Many tour operators in the region offer tours to Ostional during nesting season, or you can make arrangements with a certified, local guide. Thanks to social media, the news about *arribadas* spreads very rapidly these days, and tourists from surrounding towns show up almost immediately. Because of this, government body Minae has become particularly strict about enforcing the rules of the refuge, and visitors are strictly prohibited from entering without a guide at these times.

Minae WILDLIFE

(Ministerio de Ambiente y Energía; ☎2682-0400; ⏱8am-4pm Mon-Sat) The government agency that controls wildlife, Minae can help larger groups organize turtle-watching, because each guide is only allowed to bring 10 people (nine plus the guide) on the beach at one time. They're located in a light-green building behind the cemetery, right on the beach. Authorized guides can be identified by the government-issued ID, and a T-shirt with the proper logo.

Sleeping & Eating

Most turtle tourists come on tours or drive themselves from Nosara or Sámara; but there are a few simple guesthouses in town for those who care to spend the night (and avoid driving on the treacherous road in the dark). North of the village, there are a few fancier accommodations options.

THE PARK'S TURTLES

The olive ridley is one of the smallest species of sea turtle, typically weighing around 45kg. Although they are endangered, there are a few beaches in the world where ridleys nest in large groups that can number in the thousands. Scientists believe that this behavior is an attempt to overwhelm predators.

Prior to the creation of the park, coastal residents used to harvest and sell eggs indiscriminately (raw turtle eggs increase sexual vigor, or so they say). In recent years, however, an imaginative conservation plan has been put into place. Residents of Ostional are allowed to harvest eggs from the first laying, as these eggs are often crushed by subsequent waves of nesting turtles anyway (you can gulp down an eye-opening turtle-egg-and-hot-sauce shot at the local *mercado:* you'll likely see a signs advertising eggs on the main north–south road through town). By allowing this limited harvesting, the community maintains its economic livelihood, and the villagers in turn act as park rangers to prevent poachers from infringing on their enterprise.

Ostional Turtle Lodge LODGE $$
(☎2682-0131; www.ostionalturtlelodge.com; s/d/tr US$64/84/96, treehouse from US$87; P❄📶) A great guesthouse with only five upgraded rooms and a more spacious and stylish treehouse apartment. Guests spend most of their time in the exquisite community *rancho* or on the communal patio's sofas and easy chairs, backed by mangroves, overlooking pastureland and within earshot of the sea.

Luna Azul HOTEL $$$
(☎2682-1400; www.hotellunaazul.com; d incl breakfast US$192; P❄📶🏊) This elegant hotel is a surprise, with its spacious bungalows and inviting infinity pool. From the outdoor showers to the private terraces, this is a place for relaxing – and perhaps eyeing a monkey or a bird or two. The chef at the fine onsite restaurant has worked here for a decade. It's about 4km north of Ostional village.

The owner, Rolf, a retired Swiss biologist, is helpful in arranging turtle tours and other excursions. He buys the fish for his excellent restaurant in nearby San Juanillo.

Las Tortugas Pizzeria COSTA RICAN $$
(☎2682-0627; mains from US$10, pizza US$20; ⊙10am-10pm) About the only place to eat in town besides the *sodas*, this roadhouse restaurant has a nice lunch and drinks menu. Don't come for the pizzas, despite the name – the other food's much better. The perfect place to while away the hours, waiting for a bus or a turtle tour.

Tree Tops Inn INTERNATIONAL $$$
(☎2682-1335; www.costaricatreetopsinn.com; San Juanillo; lunch/dinner per person US$34/63; ⊙lunch 11am-2pm, dinner by reservation) Jack and Karen Hunter are renowned for their decadent five-course candlelit dinners (reserve one day in advance), potent piña coladas, fresh-picked mango margaritas, and their engaging storytelling. The prix-fixe meals feature the best of local ingredients, especially seafood and tropical fruit. It all takes place on a shaded deck with marvelous views of the forest canopy and the ocean beyond.

The couple also rents out two rooms – one that is actually in the treetops, and another bungalow on the beach (from US$158, including breakfast). Located about 8km north of Ostional in the village of San Juanillo. Cash only.

ℹ Getting There & Away

Ostional village is about 8km northwest of Nosara village. During the dry months there are two daily departures from Santa Cruz (two hours), leaving Ostional at 5:30am and 7:30am and returning from Santa Cruz at 12:30pm and 4pm. From Nosara, there are buses to Ostional at 5am, 7:15am and 3:30pm (US$1, 30 minutes) and return buses at 2:30pm and 6pm. Note that at any time of the year the road can get washed out by rain.

If you're driving, you'll need a 4WD, as the journey requires at least one river crossing. Ask locally about conditions before setting out. From the main road joining Nosara beach and village, head north and cross the bridge over the Río Nosara. After 2km, you'll reach a T-junction. Take the left fork (which is signed) and continue about 6km north to Ostional.

Beyond Ostional, the dirt road continues on to San Juanillo and Marbella before arriving in Paraíso, northeast of Junquillal. Again, inquire locally before attempting this drive, and don't be afraid to use your 4WD.

Playa Sámara

POP 4100

Is Sámara the happiest place on earth? That's what more than one expat has said after stopping here on vacation and never leaving. On the surface it's just a laid-back beach town with barefoot, three-star appeal and a bunch of craft stands. The crescent-shaped strip of pale-gray sand spans two rocky headlands, where the sea is calm and beautiful. It's not spectacular, just safe, mellow, reasonably developed, easily navigable on foot and accessible by public transportation. Not surprisingly, it's popular with vacationing Ticos, foreign families and backpackers, a somewhat rare, happy mix of visitors and locals. But be careful, the longer you stay the less you'll want to leave.

If you've got some extra time and a 4WD, explore the less frequented and incredibly gorgeous beaches north and south of Sámara.

Activities

No matter what you like to do at the beach, you can probably do it at Playa Sámara. Expert surfers might get bored by Sámara's inconsistent waves, but beginners will have a blast. Otherwise, there's hiking, horseback riding and sea kayaking, as well as snorkeling out around Isla la Chora. Take a break from the beach to explore the forested hillsides on foot or by zipline. Sámara is not far from the turtle tours up the coast in Ostional, or to the south at Playa Camaronal.

Pato Surf School SURFING

(☎8373-2281; www.patossurfingsamara.com; board rental per day US$15, lessons US$35-55; ⏰8am-6pm) Pato offers inexpensive and quality board rental, as well as beginner surf instruction, on the beach at the southwest end of town. The instructors are topnotch. Pay for a lesson and get free board rental for five days. Also on offer: stand-up paddleboard rental and lessons; kayak rental and tours; snorkel gear; and beach massages. What else could you want?

C&C Surf School SURFING

(☎8817-2203; www.facebook.com/AdolfoGomezSurf; board rentals per day US$15, lessons group/private US$50/65; ⏰8am-8pm) A great choice at the south end of the beach, offering lessons for individuals, pairs and small groups. Especially recommended for beginners. Owner Adolfo Gómez is a champion longboarder who has represented Costa Rica in the Central American Surfing Games.

Sámara Trails HIKING

(Samara Adventure Company; ☎8833-5369, 2656-0920; www.samaratrails.com; adult/child US$39/30; ⏰6:30am & 2:30pm with reservation) This hike follows a 6km route through a mango plantation and into the Werner Sauter Biological Reserve, located in the hills above Sámara. In three hours, your naturalist guide covers the history of the area and the ecology of the dry tropical forest. The office in town is on the main road.

Wingnuts ADVENTURE

(☎2656-0153; www.wingnutscanopy.com; adult/child US$65/50; ⏰tours 8am, 9am, noon & 1pm) One entrepreneurial family found a way to preserve their beautiful, wild patch of dry tropical forest: by setting up a small-scale canopy tour. Locally owned and professionally run, this 10-platform operation is unique for its personal approach, as groups max out at 10 people. The price includes transportation from your hotel in Sámara.

Flying Crocodile SCENIC FLIGHTS

(☎2656-8048; www.hotelflyingcrocodile.com; per person 20min/30min/60min US$120/160/240) Based just east of the Río Buenavista, the Flying Crocodile offers ultralight flights over the nearby beaches and mangroves. The namesake hotel, a curious collection of hobbit huts and other oddly shaped accommodations (d from US$86), is located about 2km west on the opposite side of the river. During the dry season it's easy to cross the river. Rainy season, not so much.

Carrillo Tours TOURS

(☎2656-0584, WhatsApp 8746-7567; ⏰8am-8pm) Organizes turtle tours, snorkeling, kayaking, horseback riding and trips to Palo Verde. The office is on the main road in Sámara.

Leo Tours ADVENTURE

(☎8995-6820; www.leotourssamara.com; kayak & snorkel tour US$45; ⏰7am-5pm) Leo has kayaks, fishing equipment, snorkel gear and a couple of boats. That means he'll take you out for any kind of water fun you crave, from sea kayaking to sportfishing. A favorite tour is kayaking out to Isla la Chora, where you can snorkel around the island. Find him on the beach 50m northeast of Gusto.

OFF THE BEATEN TRACK

PLAYA BARRIGONA

If the crowds in Nosara and Sámara are bumming you out, make for the oft-deserted shore of **Playa Barrigona**. The white sands of this crescent-shaped beach are powder-soft, its crashing waves translucent blue. The beach backs up to forest-covered mountains and features rocky reefs at either end. And with only a dirt access road that's impassable in the rainy season, Barrigona is rarely crowded. Even in the dry season when any vehicle can make the trip, you'll likely only spot a few other humans.

Oddly enough, one of them just might be Mel Gibson – he owns a sprawling **hacienda** (6478-6825; www.haciendabarrigona.com; d from US$300; P ❄ 📶 🏊) just inland from the beach, and it's actually possible to stay the night in one of the villas. They're lovely, with vaulted ceilings, elegant verandas, relaxing pools and delicious communal meals. But at the time of research the property was on the market (again), so this opportunity may be short-lived. In keeping with Costa Rican law, though, Playa Barrigona will always remain open to the public.

Courses

Intercultura Costa Rica Spanish Schools LANGUAGE
(2656-3000; www.interculturacostarica.com; courses per week with/without homestay US$510/325; 7:30am-5:30pm Mon-Fri) Intercultura is right on the beach, which makes for a pleasant – if not always productive – place to study. Language courses can be arranged with or without a family homestay, and activities like yoga, Latin dance, cooking and movie nights are included. Teachers are very experienced, and courses for kids are also available.

Sleeping

In town, it's nearly impossible to be more than two blocks from the beach. Many hotels, hostels and charming guesthouses are clustered in the small rectangular grid that borders the sand. If you prefer to be further away from the action, there are some real gems west of town. Generally, budget options greet you with a brisk cold morning shower, while midrange and top-end facilities have hot water.

El Cactus Hostel HOSTEL $
(2656-3224; www.samarabackpacker.com; s/d US$45/52; 📶) Brightly painted in citrus colors, El Cactus is a great option, especially for those who prefer serenity over revelry. Fresh rooms have wooden furniture, clean linens and hot-water showers. Hammocks hang around a lovely garden, and a fully fitted kitchen is also available.

Hotel Casa Paraíso GUESTHOUSE $
(2656-0741; scodinzolo@libero.it; dm/d from US$15/60; 📶) A lovely little guesthouse tucked in behind the restaurant **Ahora Sí** (www.ahorasi.isamara.co; mains US$5-12; 7:30am-10pm; P 📶 🌿). Four simple rooms and a shared dorm are brushed in deep blues and inviting pastels, with thematic murals, high ceilings and comfy beds. Ceiling fans will keep you cool while hot-water showers will warm you up. Hostess Sylvia will overwhelm you with her charm, and there's Italian cooking at the restaurant.

Sámara Palm Lodge GUESTHOUSE $$
(2656-1169; www.samarapalmlodge.com; d US$65-84; P ❄ 📶 🏊) An inviting little Swiss-owned lodge on the edge of town. Eight spotless rooms feature tropical decor, with stained-wood furniture, tiled floors and bold colorful artwork. They face a lush garden and enticing swimming pool. It's just over the bridge, a little west of town but only a five-minute walk to the beach.

La Mansion B&B B&B $$
(2265-0165; www.isamara.co/mansion; d from US$55, ste US$160; P ❄ 📶) This whitewashed concrete hacienda, twirling with fans and bursting with colorful knickknacks, is on a quiet street. There's loads of charm: rooms are spacious and bright, and ex-Arizonian hostess Marlene McCauley is proud of her huge and delicious breakfasts. Her artwork adorns the walls and you can even buy one of her cute bird-themed postcards. Air-con is US$10 extra.

Tico Adventure Lodge LODGE $$
(2656-0628; www.ticoadventurelodge.com; s/d/q/apt from US$28/86/113/192; P ❄ 📶 🏊) This dreamy lodge was constructed without cutting down a single tree, and its rooms, suites and several larger apartments are sur-

rounded by lush vegetation and old-growth evergreens. There's an outdoor kitchen and cookout area for communal use, a pool, and a yoga/spa area. It's about 200m from the beach, on the main road between Sámara and Carrillo.

Casa del Mar HOTEL $$
(☎4701-4585, 2656-0264; www.casadelmarsamara.com; incl breakfast s/d/tr US$90/90/100, without bathroom US$45/50/60; P ❄ ☎ ≋) Surrounding a big mango tree and a tiny swimming pool are 17 rooms with whitewashed stucco walls and tiled floors. The rooms that share a bathroom are fan-cooled, and a steal. The beach, for which the hotel provides towels for its guests, is right across the street. The multilingual staff are friendly and attentive. At the main Sámara intersection.

★ **LazDivaz** COTTAGE $$
(☎2656-0295; www.lazdivaz.com; d US$113-124; P ☎) They call it a B&C. No breakfast, just coffee. The rest is basically a dream: cozy and colorful, three darling cottages are perched in the sand, surrounded by tropical foliage just steps from the sea. The spunky owner has a wealth of local knowledge, though many guests opt to stick around, swing in a hammock and simply unwind. *Pura vida.*

Sámara Tree House Inn TREEHOUSE $$$
(☎2656-0733; www.samaratreehouse.com; incl breakfast d from US$147, treehouse US$192; P ❄ ☎ ≋) These four stilted tree houses and two poolside bungalows for grown-ups are so appealing that you might not want to leave. Fully equipped kitchens in most units have pots and pans hanging from driftwood racks, huge windows welcome light and breezes, and hammocks hang underneath. The pricier units face the beach.

You can't get much closer than this to the ocean without getting on a surfboard.

El Pequeño Gecko Verde BUNGALOW $$$
(☎2656-1176; www.gecko-verde.com; r incl breakfast from $120, bungalows from US$186, villa from US$271; P ❄ ☎ ≋) A hidden slice of heaven. Contemporary and classy, these bungalows have beds dressed in plush linens, artisanal carvings on the walls, private terraces with hammocks and outdoor dining areas, and outdoor stone showers. Onsite amenities include a swimming pool with waterfall, lush gardens and a fabulous open-air breakfast restaurant and bar. Located several kilometers west of town.

Eating

Sheriff Rustic BREAKFAST $
(☎8376-6565; www.facebook.com/SheriffRustic; breakfast US$4-6; ⏲7am-11pm) Locals adore this inexpensive beachfront *soda*, and truly the *gallo pinto* (with traditional add-ons like stewed beef and pork chops) hits the spot. Bonus points for breakfast served all day, but be sure to guard your food – white-throated magpie-jays apparently love *gallo pinto*.

Bouticafé Bohemia CAFE $
(☎8468-8007; brunch US$8, mains US$5-8; ⏲6:30am-3pm Mon-Fri, to noon Sat; ✎) Those in search of healthy and delicious breakfasts, brunches and lunches need look no further. This artsy little cafe serves up yummy juices and strong coffee, homemade granola, healthy salads, crepes and paninis, with plenty of vegan options. Locals tend to gather here for open mic nights and other special events; ask if anything's up during your visit, or check the Facebook page.

Luv Burger VEGETARIAN $$
(☎2656-3348; www.luvburger.com; mains US$10-15; ⏲9am-9pm; ✎) The 'Luv' has moved from the mini-mall to the beachfront, and several sister restaurants have opened in Nosara and San José. It's all veggie, all the time, from vegan pancakes for breakfast to guilt-free ice cream for dessert – all the burgers and sandwiches are meatless. Coffee drinks are made only with soy or almond milk. See for yourself how delicious animal-free can be.

Sámara Organics MARKET $$
(☎2656-3046; www.samaraorganics.com; smoothies & juices US$5; ⏲8am-7pm) It's not cheap, but self-caterers (and anybody with a dietary restriction) will appreciate this cafe and market, well stocked with organic produce and delicious prepared foods. Come get your healthy food fix, and enjoy the small seating area for a chat or read. On the main beach road, parallel to the water.

Casa Esmeralda SODA $$
(☎2656-0489; www.facebook.com/casaesmeralda.samara; mains US$9-18; ⏲7am-10pm) A favorite with locals, this is a dressed-up *soda* with tablecloths, faux-adobe walls and excellent food. The menu ranges from the expected (*arroz con pollo* – chicken with rice) to the exotic (a spicy octopus appetizer), all of which is fantastic. Be prepared to wait

when it gets busy. It's about a block from the beach at the southeast end of town.

It has rooms to rent upstairs.

El Lagarto BARBECUE **$$**

(☎2656-0750; www.isamara.co/ellagarto; mains US$11-25; ⌚3-11pm; 📶) Grilled meats are the big draw at this alfresco restaurant, studded with old trees and walking distance to the waves. Watching the chefs work their magic on the giant wood-fired oven is part of the fun. The Surf & Turf is highly recommended, as are the cocktails.

Locanda PIZZA **$$**

(☎2656-0036; www.locandasamarabeach.com; mains US$12-16; ⌚7am-11pm) Ask anyone in Sámara where the best pizza in town is and they'll point you to this enchanting, tiki-style hotel, bar and restaurant at the southern corner of the beach. With a thatched *palapa* overhead and your toes in the sand, feast on thin-crust slices and gulp two-for-one fruity cocktails as the sun dips behind the horizon.

★**Mama Gui** ITALIAN **$$$**

(☎2656-2347; http://isamara.co/mamagui/index.htm; pizza from US$11, mains US$18-30; ⌚5-11pm) Sámara's best restaurant is this cozy, contemporary Italian spot that wouldn't be out of place in New York City. And go figure, owner/chef Gigio Palazzo has two sister restaurants there. Playful dishes include 'seacuterie' options like blow torch marlin sashimi, homemade pastas (go for the tagliatelle with red snapper) and sides of truffle parmesan *patacones* (fried plantains) and beetroot arugula ginger.

Cocktails are equally adventurous, with outrageously artful garnishes. Sadly, as of 2019 Gigio was aiming to sell the place, so ask around to make sure it's still great.

Drinking & Nightlife

Microbar MICROBREWERY

(www.facebook.com/microbar.samara; ⌚11am-midnight) Not an inch of space is wasted in this smart little bar on the main road, which serves up 21 Costa Rican microbrews plus infused 'beertails' like the Terremoto (dark rum and dark beer) and the Apocatopia (vanilla, bourbon, light ale). Love the hipster chic vibe and upbeat, old-timey tunes.

L'Authentique WINE BAR

(☎8544-1691; ⌚5-11pm Mon-Sat) Step out of Latin America and into this lovely, French-owned wine bar and tapas bistro, where fabulous boards of imported cheeses and charcuterie pair exceedingly well with a carefully curated list of mostly European wines. Portions are small, service is top-notch and the ambience is romantic.

Shopping

Sámara has a more creative vibe than most beach towns on the peninsula. You'll find a handful of galleries selling handcrafted jewelry and exquisite items, as well as vendors hawking their wares at stands along the main road, and at your beachside restaurant tables.

Cocotales JEWELRY

(☎8807-7056; ⌚8am-8pm Mon-Sat) Carlos Caicedo travels around South America to procure gorgeous semiprecious stones, which he crafts into fine jewelry right here in the back of his shop, on the main north–south road. There are also plenty of clever creations from recycled materials. But his most unique and eye-catching pieces are crafted from coconut and shells.

Information

Banco Costa Rica (⌚9am-4pm Mon-Fri, ATM 24hr) Just off the main road, across from the soccer field.

Banco Nacional (☎2656-0089; ⌚8:30am-3:45pm Mon-Fri) Located next to the church.

La Vida Verde (Green Life; ☎2656-1051; per kg US$4; ⌚8am-5pm) Drop your dirty duds off at this laundry, 75m west of Banco Nacional. Or call ahead for collection and delivery.

Post Office (☎2656-0368; ⌚8am-4pm Mon-Fri) Next to the Super Olas, 75m west of the ICE building.

Samara Info Center (☎2656-2424; www.samarainfocenter.com; ⌚9am-5pm Mon-Fri, to 2pm Sat) Located in front of Lo Que Hay, the Info Center is run by the amiable Brenda and Christopher. It's basically a tour consolidator, but they can help with accommodations, restaurant recommendations, transportation and simply answering questions about Sámara and Carrillo. And they book tours.

Getting There & Away

Playa Sámara lies about 35km southwest of Nicoya on a paved road. The nearby Carrillo airstrip is now closed; the nearest flight one could book would be for Nosara, which has flights from San José and Liberia.

Alfaro has a bus stop in town, with buses departing at 4am and 8:30am to San José via the Friendship Bridge (US$8, four hours). Traroc buses go to Nicoya (US$2.20, one hour) 10 times a day from 5:30am to 6:45pm. The same company also offers buses in the opposite direction, to Playa Carrillo.

Playa Carrillo

POP 1800

About 4km southeast of Sámara, Carrillo is a wide, crescent-shaped beach with clean white sand, cracked granite headlands and a jungle backdrop. On weekends and holidays, the palm-fringed boulevard is lined with cars and the beach crowded with Tico families. At other times, it's practically deserted. The little town is on a hillside above the beach and attracts a trickle of sunbathers and surfers working their way down the coast.

Interesting and pretty tidal pools form at high tide at the southern end of the beach near town.

Activities

Kingfisher Sportfishing FISHING

(☎8834-7125, 8358-9561; www.costaricabillfishing.com; half-/full-day excursions from US$900/1250) A well-known local outfit offering deep-sea fishing on board the *Kingfisher*. Captain Rick and his crew provide top-notch service. Packages include accommodations at the luxurious Villa Oasis. The boat picks you up at the southern end of Playa Carrillo, where the boats are moored.

Sleeping & Eating

La Tropicale BUNGALOW **$$**

(☎8731-9927, 2656-0159; d/q incl breakfast from US$60/140; P❄📶🏊) Across from La Selva wildlife reserve is this delightful inn that has ramshackle charm and plenty of whimsical touches. A stony path winds around the sparkling swimming pool and through mango, papaya and coconut trees. Standalone bungalows are draped with bold linens, lit with funky light fixtures and hung with original art.

Owner Arnaud has stepped it up a notch with the onsite Chez Nous restaurant, featuring French and seafood specialties.

Hideaway Hotel BOUTIQUE HOTEL **$$$**

(☎2656-1145; www.thehideawayplayasamara.com; d/tr/q incl breakfast US$150/190/220, penthouse from US$500; P❄📶🏊) Midway between Carrillo and Sámara, this attractive whitewashed place is noteworthy for its super service and intimate atmosphere. A dozen spacious tiled suites all overlook the pleasant pool and blooming gardens. The airy restaurant is excellent. There is a small beach at the end of the road; alternatively, Playa Carrillo is a 5-minute walk. A separate 'penthouse' houses six to eight guests.

Getting There & Away

The airstrip in Carrillo is now closed, even to charter services. Buses operated by **Traroc** (☎2685-5352; www.traroc.com) originate in Estrada, just east of here. From Carrillo, the buses go to Sámara, then continue on to Nicoya (US$3, 90 minutes, 10 daily). The fare to Sámara is 60¢ for a 20-minute ride.

Islita Area

The coast southeast of Playa Carrillo remains one of the peninsula's most isolated and wonderful stretches of coastline, mainly because it is difficult to access and lacking in accommodations. But if you're willing to tackle rugged roads or venture down the coastline in a sea kayak (or possibly on foot), you'll be rewarded with abandoned beaches backed by pristine wilderness and rugged hills.

Islita is a pretty little town centered on a church and a soccer field, spruced up by artwork. There are a few small breaks in front of the Hotel Punta Islita, where you'll find a gorgeous cove punctuated with that evocative wave-thrashed boulder that is Punta Islita. At high tide the beach narrows, but at low tide it is wide and as romantic as those vistas from above.

Sights

Macaw Recovery Network WILDLIFE RESERVE

(☎8505-3336; www.macawrecoverynetwork.org; tour adult/child US$20/10, photography tour US$50; ⊙tours 7am, 7:30am, 4pm) A local NGO that is dedicated to the conservation of Costa Rica's two species of macaw: the great green macaw and the scarlet macaw. The group rehabilitates injured or rescued birds and eventually reintroduces them into the wild. Long-term volunteer opportunities are available as are hour-long tours, during which visitors can observe dozens of wild macaws as they glide in for a morning or afternoon snack. There is also an informative visitor center with lots of information about the organization.

Refugio Nacional de Vida Silvestre Camaronal WILDLIFE RESERVE
(Playa Camaronal; 2659-8375; www.fundecodes.org/refugio-nacional-de-vida-silvestre-camaronal; adult/child US$10/5; 6am-6pm) A good beach and point break, this charcoal-gray stretch north of Punta Islita is strewn with driftwood and sheltered by two headlands. This beach also happens to be a protected nesting site for leatherback, olive ridley, hawksbill and black turtles, hence its protected status. Tour operators in Sámara and Carrillo offer turtle-watching excursions to Camaronal.

Playa Corozalito BEACH
About 4km south of Punta Islita, Playa Corozalito is an entirely undeveloped beach backed by mangrove swamps and offering plenty of opportunities to spot birds and other wildlife. Several types of sea turtles nest there, and several times each year the beach draws thousands of olive ridleys for the mass *arribada* egg-laying phenomenon.

Playa Bejuco BEACH
South of Punta Islita (and not to be confused with a beach of the same name south of Jacó), Playa Bejuco has reddish-brown sand, crystal-clear water and plenty of opportunity for surfing, sunbathing and wildlife-watching. A nearby village of the same name is quaint and hospitable.

Museo Islita MUSEUM
(2661-4044; tours at 8am & 3pm) FREE Sponsored by the Hotel Punta Islita, this imaginative, open-air museum includes mosaics, carvings and paintings that adorn everything from houses to tree trunks around the center of the town Punta Islita. There's also a gallery of temporary exhibitions, a working studio and a museum shop that supports local artists.

Sleeping & Eating

Hotel Punta Islita RESORT $$$
(2231-6122; www.hotelpuntaislita.com; d incl all activities US$400-500;) This hilltop hotel has 54 fully equipped rooms with staggering ocean views. (If you spring for a suite, you'll enjoy this view from a private outdoor Jacuzzi or plunge pool.) The infinity pool and surrounding grounds are stunning, and amenities onsite simply do not stop. There's a full-service spa, a beach club with a sunken pool bar and lounges on a rolling lawn.

Pacifico COSTA RICAN $$$
(2656-3500; Hotel Punta Islita; mains US$14-28; 7am-10pm;) The restaurant at the Hotel Punta Islita showcases Tico flavors with the freshest seafood, local meats and poultry, and organic produce, with plenty of vegan and vegetarian options. A superlative ocean view complements the beautiful food presentations.

Getting There & Away

There's no public transportation to Punta Islita. In any case, you'll probably want your own vehicle to explore the coastline, preferably a 4WD.

There's a permanent bridge over the Río Ora, so the 10km journey between Puerto Carrillo and Punta Islita is a lot easier than it once was. South of the bridge, the road condition is less reliable; proceed with caution during the rainy season.

Commercial flights no longer serve this airport, but you can charter a flight from San José or Liberia.

Playas San Miguel & Coyote

Two of the most gorgeous – yet least visited – beaches in Costa Rica are on this stretch of the peninsula, just south of Bejuco. Playa San Miguel is a stunning, desolate beach buffeted by a hulking granite headland and backed by elegant coconut palms. There are a couple of restaurants near the beach, but not much more. Playa Coyote, to the south, is likewise a wilderness beach, and is split by a serene (but crocodile-filled) river. Locals know the area north of the river as Costa de Oro, and the whole coastline serves as nesting grounds for olive ridley turtles.

A number of in-the-know foreigners have settled in the area and opened accommodations and restaurants near the shoreline. If you're looking for a proper village, **La Javilla** is located 2km inland from Playa San Miguel; further south, **San Francisco de Coyote** is 4km inland from Playa Coyote. Get here before this slice of 'old' Costa Rica becomes the 'new' Costa Rica.

Sights & Activities

You can surf crowd-free beach breaks at Playa Coyote and Costa de Oro, particularly when the tide is rising. For experts, the reef at Punta Coyote offers a good left break. Boards are available for rent at Alouatta.

The beaches are also good for swimming, but beware of rip tides and steer clear of the rivers, where crocodiles hang out. If you have your own sea kayak, these beaches are ideal for coastal exploration.

The Jungle Butterfly Farm GARDENS

(☎8719-1703; www.facebook.com/junglebutterflyfarm; Nandayure, Pueblo Nuevo; tours adult/child US$25/12; ⏱by appointment 9am-3pm) Mike's beautiful 45-acre mountainside property, 10 minutes north of San Miguel, includes walking trails and a butterfly *rancho*. In addition to the butterflies, you might spot howler monkeys, agoutis and iguanas. He also raises colonies of stingless bees; you can buy their honey in the gift shop. Book ahead for a tour. Turn west at the Catholic Church/sports field in Nadayure.

Turtle Trax VOLUNTEERING

(☎2655-1179; www.turtle-trax.com; San Francisco) Turtle Trax collaborates with environmental watchdog CREMA (Rescue Center for Endangered Marine Species; www.cremacr.org) to offer opportunities to visiting volunteers who want to help monitor the turtle beaches in the area. Tasks include patrolling the beach, recording data, collecting eggs, maintaining the hatcheries and releasing the newly hatched *tortuguitas* (baby turtles). The organization also offers one-day and longer environmental tours. Located 100m south of the school in San Francisco de Coyote.

Sleeping

There's a smattering of unique and lovely lodgings spread out along this coast, though they are few and far between. Alternatively, both villages have *cabinas* that are acceptable options in which to pass a night. You can camp on either beach if you're self-sufficient, but there are no services.

★**Alouatta** CAMPGROUND $

(☎8347-4479; www.alouatta.org; Playa Coyote; camping per person US$8, shared/private tent US$17.50/48; ⏱Nov-May; P 📶) A dreamy campground offering three cozy, fan-cooled safari tents, an open-air *rancho*, a shared kitchen, and bathroom facilities with hot showers, all perched on a verdant hillside overlooking the Pacific. The place is run by a Dutch surfer couple with plenty of local knowledge and serious breakfast skills (US$6 extra). Bonus points for the books, board games and good company.

Laguna Mar BOUTIQUE HOTEL $$

(☎2655-8181; www.lagunamarhotel.com; Javilla; s/d incl breakfast from US$46/74; P ❄ 📶 🏊) In the center of unassuming La Javilla (2km from the beach), this semi-swanky hotel is incongruous with the setting, but still lovely. Rooms are simple but sophisticated, with high-thread-count linens and flat-screen TVs, set around a sublime three-in-one swimming pool. Extra props for the good international restaurant.

Casa Caletas BOUTIQUE HOTEL $$$

(☎2655-1271; www.casacaletas.com; Punta Coyote; s/d/tr/ste US$70/120/140/155; P ❄ 📶 🏊) Sitting pretty on a bank of the Río Coyote, this elegant property is blessedly intimate and blissfully isolated. The rooms are decorated with heavy wood furniture and folksy art, and most feature private terraces with ocean views. The infinity pool offers the same panoramic vista, and a walking trail leads to the beach. Friendly service, too.

Cristal Azul B&B $$$

(☎8869-6633; www.cristalazulhotel.com; d from US$155; P 📶 🏊) Spectacular panoramas surround you at this hilltop retreat, where the four *cabinas* feature floor-to-ceiling windows, open-air showers and super-comfortable beds. It's worth the treacherous journey to spend a few days swinging in a hammock or lounging around the infinity pool (which really does seem to go on forever). Happy to share their little piece of paradise, your hosts are eager to please.

Eating

Pizza Tree PIZZA $$

(☎2655-8063; pizzas US$10-12; ⏱noon-10pm; P) If there's anything more fun than eating pizza in a tree house, we'd love to hear about it. Take a seat at the top of this well-constructed, Seuss-like structure with views of the neighboring cattle ranch, and feast on thin-crust pizzas from the wood-fired brick oven. The owner is Italian but the setting feels super Tico. Situated 2km northeast of San Miguel beach.

Tanga SEAFOOD $$

(Playa Coyote; mains US$12-18; ⏲11am-6pm) Follow the odd signage depicting a woman's bikini-clad pelvis to this informal beach restaurant, where for more than 25 years the owner has been cooking up some of Costa Rica's most delectable whole fried snapper, along with other seafood and rice dishes. A goofy wooden sculpture of a mostly naked woman (sort of) explains the signs.

El Barco INTERNATIONAL $$

(☎2655-1003; www.el-barco-costarica.com; mains US$9-13; ⏲11:30am-10pm Wed-Mon; 📶✍) It looks like a boat, but it's actually a building, facing a sweet slice of sand on Playa Coyote (close to the T-intersection at the beach). Hokey, perhaps, but there's nothing gimmicky about the delicious and nutritious creations coming out of the kitchen. Fresh salads, hearty sandwiches and more substantial pasta and rice dishes will keep you sated.

LocosCocos SEAFOOD $$

(www.locoscocos.com; Playa San Miguel; mains US$10-20; ⏲11am-8pm Jan-Aug, to 4pm Sep & Oct) On a nearly deserted stretch of beach, Henner serves up his secret-family-recipe *ceviche*, along with a catch of the day and piles of seafood out of a shipping container. Ice-cold beers and fresh-fruit smoothies (rum optional) cap off this idyllic experience. If you time it right, you might get to see an amazing show (aka sunset). It's 3km downhill from Cristal Azul (p331) boutique hotel.

ℹ Getting There & Away

You can reach these beach towns by bus, but they are rather remote with minimal facilities, so you may feel stranded if you don't have your own vehicle. If your plans are limited to lounging on a deserted beach, you should be OK.

Transportes Arsa (☎2650-0954; www.transportesarsa.com) has two daily buses (US$8) from San José that take about four hours to reach the beach (optimistically). The buses depart San José at 6am and 3:30pm. Return buses leave Bejuco at 2am and 1pm, passing through San Miguel and Coyote a half-hour or an hour later. This service is sketchy in the rainy season and the trip may take longer if road conditions are bad.

SOUTHERN PENINSULA

Word has spread about Montezuma and Santa Teresa. During the dry season, packs of international surfers and wanderers arrive, hungry for the wild beauty and soul-stirring waters on either side of the peninsula. In between – at the very southern tip of the Península de Nicoya – lies the first natural reserve in Costa Rica.

It all used to require hours of sweaty bus rides and sluggish ferries from the mainland to access this tropical land's end, but these days there are more roads and regular boat shuttles, making the southern peninsula altogether more accessible. But if you have the time and money (and a thirst for adventure), embrace the gritty, arduous drive down the rugged western coast, which requires river crossings and low-tide beach traverses, muddy jungle slogs and steep narrow passes. It's hard work, but your arrival in paradise is all the sweeter for it. (Though perhaps not in the rainy season.)

Mal País & Santa Teresa

POP 3000

Santa Teresa didn't even have electricity until the mid-1990s. Then one major landowner died and his property was subdivided, and the landscape north of the Playa El Carmen intersection changed forever. These days it attracts plenty of visitors with its enchanting surf-perfect beaches, astounding technicolor sunsets, restaurants serving gob-smackingly delicious food and yoga dens with transformational ocean views.

It's still a wonderful surfing town, though no longer a secret one, and there are plenty of great places to eat as well as a modicum of nightlife. The entire area unfurls along one bumpy coastal road that rambles south from Santa Teresa through Playa El Carmen and terminates in the relaxed, sleepy fishing hamlet of Mal País.

Beaches

Playa Santa Teresa BEACH

Playa Santa Teresa is a long, stunning beach that's famous for its fast and powerful beach break. The waves are pretty consistent and can be surfed at virtually any time of day. At the north end of the beach, Roca Mar – aka Suck Rock – is an awesome point break and a local favorite. The break La Lora is named for the nightclub that marks the turnoff from the main road, which is how you find it.

Playa Hermosa BEACH

Somewhere north of town, Playa Santa Teresa ends and Playa Hermosa starts. This gorgeous beach deserves its *hermosa* (beautiful) moniker and then some. It's wide and flat and spectacular at low tide. The beach nearly disappears at high tide. Somewhere between low and high is surf tide, when you can ride the wide beach break left or right from center. You can surf the point break (at the north end of the beach) at any time.

Playa El Carmen BEACH

Playa El Carmen, downhill from the main T-intersection coming into town, is a good beach break that can be surfed anytime. The beach is wide and sandy and curls into successive coves, so it makes good beachcombing and swimming terrain too.

Playa Manzanillo BEACH

About 8km north of the Playa El Carmen intersection (past Playa Hermosa), Playa Manzanillo is a combination of sand and rock that's best surfed when the tide is rising and there's an offshore wind.

Activities

Surfing is the raison d'être for most visits to Santa Teresa and Mal País, and perhaps for the town itself. Most travelers want to do little else, except maybe stretch their muscles with a little yoga. That said, it's a gorgeous, pristine coastline: horseback riding or fishing trips can be easily arranged, as well as a fun-filled ziplining jaunt.

Freedom Riding SUP WATER SPORTS

(☎8737-8781, 2640-0939; www.sup-costarica.com; Mal País; rental half-/full day US$25/40, lessons US$50; ⏲9am-6pm) A stand-up paddle place with sharp management and excellent safety and instruction techniques. Andy offers lessons for first-timers and rentals for old pros, as well as tours that are entertaining for anyone. Located near the fishing pier in Mal País.

Canopy Mal País ADVENTURE SPORTS

(☎2640-0360; www.canopymalpais.com; Justin's Rd; US$55; ⏲8am-5pm) You don't think of ziplining when you come to a surf town? You should. Just south of Mal País, Carlos and crew provide one of the most entertaining experiences around, joking so much you'll forget your fear of heights on the 11 cables, including one that stretches 500m across the jungle below. The last cable is a surfboard ride!

Surfing

The long, flat beach stretches for many kilometers along this southwestern coast of the peninsula. The entire area is saturated with surf shops. This is a good place to pick up an inexpensive board, which you can probably sell later. Most of the local shops also do rentals and repairs; chat them up to find out about their secret surf spots.

Kina Surf Shop SURFING

(☎2640-0627; www.kinasurfcr.com; Santa Teresa; 2hr lessons US$60-80, board rentals per day US$15-20; ⏲9am-5pm) A terrific, efficient surf shop near the break in Santa Teresa. Kina claims to have the best selection of rental boards in the area, with 60-something quality boards available. The 90-minute lessons for beginner, intermediate and advanced surfers also come highly recommended. We expect owner Eric may never return to the cold Atlantic waters of New Jersey.

Around 300m north of the soccer field in Villas Solar, a small shopping complex.

Nalu Surf School SURFING

(☎2649-0391, 8358-4436; www.nalusurfschool.com; Santa Teresa; board rental per day US$10-20, 1½hr group/private lessons US$55/75) Located 300m north of the Playa El Carmen intersection (next to Ronny's Supermarket), this surf school is recommended for its fun and professional approach to instruction. Lessons usually take place at Playa El Carmen, but these guys will also transport you to other breaks in the area. The shop has a good selection of boards for rental and purchase.

Pura Vida Adventures SURFING

(☎in USA 415-465-2162; www.puravidaadventures.com; Hotel Tropico Latino, Playa El Carmen; weekly rates from US$2995) Excellent women-only and co-ed retreats that combine surfing and yoga in weeklong experiences that also include all meals. Held in Hotel Tropico Latino.

Yoga

Many surfers know that yoga is the perfect antidote to their sore flippers. Several studios in the area offer drop-in classes.

1

Surfing the Peninsula

For decades, surfers have descended to this rugged peninsula in search of the perfect wave. Now the spectacular coastline is dotted by enticing beach towns with good vibrations and epic surf. You can surf almost anywhere on the coast, but here are a few of our favorite spots.

Playa Grande

Playa Grande is across the river and a world away from tourist-jammed Tamarindo. Doubling as a national park that protects leatherback turtle nesting grounds, the wide, rambling beach is damn near pristine. The waves shape up beautifully with head-high sets year-round. The village has a little hub at either end of the beach with a handful of tasty kitchens and comfy inns catering to the visiting surfers. However, marked building plots suggest development may change things.

Playas Avellanas & Negra

South of Tamarindo are two of the most celebrated surf spots on the peninsula, but the nearby villages retain an appealing atmosphere of rusticity and remoteness. Playa Avellanas is an understated yet elegant place to nest, within reach of white-sand beaches and a break that's kind to beginners. Nearby, the surf swells big and gnarly at Playa Negra, breaking on beautiful dark sand. To dodge the crowds, seek out the still-hidden waves tucked between all the big names.

Nosara

Within striking distance of three different beach breaks, Nosara offers consistent surf and a welcome cloud of hippie-chic

JONATHAN GREGSON/LONELY PLANET ©

KRYSSIA CAMPOS/GETTY IMAGES ©

GROGL/SHUTTERSTOCK ©

1. Nosara (p318) **2.** Playa Tamarindo (p303) **3.** Surf lessons in Santa Teresa (p332)

comfort. The town is a maze of rough dirt roads, backed by lush rainforest – although it is growing and changing rapidly (the long-promised paved road into town is still underway, folks). Here, yoga studios and spa treatments are the antidote for your surf-sore body.

Mal País & Santa Teresa

At the southern end of the peninsula, Mal País and Santa Teresa are favored by young, hip and sexy surfers from around the world. The beach is long and the swell is consistent, which means you can generally find your own space – particularly if you drive to the far northern beaches. There's also a wonderful farm-to-table movement happening here, so you'll be well-fed throughout your stay.

SURF CAMPS

In addition to room and board, most surf camps include equipment and daily instruction, as well as some nonsurf activities. Camps may cater to beginners, budget travelers, families, women, yogis and more. Places specializing in all-inclusive surf camps include:

Malpaís Surf Camp & Resort (p336), Mal País

Pato Surf School (p325), Playa Sámara

Peaks & Swells Surf Camp (p342), Montezuma

Surf Simply (p319), Nosara

Casa Surf (p311), Playa Avellanas

Witch's Rock Surf Camp (p305), Tamarindo

Casa Zen YOGA

(☑ 2640-0523; www.zencostarica.com; Santa Teresa; classes US$10) Two daily classes take place in a lovely second-story, open-air studio, surrounded by trees. Most of the classes are a hatha-inspired vinyasa flow, but there's also ashtanga and other styles. Yoga by candlelight is a sublime way to transition from day to night. Multi-class packages and **lodgings** (dm/s/d/tr incl breakfast US$18/40/45/50; P 🛜) are available. Located behind the Plaza Royal.

Yoga Studio at Nautilus YOGA

(☑ 2640-0991; www.hotelnautiluscostarica.com; Santa Teresa; drop-in/private classes US$14/60; ☺ 9am & 6pm) What's not to love about rooftop yoga? Twice-daily classes are held on the deck at the **Nautilus Boutique Hotel** (villa d/q US$165/270; P ❄️🍽🛜📶) 🌱, offering lovely views of surrounding palm trees and the village. It offers vinyasa flow and kundalini, yin, hatha, ashtanga and power yoga. Multi-class packages available. Look for the Nautilus signs.

Horizon Yoga Hotel YOGA

(☑ 2640-0524; www.horizon-yogahotel.com; Calle Buenos Aires, Santa Teresa; drop-in class US$15) Offers two classes daily, in a serene environment overlooking the ocean. As with other schools, weekly and other passes are available. About 100m north of Supermarket Ronny, turn off the main road and drive 50m up the hill.

🛏 Sleeping

Frank's Place is the landmark that occupies the main corner at Playa El Carmen. Stretching to the north, Santa Teresa is a dusty hamlet that's crammed with guesthouses, cafes and surf shops ('uncontrolled development' is a phrase which comes to mind.) Stretching to the south, Mal País is more sparsely developed and more densely forested, offering a quieter, old-school hippie atmosphere.

Don Jon's BUNGALOW $$

(☑ 2640-0700; www.donjonsonline.com; Santa Teresa; dm/bungalow & tree house/apt US$20/70/110; P ❄️🛜) Just 100m from the surf, this is the perfect base for anybody looking to 'relax to the max.' Rustic teak bungalows are creatively decorated, while attractive Spanish-tiled dorms have high-beamed ceilings and plenty of hammocks

in the garden. An amazing tree-house structure not only has an appealing room but also hosts yoga classes. It's 150m past the soccer field.

The vegetarian restaurant knows its audience, serving filling breakfasts, giant burritos and sandwiches.

Villa Cacao BOUTIQUE HOTEL $$

(☑ 8400-3160; www.villacacao.com; Santa Teresa; studios from US$89, suites from US$99, 2-bedroom apt from US$134; P ❄️🍽🛜📶) 🌱 Escape from the dust and into this cozy, quiet boutique featuring just a few accommodations set before a relaxing pool and surrounded by tropical landscaping. The suites and studios offer a modern and tasteful design, with kitchenettes and darling terraces, and the beach is just a short walk across the street. Owned by a super nice, knowledgeable, multilingual family.

Hotel Meli Melo HOTEL $$

(☑ 2640-0575; www.hotelmelimelo.com; Santa Teresa; d/tr/q US$70/85/100, apt US$100-130; P ❄️🍽🛜📶) A cheerful hotel, smack dab in the center of town and close to the main surf break. Clean, colorful rooms have all the standard amenities, plus a private terrace, a common kitchen, tropical gardens and an outdoor shower. Everyone gets a shelf in the communal fridges and access to free bikes. Meli takes great pride in her hotel and it shows.

A fully equipped apartment with a kitchen is also available, and surf boards can be rented for US$15 a day. Just over 2km north of the main T-intersection on the north–south beach road.

Malpaís Surf Camp & Resort LODGE $$

(☑ 2640-0031; www.malpaissurfcamp.com; Mal País; campsite per person US$15, dm US$25, d with/without bathroom US$95/45, villa/house from US$95/175; P ❄️@🛜📶) There are comfortable, private *cabañas* and more luxurious digs, but the best deal at this surfers' lodge is the open-air *rancho,* with a tin roof and pebble floors, which you can share with three other surfers. Explore the landscaped tropical grounds, swim in the luscious pool, grab a cold beer in the open-air lounge and soak up the good vibes.

Star Mountain Jungle Lodge LODGE $$

(☑ 2640-0101; www.starmountaineco.com; Mal País; d/tr incl breakfast US$105/135, casitas US$130-160; P 🛜📶) 🌱 Set on a 90-hectare private reserve, replete with birds, butterflies and monkeys, Star Mountain is an escape back to nature. The lodge has spacious guest rooms, a wide porch with hammocks and rockers, a yoga studio and a glorious pool. There's also a traditional wooden casita that's ideal for families.

Funky Monkey Lodge BUNGALOW **$$**
(2640-0272; www.funkymonkeylodge.com; Santa Teresa; d US$60-100, apt US$130-220; P ❄ wifi pool) Located about 100m up a side road off the main drag, this funky lodge has sweet, rustic bungalows built out of bamboo. Each has an open-air shower, balcony with hammock and access to a communal kitchen. Also: table tennis, pool and board games... good times!

★ Canaima Chill House BOUTIQUE HOTEL **$$**
(2640-0410; www.hotel-canaima-chill-house.com; Santa Teresa; d/q US$100/130; P wifi pool) A 'chill house' is an apt descriptor for this eight-room boutique eco-chic hotel, set in the jungle. Super-stylish suites have breezy indoor-outdoor living areas, well-equipped kitchens, awesome hanging bamboo beds and loads of natural materials (such as stone grotto showers). Guests share the Jacuzzi and plunge pool, and commune in the sunken pillow lounge.

Located 400m uphill from the sign for Nautilus Hotel. It can be walked, but you may want a taxi.

Hotel Moana BOUTIQUE HOTEL **$$$**
(2640-0230, in USA 888-865-8032; www.moanacostarica.com; Mal País; incl breakfast r standard/deluxe US$105/150, ste US$160-250; P ❄ wifi pool) A simply stunning boutique property etched into the wooded hillside above Mal País. Standard rooms are all-wood garden cottages, decked out with African art. Make the climb to the junior suites for 180-degree views of the coast. There are wood floors throughout, rain showers inside and outside, and sliding glass doors. The top-shelf **Papaya Lounge** (tapas US$6-15; 7:30-10am Tue, 7:30-10am & 5-9pm Wed-Mon) shares that stunning perch.

Atrapasueños BOUTIQUE HOTEL **$$$**
(Dreamcatcher Hotel; 2640-0080; www.dreamcatcherhotel.com; Santa Teresa; d incl breakfast US$70-170, apt US$200; P ❄ wifi pool) Steps from the beach, this family-owned place offers the intimacy of a B&B and the luxury of a boutique hotel. With a balcony or terrace overlooking lush gardens, the rooms have hardwood floors, exotic art and tapestries, and big glass sliding doors. A lovely mosaic pool is surrounded by a sun terrace with an outdoor shower.

Florblanca VILLA **$$$**
(2640-0232; www.florblanca.com; Santa Teresa; villas incl breakfast from US$600; P ❄ wifi pool) Truly in a class of their own, these romantic villas are scattered around 3 hectares of land next to a pristine white-sand beach. Indoor-outdoor spaces are flooded with natural light, and are replete with stylish design, from the open-air bathrooms to the sunken indoor-outdoor living areas. Perks include complimentary yoga, bikes and surfboards. An isolated location, 4km north of the intersection.

Eating

Zwart Cafe CAFE **$**
(Zwart Art Cafe; 2640-0011; Santa Teresa; mains US$6-10; 7am-5pm; wifi) *Zwart* means 'black' in Dutch, but this shabby-chic, artist-owned gallery and cafe is all white (or mostly – damn dust!). You'll love the surf-inspired Technicolor canvases, the lively outdoor patio and the breakfasts, including chocolate-chip pancakes. At lunch it's all about the burritos and there are plenty of vegan options. There's a dynamite used bookstore here too.

About 2km north of the T-intersection, on the right if you're heading north.

Bakery BAKERY **$**
(2640-0560; https://the-bakery-restaurant.business.site; Playa El Carmen; bakery items US$5-10, mains US$7-12; 7am-10pm; wifi) A dainty, classic bakery and longstanding favorite brunch spot in the center of Playa El Carmen. Some naughty delights like croque monsieur and Belgian waffles are offset by more surfer-centric choices like *batidos* (fruit shakes) and healthy salads. Service is flawless.

★ Earth Café HEALTH FOOD **$$**
(8427-4928; www.facebook.com/earthcafe.st; Santa Teresa; mains US$11-13; 8am-5pm) For surfers and yogis, there is not a more perfect lunch spot. We're talking elaborate salads, savory toppings piled high on toast and big colorful bowls of tuna poke, vegetables and smoothie goodness that pop with spice and flavor. The green juices and coffee are also top-notch, and the service is super friendly.

El Carmen PIZZA $$
(☎2640-0110; Playa El Carmen; mains US$10-23; ⊙9am-10pm) The location right on the *playa* is hard to beat, and the list of *ceviche* and cooked fish shows it's more than just a pizzeria. It's a popular spot for sundowners, thanks to the happy-hour specials (two-for-one drinks) and the amazing show that takes place in the sky. Come hobnob with the locals and enjoy. Special events can be found on the Facebook page.

Caracolas SEAFOOD $$
(☎2640-0525; Mal País; mains US$7-23; ⊙8am-9pm; P ☎ ✎) The lone *soda* at this end of the coast revamped its menu in 2019 and now emphasizes seafood and paellas. But you can still eat a classic *casado* off a timber table in a garden that rolls onto the rocky beach. It also does steak, chicken and vegetarian dishes, but the best reason to come here is to feel the ocean breeze.

It also has a few fully equipped cabins (from US$50) for rent – on the beach, no less.

Burger Rancho BURGERS $$
(www.facebook.com/BurgerRancho; Santa Teresa; mains US$10-12; ⊙11am-10pm; ✎) Get your burger on at this open-air *rancho* that in 2019 found a new home just north of Kina Surf Shop. Check the blackboard for daily changing specials, including veggie choices like a portobello mushroom burger, fish options like a mahi mahi with curry sauce, and other interesting burgers such as a chorizo one. Cocktails and craft beer also available.

Koji's JAPANESE $$
(☎2640-0815; www.kojisrestaurant.com; Playa Hermosa; sushi US$5-16, mains US$9-18; ⊙5:30-9:30pm Tue-Sun) Koji Hyodo's outdoor patio is a twinkling beacon of fresh, raw excellence. The atmosphere and service are superior, of course, but his food is a higher truth. The grilled octopus is barely fried and sprinkled with sea salt, and there's a perfectly sweet crunch to his softshell crab and lobster tempura. Uphill from the main road.

Bajo El Arbol TAPAS $$
(☎2640-0302; www.facebook.com/bajoelarbolcr; Playa El Carmen; mains US$14-17; ⊙6-10pm) If you can't afford a flight to Spain, just sit down 'Beneath the Tree.' Basque chef Julio's menu changes daily, but he whips up an extraordinary *escalivada* (eggplant and pepper dish), and the *pulpo a la gallega* (octopus), topped with crunchy sea salt, is so damned good it ought to be illegal. Add a half-bottle of Spanish wine, and you're set.

There's also a convenient four-room guesthouse attached (d incl breakfast US$40-50). Just 200m north of the T-intersection, in Playa El Carmen.

Drinking & Entertainment

It's no mystery where the party is going on: Thursdays at Kika, Sundays at **Habaneros** and any night of the week – around sunset – at Banana Beach or El Carmen. **Nativos** (☎2640-0356; www.facebook.com/NativoSportsBar; Playa El Carmen; ⊙11am-midnight), a fun sports bar, is smack-dab in the middle of things.

Drift Bar BAR
(☎8496-6056; www.driftbarcr.com; Santa Teresa; ⊙noon-11pm Mon-Thu, to midnight Fri & Sat, 3-10pm Sun) Part cocktail bar, part vegetarian restaurant, part art gallery, Drift bar is wholly satisfying. Drinks are made with cold-pressed juices and are best consumed in the chic lounge or while browsing the art. If you've got other obligations, you can always order a sealed cocktail in a glass bottle (along with a reusable bag of ice) to go. Don't forget to bring the bottle back!

Banana Beach BAR
(☎2640-0320; www.bananabeachcr.com) What began as a few tables and a hut in the sand has blossomed into Santa Teresa's liveliest sunset bar. Grab a fruity cocktail and plop down in an Adirondack chair, beach lounger or an old boat repurposed as a couch, and watch surfers dance across the waves at sunset.

The property also contains seven swanky bungalows (d from US$139) of different sizes and configurations, each with air-con, wi-fi, a kitchenette and a terrace. There's also a pool. Families will dig it.

Kika LIVE MUSIC
(☎2640-0408; www.facebook.com/kika.santateresa; Santa Teresa; ⊙6-10pm) This Argentine-owned restaurant is a popular spot for dinner and drinks by candlelight (Grandma's pork gets rave reviews). But things really pick up after dark on Thursday, when live bands take the stage and attract a lively crowd for drinking and dancing. Cash only.

Information

ATMs occasionally run out of cash, so stock up before the weekend.

Banco de Costa Rica (2211-1111; Playa El Carmen; 9am-4pm Mon-Fri) Has a 24-hour ATM.

Banco Nacional (2640-0598; Playa El Carmen; 1-7pm Mon-Fri) Has an ATM. Directly across the street at the Centro Comercial Playa El Carmen.

Malpaisnet (www.malpais.net) A useful website with lots of local information, including a handy map of the area.

Getting There & Away

BUS

All buses begin and end 100m south of Cuesta Arriba hostel, but you can flag the bus down anywhere along the road in Santa Teresa. At Frank's Place, the buses turn left and head inland toward Cóbano.

A direct bus to San José via the Paquera ferry departs at 6am and 2pm (US$14, six hours). Local buses to Cóbano (US$2, 45 minutes) depart nine times a day.

Tropical Tours (2640-1900, WhatsApp 8890-9197; www.tropicaltourshuttles.com; 8am-9pm), with its main office right next to Frank's Place, offers a reliable shuttle service around the peninsula and as far as Liberia and the Nicaragua border.

CAR

Consider renting a car if you want to check out some of the more distant breaks, but beware that the town's gas station closed in 2019. The closest one is now 15km away, in Cóbano. Ask at your rental agency about where to find informal (but expensive) places to fill up in town, in a pinch.

Alamo (2642-0622; www.alamocostarica.com; Playa El Carmen; 8am-5pm) Located at Frank's Place.

Budget (2436-2084; www.budget.co.cr; Centro Comercial, Playa El Carmen; 7am-6pm Mon-Sat, to 4pm Sun) Next to Banco Nacional.

Getting Around

Santa Teresa and Mal País are dirt-road types of towns: during the dry season, life gets extremely dusty. The preponderance of ATVs stirs up more grit (and the ire of locals); consider using a bicycle to get around town, so you're not contributing to the problem. If you must drive, please go slowly. Taxis between Mal País, Playa El Carmen and Santa Teresa range from US$5 to US$10.

Cabuya

POP 200

This tiny, bucolic village unfurls along a rugged dirt road about 7km south of Montezuma. Populated by a tight-knit community of Ticos and expats, it's a gem with easy access to the Cabo Blanco reserve, ideal for those looking to chill. Don't miss the amazing banyan tree (**El Higueron**), reportedly the largest strangler fig in Costa Rica, measuring 40m high and 22m in circumference.

The beach here is rocky and not great for swimming or surfing. But you're a short walk from **Playa los Cedros**, a great surf spot halfway between Montezuma and Cabuya. Alternatively, there's a two-hour hike along Río Lajas to a swimmable pool and impressive waterfall. At low tide, you can also hike the natural bridge to **Isla Cabuya**, which has a small sandy beach and good snorkeling, as well as an evocative island cemetery. Keep an eye on the tides or you'll be swimming back.

Sleeping

L&L Aparthotel HOTEL **$$**
(8427-7578; www.ll-apart.hotelsinpuntarenas.com; Calle Delicias-Cabuya; 1-/2-bedroom chalet from US$69/86; P ❄ 📶) Tucked between Montezuma and Cabuya, these tidy little chalets look like Lincoln log cabins in the tropics. They're equipped with living rooms, kitchens, dining areas and (in some cases) terraces that look out over the pool and lush surrounding gardens. There's lots of wildlife around these parts, and the French owners are lovely. Short walk to Playa Cedros.

Howler Monkey Hotel HOTEL **$$**
(2642-0303; www.howlermonkeyhotel.com; d/tr/q US$80/90/100; P 📶 🏊) Follow the signs down the side road to these large rustic A-frame bungalows with kitchenettes (useful as eating options are limited). The place is right on a slice of very quiet, rocky beach. The friendly owner is a wealth of information, and also offers free bikes, snorkeling equipment, kayaks and laundry. It's called Howler Monkey Hotel for a reason: expect a wake-up call.

There's a good book exchange in the library.

Calala Lodge CABINA **$$**
(8480-3649; https://calalalodge.com; d/family room incl breakfast US$85/90; P 📶 🏊) This sweet spot is a collection of spacious,

stained-wood A-frame bungalows renovated in 2019 by a new set of owners to feature balconies, kitchenettes and enlarged windows. The grounds are decorated with artistic touches like coconut lamps and bamboo chandeliers, while the sun-dappled beach is gorgeous. Swimming isn't advised due to rocks, but the pool remains glorious.

A nice walk to Isla Cabuya at low tide begins about 500m south of here.

Eating & Drinking

Café Coyote PIZZA $

(☎2642-0354; www.cabuyabeach.com/restaurants/cafe-coyote.html; mains US$5-11, pizzas US$14-18; ⏰8am-10pm; 📶) Jenny can help you with just about anything, from calling a taxi to organizing an adventure outing, pouring you a cold *cerveza* or making you a tasty pizza (her specialty). She also offers delicious breakfasts and other meals to sate your appetite at any time of day. Just after the intersection where the Cabuya road turns right toward Mal País.

Pick hubby Wilfredo's brain on local birding over a pizza. There's also a funky converted trailer and apartments (US$25 to US$50) with kitchenettes to rent.

Panadería Cabuya CAFE $$

(☎2642-1184; www.facebook.com/panaderiacafeteria.cabuya; mains US$7-20; ⏰6:30am-8pm Mon-Sat, to 6pm Sun; 📶) A local landmark on the main road from Cabuya to Reserva Cabo Blanco. Set on a tropical patio, this inviting cafe serves up a stellar menu including fresh bread, pastries and strong coffee for breakfast, as well as soups and sandwiches for later. If you have a thing for tall, dark and handsome, you should meet the chocolate cake.

La Selva Brewery CRAFT BEER

(☎2642-1559; www.laselva.cr; ⏰11am-7pm Mon-Sat, 9am-4pm Sun) If there is a list of unlikely places to find a craft brewery, put Cabuya on there. But it has one! Hidden down a quiet side road, the tiny tasting room features six tap beers brewed onsite, as well as an alfresco living room, a tapas menu and facility tours. It's a perfect stop after a hike in Cabo Blanco or a swim at Río Lajas.

Getting There & Away

Driving from Montezuma, it's a straight shot 7km down the coast to the village of Cabuya. Minibuses make this run – en route to Cabo Blanco – a couple of times a day in either direction.

If you find Café Coyote you have found the road to Mal País, which is about 7km due west on the stunningly scenic Star Mountain Rd (passable only during the dry season). Make sure you have a 4WD, especially during the rainy season, as these roads are rugged and there is at least one river crossing.

Montezuma

POP 7500

Montezuma is a distinctly boho beach town that demands you abandon the car to stroll, swim and (if you can stroll a little further) surf. The warm and wild ocean and that remnant, ever-audible jungle have helped this rocky nook cultivate an inviting, mellow vibe. Typical tourist offerings such as canopy tours and waterfall hikes do a brisk trade here, but you'll also bump up against Montezuma's internationally inflected, artsy-rootsy beach culture in yoga classes, volunteer corps and veggie-friendly dining rooms.

This is a barefoot *pueblo* where itinerant travelers tend to camp on the beach, though an array of dreamy lodgings are set at all price points. Regardless of where you stay, you're never far from the rhythm and sound of the sea, and truly it's a beautiful thing.

Sights

Picture-perfect white-sand beaches are strung along the coast, separated by small rocky headlands, offering great beachcombing and ideal tide-pool contemplation. Unfortunately, there are strong riptides, so inquire locally before going for a swim.

★**Montezuma Waterfalls** WATERFALL

(parking US$2) A 40-minute river hike leads to a waterfall with a delicious swimming hole. Further along, a second set of falls offers a good 12m leap into deep water. Reach the 'diving platform' from the trail: do not try to scale the slippery rocks! Daring souls can test their Tarzan skills on the rope that swings over a third set. A lot of travelers enjoy these thrills but a few of them have died, so do it at your own risk.

To get to the parking area, head south from town and you'll see it just past Hotel La Cascada; once parked, take the trail to the right just after the bridge. You'll want proper hiking footwear. There are official rangers/guards (in official vests/hats) who

Montezuma

Sights
1 Playa Montezuma B1

Activities, Courses & Tours
Montezuma Yoga .... (see 7)
2 Peaks & Swells Surf Camp B1
3 Sun Trails A3
4 Young Vision Surf School A2
Zuma Tours .... (see 3)

Sleeping
5 El Sano Banano A2
6 Hotel Amor de Mar B5
7 Hotel Los Mangos B4
8 Luna Llena A2
9 Luz en el Cielo A1
10 Nya B2

Eating
11 Cafe Orgánico B2
12 Chia B2
13 Cocolores B2
14 Playa de los Artistas B4

Drinking & Nightlife
15 Chico's Bar B2

Transport
Montezuma Expeditions .... (see 4)
16 Zuma Tours A2

Montezuma

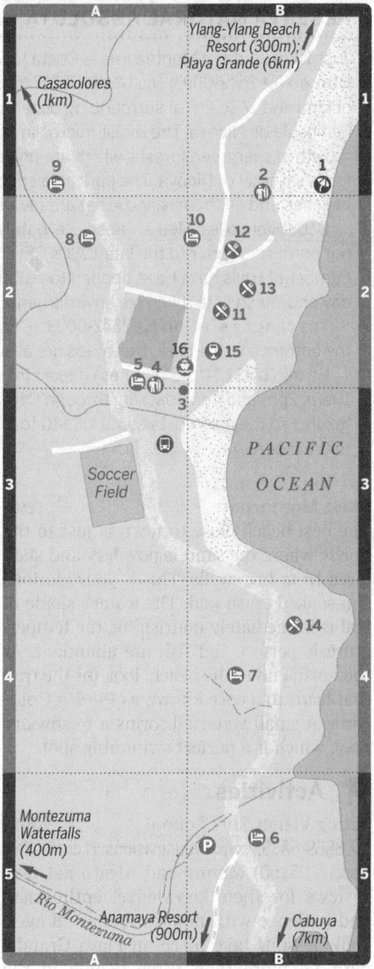

work the trail and can offer the best advice, free of charge, on the safest routes to take, particularly during rainy season. Families with children or elderly members may want to enter via Sun Trails (p342), which charges.

Playa Cocolito BEACH

Here's your chance to see a waterfall crashing down a cliff, straight onto the rocks and into the ocean. El Chorro Waterfall is the pièce de résistance of Playa Cocolito, which is itself pretty irresistible.

It's a hot, two-hour, 12km hike from Montezuma: leave at sunrise to spot plenty of wildlife along the way. Alternatively, this is a popular destination for horseback riding, or you can grab a meal at Tango Mar (p346) then make the 20-minute hike at low tide from there. Otherwise, bring water and snacks as there are no facilities on the beach.

The waters here are a dreamy, iridescent azure, with pink rocky cliffs creating two inviting swimming areas. It's far enough from the action that you are likely to have the place to yourself.

Playa Grande BEACH

About 6km north of town, Playa Grande is the best surf beach in the area. It's a 3km-plus stretch of waves and sand, which never gets too crowded as it requires a 30-minute hike to get here. But what a hike it is, wandering along between the turquoise waters of the Pacific and the lush greenery of the Montezuma Biological Reserve.

Playa Grande is sometimes a destination for topless or nude sunbathers. This is not the cultural norm in Costa Rica, so please be discreet if you're trying to get rid of your tan lines.

WORTH A TRIP

RESERVA NATURAL ABSOLUTA CABO BLANCO

Just 11km south of Montezuma is Costa Rica's oldest protected wilderness area. **Cabo Blanco** (☎2642-0093; adult/child US$12/5; ⏲8am-4pm Wed-Sun) comprises 12 sq km of land and 17 sq km of surrounding ocean, and includes the entire southern tip of the Península de Nicoya. The moist microclimate on the tip of the peninsula fosters the growth of evergreen forests, which are unique when compared with the dry tropical forests typical of Nicoya. The park also encompasses a number of pristine white-sand beaches and offshore islands that are favored nesting areas for various bird species.

Cabo Blanco is called an 'absolute' nature reserve because visitors were originally not permitted (prior to the late 1980s). Even though the name hasn't changed, a limited number of trails have been opened to visitors, but the reserve remains closed on Monday and Tuesday to minimize environmental impact.

The **ranger station** (☎2642-0093; ⏲8am-4pm Wed-Sun) is 2km south of Cabuya at the entrance to the park; trail maps are available here.

Buses (US$1.50, 45 minutes) depart from the park entrance for Montezuma at 8am, 10am, 2pm and 4pm, passing through Cabuya about 15 minutes later. A taxi from Montezuma to the park costs about US$10 to US$15 (US$10 to Cabuya itself, an extra US$5 to the reserve).

Playa Montezuma BEACH

The best beach close to town is just to the north, where the sand is powdery and sheltered from big swells. This is your glorious sun-soaked crash pad. The water's shade of teal is immediately nourishing, the temperature is perfect and fish are abundant. At the north end of the beach, look for the trail that leads to a cove known as **Piedra Colorada**. A small waterfall forms a freshwater pool, which is a perfect swimming spot.

Activities

Young Vision Surf School SURFING

(☎8669-6835; www.youngvisionsurf.com; 2hr lessons US$50) Manny and Alvaro get rave reviews for their knowledge, enthusiasm and patience with new surfers of all ages. Daily lessons take place on Playa Grande, with no more than three people in the class. Surfboard, rash guard and fresh fruit are included. They also offer weeklong camps specifically for families, surfer chicks and yogis. Inquire at Sano Banano for details.

Montezuma Yoga YOGA

(☎2642-0076; www.montezumayoga.com; per class US$15; ⏲8:30am & 6pm) Vinyasa and yin yoga classes are held in this gorgeous studio kissed by ocean breezes, sheltered by a peaked tin roof and serenaded by the sounds of nature. The Sunday-night candlelight flow class is a transformative experience. On the grounds of Hotel Los Mangos.

Peaks & Swells Surf Camp SURFING

(☎2642-0067; www.surfcamppeaksnswells.com; 7-day camp per person from US$2950) Weeklong camps that are geared to women, families and mountain bikers. If one of these is you, here's a chance to learn how to surf, following systematic methods of instruction. Located on the beach, just north of 'downtown' Montezuma.

Tours

Tour operators around town rent everything from bodyboards to bikes. The most popular tour is a boat trip to Isla Tortuga (p348), which costs around US$65 including lunch, fruit, drinks and snorkeling gear. Although the island is certainly beautiful (the *most* beautiful in Costa Rica, by many accounts), travelers complain that the outing feels like a tourist circus, especially during high season.

Also popular are guided hikes in Cabo Blanco and horseback riding to Playa Cocolito.

Sun Trails TOURS

(Montezuma Waterfall Canopy Tour; ☎2642-0808; www.montezumatraveladventures.com; tours from US$45; ⏲9am, 1pm & 3pm) Tour company Sun Trails operates a 1½-hour canopy tour. After you've flown down nine ziplines, you'll hike down – rather than up – to the waterfalls. Bring your swimsuit, so you can jump off the rocks and cool off (if the conditions are safe). Park at the canopy entrance for quick access to the falls via a suspension bridge (US$4 per person).

This company has opened a spotless new lodge on the other side of the swinging bridge, Sun Trails Hotel, with the latest amenities.

Zuma Tours TOURS
(☎2642-0024; www.zumatours.net; Tortuga snorkeling from US$65, canopy tours US$45-50; ⏱7am-8pm) Makes arrangements for transportation and tours of all sorts: snorkeling trips to Isla Tortuga, horseback riding in Cabo Blanco and more. Located on the main downhill east–west street, towards the water.

Sleeping

Montezuma offers a number of solid budget-friendly accommodations around town, as well as some stunning options of varying prices tucked into the natural surrounds. There's also a sprinkling of good guesthouses and boutique hotels north of Montezuma off the road to Cóbano, but these are only suitable if you have wheels.

★ **Luz en el Cielo** HOSTEL, B&B $
(☎2642-0030; www.luzenelcielo.com; incl breakfast dm from US$20, cabinas US$85-102, house US$125-153; P 📶) In the heart of the jungle but two minutes from town, this homey hostel and B&B is an inviting retreat. Crowded dorm rooms are super-clean with sturdy wood furniture and lockers, while the 'luxury' dorms are more spacious, with private balconies and en suite bathrooms. The treetop *cabinas* are also wonderful, as are the amazing organic breakfasts, enticing hammocks and friendly staff.

Two fully-furnished houses with kitchens are also on offer.

Luna Llena HOSTEL $
(☎2642-0390; www.lunallenahotel.com; dm US$15, s/d US$55/65, without bathroom from US$28/38; P 📶) On the northern edge of town on a hilltop overlooking the sea, this budget option is delightful. The 15 rooms and two dorms are simple but stylish, colorful and clean; many have balconies. There is one large kitchen and a breezy communal lounge featuring local art and lovely ocean views. Wildlife abounds in the surrounding trees.

Hotel Los Mangos HOTEL $
(☎2642-0076; www.hotellosmangos.com; r with/without bathroom US$75/35, bungalows US$90; P 📶 🏊) Scattered across mango-dotted gardens, this whimsical hotel has plain, painted-wood rooms in the main building and attractive (though dark) octagonal bungalows offering more privacy. Monkeys populate the mango trees and yoga classes are held in the gorgeous, ocean-view yoga pavilion, next to a pool with an accompanying Jacuzzi. On the road south of town on the way to the waterfall.

Nya BOUTIQUE HOTEL $$
(☎2642-0010; www.nyahotel.cr; dm from US$36, d from US$116, family room US$225; P ❄ 📶 🏊) The brainchild of a Swedish photographer, this minimalist boutique hotel feels a bit buttoned-up for freewheeling Montezuma. But the posh rooms (including a 'luxury dorm') are super-comfortable, with lovely outdoor green spaces and terraces, and the front desk might be the most amazing piece of driftwood we've ever seen.

Amenities are wellness-driven, with a pool, yoga deck and gourmet French restaurant, Ubin, which has earned high marks with travelers.

Casacolores BUNGALOW $$
(☎2642-0283; www.casacolores.com; 1-/2-bedroom casas US$90/120; P ❄ 📶 🏊) Nine bright houses (each painted and named for a color of the rainbow) are fully equipped with kitchens and big porches with hammocks. They're set amid blooming tropical gardens, with a stone-rimmed swimming pool onsite. The location is sort of a no-man's land (a 20-minute uphill hike from town) but there's plenty of wildlife wandering around these jungly grounds.

El Sano Banano HOTEL $$
(☎2642-0638; www.elsanobanano.com; d from US$75; P ❄ 📶) A well-run hotel in the center of town. Although its many businesses take up an entire city block, it has just 12 prim and comfortable rooms with whimsical paint jobs. Many rooms do not have windows, but the walls are adorned with trees, flowers and ocean views.

Guests may use the Ylang Ylang Resort pool for free.

The attached restaurant has appetizing baked goods and chocolates, and an inviting terrace on the main drag. It's also worth showing up in the evening when the restaurant shows nightly films and there's live music in the garden out back.

Kalapiti Luxury Jungle Suites HOTEL $$$
(2642-1361; www.kalapiti.com; d incl breakfast from US$400;) Set on jungle-shrouded former horse ranch, this Moroccan-inspired stay is defined by arching doorways and Arabesque windows, moon-shaped door handles and Marrakeshi streetscape murals. Even the baby-blue and yellow paint was imported from Morocco. Botanical gardens surround the three distinctive suites, where guests sleep in four-poster beds, take outdoor showers and soak in private whirlpools.

In case one gets an urge to leave the suite, there's a massive infinity pool (and waterslide), a steam room, a shared chef's kitchen and a Mediterranean restaurant. It's in Las Delicias, in between Montezuma and Mal País. Two-night minimum stay.

Anamaya Resort RESORT $$$
(2642-1289; www.anamayaresort.com; per week incl 3 meals from US$1125;) Billed as a 'mind, body, and soul resort,' Anamaya's perch, high above Montezuma, is pretty damn special. With ocean panoramas and weeping jungle on all sides, this environment is certainly dramatic enough to spark enlightenment, if only for a weekend. The yoga space floats off the main house and has that insane aforementioned view, as does the adjacent infinity pool.

Yoga classes, surf lessons and lots of other activities are available as 'retreat addons'. Monthlong teacher training happens here, too. You'll find it on a side road just past the waterfalls.

Ylang-Ylang Beach Resort RESORT $$$
(2642-0636, in USA 888-795-8494; www.ylangylangbeachresort.com; incl breakfast & dinner cabina/d/bungalow/ste US$198/220/295/315;) Walk 15 minutes north along the beach to this lush property, complete with beautifully appointed cabinas and bungalows, and a palm-fringed swimming pool, yoga center, gourmet organic restaurant and spa. The decor is lovely and tropical, with tiled floors, stenciled walls and colorful tapestries. All accommodations have outdoor terraces facing the glorious sea.

Hotel Amor de Mar B&B $$$
(2642-0262; www.amordemar.com; d with/without ocean view from US$120/90, villas from US$250;) A lovely B&B just south of town with nine unique rooms, replete with exquisite touches like timber-framed mirrors, organic lanterns, and rocking chairs on a terrace. Then there's the palm-dappled, hammock-strewn lawn that rolls out to the tide pools and the Pacific beyond. It's gorgeous to look at, although the back rooms get some road noise.

The breakfast (US$7 to US$12) includes home-made challah and linseed breads and jams by owner Ori.

Eating & Drinking

Montezuma is experiencing the same food revolution that is taking place on other parts of the peninsula. Local ingredients are meeting international chefs, with magnificent results. Montezuma is also good for traditional Tico fare, often with oceanside service. Most of the restaurants are clustered along the beach.

Chia INTERNATIONAL $
(8500-7651; 7am-10pm) A cozy feeling permeates this restaurant and bakery on the beach road, which in 2019 was repainted in a cheerful yellow by its new owner. The terrace seating is lovely, and the menu features breakfast items like bagels and banana bread, along with lunch and dinner dishes including burgers, pizzas, tacos, burritos, salads and poke bowls. The coffee's good, too.

Tierra y Fuego ITALIAN $$
(2642-1593; mains US$10-17; 5-10pm Thu-Sun;) Take a taxi up to this gem in the hills above Montezuma – fittingly in the Delicias neighborhood. This Italian outpost seems straight out of the Tuscan countryside, complete with brick ovens, and chickens roasting over the fire. The menu is mostly pizza and pasta, but the flavors are divine – not surprising given the ingredients are all imported or grown onsite.

Cocolores INTERNATIONAL $$
(2642-0348; mains US$9-22; 4-10pm Tue-Sun) Set on a beachside terrace lit by lanterns, Cocolores is one of Montezuma's top spots for an upscale dinner. The wide-ranging menu includes curries, pasta, fajitas and steaks, all prepared and served with careful attention to delicious details. Cash only.

Cafe Orgánico VEGETARIAN **$$**
(☎2642-1322; www.organicocostarica.com; mains US$8-10; ⏰7am-10pm; 🅥) When they say 'pure food made with love,' they mean it – this healthy cafe turns out vegetarian and vegan dishes such as veggie burgers, smoothies named for local wildlife and more (as well as meaty options too). Opposite the church square, on the road leading north to the beach.

The avocado ice cream is something everyone should try. There's live music almost nightly, including a popular open mic on Monday nights from 6:30pm to 9:30pm.

★**Playa de los Artistas** INTERNATIONAL **$$**
(☎2642-0920; mains US$9-18; ⏰4-9pm Mon-Fri, noon-4pm Sat) Most romantic dinner ever. If you're lucky, you'll snag one of the tree-trunk tables under the palms. The international menu with Mediterranean influences changes daily, though you can always count on fresh seafood roasted in the wood oven. The service is flawless, the cooking is innovative and the setting is downright dreamy. Cash only (back to reality) so bring lots.

Just past the soccer field, on the beach side of the road leading to the waterfall.

Chico's Bar BAR
(⏰11am-2am) When it comes to nightlife, Chico's is the main game in town, which means that everybody – old, young, Ticos, tourists, rowdy, dowdy – ends up here eventually, especially on Thursday night, which is reggae night. Grab a table on the back patio for a lovely view of the beach and beyond. On the main road parallel to the beach.

ℹ Information

There is no working ATM in town. Be sure to withdraw cash up the road in Cóbano, which has a few ATMs along with a full-service bank. For money exchange, tour operators in town will take US dollars or euros.

You can get your laundry done at one of the many low-cost *lavandarias* along the main road near the bus stop.

ℹ Getting There & Around

BOAT

Zuma Tours (p343) operates a fast water shuttle connecting Montezuma to Jacó in an hour. At US$45 it's not cheap, but it'll save you a day's worth of travel. From Montezuma, boats depart at 8:30am daily, and the price includes van transfer from the beach to the Jacó bus terminal. From Jacó, the departure to Montezuma is at 10am. During the high season, it may run an additional shuttle, departing Montezuma at 1:30pm and departing Jacó at 3pm. Book in advance from any tour operator. Also, dress appropriately; you will have to board the boat by walking through knee-high water, and sometimes passengers get sprayed along the way.

BUS

Buses depart Montezuma from the **sandy lot** lot on the beach, across from the soccer field. Buy tickets directly from the driver. To get to Mal País and Santa Teresa, go to Cóbano and change buses. The Paquera bus can drop you at the entrance to Refugio Nacional de Vida Silvestre Curú.

Montezuma Expeditions (☎2642-0919, WhatsApp 6483-8840; www.montezumaexpeditions.com; from US$50) and Tropical Tours (p339) operate shuttle buses to destinations including Mal País, Santa Teresa, San José, La Fortuna, Monteverde, Jacó, Manuel Antonio, Dominical, Tamarindo, Sámara and Liberia.

CAR

Although the road from Paquera to Cóbano is paved, the stretch between Cóbano and Montezuma is not, and it can be rough. During the rainy season you may need a 4WD. In the village itself, parking can be a problem, though it's easy enough to walk everywhere.

BUSES FROM MONTEZUMA

DESTINATION	PRICE (US$)	DURATION	DEPARTURES
Cabo Blanco via Cabuya	1.50	45min	8am, 10am, 2pm, 4pm
Cóbano	2	1hr	5:50am, 8pm
Paquera, via Cóbano	3	2hr	5:15am, 8:15am, 10:15am, 12;15am, 2:15pm & 4:15pm
San José	14	5hr	6:20am & 2:20pm

Playas Pochote & Tambor

POP 13,695

These two mangrove-backed, gray-sand beaches are protected by Bahía Ballena, and are surrounded by small fishing communities. In the past 20 years, the area has slowly developed as a resort destination, but for the most part, Pochote and Tambor are mellow Tico beaches, providing plenty of opportunities for hiking, swimming, kayaking and whale-watching, along with easy access to the Refugio Nacional de Vida Silvestre Curú.

The beaches begin 14km south of Paquera, at the mangrove-shrouded, fishing *pueblo* of Pochote, and stretch for about 8km southwest to Tambor. The two villages are divided by the narrow estuary of the Río Pánica.

It should also be said that there is one rather conspicuous all-inclusive mega-resort in the Tambor area – Hotel Barceló Playa Tambor. The huge place has a convention center and golf course, but once you're in the *pueblo*, you won't even know it's there.

Sleeping

Blue Zone Retreat GUESTHOUSE $$
(☎8335-5300; www.thebluezoneretreat.com; d/q US$69/89; P ❄ ☎) The location seems odd – stuck on a side road with no beach in sight – but the attentive owners and art-filled premises make it an excellent lower-cost option. A yoga deck and hammocks strung up around the property (including in a treehouse) are part of an emphasis on wellness, and the eight simple rooms feature pretty wall murals.

★ **Tambor Tropical** BOUTIQUE HOTEL $$$
(☎2683-0011; www.tambortropical.com; ste incl breakfast US$204-242; P ❄ ☎ ≋) Romantically set on the beach amid a palm-fringed garden, Tambor Tropical is a lovely boutique hotel with stunning architecture. The 12 roomy, hexagonal suites all have dark wood interiors, full kitchens and private verandas, most with sunrise views. The place is a boon for birders: nearly 300 species have been spotted around the property, including some raucous scarlet macaws.

Tango Mar HOTEL $$$
(☎2683-0001; www.tangomar.com; Playa Quizales; d from US$180; P ❄ ☎ ≋) A longstanding and secluded beachfront hotel catering mostly to domestic tourists, and the outdated design and so-so restaurant leave something to be desired. But everybody will appreciate the proximity to a gorgeous beach, which can be walked at low tide to reach the El Chorro waterfall. Sun terraces, stables, a relaxing pool and tennis courts round out the offerings.

ℹ Getting There & Around

The airport is just north of the entrance to Hotel Barceló Playa Tambor. Hotels will arrange pickup at the airport for an extra fee. Sansa (p98) has long served Tambor with seven daily flights to and from San José, and other carriers including Green (www.costaricagreenair.com), Skyway (www.skywaycr.com) and Aerobell (www.aerobell.com) began offering this route more recently.

There's a **Budget** (☎2436-2007; www.budget.co.cr; Ruta 160; ⏲8am-5pm Mon-Sat, to 4pm Sun) car-rental place 4km from the Tambor airport. It has a free shuttle to and from the 'terminal.' If you're not renting wheels, you can hop on one of the Paquera–Montezuma buses passing through here.

Refugio Nacional de Vida Silvestre Curú

Situated at the eastern end of the peninsula and only 6km south of Paquera, the tiny, 84-hectare **Refugio Nacional de Vida Silvestre Curú** (☎2641-0100; www.curuwildliferefuge.com; adult/child US$15/8; ⏲7am-4pm) holds a great variety of landscapes, including dry tropical forest, semi-deciduous forest and five types of mangrove swamp. The rugged coastline is also home to a series of secluded coves and white-sand beaches that are perfect for snorkeling and swimming, while hiking trails traverse varied but beautiful landscapes.

Activities

Visitors have access to several easy to moderate trails, and the refuge also offers horseback riding. Local fauna includes three types of monkey, deer, anteaters, armadillos, coati, agoutis and *pacas*, plus three species of wildcat. Crabs, lobsters, shellfish, sea turtles and other marine creatures can be found on the beaches and in the tide pools. Birdwatchers have recorded more than 232 avian species.

Turismo Curú TOURS
(☎2641-0004; www.curutourism.com; incl park admission snorkeling US$45, bioluminescence tour US$50; ⏰8am-9pm) Anything that you might want to do at Curú Wildlife Refuge, Luis can make it happen. A boat trip to Tortuga includes snorkeling at Islas Morteros and an optional beach lunch (US$10 extra). The most distinctive offering is the evening bioluminescence tour, which involves kayaking or boating to beautiful Quesera beach and swimming/snorkeling in the luminescent waters. The office is right on the Curú beach.

Sleeping

Refugio Nacional de Vida Silvestre Curú Cabinas CABINA $
(☎2641-0100; www.curuwildliferefuge.com; r per person US$30) There are six rustic *cabinas* on the grounds of the wildlife reserve. The accommodations are bare and the showers are cold, but they are beautifully situated about 50m from the waves. Also, you'll be in good company (white-faced capuchin monkeys, primarily). Your reserve fee is included in the cost of the room. Advance arrangements required. Meals are US$10.

Getting There & Away

The entrance to the refuge is clearly signed on the paved road between Paquera and Tambor. Alternatively, the Paquera–Montezuma bus passes this way and will drop you at the park entrance upon request.

Paquera

POP 7900

The tiny village of Paquera is about 12km by road from Playa Naranjo and 4km from the Paquera ferry terminal. Paquera can be a useful base for a few days of exploring Refugio Nacional de Vida Silvestre Curú and the offshore islands. Short of that, you might want to spend a night here if you arrive on a late ferry from Puntarenas – instead of tackling those challenging roads in the dark.

Sleeping

While there are some budget *cabinas* right in town, there's nothing to be gained by staying there. You're better off staying on the outskirts (or in the hills, if you can afford it), for a more peaceful setting.

Bahia Rica LODGE $$
(☎2641-0811; www.bahiarica.com; d incl breakfast US$70-78, extra person US$10; P 📶) Run by a couple of adventuresome Norwegians, this fishing lodge has a *Swiss Family Robinson* vibe in its jungle lodge and private bungalow, both tucked into the forest. Rooms are fan-cooled but bathrooms have hot showers, and the two-story hardwood lodge contains a full, shared kitchen. A path leads down to the water, where boat, kayak, sportfishing and SUP tours originate.

It's 1.5km east of the Paquera ferry landing. This is, in fact, the home of Costa RIca's first bioluminescence tour, and it remains the best. The area has very little light pollution, groups are kept small and the water is calm, allowing for an intimate kayaking encounter with astoundingly bright plankton.

Hotel Vista Las Islas HOTEL $$$
(Eco Boutique Hotel; ☎2641-0817; https://vistalasislas.com; d from US$145; P ❄ 📶 🏊) 🍃 As implied by the name, the amazing panoramic view of the islands is the selling point here. It really is spectacular, and you can enjoy it from your private balcony, from the restaurant or from the magnificent infinity pool. Solar panels play a key role in powering the hotel, and it's a short walk to Playa Órganos, where you can swim or surf.

The hotel can organize tours around the area, including island hops and excursions to see bioluminescence.

Getting There & Away

All transportation is geared to the arrival and departure of the Puntarenas ferry. If either the bus or the ferry is running late, the other will wait.

BOAT

Ferry Naviera Tambor (☎2661-2084; www.navieratambor.com; adult/child/bicycle/motorcycle/car US$1.50/1/4/6/20) leaves daily at 5:30am, 9am, 11am, 2pm, 5pm and 8pm. The trip to Puntarenas takes a little over an hour. Buy a ticket at the window, reboard your car and then drive on to the ferry; you can't buy a ticket on board. Show up at least an hour early on holidays and busy weekends. The terminal contains a *soda* where you can grab a bite while waiting for the boat.

BUS

Buses meet arriving passengers at the ferry terminal and take them to Paquera, Tambor and Montezuma. They can be crowded, so try to get off the ferry fast to secure a seat.

Most travelers take the bus from the terminal directly to Montezuma (US$3, two hours). Taxi drivers will sometimes tell you the bus won't come, but this isn't true. There are no northbound buses.

Islands Near Bahía Gigante

The waters in and around the isolated Bahía Gigante, 9km southeast of Playa Naranjo, are studded with rocky islets and deserted islands. Islas San Lucas, Venado and Caballo are tucked into the Golfo de Nicoya, while further south, the lovely Isla Tortuga hangs off the southeastern corner of the Nicoya Peninsula. In the the tranquil Bahía de Paquera, Isla Jesuita features a glamping operation, and just around the bend, Isla Negritos is home to a colony of squirrel monkeys. These idyllic outposts are popular destinations for snorkelers, sea kayakers and sportfishers.

Tours

In addition to party cruises (p355) departing from Jacó, tour operators in Jacó and Montezuma offer smaller-scale excursions to these islands, including Isla Tortuga, Isla Caballo, Isla Venado and Isla San Lucas. Hotels in Tambor can also make the arrangements.

Turismo Curú (p347) offers a half-day boat trip to Isla Tortuga, which is only 3km from the wildlife refuge. This unique tour makes an effort to avoid the crowds by visiting in the morning (when other boats are still en route) and hitting lesser-known spots.

Bahia Rica (p347) has the advantage of proximity to Tortuga. Its all-day tour includes snorkeling and lunch, as well as kayaking and a visit to an island inhabited by spider monkeys.

Isla Tortuga

Isla Tortuga is actually two uninhabited islands, just offshore from Refugio Nacional de Vida Silvestre Curú. This stunner – a quintessential tropical paradise – is widely regarded as the most beautiful island in Costa Rica. The pure white sand feels like baby powder; gargantuan coconut palms tower overhead; and clear turquoise waters lap up on the shores. Snorkelers usually enjoy good visibility and a wide variety of sea life, although there is no reef here. Jet Skis and kayaks are sometimes on offer, depending on your tour.

Unfortunately, Tortuga receives heavy boat traffic from tour operators from Montezuma and Jacó. If possible, avoid weekends and holidays. Even better, avoid high season.

Isla San Lucas

The largest island in Bahía Gigante (just over 600 hectares) is about 5km off the coast from Playa Naranjo. From a distance, it seems like a beautiful desert island, but the 'Island of Unspeakable Horrors' has a 400-year history as one of the most notorious prisons in Latin America. In 2001 the island was declared a national park. Visitors can expect to learn about the island's checkered history and explore the 100-year-old remains of the prison. Most tours also allow time to hike the trails and relax on the island's sandy shores.

ISLAND GLAMPING

From the hoteliers who created the magnificent Hotel Punta Islita (p330) comes **Isla Chiquita** (☎2231-6122; www.islachiquitacostarica.com; Isla Jesuita; glamping tent from US$375;), Costa Rica's first-ever island glamping operation. The exclusive, manicured grounds are set within Isla Jesuita, a government-owned island reachable with a five-minute ferry ride from the boat launch near Paquera. The 16 fan-cooled safari tents were actually a work-around, as no new structures were permitted on the island. That said, the tents are larger and more stylish than most of the country's hotel rooms, offering hardwood furnishings, private balconies and minibars.

By day, visitors laze in sun loungers, circumnavigate the island by kayak, birdwatch or head out on boating excursions. Meals are taken at one of two lovely restaurants, and evenings are spent stargazing and splashing about in bioluminescent waters. A spa and hiking trails were under construction at the time of research.

Playa Naranjo

POP 200

This tiny village next to the ferry terminal has a few sodas and small hotels that cater to travelers either waiting for the ferry or arriving from Puntarenas.

Getting There & Away

All transportation is geared to the arrival and departure of the Puntarenas ferry, so don't worry – if one is running late, the other will wait.

BOAT

The **Coonatramar ferry** (☎2661-1069; www.coonatramar.com; adult/child/bicycle/motorcycle/car US$2/1/4/6/18) to Puntarenas departs daily at 8am, 12:30pm, 4:30pm and 8:30pm, and can accommodate both cars and passengers. The trip takes 1½ hours. If traveling by car, get out and buy a ticket at the window, get back in your car and then drive on to the ferry. You cannot buy a ticket on board. Show up at least an hour early on holidays and busy weekends, as you'll be competing with a whole lot of other drivers to make it on.

BUS

Buses meet the arriving ferry and take passengers on to Jicaral, for travel on to the more northerly parts of the peninsula. If you're headed to Montezuma or Mal País, take the other ferry from Puntarenas to Paquera.

CAR

If you are driving yourself, it's unlikely that you'll need to pass this way. Heading north, you'll be better off driving over the Puente de la Amistad to the peninsula instead of taking the ferry. And heading to Mal País or Montezuma, you should take the Puntarenas–Paquera ferry. That said, Ruta 21 is a mostly paved road that connects Playa Naranjo to Nicoya (via Jicaral). It is also possible to get to Paquera (and further to Mal País or Montezuma) via a scenic, rugged and steep but passable road over three inland ridges with magical vistas of Bahía Gigante. A 4WD is recommended, especially in the rainy season when there might be rivers to cross.

AT A GLANCE

POPULATION

Puntarenas: 77,250

FAST FACT

At 16 square km, Manuel Antonio (p386) is Costa Rica's smallest national park.

BEST COSTA RICA COFFEE

Café Bohío (p369)

BEST TROPICAL COCKTAILS

Bamboo Room (p407)

BEST LOCAL BEER

Fuego Brew Co (p398)

WHEN TO GO

Jan–Feb Music and art gatherings light up Jacó and Uvita.

Apr–Nov Heavy rains make this the best time to catch some waves in Playa Hermosa and Jacó.

Dec–Mar & **Jul–Nov** Whale-watching in Uvita.

Humpback whale, Parque Nacional Marino Ballena (p404)

Central Pacific Coast

Stretching from the port of Puntarenas to tiny Uvita, the central Pacific coast is home to wet and dry tropical forests, sun-drenched beaches and a healthy dose of wildlife. On shore, national parks protect endangered squirrel monkeys and scarlet macaws, while offshore waters nurture migrating whales and pods of dolphins. With so much biodiversity packed into a small geographic area, the region is often thought of as Costa Rica in miniature. Given its close proximity to San José and easily accessible national parks via a well-developed system of paved roads, this area is a favorite weekend getaway.

INCLUDES

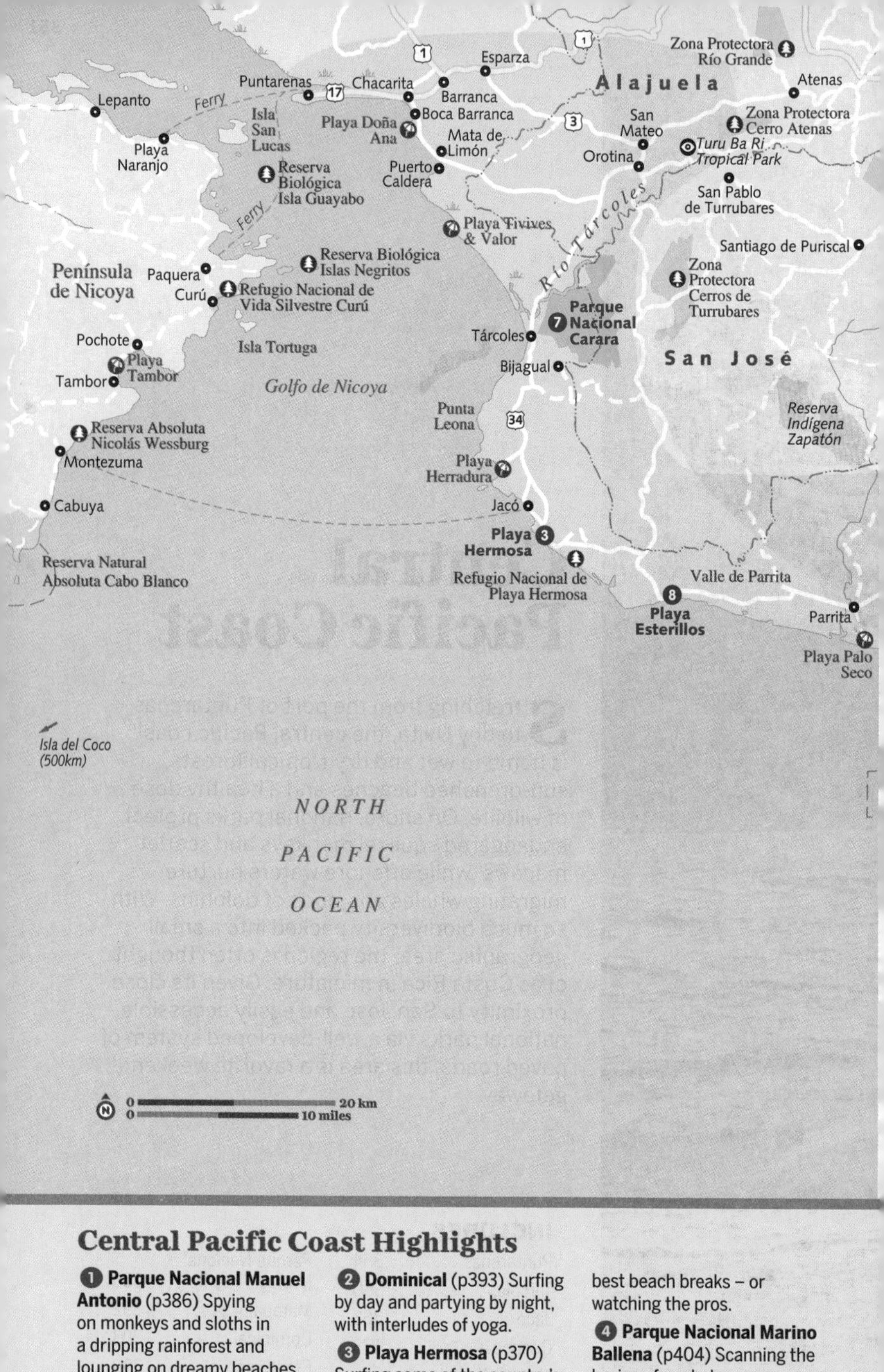

Central Pacific Coast Highlights

❶ **Parque Nacional Manuel Antonio** (p386) Spying on monkeys and sloths in a dripping rainforest and lounging on dreamy beaches.

❷ **Dominical** (p393) Surfing by day and partying by night, with interludes of yoga.

❸ **Playa Hermosa** (p370) Surfing some of the country's best beach breaks – or watching the pros.

❹ **Parque Nacional Marino Ballena** (p404) Scanning the horizon for whales.

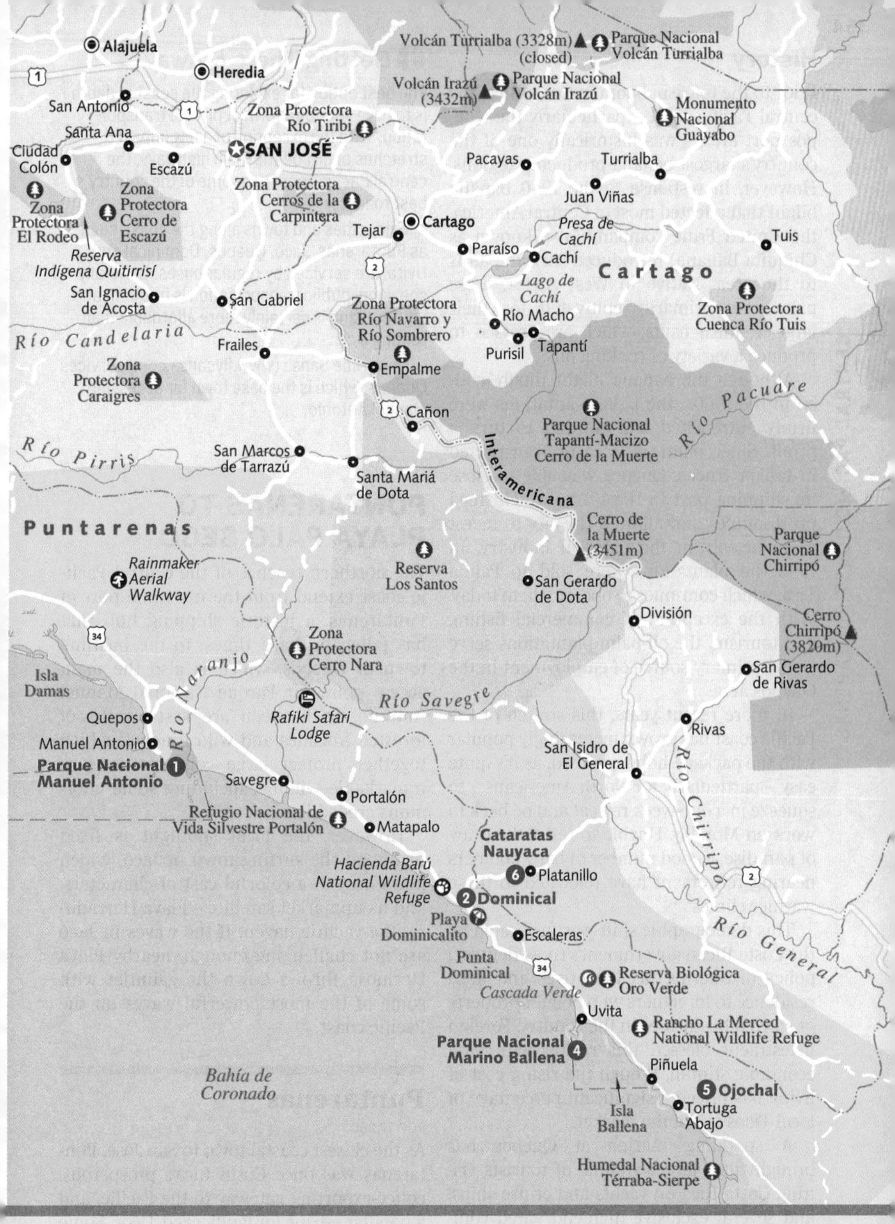

5 Ojochal (p405) Sampling some of the coast's most sophisticated cuisine.

6 Cataratas Nauyaca (p394) Swimming in a jaw-droppingly gorgeous waterfall.

7 Parque Nacional Carara (p358) Encountering giant crocodiles and squawking scarlet macaws.

8 Playa Esterillos (p372) Kickin' back with a margarita, a beautiful sunset and a book, away from it all.

History

Prior to the tourism boom in Costa Rica, the central Pacific coast – particularly the Quepos port area – was historically one of the country's largest banana-producing regions. However, in response to the 1940 banana blight that affected most of Central America, the United Fruit Company (also known as Chiquita Banana) introduced African palms to the area. Native to West Africa, these palms are primarily cultivated for their large, reddish fruits, which are pressed to produce a variety of cooking oils.

Although the banana blight finally ended in the 1960s, the palm plantations were firmly entrenched and starting to turn a profit. Since palm oil is easily transported in tanker trucks, Quepos was able to close its shipping port in the 1970s, which freed up resources and allowed the city to invest more heavily in the palm-oil industry. In 1995 the plantations were sold to Palma Tica, which continues to operate them today. With the exception of commercial fishing and tourism, the oil-palm plantations serve as the primary source of employment in the Quepos area.

In more recent years, this stretch of the Pacific coast has grown increasingly popular with the package-holiday crowd, as it's quite easy – particularly for North Americans – to squeeze in a one-week retreat and be back to work on Monday. Unable to resist the draw of paradise, a good number of baby boomers nearing retirement have relocated to these warmer climes.

This demographic shift was facilitated by the Costa Rican government's (now defunct) policy of offering tax incentives and legal residence to foreigners who bought property or started businesses in the country. Foreign investment blessed this region with vital economic stimuli, though the rising cost of living has priced a significant percentage of local Ticos out of the market.

A sparkling marina at Quepos has brought in a larger volume of tourists visiting Costa Rica on yachts and cruise ships, and several exclusive high-end gated communities continue to attract an even greater number of wealthy immigrants. Things have changed quickly along this stretch of coastline, though it's difficult to imagine that the authenticity of the coastal fishing villages, agricultural plantations and protected areas could ever be totally lost.

Getting There & Away

The best option for exploring the coast in depth is to have your own form of private transportation. With the exception of a few unpaved stretches of dirt off the main highways, the central Pacific coast has some of the country's best roads.

Major cities and towns along the coast, such as Puntarenas, Jacó, Quepos, Dominical and Uvita, are serviced by regular buses. Generally speaking, public transportation is frequent and efficient, and is certainly more affordable than renting a car.

The airline Sansa (www.flysansa.com) services Quepos, which is the base town for accessing Manuel Antonio.

PUNTARENAS TO PLAYA PALO SECO

The northern reaches of the central Pacific coast extend from the maritime port of Puntarenas, a historic shipping hub that has fallen on hard times, to the bustling town of Quepos, which is also the main access point for Parque Nacional Manuel Antonio. In between are vast swaths of forested hillsides and wild beaches, which together protect large concentrations of remarkable wildlife, including some enormous crocodiles.

However, the local spotlight is fixed firmly on the surfing town of Jacó, which plays host to a colorful cast of characters, and its upmarket satellite – Playa Herradura, the yachtie haven. If the waves in Jacó are not challenging enough, nearby Playa Hermosa throws down the gauntlet with some of the most powerful waves on the Pacific coast.

Puntarenas

POP 77,250

As the closest coastal town to San José, Puntarenas was once Costa Rica's prosperous, coffee-exporting gateway to the Pacific, and a popular escape for landlocked Ticos. Some still come here on weekends, but during the week activity along the oceanfront promenade slows to a languid pace – all the better to enjoy the beachfront *sodas* (inexpensive eateries) and market.

The city's ferry terminal is a convenient way to connect to the pristine beaches of

PARKS & RESERVES OF THE CENTRAL PACIFIC COAST

The central Pacific coast is home to a number of excellent national parks and reserves, including the most visited national park in Costa Rica.

Parque Nacional Carara (p358) Home to more than 400 species of bird, including the rare scarlet macaw, which is, amazingly, a commonly sighted species in the park.

Parque Nacional Manuel Antonio (p386) The pristine beaches, rainforest-clad mountains and dense wildlife never fail to disappoint in Costa Rica's most touristed national park.

Parque Nacional Marino Ballena (p404) A vitally important marine park shaped like a whale's tale, this is the country's premier destination for both whale- and dolphin-watching.

Hacienda Barú National Wildlife Refuge (p393) A small reserve that encompasses a number of tropical habitats and is part of a major biological corridor that protects a wide range of species.

southern Nicoya, and Puntarenas is also the jumping-off point for the almost mystical Isla del Coco.

Travelers mainly pass through here en route to somewhere else, but if you stay overnight you'll feel the vibe of a genuine working Tico town and find a couple of attractions.

Sights

Casa Fait ARCHITECTURE

(Av 3 & Calle 3) Quite possibly the most beautiful building in Puntarenas, Casa Fait is a purple-and-cream clapboard 1920s colonial building with ornate iron balconies. It's now owned by a German expat and his wife; the couple lovingly restored it a decade ago and have imported a remarkable number of antiques.

Occasionally it opens for guests (via Airbnb), and visitors can stay in one of two historic rooms (double room including breakfast from US$40). The communal facilities include glorious balconies overlooking the water, a grand dining area, a kitchen with a century-old double basin and a modern Jacuzzi at the center of the house. The breakfast is superb.

Parque Marino del Pacífico AQUARIUM

(☎2661-5272; www.parquemarino.org; Paseo de Los Turistas; adult/child 4-12yr US$10/5; ⏰9am-4:30pm Tue-Sun; P ♿) This retro marine park has seen better days, but it will certainly keep the kids entertained for a while. There's an aquarium showcasing many tropical fish, manta rays, turtles, nurse sharks and crowd-pleasing Nemos (clown fish), plus crocodiles. The park sits on the site of the old train station and has a tiny splash pool, a playground for kids and a gift shop.

Paseo de los Turistas WATERFRONT

(Tourists' Promenade) This beachside, pedestrian boulevard stretches along the southern edge of town. Cruise ships make visits to the eastern end of the road, and a variety of souvenir stalls and casual restaurants known as *kioscos* are there to greet passengers. Their specialty is the Churchill (p356), a bizarre dessert concoction of condensed milk, syrup and chopped fruit, which got its name in the 1940s from a guy who regularly ordered it and looked like the British prime minister.

Tours

Calypso Cruises BOATING

(☎2256-2727; www.calypsocruises.com; Av 3; day trips adult/child under 7yr US$150/95) With tours bookable inside El Shrimp Shack restaurant, this long-established company runs top-class catamaran trips. Boats come complete with two Jacuzzis and an underwater viewing window, and make day trips to Tortuga's brilliant white beaches. It caters mostly to Puntarenas cruise-ship crowds. There are also kayaking, sportfishing and diving trips. Many come with a picnic lunch, snacks and booze.

Sleeping

There's no shortage of accommodations in Puntarenas, though a slew of the very cheapest ones serve clientele who want to pay by

LOCAL KNOWLEDGE

THE CHURCHILL

As you wander the Paseo de Los Turistas (p355), you will inevitably encounter signs advertising something called a Churchill. This is in fact the official snack of Puntarenas. Each shop and restaurant has its own way of making one, but generally the ingredients include: shaved ice, fruit, syrup and condensed and powdered milk.

This very sweet product has been the standard treat of Puntarenas for more than six decades. According to legend, the refreshment was born in the 1940s when a store-keeper called Joaquín Aguilar Esquivel realized he wanted to eat something sweet, milky and delicious. Back then, ice cream was not available in hot Puntarenas, and milk wouldn't keep, so Aguilar worked around that by requesting the aforementioned items. He ordered this same snack so many times that eventually restaurant owners standardized it, and named it after the guy they thought Esquivel resembled: Winston Churchill.

The Churchill is an institution in Puntarenas, and there is even a 'Churchill Coloso' (colossal Churchill) including scoops of ice cream, which is available at Kiosco Mar de Plata.

the hour. Also, high humidity and lots of rain makes even the most upscale options muggy, so make sure there's a fan.

Hotel La Punta HOTEL **$$**
(☎2661-0696; www.hotellapunta.net; cnr Av 1 & Calle 35; d weekday/weekend US$50/62, extra person US$9; P ❄ 📶 🏊) For early-morning ferry departures, Hotel La Punta is an appealing choice. Conveniently located one block from the dock, its 12 rooms are arranged around a landscaped courtyard and small pool. Comfortable, clean accommodations are a little dated but perfectly pleasant, featuring terracotta floors, cable TV and fridge.

Upon check-in, guests can prebook breakfast (US$3) at the front desk, and it will be delivered to the hotel the following morning.

Fiesta Resort RESORT **$$$**
(☎2660-1600, 800-555-5555; www.fiestaresort.com; off Ruta Nacional 23; all-incl package per person from US$170; P ❄ @ 📶 🏊) Formerly the Double Tree Resort by Hilton Central Pacific, this all-inclusive, family-friendly resort comes with four restaurants, seven bars and an arsenal of amenities, from four swimming pools to water sports and around-the-clock entertainment. There's also a spa and a plethora of tours. Rooms with dark wood furnishings and tiled floors are clean, spacious and well presented, but a little old-fashioned.

While there are certainly nicer beaches down the coastline, the legendary Boca Barranca (p358) surf spot is nearby and there is excellent value to be had at this resort, especially if you book in advance online. It's around 30km from Puntarenas.

Eating

Self-caterers can head to supermarket **MegaSuper** (☎2661-5301; Calle 1 btwn Avs 1 & 3; ⏲8am-9pm) or the **Mercado Municipal** (Central Market; btwn Avs 3 & 5; ⏲6am-4pm Mon-Sat, to noon Sun), where you can find reasonably priced seafood.

Kiosco Mar del Plata DINER **$**
(Paseo de Los Turistas; Churchill Coloso US$5) A beachside place where you can try the Churchill, a traditional sickly sweet snack made of shaved ice, fruit, syrup and condensed and powdered milk. They've been making it here since the 1940s.

★ **El Shrimp Shack** SEAFOOD **$$**
(☎2661-0585; www.elshrimpshack.com; Av 3 btwn Calles 3 & 7; mains US$12-19; ⏲11am-3:30pm Mon-Thu, to 9pm Fri & Sat, to 6pm Sun; 📶) Offering the most upscale dining in Puntarenas, El Shrimp Shack's silly name belies a graceful interior – wood-paneled walls, marble-topped tables, antique light sconces and a stunning stained-glass ceiling, all within a century-old house with harbor views. Shrimp dishes feature prominently, though other options include burgers and excellent *ceviche* (seasoned lemon- or lime-marinated seafood). Old-school service. Delicious pineapple and mint smoothie.

Drinking & Nightlife

★Isla Coco's Bar & Grill BAR

(☎4700-3142, 8876-9355; www.islacocos.com; Av 3; ⊙6-11pm Tue-Fri, noon-midnight Sat, noon-9pm Sun) This social hub near the ferry port ticks a lot of boxes: it offers a tiki bar, bountiful seafood, a tour desk, live music (Thursday to Saturday) and sushi night on Thursday.

Capitán Moreno CLUB

(El Gallego; ☎2661-6888; www.facebook.com/pg/CapitanMorenoOFICIAL; cnr Paseo de los Turistas & Calle 13; ⊙11am-10pm Sun-Thu, to 2am Fri & Sat; 📶) A time-honored spot for shaking some booty, with a huge dance floor right on the beach. It's popular with a younger Tico crowd. Seafood and *ceviche* dishes are served on a wooden deck earlier in the evening (mains from US$9). Drinks deals start at US$2.

Orientation

Situated at the end of a sandy peninsula (8km long but only 100m to 600m wide), Puntarenas is just 110km west of San José by paved highway. The city has more than 50 calles (streets) running north to south, but only five avenidas (avenues) running west to east at its widest point. The southerly promenade, where you'll find the cruise-ship pier and some restaurants, is called the Paseo de los Turistas. As in all of Costa Rica, street names are largely irrelevant, and landmarks are used for orientation.

Information

There are few ATMs in town; most are located around the center of Puntarenas, and there's also a **Banco Popular** (Calle 2; ⊙8:45am-4:30pm Mon-Fri, 8:15-11am Sat) ATM near the pier on Paseo de los Turistas.

The **Puntarenas Tourism Office** (ITC – Instituto Costarricense De Turismo; ☎2299-5800; www.ict.go.cr; cnr Calle 1 & Paseo de los Turistas; ⊙8am-5pm Mon-Fri; 📶) is near the pier and opposite Paseo de los Turistas. It has English-speaking staff offering helpful information on the local area.

Getting There & Away

BOAT

Car and passenger ferries bound for Paquera and Playa Naranjo depart several times a day from the **northwestern dock** (Av 3, btwn Calles 31 & 33). If you are driving and will be taking the car ferry, arrive at the dock early to get in line. The vehicle section tends to fill up quickly and you may not make it on. In addition, make sure that you have purchased your ticket from the walk-up ticket window before driving onto the ferry. You will not be admitted onto the boat if you don't already have a ticket.

Schedules change seasonally and can be affected by inclement weather. Check with the ferry office by the dock for any changes. Many of the hotels in town also have up-to-date schedules posted.

Coonatramar (☎2661-1069; www.coonatramar.com; Av 3; adult/child/bike/car US$2/1/4/35) has daily departures to Playa Naranjo (for transfer to Nicoya and points west) at 6:30am, 10am, 2:30pm and 7pm.

Naviera Tambor (☎2661-2084; www.navieratambor.com; Av 3; adult/child/bike/car US$1.50/1/4.50/23) has daily departures to Paquera (for transfer to Montezuma and Mal País) at 5am, 9am, 11am, 2pm, 5pm and 8:30pm.

BUS

Buses for San José depart from the large navy-blue building on the north corner of Calle 2 and Paseo de los Turistas. Book your ticket ahead of time on holidays and weekends. Buses for other destinations leave from across the street, on the beachside of the Paseo.

Jacó US$2.10, 1½ hours, five daily, 6:50am to 6:30pm

Quepos US$4.40, three hours, 12 daily 4:30am-3:30pm

San José via San Ramón US$4.70, 2½ hours, hourly, 4am-9pm

Monteverde US$2.70, three hours, four daily, 8am to 2:15pm

Check the most up-to-date schedules with local bus providers (www.tqpcr.com, www.eupsacr.com, www.transmonteverde.com) before you travel.

Getting Around

Buses marked 'Ferry' run up Av Central and go to the ferry terminal, 1.5km from downtown. The taxi fare from the San José bus terminal in Puntarenas to the northwestern ferry terminal is about US$4.

Buses for the port of Caldera (also going past Playa Doña Ana and Mata de Limón) leave from the market about every hour and head out of town along Av Central.

Around Puntarenas

The road heading south from Puntarenas skirts the coastline, and a few kilometers out of town you'll start to see the forested peaks of the Cordillera de Tilarán in the distance. Just as the port city fades into the distance, the water gets cleaner, the air crisper and the vegetation lusher. At this point, you should take a deep breath and heave a sigh of relief – the Pacific coastline gets a whole lot more beautiful as you head further south, with beaches, surfing opportunities and mangroves aplenty.

Sights & Activities

Playa Doña Ana BEACH

(Calle Doña Ana; entry US$3, parking US$2; ⏲8am-4pm) The pair of beaches known as Playa Doña Ana are relatively undeveloped and have an isolated and unhurried feel. They are popular among Ticos on day trips from Puntarenas, especially on weekends in high season. There are picnic shelters and changing areas.

Playa San Isidro BEACH

(Calle 188) About 8km south of Puntarenas is Playa San Isidro, the first 'real' beach on the central Pacific coast. It's quite often empty, and preferred by Puntarenas beachcombers wanting a more chilled-out beach day and by surfers who come for one of the longest waves in Costa Rica, found at the southern end of the beach. The beach runs parallel to Transversal 202.

Boca Barranca SURFING

(Av 26, off Ruta Nacional 23) About 12km south of Puntarenas is – according to some – the third-longest left-hand surf break in the world. Conditions here are best in larger swells, at low to mid tide; it's possible to surf here year-round. There are no services, so be sure that you're confident in the water and seek local advice (on everything from pollution to crocs) before hitting the break.

Mata de Limón BIRDWATCHING

(Calle Mata de Limón) Around 20km south of Puntarenas is this picturesque little hamlet situated on a mangrove lagoon, locally famous for its birdwatching. During low tide, you'll see flocks of feathered creatures descending on the lagoon to scrounge for tasty morsels. Mata de Limón is divided by a river, with the lagoon and most facilities on the south side. Guesthouses rent out kayaks.

Eating

★Malibu Bar y Restaurante COSTA RICAN $

(☎2639-9309; www.facebook.com/maliburestaurantecr; Av Alberto Echandi Montero (Ruta 17); mains from US$5; ⏲11am-11pm) On the road going south of Puntarenas, you'll find this excellent seafood restaurant opposite the beach. It has a modern, airy, tiki feel and serves up some of the freshest *casados* (set meals) in the area, plus deliciously tangy *ceviche* and superfresh fish dishes. Everything is well presented and extremely good value.

Getting There & Away

Buses heading for the Caldera port depart hourly from the market in Puntarenas, and can easily drop you off at any of the spots along the highway. If you're driving, the break at Boca Barranca is located near the bridge on the Costanera Sur (South Coastal Hwy), while the entrance to Playa Doña Ana is a little further south (look for a sign that says 'Paradero Turístico Doña Ana'). The turnoff for Mata de Limón is located about 5.5km south of Playa Doña Ana.

Parque Nacional Carara

Situated at the mouth of the Río Tárcoles, this 52-sq-km **park** (Ruta Nacional 34; adult/child US$10/5; ⏲7am-3pm Dec-Apr, 8am-3pm May-Nov) is only 50km southeast of Puntarenas by road or about 90km west of San José via the Orotina Hwy. Straddling the transition between the dry forests of Costa Rica's northwest and the sodden rainforests of the southern Pacific lowlands, this national park is a biological melting pot. Acacias intermingle with strangler figs, and cacti with deciduous kapok trees, creating a heterogeneous habitat with a blend of wildlife to match, including the scarlet macaw and Costa Rica's largest crocodiles.

The park's four trails can easily be explored in half a day; come early to maximize wildlife sightings.

Sights

Crocodile Bridge WILDLIFE RESERVE

(Ruta 34) If you're driving from Puntarenas or San José, pull over by the Río Tárcoles bridge, also known as Crocodile Bridge, running over the river where 2000 crocodiles live. It's a top tourist attraction in the area, as the sandbanks below regularly feature a few dozen massive, basking crocodiles.

They're visible year-round, but the best time for seeing them is during low tide in the dry season. Crocodiles this large are rare in Costa Rica as they've been hunted vigorously for their leather. However, the crocs are protected here and they are the main attractions of wildlife tours that depart from Tárcoles.

SCARLET MACAWS

With a shocking bright-red body, blue-and-yellow wings, a long, red tail and a white face, the scarlet macaw *(Ara macao)* is one of the most visually arresting birds in the neotropical rainforest. It also mates for life and can live up to 75 years. They fly across the forest canopy in pairs, uttering their loud, grating squawks – there are few birds in Costa Rica with such character, presence and beauty.

Prior to the 1960s the scarlet macaw was distributed across much of Costa Rica, but trapping, poaching, habitat destruction and increased use of pesticides devastated the population. By the 1990s the distribution was reduced to two isolated pockets: the Península de Osa and Parque Nacional Carara.

Fortunately, these charismatic creatures are thriving in large colonies at both locales, and sightings are virtually guaranteed if you have the time and patience to spare. Furthermore, despite this fragmentation, the International Union for the Conservation of Nature continues to evaluate the species' status as of 'Least Concern' due to their total numbers being relatively high overall. This doesn't mean they aren't in trouble, however. Their original range is so large that, while the total numbers might be high, locally these numbers are still very low and many fragmented populations are still in decline.

Activities

Wildlife-Watching

Dominated by open secondary forest punctuated by patches of dense, mature forest and wetlands, Carara offers some superb birdwatching. More than 400 species of bird inhabit the reserve, though your chances of spotting rarer species will be greatly enhanced with the help of an experienced guide. Some commonly sighted species include orange-billed sparrows, five kinds of trogon, crimson-fronted parakeets, blue-headed parrots, golden-naped woodpeckers, rose-throated becards, gray-headed tanagers, red-capped manikins, rufous-tailed jacamars and royal flycatchers (just to name a few!).

The most exciting birds for many visitors to see, especially in June or July when chicks may be present, are the brilliantly patterned scarlet macaws. These rare birds are nonetheless commonly seen in the Parque Nacional Carara, and their distinctive call echoes loudly through the canopy, usually moments before a pair appears against the blue sky. If you're having problems spotting them, it may help to inquire at the ranger station; the staff keeps tabs on where nesting pairs are located.

Birds aside, the trails at Carara are home to several mammal species, including red brockets, white-tailed deer, collared peccaries, monkeys, sloths and agoutis. The national park is also home to one of Costa Rica's largest populations of tayras, weasel-like animals that scurry along the forest floor. And although most travelers aren't too keen to stumble upon an American crocodile, some truly monstrous specimens can be viewed from a safe distance at the nearby Crocodile Bridge.

According to the park rangers, the best time to spot wildlife is as soon as the park opens (7am December to April, or 8am May to November).

Hiking

Some 600m south of the Crocodile Bridge on the left-hand side is a locked gate leading to the **Sendero Laguna Meándrica**. This trail penetrates deep into the reserve and passes through open secondary forest and patches of dense mature forest and wetlands. About 4km from the entrance is Laguna Meándrica, which has large populations of heron, smoothbill and kingfisher. If you continue past the lagoon, you'll have a good chance of spotting mammals and the occasional crocodile, though you will have to turn back to exit. Note that this trail closes in September and October due to occasional flooding and can be very muddy after the rainy season.

Another 2km south of the trailhead is the Carara ranger station (p360), where there are restrooms. There are short trail loops within the park that pass through the sultry semi-gloom of the rainforest, characteristic of most of the park. They are accessed via the easy, paved, wheelchair-accessible **Interpretative Trail**, also known as the Universal Trail, which begins at the ranger station. The first, **Sendero Las Aráceas**, is 1.2km long and links up with the second, **Sendero Quebrada Bonita** (another 1.5km). Sendero Quebrada Bonita is your best bet for seeing wildlife such as agoutis and ample birdlife, as it's furthest from the main road.

Guides can be hired at the ranger station for US$25 per person (minimum of two people; deals available for groups) for a two-hour hike. Particularly knowledgeable guides are **Victor Mora Chaves** (☎8723-3008; www.victourscostarica.com; group/private jungle tours from US$45/65) and **Antonio Tours** (☎5704-7077; nature walks min 2 people from US$50), both of whom specialize in birding and photography.

Information

Carara ranger station (Ruta 34; 7am-4pm Dec-Apr, 8am-4pm May-Nov) Info on the park and the possibility of hiring guides; 3km south of Río Tárcoles.

SAFE TRAVEL

Heavy tourist traffic along the Pacific coast has also been a draw for petty theft in the area. In years past, vehicles parked at the Laguna Meándrica trailhead were sometimes broken into. There are now parking attendants here (who watch cars for a tip), but it is still safer to leave your car by the Carara ranger station and walk along the Costanera Sur for 2km north or 1km south. Alternatively, park beside Restaurante Los Cocodrilos (remember to tip the parking attendants on your return).

Getting There & Away

Any bus traveling between Puntarenas and Jacó can leave you at the park entrance. You can also catch buses headed north or south in front of Restaurante Los Cocodrilos. This may be a bit problematic on weekends, when buses are full, so go midweek if you are relying on a bus ride. If you're driving, the entrance to Carara is right on the Costanera and is clearly marked. Avoid traveling north towards San José from here on a Sunday afternoon or evening, when traffic from weekend beachgoers heading back to the city is shockingly bad.

Tárcoles

POP 4500

The small, unassuming town of Tárcoles is little more than a few rows of houses strung along a series of dirt roads parallel to the ocean. As you'd imagine, this tiny, dusty Tico town isn't much of a tourist draw, though the surrounding area is perfect for fans of the superlative, especially if you're interested in seeing one of the country's tallest waterfalls and some of its biggest crocodiles.

A handful of river-tour operators line the road leading towards the banks of the Río Tárcoles, where you can explore the wildlife- and bird-rich mangroves by boat.

Sights

★Catarata Manantial de Agua Viva WATERFALL

(Ruta Nacional 320; US$20; 7am-4pm) This 200m-high waterfall is claimed to be the highest in the country. From the entrance, it's a steep 3km (45-minute) hike down into the valley (an hour back up); at the bottom, the river continues through a series of natural swimming holes. The falls are most dramatic during the rainy season, though the serene rainforest setting is beautiful any time of year. A 5km dirt road past Hotel Villa Lapas leads to the primary entrance to the falls.

Pura Vida Gardens & Waterfalls GARDENS

(☎8352-9419, 2645-1001; Ruta Nacional 320; adult/child under 12yr US$20/10; 7:30am-4pm Mon-Sat) Just before the village of Bijagual, this private botanical garden offers great vistas of Manantial de Agua Viva cascading down the side of a cliff, and there are some pleasant hiking trails where you might see nesting toucans, monkeys and other wildlife.

The onsite restaurant caters to the **Adventure Dining** (www.adventurediningcostarica.com) crowds. Dining is by reservation only, starting at 4:30pm, ready for sunset.

Tours

Crocodile Man Tour WILDLIFE-WATCHING

(☎2637-0426, 2637-0771; www.crocodilemantour.com; Calle La Barca; adult/child US$35/25, under 5yr free; 8am-4pm) This locally owned tour company takes guests out on the Río Tárcoles for a close encounter with 15ft-long, 800lb American crocodiles. Guides are bilingual and highly entertaining, humorously naming the crocs after various celebrities such as the one called Angelina Jolie, because she 'loves kids'. Tours include 'birdwatching bingo' with more than 200 species to be spotted on this river.

The best tours leave at 4pm, just before sunset, and include a trip to the mangroves

DON'T MISS

PUNTA LEONA

Punta Leona is a closely held secret, with 'close' being the key word. Behind a couple of easy-to-miss entrances and long, winding driveways, its serene beaches – Playa Mantas and Playa Blanca – are the first a traveler can visit when headed from San José down the central Pacific coast, just an hour's drive from the capital.

The turnoff for Playa Mantas, where the public has access, is a right just after the small restaurant called Soda Nimar onto an unmarked dirt road, a 12-minute drive south of the Crocodile Bridge (p358). On the 10-minute ride down this road, security guards may take your license plate number and ask your destination. The guards are working for **Punta Leona Hotel & Club** (☎2231-3131; www.hotelpuntaleona.com; Calle Vieja Punta Leona; r incl breakfast from US$176, all-incl weekday/weekend from US$218/239, day pass incl lunch US$85), a sprawling complex with a country-club vibe, some restaurants, exclusive parking and beach access. Some beachgoers have memberships and a day pass costs a whopping US$85, but there's no need to pay this because all beaches in Costa Rica are public by law.

At the end of the entry road, you can park for around US$4, grab a swim in the tranquil, azure waters of Playa Mantas, and then set off on foot to the south, over some rocks, to your true destination – majestic Playa Blanca. At low tide, the flat rocks on the far end of the point are easy to traverse. At hide tide those will be submerged, but you should not attempt to swim over them (waves will bash you against the rocks). The best plan is to time the trip so that you can get to and from Playa Blanca when the tide is as low as possible. The reward for your efforts is a massive cove featuring soft white sand, bathtub-calm water and swaying coconut palms. Scarlet macaws will soar overhead in couples, and you can explore a network of tide pools for fish, crabs and even octopus.

This stretch of paradise is something of a local family affair, particularly on holidays. You'll want to arrive early to ensure a parking spot, and consider stopping on the way in or out at the rather good **Chanchitos** (☎2637-0000; www.facebook.com/chanchitoscr; Ruta 34; mains US$11-31; ⏲11am-10pm Mon-Fri, 7am-11pm Sat, 7am-10pm Sun; P), a restaurant just a bit north of the public entrance to Punta Leona (and just beside a separate entrance for club members and those with day passes). It serves up the tastiest seafood enchiladas we've ever tried. All-inclusive enthusiasts may also appreciate Punta Leona's other stay, **Hotel Arenas** (☎2529-0505, 2105 2100; Calle Vieja Punta Leona; all-incl per person US$120; 🏊), which offers a pool and entertainment to make sure everybody's having fun.

where the river meets the sea, and a beautiful view of the sun as it dips on the horizon.

Crocodile Man Tour is notorious for hand-feeding the crocodiles. The feedings are controversial: although entertaining, some believe they are dangerous for the crocs, and might make them become more aggressive and associate humans with food. Others claim it keeps the crocs fed and lazy, therefore reducing attacks on humans.

Jungle Crocodile Safari WILDLIFE
(☎2637-0656; www.junglecrocodilesafari.com; Calle La Barca; tours from US$35; ⏲tours 8:30am, 10:30am, 1:30pm, 3:30pm) Two-hour boating tours to see and get up close to the enormous crocodiles along the mangrove-lined Río Tárcoles. There are many birdwatching opportunities here; bring your binoculars.

Sleeping

Hotel Villa Lapas RESORT $$$
(☎2637-0232; www.villalapas.com; off Ruta Nacional 320; d incl breakfast from US$135; P ❄ 📶 🏊) 🌿 Located on a 500-acre private reserve, comprising both secondary rainforest and tropical gardens, this eco-resort offers 70 rooms housed in an attractive Spanish colonial–style lodge. Guests can unwind in comfort between guided hikes along the onsite trail network, birdwatching trips, canopy tours and soaks in two pools. Geared towards a birding crowd, the pace here is slow and low-key.

Getting There & Away

Any bus between Puntarenas and Jacó can leave you at the entrance to Tárcoles. If you're driving, the entrance to the town is right on the Costanera Sur and is clearly marked. Local buses between Orotina and Bijagual can drop you off at the entrance to the Parque Nacional Carara.

Playa Herradura

Until the mid-1990s, Playa Herradura was a rural, palm-sheltered beach of grayish-black sand that was popular mainly with campers and local fishers. In the late 1990s, however, Herradura was thrown into the spotlight having been used as the stage for the Ridley Scott movie *1492: Conquest of Paradise*. Rapid development ensued, resulting in the construction of Los Sueños marina, one of the most high-profile marinas in the country.

Playa Herradura represents one possible future for the central Pacific coast. Sprawling complexes of condos, fancy hotels and high-rise apartments are slowly encircling the bay and snaking up the mountainside, while the marina features rows of luxury yachts and sportfishing vessels. The southern half of the beach at the end of the Playa Herradura road, however, is a world apart from the landscaped grounds traversed by golf buggies: it remains stubbornly local, with picnicking Ticos, and local bars and restaurants.

Activities

SupHerr WATER SPORTS
(☎2637-6032; www.supherr.com; Calle Herradura; 1hr SUP rental US$22, 1/2hr kayak US$22/32; ⏰7am-6pm) Offers good-quality water-sport rentals, including kayaks, boogie boards and stand-up paddleboards (SUP), on which you can explore the calm waters around Playa Herradura. It also does lessons and tours, including a beautiful sunset tour. There are showers and changing facilities onsite.

Sleeping

★Hotel Villa Caletas BOUTIQUE HOTEL $$$
(☎2630-3000; www.hotelvillacaletas.com; off Hwy 34; d/ste from US$260/480; P❄📶🏊) 🍃 Although the views of the Pacific are amazing, what makes this bluff-top hotel truly unique is its architectural fusion, incorporating elements as varied as tropical Victorian, Hellenistic and French colonial. The ultra-exclusive accommodations are located on the tiny headland of Punta Leona, perched high on a dramatic hillside at the end of a serpentine driveway just north of Playa Herradura.

Each room is arranged amid the tropical foliage of the terraced property, affording a singular sense of privacy and isolation. The room interiors are tastefully decorated with art and antiques, with windows looking onto spectacular views. There is also a French-influenced restaurant, several semi-private infinity pools, and a private 1km trail leading down the hillside to the beach. Folks from Jacó come here especially for a romantic dinner or sunset happy hour (4pm to 5pm daily). The lush views from the hotel's Greek-style amphitheater are simply jaw-dropping.

Zephyr Palace BOUTIQUE HOTEL $$$
(☎2630-3000; www.zephyrpalace.com; off Hwy 34; ste from US$532; P❄@📶🏊) On the same property as the elegant Villa Caletas, its over-the-top sibling takes the decadence to another level of luxury. At this marble palace, seven individually decorated suites that wouldn't look out of place in Las Vegas evoke the splendor of ancient Rome and pharaonic Egypt amongst other themes. Three-night minimum. The turnoff is signposted just north of Playa Herradura.

Los Sueños Marriott Ocean & Golf Resort RESORT $$$
(☎2630-9000; www.marriott.com/sjols; Calle Los Sueños; d from US$350, ste US$640; P⊖❄@📶🏊) With a golf course behind and marina in front, this sprawling resort embodies the upscale comfort envisioned for the development, all wrapped up in a hacienda-style aesthetic. Interconnected pools meander through the landscaped property, while modern design-led rooms are minimalist, with natural tones and sleek lines. Service could be better, though, and in-room wi-fi isn't free.

Eating

Dolce Vita CAFE $
(☎2630-4050; www.lsrestaurants.com; Los Sueños Marina Village; cakes from US$3, mains from US$8; ⏰6am-10pm; ❄📶) Good coffee, quiches, pastries, proper bagels and outstanding gelato are found inside this little Italian-style cafe right on the marina. The menu also includes breakfast mains and a bunch of Costa Rican and Mediterranean favorites, including a house lasagna,

pizza, panini and *ceviche*. It's part of the Los Sueños Marina Village complex.

Jimmy T's Provisions SUPERMARKET **$$**
(☎2637-8636; www.jimmytsprovisions.com; Los Sueños Marina; ⏲6:30am-8:30pm) Jimmy T's is a small deli store on the docks of Los Sueños marina catering mostly to the yachting set. It's stacked floor to ceiling with organic, imported and rare-in–Costa Rica delicacies. Italian cheeses, grass-fed meat, Asian foods – it's a dream come true for self-caterers with *mucho* cash.

Grab the deli-made lunch specials before they sell out: they rotate dishes such as meatballs, grilled chicken breast and pepper onion sausage.

★**El Pelicano** SEAFOOD **$$$**
(☎2637-8910; www.elpelicanorestaurante.com; Calle Herradura; ceviche from US$10, mains US$18-60; ⏲11:30am-10pm; ❄📶) Right on Playa Herradura's pretty oceanfront, this simple Tico restaurant with white tablecloths and fairy lights holds its own next to the polished eateries of the marina. The menu is all about fish, and it's as fresh as it comes. The yellowfin tuna poke is exceptional. Most dishes are served with a side and warm soup, plus free salad from the salad bar.

Fishers can bring their catch of the day and the chef will prepare and cook it. There are also steak and chicken dishes.

Bambú Sushi SUSHI **$$$**
(☎2630-4333; www.lsrestaurants.com; Los Sueños Marina Village; sushi rolls/mains from US$9/15; ⏲11am-10pm; ❄📶) On the waterfront overlooking the rows of gleaming yachts, this upmarket spot decorated in dark tones with nice lighting serves an appropriate selection of Poseidon's subjects. We're particularly partial to the spicy tuna and the 'pimpin' shrimp' roll, which comes with avocado, tempura shrimp and volcano sauce. The lunchtime bento boxes are the best value. Pair one with a cold Asahi beer.

ℹ Getting There & Away

There are frequent local buses (less than US$1, 20 minutes) connecting Playa Herradura to Jacó. If you're driving, the Herradura turnoff is on the Costanera Sur, about 6km after the Costanera Sur leaves the edge of the ocean and heads inland. From here, a paved road leads 3km west to Playa Herradura.

Jacó

POP 10,000

Few places in Costa Rica generate such divergent opinions as Jacó. Partying surfers, North American retirees and international developers laud it for its devil-may-care atmosphere, bustling streets and booming real-estate opportunities. Observant ecotourists, marginalized Ticos and loyalists of the 'old Costa Rica' absolutely despise the place for the exact same reasons.

Jacó was the first town on the central Pacific coast to explode with tourist development and it remains a major draw for backpackers, surfers, snowbirds and city-weary *josefinos* (inhabitants of San José). Although working-class Tico neighborhoods are nearby, open-air trinket shops and tour operators line the main drag which, at night, is given over to a safe but somewhat seedy mix of binge-drinking students, surfers and sex workers.

While Jacó's lackadaisical charm is not for everyone, the surfing is excellent, and the restaurants and bars are great, particularly those lining polished **Jacó Walk** (www.jacowalk.com; Av Pastor Díaz; 👪).

Activities

Surfing

Although the rainy season is considered best for Pacific-coast surfing, Jacó is blessed with consistent year-round breaks. Advanced surfers head further south to Playa Hermosa, but the waves at Jacó are strong, steady and a lot of fun for intermediate surfers. Jacó is also a great place to learn to surf or start a surf trip, as many places offer lessons and it's easy to buy and sell boards here.

If you're looking to rent a board for the day, shop around as board quality can vary. Rental charges range from US$10 to US$20 for 24 hours.

Tortuga Surf Camp SURFING
(☎8847-6289, 2463-3348; www.tortugasurfcamp.com; off Av Pastor Díaz; 2hr private surfing lesson incl equipment from US$50; ⏲9am-5pm) Regardless of your age or ability, this is one of the top places in Jacó to learn to surf or improve your technique. Michael and his crew are very patient and encouraging. Lessons should be booked at least 24 hours in advance. Find it south of town on a road off Av Pastor Díaz.

Jacó Center

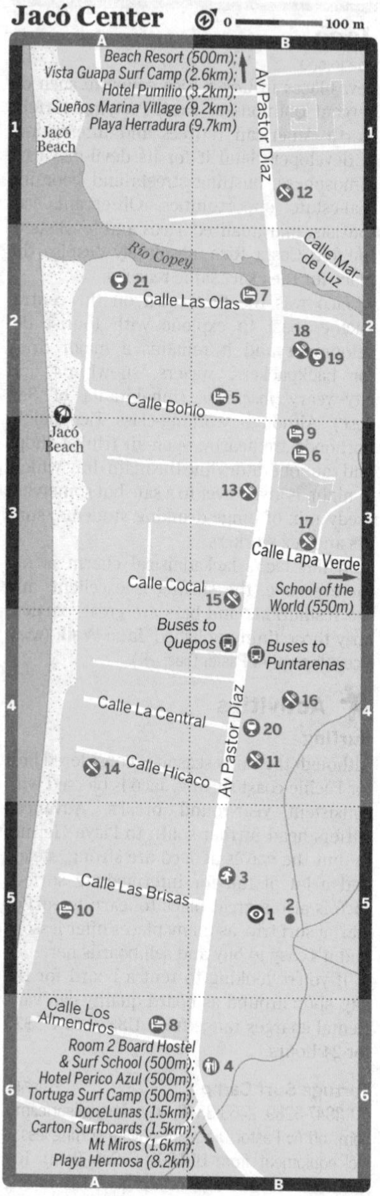

Jacó Center

Sights
1 Jacó Walk B5

Activities, Courses & Tours
2 Costa Rica Waterfall Tours B5
3 Escape Bus B5
4 Surfer Factory B6

Sleeping
5 Beds on Bohio B2
6 Buddha House B3
7 Hotel Ibiza B2
8 Hotel Tuanis Jacó Beach A6
9 Jacó Inn B3
10 Selina Jacó A5

Eating
11 Amancio's Pizza B4
12 Amara B1
13 Caliche's Wishbone B3
14 El Hicaco Seafood Restaurant A4
Graffiti .... (see 1)
15 Green Room B3
Lemon Zest .... (see 11)
16 Más x Menos B4
17 TacoBar B3
18 The Pizza Shop B2
Tsunami Sushi .... (see 1)

Drinking & Nightlife
19 Beer House B2
Café Bohío .... (see 9)
20 Jaco Bar B4
PuddleFish Brewery .... (see 1)
21 Samudio's Sunset Restobar A2

Vista Guapa Surf Camp Lodge SURFING
(☎2643-0244; www.vistaguapa.com; 5-night packages per person from US$1199) Secluded on five acres of landscaped hillside, with manicured lawns and three lovely wooden bungalows with hardwood floors and terraces, Vista Guapa Surf Camp is a higher-end surf camp experience for those who love surfing but are not hostel goers. This spot is the ideal place to unwind and hone your board riding skills, whether a beginner, intermediate or expert surfer.

Carton Surfboards SURFING
(☎2643-3762; www.cartonsurfboards.com; Calle Madrigal; surfboard rental per day US$15-20; ⏲8am-6pm) A good place to rent boards, run by friendly local shapers the Villalobos brothers. It's near the beach at the southern end of the main drag on Calle Madrigal.

Surfer Factory SURFING
(☎6068-7636; www.surferfactory.com; cnr Calle Sol de Oro & Av Pastor Díaz; 2hr surf lesson from US$49, board rental per day from US$10; ⏲6am-6pm) Highly recommended surf school and board rental shop, with great-quality boards and a good location near the beginners' break on Jacó Beach. The instructors guarantee you will stand up and surf your

first waves in just one lesson. If you don't, the lesson is free. Find it at the southern end of Av Pastor Díaz.

School of the World LANGUAGE
(☎2643-2462; www.schooloftheworld.org; off Calle Lapa Verde; 1-/2-/3-week packages from US$595/1190/1785) This popular school and cultural-studies center offers classes in Spanish, surfing, yoga, art, GoPro and photography (choose your ideal combo). The impressive building and activities center also houses a cafe and art gallery. Onsite lodgings and homestays can be arranged, either in shared or private rooms.

Swimming

Jacó Beach is generally safe for swimming, though you should avoid the areas near the estuaries, which are polluted and may have crocodiles in the rainy season. Be advised that the waves can get crowded with beginner surfers who don't always know how to control their boards, so keep your wits about you and stay out of their way. Riptides can occur, especially when the surf gets big, so inquire about local conditions and keep an eye out for red flags marking the paths of rips.

Hiking

Mt Miros HIKING
(Ruta Nacional 34, opposite Delta gas station) A walk that few tourists are aware of is the trail up Mt Miros at the southern end of Jacó Beach. The roughly 2.5km round trip winds up the hillside through primary and secondary rainforest and offers seriously spectacular views of Jacó and Playa Hermosa, plus an atmospheric ruin. The trail is unmarked, but fairly well trafficked by dog walkers in the morning.

It starts on a paved road opposite the Delta gas station on Ruta National 34 heading towards Playa Hermosa. Pass Villa Mariposa and head up the hill. The views out to the ocean start almost immediately from here and just get better as you go along. The trail turns to dirt and becomes narrower, opening onto a columned viewpoint overlooking Jacó. Higher up, the forest gets denser and it's possible to see poison-dart frogs, monkeys and other wildlife. You'll pass lots of colorful art on a section of concrete wall along the trail. The best view is near a fork in the road: take the first left at the fork and stay left until you see white banisters on the far left (easy to miss – keep your eyes peeled), then walk alongside the banisters and you'll reach what looks like the spooky ruins of a dream hotel. Now covered with creative graffiti, you can walk the labyrinthine staircases and explore two levels, complete with the ruin of a fountain and rooms. The best bit is the to-die-for view over the ocean and town below. The trail used to continue higher, but it's currently unmaintained and off-limits, with 'no entry' signs.

Indoor

Escape Bus LIVE CHALLENGE
(☎8524-7658; www.costaricaescapebus.com; Jacó Walk, Av Pastor Díaz; adult/child US$25/20; ⏲2-10pm) Ideal for rainy days, this fun two-to-six player escape game is housed inside a converted bus with air-con. In this scenario, you and your team have been kidnapped and locked in the hull of a 300-year-old pirate ship. Can you escape the capture of murderous Captain Jorge Cacique and steal his treasure before your time runs out?

Tours

Tour companies offer a huge array of activities in and around Jacó, from surfing (there are numerous surfing schools) and sea kayaking to horseback riding, canopy tours, all-terrain vehicle (ATV) tours and more extreme canyoning and waterfall-jumping adventures.

Virtually every shop, hotel and restaurant in town books tours, as Jacó operates on a lucrative commission-based system. As you'd imagine, it's hard to know who is greasing whose palms and who is running tours. Still, you shouldn't book anything from touts on the streets, and if an offer from a vendor seems too good to be true, then most likely it is. Talk to your lodgings and fellow travelers for recommendations. It's usually better to go for companies that specialize in one activity or a small handful, rather than a catch-all operator that claims it can arrange everything under the sun.

Kayak Jacó KAYAKING
(☎2643-1233; www.kayakjaco.com; Calle Agujas; kayak tours with/without transport from $90/65, kayak fishing tours from US$100; ⏲7:30am-8pm, tours 8am & 1pm) This reliable, responsible company facilitates kayaking and sea-canoeing trips that include snorkeling excursions to tropical islands in a wide variety of customized day and multiday trips. Though it does have a presence at Playa Agujas, 250m east of the beach, it's best to phone or email in advance. Kayak fishing is also available with advance notice.

Discovery Horseback Tours HORSEBACK RIDING
(☎8838-7550; www.horseridecostarica.com; off Calle Rio Seco; 2½hr group tours from US$85; ⊙tours 8:30am & 2pm Mon-Fri, 8:30am Sat) Nearby beach and rainforest rides are available through this highly recommended outfit, run by an expat couple who offer an extremely high level of service and professionalism and who clearly take excellent care of their horses. Advance booking required. Cash only.

Costa Rica Waterfall Tours ADVENTURE
(Costa Rica Holiday Rentals; ☎2643-1834; www.costaricawaterfalltours.com; Jacó Walk, Av Pastor Díaz; rafting from US$93, crocodile tours from US$50, ziplining from US$65, waterfall tours from US$79; ⊙9am-5pm) This experienced, safety-conscious operator arranges some of the most adrenaline-charged excursions in town, from tamer ziplining or crocodile tours to waterfall rappelling and rafting.

Vista Los Sueños Rainforest Tours ADVENTURE
(☎2637-6020, in USA 321-220-9631; www.canopyvistalossuenos.com; ziplining from US$65, ATV tours US$70, horseback-riding tours US$70, chocolate tours US$40; ⊙7am-5pm, hourly tours 8am-3pm) The longest ziplines in the area belong to Vista Los Sueños, which offers 12 cables through the lush hillside with some sea views, accessed by tractor cart. It also arranges recommended horseback-riding and waterfall tour combos, plus ATV adventures (minumum four people) and chocolate tours. Find it 1.7km east of the Herradura intersection on Ruta 34.

Festivals & Events

Jacó Christmas Carnival CARNIVAL
(Av Pastor Díaz; ⊙Dec; 👪) FREE The whole town comes out for this family-friendly mega-festive Christmas celebration with more brass bands than you've ever seen. Troupes parade in various outfits along the main street through town creating a merry spirit as they go, with dances, loud brass classics, Christmas songs and even rock numbers. Dates are advertised locally, ask around town for details.

Sleeping

★**Buddha House** GUESTHOUSE $
(☎2643-3615; www.hostelbuddhahouse.com; Av Pastor Díaz; dm from US$20, r with fan & without bathroom from US$30, r with air-con & with/without bathroom from US$50/45; P❄📶🏊) Bold colors and modern art create an artistic atmosphere at this 'boutique hostel,' where the best private rooms are spacious suites. The staff are lovely, and the communal areas include a breezy patio, a spotless kitchen and even a small pool. Ask for rooms away from the neighboring bar, which can get noisy.

Beds on Bohio HOSTEL $
(☎2643-5251; www.bedsonbohio.com; Calle Bohío; dm/r from US$10/40; ❄📶) This chill hostel is steps from the beach, with surfers hanging around in a courtyard strung with hammocks (surfboard rental US$10 per day). There's a decent restaurant onsite serving burgers and breakfast. Rooms are bright and airy with colorful details and natural features. Some private rooms have air-con. It can be quite the party hostel, depending on the crowd in residence.

Room 2 Board Hostel & Surf School HOSTEL $
(☎2643-4949, in USA 310-956-1772; www.room2board.com; dm from US$15, d with/without bathroom from US$73/68; P❄@📶🏊) In a modern white-and-green complex a few minutes' walk from the beach, this hostel is spacious and professionally run. It has a buzzy pool-side cafe, dedicated staff who arrange tours and surfing lessons, and various configurations of rooms spread over three floors. Roof-terrace hammocks catch the breeze, and dorms come with excellent mattresses, solar-heated rain showers and lockers.

Jacó Inn HOSTEL $
(☎2643-1935; www.facebook.com/jacoinn; Av Pastor Díaz near Calle Bohío; dm US$15, r US$28-45; P📶) Down a shaded alley in the middle of town, dorms and private rooms share a relaxed TV living area and fully equipped kitchen in the main house. Four private rooms were created in a recycled airplane hangar, and have a hip industrial vibe. Rooms are spotless but, disappointingly, they have polyester sheets. Free yoga classes take place in an open-air studio.

★**Selina Jacó** HOSTEL $$
(☎8304 2994; www.selina.com/jaco; Calle Las Brisas; dm/d from $12/64; P❄📶🏊) Part of the Selina hostel empire, this latest edition was added in the fall of 2017 and has since become one of the best places to stay in town. It has a pool and bar overlooking Jacó's best

surf break and nicely decorated rooms with cleverly thought-out details. Options range from privates and dorms to Insta-worthy upcycled-concrete-cylinder rooms.

Facilities include a reading room with books and free-to-use guitars for guests, and a somewhat grubby communal kitchen. The bar and cafe serves a mean cocktail at happy hour, plus a small menu of bites, with items like fresh poke or shrimp and rice bowls. The breakfast is also decent. Selina's surf and SUP lessons (from US$50) are regarded as some of the best in town and come with a video deconstruction of the lesson you've just had, so you can improve your technique.

Hotel Ibiza HOTEL **$$**
(☎2643-1318; www.jacohotelibiza.com; Calle Bohío; d from US$55; ❄📶🏊) A Mediterranean-style boutique hotel with spacious, clean, marble-tiled rooms with chunky wooden headboards, and lots of amenities including a hairdryer, fridge, TV, coffeemaker, safe and toiletries. Larger rooms have couches and desks. There's a communal kitchen, pleasant grounds and a central pool, plus a tour desk for booking activities.

Hotel Perico Azul HOTEL **$$**
(☎2643-1341; www.hotelpericoazuljaco.com; off Av Pastor Díaz; r/studio US$60/75; P❄📶🏊) Tucked away off a quiet side street, this small, adults-only seven-room hotel is difficult to fault. Studios, double rooms and suites (some with kitchenette) are light and spotless, with bright splashes of color. There's a small pool to relax around and a communal kitchen. Staff go out of their way to make you feel welcome. Owner Mike runs the recommended Tortuga Surf Camp (p363); surfing packages can be arranged.

Hotel Tuanis Jacó Beach HOTEL **$$**
(☎2643-2094; www.hoteltuanisjacobeach.com; Calle Los Almendros; d/studio/1-bed apt/2-bed apt from US$74/95/107/146; ❄📶🏊) 🍃 In a good location just steps from the beach, this well-maintained hotel has clean rooms with dark wooden furnishings. Apartments come with a kitchen, and one has a large terrace. There are plenty of amenities (TV, hairdryer, safe), and solar panels supply power to the hotel. Downsides? The cheapest room is street-facing, with a front door onto the sidewalk.

★**Hotel Pumilio** BOUTIQUE HOTEL **$$$**
(☎2643-5678; www.hotelpumilio.com; r incl breakfast from US$223; P❄📶🏊) In a wonderfully peaceful location along an unpaved road 2.5km north of Jacó, this intimate hotel caters to travelers who want to do their own thing and still repose in style. The luxurious rooms come with comfy beds, a rain shower and outdoor kitchenette. The waterfall-fed pool and spa are surrounded by lush greenery. There's free transport to downtown Jacó.

Eden Retreat Center SPA HOTEL **$$$**
(☎8718-5258, 2643-2046; www.edenretreatcenter.com; Calle Marvin; r incl breakfast from US$150) Doctor of Integrative Medicine and super-cool woman Randi Raymond runs what she calls a 'purposely unstructured environment' for de-stressing and unwinding. Relax into a health-focused vacation involving organic meals, yoga, meditation, oxygen therapy, nutrition counseling, colonics and more at this six-room retreat. The sea and jungle views are stunning, while rooms are bright, plush and spacious. Day-spa passes available (9am to 5pm).

DoceLunas HOTEL **$$$**
(☎2643-2211; www.docelunas.com; Costanera Sur; r/ste incl breakfast from US$147/183; P⊖❄📶🏊) Situated in the foothills across the highway, 'Twelve Moons' is a heavenly mountain retreat consisting of 20 rooms sheltered in a pristine landscape of tropical rainforest. Each teak-accented room is uniquely decorated with original artwork, and the luxurious bathrooms feature double sinks and bathtubs. Yoga classes, offered regularly, are included in room rates.

Eating

For self-caterers, there's a **Más x Menos** (☎2643-2528; Av Pastor Díaz; ⊙8am-10pm Mon-Sat, to 9pm Sun) supermarket.

The Pizza Shop PIZZA **$**
(☎2643-2643; www.pizzajaco.com; Av Pastor Díaz; pizzas from US$10; ⊙11am-11pm Tue, to midnight Wed & Thu, to 2:30am Fri & Sat, 5pm-11am Sun) For a decent late-night snack of NYC-style pizzas it's got to be this open-plan joint. Pizzas are cooked from scratch; create your own or order from the 11 house options. Its take on the Hawaiian is cheekily named and comes with mozzarella and maple-smoked bacon, pineapple and shaved coconut.

★Green Room FUSION **$$**

(☎2643-4425; www.facebook.com/Green-Room-Cafe-325667240786166/; Calle Cocal; mains US$9-20; ⊙9am-1am Sun-Thu, until 2am Fri & Sat; 📶) With an emphasis on creativity and fresh ingredients (these guys work with local organic farms), Green Room serves excellently executed dishes such as sweet-potato-crusted mahi-mahi, herby seared tuna, and ribs with spicy passionfruit BBQ sauce, along with a supporting cast of salads, melts, wraps and burgers. Twenty local craft brews are on tap, and there's live music every night.

★Graffiti INTERNATIONAL **$$**

(☎2643-1708; www.graffitirestro.com; Jacó Walk, Av Pastor Díaz; bocas & tapas from US$3, mains US$16-27; ⊙5-10pm; 📶✎) Housed in a hip spot with colorful art and black metal French windows, this longtime favorite has beautifully presented creative dishes made with fresh local ingredients. Highlights include cacao-and-coffee-encrusted filet mignon, candied pork belly, and bowls of superfresh poke. Save room for a decadent dessert. Reservations recommended.

Lemon Zest FUSION **$$**

(☎2643-2591; www.lemonzestjaco.com; Av Pastor Díaz; mains US$11.50-23; ⊙5-10pm; ❄📶✎) Chef Richard Lemon (a former instructor at Le Cordon Bleu Miami) has been inspiring with one of Jacó's swishest and most imaginative menus for more than a decade. Order up dishes like organic Delmonico steak with caramelized onions and brie, or spicy togarashi ahi tuna with pickled ginger, teriyaki and spinach. Meanwhile the fresh salads are contenders for Best in Town.

Amancio's Pizza ITALIAN **$$**

(☎2643-2373; Av Pastor Díaz; pizza from US$9, mains US$9-28; ⊙12:30pm-10pm Thu-Tue) If you're craving Mediterranean comfort food in Jacó, this luscious Italian joint will hit the spot. The pizza is delish, the salads are fresh and the classic pasta dishes (from penne arrabiata and lasagna to rigatoni carbonara) are done well.

Tsunami Sushi JAPANESE **$$**

(☎2643-1635; www.tsunamisushi.com; Jacó Walk, Av Pastor Díaz; meals US$10-30; ⊙noon-10pm Sun-Tue & Thu, to 11pm Wed, Fri & Sat; ❄📶) This sleek and popular sushi spot has expanded from the central Pacific coast to open at three more locations in and around the capital. We're particularly partial to its spicy lobster rolls and cucumber martinis. Inquire about various specials throughout the week to save you serious colones, otherwise it's very pricey.

TacoBar INTERNATIONAL **$$**

(☎2643-0222; https://tacobar-jaco.business.site; Calle Lapa Verde; meals US$7-15; ⊙11am-10pm Mon, 7am-10pm Tue-Sun; 📶✎) Head here for great-value mixed tacos and health-conscious plates. First choose your carb (tortilla, rice etc), then your protein (grilled fish, shrimps, beef and more), then add your flavor (from lemon to Mexican spice), and load up on the free salad bar with 20 pots of fresh veggies. Wash it down with a smoothie or fresh juice.

Caliche's Wishbone INTERNATIONAL **$$**

(☎2643-3406; Av Pastor Díaz; pizza from US$12, meals US$8-21; ⊙noon-10pm Thu-Tue; ❄📶) Overseen by the charming Caliche, this has been a Jacó favorite for years. The eclectic, Mexican-inspired menu includes pitas, blackened tuna sashimi, pan-seared sea bass, and fish and shrimp tacos, plus pizza made in a wood-fired oven. Its justifiable fame comes from the fact that everything is fresh, delicious and good value. It's south of Calle Bohío.

Amara MEDITERRANEAN **$$**

(☎2438-4099; www.amaracostarica.com; Av Pastor Díaz, next to Hotel Tangeri; mains US$9-20; ⊙5pm-10:30pm Mon, Wed & Fri, noon-11pm Sat, noon-10pm Sun) Upmarket yet casual, with tasteful pink-tiled walls, marble tables and vintage pendant lights, Amara is a cute spot serving healthy Mediterranean dishes made with Costa Rican ingredients. Small tapas-like appetizers include the superb tomato gazpacho (which arrives on colorful crockery) and the flavorsome sautéed shrimp with Sicilian sausage. Second courses span gyros to grilled octopus with gremolata.

El Hicaco Seafood Restaurant SEAFOOD **$$$**

(☎2643-3226; www.elhicaco.com; Calle Hicaco; mains US$21-57; ⊙11am-10pm) This oceanside spot brims with casual elegance and is regarded as one of the finer dining experiences in Jacó. The menu is entirely dependent on seasonal offerings, both from the land and the sea – order up a salmon steak or lobster tail, perhaps. Everything is prepared with a variety of sauces highlighted by Costa Rica's tropical produce. Service can be glacially slow.

Drinking & Nightlife

★Café Bohío COFFEE
(☎2643-5915; www.cafebohio.com; Av Pastor Díaz; ⏰7am-7pm Sun-Wed, to 8:30pm Thu-Sat) Farmed and harvested in Tarrazú and roasted in Jacó, this is some of the finest-tasting coffee in Costa Rica. This small artisan coffee shop has no gimmicks, just a few tables and excellent brews with an abundance of flavor. Buy bags of their beans to take home here too for US$12 (tip: they're cheaper in nearby Más x Menos supermarket; p367).

★Samudiós Sunset Restobar BAR
(☎8928-6266; Jacó Beach, Calle Bohío, beside Río Copey; ⏰3pm-11pm Wed-Fri, noon-11pm Sat, Sun & Tue) The best place to sip on artisan mixed drinks and watch the sunset is this mellow, palm-tree-fronted place with minimalist airy design and pops of turquoise. Cocktails are pricey but mega: signature creations (from US$8) include the house piña colada in a frozen carved-out pineapple, a zingy passionfruit mojito, and the spicy ginger margarita with its wicked chili kick.

PuddleFish Brewery CRAFT BEER
(☎2643-1659; www.puddlefishbrewery.com; Av Pastor Díaz; ⏰4-11pm) Stationed in the glitzy Jacó Walk, this microbrewery is the city's first. Try PuddleFish's own rotating brews, like Fatty Knees IPA, The Nut Smuggler Brown Ale and Fest Orange Spiced Marzen. There's regular live music at the weekends and a bistro-style pub menu, including beer-battered fish and chips, and slider trios.

Beer House BREWERY
(☎7199-2381; www.facebook.com/pg/thebeerhousecr; Av Pastor Díaz; ⏰5pm-midnight Wed-Mon) Tucked into a nondescript plaza, this little watering hole features 10 craft beers on tap; it's a welcome alternative to some of the grimier nightlife options around town. When there's no live music, funk and rock 'n' roll plays on the stereo. 'Hoppy Hour' runs from 5pm to 7pm with US$4.50 deals on beers, or get flights of three to five samplers.

Jaco Bar BAR
(www.jacobar.com; Av Pastor Díaz; ⏰noon-2am; 📶) Popular nonseedy 2nd-floor bar on the main drag with daily drink deals like Craft Beer Mondays, and a good daily happy hour (4pm to 6pm with all drinks half price and beers around US$2). It has DJs Friday to Wednesday, live music on Thursday from 9:30pm, plus a good bar menu.

Information

There's no independent tourist information office, though several tour offices will give information. Look for the free *Howler* magazine for listings and visit www.infojaco.com for useful local info.

SAFE TRAVEL

Aside from occasional petty crime such as pickpocketing and breaking into cars, Jacó is not a dangerous place. But keep the following in mind:

- The high concentration of wealthy foreigners and comparatively poor Ticos has resulted in a visible sex and drugs industry. The local council has cleaned things up in recent years, but not entirely.
- Jacó is the epicenter of Costa Rica's prostitution scene. Travelers who wish to explore this dark corner of Costa Rican nightlife should consider the health and safety risks and negative social impacts.
- Locals warn against walking alone on the beach at night due to muggings.

Getting There & Away

BOAT

The jet-boat transfer service that connects Jacó to Montezuma is far and away the most efficient way to get between the central Pacific coast and the Península de Nicoya. The journey across the Golfo de Nicoya only takes about an hour (compared to about seven hours overland), though at US$45 (child US$35; for US$10-20 you can bring a surfboard) it's not cheap. The bonus? Sometimes travelers see dolphins along the ride. Several boats leave daily from Playa Herradura, 2km north of town. Reservations are required and the most consistent departures are with **Zuma Tours** (☎2642-0050, 2642-0024; www.zumatours.net; ⏰8am-8pm) at 10am. It's a beach landing, so wear the right shoes.

BUS

Gray Line, Easy Ride and Monkey Ride run shared shuttles from Jacó to popular destinations such as San José (from around US$42), Manuel Antonio (from US$47), Dominical/Uvita (from US$50), Sierpe (from US$65), Puerto Jiménez (US$89) and Monteverde (from US$59). Easy Ride runs shuttles from Jacó to Rivas San and Juan del Sur, Nicaragua (US$99).

Buses for San José stop at the Plaza Jacó mall, north of the center. The bus stops for other destinations are on Av Pastor Díaz, opposite the Más x Menos supermarket (p367): stand at the bus stop in front of the supermarket if you're headed north; stand at the bus stop across the street if you're headed south.

Buses originate in Puntarenas or Quepos, so consult your lodgings or visit the bus company websites to check the latest schedule and get to the stop early.

Puntarenas Around US$3, 1½ hours, several daily between 5:30am and 5:50pm (www.tqpcr.com).

Quepos Around US$3, 1½ hours, several daily between 6am and 7pm (www.tqpcr.com and www.tracopacr.com).

San José Around US$5.50, 2½ hours, several daily between 5am and 7pm (www.transportesjacoruta655.com and www.tracopacr.com).

Getting Around

Getting around is easy on foot; strolling the far lengths of town in flip-flops takes about 30 minutes. Uber also now operates in Jacó and, at the time of research, fares were more competitive than taxis, with short trips around town for a few dollars.

BICYCLE

Accommodations around town, such as Selina Jacó (p366), rent out bicycles. Bikes can usually be rented for about US$5 an hour or US$10 to US$15 per day, though prices change depending on the season.

CAR

There are several rental agencies in town, so shop around for the best rates.

Budget (2436-2082; Av Pastor Díaz, near Calle Bohío; 8am-5pm Mon-Sat, to 4pm Sun) International car-rental company.

Economy (2299-2000; Av Pastor Díaz; 8am-6pm) Northwest of Calle Ancha.

Playa Hermosa

Regarded as one of the most consistent and powerful breaks in the whole country, Hermosa serves up serious surf that commands the utmost respect. You really need to know what you're doing in these parts – huge waves and strong riptides are unforgiving, and countless surfboards here have wound up broken and strewn about on the shoreline. Unless you're a hardcore surfer, it's best to stick to gentler breaks near Jacó, but there's nothing to stop you from coming up here and watching the action.

Billed as an upscale alternative to Jacó, minus the seediness and the traffic, Hermosa hasn't quite avoided development, with condos popping up along the beach like mushrooms. Still, for now, it is very much a slow-paced beach village.

Sights & Activities

Royal Butterflies NATURE CENTER

(8409-5638; www.royalbutterflygarden.com; Calle Río Seco; US$10; 8am-1pm Mon-Sat; P) This local butterfly farm run by American expat Dan is set on 1.2 hectares with 70 kinds of fruit tree and 15 species of butterfly, including the enormous *Caligo memnon* (giant owl), whose wingspan can reach 150mm. Dan's enjoyable 45-minute tour explains the delicate farming processes. At the time of research there were plans to open treehouse accommodation.

Surfing

Most of the surfing action takes place at the northern reaches, where there are no fewer than six clearly defined beach breaks. These have tons of power and break very near the shore, particularly in the rainy season between May and August. Conditions are highly variable, but you can expect the maximum height to top out around high tide. Swell size is largely dependent on unseen factors such as current and offshore weather patterns, but when it gets big, you'll know. At times like these, you really shouldn't be paddling out unless you have some serious experience under your belt. Playa Hermosa is not for beginners, and even intermediate surfers can get chewed up and spat out here. To watch and appreciate, park at the small road by the **Backyard Hotel** (2643-7011; www.backyardhotel.com; Ruta 34; r/ste incl breakfast from US$150/250; P) and wander out to the beach.

Yoga

Vida Asana School of Yoga YOGA

(8483-7603, in USA 201-603-3602; www.vidaasana.com; off Calle Hermosa; drop-in yoga classes US$10, 2-night yoga and surf retreats incl meals from US$395; yoga classes 10am) This hillside retreat offers packages combining yoga, surfing, healthy organic meals and permaculture design workshops. Reservations for 'weekend recharge retreats' are highly recommended, and prices are dependent on the size of your party, the season and the extent of instruction. Drop-in classes are also available. Accommodations are charming and set amid lush jungle.

✦ Festivals & Events

National Surfing Championship
SPORTS

(☉ Jul/Aug) If you don't think you can hack it with the aspiring pros, you might want to give the surf on this beach a miss. However, consider stopping by in late July or late August, when local pro surfers descend for the annual national surf competition. Dates vary depending on swells, but the event is heavily advertised around the country, especially in neighboring Jacó.

🛏 Sleeping

Cabinas Brisa del Mar
CABINA $

(☑ 2643-7023; www.cabinasbrisadelmar.com; Calle Oeste; s/d/tr US$35/45/55; P❄🛜🏊) A classic no-frills surfers' crash pad popular with Ticos, this spot has basic rooms with air-con, hot showers, refrigerators, and cable TV, as well as a communal kitchen for self-caterers. If the surf is looking too small (or too big!), you can pass the time at the pool or join in the yoga sessions at the Hermosa Beach House (☑ 2643-7178; www.hbhcr.com; Calle Oeste; d from US$72; P❄🛜) nearby.

Tortuga del Mar
LODGE $$

(www.tortugadelmar.net; Calle Oeste; d from US$67; P❄@🛜🏊) Sheltered amid shady grounds, this beachfront lodge has nine clean and stylish beach-themed rooms housed in a two-story building. 'Tropical modern' is the style, with white walls, pops of color, and lofty ceilings constructed from hardwoods, catching every gust of the Pacific breezes. The best bit? The wooden deck out front to watch the surfing action.

Sandpiper Hotel
HOTEL $$

(☑ 2643-7042; www.sandpipercostarica.com; Calle Oeste; d with/without breakfast from US$70/65; P❄🛜🏊) A central waterfront location with hammocks strung up so that guests can watch the surfing in comfort, a little pool with a miniature waterfall, plus comfortable (but slightly dated) rooms with kitchens make this a decent choice. The grounds are full of iguanas and other local wildlife. Day trips, surf lessons and board rental are bookable in advance.

Marea Brava
RESORT $$$

(☑ 2643-7055; www.mareabravacostarica.com; Calle Oeste; studio/r/condo from US$65/120/180;

P❄🛜🏊) Tucked away in the northernmost corner of Hermosa's beachfront road, this creeper-clad hotel is one of the more characterful places in the village. The tropical-style rooms are spacious and comfortable but could do with some modernizing. Very popular with weekending Ticos.

🍴 Eating

★ Vida Hermosa
COSTA RICAN $

(☑ 2643-6215; www.facebook.com/VidaHermosa PlayaHermosa; Ruta 34; mains US$8-15; ☉ 7am-10pm) Vida Hermosa has a sweet surf view and outrageously delicious cuisine. At breakfast, the hearty surfer's burrito is the ideal fuel for Hermosa's gigantic waves, and the coffee's great too. For lunch, tuck into one of the nine healthy salad, noodle or poke bowls, or go for a fresh fish plate.

With fruity cocktails, open mic nights on Tuesdays (from 7pm), acoustic sessions on Friday (from 8pm), rock 'n' roll on Saturdays (from 8pm) and roots on Sunday (from 1pm), Vida Hermosa is the most fun hangout spot in the area.

There are a couple of charming, tidy rooms available from US$80 per night including breakfast.

Falafel Hermosa
MIDDLE EASTERN $

(☑ 8482-6867; www.falafelhermosa.wordpress.com; Ruta Nacional 34; mains from US$7; ☉ 11am-9pm; P🛜) Your one-stop shop for falafel, this open-air beachy place serves homemade pitas stuffed with deep-fried chickpea goodness, smothered with garlicky tzatziki and red cabbage salad. Flavorsome shakshuka, souvlaki skewers and gyros are also available. Wash it down with a fresh smoothie and finish off with some of the house's yummy sticky baklava. It's on the main road before Playa Hermosa.

Backyard Bar
INTERNATIONAL $$

(☑ 2643-7011; www.backyardhotel.com/bar.html; Ruta 34; mains US$6-21; ☉ 7am-11pm; P🛜) The expansive menu has the usual bar fare (tacos, pizza, burritos), but none of it is likely to set your taste buds alight. As the town's de facto nightspot, the Backyard Bar hosts live music, and a local surf contest every Friday and Saturday from 4pm until sunset (no entry fee and a cash prize of US$300).

OFF THE BEATEN TRACK

LAID-BACK BEACH LIFE

Playa Palo Seco, also known as Isla Palo Seco, is a quiet, unhurried black-sand beach that's away from the main tourist spots. It's located near mangrove swamps with good opportunities for birdwatching. Just south of the Río Parrita, a 6km dirt road connects the eastern edge of Parrita to the beach. Another popular excursion is to visit **Isla Damas**, which is actually the tip of a mangrove peninsula that becomes an island at high tide. Most people arrive here on package tours from Jacó or Quepos, though you can hire a boat to take you to and from the island.

Places to stay include a couple of secluded upmarket options off Playa Palo Seco. It's worth making a detour to stay at **Beso del Viento** (2779-9674; www.besodelviento.com; r incl breakfast with/without air-con from US$123/105; P ❄ ☎ ≋), a lovely adults-only B&B located across the road from an isolated beach. Charming rooms are comfortably outfitted and decorated with an elegant eye for detail, with hardwood floors, tiled bathrooms and immaculate linens. The hosts serve superb French meals and can arrange tours. Bare feet only in the main house, please!

Sandwiched between a mangrove-lined canal and a jungle-fringed, chocolate-sand beach, **Clandestino Beach Resort** (2779-8806; www.clandestinobeachresort.com; d US$175-410; ❄ ☎ ≋) is one secluded stretch of paradise. Twelve comfortable private bungalows are strewn around a large, open-air restaurant with a thatched roof. There are lots of homey-tropical touches, hand-selected by the friendly expat owner who claims to have visited every beach in Costa Rica before choosing to build her paradise here.

Parrita is about 40km south of Jacó, and can be reached on any bus heading south from there. After Parrita, the coastal road dips inland through more palm-oil plantations on the way to Quepos. A taxi from Parrita to Playa Palo Seco costs around US$10 to US$14.

Getting There & Away

Playa Hermosa can be accessed by any bus heading south from Jacó, 5km away. Frequent buses running up and down the Costanera Sur can easily pick you up, though determined surfers sometimes hail a taxi (with surf racks) or hitchhike.

Playa Esterillos

Only 15 minutes south of Jacó but worlds away, Playa Esterillos lures those who simply want to catch some sun, empty surf, and scenery (sans scene), as there isn't much else to do along this miles-long expanse of beach. Playa Esterillos is signposted off the highway in several sections: Esterillos Oeste (West), Centro (Central) and Este (East). Esterillos Oeste has a mini-supermarket, a couple of *sodas,* a tiny tour office and a Tico-village vibe, while Esterillos Este has more of a resort feel, with upscale accommodations and a string of holiday homes along the beachfront.

Sleeping

Hotel La Dolce Vita HOTEL $$
(2778-7015; www.hotel-ladolcevita.biz; Esterillos Oeste; s/d incl breakfast from US$62/89; P ❄ ☎ ≋) The intimate and quiet Hotel La Dolce Vita is just meters away from the beach. The pool may be small, but you can fall asleep lulled by the sound of the waves, and in the morning have your breakfast served on your private terrace at a time of your choosing. The almond trees by the hotel attract scarlet macaws.

★ **Alma del Pacífico** RESORT $$$
(2778-7070; www.almadelpacificohotel.com; Esterillos Este; bungalow/villa from US$186/422; P ❄ ☎ ≋) Each individually designed villa at this remarkable resort encompasses intriguing bright and colorful design elements, including wooden-lattice ceilings, sheer walls of glass framing private gardens, concrete-poured furniture done up with custom leatherwork, and impossibly intricate mosaics. There is also a spa and onsite restaurant specializing in healthy gourmet organic fare, and an immaculate palm-fringed infinity pool.

Encantada Ocean Cottages COTTAGE $$$
(☎2778-7048; www.encantadacostarica.com; Esterillos Este; cottage/villa incl breakfast from US$158/203;) With verdant grounds and a collection of smart and airy Dutch-looking cottages surrounding a relaxing pool by the sea, Encantada is a sanctuary. Solidifying the wellness angle, the owners have constructed an oceanfront yoga deck. Classes are held at 10am daily for guests and drop-ins (US$10 per class).

Hotel Pelicano HOTEL $$$
(☎2778-8105; www.pelicanbeachcostarica.com; Esterillos Este; d/ste from US$105/186;) The long-standing beachside Hotel Pelicano hits a sweet spot: it's affordable, safe, homey and on a dreamy stretch of the Pacific. The 13 rooms are on the rustic side, but open to balconies overlooking a small pool. Guests can take in magnificent sunsets, go surfing or splash around in the waves.

Eating

★Los Almendros INTERNATIONAL $$
(☎2778-7322; www.facebook.com/LosAlmendrosRestaurant; Esterillos Oeste; mains from US$8; 4-10pm Mon-Sat) Around 50m west of the soccer field, this cozy restaurant serves delectable international favorites from falafel and Caribbean-style curry to pad thai, black-bean soup and whole red snapper with homemade salsa. The dishes are beautifully executed, the atmosphere convivial and the service sweet. Wash it down with a juicy IPA, summer ale or a chocolate stout.

El Chiringuito MEDITERRANEAN $$
(☎4702-4703; www.facebook.com/crchiringuito; Esterillos Town Center; mains US$10-19; noon-9pm) Sit on the lovely open-air patio with a glass of European wine and enjoy delights like Spanish-style tapas, Italian pasta dishes, and fresh fish and seafood dishes. The lobster bisque and mixed rice with shrimp are wonderfully flavorsome. Superbly prepared specials include homemade ricotta and spinach ravioli, and blackened Cajun tuna served with fresh veggies.

Getting There & Around

While buses connecting Jacó with Quepos can drop you off at the access roads into Playa Esterillos, getting there and around is easiest with your own set of wheels.

PARQUE NACIONAL MANUEL ANTONIO & AROUND

At this small outcrop of land jutting into the Pacific, the air becomes heavy with humidity, scented with thick vegetation and alive with the calls of birds and monkeys, making it suddenly apparent that *this* is the tropics. The reason to come here is the wonderful Parque Nacional Manuel Antonio, one of the most picturesque bits of tropical coast in Costa Rica. If you get bored of cooing at the baby monkeys scurrying in the canopy and scanning for birds and sloths, the turquoise waves and perfect sand provide endless entertainment. However, as it's one of the country's most popular national parks, little Quepos, the once-sleepy fishing and banana village on the park's perimeter, has ballooned in this tourism-based economy, and the road from Quepos to the park is overdeveloped. Despite this, the rainforested hills and the blissful beaches make the park a stunning destination worthy of the hype.

Quepos

POP 22,000

Just 7km from the entrance to Manuel Antonio, the small, busy town of Quepos serves as the gateway to the national park, as well as a convenient port of call for travelers flying in or those in need of goods and services. Although the Manuel Antonio area was

DON'T MISS

RAINMAKER AERIAL WALKWAY

Rainmaker (☎2777-3565, 8960-3836; www.rainmakercostarica.org; US$20, guided tours US$30-35; 7am-4pm) is a privately owned rainforest that offered the first aerial walkway through the forest canopy in Central America. Although its star has faded a bit, the place is still regarded as one of the region's best. Experience the walkway's tree-to-tree platforms, spectacular hanging bridges and panoramic views of the surrounding primary and secondary rainforest.

Quepos

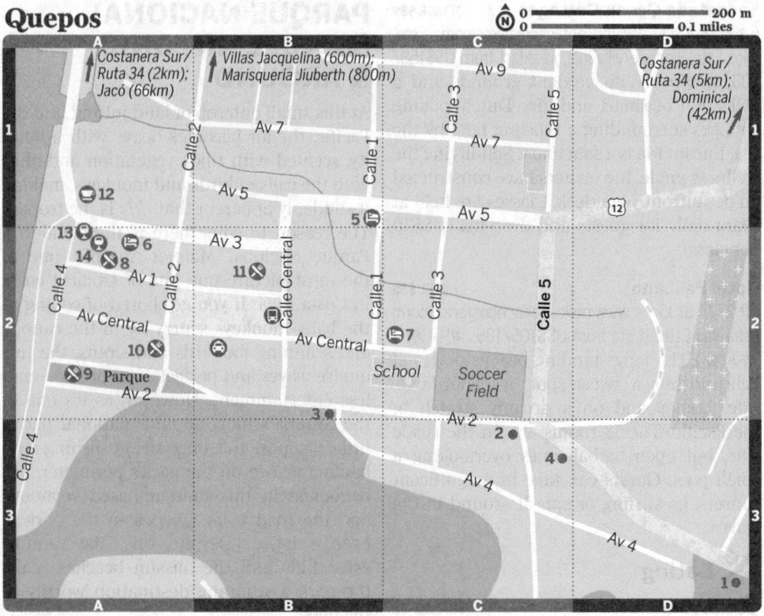

Quepos

Activities, Courses & Tours

1 H2O Adventures D3
2 Iguana Tours C3
3 Jade Tours B2
4 Paddle 9 .... C3

Sleeping

5 Hotel Boutique Puerta Del Cielo B1
6 Serenity A2
7 Wide Mouth Frog Backpackers C2

Eating

8 Brooklyn Bakery A2
9 Farmers Market A2
10 L'Angolo A2
11 Soda Come Bien B2

Drinking & Nightlife

12 Café Milagro Coffee Roasters A1
13 Cuban Republik Disco Lounge A2
14 El Gran Escape A2

rapidly and irreversibly transformed following the ecotourism boom, Quepos has largely retained its charm.

Many visitors to the Manuel Antonio area prefer to stay outside Quepos, but accommodations in town are comparatively good value, and there are many eateries.

Activities

Diving

Oceans Unlimited DIVING
(2519-9544; www.scubadivingcostarica.com; Marina Pez Vela; 2-tank dive US$110; 7am-5pm, dives 8am-noon) This shop takes its diving very seriously, and runs most of its excursions out to Isla Larga and Isla del Caño, which are to the south in Bahía Drake (connected via a two-hour bus trip). It also has a range of specialized PADI certifications, and regular environmental-awareness projects that make it stand out from the pack.

Sportfishing

Quepos Sailfishing Charters FISHING
(8746-3970, in USA 800-388-9957; www.queposfishing.com; charters per day from US$1250) This Quepos-based outfitter runs sportfishing trips and charters on a fleet of variously sized boats, whether you're after sailfish, marlin, dorado or wahoo. Trip rates vary significantly depending on the season, number of people and size of boat. It also offers packages that include accommodations and transfers.

Tours

★Paddle 9 WATER SPORTS
(☎2777-7436; www.paddle9sup.com; Ruta Nacional 618; 3hr tours from US$65, full-day tours from US$143; ⏲8:30am-4pm) This passionate, safety-conscious team introduced SUP to Quepos and delights in showing visitors around the Pacific coast. Apart from the two-hour mangrove or ocean paddleboarding tours, the most popular outing is an eight-hour journey involving paddleboarding, lunch at a tilapia fish farm and swimming in various waterfalls.

Unique Tours ADVENTURE
(☎2777-1119; www.costaricauniquetours.com; rafting & waterfalls/ziplining/catamaran/horseback riding/kayaking from US$95/75/75/65/65) This established local operator organizes entertaining rafting tours on the Río Savegre, plus ocean and mangrove kayaking outings. It also does coastal hikes to Parque Nacional Manuel Antonio, ziplining, catamaran and horseback-riding tours plus much more. Prices vary depending on group size.

H2O Adventures ADVENTURE
(Ríos Tropicales; ☎2777-4092; www.h2ocr.com; Ruta Nacional 618; rafting with/without lunch US$95/85) The venerable Costa Rican rafting company Ríos Tropicales has a hugely popular franchise in Quepos called H2O Adventures, which organizes rafting outings on the Naranjo, El Chorro and Savegre rivers (the latter with a waterfall stop), as well as kayaking and tubing outings. Rapids range from Class II to Class IV.

Titi Canopy Tours ADVENTURE
(☎2777-3130; www.titicanopytour.com; Costanera Sur at La Foresta Nature Resort; adult/child US$80/65; ⏲tours 7:30am, 11am & 2:30pm) This outfit has friendly, professional guides, who take adventure seekers on 12 ziplines (reaching up to 450m), 22 platforms, one rappel and a Tarzan swing. The lines are situated in the 37-acre grounds of a private reserve filled with nature and they offer lovely mountain and valley views. Rates include a Tico meal, fruit, drinks and local transportation.

Iguana Tours ADVENTURE
(☎2777-2052; www.iguanatours.com; cnr Av 2 & Calle 5; rafting from US$70, sea kayaking and snorkeling from US$65, horseback riding from US$80, catamaran from US$70; ⏲6:30am-9pm) With tours that leave for destinations all over the central Pacific coast, this adventure-travel shop offers reputable river rafting, sea kayaking, horseback riding, mangrove tours and dolphin-watching excursions. It's no fly-by-night operation – it's been around since '89 – and has a proven commitment to ecotourism principles.

Tico Loco Adventures OUTDOORS
(☎2777-0010; www.ticolocoadventures.com; Ruta Nacional 235; waterfall party tour min 4 people US$110, rafting from US$70) With a local office on the way into Quepos, this welcoming tour company offers rafting on the Naranjo river with Class III–IV rapids, and Savegre on Class II–III rapids, plus outdoor adventures that double as parties. The waterfall party tour involves a hike to majestic falls with a cooler of drinks.

Jade Tours ADVENTURE
(☎2777-0932; www.costaricajadetours.com; Av 2; nature tours from US$59; ⏲9am-8pm Sun-Tue, 7am-8pm Wed-Sat) Recommended agency for nature tours in Parque Nacional Manuel Antonio. Trips include transport and a guide with a telescope (through which you can take pictures of sloths, monkeys and insects for your preferred social media profile). Also offers adventure day trips and private transportation. Prices listed online are more expensive than for walk-ins.

Sleeping

★Wide Mouth Frog Backpackers HOSTEL $
(☎2777-2798; www.widemouthfrog.org; Av Central; dm US$14, s/d without bathroom from US$25/37 d with bathroom US$53; P ❄ @ 📶 ≋) Secure and cozy, this good-value gated backpacker outpost centered around a tranquil pool has spacious doubles and clean shared bathrooms. There are hammocks, a well-equipped kitchen and a large, open-air dining area that encourages socializing. The recently refurbished rooms are bright, with a smart, clean, tiled bathroom, refrigerator and TV. The cheaper rooms could do with modernizing.

There's also a TV lounge, book exchange and a Budget car rental reservation center onsite.

★Villas Jacquelina GUESTHOUSE $$
(☎8345-1516; www.villasjacquelina.com; Calle 2; d US$42-70; P ❄ 📶 ≋) By far the best budget-to-mid-range option in Quepos, this large,

rambling building just out of town offers various configurations of bright simple rooms. Best for groups is the 3rd-story open-air 'Birds Nest', complete with secret toilet (see if you can find it).

The place is run by Steve, an expat with tons of local knowledge, who can help arrange tours. There are large hangout spaces with hammocks, and a vibe of friendly camaraderie prevails. Several rooms are geared toward families with kids, and there's a child-friendly pool.

Serenity BOUTIQUE HOTEL $$

(☑2777-0572; www.serenityhotelcostarica.com; Av 3; r incl breakfast from US$92; P ❋ 🛜 🐾) This intimate boutique hotel is a welcome part of the Quepos scene, and is a good midrange option in the center of town. The whitewashed walls and blue trim offer a slice of breezy Mediterranean calm. In the slightly dated rooms are crisp white linens, a TV and minifridge. Rooms upstairs get much better light but some windows face the corridor.

Hotel Boutique

Puerta Del Cielo BOUTIQUE HOTEL $$$

(☑7011-0551; www.puertadelcieloquepos.com; cnr Av 5 & Calle 1; d from US$132; ❋ 🛜) This cozy, well-situated seven-room boutique hotel in the center of Quepos doesn't have the glam of places nearer to Manuel Antonio, but is one of the better high-end options in town. Rooms are finished well, with bright and tasteful hardwood furnishings and large balconies with city views. Amenities include a minifridge, toiletries, TV and a good breakfast.

✖ Eating

★Marisquería Jiuberths SEAFOOD $

(☑2777-1292; off Ruta Nacional 235; mains US$6-21; ⊙11am-9:30pm) Run by a hardworking fisherman's family, this institution with brightly tiled floors serves the best seafood in town, yet is practically unknown to visitors because it's tucked away in the back streets of Quepos. Whether you have the catch of the day or the satisfying fish soup, *ceviche* or seafood mains, the portions are generous and the service attentive. Cash only.

Follow Ruta 235 out of town and it will be signposted on the left; it's a few minutes up an unpaved road. If in doubt, ask locals for directions as it's well known.

★Brooklyn Bakery BAKERY $

(☑8583-0541; www.facebook.com/TheBrooklyn BakeryCR; Av 1; bagels US$2, mains US$6-8; ⊙6am-3pm Mon-Sat; 🛜🐾) Real New York–style bagels, lox salmon (a real rarity in Costa Rica) and rye bread! This adorable little bakery bakes its fresh wares every morning, and light bites continue throughout the day, plus there's good iced coffee. Order amazing salads and bagels, ciabatta or soughdough sandwiches with fillings from guacamole to tuna. Grab a delicious slice of lemon pie to go.

L'Angolo DELI $

(Restorante L'Angolo Gastronomia Italian Deli; ☑2777-7865; Calle 2; sandwiches US$6-7; ⊙11am-10pm Mon-Sat) This tiny deli with a couple of tables makes rather good pastas, salads and sandwiches with imported Italian meats and cheeses – the perfect picnic for the beach or a fishing trip.

Soda Come Bien CAFETERIA $

(☑2777-2550; Av 1, Mercado Central; mains US$3.50-6; ⊙6am-5pm Mon-Sat, to 11am Sun) The daily rotation of delicious cafeteria options here might include fish in tomato sauce, *olla de carne* (beef soup with rice) or chicken soup. Everything is fresh, the women behind the counter are friendly and the burly portions are a dream come true for hungry shoestringers. Or pick up a fresh *empanada* before or after a long bus ride.

Farmers Market MARKET $

(Calle 4; ⊙4-11pm Fri, 6am-noon Sat) Self-caterers should check out the farmers market near the waterfront, where you can buy directly from farmers, fisherfolk, bakers and other food producers.

Sunrice SUSHI $$

(☑2519-9955; www.sunricerestaurant.com; Marina Pez Vela; poke bowls from US$12, dumplings US$9, sushi rolls from US$12; ⊙noon-9pm Tue-Sun) A Latin-influenced sushi and sake bar that fills its rolls with fresh tropical produce and local seafood. The spicy tuna served on crispy rice cakes is a big hit, along with the salmon, avocado and mango poke bowl and the *omusubi* (Japanese rice balls). Dishes tend to be on the smaller side. Enjoy your food on the outside tables.

Runaway Grill AMERICAN **$$**
(☎2519-9095; www.runawaygrill.com; Marina Pez Vela; mains US$12-30; ⏲10am-10pm Mon-Fri, 8am-11pm Sat & Sun; P ❄ 📶) An all-round crowd pleaser, casual open-air Runaway Grill looks out on the yachts of the marina and its ceiling is covered in fishing hats. The menu spans fish, Mexican, Costa Rican, steaks, wraps, salads and more. Portions are sizeable and the service is friendly, but due to its upmarket location it's a little on the pricey side.

Pesca Seafood SEAFOOD **$$**
(☎2519-9422; www.facebook.com/Pescaseafood; Marina Pez Vela; mains US$11-26, sharing platters US$80; ⏲11:30am-10pm; P) This new kid on the block, with fish shapes hanging from the ceiling, is a good choice for seafood lovers. It serves up fresh morsels in various styles: the crowd-pleasing salmon *ceviche* arrives in a coconut, while the paella or seafood platter with tuna steak, shrimp, octopus, clams, and a whole lobster are fun sharing options for bigger groups.

★ **Gabriella's** SEAFOOD **$$$**
(☎2519-9300; www.gabriellassteakhouse.com; Marina Pez Vela; mains US$23-53; ⏲4-10pm; P ❄ 📶) A contender for the region's best restaurant, Gabriella's does many things well: the veranda catches the sunset and overlooks a gorgeous marina, and the service is attentive. But the food is the real star, with great emphasis on fresh fish and mouth-watering steak. We're fans of the seared tuna with chipotle sauce and the spicy sausage and shrimp pasta. In a word: terrific.

Drinking & Entertainment

Café Milagro Coffee Roasters CAFE
(☎2777-1707; www.cafemilagro.com; Calle 4; ⏲9am-5pm Mon-Sat) Café Milagro sources its coffee beans from all over Costa Rica and produces a variety of estate, single-origin and blended roasts to suit any coffee fiend's palate.

Cuban Republik Disco Lounge CLUB
(☎8345-9922; www.facebook.com/cubanrepublik.quepos; cnr Ruta Nacional 235 & Av 3; cover charge Fri & Sat US$2-4; ⏲10pm-2:30am Thu-Sat) Cuban Republik hosts the most reliable party in central Quepos, and has various drink specials. The DJs get loud late into the night and women get in at a discount on certain nights. It's a nice mixed Tico and gringo scene.

El Gran Escape BAR
(☎2777-7850; www.elgranescapequepos.com; Av 3; ⏲11am-11pm; 📶) This well-established pub offers a good happy hour (4:30pm to 6:30pm) with two-for-one cocktails, plus excellent fresh seafood, sports on the screen and delicious (though pricey) burgers. Prompt bar staff too. Bring your catch after your fishing trip and they will prepare it, cook it and serve it back to you with two sides for US$14.

ℹ Orientation

Downtown Quepos is a small checkerboard of dusty streets that are lined with a mix of local- and tourist-oriented shops, businesses, markets, restaurants and cafes. The town loses its well-ordered shape as it expands outward, but the sprawl is kept relatively in check by the mountains to the east and the water to the west.

South of the town center is the **Marina Pez Vela** (☎2774-9000; www.marinapezvela.com; Paseo del Mar, Calle 4); its marine slips opened to much fanfare in 2010, and it now features some of the best restaurants in town.

ℹ Information

Look out for *Quepolandia*, a free English-language monthly magazine that can be found at many of the town's businesses and online at www.quepolandia.com.

SAFE TRAVEL

- Theft can be a problem, and the usual common-sense precautions apply: lock valuables in a hotel safe and never leave anything in a car.
- When leaving bars late at night, walk in a group or take a taxi. The town's bars attract rowdy crowds of plantation workers on weekends.
- Note that the beaches in Quepos are polluted and not recommended for swimming. Go over the hill to Manuel Antonio instead, where some of the dreamiest waters in Costa Rica await.

ℹ Getting There & Away

AIR

Sansa (www.flysansa.com) and Skyway (www.skywaycr.com) airlines service Quepos. Prices vary according to season and availability; destinations include San José and Liberia. Flights are packed in the high season, so book (and pay) for your ticket well ahead of time and reconfirm often. Quepos La Managua airport is 5km out of town, and taxis make the trip for around US$10.

There's also a US$3 entry/exit fee at the airport.

BUS

Scheduled private shuttles, operated by Gray Line, Easy Ride and Monkey Ride, run between Quepos and Manuel Antonio, and popular destinations such as Jacó (US$39), Monteverde (US$59), Puerto Jiménez (US$79), San José (US$55) and Uvita (US$359).

Uber is another option; depending on the surge in fares, a private car can work out only slightly more expensive than a shuttle. All buses arrive at and depart from the busy, chaotic main **terminal** (Calle Central) in the center of town. If you're coming and going in the high season, check schedules and buy tickets for San José in advance at the **Tracopa ticket office** (☎2221-4214; www.tracopacr.com; Calle Central; ⏰6am-6pm) at the bus terminal or online at www.blancotiquete.com/venta and www.tracopacr.com.

Jacó: US$3, 1½ hours, 12 daily from 4:30am to 6pm.

Puntarenas: US$5, three hours, 12 daily from 4:30am-5:30pm.

San Isidro de El General via Dominical: US$5; three hours, four daily at 5am, 11:30am, 3:30pm, 8pm.

San José: US$7, 3½ hours, six direct daily from 4am-5pm.

Uvita via Dominical: US$4, two hours, four daily at 6am, 9:30am, 2:30pm, 5:30pm.

Buses to local destinations cost around US$1 to US$3 and are more frequent.

Buses between Quepos and Manuel Antonio (less than US$1) depart roughly every 30 minutes from the main terminal between 7am and 7pm, and less frequently after 7:30pm.

TAXI

Colectivo taxis run between Quepos and Manuel Antonio (around US$1 for short local distances). A private taxi will cost a few thousand colones. Catch one at the **taxi stand** (Av Central) south of the market. The trip between Quepos and the park should cost about US$15.

ℹ Getting Around

A number of international car-rental companies operate in Quepos, such as **Budget**, which has branches at the **airport** (www.budget.co.cr; Quepos La Managua Airport; ⏰8am-5pm Mon-Sat, to 4pm Sun) and in **Quepos town** (☎2774-0558; www.budget.co.cr; cnr Av 5 & Calle 1; ⏰8am-5pm Mon-Sat, to 4pm Sun); reserve ahead and reconfirm to guarantee availability.

Quepos to Manuel Antonio

From the Quepos waterfront, the steep, narrow, winding road swings uphill and inland for 7km before reaching the beaches of Manuel Antonio village and the entrance to the national park. This route passes over a number of hills awash with picturesque views of jungle slopes leading down to the palm-fringed coastline.

This area is home to some of Costa Rica's finest hotels and restaurants, and while shoestringers and budget travelers are catered for, this is one part of the country where those with deep pockets can bed down and dine out in the lap of luxury.

Drive and walk with care, especially at night, and avoid the evening rush between around 6pm to 7pm.

LGBTIQ+ MANUEL ANTONIO

For jet-setting LGBTIQ+ travelers the world over, Manuel Antonio has a reputation as something of a tolerant destination in comparison to its neighbors. Homosexuality has been decriminalized in Costa Rica since the 1970s – a rarity in all-too-often machismo-fueled, conservative Central America. Same-sex marriage became legal in May 2020. A well-established rainbow community (made up predominantly of gay men) has blossomed in Manuel Antonio and it's not hard to understand why.

Not only is the area stunningly beautiful, but it has also long attracted liberal-minded individuals, creating a burgeoning artist community and a sophisticated restaurant scene. And with the recent Supreme Court ruling against the country's same-sex marriage ban, this area is set to become one of Costa Rica's premier destinations for same-sex weddings. Check out www.gaymanuelantonio.com for a full list of LGBTIQ+ and LGBTIQ-friendly accommodations, events, restaurants and bars.

During daylight hours, the epicenter of gay Manuel Antonio is the famous La Playita, a beach with a long history of nude sunbathing for gay men. Alas, the days when you could sun in the buff are gone, but the end of La Playita is still widely regarded as a playful pickup spot.

◉ Sights

La Playita
BEACH
At the far western end of Playa Espadilla, beyond a rocky headland (wear sandals), this former nude beach remains one of Costa Rica's most famous gay beaches and a particular draw for young men. The beach is inaccessible around high tide, so time your walk, or access it via the ultra-luxury Arenas del Mar (p380) hotel.

Greentique
Wildlife Refuge
WILDLIFE RESERVE
(☑2777-0850; www.greentiquehotels.com/nature -reserves/#wlr; Ruta Nacional 618; 1hr tours adult/ child US$25/15, 2hr tours adult/child US$35/25, 2hr night tour adult/child US$39/29; ☺day tours 8am-4pm, night tours 5:30pm-7:30pm; 🚶) Biologist Jimmy Mata leads magical one- and two-hour sojourns through the Butterfly Atrium, Reptile & Amphibian Water Gardens and Crocodile Lagoon, as well as a night tour, in this 12-acre haven of second-growth Pacific coast wet forest. Sloths, monkeys, baby crocodiles, armadillos and coatis are among the creatures you might see from the forest floor to the dripping canopy. Across from Sí Como No Resort (p381).

🏃 Activities

Manuel Antonio Surf School
SURFING
(MASS; ☑2777-4842, 2777-1955; www.manuel antoniosurfschool.com; Ruta Nacional 618; 1hr lesson US$30, 3hr lesson group/private US$70/95, surf tour incl lunch & waterfall US$89) MASS offers friendly, safe and fun small-group surfing lessons daily, lasting for three hours and with a three-to-one student–instructor ratio. Find its stand about 500m up the Manuel Antonio road south of Quepos.

Zip Coaster
ZIPLINING
(☑4000-1379; Hwy 618; US$12; ☺9am-5pm) This rollercoaster zipline dives through the jungle off the side of the main road through town. There's also a canopy bike that you sit in and slowly (and loudly) throttle your way through the canopy on a 500m loop. Lucky riders will get up close to the monkeys (if you've not scared them away with your motor). South of El Avion (p383).

➸ Courses

Mamá Cacao
FOOD
(☑8383-5910; thechocolatemakingworkshopma@ gmail.com; per person US$40, min 3 participants) Manuel Antonio chocolate maker Mamá

Cacao runs this traveling chocolate-making workshop in Manuel Antonio hotels and around the Pacific coast using beans she's gathered up from local farms. The workshop lasts two hours, during which guests prepare their own vegan and dairy truffles, sample homemade chocolates and discuss the history and nutritional value of cacao. Discounts available for larger groups.

☞ Tours

Amigos del Río
ADVENTURE
(☑2777-0082; www.adradventurepark.com; Ruta Nacional 618; '10-in-One Adventure' US$139, rafting from US$70, kayaking from US$69) Pack all of your canopy-tour jungle fantasies into one day on Amigos del Río's '10-in-One Adventure,' featuring ziplining, a Tarzan swing, rappelling down a waterfall and more. The seven-hour adventure tour includes a free transfer from the Quepos and Manuel Antonio area as well as breakfast and lunch. Amigos del Río is also a reliable outfit for kayaking and white-water-rafting trips.

🛌 Sleeping

Hostel Plinio and
Bed & Breakfast
HOSTEL $
(☑2777-6123; www.pliniocr.com; Ruta Nacional 618; dm/s/d from US$12/30/60; 🅿❄🛜❄) From afar, Hostel Plinio feels like a giant treehouse surrounded by jungle. This backpacker haven is in a convenient location near Quepos and has a large pool, common areas with hammocks and sofas for socializing, an efficient tour desk, plus dorms and rooms with jungle views. Mosquito nets in place of glass mean rooms facing the roadside can be noisy.

Vista Serena Hostel
HOSTEL $
(☑2777-5162; www.vistaserena.com; Ruta Nacional 618; dm US$10-18, bungalows with/without air-con US$60/50; 🅿@🛜) Perched on a seriously scenic hillside, this memorable, quiet hostel has spectacular ocean and sunset views from its hammock-filled terrace. Rustic accommodations range from spartan econodorms and plusher dorms to bungalows for those who want a bit more privacy. Guests can use a kitchen. Rates fluctuate depending on occupancy. For breakfast, tea, coffee, toast and jam are complimentary.

Hostel Manuel Antonio
HOTEL $
(☑2777-2507; www.hostelmanuelantonio.com; Ruta Nacional 618; dm US$10-15, d US$24-36; 🅿❄

) Off the main drag on the ocean side, this hostel's entrance is hidden next to a corrugated-iron fence. Don't let first impressions dissuade you: once you're in, the atmosphere is friendly and views are staggering, with a pool overlooking the jungle and the ocean. Rooms are small, basic and clean with tiled floors. Privates come with or without bathroom and air-con.

★Selina Manuel Antonio HOSTEL **$$**
(www.selina.com/manuel-antonio; Ruta Nacional 618; dm US$20-25, r US$76-202;) Part of the Selina empire of dozens of hostels across Central America, this place is already a legend. Check in at the VW campervan desk, then find your dorm or private room scattered among rainforested cliffs in elegant white buildings livened up with rotating art exhibits. The bar has become the area's best nightlife spot.

There's frequent live music from some of the hottest local talent, plus happy hour from 5pm to 7pm (with two-for-one deals on classic drinks). Plus there are two pools, sweet views and a good restaurant.

Hotel Mimos HOTEL **$$**
(2777-0054; www.mimoshotel.com; Ruta Nacional 618; d from US$55;) Run by kind and attentive staff, this hotel has rooms of various styles and configurations. The nicest are newer with graphite designs; older, more dated rooms have tiled floors and wacky wood designs. The property has lovely stone paths, bringing guests to two palm-fringed swimming pools and a hot tub (though the water is not kept hot).

Hotel Mono Azul HOTEL **$$**
(2777-2572; www.hotelmonoazul.com; Ruta Nacional 618; s from US$45, d US$68-147;) The Mono Azul is decent value and a good family option. Nestled in a tropical garden and decorated throughout in a rainforest theme, rooms are arranged around two pools. Nicer rooms include a TV, air-con units and murals. Double rooms come with two big beds. We love the bamboo memory-foam pillows.

The restaurant serves comfort food like pizzas, fish and chips and house-made meatloaf. Conveniently, the bus to Parque Nacional Manuel Antonio stops right outside the hotel and leaves every 30 minutes between 6am and 6pm.

★Gaia Hotel & Nature Reserve BOUTIQUE HOTEL **$$$**
(2777-9797, in USA 800-226-2515; www.gaiahr.com; Ruta Nacional 618; studios from US$305;) This luxurious retreat comprises immaculately furnished studios, terrace suites and three-story villas. It offers free nature tours for guests within its expansive tropical grounds, a former wildlife rehabilitation center where scarlet macaws are being reintroduced through a hotel program. The restaurant, La Luna, is one of the best in the region and uses fresh local produce. Adults only.

Guests are golf-buggied around the reserve on the small jungle-lined paths. Escapism and relaxation are greatly aided by the cascading pools and spa treatments. Bonus: you get a welcome cocktail and a US$20 spa voucher with your room (guests staying longer than three nights get a free 20-minute treatment). There are free shuttles to Parque Nacional Manuel Antonio for guests and a delicious breakfast.

★Hotel Villa Roca BOUTIQUE HOTEL **$$$**
(2777-1349; www.villaroca.com; Ruta Nacional 618; r/apt incl breakfast from $187/305;) The gay owners of this intimate hotel cater to many of Manuel Antonio's LGBTIQ+ travelers; it's particularly popular with men. The upstairs rooms are breezier. All guests and visitors must be 18 years or older. You can sun your buns around the beautiful, clothing-optional, 24-hour pool and hot tubs, where you may be joined by a couple of resident iguanas.

The 12 rooms are white, airy and tiled with blue splashes of color. Four apartments sleep up to four people. They're centered around a rainforest garden with exotic plants and wildlife, and sit on a hillside with an infinity pool and 180-degree views of the ocean. At the time of research, a new owner had just taken over, who is set to keep the current vibe and clientele of the hotel but also add improvements.

Manuel Antonio has always been open-minded when it comes to same-sex couples and the hotel has hosted same-sex marriages since 2020.

★Arenas del Mar BOUTIQUE HOTEL **$$$**
(4040-0422; www.arenasdelmar.com; r incl breakfast US$497-1130;) This visually arresting hotel and resort complex is consistently shortlisted among Costa Rica's

finest upscale hotels. The earthy, luxury rooms with large rain showers have been designed to incorporate the beauty of the natural landscape to great effect, especially when you're staring down the coastline from the lofty balcony of your sumptuous digs. The top-tier accommodations feature ocean-view Jacuzzis.

The golf car service whizzes guests around the property and to a 'private' beach (only accessible to the public when the tide is out). A dreamy pool overlooks the ocean. Boons include roaming wildlife, and nature-spotters can enjoy the property's short 10-minute trail into the surrounding jungle. Expertly prepared dishes and seafood can be sampled at the large tiki-thatched Mirador restaurant, also with great views and an inviting pool. Happy hour at the bar runs from 5:30pm to 7pm, with US$6 cocktails and vino.

Makanda by the Sea VILLA **$$$**
(2777-1032, 2777-0442; www.makanda.com; studio/villa incl breakfast from US$391/632; P ❄ 📶 ≋) A 2017 face-lift elevated this already spectacular property to a veritable Shangri-la, featuring uniquely glamorous design elements, beautifully textured surfaces and hangout spaces that simply drip with style. Makanda comprises six villas, four studios, a suite, and a smattering of ocean-view hotel rooms, all perched in a stellar bluff-top location with an unmatched air of intimacy and privacy.

Villa 6 (with its 4m-deep private pool) will take your breath away, and Villa 1 has an entire wall open to the rainforest and the ocean. The other villas and studios are air-conditioned and enclosed, though they draw upon the same Eastern-infused design schemes.

The grounds are also home to two saltwater infinity pools, two Jacuzzis, a gastronomic restaurant that uses seasonal products from Central Pacific farmers and fishers, and the Shanti Spa. If somehow you're still not impressed, you can access a private beach by taking either a golf cart or walking a few hundred steps down the side of the mountain – bliss! Note that guests must be 16 years or older.

Hotel Sí Como No HOTEL **$$$**
(2777-0777; www.sicomono.com; Ruta Nacional 618; r US$276-497, child under 6yr free; P ❄ 📶 ≋) This flawlessly designed 10-acre hotel is an example of how to build an ecofriendly resort. The 58 rooms are built into the jungle hillside and accented by rich woods and bold splashes of tropical colors. They come with balconies offering magnificent views across the jungle and ocean. All guests get free shuttles to Parque Nacional Manuel Antonio and the beach.

The hotel has two pools, one with a waterslide for kids and one for adults only; both have swim-up bars. There are also two Jacuzzis, a superb health spa and two excellent restaurants, each with a barefoot luxury vibe and serving fresh, locally sourced artisan food. There's a butterfly garden, a **cinema** (screenings 5pm & 8pm) and **spa** (treatments US$40-147; 10am-7pm).

Sustainable construction and practices include energy-efficient air-con units, recycling water for landscaping use, solar-powered water heaters, and biodegradable cleaning and laundry products. No surprise, then, that Sí Como No is one of a few dozen hotels in the country to have been awarded five out of five leaves by the government-run Certified Sustainable Tourism (CST) campaign.

Hotel Costa Verde HOTEL **$$$**
(2777-0187, 2777-0584; www.costaverde.com; Ruta Nacional 618; efficiency units/studios from US$160/200, Boeing 727 home US$593, cockpit cottage US$290; P ❄ @ 📶 ≋) This collection of rooms and studios occupies a verdant setting frequented by troops of monkeys. Efficiency units incorporating teak trim and furnishings face the encroaching forest, while more expensive studios have full ocean views. FYI: the cheapest units are near the road! The most coveted and spectacular accommodations are inside a

GOT KIDS?

The Quepos to Manuel Antonio stretch of road is home to the lion's share of accommodations and restaurants in these parts, but it's worth pointing out that many of the high-end boutique hotels and upscale eateries are not always very welcoming to babies and young children, so check your accommodation's policy.

If you find yourself walking along the narrow, winding road (there is no shoulder), keep a close eye on your children at all times.

decommissioned Boeing 727 fuselage and in a cockpit cottage.

The 727, which juts out of the jungle in the most surreal way, has two bedrooms with three queen-sized beds, two bathrooms, a kitchenette and a private terrace. The cockpit cottage is accessed by a suspension bridge and sleeps two, with panoramic ocean views and a bathroom open to the jungle. (It's popular with honeymooners.)

The owners of Costa Verde are also the masterminds behind several eateries along the road to Manuel Antonio, including El Avión bar and restaurant (also fashioned from a retired fuselage).

Eating

Falafel Bar MEDITERRANEAN $

(2777-4135; Ruta Nacional 618; mains US$6.50-12.50; 11am-8pm Tue-Sun;) Adding to the diversity of cuisine along the road, this falafel spot dishes up authentic Middle Eastern favorites. You'll also find plenty of vegetarian options, including couscous and fresh salads, stuffed grape leaves, fab fruit smoothies and even French fries for the picky ones. For the meat-eaters there are shawarmas and schnitzels. Yum.

★Café Milagro FUSION $$

(2777-2272; www.cafemilagro.com; Ruta Nacional 618; mains from US$7; 7am-9pm) This is a fine stop for fancy coffee drinks and a satisfying full breakfast, lunch or dinner (eggs, quesadillas, sandwiches, salads and Tico plates), and there are plenty of vegan and veggie options on the menu. You can enjoy your food on the patio surrounded by tropical gardens or order a sandwich for the park. Live music every night (7:30pm to 9:30pm).

Samui Thai THAI $$

(2101-7058; www.facebook.com/samuicr; Ruta Nacional 618; mains US$10-13; 12:30-9:30pm) This cute wood-decked corner restaurant with jungle and ocean views does Thai classics well, from the zingy salads to the satay or tom yum soup. House main specialties include tasty crispy ginger fish and tastebud-tingling volcano chicken (half a chicken marinated in herbs and spices).

Happy hour runs from 2pm to 6pm with two-for-one offers on cocktails and three-for-two on draft beers.

Agua Azul INTERNATIONAL $$

(2777-5280; www.cafeaguaazul.com; Ruta Nacional 618; breakfast from US$5, lunch mains US$9-24; 11am-10pm Thu-Tue;) Perched on the 2nd floor with uninterrupted ocean views, Agua Azul is a marvelous casual lunch spot on this stretch of road – perfect for early-morning park visitors who are heading back to their hotel. The breezy, unpretentious open-air restaurant, renowned for its 'big-ass burger,' also serves up the likes of fajitas, panko-crusted tuna and a tasty fish salad.

Barba Roja Restaurant SEAFOOD $$

(2777-0331; www.barbarojarestaurante.com; Ruta Nacional 618; mains US$12-28; 6:30am-10pm Tue-Sun) A Manuel Antonio area institution, the Barba Roja is both a lively pirate-themed bar and a seafood-and-steak spot with a respectable menu (try the coconut shrimp with mango or smoked meats). The terrace affords fantastic ocean views, best enjoyed with a local craft brew (from US$6), 'loco mojito' or sangria.

★La Luna INTERNATIONAL $$$

(2777-9797; www.gaiahr.com; Gaia Hotel; mains US$13-39; 6am-11pm;) Unpretentious and friendly La Luna, inside the five-star Gaia Hotel, makes a lovely spot for a special-occasion dinner or sundowner, with fabulous martinis and a spectacular backdrop of jungle and ocean. An international menu offers everything from plantain and coconut-crusted mahi-mahi to grilled ginger chicken, and jumbo shrimp with tagliatelle. Separate vegetarian and vegan menu available.

Claro Que Sí SEAFOOD $$$

(2777-0777; www.sicomono.com/dining; Hotel Sí Como No; salads from US$8, mains US$18-39; noon-10pm;) A family-friendly restaurant that manages to tread the line between upscale and casual, Claro Que Sí proudly serves organic and locally sourced food items that are in line with the philosophy of its parent hotel, Sí Como No (p381). Sustainably sourced meats and fish are expertly complemented with fresh produce, resulting in flavorful dishes typical of both the Pacific and Caribbean coasts.

Dishes range from the fresh catch of the day to range-grown chicken and fresh homemade pasta. There's a separate kids' menu. Live music takes place between 6pm and 9pm on some evenings. Hotel nonguests must spend a minimum of US$10; after doing so ask your waiter for a free 'cine-pass' for the cinema (p381) next door.

Drinking & Nightlife

Karma Lounge GAY & LESBIAN

(☎2777-7230; www.facebook.com/karmaloungema; off Ruta National 618; ⊙8pm-2:30am Fri & Sat, until 1am Sun) Popular gay mingling spot, which is straight-friendly. Usually plays pop, disco and dance music.

El Avión BAR

(☎2183-7953, 2777-3378; www.elavion.net; Ruta Nacional 618; ⊙noon-10pm; ⓦ) Constructed around a 1954 Fairchild C-123 plane (allegedly purchased by the US government in the '80s for the Nicaraguan Contras but never used), this striking bar-restaurant is a great spot for a beer, cocktail or wine and stellar sunset-watching. The Tico and international menu is overpriced, and the service could be improved, but you can't beat the setting.

In 2000 the enterprising owners of El Avión purchased the plane for the surprisingly reasonable sum of US$3000 (it never made it out of its hangar in San José because of the Iran–Contra scandal that embroiled Oliver North and his cohorts), and proceeded to cart it piece by piece to Manuel Antonio. It now sits on the side of the main road, where it looks as if it crash-landed into the side of the hill.

Ronny's Place BAR

(☎2777-5120; www.ronnysplace.com; ⊙noon-10pm) The insane views of two pristine bays and jungle on all sides at Ronny's Place make it worth a detour for a drink and a tasty meal (mains US$14-70). While plenty of places along this stretch of road boast similar views, the off-the-beaten-path location makes it feel like a secret find. Look for the well-marked dirt road off the main drag.

There's a long cocktail list of around two-dozen favorites, plus imported beers. Order special mains like coconut breaded shrimp, whole red snapper or a seafood platter for two with lobster, tuna, mahi-mahi and calamari with garlic sauce. The stone tables out front are the best for sunset viewing.

Z Poolside Bistro BAR

(☎2777-6948; Ruta Nacional 618; ⊙7am-10pm) With one of the longest happy hours in town (noon to 6pm), Z Poolside Bistro is a mellow afternoon drinking spot. Centered around a big pool, you can catch some rays and take a dip while sipping on cocktails. On Sunday evenings (5pm to 9pm), it's more of a party scene: a DJ plays and deals mean drinks are flowing.

On Sundays get two-for-one margaritas, sangria and daiquiris, 40% off champagne, and US$3 craft beers. There's also a full menu of poolside mains like burgers, grilled meats and snacks.

Shopping

Organic Market FOOD & DRINKS

(☎2101-0166; Ruta Nacional 618; ⊙7am-9pm) It's pricey and geared towards monied tourists, but the products are top quality. Stock up on local chocolate and all manner of local and imported organic goodies, from ice cream and skin products to coffee, chocolate, craft beers, wine and general groceries.

Getting There & Away

Every 30 minutes or so local buses and shared taxis connect Quepos with Manuel Antonio (20 minutes). The public bus from Quepos will let you off anywhere along the road.

A word of caution: driver visibility is limited along parts of the narrow, steep and winding road, particularly during low-light and foul-weather conditions.

Manuel Antonio Village

As you travel the road between Quepos and Parque Nacional Manuel Antonio, the din from roaring buses, packs of tourists and locals hunting foreign dollars becomes increasingly loud, reaching its somewhat chaotic climax at Manuel Antonio village. Hordes descend on this tiny oceanside village at the entrance to the country's most visited national park. Don't show up all bright-eyed and bushy tailed, expecting deserted beaches and untouched tropical paradise. Higher primates tend to be the most frequently sighted species, especially during the congested dry season, when tour groups arrive en masse.

But come here in low season or on a Monday (when the park is closed), and you'll find a tranquil little village with waves sedately lapping at the white sand. And when troops of monkeys climb down from the forest canopy to the tropical sands, you can get up close and personal with some marvelous wildlife.

Manuel Antonio Area

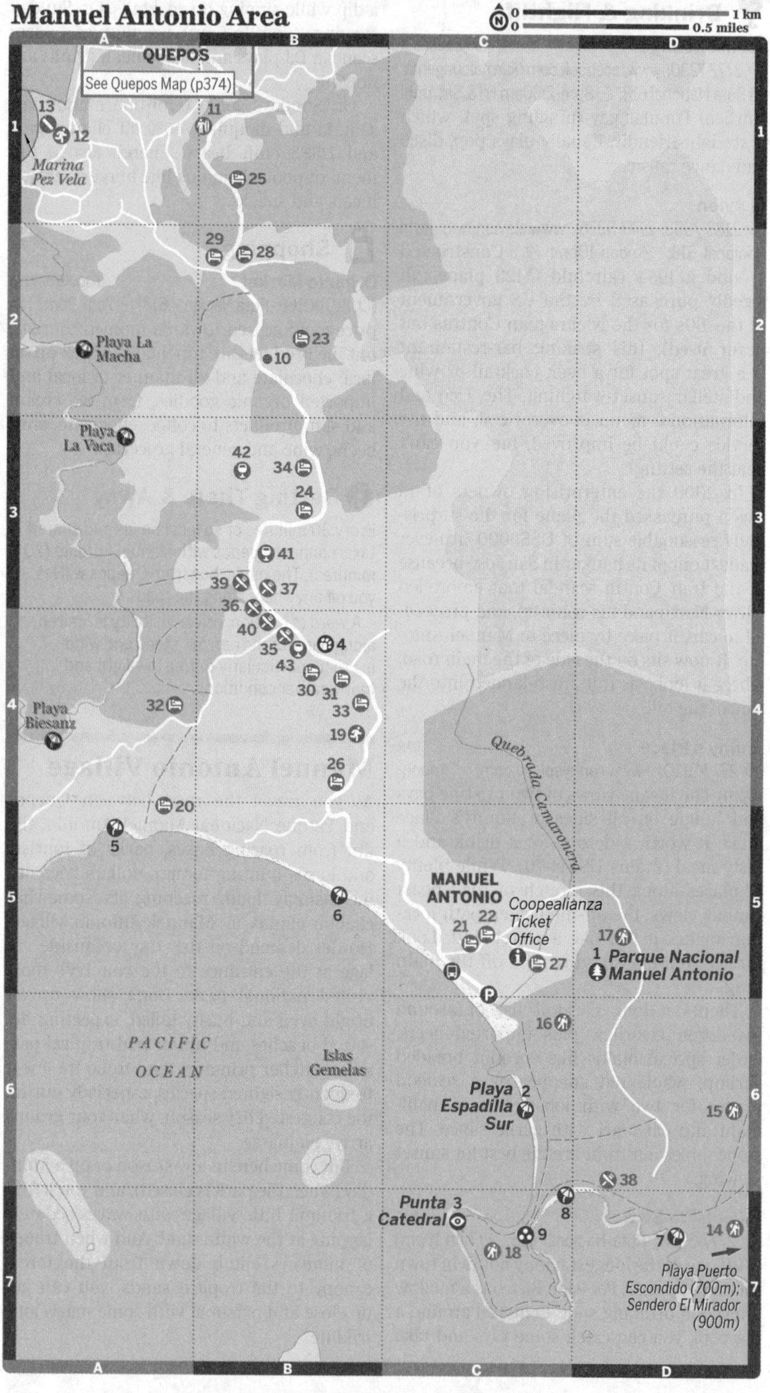

Manuel Antonio Area

Top Sights
1 Parque Nacional Manuel Antonio D5
2 Playa Espadilla Sur C6
3 Punta Catedral........C7

Sights
4 Greentique Wildlife Refuge B4
5 La Playita........A5
6 Playa Espadilla........B5
7 Playa Gemelas........D7
8 Playa Manuel Antonio........C7
9 Turtle Trap C7

Activities, Courses & Tours
10 Amigos del Río........B2
Cala Spa ....(see 30)
11 Manuel Antonio Surf School........B1
12 Marina Pez Vela........A1
13 Oceans Unlimited........A1
14 Sendero El Escondido D7
15 Sendero El Mirador D6
16 Sendero El Perezoso C6
17 Sendero La Catarata D5
Sendero Playa Gemelas ....(see 7)
18 Sendero Punta Catedral........C7
19 Zip Coaster........B4

Sleeping
20 Arenas del Mar A5
21 Art Hostel Costa Linda C5
22 Cabinas & Hotel Playa Espadilla C5
23 Gaia Hotel & Nature Reserve........B2
24 Hostel Manuel Antonio........B3
25 Hostel Plinio and Bed & Breakfast........B1
26 Hotel Costa Verde........B4
27 Hotel La Posada........C5
28 Hotel Mimos B2
29 Hotel Mono Azul........B2
30 Hotel Sí Como No B4
Hotel Vela........(see 22)
31 Hotel Villa Roca B4
32 Makanda by the Sea........A4
33 Selina Manuel Antonio B4
34 Vista Serena Hostel........B3

Eating
35 Agua Azul B4
36 Barba Roja Restaurant........B3
37 Café Milagro B3
Claro Que Sí........(see 30)
38 Coffee Shop........D6
39 Falafel Bar B3
Gabriella's........(see 13)
La Luna........(see 23)
Pesca Seafood ....(see 13)
Runaway Grill ....(see 13)
40 Samui Thai........B4
Sunrice ....(see 13)

Drinking & Nightlife
El Avión........(see 31)
41 Karma Lounge........B3
42 Ronny's Place........B3
43 Z Poolside Bistro........B4

Entertainment
Sí Como No Cinema ....(see 30)

Shopping
Organic Market ....(see 37)

Activities

Surfboards (in rainy season), body boards and kayaks can be rented all along the beach at Playa Espadilla. Paragliding, white-water rafting and sea kayaking are also popular in this area.

Sleeping

Art Hostel Costa Linda HOSTEL $
(☎2777-0304; www.arthostel-cr.com; r per person from US$12; P❄@🛜) You can't beat the prices here when you can amble out to the beach or the national park in five minutes. While the staff are a bit harried, and the shared bathrooms could be cleaner, the cocktail and beer prices are easy on the wallet and the tropically painted digs are jovial.

A big breakfast of fruit, pancakes, *pinto*, eggs, bread and coffee is a mere US$5.

★Hotel Vela HOTEL $$$
(☎2777-0413; www.velabar.com; d US$130-175, ste US$225; P❄@🛜🏊) This attractive little adults-only hotel offers light, bright, spacious and contemporary rooms and suites, set around an oval pool and overlooking lush gardens. It's one of the most polished places to stay right next to the park, which is two minutes away. Room amenities are plentiful, including Egyptian-cotton sheets, a coffee machine, safe, hairdryer, minibar, air-con and TV. The breakfast buffet is very satisfying.

Hotel La Posada BUNGALOW $$$
(☎2777-1446; www.laposadajungle.com; ste US$140-170, r US$140-240; P❄🛜🏊) These secluded jungle bungalows and fully equipped apartments (sleeping four to five guests) all come with kitchenette, TV with DVD player, safe and terrace, and are clustered around a small pool. But the real beauty of staying here is the location right next to the park – from your lodgings you'll see squirrel monkeys and other wildlife crisscrossing the trees and rooftops.

Cabinas & Hotel
Playa Espadilla HOTEL $$$
(☑ cabinas 2777-0416, hotel 2777-0903; www.
espadilla.com; d from US$220; P ❄ 🛜 🏊) Two
favorably located properties in one: the
hotel has a smallish swimming pool and
tennis courts, and the more affordable *ca-
binas* across the road are slightly closer to
the beach. Rooms include air-con, TV, re-
frigerator, and a hairdryer. Some units have
been recently renovated and both properties
have extremely convenient park and beach
access.

❶ Getting There & Away

BUS

The **bus stop** (Ruta Nacional 618) in Manuel
Antonio is at the end of the road into the village
that runs along the beach. Buses depart Manuel
Antonio beach direct for San José (US$9, 3½
hours) nine times daily between 4am and 5pm.
Buy tickets well in advance at the Quepos bus
terminal (p378).

Buses for destinations other than San José
leave from the main terminal in Quepos.

Local buses (less than US$1, 20 minutes,
every 30 minutes) and shared taxis connect
Manuel Antonio village with Quepos.

CAR & MOTORCYCLE

Driving the winding 7km road between Quepos
and Manuel Antonio village often means spend-
ing time in traffic jams and paying for parking
(from US$4 to US$20; negotiate for a better
price) near the park. Leave at the crack of dawn
for a quieter drive and your pick of parking spac-
es right outside the park.

Parque Nacional
Manuel Antonio

A place of swaying palms and playful mon-
keys, thick unspoiled forest, sparkling blue
water and a riot of tropical birds, **Parque
Nacional Manuel Antonio** (☑ 2777-8551;
US$16; ⏱ 7am-3:30pm Tue-Sun) is the country's
smallest and most popular national park. It
became a protected area in 1972, preserv-
ing it from being razed to make room for
a coastal development project. It's a truly
lovely place; the clearly marked trail system
winds through rainforest-backed white-sand
beaches and rocky headlands, the wildlife
(iguanas, sloths, monkeys) is plentiful, and
the views across the bay to the pristine outer
islands are gorgeous.

Get here early (7am) and head for the
furthest reaches of the park for a bit of
tranquillity and the best chances to spot
wildlife.

◉ Sights

There are several beautiful beaches – two of
which are just outside the entrance. There's
Playa Espadilla (outside the park), Playa
Espadilla Sur, Playa Manuel Antonio, Pla-
ya Puerto Escondido, Playa Gemelas, and
Playa Playitas (outside the park). They're
all equally pristine and provide sunbath-
ing opportunities; check conditions with
the rangers to see which ones are safe for
swimming.

Rangers indefinitely closed Playa Puerto
Escondido to visitors in 2017, but its beauty
can still be admired from a lookout point at
the end of the short 350m Puerto Escondido
trail.

★ Punta Catedral AREA
Geography fun fact: this isthmus, which is
the centerpiece of the park, is called a tom-
bolo and was formed by the accumulation of
sand between the mainland and the penin-
sula beyond, which was once an island. At
its end, the isthmus widens into a rocky pen-
insula, with thick forest in the middle, encir-
cled by Sendero Punta Catedral. There are
good views of the Pacific Ocean and various
rocky islets – nesting sites for brown boobies
and pelicans.

★ Playa Espadilla Sur BEACH
A half-hour hike from the park entrance,
the exposed Playa Espadilla Sur is to the
north of Punta Catedral and gorgeous with
pinch-me scenes of white sand backed by
lush tropical forest. As tempted as you may
be, swimming here can be dangerous – be
aware of currents. There's drinking water,
bathrooms and showers in the middle of the
beach.

Playa Manuel Antonio BEACH
With its turquoise waters, this lovely forest-
backed beach fronts a deep bay, sheltered
by the Punta Catedral on the west side and
a promontory on the east. Families love to
watch the monkeys playing in the trees be-
hind the beach; ropes have been set up for
them to walk on. This is the best beach for
swimming.

Playa Espadilla BEACH
(off Ruta Nacional 618) This wide stretch of white sand is found just outside the park entrance, in front of Manuel Antonio village. It's a popular place for families and beach activities like parasailing. There's surfboard rental here (from US$10 per day), though waves tend to be smaller than other spots nearby (the breaks work in the winter months, not in the summer).

Playa Gemelas BEACH
Clasped by volcanic rock and jungle, Playa Gemelas is smaller than the other beaches, but no less spectacular: this place could be a desert island beach from the movies. If you find it early in the morning it will likely be empty. It's a special place and feels almost like it's been forgotten in time. Watch your footing as you wander, iguanas like to bask in the sun here. Access via Sendero Playa Gemelas (p388).

Turtle Trap ARCHAEOLOGICAL SITE
At the western end of Playa Manuel Antonio you can see a semicircle of rocks at low tide. Archaeologists believe that these were arranged by pre-Columbian indigenous people to function as a turtle trap. (Turtles would swim in during high tide, but when they tried to swim out after the tide started receding, they'd be trapped by the wall.)

Activities

The average daily temperature is 27°C (80°F) and average annual rainfall is 3875mm. The dry season is not entirely dry, merely less wet, so you should be prepared for rain (although it can also be dry for days on end). Make sure you carry plenty of drinking water, sun protection and insect repellent.

Hiking

★Sendero Punta Catedral HIKING
This moderate up-and-down trail along a 1.4km loop first goes over a natural bridge between Playa Manuel Antonio and Playa Espadilla Sur, then into dense vegetation via concrete and gravel steps and low wooden walkways. There are a few stops at viewpoint platforms with glorious scenes of the Pacific and the offshore islands where frigate birds nest.

This is a whale-crossing area, so keep your eyes peeled during migration season (August to October) when they make their annual journey from Alaska to Costa Rica.

Sendero El Mirador HIKING
Heading inland and into the jungle from the east side of Playa Manuel Antonio, this primary forest and step-filled 1.3km trail will get your heart racing as you take a moderate climb to a wooden viewpoint platform on a bluff overlooking Puerto Escondido and Punta Serrucho beyond. The vista is simply stunning. Humpback whales can occasionally be spotted in these waters.

Punta Serrucho (or Saw Point), was named for its serrated edge, created due to the fact it sits right on a tectonic fault line.

Sendero El Perezoso HIKING
The main trail (1.3km) that connects the park entrance with the other trails. It's flat,

MONKEY BUSINESS

Your bag will be searched for snacks upon entering Parque Nacional Manuel Antonio – cigarettes, chips, junk food, alcohol, nuts, seeds and cans are prohibited. Water and soft drinks in reusable bottles, packed sandwiches and ready-cut fruit are allowed. There is now a **cafe** (www.sinac.go.cr; intersection of Playa Gemelas and Puerto Escondido; pastries from US$3, sandwiches US$8, ice cream US$6; ⏲7am-4pm) inside the park serving refreshments and hot foods. However, do not even think about feeding any food scraps to the monkeys, as this risks their health and negatively impacts the monkey population in the following ways:

- Monkeys are susceptible to bacteria transmitted by human hands.
- Irregular feeding will lead to aggressive behavior as well as create a dangerous dependency.
- Bananas are not their preferred food, and can cause serious digestive problems.
- Increased exposure to humans facilitates illegal poaching as well as attacks from dogs.

If you do happen to see someone feeding the monkeys, take the initiative and ask them politely to stop.

WORTH A TRIP

RAFIKI SAFARI LODGE

The expat owners of **Rafiki Safari Lodge** (☑8419-6832, 8583-5104; www.rafikisafari.com; r incl all meals per person for 1/2/3/4 persons from US$285/180/145/127.50; ⓟ @ 🛜 🆑) have combined all the comforts of a hotel with the splendor of a jungle safari in a prime spot right by the Río Savegre, with several luxury tents equipped with beds, bathroom, hot water, private porch and hydroelectric power. Kids will love the spring-fed pool and waterslide. Activities include horseback riding, birdwatching, hiking and white-water rafting.

All units are screened in, which allows you to see and hear the rainforest without actually having creepy-crawlies in your bed.

The owners are also masters on the *braai* (South African for BBQ), so you know that you'll eat well alongside other guests in the *rancho*-style restaurant. It's too remote to warrant the transport for only one night, but three days is perfect to exhaust all the activities on offer.

The entrance to the lodge is about 15km south of Quepos on Hwy 34, and the turnoff is just south of a bridge. From here, a dirt road (4WD necessary) parallels the Río Savegre and leads 16km inland, past the towns of Silencio and Santo Domingo, to the lodge. If you don't have private transportation, the lodge can arrange all of your transfers with advance reservations.

paved and wheelchair accessible. A vehicle evacuation access trail runs parallel. Along both you'll find numerous tour groups trying to spot birds and sloths through their guides' telescopes.

The numerous guides along this stretch can provide lessons on the many birds, sloths and monkeys along the way.

Sendero La Catarata HIKING
Just beyond the park entrance, on the left, this 900m trail branches off Sendero El Perezoso and leads to a little waterfall – during the summer months (December to March) it's just a trickle. Visit after the rainy season (June to November). However, there are more impressive waterfalls to be seen on day trips from the Parque Nacional Manuel Antonio area.

Sendero El Escondido HIKING
Accessed via Sendero Playas Gemelas, this moderate quarter-mile descent down wooden steps leads to a viewing platform overlooking Playa Escondido. The beach is off-limits, but the view is lovely. At low tide it is possible to spy the sand bridge that connects to the continental coast.

Sendero Playa Gemelas HIKING
This quarter-mile walk connecting to Sendero Los Congos and Sendero El Mirador leads to a glorious, less-trafficked and almost secret beach. If you arrive at the park early, come here first and you'll likely have the place to yourself.

Wildlife-Watching
Though visitors are funneled along the main access road, you should have no problem seeing animals here, even as you line up at the gate. White-faced capuchins are very used to people, and normally troops feed and interact within a short distance of visitors; they can be encountered anywhere along the main access road and around Playa Manuel Antonio. The capuchins are the worst culprits for snatching bags, so watch your stuff. It's less likely if you have no food or scented products in your bag.

You'll probably also hear mantled howler monkeys soon after sunrise. Like capuchins, they can be seen virtually anywhere inside the park and even along the road to Quepos – watch for them crossing the monkey bridges (like those at Playa Manuel Antonio) that were erected by local conservation groups.

Coatis can be seen darting across various paths and can get aggressive on the beach if you're eating. Three-toed and two-toed sloths are also common in the park. Guides are extremely helpful in spotting sloths, as they tend not to move around all that much.

However, the movements of the park's star animal and Central America's rarest primate, namely the Central American squirrel monkey, are far less predictable. These adorable monkeys are more retiring than capuchins, and though they are occasionally seen near the park entrance in the early morning, they usually melt into the forest well before opening time. With luck, however, a troop could be encountered during a morning walk, and they often reappear in beachside trees and on the fringes of Manuel Antonio village in the early evening.

Offshore, keep your eyes peeled for pantropical spotted and bottlenose dolphins, as well as humpback whales passing by on their regular migration routes. Other possibilities include orcas (killer whales), false killers and rough-toothed dolphins.

Big lizards are also a featured sighting at Manuel Antonio – it's hard to miss the large spiny-tailed and green iguanas that bask along the beach at Playa Manuel Antonio and in the vegetation behind Playa Espadilla Sur. To spot the well-camouflaged basilisk, listen for the rustle of leaves along the edges of the trails, especially near the lagoon.

Manuel Antonio is not usually on the serious birdwatchers' trail of Costa Rica, though the list of birds here is respectable. The usual suspects include the blue-gray and palm tanagers, great-tailed grackles, bananaquits, blue dacnises and at least 15 species of hummingbird. Among the regional endemics you should look out for are the fiery-billed aracaris, black-hooded antshrikes, Baird's trogons, black-bellied whistling ducks, yellow-crowned night herons, brown pelicans, magnificent frigate birds, brown boobies, spotted sandpipers, green herons and ringed kingfishers.

Tours

Group tours with a wildlife guide can be booked online ahead of your visit from many tour companies. Tours usually include entry to the park, transport and water. 'Guides' outside the park also hover around, looking official in ranger-like uniforms. They can be a nuisance and often stand in the road beckoning drivers into their parking areas and trying to charge exorbitant rates to 'look after your car' and for their 'guiding services'. Don't feel intimidated, simply drive past them and up to the entrance to the park for a shorter walk to the gates. If you do go for a guide outside the park, you should be paying roughly US$15 to US$25 per person (two-person minimum; more people and some negotiating ensures a better price; park entrance fee not included) for a two-hour tour. Many, though, are simply charging money for the privilege of looking through their telescope – don't expect detailed knowledge of the park's wildlife.

That said, some freelance guides are excellent and are able to spot animals and birds and explain their role in the park's ecosystem. Opt for recommended guides such as **Lenny Montenegro** (☎8875-0437; 2hr group/private tour per person from US$25/40), or else ask to see the guide's Costa Rican Tourism Board (ICT) license to be sure that they're the real deal.

We can testify to the fact that hiring a good guide dramatically improves your chances of wildlife sightings and lets you see animals and birds that you most likely would not have spotted by yourself.

Information

The park **ticket office** (; ☎2785-3000, 2777-6208; park entrance US$16; ⏲7am-3:30pm) is in Manuel Antonio village, a few hundred meters before the park entrance. The ranger station is just before Playa Manuel Antonio.

SAFE TRAVEL

Watch out for the manzanillo tree *(Hippomane mancinella)* – it has poisonous fruits that look like little crab apples, and the sap exuded by the bark and leaves is toxic, causing the skin to itch and burn. Warning signs are prominently displayed beside examples of this tree near the park entrance. Stay on the trails and don't touch the wildlife – poisonous frogs, deadly snakes, predatory arachnids and more can be found in the undergrowth.

Getting There & Away

BUS

The entrance and exit to Parque Nacional Manuel Antonio lies in Manuel Antonio village, connected to Quepos by frequent daily buses (20 minutes, every 30 minutes). Direct buses also depart for San José (US$9, 3½ hours) nine times daily between 4am and 5pm; some stop in Quepos, some don't.

CAR

Note that the road to Manuel Antonio is very narrow and congested, so it's recommended that you leave your car at your hotel and take an early-morning bus to the park entrance instead, then simply walk in. Alternatively, there are a few parking areas before the entrance, these will charge US$4 to US$20 per day, depending on the season and your negotiating skills. Get there early if you intend to use these.

1. Tent-making bats, Hacienda Barú National Wildlife Refuge (p393) **2.** Orange iguana **3.** Humpback whale breaching, Parque Nacional Marino Ballena (p404) **4.** Catarata Manantial de Agua Viva (p360)

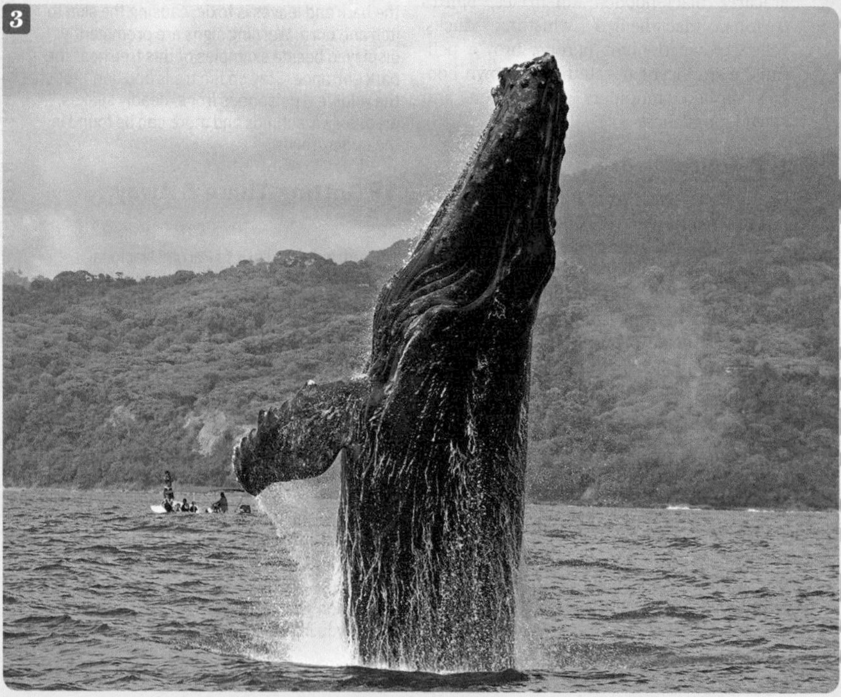

ONDREJ PROSICKY/SHUTTERSTOCK ©

Reserves of the Central Pacific Coast

Costa Rica's best road trip follows the Costanera Sur (Ruta 34), along a string of fantastic natural parks. Replete with wet and dry tropical forests and long beaches, these parks are alive with brightly colored birds, curious monkeys and a veritable army of iguanas – all of which show off the country's stunning biodiversity.

Rancho La Merced National Wildlife Refuge

Surrounding Parque Nacional Marino Ballena on the southern part of the central Pacific coast, this former cattle ranch (p400) has excellent horse trails, primary and secondary forest, and miles of mangrove channels.

Parque Nacional Marino Ballena

It's appropriate that this lovely, increasingly touristed national park (p404) has a sandbar shaped like a whale's tail; from the beaches it's possible to spot the migrating giants as they swim near the shore.

Hacienda Barú National Wildlife Refuge

Excellent trails and naturalist-led hikes make this (p393) the best birdwatching spot on the central Pacific coast. If spotting rare tropical birds doesn't thrill you enough, there's also a zipline.

Catarata Manantial de Agua Viva

With macaws overhead, this picture-perfect jungle waterfall (p360) drops 183m from one swimming pool to the next. It's best during the rainy season, when the flows are full.

QUEPOS TO UVITA

South of Quepos, the well-trodden central Pacific tourist trail begins to taper off, evoking of the Costa Rica of yesteryear – surf shacks and empty beaches, roadside *ceviche* vendors and a little more space. Intrepid travelers can have their pick of any number of deserted beaches and great surf spots. The region is also home to the great bulk of Costa Rica's African-palm-oil industry, which should be immediately obvious after the few dozen kilometers of endless plantations lining the sides of the Costanera.

Known as the Costa Ballena, the beauteous length of coastline between Dominical and Ojochal has three main reasons to visit: surfing (Dominical), whale-watching (Uvita) and gourmet cuisine (Ojochal). For the time being, the area largely retains an easygoing, unspoiled allure despite the growing numbers discovering its appeal.

Matapalo

Off the Quepos–Dominical stretch of highway, Matapalo has been off most travelers' radars, though without good reason: this vast, palm-fringed, gray-sand beach has some awesome, and usually empty, surf. With two river-mouth breaks generating some wicked waves, Matapalo is recommended for intermediate to advanced surfers who are comfortable dealing with rapidly changing conditions, though there may be a local lifeguard on duty.

Matapalo is not the best beach for swimming as the transient rips here are about as notorious as they come, but it's perfect for sunbathing and watching the action.

🛏 Sleeping

★ **Rafiki Beach Camp**　　　CABINA $$
(☑ 8368-9944, 2787-5014; www.rafikibeach.com; tent incl breakfast US$135-155, cabins with air-con/ fan US$80/70; ❋ 🐾 ≋) On the beach road you'll find this friendly and laid-back place with luxury safari-style beachfront tents – all with electricity, tiled bathroom with hot shower and ocean views. There are also cabins with air-con or fans and a pool overlooking the ocean, adjacent to a *rancho* with a communal kitchen. Guests can stay here in conjunction with Rafiki Safari Lodge, kayaking down to Matapalo.

Charlie's Jungle House　　GUESTHOUSE $$
(☑ 2787-5005; www.charliesjunglehouse.com; r US$65-125; P❋🐾≋🐕) Run by the effusive Charlie, this guesthouse halfway along the beach road has eight spacious jungle-themed and colorful rooms, the largest with kitchenettes and refrigerators. Campers have access to a full bathroom and a common, shaded space to relax, while the onsite Jungle Cafe serves wholesome meals. Charlie is hugely knowledgeable about Matapalo, and arranges waterfall hikes, horseback rides and surf lessons.

Dreamy Contentment　　BUNGALOW $$
(☑ 2787-5223; www.dreamycontentment.com; budget/standard bungalow from US$78/95 villa from US$280; P❋🐾) Right on the beach, this Spanish-colonial-style property with towering trees and impressive woodwork throughout offers comfy but slightly dated bungalows equipped with functional kitchenettes and terraces; some have hammocks. The real star attraction is the villa, which has a large kitchen, a beachfront veranda and a princely bathroom complete with hot tub. There may be a two-night minimum if you book online.

Jardin de los Monos　　B&B $$$
(☑ 8826-1794; www.bnbbythebeach.com; d from US$112; P❋🐾🐕≋) If you're looking for a quiet and relaxing stay, this pleasant, adult-only bed and breakfast is just the ticket. Moments from the beach, it's surrounded by a peaceful tropical garden with a resident sloth (during research). Well-finished and spacious rooms have a minifridge, locker, large shower and private patio with a hammock. The pool has a swim-up bar.

Try the homemade Dutch pancakes for breakfast. Find it north of Charlie's Jungle House.

🍴 Eating

Most accommodations offer meals. There's also the excellent **Langosta Feliz** (Happy Lobster; ☑ 2287-5214; mains US$8-20; ⏱ 11am-9:30pm) seafood restaurant across the highway from the entrance to Matapalo.

❶ Getting There & Away

Buses between Quepos and Dominical can drop you off at the turnoff to the village; from there it's a couple of kilometers to this off-the-beaten-track beach.

There are a few buses daily that stop in the village (at the top of the road into town, still a walk to the beach) on their routes. Those coming from the north continue on to Dominical (around US$1, 20 minutes) or Uvita (around US$1.50, 45 minutes). Others arrive in Matapalo from the south and continue to Quepos (around US$2, one hour) and San José (around US$10, four hours). The stop is in front of the village *pulpería* (convenience store), and you can ask about bus times there or at your guesthouse.

Hacienda Barú National Wildlife Refuge

Located on the Pacific coast 3km northeast of Dominical on the road to Quepos, this **wildlife refuge** (☎2787-0003; www.haciendabaru.com; off Carretera Pacifica Fernandez Oreamundo (Ruta 34); self-guided trails US$15, 2hr nature tours US$29, Ecotram US$30; ⏲7am-6pm) forms a key link in a major biological corridor called the Path of the Tapir, and is thought to have been inhabited by a large population of indigenous people. It comprises around 330 hectares of private and state-owned land that have been protected from hunting since 1976. The range of tropical habitats here includes pristine beaches, riverbanks, mangrove estuaries, wetlands, primary and secondary forests, tree plantations and pastures.

This diversity of habitats, plus its key position in the Path of the Tapirs, account for the multitude of species that have been identified in Hacienda Barú. These include 365 birds, 69 mammals, 94 reptiles and amphibians, 87 butterflies, 158 trees and around 250 orchids. Ecological tourism provides this wildlife refuge with its only source of funds, meaning money spent here helps conserve tropical rainforests.

Tours

There is an impressive number of guided tours on offer. You can experience the rainforest canopy by 'Ecotram' – a motorized chair that goes through the treetop canopy and turns 340 degrees for nature viewing – or a zipline course called 'Flight of the Toucan.' In addition to the canopy activities, Hacienda Barú offers birdwatching tours, hiking tours, and an overnight camping tour in the tropical rainforest. Hacienda Barú's naturalist guides come from local communities and have lived near the rainforest all of their lives. Even if you don't stop here for the sights, the onsite store carries an excellent selection of specialist titles for birdwatchers.

Sleeping

Hacienda Barú Lodge LODGE $$$
(☎2787-0003; d incl breakfast $146, additional adult/child under 11yr US$15/10; P 📶) Hacienda Barú Lodge consists of six fan-cooled, two-bedroom cabins located 350m from Barú beach. Accommodations have kitchenettes with coffee makers, but are basic overall, and worn and a bit buggy; the upside is that guests staying here receive free admission to the refuge.

Getting There & Away

BUS

The Quepos–Dominical–San Isidro de El General bus stops outside the hacienda entrance. The San Isidro de El General–Dominical–Uvita bus will drop you off at the Río Barú bridge, 2km from the hacienda office, or you may be able to ask the driver on a bus heading north or south along the highway to make a stop for you.

CAR

If you're driving it's very easy to reach. Fuel up at the El Ceibo gas station, 50m north of the Hacienda Barú Lodge – it's the only one for a good distance in any direction.

TAXI

A taxi from Dominical should cost around US$10.

Dominical

For as long as anybody could remember, Dominical was a lazy little town that drew a motley crew of surfers and backpackers, a place where a traveler could wander the dusty roads, surfboard tucked under an arm, balancing the day's activities between wave riding and hammock hang time.

Those days aren't entirely gone, but in 2015 a bunch of paving stones laid along the beach became the town's first real road. And as an increasing population of expats and gringos began to hunker down, some more sophisticated (though decidedly ecofriendly) businesses began to sprout. The place gets busiest in high season, particularly February around the time of neighboring Uvita's hippie festival Envision (p401). Rainier months remain as languidly 'old Costa Rica' as ever.

SURF DOMINICAL

Dominical owes its fame to its seriously sick point and beach breaks, though surf conditions here are variable. On smaller days at the right tide, it's possible to learn surfing here in the white-water, but beware of getting too deep, as currents are strong and when swells are big you can really get trashed if you don't know what you're doing. Some beginners and surf schools head for nearby Playa Dominicalito, which is always tamer.

Sunset Surf (☎8917-3143; www.sunsetsurfdominical.com; all-incl packages per week from US$1200; ⏲8am-4:30pm) Operated by Dylan Park, who grew up surfing the waves of Hawaii and Costa Rica, Sunset offers a variety of packages (including one for women only, and day lessons). It has a three students to every instructor and Park is an excellent teacher. Organic, all-natural sunblock is provided and 1% of proceeds go toward 'the planet.' Located on the main road into town.

Costa Rica Surf Camp (☎8812-3625, 2787-0393; www.crsurfschool.com; opposite Playa Dominical behind Hotel DiuWak; all-incl packages per week US$1717, group surf lessons from US$60, 2hr board hire US$6) This fantastic locally owned surf school prides itself on having only two students to each teacher, with teachers who have CPR and water-safety training and years of experience. The amiable owner, Cesar Valverde, runs a friendly, warm-hearted program including surf lessons and accommodation. Single lessons and board rental are also available, and boards are great quality.

Sights

★Cataratas Nauyaca WATERFALL
(☎2787-0541; www.cataratasnauyaca.com; Ruta Nacional 243; horseback tour US$79, 4WD tour US$32, self-guided hike US$9, parking US$3; ⏲7am-5pm Mon-Fri, 7am-4pm Sat, 8am-4pm Sun; P) Owned and operated by a Costa Rican family, this center is home to the coast's most impressive waterfalls. Two falls cascade through a protected reserve of both primary and secondary forest, and are reached by hiking, 4WD or on horseback. Visitors can swim in the inviting natural pools at the lower falls, and the family runs horseback-riding tours and tours by pickup truck to the falls (reservations required; Dominical pick-up available).

The cheapest option is to hike in; those in decent shape can visit the falls on a walk (around two hours one way). It's a full 12km round-trip hike from the booking office. Alternatively, if you have a 4WD you can drive the first 2km and pay to park in the parking area, then it's a moderate 4km uphill to the falls and 4km back down. There are rest benches along the trail and a first toilet break around 2km from the falls, with peacocks and monkeys nearby. Bring swimming gear (changing area and toilets available at the waterfall), plus sunscreen, a towel, and proper sneakers or hiking shoes. The path is wide and well marked but uneven and muddy in places, especially during or just after the rainy season.

★Alturas Wildlife Sanctuary NATURE RESERVE
(☎2200-5440; www.alturaswildlifesanctuary.org; Calle San Martin, off Ruta 34; 1-1½hr tours min donation adult/child under 12yr US$25/15, tour & lunch combo adult/child US$35/22; ⏲tours 9am, 11am, 1pm & 3pm Tue-Sun) Around 1.5km east and uphill from Dominical, this wildlife sanctuary takes in injured and orphaned animals as well as illegal pets. Its mission is to rehabilitate and reintroduce to the wild those that can be, and look after those that cannot. It has an 85% success rate. During the tour you meet its residents: a macaw missing an eye, three types of monkey, Bubba the famous coati, a toucan, sloths and more. Entertaining, educational and a terrific cause. Reserve a tour ahead of time.

Playa Dominicalito BEACH
(Carretera Pacifica Fernández Oreamuno/Ruta 34) Three kilometers south of Dominical, this sheltered bay is favored by beginners when the surf is big in Dominical. Surf schools from Dominical frequently do lessons here on the mellower waves, and surf rental is often available on the beach.

Parque Reptilandia ZOO
(☎8308-8855, 2787-0343; www.crreptiles.com; Ruta Nacional 243; adult/child US$12/6; ⏲9am-4:30pm; P 👪) Near the entrance to Nauyaca Waterfall, this weathered reptile park sits on an acre of land and is a mini Jurassic Park. It's got everything from crocodiles and

turtles to snakes and poison-dart frogs in glass-fronted terrariums. Our favorite is the viper section, where you can see Costa Rica's deadliest creatures, such as the fer-de-lance, pit viper and the black-headed bushmaster. Friday is feeding day, when live mice are introduced into snake enclosures, which spectators may or may not love.

Don't miss Langka the Komodo dragon, Jumbo the enormous tortoise and Shakira the anaconda.

Activities

★ Airborne Arts CIRCUS

(☎8302-4241, 8320-0929; 2hr group trapeze session per person from $75, shared r incl meals from US$113; ⊙hours vary, booking required) Ever felt like learning the flying trapeze in the middle of the Costa Rican countryside, with a view of a 100m waterfall? Do it with world-renowned acrobat couple Jonathon Conant and Christine Van Loo, who have constructed a circus-themed paradise south of the remote town of Las Tumbas. It's the perfect escape for those looking to learn how to fly.

Packages with trapeze classes, aerial silks and partner acrobatics courses are all available (prices vary depending on the length of stay and group size), and the restaurant's veggies come from the couple's onsite garden. Waterfall hikes abound in the area, as do friendly locals. It's around 25km from Dominical in the hills and is tricky to find; check the website for GPS directions. A 4WD is recommended.

Alegria Soul Spa SPA

(☎2787-0210; www.alegriasoulspa.com; Main St; massages from US$30; ⊙10am-6pm) Unwind after a surf session at this good-value day spa. Choose from relaxing Swedish-style, herbal, bamboo, reflexology, stone and lymphatic drainage massages.

Danyasa Yoga Arts School YOGA

(☎2787-0229; www.danyasa.com; Main St; classes from US$10; ⊙shop 9:30am-8pm) This lovely Dominical yoga studio offers a variety of classes for all levels, including unique dance-yoga-flow hybrid styles and even ecstatic moon dance. The studio also serves as a center for retreats.

Dominical Surf Adventures RAFTING, SURFING

(☎2787-0431; www.dominicalsurfadventures.com; private surf lesson incl 2hr board rental US$70; ⊙8am-5pm Mon-Sat, 9am-3pm Sun) A bit of an adventurer's one-stop shop: visitors can book white-water rafting, kayaking, snorkeling and dive trips, as well as surf lessons (from US$55), from an office on the main drag. Rafting trips start at US$100 (for runs on the Class II and III Guabo) and include a more challenging run on the Río Coto Brus' Class IV rapids.

Pineapple Tours KAYAKING

(☎8362-7655, 8873-3283; www.pineapplekayaktours.com; mangrove kayak tour US$75, Río Barú paddleboarding US$60, snorkeling US$80, 2hr surf rental US$5) With friendly guides, Pineapple Tours runs kayaking and stand-up paddleboarding (SUP) trips to local caves, rivers and mangrove forests. It also does snorkeling tours to the 'whale's tail' in Parque Nacional Marino Ballena, and rents SUP gear, surfboards, kayaks, beach chairs and umbrellas. Find its office next to the police station in Dominical.

Courses

Adventure Education Center LANGUAGE

(☎2787-0023, 8866-6042; www.adventurespanishschool.com; ⊙classes 9am-1:30pm) This school runs various language courses – from medical Spanish to kids' lessons – of varying lengths. A standard group Spanish class for one week (16 hours) starts from US$280 without accommodations. Homestays are US$180 per week; other accommodation options are available, as are private lessons and discounts for longer periods of study.

Sleeping

Cool Vibes Hostel HOSTEL $

(☎8353-6428; www.hosteldominical.com; dm from US$13, d with/without air-con from US$58/38; P@🛜≋) On the road at the southern end of town, this two-story sanctuary features a relaxing lounge, shared kitchen and attractive (but occasionally malfunctioning) plunge pool lined with potted plants. Tile-floored rooms are spacious and clean, with solid beds and bamboo furniture. Catch rays on the hammocks in the garden, and there's a communal TV room upstairs. Free coffee. Cash only. Surfboard rentals are $10 for 24 hours.

Posada del Sol HOTEL $

(☎2787-0085; d from US$40; P🛜) Maintained by the charming Latishia, there are only five rustic rooms at this lovely, secure, tidy little place on the main drag. Comforts include a hammock outside each room, a basic kitchen, a sink to rinse out your salty beach gear and a clothesline for drying. Single travelers should check out the tiny place in the back. No advance reservations.

Rainbow Beach Hostel HOSTEL $

(☑ 8722-5229; www.facebook.com/therainbowbeach hostel; Beach Rd; dm $20, d US$30-40) At the northern end of the beach is this attractive, psychedelic building painted purple with rainbow-colored banisters and beach art on the walls. Comfortable four-bed dorms are bright with tasteful patterned bedspreads. Basic privates with shared bathrooms are small and simple with white walls and wooden beds. There's a sociable shared kitchen and a nice communal balcony for ocean-gazing.

★ Danyasa Yoga Retreat GUESTHOUSE $$

(☑ 2787-0229; www.danyasa.com; d/tr US$88/128; ✱ 🛜 🌊) 🌿 To visualize Danyasa, imagine eight refurbished cargo containers set amid tranquil greenery, each turned into a snug room or grander suite, with shared outdoor bamboo showers and a guest kitchen. Now imagine water features in the shape of Buddha's head, a relaxing pool, yoga and dance classes (from US$10) designed to unleash your inner goddess and align your chakras, and you're there.

Tropical Sands Dominical Eco Inn HOTEL $$

(☑ 2787-0200; www.tropicalsandsdominical.com; d with/without air-con US$85/62; P ✱ 🛜) A lovely, secure hotel option hidden amid lush foliage on the southern end of town, this place offers smart, comfortable rooms with tiled floors, wide-plank ceilings and small porches strung with hammocks. The grounds are beautiful and the expat owners (who speak Spanish, French and English) lovingly maintain them. It's also just steps from the beach.

Hotel Rio Lindo HOTEL $$

(☑ 8857-4937; www.riolindocostarica.com; 🕒 d/tr/q from US$102/107/158; ✱ 🌊) On the main drag at the northern end of town, this friendly hotel has three suites and five double rooms centered around a tropical garden and large pool. Rooms are comfortable with tiled floors but could do with modernizing. They come with plenty of amenities, a TV and outdoor sitting area (most with hammocks). The largest suite has a kitchen.

There's a good tiki bar-restaurant with a pool table, where locals drink with tourists, plus there's a live-music pool party from 3pm on Sunday.

★ Mavi Surf Hotel BOUTIQUE HOTEL $$$

(☑ 2787-0429; www.mavi-surf.com; r incl breakfast US$146; P ⊖ ✱ 🛜 🌊) At the top end of the surfer market is this delightful and smart lime-green hotel. It's a two-minute walk to the beach, but far enough from the 'doof doof doof' of main-street bars. There's a clean pool, surfing racks by each spacious, tiled, air-conditioned room, plus a kitchenette and bamboo partitions offering some privacy on the breezy terrace. Excellent breakfast.

Hotel y Restaurante Roca Verde HOTEL $$$

(☑ 2787-0036; www.facebook.com/RocaVerdeHo tel; Carretera Pacifica Fernández Oreamuno (Ruta 34); d incl breakfast US$135-145; P ✱ @ 🛜 🌊) Overlooking the beach about 1km south of town, this slightly weathered but atmospheric hotel has a hippy feel and common spaces with tile mosaics, festive murals and rock inlays. The 10 comfortable, tropical-themed rooms have terracotta-tiled floors and pretty hand-painted flora and fauna decorating the walls. The real action takes place in the open-air bar, which is covered with whale wall art.

Costa Paraíso BOUTIQUE HOTEL $$$

(☑ 2787-0025; www.costa-paraiso.com; d US$140-220; P ✱ 🛜 🌊 🌊) In a prime spot overlooking a rocky cove in Playa Dominicalito, this snug hideaway lives up to its name. Each of the five rooms is beautifully appointed in a modern tropical style, with tiled floors, wood beams and windows oriented to catch ocean breezes and views. There were renovations during research – check these have been completed before you book.

All but two rooms have a kitchenette. Keep an eye out for the tiny sign on the ocean side, 2km south of Dominical – it's a sharp turn that goes steeply downhill.

Villas Alturas VILLA $$$

(☑ 2200-5440; www.villasalturas.com; 1-/2-bedroom villa US$195/295; P ✱ 🛜 🌊) Just down the mountain from the eponymous wildlife sanctuary (p394), this gorgeous place has a posh collection of seven villas perched on the hillside, each with balconies and stunning panoramic views of the Pacific. The relaxing communal terrace comes complete with pool, bar and restaurant. Self-caterers will appreciate the full kitchen in the well-kept, stylish units. Nature tours from US$25. 4WD required.

OVERNIGHT AT THE WATERFALL

Waterfall hikes are a dime a dozen in Costa Rica, and most include a familiar itinerary: hike, swim, eat lunch, maybe rappel, head home. Over at family-owned tour company **Pacific Journeys** (8325-9818, 2266-1717; www.pacificjourneyscr.com; overnight waterfall tour per person from US$159, with rappelling US$229, day trek US$89 per person), based out of the tiny town of Las Tumbas, there's something better on offer.

The experienced bilingual guides at Pacific Journeys lead people up to the top of 600ft **Diamante Falls**, one of the highest, most jaw-droppingly beautiful cascades in the country. To get there, travelers scale hundreds of stairs up through the company's private reserve, amid lush primary forest and past a botanical garden. Upon arrival (which takes about three hours and is moderately difficult), the group unpacks and selects mats within an open-air cavern behind the waterfall – where everybody sleeps for the night. Yep, this waterfall doubles as a hotel, and there are actually three massive waterfalls visible from the campsite.

Candles and solar-powered lights illuminate the paths and the kind and knowledgeable guides prepare yummy vegetarian meals in an open-air kitchen. The place is decidedly rustic but features flush toilets and picnic benches and is protected from the elements – what else do you really need? Rappelling excursions and hikes to nearby swimming holes and cliff-jumping sites get the adrenalin pumping to the point that few will mind the cold, waterfall-fed showers. Those who do can warm up with hot tea the guides prepare from spices picked from the botanical garden. A car is required to get to the meeting point at the booking office in the village of Las Tumbas. No pickups.

Cascadas Farallas LODGE $$$
(8882-7687, in USA 888-986-0086; www.waterfallvillas.com; Ruta Nacional 243; ste/villa from US$165/300; P) On the San Isidro road, this spiritual retreat is located beside a series of cascading waterfalls. Balinese-style suites and villas are decked out from floor to ceiling with Asian art, and all have balconies facing the waterfalls – one has a Jacuzzi. Yoga and meditation sessions are balanced with exclusively vegan cuisine. This eco-retreat has no TV and no wi-fi.

Eating

The restaurant scene in Dominical is varied and of a high standard, catering mostly to foreign guests and including many international options. Self-caterers will appreciate the fabulous health-food store Mama Toucan's (p398).

★ **Cafe Mono Congo** CAFE $
(www.cafemonocongo.com; mains US$4-9; 7am-5pm;) Perch on a swing at the bar or at a riverside table to enjoy an espresso. This open-air cafe also dishes up tasty, simple breakfasts like *gallo pinto* and *huevos rancheros* and (largely veggie) lunches, using organic local produce. Find it at the junction of the road into town and the main drag.

Sol Frozen Yogurt, Gelato & Drinks ICE CREAM $
(8567-0607; www.facebook.com/SolDominical; one gelato scoop US$3; 11am-8pm;) Organic Dominical homemade artisan ice cream and fro-yo, with lots of tasty vegan varieties. Our faves are the pistachio, coconut and vegan mint-choc-chip gelato. The low-key stand also sells frappés, milkshakes and hot drinks.

Del Mar Taco Shop TACOS $
(8428-9050; tacos US$4; 11:30am-9pm) On the approach to the beach this casual surfer hangout serves some of the area's best tacos (fresh fish, shrimp, beef, chicken or veggie). The chips are mixed with handmade nachos – pair them with the superb guacamole. There's a variety of hot sauces to slather over your order. On Taco Tuesday (April to November) all tacos cost just US$2.

El Pescado Loco SEAFOOD $
(8303-9042; www.facebook.com/elpescadoloco.dominical; tacos US$7, fish & chips US$8; 11:30am-8pm Mon-Sat) This little open-air shack has only a handful of menu items, but it knows what it's doing when it comes to fish tacos with spicy mango salsa and chunky guacamole. The onion rings and fish and chips are tasty too.

Phat Noodle THAI $

(☎2787-0017; www.phatnoodlecostarica.com; mains US$9-11; ⊙4:30pm-9pm Tue-Sun, 5-9pm Mon; ✎) Set in a pretty garden, this Thai restaurant and bar serves up tasty, piping-hot bowls of rice and noodles, along with spicy margaritas, all from inside a converted school bus. Skillfully prepared menu items range from shrimp and crab rangoon to Thai coconut *ceviche* and green curry. There are a great many vegan and gluten-free options as well.

Cafe Delicias CAFE $

(☎2787-0097; www.cafedelicias.com; breakfast from US$4, casados from US$6; ⊙7:30am-6pm; 📶) This Costa Rican coffee shop chain is a solid, good-value place to grab breakfast or a snack. The cake counter is always stuffed with sweet goodies and the *casados* are pretty good too. There's better coffee in town though. It's on the right on the way into Dominical.

Mama Toucan's HEALTH FOOD $

(☎8433-4235; www.mamatoucans.com; pizzas from US$6; ⊙9:30am-6:30pm; ✎) Selling gourmet, organic and vegan products and those free of 'artificial flavors, chemicals and bad vibes,' this super health-food store is ideal for self-catering. While groceries are a bit pricey, the 12-inch deli pizzas are a steal. Plus, grab a coconut for less than a dollar – they'll cut it open and put a straw in it for you.

Ricar 2 Restaurant COSTA RICAN $$

(Cataratas Nauyaca; ☎8847-5604; Ruta Nacional 243; mains US$7-14; ⊙10am-10pm) This Costa Rican restaurant 1.5km north of Dominical on the way to Cataratas Nauyaca serves yummy *comida típica* (regional specialties), but is better known for the old, hollowed-out Allegro airplane parked beside it: supposedly it's being converted into a cocktail bar (or so staff members have been claiming for years). The *casados* and mixed rice dishes hit the spot.

Dominical Sushi SUSHI $$

(☎8826-7946; sushi rolls from US$7; ⊙1-10pm Sun-Thu, 1-5pm Fri, 5-10pm Sat) Set back from the main road through town in an open-air setting overlooking the Río Barú, this sushi place takes advantage of the fresh tuna and other fish caught daily in Dominical. We're big fans of its ahi poke salad and tuna sashimi, plus the *unagi* and rainbow rolls. The menu is complemented by a selection of Japanese beers and sake.

Drinking & Nightlife

★ **Fuego Brew Co** CRAFT BEER, COFFEE

(☎8992-9559; www.fuegobrew.com; Main St; ⊙breakfast from 7am, bar 11:30am-10:30pm) In the center of Dominical, with a doorway decorated with two mini-flamethrowers, this sleek establishment with a coffee shop, glistening hardwood bar and restaurant is the town's first craft brewery and coffee roastery. Here you can sip mango pale or wina guanabana ale all day long. Bartenders are friendly and the meals (mains US$11-28) and java are tasty.

Downstairs is the seven-barrel brewing system and coffee roaster with take-out service counter. Happy hour runs 4:30pm to 5:30pm. There are plenty of cocktails and a dozen imported wines to try too.

Rum Bar BAR

(☎2787-0287; www.facebook.com/rumbarcostarica; ⊙4:30pm-2am) On the road into town, this lively, divey spot plays reggae, has live music or DJs nightly and does a ladies' night on Wednesday, when women get free shots and other promotions.

Tortilla Flats BAR

(☎2787-0033; ⊙8am-9pm Mon-Fri, to midnight Fri & Sat) The beachfront Tortilla Flats is the de facto place for surfers to enjoy sunset beers after a day in the water (skip the food, though). Its open-air atmosphere and easy vibes reflect the clientele, with regular live music, DJs and karaoke. When it's busy continents may drift before you get served.

Shopping

Eco Feria Dominical FAIR

(Eco Farmers Market; ☎8935-3037; www.facebook.com/Ecoferiadominical; Main St; ⊙8:30am-2:30pm Fri) Self-caterers can stock up on local organic groceries and goodies. Vendors range from chocolatiers, bakers and nut roasters to dairy producers and craft kombucha stalls. However, it's more than a food market. There's usually music, dancing and activities like yoga. The general ethos of the fair is to spread the message about living a more sustainable lifestyle. It's next to the soccer pitch.

Orientation

The Costanera Sur (Ruta 34) bypasses the town entirely; the entrance to the village is immediately past the Río Barú bridge. There's an unpaved main road through the village, where many of the services are found, and a paved beach road parallel to the ocean.

ℹ Information

Dominical Information Center (☑2787-0454; www.dominicalinformation.com; ⊘9:30am-5pm) On the main strip near the entrance to Dominical, this info center and tour provider has useful maps of town and bus timetables for the entire region. Bus-ticket, shuttle and tour booking services available.

There is an ATM outside Mama Toucan's.

SAFE TRAVEL

➤ Waves, currents and riptides in Dominical are very strong, and there have been drownings in the past. Watch for red flags (which mark riptides), follow the instructions of posted signs and swim at beaches that are patrolled by lifeguards. If you're a competent surfer or a smart visitor (checking ocean conditions), the beach is no problem, but people do die here every year.

➤ Dominical attracts a party crowd, which in turn has led to a burgeoning drug problem.

➤ Petty theft has been known to occur in the less-secure hostels around town and to affect those camping on the beach. Lock away your valuables where possible and don't leave them on display in your car.

ℹ Getting There & Away

BUS

Gray Line, Easy Ride and Monkey Ride offer private and shared shuttle services from Dominical to popular destinations such as Jacó, San José, Monteverde, Tamarindo and Sierpe; Easy Ride has direct services to Rivas and San Juan del Sur, Nicaragua.

Buses pick up and drop off passengers along the main road in Dominical.

San Isidro US$2, 1½ hours, six daily at 6am, 6:30am, 9am, 12:45pm, 2:35pm, 4:45pm.

Quepos US$6, one hour, seven daily at 6am, 9am, 12pm, 1pm, 3pm, 4:35pm, 4:45pm.

San José US$10, 4½ hours, four daily at 5:45am, 7:02am, 7:25pm, 1:30pm.

Uvita US$1, 20min, nine daily at 4:45am, 7:30am, 10:20am, 11am, 12:15pm, 3:30pm, 4pm, 5:15pm, 6:30pm.

Schedules change frequently; contact Dominical Information Center for up to date timetables.

TAXI

Taxis to Uvita cost US$10 to US$25. The ride to Quepos costs around US$60 and to Manuel Antonio it's around US$70. Cars accommodate up to five people, and can be hailed in town from the main road.

Escaleras

Escaleras, a small community scattered around a steep and narrow dirt loop road that branches off the Costanera, is famed for its sweeping views of the coastline. If you want to make it up here, you're going to need a 4WD to navigate one of the country's most notoriously difficult roads. Needless to say, the locals weren't kidding when they named the place *escaleras* (staircase). Aside from the scenic views, travelers primarily brave the road to relax in a mountain retreat that's still close enough to the action in Dominical and Uvita.

🍴 Sleeping & Eating

Pacific Edge CABINA $$
(☑2200-5428; www.pacificedge.info; cabin US$90-115, bungalow from US$150; P❋🛜🏊) Pacific Edge is located on an access road 1.2km south of the first entrance to Escaleras. The owners are a worldly couple who delight in showing guests their slice of paradise. Four cozy weathered cabins are perched on a knife-edge ridge about 200m above sea level, while larger, fully equipped bungalows including mini-kitchens, accommodate up to six. 4WD only.

Villa Escaleras VILLA $$$
(☑8823-0509, in USA & Canada 866-658-7796; www.villa-escaleras.com; Calle Escaleras, off Calle San Martin Sur; villa for 4/6/8 people US$240/280/320, casa US$70; P❋🛜🏊) About 2km up the Escaleras road, Villa Escaleras has a spacious four-bedroom villa accented by cathedral ceilings, tiled floors, colonial furnishings and a palatial swimming pool. A wraparound balcony awash with panoramic views makes the setting complete. There's also a smaller casa; both have a three-night minimum stay. 4WD essential.

Bar Jolly Roger AMERICAN $
(☑8858-8841; www.facebook.com/BarJollyRoger CostaRica; Calle Cuesta Del Diablo; 10 wings US$10; ⊘noon-10pm) If you have a hankering for delicious chicken wings, Bar Jolly Roger offers 24 varieties, in addition to burgers, pizzas, cold beers and good margaritas and other cocktails. This friendly expat outpost is up the southern entrance to Escaleras and has live music on Friday and sometimes other nights from 6pm to 9pm. Look for the smiley-face Jolly Roger sign. Cash or PayPal only.

Getting There & Away

The first entrance to Escaleras is 4km south of the San Isidro de El General turnoff before Dominical, and the second is 4.5km past the first one. Both are on the left-hand side of the road and poorly signposted. 4WD essential.

Uvita

POP 2000

Just 17km south of Dominical, this growing village consists of some dirt roads lined with farms, guesthouses and shops, a cluster of strip malls by the main Costanera Sur (Ruta 34) entrance, and a scattering of hotels in the jungle-covered hills above. Uvita has retained its gentle pace of life during the low season, but otherwise has become quite a popular and buzzing travel destination thanks to its increasingly sought-after main attraction, Parque Nacional Marino Ballena. The marine reserve has become famous for its migrating pods of humpback whales and its virtually abandoned wilderness beaches, but there are also good waterfalls nearby.

Two of the country's most important tourist events happen yearly in Uvita: a popular Whale and Dolphin Festival celebrating the arrival of the humpbacks, and the country's biggest hippie gathering, the Envision Festival (Costa Rica's answer to Burning Man at the beach).

Sights

★Cascada Verde WATERFALL

(Calle Bejuco; US$2; ⏲8am-4pm; P) Around 2.5km inland and uphill (toward Cascada Verde hostel), this waterfall plunges into an inviting deep pool, perfect for a refreshing dip. Visitors may see daredevils lie down at the top and slide some 5m down the cascade. This isn't recommended; the official path to the top is in disrepair and fenced off (rule breakers use the obvious hole in the fence).

A trail leads down the hill to a smaller waterfall and Poza Pool beneath, also suitable for swimming. Keep walking along the path and you'll come to a tropical garden and the lower car park for the falls. A bar at the top entrance serves hot and cold drinks (from US$2-5), plus tacos, hummus, pasta and falafel (from US$6).

Farmers Market MARKET

(☎8680-9752; ⏲8am-noon Sat) Held a short distance from the main entrance to Uvita, along the unpaved road, this sweet little farmers market is a good place to mingle with locals and longtime expats, and purchase psychedelic jewelry, locally grown fruit and vegetables, honey and home-cooked foods.

Rancho La Merced National Wildlife Refuge NATURE RESERVE

(☎8861-5147, 2743-8032; www.rancholamerced.com; Ruta Nacional 34; horseback-riding tours US$50, sunset rides US$57, nature walks from US$40; ⏲7am-4pm) Opposite the turnoff to Oro Verde, a few kilometers before Uvita, is this 506-hectare national wildlife refuge (and former cattle ranch), with primary and secondary forests and mangroves lining the Río Morete. Here you can go on guided nature hikes and birdwatching walks, ride on horseback to Punta Uvita or opt for the 'cowboy experience', which involves cattle roping, herding cows and riding around with real cowboys.

Reserva Biológica Oro Verde NATURE RESERVE

(☎2743-8072, 8843-8833; www.uvita.info/en/activity/230201/bird-watching-oro-verde; US$40; ⏲tours 6:30am) A few kilometers before Uvita is a signed turnoff to the left. A rough dirt road (4WD only) leads 3.5km up the hill to this private reserve on the farm of the Duarte family, who have lived in the area for more than three decades. Two-thirds of the 155-hectare property is rainforest, where visitors can do a two- to three-hour guided birdwatching walk with a bilingual naturalist guide with birding equipment, followed by a Costa Rican breakfast. Reserve via Uvita Information Center (p403).

Activities

Whale-Watching

Whale-watching is a huge attraction here, with humpback whales visiting the waters surrounding Parque Nacional Marino Ballena twice a year (December to April and July to November).

Bahía Aventuras ADVENTURE

(☎8846-6576, 2743-8362; www.bahiaaventuras.com; near Calle Bahía Ballena; adult/child snorkeling Marino Ballena from US$75/35, hiking Corcovado US$145/90, snorkeling Isla del Caño US$145/90;

⊙6:30am-5:30pm) An experienced tour operator in Uvita, running the gamut of tours, including a combo of snorkeling and whale-watching in Parque Nacional Marino Ballena, snorkeling around Isla del Caño in Bahía Drake, and hiking in Costa Ballena and Corcovado. The office is on the road parallel and north of Calle Bahía Ballena.

Surfing

Surfers passing through the area tend to push on to more extreme destinations further north or south, though there are occasionally some swells at Playa Hermosa (not to be confused with the world-class spot south of Jacó) to the north and Playa Colonia to the south. However, if you're a beginner, this can sometimes be a good place to practice.

Diving

★Mad About Diving DIVING
(☑2743-8019; www.madaboutdivingcr.com; Calle Playa Bahía; 2-tank dives from US$130) A friendly, safe and professional diving operator offering dives in the Parque Nacional Marino Ballena and full-day scuba excursions to Isla del Caño in Bahía Drake. The office operates irregular hours; book via the website or phone.

☞ Tours

★Rancho DiAndrew OUTDOORS
(☑8475-1287; www.facebook.com/rancho.diandrew; Calle Río Morete; tours from US$69) A fun tour operator specializing in surf retreats and nature tours, the most popular of which involves navigating a hidden gorge, plunging off a cliff and feasting on BBQ by the river. The *rancho* is perched in a patch of jungle near the town of San Josecito, and features tented cabins (summer only; single/double per night from US$75/85). Sweet views.

Uvita 360 ADVENTURE
(☑8586-8745; surfing, kayaking & snorkeling from US$65, waterfalls & Manuel Antonio from US$95) Set up by friendly local Alvaro 'Tito' Azofeifa, this professional tour company will arrange all the fine details for exploring the major sights in the area. Visit Nauyaca Waterfall and Parque Nacional Manuel Antonio, see the mangroves by kayak, snorkel the 'whale's tail' at Parque Nacional Marino Ballena or arrange surf lessons.

☆ Festivals & Events

Envision Festival ART, MUSIC
(www.envisionfestival.com; 4-day admission from US$389; ⊙late Feb) Four days of spoken word, music, yoga, performance art, permaculture and a full line-up of DJs happen in Uvita in late February for Costa Rica's take on the Burning Man festival. Attendees set up camp in a jungle setting near the beach in Uvita where you might spot thousands of naked hippies.

Whale and Dolphin Festival WILDLIFE
(☑8729-3624; www.festivaldeballenasydelfines.com; ⊙Sep-Oct) Tens of thousands descend on Uvita for this responsibly organized two-weekend oceanic extravaganza celebrating the arrival of humpback whales with cultural events, concerts, parades, performances and lectures. Visitors take boat tours (adult/child US$32/26) to view the marine mammals and enjoy the national marine park.

🛌 Sleeping

★Flutterby House HOSTEL $
(☑8341-1730, 2743-8221; www.flutterbyhouse.com; Calle La Curinga; dm US$15-18, d US$40-120; P @🗟) 🏄 Is it possible to fall in love with a hostel? If so, this ramshackle collection of colorful *Swiss Family Robinson*-style tree houses and dorms has beguiled us. It's run by a pair of expat sisters, and the clientele here tends to be of the barefoot, surfing variety. The bar is a social hub. Breakfast is extra, but delicious, local and organic.

Flutterby also rents out boards and bikes, sells beer for a pittance, and has a tidy, open-air communal kitchen as well as a restaurant which offers many vegan and vegetarian options. It employs downright visionary sustainability practices; single-use plastics are banned.

It's in a great location a short stroll from Marino Ballena's beaches, near the south entrance gate of the park. Follow the signs from the Costanera Sur.

Cascada Verde HOSTEL $
(☑2743-8191; www.cascadaverde-costarica.com; Calle Bejuco; dm US$10-15, r US$16-80; P @🗟) 🏄 If you're looking for a jungle retreat that's a bit like a treehouse adventure, this awesome hostel run by a young expat couple is for you. About 2km uphill from Uvita, it features jaw-dropping jungle views from the

dining terrace, a large communal kitchen, plenty of indoor and outdoor spaces for relaxing, rooms with bamboo partitions, and a waterfall a short walk away.

The open architecture style means there's a great atmosphere among guests and you'll hear the glorious jungle symphony surrounding you; however, be aware that there's very little noise privacy. Breakfast is extra (US$7 per person). Rooms can be configured to accommodate kids and child-friendly tours can be organized. Yoga sessions (US$10) take place regularly, and there are snorkels and boogie boards for rent (US$5 per day). Shuttles bookable at reception.

Tucan Hotel HOSTEL $

(☎2743-8140; www.tucanhotel.com; Calle Uvita; dm US$12, d with/without bathroom from US$29/25; P ❄ @ ☎) Located 100m inland from the main highway, this cheapie is popular with international travelers of all ages. The rustic rooms are arranged around a semi-open communal area, and there's a house in the trees. Bonuses include a shared kitchen, book exchange, bicycles, pool table and movie evenings, plus an Italian restaurant and cheap beer.

Ú Kiñca Hostel HOSTEL $

(☎8810-5862; www.ukinca.com; Ruta Nacional 34; dm/s/d from US$14/24/30; P ❄ ☎) If you just want a quiet place to rest your head, these extremely good-value, comfortable motel-like rooms will do the trick. Tiled, cream-colored accommodations are clean and in good order, but lack charm. Doubles come with a TV, air-con and private bathroom; dorms have three bunks (six beds). It's a two-minute drive to town and five to Parque Nacional Marino Ballena.

Cabinas Los Laureles CABINA $$

(☎2743-8008, 2743-8235; www.facebook.com/laureleslodge; s/d from US$35/55; P @ ☎) Set on a forested property with a short trail running through it, this 14-room spot slightly uphill from the Costanera Sur offers basic abodes with authentic Costa Rican hospitality. The restaurant serves delicious meals.

Finca Bavaria BOUTIQUE HOTEL $$

(☎8355-4465; www.finca-bavaria.de; Calle Bavaria; s/d from US$75/87; P ☎ ≋) This German-run inn comprises a handful of appealing, tidy, tiled rooms with wooden accents, bamboo furniture, romantic mosquito-net-draped beds and one of the best breakfasts along the coast (US$10). The grounds are lined with walkways and hemmed in by jungle. You can take in sweeping views of the ocean from the hilltop pool. Look for the signed dirt road at Km 167.

Arboura Eco Cabins CABAÑAS $$

(☎8482-8014; Calle La Curinga; cabins from US$50; ❄ ☎ ≋) Right next to Flutterby House (p401), this funky little newcomer offers four A-frame cabin hideaways with big windows. Surrounded by a lush garden, each comes with a couch area, kitchen and an outside shower, and some have air-con. Guests can use a gorgeous pool, ping pong table, and the house bikes. Cash only. It's three minutes from the Marino Ballena beaches.

★ **Oxygen Jungle Villas** VILLA $$$

(☎8322-4773, 8314-7371; www.oxygenjunglevillas.com; off Calle Bejuco; villas US$337-427; P ❄ ☎ ≋) Twelve smart mountaintop cabins constructed almost entirely of glass overlook the mountains and sea. The transparent and sumptuous digs allow guests to feel like part of the rainforest even from a plush, four-poster king bed. After a waterfall trail, have a spa treatment, then retire to the sundeck's infinity pool or the alfresco restaurant.

Hotel Cristal Ballena BOUTIQUE HOTEL $$$

(☎2786-5354; www.cristal-ballena.com; Calle El Tigre, Costanera Sur; d from US$255; P ❄ ☎ ≋) About 7km south of Uvita, surrounded by 12 hectares of private nature reserve and with sweet views of the coast from its hillside location, this blue-and-white boutique hotel is a top birding destination, with knowledgeable guides arranging birdwatching excursions. An excellent restaurant, bright, comfortable rooms, vast, gorgeous suites and a tranquil ambience complete the picture.

Bungalows Ballena BUNGALOW $$$

(☎8309-9631, 2743-8543; www.bungalowsballena.com; Calle Playa Bahía; apt/bungalow from US$125/250; P ❄ ☎ ≋) These apartments and standalone bungalows are popular with Tico families and large groups. All have a kitchen, wi-fi and satellite TV. The place is outfitted for kids – there's a playground and a big, welcoming pool in the shape of a whale's tail. Find it 300m north of the park's main entrance.

Eating

★Sibu Cafe CAFE $

(☎2743-8674; Ruta Nacional 34; coffee US$2-5, mains from US$6; ⏰7am-9pm Mon-Sat, 9am-9pm Sun; ❄📶🌶) Serving the best coffee for miles around, this little cafe hides in an Uvita strip mall. Latte art, eggs Benedict, chunky brownies and homemade lemon pie are all on the menu. Want something more substantial? The hardworking couple here also makes excellent salads, thin-and-crispy pizza, plus 10 hormone- and additive-free cuts of steak from a local farm in San Carlos.

Bar y Restaurante Los Laureles COSTA RICAN $

(☎2743-8008; mains US$7-13; ⏰11am-8:30pm Mon-Sat) Adorable casual family-run restaurant serving mainly Costa Rican and Tex-Mex cuisine, with innovative favorites such as avocado hummus and nacho *patacones* (fried green plantains cut in thin pieces), and staples like chicken wings, chili fries and quesadillas. The margaritas are great, the service is top-notch and the open-air setting, amid tropical foliage, is super *tranquilo*.

★Sabor Español SPANISH $$

(☎8367-7930, 8768-9160; Calle Esmo; tapas from US$7, mains US$13-35; ⏰6-9:30pm Tue-Sun; 📶) After a successful run in Monteverde, charming Spanish couple Heri and Montse realized that they wanted to live by the ocean – to Uvita's good fortune. Thus, their sublime gazpacho, paella, *tortilla española* (Spanish omelet) and other Spanish specialties can now be savored with sangria and imported wine in a lovely *rancho* setting. Don't expect fast food; this is a leisurely experience.

Reservations advised. It's at the end of a dirt road near the beach in Playa Uvita.

Pizza Time PIZZA $$

(☎2201-5300; Ruta Nacional 34; pizzas US$11-26; ⏰noon-9pm Tue-Sun; P) South of Uvita on the road to Ojochal is this casual pizza joint, serving authentic Neapolitan pizzas cooked in a proper wood-fired brick oven. The dining area is very simple and many choose to take out. Flavours are mostly classic (margherita, pepperoni, chicken) with a couple of wild cards, such as shrimp or eggplant, thrown into the mix.

El Ancla SEAFOOD $$

(☎2101-2489; https://el-ancla-seafood.business.site; Ruta Nacional 34; ceviche from US$8, mains from US$13; ⏰11am-9pm; P📶) Off the main road into Uvita is this container-cum-seafood restaurant, with a simple deck out front with tables and chairs. It serves delectable *ceviche* made with high-quality white marlin, and satisfying fishy mains from tacos and mixed rice with shrimp to pastas with mussels, shrimp and octopus. Wash it down with a smoothie, cocktail or craft beer.

Drinking & Nightlife

Mosaic WINE BAR

(☎2215-0068; www.mosaiccr.com; Calle Uvita; ⏰10am-10pm) A pleasant open-plan wine bar serving a long list of imported wines from South America and Europe. You can also dabble in potent craft drinks like Malfy Gin with pink grapefruit and blood orange, or Cava sangria with brandy, triple sec, orange juice and lemon. Tuck into good sushi and Mediterranean-style tapas while you sip. Live music takes place on Thursday nights.

Orientation

The area off the main highway is referred to locally as Uvita, while the area next to the beach is called Playa Uvita and Playa Bahía Uvita (the southern end of the beach). The beach area is reached via two parallel roads that are roughly 500m apart – they make a C-shape connecting back to the road. The first entrance is just south of the bridge over the Río Uvita and the second entrance is in the center of town. At low tide you can walk out along Punta Uvita and onto the whale's-tail stretch of beach, but ask about tide times at the ranger station before heading out so that the rising water doesn't cut you off.

Information

Uvita Information Center (☎2743-8072; www.uvita.info; Ruta Nacional 34; ⏰9am-1pm & 2-6pm Mon-Sat) is a fine place to book tours and transport.

Also keep an eye out for the free print magazine *Ballena Tales*, a wonderful resource for visitors, with bilingual articles, tide charts and listings of local businesses from Dominical to the Península de Osa.

SAFE TRAVEL

➡ When enjoying the local beaches, be aware that personal possessions that are left unattended have been known to melt away into the jungles that fringe the shorelines.

➡ In fact, it's best not to bring anything valuable to the beach with you at all. Until recently, petty theft was the worst problem around the national park and area beaches and, unfortunately, a few in-person (but nonviolent) robberies have taken place in the past. Get the latest word from the staff at your accommodations.

Getting There & Away

Most buses depart from the sheltered bus stops on the Costanera (Ruta 34) in the main village. Check with Uvita Information Center (p403) for up-to-date departure times.

Dominical US$1, 30 minutes, nine daily between 4:45am and 5:30pm.

Quepos US$4, two hours, departs 5:30am, 11:40am, 1pm and 4pm.

San José Around US$10, 3½ hours, eight daily between 5:30am and 7pm.

Private shuttle companies – Grayline, Easy Ride and Monkey Ride – offer pricier transfers from Uvita to Dominical, San José, Quepos, Jacó, Puerto Jiménez and other popular destinations.

Parque Nacional Marino Ballena

This stunner of a **marine park** (☎2743-8141; Calle Playa Bahía; adult/child under 11yr US$6/free; ⏰7am-4pm), created in 1989, protects coral and rock reefs surrounding several offshore islands. Its name comes not only from the humpback whales that breed here but also because of the Punta Uvita 'Whale Tail,' a distinctive sandbar extending into a rocky reef that, at low tide, forms the shape of a whale's tail. Despite its small size, the importance of this area cannot be overstated, especially since it protects migrating humpback and pilot whales, three types of dolphin and nesting sea turtles, not to mention colonies of seabirds and several terrestrial reptiles.

Although Ballena was once ignored by many coastal travelers, its rewards have recently lured an increasing number of beach-lovers and wildlife-watchers. Beat the crowds by arriving early – you might even see dolphins in the surf or a humpback breaching.

Activities

Swimming

The beaches at Parque Nacional Marino Ballena are a stunning combination of golden sand and polished rock. All of them are virtually deserted and many spots are perfect for peaceful swimming and sunbathing. Check with the ranger for current conditions and the safest spots to swim.

Diving & Snorkeling

The coral reefs around the offshore islands are a good place to experience the park's underwater world, unlike the coral reefs near the shore that were heavily damaged by sediment runoff from the construction of the coastal highway. To delve into the underwater beauty of the park, go on a diving or snorkeling trip with local providers like Mad About Diving (p401).

Wildlife-Watching

Heading southeast from Punta Uvita, the park includes mangrove swamps, estuaries and rocky headlands. In the early morning, before other visitors arrive, you'll have the best opportunity for good birdwatching.

The park is home to, or frequently visited by, a number of wildlife species, including common, bottlenose and pantropical spotted dolphins and a variety of lizards. The offshore islands are important nesting sites for frigate birds, brown boobies and brown pelicans, and from May to November, with a peak in September and October, olive ridley and hawksbill turtles bury their eggs in the sand nightly. However, the star attraction is the pods of humpback whales that pass through the national park from July to November and December to April, as well as occasional pilot whales.

Scientists are unsure why humpback whales migrate here, though it's possible that Costa Rican waters may be one of only a few places in the world where the whales mate. There are actually two different groups of humpbacks that pass through the park – whales seen in the fall migrate from Californian waters, while those seen in the spring originate from Antarctica and come here to breed and rear their babies.

Whale- and dolphin-watching trips are run by several tour companies in Uvita, including Bahía Aventuras (p400).

Information

There are four entrances to the park, the most commonly used being the one by the **ranger station** (☎2743-8141; Calle Playa Bahía; ⏰7am-4pm) in Playa Uvita (follow the main road through Uvita). Park entrances are open from 7am to 4pm.

SAFE TRAVEL

➡ The beaches of Parque Nacional Marina Balleno are notorious for bag theft. If you leave your bag on the sand near the bushes for a second, you're unlikely to ever see it again.

Local residents are putting pressure on the park authorities to improve security in the park and also to provide working toilet facilities.

➡ Another annoyance is the enterprising parking touts who charge visitors around US$4 to park near the main entrance to the park. If you park on the street, you're not legally obliged to pay them anything. Better still, park nearby and walk to the entrance.

Getting There & Away

Parque Nacional Marino Ballena is best accessed from Uvita or Ojochal, by private vehicle, a quick taxi ride or by walking.

Ojochal

Of the trio of villages that make up the Costa Ballena (Dominical, Uvita and Ojochal), this laid-back, spread-out village is the culinary epicenter, with a multicultural expat population. Its friendly, well-integrated vibe has a distinctly different feel from that of surfer-dominated Dominical, although just north of Ojochal the largely undiscovered wilderness beach of Playa Tortuga is home to occasional bouts of decent surf.

Its excellent dining scene aside, Ojochal also serves as a convenient base for exploring nearby Parque Nacional Marino Ballena, and despite its small size there are plenty of accommodations in and around the village to choose from. Wildlife lovers may wish to linger a while to learn more about the locally based turtle conservation project.

Sights

Playa Ventanas BEACH

(parking until 2pm/after 2pm US$3.50/2.50; sunrise to 5:30pm) Tucked behind a grove of coco palms, this crescent-shaped, black-sand-and-pebble beach has elaborate rock formations at either end, and is called Ventanas (Windows) because there are a couple of caves large enough to walk into on the northern side. The ocean roars and crashes through the caves as the tide comes in – it's pretty spectacular to watch. There are no services here, but you can pick up some roadside coconut water, and snacks from vendors on the beach.

During or after rainy season you may have to negotiate a ford on the road to the beach. A 4WD is advisable, but many locals will cross the water in their cars if the levels are low. Check water levels before driving through. Find the dirt road to the beach off Ruta Nacional 35.

Reserva Playa Tortuga NATURE RESERVE

(2786-5200; www.reservaplayatortuga.org; Calle Tortuga, off Ruta Nacional 34; turtle rescue/crocodile monitoring project US$75/30; 9am-3pm Mon-Fri) FREE Set up in 2009 by Costa Rican scientists, this excellent center conducts several important projects, including an inventory of local mammals and monitoring scarlet macaw, monkey and bat populations in the reserve. There's a butterfly garden and educational outreach to show children the importance of protecting wildlife. With advance booking, visitors can get involved in various volunteer activities each day.

Stop by the office to see interesting artefacts, from monkey skulls and toucan beaks to species of snakes in lab containers. The office has a full schedule of upcoming projects, including crocodile monitoring (which involves night patrols, sometimes capturing crocodiles to tag them) and turtle rescue, during which eggs are brought to the hatchery and, once they are hatched, released back into the wild. Longer research projects with accommodation are also possible; email the office for tailor-made options. The office is along the public road to Playa Tortuga.

Sleeping

Hotel El Mono Feliz HOTEL $$

(2786-5146; www.elmonofeliz.com; Calle del Jardin; d incl breakfast from US$88, bungalow US$112-133;) Around 3km inland from Ojochal's entrance, this sweet little spot has well-finished, tropical-styled rooms, each with a round stone sink, refrigerator and air-con. The forested property is hemmed in by a trickling brook that guests can paddle in. Smart higher-end bungalows come with a kitchenette, dining table and forest views. Bonuses include a deck for yoga and reading, and a relaxing pool.

Diquis del Sur B&B $$

(2786-5012; www.diquis.com; Calle Papagayo; d incl breakfast with/without air-con from US$96/63; P) In Ojochal proper, around 1.5km in, this B&B is like a home away from home. Accommodations consist of a variety of fairly modest rooms, though some have a kitchenette for self-catering. There's also a good restaurant onsite (only open in the high season), and the well-maintained property is landscaped with flowers and fruit trees.

★**El Castillo** BOUTIQUE HOTEL $$$
(☎2786-5543; www.elcastillocr.com; Calle Perezoso; d from US$326; P❄📶≋) Even the most jaded of guests will give an involuntary gasp of surprise when faced with the tremendous view from the infinity pool at this bluff-top hotel. Perched nearly 200m above the Pacific Ocean, it has a handful of rooms and a few suites, decked out with four-poster beds and rain showers. Planning to propose to your sweetie? Do it here.

★**La Cusinga** LODGE $$$
(☎2770-2549; www.lacusingalodge.com; Ruta Nacional 34, Km 166, Finca Tres Hermanas; r incl breakfast from US$201; P) 🍃 This lovely ecolodge has breezy wood-and-stone rooms and sustainable practices. It's also a relaxing place to unplug, with gorgeous sweeping ocean views. In place of TVs are yoga classes. It's located on a 60-acre private reserve, with over 4km of hiking trails, a natural swimming hole, birdwatching, snorkeling and swimming at Parque Nacional Marino Ballena. It's about 5km south of Uvita.

Casa Blanca VILLA $$$
(☎8399-3207; www.casablancavillasojochal.com; Calle Tortuga Abajo; d/q from US$170/340; P❄📶≋) This stylish French-owned complex of boutique villas is the chicest option in town. Immaculate units are centered around a pool. Each comes with a kitchen and dining area, a separate bedroom, hardwood floors, plus colorful wood headboards and beachy decor throughout. The porches or conservatories are lovely places to unwind.

Eating

Ballena Bistro FUSION $
(☎2786-5407; www.ballenabistro.com; cnr Ruta Nacional 34 & Calle Playa Ballena; mains US$8-13; ⏲11am-4pm Tue-Sun; P📶🖉) In a well-decorated, barnlike structure with hardwood floors, this bistro offers diverse fodder for your belly and Instagram feed. Feast on garlic hummus, lentil and beet salad, pulled-pork burgers and mango chicken curry. Passion-fruit pie, craft kombucha on tap and local beers round out the menu. It's a smashing spot to break up a long drive.

Pancito Cafe CAFE $
(☎8729-4115, 2786-5774; cnr Calle Tortuga Abajo & Calle Soluna; pastries from US$3; ⏲7am-5pm Mon-Sat) This truly excellent bakery and cafe is both inexpensive and tasty. Stop by for a tasty ham-and-cheese quiche, dreamy cocoa-dusted truffle or a divine spicy chicken empanada. Enjoy breakfasts, sandwiches and crepes on the laid-back dining porch, or get items to go at the counter.

★**Citrus** MEDITERRANEAN $$
(☎2786-5175; www.facebook.com/CitrusOjochal; Calle Tortuga Abajo; mains US$8-27; ⏲8am-9pm Mon-Sat; P❄📶) Open-air, facing a courtyard and with a gorgeous patterned tiled floor, elegant velvet furnishings and beautiful light fixtures, Citrus feels upmarket yet casual and welcoming. Most importantly, the unstuffy Mediterranean-inspired gourmet fare is exceptional. Order a perfectly prepared *croque madame* for breakfast, *fattoush* salad (toasted bread, tomatoes, onions and mint) for lunch, and moules Madagascar or half a lobster for dinner.

Azul FUSION $$
(☎2786-5543; Calle Perezoso; mains US$10-28; ⏲5-10pm; 📶🖉) The perfect date spot, this chic little restaurant inside El Castillo has dreamy views of the Pacific coast. Your tastebuds will be singing when you treat them to tempura shrimp, goat-cheese ravioli and expertly seared steak. There's terrific attention to presentation and taste, and the Mediterranean-style three-course dinners are worth a splurge. Great cocktails and wine list too.

Restaurante Terraba COSTA RICAN $$
(☎4702-9868; Ruta Nacional 34; mains from US$7; ⏲11am-9pm Wed-Mon; P) This unassuming, open-plan roadside eatery with a corrugated steel roof offers local cuisine with giant flavors at tiny prices (relative to the rest of Ojochal). How did this happen? Well, the kind owners picked up their kitchen skills in some of the area's top restaurants before opening this one. Order from a strong list of seafood mains and Tico favorites.

★**Exotica** INTERNATIONAL $$$
(☎2786-5050; Calle Tortuga Abajo; mains US$11-46; ⏲5-9pm Mon-Sat) This phenomenal gourmet restaurant is worth planning your evening around. With a sultry jungle ambiance and orchids everywhere, the nouveau-French dishes each emphasize a breadth of ingredients brought together in masterful combinations. Some of the highlights include Tahitian fish carpaccio, wild

duck breast with port-pineapple reduction, and its signature dessert – the chili-tinged chocolate Devil's Fork. Reservations recommended.

There's also a long wine list of imported bottles from Chile, Argentina, France, Spain and even South Africa and Israel.

Shopping

L'Epicerie Super & Deli FOOD & DRINKS
(☎4702-7430; Calle Tortuga Abajo; ⊙7am-7pm Mon-Sat, 8am-6pm Sun) This upmarket deli is for self-caterers with cash to burn. It's packed with salivatingly good artisan creations from the area and abroad, from cheese and pastries to homemade meals.

Drinking & Nightlife

★**Bamboo Room** COCKTAIL BAR
(☎2786-5295; www.almacr.com; Calle Perezoso; ⊙noon-9pm Mon-Sat) This epic hilltop bar and restaurant, with steps painted like the keys of a piano and musical instruments on the walls, has raised the bar for nightlife in an otherwise food-focused beach enclave. Sunset views are a beautiful thing here, particularly with a signature Ginger Zinger 'shocktail' in hand. Great live music (including dueling pianos) goes on nightly.

Getting There & Away

Daily buses between Dominical and Palmar can drop you off near any of the places along the highway and also at the entrance of Ojochal village. However, to reach most places in Ojochal proper, it's best to have a car.

Gray Line, Easy Ride and Monkey Ride shuttles connect Ojochal with popular destinations along the Pacific coast and the Península de Osa.

AT A GLANCE

POPULATION
San Isidro de El General: 45,000

FAST FACT
Spanning the Costa Rica–Panama border, La Amistad (p429) is the largest nature reserve in Central America.

BEST RAINFOREST ADVENTURE
Río Claro Tours (p439)

BEST ECOLODGE
Playa Nicuesa Rainforest Lodge (p459)

BEST ECO HOSTEL
Osa Jungle Hostel (p449)

WHEN TO GO

Jan–Mar Less rain makes this the best time for trekking in Corcovado and climbing Cerro Chirripó.

Apr–Oct Surf's up in Pavones.

Feb–May Quetzal sightings in San Gerardo de Dota.

Parque Nacional Corcovado (p440)

Southern Costa Rica & Península de Osa

From the chilly heights of Cerro Chirripó (3820m) to the steamy coastal jungles of the Península de Osa, southern Costa Rica encompasses some of the country's more remote land. Vast tracts of wilderness remain untouched in Parque Internaciopnal La Amistad, and the country's most visible indigenous groups – the Bribrí, Cabécar, Boruc and Ngöbe – maintain traditional ways of living in remote territories. Monkeys, sloths and coatis roam the region's parks and reserves, and in Parque Nacional Corcovado there's a rare chance to spy on slumbering tapir. Meanwhile, the rugged coasts of the Golfo Dulce and Península de Osa captivate travelers with abandoned wilderness beaches, world-class surf and countless opportunities for rugged exploration.

INCLUDES

Southern Costa Rica & Península de Osa Highlights

❶ **Parque Nacional Corcovado** (p440) Hiking the remote coast and rich rainforest in the country's premier wilderness experience.

❷ **Cerro Chirripó** (p421) Summitting Costa Rica's tallest peak at sunrise.

❸ **Reserva Biológica Isla del Caño** (p434) Snorkeling or scuba diving with sea turtles, sharks and a host of sea creatures.

❹ **San Gerardo de Dota** (p412) Spotting the resplendently feathered quetzal in the cool highlands.

❺ **Pavones** (p459) Riding on one of the world's longest left breaks at this laid-back surfing paradise.

❻ **Fiesta de los Diablitos** (p425) Celebrating this vibrant festival at the Reserva Indígena Boruca.

❼ **Puerto Jiménez** (p447) Lying on the deserted beach at Playa Platanares while scarlet macaws soar overhead.

❽ **Dos Brazos** (p452) Immersing yourself in rural tourism at a gold-mining village.

❾ **Humedal Nacional Térraba-Sierpe** (p431) Discovering the mysterious mangroves, the ecosystem between land and sea.

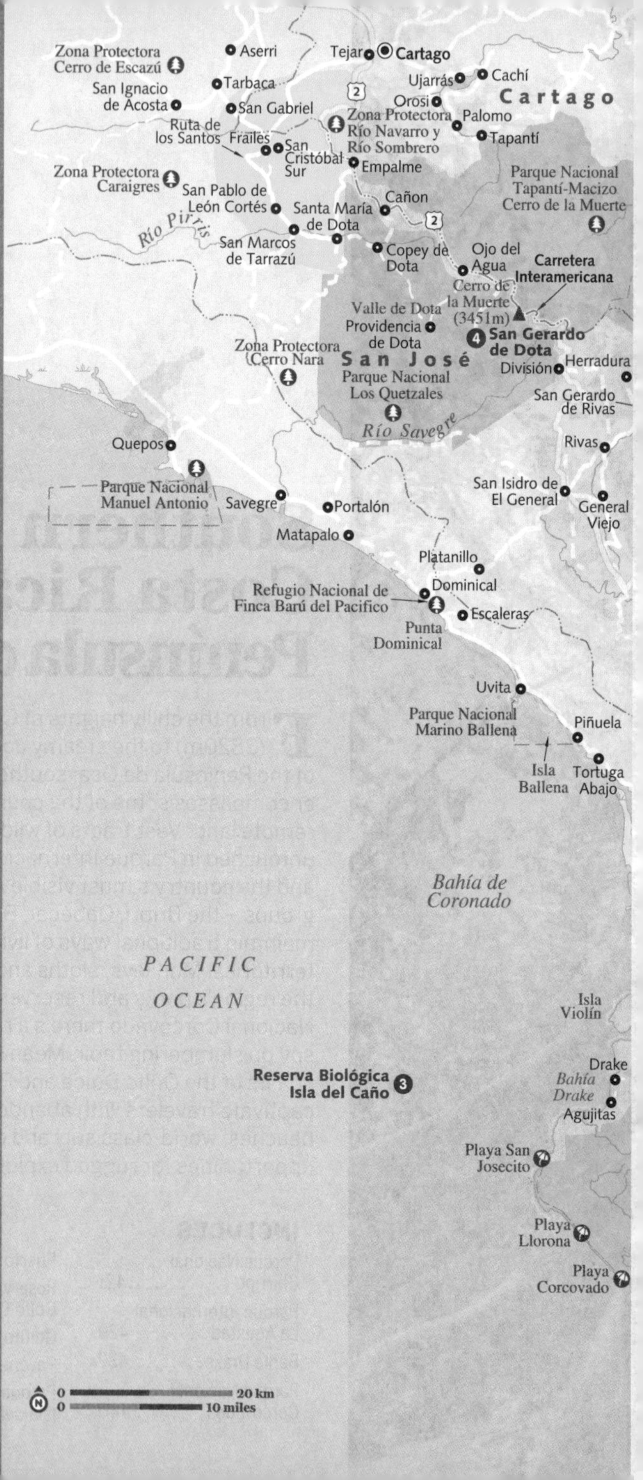

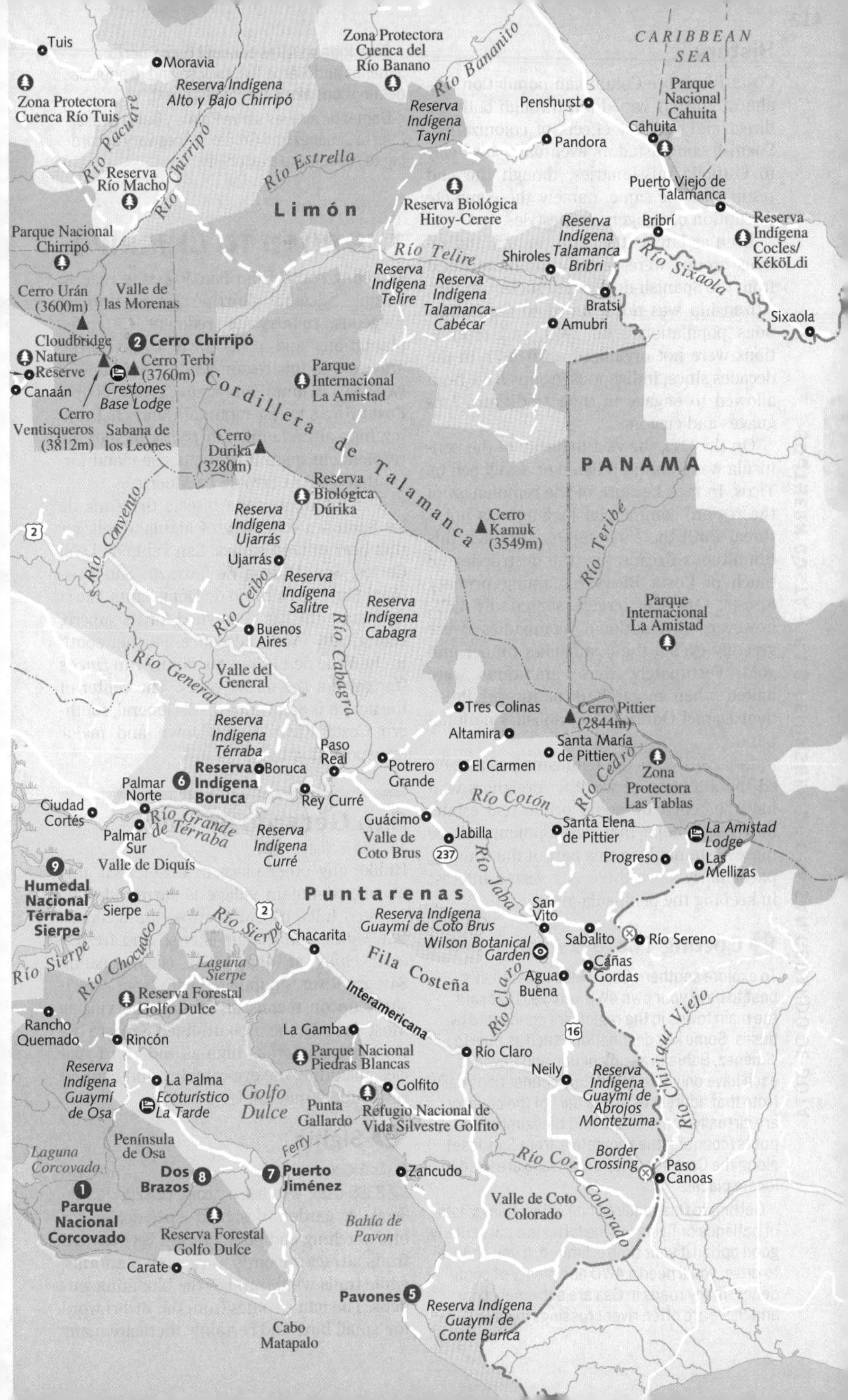

CARIBBEAN SEA
Tuis
Moravia
Zona Protectora Cuenca del Río Banano
Río Bananito
Zona Protectora Cuenca Río Tuis
Río Pacuare
Reserva Indígena Alto y Bajo Chirripó
Reserva Indígena Tayní
Penshurst
Parque Nacional Cahuita
Cahuita
Pandora
Río Chirripó
Río Estrella
Reserva Río Macho
Limón
Reserva Biológica Hitoy-Cerere
Puerto Viejo de Talamanca
Parque Nacional Chirripó
Reserva Indígena Talamanca Bribri
Bribrí
Reserva Indígena Cocles/ KéköLdi
Río Telire
Shiroles
Río Sixaola
Reserva Indígena Telire
Reserva Indígena Talamanca-Cabécar
Bratsi
Cerro Urán (3600m)
Valle de las Morenas
Amubri
Sixaola
Cloudbridge Nature Reserve
Cerro Chirripó
Cerro Terbi (3760m)
Canaán
Crestones Base Lodge
Parque Internacional La Amistad
Cerro Ventisqueros (3812m)
Sabana de los Leones
Cordillera de Talamanca
Cerro Durika (3280m)
PANAMA
Reserva Biológica Dúrika
Río Convento
Cerro Kamuk (3549m)
Reserva Indígena Ujarrás
Río Teribé
Ujarrás
Reserva Indígena Salitre
Reserva Indígena Cabagra
Río Ceibo
Buenos Aires
Parque Internacional La Amistad
Río Cabagra
Río General
Valle del General
Tres Colinas
Cerro Pittier (2844m)
Reserva Indígena Térraba
Altamira
Santa María de Pittier
Paso Real
Zona Protectora Las Tablas
Reserva Indígena Boruca
Boruca
Potrero Grande
El Carmen
Palmar Norte
Río Cedro
Rey Curré
Ciudad Cortés
Río Cotón
Río Grande de Térraba
Guácimo
Santa Elena de Pittier
La Amistad Lodge
Palmar Sur
Reserva Indígena Curré
Valle de Coto Brus
Jabilla
237
Progreso
Las Mellizas
Valle de Diquís
Humedal Nacional Térraba-Sierpe
Río Jaba
Puntarenas
Sierpe
2
San Vito
Río Sierpe
Reserva Indígena Guaymí de Coto Brus
Sabalito
Río Sereno
Chacarita
Wilson Botanical Garden
Fila Costeña
Cañas Gordas
Río Chocuaco
Laguna Sierpe
Agua Buena
Río Claro
Reserva Forestal Golfo Dulce
Interamericana
Río Chiriquí Viejo
Rancho Quemado
La Gamba
16
Rincón
Parque Nacional Piedras Blancas
Río Claro
Neily
Reserva Indígena Guaymí de Osa
La Palma
Golfito
Reserva Indígena Guaymí de Abrojos Montezuma
Ecoturístico La Tarde
Golfo Dulce
Punta Gallardo
Refugio Nacional de Vida Silvestre Golfito
Península de Osa
Ferry
Río Coto
Border Crossing
Paso Canoas
Laguna Corcovado
Dos Brazos
Puerto Jiménez
Zancudo
Parque Nacional Corcovado
Valle de Coto Colorado
Río Coto Colorado
Reserva Forestal Golfo Dulce
Bahía de Pavon
Carate
Pavones
Reserva Indígena Guaymí de Conte Burica
Cabo Matapalo

History

Costa Rica's pre-Columbian population was almost entirely wiped out through both the direct and indirect effects of colonization. Spanish conquistadors eventually gave way to Catholic missionaries, though the end result was the same, namely the complete disruption of indigenous lifestyles.

Even as late as the 20th century, indigenous groups were actively disenfranchised from the Spanish-dominated society. In fact, citizenship was not granted to the indigenous population until 1949, and reservations were not organized until 1977. In the decades since, indigenous groups have been allowed to engage in their traditional languages and customs.

On the Osa, the vast majority of the peninsula was never populated or developed by Ticos. In fact, because of the remoteness of the region, commercial logging was not a threat until the early 1960s. Although this tumultuous decade saw the destruction of much of Costa Rica's remaining primary forests, Osa was largely spared. By 1975, however, international companies were greedily eyeing the peninsula's timber and gold. Fortunately, these ambitions were halted when researchers petitioned President Daniel Oduber to establish a national park.

In recent years the peninsula has attracted the attention of wealthy foreigners who have snatched up some prime real estate, but there's hope that development will be more sustainable in this part of the country, particularly since there is a vested interest in keeping the peninsula green.

Getting There & Away

To explore southern Costa Rica in depth, it's best to have your own 4WD vehicle. That said, the main towns in the region are connected by buses. Some key destinations such as Puerto Jiménez, Bahía Drake, Zancudo and Pavones each have only a couple of bus connections daily. Note that addresses in this part of the country are virtually nonexistent, and the numbered posts (counting the kilometers from San José) along the Carretera Interamericana are used to locate places.

Getting to Osa requires one of two things: lots of patience or flying in. The latter is a particularly good option if your time is limited. If you choose to drive, you'll need a 4WD and plenty of confidence: many roads in Osa are extremely poor and there are often river crossings involved.

Easy Ride shuttles connect both Puerto Jiménez and Sierpe to San José and to popular destinations along the Pacific coast.

Domestic airlines serve Palmar, Bahía Drake, Puerto Jiménez and Golfito. Prices vary according to season and availability.

THE ROAD TO CHIRRIPÓ

Traveling south from San José, the road to Parque Nacional Chirripó passes through gorgeous countryside redolent of coffee plantations and cool, misty cloud forest. Travelers to this region tend to have one of two goals in mind: hiking up Cerro Chirripó, Costa Rica's tallest mountain and challenging high-altitude hike; or trying to spot the resplendent quetzal in the dense cloud forest that cloaks Cerro de La Muerte.

The Interamericana bisects the Zona de los Santos, a collection of highland villages that bear sainted names: San Pablo de León Cortés, San Marcos de Tarrazú, San Cristóbal Sur, San Gerardo de Dota, Santa María de Dota – the last renowned for its superb, ecologically produced coffee. Further south in the Valle de El General, family-run *fincas* (farms) dot the fertile valley. The center of the action is San Isidro de El General, southern Costa Rica's largest town and major transportation hub.

San Gerardo de Dota

POP 220 / ELEV 2194M

Unlike any other place in Costa Rica, this bucolic mountain village is surrounded by forested hills. It's set deep within a mountain valley, and the air is crisp and fresh – even chilly at night. The clear, rushing Savegre River is populated with trout, which show up on menus all around the village. Most notably, the orchard-lined Savegre basin hosts numerous high-altitude bird species, including the eye-catching and beloved resplendent quetzal.

Sights

Batsù Garden GARDENS

(☎8395-0115; www.batsucr.com; US$20; ⏲5am-8pm) A garden designed specifically for birdwatching and photography. Feeders and fruits attract the birds to viewing platforms, while trails wind through the blooming gardens. The name comes from the Bribri word for 'small bird' and certainly there are many

PARKS & RESERVES OF SOUTHERN COSTA RICA & PENINSULA DE OSA

As the country's premier ecotourism destination, the Península de Osa has a plethora of parks, reserves and wildlife refuges. Beyond the Osa, the southern zone has additional less visited protected lands. The following is a list of highlights only.

Parque Internacional La Amistad (p429) This enormous binational park is shared with Panama and protects a biological corridor of incredible ecological significance.

Parque Nacional Chirripó (p421) Home to Costa Rica's highest and most famous peak, Cerro Chirripó, which on a clear day offers views of both the Pacific and the Caribbean.

Parque Nacional Corcovado (p440) Osa's shining crown jewel, and one of Costa Rica's last true wilderness areas.

Reserva Biológica Isla del Caño (p434) A tiny but spectacular marine and terrestrial park, popular with snorkelers, divers and biologists.

hummingbirds, parakeets, flycatchers and tanagers fluttering among the wonderfully natural backdrops. Check in and pay admission at Alma de Árbol (p415).

Parque Nacional Los Quetzales NATIONAL PARK
(☎2514-0403; US$10; ⏰7:30am-3:30pm) Spread along both banks of the Río Savegre, Parque Nacional Los Quetzales covers 50 sq km of rainforest, cloud forest and premontane forest lying along the slopes of the Cordillera de Talamanca. At an altitude of 2000m to 3000m, Los Quetzales is all jagged peaks and glacial lakes. True to the park's name, the beautiful quetzal is here (best spotted during the March to June nesting season), along with trogons, hummingbirds and sooty robins.

Two trails are open for birders and hikers – the 4km (round-trip) Ojo de Agua and the longer Sendero Zeledonia, which includes a 400m accessible paved section near the ranger station.

The entrance is just past Km 76 on the Interamericana. Any bus along this route can drop you off at the ranger station, though most people arrive in a private car or coach.

Activities

There are many places to go birdwatching and hiking in the area. Parque Nacional Los Quetzales is a good option, but there are also private trails in the grounds of most local lodges. Savegre Hotel (p414), Dantica Cloud Forest Lodge (p414) and Paraíso Quetzal Lodge (p415; a little way from San Gerardo) all allow access to nonguests.

Quetzals are easily spotted in April and May (during breeding season) and are fairly common throughout the rest of the year. Most accommodations offer early-morning quetzal walks, on which you are likely to spot at least one of these beauties. There are a few well-known quetzal hangout spots along the river and right in the village: ask at your lodging for details or look for signs along the road. There is also a decent chance to spot a quetzal from the observation deck behind La Comida Típica Miriam (p414), especially in the morning.

Of course, the cloud forest is home to many spectacular avian species, not just the quetzal. Keep your eyes open for collared trogons, emerald toucanets and plenty of hummingbirds. Photographers will appreciate the lovely Batsù Garden, which is specially designed with flowers and fruit to lure the birds into the range of the camera lens.

For those interested in hiking, a challenging 9km trail runs up from San Gerardo to Cerro de la Muerte; the trailhead is in the Savegre Hotel grounds. It's easier to hike down (five hours), but best done with a guide as the trailhead down is not as easy to find as the one going up. Less ambitious hikers can follow an easy 1km trail that rambles along the Río Savegre to a pretty waterfall at the south end of the San Gerardo valley.

Sleeping

★**Sueños del Bosque Lodge** LODGE $$
(☎2740-1023; www.bosquesangerardo.com; d incl breakfast US$65-84; P 📶) Simple but sweet chalets are lined up along a small lake, surrounded by beautiful gardens and trails

DON'T MISS

COFFEE CO-OP TOUR

Coopedota (☎2541-2828; www.coopedota.com; tours US$27-39; ⏱tours 9am, 11am & 2pm daily, plus 4pm Mon-Sat) shows you where your caffeine fix comes from. The 1½-hour tour visits the coffee farm and the production facility. Or opt for a longer tour that includes tastings and/or a barista demonstration. Harvest season (November to March) is the best time to visit. It's on the south side of the Coopedota Building, across from the soccer field in Santa María de Dota.

Coopedota is the first coffee co-op in the world to be certified carbon-neutral by the British Standards Institution, and you'll learn about the steps it takes to reduce its environmental impact during the course of the tour. You can buy bags of freshly roasted coffee at the cafe next to the processing facility.

through the forest. The digs are not fancy, but service is extra accommodating, even by Tico standards. Some of the chalets have fireplaces, which are appreciated when the sun goes down.

Hotel Suria LODGE $$
(☎2740-1004; www.hotelsuria.com; s/d incl breakfast from US$105/125; 📶) At the southern end of the San Gerardo road, rustic wood bungalows offer views of the flower-filled gardens or verdant mountains from their front porches. A plethora of activities and accommodating service are the hallmarks of this friendly, family-run mountain lodge.

Cabinas El Quetzal CABINA $$
(☎2740-1036; www.cabinaselquetzal.com; per person incl 2 meals US$70; P📶) This cluster of simple riverside *cabinas* (cabins) has a homespun feel. Frills are few, but the cabins are clean, comfortable and stocked with piles of blankets. Some are even equipped with wood-burning stoves for the likely event of a chilly night. The included meals are prepared with love.

★**Dantica Cloud Forest Lodge** LODGE $$$
(☎2740-1067; www.dantica.com; d incl breakfast from US$208; P❄📶) The most elegant place in San Gerardo, this upscale lodge consists of lovely stucco bungalows with colorful Colombian architectural accents. The leather sofas and Jacuzzi tubs are nice, but the floor-to-ceiling windows overlooking the cloud forest steal the scene. A nature reserve complete with private trails is just steps away, as is a spa for post-hike pampering.

If the price tag is too steep, it's worth stopping by to browse the gallery's collection of art from all over Latin America or to enjoy a romantic dinner at the fabulous Restaurant Le Tapir.

Savegre Hotel LODGE $$$
(☎2740-1028, in USA & Canada 866-549-1178; www.savegre.com; d from US$162; P@📶) Operated by the Chacón family since 1957, this lodge is beautifully landscaped and hugely popular with birdwatchers, since quetzals nest along the 20km of trails on the 400-hectare property. The gorgeous, wood-paneled rooms and suites have wrought-iron chandeliers and wooden furniture surrounding a stone fireplace. The onsite spa provides pampering and the professional guides organize birding, horseback riding and hiking outings.

Trogon Lodge LODGE $$$
(☎2293-8181; www.trogonlodge.com; s/d incl breakfast from US$140/167; P📶) Hemmed in by cloud forest and with the Río Savegre crossing the property, Trogon Lodge is home to over 190 bird species, including that feathered prize – the quetzal – found along the marked hiking trails. Beautifully landscaped gardens and the excellent farm-to-table restaurant make this a superb choice, as do other delightful touches, such as hot-water bottles delivered to your cabin.

Eating

La Comida Típica Miriam COSTA RICAN $
(☎8593-6032, 2740-1049; www.miriamquetzals.com/restaurant.html; meals US$6-10; ⏱7am-7pm; P) One of the first places you will pass on the San Gerardo road, this cozy house specializes in *comida típica* (regional cooking). Eating here is almost like being welcomed into a Tico home: the food is delicious and abundant, and the hospitality even more so. Catch a glimpse of many birds from the viewing platform out back, including (occasionally) the quetzal.

Miriam also rents a few cabins (US$40) in the woods behind the restaurant: a modest but comfortable place to spend a night or two.

Café Kahawa
CAFE $

(☑2740-1081; www.kahawa.co; mains US$8-10; ⏱7:30am-6pm; P) With alfresco tables sitting above the river, funky skull art and sparkling fish tanks filled with fingerling trout, this atmospheric spot prepares trout in many excellent ways (and there are a few non-fishy dishes). Here's a chance to sample some unique variations on the theme, such as trout in coconut sauce and trout *ceviche*.

Restaurante Los Lagos
COSTA RICAN $

(☑2740-1009; mains US$7-10; ⏱7am-7pm) Set amid gardens, ponds and a splashing fountain, this is the place to catch your own trout and have it seasoned, lightly breaded and then deep-fried for lunch, alongside some french fries made from locally grown potatoes. The complimentary dessert, *papaya chilena* (sweet glacé papaya), is also a regional favorite and is served with a scoop of ice cream.

Alma de Árbol
CAFE $$

(☑2740-1003; mains US$8-13; ⏱11:30am-8pm Wed-Mon) This sunny cafe is a perfect stop for lunch or a light dinner, with an eclectic menu highlighting all the local goodness, from fruits to cheeses to homemade breads and (of course) fresh caught trout. Don't miss the specialty cocktail, a mixture of peach, gooseberries and spices, with Costa Rican sugarcane liqueur.

★ Restaurant Le Tapir
COSTA RICAN $$$

(☑2740-1069; www.dantica.com; Dantica Cloud Forest Lodge; pasta US$10-13, mains US$16-23; ⏱7am-9pm) With 270-degree views of the valley, this glass-encased restaurant specializes in homemade pasta, rainbow trout and mouthwatering steaks, all garnished with organic herbs fresh from the onsite garden. The house specialties are unusual and delectable preparations, such as blackberry tenderloin with ground pepper and rosemary and chicken breast in passion fruit sauce.

❶ Getting There & Away

If you're driving, the turnoff to San Gerardo de Dota is near Km 80 on the Interamericana. From here, the steep road down into the valley alternates between paved and dirt; you'll appreciate your 4WD. Take it slowly, as two-way traffic necessitates a bit of negotiation. Buses between San José and San Isidro de El General can drop you at the turnoff, but bear in mind that the village spreads along 9km of road, so you may have a fair hike ahead of you. Taxis sometimes wait at the drop-off ($25 to Savegre, for example).

Cerro de La Muerte

Around Km 89, between Empalme and San Isidro de El General, the Interamericana reaches its highest point along the famed Cerro de la Muerte (3451m). The 'Hill of Death' received its moniker during its prehighway days, when crossing the mountains required travel on foot or horseback and many travelers succumbed to exposure.

It's still a harrowing journey, snaking the fog-shrouded spine along a path riddled with blind corners, hair-raising cliffs and careless drivers who take huge risks to overtake slower road users. The upside? Exquisite panoramic views of the Cordillera de Talamanca.

Cerro de la Muerte marks the northernmost extent of the *páramo,* a highland shrub and tussock grass habitat typical of the southern zone. This Andean-style landscape is rich in wildlife and home to many of the same species found in nearby Parque Nacional Chirripó. On the way to San Isidro the road also descends through cloud forests, montane and premontane forest.

There are several lodges spread out along this stretch of highway between Empalme and San Isidro de El General. Note that addresses in this part of Costa Rica are nonexistent, so accommodations tend to be listed by their 'Km' distance marker.

Bosque del Tolomuco
B&B $$

(☑8847-7207; www.bosquedeltolomuco.com; Interamericana Km 118; d US$65-75, extra person $25; P🛜❄) Named for the sly tayra (tree otter) spotted on the grounds, this cutesy B&B is run by a lovely, chatty expat couple. There are five spacious, light-filled cabins, the most charming of which is the secluded 'Hummingbird Cabin.' The grounds offer 5km of hiking trails, ample opportunities to indulge in birdwatching and some magnificent views of Los Cruces and Chirripó.

Delicious home-cooked meals are available for an additional price.

Paraíso Quetzal Lodge
LODGE $$

(☑2200-0241; www.paraisoquetzal.com; Interamericana Km 70; d incl breakfast US$116-145, half-board US$157-189) Birders rave about this lodge, surrounded by 13km of walking trails and viewing platforms that provide an excellent chance of spotting the resplendent quetzal. The scattering of wooden cabins is kept warm by a generous collection of space heaters and woollen blankets. Superior cabins come with Jacuzzis and superb valley views, ideal for canoodling with your sweetie.

The lodge offers **quetzal tours** three times a day (open to nonguests, US$60 per couple), cooperating with local farmers who monitor and report on the birds' whereabouts.

Mirador Valle del General LODGE **$$**
(☎2200-5465; www.valledelgeneral.com; Interamericana Km 119; d incl breakfast US$50-80; P 📶) This aptly named lodge features a panoramic view from its charming reception area and restaurant, which serves local specialties such as fried trout. Below, spotless rooms and bungalows built from cultivated wood are brightened by colorful indigenous tapestries and also offer spectacular valley views. Nature trails through the cloud forest often receive visits from tanagers and other feathered life.

Offering a different perspective on the mountainside and valley, there is also a **canopy tour** (US$37, open 8am to 2pm) on the grounds of the lodge. With seven ziplines, a swinging bridge and a 32m rappel, it's less of a destination and more of a fun driving break.

Mirador de Quetzales CABINA **$$**
(☎2200-4185, 8381-8456; www.elmiradordequetzales.com; Interamericana Km 70; d incl breakfast US$96; P) About 1km west of the Interamerican, a cluster of 15 wooden cabins, warmed by electric heaters, overlook the forest-cloaked valley. Four kilometers of trails weave among the immense cypress trees – which provide a year-round home to the namesake quetzal. Expert guides lead an early-morning 'quetzal quest' for US$25 per person.

Getting There & Away

Frequent buses running between San José and San Isidro de El General can drop you off near any of these lodges.

San Isidro de El General

POP 45,000

San Isidro de El General is a sprawling, utilitarian market town at the crossroads between some of Costa Rica's prime destinations. It's a place where few travelers choose to linger, but as the fastest-growing urban area outside the capital, it is an authentic, bustling Tico town that does not revolve around tourism.

'El General' (often referred to as Pérez Zeledón, the name of the municipality) is the southern sector's largest population center and major transportation hub. If you're traveling by public transportation to the southern Pacific beaches or Chirripó, a brief stop is inevitable. Some accommodations options just outside of the town environs are worthy destinations in their own right.

Festivals & Events

Agricultural Festival CULTURAL
(early Feb) This fair is a chance for local farmers to strut their stuff – and that they do, by taking over the agricultural showgrounds 4km south of the city with regional culinary delights. There are also bullfights, horsemanship events, an orchid exhibition, livestock competitions and concerts in the evening.

Sleeping

Hotel Los Crestones HOTEL **$**
(☎2770-1200, 2770-1500; www.hotelloscrestones.com; cnr Calle Central & Av 14; s/d/tr from US$40/50/65, plus US$10 for air-con; P ❄ 📶 🏊) This sharp motor court is decked with blooming hedges and climbing vines outside – indeed a welcome sight to the road-weary traveler. Inside, functional rooms feature modern furnishings and fixtures, which are made all the better by the staff who keep this place running efficiently.

Hotel Chirripó HOTEL **$**
(☎2771-0529; Av 2, btwn Calles Central & 1; d incl breakfast US$46; P ❄ 📶) Let's put it bluntly: if you're traveling through town, weary and cash poor, this is the cheapest choice. The centrally located hotel is a two-minute stroll from the bus terminals and filled with bare, whitewashed rooms that are barren but utterly dirt- and grime-free.

Talari Mountain Lodge LODGE **$$**
(☎2771-0341; www.talari.co.cr; Rivas; s/d/tr incl breakfast from US$80/96/118; P 📶 🏊) This secluded mountain lodge is a birdwatcher's haven, with over 200 species spotted along the three well-maintained trails on the riverside property. Accommodations are in simple wooden cabins hemmed in by the forest, and there's also a pool and a tennis court. From San Isidro, follow the road to San Gerardo de Rivas for 7km and look for the driveway on the right.

Best Western Hotel Zima HOTEL $$

(2770-1114; www.bestwesternhotelzima.com; Interamericana; d incl breakfast from US$76; P) This Best Western benefits from a central location, yet it is far enough from the main highway to avoid the traffic noise. The rooms are of a standard, business variety – not hugely memorable, but very comfortable, and equipped with TV, refrigerator and coffee maker. Staff are friendly and eager to please.

Hacienda AltaGracia RESORT $$$

(2105-3000, in USA 815-812-2212; http://altagracia.aubergeresorts.com; Santa Teresa de Cahón; ste US$666-1366; P) A hillside hacienda overlooking the lush Valle de General, this Auberge Resort consists of self-contained *casitas* (cottages) and suites, their decor stylish and understated (neutral shades, dark leather), surrounded by 350 hectares – ideal for hiking, horseback riding and observing from the air from one of the resort's own ultralights. Dining focuses on the farm-to-table concept, and there's a world-class spa.

Eating & Drinking

★ **Urban Farm Cafe** INTERNATIONAL $

(2771-2442; Calle Central; mains US$5-8; 7am-7pm Mon-Fri, to 4pm Sat) With its 'from farm to table' motto, this delightful cafe single-handedly pushes San Isidro's dining scene up a big notch. Breakfast options range from 'Hawaiian-style' macadamia pancakes with banana to veggie omelets, while its lunchtime wraps and salads are overflowing with fresh vegetables. Dine out back on a covered terrace, surrounded by the garden where many ingredients are growing.

Antojos de Maíz COSTA RICAN $

(2772-4381; chorreadas US$3, mains US$5; 7:30am-7:30pm Wed-Mon) For all things corn, stop at this traditional roadside restaurant on your way to or from the mountain. Our favorite here is the *chorreada,* a traditional sweet pancake made with fresh white or yellow corn and served with sour cream. Pairs very well with strong, organic coffee.

Located halfway between San Isidro de El General and San Gerardo de Rivas. The open-air deck overlooks a wonderful, tree-filled valley.

San Isidro de El General

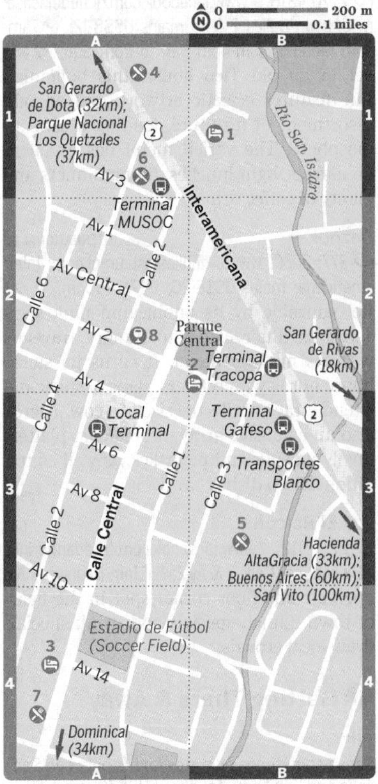

San Isidro de El General

Sleeping

1 Best Western Hotel Zima B1
2 Hotel Chirripó B2
3 Hotel Los Crestones A4

Eating

4 Bazookas A1
5 Farmers Market B3
6 Kafe de la Casa A1
7 Urban Farm Cafe A4

Drinking & Nightlife

8 Bar El Balcón A2

Farmers Market MARKET $

(off Calle 3) The largest *feria* (fair) in the region, this farmers market starts early Thursday morning and usually winds down by early afternoon on Friday; organic produce, prepared foods and goods are bountiful.

Kafe de la Casa CAFE $

(☎2770-4816; www.facebook.com/kafedelacasa; Av 3, btwn Calles 2 & 4; mains US$8-12; ⊙7am-7pm Mon-Fri, 8am-4pm Sat, to 2pm Sun;) Set in an old Tico house, this bohemian cafe features eclectic artwork and an odd assortment of furniture, lending a cozy atmosphere. The varied menu has excellent breakfasts, light lunches, filling dinners and plenty of coffee drinks.

Bazookas INTERNATIONAL $$

(☎2771-2050; www.bazookasrestaurant.com; Interamericana; mains US$8-20; ⊙7am-10pm;) Recognizable by its bubblegum pink signage, this diner caters to hungry travelers with its massive menu. It earns its steakhouse horns with burgers, slaps of steak and a tender rack of ribs the size of a cow. There's also an extensive array of breakfast platters involving eggs and pancakes, as well as traditional Tico dishes.

Bar El Balcón BAR

(☎2771-1112; www.facebook.com/FoodanddrinkselBalcon; cnr Calle 2 & Av 2; ⊙11am-midnight) An open-air 2nd-floor corner spot in the heart of town. Lunch specials and drink specials draw local crowds.

Getting There & Away

AIR

Sansa sometimes operates flights between San José and San Isidro for about US$70 one way, although these flights were not running at the time of research.

BUS

In San Isidro the **local bus terminal** (Mercado; Av 6;) is on Av 6 and serves nearby villages. The bus to San Gerardo de Rivas (for Parque Nacional Chirripó; US$4, 1½ hours) departs from the local terminal six times daily from 5:45am.

Local buses from **Terminal Gafeso** (☎2771-1523) serve Buenos Aires (nine daily, US$2.50), with onward connections to Reserva Biológica Dúrika.

Long-distance buses leave from dedicated terminals near the Interamericana and frequently fill up, so buy tickets early. Note that buses heading south to Golfito or Ciudad Neily will go through Palmar Norte.

Terminals Tracopa & MUSOC

You will find **Terminal Tracopa** (☎2771-0468; www.tracopacr.com) on the Interamericana, just southwest of Av Central, and **Terminal MUSOC** (☎2771-0414), which only serves San José, just beside Kafe de la Casa. If heading for Paso Canoas, Golfito or Palmar Norte, try to catch a bus that originates from San Isidro, or risk standing room only.

Terminal Quepos

Transportes Blanco (☎2771-4744) is on the side street west of the Interamericana. Destinations include the following:

Dominical (US$3; 1½ hours; daily 5am, 8am, 9am, 11:30am, 3:30pm and 4pm)

Puerto Jiménez (via Palmar Norte; US$9.30; five hours; daily 6:30am, 11am and 3pm)

Quepos (US$4.75; 2½ hours; daily 5am, 8am, 11:30am and 3.30pm)

Uvita (US$3.50; two hours; daily 5am, 8am, 9am and 4pm)

BUSES FROM TERMINALS TRACOPA & MUSOC

DESTINATION	COST (US$)	DURATION (HR)	DEPARTURES (DAILY)
Golfito	8	4	10am
Neily	7	4½	4:45am, 7am, 10:40am, 12:30pm, 3pm, 4:10pm, 6:30pm
Palmar Norte	10	2½	4:45am, 7am, 8am, 10am, 10:40am, 12:30pm, 1pm, 3pm, 4:10pm
Paso Canoas	9	4¾	8am, 10:40am, 4:10pm, 6:30pm, 9:30pm
San José	6	3	hourly
San Vito	6.50	3½	5:30am, 9am, 11am, 2pm, 3:20pm, 7pm

San Gerardo de Rivas

POP 350 / ELEV 1219M

If you plan to climb Chirripó, you're in the right place – the tiny, tranquil, spread-out town of San Gerardo de Rivas is at the doorstep of the national park. Here you can get supplies, have a good night's rest and take a hot shower before and after the trek. Be aware that all arrangements for hiking permits and accommodations must be made well in advance, using the park's online reservation system.

For those who don't have the time or energy to summit Chirripó, there are also lovely, less difficult hikes in private nature reserves, and rural tourism aplenty, from the local **trout farm** (☎2742-5054; www.facebook.com/trucherolos.cocolisos; ⏲9am-6pm Sat & Sun & by appointment) to producers of **cheese** (☎2742-5125; www.quesoscanaan.com; ⏲9am-5pm Mon-Sat) and **chocolate** (☎8820-7095; www.samaritanxocolata.com; ⏲10am-4pm Mon-Sat) in nearby **Canaán**. San Gerardo's bird-filled alpine scenery makes it a beautiful place to linger, hike or no hike.

The road to San Gerardo de Rivas winds its way 22km up the valley of the Río Chirripó from San Isidro.

Sights & Activities

★Cloudbridge Nature Reserve NATURE RESERVE
(☎in USA 917-494-5408; www.cloudbridge.org; admission by donation, tours from US$35; ⏲6am-6pm) About 2km past the trailhead to Cerro Chirripó you will find the entrance to the mystical, magical Cloudbridge Nature Reserve. Covering 283 hectares on the side of Cerro Chirripó, this private reserve is an ongoing reforestation and preservation project founded by Genevieve Giddy and her late husband Ian. A network of trails traverses the property, which is easy to explore independently. Even if you don't get far past the entrance, you'll find two waterfalls, including the magnificent Catarata Pacifica.

The trails range from the moderate but stunning Waterfall Trail to the more strenuous Sendero Montaña Loop, which joins the main Chirripó trail. Guided tours in English include birdwatching, night hikes and strolls through old-growth forest. Volunteer reforestation and conservation opportunities are listed on the reserve's website.

Talamanca Reserve NATURE RESERVE
(☎2742-5080; www.talamancareserve.com; US$15) With over 1600 hectares of primary and secondary cloud forest, this private reserve has miles of hiking trails to explore. Visitors will be rewarded with spectacular mountain vistas, 10 different waterfalls and sightings of countless bird species. Bordering the Parque Nacional Chirripó, Talamanca is a viable alternative for hikers who do not care to summit the mountain.

Jardines Secretos GARDENS
(☎2742-5086, 8451-3001; www.sangerardocostarica.com/es/activities/gardens; US$5; ⏲8am-4pm) These not-so-secret gardens make for a tranquil pre- or post-Chirripó pastime as the owners talk you through their collection of orchids and other tropical plants. Find the turnoff just after the ranger station but before the first bridge.

Thermal Hot Springs HOT SPRINGS
(Gevi Aguas Termales; ☎2742-5210; Herradura; US$8; ⏲7am-5:30pm) After climbing a mountain, what could be more enticing than soothing your tired muscles in thermal pools, naturally heated to 37°C (98.6ºF)? Two pools provide ample space for soaking.

Just north of the ranger station, take the left-hand turnoff (before the first bridge) and continue 700m on the paved road. Look for a signed turnoff on the right and cross the suspension bridge over the river. A steep switchback road climbs for another 1km to a small house and the entrance to the hot springs.

Festivals & Events

Carrera Chirripó SPORTS
(www.carrerachirripo.com; ⏲Feb) This grueling race from San Gerardo de Rivas to Crestones Base Lodge and back (34km) takes place at the end of February, with up to 225 participants. If you're trekking up the mountain, you may be disheartened (or inspired) to know that the fastest person covered the distance in three hours and nine minutes.

Sleeping

★Hostel Cabaña Mis Ojos GUESTHOUSE $
(☎8349-6842; www.facebook.com/MisOjos2015; r incl breakfast US$25) This charming wooden cottage overlooks the river, northeast of the soccer field. Guests rave about the warm welcome and tasty meals prepared by the owner Laura, who lives onsite, speaks

decent English and personally retrieves her guests from the bus station. There's no sign (other than 'Rooms Available'), but look for the funky mural just before the road forks.

Hotel Uran HOSTEL $

(2742-5003; www.hoteluran.com; s/d US$45/58, without bathroom US$30/48; P) Just 70m below the trailhead, these no-nonsense digs are a longtime mecca for hikers heading to/from Chirripó. Budget-friendly rooms are fine for a restful snooze, while the onsite restaurant and laundry facilities cater to the hiker set. Note that it's possible to buy beer here (the *pulpería* – corner store – in town doesn't sell alcohol).

Casa Hostel Chirripó HOSTEL $

(8814-8876, 2742-5020; www.facebook.com/Hostel-Casa-Chirripó-417397658422067; dm US$17, d US$48, without bathroom US$32;) Near the soccer field, this colorful hostel gives guests a space to cook and socialize, as well as basic but clean rooms and dorms to lay their weary heads. Taxis to the trailhead cost US$10, which can be split among groups.

Hotel Roca Dura CABINA $

(2742-5071; www.facebook.com/RocaDuraHotel; d incl breakfast from $US22; P) Located in the center of town just opposite the soccer field, this hip hostel is built right into the side of a giant boulder, lending a *Flintstones* ambience to the quarters. Wall murals brighten the smallest stone rooms, while pricier rooms have tree-trunk furniture and fixtures plus views of forested hillsides. The onsite restaurant serves decent pizza and cold beer.

★Casa Mariposa HOSTEL $$

(2742-5037; www.casamariposachirripo.net; dm US$22, s/d US$56/70, without bathroom from US$34/50; P@) Just 50m from the Chirripó trailhead, this adorable hostel is built into the side of the mountain and is characterized by the warmth and knowledge of owners John and Jill. Traveler-oriented benefits – warm clothes to borrow for the hike, laundry service and tips on alternative activities in the area – make it a top spot.

In the evening, guests gather around the wood stove in the communal living room to read, plan hikes and welcome weary hikers returning from the summit. There's a tidy kitchen, a lookout with hammocks on the roof and a stone hot tub. Advance booking is recommended. Parking here is $2 per night.

Hotel de Montaña El Pelícano HOTEL $$

(2742-5050; www.hotelpelicano.net; d incl breakfast US$72-82, ste US$98; P) About 300m south of the ranger station, a steep driveway leads uphill from the main road to this simple, functional lodge. Surrounded by gorgeous vegetation, the lodge has a spacious restaurant and a collection of spartan but spotless rooms overlooking the river valley. The highlight of the property is the gallery of the owner, a late-blooming artist who sculpts whimsical wood pieces.

★Talamanca Reserve HOTEL $$$

(2742-5080; www.talamancareserve.com; d US$140-160, apt US$195; P) Set within the eponymous reserve, these appealing garden and river cabins all show off beautifully embellished wood and tile interiors, with indigenous and animal motifs adorning the walls. Private terraces overlook the surrounding cloud forest. There's a good onsite restaurant. The main attraction, of course, is access to the many trails and natural attractions of the Talamanca Reserve (p419).

The accommodations and hiking tours are managed by the friendly, bilingual Kenneth, who was born and raised on the reserve, and whose family still maintains the gardens, fruit trees, trails and a reforestation project here.

Río Chirripó Retreat HOTEL $$$

(2742-5109; www.riochirripo.com; d US$173-195, ste US$234-305, all incl breakfast; P) This gorgeous spot is 1.5km from San Gerardo, in Canaán. The good-vibe retreat is centered on an open-air, Santa Fe–style communal area, with a a yoga studio overlooking the river. You can hear the rush of the river from 10 light-filled cabins, where woven blankets and stenciled walls evoke the southwest USA.

On the grounds are a private reserve with a 30-minute hiking trail, a couple of glorious pools, a hot tub and a relaxing spa.

Eating

Eating options in the village are sparse, but some hotels have restaurants attached, including Hotel Roca Dura and Hotal Uran.

★Garden House Observatory CAFE $

(8524-6857; www.facebook.com/gardenhousecr; mains US$6-8; 7am-6pm;) Come for breakfast or lunch and while away the day, sipping coffee, sampling baked goodies and watching the feathered friends flitting about the grounds. A short trail meanders through the gardens, but there's plenty to keep your attention if you prefer to sit still on the delightful terrace. The menu is short (juices, snacks, salads) but it's all fresh and delicious.

Batsú Gastropub GASTROPUB **$$**
(www.facebook.com/batsugastropub; Canaán; mains US$8-26; ⏲11am-9pm; 📶) The tiny village of Canaán is not the type of place you would expect to find a 'gastropub' yet here it is. The menu is eclectic and delicious, featuring items like sesame-crusted tuna, grilled chicken with Gruyère and figs, sandwiches served on homemade bread, and an extremely tasty veggie burger.

There is a small selection of beers on tap and live music on Friday and Saturday nights. Nightlife!

Information

The **Chirripó Ranger Station** (Sinac; ☎905-244-7747, in USA 506-2742-5348; ⏲8am-noon & 1-4:30pm) is 1km below the soccer field, at the entrance to San Gerardo de Rivas. If you're planning to hike up Cerro Chirripó, you must stop by the ranger station before you start the hike to confirm your permit and obtain a wrist band. If you haven't booked your park permit in advance, there's a slim chance of availability.

After obtaining your wrist band, you must also stop at the office of the Consorcio Aguas Eternas (p422), the concessionaire of nonessential services in Parque Nacional Chirripó. The office is right next to the soccer field. This is to confirm your lodging and food at Crestones Base Lodge. Note that you must reserve and pay for lodging and food in advance online, within a few days of purchasing your park permit, or your park permit will be canceled. But you *also* must stop at the consortium office prior to entering the park to confirm your reservation.

Note that the concession is subject to change, and current instructions for how to reserve lodgings are always available through the online reservation system (https://serviciosenlinea.sinac.go.cr).

Getting There & Away

Arriving via public transportation requires a connection through San Isidro. Buses to San Isidro (US$2, 1½ hours) depart from the soccer field six times daily (four daily on Sunday) between 5:15am and 6:45pm.

Driving from San Isidro, head south on the Interamericana and cross Río San Isidro south of town. About 500m further on, cross the unsigned Río Jilguero and take the first, steep turn up to the left, about 300m beyond the Jilguero. Note that this turnoff is not marked (if you miss the turn, it is signed from the northbound side).

The ranger station is on this road at the start of San Gerardo de Rivas, about 18km from the Interamericana. Past the ranger station, the road passes through the village and continues up to the Chirripó trailhead and Cloudbridge Nature Reserve. The road is passable for ordinary cars, but a 4WD is recommended if you are driving to Hotel Urán or to Cloudbridge Nature Reserve, as the unpaved road is steep and truly hideous.

Parque Nacional Chirripó

Costa Rica's mountainous spine runs the length of the country in four distinct mountain ranges, of which the Cordillera de Talamanca is the highest, longest and most remote. The cordillera's highlight and the focus of the high-altitude Parque Nacional Chirripó is Costa Rica's highest peak, **Cerro Chirripó** (3820m).

The only way up Chirripó is on foot. Although the trekking routes are challenging, watching the sunrise from such lofty heights is one of the country's undeniable highlights.

Parque Nacional Chirripó is a welcome respite from lowland heat. Above 3400m, the landscape is *páramo,* comprising scrubby trees and grasslands. Rocky outposts punctuate the otherwise barren hills, and feed a series of glacial lakes that earned the park its iconic name: Chirripó means 'Eternal Waters.'

The bare *páramo* contrasts with the lush cloud forest, which dominates the hillsides between 2500m and 3400m. Oak trees tower over the dense undergrowth and the evergreen canopy.

Activities

Wildlife-Watching

The varying altitude means an amazing diversity of fauna in Parque Nacional Chirripó. Particularly famous for its extensive birdlife, the national park is home to several endangered species, including the harpy eagle (the largest, most powerful raptor in the Americas) and the resplendent quetzal (especially visible between March and May). Even besides these highlights, you might see highland birds including the three-wattled bellbird, black guan and tinamou. The Andean-like *páramo* guarantees volcano junco, sooty robin, slaty finch, large-footed finch and the endemic volcano

PLANNING YOUR HIKE

Hiking up Chirripó requires a bit of planning, though the process has become significantly easier with the implementation of online booking systems for park permits, lodging and food. Make arrangements well in advance (especially during the dry season), as space is limited.

➡ First, purchase your park permits through SINAC at www.sinac.go.cr. (Click on 'Online booking' and then 'Check In.') You'll need to purchase a permit for each day you'll be in the park, which can be done up to six months in advance.

➡ After you purchase your permits, you will receive an email from **Consorcio Aguas Eternas** (Consortium Office; ☎2742-5097, 2742-5200; www.chirripo.org; ⏲8am-5pm Mon-Sat, from 9am Sun), which currently handles lodging and food inside the park. Follow the link to reserve your bed at Crestones Base Lodge, as well as meals. Note that you have a limited time to reserve your lodging (about four days) before your park permit is canceled.

➡ *Don't forget!* You still have to check in at the Chirripó ranger station (p421) and at the Consorcio Aguas Eternas office in San Gerardo de Rivas before you start your hike. Ideally do it the day before you hike; otherwise you will get a late start, as the offices do not open until 8am.

When to Go

The dry season (from late December to April) is the most popular time to visit Chirripó. February and March are the driest months with the clearest skies, though it may still rain. On weekends, and especially during holidays, the trails can get crowded with Tico hiking groups. The park is open year-round, and the early months of the rainy season are good for climbing as it usually doesn't rain in the morning.

In any season, temperatures can drop below freezing at night, so warm clothes (including hat and gloves) and rainwear are necessary. Wear sturdy boots and bring good second-skin blister plasters. In exposed areas, high winds seem even colder. The ranger station in San Gerardo de Rivas is a good place to check on the weather conditions.

Chirripó's trails are well marked and do not require maps.

hummingbird, which is found only in Costa Rica's highlands.

In addition to the prolific birdlife, the park is home to some unusual high-altitude reptiles, such as the green spiny lizard and the highland alligator lizard. Mammals include pumas, Baird's tapirs, mountain peccaries, spider monkeys, capuchin monkeys, and – at higher elevations – Dice's rabbits and the coyotes that feed on them.

Spotting the rarer animals is unlikely, but here are a few tips. Pumas stick to the savanna areas and use the trails at dawn and dusk to move about. Baird's tapirs gravitate to various highland lagoons, mainly in the rainy season, so stake out the muddy edges at dawn or dusk if you see recent tracks. Coyotes sometimes feed at night at the rubbish bins near Crestones Base Lodge.

Climbing Chirripó

The park entrance is at San Gerardo de Rivas, which lies 1219m above sea level; the altitude at the summit is 3820m, which makes it 2.6km straight up! A well-marked 19.6km trail leads all the way to the top, with trail markers every kilometer, and no technical climbing is required. It would be nearly impossible to get lost.

Altitude sickness can be an issue as you get higher up. Watch out for nausea, shortness of breath, headaches and exhaustion. If you start feeling unwell, rest for a little while; if the symptoms persist, descend immediately.

The amount of time it takes to get up varies greatly – it can take as little as five and as many as 12 hours to cover the 14.5km from the start of the trail to the Crestones Base Lodge, depending on how fit you are; bank on at least seven hours. From the lodge it's another 5.1km to the summit, which takes around two hours one way.

Most hikers start the hike between 4am and 5am, though there's nothing to stop you from leaving earlier. The start of the trail is just past Casa Mariposa (and about 4km from the ranger station). The actual entrance to the park is a further 4km along the trail.

The first 6km or so are mostly uphill, over uneven, rocky ground, with some relatively flat stretches. You pass through dense cloud forest, so keep an eye out for quetzals.

Then there's a gentle descent toward the shelter at **Llano Bonito** (7.5km), which is a good place for a break. Here you can stock up on drinking water, use the flushing toilets and buy snacks and even aspirin. This place is not equipped for overnight stays.

Just beyond begins the **Cuesta de los Arrepentidos** (Hill of the Repentants) and boy, will you repent! (At this point, try not to think about the long-distance runners who run from San Gerardo to Crestones and back again in around four hours.) It's a steep uphill slog until you reach the top of **Monte Sin Fe** (which translates as 'Mountain Without Faith'), a preliminary crest that reaches 3200m at around Km 10. By then you're on exposed ground, flanked by stunted tree growth, with gorgeous mountain views around you. The trail then descends gently for around 1.5km, making you grind your teeth, since what goes down must come up! The last section is an interminable, steep ascent before you see the green roofs of the **Crestones Base Lodge** just downhill from you; breathe a sigh of relief before descending to 3400m.

Reaching the lodge is the hardest part. From here the hike to the **summit** is 5.1km on relatively flatter terrain. Carry a warm jacket, rainwear, water, snacks and a flashlight, but leave most of your gear at the lodge. There is one tricky spot where it's possible to lose the trail if you are hiking in the dark. When you come to an open area where the trail is not clear, look for arrows painted on the rocks to point you in the right direction. The last couple hundred meters is very steep, requiring scrambling on all fours. From the summit on a clear day, the vista stretches to both the Caribbean Sea and the Pacific Ocean. The deep-blue lakes and the plush-green hills carpet the Valle de las Morenas in the foreground.

Most hikers reach the lodge around lunchtime on the first day, then leave for the summit at around 3am the next morning to arrive in time to watch the sunrise – a spectacular experience.

A minimum of two days is recommended to climb from the ranger station in San Gerardo to the summit and back. This leaves no time for additional exploration, however. During peak season you're allowed to book a maximum of two nights at the lodge, and at all other times the max is three nights. This gives you extra time to explore the trails around the summit and/or the Base Lodge.

Hiking Other Trails

There are several attractive destinations that are accessible by trails from the Crestones Base Lodge. These will require at least another day and real topographical maps. An alternative, longer route between the Base Lodge and the summit goes via **Cerro Terbi** (3760m), as well as **Los Crestones**, the moonlike rock formations that adorn many postcards. If you are hanging around for a few days, the glorious, grassy **Sabana de los Leones** is a popular destination that offers a stark contrast to the otherwise alpine scenery. Peak-baggers will want to visit **Cerro Ventisqueros** (3812m), which is also within a day's walk of Crestones. These trails are fairly well maintained, but it's worth inquiring about conditions before setting out.

For hard-core adventurers, an alternative route is to take a guided three- or five-day loop trek that begins in the nearby village of Herradura and spends a day or two traversing cloud forest and *páramo* on the slopes of Fila Urán. Hikers ascend **Cerro Urán** (3600m) before the final ascent of Chirripó and then descend through San Gerardo. This trip requires bush camping and carrying a tent. **Costa Rica Trekking Adventures** (☎2771-4582; www.chirripo.com) can make arrangements for this tour or the other trails in Parque Nacional Chirripó.

Sleeping & Eating

Crestones Base Lodge (☎2742-5097; www.chirripo.org/hospedaje; dm US$37;) is the only accommodations in the park. Visitors may stay a maximum of three nights most of the year, and only two nights during peak season. The price for a dorm bed includes sheets, a pillow and a blanket. The lodge is not heated and it gets cold at night, so bring warm clothes to sleep in. Solar panels provide electric light for limited hours, though showers are cold.

Space is at a premium during holiday periods and on weekends during the dry season. Your chances of getting a last-minute place are best when you have days to spare or come in low season.

DAY HIKING CHIRRIPÓ

It's not recommended, but it is done. For the masochistically inclined or the super fit, it's feasible to summit Chirripó and return to town in a single day.

The strategy here is to start early – around 1am or 2am. That way you can get to Crestones Base Lodge by midmorning, have time to rest, summit, and then head back down again in the afternoon. Walking part of the way in the dark is not a problem, since the trail is clearly marked and it's almost impossible to get lost. Make sure you take food, water, a flashlight with spare batteries and warm clothes.

That said, keep in mind that this is a 39.2km round trip that involves a climb of 2000m into high-altitude territory. It is an exhausting uphill slog most of the way. The summit is more likely to be cloudy in the afternoons, meaning you probably won't get much of a view. Summiting and returning on the same day almost invariably means descending at least part of the way in the dark (which is not dangerous in this case, but it's not that fun).

There are several excellent alternatives to summiting Chirripó, including fantastic day hikes in the Cloudbridge Nature Reserve (p419) or Talamanca Reserve (p419). Whatever you do, don't underestimate the mountain.

There's a good cafeteria serving three meals per day (US$10 to US$13 per meal) at Crestones Base Lodge. Hikers are not permitted to cook their own meals but they may bring cold food and snacks.

Information

To climb Chirripó, you must purchase your park permits and reserve your lodging well in advance (p422)!

It is essential that you stop at the ranger station (p421) in San Gerardo de Rivas the day before you intend to climb Chirripó to confirm your park permit and obtain a wrist band (bring your passport and reservation confirmation).

Afterwards, you must confirm your Crestones Base Lodge reservation at the Consorcio Aguas Eternas (p422). You can also make arrangements to hire a porter (a fixed fee of US$100 for up to 15kg of luggage), though it's now less necessary than ever. Since Crestones offers meals and includes bedding in the accommodations price, you can travel light, without cooking gear or a sleeping bag.

Getting There & Around

Travelers connect to the trails via the mountain village of San Gerardo de Rivas, which is also home to the ranger station. Most hotels offer early-morning transportation to the trailhead for their guests.

While supplies are brought to Crestones Base Lodge by horse, the only way you can get up and down the mountain is on your own two legs (don't underestimate the challenge).

THE ROAD TO LA AMISTAD

From San Isidro de El General, the Interamericana winds its way southeast through glorious rolling hills and coffee and pineapple plantations backed by striking mountain facades, towering as much as 3350m above. Along this stretch, a series of narrow, steep, dirt roads leads to some of the country's most remote areas – some nearly inaccessible due to the prohibitive presence of the Cordillera de Talamanca. But it's worth enduring the thrilling road for the chance to visit Parque Internacional La Amistad, a true wilderness of epic scale. This part of the country is rich in indigenous culture, and Italian immigrants have left their mark on the mountain town of San Vito, which has the best dining in the area.

Reserva Indígena Boruca

POP 430

The picturesque valley of the Río Grande de Térraba cradles several mostly indigenous villages that comprise the reserve of Boruca (Brunka) peoples. At first glance it is difficult to differentiate these towns from typical Tico villages, aside from a few artisans selling their handiwork. These towns hardly cater to the tourist trade, which is one of the main reasons why traditional Boruca life has been able to continue without much distraction. The village does have a small **community museum** (☎2730-2514, 2730-0045; ⏰9am-4pm) **FREE**, with simple exhibits about the Boruca lifestyle, language and crafts. The best way to engage with the community is to come here on a culturally sensitive tour, or else contact the community directly to arrange an overnight stay and activities. More information is available at the Boruca communitiy website, Beyond the Mask (www.boruca.org).

Be thoughtful when visiting these communities – avoid taking photographs of people without asking permission, and respect the fact that these communities are struggling to maintain traditional culture in a changing world.

Tours

Galería Namu (p96) in San José can arrange eco-ethno tours of the Boruca area, which include homestays, hiking to waterfalls, handicraft demonstrations and storytelling. These cost US$62 per person per day, and include meals, but not transportation to the village itself, which is relatively simple to work out by bus or taxi via Buenos Aires. Visit the website for more details.

Festivals & Events

Fiesta de los Diablitos CULTURAL

(Boruca Dec 30-Jan 2, Curré Feb 5-8) This raucous three-day festival, held in Boruca and Curré, symbolizes the historical struggle between the Spanish and the indigenous population. Villagers wearing wooden devil masks and burlap costumes role-play the native peoples in their fight against the Spanish conquerors and the festival culminates in a choreographed battle, which the Spanish lose.

Fiesta de los Negritos RELIGIOUS

(Dec) This festival is held during the second weekend of December to celebrate the Virgin of the Immaculate Conception. Traditional indigenous music (mainly drumming and bamboo flutes) accompanies dancing and costumes.

Sleeping & Eating

Travelers can find rooms to rent by inquiring locally in Boruca village. **Mileni Gonzalez** (2730-5178; www.boruca.org), a local community organizer, can help arrange rustic *cabina* and traditional *rancho* accommodations and also homestays, which are an excellent way to connect with the community and contribute to the local economy.

Shopping

The Boruca are celebrated craftspeople and their traditional art plays a leading role in the survival of their culture. While most make their living from agriculture, some Boruca began producing fine handicrafts for tourists a couple of decades ago, at the initiative of a female community leader.

The tribe is most famous for its ornate masks featuring jungle birds and animals as well as devil faces, carved from balsa or cedar, and often colored with natural dyes and acrylics. Boruca women also use pre-Columbian backstrap looms to weave colorful, natural cotton bags, placemats and other textiles. These crafts are available along the Pacific coast, in the Península de Osa and the capital, with particularly good selections at Hotel Cristal Ballena (p402) in Uvita, Jagua Arts & Crafts (p451) in Puerto Jiménez and Galería Namu (p96) in San José.

Curré is about 30km south of Buenos Aires, right on the Interamericana. Drivers can stop to visit a small **cooperative** (8846-8786, 8890-3138; 9am-5pm Mon-Fri, from 2pm Sat) that sells handicrafts. In Boruca, local artisans post signs outside their homes advertising their handmade balsa masks and woven bags, but the best selection of masks and woven goods is found at **Bisha Cra** (2730-0854, 8366-8606; 10am-5pm), near the entrance to the village (coming from Curré).

Information

The community operates an excellent website, www.boruca.org, with historical information and more. Community leader Mileni Gonzalez is an excellent source of local information.

Getting There & Away

Buses (US$1.70, one hour) leave the central market in Buenos Aires at 11:30am and 3:30pm daily, traveling to Boruca via a bumpy, partially paved road. The bus returns at 6am and 11am the following morning, which makes an overnight stay necessary if you're relying on public transportation. A taxi from Buenos Aires to Boruca is about US$30.

Drivers will find a better road that leaves the Interamericana about 3km south of Curré; look for the sign to Boruca. This dusty, unpaved route climbs a ridgeline and affords spectacular views of the valleys below. It's about 8km to Boruca from Curré, though the going is slow. A 4WD is recommended, though not strictly necessary. If you're heading toward San Isidro or Buenos Aires, you can follow this road all the way through the village of Térraba, with more glimpses of indigenous community life along the way.

WORTH A TRIP

DIQUÍS SPHERES

The Diquís Delta is believed to have been the most developed and historically significant part of Costa Rica, heavily populated in pre-Columbian times. Jade and gold artifacts found in the delta and created elsewhere suggest that the region played a vital role as a trading post between the other important cultures in Latin America (the Incas to the south and the Maya to the north). While other pre-Columbian cultures left behind vast pyramid-like monuments, unparalleled stonework and sophisticated languages, the Diquís left behind immense stone spheres and little else.

It is known that the civilization invested great efforts in their creation (over 300 spheres have been found in the Diquís Delta). Ancient people crafted the spheres out of sandstone, limestone, gabbro and granodiorite from the Costeña coastal range, using nothing but stone tools, and transporting them great distances, including over water (some have been found on Isla del Caño).

Their function remains unclear. Theories suggest that those spheres found in sets or alignments may represent celestial phenomena or function as solar calendars. Others have been interpreted as territorial markers or symbols of an individual's power (the bigger the sphere, the more powerful the individual). Spheres range from a few centimeters to 2.54m in diameter; the largest and heaviest found at the El Silencio site weighs a staggering 24 tons. Smaller spheres have been found in some graves, presumed to be of particularly important chiefs.

In 2014 the Diquís spheres were included on Unesco's list of World Heritage sites, and efforts are underway to excavate other significant sites in the Diquís Delta and to educate both visitors and the local population about the region's unique history. Communities also hope that this Unesco endorsement will bring more tourism to the Delta and revitalize the area.

While a number of spheres were whisked away from the area in the past to be used as decorative elements in people's gardens, and the most important archaeological finds grace San José museums, there are a few excellent examples of these spheres that can easily be seen in parks in Palmar Sur and Sierpe.

Sitio Arqueológico Finca 6 (☎2100-6000; finca6@museocostarica.go.cr; US$6; ⏲8am-4pm Tue-Sun), 4km north of Sierpe, offers the best opportunity to view these mysterious spheres, and the onsite museum screens a good video on the spheres' significance and purpose. The site on which the Finca 6 museum is located is thought to have been a large settlement in pre-Columbian times, with trade links throughout the region.

Palmar

POP 4900

At the intersection of the country's two major highways, this crossroads town serves as a gateway to the Península de Osa and Golfo Dulce. The functional banana-growing settlement is mostly a transit town. But it makes a convenient base for exploring the Sierpe area if you have a particular interest in pre-Columbian stone spheres, which the area is newly famous for; it was declared a World Heritage Site by Unesco in 2014. The **Festival de la Luz** during the week before Christmas is also an attraction.

Palmar is actually split in two – to get from Palmar Norte to Palmar Sur, take the Interamericana southbound over the Río Grande de Térraba bridge, then take the first right. Most facilities are in Palmar Norte, clustered around the intersection of the Interamericana and the Costanera Sur; if you're heading to Bahía Drake via Sierpe, this is your last chance to hit an ATM. Palmar Sur is home to the airstrip and a little park with several examples of the famous stone spheres.

Sleeping & Eating

Self-caterers will want to hit the **Supermercado BM** (☎2786-6556; ⏲8am-9pm), 200m north of the Interamericana–Costanera intersection, before heading to the Osa, as shopping opportunities are limited in Bahía Drake. The nicest place to eat is the onsite restaurant at Brunka Lodge.

Hotel El Teca HOTEL $

(☎2786-8010, 8950-8562; www.hotelelteca.com; Ruta 2; s/d/tr from US$27/34/48; P ❄) Run by a hospitable local family, this small hotel offers a clutch of tidy, tiled rooms, complete with coffee makers and mini-fridges. The owners can provide information on the pre-Columbian stone spheres and where best to find them, and also organize trips to Parque Nacional Corcovado, Térraba mangroves and more. Located just east of the main intersection.

Brunka Lodge HOTEL $

(☎2786-7489; www.facebook.com/BrunkaLodge; s/d from US$36/50; P ❄) The Brunka Lodge is the most inviting option in Palmar Norte, though there is wide variation in the lodgings onsite. Most are sun-filled, clean-swept bungalows, clustered around a swimming pool and a popular open-air restaurant. All rooms have hot-water bathrooms, cable TV and high-speed internet.

ℹ Getting There & Away

Sansa, Skyway and Aerobell have daily flights from San José to the Palmar airstrip. Prices vary by season and availability, though you can expect to pay US$100 to US$140 to/from San José.

Taxis meet incoming flights and charge up to US$10 to Palmar Norte and US$15 to US$30 to Sierpe. Otherwise, the infrequent Palmar Norte–Sierpe bus goes through Palmar Sur – you can board it if there's space available.

BUS

Most buses leave from the **Tracopa window** (www.tracopacr.com; cnr Calle 143 & Av 11) attached to the Monge store.

For coastal destinations (Dominical, Puerto Jiménez and Uvita), buses depart from the **Blanco office** (cnr Calle 143 & Av 7) across from Super Sur.

Buses to Sierpe depart from the bus stop on Calle 143, opposite the Monge store.

Neily

POP 19,600

Although it is southern Costa Rica's second-largest 'city,' Ciudad Neily has retained the friendly atmosphere of a rural town. At just 50m above sea level, steamy Neily serves as a regional transportation hub and agricultural center.

Neily has several unexciting budget hotels. If you wind up stranded here, the one good option is **Hotel Andrea** (☎2783-3784; www.hotelandreacr.com; r with/without air-con US$45/37; P ❄).

ℹ Getting There & Away

Buses leave from the **bus station** (☎2221-4214), which is attached to a *mercado* (market), two blocks east of Hwy 237.

Trasportes Blanco offers services to **Dominical** (US$6; 3 hours; daily 6am, 11am & 2:30pm), **Puerto Jiménez** (US$11, 6 hours, daily 7am & 2:30pm), **Palmar** (US$1.20; 1½ hours; 12 daily 4:45am to 5:45pm) and **Uvita** (US$6; 2½ hours; daily 4:45am, 6am, 8am, 11am & 2:30pm).

Tracopa buses go to **Paso Canoas** (US$0.70; 30 minutes; 9 daily 5am to 6pm), **San Isidro** (US$7.60; 4 hours; 5 daily 4.20am to 5pm) and **San José** (US$12.80; 7 hours; 11 daily 4am to 5pm).

Other destinations include **Golfito** (US$1; 1½ hours; daily 6am, 11am & 2:30pm) and **San Vito** (US$1.30; 1½ hours; 8 daily 6am to 5pm).

Paso Canoas

POP 9550

The main port of entry between Costa Rica and Panama is a straightforward border crossing, with most travelers quickly passing through.

BUSES FROM PALMAR

DESTINATION	COST (US$)	DURATION (HR)	FREQUENCY (DAILY)
Dominical via Uvita	2	1½	6:30am, 7:45am, 9:45am, 12:45pm, 4:15pm
Golfito	3.20	1½	11:30am, 12:30pm
Neily	3.20	1½	7:30am, 9:30am, 3pm, 5pm
Paso Canoas	3.80	2	10:30am, 2:45pm, 6:30pm
Puerto Jiménez	6	4	9:30am
San Isidro	6.36	2½	hourly 4:45am-6:30pm
San José	11	5½	hourly 4:45am-6:30pm
Sierpe	0.70	40min	7 daily, 5am-5:15pm

Information

If leaving Costa Rica, you'll be charged an exit tax of $9 here ($8 for the actual exit tax, plus $1 'commission' because you didn't pay through a national bank before you arrived at the border). You'll pay this tax in cash at a window across from the **Migración & Aduana office** (☎2732-2150, 2732-2801, 2732-2804; ⏲8am-noon & 1-4pm).

BCR (Banco de Costa Rica; ☎2732-2613; ⏲9am-4pm Mon-Sat, to 1pm Sun) has an office near the Tracopa bus terminal, as well as an ATM near the Migración & Aduana office. Street vendors' rates for converting excess colones into US dollars are not great. Colones are accepted at the border, but are difficult to get rid of further into Panama.

The **Autoridad de Turismo de Panamá** (☎507-526-7000; ⏲8am-4pm), in the Panamanian immigration post, has basic information on travel to Panama.

Getting There & Away

Tracopa buses leave for San José (US$15, 7½ hours) at 4am, 8am, 11am and 4:30pm. The **Tracopa bus terminal** (☎2732-2119; ⏲7am-4pm), a window really, is north of the border post, on the east side of the main road. Sunday-afternoon buses are full of weekend shoppers, so buy tickets as early as possible. For transfer to other southern destinations, buses for Neily (US$0.70, 30 minutes) leave from the **Terminal de Buses Transgolfo** every hour from 5am to 6:30pm. Taxis to Neily cost about US$10.

Just across the border, buses run to David, the nearest city in Panama, from where there are onward connections to Panama City and elsewhere. Crossing the border, you may be required to show proof of your intended departure from Panama. If you don't have an airplane ticket (or something) on hand, you can purchase a David–San José bus ticket at the Tracopa bus terminal in Paso Canoas.

San Vito

POP 5500

Although the Italian immigrants who founded little San Vito in the 1850s are long gone, this hillside village proudly bears traces of their legacy in linguistic, cultural and culinary echoes. As such, the town serves as a base for travelers in need of a steaming plate of pasta and a good night's sleep.

The proximity of the town to the Reserva Indígena Guaymí de Coto Brus means that indigenous peoples pass through this region (groups of Ngöbe – also known as Guaymí – move back and forth across the border with Panama).

Tucked in between the Cordillera de Talamanca and the Fila Costeña, the Valle de Coto Brus offers some glorious geography, featuring the green, rolling hills of coffee plantations backed by striking mountain facades.

★ Wilson Botanical Garden — GARDENS

(Las Cruces Biological Station; ☎2773-4004; www.tropicalstudies.org; US$10, guided walks short/long US$30/40; ⏲7am-5pm) The world-class Wilson Botanical Garden is internationally known for its collection of more than 2000 native Costa Rican species. Species threatened with extinction are preserved here for possible reforestation in the future. A trail map is available for self-guided walks amid exotic species such as orchids, bromeliads and medicinal plants. Guided walks are at 7:30am and 1:30pm. The botanical garden is a choice spot for birders, as it draws hundreds of Costa Rican and migrating species, as well numerous butterfly species.

Wilson Garden is 6km south of San Vito. Buses between San Vito and Neily (via Agua Buena not Cañas Gordas) pass the entrance to the garden.

If you want to stay overnight at the botanical garden, make reservations well in advance: facilities often fill with researchers. Accommodations are in comfortable cabins (singles/doubles including meals and a tour US$105/180) in the midst of the gorgeous grounds. The rooms are simple, but they each have a balcony with an amazing view.

Finca Cántaros — PARK

(☎2773-3760, 2773-5530; www.fincacantaros.com; adult/child 12-17yr $6.50/3.25; ⏲6:30am-5pm) About 3km south of San Vito, Finca Cántaros is a recreation center and reforestation project. Over 7 hectares of grounds – formerly coffee plantations and pastureland – are now a lovely nature reserve with trails, picnic areas and a dramatic lookout over the city. Especially interesting are the pre-Columbian cemetery and a large petroglyph that was discovered on the property in 2009. Though its meaning and age are unclear, the petroglyph is estimated to be around 1600 years old.

Another point of interest is the 3000-year-old Laguna Zoncho: picnic at one of the small shelters and watch for rare birds.

If birders wish to visit the *finca* before 6:30am, arrangements can be made in advance. The reserve's reception contains a small but carefully chosen selection of local and South American crafts.

Camping on the property is allowed (US$10 per person); call ahead if arriving on a Sunday.

Cascata del Bosco BUNGALOW **$$**
(☎2773-3208; www.cascatasanvito.com; cabins from US$75; 🅿📶) The four round cabins at Cascata del Bosco overlook the forested valley below and enclose guests in tree-house-like comfort. Each cabin has a terrace, skylight, kitchenette and bamboo-and-tile interior. Several nature trails wind through the property, and the roadside restaurant (mains US$5 to US$10) is a convivial gathering spot for locals and expats, serving delicious BBQ. Located just north of Wilson Botanical Garden.

ℹ Getting There & Away

BUS

The main **Tracopa bus terminal** (☎2773-3410) is about 150m down the road to Sabalito from San Vito's main intersection. Destinations include the following:

San Isidro (US$7; 3 hours; daily 6:45am & 1:30pm)

San José (US$13; 7 hours; daily 5am, 7am, 7:30am, 10am, 3pm)

A local bus terminal at the northwest end of town runs buses to Neily (US$1.50, 1½ hours, eight daily) and other destinations.

CAR

The drive north from Neily is a scenic one, with superb views of the lowlands dropping away as the road winds up the hillside. The paved road is steep, narrow and full of hairpin turns. You can also get to San Vito from San Isidro via the Valle de Coto Brus – an incredibly scenic and less used route with fantastic views of the Cordillera de Talamanca to the north and the lower Fila Costeña to the south.

Parque Internacional La Amistad

The 4070-sq-km Parque Internacional La Amistad – by far the largest protected area in Costa Rica – is an enormous patch of green sprawling across the borders of Panama and Costa Rica (hence its Spanish name La Amistad – 'Friendship'). Standing as a testament to the possibilities of international cooperation and environmental conservation, the park was established in 1982 and declared a Unesco World Heritage Site in 1990. It then became part of the greater

OFF THE BEATEN TRACK

BIOLLEY

Below the wilderness of Parque Internacional La Amistad, a network of rural villages is signposted by Gaudí-esque mosaic navigation markers made by a local artist. These farming villages went about their business mostly unperturbed by tourists until 1997, when an enterprising group of local women in the village of Biolley (bee-oh-*lay;* named for a Swiss biologist who settled here) set up a cooperative, Asociación de Mujeres Organizadas de Biolley (Asomobi). It has 37 members and is designed to promote rural tourism in the area and to generate funds for the cooperative's various sustainable projects, such as organic coffee growing.

Asomobi (☎8916-4638, 8492-4020; www.asomobi-costarica.com) organizes coffee tours that let you visit the *beneficio* (processing plant) in Biolley that processes delicious locally grown coffee. It uses ecofriendly methods that conserve water and compost organic waste for use as fertilizer. Other tours are on offer, from birding outings and hot-springs tours to hiking the Valle del Silencio in Parque Internacional La Amistad.

The cooperative operates a simple hotel, **Posada Cerro Biolley** (☎2200-4250; per person incl breakfast US$20; 🅿📶), and can also make arrangements for homestays in the local community. Down the road, **Hotel Finca Palo Alto** (☎2743-1063; www.hotelfincapaloalto.com; d US$59-89; 🅿❄) is also a decent place to stay.

Biolley is 6km west of the crossroads in Altamira village, but the way there zigzags and is poorly signed; get detailed directions at AsoProLA (p430) or by calling Asomobi if traveling independently.

Mesoamerican Biological Corridor, which protects a great variety of endangered habitats and animals. Its cultural importance is also significant as it includes several scattered indigenous reserves.

The largest chunk of the park is high up in the Cordillera de Talamanca, and remains virtually inaccessible. There's very little tourist infrastructure within the park, although hard-core exploration of some of the country's most rugged terrain is possible with an experienced guide.

Activities

Hiking

Except for the specialized guided hikes, park visitors are limited to the two trails that leave from the Altamira Ranger Station: **Sendero Gigantes del Bosque** and **Sendero Valle del Silencio**.

Contact the association of guides, AsoProLA, to inquire about arrangements for guided hikes. Rates vary depending on the size of your party and your intended course.

Wildlife-Watching

Parque Internacional La Amistad is home to a recorded 90 mammal species and more than 400 bird species. The park has the nation's largest population of Baird's tapirs, as well as giant anteaters, all six species of neotropical (and endangered) cats – jaguar, puma (mountain lion), margay, ocelot, oncilla (tiger cat) and jaguarundi – and many more common mammals.

Bird species (49 unique) that have been sighted – more than half of the total in Costa Rica – include the majestic but extremely rare harpy eagle, now feared extinct in the country. In addition, the park protects 115 species of fish, 215 different reptiles and amphibians, as well as innumerable insect species.

Sleeping & Eating

In addition to the AsoProLA lodge in the village of Altamira, it's also possible to camp at the Altamira Ranger Station and at the base of Cerro Kamuk.

AsoProLA Lodge LODGE $

(La Asociación de Productores La Amistad; ☎8616-1647, 8621-5559; www.facebook.com/AsoProLA; r incl breakfast from US$25; P) The AsoProLA guiding association runs a simple lodge and restaurant in Altamira village, ideal for the night before or after your trek in La Amistad. The mosaic-covered common areas are much more elaborate and artistic than you would expect in this remote location. By contrast, the rooms are rustic but adequate. Staff are enthusiastic and ever helpful.

Heladería Biolley ICE CREAM $

(☎8515-9267; www.facebook.com/heladeriabiolley; ice cream US$1-3; ⏰9am-6pm) This purple-and-green, mushroom-shaped, artisanal ice-cream shop is an unexpectedly weird installment near the AsoProLa Lodge. The ice cream is all natural and flavored with fruit grown nearby.

Drinking

Coffea Diversa COFFEE

(☎8457-6814, 2297-5904; www.coffeadiversa.com; 2hr tour adult/child US$10/5) Coffea Diversa is equal parts coffee shop, coffee farm and coffee academy. Folks come from all over the world to learn about the cultivation and production of the highest-quality coffee during multiday courses. For the less academically inclined, there is a two-hour tour. Or, just relax on the terrace, enjoy the spectacular view and sip a cuppa.

Information

The primary jumping-off point by which visitors launch into the deepest parts of the park is the tiny mountain village of Altamira, 25km northwest of San Vito. There are three other official entrances to the park: one near Buenos Aires, one near Helechales, and one near San Vito. But Altamira Ranger Station is the only year-round, staffed facility, and the other entrances are accessed by horrifically bad roads.

To make reservations to camp, call the park headquarters at Altamira Ranger Station directly. This is the best-developed area of the park, with a camping area, showers, drinking water, electricity and a lookout tower.

Altamira Ranger Station (☎8616-1647; park fee US$10, campsite per person US$6; ⏰8am-4pm) Collects entrance fees and provides information on the park.

AsoProLA (☎8651-7324, 8616-1647, 8621-5559; www.asoprola.com; Altamira; ⏰7am-8pm) Can arrange guided hikes within the park.

Getting There & Away

To reach Altamira, you can take any bus that runs between San Isidro and San Vito and get off in the town of Guácimo (often called Las Tablas). From Guácimo buses generally depart at 1pm and 5pm for El Carmen; if the road conditions permit, they continue 4km to the village of Altamira. From Altamira, follow the Minae sign (near the church) leading to the steep 2.5km hike to the ranger station.

It's considerably more convenient to explore the area by 4WD rather than with public transportation; the roads are rough and bumpy and the buses are not hugely reliable. The turnoff for the park is signposted after the town of Guácimo if you're driving from San Vito. The park entrance at Altamira is 21km (around an hour's drive) along the unpaved, bone-jarring road from Hwy 237.

TO CORCOVADO VIA BAHÍA DRAKE

On the western side of the Península de Osa, the Bahía Drake route is one of two principal ways to reach Parque Nacional Corcovado. The route starts in the town of Sierpe in the Valle de Diquís, at the northern base of the peninsula, from where the Río Sierpe flows out to Bahía Drake. Most travelers opt for the exhilarating boat ride through the mangroves from Sierpe to Drake, with a potential detour via the Humedal Nacional Térraba-Sierpe. Alternatively, there's a rough road to Drake via the former gold-mining settlement of Rancho Quemado, which allows for a spot of *agroturismo* along the way. (Note: this road is often impassable during the rainy season.) Either way, the Bahía Drake route offers a chance to experience rural Tico life, while the wilderness lodges offer many creature comforts (or at least creatures).

Sierpe

POP 800

This sleepy village on the Río Sierpe is the gateway to Bahía Drake. If you've made a reservation with any of the jungle lodges further down the coast, you will be picked up here by boat. Otherwise, there is little reason to linger, except to catch a glimpse of a Unesco-recognized archaeological artifact. You can see some of the pre-Columbian stone spheres in the main square, or visit the excellent museum at Sitio Arqueológico Finca 6 nearby.

If you're not continuing on to Bahía Drake, this is your chance to take a boat trip through the mangroves with La Perla del Sur or **Kokopelli** (☎8897-1678; www.sierpemangrovetour.com; tour US$68).

Hotel River Sierpe HOTEL **$**
(Hotel Oleaje Sereno; ☎2788-1082; www.oleajeserenohotel.com; s/d incl breakfast from US$36/55; P ❄ wi-fi) Attached to La Perla del Sur, this riverside motel is a place to lay your head before or after your boat trip. You'll find dusty rooms with wooden floors, sturdy furniture and hot showers. The onsite restaurant is popular with boat-catching gringos.

Information

La Perla del Sur (☎2788-1082; info@perladelsur.net; ⏲6am-10pm; wi-fi) This info center and open-air restaurant next to the boat dock is the hub of Sierpe – arrange your long-term parking (US$6 per night), book a tour and take advantage of the free wi-fi before catching your boat to Drake.

OFF THE BEATEN TRACK

HUMEDAL NACIONAL TÉRRABA-SIERPE

The Ríos Térraba and Sierpe begin on the southern slopes of the Talamanca mountains and, nearing the Pacific Ocean, they form a network of channels and waterways that weave around the country's largest mangrove swamp. This river delta comprises the Humedal Nacional Térraba-Sierpe, which protects approximately 330 sq km of wetland and is home to red, black and tea mangrove species. The reserve also protects a plethora of birdlife, especially waterbirds such as herons, egrets and cormorants, and larger denizens of the murky waters and tangled vegetation such as caimans and boas. An exploration of this watery world by boat gives you a unique insight into this very special and fragile ecosystem.

The Térraba-Sierpe reserve has no facilities for visitors, though lodges and tour companies can organize tours to help you explore the wetlands. Book a tour through Bahía Aventuras (p400) in Uvita (US$85 per person), as well as La Perla del Sur or Kokopelli in Sierpe.

Getting There & Away

Scheduled flights (Sansa, Skyway and Aerobell) and charters fly into Palmar Sur, 14km north of Sierpe. If you are heading to Bahía Drake, most upmarket lodges will arrange the boat transfer. Regularly scheduled *colectivo* (shared) boats depart Sierpe for Drake at 11:30am (US$15) and 4:30pm (US$20). Should things go awry or if you're traveling independently, there's no shortage of water taxis milling about – be prepared to negotiate.

Buses to Palmar Norte (US$0.70, 40 minutes) depart from in front of Pulpería Fenix six times a day between 5:30am and 6pm. A shared taxi to Palmar costs about US$10 per person.

Bahía Drake

POP 1000

One of Costa Rica's more isolated destinations, Bahía Drake *(drah-kay)* is a veritable Lost World, bordered by Parque Nacional Corcovado to the south. In the rainforest canopy, howler monkeys greet the rising sun with their haunting bellows, while pairs of macaws soar between the treetops, filling the air with their cacophonous squawking. Offshore in the bay, pods of migrating dolphins glide through turquoise waters near the beautiful Isla del Caño marine reserve.

One of the reasons Bahía Drake is brimming with wildlife is that it remains largely cut off from the rest of the country. Life is centered on the sedate village of **Agujitas**, the area's transport hub, which attracts increasing numbers of backpackers and nature lovers with inexpensive digs and plenty of snorkeling, diving and wildlife-watching opportunities. The more remote corners of Bahía Drake are home to some of Costa Rica's best (and priciest) wilderness lodges.

Activities

Swimming & Snorkeling

About 20km west of Agujitas, Isla del Caño (p434) is considered the best place for snorkeling in this area. Lodges and tour companies offer day trips to the island (from US$80 per person), usually including the park fee, snorkeling equipment and lunch on Playa San Josecito. The clarity of the ocean and the variety of the fish fluctuate according to water and weather conditions: it's worth inquiring before booking.

Along the coast between Agujitas and Corcovado, Playa San Josecito (p438) and **Playa Caletas** attract many tropical fish, while Playa Cocalito (p438), a small, pretty beach near Agujitas, is pleasant for swimming and sunbathing.

Diving

Isla del Caño (p434) is one of Costa Rica's top spots for diving, with attractions including intricate rock and coral formations and an amazing array of underwater life. Hawksbill turtles and white-tipped sharks are common highlights, as well as rays, jacks, eels and a host of reef fish. Divers report that the schools of fish swimming overhead are often so dense that they block the sunlight from filtering down. A two-tank dive usually runs around US$140. Popular dive sites include **Bajo del Diablo** (Devil's Rock) and Sunken Ship.

Birdwatching & Wildlife-Watching

With almost 400 species recorded in the area, Bahía Drake and nearby Corcovado are hands down the best places to spot Costa Rica's Pacific lowland rainforest species, including such feathered beauties as scarlet macaws, chestnut-mandibled toucans, honeycreepers, hawk-eagles and the black-cheeked ant tanager (endemic to the Península de Osa). All upscale lodges organize birding walks, as do the bay's independent tour operators and specialist birding guides.

All of the lodges and most tour companies offer tours to Parque Nacional Corcovado, usually a full-day trip to San Pedrillo or Sirena Ranger Stations (US$80 or US$90 per person, respectively), including boat transportation, lunch and guided hikes.

Some travelers, however, are disappointed by these tours, particularly with boating all the way to Sirena, which takes a while and can be treacherous in rough seas. The trails around Sirena attract many groups of people, which inhibit animal sightings. Furthermore, most tours arrive at the park well after sunrise, so activity in the rainforest has already quieted down. If you have your heart set on seeing wildlife, it's worth the extra investment to stay overnight at Sirena.

Note that all park visitors are required to be accompanied by a guide certified by the Costa Rican Tourism Board (ICT). Even if you're not entering the park, exploring the beaches and jungles with an eagle-eyed guide will reveal much more than you would likely discover on your own.

Bahía Drake & Around

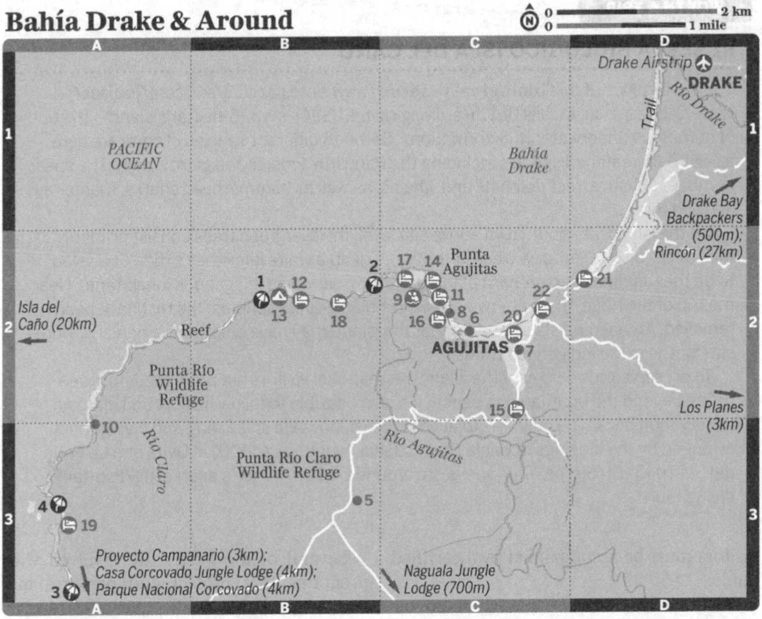

Bahía Drake & Around

Sights
1 Playa Caletas B2
2 Playa Cocalito B2
3 Playa Rincon de San Josecito A3
4 Playa San Josecito A3

Activities, Courses & Tours
5 Corcovado Canopy Tour B3
6 Corcovado Info Center C2
7 Drake Divers C2
8 Original Canopy Tour C2
Pacheco Tours .... (see 20)
9 Río Agujitas C2
10 Río Claro Tours A3

Sleeping
11 Aguila de Osa C2
12 Copa de Arbol B2
13 Corcovado Adventures Tent Camp B2
14 Drake Bay Wilderness Resort C2
15 Finca Maresia C2
16 Hotel Jinetes de Osa C2
17 La Paloma Lodge C2
18 Las Caletas Lodge B2
19 Life for Life Hostel A3
20 Martina's Place C2
Ocean Forest Ecolodge .... (see 4)
21 Pirate Cove D2
22 Sunset Lodge C2

Eating
Bahía Azul .... (see 20)
Drake's Kitchen .... (see 22)
Heladería Popis .... (see 20)
Kalaluna Bistró .... (see 16)
Soda Mar y Bosque .... (see 20)

Canoeing & Kayaking

Río Agujitas KAYAKING

The idyllic Río Agujitas attracts a huge variety of birdlife and lots of reptiles. The river conveniently empties out into the bay, which is surrounded by hidden coves and sandy beaches ideal for exploring in a sea kayak, best done at high tide. Some accommodations have kayaks and canoes for rent; or else kayaks can be rented along Agujitas beach (around US$15 per hour).

Hiking

Parque Nacional Corcovado is a popular destination for long-distance hikes, although the trek normally starts and ends on the opposite side of the park (at Carate or Los Patos, both accessible from Puerto Jiménez). Coming from Bahía Drake, it is possible to take a boat to Sirena station and hike out the following day to either Carate or Los Patos. But there is no long-distance trekking around San Pedrillo. Note that all park

WORTH A TRIP

RESERVA BIOLÓGICO ISLA DEL CAÑO

The centerpiece of this **biological reserve** (www.sinac.go.cr/ES/ac/acosa/Paginas/IsladelCaño.aspx; adult/child US$15/5, diving charge US$4) is a 326-hectare island – the tip of numerous underwater rock formations. Some 15 different species of coral are here, as well as threatened species including the Panulirus lobster and giant conch. The sheer numbers of fish attract dolphins and whales, as well as hammerhead sharks, manta rays and sea turtles.

On the island, at about 110m above sea level, the evergreen trees consist primarily of milk trees (also called 'cow trees' after the drinkable white latex they exude), believed to be the remains of an orchard planted by pre-Columbian indigenous inhabitants. Near the top of the ridge, there are two pre-Columbian granite spheres; the rest have been removed. Archaeologists speculate that the island may have been a ceremonial or burial site for the same indigenous tribes.

To preserve the ecology of the island, recreational visitors are prohibited from venturing beyond the boat-landing beach. It's also possible to follow a short trail up to an observation deck. The only way to access the island is via snorkeling and diving tours, arranged by the lodgings in Bahía Drake, Bahía Aventuras (p400) in Uvita and La Perla del Sur (p431) in Sierpe. Tour prices are around US$90/40 for a snorkeling/two-tank diving tour.

visitors must be accompanied by a certified guide.

Fortunately, there are plenty of opportunities for hiking outside the park. The easiest and most obvious route is the 17km coastal trail from Agujitas to San Pedrillo (p438). A determined, reasonably fit hiker could make it all the way to San Pedrillo Ranger Station in six to seven hours (though visitors intending to enter or spend the night in the park must have secured reservations in advance and be accompanied by a guide). Any section of this trail offers opportunities for animal spotting, ocean dips and beach picnics.

Spend a day at Naguala Jungle Lodge for a fabulous waterfall hike. There are two trails and three waterfalls on the property, as well as an inviting hammock hut for recovery. Natural plunge pools are perfect for jumping, diving and frolicking in the spray.

Dolphin- and Whale-Watching

Bahía Drake is rife with marine life, including more than 20 species of dolphin and whale that pass through on their migrations throughout the year. This area is uniquely suited for whale-watching: humpback whales come from both the northern and the southern hemispheres to calve, resulting in the longest humpback-whale season in the world. Humpbacks can be spotted in Bahía Drake from December to March, and then from July until October.

Several of the lodges are involved with programs that protect and preserve marine life in Bahía Drake, and offer tourists a chance for a close encounter, as do independent, knowledgeable operators in Agujitas. Tours generally start at about US$110 per person.

Tours

★ Pacheco Tours OUTDOORS
(☎8906-2002; www.pachecotours.com) Very competent all-rounder organizing snorkeling tours to Isla del Caño, day trips to Corcovado, daylong tours combining jungle trekking with waterfall swimming (The Floating Tour, US$65), and whale-watching excursions.

★ Tracie the Bug Lady WILDLIFE
(☎8701-7356, 8701-7462; www.thenighttour.com; tours per person US$45; ⏲7:30-10:15pm) Tracie the 'Bug Lady' has created quite a name for herself with this fascinating nighttime walk in the jungle that takes in bugs, reptiles and birds. Tracie is a walking encyclopedia on bug facts – one of her fields of research is the military use of insects! Her naturalist-photographer husband Gian also leads the night tours; reserve in advance.

Corcovado Info Center OUTDOORS
(☎2775-1760, 8846-4734; www.corcovadoinfocenter.com; whale-watching US$110-130, Corcovado day tours US$80-90, Corcovado overnight from US$280) Leading tours into Corcovado and

Isla del Caño, all guides with this outfit are local, bilingual and ICT-certified. They're at the beach end of the main road in Agujitas.

Drake Bay Birdwatching BIRDWATCHING
(www.drakebaybirdwatching.com; tours from US$45) Let the experts help you spot that one special species. Tours range from morning and evening bird walks (US$45) to avian-focused boat trips, mangrove tours and Corcovado hikes.

Drake Divers DIVING
(☎2775-1818; www.drakediverscr.com; snorkeling US$85, 2-tank dive US$140; ⏰7am-7pm) This friendly outfit takes divers and snorkelers to Isla del Caño. Experienced dive masters point out the resident sharks, turtles, eels and more, while the onboard crew is helpful with setting up equipment. The outing is followed by a tasty picnic lunch at Playa San Josecito. Prices include equipment.

Corcovado Canopy Tour CANOPY TOUR
(www.corcovadocanopytour.com; US$73; ⏰7:30am, 10:30am, 1:30pm & 4pm) With 11 cables and two suspension bridges, this is the biggest and best canopy tour in the area. Zip through primary and secondary rainforest at this excellent facility that borders the national park.

Sleeping

Bahía Drake accommodations are skewed toward the top end, but Agujitas has an ever-growing number of budget and midrange options. This area is off the grid, so a few places do not have 24/7 electricity. Reservations are recommended in the dry season (mid-December to mid-April).

For more accommodations check out the stretch of coastline from Bahía Drake to Corcovado.

★ **Drake Bay Backpackers** HOSTEL $
(☎8570-6058, 8959-4067; www.drakebaybackpackers.com; dm from US$13, d with/without bathroom US$45/34; P ❄ 📶) 🍃 This excellent nonprofit, off-the-beaten-track hostel is a boon for budget travelers wanting to connect with the local community. All rooms have sturdy wood furniture, fans and hot-water showers; there's a nice hangout area and a BBQ patio. Profits are donated to local environmental groups.

The hostel is in the village of El Progreso, near the airstrip, straight after the river crossing. Free transfer from Drake Bay airport!

Martina's Place GUESTHOUSE $
(☎8720-0801; www.puravidadrakebay.com; dm US$15, d with bathroom US$68, s/d without bathroom US$22/45; 📶) With a few simple fan-cooled dorms, this budget spot is a friendly and economical place to lay your head in the middle of Agujitas. It's also an excellent place to meet other travelers, tap into Martina's wealth of Corcovado intel and arrange a variety of local tours. Guests have access to a clean, thoroughly equipped communal kitchen.

★ **Finca Maresia** LODGE $$
(☎8888-1625; www.fincamaresia.com; Camino a Los Planes; s/d/tr incl breakfast from US$68/79/90; 📶) This absolute gem of a *finca* hotel stretches across the hills 2km south of Agujitas. Cost-conscious travelers are drawn by the excellent value-to-price ratio and superb wildlife-watching opportunities. Besides the show-stopping natural setting, the cabins feature eye-catching design elements such as shiny wood floors, rice paper walls and spacious balconies. The family-style dinners are a highlight.

Naguala Jungle Lodge LODGE $$
(☎6097-8675; www.nagualajunglelodge.com; Los Planes; dm US$75, d US$200-250, all incl meals; 📶) 🍃 It's not easy to reach Naguala Jungle Lodge (ATVs required) but it's worth it. Set on 15 hectares in Los Planes, 7km from Agujitas, the family-run lodge is interlaced with walking trails and waterfalls and dotted with simple, secluded cabins. Much love goes into this operation, from the home-cooked meals, to the flower-filled gardens and the open-air hammock hut.

Naguala is also open to day visitors, who come to swim in the waterfalls, swing in the hammocks and perhaps stay for lunch (adult/child US$15/10 admission only or US$45/35 with transportation and lunch).

Hotel Jinetes de Osa HOTEL $$
(☎8996-6161, in USA 866-553-7073; www.jinetesdeosa.com; s/d/tr from US$95/110/115, ste from US$165, all incl breakfast; 📶) Ideal for divers, the reasonably priced Jinetes de Osa boasts a choice bayside location that is literally steps from the ocean. The resort has nine simple rooms of tile and wood, and a dining room serving tasty meals of fresh fish and local fruits. Just outside of Agujitas, this sweet collection of rooms strikes the perfect balance between village and jungle.

Jinetes also has a **canopy tour** (☑2775-0438; US$65; ⊙8am-4pm), as well as one of the peninsula's top Professional Association of Diving Instructors (PADI) dive facilities.

Pirate Cove LODGE $$
(☑2234-6154; www.piratecovecostarica.com; d incl breakfast/full board from US$125/250; ❉🛜❄) On the northeastern edge of town, along the road to the airport, Pirate Cove is a laidback resort with a friendly vibe and a quiet location. There are sharp standard rooms with air-con, cozy bungalows with private terraces and spacious, secluded cabins. All enjoy a beachfront location and beautiful gardens. Onsite PADI dive shop. It's a 30-minute walk into town.

Sunset Lodge CABIN $$
(☑8580-5154, 6131-5738; www.sunsetlodgedrake bay.com; cabin incl breakfast US$109; 🅿🛜) Ascend the punishingly steep flight of steps from the coastal road and be rewarded with absolutely stellar views of Drake Bay. Enjoy them from your terrace at one of the four wooden cabins on the property. The accommodations are simple, but the Tico owner is enthusiastic and kind. His family were among the original pioneers who came to settle in Bahía Drake.

Aguila de Osa LODGE $$$
(☑8840-2929, in USA 866-924-8452; www.aguila deosa.com; d/q from US$300/500; 🅿❉🛜) 🏊 On the east side of the Río Agujitas, this swanky lodge offers spacious bungalows with cathedral ceilings and private decks with expansive ocean views. Delicious, four-course meals make use of fresh fruits and veggies from the property's hydroponic garden. Service is a priority: everyone from hotel to tour guides is attuned to guest needs. Packages cater to families, divers and fisher folk.

La Paloma Lodge LODGE $$$
(☑2293-7502, 2775-1684, in USA 1-303-719-8305; www.lapalomalodge.com; 3-/4-/5-day package per person from US$1150/1420/1690, beach house per person $925; ❉🛜❄) This hillside lodge provides guests with an incredible panorama of ocean and forest, all from the comfort of the sumptuous, stylish quarters. Rooms feature queen-sized orthopedic beds and ocean-view balconies, while shoulder-high walls in the bathrooms offer rainforest views.

Three-day minimum; rates include a tour to both Isla del Caño and Corcovado. Family rates available.

Drake Bay Wilderness Resort CABIN $$$
(☑2775-1716; www.drakebay.com; 3-night package per person US$926; ❉🛜❄) Sitting pretty on Punta Agujitas, Drake's oldest resort comprises comfortable cabins with mural-painted walls and ocean-view terraces, more functional than luxurious. Naturalists will be won over by the lovely landscaping, from flowering trees to the rocky oceanfront outcroppings, while history buffs will appreciate the memorial to Drake's landing. Prices include three meals day, two tours and airport transfers.

🍴 Eating

⭐**Drake's Kitchen** COSTA RICAN $
(Casa el Tortugo; ☑6161-3193, 2775-1405; mains US$8-12; ⊙noon-9pm; 🅿) This small, friendly local restaurant is along the main dirt road from Agujitas to the airstrip. The capable and passionate chef prepares tasty *casados* (set meals) featuring the catch of the day with fried plantains and avocado. Wash it down with a *fresco* (fresh juice) and soak up the mellow ambience.

Heladería Popis ICE CREAM $
(☑8529-6750; ice cream US$2-4; ⊙1-9pm) In hot and dusty Bahía Drake, there isn't a more refreshing midday treat than a vanilla milkshake from this open-air ice-cream parlor. It also does banana splits, coffee and ice cappuccinos, as well as tacos and other fast food.

Soda Mar y Bosque COSTA RICAN $$
(☑5002-7554, 2775-1639; mains US$5-16; ⊙6am-9pm; 🛜) This restaurant up the hill in Agujitas serves typical Tico cuisine on Tico time. The downstairs bakery is perfect for an early-morning breakfast or an afternoon snack. From the spacious terrace and a recently added upstairs seating area, it's possible to catch a cool breeze and spot pairs of scarlet macaws coasting over the sea.

Bahía Azul CARIBBEAN $$
(☑8360-5715; mains US$8-16; ⊙11am-8pm) It's not much to look at, but your mouth and stomach will thank you after a meal of fresh fish served Caribbean style. A selection of mojitos and margaritas washes it down nicely. The diverse menu also includes pizza, pasta and some mouthwatering desserts.

★**Kalaluna Bistró** LATIN AMERICAN $$$
(☎6030-2615, 8355-8237; www.kalalunabistro.com; mains US$18-30; ⏲11am-8pm) Located at the Hotel Jinetes de Osa, Kalaluna is a gourmet affair that uses fresh local ingredients and highlights them with artistic flair. Feast your senses on a filet of pork with coffee sauce, fish filet cooked in coconut milk, or the famous guacamole made with black olives and fresh basil. There's also homemade pasta, several *ceviche* options and cocktails.

Getting There & Away

AIR

Departing from San José, Sansa, Skyway and Aerobell all have daily flights to the **Drake airstrip**, which is 6km north of Agujitas. Prices vary according to season and availability, though you can expect to pay around US$100 to US$140 one way.

Most lodges provide transportation to/from the airport or Sierpe, which involves a jeep or a boat or both, but advance reservation is necessary.

BOAT

An exhilarating boat ride from Sierpe is one of the true thrills of visiting Bahía Drake. Boats travel along the river through the rainforest and the mangrove estuary. Captains then pilot boats through tidal currents and surf the river mouth into the ocean. All of the hotels offer boat transfers between Sierpe and Bahía Drake with prior arrangements. Most hotels in Drake have beach landings, so wear appropriate footwear.

If you have not made advance arrangements with your lodge for a pickup, two *colectivo* boats depart daily from Sierpe at 11:30am and 4:30pm, and from Bahía Drake back to Sierpe at 7:15am (US$15) and 2:30pm (US$20).

BUS

A bus to La Palma (where you can connect to a bus to Puerto Jiménez) picks passengers up along the beach road and in front of the supermarkets at around 8am and 1:30pm (US$10, two hours). The return journey from La Palma is at 11am and 4:30pm. The bus does not run consistently during the rainy season, when the road is often impassable. Double-check departure times locally.

CAR

Rincón, on the main road between Puerto Jiménez and the Interamericana, is linked to Agujitas in Bahía Drake by a decent dirt road, although a 4WD is absolutely necessary for this route, which can be impassable during the rainy season as there are several river crossings. The most hazardous crossing is the Río Drake – locals fish many a water-logged vehicle out of the river. Even high-clearance 4WD vehicles have difficulty after it's been raining. If in doubt, wait until a local car appears, watch where it crosses and follow its lead. The construction of a bridge has been approved, but it may be some years yet until it's actually built.

Between Rincón and Rancho Quemado there's also a very narrow bridge with no safety railings; proceed with caution.

Fill up your tank before driving to Drake; there is no gas station here, though in a pinch you can buy some pricey gas at the supermarket.

Once in Agujitas, you will likely have to abandon your car as most places are accessible only by boat or on foot. Park your car in a secure place, such as a guesthouse. There are several small supermarkets where the management will be happy to watch over your 4WD for a nice tip.

> **LOCAL KNOWLEDGE**
>
> **SIR FRANCIS DRAKE SLEPT HERE**
>
> During his 1579 circumnavigation of the globe in the *Golden Hind*, Sir Francis Drake visited this area and left his mark (or at least his name). History has it that he stopped on the nearby Isla del Caño, but locals speculate that he probably landed on the continent as well. A monument at Punta Agujitas, located on the grounds of the Drake Bay Wilderness Resort, states as much.

Rancho Quemado

POP 200

This small village, some 15km east of Bahía Drake, was founded by gold miners in the 1940s. When gold mining dried up and became illegal, most residents turned to farming and raising cattle for their existence (though some gold-panning still goes on in the nearby rivers). In recent years, the community has begun to look at rural tourism as an alternative means of making a living and protecting the natural environment at the same time. These locals enthusiastically welcome visitors, who come here to learn about gold-panning and farming, or to enjoy some terrific rural hospitality and hearty Tico food, en route to or from Bahía Drake.

Trapiche Don Carmen FARM

(☎8455-9742; tours per adult/child US$25/12) The Rodríguez family proudly demonstrates the workings of their sugarcane mill. Visitors see (and taste) the fresh sugarcane juice when the stalks pass through the grinder, watch the boiling of the juice and cooling in special molds, and then behold the finished product – delicious cane sugar. The tour is 1½ hours and it's best to call ahead.

Finca Las Minas de Oro CULTURAL

(☎8621-6531; tour US$33) A two-hour tour at this farm brings visitors to a creek where they learn to pan for gold, and then try their luck at this time-honored profession. The lunch here, consisting of fresh, typical Costa Rican cuisine served atop grape leaves, is enormous and outstanding.

Rancho Verde CABIN $

(☎8646-5431; cabin per person US$28) Right by the road winding through Rancho Quemado, this welcoming little place has a couple of tidy wooden guest cabins. The friendly proprietor cooks up monumental portions of grilled pork or fish with rice, beans and plantains (meals US$8 to US$11). Discounts are available for groups and volunteers.

Information

The **Rancho Quemado information** (☎Alice 8552-1822, Jessica 8667-2535; www.visitranchoquemado.com) website details the opportunities for rural tourism in Rancho Quemado. Tours give visitors a chance to learn how local families survive and thrive in this industrious village, including visits to a sugar mill and a dairy, as well as observation of gold mining, cacao production and other unique immersive learning experiences. The information center also serves as a first point of contact for visitors who wish to make arrangements to visit the farms.

Getting There & Away

Buses leave Bahía Drake at 8am and 1:30pm, Monday through Saturday, passing Rancho Quemado on the way to La Palma. In the opposite direction, the bus departs La Palma at 11:30am and 4:30pm. Low-season buses can run irregularly. If you're driving, you'll need a 4WD to get here as there are a couple of shallow rivers to cross.

Bahía Drake to Corcovado

This craggy stretch of coastline is home to sandy inlets that disappear at high tide, leaving only the rocky outcroppings and luxuriant rainforest. Virtually uninhabited and undeveloped beyond a few tourist lodges, the setting here is magnificent and wild. If you're looking to spend a bit more time along the shores of Bahía Drake before penetrating the depths of Parque Nacional Corcovado, consider a night or two in some of the country's most remote accommodations, with plenty of wildlife sightings in the surrounding jungle.

The only way to get around the area is by boat or by foot, which means that travelers are more or less dependent on their lodges unless they're close to Agujitas.

Sights

Playa Cocalito BEACH

Just west of Punta Agujitas, a short detour off the main trail leads to the picturesque Playa Cocalito, a secluded cove perfect for sunning, swimming and body surfing.

Playa San Josecito BEACH

South of Río Claro, Playa San Josecito is one of the longest stretches of white-sand beach on this side of the Península de Osa. It is popular with swimmers, snorkelers and sunbathers, though you'll find it crowded at lunchtime since it's the favorite post-snorkeling picnic spot for tour companies coming back from Isla del Caño. Watch out for capuchin monkeys!

Playa Rincon de San Josecito BEACH

Just past Playa San Josecito is the less famous but more impressive beach, Playa Rincon de San Josecito. It's a vast stretch of sand – 1km or more – backed by palm trees swaying in the breeze. There's one lodge fronting the beach, and little else. Picturesque rocky outcrops punctuate either end, completing the idyllic scene. Fabulous spot to watch the sunset, with the added advantage that it's accessible by car.

Activities

★**Agujitas–Corcovado Trail** HIKING

This 17km public trail follows the coastline from Agujitas to the San Pedrillo Ranger Station for the entire spectacular stretch, and it's excellent for wildlife-spotting (particularly early in the morning), beach-hopping and canoe tours with Río Claro Tours. Tour operators can drop you off by boat at a point of your choosing and you can walk back to Agujitas.

★Río Claro Tours CANOEING

(☎8450-7198; www.lifeforlifehosteldrakebay.com; 2/4hr tour US$28/45) A 20-minute walk east from Playa San Josecito, a man called Ricardo (aka 'Clavito') lives by the Río Claro and runs hugely entertaining canoeing tours. The adventure starts with a rope-swing plunge in the river and continues to some waterfalls with refreshing plunge pools. Various tour operators can drop you off by boat, leaving you to walk back to Agujitas afterward.

Sleeping

Reservations are recommended in the dry season (mid-December to mid-April). Some places in this area don't have 24-hour electricity (pack a flashlight) or hot water.

With prior arrangements, accommodations provide transportation (free or for a charge) from Agujitas, Sierpe or the airstrip in Drake.

Life for Life Hostel HOSTEL $

(☎4702-7209, WhatsApp 8450-7198; www.lifeforlifehosteldrakebay.com; Playa San Josecito; dm/r incl full board per person US$60/72) This is a beachfront, jungle-shrouded hostel and turtle-conversation project, beloved by travelers for the relaxed atmosphere, home-cooked meals and proximity to local wildlife. The activity of choice is relaxing in a hammock as exotic birds and monkeys stop by, though hanging at the beach, hiking and visiting waterfalls are also popular. Dorms are basic but adequate, and there's no wi-fi whatsoever.

Turtle-project volunteers are accepted to excavate nests, rebury eggs, input data, patrol the beach, do hatchery maintenance and participate in turtle releases. Volunteers work six hours a day and pay US$35 per night for a room and full board.

★Las Caletas Lodge LODGE $$

(☎2560-6602, 8826-1460, 8863-9631; www.caletaslodgedrake.com; Playa Caletas; tent/d per person incl 2 meals US$85/105; @) This adorable lodge consists of colorful wooden cabins and safari tents, located near the picturesque beach of the same name. The owners are warm hosts who established this convivial spot before there was phone access or electricity (now mostly solar- and hydro-powered). The food is delicious and bountiful, the staff friendly and the environment beautifully chill.

Proyecto Campanario CAMPGROUND $$

(☎2289-8708, 2289-8694; www.campanario.org; 3-day package per person US$511, minimum 2 people) This biological reserve is an education center rather than a tourist facility, aimed at those wanting to learn about the importance of various tropical ecosystems, as evidenced by the dormitory, library and field station. Ecology courses and conservation camps are scheduled throughout the year, attracting individuals passionate about these issues, from university students and field biologists to concerned tourists.

Corcovado Adventures Tent Camp CAMPGROUND $$

(☎8386-2296, in USA 866-498-0824; www.corcovado.com; d from US$110;) Less than an hour's walk from Agujitas brings you to this rugged spot, with spacious safari tents with beds set up on covered platforms. Twenty hectares of rainforest offer plenty of opportunity for exploration, and the beachfront setting is excellent for kayaking, snorkeling and bodyboarding (equipment use is free). Full-board packages also available.

★Copa de Arbol LODGE $$$

(☎8935-1212, in USA 831-246-4265; www.copadearbol.com; Playa Caletas; cabin per adult/child incl full board US$340/203;) They might look rustic from the outside with their thatch roofs and stilts, but these 10 hillside *cabinas* are gorgeously outfitted inside. Built with recycled materials and reforested wood, each has private terraces overlooking the forest or sea. Steps from the beach, the lodge offers laid-back luxury, spectacular views from the restaurant and a top-notch infinity pool. Paddleboards and kayaks are free for guests.

Ocean Forest Ecolodge LODGE $$$

(☎2235-4313, in USA 510-235-4313; www.oceanforest.org; s/d/tr incl full board from US$215/310/385;) Sitting pretty on Playa San Josecito, this ecolodge and yoga retreat center offers nine light-filled rooms with polished wood floors, colorful tapestries and glorious views all around. The lovely grounds include an ethnobotanical garden, which features exotic local species. Also on site: hiking trails, a labyrinth and a fantastic yoga shala.

Casa Corcovado Jungle Lodge LODGE $$$
(☎2256-3181, in USA 888-896-6097; www.casacorcovado.com; 2-day package per person from US$960;) A spine-tingling boat ride takes you to this luxurious lodge on 175 hectares of rainforest bordering Parque Nacional Corcovado. Each bungalow is tucked away in its own private tropical garden, and artistic details include antique Mexican tiles and handmade stained-glass windows. Guests can stretch their legs on the lodge's extensive network of trails and end the day at the Margarita Sunset Bar.

Parque Nacional Corcovado

Parque Nacional Corcovado takes up 40% of the Península de Osa and is the last great original tract of tropical rainforest in Pacific Central America. The bastion of biological diversity is home to *half* of Costa Rica's species, including the largest population of scarlet macaws, and countless other endangered species, including Baird's tapir, the giant anteater and the world's largest bird of prey, the harpy eagle.

Corcovado's amazing biodiversity, as well as the park's demanding, multiday hiking trails, attract a devoted stream of visitors who descend from Bahía Drake and Puerto Jiménez to see the wildlife and experience a bona fide jungle adventure.

Activities

Hiking

There are three main trails in the park that are open to visitors, as well as shorter trails around the ranger stations. Trails are primitive and the hiking is hot and humid, but the challenge of the trek and the interaction with wildlife at Corcovado are thrilling. Carry plenty of snacks, water and insect repellent.

One trail traverses the park from **La Leona to Sirena** (or vice versa); another trail leads from **Sirena to Los Patos** (or vice versa). Completed in either direction, these two legs allow hikers to make a sort of loop, beginning and ending their journey in or near Puerto Jiménez, which offers easy access to both La Leona and Los Patos.

The most popular single-day hike is **La Leona to Sirena**, with its glorious beach and forest scenery and plenty of wildlife-sighting opportunities. Many hikers opt to complete this one-day route, spend the night at Sirena and then boat out the next day.

At times, high water makes it impossible for vehicles to reach Los Patos to drop or retrieve hikers. In this case, hikers must tag on an additional 5km to or from the village of **La Tarde**. This results in the toughest day trek – from the village of La Tarde to Sirena via Los Patos (or vice versa) – a whopping 30km.

A one-day option is the newish **El Tigre trail loop**, which starts in Dos Brazos and dips into the park but doesn't join up with the rest of the trail network. You still have to pay the full US$15 park fee to hike it, though.

Hiking is best in the dry season (December to April), when there is still regular rain but all of the trails are open. It remains muddy, but you won't sink quite as deep.

La Leona to Sirena HIKING
The largely flat 16km hike (five to seven hours) follows the shoreline through coastal forest and along deserted beaches. Take plenty of water, a hat and sunscreen. It involves one major river crossing at Río Claro, just south of Sirena, and there's an excellent chance of seeing monkeys, tapirs and scarlet macaws en route.

This leg requires an additional 3.5km hike between La Leona and Carate, which is the closest access for vehicles. Some hot and sandy beach trekking is required, but much of the hike takes place on a parallel forest trail, which allows you to avoid the sizzling sun for part of the time.

Sirena to Los Patos HIKING
This trail goes 24km through the heart of Corcovado, passing through primary and secondary forest, and is relatively flat for the first 12km. After you wade through two river tributaries before reaching the Laguna Corcovado, the route undulates steeply (mostly uphill!) for the second half. It's less punishing to do this trek in the opposite direction, from Los Patos to Sirena.

Wildlife is not as easy to spot in the dense forest as it is along the coast, but in eight-plus hours of hiking you're bound to see some creatures. The largest herds of peccaries are reportedly on this trail. Local guides advise that peccaries sense fear, but

Hiking in Parque Nacional Corcovado

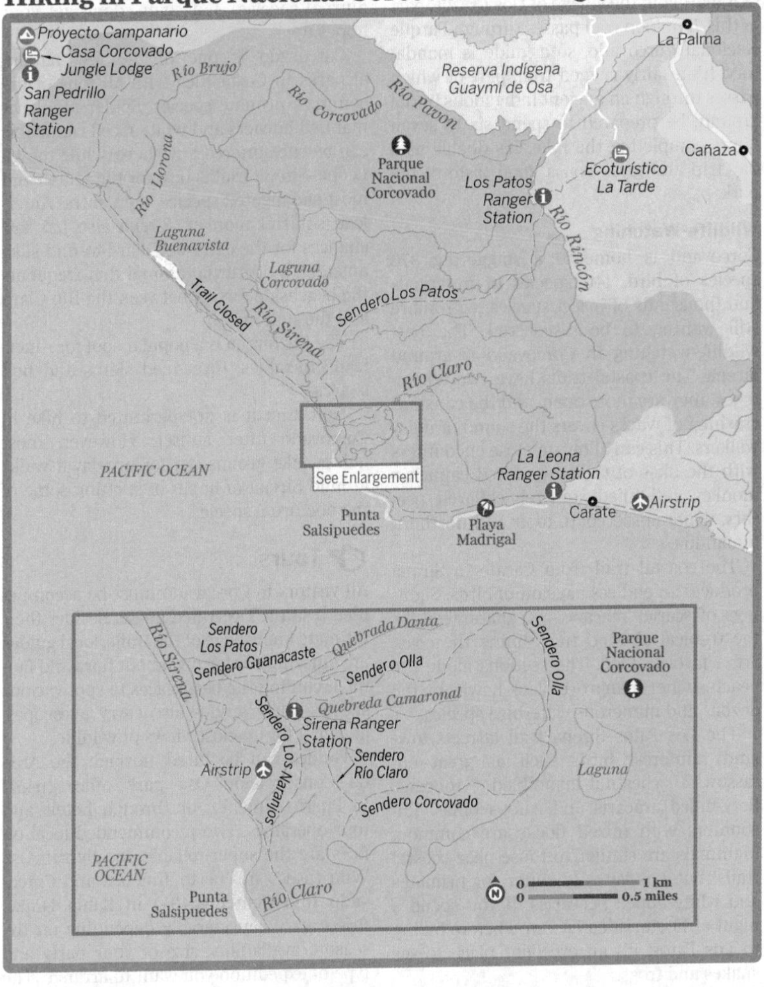

they will back off if you act aggressively. Alternatively, if you climb up a tree – about 2m off the ground – you'll avoid being bitten or trampled in the event of running into a surly squadron. Fun fact: peccaries emit a strong smell of onions, so you usually have a bit of a heads-up before they come crashing through the bush.

La Tarde to Los Patos HIKING

This 5km hike starts (or finishes) outside the Corcovado park boundary, in the village of La Tarde. Coming from the village, it consists of fairly steep downhills through dense secondary forest, where you're likely to see different monkey species, numerous birds and the Golfo Dulce poison-dart frog, endemic to Costa Rica. A little way past Los Patos Ranger Station there's an enticing waterfall with a deep pool to swim in.

There are no facilities for camping or lodging at Los Patos Ranger Station. That means that this 5km hike is a necessary same-day add-on to the 24km trek between Los Patos and Sirena, if the road to Los Patos is impassable to vehicles (often the case during heavy rains).

Sendero El Tigre HIKING

Originating in the village of Dos Brazos, part of this 7km loop trail passes through Parque Nacional Corcovado, so a guide is mandatory. It's a fairly rugged trail, part of which passes through an ancient indigenous burial ground; be prepared to spend six to seven hours completing the hike. It's doable as a day trip and gives you a good taste of the park.

Wildlife-Watching

Corcovado is home to a staggering 370 species of bird, 140 species of mammals and thousands of insect species, with more still waiting to be discovered. The best wildlife-watching in Corcovado is around Sirena. The coastal trails have two advantages: they are more open, and the constant crashing of waves covers the sound of noisy walkers. This can allow up-close encounters with the likes of the white-faced capuchin monkey, red-tailed squirrel, collared peccary, white-nosed coati, tapir and northern tamandua.

The coastal trail from Carate to Sirena produces an endless pageant of birds. Sightings of scarlet macaws are guaranteed, as the tropical almond trees lining the coast are a favorite food. The sections along the beach shelter mangrove black hawks by the dozens and numerous waterbird species.

The Los Patos–Sirena trail attracts lowland rainforest birds such as great curassows, chestnut-mandibled toucans, fiery-billed aracaris and rufous pihas. Encounters with mixed flocks are common. Mammals are similar to those near coastal trails, but Los Patos is better for primates and white-lipped peccaries. If you spend a night at Ecoturístico La Tarde before hiking to Los Patos, it's an excellent place to see snakes and frogs.

For wildlife-watchers frustrated by the difficulty of seeing rainforest mammals, a stay at Sirena Ranger Station is a must. If you get up for an early-morning walk, a sighting of a Baird's tapir is almost guaranteed – a statement that can be made at few other places in the world. Sirena is excellent for other herbivores, particularly red brocket and both species of peccary. Agouti and tayra are also common.

Jaguars are rarely spotted, as their population in the Osa is suspected to be in the single digits. Look for kinkajous and crab-eating skunks (especially at the mouth of the Río Sirena). Pumas represent your best chance for observing a cat (the only diurnal species), but again, don't get your hopes up.

Corcovado is one of the few national parks in Costa Rica with all four of the country's primate species. Spider monkeys, mantled howlers and white-faced capuchins can be encountered anywhere, while the La Leone–Sirena trail is best for the fourth and most endangered species, the Central American squirrel monkey. Sirena also has fair chances for the extremely hard-to-find silky anteater, a nocturnal animal that frequents the beachside forests between the Río Claro and the station.

The Río Sirena is a popular spot for American crocodiles, three-toed sloths and bull sharks.

Note that it is not permitted to hike in Corcovado after sunset. However, most guides take groups out for pre-dawn walks around Sirena in hopes of spotting some of the nocturnal species.

Tours

All visitors to Corcovado must be accompanied by an ICT-certified guide. Besides their intimate knowledge of the trails, local guides are amazingly informed about flora and fauna, including the best places to spot various species. Most guides also carry telescopes, allowing for up-close views of wildlife.

Guides can be hired through the Área de Conservación Osa park office (p451) in Puerto Jiménez, or through hotels and tour operators. Two recommended local offices are the super-reliable, locally run Osa Wild (p447) in Puerto Jiménez and Corcovado Info Center (p434) in Bahía Drake. Prices vary considerably depending on the season, availability, size of your party and type of expedition you want to arrange. The price should include park fees, meals and transportation.

Sleeping & Eating

Camping costs US$6 per person per day at the **San Pedrillo** (per person US$6) and **La Leona** (per person US$6) Ranger Stations, but is no longer allowed elsewhere in the park. Facilities include potable water and latrines. Remember to bring a flashlight or a headlamp, as the campgrounds are dark at night.

Note that all visitors are required to pack out all of their trash.

POISON DARTS & HARMLESS ROCKETS

Traversed by many streams and rivers, Corcovado is a hot spot for exquisitely beautiful poison-dart frogs. Two species here, the granular poison-dart frog and the Golfo Dulce poison-dart frog, are Costa Rican endemics – the latter only occurs in and around Corcovado. A search of the leaf litter near Sirena Ranger Station readily turns up both species, as well as the more widespread green and black poison-dart frog.

You might also find some other members of the family that have one important difference: they're not poisonous! Called rocket frogs because of their habit of launching themselves into streams when disturbed, they are essentially poison-dart frogs without the poisonous punch.

The difference is likely in their diets. Poison-dart frogs have a diet dominated by ants, which are rich in alkaloids, and are thought to give rise to their formidable defenses. Rocket frogs also eat ants but in lower quantities, and rely instead on their astounding leaps to escape predators. They also lack the dazzling warning colors of their toxic cousins.

Costa Rica's poison-dart frogs are not dangerous to humans unless their toxins come into contact with a person's bloodstream or mucous membranes. It's probably best to admire their cautionary colors without touching.

Sirena Ranger Station LODGE **$**
(dm US$30) Facilities at Sirena Ranger Station include bunk beds with mosquito nets, sheets and pillowcases, clean bathrooms and cool showers. Sirena serves large meals (US$20 to US$25 per meal) by advance reservation only. Snacks and potable water are also available. There are no cooking facilities.

★Ecoturístico La Tarde LODGE **$$**
(☎2200-9617; www.ecoturisticolatarde.com; per person incl 3 meals US$80-85; wi-fi) This wonderful, farm-based rural-tourism project is run by Eduardo and his hospitable family. There are various nature trails on the property, and it's a great place to stay prior to your hike to Sirena in Parque Nacional Corcovado (or on your way out). Accommodations are either in a dorm or in rustic cabins.

Guides lead day hikes to Los Patos Ranger Station (US$75) and a resident herpetologist leads excellent night tours (US$50) in search of rare frogs and fer-de-lance snakes.

Information

SAFE TRAVEL

The main danger in the park comes from the wildlife. Pay attention to your guide, who will be on the lookout for venomous snakes and other dangerous creatures. Don't get too close to peccaries because they are very aggressive; climb a tree if in doubt.

Guides no longer run night hikes around Sirena for the sake of safety. (If anyone gets a snakebite, there is no way to transport them to a hospital in the dark.)

The San Pedrillo to Sirena trail remains closed indefinitely, since it was deemed too dangerous. Again, this trail was particularly precarious at night, when predatory wildlife is most active. Also, there is no way to cross the Río Llorona except by swimming – and the river estuary is home to both crocodiles and bull sharks.

TOURIST INFORMATION

Information and maps are available at the office of Área de Conservación Osa (p451) in Puerto Jiménez, where you also have to pay your park entry fee of US$15 per day. If you hire a guide through a tour agency, the agency will make all the arrangements and include the required fees in the package price. If you hire a guide independently, you may have to obtain your permit and make the reservations for lodging and meals yourself. Be sure to make these arrangements in advance, especially in the dry season, as there's a daily limit to the number of visitors allowed in the park and facilities often hit their maximum capacity. Note that you cannot secure a permit more than 30 days in advance.

Park headquarters are at Sirena Ranger Station on the coast in the middle of the park. Other ranger stations are located on the park boundaries: San Pedrillo in the northwest corner on the coast; La Leona in the southeast corner on the coast (near the village of Carate); and Los Patos (near the village of La Tarde). The newest ranger station is in Dos Brazos village, north of Puerto Jiménez.

Getting There & Away

FROM BAHÍA DRAKE

From Bahía Drake, you can walk the coastal trail that leads to San Pedrillo Ranger Station (about seven hours from Agujitas). Remember that you must be accompanied by an ICT-certified guide to enter the park. There is camping (and potable water) at San Pedrillo, but you must bring your own food and camping equipment.

Many lodges and tour companies offer tours into Corcovado. The most popular trips are one-day boat tours to San Pedrillo (US$80) or Sirena (from US$90), or a boat tour with an overnight stay at Sirena (from US$335), which is highly recommended.

FROM CARATE

In the southeast, the closest point of access is the so-called village of Carate, from where La Leona Ranger Station is a one-hour, 3.5km hike west along the beach.

Carate is accessible from Puerto Jiménez via a poorly maintained, 45km dirt road. This journey is an adventure in itself, and often allows for some good wildlife-spotting along the way. A 4WD *colectivo* travels this route twice daily for US$10, departing Puerto Jiménez for Carate at 6am and 1:30pm, returning at 8:30am and 4pm. Otherwise you can hire a 4WD taxi for around US$80.

If you have your own car, the *pulpería* in Carate is a safe place to park for a few days, though you'll have some extra peace of mind if you tip the manager before setting out.

FROM LA PALMA

From the north, the closest point of access to Corcovado is the town of La Palma, which is accessible by bus or taxi from Puerto Jiménez. La Palma is 14km from Los Patos Ranger Station.

When road conditions permit, tour companies will drop hikers or pick them up directly at Los Patos Ranger Station. If you're making your own arrangements, it's sometimes possible to hire a taxi all the way to Los Patos. However, the road is only passable to 4WD vehicles (and not always), so be prepared to hike at least part of the way to the ranger station. The road crosses the river about 20 times in the last 6km, so not only do you need a rugged vehicle, but your driver must be experienced at driving through rivers.

Another possibility is to get a lift to the village of La Tarde and hike the 5km to Los Patos from there. Note that there's no lodging or camping at Los Patos, so you have to either limit yourself to a day hike or walk all the way to Sirena.

FROM DOS BRAZOS

Dos Brazos is 10km from Puerto Jiménez. The trailhead is signposted in the Dos Brazos village. A *colectivo* travels this route twice daily for US$3.50, departing Dos Brazos at 6am and noon, and returning from Puerto Jiménez at 11am and 4pm.

TO CORCOVADO VIA PUERTO JIMÉNEZ

Of the two principal overland routes to Parque Nacional Corcovado, the Puerto Jiménez route on the eastern side of the peninsula has more going on. There is just single road and a sprinkling of villages, cattle pastures and palm-oil plantations along the coast of Golfo Dulce. The Reserva Forestal Golfo Dulce protects much of the inland area and encompasses the former gold-mining community of Dos Brazos, now the newest entrance to Corcovado and *agroturismo* epicenter. The largest settlement in the area is the town of Puerto Jiménez, which has transitioned from a gold mining boomtown to an ecotourism hot spot. South of Jiménez, the surfer haven of Cabo Matapalo and the jungle lodges of Carate beckon travelers in search of nature and solitude.

Carate

Carate, where the dirt road rounds the peninsula and comes to an abrupt end, is the southwestern gateway for anyone hiking into Sirena Ranger Station in Parque Nacional Corcovado. A handful of well-designed wilderness lodges in the area make a good night's rest for travelers heading to/from Corcovado or those in search of a quiet retreat surrounded by jungle. The bone-rattling 45km ride from Puerto Jiménez to Carate is also its own adventure as the narrow, bumpy road winds its way around dense rainforest, through gushing rivers and across windswept beaches. Birds and other wildlife are prolific along this stretch: keep your eyes peeled and hang on tight.

Sleeping & Eating

Some places in Carate don't have 24-hour electricity or hot water. Reservations are recommended in the dry season – communication is often through Puerto Jiménez, so messages may not be retrieved every day. All accommodations provide meals. For shoestringers, it's possible to camp in the yard in front of the *pulpería* for US$5 a day.

★Finca Exotica BUNGALOW $$$
(☎8359-8408; http://fincaexotica.com; tent s/d US$50/120, bungalow s/d/tr US$140/220/300, all incl breakfast) To stay at Finca Exotica is to glamp in a tropical Eden, surrounded by 90 hectares of farmland that include more than 125 species of fruit and vegetables, as well as farm animals. Guests sleep in open-air, designer cabins and tents, feast on organic, communal meals and relax in hammocks overlooking mountains and the sea.

Luna Lodge LODGE $$$
(☎4070-0010, in USA & Canada 888-760-0760; www.lunalodge.com; tent/d/bungalow incl all meals US$330/450/580; P ᯤ ≋) A steep road crisscrosses the Río Carate and up the valley to this enchanting mountain retreat on the border of Parque Nacional Corcovado. Accommodations range from tent cabins to thatched bungalows with open-air garden showers and private terraces, all of which stunning views of the pristine jungle rolling down to the ocean. Luna Lodge is the furthest-flung of Carate's accommodations.

The open-air restaurant is a marvelous place to indulge in the expansive views, while a rooftop yoga deck provides an even higher vantage point. Lana, the founder and owner of the lodge, is passionate about conservation and sustainability and has made the lodge a working practice in both. There are accommodations discounts for under-12s.

Lookout Inn GUESTHOUSE $$$
(☎2735-5431; www.lookout-inn.com; s/d/q incl breakfast US$150/204/300; P @ ≋) Near the airstrip and perched up the side of a steep hill overlooking the ocean, Lookout Inn attracts younger travelers with its comfortable, open-air quarters with mural-painted walls and unbeatable views. Accommodations are accessible by a wooden walkway winding through the trees. The 'Stairway to Heaven' (360 steps) leads up to four observation platforms and a waterfall trail.

La Leona Eco-Lodge LODGE $$$
(☎2735-5704; www.laleonaecolodge.com; d from US$146; ᯤ) This friendly lodge offers all the thrills of camping without the hassles. The 16 fully screened forest-green tents with beds are nestled between palm trees, with decks facing the beach and allowing frequent wildlife sightings. Solar power provides electricity in the restaurant.

All guests must hike the 2.5km in from the Carate airstrip, but the lodge offers a new base camp in Carate where guests may drop their bags. From here, the bags are transported via horse-drawn carriage so guests can hike the beach with a lighter load.

ℹ Getting There & Away

BUS

The *colectivo* (US$10) departs Puerto Jiménez for Carate at 6am and 1:30pm, returning at 8:30am and 3:30pm. Note that it often fills up on its return trip to Puerto Jiménez, especially during the dry season. Arrive at least 30 minutes ahead of time or you might find yourself stranded. Alternatively, catch a taxi from Puerto Jiménez (US$80).

CAR

If you're driving you'll need a 4WD, even in the dry season, as there are several streams to ford, as well as a river. Assuming you don't have valuables in sight, you can leave your car at the *pulpería* (per night US$5) and hike to La Leona Ranger Station (1½ hours).

Cabo Matapalo

If you didn't know that it was here, you would hardly suspect that the jungle-obscured community of Matapalo existed. There isn't much to the southern tip of the Península de Osa save some surfing digs and homes at the entrance to the Golfo Dulce. Matapalo lies just 17km south of Puerto Jiménez, but this heavily forested and beach-fringed cape is a vastly different world. A network of trails traverses the foothills, uninhabited except for migrating wildlife from the Reserva Forestal Golfo Dulce. Along the coastline, miles of beaches are virtually empty, except for a few surfers in the know.

Cabo Matapalo is home to wilderness lodges that cater to travelers searching for seclusion and wildlife. Scarlet macaws, brown pelicans and herons are frequently sighted on the beaches, while all four species of Costa Rican monkey, several wildcat species, plus sloths, coatis, agoutis and anteaters roam the woods.

Activities

Playa Matapalo SURFING

There are three excellent right point breaks off this beach, not far from Encanta La Vida. If there's a south or west swell, this is the best time to hit the waves.

Playa Pan Dulce SURFING

Good for beginners and intermediate surfers, Pan Dulce gets some nice longboard waves most days. You can also go swimming here, but be careful of rip tides.

Tours

★Psycho Tours ADVENTURE

(Everyday Adventures; ☎8428-3904; www.psychotours.com; tours US$55-130) Witty, energetic naturalist Andy Pruter runs Psycho Tours, which offers high-adrenaline adventures in Cabo Matapalo. His signature tour is tree climbing (US$65 per person): scaling a 60m ficus tree, aptly named 'Cathedral.' Also popular – and definitely adrenaline-inducing – is waterfall rappelling (US$95) down cascades ranging from 15m to 30m. The best one? The tree-climbing/waterfall combo tour (US$130).

For the tamer of heart, excellent three- to four-hour guided nature walks (US$55) tap into the extensive knowledge base of Andy and his staff members.

Sleeping

★Ojo del Mar BUNGALOW $$

(☎8378-5246; www.ojodelmar.com; road to Carate, Km 16; s/d beach nests US$79/104, bungalows from US$135/145, all incl breakfast; P 📶 ≋) 🍃 Tucked in amid a good surfing beach and lush jungle, the six beautifully handcrafted, thatch-roofed bamboo bungalows are open-air, allowing for all the natural sounds and scents to seep in. There are also two cozy 'beach nests' that are the next best thing to sleeping on the sand. Surfers chill in palm-strung hammocks, and yogis salute the rising sun from the gorgeous yoga shala.

A fantastic seasonally inspired buffet is served nightly (US$25). Guests dine by candlelight and share stories of their adventures from the day.

★Lapa Ríos LODGE $$$

(☎4070-0420, 800-963-1195; www.laparios.com; road to Carate, Km 17; d incl 3 meals from US$1140; P 📶 ≋) 🍃 One of Costa Rica's best all-inclusive wilderness lodges, Lapa Ríos combines luxury with a rustic, tropical ambience. It comprises 17 spacious, thatched bungalows, all decked out with king- and queen-sized beds, bamboo furniture, garden showers and private decks with panoramic views. An extensive trail system allows exploration of the 400-hectare reserve, with onsite tours included in the price.

Encanta La Vida LODGE $$$

(☎8376-3209; www.encantalavida.com; Cabo Matapalo; s/d incl 3 meals from US$172/300; P 📶 ≋) The enchanted life, indeed. Lodging is in romantic, wood-beamed *casitas*, all equipped with breezy verandas overlooking the jungle-clad backdrop. Howlers and spider monkeys regularly travel the treetops, while pairs of great currasows stroll shyly below.The location is a perfect base for exploring the cape. Surfboards, ocean-view yoga terrace and spa treatments are at your disposal.

Bosque del Cabo BUNGALOW $$$

(☎2735-5206; www.bosquedelcabo.com; s/d incl 3 meals from US$270/440, rental houses without food US$595; P 📶 ≋) 🍃 Dreamy, far-flung cabins overlook the jungle and sea at this expansive property tucked away on Cabo Matapalo. Amenities include two pools, The grounds feel a bit manicured in comparison to wilder, neighboring properties, but there's a vast system of hiking trails to bring guests into contact with an abundance of rainforest flora and fauna.

One unique feature on the grounds: a 110ft-high tree platform gives guests a bird's eye view of the surrounding forest.

El Remanso Lodge LODGE $$$

(☎2735-5569; www.elremanso.com; road to Carate, Km 21; s/d incl 3 meals from US$335/450; P 📶 ≋) 🍃 Set on 72 hectares of rainforest, this bluff-top lodge is constructed from fallen tropical hardwoods, with secluded, sumptuous, modern cabins and an open-air dining room with a wonderful vista. Private trails lead through jungle to the beach, a waterfall and tide pools. Thrill-seekers can also go ziplining or waterfall rappelling on the grounds.

Eating & Drinking

Martina's Bar BAR

(Buena Esperanza Bar; ☎8360-9979; road to Carate, Km 17; mains US$8-18; ⊙9am-9pm Sat-Thu, to 1am Fri) The sign says 'Buena Esperanza Bar' but it's known as Martina's, named for the charismatic owner who is a local legend. This festive, open-air tropical bar is about 1km before the Matapalo turnoff. The changing menu usually features three or four options, including fresh seafood, pasta and other gourmet fare. The food is excellent and the bartenders are sassy.

Martina's is always hopping on Friday nights, when local artisans and vendors set up a sort of artist market and folks come out from Puerto Jiménez to join the party.

Getting There & Away

If you are driving, a 4WD is essential even in the dry season, as roads frequently get washed out. There are several streams and a river to cross on the way here. From the Puerto Jiménez–Carate road, the poorly marked turnoff for Cabo Matapalo is on the left-hand side, then through a crumbling cement gate (called 'El Portón Blanco').

Otherwise, the *colectivo* (US$6) will drop you at the turnoff; it passes by at about 7:15am and 2:45pm heading to Carate, and 9:15am and 4:45pm heading back to Jiménez. A taxi will come here from Puerto Jiménez for about US$55.

Puerto Jiménez

POP 6815

Sliced in half by the swampy, overgrown Quebrada Cacao, and flanked on one side by the emerald waters of the Golfo Dulce, Puerto Jiménez is shared by local residents and wildlife. While walking through the streets of Jiménez (as it's known to locals), it's not unusual to spot scarlet macaws roosting on the soccer field, or white-faced capuchins traversing the treetops along the main street.

On the edge of Parque Nacional Corcovado, Jiménez is the preferred jumping-off point for travelers heading to the famed Sirena Ranger Station, and a great place to organize an expedition, stock up on supplies and get a good night's rest before hitting the trails.

And even besides Corcovado, there are beaches to swim and sun, mangroves to kayak and fish to catch. This is a Tico town with tourist appeal, and an adventure to fit every palate.

Sights

Playa Platanares BEACH

About 5km southeast of town, the long, secluded – and often deserted – Playa Platanares is excellent for swimming, sunning and recovering from too much adventure. The nearby mangroves of Río Platanares are a paradise for kayaking and birdwatching. Take the road that runs parallel to the airstrip.

Tours

Puerto Jiménez has a host of tour operators, taxi drivers and touts hungry for the tourist dollar. Ask lots of questions, consult with fellow travelers and choose carefully.

★**Osa Wild** TOURS

(2735-5848; www.osawildtravel.com; tours from US$40, 1-day Corcovado tour US$85-105; 8am-noon & 2-7pm Mon-Fri, 9am-noon &1-4pm Sat & Sun) Osa Wild is *the* way to connect with Corcovado park and Osa. It's just what the area so desperately needed: a resource for travelers to connect with community-oriented initiatives that go to the heart of the real Osa through homestays, farm tours and

DAY-TRIPPER

You've got a free day in Puerto Jiménez and you don't want to hang around town? Here's what you can do:

- Take a trip to meet a local farmer or learn about rainforest medicine with Osa Wild.
- Kayak through the mangrove estuary to look for caimans, birds and monkeys with Aventuras Tropicales (p449).
- Indulge your sweet tooth; see (and taste) where chocolate comes from at Finca Köbö (p453).
- Slow down and get some sun; have a picnic and play in the waves at Playa Platanares.
- Head to Dos Brazos (p452) to try your hand at panning for gold.

Puerto Jiménez

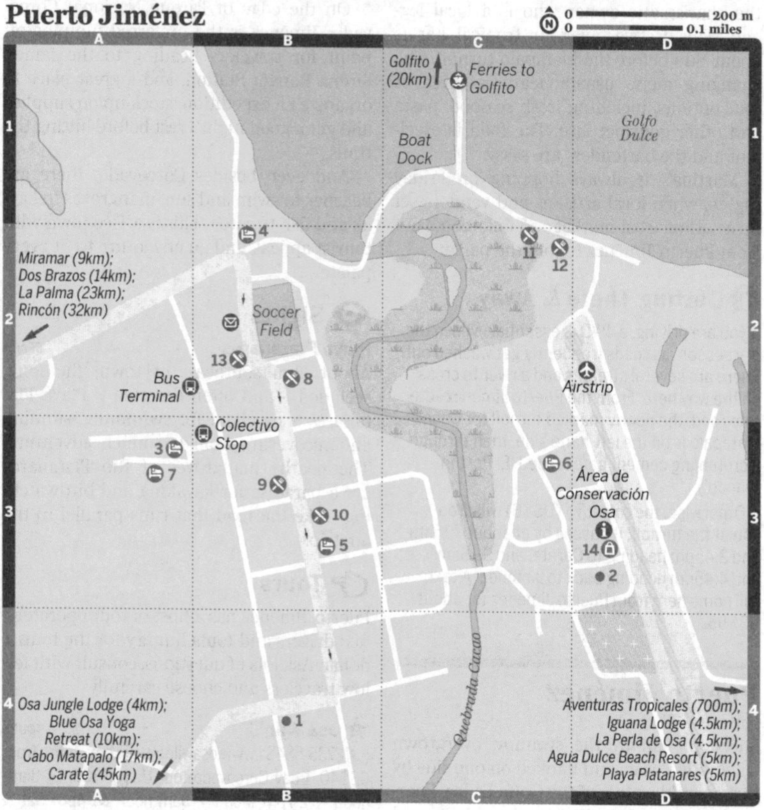

Puerto Jiménez

Activities, Courses & Tours
1 Osa Wild B4
2 Surcos Tours D3

Sleeping
3 Cabinas Back Packer A3
4 Cabinas Jiménez B2
5 Cabinas Marcelina B3
6 Cabinas Tropicales C3
7 Refugio Turistico A3

Eating
8 Cafetería Monka B2
9 Dog House B3
10 Hellen's Chill House B3
11 Il Giardino C2
12 Marisquería Corcovado C2
13 Pizzamail.it B2

Shopping
14 Jagua Arts & Crafts D3

sustainable cultural exchanges. It also offers more typical stuff like kayaking tours and guided trips through Corcovado.

Run by university-trained biologist Ifi and her husband Daniel, Osa Wild's focus on sustainability, environmental protection and community development put it in a league of its own. It also sets up volunteer programs.

Surcos Tours TOURS
(☎8550-1089, 2235-5355; www.surcostours.com)
A team of excellent guides make Surcos a great option, especially for wildlife and birdwatching tours. Surcos offers all the options for multiday treks in Corcovado, as well as shorter wildlife outings at Cabo Matapalo or around La Leona.

Aventuras Tropicales
KAYAKING

(☑ 2735-5195; www.aventurastropicales.com) Aventuras Tropicales is your specialist in water-based adventures. Its main thing is kayak tours, which might include mangrove exploration, fishing or bioluminescent paddling. Located 2km east on the road to Platanares.

If you're into culinary adventure, check out the Aventura Coco Dulce (US$35), which is a sort of cooking course where you learn all about the coconut – how to choose a good one, open it and use it to make coconut *cajeta* (candy).

Osa Aventura
ADVENTURE

(☑ 2735-5670, 8372-6135; www.osaaventura.com; 1-/2-day Corcovado hikes US$105/350) ✦ Run by Mike Boston, a biologist with a real passion for nature, Osa Aventura aims to introduce travelers to the beauty of rainforest life and to raise awareness of the need to preserve Osa's unique environment. Mike specializes in designing educational activities for classes and groups, but he also leads multiday treks in Corcovado.

🛏 Sleeping

There's usually a plethora of lodging options in Puerto Jiménez proper, but reservations are a good idea on weekends and during holidays. You'll find the greatest diversity of accommodations at the budget and midrange levels here, more so than in other parts of the Osa. Top-end options tend to be located on the outskirts of town.

★ Osa Jungle Hostel
HOSTEL $

(☑ 8834-4963, 8983-0950; www.osajunglehostel.com; dm US$15; 🖧) ✦ Here is a supercool way for budget travelers to experience all the adventure and wildness of a jungle lodge without the hefty price tag. This property is completely off the grid and surrounded by forest, home to birds, monkeys and wildlife galore. Two new purpose-built bunk houses have mosquito-netted beds, communal kitchens and hammock-strung hangout lounges. Meals are available at the onsite restaurant.

Osa Jungle Hostel is 4km south of Puerto Jiménez. The Carate *collectivo* will drop you at the turnoff, from where it's a 1.5km walk uphill to the hostel. Or, call ahead to make arrangements for a pickup from the bus station.

Cabinas Marcelina
HOTEL $

(☑ 2735-5007; www.facebook.com/cabinasmarcelina.puertojimenez; s/d US$30/44; 🅿❄🖧) Marcelina's place is a long-standing favorite among budget travelers looking for a peaceful night's sleep. In a cheerful pink concrete building, the rooms are clustered around a courtyard filled with blooming flowers. Rooms have modern furniture, TV and air-con, not to mention fluffy towels and hot-water tile bathrooms. The guarded parking is also reassuring.

Cabinas Tropicales
CABINA $

(☑ 8997-1445, 2735-5298; www.cabinas-tropicales.com; s/d/tr US$45/55/70; 🅿❄🖧) Six tidy rooms at Cabinas Tropicales range from simple standards to roomy lofts and a deluxe suite, some of which have lovely outdoor showers. Each is unique, but they all have sturdy furniture, air-con and access to a well-stocked open-air kitchen. Your host, Mark, is both personable and knowledgeable. One of the best-value options in town.

Cabinas Back Packer
GUESTHOUSE $

(☑ 2735-5181; www.facebook.com/cabinasbackpackers; s/d without bathroom US$20/30; ❄🖧) On the edge of town, these budget digs are squeaky clean and relatively quiet. Rooms share clean bathrooms and a brightly tiled kitchen (available for a fee). Bicycles are available for guest use. But the best feature is the front garden strung with hammocks. Air-con available for an additional US$10.

Refugio Turistico
CABINAS $

(☑ 8342-4304, 2735-5079; www.facebook.com/cabinasrefugiopj; d/apt US$45/72; 🅿❄🖧) Here are some shiny new *cabinas* on the edge of town. The rooms are spartan, with cinder block walls and tile floors, but sheets are crisp and clean and the bathrooms sparkle. Adirondack chairs and potted plants create an inviting outdoor seating area out front.

★ Cabinas Jiménez
CABINA $$

(☑ 2735-5090; www.cabinasjimenez.com; s/d from US$80/95, with kitchen US$105/120; 🅿❄🖧🏊) The most appealing place to stay in Puerto Jiménez proper, Cabinas Jiménez combines the convenience of a central location with the ambience and amenities of a vacation destination. The *cabinas* are all decorated with colorful murals featuring jungle scenes or underwater themes. Some have private balconies, lagoon views or poolside patios. Free bikes and kayaks are a bonus.

Agua Dulce Beach Resort RESORT $$
(☎8310-6304, 8599-9499; www.aguadulcehotel.com; Playa Platanares; d US$100-112, ste US$135-180, all incl breakfast; P❄📶🏊) A stone's throw from Playa Platanares, this resort offers spacious and attractive rooms with white-washed walls and wicker furniture. Sliding glass doors open onto a terrace facing the garden or pool. Monkeys and macaws haunt the grounds, and the beautiful (often deserted) beach is just steps away.

The breezy restaurant is a trusted spot for imaginative pasta dishes, grilled fish and ample breakfasts, although the service is positively languid.

★**Iguana Lodge** HOTEL $$$
(☎8848-0752, in USA & Canada 800-259-9123; www.iguanalodge.com; d incl breakfast US$169-183, casitas per person incl 2 meals US$211; P❄📶🏊) Here are the most architecturally alluring cabins in the area: two-story bungalows with breezy decks, bamboo furniture, orthopedic beds draped in mosquito netting and lovely stone bathrooms with garden showers. The club rooms are more straightforward, but still appealing and airy, with lofty ceilings and private porches. The whole lodge benefits from a fabulous location fronting spectacular Playa Platanares.

The excellent restaurant, La Perla de Osa, is open to nonguests. On the beach there are *palapas* (shelters with a thatched, palm-leaf roof and open sides), hammocks and a volleyball court.

Blue Osa Yoga Retreat BOUTIQUE HOTEL $$$
(☎in USA 917-400-9797; www.blueosa.com; s/d incl 3 meals from US$295/398; P⊖❄📶🏊) 🌿 Emphasizing rejuvenation, this intimate oceanfront retreat center attracts those looking to unwind, through yoga, swimming in the chemical-free pool or getting pampered in the solar-powered eco-spa. Communal meals include organic produce from the onsite garden and lodgings are harmonious, with rustic furnishings and screened windows. Prices include daily yoga classes. Located 12km south of Puerto Jiménez on the road to Carate.

Eating

★**Cafetería Monka** COSTA RICAN $
(☎2735-5051; www.facebook.com/monkascafe; mains US$6-10; ⏲6am-8pm; 📶🌿) The best breakfast spot in town, Monka makes excellent coffee drinks and smoothies, as well as extensive breakfast platters, ranging from tropical French toast topped with fruits to tasty breakfast burritos. The rest of the day you can fill up on sandwiches, salads and inexpensive *casados*.

Hellen's Chill House INTERNATIONAL $
(☎8359-5203; www.facebook.com/Hellenschillhouse; mains US$5-10; ⏲5am-8pm; 📶🌿) Hellen's is supremely popular with pretty much everyone, for wake-me-up coffee drinks, filling breakfasts, excellent burgers (including veggie burgers) and more. The homemade bread means the sandwiches are hard to beat. Order one to go and you've got a perfect picnic for your hike or beach outing.

Pizzamail.it PIZZA $
(☎2735-5483; pizzas US$10-20; ⏲4-10:30pm; 📶🌿) While this pizzeria's name sounds more like a website, all doubts will be cast aside when a server at Pizzamail.it brings out the pie: a thin-crust, wood-fired piece of Italy in the middle of the jungle. From its small patio diners can watch squawking macaws in the trees over the soccer pitch. Several pizza options are meat-free. *Bellissimo!*

Dog House AMERICAN $
(☎2735-5138; www.facebook.com/doghouse.ptojimenez; mains US$5-8; ⏲11am-midnight) We love *gallo pinto* (a common meal of blended rice and beans) as much as the next person, but sometimes you gotta get your fix of burgers and dogs. Make your way to the Dog House for specialty hamburgers like La Tica (with cheese, avocado and a fried egg) and hot dogs like the Mexicana (with chili and guacamole). There's also French fries, onion rings and, um, salad.

La Perla de Osa INTERNATIONAL $$
(☎8829-5865; mains US$10-17; ⏲11am-8pm; P📶🌿) On the grounds of Iguana Lodge, this jungle-fringed restaurant-bar is locally (and justifiably) famous for its cocktails, accompanied by such delectable nibbles as pulled-pork tacos, grilled Asian-style tuna and shrimp plates. This is a sweet spot for a snack after a day on Playa Platanares.

Marisquería Corcovado SEAFOOD $$
(☎2735-5659; mains US$8-20; ⏲11am-9pm) A spacious, covered, waterfront deck – ceiling fans spinning overhead – is the perfect place to feast on fresh grilled tuna, whole red snapper or tangy *ceviche* served with

patacones (fried green plantains cut in thin pieces). There is a selection of cocktails and craft beer, in addition to the typical fresh fruit *batidos*. The servers are quite charming, though not in any hurry!

Il Giardino ITALIAN $$
(☎2735-5129; www.ilgiardinoitalianrestaurant.com; meals US$11-16; ⊙7am-10pm) A sweet Italian restaurant with a romantic candlelit ambience. The rather long menu features pizza, pasta and other exquisite Italian dishes. Especially tantalizing are the house inventions such as Loreto pizza (with guacamole and mozzarella) and crab ravioli. Be forewarned that the Ranalli family subscribes to the 'slow food' movement: there's no rushing good cooking, especially when it's on Tico time.

Shopping

★**Jagua Arts & Crafts** ARTS & CRAFTS
(☎2735-5267; ⊙7am-3pm Mon-Sat) A terrific, well-stocked crafts shop, featuring local art and jewelry, a wonderful collection of colorful Boruca masks and black-and-ocher Guaitil pottery, as well as woven goods by the Emberá and Wounaan people. Kuna weavings technically belong across the border in Panama, but they make excellent gifts.

Information

Área de Conservación Osa (ACOSA; Osa Conservation Area Headquarters; ☎2735-5036; Corcovado park fee per person per day US$15; ⊙8am-4pm Mon-Fri) Information about Parque Nacional Corcovado, Isla del Caño, Parque Nacional Marino Ballena and Golfito parks and reserves.
Banco Nacional (☎2735-5020; ⊙8:30am-3:30pm Mon-Fri) Has an ATM.
BCR (Banco de Costa Rica; ☎2211-1111; ⊙9am-4pm Mon-Fri) Across from the church; it also has an ATM.
Police Near the soccer field.
Post office (☎2735-5045; ⊙8am-noon & 1-5pm Mon-Fri) Near the soccer field.

Getting There & Away

AIR

The **airstrip** is to the east of town. **Sansa** (☎2735-5890; www.flysansa.com), Skyway and Aerobell all have flights to/from San José (50 minutes); one-way flights are anywhere from US$80 to US$150.

BOAT

Several fast **ferries** (☎8839-8497, 2735-5095) travel to Golfito (US$6, 30 minutes), departing at 6am, 8:45am, 11:30am, 2pm and 4:20pm daily. Double-check current schedules, as they change often and without notice. On Sundays, ferries depart less frequently.

Alternatively, you could opt to hire a private water taxi to shuttle you across to Golfito or Zancudo. You will have to negotiate, but prices are generally reasonable, especially considering that you set the schedule.

BUS

Most buses arrive at the blue **terminal** (☎2735-5189) behind the green paint store on the west side of town.

CAR

Puerto Jiménez is now connected to the rest of the country by a beautifully paved road. If you're driving to Carate or Matapalo, you'll need a 4WD; be sure to fill up at the **gas station** in Jiménez.

TAXI

The *colectivo* (shared truck taxi) runs daily to Cabo Matapalo (US$5, 1½ hours) and Carate (US$10, 2½ hours) on the southern tip of the national park. Departures are from the **colectivo stop** (☎8832-8680) at Soda Deya at 6am and 1:30pm, returning at 8:30am and 4pm.

Otherwise, you can call and hire a 4WD taxi. Taxis usually charge from US$60 for the ride to Carate and from US$70 for the ride to Matapalo, and more than US$120 for the overland trek to Bahía Drake.

BUSES FROM PUERTO JIMÉNEZ

DESTINATION	COST (US$)	DURATION (HR)	FREQUENCY (DAILY)
Neily	4.60	3	5:30am, 2pm
La Palma	2.60	1	hourly
San Isidro de El General	10	5½	1pm
San José	13	8	5am, 9am

Dos Brazos

POP 300

Clustered along two branches of Río Tigre (which gives the village its full name: Dos Brazos de Río Tigre), this appealing village that lives on 'Tico time' is surrounded by secondary forest near the edge of Parque Nacional Corcovado. In the 1970s there was a gold rush here, with miners coming from all over to seek their fortune. While small-scale gold-panning still goes on, Dos Brazos is now looking toward rural tourism and ecotourism as the way forward for its close-knit community.

Activities

A rugged 7km trail loop, which passes through Parque Nacional Corcovado, has its trailhead in Dos Brazos. Known as Sendero El Tigre (p442), the trail opened in early 2015. The idea is that the trail generates tourism in the village, and profits are reinvested in the local community. It takes about six hours to complete the Sendero El Tigre loop, and it does require a guide (US$102 for one person, plus US$68 per additional person); book through the Dos Brazos Oficina de Turismo.

For independent hiking and wildlife-watching, day hikers can explore the walking trails and waterfalls at Bolita Rainforest Hostel for US$10 (starting with the monkey-filled walk into the property). Stop at the office in the village for directions.

Tours

In addition to the Sendero El Tigre, the Dos Brazos Oficina de Turismo offers many other tours and activities in Dos Brazos and the surrounding countryside. A unique option is the gold-panning tour (per person US$40), where you can learn how it's done from real *oreros*. There's also horseback riding, waterfalls hikes, cooking classes and more.

Sleeping & Eating

There's no restaurant in the village but all accommodations provide meals on request and some offer cooking facilities.

★ Bolita Rainforest Hostel HOSTEL $

(☎8549-9898; www.bolita.org; dm/cabina/house US$12/35/89) For total immersion in rural life, stay at this rustic farmhouse in the midst of 25 hectares of rainforest. There's no electricity, so you'll be up with the howler monkeys and eating dinner by candlelight (though there are solar-powered USB charging stations). Attractive open-air rooms come with mosquito nets and fresh linens, as well as access to walking trails and waterfalls.

Day hikers are welcome to explore the 15km of trails for US$10. Stop at the Bolita office in the village for directions.

Los Mineros Guesthouse GUESTHOUSE $

(☎8721-8087; www.losminerosguesthouse.com; cabina with bathroom US$21, per person hut without bathroom US$16) This is a characterful place to stay, with a historical bar frequented by miners during the gold rush. Most of the *cabinas* were part of the village brothel. There are also rustic bamboo A-frame huts, with shared bathrooms that were once prison cells. Communal kitchen, yoga deck and river swimming hole available for guest use.

Yejos B&B B&B $

(☎8554-7381; www.Yejosbb.com; tent cabana US$24, d/ste US$34/54; P❄🛜) This newish B&B has four simple rooms and suites, plus the tent-like open-air Garden Cabana. It's a sweet spot, surrounded by blooming gardens and frog-croaking ponds. Birders will be in heaven, thanks to the observation deck and feeders attracting many feathered friends. Guests have access to a shared kitchen, or prepared food is available on request (preferably in advance).

Air-con is available for an additional US$10.

Amazonita BUNGALOW $$

(☎8501-9608, 8982-9513; www.amazonitaecolodge.com; cabinas US$70-80, house US$100) A five-minute walk from the Sendero El Tigre trailhead, on a steep hillside, Amazonita consists of two *cabinas* and a house open to the wilderness. There are wonderful views over the treetops from the hammocks on the porches. Kitchens are well equipped, but there is also a restaurant onsite.

Bosque del Río Tigre LODGE $$$

(☎8705-3729; www.bosquedelriotigre.com; s/d incl 3 meals US$218/356, 4-day package per person US$692; P) 🌿 In the midst of a 13-hectare private reserve, this ecolodge is a bird-watcher's paradise; guests can opt for unlimited birding and herping packages. Liz and Abraham are effusive hosts, the food is outstanding and wildlife comes up to your door. Four well-appointed guest rooms and one private cabin have huge windows for wildlife-watching.

Getting here involves a river crossing, which can become impassable during rain.

Information

There's a helpful tourist office, **Dos Brazos Oficina de Turismo** (☎6098-7616, 8691-4545; www.corcovadoeltigre.com; ⏲6am-6pm), near the entrance to the village. Here visitors can book various tours, pay the park entry fee (US$15) if they wish to hike the Sendero El Tigre, and book a guide – mandatory for hiking inside the national park.

The comprehensive website www.corcovadoeltigre.com offers useful info on what to do and where to stay in the village.

Getting There & Away

A minibus runs from Puerto Jiménez to Dos Brazos twice daily on weekdays at 11am and 4pm (US$3.50, 30 minutes), returning to Puerto Jiménez at 6am and noon. If driving, Río Tigre is well signposted off the main highway, around 10km north of Puerto Jiménez.

Reserva Forestal Golfo Dulce

The northern shore of the Golfo Dulce is home to this vast forest reserve, which links Parque Nacional Corcovado to the Parque Nacional Piedras Blancas. This connecting corridor plays an important role in preserving the biodiversity of the peninsula, and in allowing the wildlife to migrate to the mainland. Although much of the reserve is not easily accessible, there are several lodges in the area doing their part to preserve this natural resource by protecting their own little pieces of this wildlife wonderland.

Sights

Finca Köbö FARM

(☎8398-7604; www.fincakobo.com; 2hr tour US$32; P) About 8km south of La Palma, Finca Köbö is a chocolate-lover's dream come true (in fact *köbö* means 'dream' in Ngöbere). The 20-hectare *finca* is dedicated to the organic cultivation of fruits and vegetables and – the product of choice – cacao. Tours in English give a comprehensive overview of the life cycle of cacao plants and the production of chocolate (with degustation!). More than half of the territory is dedicated to protecting and reforesting natural ecosystems.

To really experience the beauty and vision of this *finca*, you can stay in simple, comfortable teak cabins and bungalows (US$95 to US$105, including breakfast; dinner available for US$15), with lovely open-air bathrooms and quality linens.

Activities

Kayaking

At the east end of La Palma, **Playa Blanca** is ideal for sea kayaking. The owner of Lapamar (p454) also arranges independent sea-kayaking outings, and this ecolodge is an overnight stop for participants in multiday kayaking trips run by Tropical Sea Kayaking.

Tropical Sea Kayaking KAYAKING

(☎2249-0666, in USA 719-581-9891; www.tropicalseakayaking.com; 8-day trip US$2200) This experienced, reliable operator organizes in-depth eight-day sea-kayaking adventures on the Golfo Dulce, looking for wildlife in the mangroves and dolphin-spotting along the way, stopping on tiny islands and Playa Blanca, seeking out secret spots that few visitors get to see and staying in lodges only accessible by water. Prices include accommodations, meals, kayaking and all arrangements.

Wildlife-Watching

Most travelers skip the northern part of the peninsula and beeline for Puerto Jiménez to get to Parque Nacional Corcovado. If you have time to dawdle, there's lots of DIY wildlife-watching to be had. About 9km southeast of Rincón, the town of **La Palma** is the origin of the rough road that turns into the trail to Corcovado's Los Patos Ranger Station. If you're through-hiking Corcovado, this will likely be the start or end point of your trek.

Río Nuevo is a hamlet reachable via a 16km unpaved road from a turnoff just before entering Puerto Jiménez. A good trail network leads to spectacular mountain viewpoints, some with views of the gulf. Birdwatching is excellent around Rio Nuevo.

Tours

Reserva Indígena Guaymí de Osa CULTURAL

The Reserva Indígena Guaymí de Osa is southwest of La Palma town, on the border of Parque Nacional Corcovado. A few lodges offer tours into the reserve to learn more about the Ngöbe, including Ojo del Mar (p446) in Cabo Matapalo and Danta Corcovado Lodge (p454) in La Palma.

KNOWING THE NGÖBE

The earliest inhabitants of Costa Rica's far southern corner were the Ngöbe, historically referred to as the Guaymí. The name Guaymí was a Spanish transliteration of what another indigenous group had dubbed the Ngöbe – and while 'Guaymí' is not considered offensive, necessarily, the Ngöbe rightly prefer the name that they call themselves.

Having migrated over generations from neighboring Panama, the Ngöbe now inhabit indigenous reserves in the Valle de Coto Brus, the Península de Osa and southern Golfo Dulce; however, they retain some seminomadic ways and are legally allowed to pass freely over the border into Panama. This occurs frequently during the coffee-harvesting season, when many travel to work on plantations.

More so than many tribes in Costa Rica, the Ngöbe have been able to preserve their customs and culture, and it is not unusual to see women wearing the traditional brightly colored, ankle-length *nagua* dress. Unlike other indigenous groups, the Ngöbe still speak Ngöbere, their native language, and teach it in local schools.

One reason the culture has been able to preserve its traditional ways is that the Ngöbe reserves are largely inaccessible. But as tourism filters into the furthest reaches of the country, the growing interest in indigenous traditions and handicrafts may actually encourage their preservation, so long as it is managed with community participation and visitor respect.

The easiest way to visit a Ngöbe reserve is to visit the **community museum** (open 8am to 5pm) at Villa Palacios in the Coto Brus reserve, about 8km north of San Vito and another 8km off the Interamericana.

Sleeping

Lapamar CABINA $

(☎8339-1458, 2735-1347; r per person incl breakfast US$18; P) This clutch of shiny wooden cabins is just a few steps away from the beach at Playa Blanca. The lodgings are decorated with murals of local flora and fauna. Guests can sit on their private porches and watch the scarlet macaws in all their squawky glory, as they nest in the trees above the cabins.

The owner of the ecolodge runs excellent sea-kayaking tours (US$25 per person) and is very knowledgeable about local wildlife. If you call ahead when arriving by bus, you can get picked up from the Playa Blanca turnoff.

Manglares del Golfo CABIN $

(☎8989-7246; cabin per person US$9) Fronting Playa Blanca, this friendly place has simple wooden cabins. Mural-painted walls and floors brighten up the otherwise dark accommodations.

★**Danta Corcovado Lodge** LODGE $$

(☎2735-1111; www.dantalodge.com; d/bungalow incl breakfast US$110/140; P 📶) Midway between the Los Patos Ranger Station and La Palma, this low-key lodge is a fantastic base to visit Corcovado and explore the surrounding forest. The delightful room designs are inventions of the staff, featuring unique furniture, open-air bathrooms and some truly whimsical flair. Excellent meals are served underneath the soaring roof of the open-air *ranchito*.

Tours to Los Patos are conducted in a special high-clearance, open-air contraption with benches that's attached to a tractor – the best way to navigate the rough road crisscrossed by a river and ideal for wildlife-viewing. There is also 4km of trails on the property to explore independently.

Suital Lodge LODGE $$

(☎2200-4662; www.suital.com; s/d/tr US$51/75/86) Lots of love has gone into this tiny clutch of four *cabinas* on the northern shores of Golfo Dulce. They are all decked out with polished wood floors and ceiling fans, and situated on 30 hectares of hilly, forested property. A network of birdwatching trails winds through the property and down to the beach.

Suital is located about 15km northeast of Rincón, just off Hwy 245.

Getting There & Away

The easiest way to travel on the eastern coast of the peninsula is by car. Otherwise, frequent buses ply the sole road between La Palma and Puerto Jiménez (US$2.50, 30 minutes).

GOLFO DULCE

While the Golfo Dulce is certainly less celebrated than the Península de Osa, an increasing number of travelers are making the arduous journey in search of one of the world's longest left-hand breaks at Pavones. The region is also home to Parque Nacional Piedras Blancas, a stunning tract of rainforest that used to be part of Corcovado, and still protects the same amazing biodiversity, with some wonderful lodges on its outskirts. This far corner of Costa Rica is also home to significantly large indigenous communities, who live in the Reserva Indígena Guaymí de Conte Burica near Pavones.

Golfito

POP 11,800

Golfito is largely a transportation hub for hikers heading to Corcovado, surfers heading to Pavones, and sportfishers, though nearby attractions include hiking or horseback riding in a wildlife refuge or kayaking to nearby mangrove forests and islands.

In an attempt to boost the region's economy, the federal government built the duty-free Zona Americana in Golfito. The surreal shopping mall Depósito Libre attracts people from around the country, who descend on the town for 24-hour shopping sprees.

⊙ Sights

Refugio Nacional de
Vida Silvestre Golfito NATURE RESERVE

(☑ 2775-1210, Sinac office in Golfito 2775-2620; US$10; ⊙ 8am-4pm) This small, 28-sq-km reserve encompasses most of the steep hills surrounding Golfito, though it's easy to miss. There are no facilities for visitors, save some poorly maintained trails. About 2km south of Golfito's center, a gravel road heads inland, past a soccer field, and winds 7km up to some radio towers (Las Torres) 486m above sea level. A very steep hiking trail (two hours), almost opposite the Samoa del Sur hotel, brings you out near the radio towers.

Playa Cacao BEACH

Just a quick trip across the bay, this small beach offers a prime view of Golfito, with the rainforest as a backdrop. It's a pleasant spot to spend the day, and there are a couple of tasty seafood shacks where you can have lunch. To reach the beach, catch a water taxi from Golfito for around US$6 per person. You can also get to Playa Cacao by taking the 6km dirt road west and then south from the airport – a 4WD is recommended.

🏊 Activities

Golfito is home to several full-service marinas that attract coastal-cruising yachties. If you didn't bring your own boat, you can hire local sailors for tours of the gulf at any of the docks. You can fish year-round, but the best season for the sought-after Pacific sailfish is from November to May.

Banana Bay Marina FISHING

(☑ 2775-0003, in USA 512-431-4187; www.banana baymarinagolfito.com) Charters can be arranged, and a full day of all-inclusive inshore fishing starts at US$650; all-inclusive offshore fishing starts at US$800.

🛏 Sleeping

Domestic tax-free shoppers usually spend the night in Golfito, so hotel rooms can be in short supply on weekends and during holiday periods. The digs aren't particularly appealing, but there are some lovely ecolodges along the nearby coastline.

Note that the area around the soccer field in town is Golfito's red-light district.

La Purruja Lodge CABINAS $

(☑ 2775-5054; www.purrua.com; s/d/tr US$30/ 40/48, breakfast US$5) About 5km south of Golfito's center, these family-run *cabinas* are far enough out of town to be noticeably quiet (and wildlife-friendly – birds and agoutis frolic about the landscaped grounds) and close enough to be convenient to restaurants and other amenities. The *cabinas* are super basic with tile floors; the showers are cold but the welcome is warm.

Fish Hook LODGE $$

(☑ 2775-1624, 2775-0592; www.fishhookcr.com; d/ ste incl breakfast US$75/105; ❄🛜) This attractive fishing lodge on the main drag has spacious but plain rooms and suites overlooking the marina. The attached bar-restaurant draws a good crowd with its tasty food and friendly vibe. All around good value.

Samoa del Sur HOTEL $$

(☑ 2775-0233; www.samoadelsur.com; s/d incl breakfast US$50/64; 🅿❄🛜🏊) This orange, hard-to-miss facility offers 19 dated rooms outfitted with tiled floors, wood furniture and thick towels. The bar, with its huge dome ceiling, is a popular spot in the evenings, and the restaurant serves a wide-ranging menu. There's a children's pool and a canopy tour and nature walk suitable for older children.

Casa Roland Marina Resort RESORT $$$
(2775-0180; www.casarolandgolfito.com; s/d from US$100/120; P ❄ 📶 ≋) Golfito's swishest hotel primarily caters to duty-free shoppers looking for an amenity-laden base. You can expect to find such facilities as a swimming pool, a restaurant, a bar and a health spa. The hotel is arguably overpriced, but the rooms are comfortable and you won't get any surprises.

Eating

The small, walkable district of the Pueblo Civil has about a dozen *sodas* of reputable quality, and all of the larger hotels and marinas have restaurants serving international fare. But the best place to eat is likely the seafood shacks over at Playa Cacao.

Restaurante Buenos Días COSTA RICAN $
(2775-1124; meals US$6-10; 6am-10pm; P ❄) Rare is the visitor who passes through Golfito without stopping at this cheerful spot opposite the Muellecito (Small Dock). Brightly colored booths, bilingual menus and a convenient location ensure a constant stream of guests – whether for an ample early breakfast, a typical Tico *casado* or a good old-fashioned burger, accompanied by tamarind and other fresh juices.

Orientation

The southern part of town is where you'll find most of the bars and businesses, including a seedy red-light district. Nearby is the so-called Muellecito (Small Dock), from where the daily ferry to Puerto Jiménez departs. The northern part of town was the old United Fruit Company headquarters, and it retains a languid air with its large, veranda-decked homes. Now, the Zona Americana is home to the airport and the duty-free zone.

Getting There & Away

AIR

The airport is 4km north of the town center near the duty-free zone. Sansa has daily flights to/from San José.

BOAT

There are two main boat docks for passenger service: the **Muellecito** is the main dock in the southern part of town. There is a smaller dock north of the Muelle Bananero (opposite the ICE building) where you'll find the **Asociación de Boteros** (Abocap; 8824-6571; www.facebook.com/boterosdegolfito), an association of water taxis that can provide services anywhere in the Golfo Dulce area.

Fast ferries travel to Puerto Jiménez from the Muellecito (US$6, 30 minutes), departing at 7am, 10am, 11:30am, 1pm, 3pm and 5pm daily. This schedule is subject to change, so it's best to check for current times at the dock; in any event, show up early to ensure a spot.

You can also take a private water taxi to Puerto Jiménez. You'll have to negotiate, but prices usually cost US$25 to US$30 per person (sometimes with a US$60 minimum).

At research time there was no scheduled shared *lancha* (small motorboat) to Zancudo, but you can negotiate with loitering boatmen to run you over for around US$30 per person. If you're staying at a coastal lodge north of Golfito and you've made prior arrangements for transportation, the lodge will pick you up at the docks.

BUS

Tracopa buses depart from the **stop** (2775-0365; www.tracopacr.com) across from the fire station. The bus to Pavones and Zancudo leaves from a bus stop across from the hospital in the northern part of town. It will make additional stops in town, but if you get on at the beginning you will be more likely to get a seat.

BUSES FROM GOLFITO

DESTINATION	COST (US$)	DURATION (HR)	FREQUENCY (DAILY)
Neily	3	1½	every 30min 6am-7pm
Pavones	4	2½	10am & 3pm
San José, via San Isidro de El General and the Costanera (Tracopa)	15	7	5am & 1:30pm (2pm Sun)
Zancudo	4	3	10am & 3pm

OFF THE BEATEN TRACK

PLAYAS SAN JOSECITO, NICUESA & CATIVO

Idyllic deserted beaches, backed by the pristine rainforest of Parque Nacional Piedras Blancas, define the northeastern shore of the Golfo Dulce. The appeal of this area is enhanced by its inaccessibility, as it can be reached only by boat. If you're looking for a romantic retreat or a secluded getaway, all of the lodges along this stretch of coastline are completely isolated and serve as perfect spots for quiet reflection.

The lodges also provide kayaks for maritime exploration and transport to **Casa Orquideas** (8829-1247; self-guided tour US$10; 7am-5pm Sat-Thu), a vibrant botanical garden that can only be reached by boat, along with direct access to the wilds of Piedras Blancas. Miles of trails lead to secluded beaches, waterfalls and other attractions.

Parque Nacional Piedras Blancas

One of the last remaining stretches of lowland rainforest on the Pacific, Piedras Blancas is home to a mindboggling array of flora and fauna, including many of Costa Rica's most exciting animals: pumas, jaguars, monkeys, two-toed sloths and numerous species of bats. Dozens of species of migrating birds stop by here also. According to a study conducted at the biological station at La Gamba, the biodiversity of trees in Piedras Blancas is the densest in all of Costa Rica, even surpassing Corcovado.

Consisting of parcels of land purchased by benefactors as diverse as the Nature Conservancy and the Austrian government, this national park was established in 1992 as an extension of Parque Nacional Corcovado, though it's now independent. Piedras Blancas has 120 sq km of tropical primary rainforest, as well as 20 sq km of secondary forests, pastureland, coastal cliffs and beaches.

Activities

Any would-be hikers must stop first at the **La Gamba Ranger Station** (2741-8067; park admission US$10; 8am-4pm) to pay the park admission fee and to inquire about trail conditions and access points. This is the only ranger station that is staffed year-round. Facilities for tourists in Piedras Blancas are quite limited, but they are improving, thanks in large part to the efforts of the folks at Esquinas Rainforest Lodge.

There are two options for independent hiking in the park. **El Tajo** is a 5km foray into the park (10km round trip) that climbs into the mountains and then connects to the more extensive trail network. It requires at least one river crossing and the terrain is challenging. Find the trailhead off the highway between La Gamba and Golfito.

At research time a second access point known as the **Ocelot Trail** was soon to open, with the trailhead near the entrance to Esquinas Rainforest Lodge. This new trail should be be well marked and easily accessible, connecting the network of existing trails in the park. Look for a trail map near the entrance.

Sleeping

★Finca Bellavista TREEHOUSE **$$**
(www.fincabellavistacommunity.com; tree house US$50-275;) Finca Bellevista is a 242-hectare community of arboreal abodes near Parque Nacional Piedras Blancas. Tree house and canopy dwellings are individually owned and rented when unoccupied. Each unique design conforms to established sustainable principles. There's a zipline, a yoga studio and hiking trails on the grounds for guests, and the communal *rancho* offers a restaurant, a bar and a hang-out zone.

Many of the homes offer kitchens, electricity and running water, although some don't. Two-night minimum.

Esquinas Rainforest Lodge LODGE **$$$**
(2741-8001; www.esquinaslodge.com; s/d/tr incl meals US$203/338/423;) Esquinas consists of 16 spacious, high-ceilinged, fan-cooled cabins with indigenous textiles on the walls. The lodge's extensive grounds include birdwatching trails and an inviting stream-fed pool. It was founded by the nonprofit Rainforest of the Austrians, vital in the establishment of Piedras Blancas as a national park. Esquinas is located in Gamba, 7km west of Km 37 on the Interamericana.

Surrounded by the primary rainforest of the park, Esquinas is integrally connected with the community of Gamba, employing local workers and reinvesting profits in community projects. By offsetting development with tree planting, it has become 100% carbon neutral.

Getting There & Away

Hiking in Piedras Blancas requires driving a private vehicle (or hiring a taxi) in order go to the La Gamba Ranger Station and double back and find the trailhead. It is possible to take any northbound bus from Golfito and get dropped off at the entrance of Esquinas Rainforest Lodge (p457). With the opening of the Ocelot Trail, it will be possible for Esquinas guests to hike in the park.

Zancudo

POP 450

Occupying a slender finger of land that juts into the Golfo Dulce, this tiny village is about as laid-back a beach destination as you'll find in Costa Rica. On the west side of town, gentle, warm Pacific waters lap onto black sands, and seeing more than a handful of people on the beach means it's crowded. On the east side, a tangle of mangrove swamps attracts birds, crocodiles and plenty of fish, which in turn attract fishers hoping to reel them in.

Aside from fishing, the main activities at Zancudo are undoubtedly swinging on hammocks, strolling on the beach and swimming in the aqua-blue waters of the Golfo Dulce. Here, the surf is gentle, and at night the water sometimes sparkles with bioluminescence – tiny phosphorescent marine plants and plankton that light up if you sweep a hand through the water.

Sleeping & Eating

Be aware that life goes into hibernation mode in low season – accommodations are discounted up to 50% and some may be closed altogether.

★Cabinas Coloso Del Mar CABINA $

(☎2776-0050; www.colosodelmar.com; s/d/tr incl breakfast US$52/58/68; P 📶) A large thatch-roof *rancho,* strung with hammocks, is the centerpiece of this property. Behind it, shiny wooden *cabinas* face the waves. They are dimly lit but they have porches and cute, beachy decor. The included breakfast is phenomenal, as is all food and cocktails served at the onsite restaurant.

Cabinas Sol y Mar CABINA $

(☎2776-0014; www.zancudo.com; cabins d from US$50; P @ 📶) The darkish wood cabins are plain, with no decoration to brighten the mood. But they are clean and the tile showers with stone drains are funky cool. Even if you're not staying here, the open-air restaurant, serving fish burgers and chicken cordon bleu (mains US$3 to US$12), and thatched bar are Zancudo favorites.

Cabinas Pura Vida HOSTEL $

(☎2776-0029; www.cabinaspuravida.com; ⏲per person US$7-12) This Zancudo cheapie proves that Costa Rica is still a friend to backpackers, while providing a fun gathering spot for travelers from the far reaches of the Earth. These are the most basic of rooms, but they are adequate. Guests gather for rowdy group dinners and drinks on weekends.

Cabinas Au Coeur du Soleil CABINA $$

(☎2776-0112; www.aucoeurdusoleil.com; cabins US$50-80; P 📶) These three brightly painted, lovingly maintained cabins have fans, fridges and kitchenettes, along with hammock-strung porches and tons of homey charm. The young French-Canadian hosts Joanne and Daniel are warm and gregarious, offering guests the use of bikes for cruising around Zancudo and kayaks and bodyboards for hitting the sea.

Cabinas Los Cocos CABINA $$

(☎2776-0012; www.loscocos.com; cabins US$89; P) Capuchin monkeys swing through the coco trees at this beachfront property. Los Cocos is home to two historical cabins that used to be banana-company homes in Palmar, until they were transported here and restored. The other two *rancho* cabins are also charming, with loft sleeping areas under palm-frond roofs, plus wide porches with hammocks.

Dolphin Quest LODGE $$

(☎8669-4688, 8811-2099; www.dolphinquestcostarica.com; Playa San Josecito; per person incl 3 meals US$85-115; P 📶) This jungle lodge offers a mile of beach and 300 secluded hectares of mountainous rainforest, with accommodations in round, thatched-roof cabins. Meals – featuring organic ingredients from the garden – are served in an open-air pavilion near the shore. Beachcombing, horseback riding, snorkeling and fishing are on offer, and there's a real timelessness to the place. The hotel is only reachable by private boat.

Zancudo Lodge LODGE $$$

(☎2776-0008; www.zancudolodge.com; r/ste from US$350/450; P ❄ 📶 🏊) The most luxurious retreat in Zancudo by a long shot, this 16-room lodge sits amid landscaped grounds, complete with trickling water features, bamboo stockades, and spacious, tranquil rooms fitted out with fine linens and other creature comforts. Sportfishing outings and boat pickup from Golfito arranged.

The onsite gourmet restaurant (open to nonguests), Gamefisher, prides itself on its commitment to super-fresh produce and creative preparations. Specialties include the best fish tacos for miles around and tuna smoked in-house.

★ Playa Nicuesa Rainforest Lodge LODGE $$$
(☎ 2258-8250, in USA 866-504-8116; www.nicuesalodge.com; Playa Nicuesa; s/d incl 3 meals from US$320/510;) Nestled into a 65-hectare private reserve, Nicuesa is a wonderful retreat and ecolodge. The dreamy accommodations come with canopied beds, indigenous textile spreads and garden showers. On the grounds, guests can explore 6km of jungle trails, swim and snorkel along a deserted beach, and take advantage of daily yoga classes. A fascinating site tour showcases the lodge's impressive efforts toward sustainability.

Getting There & Away

BOAT

The boat dock is near the north end of the beach on the inland, estuary side. *Cabinas* and hotels in Zancudo can arrange private water taxis at the time of your choosing, starting at US$60 for two people and becoming cheaper per person as the group size increases. For US$80, a boat captain will take you to Puerto Jiménez.

BUS

A bus to the border at Paso Canoas passes through Zancudo at around 6am each morning (two hours). In Conte, passengers may switch to a bus to Golfito. Those continuing to the border will exit the bus at Laurel and catch a *colectivo* (shared taxi) the rest of the way.

CAR

From both Golfito and Paso Canoas, roads to Zancudo are well signposted. The main roads are paved, but as you get closer to Zancudo, long stretches of road are not. Outside of the dry season a 4WD is recommended. The coastal road to Pavones is a straight shot. It's bumpy, but newly constructed bridges mean that the trip no longer requires river crossings. It takes around 1¼ hours to drive from Golfito and about 45 minutes to drive to Pavones.

Pavones

POP 2500

Pavones is legendary for surfers the world over. This is Costa Rica's southernmost point, and it takes some effort to get down here. Indeed, the journey is an adventure in its own right, especially since the best months for surfing coincide with the rainy season.

Pavones is not the backwater it once was, but it has not lost its adventurous edge. Though visitors are heading to the village more frequently than in the past, it remains relatively off the beaten path – the pace of life is slow and the overall atmosphere is tranquil and New Agey.

Activities

Surfing

Pavones is legendary among surfers for being one of the longest left breaks in the world (up there with a 2km-long break in Chicama, Peru, and an even longer sand-bottomed left in Namibia's Skeleton Bay). On the best days, your ride can last over two minutes!

Conditions are best with a southern swell, usually during the rainy season from April to October, but the rest of the year the waves are ideal for beginners. **Sea Kings Surf Shop** (☎ 2776-2015; www.yogapavones.comSeaKingsShop.htm; ⏲ 9am-5pm Mon-Sat) carries accessories, rents boards and arranges surfing lessons.

When Pavones has nothing (or when it's too crowded), head south to Punta Banco, a reef break with decent rights and lefts. The best conditions are at mid- or high tide, especially with swells from the south or west.

Yoga

Surfing goes hand in hand with yoga, and there are several yoga studios in Pavones where you can stretch your knotted limbs.

Shooting Star Studio YOGA
(☎ 8829-2409, 2776-2107; www.yogapavones.com; drop-in class US$15) Only 30m from the beach, this open-air yoga studio offers walk-in classes several times a week. Private instruction is also available.

Sleeping

Accommodations are scattered along the main road in Playa Río Claro and along the coastal road to Punta Banco. When the surf's up, shoestringers and locals camp along the coastal road to Punta Banco.

Playa Río Claro

Cabinas & Café de la Suerte GUESTHOUSE $
(☎ 2776-2388; s/d/tr US$75/85/95; ⏲ cafe 8am-5pm Mon-Sat;) These three *cabinas* are colorful, with bold patterned linens and brightly painted walls. The upstairs rooms share the hammock-hung terrace, while the downstairs room has a secluded garden corner. The place is just 50m from the beach.

From the supermarket crossroads, follow the beach road to the left.

Vegetarians are in luck at the attached Café de la Suerte, serving a menu of omelets and veggie dishes. There's usually a daily special such as veggie burgers or lasagna, plus tropical-fruit smoothies and brownies.

Surf House HOSTEL $
(☎8508-7779; www.facebook.com/pavonesrooms; dm/d incl breakfast & surf board from US$20/40; P 📶) Get back to basics at this ecofriendly surfer crash pad right near the beach. Dark rooms have rough wood walls, few windows and shared bathrooms, but comfy beds and good vibes. There are plenty of relaxing common areas, where you can pass the time between waves. A chilled-out atmosphere pervades the place, especially during the community vegan dinner (US$8).

Cabinas Mira Olas CABINA $
(☎8393-7742, 2776-2006; www.miraolas.com; d/tr from US$40/50; P 📶) This 4.5-hectare farm is full of wildlife and fruit trees, with a lookout at the top of a hill. A sweet duplex with comfortable tiled cabins has a terrace in front, while the 'Jungle Deluxe' is a beautiful, open-air lodging with a huge balcony, kitchen and elegant cathedral ceiling. A walking trail leads down to the Río Claro swimming hole.

Turn off the Río Claro road, just before the bridge.

Riviera Riverside Villas VILLA $$
(☎2776-2396; www.pavonesriviera.com; d/house US$115/160; P ❄ 📶) This clutch of upmarket *cabinas* and homes in Pavones proper offers fully equipped kitchens, cool tile floors and attractive hardwood ceilings. Big shady porches overlook the landscaped fruit gardens, which are visited by birds and monkeys. These villas offer a degree of luxury found at few other places in town.

Punta Banco

★Rancho Burica LODGE $
(☎2776-2223; www.ranchoburica.com; dm US$15, s/d US$40/70, without bathroom US$25/45; P ❄ 📶) This legendary Dutch-run outpost is literally the end of the road in Punta Banco. Here, surfers gather to socialize in the evenings, sharing family-style meals and stories of the wave that got away (or didn't). Dark comfortable rooms are cooled with fans, hammocks are interspersed around the property and a trail leads to a romantic jungle lookout.

Clientele mainly includes surfers, but those interested in relaxation, wildlife and yoga will also land well here, as there's a newly constructed yoga deck and lots of rare birds flitting around. The owners are also involved in a community turtle conservation project.

Yoga Farm LODGE $$
(www.yogafarmcostarica.org; dm/r/cabin per person incl meals & yoga US$55/65/75) This tranquil retreat has simple rooms and dorms with shared bathroom facilities, as well as more private cabins. Prices include three fantastic vegetarian meals prepared with ingredients from the organic garden, as well as daily yoga classes in an open-air studio overlooking the ocean. This place is all about rejuvenation and sustainable living; no wi-fi or phones.

★Tiskita Jungle Lodge LODGE $$$
(☎2296-8125; www.tiskita.com; r/ste incl all meals from US$246/380; P 📶 🏊) Set amid extensive gardens and orchards, this lodge is arguably the most beautiful and intimate in all of Golfo Dulce. Stunning modern wooden cabins are accented by wide porches and stone garden showers. Daily yoga classes and surf lessons are available, as well as guided birding walks, horseback riding and night tours. Three-night minimum.

Eating

Restaurante Ebenezer SODA $
(☎2776-2052; mains US$5-10; ⏰7am-9pm Mon-Sat; 📶 🖉) Ebenezer's place is an essential stop after a morning at the beach. Satisfying breakfasts and hot coffee get your day going in the right direction. Later on, there are delicious fish sandwiches and standard *casados,* as well as ice cream to sate your sweet tooth.

Soda Doña Dora COSTA RICAN $
(☎2776-2021; meals US$4-8; ⏰6am-10pm) This long-standing family-run spot serves huge breakfasts of *gallo pinto,* eggs and toast; banana pancakes; *casados* with fresh seafood; burgers and fries; and cheap beer. Look for the Bar La Plaza sign just inland from the soccer field; the *soda* and bar share this space.

★La Bruschetta ITALIAN $$
(La Piña; ☎2776-2174; mains US$8-20; ⏰10am-10pm; 📶 🖉) A couple of kilometers along the beach road to Punta Banco, this cheerful place decked out with fairy lights is the most happenin' spot in town. Ample portions of homemade pasta, wood-fired pizza and Italian desserts are made with fresh ingredients, authentic preparations and plenty of love. The sign says 'La Piña' and many still call it that.

Orientation

The name Pavones is used to refer to both Playa Río Claro de Pavones and Punta Banco, which is 6km south.

The road into Pavones first arrives at Río Claro, where you'll find a crossroads with two small supermarkets. One road leads straight to the beach, and the other crosses a bridge and carries straight on. Playa Río Claro's accommodations are located near the beach and around this intersection.

Straight after the bridge, another road branches right and runs parallel to the waterfront for 6km to Punta Banco where, as the locals say, 'the bad road ends and the good life begins.' The rest of the accommodations are spread out along this coastal road.

Information

We cannot stress this enough: Pavones has no bank or gas station, so make sure you have plenty of money and gas prior to arrival. Very few places accept credit cards and the nearest ATM and gas station are in Laurel, an hour's drive away. In an emergency, you can buy gas at either of the supermarkets (for a high price).

Getting There & Away

AIR

Sansa offers charter flights to the airstrip at Tiskita Jungle Lodge. Prices are dependent on the number of passengers, so it's best to try to organize a larger group if you're considering this option.

BUS

Two daily buses go to Golfito (US$3.80, two hours). The first leaves at 5:15am, departing from the end of the road in Punta Banco and stopping by the supermarket intersection. The second leaves at 12:30pm from this intersection.

CAR

The turnoff to Pavones and Zancudo is well signposted from the main road leading south from Golfito to Laurel. The main road is partially paved; the 32km of minor road that leads to Pavones is not. There's a decent coastal road connecting Pavones to Zancudo that no longer requires driving through rivers, thanks to some new bridges. It takes around 1¼ hours to drive from Golfito and about 45 minutes to drive to Zancudo.

TAXI

A 4WD taxi will charge about US$80 from Golfito and US$70 from Paso Canoas. One of the locals operates a shared-van service to Paso Canoas and Golfito on demand for US$16 per person; ask around to see if it's operating during your visit.

PARQUE NACIONAL ISLA DEL COCO

A tiny speck of green amid the endless Pacific, Isla del Coco looms large in the imagination of the adventurer: jagged mountains and tales of treasure, a pristine and isolated ecosystem filled with wildlife and some of the world's best diving. Remember the opening aerial shot of *Jurassic Park,* where the helicopter sweeps over the sea to a jungle-covered island? That was here.

As beautiful as the island may be, its terrestrial environs pale in comparison to what lies beneath. Named by PADI as one of the world's top 10 dive spots, the surrounding waters of Isla del Coco harbor abundant pelagics, including one of the largest known schools of hammerhead sharks in the world.

Isla del Coco (aka Cocos Island) is around 500km southwest of the mainland in the middle of the eastern Pacific, making it Costa Rica's most remote destination.

History

In 1526 Spanish explorer Joan Cabezas stumbled onto Isla del Coco, though it wasn't noted on maps until its second discovery by French cartographer Nicolás Desliens in 1541; prior to being 'discovered' by Europeans, Isla del Coco received pre-Columbian seafaring visitors from Latin America. In the centuries that followed, heavy rainfall attracted the attention of sailors, pirates and whalers, who frequently stopped by for fresh water, seafood and coconuts.

Between the late 17th and early 19th centuries, Isla del Coco became a way station for pirates who are rumored to have hidden countless treasures here. The most famous was the storied Treasure of Lima, a trove of gold and silver ingots, gold laminae scavenged from church domes and a solid-gold, life-sized sculpture of the Virgin Mary. 'X marks the spot,' right? Not really. More than 400 treasure-hunting expeditions have found only failure. In fact, in 1869 the government of Costa Rica organized an official treasure hunt. They didn't find anything, but the expedition resulted in Costa Rica taking possession of the island, a treasure in itself, and it was declared a national park in 1978.

German settlers arrived on the island in the late 19th and early 20th centuries, though their stay on Isla del Coco was short-lived. However, they did leave behind a host of invasive plants and domestic animals that have since converted into feral populations of pigs, goats, cats and rats – all of which threaten the natural wildlife.

Activities

Diving

The diving is excellent, and is regarded by most as the main attraction of the island. But strong oceanic currents can lead to treacherous underwater conditions, and Isla del Coco can only be recommended to intermediate and advanced divers with sufficient experience. Divers are wise to bring gloves to cling onto the rocks.

The island has two large bays with safe anchorages and sandy beaches: Chatham Bay is located on the northeast side and Wafer Bay is on the northwest.

The island's marine life is hugely varied, with more than a dozen species of coral, more than 50 types of crustaceans and more than 270 species of fish. Sea turtles, manta rays, marble rays, dolphins and sharks are also abundant. Just off Cocos are a series of smaller basaltic rocks and islets, which constitute some of the best dive sites.

Isla Manuelita is a prime spot, home to a wide array of fish, rays and eels, as well as schools of manta rays. Eleven species of shark also inhabit these waters, including huge schools of scalloped hammerheads as well as whitetips, which are best spotted at night. Dirty Rock is another main attraction – a spectacular rock formation that harbors all kinds of sea creatures.

Diving is possible year-round, and tiger sharks, Galapagos sharks and whitetip sharks are always around, but the best time to see hammerhead sharks is the May–November rainy season.

Undersea Hunter DIVING

(☎2228-6613, in USA 800-203-2120; www.underseahunter.com) Runs liveaboard 10- and 12-day land and sea expeditions to Isla del Coco from Puntarenas, with room for 14 to 18 people, from US$5795 per person. Undersea Hunter passengers can also experience life at 305m below the ocean's surface, in the **DeepSee Submersible** (80/300m dive US$1450/1850).

Aggressor DIVING

(☎in USA & Canada 800-348-2628; www.aggressor.com) Operates a fleet of liveaboard diving boats in different destinations around the world. Offers eight- and 10-day land and sea expedition charters on *Okeanos Aggressor I* and *Okeanos Aggressor II* from Puntarenas to Isla del Coco from US$5099 per person.

Hiking

Even though this is the turf of hard-core divers, making landfall and exploring is worth the time and effort.

Rugged, heavily forested and punctuated by cascading waterfalls, Cocos is ringed and transected by an elaborate network of trails. The highest point is at **Cerro Iglesias** (575m), where you can soak up spectacular views of the lush, verdant island and the deep blue Pacific.

Note that visitors to the island must first register with the park rangers, though your tour company will most likely make all the necessary arrangements well in advance.

Because of its remote location, Isla del Coco is the most pristine national park in the country and one of Costa Rica's great wildlife destinations. Since the island was never linked to the Americas during its comparatively short geological history, Cocos is home to a very large number of rare endemic species.

Heading inland from the coastal forests up to the high-altitude cloud forests, it is possible to find around 235 unique species of flowering plants, 30% of which are found only on the island. This incredible diversity of flora supports more than 400 known insect species – 65 endemics, as well as a striking range of butterflies and moths, are included in this count. Scientists believe that more remain to be discovered.

Of the 87 recorded bird species on the island and neighboring rocks, the most pronounced are the aquatic birds: brown and red-footed boobies, great frigatebirds, white terns and brown noddies. There are also three terrestrial endemics, namely the Cocos cuckoo, Cocos flycatcher and Cocos finch.

Information

In order to protect the conservation status of the island, all visitors must apply for a permit at the **Área de Conservación Marina Isla del Coco** (Acmic; Map p76; ☎in San José 2250-7295, in San José 2258-8750; www.sinac.go.cr; ⏲8am-3pm Mon-Fri) in San José (which costs a whopping US$70 per day). However, unless you're sailing to the island on a private boat, tour operators will make all the necessary arrangements for you.

Getting There & Away

The only way to get here is via a liveaboard diving boat. With advance reservations, both of the liveaboard diving tour companies in Puntarenas will arrange transfers from either San José or Liberia to Puntarenas, which is the embarkation/disembarkation point for tours. It takes 32 hours by boat from Puntarenas to Isla del Coco.

Understand Costa Rica

History

Like other Central American countries, Costa Rica's history remains a loose sketch during the reign of its pre-Columbian tribes, and European 'discovery' of the New World was followed by the subjugation and evangelization of Costa Rica's indigenous peoples. But in the mid-20th century, Costa Rica radically departed from the standard Central American playbook by abolishing its army, diversifying its economy and brokering peace in the region, paving the way for today's stable and environmentally progressive nation.

Lost Worlds of Ancient Costa Rica

The coastlines and rainforests of Central America have been inhabited by humans for at least 10,000 years, but ancient civilizations in Costa Rica are largely the subject of speculation. It is thought that the area was something of a backwater straddling the two great civilizations of the Andes and Mesoamerica, with the exception of the Diquís Valley along the Pacific coast, where archaeological finds suggest that a great deal of trading took place between early inhabitants of Costa Rica and their more powerful neighbors. Costa Rica had around 400,000 inhabitants on the eve of European discovery some 500 years ago.

Unlike the grand pyramid complexes found throughout other parts of Latin America, the ancient towns and cities of Costa Rica (with the exception of Guayabo) were loosely organized and had no centralized government or ceremonial centers. Settlements fought each other, but to get slaves rather than to extend their territory. They didn't build edifices that would stand the test of time, but inhabitants did leave behind mysterious relics: enormous stone spheres around the Diquís Valley.

Ancient Sites

Guayabo (Turrialba)

Hacienda Barú (Dominical)

Sitio Arqueológico Finca 6 (Sierpe)

Finca Cántaros (San Vito)

Heirs of Columbus

On his fourth and final voyage to the Americas in 1502, Christopher Columbus was forced to drop anchor near present-day Puerto Limón after a hurricane damaged his ship. While awaiting repairs, Columbus ventured into the verdant terrain and exchanged gifts with hospitable and welcoming chieftains. He returned from this encounter claiming to have seen 'more gold in two days than in four years in Española.' Columbus

TIMELINE

11,000 BCE

The first humans occupy Costa Rica and populations quickly flourish due to the rich land and marine resources found along both coastlines.

1000 BCE

The Huetar power base in the Central Valley is solidified following construction and habitation of the ancient city of Guayabo, continuously inhabited until its mysterious abandonment in 1400 CE.

100 BCE

Costa Rica becomes part of an extensive trade network that moves gold and other goods and extends from present-day Mexico down to the Andean empires.

dubbed the stretch of shoreline from Honduras to Panama 'Veraguas,' but it was his excited descriptions of the *'costa rica'* (the 'rich coast') that gave the region its lasting name. At least that's how the popular story goes.

Anxious to claim the country's bounty, Columbus petitioned the Spanish Crown to have himself appointed governor. But by the time he returned to Seville, his royal patron Queen Isabella was on her deathbed, which prompted King Ferdinand to award the prize to Columbus' rival, Diego de Nicuesa. Although Columbus became a very wealthy man, he never returned to the Americas. He died of heart failure in 1506 after being worn down by ill health and court politics.

To the disappointment of his conquistador heirs, Columbus' tales of gold were mostly lies and the locals were considerably less than affable. Nicuesa's first colony in present-day Panama was abruptly abandoned

PRE-COLUMBIAN COSTA RICA

The early inhabitants of Costa Rica were part of an extensive trading zone that extended as far south as Peru and as far north as Mexico. The region hosted roughly 20 small tribes, organized into chiefdoms with a *cacique* (permanent leader), who sat atop a hierarchical society that included shamans, warriors, toilers and enslaved people.

Adept at seafaring, the Carib dominated the Atlantic coastal lowlands and served as a conduit of trade with the South American mainland. In the northwest, several tribes were connected to the great Mesoamerican cultures. Aztec religious practices and Maya jade have been found in the Península de Nicoya, while Costa Rican quetzal feathers and golden trinkets have been found in Mexico. In the southwest, three chiefdoms showed the influence of Andean indigenous cultures with coca leaves, yucca and sweet potatoes.

There is also evidence that the language of the Central Valley, Huetar, was known by all of Costa Rica's indigenous groups, which may be an indication of their power and influence. The Central Valley is home to Guayabo, the only major archaeological site uncovered in Costa Rica thus far.

Thought to be an ancient ceremonial center, Guayabo once featured paved streets, an aqueduct and decorative gold. Here archaeologists uncovered exquisite gold ornaments and unusual life-size stone statues of human figures, as well as distinctive types of pottery and metates (stone platforms that were used for grinding corn). Today the site consists of little more than ancient hewed rock and stone, though Guayabo continues to stand as a testament to a once-great civilization.

Still a puzzle, however, are the hundreds of hand-sculpted, monolithic stone spheres that dot the landscape of the Diquís Valley in Palmar and the Isla del Caño. Weighing up to 16 tons and ranging from the size of a baseball to the size of a Volkswagen, the spheres have inspired many theories: an ancient calendar, symbols of power, extraterrestrial meddling or pieces of a giant game.

1502

Christopher Columbus docks off the coast and, due to all the gold he sees, dubs it *'costa rica'* ('rich coast'). The name sticks.

1522

Spanish settlement develops in Costa Rica, though it will be several decades before the colonists can get a sturdy foothold on the land.

1540

The Kingdom of Guatemala is established by the Spanish and includes much of Central America: Costa Rica, Nicaragua, Honduras, El Salvador, Guatemala and the Mexican state of Chiapas.

1562

Spanish conquistador Juan Vásquez de Coronado arrives in Costa Rica under the title of governor, determined to move the fringe communities of Spanish settlers to the more hospitable Central Valley.

when tropical disease and warring tribes decimated its ranks. Successive expeditions launched from the Caribbean coast also failed as pestilent swamps, oppressive jungles and volcanoes made Columbus' paradise seem more like a tropical hell.

In 1513, Vasco Núñez de Balboa heard rumors about a large sea and a wealthy, gold-producing civilization across the mountains of the isthmus – likely referring to the Inca empire of present-day Peru. Driven by ambition and greed, Balboa scaled the continental divide and, in 1513, he became the first European to set eyes upon the Pacific Ocean. Balboa proceeded to claim the ocean and all the lands it touched for the king of Spain.

The thrill of discovery aside, the conquistadors now controlled a strategic western beachhead from which to launch their conquest of Costa Rica. In the name of God and king, aristocratic adventurers plundered indigenous villages, executed resisters and enslaved survivors throughout the Península de Nicoya. However, none of these bloodstained campaigns led to a permanent presence, as intercontinental germ warfare caused outbreaks of feverish death on both sides. The indigenous people mounted a fierce resistance to the invaders, which included guerrilla tactics, destroying their own villages and killing their own children rather than letting them fall into Spanish hands.

New World Order

The indigenous people of Costa Rica make up only about 2% of the population. They represent several ethnic groups (the Boruca, Bribrí, Cabécar, Chorotega, Huetar, Kéköldi, Maleku, Ngöbe-Buglé and Térraba) speaking six surviving languages.

It was not until the 1560s that a Spanish colony was firmly established in Costa Rica. Hoping to cultivate the rich volcanic soil of the Central Valley, the Spanish founded the village of Cartago on the banks of the Río Reventazón. Although the fledgling colony was extremely isolated, it miraculously survived under the leadership of its first governor, Juan Vásquez de Coronado. Some of Costa Rica's demilitarized present was presaged in its early colonial government: preferring diplomacy over firearms to counter the indigenous threat, Coronado used Cartago as a base to survey the lands south to Panama and west to the Pacific, and secured deed and title over the colony.

Though Coronado was later lost in a shipwreck, his legacy endured. Costa Rica was an officially recognized province of the Virreinato de Nueva España (Viceroyalty of New Spain), which was the name given to the viceroy-ruled territories of the Spanish empire in North America, Central America, the Caribbean and Asia.

For roughly three centuries, the Captaincy General of Guatemala (also known as the Kingdom of Guatemala), which included Costa Rica, Nicaragua, Honduras, El Salvador, Guatemala and the Mexican state of Chiapas, was a loosely administered colony in the vast Spanish empire. Since the political and military headquarters of the kingdom were in

1563

The first permanent Spanish colonial settlement in Costa Rica is established in Cartago by Juan Vásquez de Coronado, who chooses the site based on its rich and fertile volcanic soils.

1737

The future capital of San José is established, sparking a rivalry with neighboring Cartago that will culminate in a civil war between the two dominant cities.

1808

Coffee, set to become the nation's main agricultural crop, arrives from Cuba.

1821

Following a unanimous declaration by Mexico on behalf of all of Central America, Costa Rica finally gains its independence from Spain after centuries of colonial occupation.

Guatemala, Costa Rica became a minor provincial outpost that had little if any strategic significance or exploitable riches.

As a result of its status as a swampy, largely useless backwater, Costa Rica's colonial path diverged from the typical pattern in that a powerful landholding elite and slave-based economy never gained prominence. Instead of large estates, mining operations and coastal cities, modest-sized villages of smallholders developed in the interior Central Valley. According to national lore, the stoic, self-sufficient farmer provided the backbone for 'rural democracy' as Costa Rica emerged as one of the only egalitarian corners of the Spanish empire.

Equal rights and opportunities were not extended to the indigenous groups and, as Spanish settlement expanded, the local population decreased dramatically. From 400,000 at the time Columbus first sailed, the population was reduced to 20,000 a century later, and to 8000 a century after that. While disease was the main cause of death, the Spanish were relentless in their effort to exploit the natives as an economic resource by establishing the *encomienda* system that applied to indigenous males and gave the Spaniards the right to demand free labor. Many were worked to death. Central Valley groups were the first to fall, though outside the valley several tribes managed to survive longer under forest cover, staging occasional raids. However, as in the rest of Latin America, repeated military campaigns eventually forced them into submission and slavery, though throughout that period many clergy protested the brutal treatment of indigenous people and implored the Spanish Crown to protect them.

British explorer, government-sponsored pirate and slaver Sir Francis Drake is believed to have anchored in Bahía Drake in 1579. Rumor has it that he buried some of his plundered treasure here, but the only solid memorial to the man is a monument that looks out to his namesake bay.

Fall of an Empire

Spain's costly Peninsular War with France from 1808 to 1814 – and the political turmoil, unrest and power vacuums that it caused – led Spain to lose all its colonial possessions in the first third of the 19th century.

In 1821 the Americas wriggled free of Spain's imperial grip following Mexico's declaration of independence for itself as well as the whole of Central America. Of course, the Central American provinces weren't too keen on having another foreign power reign over them and subsequently declared independence from Mexico. These events hardly disturbed Costa Rica, which learned of its liberation a month after the fact.

The newly liberated colonies pondered their fate: stay together in a United States of Central America or go their separate national ways. At first they came up with something in between, namely the Central American Federation (CAF), though it could neither field an army nor collect taxes. Accustomed to being at the center of things, Guatemala also attempted to dominate the CAF, alienating smaller colonies and hastening the CAF's demise. Future attempts to unite the region would likewise fail.

Thirty-three out of 44 Costa Rican presidents prior to 1970 were descended from just three original colonizing families.

1823

The capital officially moves to San José. Later the United Provinces of Central America is formed between Costa Rica, El Salvador, Guatemala, Nicaragua and Honduras.

1838

Costa Rica becomes entirely independent.

1856

Costa Rica quashes the expansionist aims of hawks in the US by defeating William Walker and his invading army at the epic Battle of Santa Rosa.

1889

Costa Rica's first democratic elections are held – a monumental event given the long history of colonial occupation – though the black population and women are prohibited from voting.

Meanwhile, an independent Costa Rica was taking shape under Juan Mora Fernández, the first head of state (1824–33). He tended toward nation building, and organized new towns, built roads, published a newspaper and coined a currency. His wife even partook in the effort by designing the country's flag.

Life returned to normal, unlike in the rest of the region, where post-independence civil wars raged on. In 1824 the Nicoya-Guanacaste region seceded from Nicaragua and joined its more easygoing southern neighbor, defining the territorial borders. In 1852 Costa Rica received its first diplomatic emissaries from the US and Great Britain.

The coffee-processing cooperative Coopedota, located in Costa Rica's Valley of the Saints (famous for growing delicious highland coffee), launched the country's first carbon-neutral coffee in 2011, certified to the British Standards Institution's PAS2060 specifications for carbon neutrality.

Coffee Rica

In the 19th century, the riches that Costa Rica had long promised were uncovered when farmers realized that the soil and climate of the Central Valley highlands were ideal for coffee cultivation. Costa Rica led Central America in introducing the caffeinated bean, which transformed the impoverished country into the wealthiest in the region.

By the 1840s, local merchants had already built up domestic capacity and learned to scope out their own overseas markets. Their big break came when they persuaded the captain of HMS *Monarch* to transport several hundred sacks of Costa Rican coffee to London, percolating the beginning of a beautiful friendship.

The Costa Rican coffee boom was on. The drink's quick fix made it popular among working-class consumers in the industrializing north. The aroma of riches lured a wave of enterprising German immigrants, enhancing technical and financial skills in the business sector. By the century's end, more than one-third of the Central Valley was dedicated to

THE LITTLE DRUMMER BOY

As you travel through the countryside, you may notice statues of a drummer boy from Alajuela named Juan Santamaría. He is one of Costa Rica's most beloved national heroes.

In April 1856 the North American mercenary William Walker and his ragtag army attempted to invade Costa Rica during an ultimately unsuccessful campaign to conquer all of Central America. Walker had already managed to seize control of Nicaragua, taking advantage of the civil war that was raging there. It didn't take him long after that to march on Costa Rica, though Costa Rican president Juan Rafael Mora Porras guessed Walker's intentions and managed to recruit a volunteer army of 9000 civilians. They surrounded Walker's army in an old hacienda in present-day Parque Nacional Santa Rosa. The Costa Ricans won the battle and Walker was forever expelled from Costa Rican soil. During the fighting, Santamaría was killed while daringly setting fire to Walker's defenses – and a national legend was born.

1900
The population of Costa Rica reaches 50,000 as the country begins to develop and prosper due to the increasingly lucrative international coffee and banana trades.

1914
Costa Rica is given an economic boost following the opening of the Panama Canal. The canal was forged by 75,000 laborers, many thousands of whom died during construction.

1919
Federico Tinoco Granados is ousted as the dictator of Costa Rica in one of the few violent episodes in an otherwise peaceful political history.

1940
Rafael Ángel Calderón Guardia is elected president and proceeds to improve working conditions in Costa Rica by enacting minimum-wage laws as well as an eight-hour day.

coffee cultivation, and coffee accounted for more than 90% of all exports and 80% of foreign-currency earnings.

Coffee wealth became a power resource in politics. Costa Rica's traditional aristocratic families were at the forefront of the enterprise. At mid-century, three-quarters of the coffee barons were descended from just two colonial families. The country's leading coffee exporter at this time was President Juan Rafael Mora Porras (1849–59), whose lineage went back to the colony's founder, Juan Vásquez de Coronado. Mora was overthrown by his brother-in-law after the president proposed to form a national bank independent of the coffee barons. The economic interests of the coffee elite become a priority in Costa Rican politics.

Banana Empire

The coffee trade unintentionally gave rise to Costa Rica's next export boom: bananas. Getting coffee out to world markets necessitated a rail link from the central highlands to the coast, and Limón's deep harbor made an ideal port. Inland was dense jungle and insect-infested swamps, and the government contracted the task to Minor Keith, the nephew of an American railroad tycoon.

The project was a disaster. Malaria and accidents churned through workers. In 1890 the line was finally completed and running at a loss. Keith had grown banana plants along the tracks as a cheap food source for the workers and, desperate to recoup his investment, he shipped some bananas to New Orleans in the hope of starting a side venture. He struck gold, or rather yellow. Consumers went crazy for the elongated finger fruit. By the early 20th century, bananas surpassed coffee as Costa Rica's most lucrative export and the country became the world's leading banana exporter. Unlike in the coffee industry, though, the profits were exported along with the bananas.

In its various incarnations as the United Brands Company (Yunai) and, later, Chiquita, the United Fruit Company was virulently anti-union and maintained control over its workforce by paying them in redeemable scrip rather than cash for many years. The company drew a wave of migrant laborers from Jamaica, changing the country's ethnic complexion and provoking racial tensions. The marks left on Costa Rica are still present, including the rusting train tracks.

For details on the role of Minor Keith and the United Fruit Company in lobbying for a CIA-led coup in Guatemala, pick up a copy of the highly readable *Bitter Fruit*, by Stephen Schlesinger and Stephen Kinzer.

Birth of a Nation

The inequality of the early 20th century led to the rise of José Figueres Ferrer, a self-described farmer-philosopher. The son of Catalan immigrant coffee planters, Figueres excelled in school and went to Boston's MIT to study engineering. Upon returning to Costa Rica to set up his own coffee plantation, he organized the hundreds of laborers on his farm

1940s

José Figueres Ferrer champions social-democratic policies, becomes involved in national politics and opposes the ruling conservatives.

1948

Conservative and liberal forces clash, resulting in a six-week civil war that leaves 2000 Costa Ricans dead and many more wounded, and destroys much of the country's fledgling infrastructure.

1949

Hoping to heal old wounds and look forward, the temporary government enacts a new constitution abolishing the army, desegregating the country, and granting women and black people the right to vote.

1977

The Indigenous Law of 1977 is passed, protecting indigenous communities' right to ownership of their territories.

into a utopian socialist community and appropriately named the property La Lucha Sin Fin (The Struggle Without End).

In the 1940s Figueres became involved in national politics as an outspoken critic of President Calderón. In the midst of a radio interview in which he bad-mouthed the president, police broke into the studio and arrested Figueres. He was accused of having fascist sympathies and was banished to Mexico. While in exile he formed the Caribbean League, a collection of students and democratic agitators from all over Central America who pledged to bring down the region's military dictators. When he returned to Costa Rica, the Caribbean League, now 700 strong, went with him and helped protest against those in power.

When government troops descended on the farm with the intention of arresting Figueres and disarming the Caribbean League, it sparked a civil war. The moment had arrived: the diminutive farmer-philosopher now played the man on horseback. Figueres emerged victorious from the brief conflict and seized the opportunity to put into place his vision of Costa Rican social democracy. After dissolving the country's military, Figueres quoted HG Wells: 'The future of mankind cannot include the armed forces.'

As head of a temporary junta government, Figueres enacted nearly a thousand decrees. He taxed the wealthy, nationalized the banks and built a modern welfare state. His 1949 constitution granted full citizenship and voting rights to women, African Americans, indigenous groups and Chinese minorities. Today Figueres' revolutionary regime is regarded as the foundation of Costa Rica's unarmed democracy.

The American Empire

Throughout the 1970s and '80s, the sovereignty of the small nations of Central America was limited by their northern neighbor, the US. Big sticks, gunboats and dollar diplomacy were instruments of a Yankee policy to curtail socialist politics, especially the military oligarchies of Guatemala, El Salvador and Nicaragua.

In 1979 the rebellious Sandinistas toppled the US-backed Somoza dictatorship in Nicaragua. Alarmed by the Sandinistas' Soviet and Cuban ties, fervently anticommunist president Ronald Reagan decided to intervene. Just like that, the Cold War arrived in the hot tropics.

The organizational details of the counterrevolution were delegated to Oliver North, an eager-to-please junior officer working out of the White House basement. North's can-do creativity helped to prop up the Contra rebels to incite civil war in Nicaragua. While both sides invoked the rhetoric of freedom and democracy, the war was really a turf battle between left-wing and right-wing forces.

Under intense US pressure, Costa Rica was dragged in. The Contras set up camp in northern Costa Rica, from where they staged guerrilla

1987	1994	2010	2010
President Óscar Arias Sánchez wins the Nobel Peace Prize for his work on the Central American peace accords, which brought about greater political freedom throughout the region.	The indigenous people of Costa Rica are finally granted the right to vote.	Costa Rica elects its first female president, National Liberation Party candidate Laura Chinchilla.	Volcán Arenal, the country's most active volcano for over four decades, stops spitting lava and enters a resting phase.

raids. Not-so-clandestine CIA operatives and US military advisors were dispatched to assist the effort. A secret jungle airstrip was built near the border to fly in weapons and supplies. To raise cash for the rebels, North allegedly used this covert supply network to traffic illegal narcotics through the region.

The war polarized Costa Rica. From conservative quarters came a loud call to re-establish the military and join the anticommunist crusade, which was largely underwritten by the US Pentagon. In May 1984 more than 20,000 demonstrators marched through San José to give peace a chance, though the debate didn't climax until the 1986 presidential election. The victor was 44-year-old Óscar Arias Sánchez, who, despite being born into coffee wealth, was an intellectual reformer in the mold of José Figueres Ferrer, his political patron.

Prior to his re-election, Óscar Arias Sánchez founded the Arias Foundation for Peace and Human Progress (www.arias.or.cr).

Once in office, Arias affirmed his commitment to a negotiated resolution and reasserted Costa Rican national independence. He vowed to uphold his country's pledge of neutrality and to vanquish the Contras. The sudden resignation of the US ambassador around this time was suspected to be a result of Arias' strong stance. In a public ceremony, Costa Rican schoolchildren planted trees on top of the CIA's secret airfield. Most notably, Arias became the driving force in uniting Central America around a peace plan, which ended the Nicaraguan war and earned him the Nobel Peace Prize in 1987.

In 2006 Arias once again returned to the presidential office, winning the popular election by a 1.2% margin and subsequently ratifying the controversial Central American Free Trade Agreement (Cafta), which Costa Rica entered in 2009.

When Laura Chinchilla became the first female president of Costa Rica in 2010, she promised to continue with Arias' free-market policies. She also pledged to tackle the rise of violent crime and drug trafficking. Ironically, Chinchilla herself became embroiled in a drug-related scandal over the use of a private jet belonging to a man under investigation for possible links to international drug cartels.

Costa Rica Goes Green

Costa Rica has long had a reputation for being green. In 2009, then-president Arias set an over-ambitious goal: that Costa Rica would achieve carbon neutrality by the year 2021. Ten years later Environment Minister Carlos Manuel Rodríguez revised that time frame and has said he plans to combat climate change by achieving zero emissions by 2050.

Proposed changes to the energy sector include completely reforming transport, energy, waste and land use in Costa Rica. In 2019, the nation was running on 98% renewable energy and Costa Rica's forested areas totaled 53%, after highly commendable work to counteract decades of

2011

Central American drug wars encroach on Costa Rica's borders, and the country is listed among the US' major drug-trafficking centers.

2014

Luis Guillermo Solís is elected president by default when his opponent withdraws from the race.

2015

The International Court of Justice in the Hague settles the long-standing land dispute between Costa Rica and Nicaragua in Costa Rica's favor.

2016

Volcán Turrialba erupts, engulfing the country's major cities in a toxic ash cloud. The national park is closed until further notice.

deforestation. In 2017, Costa Rica ran without fossil-fuel-generated electricity for 300 days – a feat achieved using geothermal, hydro and wind power to produce household electricity. The next target is to achieve 100% renewable electricity by 2030, and to make the majority of public transport services electric, with full electrification projected for 2050.

According to the UN, Costa Rica's population of 4.09 million produces just 0.4% of global emissions. In 2019 the country received the UN's highest environmental honor, the 'Champions of the Earth' award, for its focus on green policy and measures to combat climate change.

The Government Today

On April 1, 2018, Costa Rica elected President Carlos Alvarado Quesada, of the center-left Citizen Action Party (PAC). His second-in-command, Epsy Campbell Barr, became the first female vice president of African descent in Latin America. Alvarado took over from President Luis Guillermo Solís, also a member of PAC. Solís was Costa Rica's first president in half a century not to come from the two-party system, under which the social-democratic National Liberation Party and the center-right Social Christian Unity Party took turns holding power.

Although polls predicted the run-off would be close, it wasn't. Alvarado – a 38-year-old novelist, musician and former cabinet minister – won more than 60% of the vote, becoming the youngest serving president for a century. The decisive victory was particularly good news for progressives, environmentalists and proponents of equal rights, with same-sex marriage becoming legal in mid-2020, and ambitious environmental policies.

Key challenges the president faces before the next election in 2022 include a widening national deficit; tensions between indigenous and non-indigenous peoples following the murder of Sergio Rojas, the leader of the indigenous Bribrí community, in 2019; and an escalating crime rate against tourists, resulting in the US increasing their travel advisory to Level 2 ('exercise increased caution') for US citizens. All of these issues were largely overshadowed by the Covid-19 global pandemic, which closed Costa Rica borders for five months in 2020 and reduced hotel and restaurant business nearly by half. Although the country earned plaudits for its handling of the health crisis, the economic recovery is expected to be slow.

2017
The Costa Rican government files a new case with the International Court of Justice concerning Nicaraguan military presence on its territory.

2018
Novelist and former Solís Labor Minister Carlos Alvarado Quesada, 38, is elected as the country's second-youngest president ever.

2020
The ban on same-sex marriage is fully abolished in May, and joint adoption by same-sex couples becomes legal.

2020-21
Covid-19 causes Costa Rica to temporarily close its international borders, resulting in a drastic reduction in tourism and a devastating economic downturn.

Landscapes & Ecology

Despite its diminutive size – at 51,100 sq km, it's slightly smaller than West Virginia in the US – Costa Rica's land is an astounding collection of habitats. On one coast are the breezy skies and big waves of the Pacific, while only 119km away lie the languid shores of the Caribbean. In between, there are active volcanoes, alpine peaks and crisp high-elevation forests. Few places on earth can compare with this little country's spectacular interaction of natural, geological and climatic forces.

The Land

The Pacific Coast

Two major peninsulas hook out into the ocean along the 1016km-long Pacific coast: Nicoya in the north and Osa in the south. Although they look relatively similar from space, on the ground they could hardly be more different. Nicoya is one of the driest places in the country and holds

Above Catarata del Toro (p118)

some of Costa Rica's most developed tourist infrastructure; Osa is wet and rugged, run through by wild, seasonal rivers and rough dirt roads that are always encroached upon by the creeping jungle.

Just inland from the coast, the Pacific lowlands are a narrow strip of land backed by mountains. This area is equally dynamic, ranging from dry deciduous forests and open cattle country in the north to misty, mysterious tropical rainforests in the south.

Central Costa Rica

Move a bit inland from the Pacific coast and you immediately ascend the jagged spine of the country: the majestic Cordillera Central in the north and the rugged, largely unexplored Cordillera de Talamanca in the south. Continually being revised by tectonic activity, these mountains are part of the majestic Sierra Madre chain that runs north through Mexico.

Costa Rica's national tree is the guanacaste, commonly found in the lowlands of the Pacific slope.

Home to active volcanoes, clear, trout-filled streams and ethereal cloud forest, these mountain ranges generally follow a northwest to southeast line, with the highest and most dramatic peaks in the south near the Panamanian border. The highest peak in the country is windswept Cerro Chirripó (3820m).

In the midst of this powerful landscape, surrounded on all sides by mountains, are the highlands of the Meseta Central – the Central Valley. This fertile central plain, some 1000m above sea level, is the agricultural heart of the nation and enjoys abundant rainfall and mild temperatures. It includes San José and cradles three more of Costa Rica's five largest cities, accounting for more than half of the country's population.

The Caribbean Coast

Cross the mountains and drop down the eastern slope and you'll reach the elegant line of the Caribbean coastline – a long, straight 212km along low plains, brackish lagoons and waterlogged forests. A lack of strong tides allows plants to grow right over the water's edge along coastal sloughs. Eventually, these create the walls of vegetation along the narrow, murky waters that characterize much of the region. As if taking cues from the slow-paced, Caribbean-influenced culture, the rivers that rush out of the central mountains take on a languid pace here, curving through broad plains toward the sea.

While there are smoothly paved main roads along the southern Caribbean coast, the northern Caribbean is still largely inaccessible except by boat or plane.

The Geology

If all this wildly diverse beauty makes Costa Rica feel like the crossroads between vastly different worlds, that's because it is. As it's part of the thin strip of land that separates two continents with hugely divergent wildlife and topographical characters, and right in the middle of the world's two largest oceans, it's little wonder that Costa Rica boasts such a colorful collision of climates, landscapes and wildlife.

DON'T DISTURB THE DOLPHINS

Swimming with dolphins has been illegal since 2006, although shady tour operators out for a quick buck may encourage it. Research indicates that in some heavily touristed areas, dolphins are leaving their natural habitat in search of calmer seas. When your boat comes across these amazing creatures of the sea, avoid the temptation to jump in with them – you can still have an unforgettable experience peacefully observing them without disturbing them.

Volcán Arenal (p261)

The country's geological history began when the Cocos Plate, a tectonic plate that lies below the Pacific, crashed headlong into the Caribbean Plate, which is off the isthmus' east coast. Since the plates travel about 10cm every year, the collision might seem slow by human measure, but it was a violent wreck by geological standards, creating the area's subduction zone. The plates continue to collide, with the Cocos Plate pushing the Caribbean Plate toward the heavens and making the area prone to earthquakes and volcanic activity.

Despite all the violence underfoot, these forces have blessed the country with some of the world's most beautiful and varied tropical landscapes.

Coral Reefs

Compared with the rest of the Caribbean, the coral reefs of Costa Rica are not a banner attraction. Heavy surf and shifting sands along most of the Caribbean coast produce conditions that are unbearable to corals. The exceptions are two beautiful patches of reef in the south that are protected on the rocky headlands of Parque Nacional Cahuita and Refugio Nacional de Vida Silvestre Gandoca-Manzanillo. These diminutive but vibrant reefs are home to more than 100 species of fish and many types of coral and make for decent snorkeling and diving.

Few organizations are as involved in building sustainable rainforest-based economies as the Rainforest Alliance (www.rainforest-alliance.org).

Unfortunately, the reefs themselves are in danger due to climate change and tourism (divers and snorkelers damage the reefs with sunscreen and contact), plus pollutants like sediments washing downriver from logging operations and toxic chemicals that wash out of nearby agricultural fields. Although curbed by the government, these factors persist. In addition, a major earthquake in 1991 lifted the reefs as much as 1.5m, stranding and killing large portions of this fragile ecosystem. Scientists are experimenting with 'reforesting' and reviving coral reefs,

JOHN COLETTI/GETTY IMAGES ©
Playa Blanca (p168), Cahuita

like those off Península de Osa. It's a slow process; only time will tell if it's a viable solution to Costa Rica's dying coral.

Wildlife

Nowhere else has so many types of habitats squeezed into such a tiny area, and species from different continents have been commingling here for millennia. Costa Rica has the world's largest number of species per 10,000 sq km – more than 615. This simple fact alone makes Costa Rica the premier destination for nature lovers.

The number-one reason for forest clearing in Central America is to graze cattle, mostly for export. Can't give up eating beef? Consider opting for more environmentally friendly grass-fed beef instead.

The large number of species here is also due to the country's relatively recent appearance. Roughly three million years ago, Costa Rica rose from the ocean and formed a land bridge between North and South America. Species from these two vast biological provinces started to mingle, and the number of species essentially doubled in the area where Costa Rica now sits.

Flora

Simply put, Costa Rica's floral biodiversity is mind-blowing – there are more than 500,000 species in total, including close to 12,000 species of vascular plant, and the list gets more and more crowded each year. Orchids alone account for about 1400 species. The diversity of habitats created when this many species mix is a wonder to behold.

Rainforest

The humid, vibrant mystery of the tropical rainforest connects acutely with a traveler's sense of adventure. These forests, more dense with plant life than any other environment on the planet, are leftover scraps of prehistoric jungles that once covered the continents. Standing in the midst of it and trying to take it all in can be overwhelming: tropical rainforests contain more than half of the earth's known living organisms. Naturally, this riotous pile-up of life requires lots of water – the forest typically gets between 5m and 6m of rainfall annually (yes, that's *meters*!).

Classic rainforest habitats are well represented in the parks of southwestern Costa Rica and in the mid-elevation portions of the central mountains. Here you will find towering trees that block out the sky, long, looping vines and many overlapping layers of vegetation. Large trees often show buttresses – wing-like ribs that extend from their trunks for added structural support. Plants climb atop other plants, fighting for a bit of sunlight. The most impressive areas of primary forest – a term designating completely untouched land that has never been disturbed by humans – exist on the Península de Osa.

Due to deforestation it is best to avoid products made from tropical hardwoods if you're uncertain of their origin.

Cloud Forest

Visiting the unearthly terrain of a cloud forest is a highlight for many visitors; there are amazing swaths of it in Monteverde, along the Cerro de la Muerte and below the peaks of Chirripó. In these regions, fog-drenched trees are so thickly coated in mosses, ferns, bromeliads and orchids that you can hardly discern their true shapes. These forests are created when humid trade winds off the Caribbean blow up into the highlands, then cool and condense to form thick, low-hanging clouds. With constant exposure to wind, rain and sun, the trees here are crooked and stunted.

Cloud forests are widespread at high elevations throughout Costa Rica and any of them warrant a visit. Be forewarned, though, that in these habitats the term 'rainy season' has little meaning, as it's always dripping wet from the fog – humidity in a cloud forest often hovers around 100%.

Tropical Dry Forest

Along Costa Rica's northwestern coast lies the country's largest concentration of tropical dry forest – a stunningly different scene to the country's wet rainforests and cloud forests. During the dry season, many trees drop their foliage, creating carpets of crackling, sun-drenched leaves and a sense of openness that is largely absent in other Costa Rican habitats. The large trees here, such as Costa Rica's national tree, the guanacaste, have broad, umbrella-like canopies, while spiny shrubs and vines or cacti dominate the understory. At times, large numbers of trees erupt into spectacular displays of flowers, and at the beginning of the rainy season everything is transformed with a wonderful flush of new, green foliage.

This type of forest was native to Guanacaste and the Península de Nicoya, but it suffered generations of destruction for its commercially valuable lumber. Most was clear-cut or burned to make way for ranching. Guanacaste and Santa Rosa national parks are good examples of the dry forest and host some of the country's most accessible nature hiking.

Mangroves

Along brackish stretches of both coasts, mangrove swamps are a world unto themselves. Growing on stilts out of muddy tidal flats, five species of tree crowd together so densely that no boats and few animals can penetrate. Striking in their adaptations for dealing with salt, mangroves thrive where no other land plant dares to tread and are among the world's most relentless colonizers. Mangrove seeds are heavy and fleshy, blooming into flowers in the spring before falling off to give way to fruit. By the time the fruit falls, it is covered with spiky seedlings that anchor in the soft mud of low tides. In only 10 years, a seedling has the potential to mature into an entire new colony.

Mangroves survive in highly saline environments by filtering salt.

Mangrove swamps play extremely important roles in the ecosystem and are protected by Costa Rican law. Not only do they buffer coastlines

Top Horseback-riding on Playa Nosara, Refugio Nacional de Vida Silvestre Ostional (p323)

Bottom Bahía Drake (p432)

Parque Nacional Volcán Poás (p113)

from the erosive power of waves but they also have high levels of productivity because they trap nutrient-rich sediment and serve as spawning and nursery areas for innumerable species of fish and invertebrates. The brown waters of mangrove channels – rich with nutrients and filled with algae, shrimp, crustaceans and caimans – form tight links in the marine food chain and are best explored in a kayak, early in the morning.

There are miles of mangrove channels along the Caribbean coast, and a vast mangrove swamp around the Río Tárcoles, and on the Pacific near Bahía Drake.

Fauna

Though tropical in nature – with a substantial number of tropical animals such as poison-dart frogs and spider monkeys – Costa Rica is also the winter home for more than 200 species of migrating birds that arrive from as far away as Alaska and Australia. Don't be surprised to see one of your familiar backyard birds feeding alongside trogons and toucans. Birds are one of the primary attractions for naturalists, who scan endlessly for birds of every color, from strawberry-red scarlet macaws to the iridescent jewels called violet sabrewings (a type of hummingbird). Because many birds in Costa Rica have restricted ranges, you are guaranteed to find different species everywhere you travel.

Two-toed sloths descend from the trees once a week to defecate, risking their lives every time.

The extensive network of national parks, wildlife refuges and other protected areas are prime places to spot wildlife. Visitors to national parks will almost certainly see one of Costa Rica's four types of monkey or two types of sloth, but there are an additional 230 types of mammal awaiting the patient observer. More exotic sightings might include the amazing four-eyed opossum or the silky anteater, while a lucky few might spot the elusive tapir or have a jaguarundi cross their path.

Owl butterfly, Parque Nacional Tortuguero (p155)

If you are serious about observing birds and animals, the value of a knowledgeable guide cannot be underestimated. Their keen eyes are trained to notice the slightest movement in the forest, and they recognize the many exotic sounds. Bird guides are proficient in the dialects of local birds, greatly improving your chances of hearing or seeing these species.

No season is a bad one for exploring Costa Rica's natural environment, though most visitors arrive during the peak dry season, when trails are less muddy and more accessible. A bonus of visiting between December and February is that many of the wintering migratory birds are still hanging around. A trip after the peak season means fewer birds, but this is a stupendous time to see dry forests transform into vibrant greens and it's also when resident birds begin nesting.

For more on Costa Rica's animals,, see the our wildlife guide (p487).

The world-famous Organization for Tropical Studies (www.tropicalstudies.org) runs three field stations in Costa Rica.

Endangered Species

As expected in a country with unique habitats and widespread logging, there are numerous species whose populations are declining or in danger of extinction. Currently, the number-one threat to most of Costa Rica's endangered species is habitat destruction, followed closely by hunting and trapping.

Costa Rica's four species of sea turtle – olive ridley, leatherback, green and hawksbill – deservedly get a lot of attention. All four species are classified as endangered or critically endangered, meaning they face an imminent threat of extinction. While populations of some species are increasing thanks to various protection programs along both coasts, the risk for these *tortugas* (turtles) is still very real.

Destruction of habitat is a huge problem. With the exception of the leatherbacks, all of these species return to their natal beach to nest, which means that the ecological state of the beach directly affects that turtle's ability to reproduce. All of the species prefer dark, undisturbed beaches, and any sort of development or artificial lighting (including flashlights) will inhibit nesting.

Hunting and harvesting eggs are two major causes of declining populations. Green turtles are hunted for their meat. Leatherbacks and olive ridleys are not killed for meat, but their eggs are considered a delicacy – an aphrodisiac, no less. Hawksbill turtles are hunted for their unusual shells, which are sometimes used to make jewelry and hair ornaments. Any trade in tortoiseshell products and turtle eggs and meat is illegal, but a significant black market exists.

The ultra-rare harpy eagle and the legendary quetzal – the birds at the top of every naturalist's must-see list – teeter precariously as their home forests are felled at an alarming rate. Seeing a noisy scarlet macaw could be a birdwatching highlight in Costa Rica, but trapping for the pet trade has extirpated these magnificent birds from much of their former range. Although populations are thriving on the Península de Osa, there are fewer than 1500 remaining in Central America and the species is now extinct in most of the region, including the entire Caribbean coast.

The eight species of poison-dart frog in Costa Rica are beautiful but have skin secretions of varying toxicity that cause paralysis and death if they get into your bloodstream.

A number of Costa Rica's mammals are highly endangered, including the elusive jaguar and the squirrel monkey, both due to habitat destruction. Both survive in the depths of Parque Nacional Corcovado, with the latter also found in some numbers in Parque Nacional Manuel Antonio.

Harassment and intimidation of conservationists in Costa Rica is nothing new, an issue brought to international attention by the brutal murder (p154) of 26-year-old environmentalist Jairo Mora Sandoval in Limón Province in 2013. In 2015, seven men were accused of Sandoval's murder. Four of the men were acquitted on the murder charge but convicted for assault, kidnapping and aggravated robbery for a crime that took place after Mora's murder. Then in 2016, after an appeal, the not-guilty verdict was overturned. Each of the men is serving 50 years in prison, the maximum sentence in Costa Rica.

National Parks & Protected Areas

The national-park system began in the 1960s, and has since been expanded into the Sistema Nacional de Areas de Conservación (National System of Conservation Areas; Sinac), with an astounding 186 protected areas, including 27 national parks, eight biological reserves, 32 protected zones, 13 forest reserves and 58 wildlife refuges. At least 10% of the land is strictly protected and another 17% is included in various multiple-use preserves. Costa Rican authorities take pride in the statistic that more than 27% of the country has been set aside for conservation, but multiple-use zones still allow farming, logging and other exploitation, so the environment within them is not totally protected. The smallest number might be the most amazing of all: Costa Rica's parks are a safe haven to approximately 5% of the world's wildlife species.

In addition to the system of national preserves, there are hundreds of small, privately owned lodges, reserves and haciendas (estates) that have been set up to protect the land. Many belong to longtime Costa Rican expats who decided that this country was the last stop in their journey along the 'gringo trail' in the 1970s and '80s. The abundance of foreign-owned protected areas is a bit of a contentious issue with Ticos. Although these are largely nonprofit organizations with keen interests in conservation, they are private and often cost money to enter. There's also a number of animal rescue and rehabilitation centers (also largely set up by expats), where injured and orphaned animals and illegal pets are rehabilitated and released into the wild, or looked after for life if they cannot be released.

Mushrooms, Reserva Biológica Bosque Nuboso Monteverde (p213)

Although the national-park system appears glamorous on paper, the Sinac authority still sees much work to be done. A report from several years ago amplified the fact that much of the protected area is, in fact, at risk. The government doesn't own all of this land – many of the areas are in private hands – and there isn't the budget to buy it. Technically, the private lands are protected from development, but there have been reports that many landowners are finding loopholes in the restrictions and selling or developing their properties, or taking bribes from poachers and illegal loggers in exchange for access.

Excellent, contemplative tomes include *A Naturalist in Costa Rica* and *The Minds of Birds* by the esteemed Dr Alexander Skutch.

On the plus side is a project by Sinac that links national parks and reserves, private reserves and national forests into 13 conservation areas. This strategy has two major effects. First, these 'megaparks' allow greater numbers of individual plants and animals to exist. Second, the administration of the national parks is delegated to regional offices, allowing a more individualized management approach. Each conservation area has regional and subregional offices charged with providing effective education, enforcement, research and management, although some regional offices appear to play only an obscure bureaucratic role.

In general, support for land preservation remains high in Costa Rica because it provides income and jobs to so many people, plus important opportunities for scientific investigation.

Environmental Issues

No other tropical country has made such a concerted effort to protect its environment, and a study published by Yale and Columbia Universities in 2012 ranked Costa Rica in the top five nations for its overall environmental performance. At the same time, as the global leader in the burgeoning ecotourism economy, Costa Rica is proving to be a case study in the pitfalls and benefits of this kind of tourism. Costa Rica has slipped in

Catarata de Río Celeste (p221)

the rankings and the pressures of overpopulation, global climate change and dwindling natural resources have further highlighted the urgency of environmental protection.

Deforestation

Sometimes, when the traffic jams up around the endless San José sprawl, it is hard to keep in mind that this place was once covered in a lush, unending tropical forest. Tragically, after more than a century of clearing for plantations, agriculture and logging, Costa Rica lost about 80% of its forest cover before the government stepped in with a plan to protect what was left. Through its many programs of forest protection and reforestation, 51% of the country is forested once again – a stunning accomplishment.

Tales of the green turtle's resurgence in Tortuguero are told by Archie Carr in *The Windward Road: Adventures of a Naturalist on Remote Caribbean Shores*.

Despite protection for two-thirds of the remaining forests, cutting trees is still a major problem for Costa Rica, especially on private lands that are being cleared by wealthy landowners and multinational corporations. Even within national parks, some of the more remote areas are being logged illegally because there is not enough money for law enforcement.

Apart from the loss of tropical forests and the plants and animals that depend on them, deforestation leads directly or indirectly to a number of other severe environmental problems. Forests protect the soil beneath them from the ravages of tropical rainstorms. After deforestation, much of the topsoil is washed away, lowering the productivity of the land and silting up watersheds and downstream coral reefs.

Cleared lands are frequently planted with a variety of crops, including acres of bananas, the production of which involves pesticides as well as blue plastic bags to protect the fruit. Both the pesticides and the plastic end up polluting the environment. Cattle ranching has been another historical motivator for clear-cutting. It intensified during the 1970s, when Costa Rican coffee exports were waning in the global market.

For detailed information on national parks and conservation areas, visit www.sinac.go.cr.

Because deforestation plays a role in global warming, there is much interest in rewarding countries such as Costa Rica for taking the lead in protecting their forests. The US has forgiven millions of dollars of Costa Rica's debt in exchange for increased efforts to preserve rainforests. The Costa Rican government itself sponsors a program that pays landowners for each hectare of forest they set aside, and for adopting sustainable land management practices. It also petitioned the UN for a global program that would pay tropical countries for their conservation efforts – and they listened. The UN, under the REDD+ initiative, has helped begin a system for tropical-forest countries to be paid for their positive actions to combat deforestation. Travelers interested in taking part in projects that can help protect Costa Rica's trees should look at volunteer opportunities (p515) in conservation and forestry.

Tourism

The other great environmental issue facing Costa Rica comes from the country being loved to death, directly through the passage of around two million foreign tourists a year, and less directly through the development of extensive infrastructure to support this influx. For years, resort hotels and lodges continued to pop up, most notably on formerly pristine beaches or in the middle of intact rainforest. Too many of these projects were poorly planned, and they necessitate additional support systems, including roads and countless vehicle trips, with much of this activity unregulated and largely unmonitored.

The tallest tree in the rainforest is usually the ceiba (silk-cotton tree); the most famous example is a 80m elder with a 3m radius in Corcovado.

As tourism continues to become a larger piece of the Costa Rican economy, the bonanza invites more and more development. Taking advantage of Costa Rica's reputation as a green destination, developers promote mass tourism by building large hotels and package tours that, in turn, drive away wildlife, hasten erosion and strain local sewer and water systems. The irony is painful: these businesses threaten to ruin the very environment that they're selling.

It's worth noting that many private lodges and reserves are also doing some of the best conservation work in the country, and it's heartening to run across the ever-increasing homespun efforts to protect Costa Rica's environment, spearheaded by hardworking families or small organizations tucked away in quiet corners of the country. These include projects to boost rural economies by raising native medicinal plants, efforts by villagers to document their local biodiversity, and resourceful fundraising campaigns to purchase endangered lands.

Sustainable Travel

Costa Rica's visitors presently account for the largest sector of the national economy and thus have unprecedented power to protect this country. How? By spending wisely, asking probing questions about sustainability claims and simply avoiding businesses that threaten Costa Rica's future.

Green Phoenix, by science journalist William Allen, is an absorbing account of his efforts, alongside scientists and activists, to conserve and restore the rainforest in Guanacaste.

In its purest form, sustainable tourism simply means striking the ideal balance between the traveler and their surrounding environment. This often includes being conscientious about energy and water consumption, and treading lightly on local environments and communities. Sustainable tourism initiatives support their communities by hiring local people for decent wages, furthering women's and civil rights, and supporting local schools, artists and food producers.

On the road, engage with the local economy as much as possible; for example, if a local artisan's handiwork catches your eye, make the purchase – every dollar infuses the micro-economy in the most direct (and rewarding) way.

Top Green basilisk, Parque Nacional Tortuguero (p155)
Bottom Orchids

Hot springs, Parque Nacional Volcán Arenal (p261)

The National Biodiversity Institute's database is managed by the Costa Rica National Museum (NMCR).

Ecofriendly Credentials

Interpreting the jargon – 'green,' 'sustainable,' 'low carbon footprint,' 'ecofriendly' etc – can be confusing when every souvenir stall and tour operator claims to be ecofriendly. Since sustainable travel has no universal guidelines, here are some things to look for:

- For hotels and restaurants, expect obvious recycling programs, effective management of wastewater and pollutants, and alternative energy systems and natural illumination, at a bare minimum.
- A high rating from a legitimate sustainability index. In Costa Rica, the government-sanctioned Certificado para la Sostenibilidad Turística (CST; www.turismo-sostenible.co.cr) offers a 'five-leaf' rating system. Factors considered by the CST include physical-biological parameters, infrastructure and services, and the socioeconomic environment, including interaction with local communities. Its website has a complete directory.
- Partnership with environmental conservation programs, education initiatives, or regional or local organizations that work on solving environmental problems.
- Grassroots connections: sourcing a majority of employees from the local population, associating with locally owned businesses, providing places where local handicrafts can be displayed for sale, serving foods that support local markets, and using local materials and products in order to maintain the health of the local economy.

Costa Rica Wildlife Guide

Costa Rica's reputation as a veritable Eden precedes it – see its iconic blue morpho butterflies, four species each of monkey and sea turtle, scarlet and great green macaws, two- and three-toed sloths, a rainbow of poison-dart frogs, mysterious tapirs and cute coatis.

They might be adorable, but please heed the '#stopanimalselfies' campaign introduced by the government in 2019; designed to protect both tourists and wildlife.

Contents

Above Red-eyed tree frog

1

MACIEJ CZEKAJEWSKI/SHUTTERSTOCK ©

1. Scarlet macaw **2.** Roseate spoonbill and ducks **3.** Golden-hooded tanager **4.** Resplendent quetzal

3

ONDREJ PROSICKY/SHUTTERSTOCK ©

2

JORGE A. RUSSELL/SHUTTERSTOCK ©

4

BRANDON LINDBLAD/SHUTTERSTOCK ©

Birds

Toucan

Six species of this classic rainforest bird are found in Costa Rica. Huge bills and vibrant plumage make the commonly sighted chestnut-mandibled toucan (aka yellow-throated toucan) and keel-billed toucan hard to miss. Listen for the keel-billed's song: a repetitious 'carrrick!'

Scarlet Macaw

Of more than a dozen parrot species in Costa Rica, none is as spectacular as the scarlet macaw. Unmistakable for its large size, bright-red body and ear-splitting squawk, it's common in Parque Nacional Carara (p358) and the Península de Osa. Its cousin, the rarer great green macaw, inhabits the Caribbean coast; visit Ara Manzanillo (p191) for a good glimpse. Macaws have long, monogamous relationships and can live for 50 years.

Resplendent Quetzal

The most dazzling bird in Central America, the quetzal held great ceremonial significance for the Aztecs and the Maya. Look for its iridescent-green body, red breast and long green tail at high elevations and near Parque Nacional Los Quetzales (p413).

Roseate Spoonbill

This wading bird has a white head and a distinctive spoon-shaped bill, and feeds by touch. It's common around the Península de Nicoya, the Pacific lowlands and on the Caribbean side at the Refugio Nacional de Vida Silvestre Caño Negro (p272).

Tanager

There are 42 species of tanager in the country – many are brightly colored and all have bodies about the size of an adult fist. Look for them everywhere except at high elevation. The blue-grey tanager, quite common, is known as the *'viuda'* (widow) for its appearance.

Hummingbird

More than 50 species of hummingbird have been recorded in Costa Rica – and most live at high elevations. The largest is the violet sabrewing, with a striking violet head and body and dark-green wings.

MLORENZPHOTOGRAPHY/GETTY IMAGES ©

1. Strawberry poison-dart frog **2.** Green iguana **3.** Caiman
4. Eyelash pit viper

JOSH MILLER PHOTOGRAPHY/GETTY IMAGES ©

2

FRANCIS WONG/500PX ©

Reptiles & Amphibians

Green Iguana

The stocky green iguana is regularly seen draping its 2m-long body along a branch. Despite their bulk, iguanas are vegetarians, and eat young shoots and leaves. You'll see them almost everywhere in Costa Rica – if you're driving, beware of iguanas skittering across or sunbathing on the roads. Learn more at the breeding and educational centers at Tree House Lodge (p187) and the Kéköldi indigenous territory (p183).

Red-Eyed Tree Frog

The unofficial symbol of Costa Rica, the red-eyed tree frog has red eyes, a green body, yellow and blue side stripes, and orange feet. Despite this vibrant coloration, they're well camouflaged in the rainforest and rather difficult to spot, but they are widespread apart from on the Península de Nicoya, which is too dry for them. You have a good chance of seeing them at Estación Biológica La Selva (p285).

4

KEVIN WELLS PHOTOGRAPHY/SHUTTERSTOCK ©

Poison-Dart Frog

Among the several species found in Costa Rica, the blue-jeans or strawberry poison-dart frog is the most commonly spotted, from Arenal to the Caribbean coast. The colorful frogs' toxic excretions were once used as poison on the arrowheads of indigenous peoples. The Golfo Dulce poison-dart frog is endemic to Costa Rica.

Crocodile

Impressive specimens can be seen from Crocodile Bridge (p358) on the central Pacific coast or in a more natural setting on boat trips along the Tortuguero canals. Avoid swimming in these areas.

Viper

Three serpents you'll want to avoid are the fer-de-lance pit viper, which lives in agricultural areas of the Pacific and Caribbean slopes, the black-headed bushmaster (endemic to Costa Rica) and the beautiful eyelash pit viper, which lives in low-elevation rainforest. To avoid serious or fatal bites, wear boots. watch your step and look before you grab onto any vines when hiking.

LEN DEELEY/GETTY IMAGES ©

1. Whale shark **2.** Bottlenose dolphins **3.** Young olive ridley turtle
4. Hammerhead shark

DUSSEAU PHOTO/SHUTTERSTOCK ©

2

PHOTOBOTOS IMAGE/GETTY IMAGES ©

Marine Animals

Olive Ridley Turtle

The smallest of Costa Rica's sea turtles, the olive ridley is easy to love – it has a heart-shaped shell. Between September and October they arrive to nest at Ostional beach in Guanacaste province and near Ojochal on the Pacific coast.

Leatherback Turtle

The gigantic, 360kg leatherback sea turtle is distinguished by its soft, leathery carapace, which has seven ridges. It nests on the Pacific beaches of the Osa and Nicoya peninsulas, and on the Caribbean side at Parismina.

Whale

Migrating whales, which arrive from both the northern and southern hemispheres, include orca, blue and sperm whales and several species of relatively unknown beaked whale. Humpback whales are commonly spotted along the Pacific coast and off the Península de Osa.

4

DMITRY MIROSHNIKOV/GETTY IMAGES ©

Bottlenose Dolphin

These charismatic, intelligent cetaceans are commonly sighted, year-round residents of Costa Rica. Keep a lookout for them on the boat ride to Bahía Drake.

Whale Shark

Divers may encounter this gentle giant in the waters off Reserva Biológica Isla del Caño, the Golfo Dulce or Isla del Coco. The world's biggest fish, whale sharks can reach 6m and weigh more than 2000kg.

Manta Ray

With wings that can reach 7m, the elegant manta ray is common in warm Pacific waters, especially off the coast of Guanacaste and around the Bat and Catalina islands.

Hammerhead Shark

The intimidating hammerhead has a unique cephalofoil that enables it to maneuver with incredible speed and precision. Divers can see enormous schools of hammerheads around the remote Isla del Coco.

CYNTHIA KIDWELL/SHUTTERSTOCK ©

1. White-nosed coati **2.** Baby sloth **3.** Jaguar **4.** Squirrel monkeys

EDWIN BUTTER/SHUTTERSTOCK ©

JONATHAN FIFE/GETTY IMAGES ©

ZORAN KOLUNDZIJA/GETTY IMAGES ©

Land Mammals

Sloth

Costa Rica is home to the brown-throated three-toed sloth and Hoffman's two-toed sloth (nocturnal). Both species tend to hang seemingly motionless from branches, their coats growing moss. Find them in Parque Nacional Manuel Antonio (p386) and anywhere the cecropia tree flourishes.

Howler Monkey

The loud vocalizations of a male mantled howler monkey can carry for over 1km, even in dense rainforest; they echo through many of the country's national parks.

White-Faced Capuchin Monkey

The small and inquisitive white-faced capuchin has a prehensile tail typically carried with the tip coiled – one is likely to steal your lunch near Volcán Arenal or Parque Nacional Manuel Antonio.

Squirrel Monkey

The diminutive squirrel monkey travels in small- to medium-sized groups during the day, in search of insects and fruit. They live along the Pacific coast and are common in Parque Nacional Manuel Antonio and on the Península de Nicoya.

Jaguar

The king of Costa Rica's big cats, the jaguar is extremely rare, shy and well camouflaged, so the chance of seeing one is virtually nil (but the likeliest place is Parque Nacional Corcovado).

White-Nosed Coati

A frequently seen member of the raccoon family, the white-nosed coati has a longer, slimmer and lighter body than the average raccoon. It has a distinctive pointy, whitish snout and a perky striped tail. It's tempting, but don't feed them.

Baird's Tapir

A large browsing mammal related to the rhinoceros, the tapir has a characteristic prehensile snout and lives deep in forests ranging from the Península de Osa to Parque Nacional Santa Rosa.

Blue morpho butterfly

Insects & Arachnids

Blue Morpho Butterfly

The blue morpho butterfly flutters along tropical rivers and through openings in the forests. When it lands, the electric-blue upper wings close, and only the mottled brown underwings become visible, an instantaneous change from outrageous display to modest camouflage.

Tarantula

Easily identified by its enormous size and hairy appendages, the Costa Rican red tarantula is an intimidating arachnid that can take down a mouse, but although its bite may cause as much pain as a bee sting, its venom is harmless to humans. They are most active at night while foraging and seeking mates.

Hercules Beetle

Turn on your flashlight while visiting one of Costa Rica's old-growth forests and you might draw out the Hercules beetle, one of the largest bugs in the world, a terrifying-looking but utterly harmless scarab beetle that can be as big as a cake plate. Fun fact: it can carry over 100 times its own body weight.

Leaf-Cutter Ant

Long processions of busy leaf-cutter ants traverse the forest floors and trails of Costa Rica, appearing like slow-moving rivulets of green leaf fragments. Leaf-cutter ants are actually fungus farmers – in their underground colonies, the ants chew the harvested leaves into a pulp to precipitate the growth of fungus, which feeds the colonies. Don't confuse them with the predatory army ants!

King Cricket

Evidence of how bountiful (and unknown) the rainforest is, a new species of King cricket was only discovered in 2018 at the Soltis Center in San Isidro.

MARCUS GRIP/SHUTTERSTOCK ©

The Tico Way of Life

Blessed with natural beauty and a peaceful, army-less society, it's no wonder Costa Rica has long been known as the Switzerland of Central America. While nowadays the country is certainly challenged by its lofty eco-conscious goals and modern intercontinental maladies (such as border control and drug trafficking), the Tico attitude remains sunny and family-centered, with a good balance between work and quality of life.

The Pura Vida

Pura vida – pure life – is more than just a slogan that rolls off the tongues of Ticos and emblazons souvenirs. In the laid-back tone in which it is constantly uttered, the phrase is a bona fide mantra for the Costa Rican way of life. Perhaps the essence of the pure life is something better lived than explained, but hearing *'pura vida'* again and again while traveling across this beautiful country – as a greeting, a stand-in for goodbye, 'cool,' and an acknowledgment of thanks – makes it evident that the concept lives deep within the DNA of this country.

The living seems particularly pure when Costa Rica is compared with its Central American neighbors such as Nicaragua and Honduras; there's little poverty, illiteracy or political tumult, the country is crowded with ecological jewels, and the standard of living is high. What's more, Costa Rica has flourished without an army for the past 60 years. The sum of the parts is a country that's an oasis of calm in a corner of the world that has been continuously degraded by warfare. And though the Costa Rican people are justifiably proud hosts, a compliment to the country is likely to be met simply with a warm smile and an enigmatic two-word reply: *pura vida.*

One of the most comprehensive and complete books on Costa Rican history and culture is *The Ticos: Culture and Social Change in Costa Rica*, by Mavis, Richard and Karen Biesanz.

Daily Life

With its lack of war, long life expectancy and relatively sturdy economy, Costa Rica enjoys the highest standard of living in Central America. For the most part, Costa Ricans live fairly affluent and comfortable lives.

As in many places in Latin America, the family unit in Costa Rica remains the nucleus of life. Families socialize together and extended families often live near each other. When it's time to party it's also largely a family affair; celebrations, vacations and weddings are a social outlet for rich and poor alike, and those with relatives in positions of power – nominal or otherwise – don't hesitate to turn to them for support.

Given this mutually cooperative environment, it's no surprise that life expectancy in Costa Rica is slightly higher than in the US. In fact, most Costa Ricans are more likely to die of heart disease or cancer as opposed to the childhood diseases that plague many developing nations. A comprehensive socialized healthcare system and excellent sanitation systems account for these positive statistics, as do tropical weather, a healthy, varied diet and a generally stress-free lifestyle – the *pura vida*.

Still, the divide between rich and poor is evident. The middle and upper classes largely reside in San José, as well as in the major cities of the Central Valley highlands (Heredia, Alajuela and Cartago), and enjoy a level of comfort similar to their economic brethren in Europe and the US. City dwellers are likely to have a maid and a car or two, and the lucky few have a second home on the beach or in the mountains.

The home of an average Tico is a one-story construction built from concrete blocks, wood or a combination of both. In the poorer lowland areas, people often live in windowless houses made of *caña brava* (a local cane). For the vast majority of *campesinos* (farmers) and *indígenas* (people of indigenous origin), life is harder than in the cities, poverty levels are higher and standards of living are lower than in the rest of the country. This is especially true in indigenous reservations and along the Caribbean coast, where the descendants of Jamaican immigrants have long suffered from lack of attention from the federal government. However, although poor families have few possessions and little financial security, every member assists with working the land or contributing to the household, which creates a strong safety net.

The expression *matando la culebra* (meaning 'to be idle' or 'to waste time' – literally 'killing the snake') originates with *peones* (laborers) from banana plantations. When foremen would ask what they were doing, the response would be '*¡Matando la culebra!*'

As in the rest of the world, globalization is having a dramatic effect on Costa Ricans, who are increasingly mobile, international and intertwined in the global economy – for better or for worse. These days, society is increasingly geographically mobile – the Tico who was born in Puntarenas might end up managing a lodge on the Península de Osa. And, with the advent of better-paved roads, cell coverage and the increasing presence of North American and European expats (and the accompanying malls and big-box stores), the Tico family unit is somewhat influenced by the changing tides of a global society.

SAME-SEX RELATIONSHIPS

Legal recognition of same-sex partnerships has been a hot topic since 2006 and was a major point of contention in the 2010 and 2018 presidential races. In January 2012 Costa Rica's primary newspaper, *La Nación*, conducted a poll in which 55% of the respondents believed that same-sex couples should have the same rights as heterosexual couples. Then, in July 2013, the Costa Rican legislature 'accidentally' passed a law legalizing same-sex marriage, due to a small change in the bill's wording. In 2015 a Costa Rican judge granted a same-sex common-law marriage, making Costa Rica the first country in Central America to recognize gay relationships. The previous president, Luis Guillermo Solís, expressed support for equal rights, and he even flew the rainbow flag at the presidential house. His successor, Carlos Alvarado Quesada, elected in May 2018, continues this spirit of tolerance and in August 2018 the Supreme Court ruled that a ban on same-sex marriage was unconstitutional. The Legislative Assembly was given 18 months to change the law or it would be automatically overturned, meaning that from May 26, 2020 same-sex marriage became legal in Costa Rica. Costa Rica is firmly on the map for the international LGBTIQ+ community, and is slowly becoming a destination for same-sex weddings – the liberal-minded Manuel Antonio, with its gay-friendly clubs and hotels, is a hotspot for ceremonies. Adoption by same-sex couples was also made legal in May 2020.

Women in Costa Rica

By the letter of the law, Costa Rica's progressive stance on women's issues makes the country stand out among its Central American neighbors. A 1974 family code stipulated equal duties and rights for men and women. Additionally, women can draw up contracts, assume loans and inherit property. Sexual harassment and sex discrimination are also against the law, and in 1996 Costa Rica passed a landmark law against domestic violence that was one of the most progressive in Latin America. With women holding more and more roles in political, legal, scientific and medical fields, Costa Rica has been home to some historic firsts: in 1998 both vice presidents (Costa Rica has two) were women, and in February 2010 Arias Sánchez's former vice president, Laura Chinchilla, became the first female president. The elected vice president in 2018 was another historic milestone for the country: a woman of Afro–Costa Rican descent, Epsy Campbell Barr.

Still, the picture of sexual equality is much more complicated than the country's bragging rights might suggest. Unwanted byproducts of the legal prostitution trade include illicit underground activities such as child prostitution and the trafficking of women (despite pimping being illegal). Despite the cultural reverence for the matriarch (Mother's Day is a national holiday), traditional Latin American machismo is hardly a thing of the past and anti-discrimination laws are rarely enforced. Particularly in the countryside, many women maintain traditional societal roles: raising children, cooking and running the home.

In conjunction with two indigenous women, Juanita Sánchez and Gloria Mayorga, Paula Palmer wrote *Taking Care of Sibö's Gifts*, an inspiring account of the intersection between the spiritual and environmental values of the Bribrí community, from the Talamanca region.

Sports

From the scrappy matches that take over the village pitch to the breathless exclamations of 'Goal!' that erupt from San José bars on the day of a big game, no Costa Rican sporting venture can compare with *fútbol* (soccer). Every town has a soccer field (which usually serves as the most conspicuous landmark) where neighborhood athletes play in heated matches.

The *selección nacional* (national team) is known affectionately as La Sele. Legions of Tico fans still recall La Sele's most memorable moments, including an unlikely showing in the quarterfinals at the 1990 World Cup in Italy and a solid (if not long-lasting) performance in the 2002 World Cup. More recently, La Sele's failure to qualify for the 2010 World Cup led to a top-down change in leadership and the reinstatement of one-time coach Jorge Luis Pinto, a Colombian coach who has had mixed results

JOSHUA TEN BRINK/SHUTTERSTOCK©

Estadio Nacional de Costa Rica (p95), San José

on the international stage. Pinto seemed to be a good fit for the team's ferocious young leaders such as record-setting scorer Álvaro Saborío, goalkeeper Keylor Navas and forward Bryan Ruiz. In fact, Pinto led the team to qualify for the 2014 World Cup in Brazil, where the team reached the quarterfinals, making them national heroes. The country qualified for the 2018 World Cup in Russia but, this time led by former Tico legend Óscar Ramírez as coach, they did not advance past the first round, managing just one draw in three matches.

Get player statistics and game schedules, and find out everything you ever needed to know about La Sele, the Costa Rican national soccer team, at www.fedefutbol.com.

The women's national *fútbol* team proved their mettle in 2018, though, making it to the final of the Caribbean and Central American Games.

With such perfect waves, surfing has steadily grown in popularity among Ticos, especially those who grow up in surf towns. Costa Rica hosts numerous national and international competitions annually that are widely covered by local media, and holds regular local competitions such as the weekly contest at Playa Hermosa (south of Jacó).

For a nation that values its wildlife, it may be surprising that the controversial sport of bullfighting is still popular, particularly in the Guanacaste region, though the bull isn't killed in the Costa Rican version of the sport. It might be more apt to describe bullfighting here as a ceremonial opportunity to watch an often tipsy cowboy run around with a bull.

Arts

Literature

Costa Rica has a relatively young literary history and few works by Costa Rican writers or novelists are available in translation. Carlos Luis Fallas (1909–66) is widely known for *Mamita Yunai* (1940), an influential 'proletarian' novel that took the banana companies to task for their labor practices, and he remains very popular among the Latin American left.

Carmen Naranjo (1928–2012) is one of the few contemporary Costa Rican writers to have risen to international acclaim. She was a novelist, poet and short-story writer who also served as ambassador to India in the 1970s, and a few years later as minister of culture. In 1996 she was awarded the prestigious Gabriela Mistral medal by the Chilean government. Her collection of short stories, *There Never Was a Once Upon a Time,* is widely available in English. Two of her stories can also be found in *Costa Rica: A Traveler's Literary Companion.*

José León Sánchez (b 1929) is an internationally renowned memoirist of Huetar descent, hailing from the border of Costa Rica and Nicaragua. After being convicted for stealing from the famous Basílica de Nuestra Señora de Los Ángeles in Cartago, he was sentenced to serve his term at Isla San Lucas, one of Latin America's most notorious jails. Illiterate when he was incarcerated, Sánchez taught himself how to read and write, and clandestinely wrote one of the continent's most poignant books: *La isla de los hombres solos* (called *God Was Looking the Other Way* in the translated version).

Music & Dance

Although there are other Latin American musical hotbeds of more renown, Costa Rica's central geographical location and colonial history have resulted in a varied musical culture that incorporates elements from North and South America and the Caribbean islands.

San José features a regular lineup of domestic and international rock, folk and hip-hop artists, but you'll find that regional sounds also survive, each with their own special rhythms, instruments and styles. For instance, the Península de Nicoya has a rich musical history, with its sounds of guitars, maracas and marimbas. The common sounds on the Caribbean coast are reggae, reggaetón (a newer version of reggae mixed with hip-hop beats) and calypso, which has roots in Afro-Caribbean slave culture.

Popular dance music includes Latin dances, such as salsa, merengue, bolero and *cumbia.* Guanacaste is also the birthplace of many traditional dances, most of which depict courtship rituals between country folk. The most famous – sometimes considered the national dance – is the *punto guanacasteco.* What keeps it lively is the *bomba,* a funny (and usually racy) rhymed verse shouted by the male dancers during the musical interlude.

STADIUM DIPLOMACY

As in many Latin American nations, *fútbol* dominates the sports conversation in Costa Rica. So imagine the wonderment when a brand-new, state-of-the-art national stadium was proposed – and at no cost to Costa Rica.

China was the font of this magnanimity, asking in return that Costa Rica establish trade relations with the Asian giant while cutting ties with Taiwan. As recently as 2003, the Costa Rican and Taiwanese governments were the closest of allies, with Taiwan funding the construction of the Puente de la Amistad (Friendship Bridge) in Puntarenas. That was a trade, too, for fishing rights. With the new stadium, Taiwan is out and China is in. Ironic commentators dubbed the structure Puente de la Apuñalada (Backstabbing Bridge).

Opened in 2011, the San José stadium (Estadio Nacional de Costa Rica) was built entirely with Chinese materials and labor (800 workers in all), and violated Costa Rican labor law in the forced overtime of workers. It did not sit well with all in the country. One worker died during construction.

Costa Rica is now China's second-biggest trading partner in Central America, and China has used this 'stadium diplomacy' to forge friendships across Latin America, the Caribbean, Asia and Africa.

For most Costa Ricans, the stadium has been a bonus – a cutting-edge place to watch the national team play world-class competition such as Argentina, Brazil and Spain. Miley Cyrus, the Red Hot Chili Peppers, Paul McCartney, Shakira and Guns N' Roses have all played shows there.

Visual Arts

The visual arts in Costa Rica first took on a national character in the 1920s, when Teodórico Quirós, Fausto Pacheco and their contemporaries began painting landscapes that differed from traditional European styles, depicting the rolling hills and lush forest of the Costa Rican countryside, often sprinkled with characteristic adobe houses.

The contemporary scene is more varied and it's difficult to define a unique Tico style. The work of several artists has garnered acclaim, including the magical realism of Isidro Con Wong, the surreal paintings and primitive engravings of Francisco Amighetti and the mystical female figures painted by Rafa Fernández. The Museo de Arte y Diseño Contemporáneo (p67) in San José is the top place to see this type of work, and its permanent collection is a great primer.

Many galleries are geared toward tourists and specialize in 'tropical art' (for lack of an official description): brightly colored, whimsical folk paintings depicting flora and fauna that evoke the work of French artist Henri Rousseau.

Folk art and handicrafts are not as widely produced or readily available here as in other Central American countries. However, the dedicated souvenir hunter will have no problem finding the colorful handmade Sarchí oxcarts that have become a symbol of Costa Rica – there are many skilled oxcart-makers in the Central Valley. Indigenous crafts, which include intricately carved and painted masks made by the Boruca, as well

COSTA RICA BY THE BOOK

Costa Rica's history and culture have been detailed in a number of books.

Tycoon's War, by Stephen Dando-Collins, is a well-told tale of US business tycoon Cornelius Vanderbilt's epic struggle to maintain his economic stranglehold over the Central American isthmus. There are hair-raising battle scenes and intriguing personal sketches of protagonists Vanderbilt and William Walker.

Bananas: How United Fruit Company Shaped the World, by Peter Chapman, tells the story of the meteoric rise and inevitable collapse of the megalith known to locals as '*el pulpo*' (the octopus) for its far reach into the echelons of power in Costa Rica and Central America.

Nation Thief, by Robert Houston, is a novelistic telling of William Walker's excursions into Central America, narrated by several of his 'immortals' in the vernacular of the time.

Green Phoenix, by William Allen, details the ultimate victory of a cohort of Costa Rican and US scientists and volunteers in halting deforestation and establishing the over-600-sq-mile Guanacaste Conservation Area.

Walking with Wolf, by Kay Chornook and Wolf Guindon, recounts the life of one of Monteverde's pioneering Quakers and his decades-long dedication to preserving and sharing his adopted cloud-forest home.

Cocorí, by Joaquín Guitiérrez, is an illustrated tapestry of life lessons gleaned by a young boy in the rainforest. Recounted by Costa Rica's most famous author, this children's book, first published in 1947 and translated worldwide, is required reading for Tico students, though some Afro-Caribbean Costa Ricans find the portrayal of the young protagonist offensive and racist.

Monkeys Are Made of Chocolate: Exotic and Unseen Costa Rica, by Jack Ewing, presents evocative descriptions of Costa Rica's natural world alongside details of ecosystems, environmentalism, and the author's observations from living in the country for more than 30 years.

Guanacaste: Rutas de Viaje (Travel Routes), by Luciano Capelli and Yazmin Ross, is a stunning coffee-table book of the province's festivals, farmers and frogs, among other things. It's a lovely record of your trip here.

DGPHOTO/GETTY IMAGES ©

YANNICK MARTINEZ/SHUTTERSTOCK ©

Top Painted *carreta* (oxcart) wheel, Sarchí (p116)

Bottom Boruca wood carving

Chorotega pottery

as handwoven bags and linens and colorful Chorotega pottery, can also be found in San José and more readily along Costa Rica's Pacific coast.

Film

Artistically, while film is not a new medium in Costa Rica, young filmmakers have been upping the country's ante in this arena. Over the last decade or so, a handful of Costa Rican filmmakers have submitted their work for Oscar consideration, and many others have received critical acclaim for their pictures nationally and internationally. Films include the adaptation of Gabriel García Márquez's magical-realism novel *Del amor y otro demonios* (Of Love and Other Demons, 2009), directed by Hilda Hidalgo; a comedic coming-of-age story of young Ticos on the cusp of adulthood in contemporary Costa Rica in *El cielo rojo* (The Red Sky, 2008), written and directed by Miguel Alejandro Gomez; and the light-hearted story of a Costa Rican farmer who embarks on the journey to Europe to raise money to avoid losing his farm in *Maikol Yordan de viaje perdido* (Maikol Yordan Traveling Lost, 2014), also directed by Gomez. More recently, the 2016 rom-com *About Us (Entonces nosotros)*, directed by Hernan Jimenez, sees a couple trying to repair their relationship on a beach getaway, simultaneously making you laugh, cringe and somehow want to be on that beach.

Little of his work is translated into English, but poet Alfonso Chase is a Fulbright scholar and a contemporary literary hero. In 1999 he won the nation's highest literary award, the Premio Magón.

A film-festival calendar has also been blossoming in Costa Rica, though dates vary year on year. Sponsored by the Ministerio de Cultura y Juventud, the Costa Rica Festival Internacional de Cine (www.costaricacinefest.go.cr) takes place in San José (check the website for current dates) and features international films fitting the year's theme. The longer-running Costa Rica International Film Festival (CRIFF; www.filmfestivallife.com) takes place annually, check the website for dates.

Survival Guide

Directory A–Z

Accessible Travel

Independent travel in Costa Rica is difficult for anyone with mobility constraints. Although Costa Rica has an equal-opportunity law, the law applies only to new or newly remodeled businesses and is loosely enforced. Therefore, some hotels and restaurants have features specifically suited to wheelchair use. However, many don't have ramps, and room or bathroom doors are rarely wide enough to accommodate a wheelchair.

Streets and sidewalks are potholed and poorly paved, making wheelchair use frustrating at best. Public buses don't have provisions to carry wheelchairs, and most national parks and outdoor tourist attractions don't have trails suited to wheelchair use. Notable exceptions include Carara National Park and Manuel Antonio National Park (both of which have a wheelchair-accessible trail) and Poás Volcano National Park.

The hearing-impaired will find most museums have signs and info boards explaining exhibits. However, at most museums, these will be in Spanish only. Audio guides are available at few museums for the visually impaired.

Download Lonely Planet's free Accessible Travel guide from https://shop.lonelyplanet.com/categories/accessible-travel.

Climate

San José

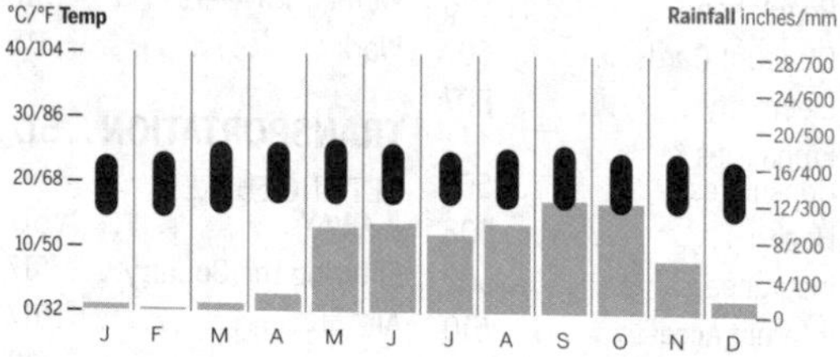

Puerto Limón

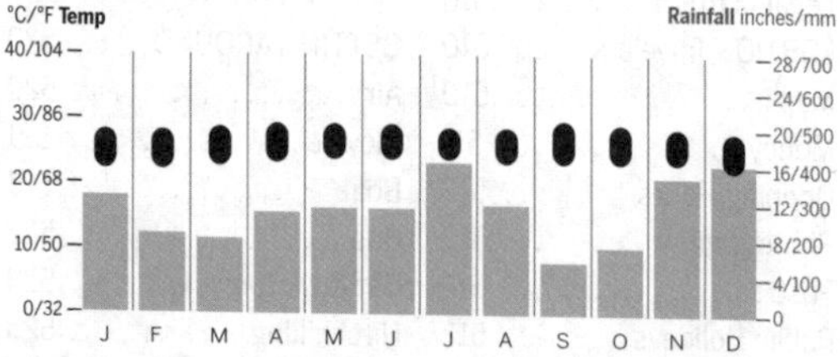

Puntarenas

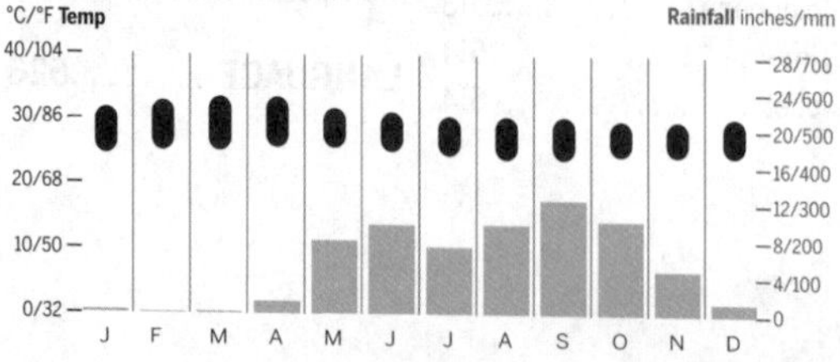

Customs Regulations

- All travelers over the age of 18 are allowed to enter the country with 5L of wine or spirits and 500g of processed tobacco (roughly 400 cigarettes or 50 cigars).
- Camera gear, binoculars, and camping, snorkeling and other sporting equipment

are readily allowed into the country.

- Dogs and cats are permitted entry to Costa Rica providing they have obtained both general-health and rabies-vaccination certificates.
- Pornography and illicit drugs are prohibited.

Discount Cards

Note that discount cards are not universally accepted at museums and parks.

International Student Identity Card (ISIC; www.isic.org; around US$16 depending on country of origin) Discounts on museum and tour fees for any full-time student.

International Student Exchange (ISE; www.isecard.com; from US$9 depending on country of origin) Discounts on museums and tour fees for full-time and part-time students between 12 and 26 years old, and also for faculty.

Electricity

Embassies & Consulates

Australia and New Zealand do not have consular representation in Costa Rica; their closest embassies are in Mexico City. Most countries are represented in San José. Mornings are the best time to go to embassies and consulates.

Canadian Embassy (2242-4400; www.costarica.gc.ca; Oficentro Ejecutivo La Sabana, 3rd fl, Edificio 5, Sabana Sur; 7:30am-4pm Mon-Thu, to 1pm Fri) Behind La Contraloría.

Dutch Embassy (Netherlands Embassy; 2296-1490; www.nederlandwereldwijd.nl/landen/costa-rica; Oficentro La Sabana, Edificio 3, 3rd fl, Sabana Sur; 7:30am-4:30pm Mon-Thu, to 12:30pm Fri)

French Embassy (2234-4201, 2234-4167; www.ambafrance-cr.org; Av 22, Curridabat; 7:30am-12:30pm Mon-Fri) On the A022, off the D022 (a smaller road off Rte 2, the road to Curridabat).

German Embassy (2290-9091; www.san-jose.diplo.de; 8th fl, Edificio Torre Sabana, Sabana Norte; 8am-noon Mon-Fri) Northwest of Parque Metropolitano La Sabana.

Guatemalan Embassy (2220-1297, 2291-6172; www.minex.gob.gt; Calle 64, Sabana Sur; 9am-1pm Mon-Fri) Southwest Parque Metropolitano La Sabana.

Honduran Embassy (2231-5145, 2231-9506; www.embajadahonduras.co.cr; Blvr Rohrmoser, Av 1, near Calle 72; 9am-noon & 1:30-4pm Mon-Fri)

Israeli Embassy (2221-6444; 11th fl, Edificio Colón, Paseo Colón, btwn Calles 38 & 40; 9am-noon Mon-Fri)

Italian Embassy (2224-6574, 2224-1082; www.ambsanjose.esteri.it; Calle 43, Los Yoses; 9am-noon Mon-Fri) Between Avs 2 and 8.

Mexican Embassy (2257-0633; https://embamex.sre.gob.mx/costarica; Av 7, btwn Calles 13 & 15, 50m east of Casa Amarilla; 8am-5pm Mon-Fri) Northwest of Parque National.

Nicaraguan Embassy (2222-7896, 2233-8001; Av Central 2540, btwn Calles 25 & 27; 8am-4pm Mon-Fri) On the corner of 25A, in Carmen (San José).

Panamanian Embassy (2281-2442; www.facebook.com/EmbajadadePanamaenCostaRica; cnr Av 10 & Calle 69, Barrio La Granja; 9am-2pm Mon-Fri) A block north of Parque El Retiro in San Pedro (San José).

Spanish Embassy (2222-1933, 2222-5745; www.exteriores.gob.es; Calle 32, btwn Paseo Colón & Av 2; 8am-3:30pm Mon-Fri)

Swiss Embassy (2221-4829; www.eda.admin.ch/sanjose; 10th fl, Edificio Centro Colón, Paseo Colón, btwn Calles 38 & 40; 8am-noon Mon-Fri)

UK Embassy (2258-2025; www.gov.uk/government/world/organisations/british-embassy-in-costa-rica; 11th fl, Edificio Centro Colón, Paseo Colón, btwn Calles 38 & 40; 8am-noon & 12:15-4pm Mon-Thu, 8am-1pm Fri)

EATING PRICE RANGES

The following price ranges refer to a standard meal. Unless otherwise stated, tax is included in the price.

$ less than US$10

$$ US$10–20

$$$ more than US$20

US Embassy (☎2519-2000; https://cr.usembassy.gov; Pavas, cnr Calle 98 & Via 104; ⊗8am-noon & 1-4pm Mon-Fri)

Health

Travelers to Central America need to be vigilant about food- and mosquito-borne infections. The majority of the illnesses most frequently caught while on holiday here are not life-threatening, but they can certainly ruin your trip. Besides getting the proper vaccinations, it's important to use a good insect repellent and exercise care in what you eat and drink.

Before You Go

HEALTH INSURANCE

High-risk adventure activities or water sports such as diving are not covered on all travel policies, so make sure you pay for the appropriate level of insurance coverage. Yours may cover basic activities, such as walking, but not ziplining or surfing. If diving, some companies may only cover you up to a certain number of dives or a certain depth. If unsure, check with your insurer before leaving your home country.

A list of medical-evacuation and travel-insurance companies can be found on the US State Department (www.travel.state.gov) website under the International Travel 'Before You Go' tab.

RECOMMENDED VACCINATIONS

➡ Get necessary vaccinations four to eight weeks before departure.

➡ Ask your doctor for an International Certificate of Vaccination (otherwise known as the 'Yellow Card'), which will list all the vaccinations you've received. This is mandatory for countries that require proof of yellow-fever vaccination upon entry (Costa Rica only requires such proof if you are entering from a country that carries a risk of yellow fever – check if your country of origin has a risk of yellow fever before you travel).

In Costa Rica

AVAILABILITY & COST OF HEALTH CARE

➡ Good medical care is available in most major cities but may be limited in rural areas.

➡ For an extensive list of physicians, dentists and hospitals, visit https://cr.usembassy.gov and look under 'U.S. Citizen Services/Medical Assistance/Medical Practitioners List.'

➡ Most pharmacies are well supplied and a handful are open 24 hours. Pharmacists are licensed to prescribe medication. If you're taking any medication on a regular basis, make sure you know its generic (scientific) name, since many pharmaceuticals go under different names in Costa Rica.

INFECTIOUS DISEASES

Chikungunya virus The newest mosquito-borne viral disease was accidentally introduced to Costa Rica from Africa, and carried from *Aedes albopictus* (Tiger mosquitoes). The symptoms are similar to those of dengue fever (high fever, joint inflammation, a skin rash, headache, muscle aches, nausea), and so are the treatments – replace fluids, reduce fever and wait it out. Unlike dengue, it's very unlikely to be fatal, and once you get it you'll probably develop an immunity. The best prevention is to cover up with long sleeves and DEET.

Dengue fever (breakbone fever) Dengue is transmitted by *Aedes aegypti* mosquitoes, which often bite during the daytime and are usually found close to human habitations, often indoors. Dengue is especially common in densely populated urban environments. It usually causes flu-like symptoms including fever, muscle aches, joint pains, headaches, nausea and vomiting, often followed by a rash. Most cases resolve uneventfully in a few days. There is no treatment for dengue fever except taking analgesics such as acetaminophen/paracetamol (Tylenol) and drinking plenty of fluids. Severe cases may require hospitalization for intravenous fluids and supportive care. There is no vaccine. The key to prevention is taking insect-protection measures.

Hepatitis A The second most common travel-related infection (after traveler's diarrhea). It's a viral infection of the liver that is usually acquired by ingestion of contaminated water, food or ice, though it may also be acquired by direct contact with infected persons. Symptoms may include fever, malaise, jaundice, nausea, vomiting and abdominal pain. Most cases resolve without complications, though hepatitis A occasionally causes severe liver damage. There is no treatment. The vaccine for hepatitis A is extremely safe and highly effective.

Leishmaniasis This is transmitted by sand flies. Most cases occur in newly cleared forest or areas of secondary growth; the highest incidence is in Talamanca. It causes slow-growing ulcers on overexposed parts of the body. There is no vaccine. To protect yourself from sand flies, follow the same precautions as for mosquitoes.

Malaria Malaria is very rare in Costa Rica, occurring only occasionally in rural parts of Limón Province. It's transmitted by mosquito bites, usually between dusk and dawn. Taking malaria pills is not necessary unless you are making a long stay in the province of Limón (not Puerto Limón). Protection against mosquito bites is most effective.

Traveler's diarrhea Tap water is safe and of high quality in Costa Rica, but when you're far off the beaten path it's best to avoid tap water unless it has been boiled, filtered or chemically disinfected (with iodine tablets). To prevent diarrhea, be wary of dairy products that might contain unpasteurized milk and be highly selective when eating food from street vendors. If you develop diarrhea, be sure to drink plenty of fluids, preferably with an oral rehydration solution containing lots of salt and sugar. If diarrhea is bloody or persists for more than 72 hours, or is accompanied by fever, shaking chills or severe abdominal pain, seek medical attention.

Typhoid Caused by ingestion of food or water contaminated by a species of salmonella known as *Salmonella typhi*. Fever occurs in virtually all cases. Other symptoms may include headache, malaise, muscle aches, dizziness, loss of appetite, nausea and abdominal pain. Possible complications include intestinal perforation, intestinal bleeding, confusion, delirium or (rarely) coma. A pre-trip vaccination is recommended.

Zika virus At the time of research, there was no evidence of Zika virus, which has been linked to microcephaly, a birth defect that affects a baby's brain development. Zika is primarily transmitted by mosquitoes, but it can also be transmitted by a man to his sexual partner or by a woman to her fetus. Be aware that symptoms are usually mild in adults, and many people may not realize that they are infected.

For a full list of potential risks, see the CDC website's Costa Rica page at https://wwwnc.cdc.gov/travel/destinations/traveler/none/costa-rica.

ENVIRONMENTAL HAZARDS

Animal bites Do not attempt to pet, handle or feed any animal. Any bite or scratch by a mammal, including bats, should be promptly and thoroughly cleansed with large amounts of soap and water, and an antiseptic such as iodine or alcohol should be applied. Contact a local health authority in the event of such an injury. Rabies cases are rare but do happen.

Poison-dart frogs They are very colorful and may be tempting to touch, but don't. These colors serve as a warning. Their skin secretes toxins and may cause swelling, nausea and even muscular paralysis, and sometimes death, depending on the species of the frog.

Snakes When trekking in thick forest terrain wear long pants (trousers) and closed-toed shoes to help prevent encounters with camouflaged snakes on grass and tree branches.

Insect bites No matter how much you safeguard yourself, getting bitten by mosquitoes is part of every traveler's experience here. The best prevention is to stay covered up – wear long pants, long sleeves, a hat and shoes, not sandals. Invest in a good insect repellent, preferably one containing 20% DEET. Apply to exposed skin and clothing (but not to eyes, mouth, cuts, wounds or irritated skin). Compounds containing DEET should not be used on children under the age of two and should be used sparingly on children under 12 years. Invest in a bug net to hang over beds (along with a few thumbtacks or nails with which to hang it). Many hotels in Costa Rica don't have windows (or screens), and a cheap little net will save you plenty of nighttime aggravation. The mesh size should be less than 1.5mm. Dusk is the worst time for mosquitoes, so take extra precautions then.

Sun Stay out of the midday sun, wear sunglasses and a wide-brimmed hat, and apply sunblock with SPF 15 or higher, with both UVA and UVB protection and reapply often, especially if getting in the sea or rivers. Drink plenty of fluids and avoid strenuous exercise when the temperature is high.

Insurance

It's vital that travelers purchase the right type of travel insurance before coming to Costa Rica. Basic insurance tends to cover medical expenses, baggage loss, trip cancellation, accidents and personal liability, but it's worth spending extra to make sure you're covered in the event of natural disasters. If you intend to take part

TAP WATER

➡ It's generally safe to drink tap water in Costa Rica, except in the most rural and undeveloped parts of the country. However, if you prefer to be cautious, buying bottled water is your best bet.

➡ If you have the means, vigorous boiling for one minute is the most effective means of water purification. At altitudes greater than 2000m, boil for three minutes.

➡ Another option is to disinfect water with iodine pills: add 2% tincture of iodine to 1L of water (five drops to clear water, 10 drops to cloudy water) and let stand for 30 minutes. If the water is cold, longer times may be required.

➡ Alternatively, carry a SteriPen that destroys most bacteria, viruses and protozoa with UV light or a purifying water bottle or straw.

WHAT'S THAT ADDRESS?

Though some larger cities have streets that have been dutifully named, signage is rare in Costa Rica and finding a Tico who knows what street they are standing on is even rarer. Everybody uses landmarks when providing directions; an address may be given as 200m south and 150m east of a church. A city block is *cien metros* – literally 100m – so 250 *metros al sur* means '2½ blocks south,' regardless of the distance. Churches, parks, office buildings, fast-food joints and car dealerships are the most common landmarks used – but these are often meaningless to the foreign traveler, who will have no idea where the Subaru dealership is to begin with. Even more confusingly, Ticos frequently refer to landmarks that no longer exist. In San Pedro, outside San José, locals still use the site of an old fig tree *(el antiguo higuerón)* to provide directions.

Confused? Get used to it...

in adventure sports, make sure that those particular sports are covered by your policy; for divers, some policies only cover you up to a certain depth.

Internet Access

- The number of internet cafes in Costa Rica has greatly decreased with the advent of smartphones, and wi-fi in restaurants and cafes.
- Expect to pay US$1 to US$2 per hour at internet cafes in San José and tourist towns.
- Wi-fi is common in all midrange and top-end hotels, and in the vast majority of cafes, budget hotels and hostels. Some hostels still have computers for guest use and/or wi-fi.

Language Courses

- Spanish-language schools operate all over Costa Rica and charge by the hour for instruction.
- Many courses can be found in central San José and the suburb of San Pedro, and the Central Valley.
- It's best to arrange classes in advance. A good clearinghouse is the **Institute for Spanish Language Studies** (ISLS; ☎505-404-0736, in USA 866-391-0394; www.isls.com; 16hr group courses per week from US$280), which has eight schools in Costa Rica.

Legal Matters

- If you are arrested, your embassy can offer limited assistance. Embassy officials will not bail you out, but can contact a lawyer on your behalf. You are subject to Costa Rican laws, not the laws of your own country.
- The use of recreational substances other than tobacco and alcohol is illegal in Costa Rica and punishable by imprisonment.

LGBTIQ+ Travelers

Costa Rica is miles ahead in terms of tolerance compared with other Central American countries, and some areas of the country – particularly Quepos and Parque Nacional Manuel Antonio – have been gay vacation destinations for two decades. Homosexual acts are legal, and in 2015 Costa Rica became the first country in Central America to recognize same-sex relationships. On 26 May 2020, same-sex marriage became legal. Same-sex couples are unlikely to be the subject of harassment, though same-sex affection is rarely seen in smaller towns and might attract unwanted attention, as some cultural attitudes remain behind the times.

The undisputed gay and lesbian capital of Costa Rica is Manuel Antonio; visit https://gaymanuelantonio.com for info on the scene.

Center of Investigation & Promotion of Human Rights in Central America (CIPAC; ☎2280-7821; www.cipacdh.org) The leading gay activist organization in Costa Rica.

Toto Tours (☎USA 773-274-8686; www.tototours.com) Gay-travel specialist that organizes regular trips to Costa Rica, among other destinations.

Maps

Detailed maps are hard (but not impossible) to come by in Costa Rica, so for ease it's best to purchase one online before your trip.

- The excellent, water-resistant 1:350,000 *Costa Rica Adventure Map* published by National Geographic also has an inset map of San José. Available online or in various book and gift shops in San José.
- Another quality option is the 1:330,000 *Costa Rica* sheet produced by International Travel Map, which is waterproof and includes a San José inset.
- Few national-park offices or ranger stations have maps for hikers.
- *Waterproof Travel Map Of Costa Rica* by Toucan Maps is a robust overview map of the country, with detailed 4WD seasonal roads marked, plus highlighted beaches, national parks and attractions. It also has zoomed-in maps of

Arenal, Monteverde, Manuel Antonio. Available online.

➡ **Instituto Geográfico Nacional** (IGN; ☎2202-0777; www.registronacional.go.cr/instituto_geografico/index.htm; Ruta 215, San Gerardo, Zapote District; ⏲8:30am-3:30pm Mon-Fri) in San José has topographical maps available for purchase.

➡ Incafo formerly published the *Mapa-Guía de la Naturaleza Costa Rica*, an atlas that included 1:200,000 topographical sheets, as well as English and Spanish descriptions of Costa Rica's natural areas. Used copies can be purchased online.

Money

ATMs

ATMs are ubiquitous, typically dispensing colones; many dispense US dollars. They are not as easily found in rural and remote areas.

Bargaining

➡ A high standard of living along with a stream of international tourist traffic means that the Latin American tradition of haggling is uncommon in Costa Rica.

➡ Negotiating prices at outdoor markets is acceptable, as is bargaining when arranging informal tours or hiring long-distance taxis.

Cash & Currency

➡ The Costa Rican currency is the colón (plural colones), named after Cristóbal Colón (Christopher Columbus).

➡ Bills come in 1000-, 2000-, 5000-, 10,000-, 20,000- and 50,000-colón notes, while coins come in denominations of five, 10, 20, 25, 50, 100 and 500 colones.

➡ Paying for things in US dollars is common, and at times is encouraged, since the currency is viewed as being more stable than the colón.

➡ In US-dollar transactions the change will usually be given in colones.

➡ Newer US dollars are preferred throughout Costa Rica; if your note has a rip in it, it may not be accepted.

➡ When paying in US dollars at a local restaurant, bar or shop, the exchange rate can be unfavorable.

Changing Money

All banks will exchange US dollars, and some will exchange euros and British pounds; other currencies are more difficult. Most banks have excruciatingly long lines, especially at the state-run institutions (Banco Nacional, Banco de Costa Rica, Banco Popular). Make sure the bills you want to exchange are in good condition or they may be refused.

Credit Cards

➡ Cards are widely accepted at midrange and top-end hotels, as well as at top-end restaurants and some travel agencies; they are less likely to be accepted in small towns and in remote areas.

➡ A transaction fee (around 3% to 5%) on all international credit-card purchases is often added.

➡ Holders of credit and debit cards can buy colones in some banks, though expect to pay a high transaction fee.

➡ All car-rental agencies require drivers to have a credit card. It's possible to hire a car with just a debit card, but only on the condition that you pay for full insurance and leave a large deposit for traffic violations (check with the car-rental company ahead of time).

Taxes & Refunds

Travelers will notice an extra 13% sales tax at hotels and restaurants, although many smaller budget and midrange businesses have been known to waive the tax if you pay in cash, others simply include it in the price.

Some basic foods will incur a 1% tax, while a 4% value-added tax (VAT) applies to airfares, health-care services and medical products.

Tipping

Guides Tip guides US$5 to US$20 per person per day. Tip the tour driver about half of what you tip the guide.

Hotels Tip the bellhop/porter US$1 to US$5 per service and the housekeeper US$1 to US$2 per day in top-end hotels; less in budget places.

Restaurants Bills usually include a 10% service charge. If not, you might leave a small tip.

Taxis Tip only if special service is provided.

DOLLARS VERSUS COLONES

While colones are the official currency of Costa Rica, US dollars are virtually legal tender. Case in point: most ATMs in large towns and cities will dispense both currencies. However, it pays to know where and when you should be paying with each currency.

In Costa Rica you can use US dollars to pay for hotel rooms, midrange to top-end meals, admission fees for sights, tours, domestic flights, international buses, car rental, private shuttle buses and big-ticket purchases. Local meals and drinks, domestic bus fares, taxis and small purchases should be paid for in colones.

Traveler's Checks

With the popularity of ATMs and credit cards, traveler's checks are increasingly uncommon in Costa Rica and difficult to exchange outside big cities. They can be exchanged at banks, typically only for US dollars or Costa Rican colones.

Opening Hours

The following are high-season opening hours; hours will generally shorten in the shoulder and low seasons. Generally, sights, activities and restaurants are open daily.

Banks 9am–4pm Monday to Friday, sometimes 9am–noon Saturday

Bars and clubs 8pm–2am

Government offices 8am–5pm Monday to Friday; often closed 11:30am–1:30pm

Restaurants 7am–9pm; upscale places may open only for dinner and in remote areas even the small *sodas* (inexpensive eateries) might open only at specific mealtimes

Shops 9am–6pm Monday to Saturday

Photography

➡ Always ask permission to take someone's photo.

➡ With the prominence of digital cameras, it is increasingly difficult to purchase high-quality film in Costa Rica.

➡ *Lonely Planet's Guide to Travel Photography* is full of helpful tips for photography while on the road.

Post

➡ Mailing smaller parcels (less than 2kg) internationally is quite reliable; for example, a 1kg package costs upwards of US$30 to ship to North America and takes one to two weeks to arrive.

➡ EMS (Express Mail Service) courier service tends to cost a bit more but includes tracking and is speedier.

Public Holidays

Días feriados (national holidays) are taken seriously in Costa Rica. Banks, public offices and many stores close. During these times, public transport is tight and hotels are heavily booked. Many festivals coincide with public holidays.

New Year's Day January 1

Semana Santa Holy Week; March or April. The Thursday and Friday before Easter Sunday is the official holiday, though most businesses shut down for the whole week. From Thursday to Sunday bars are closed and alcohol sales are prohibited; on Thursday and Friday buses stop running.

Día de Juan Santamaría April 11. Honors the national hero who died fighting William Walker in 1856; major events are held in Alajuela, his hometown.

Labor Day May 1

Día de la Madre Mother's Day; August 15. Coincides with the annual Catholic Feast of the Assumption.

Costa Rican Independence Day September 15

Día de la Raza Columbus Day; October 12.

Christmas Day December 25. Christmas Eve is also an unofficial holiday.

Last week in December The week between Christmas and New Year is an unofficial holiday; businesses close and beach hotels are crowded.

PRACTICALITIES

Media

La Nación (www.nacion.com) Spanish-language daily newspaper.

La Prensa Libre (www.laprensalibre.cr) Launched in 1889, this is the oldest continually published daily newspaper in Costa Rica. Spanish language.

Tico Times (www.ticotimes.net) Costa Rica's online English-language newspaper. It's high quality. News and views are often geared toward the expat community.

Costa Rican Times (www.costaricantimes.com) This online, English-language newcomer focuses on Costa Rican happenings but also features international news.

DVDs In Costa Rica DVDs are region 4.

Weights & Measures

➡ The metric system is used.

Safe Travel

Costa Rica is a largely safe country, but petty crime (bag snatchings, car break-ins etc) is common and muggings do occur, so it's important to be vigilant.

➡ Many of Costa Rica's dangers are nature-related: riptides, earthquakes and volcanic eruptions are among them.

➡ Predatory and venomous wildlife can also pose a threat, so a wildlife guide is essential if trekking in the jungle.

Earthquakes & Volcanic Eruptions

Costa Rica lies on the edge of active tectonic plates, so it is decidedly earthquake-prone. Recent major quakes occurred in 1990 (7.1 on the Richter scale), 1991 (7.4) and 2012 (7.6). Smaller quakes and tremors happen quite often (one area that sees particularly frequent seismic activity is the Península de Nicoya), cracking roads and knocking down telephone lines.

Two of the most popular volcanoes in Costa Rica, Poás and Turrialba, have been very active recently with a number of eruptions of varying degrees since 2014 and 2018. Due to safety concerns, the national parks surrounding Turrialba were closed at the time of research. Check the status of each volcano before you visit.

Hiking Hazards

Hikers setting out into the wilderness should be adequately prepared.

- Know your limits and don't attempt a hike you can't reasonably complete.
- Carry plenty of water, even on very short trips.
- Take maps, extra food and a compass.
- Let someone know where you are going, so they can narrow the search area in the event of an emergency.
- Be aware that Costa Rica's wildlife can pose a threat to hikers, particularly in Parque Nacional Corcovado. The best policy is to look at but not touch or feed the wildlife.

Riptides

Each year Costa Rican waters see more than 100 drownings, many of which are caused by riptides (strong currents that pull the swimmer in different directions). Many deaths due to riptides are caused by panicked swimmers struggling to the point of exhaustion. If you are caught in a riptide, do not struggle. Swim parallel to shore; eventually the riptide will dissipate. Alternatively, you can float until the riptide dissipates, then swim parallel to shore and back in where there is no riptide.

Thefts & Muggings

The biggest danger that most travelers face is theft, primarily from pickpockets, but also when personal possessions are left in parked cars. There is a lot of petty crime in Costa Rica, so keep an eye on your belongings and your surroundings at all times.

GOVERNMENT TRAVEL ADVICE

The following government websites offer travel advisories and information on current hot spots.

Australian Department of Foreign Affairs (http://smartraveller.gov.au)

British Foreign Office (www.gov.uk/foreign-travel-advice)

Canadian Department of Foreign Affairs (www.dfait-maeci.gc.ca)

Dutch government (www.nederlandwereldwijd.nl)

French Ministry for Foreign Affairs (www.diplomatie.gouv.fr/en/country-files/costa-rica)

German Federal Foreign Office (www.auswaertiges-amt.de/de)

Japanese Ministry of Foreign Affairs (www.anzen.mofa.go.jp)

New Zealand government (www.safetravel.govt.nz)

US State Department (http://travel.state.gov)

Telephone

- To call Costa Rica from abroad, use the country code (☎506) before the eight-digit number. Costa Rica has no area codes.
- Due to the widespread popularity of internet-based services, such as Skype, WhatsApp and iChat, calls with a smartphone or tablet can be free over wi-fi (or cheapest using a local internet provider) and are the easiest way to call internationally.
- SIM cards are available at large supermarkets and phone shops; providers include Kolbi (state-owned), Claro, Movistar and TuYo. Some networks have better coverage than others. Top-ups are easy and possible with numerous recharge services in English online.
- To buy an internet package SIM you may need your passport to register. Your phone will also need to be unlocked before you arrive in Costa Rica.
- Cell (mobile) service now covers most of the country and nearly all of the country that is accessible to tourists.
- Public phones are slowly being retired, but if you search they can still be found around Costa Rica. Chip phone cards are available from local shops. Payphones cannot receive international calls.
- Chip cards are inserted into the phone and scanned. Colibrí cards (more common) require you to dial a toll-free number (☎199) and enter an access code.

SEX TRADE

Exit the baggage claim at the international airport in San José and you may be welcomed by signs that read 'In Costa Rica sex with children under 18 is a serious crime. Should you engage in it we will drive you to jail.' For decades, travelers have arrived in Costa Rica in search of sandy beaches and lush mountainscapes; unfortunately, an unknown percentage of them also come in search of sex – not all of it legal.

Prostitution by men and women over the age of 18 is legal. With the tourist juggernaut of the last few decades has come unwanted illicit activities at its fringes – namely child prostitution and human trafficking. Sex with a minor in Costa Rica is illegal, carrying a penalty of up to 10 years in jail, but child prostitution is rife. In fact, a number of aid groups, along with the country's national child-welfare agency (Patronato Nacional de la Infancia; PANI), estimate that there may be thousands of child prostitutes in San José alone. In turn, this has led to women and children being trafficked for the purpose of sexual exploitation, as documented in a 2008 report issued by the US Department of State.

Alarm over the problem has increased steadily since 1999, when the UN Committee on Human Rights issued a statement saying that it was 'deeply concerned' about child-sex tourism in Costa Rica. Since then, the government has established national task forces to combat the problem, trained the police force in how to deal with issues of child exploitation and formed a coalition against human trafficking. But enforcement remains weak – largely due to lack of personnel and lack of funding. Meanwhile the US – the principal source of sex tourists to Costa Rica – has made it a prosecutable crime for its citizens to have sex with minors anywhere in the world.

Along with Thailand and Cambodia, Costa Rica is one of the most popular sex-tourism destinations in the world, according to Ecpat International, a nonprofit dedicated to ending child prostitution. The phenomenon has been magnified by the internet: entire sex-tourism websites chronicle – in detail – where and how to find sex. In all of these, Costa Rica figures prominently.

Various organizations fight the sexual exploitation of children in Costa Rica. See the websites of Ecpat International (www.ecpat.org) and Cybertipline (www.cybertip.org) to learn more about the problem or to report any incidents you encounter.

Instructions are provided in English or Spanish.

- Cheap international calls from Costa Rica can be direct-dialed using a phone card. To make international calls, dial '☎00' followed by the country code and number.

Time

Costa Rica is six hours behind GMT, so Costa Rican time is equivalent to Central Time in North America. There is no daylight saving time.

Toilets

- Public restrooms are rare, but most restaurants and cafes will let you use their facilities, sometimes for a small charge – never more than 500 colones.
- Bus terminals and other major public buildings usually have toilets, also at a charge.
- Don't flush your toilet paper. Costa Rican plumbing is often poor and has very low pressure.
- Dispose of toilet paper in the rubbish bin inside the bathroom.

Tourist Information

- The government-run Costa Rica Tourism Board, the ICT (www.ict.go.cr/en), has an office in the capital; English is spoken.
- The ICT can provide you with free maps, a master bus schedule, information on road conditions in the hinterlands and a helpful brochure with up-to-date emergency numbers for every region.
- Consult the ICT's English-language website for information.

Visas

Passport-carrying nationals from the following countries are allowed 90 days' stay with no visa: Argentina, Australia, Brazil, Canada, Chile, Ireland, Israel, Japan, Mexico, New Zealand, Panama, South Africa, UAE, USA and most Western European countries.

Some visitors from other nations require a visa from a Costa Rican embassy or consulate.

For the latest info on visas, check the websites of the ICT (www.ict.go.cr/en) or the Costa Rican embassy (www.costarica-embassy.org).

Extensions

- Extending your stay beyond the authorized 30 or 90 days is time-consuming; it's often easier to leave the country for 72 hours via land and then re-enter.
- Extensions can be handled by **migración offices** (Juan Santamaria International Airport 2299-8001, Puerto Limón 2798-2097, Puntarenas 2661-1446, San José 2299-8100; www.migracion.go.cr).
- Requirements for extensions change, so allow several working days.

Volunteering

Costa Rica offers a huge number of volunteer opportunities. Word of mouth is a powerful influence on future participants, so the majority of programs in Costa Rica are very conscientious about pleasing their volunteers. Almost all placements require a commitment of two weeks or more.

Lonely Planet does not vouch for any organization that we do not work with directly, and we strongly recommend travelers always investigate a volunteer opportunity themselves to assess the standards and suitability of the project.

Teaching & Training Abroad

Amerispan Study Abroad (www.amerispan.com) Offers a variety of educational travel programs in specialized areas.

One World (www.oneworld365.org) Arranges teaching gigs in Costa Rica and other destinations.

Projects Abroad (www.projects-abroad.co.uk) Organizes work placements for people seeking work experience in different fields.

Forestry Management

Cloudbridge Nature Reserve (www.cloudbridge.org) Trail building, construction, tree planting and projects monitoring the recovery of the cloud forest are offered to volunteers, who pay for their own housing with a local family. Preference is given to biology students, but all volunteers can apply.

Fundación Corcovado (www.corcovadofoundation.org) A network of people and organizations committed to preserving Parque Nacional Corcovado.

Monteverde Institute (www.monteverde-institute.org) A nonprofit educational institute offering training in tropical biology, conservation and sustainable development.

Tropical Science Center (www.cct.or.cr) This long-standing NGO offers volunteer placement at Reserva Biológica Bosque Nuboso Monteverde. Projects can include trail maintenance and conservation work.

Organic Farming

Alegria Village (www.alegriavillage.com) A community growing organic produce that invites the public for tours and big dinners using produce from the farm.

Finca La Flor de Paraíso (www.fincalaflor.org) Offers programs in a variety of disciplines, from animal husbandry to medicinal-herb cultivation.

Punta Mona (www.puntamona.org) An organic farm and retreat center that focuses on organic permaculture and sustainable living.

Rancho Margot (www.ranchomargot.com) This self-proclaimed 'life-skills university' offers a natural education emphasizing organic farming and animal husbandry.

WWOOF Costa Rica (https://wwoofindependents.org) This loose group of farms is part of the large international network of Willing Workers on Organic Farms (WWOOF). Placements are incredibly varied. WWOOF Mexico, Costa Rica, Guatemala and Belize have a single/joint US$26/40 membership, which gives potential volunteers access to all placement listings.

Wildlife Conservation

Be aware that conservationists in Costa Rica occasionally face harassment or worse from local poachers and that police are pretty ineffectual in following up incidents.

Asociacion Salvemos las Tortugas de Parismina (ASTOP, Save the Turtles of Parismina; 2798-2220, 8357-2862; www.parisminaturtles.org; by arrangement Mar-Sep) Helps to protect turtles and their eggs, and improve quality of life for villagers in this tiny community.

Earthwatch (www.earthwatch.org) This broadly recognized international volunteer organization works in sea-turtle conservation in Costa Rica.

Las Pumas (www.centrorescatelaspumas.org) A feline-conservation program that takes care of confiscated wild cats, both big and small.

Reserva Playa Tortuga (www.reservaplayatortuga.org) Assists with olive-ridley-turtle conservation efforts near Ojochal.

Sea Turtle Conservancy (www.conserveturtles.org). This Tortuguero organization hosts 'eco-volunteer adventures' working with sea turtles and birds.

Women Travelers

- Most female travelers will experience a 'mi amor' ('my love') or unwanted glances from local men. Ticas (female Costa Ricans) ignore these advances completely. Many Costa Rican men consider foreign women to have looser morals and to be easier conquests than Ticas, and blondes and single women might have the worst of it, though women traveling together are not exempt.

- In small highland towns, the dress is usually conservative. Women rarely wear shorts, but belly-baring tops are all the rage. Bathing suits are common on public beaches; topless and nude bathing is not allowed.
- We don't recommend hitchhiking (p525). There have been cases of solo women being attacked when hitchhiking.
- Assaults on women by unlicensed taxi drivers have taken place. Travelers should avoid unlicensed 'pirate' taxis where possible (licensed taxis are red and have medallions).
- Some travelers have reported that their drinks have been spiked in bars. It's advisable for travelers to keep a watchful eye on open drinks, and don't leave them unattended, with strangers or accept drinks from strangers. There have been recent reports of spiked drinks in touristy places such as Jacó.

Work

It is difficult for foreigners to find work in Costa Rica. The only foreigners legally employed in Costa Rica are those who work for their own businesses, possess skills not found in the country, or work for companies that have special agreements with the government.

Getting a bona fide job necessitates obtaining a work permit, which can be a time-consuming and difficult process. The most likely source of paid employment is as an English teacher at one of the language institutes, or working in the hospitality industry in a hotel or resort. Naturalists or river guides may also be able to find work with private lodges or adventure-travel operators, though you shouldn't expect to make more than survival wages.

Transportation

GETTING THERE & AWAY

Costa Rica can be reached via frequent, direct international flights from the US and Canada and from other Central American countries. You can also cross a land border into Costa Rica from Panama or Nicaragua. Flights, cars and tours can be booked online at lonelyplanet.com/bookings.

Entering the Country

- Entering Costa Rica is mostly free of hassle, with the exception of some long queues at the airport.
- The vast majority of travelers enter the country by plane, and most international flights arrive at Aeropuerto Internacional Juan Santamaría, just outside San José.
- Liberia is a growing destination for international flights; it is in the Guanacaste province and serves travelers heading to the Península de Nicoya.
- Overland border crossings (p518) are straightforward and, with the correct documentation, travelers can move freely between Panama to the south and Nicaragua to the north.
- Some foreign nationals will require a visa (p514). Be aware that you cannot get a visa at the border.

Passports

- Citizens of all nations are required to have a passport that is valid for at least six months beyond the dates of their trip.
- The law requires that you carry your passport at all times; if you're driving, you must have your passport handy, but otherwise the law is seldom enforced.

Onward Ticket

- Officially, travelers are required to have a ticket out of Costa Rica before they are allowed to enter. This is rarely and erratically enforced.
- Those arriving overland with no onward ticket can purchase one from international bus companies in Managua (Nicaragua) and Panama City (Panama).

Air

Costa Rica is well connected by air to other Central and South American countries, as well as the US.

Airports & Airlines

Aeropuerto Internacional Juan Santamaría (SJO; ☎2437-2400; www.fly2sanjose.com) International flights arrive here, 17km northwest of San José, in the town of Alajuela.

Aeropuerto Internacional Daniel Oduber Quirós (LIR; ☎2666-9600; www.lircr.com)

CLIMATE CHANGE & TRAVEL

Every form of transport that relies on carbon-based fuel generates CO_2, the main cause of human-induced climate change. Modern travel is dependent on airplanes, which might use less fuel per mile per person than most cars but travel much greater distances. The altitude at which aircraft emit gases (including CO_2) and particles also contributes to their climate change impact. Many websites offer 'carbon calculators' that allow people to estimate the carbon emissions generated by their journey and, for those who wish to do so, to offset the impact of the greenhouse gases emitted with contributions to portfolios of climate-friendly initiatives throughout the world. Lonely Planet offsets the carbon footprint of all staff and author travel.

DEPARTURE TAX

➡ There is a US$29 departure tax on all international outbound flights, payable in dollars or colones, though most carriers now include it in the ticket price.

➡ If fees are not included in your ticket, travelers will not be allowed through airport security without paying.

This airport in Liberia also receives international flights from the USA, the Americas and Canada. It serves a number of US and Canadian airlines and some charters from London, as well as regional flights from Panama and Nicaragua.

Avianca (part of the Central American airline consortium Grupo TACA; www.avianca.com) The Colombian-owned airline is regarded as the national airline of Costa Rica and flies to the USA, plus Central and Latin America.

Tickets

Airline fares are usually more expensive during the Costa Rican high season (December through April); December and January are the most expensive months to travel.

TO/FROM CENTRAL AMERICA

➡ American Airlines (www.aa.com), Delta (www.delta.com) and United (www.united.com) have connections to Costa Rica from many Central and Latin American countries. Avianca usually offers the most flights on these routes.

➡ Green Airways (https://costaricagreenair.com) was set to launch at the time of research. This carrier intends to plant a tree seed around the Bongo and Ario Rivers for every passenger that flies with them.

➡ Avianca (which subsumed the former TACA airline) offers direct flights to Guatemala City (Guatemala), Panama City (Panama) and San Salvador (El Salvador).

➡ AeroMexico (https://aeromexico.com) has daily flights to Mexico City, and COPA also has multiple flights a day to Panama City. Rates vary considerably according to season and availability.

TO/FROM OTHER COUNTRIES

➡ Flights from Houston, Miami and New York are most common.

➡ From Canada, most travelers to Costa Rica connect through US gateway cities, though Air Canada has direct flights from Toronto.

➡ From the UK, Costa Rica is served by British Airways (two direct flights per week, or daily with typically with at least one stop).

➡ Flights from the UK and Europe connect either in the US, Mexico City or Toronto. High-season fares may still apply during the northern summer, even though this is the beginning of the Costa Rican rainy season.

➡ From Australia and New Zealand, routes usually go through the US or Mexico. Fares are highest in June and July, even though this is the beginning of the rainy season in Costa Rica.

Land

Border Crossings

Costa Rica shares land borders with Nicaragua and Panama. Visas (p514) may be required for certain nationalities, and passports need a six-month validity. There have been reports of towns adding their own entry and exit fees, usually US$1. Some borders require the exact change of US dollar bills; bring them with you as ATMs at the borders are scarce and sometimes empty or out of order.

NICARAGUA

A land border crossing opened in 2015 linking Los Chiles (Nicaragua) to Las Tablillas (Costa Rica). A bridge crosses the Río San Juan just north of the Nicaraguan border.

➡ The **Los Chiles–Las Tablillas border crossing** (2471-1233; www.migracion.go.cr) is open from 8am to 5pm daily (it is advisable to arrive by 4pm).

➡ Hourly buses connect Los Chiles and Las Tablillas (US$1, 15 minutes). There are also direct buses from San José and Ciudad Quesada (San Carlos).

➡ A Costa Rican land exit fee of US$8 is payable at immigration by credit or debit card only (no cash).

➡ After walking across the border, you'll go through Nicaraguan immigration. The entrance fee is US$12, payable in US dollars or cordobas.

➡ After exiting immigration, you can catch a boat up the river or hop on a bus or a *collectivo* (shared transport) to San Carlos (roughly US$2.50, 30 minutes).

➡ If you are entering Costa Rica from Nicaragua, there are three lines in Nicaragua: one for payment (go there first and pay the US$3 municipal tax/exit tax); one for entrance; and one for exiting the country. Situated on the Carretera Interamericana (Pan-American Hwy), Sapoá–Peñas Blancas is a heavily trafficked border station between Nicaragua and Costa Rica.

➡ The **Sapoá–Peñas Blancas border crossing** (2677-0230, www.migracion.go.cr) is open from 6am to midnight.

➡ Crossing the border into Nicaragua at Peñas

Blancas is a highly variable experience, sometimes taking a half hour or less, sometimes taking many hours.

➡ You cannot cross into Nicaragua with a rental car; however, you can leave it at the customs office if you're just going for a quick visit – it'll cost around US$10 per day to have your vehicle watched. However, don't leave anything of value inside.

➡ Costa Rica charges a US$9 land exit fee; be sure to have that cash on hand. You will need a passport with at least six months' validity.

➡ The border posts are about 1km apart. If you're on an international bus (TicaBus), you'll get a lift between posts. Otherwise, you'll have to hoof it. Hordes of generally useless touts will offer to 'guide' you through the simple crossing – let them carry your luggage if you like (keep your eyes on your luggage), but agree on a fee beforehand.

➡ Entering Nicaragua costs US$12, and leaving Nicaragua costs US$3, which must be paid in US dollars. You may be asked to show a proof of exit, such as a return bus ticket or a flight reservation out of Nicaragua. Keep your passport handy but stowed safely away – officials from both countries may ask to see it, and may also ask you where you are staying in Nicaragua.

➡ There are no banks at the border, but there are plenty of money changers hanging around. Rates will be not be to your advantage.

➡ Do not pay anyone for customs forms; this is a scam. The forms are free, but do bring a pen to avoid the hassle of borrowing one.

➡ There's a fairly fabulous duty-free shop waiting for you in Sapoá, the Nicaraguan equivalent of Peñas Blancas. Relax with your purchases on the 45-minute bus ride to Rivas (departing every 45 minutes or so, approximately US$1 – bring small bills, several daily). Rivas is a quiet transport hub, though its well-preserved 17th-century center is worth exploring. If you're good at bargaining (and you will have to bargain hard), there are taxis waiting on the Nicaraguan side of the border to whisk you to Rivas (US$30).

➡ You'll also be charged US$1 to enter the state of Rivas.

➡ Theoretically, if you've already stayed in Costa Rica for 90 days you're supposed to stay in Nicaragua for three days before returning to Costa Rica. Coming back into Costa Rica, you'll pay a US$3 municipal tax/exit tax. Costa Rican officials may query you about how long you plan to stay and base your visa (60 or 90 days) on this information. Importantly, you should have a return ticket home or out of Costa Rica, dated within 90 days.

➡ **Tica Bus** (☎2296-9788, Nicaragua 2298-5500, Panama 314-6385; www.ticabus.com), **Nica Bus** (☎2221-2679, Nicaragua 2222-2276; www.nicabus.com.ni) and **TransNica** (Map p68; ☎2223-4242; www.transnica.com; Calle 22, btwn Avs 3 & 5) all have daily buses that serve points north and south. Regular buses depart Peñas Blancas, on the Costa Rican side, for La Cruz, Liberia and San José.

➡ Note that Peñas Blancas is only a border post, not a town, so there is nowhere to stay.

PANAMA

Note that Panamanian time is one hour ahead of Costa Rican time.

At the time of writing, entry to Panama required proof of US$500 (per person) or a credit card, plus proof of onward travel from Panama (including a bus ticket from Panama back to Costa Rica, if you're not flying out of Panama) and a passport valid for at least six months. If you don't have an onward plane ticket yet, it's possible to purchase a David–San José ticket at the Tracopa office in Paso Canoas.

The Carretera Interamericana at **Paso Canoas** (2732-2150, www.migracion.go.cr) is by far the most frequently used entry and exit point with Panama, and it's open 6am to 10pm Monday to Friday, and to 8pm on weekends.

➡ The border crossing in either direction is at times chaotic and slow.

➡ Get an exit stamp from Costa Rica at the immigration office before entering Panama; do the same on the Panamanian side when entering Costa Rica.

➡ There is no charge for entering Costa Rica. Entry to Panama costs US$1.

➡ The departure tax in Costa Rica is US$8, plus an admin charge that goes to the company that handles the transaction – a US$1 commission. You pay this through the window of a storage container across the highway from the Costa Rica Migration office. Panama has no departure tax.

➡ Northbound buses usually stop running at 6pm. Travelers without a private vehicle should arrive during the day.

➡ Those with a private vehicle are likely to encounter long lines.

➡ Tica Bus goes daily between San José and Panama City (US$40, 16 to 17 hours) and Tracopa (www.tracopacr.com) has a route from San José to David (eight hours, US$20) running twice daily. Both buses cross this border post. In David you'll also find frequent buses to the border at Paso Canoas.

➡ Situated on the Caribbean coast, **Guabito–Sixaola** (2754-2044, www.migracion.go.cr) is a fairly tranquil and hassle-free border crossing open between 7am and 5pm.

➡ If you're coming from Bocas del Toro in Panama, you'll first have to take the frequent boat to Almirante (around US$2), then a public bus or shuttle to Changuinola (roughly 40 minutes), from where you can take a quick taxi to the border or to the bus station (roughly US$5).

➡ You can walk over the border and catch one of the hourly buses that go up the coast from Sixaola.

➡ **Río Sereno–San Vito/Sabalito** (2784-0130, www.migracion.go.cr) is a rarely used crossing in the Cordillera de Talamanca, with few wait lines. The border is open 8am to 4pm on the Costa Rican side and 9am to 5pm on the Panamanian side. The small village of Río Sereno on the Panamanian side has a hotel and a place to eat; there are no facilities on the Costa Rican side.

➡ Regular buses depart Concepción and David in Panama for Río Sereno. Local buses (around US$2, 40 minutes, six daily) and taxis (about US$30) go from the border to San Vito.

➡ For travelers departing Costa Rica, there is a US$8 exit tax, plus a US$1 admin fee, payable at a kiosk at the border crossing.

Bus

➡ If crossing a border by bus, note that international buses may cost slightly more than taking a local bus to the border, then another local bus onward from the border, but they're worth it. These companies are familiar with border procedures and will tell you what's needed to cross efficiently.

➡ There will be no problems crossing borders provided your papers are in order. If you are on an international bus, you'll have to exit the bus and proceed through both border stations. Bus drivers will wait for everyone to be processed before heading on.

➡ If you choose to take local buses, it's advisable to get to border stations early in the day to allow time for waiting in line and processing. Note that onward buses tend to wind down by the afternoon.

➡ International buses go from San José to Changuinola (Bocas del Toro), David and Panama City in Panama; Guatemala City in Guatemala; Managua in Nicaragua; San Salvador in El Salvador; and Tegucigalpa in Honduras.

Car & Motorcycle

The cost of insurance, fuel and border permits makes a car journey significantly more expensive than buying an airline ticket. To enter Costa Rica by car, you'll need the following items:

➡ valid registration and proof of ownership

➡ valid driver's license or International Driving Permit (IDP)

➡ valid license plates

➡ recent inspection certificate

➡ passport

➡ multiple photocopies of all these documents in case the originals get lost.

Before departing, check that all of the following elements are present and in working order:

➡ blinkers and head- and taillights

➡ spare tire

➡ jerrycan for extra gas (petrol)

➡ well-stocked toolbox including parts, such as belts, that are harder to find in Central America

➡ emergency flares and roadside triangles.

Insurance from foreign countries isn't recognized in Costa Rica, so you'll have to buy a policy locally. At the border it will cost about US$15 to US$45 a month. In addition, you'll have to pay a fumigation fee of about US$5. If you have an accident, you must leave your car where the accident occurred and call the police (then wait for them to arrive) or your insurance will be invalid.

You are not allowed to sell the car in Costa Rica. If you need to leave the country without the car, it must be left in a customs warehouse in San José.

Sea

Cruise ships stop in Costa Rican ports and enable passengers to make a quick foray into the country. Typically, ships dock at either the Pacific ports of Caldera, Puntarenas, Quepos and Bahía Drake, or the Caribbean port of Puerto Limón.

It is also possible to arrive in Costa Rica by private yacht.

GETTING AROUND

Air

Airlines in Costa Rica

➡ Costa Rica's domestic airlines are **Sansa** (☎2290-4100, in USA 877-767-2672; www.flysansa.com), **Aerobell** (www.aerobell.com) and **Skyway** (https://skywaycr.com), plus a new carrier named **Green Airways** (https://costaricagreenair.com) was due to launch at the time of research.

➡ Airlines fly small passenger planes. Check your luggage allowance, as some only allow around 12kg.

➡ Space is limited and demand is high in the dry season, so reserve and pay for tickets in advance.

Charter Flights

➡ Travelers on a larger budget or in a larger party should consider chartering a private plane, which is by far the quickest way to travel around the country.

➡ It takes under 90 minutes to fly to most destinations, though weather conditions can significantly speed up or extend travel time.

➡ Charter companies in the country include Carmon Air (www.carmonair.com), and Aero Caribe Air Charter (https://aerocaribecr.com). Flights can be booked directly through the company, a tour agency or some high-end accommodation.

➡ Luggage space on charters is extremely limited.

NATURE AIR ACCIDENTS & SUSPENSION

In late 2017, in separate incidents, two planes operated by the Costa Rican airline Nature Air crashed, resulting in 14 deaths. The Civil Aviation Administration temporarily suspended the airline shortly after the second crash, reportedly due to personnel shortages and route changes. Nature Air had not reactivated its routes at time of research and the airline's operating license was indefinitely suspended by the Costa Rica General Directorate of Aviation. Nature Air was the world's first carbon-neutral airline.

Bicycle

With an increasingly large network of paved secondary roads and heightened awareness of cyclists, Costa Rica is emerging as one of Central America's most exciting cycle-touring destinations. In the Central Valley & Highlands, there's a burgeoning road biking scene and visitors are likely to see Lycra-clad cyclists climbing and zooming down the attractive winding roads, taking in the epic scenery. That said, many roads are narrow, potholed and winding and there are no designated cycle lanes, so there's an element of risk involved.

Bikes, mostly mountain bikes and beach cruisers, can be rented in towns with a significant tourist presence for US$10 to US$20 per day. A few companies organize bike tours around Costa Rica.

Boat

➡ In Costa Rica there are some regular coastal services, and safety standards are generally good.

➡ Ferries cross the Golfo de Nicoya, connecting the central Pacific coast with the southern tip of the Península de Nicoya.

➡ The ferry **Coonatramar** (☎2661-1069; www.coonatramar.com; adult/child/bicycle/motorcycle/car US$2/1/4/6/18) links the port of Puntarenas with Playa Naranjo several times daily. The ferry **Naviera Tambor** (☎2661-2084; www.navieratambor.com; adult/child/bicycle/motorcycle/car US$1.50/1/4/6/20) travels between Puntarenas and Paquera frequently each day, for a bus connection to Montezuma.

➡ On the Golfo Dulce a daily passenger ferry links Golfito with Puerto Jiménez on the Península de Osa. On the other side of the Península de Osa, water taxis connect Bahía Drake with Sierpe.

➡ On the Caribbean coast there are various bus and boat services that run several times a day, linking Cariari and Tortuguero via La Pavona, while another links Parismina and Siquirres (transfer in Caño Blanco).

AIRLINE DEPARTURES FROM SAN JOSÉ

DEPARTURE CITY	DESTINATION CITY	AIRLINE
San José	Arenal (La Fortuna)	Aerobell, Sansa, Skyway
San José	Manuel Antonio/ Quepos	Sansa, Skyway
San José	Bahía Drake	Skyway, Sansa, Aerobell
San José	Golfito	Sansa
San José	Liberia	Sansa, Skyway
San José	Limón	Sansa
San José	Palmar Sur	Sansa, Aerobell
San José	Playa Nosara	Sansa, Aerobell
San José	Puerto Jiménez	Aerobell, Sansa, Skyway
San José	Tortuguero	Sansa, Aerobell
San José	San Isidro	Sansa
San José	Tamarindo	Sansa, Skyway
San José	Tambor	Aerobell, Sansa, Skyway

Domestic Air Routes

➡ Boats ply the canals that run along the coast from Moín to Tortuguero; although no regular service exists, tourists can prebook water taxis to transport them around these waterways. Costa Rica and Nicaragua have disputed the San Juan as territory, so take your passport if you want to explore these waters. You can try to arrange boat transportation for Barra del Colorado from Tortuguero.

Bus

Local Buses

➡ Local buses are a cheap and reliable way of getting around Costa Rica. Fares range from less than US$1 to around US$20.

➡ San José is the transportation center for the country, though there is no central terminal. Bus offices are scattered around the city: some large bus companies have big terminals that sell tickets in advance, while others have little more than a stop – sometimes unmarked.

➡ Buses can be very crowded but don't usually pass up passengers on account of being too full. Note that there are usually no buses from Thursday to Saturday before Easter Sunday.

➡ There are two types of bus: *directo* and *colectivo*. The *directo* buses should go from one destination to the next with few stops; the *colectivos* make more stops and are very slow going.

➡ Trips longer than four hours usually include a rest stop as buses do not have toilets.

➡ Space is limited on board, so if you have to check luggage be watchful. Theft from overhead racks is rampant, though it's much less common than in other Central American countries.

➡ Bus schedules fluctuate wildly, so always confirm the time when you buy your ticket. If you are catching a bus that picks you up somewhere along a road, get to the roadside early.

➡ For information on departures from San José, see www.visitcostarica.com/en/costa-rica/bus-itinerary

for a reasonably up-to-date copy of the master schedule, or check www.thebusschedule.com/cr for route planning. Another useful site for planning point-to-point bus trips is www.yoviajocr.com, which has a phone app as well.

Shuttle Buses

The tourist-van shuttle services (aka gringo buses) are a pricier alternative to the standard intercity buses. Shuttles are provided by **Gray Line** (☎2220-2126, in USA 800-719-3905; www.graylinecostarica.com), **Easy Ride** (☎8812-4012, in USA 703-879-2284; www.easyridecostarica.com), **Monkey Ride** (☎2787-0454; www.monkeyridecr.com), **Tropical Tours** (☎2640-1900; www.tropicaltourshuttles.com) and **Interbus** (☎6050-6500, 4100-0888; www.interbusonline.com).

➡ All five companies run overland transportation from San José to the most popular destinations, as well as directly between other destinations (see the websites for comprehensive lists).

➡ These services will pick you up at your hotel, and reservations can be made online or through local travel agencies and hotel owners.

➡ Popular destinations include Quepos/Manuel Antonio, Monteverde/Santa Elena, Jacó, Dominical, Uvita, Puerto Jiménez, Arenal, Montezuma and Mal País.

➡ Easy Ride offers international services directly from Jacó, Tamarindo and Liberia to Granada and Managua in Nicaragua and from Monteverde to Managua.

Car & Motorcycle

➡ Foreign drivers in Costa Rica are required to have a valid driver's license from their home country. Many places will also accept an International Driving Permit (IDP), issued by the automobile association in your country of origin. After 90 days, however, you will need to get a Costa Rican driver's license.

➡ Gasoline (petrol) and diesel are widely available, and there are 24-hour service stations along the Interamericana. At the time of research, fuel prices averaged around US$1.10 per liter.

➡ In more remote areas, fuel will be more expensive and might be sold at the neighborhood *pulpería* (corner store).

➡ Spare parts may be hard to find, especially for vehicles with sophisticated electronics and emissions-control systems.

Rental & Insurance

➡ There are car-rental agencies in San José and in popular tourist destinations on the Pacific coast.

➡ All of the major international car-rental agencies have outlets in Costa Rica, though you can sometimes get better deals from local companies.

DRIVING THROUGH RIVERS

If you are driving in Costa Rica, it is likely that you will have to cross a river at some point. Unfortunately, too many travelers have picked up their off-road skills from watching TV, and every season Ticos get a good chuckle out of the number of dead vehicles they help wayward travelers fish out of waterways.

If you're driving through water, follow these rules:

Only do this in a 4WD, with 4WD turned on Don't drive through a river in a car. (It may seem ridiculous to have to say this, but it's attempted all the time.) Getting out of a steep, gravel riverbed requires a 4WD. Besides, car engines flood very easily.

Check the depth of the water before driving through To accommodate an average rental 4WD, the water should be no deeper than the knee. In a sturdier vehicle (Toyota 4Runner or equivalent), water can be waist deep. If you're nervous, wait for a local car to come along, and follow their lead.

The water should be calm If the river is gushing so that there are white crests on the water, do not try to cross. The force of the water will not only flood the engine but could also sweep the car away.

Drive very, very slowly The pressure of driving through a river too quickly will send the water right into the engine and will impair the electrical system. Keep steady pressure on the accelerator so that the tailpipe doesn't fill with water, but go slowly; if driving a stick shift, go in first gear.

Err on the side of caution Car-rental agencies in Costa Rica do not insure for water damage, so ruining a car in a river can come at an extremely high cost.

➡ Due to road conditions, it's necessary to invest in a 4WD unless travel is limited to the Interamericana.

➡ Many agencies will insist on 4WD in the rainy season, when driving through rivers is a matter of course.

➡ To rent a car you'll need a valid driver's license, a major credit card and a passport. The minimum age for car rental is 21 years. It's possible to rent with a debit card, but only if you agree to pay full insurance and leave a deposit for traffic violations (check with your agency ahead of time).

➡ Carefully inspect rented cars for minor damage and make sure that any damage is noted on the rental agreement. If your car breaks down, call the rental company. Don't attempt to get the car fixed yourself – most companies won't reimburse expenses without prior authorization.

➡ Prices vary considerably; on average you can expect to pay more than US$250 per week for a standard SUV, including *kilometraje libre* (unlimited mileage). Economy cars are much cheaper (upwards of US$150 a week); prices do not include mandatory local insurance.

➡ Costa Rican insurance is mandatory, even if you have insurance at home. Expect to pay about US$10 to US$40 per day. Many rental companies won't rent you a car without it. The basic insurance that all drivers must buy is from a government monopoly, the Instituto Nacional de Seguros. This insurance does not cover your rental car at all, only damages to other people and their car or property. It is legal to drive with this insurance only, but it can be difficult to negotiate with a rental agency to allow you to drive away with just this minimum standard. Full insurance through the rental agency can be up to US$60 a day.

➡ Some roads in Costa Rica are rough and rugged, meaning that minor accidents or car damage are common.

➡ If you pay basic insurance with a gold or platinum credit card, the card company may take responsibility for damage to the car, in which case you can forgo the cost of the full insurance. Make sure you verify this with your credit-card company ahead of time.

➡ Most insurance policies do not cover damage caused by flooding or driving through a river, so be aware of the extent of your policy.

➡ Rental rates fluctuate wildly, so shop around. Some agencies offer discounts for extended rentals. Note that rental offices at the airport charge an extra fee in addition to regular rates.

➡ Thieves can easily recognize rental cars. Never leave anything in sight in a parked car – nothing! – and remove all luggage from the trunk overnight. If possible, park in a guarded parking lot rather than on the street.

➡ Motorcycles (including Harley-Davidsons) can be rented in San José and Escazú, but considering the condition of the roads, it's not recommended.

FLAT-TIRE SCAM

For years Aeropuerto Internacional Juan Santamaría has suffered from a scam involving sudden flat tires on rental cars. Though it's commonly reported, it continues to happen.

It goes like this: after you pick up a rental car and drive out of the city, the car gets a flat; as you pull over to fix it, the disabled vehicle is approached by a group of locals, ostensibly to help. There is inevitably some confusion with the changing of the tire, and in the commotion you are relieved of your wallet, luggage or other valuables.

This incident has happened enough times to suggest that you should be very wary if somebody pulls over to help after you get a flat on a recently rented car. Keep your wallet and passport on your person whenever you get out of a car.

Road Conditions & Hazards

➡ The quality of roads varies, from the quite smoothly paved Interamericana to the barely passable, bumpy, potholed, rural back roads. Any can suffer from landslides, sudden flooding and fog.

➡ Many roads are single lane and winding; mountain roads have huge gutters at the sides and lack hard shoulders; other roads are rock-strewn, dirt-and-mud affairs that traverse rivers.

➡ Drive defensively and expect a variety of obstructions, from cyclists and pedestrians to broken-down cars and cattle. Unsigned speed bumps are placed on some roads.

➡ Roads around major tourist areas are adequately marked; all others are not.

➡ Always ask about road conditions before setting out, especially in the rainy season, when a number of roads become impassable.

Road Rules

➡ There are speed limits of 100km/h to 120km/h or less on highways; limits will be posted. The minimum driving speed on highways is 40km/h. The speed limit is 60km/h or less on secondary roads. In urban areas, the speed limit is usually 40m/h.

➡ Traffic police use radar, and speed limits are sometimes enforced with speeding tickets.

➡ Tickets are issued to drivers operating vehicles without a seat belt.

➡ It's illegal to stop at an intersection or make a right turn on a red.

➡ At unmarked intersections, yield to the car on your right.

➡ Drive on the right. Passing is allowed only on the left.

➡ If you are issued with a ticket, you have to pay the fine at a bank; instructions are given on the ticket. If you're driving a rental car, the rental company may be able to arrange your payment for you – the amount of the fine should be on the ticket.

➡ Police have no right to ask for money, and they shouldn't confiscate a car unless: a) the driver cannot produce a license or ownership papers/rental agreement, b) the car lacks license plates, or c) the driver is drunk or the driver has been involved in an accident causing serious injury.

➡ If you're driving and see oncoming cars with headlights flashing, it often means that there is a road problem or a radar speed trap ahead. Slow down immediately.

Hitchhiking

Hitchhiking is never entirely safe, and we don't recommend it. Travelers who hitchhike should understand that they are taking a small but potentially serious risk. People who do hitchhike will be safer if they travel in pairs and let someone know where they are planning to go. Solo women should use even greater caution.

Hitchhiking in Costa Rica is unusual on main roads that have frequent buses. On minor rural roads, hitchhiking is more common. To get picked up, most locals wave down passing cars. If you get a ride, offer to pay when you arrive by saying *'¿Cuánto le debo?'* ('How much do I owe you?'). Your offer may be waved aside, or you may be asked to help with money for gas.

Local Transportation

Bus

Local buses operate chiefly in San José, Puntarenas, San Isidro de El General, Golfito and Puerto Limón, connecting urban and suburban areas. Most local buses pick up passengers on the street and on main roads. For years these buses were converted school buses imported from the US, but they have slowly been upgraded and are now mainly coaches.

Taxi

In San José, taxis have *marías* (meters) and it's illegal for drivers not to use them. Outside San José, most taxis don't have meters and fares tend to be agreed upon in advance. Bargaining is acceptable.

In some towns there are *colectivos* (shared taxis). Although *colectivos* are becoming increasingly difficult to find, the basic principle is that the driver charges a flat fee (usually about US$1) to take passengers from one end of town to the other.

In rural areas, 4WDs are often used as taxis and are a popular means for surfers (and their boards) to travel from their accommodations to the break. Prices vary wildly depending on how touristy the area is, though generally speaking a 10-minute ride costs US$5 to US$20.

Taxi drivers are not normally tipped unless they assist with your luggage or have provided an above-average service.

It's possible to rent a taxi for the day if you agree on a price in advance. Prices vary depending on where you want to visit and how long you need the car. This is often an easier way to see further-afield sights without renting a car. A trip to a volcano followed by a long-distance trip to the beach from San José, for example, will cost around US$200 (quite reasonable with four people in the car).

Language

Spanish pronunciation is easy, as most sounds have equivalents in English. Also, Spanish spelling is phonetically consistent, meaning that there's a clear and consistent relationship between what you see in writing and how it's pronounced. If you read our colored pronunciation guides as if they were English, you'll be understood. Note that kh is a throaty sound (like the 'ch' in the Scottish *loch*), v and b are like a soft English 'v' (between a 'v' and a 'b'), and r is strongly rolled. The stressed syllables are in italics in our pronunciation guides.

The polite form is used in this chapter; where both polite and informal options are given, they are indicated by the abbreviations 'pol' and 'inf'. Where necessary, both masculine and feminine forms of words are included, separated by a slash and with the masculine form first, eg *perdido/a* (m/f).

BASICS

Hello.	*Hola.*	o·la
Goodbye.	*Adiós.*	a·*dyos*
How are you?	*¿Cómo va?* (pol) *¿Cómo vas?* (inf)	*ko*·mo va *ko*·mo vas
Fine, thanks.	*Bien, gracias.*	byen *gra*·syas
Excuse me.	*Con permiso.*	kon per·*mee*·so
Sorry.	*Perdón.*	per·*don*
Please.	*Por favor.*	por fa·*vor*
Thank you.	*Gracias.*	*gra*·syas
You're welcome.	*Con mucho gusto.*	kon *moo*·cho *goo*·sto
Yes.	*Sí.*	see
No.	*No.*	no

My name is ...
Me llamo ... — me *ya*·mo ...

What's your name?
¿Cómo se llama Usted? — *ko*·mo se *ya*·ma oo·*ste* (pol)
¿Cómo te llamas? — *ko*·mo te *ya*·mas (inf)

Do you speak English?
¿Habla inglés? — a·bla een·*gles* (pol)
¿Hablas inglés? — a·blas een·*gles* (inf)

I don't understand.
Yo no entiendo. — yo no en·*tyen*·do

WANT MORE?

For in-depth language information and handy phrases, check out Lonely Planet's *Latin American Spanish Phrasebook*. You'll find it at **shop.lonelyplanet.com**, or you can buy Lonely Planet's iPhone phrasebooks at the Apple App Store.

ACCOMMODATIONS

Do you have a ... room?	*Tiene una habitación ...?*	tye·ne oo·na a·bee·ta·*syon* ...
single	*sencilla*	sen·*see*·ya
double	*doble*	*do*·ble

How much is it per night/person?
¿Cuánto es por noche/persona? — *kwan*·to es por *no*·che/per·*so*·na

Is breakfast included?
¿Incluye el desayuno? — een·*kloo*·ye el de·sa·*yoo*·no

campsite	*área para acampar*	a·re·a *pa*·ra a·kam·*par*
hotel	*hotel*	o·*tel*
hostel	*hospedaje*	os·pe·*da*·khe
guesthouse	*casa de huéspedes*	*ka*·sa de *wes*·pe·des
youth hostel	*albergue juvenil*	al·*ber*·ge khoo·ve·*neel*

TIQUISMOS

These colloquialisms and slang terms *(tiquismos)* are frequently heard, and are for the most part used only in Costa Rica.

¡Adiós! – Hi! (used when passing a friend in the street, or anyone in remote rural areas; also means 'Farewell!' but only when leaving for a long time)

bomba – gas station

buena nota – OK/excellent (literally 'good note')

chapulines – a gang, usually of young thieves

chunche – thing (can refer to almost anything)

cien metros – one city block

¿Hay campo? – Is there space? (on a bus)

machita – blonde woman (slang)

mae – buddy (pronounced 'ma' as in 'mat' followed with a quick 'eh'; it's mainly used by boys and young men)

mi amor – my love (used as a familiar form of address by both men and women)

pulpería – corner grocery store

¡Pura vida! – Super! (literally 'pure life,' also an expression of approval or even a greeting)

sabanero – cowboy, especially one who hails from Guanacaste Province

salado – too bad; tough luck

soda – cafe or lunch counter

¡Tuanis! – Cool!

¡Upe! – Is anybody home? (used mainly in rural areas at people's homes, instead of knocking)

vos – you (singular and informal, same as *tú*)

air-con	*aire acondicionado*	ai·re a·kon·dee·syo·*na*·do
bathroom	*baño*	*ba*·nyo
bed	*cama*	*ka*·ma
window	*ventana*	ven·*ta*·na

DIRECTIONS

Where's ...?
¿Adónde está ...? — a·*don*·de es·*ta* ...

What's the address?
¿Cuál es la dirección? — kwal es la dee·rek·*syon*

Could you please write it down?
¿Podría escribirlo? — po·*dree*·a es·kree·*beer*·lo

Can you show me (on the map)?
¿Me puede enseñar (en el mapa)? — me *pwe*·de en·se·*nyar* (en el *ma*·pa)

at the corner	*en la esquina*	en la es·*kee*·na
at the traffic lights	*en el semáforo*	en el se·*ma*·fo·ro
behind ...	*detrás de ...*	de·*tras* de ...
far	*lejos*	*le*·khos
in front of ...	*en frente de ...*	en *fren*·te de ...
left	*a la izquierda*	a la ees·*kyer*·da
near	*cerca*	*ser*·ka
next to ...	*a la par de ...*	a la par de ...
opposite ...	*opuesto a ...*	o·*pwes*·to a ...
right	*a la derecha*	a la de·*re*·cha
straight ahead	*aquí directo*	a·*kee* dee·*rek*·to

EATING & DRINKING

Can I see the menu, please?
¿Puedo ver el menú, por favor? — *pwe*·do ver el me·*noo* por fa·*vor*

What would you recommend?
¿Qué me recomienda? — ke me re·ko·*myen*·da

Do you have vegetarian food?
¿Tienen comida vegetariana? — *tye*·nen ko·*mee*·da ve·khe·ta·*rya*·na

I don't eat (red meat).
No como (carne roja). — no *ko*·mo (*kar*·ne *ro*·kha)

That was delicious!
¡Estuvo delicioso! — es·*too*·vo de·lee·*syo*·so

Cheers!
¡Salud! — sa·*lood*

The bill, please.
La cuenta, por favor. — la *kwen*·ta por fa·*vor*

I'd like a table for ...	*Quisiera una mesa para ...*	kee·*sye*·ra *oo*·na *me*·sa *pa*·ra ...
(eight) o'clock	*las (ocho)*	las (*o*·cho)
(two) people	*(dos) personas*	(dos) per·*so*·nas

Key Words

appetisers	*aperitivos*	a·pe·ree·*tee*·vos
bar	*bar*	bar
bottle	*botella*	bo·*te*·ya
bowl	*plato hondo*	*pla*·to *on*·do
breakfast	*desayuno*	de·sa·*yoo*·no
cafe	*café*	ka·*fe*
(too) cold	*(muy) frío*	(mooy) *free*·o
dinner	*cena*	*se*·na

food	*comida*	ko·*mee*·da
fork	*tenedor*	te·ne·*dor*
glass	*vaso*	*va*·so
hot (warm)	*caliente*	kal·*yen*·te
knife	*cuchillo*	koo·*chee*·yo
lunch	*almuerzo*	al·*mwer*·so
main course	*plato fuerte*	*pla*·to *fwer*·te
market	*mercado*	mer·*ka*·do
menu	*menú*	me·*noo*
plate	*plato*	*pla*·to
restaurant	*restaurante*	res·tow·*ran*·te
spoon	*cuchara*	koo·*cha*·ra
supermarket	*supermercado*	soo·per·mer·*ka*·do
with/without	*con/sin*	kon/seen

Meat & Fish

beef	*carne de vaca*	*kar*·ne de *va*·ka
chicken	*pollo*	*po*·yo
duck	*pato*	*pa*·to
fish	*pescado*	pes·*ka*·do
lamb	*cordero*	kor·*de*·ro
pork	*cerdo*	*ser*·do
turkey	*pavo*	*pa*·vo
veal	*ternera*	ter·*ne*·ra

Fruit & Vegetables

apple	*manzana*	man·*sa*·na
apricot	*albaricoque*	al·ba·ree·*ko*·ke
asparagus	*espárragos*	es·*pa*·ra·gos
banana	*banano*	ba·*na*·no
bean	*frijol*	free·*khol*
cabbage	*repollo*	re·*po*·yo
carrot	*zanahoria*	sa·na·*o*·rya
cherry	*cereza*	se·*re*·sa
corn	*maíz*	ma·*ees*
cucumber	*pepino*	pe·*pee*·no
fruit	*fruta*	*froo*·ta
grapes	*uvas*	*oo*·vas
lemon	*limón*	lee·*mon*
lentils	*lentejas*	len·*te*·khas
lettuce	*lechuga*	le·*choo*·ga
mushroom	*hongo*	*on*·go
nuts	*nueces*	*nwe*·ses
onion	*cebolla*	se·*bo*·ya
orange	*naranja*	na·*ran*·kha
peach	*melocotón*	me·lo·ko·*ton*
pea	*petipoa*	pe·tee·*po*·a
pepper (bell)	*pimentón*	pee·men·*ton*
pineapple	*piña*	*pee*·nya
plum	*ciruela*	seer·*we*·la
potato	*papa*	*pa*·pa
pumpkin	*calabaza*	ka·la·*ba*·sa
spinach	*espinaca*	es·pee·*na*·ka
strawberry	*fresa*	*fre*·sa
tomato	*tomate*	to·*ma*·te
vegetable	*vegetal*	ve·khe·*tal*
watermelon	*sandía*	san·*dee*·a

SIGNS

Abierto	Open
Cerrado	Closed
Entrada	Entrance
Hombres/Varones	Men
Mujeres/Damas	Women
Prohibido	Prohibited
Salida	Exit
Servicios/Baños	Toilets

Other

bread	*pan*	pan
butter	*mantequilla*	man·te·*kee*·ya
cheese	*queso*	*ke*·so
egg	*huevo*	*we*·vo
honey	*miel*	myel
jam	*jalea*	kha·*le*·a
oil	*aceite*	a·*sey*·te
pastry	*pastel*	pas·*tel*
pepper	*pimienta*	pee·*myen*·ta
rice	*arroz*	a·*ros*
salt	*sal*	sal
sugar	*azúcar*	a·*soo*·kar
vinegar	*vinagre*	vee·*na*·gre

Drinks

beer	*cerveza*	ser·*ve*·sa
coffee	*café*	ka·*fe*
(orange) juice	*jugo (de naranja)*	*khoo*·go (de na·*ran*·kha)
milk	*leche*	*le*·che
tea	*té*	te
(mineral) water	*agua (mineral)*	*a*·gwa (mee·ne·*ral*)
(red/white) wine	*vino (tinto/ blanco)*	*vee*·no (*teen*·to/ *blan*·ko)

EMERGENCIES

Help!	*¡Socorro!*	so·*ko*·ro
Go away!	*¡Váyase!*	*va*·ya·se

Call ...!	*¡Llame a ...!*	*ya*·me a ...
a doctor	*un doctor*	oon dok·*tor*
the police	*la policía*	la po·lee·*see*·a

I'm lost.
Estoy perdido/a. es·*toy* per·*dee*·do/a (m/f)

I'm ill.
Estoy enfermo/a. es·*toy* en·*fer*·mo/a (m/f)

It hurts here.
Me duele aquí. me *dwe*·le a·*kee*

I'm allergic to (antibiotics).
Soy alérgico/a a (los antibióticos). soy a·*ler*·khee·ko/a a (los an·tee·*byo*·tee·kos) (m/f)

Where are the toilets?
¿Dónde está el baño? *don*·de es·*ta* el *ba*·nyo

SHOPPING & SERVICES

I'd like to buy ...
Quiero comprar ... *kye*·ro kom·*prar* ...

I'm just looking.
Sólo estoy viendo. *so*·lo es·*toy* *vyen*·do

Can I look at it?
¿Lo puedo ver? lo *pwe*·do ver

How much is it?
¿Cuánto cuesta? *kwan*·to *kwes*·ta

That's too expensive.
Está muy caro. es·*ta* mooy *ka*·ro

Can you lower the price?
¿Podría bajarle el precio? po·*dree*·a ba·*khar*·le el *pre*·syo

There's a mistake in the bill.
Hay un error en la cuenta. ai oon e·*ror* en la *kwen*·ta

ATM	*cajero automático*	ka·*khe*·ro ow·to·*ma*·tee·ko
credit card	*tarjeta de crédito*	tar·*khe*·ta de *kre*·dee·to

QUESTION WORDS

How?	*¿Cómo?*	*ko*·mo
What?	*¿Qué?*	ke
When?	*¿Cuándo?*	*kwan*·do
Where?	*¿Dónde?*	*don*·de
Who?	*¿Quién?*	kyen
Why?	*¿Por qué?*	por ke

market	*mercado*	mer·*ka*·do
post office	*correo*	ko·*re*·o
tourist office	*oficina de turismo*	o·fee·*see*·na de too·*rees*·mo

TIME & DATES

What time is it?	*¿Qué hora es?*	ke *o*·ra es
It's (10) o'clock.	*Son (las diez).*	son (las dyes)
It's half past (one).	*Es (la una) y media.*	es (la *oo*·na) ee *me*·dya

morning	*mañana*	ma·*nya*·na
afternoon	*tarde*	*tar*·de
evening	*noche*	*no*·che
yesterday	*ayer*	a·*yer*
today	*hoy*	oy
tomorrow	*mañana*	ma·*nya*·na

Monday	*lunes*	*loo*·nes
Tuesday	*martes*	*mar*·tes
Wednesday	*miércoles*	*myer*·ko·les
Thursday	*jueves*	*khwe*·ves
Friday	*viernes*	*vyer*·nes
Saturday	*sábado*	*sa*·ba·do
Sunday	*domingo*	do·*meen*·go

January	*enero*	e·*ne*·ro
February	*febrero*	fe·*bre*·ro
March	*marzo*	*mar*·so
April	*abril*	a·*breel*
May	*mayo*	*ma*·yo
June	*junio*	*khoon*·yo
July	*julio*	*khool*·yo
August	*agosto*	a·*gos*·to
September	*septiembre*	sep·*tyem*·bre
October	*octubre*	ok·*too*·bre
November	*noviembre*	no·*vyem*·bre
December	*diciembre*	dee·*syem*·bre

TRANSPORTATION

boat	*barco*	*bar*·ko
bus	*bús*	boos
plane	*avión*	a·*vyon*
train	*tren*	tren

first	*primero*	pree·*me*·ro
last	*último*	*ool*·tee·mo
next	*próximo*	*prok*·see·mo

A ... ticket, please.	*Un pasaje de ..., por favor.*	oon pa·*sa*·khe de ... por fa·*vor*
1st-class	*primera clase*	pree·*me*·ra *kla*·se
2nd-class	*segunda clase*	se·*goon*·da *kla*·se
one-way	*ida*	ee·da
return	*ida y vuelta*	ee·da ee *vwel*·ta

I want to go to ...
Quisiera ir a ... kee·*sye*·ra eer a ...

Does it stop at ...?
¿Hace parada en ...? a·se pa·*ra*·da en ...

What stop is this?
¿Cuál es esta parada? kwal es es·ta pa·*ra*·da

What time does it arrive/leave?
¿A qué hora llega/ sale? a ke o·ra *ye*·ga/ *sa*·le

Please tell me when we get to ...
Por favor, avíseme cuando lleguemos a ... por fa·*vor* a·*vee*·se·me *kwan*·do ye·*ge*·mos a ...

I want to get off here.
Quiero bajarme aquí. *kye*·ro ba·*khar*·me a·*kee*

airport	*aeropuerto*	a·e·ro·*pwer*·to
aisle seat	*asiento de pasillo*	a·*syen*·to de pa·*see*·yo
bus stop	*parada de autobuses*	pa·*ra*·da de ow·to·*boo*·ses
cancelled	*cancelado*	kan·se·*la*·do
delayed	*atrasado*	a·tra·*sa*·do
platform	*plataforma*	pla·ta·*for*·ma
ticket office	*taquilla*	ta·*kee*·ya
timetable	*horario*	o·*ra*·ryo
train station	*estación de trenes*	es·ta·*syon* de *tre*·nes
window seat	*asiento junto a la ventana*	a·*syen*·to *khoon*·to a la ven·*ta*·na

I'd like to hire a ...	*Quiero alquilar ...*	*kye*·ro al·kee·*lar* ...
4WD	*un cuatro por cuatro*	oon *kwa*·tro por *kwa*·tro
bicycle	*una bicicleta*	*oo*·na bee·see·*kle*·ta
car	*un carro*	oon *ka*·ro
motorcycle	*una moto-cicleta*	*oo*·na mo·to·see·*kle*·ta

NUMBERS

1	*uno*	*oo*·no
2	*dos*	dos
3	*tres*	tres
4	*cuatro*	*kwa*·tro
5	*cinco*	*seen*·ko
6	*seis*	seys
7	*siete*	*sye*·te
8	*ocho*	o·cho
9	*nueve*	*nwe*·ve
10	*diez*	dyes
20	*veinte*	*veyn*·te
30	*treinta*	*treyn*·ta
40	*cuarenta*	kwa·*ren*·ta
50	*cincuenta*	seen·*kwen*·ta
60	*sesenta*	se·*sen*·ta
70	*setenta*	se·*ten*·ta
80	*ochenta*	o·*chen*·ta
90	*noventa*	no·*ven*·ta
100	*cien*	syen
1000	*mil*	meel

child seat	*asiento de seguridad para niños*	a·*syen*·to de se·goo·ree·*da* *pa*·ra *nee*·nyos
diesel	*diesel*	dee·*sel*
helmet	*casco*	*kas*·ko
mechanic	*mecánico*	me·*ka*·nee·ko
petrol/gas	*gasolina*	ga·so·*lee*·na
service station	*bomba*	*bom*·ba
truck	*camión*	ka·*myon*

Is this the road to ...?
¿Por aquí se va a ...? por a·*kee* se va a ...

(How long) Can I park here?
¿(Cuánto tiempo) Puedo parquear aquí? (*kwan*·to *tyem*·po) *pwe*·do par·ke·*ar* a·*kee*

The car has broken down (at ...).
El carro se varó en ... el *ka*·ro se va·*ro* en ...

I've had an accident.
Tuve un accidente. *too*·ve oon ak·see·*den*·te

I've run out of petrol.
Me quedé sin gasolina. me ke·*de* seen ga·so·*lee*·na

I have a flat tyre.
Se me estalló una llanta. se me es·ta·*yo* *oo*·na *yan*·ta

GLOSSARY

adiós – means 'goodbye' universally, but used as a greeting in rural Costa Rica
alquiler de automóviles – car rental
apartado – post-office box (abbreviated 'Apdo')
artesanía – handicrafts
ATH – *a toda hora* (open all hours); used to denote ATMs
automóvil – car
avenida – avenue
avión – airplane

bahía – bay
barrio – district or neighborhood
biblioteca – library
bomba – short, funny verse; also means 'gas station' and 'bomb'
bosque – forest
bosque nuboso – cloud forest
buena nota – excellent, OK; literally 'good note'

caballo – horse
cabaña – cabin; see also *cabina*
cabina – cabin; see also *cabaña*
cajero automático – ATM
calle – street
cama, cama matrimonial – bed, double bed
campesino – peasant, farmer or person who works in agriculture
carreta – colorfully painted wooden oxcart, now a form of folk art
carretera – road
casado – inexpensive set meal; also means 'married'
casita – cottage or apartment
catedral – cathedral
caverna – cave; see also *cueva*
cerro – mountain or hill
Chepe – affectionate nickname for José; also used when referring to San José
cine – cinema
ciudad – city
cocina – kitchen or cooking
colectivo – bus, minivan or car operating as shared taxi
colibrí – hummingbird
colina – hill
colón – Costa Rican unit of currency; plural colones
cordillera – mountain range
correo – mail service
Costarricense – Costa Rican; see also Tico/a
cruce – crossing
cruda – often used to describe a hangover; literally 'raw'
cueva – cave; see also *caverna*
culebra – snake; see also *serpiente*

Dios – God
directo – direct; refers to long-distance bus with few stops

edificio – building
estación – station, eg ranger station or bus station; also means 'season'

farmacia – pharmacy
fauna silvestre – wildlife
fiesta – party or festival
finca – farm or plantation
floresta – forest
frontera – border
fútbol – soccer (football)

garza – cattle egret
gasolina – gas (petrol)
gracias – thanks
gringo/a (m/f) – US or European visitor; can be affectionate or insulting, depending on the tone used

hacienda – rural estate
hielo – ice

ICT – Instituto Costarricense de Turismo; Costa Rica Tourism Board
iglesia – church
indígena – indigenous
Interamericana – Pan-American Hwy; the nearly continuous highway running from Alaska to Chile (it breaks at the Darién Gap between Panama and Colombia)
invierno – winter; the rainy season in Costa Rica
isla – island

jardín – garden
josefino/a (m/f) – resident of San José

lago – lake
lavandería – laundry facility, usually offering dry-cleaning services
librería – bookstore
llanura – tropical plain

machismo – an exaggerated sense of masculine pride
macho – literally 'male'; figuratively also 'masculine,' 'tough.' In Costa Rica *macho/a* (m/f) also means 'blonde.'
maría – local name for taxi meter
mercado – market
mercado central – central town market
Meseta Central – Central Valley or central plateau
mestizo/a (m/f) – person of mixed descent, usually Spanish and indigenous
metate – flat stone platform, used by Costa Rica's pre-Columbian populations to grind corn
migración – immigration
Minae – Ministerio de Ambiente y Energía; Ministry of Environment and Energy, in charge of the national park system
mirador – lookout point
mole – rich chocolate sauce
mono – monkey
mono tití – squirrel monkey
motocicleta – motorcycle
muelle – dock
museo – museum

niño – child
normal – refers to long-distance bus with many stops

obeah – spiritual rituals of African origin
ola(s) – wave(s)
OTS – Organization for Tropical Studies

pájaro – bird
palapa – shelter with a thatched, palm-leaf roof and open sides
palenque – indigenous settlement
páramo – habitat with highland shrub and tussock grass
parque – park
parque central – central town square or plaza
parque nacional – national park
perezoso – sloth
perico – mealy parrot
playa – beach
posada – country-style inn or guesthouse
puente – bridge
puerto – port
pulpería – corner grocery store
punta – point
pura vida – super; literally 'pure life'

quebrada – stream

rana – frog or toad
rancho – small house or house-like building
río – river

sabanero – cowboy from Guanacaste
selva – jungle
Semana Santa – the Christian Holy Week that precedes Easter
sendero – trail or path
serpiente – snake
Sinac – Sistema Nacional de Areas de Conservación; National System of Conservation Areas
supermercado – supermarket

telenovela – Spanish-language soap opera
Tico/a (m/f) – Costa Rican; see also *Costarricense*
tienda – store
tiquismos – typical Costa Rican expressions or slang
tortuga – turtle

valle – valley
verano – summer; the dry season in Costa Rica
volcán – volcano

zoológico – zoo

Food Glossary

a la plancha – grilled or pan-fried
agua – water
agua de sapo – literally 'toad water,' a lemonade made with fresh ginger and brown sugar
agua dulce – sugarcane juice
aguacate – avocado
almuerzo – lunch
almuerzo ejecutivo – literally 'executive lunch'; a more expensive version of a set meal or *casado*
arroz – rice

batido – fruit shake made with milk or water
bocas – small savory dishes served in bars; tapas

café – coffee
camaron – shrimp
carambola – starfruit
cas – a type of tart guava
casado – inexpensive set meal; also means 'married'
cena – dinner
cerveza – beer; also known as birra
ceviche – seafood marinated in lemon or lime juice, garlic and seasonings
chan – drink made from chia seeds
chuleta – pork chop
comida típica – typical local food

desayuno – breakfast
dorado – mahi-mahi

empanada – savory turnover stuffed with meat or cheese
ensalada – salad

frito – fried

gallo pinto – stir-fry of rice and beans
guanabana – soursop or cherimoya
guaro – local firewater made from sugarcane

leche – milk
linaza – drink made from flaxseeds
lomito – fillet; tenderloin

macrobiótica – health-food store
maracuya – passion fruit
mariscos – seafood
melón – cantaloupe
mora – blackberry

natilla – sour cream

olla de carne – beef stew

palmito – heart of palm
pargo – red snapper
pan – bread
pan tostada – toast
panadería – bakery
pastelería – pastry shop
patacones – twice-fried green plantains
patí – Caribbean version of empanada
pescado – fish
piña – pineapple
pipa – young green coconut; harvested for refreshing coconut water
plátanos maduros – ripe plantain cut in slices lengthwise and baked or broiled with butter, brown sugar and cinnamon
pollo – chicken

queso – cheese

resbladera – sweet barley and rice drink
ron – rum
rondón – seafood gumbo

Salsa Lizano – Costa Rican version of Worcestershire sauce; a key ingredient in *gallo pinto*
sandía – watermelon
soda – informal lunch counter or inexpensive eatery

tamarindo – fruit of the tamarind tree
tapa de dulce – brown sugar

vino – wine

Behind the Scenes

SEND US YOUR FEEDBACK

We love to hear from travelers – your comments keep us on our toes and help make our books better. Our well-traveled team reads every word on what you loved or loathed about this book. Although we cannot reply individually to your submissions, we always guarantee that your feedback goes straight to the appropriate authors, in time for the next edition. Each person who sends us information is thanked in the next edition – the most useful submissions are rewarded with a selection of digital PDF chapters.

Visit **lonelyplanet.com/contact** to submit your updates and suggestions or to ask for help. Our award-winning website also features inspirational travel stories, news and discussions.

Note: We may edit, reproduce and incorporate your comments in Lonely Planet products such as guidebooks, websites and digital products, so let us know if you don't want your comments reproduced or your name acknowledged. For a copy of our privacy policy visit lonelyplanet.com/privacy.

OUR READERS

Many thanks to the travelers who used the last edition and wrote to us with helpful hints, useful advice and interesting anecdotes: Anne McGuire, Greg Brenholdt, Natascha Heidari, Sheila Hutchison, Stephane Duguay

WRITER THANKS

Jade Bremner

Gracias to editor Martine Power for all her expertise and patience on this project. Thanks to Jo Walton for playing crash test dummy with me in the jungles of Costa Rica and relentlessly walking the streets of Jacó. Thanks to the chefs at Citrus and Pesquería da Limonta for the dreams about your food. A big thanks to Harriet Sinclair for holding the fort. Last but not least, *gracias* to everyone working hard behind the scenes at Lonely Planet.

Ashley Harrell

Thanks to: editor Martine Power and co-authors for all their diligent work on this title; Stacey Auch for being a true friend and a warrior; to Genna (and Sean) Davis for the hospitality, the trampoline and the racy engagement photos; Thomas Francis for being such a good sport; Lauren Smiley and Harshal Ingole for enduring vacation rain and mediocre Italian; and Steven Sparapani for the enchanting company on this usually blissful, sometimes grueling journey.

Brian Kluepfel

My wife, Paula: even in a lovely place like Costa Rica, *me muero sin ti.* My editor, Martine – thanks for your patience. The previous writers of my chapters – Jade, Ashley, and Mara – I stand on the shoulders of giants. Lonely Planet Tech Support: Dianne and Eimear, you rock. In San José: Alejandro Regidor, Mellissa Lozado and Leonardo (Bergerac). In Fortuna and Sarapiqui: Sonia Escalante and Alex Martinez. In Cahuita: Richard Robinson and Marise. To every Tico bus driver and Lonely Planet reader: bless you all.

Mara Vorhees

Thanks to my hiking companions on this trip, especially Bart and Simone, for the excellent company and extra courage on Chirripó. In Corcovado, my intrepid guide Bolivar never led me astray. Andy Pruter was a delightful host and a font of wisdom about the Osa, while Eddy and Francesca and their team took great care of my family at Naguala Jungle Lodge. So much gratitude to my three guys for accompanying me on this grand adventure. *Pura vida!*

ACKNOWLEDGEMENTS

Climate map data adapted from Peel MC, Finlayson BL & McMahon TA (2007) 'Updated World Map of the Köppen-Geiger Climate Classification', Hydrology and Earth System Sciences, 11, 163344.

Cover photograph: Hummingbird, Francesco Riccardo Iacomino/AWL Images ©

THIS BOOK

This 14th edition of Lonely Planet's *Costa Rica* guidebook was researched and written by Jade Bremner, Ashley Harrell, Brian Kluepfel and Mara Vorhees. Jade, Ashley and Brian also wrote the previous edition. This guidebook was produced by the following:

Senior Product Editors Martine Power, Sandie Kestell

Senior Cartographer Corey Hutchison

Product Editors Joel Cotterell, James Appleton

Book Designers Jessica Rose, Fergal Condon

Coordinating Editor Gemma Graham

Assisting Cartographers Michael Garrett, Rachel Imeson

Assisting Editors Ronan Abayawickrema, Daniel Bolger, Amy Lynch, Kristin Odijk, Tamara Sheward, James Smart

Cover Researcher Brendan Dempsey-Spencer

Thanks to Karen Henderson, Andi Jones, Virginia Moreno, Genna Patterson, Angela Tinson

Index

Map Pages **000**
Photo Pages **000**

Map Pages **000**
Photo Pages **000**

Map Legend

Sights
- Beach
- Bird Sanctuary
- Buddhist
- Castle/Palace
- Christian
- Confucian
- Hindu
- Islamic
- Jain
- Jewish
- Monument
- Museum/Gallery/Historic Building
- Ruin
- Shinto
- Sikh
- Taoist
- Winery/Vineyard
- Zoo/Wildlife Sanctuary
- Other Sight

Activities, Courses & Tours
- Bodysurfing
- Diving
- Canoeing/Kayaking
- Course/Tour
- Sento Hot Baths/Onsen
- Skiing
- Snorkeling
- Surfing
- Swimming/Pool
- Walking
- Windsurfing
- Other Activity

Sleeping
- Sleeping
- Camping
- Hut/Shelter

Eating
- Eating

Drinking & Nightlife
- Drinking & Nightlife
- Cafe

Entertainment
- Entertainment

Shopping
- Shopping

Information
- Bank
- Embassy/Consulate
- Hospital/Medical
- Internet
- Police
- Post Office
- Telephone
- Toilet
- Tourist Information
- Other Information

Geographic
- Beach
- Gate
- Hut/Shelter
- Lighthouse
- Lookout
- Mountain/Volcano
- Oasis
- Park
- Pass
- Picnic Area
- Waterfall

Population
- Capital (National)
- Capital (State/Province)
- City/Large Town
- Town/Village

Transport
- Airport
- Border crossing
- Bus
- Cable car/Funicular
- Cycling
- Ferry
- Metro station
- Monorail
- Parking
- Petrol station
- Subway/Subte station
- Taxi
- Train station/Railway
- Tram
- Underground station
- Other Transport

Routes
- Tollway
- Freeway
- Primary
- Secondary
- Tertiary
- Lane
- Unsealed road
- Road under construction
- Plaza/Mall
- Steps
- Tunnel
- Pedestrian overpass
- Walking Tour
- Walking Tour detour
- Path/Walking Trail

Boundaries
- International
- State/Province
- Disputed
- Regional/Suburb
- Marine Park
- Cliff
- Wall

Hydrography
- River, Creek
- Intermittent River
- Canal
- Water
- Dry/Salt/Intermittent Lake
- Reef

Areas
- Airport/Runway
- Beach/Desert
- Cemetery (Christian)
- Cemetery (Other)
- Glacier
- Mudflat
- Park/Forest
- Sight (Building)
- Sportsground
- Swamp/Mangrove

Note: Not all symbols displayed above appear on the maps in this book

OUR STORY

A beat-up old car, a few dollars in the pocket and a sense of adventure. In 1972 that's all Tony and Maureen Wheeler needed for the trip of a lifetime – across Europe and Asia overland to Australia. It took several months, and at the end – broke but inspired – they sat at their kitchen table writing and stapling together their first travel guide, *Across Asia on the Cheap*. Within a week they'd sold 1500 copies. Lonely Planet was born.

Today, Lonely Planet has offices in Tennessee, Dublin and Beijing, with a network of over 2000 contributors in every corner of the globe. We share Tony's belief that 'a great guidebook should do three things: inform, educate and amuse'.

OUR WRITERS

Jade Bremner

Central Valley & Highlands, Central Pacific Coast Jade has been a journalist for more than 15 years. She has lived in and reported on four different regions. It's no coincidence many of her favorite places have some of the best waves in the world. Jade has edited travel magazines and sections for *Time Out* and *Radio Times* and has contributed to the *Times*, CNN and the *Independent*. She feels privileged to share tales from this wonderful planet we call home and is always looking for the next adventure. Jade also wrote the Understand and Survival Guide sections.

Ashley Harrell

Península de Nicoya, Northwestern Costa Rica After a brief stint selling day spa coupons door-to-door in South Florida, Ashley decided she'd rather be a writer. She went to journalism grad school, convinced a newspaper to hire her, and started covering wildlife, crime and tourism, sometimes all in the same story. Fueling her zest for storytelling and the unknown, she traveled widely and moved often, from a tiny NYC apartment to a vast California ranch to a jungle cabin in Costa Rica, where she started writing for Lonely Planet. From there her travels became more exotic and farther flung, and she still laughs when paychecks arrive.

Brian Kluepfel

San José, Caribbean Coast, Arenal & Northern Lowlands Brian has lived in Berkeley, Bolivia, the Bronx and the 'burbs, among other places. His journalistic work across the Americas has ranged from the Copa America soccer tournament in Paraguay to an accordion festival in Quebec. His titles for LP include *Venezuela, Costa Rica, Belize, Guatemala, Bolivia* and *Ecuador*. An avid birder and musician, he blogs at www.brianbirdwatching.blogspot.com.

Mara Vorhees

Southern Costa Rica & Península de Osa Mara writes about food, travel and family fun around the world. Her work has been published by *BBC Travel*, *Boston Globe*, *Delta Sky*, *Vancouver Sun* and more. For Lonely Planet, she regularly writes about destinations in Central America and Eastern Europe, as well as New England, where she lives. She often travels with her twin boys in tow, earning her expertise in family travel. Follow their adventures and misadventures at www.havetwinswilltravel.com. Mara also wrote the Plan Your Trip section.

Published by Lonely Planet Global Limited
CRN 554153
14th edition – Nov 2021
ISBN 978 1 78701 683 5

10 9 8 7 6 5 4 3 2 1
Printed in Singapore